W9-CEK-243

American Government
Institutions and Policies

NINTH EDITION

James Q. Wilson

University of California, Los Angeles
Pepperdine University

John J. DiIulio, Jr.

University of Pennsylvania

Houghton Mifflin Company   Boston New York

**For Roberta, Matthew, Rebecca, Annie, and Bob
and Winston, Clementine, and Sarah
J.Q.W.**

**Dedicated to the memory of Aaron H. Crasner
J.J.D.**

Publisher: Charles Hartford
Editor-in-chief: Jean L. Woy
Sponsoring editor: Katherine Meisenheimer
Associate editor: Julie Hassel
Senior project editor: Carol Newman
Editorial assistant: Kendra Johnson
Senior production/design coordinator: Jennifer Meyer Dare
Senior designer: Henry Rachlin
Senior manufacturing coordinator: Jane Spelman
Marketing manager: Nicola Poser

Cover image: Capitol Building © Larry Lee Photography/CORBIS

Printed in U.S.A.

Library of Congress Catalog Number: 2002109456

ISBN: 0-618-29982-3

5 6 7 8 9—DOW—2007 2006 2005

CONTENTS

4

American Political Culture

76

PART II

Opinions, Interests, and Organizations

101

5

Public Opinion

102

6

Political Participation

130

7

Political Parties

150

8

Elections and Campaigns

184

9

Interest Groups

222

10

The Media

250

PART III

Institutions of Government
279

Congress
280

The Presidency
328

13

The Bureaucracy

372

14

The Judiciary

402

PART IV

The Politics of Public Policy
433

15

The Policy-Making Process

434

20
Foreign and Military Policy
552

21
Environmental Policy
584

PART V
The Nature of American Democracy
601

22
Who Governs? To What Ends?
602

Appendix
A1

Times change. Since the Eighth Edition of this book was published, massive terrorist attacks were inflicted on this country. Unlike many other political events, these attacks made a great and immediate difference. Congress passed the USA-Patriot Act, a law that strengthens in significant ways American law enforcement. There was an outburst of American patriotism. It will be a while before we know how the new law works and whether the heightened patriotism will endure.

Under President George W. Bush a new military doctrine has emerged, one that authorizes the United States preemptively to attack a nation that threatens to attack us with weapons of mass destruction. At the time of this writing, there is talk of military action against Iraq.

The brief era of balanced budgets that emerged by the end of the 1990s turned out to be even briefer than we had imagined. The decisions to spend money to rebuild parts of New York City, compensate the victims of terrorism, improve law enforcement and intelligence agencies, and strengthen the military have contributed to the return of budget deficits to Washington. A slowdown in the economy has made the exuberance of the dot-com years a distant memory.

Beneath these changes, of course, the enduring features of American politics, shaped by our Constitution and habits, have remained unchanged. This book traces one of the lasting themes of government: who governs, and what difference—in policies adopted or rejected—it makes who governs. Current events may change but this profoundly important question will continue to shape the way our democracy works.

In the Ninth Edition we continue our effort to structure the book in the most effective way for teaching. To that end we have combined the two old concluding chapters on political theory into one new one. The resulting new chapter is a concise but comprehensive look at political power and the changing scope of government. It takes the questions "who governs? and to what ends?" into new directions.

Another structural change we have made is in the chapters on Congress and elections. To help students understand the workings of Congress, an important institution that requires a lot of description, we have reorganized and shortened that chapter by moving material on congressional elections to the chapter on elections.

For this edition we have included a new feature: Each chapter now ends with a section called "Reconsidering the Enduring Questions" that gives contemporary responses to the Enduring Questions with which each chapter begins. These brief essays should help students focus in a novel way on what many people think are the perennial puzzles of American politics.

The very popular features "Politically Speaking," "The Rules of Politics," "Trivia," "How Things Work," "What Would You Do?," and "Who Governs? To What Ends?" have been retained in strengthened form. We have also added a list of useful World Wide Web addresses so that students with access to computers can do their own research on facts and opinions about American politics.

Finally, the text has been updated through the 2002 election and all of the relevant figures and tables made current.

This is the same book that is used in colleges and universities across the country, with a few new features specially designed for advanced high school students.

The new end of chapter feature **Reconsidering the Enduring Questions** augments the traditional summary to help students review each chapter and synthesize what they have learned. This unique approach should help students think critically about the material.

For the Teacher

AP Teachers will benefit from the outstanding ancillary program that has always supported *American Government*, which features the following for the Ninth Edition:

A correlation from the text to the Advanced Placement course description ("acorn book") is available from your McDougal Littell representative.

The **Instructor's Resource Manual** helps teachers plan their course, lectures, and discussion sections. Professor MaryAnne Borrelli (Connecticut College) has thoroughly integrated the IRM with the textbook so instructors can capitalize upon the richness of *American Government*. Elements new to this edition have been summarized, and the resources and references sections have been thoroughly updated.

The **Test Item File**, revised by P. S. Ruckman, Jr. (Rock Valley College) contains over 4,000 multiple choice, true/false, and essay questions and has been updated to help students prepare for the AP exam. The multiple-choice section now offers five possible answers for each question, which is consistent with the format of the AP exam.

These printed test items are also available in electronic format for both Windows and Macintosh platforms. **HM Testing** software provides a complete testing solution, with test generation, classroom administration, and online testing features.

The **Transparency Package** contains fifty full-color transparencies from the illustration program of *American Government*, Ninth Edition.

The illustrations in the transparency package are also available as **PowerPoint Slides**, downloadable from the *American Government*, Ninth Edition web site **Instructor's Resource Page** (go to http://politicalscience.college.hmco.com/instructors). Adopters of the text may obtain the password for this page from their McDougal Littell sales representative.

For instructors who wish to include a unit on state and local politics in their course, a newly revised chapter-length **State and Local Government Supplement** is also available.

For the Student

The **Student Handbook** has been thoroughly updated by P. S. Ruckman, Jr. (Rock Valley College) to help students using *American Government* master the facts and principles introduced in the text and prepare for examinations. For each chapter, the handbook includes focus points, a study outline, key terms, notes about possible misconceptions, a data check, practice exam questions, and special application projects, as well as answers to all chapter exercises (excluding the essay questions).

The *American Government*, **Ninth Edition Web Site**, accessible via the Houghton Mifflin College Division web site at http://politicalscience.college.hmco.com/students, contains other student study aids, including chapter outlines, ACE self-quizzes, *What Would You Do?* interactive simulations, additional "Trivia" features, and chapter-specific web links. The Ninth Edition web site also links to **Political SourceNet**, Houghton Mifflin's American Government resource, containing primary source documents, Internet exercises, and other interactive activities.

Acknowledgements

A number of scholars reviewed the Eighth Edition and made many useful suggestions for the Ninth. They include Dr. Paul Davis, Truckee Meadows Community College; Femi Ferreira, Hutchinson Community College; Susan B. Hansen, University of Pittsburgh; Tseggai Isaac, University of Missouri-Rolla; Mark R. Joslyn, University of Kansas; Joshua Kaplan, University of Notre Dame; Sam Wescoat McKinstry, East Tennessee State University; Marie Natoli, Emmanuel College; Bruce Newman, Western Oklahoma State College; Dennis L. Plane, University of Texas at Austin; P. S. Ruckman, Jr., Rock Valley College; and Edward R. Wagner, Jr., University of Wisconsin, Milwaukee.

Special thanks go to the following AP instructors whose thoughtful reviews helped guide this revision: Lesley S. Battaglia, Williamsville South High School; David Kiyoshi Irie, San Marino High School; Stephen J. Kohut, Oceanside High School; Douglas Olson, Timpanogas High School; Gina M. Passantino, Canisius High School; Jeffrey Thomas Pike, Saline High School; Ray Richardson, Aberdeen High School; Jim Sharp, Ardsley High School; and Donald M. Smith, Gonzaga College High School.

James Q. Wilson now teaches at Pepperdine University. He is an emeritus professor of management and public policy at the University of California, Los Angeles, and from 1961 to 1987 was a professor of government at Harvard University. Raised in California, he received a B.A. degree from the University of Redlands and Ph.D. from the University of Chicago. Wilson is the author or coauthor of fourteen books, including *The Marriage Problem* (2002), *Moral Judgment* (1997), *The Moral Sense* (1993), *Bureaucracy* (1989), *Crime and Human Nature* (1985, with Richard J. Herrnstein), *Thinking about Crime* (1983), and *Political Organizations* (1974).

Wilson has served in a number of advisory posts in the federal government. He was chairman of the White House Task Force on Crime in 1967, chairman of the National Advisory Council on Drug Abuse Prevention in 1972–1973, a member of the Attorney General's Task Force on Violent Crime in 1981, and a member of the President's Foreign Intelligence Advisory Board in 1986–1990.

In 1977 the American Political Science Association conferred on him the Charles E. Merriam Award for advancing the art of government through the application of social science knowledge and in 1990 the James Madison Award for distinguished scholarship. In 1991–1992 he was President of the Association.

He is a Fellow of the American Academy of Arts and Sciences and a member of the American Philosophical Society. When not writing, teaching, or advising, he goes scuba diving. He says that it clears the brain.

John J. DiIulio, Jr. is a professor of political science at the University of Pennsylvania. and a senior fellow at the Brookings Institution. From 1986 to 1999, he was a professor of politics and public affairs at Princeton University's Woodrow Wilson School of Public and International Affairs. He received B.A. and M.A. degrees from the University of Pennsylvania and M.A. and Ph.D. degrees from Harvard University. He is the author, coauthor, or editor of a dozen books, including *What's God Got to Do with the American Experiment?* (2000, with E.J. Dionne); *Medicaid and Devolution* (1998, with Frank Thompson); and *Deregulating the Public Service* (1994).

DiIulio advised both Vice President Al Gore and Governor George W. Bush during the 2000 Presidential campaign. While on leave in academic year 2000–2001, he served as Assistant to the President of the United States. Over the last decade, he has advised officials at the National Performance Review, the Office of Management and Budget, the General Accounting Office, the U.S. Department of Justice, and other federal agencies. He has served on the boards of Big Brothers Big Sisters of America and other national nonprofit organizations.

In 1995 the Association of Public Policy Analysis and Management conferred on him the David N. Kershaw Award for outstanding research achievements and in 1987 he received the American Political Science Association's Leonard D. White Award in public administration. In 1991–1994 he chaired the latter association's standing committee on professional ethics.

PART I

The American System

*In framing a government which is to be
administered by men over men,
the great difficulty lies in this:
You must first enable the government
to control the governed; and in the
next place oblige it to control itself.*

FEDERALIST NO. 51

The Study of American Government

Enduring Questions

1. If average citizens are fit to select their leaders (representative democracy), how can they be unfit to govern themselves directly (direct democracy)?

2. What is political power, and how is it actually distributed in America?

There are two questions about politics: Who governs? To what ends?

We want to know the answer to the first question because we believe that those who rule—their personalities and beliefs, their virtues and vices—will affect what they do to and for us. Many people think they already know the answer to the question, and they are prepared to talk and vote on that basis. That is their right, and the opinions they express may be correct. But they may also be wrong. Indeed, many of these opinions *must* be wrong because they are in conflict. When asked, "Who governs?" some people will say "the unions" and some will say "big business"; others will say "the politicians," "the people," or "the special interests." Still others will say "Wall Street," "the military," "crackpot liberals," "the media," "the bureaucrats," or "white males." Not all these answers can be correct—at least not all of the time.

The answer to the second question is important because it tells us how government affects our lives. We want to know not only who governs, but what difference it makes who governs. In our day-to-day lives we may not think government makes much

Why Government Matters: A Top Ten List

Based on a survey of 450 history and political science professors and an analysis of over 500 public statutes, here is one list of the government's top ten post-1950 achievements.

10. Promoted financial security in retirement
9. Reduced the federal budget deficit
8. Increased access to health care for older Americans
7. Strengthened the nation's highway system
6. Ensured safe food and drinking water
5. Reduced workplace discrimination
4. Reduced disease
3. Promoted equal access to public accommodations
2. Expanded the right to vote
1. Rebuilt Europe after World War II

As you read this book (especially Chapters 15 through 21 on public policy issues) and study American government, ponder what might be on the top ten list for the first quarter of the twenty-first century.

Source: Adapted from Paul C. Light, "Government's Greatest Achievements of the Past Half Century," Reform Watch Brief #2, Brookings Institution, Washington, D.C., November 2000. Reprinted by permission of the Brookings Institution.

---

difference at all. In one sense that is right, because our most pressing personal concerns—work, play, love, family, health—are essentially private matters on which government touches but slightly. But in a larger and longer perspective government makes a substantial difference. Consider: in 1935, 96 percent of all American families paid no federal income tax, and for the 4 percent or so who did pay, the average rate was only about 4 percent of their incomes. Today almost all families pay federal income taxes, and the average rate is 21 percent of their incomes. Through laws that have been enacted since the 1930s, the federal government has taken charge of an enormous amount of the nation's income, with results that are still being debated. Or consider: in 1960, in many parts of the country, African Americans could ride only in the backs of buses, had to use washrooms and drinking fountains that were labeled "colored," and could not be served in most public restaurants. Such restrictions have been almost eliminated, in large part because of decisions by the federal government.

It is important to bear in mind that we wish to answer two different questions, and not two versions of the same question. You cannot always predict what goals government will establish knowing only who governs, nor can you always tell who governs by knowing what activities government undertakes. Most people holding national political office are middle-class, middle-aged, white Protestant males, but we cannot then conclude that the government will adopt only policies that are to the narrow advantage of the middle class, the middle-aged, whites, Protestants, or men. If we thought that, we would be at a loss to explain why the rich are taxed more heavily than the poor, why the War on Poverty was declared, why constitutional amendments giving rights to African Americans and women passed Congress by large majorities, or why Catholics and Jews have been appointed to so many important governmental posts.

This book is chiefly devoted to answering the question, Who governs? It is written in the belief that this question cannot be answered without looking at how government makes—or fails to make—decisions about a large variety of concrete issues. Thus in this book we shall inspect government policies to see what individuals, groups, and institutions seem to exert the greatest power in the continuous struggle to define the purposes of government. We shall see that power and purpose are inextricably intertwined.

What Is Political Power?

By **power** we mean the ability of one person to get another person to act in accordance with the first person's intentions. Sometimes an exercise of power is obvious, as when the president tells the air force that it can or cannot build the B-1 bomber. More often power is exercised in subtle ways that may not be evident even to the participants, as when the president's economic advisers persuade him to impose or lift wage and price controls. The advisers may not think they are using power—after all, they are the president's subordinates—but if the president acts in accord with their intentions as a result of their arguments, they have used power.

Power is found in all human relationships, but we shall be concerned here only with power as it is used to affect who will hold government office and how government will behave. This fails to take into account many important things. If a corporation closes a factory in a small town where it was the major employer, it is using power in ways that affect deeply the lives of people. When a university refuses to admit a student or a medical society refuses to license a would-be physician, it is also using power. But to explain how all these things happen would be tantamount to explaining how society as a whole, and in all its particulars, operates. We limit our view here to government, and chiefly to the American federal government. However, we shall repeatedly pay special attention to how things once thought to be "private" matters become "public"—that is, how they manage to become objects of governmental action. Indeed, one of the most striking transformations of American politics has been the extent to which, in recent decades, almost every aspect of human life has found its way onto the governmental agenda. In the 1950s the federal government would have displayed no interest in a factory closing its doors, a university refusing an applicant, or a profession not accrediting a member. Now government actions can and do affect all these things.

People who exercise political power may or may not have the authority to do so. By **authority** we mean the right to use power. The exercise of rightful power—that is, of authority—is ordinarily easier than the exercise of power that is not supported by any persuasive claim of right. We accept decisions, often without question, if they are made by people who we believe have the right to make them; we may bow to naked power because we cannot resist it, but by our recalcitrance or our resentment we put the users of naked power to greater trouble than the wielders of authority. In this book we will on occasion speak of "formal authority." By this we mean that the right to exercise power is vested in a governmental office. A president, a senator, and a federal judge have formal authority to take certain actions.

What makes power rightful varies from time to time and from country to country. In the United

The terrorist attack on 9/11 led to tougher security arrangements at American airports. Most Americans are willing to live with these new rules.

States we usually say that a person has political authority if his or her right to act in a certain way is conferred by a law or by a state or national constitution. But what makes a law or constitution a source of right? That is the question of **legitimacy**. In the United States the Constitution today is widely, if not unanimously, accepted as a source of legitimate authority, but that was not always the case.

Much of American political history has been a struggle over what constitutes legitimate authority. The Constitutional Convention in 1787 was an effort to see whether a new, more powerful federal government could be made legitimate; the succeeding administrations of George Washington, John Adams, and Thomas Jefferson were in large measure preoccupied with disputes over the kinds of decisions that were legitimate for the federal government to make. The Civil War was a bloody struggle over the legitimacy of the federal union; the New Deal of Franklin Roosevelt was hotly debated by those who disagreed over whether it was legitimate for the federal government to intervene deeply in the economy.

In the United States today no government at any level would be considered legitimate if it were not in some sense democratic. That was not always the prevailing view, however; at one time people disagreed over whether democracy itself was a good idea. In 1787 Alexander Hamilton worried that the new government he helped create might be too democratic, while George Mason, who refused to sign the Constitution, worried that it was not democratic

Encouraging democracy in other countries is often a tough struggle, as when United Nations forces safeguard voting in Sierra Leone.

enough. Today virtually everyone believes that "democratic government" is the only proper kind. Most people probably believe that our existing government is democratic; and a few believe that other institutions of public life—schools, universities, corporations, trade unions, churches—should be run on democratic principles if they are to be legitimate. We shall not discuss the question of whether democracy is the best way of governing all institutions. Rather we shall consider the different meanings that have been attached to the word *democratic* and which, if any, best describes the government of the United States.

What Is Democracy?

Democracy is a word with at least two different meanings. First, the term *democracy* is used to describe those regimes that come as close as possible to Aristotle's definition—the "rule of the many."[1] A government is democratic if all, or most, of its citizens participate directly in either holding office or making policy. This is often called **direct or participatory democracy.** In Aristotle's time—Greece in the fourth century B.C.—such a government was possible. The Greek city-state, or *polis,* was quite small, and within it citizenship was extended to all free adult male property holders. (Slaves, women, minors, and those without property were excluded from participation in government.) In more recent times the New England town meeting approximates

the Aristotelian ideal. In such a meeting the adult citizens of a community gather once or twice a year to vote directly on all major issues and expenditures of the town. As towns have become larger and issues more complicated, many town governments have abandoned the pure town meeting in favor of either the representative town meeting (in which a large number of elected representatives, perhaps two or three hundred, meet to vote on town affairs) or representative government (in which a small number of elected city councillors make decisions).

The second definition of democracy is the principle of governance of most nations that are called democratic. It was most concisely stated by the economist Joseph Schumpeter: "The democratic method is that institutional arrangement for arriving at political decisions in which individuals [that is, leaders] acquire the power to decide by means of a competitive struggle for the people's vote."[2] Sometimes this method is called, approvingly, **representative democracy;** at other times it is referred to, disapprovingly, as the elitist theory of democracy. It is justified by one or both of two arguments: First, it is impractical, owing to limits of time, information, energy, interest, and expertise, for the people to decide on public policy, but it is not impractical to expect them to make reasonable choices among competing leadership groups. Second, some people (including, as we shall see in the next chapter, many of the Framers of the Constitution) believe that direct democracy is likely to lead to bad decisions, because people often decide large issues on the basis of fleeting passions and in response to popular demagogues. This concern about direct democracy persists today, as can be seen from the statements of leaders who do not like what voters have decided. For example, in 2000 voters in Michigan overwhelmingly rejected a referendum that would have increased public funding for private schools. Politicians who opposed the defeated referendum spoke approvingly of the "will of the people," but politicians who favored it spoke disdainfully of "mass misunderstanding."

Direct Versus Representative Democracy: Which Is Best?

Whenever the word *democracy* is used alone in this book, it will have the meaning Schumpeter gave it.

Can a Democracy Fight a War Against Terrorists?

Americans felt powerfully connected to their fellow citizens in the immediate aftermath of 9/11.

On September 11, 2001, a date that will forever more be referred to as 9/11, war came to the United States when terrorists crashed four hijacked airliners, filled with passengers, into the two towers of the World Trade Center in New York City, into the Pentagon in Washington, D.C., and into some empty land in Pennsylvania. About three thousand people were killed.

How can a democratic nation respond to a war waged, not by an enemy nation, but by a loose collection of terrorists with cells in many parts of the world? America's new war against terrorism is much more difficult to fight than the one against Nazi Germany and the Japanese warlords in 1941.

- How can we reorganize the military so that it can respond swiftly and effectively against small targets?
- Is it constitutional to try captured terrorists in military tribunals?
- How much new law enforcement authority should be given to police and investigative agencies?
- Should America invade nations that support terrorists?

In the years ahead, these questions will raise profound challenges for American democracy.

As we shall see in the next chapter, the men who wrote the Constitution did not use the word *democracy* in that document. They wrote instead of a "republican form of government," but by that they meant what we call "representative democracy." Whenever we refer to that form of democracy involving the direct participation of all or most citizens, we shall use the term *direct* or *participatory* democracy.

For representative government to work, there must, of course, be an opportunity for genuine leadership competition. This requires in turn that individuals and parties be able to run for office, that communication (through speeches or the press, and in meetings) be free, and that the voters perceive that a meaningful choice exists. Many questions still remain to be answered. For instance: How many offices should be elective and how many appointive?

How many candidates or parties can exist before the choices become hopelessly confused? Where will the money come from to finance electoral campaigns? There is more than one answer to such questions. In some European democracies, for example, very few offices—often just those in the national or local legislature—are elective, and much of the money for campaigning for these offices comes from the government. In the United States many offices—executive and judicial as well as legislative—are elective, and most of the money the candidates use for campaigning comes from industry, labor unions, and private individuals.

Some people have argued that the virtues of direct or participatory democracy can and should be reclaimed even in a modern, complex society. This can be done either by allowing individual neighborhoods in big cities to govern themselves (community control) or by requiring those affected by some government program to participate in its formulation (citizen participation). In many states a measure of direct democracy exists when voters can decide on referendum issues—that is, policy choices that appear on the ballot. The proponents of direct democracy defend it as the only way to ensure that the "will of the people" prevails.

The Framers of the Constitution did not think that the "will of the people" was synonymous with the "common interest" or the "public good." They strongly favored representative democracy over direct democracy. They believed that government should mediate, not mirror, popular views, and that elected officials should represent, not register, majority sentiments. They supposed that most citizens did not have the time, information, interest, and expertise to make reasonable choices among competing policy positions. They suspected that even highly educated people could be manipulated by demagogic leaders who played on their fears and prejudices. They granted that representative democracy often proceeds slowly and prevents sweeping changes in policy, but they cautioned that a government capable of doing great good quickly also can do great harm quickly. They agreed that majority opinion should figure in the enactment of many or most government policies, but they insisted that the protection of civil rights and civil liberties—the right to a fair trial; the freedom of speech, press, and religion; or the right to vote itself—ought never to hinge on a popular vote. Above all, they embraced representative democracy because they saw it as a way of minimizing the chances that power would be abused either by a tyrannical popular majority or by self-serving officeholders.

How Is Power Distributed in a Democracy?

Representative democracy is any system of government in which leaders are authorized to make decisions by winning a competitive struggle for the popular vote. It is obvious then that very different sets of hands can control political power, depending on what kinds of people can become leaders, how the struggle for votes is carried on, how much freedom to act is given to those who win the struggle, and

what other sorts of influence (besides the desire for popular approval) affect the leaders' actions.

In some cases the leaders will be so sharply constrained by what most people want that the actions of officeholders will follow the preferences of citizens very closely. We shall call such cases examples of *majoritarian politics.* In this case elected officials are the delegates of the people, acting as the people (or a majority of them) would act were the matter put to a popular vote. The issues handled in a majoritarian fashion can be only those that are sufficiently important to command the attention of most citizens, sufficiently clear to elicit an informed opinion from citizens, and sufficiently feasible to address so that what citizens want done can in fact be done.

When circumstances do not permit majoritarian decision-making, then some group of officials will have to act without knowing (and perhaps without caring) exactly what people want. Indeed, even on issues that do evoke a clear opinion from a majority of citizens, the shaping of the details of a policy will reflect the views of those people who are sufficiently motivated to go to the trouble of becoming active participants in policy-making. These active participants usually will be a small, and probably an unrepresentative, minority. Thus the actual distribution of political power, even in a democracy, will depend importantly on the composition of the political elites who are actually involved in the struggles over policy. By **elite** we mean an identifiable group of persons who possess a disproportionate share of some valued resource—in this case, political power.

Four Theories of Elite Influence

At least four theories purport to describe and explain the actions of political elites. One theory is associated with the writings of Karl Marx. To **Marxists**—or at least to some of them, since not all Marxists agree—government, whatever its outward form, is merely a reflection of underlying economic forces, primarily the pattern of ownership of the means of production. All societies, they claim, are divided into classes on the basis of the relationships of people to the economy—capitalists (the bourgeoisie), workers, farmers, intellectuals. In modern society two major classes contend for power—capitalists and workers. Whichever class dominates the economy also controls the government, which is nothing more than a piece of machinery designed to express and give legal effect to underlying class interests. In the United

Karl Marx (left, 1818–1883), a German philosopher and radical political leader, was the founder of modern socialist thought. Max Weber (right, 1864–1920), a German scholar, was a founder of sociology.

States the government "is but a committee for managing the common affairs of the whole bourgeoisie."[3]

A second theory, closely related to the first, argues that a nongovernmental elite makes most of the major decisions but that this elite is not composed exclusively, or even primarily, of corporate leaders. C. Wright Mills, an American sociologist, expresses this view in his book *The Power Elite.*[4] To him the most important policies are set by a loose coalition of three groups—corporate leaders, top military officers, and a handful of key political leaders. Different people have different versions of the "power elite" theory. Some would add to the triumvirate listed by Mills the leaders of the major communications media; others would add major labor leaders or the heads of various special-interest groups. The essential argument is the same, however: Government is dominated by a few top leaders, most of whom are outside the government and enjoy great advantages in wealth, status, or organizational position. They act in concert, and the policies they make serve the interests of the elite.

A third theory directs attention to the appointed officials—the **bureaucrats**—who operate government agencies from day to day. Max Weber, a German historian and sociologist who wrote in the early years of last century, criticized the Marxist position because it assigned exclusive significance to economic power. Weber thought Marx had neglected the dominant social and political fact of modern times—that all institutions, governmental and nongovernmental, have fallen under the control of large bureaucracies whose expertise and specialized competence are essential to the management of contemporary affairs. Capitalists or workers may come to power, but the government agencies they create will be dominated by those who operate them on a daily basis. This dominance would have advantages, Weber thought, because decisions would be made more rationally; but it would also have disadvantages, because the political power of the bureaucrats would become "overtowering."[5]

A fourth answer has no single intellectual parent but can be described loosely as the **pluralist** view.

Political resources, such as money, prestige, expertise, organizational position, and access to the mass media, are so widely scattered in our society and in the hands of such a variety of persons that no single elite has anything like a monopoly on them. Furthermore, there are so many governmental institutions in which power may be exercised—city, state, and federal governments and, within these, the offices of mayors, managers, legislators, governors, presidents, judges, bureaucrats—that no single group, even if it had many political resources, could dominate most, or even much, of the political process. Policies are the outcome of a complex pattern of political haggling, innumerable compromises, and shifting alliances.[6] Pluralists do not argue that political resources are distributed equally—that would be tantamount to saying that all decisions are made on a majoritarian basis. They believe that political resources are sufficiently divided among such different kinds of elites (business people, politicians, union leaders, journalists, bureaucrats, professors, environmentalists, lawyers, and whomever else) that all, or almost all, relevant interests have a chance to affect the outcome of decisions. Not only are the elites divided, they are responsive to their followers' interests, and thus they provide representation to almost all citizens affected by a policy.

Beyond Self-Interest

Contemplating these contending theories may lead some people to the cynical conclusion that, whichever theory is correct, politics is a self-seeking enterprise in which everybody is out for personal gain. Though there is surely plenty of self-interest among political elites (at least as much as there is among college students!), it does not necessarily follow that the resulting policies will be wholly self-serving. For one thing, a policy may be good or bad independent of the motives of the person who decided it, just as a product sold on the market may be useful or useless regardless of the profit-seeking or wage-seeking motives of those who produced it. For another thing, the self-interest of individuals is often an incomplete guide to their actions. People must frequently choose between two courses of action, neither of which has an obvious "payoff" to them. We caution against the cynical explanation of politics that Americans seem especially prone to adopt. Alexis de Tocqueville, the French author of a perceptive account of American life and politics in the early nineteenth century, noticed this trait among us.

Americans . . . are fond of explaining almost all the actions of their lives by the principle of self-interest rightly understood. . . . In this respect I think they frequently fail to do themselves justice; for in the United States as well as elsewhere people are sometimes seen to give way to those disinterested and spontaneous impulses that are natural to man; but the Americans seldom admit that they yield to emotions of this kind; they are more anxious to do honor to their philosophy than to themselves.[7]

The belief that people will usually act on the basis of their self-interest, narrowly defined, is a theory to be tested, not an assumption to be made. Sometimes, as happened in New York City on September 11, 2001, elected officials, government workers, and average citizens behave in ways that plainly transcend personal or professional self-interest. There are countless other far less dramatic but still telling examples of people acting publicly in ways that seem anything but self-interested. For example, in the 1960s leaders of the AFL-CIO in Washington were among the most influential forces lobbying Congress for the passage of certain civil rights bills. Yet at the time they did this, the leaders did not stand to benefit either personally (they were almost all white) or organizationally (rank-and-file labor union members were not enthusiastic about such measures).[8] Another example: In the late 1970s many employees of the Civil Aeronautics Board worked hard to have their agency abolished, even though this meant that they would lose their jobs. To understand why they took these positions, it is not enough to know their incomes or their jobs; one must also know something about their attitudes, their allies, and the temper of the times. In short, political preferences cannot invariably be predicted simply by knowing economic or organizational position.

Yet another reason to resist interpreting American politics as if it were always and everywhere driven by narrowly self-interested individuals and groups is that many of the most important political happenings in U.S. history—the revolutionary movement of the 1770s and 1780s, the battle for civil rights in the 1950s and 1960s, to name just two—were led against long odds by people who risked much knowing that they might not succeed and suspecting that, even if they did succeed, generations might pass before their efforts truly benefited anyone. As we shall see, self-

New York City Mayor Rudy Giuliani discusses the fallen World Trade Center towers with President George Bush, Senator Charles Schumer, and New York Fire Commissioner Thomas Van Essen.

interest figures mightily in politics, but so do ideas about the common good and public-spirited behavior.

Political Change

The question of who governs will be answered differently at different times. Circumstances change, as does our knowledge about politics. As we shall see in Part III, the presidency and Congress in the second half of the nineteenth century were organized rather differently from how they are today. Throughout this book we shall make frequent reference to the historical evolution of institutions and policies. We shall do this partly because what government does today is powerfully influenced by what it did yesterday, and partly because the evolution of our institutions and policies has not stopped but is continuing. If we get some sense of how the past has shaped the government, we may better understand what we see today and are likely to see tomorrow.

When we view American government from the perspective of the past, we will find it hard to accept as generally true any simple, mechanistic theory of politics. Economic interests, powerful elites, entrenched bureaucrats, and competing pressure groups have all played a part in shaping our policies, but the great shifts in the direction of that policy respond to changing *beliefs* about what government is supposed to do.

In the 1920s it was widely assumed that the federal government would play a small role in our lives. From the 1930s through the 1970s it was generally believed that the federal government would try to solve whatever social or economic problem existed. From 1981 through 1988 the administration of Ronald Reagan sought to reverse that assumption and to cut back on the taxes Washington levied, the money it spent, and the regulations it imposed. It is clear that no simple theory of politics is likely to explain both the growth of federal power after 1932 and the effort to cut back on that power starting in 1981. Every student of politics sooner or later learns that the hardest things to explain are usually the most important ones.

Take the case of foreign affairs. During certain periods in our history we have taken an active interest in the outside world—at the time the nation was founded, when France and England seemed to have it in their power to determine whether or not America would survive as a nation; in the 1840s, when we sought to expand the nation into areas where Mexico and Canada had claims; in the late 1890s, when many leaders believed we had an obligation to acquire an overseas empire in the Caribbean and the Pacific; and in the period from the 1940s to the 1960s, when we openly accepted the role of the world's police officer. At other times America has looked inward, spurning opportunities for expansion and virtually ignoring events that in other periods would have been a cause for war, or at least mobilization. Today, America seems to be looking outward once again, spurred, on the one side, by unprecedented terrorist attacks against the country and, on the other side, by historic opportunities to make new friends with old foreign foes.

Deep-seated beliefs, major economic developments, and widely shared (or competing) opinions about what constitutes the dominant political problem of the time shape the nature of day-to-day political conflict. What this means is that, in any broad historical or comparative perspective, politics is not just about "who gets what," though that is part of the story. It is about how people, or elites claiming to speak for people, define the public interest. Lest one think that such definitions are mere window dressing, signifying nothing of importance, bear in mind that on occasion men and women have been prepared to fight and die for one definition or another. Suppose you had been alive in 1861. Do you think you would have viewed slavery as a matter of gains and losses, costs and benefits, winners and losers? Some people did. Or do you think you would have been willing to fight to abolish or preserve it? Many others did just that. The differences in these ways of thinking about such an issue are at least as important as how institutions are organized or elections conducted.

Finding Out Who Governs

Ideally political scientists ought to be able to give clear answers, amply supported by evidence, to the questions, How is political power distributed? And to what purposes will it be used under various circumstances? In reality they can (at best) give partial, contingent, and controversial answers. The reason is to be found in the nature of our subject. Unlike economists, who assume that people have more or less stable preferences and can compare ways of satisfying those preferences by looking at the relative prices of various goods and services, political scientists are interested in how preferences are formed, especially for those kinds of services, such as national defense or pollution control, that cannot be evaluated chiefly in terms of monetary costs.

Understanding preferences is vital to understanding power. Who did what in government is not hard to find out, but who wielded power—that is, who made a difference in the outcome and for what reason—is much harder to discover. *Power* is a word that conjures up images of deals, bribes, power plays, and arm-twisting. In fact, most power exists because of shared understanding, common friendships, communal or organizational loyalties, and different degrees of prestige. These are hard to identify and almost impossible to quantify.

Nor can the distribution of political power be inferred simply by knowing what laws are on the books or what administrative actions have been taken. The enactment of a consumer protection law does not mean that consumers are powerful, any more than the absence of such a law means that corporations are powerful. The passage of such a law could reflect an aroused public opinion, the lobbying of a small group claiming to speak for consumers, the ambitions of a senator, or the intrigues of one business firm seeking to gain a competitive advantage over another. A close analysis of what the law entails and how it was passed and administered is necessary before much of anything can be said.

This book will avoid sweeping claims that we have an "imperial" presidency (or an impotent one), an "obstructionist" Congress (or an innovative one), or "captured" regulatory agencies. Such labels do an injustice to the different roles that presidents, members of Congress, and administrators play in different kinds of issues and in different historical periods.

The view taken in this book is that judgements about institutions and interests can be made only after one has seen how they behave on a variety of important issues or potential issues, such as economic policy, the regulation of business, social welfare,

Legal and Policy Experts Call for a Ban on Ballot Initiatives

December 11
SACRAMENTO, CA

A report released yesterday and signed by more than 100 law and public policy professors statewide urges that the state's constitution be amended to ban legislation by initiative. The initiative allows state voters to place legislative measures directly on the ballot by getting enough signatures. The initiative "has led to disastrous policy decisions on taxes, crime, and other issues," the report declared . . .

MEMORANDUM

To: Governor Steve Finore
From: Edward Heron, chief policy adviser
Subject: Initiative Repeal

You have supported several successful initiatives (life imprisonment for thrice-convicted violent felons, property tax limits), but you have never publicly stated a view on the initiative itself, and the repeal proposal will probably surface during tomorrow's press briefing.

Arguments for a ban:

1. Ours is a representative, not a direct, democracy in which voters elect leaders and elected leaders make policy decisions subject to review by the courts.
2. Voters are often neither rational nor respectful of constitutional rights. For example, many people demand both lower taxes and more government services, and polls find that most voters would prohibit people with certain views from speaking and deprive all persons accused of a violent crime from getting out on bail while awaiting trial.
3. Over the past 100 years nearly 800 statewide ballot initiatives have been passed in 24 states, including 35 in 1998 alone. Rather than giving power to the people, special-interest groups have spent billions of dollars manipulating voters to pass initiatives that enrich or benefit them, not the public at large.

Arguments against a ban:

1. When elected officials fail to respond to persistent public majorities favoring tougher crime measures, lower property taxes, and other popular concerns, direct democracy via the initiative is legitimate, and the courts can still review the law.
2. More Americans than ever have college degrees and easy access to information about public affairs. Studies find that most average citizens are able to figure out which candidates, parties, or advocacy groups come closest to supporting their own economic interests and personal values.
3. All told, the 24 states that passed 35 laws by initiative in 1998 also passed more than 14,000 laws by the regular legislative process (out of more than 70,000 bills they considered). Studies find that special-interest groups are severely limited in their ability to pass new laws by initiative, while citizens' groups with broad-based public support are behind most initiatives that pass.

Your decision:
Favor ban _____ Oppose ban _____

civil rights and liberties, and foreign and military affairs. The policies adopted or blocked, the groups heeded or ignored, the values embraced or rejected—these constitute the raw material out of which one can fashion an answer to the central questions we have asked: Who governs? and To what ends?

The way in which our institutions of government handle social welfare, for example, differs from the way other democratic nations handle it, and it differs as well from the way our own institutions once treated it. The description of our institutions in Part III will therefore include not only an account of how they work today but also a brief historical background on their workings and a comparison with similar institutions in other countries. There is a tendency to assume that how we do things today is the only way they could possibly be done. In fact, there are other ways to operate a government based on some measure of popular rule. History, tradition, and belief weigh heavily on all that we do.

Although political change is not always accompanied by changes in public laws, the policy process is arguably one of the best barometers of changes in who governs. In Chapter 15, we offer a way of classifying and explaining the politics of different policy issues. The model we present there has been developed, refined, and tested over more than two decades (longer than most of our readers have been alive!). Our own students and others have valued it mainly because, they have found, it helps to answer such questions about who governs: How do political issues get on the public agenda in the first place? How, for example, did sexual harassment, which was hardly ever discussed or debated by Congress, burst onto the public agenda? Once on the agenda, how does the politics of issues like income security for older Americans—for example, the politics of Social Security, a program that has been on the federal books since 1935 (see Chapter 17)—change over time? And if, today, one cares about expanding civil liberties (see Chapter 18) or protecting civil rights (see Chapter 19), what political obstacles and opportunities are you likely to face, and what role are public opinion, organized interest groups, the media, the courts, political parties, and other institutions likely to play in frustrating or fostering your particular policy preferences, whatever they might be?

Peek ahead, if you wish, to the book's policy chapters, but understand that the place to begin a search for how power is distributed in national politics and what purposes that power serves is with the founding of the federal government in 1787: the Constitutional Convention and the events leading up to it. Though the decisions of that time were not made by philosophers or professors, the practical men who made them had a philosophic and professorial cast of mind, and thus they left behind a fairly explicit account of what values they sought to protect and what arrangements they thought ought to be made for the allocation of political power.

Summary

There are two major questions about politics: Who governs? To what ends? This book focuses mainly on answering the first.

Four answers have traditionally been given to the question of who governs.

- The *Marxist*—those who control the economic system will control the political one.
- The *elitist*—a few top leaders, not all of them drawn from business, make the key decisions without reference to popular desires.
- The *bureaucratic*—appointed civil servants run things.
- The *pluralist*—competition among affected interests shapes public policy.

To choose among these theories or to devise new ones requires more than describing governmental institutions and processes. In addition one must examine the kinds of issues that do (or do not) get taken up by the political system and how that system resolves them.

The distinction between different types of democracies is important. The Framers of the Constitution intended that America be a representative democracy in which the power to make decisions is determined by means of a free and competitive struggle for the citizens' votes.

Reconsidering the Enduring Questions

1. *If average citizens are fit to select their leaders (representing democracy), how can they be unfit to govern themselves directly (direct democracy)?*

   The Founding Fathers' case against direct democracy rests largely on three assumptions. First, direct democracy is impractical. Citizens are too numerous, and most people lack the time, information, energy, interest, and expertise to decide on public policy. Second, since most citizens are not well educated, they are highly susceptible to popular demagogues. Third, bargaining and compromise are harder to achieve in a large group of people than in a small group of representatives. That is pretty much the classical argument against direct democracy, but is it as strong today as it was in 1787? How, if at all, does wide public access to political information, including through the Internet, affect the first assumption? To what, if any, degree does the fact that more Americans than ever now attend college challenge the second assumption? Finally, how valid is the third assumption given that Congress often produces bitter disagreements among members rather than legislative actions in the public interest?

2. *What is political power, and how is it actually distributed in America?*

   Power is the ability of one person to get another person to act in accordance with the first person's intentions. Political power is used to affect who will hold office and how government will behave. Some say that political power in America is monopolized, or nearly so, by economic elites or government bureaucrats. Others insist that political resources (money, prestige, expertise, organizational position, access to the media) are normally so dispersed that no single elite has anything like a monopoly on them. It is best to avoid any such sweeping claims. American politics involves complex processes by which citizens' political preferences are formed. The distribution of political power in America cannot be inferred simply by knowing what laws are on the books or what administrative actions have been taken. Rather, the policies adopted or blocked, the groups heeded or ignored, the values embraced or rejected—in sum, who governs, and to what ends—will vary from issue to issue and over time.

Key Terms

power *p. 4*
authority *p. 5*
legitimacy *p. 5*
democracy *p. 6*

direct or participatory democracy *p. 6*
representative democracy *p. 6*

elite *p. 8*
Marxists *p. 8*
bureaucrats *p. 9*
pluralist *p. 9*

Suggested Readings

Banfield, Edward C. *Political Influence.* New York: Free Press, 1961. A method of analyzing politics—in this case, in the city of Chicago—comparable to the approach adopted in this book.

Crick, Bernard, *The American Science of Politics.* London: Routledge & Kegan Paul, 1959. A critical review of the methods of studying government and politics.

Marx, Karl, and Friedrich Engels. "The Manifesto of the Communist Party." In *The Marx-Engels Reader*, 2nd ed., edited by Robert C. Tucker. New York: Norton, 1978, 469–500. The classic statement of the Marxist view of history and politics. Should be read in conjunction with Engels, "Socialism: Utopian and Scientific," in the same collection, 683–717.

Mills, C. Wright. *The Power Elite.* New York: Oxford University Press, 1956. An argument that self-serving elites dominate American politics.

Schumpeter, Joseph A. *Capitalism, Socialism, and Democracy.* 3rd ed. New York: Harper Torchbooks, 1950, chs. 20–23. A lucid statement of the theory of representative democracy and how it differs from participatory democracy.

Truman, David B. *The Governmental Process.* 2nd ed. New York: Knopf, 1971. A pluralist interpretation of American politics.

Weber, Max. *From Max Weber: Essays in Sociology.* Translated and edited by H. H. Gerth and C. Wright Mills. London: Routledge & Kegan Paul, 1948, ch. 8. A theory of bureaucracy and its power.

The Constitution

Enduring Questions

1. What view of human nature is embodied in the Constitution?

2. Is representative democracy possible without political compromise?

3. Has the system of separate institutions sharing powers protected liberty and promoted equality as the Framers envisioned it would?

The goal of the American Revolution was liberty. It was not the first revolution with that object; it may not have been the last; but it was perhaps the clearest case of a people altering the political order violently, simply in order to protect their liberties. Subsequent revolutions had more complicated, or utterly different, objectives. The French Revolution in 1789 sought not only liberty, but "equality and fraternity." The Russian Revolution (1917) and the Chinese Revolution (culminating in 1949) chiefly sought equality and were little concerned with liberty as we understand it.

The Problem of Liberty

What the American colonists sought to protect when they signed the Declaration of Independence in 1776 were the traditional liberties to which they thought they were entitled as British subjects. These liberties included the right to bring their legal cases before truly independent judges rather than ones subordinate to the king; to be free of the burden of having British troops quartered in their homes; to engage in

17

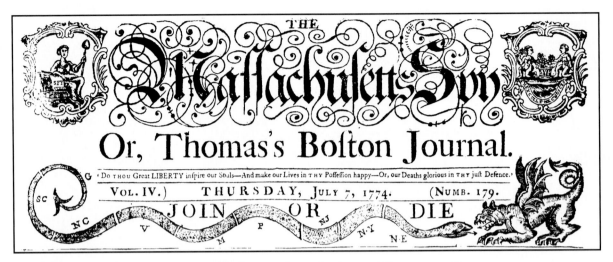

Even before the Revolutionary War, many felt that some form of union would be necessary if the rebellious colonies were to survive. In 1774, the Massachusetts Spy *portrayed the colonies as segments of a snake that must "Join or Die."*

trade without burdensome restrictions; and, of course, to pay no taxes voted by a British Parliament in which they had no direct representation. During the ten years or more of agitation and argument leading up to the War of Independence, most colonists believed that their liberties could be protected while they remained a part of the British Empire.

Slowly but surely opinion shifted. By the time war broke out in 1775, a large number of colonists (though perhaps not a majority) had reached the conclusion that the colonies would have to become independent of Great Britain if their liberties were to be assured. The colonists had many reasons for regarding independence as the only solution, but one is especially important: they no longer had confidence in the English constitution. This constitution was not a single written document but rather a collection of laws, charters, and traditional understandings that proclaimed the liberties of British subjects. Yet these liberties, in the eyes of the colonists, were regularly violated despite their constitutional protection. Clearly, then, the English constitution was an inadequate check on the abuses of political power. The revolutionary leaders sought an explanation of the insufficiency of the constitution and found it in human nature.

The Colonial Mind

"A lust for domination is more or less natural to all parties," one colonist wrote.[1] Men will seek power,

many colonists believed, because they are ambitious, greedy, and easily corrupted. John Adams denounced the "luxury, effeminacy, and venality" of English politics; Patrick Henry spoke scathingly of the "corrupt House of Commons"; and Alexander Hamilton described England as "an old, wrinkled, withered, worn-out hag."[2] This was in part flamboyant rhetoric designed to whip up enthusiasm for the conflict, but it was also deeply revealing of the colonial mind. Their belief that English politicians—and by implication, most politicians—tended to be corrupt was the colonists' explanation of why the English constitution was not an adequate guarantee of the liberty of the citizens. This opinion was to persist and, as we shall see, profoundly affect the way the Americans went about designing their own governments.

The liberties the colonists fought to protect were, they thought, widely understood. They were based not on the generosity of the king or the language of statutes but on a "higher law" embodying "natural rights" that were ordained by God, discoverable in nature and history, and essential to human progress. These rights, John Dickinson wrote, "are born with us; exist with us; and cannot be taken away from us by any human power."[3] There was general agreement that the essential rights included life, liberty, and property long before Thomas Jefferson wrote them into the Declaration of Independence. (Jefferson changed "property" to "the pursuit of happiness," but almost everybody else went on talking about property.)

The American colonists' desire to assert their liberties led in time to a deep hostility to British government, as when these New Yorkers toppled a statue of King George III, melted it down, and used the metal to make bullets.

This emphasis on property did not mean that the American Revolution was thought up by the rich and wellborn to protect their interests or that there was a struggle between property owners and the propertyless. In late-eighteenth-century America most people (except the black slaves) had property of some kind. The overwhelming majority of citizens were self-employed—as farmers or artisans—and rather few people benefited financially by gaining independence from England. Taxes were higher during and after the war than before, trade was disrupted by the conflict, and debts mounted perilously as various expedients were invented to pay for the struggle. There were, of course, war profiteers and those who tried to manipulate the currency to their own advantage, but most Americans at the time of the war saw the conflict clearly in terms of political rather than economic issues. It was a war of ideology.

Everyone recognizes the glowing language with which Jefferson set out the case for independence in the second paragraph of the Declaration:

> We hold these truths to be self-evident, that all men are created equal, that they are endowed by their Creator with certain unalienable

Rights, that among these are Life, Liberty, and the pursuit of Happiness.—That to secure these rights, Governments are instituted among Men, deriving their just powers from the consent of the governed—that whenever any Form of Government becomes destructive of these ends, it is the Right of the People to alter or to abolish it, and to institute new Government, having its foundation on such principles, and organizing its powers in such form, as to them shall seem most likely to effect their Safety and Happiness.

What almost no one recalls, but what are an essential part of the Declaration, are the next twenty-seven paragraphs, in which Jefferson listed, item by item, the specific complaints the colonists had against George III and his ministers. None of these items spoke of social or economic conditions in the colonies; all spoke instead of specific violations of political liberties. The Declaration was in essence a lawyer's brief prefaced by a stirring philosophical claim that the rights being violated were **unalienable**—that is, based on nature and Providence, and not on the whims or preferences of people. Jefferson, in his original draft, added a

North America in 1787

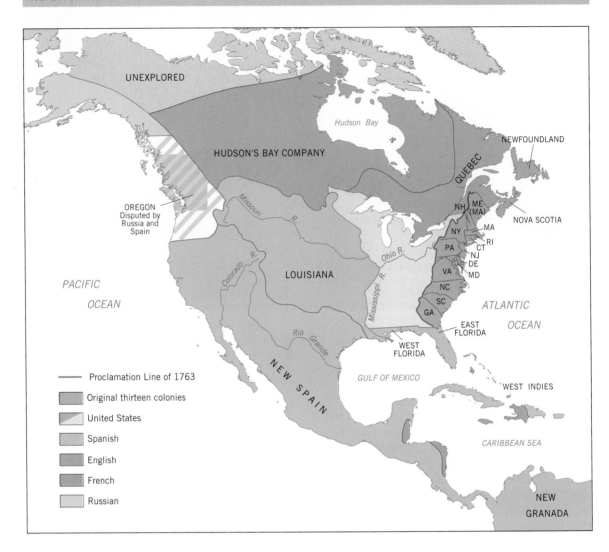

twenty-eighth complaint—that the king had allowed the slave trade to continue *and* was inciting slaves to revolt against their masters. Congress, faced with so contradictory a charge, decided to include a muted reference to slave insurrections and omit all reference to the slave trade.

The Real Revolution

The Revolution was more than the War of Independence. It began before the war, continued after it, and involved more than driving out the British army by force of arms. The *real* Revolution, as John Adams afterward explained in a letter to a friend, was the "radical change in the principles, opinions, and sentiments, and affections of the people."[4] This radical change had to do with a new vision of what could make political authority legitimate and personal liberties secure. Government by royal prerogative was rejected; instead legitimate government would require the consent of the governed. Political power could not be exercised on the basis of tradition but only as a result of a direct grant of power contained in a written constitution. Human liberty existed before government was organized, and government must respect that liberty. The legislative branch of government, in which the people were directly represented, should be superior to the executive branch.

These were indeed revolutionary ideas. No government at the time had been organized on the basis of these principles. And to the colonists such notions were not empty words but rules to be put into immediate practice. In 1776 eight states adopted written constitutions. Within a few years every former colony had adopted one except Connecticut and Rhode Island, two states that continued to rely on their colonial charters. Most state constitutions had detailed bills of rights defining personal liberties, and most placed the highest political power in the hands of elected representatives.

Written constitutions, representatives, and bills of rights are so familiar to us now that we forget how bold and unprecedented those innovations were in 1776. Indeed, many Americans did not think they would succeed: such arrangements would be either so strong that they would threaten liberty or so weak that they would permit chaos.

The eleven years that elapsed between the Declaration of Independence and the signing of the Constitution in 1787 were years of turmoil, uncertainty, and fear. George Washington had to wage a bitter, protracted war without anything resembling a strong national government to support him. The supply and financing of his army were based on a series of hasty improvisations, most badly administered and few adequately supported by the fiercely independent states. When peace came, many parts of the nation were a shambles. At least a quarter of New York City was in ruins, and many other communities were nearly devastated. Though the British lost the war, they still were powerful on the North American continent, with an army available in Canada (where many Americans loyal to Britain had fled) and a large navy at sea. Spain claimed the Mississippi River valley and occupied what are now Florida and California. Men who had left their farms to fight came back to discover themselves in debt with no money and heavy taxes. The paper money printed to finance the war was now virtually worthless.

Weaknesses of the Confederation

The thirteen states had formed only a faint semblance of a national government with which to bring order to the nation. The **Articles of Confed-**

The Articles of Confederation had made it plain that the United States was not to have a true national government but was to be governed by a compact among sovereign and independent states.

eration, which went into effect in 1781, created little more than a "league of friendship" that could not levy taxes or regulate commerce. Each state retained its sovereignty and independence, each state (regardless of size) had one vote in Congress, nine (of thirteen) votes were required to pass any measure, and the delegates who cast these votes were picked and paid for by the state legislatures. Congress did have the power to make peace, and thus it was able to ratify the treaty with England in 1783. It could coin money, but there was precious little to coin; it could appoint the key army officers, but the army was small and dependent for support on independent state militias; it was allowed to run the post office, then, as now, a thankless task that nobody else wanted. John Hancock, who in 1785 was elected to the meaningless office of "president" under the Articles, never showed up to take the job.

John Hancock was proud to have signed the Declaration of Independence but thought so little of the presidency under the Articles of Confederation that he never bothered to accept the job.

Several states claimed the unsettled lands in the West, and they occasionally pressed those claims with guns. Pennsylvania and Virginia went to war near Pittsburgh, and Vermont threatened to become part of Canada. There was no national judicial system to settle these or other claims among the states. To amend the Articles of Confederation, all thirteen states had to agree.

Many of the leaders of the Revolution, such as George Washington and Alexander Hamilton, believed that a stronger national government was essential. They lamented the disruption of commerce and travel caused by the quarrelsome states and deeply feared the possibility of foreign military intervention, with England or France playing one state off against another. A small group of men, conferring at Washington's home at Mount Vernon in 1785, decided to call a meeting to discuss trade regulation. That meeting, held at Annapolis, Maryland, in September 1786, was not well attended (no delegates arrived from New England), and so another meeting, this one in Philadelphia, was called for the following spring—in May 1787—to consider ways of remedying the defects of the Confederation.

The Constitutional Convention

The delegates assembled at Philadelphia at the **Constitutional Convention**, for what was advertised (and authorized by Congress) as a meeting to revise the Articles; they adjourned four months later having written a wholly new constitution. When they met, they were keenly aware of the problems of the confederacy but far from agreeing as to what should be done about those problems. The protection of life, liberty, and property was their objective in 1787 as it had been in 1776, but they had no accepted political theory that would tell them what kind of national government, if any, would serve that goal.

The Lessons of Experience

They had read ancient and modern political history, only to learn that nothing seemed to work. James Madison spent a good part of 1786 studying books sent to him by Thomas Jefferson, then in Paris, in hopes of finding some model for a workable American republic. He took careful notes on various confederacies in ancient Greece and on the more modern confederacy of the United Netherlands. He reviewed the history of Switzerland and Poland and the ups and downs of the Roman republic. He concluded that there was no model; as he later put it in one of the *Federalist* papers, history consists only of beacon lights "which give warning of the course to be shunned, without pointing out that which ought to be pursued."[5] The problem seemed to be that confederacies were too weak to govern and tended to collapse from internal dissension, while all stronger forms of government were so powerful as to trample the liberties of the citizens.

■ **State Constitutions**   Madison and the others did not need to consult history, or even the defects of the Articles of Confederation, for illustrations of the problem. These could be found in the government of the American states at the time. Pennsylvania and Massachusetts exemplified two aspects of the problem. The Pennsylvania constitution, adopted in 1776, created the most radically democratic of the new state regimes. All power was given to a one-house (unicameral) legislature, the Assembly, the members of which were elected annually for one-year terms. No legislator could serve more than four years. There was no governor or president, only an Executive Council that had few powers. Thomas

Paine, whose pamphlets had helped precipitate the break with England, thought the Pennsylvania constitution was the best in America, and in France philosophers hailed it as the very embodiment of the principle of rule by the people. Though popular in France, it was a good deal less popular in Philadelphia. The Assembly disfranchised the Quakers, persecuted conscientious objectors to the war, ignored the requirement of trial by juries, and manipulated the judiciary.[6] To Madison and his friends the Pennsylvania constitution demonstrated how a government, though democratic, could be tyrannical as a result of concentrating all powers into one set of hands.

The Massachusetts constitution, adopted in 1780, was a good deal less democratic. There was a clear separation of powers among the various branches of government, the directly elected governor could veto acts of the legislature, and judges served for life. Both voters and elected officials had to be property owners; the governor, in fact, had to own at least £1,000 worth of property. The principal officeholders had to swear that they were Christians.

■ **Shays's Rebellion** But if the government of Pennsylvania was thought to be too strong, that of Massachusetts seemed too weak, despite its "conservative" features. In January 1787 a group of ex-Revolutionary War soldiers and officers, plagued by debts and high taxes and fearful of losing their property to creditors and tax collectors, forcibly prevented the courts in western Massachusetts from sitting. This became known as **Shays's Rebellion,** after one of the officers, Daniel Shays. The governor of Massachusetts asked the Continental Congress to send troops to suppress the rebellion, but it could not raise the money or the manpower. Then he turned to his own state militia, but discovered he did not have one. In desperation private funds were collected to hire a volunteer army, which marched on Springfield and, with the firing of a few shots, dispersed the rebels, who fled into neighboring states.

Shays's Rebellion, occurring between the aborted Annapolis and the coming Philadelphia conventions, had a powerful effect on opinion. Delegates who might have been reluctant to attend the Philadelphia meeting, especially those from New England, were galvanized by the fear that state governments were about to collapse from internal dissension. George Washington wrote a friend despairingly: "For God's sake, if they [the rebels] have *real* grievances, redress them; if they have not, employ the force of government against them at once."[7] Thomas Jefferson, living in Paris, took a more detached view: "A little rebellion now and then is a good thing," he wrote. "The tree of liberty must be refreshed from time to time with the blood of patriots and tyrants."[8] Though Jefferson's detachment might be explained by the fact that he was in Paris and not in Springfield, there were others, like Governor George Clinton of New York, who shared the view that no strong central government was required. (Whether Clinton would have agreed about the virtues of spilled blood, especially his, is another matter.)

The presiding officer at the Constitutional Convention was George Washington (1732–1799). He participated just once in the debates, but the effect of his presence was great. He was a national military hero, and it was generally expected that he would be the nation's first president.

The Framers

The Philadelphia convention attracted fifty-five delegates, only about thirty of whom participated regularly in the proceedings. One state, Rhode Island, refused to send anyone. The convention met during a miserably hot Philadelphia summer, with the delegates pledged to keep their deliberations secret. The talkative and party-loving Benjamin Franklin was often accompanied by other delegates to make sure

Shays's Rebellion in western Massachusetts in 1786–1787 stirred deep fears of anarchy in America. The ruckus was put down by a hastily assembled militia, and the rebels were eventually pardoned.

that neither wine nor his delight in telling stories would lead him to divulge delicate secrets.

Those who attended were for the most part young (Hamilton was thirty; Madison thirty-six) but experienced. Eight delegates had signed the Declaration of Independence, seven had been governors, thirty-four were lawyers and reasonably well-to-do, a few were wealthy. They were not "intellectuals," but men of practical affairs. Thirty-nine had served in the ineffectual Congress of the Confederation; a third were veterans of the Continental Army.

Some names made famous by the Revolution were conspicuously absent. Thomas Jefferson and John Adams were serving as ministers abroad; Samuel Adams was ill; Patrick Henry was chosen to attend but refused, commenting that he "smelled a rat in Philadelphia, tending toward monarchy."

The convention produced not a revision of the Articles of Confederation, as it had been authorized to do, but instead a wholly new written constitution creating a true national government unlike any that had existed before. That document is today the world's oldest written national constitu-

tion. Those who wrote it were neither saints nor schemers, and the deliberations were not always lofty or philosophical—much hard bargaining, not a little confusion, and the accidents of personality and time helped shape the final product. The delegates were split on many issues—what powers should be given to a central government, how the states should be represented, what was to be done about slavery, the role of the people—each of which was resolved by a compromise. The speeches of the delegates (known to us from the detailed notes kept by Madison) did not explicitly draw on political philosophy or quote from the writings of philosophers. Everybody present was quite familiar with the traditional arguments and, on the whole, well read in history. But though the leading political philosophers were only rarely mentioned, the debate was profoundly influenced by philosophical beliefs, some formed by the revolutionary experience and others by the eleven-year attempt at self-government.

From the debates leading up to the Revolution, the delegates had drawn a commitment to liberty, which, despite the abuses sometimes committed in its name, they continued to share. Their defense of liberty as a natural right was derived from the writings of the English philosopher John Locke and based on his view that such rights are discoverable by reason. In a "state of nature," Locke argued, all men cherish and seek to protect their life, liberty, and property. But in a state of nature—that is, a society without a government—the strong can use their liberty to deprive the weak of theirs. The instinct for self-preservation leads people to want a government that will prevent this exploitation. But if the government is not itself to deprive its subjects of their liberty, it must be limited. The chief limitation on it, he said, should derive from the fact that it is created, and governs, by the consent of the governed. People will not agree to be ruled by a government that threatens their liberty; therefore the government to which they freely choose to submit themselves will be a limited government designed to protect liberty.

The Pennsylvania experience as well as the history of British government led the Framers to doubt whether popular consent alone would be a sufficient guarantor of liberty. A popular government may prove too weak (as in Massachusetts) to prevent one faction from abusing another, or a popular majority can be tyrannical (as in Pennsylvania). In fact the tyranny of the majority can be an even graver threat than rule by the few. In the former case there may be no defenses for the individual—one lone person cannot count on the succor of public opinion or the possibility of popular revolt.

The problem, then, was a delicate one: how to devise a government strong enough to preserve order but not so strong that it would threaten liberty. The answer, the delegates believed, was not "democracy" as it was then understood. To many conservatives in the late eighteenth century, democracy meant mob rule—it meant, in short, Shays's Rebellion (or, if they had been candid about it, the Boston Tea Party). On the other hand, *aristocracy*—the rule of the few—was no solution, since the few were likely to be self-seeking. Madison, writing later in the *Federalist* papers, put the problem this way:

> If men were angels, no government would be necessary. If angels were to govern men, neither external nor internal controls on government would be necessary. In framing a govern-

ment which is to be administered by men over men, the great difficulty lies in this: you must first enable the government to control the governed; and in the next place oblige it to control itself.[9]

Striking this balance could not be done, Madison believed, simply by writing a constitution that set limits on what government could do. The example of British rule over the colonies proved that laws and customs were inadequate checks on political power. As he expressed it, "A mere demarcation on parchment of the constitutional limits [of government] is not a sufficient guard against those encroachments which lead to a tyrannical concentration of all the powers of government in the same hands."[10]

The Challenge

The resolution of political issues, great and small, often depends crucially on how the central question is phrased. The delegates came to Philadelphia in general agreement that there were defects in the Articles of Confederation that ought to be remedied. Had they, after convening, decided to make their business that of listing these defects and debating alternative remedies for them, the document that emerged would in all likelihood have been very different from what in fact was adopted. But immediately after the convention had organized itself and chosen Washington to be its presiding officer, the Virginia delegation, led by Governor Edmund Randolph but relying heavily on the draftsmanship of James Madison, presented to the convention a comprehensive plan for a wholly new national government. The plan quickly became the major item of business of the meeting; it, and little else, was debated for the next two weeks.

The Virginia Plan

When the convention decided to make the Virginia Plan its agenda, it had fundamentally altered the nature of its task. The business at hand was not to be the Articles and their defects, but rather how one should go about designing a true national government. The Virginia Plan called for a strong national union organized into three governmental branches—the legislative, executive, and judicial. The legislature was to be composed of two houses, the first elected directly by the people and the second chosen by the first house from among the people nominated by state legislatures. The executive was to be chosen by the national legislature, as were members of a national judiciary. The executive and some members of the judiciary were to constitute a "council of revision" that could veto acts of the legislature; that veto, in turn, could be overridden by the legislature. There were other interesting details, but the key features of the Virginia Plan were two: (1) a national legislature would have supreme powers on all matters on which the separate states were not competent to act, as well as the power to veto any and all state laws, and (2) at least one house of the legislature would be elected directly by the people.

The New Jersey Plan

As the debate went on, the representatives of New Jersey and other small states became increasingly worried that the convention was going to write a constitution in which the states would be represented in both houses of Congress on the basis of population. If this happened, the smaller states feared they would always be outvoted by the larger ones, and so, with William Paterson of New Jersey as their spokesman, they introduced a new plan. The New Jersey Plan proposed to amend, not replace, the old Articles of Confederation. It enhanced the power of the national government (though not as much as the Virginia Plan), but it did so in a way that left the states' representation in Congress unchanged from the Articles—each state would have one vote. Thus not only would the interests of the small states be protected, but Congress itself would remain to a substantial degree the creature of state governments.

If the New Jersey resolutions had been presented first and taken up as the major item of business, it is quite possible that they would have become the framework for the document that finally emerged. But they were not. Offered after the convention had been discussing the Virginia Plan for two weeks, the resolutions encountered a reception very different from what they would have received if introduced earlier. The debate had the delegates already thinking in terms of a national government that was more independent of the states, and thus it had accustomed them to proposals that, under other cir-

Independence Hall in Philadelphia, where the Declaration of Independence and the Constitution were signed.

cumstances, might have seemed quite radical. On June 19 the first decisive vote of the convention was taken: seven states preferred the Virginia Plan, three states the New Jersey Plan, and one state was split.

With the tide running in favor of a strong national government, the supporters of the small states had to shift their strategy. They now began to focus their efforts on ensuring that the small states could not be outvoted by the larger ones in Congress. One way was to have the members of the lower house elected by the state legislatures rather than the people, with each state getting the same number of seats rather than seats proportional to its population.

The debate was long and feelings ran high, so much so that Benjamin Franklin, at eighty-one the oldest delegate present, suggested that each day's meeting begin with a prayer. It turned out that the convention could not even agree on this: Hamilton is supposed to have objected that the convention did not need "foreign aid," and others pointed out that the group had no funds with which to hire a minister. And so the argument continued.

The Compromise

Finally, a committee was appointed to meet during the Fourth of July holidays to work out a compromise, and the convention adjourned to await its report. Little is known of what went on in that committee's session, though some were later to say that Franklin played a key role in hammering out the plan that finally emerged. That compromise, the most important reached at the convention, and later called the **Great Compromise** (or sometimes the Connecticut Compromise), was submitted to the full convention on July 5 and debated for another week and a half. The debate might have gone on even longer, but suddenly the hot weather moderated, and Monday, July 16, dawned cool and fresh after a month of misery. On that day the plan was adopted: five states were in favor, four were opposed, and two did not vote.* Thus, by the narrowest of margins, the structure of the national legislature was set as follows:

- A House of Representatives consisting initially of sixty-five members apportioned among the states roughly on the basis of population and elected by the people
- A Senate consisting of two senators from each state to be chosen by the state legislatures

The Great Compromise reconciled the interests of small and large states by allowing the former to predominate in the Senate and the latter in the House. This reconciliation was necessary to ensure that there would be support for a strong national government from small as well as large states. It represented major concessions on the part of several groups. Madison, for one, was deeply opposed

to the idea of having the states equally represented in the Senate. He saw in that a way for the states to hamstring the national government and much preferred some measure of proportional representation in both houses. Delegates from other states worried that representation on the basis of population in the House of Representatives would enable the large states to dominate legislative affairs. Although the margin by which the compromise was accepted was razor-thin, it held firm. In time most of the delegates from the dissenting states accepted it.

After the Great Compromise many more issues had to be resolved, but by now a spirit of accommodation had developed. When one delegate proposed having Congress choose the president, another, James Wilson, proposed that he be elected directly by the people. When neither side of that argument prevailed, a committee invented a plan for an "electoral college" that would choose the president. When some delegates wanted the president chosen for a life term, others proposed a seven-year term, and still others wanted the term limited to three years without eligibility for reelection. The convention settled on a four-year term with no bar to reelection. Some states wanted the Supreme Court picked by the Senate; others wanted it chosen by the president. They finally agreed to let the justices be nominated by the president and then confirmed by the Senate.

Finally, on July 26, the proposals that were already accepted, together with a bundle of unresolved issues, were handed over to the Committee of Detail, consisting of five delegates. This committee included Madison and Gouverneur Morris, who was to be the chief draftsman of the document that finally emerged. The committee hardly contented itself with mere "details," however. It inserted some new proposals and made changes in old ones, drawing for inspiration on existing state constitutions and the members' beliefs as to what the other delegates might accept. On August 6 the report—the first complete draft of the Constitution—was submitted to the convention. There it was debated, item by item, revised, amended, and finally, on September 17, approved by all twelve states in attendance. (Not all *delegates* approved, however; three, including Edmund Randolph, who first submitted the Virginia Plan, refused to sign.)

---

*The states in favor were Connecticut, Delaware, Maryland, New Jersey, and North Carolina. Those opposed were Georgia, Pennsylvania, South Carolina, and Virginia. Massachusetts was split down the middle; the New York delegates had left the convention. New Hampshire and Rhode Island were absent.

The Constitution and Democracy

A debate continues to rage over whether the Constitution created, or was even intended to create, a democratic government. The answer is complex. The Framers did not intend to create a "pure democracy"—one in which the people rule directly. For one thing the size of the country and the distances between settlements would have made that physically impossible. But more important the Framers worried that a government in which all citizens directly participate, as in the New England town meeting, would be a government excessively subject to temporary popular passions and one in which minority rights would be insecure. They intended instead to create a **republic,** by which they meant a government in which a system of representation operates. In designing that system the Framers chose, not without argument, to have the members of the House of Representatives elected directly by the people. Some delegates did not want to go even that far. Elbridge Gerry of Massachusetts, who refused to sign the Constitution, argued that though "the people do not want [that is, lack] virtue," they are often the "dupes of pretended patriots." Roger Sherman of Connecticut agreed. But George Mason of Virginia and James Wilson of Pennsylvania carried the day when they argued that "no government could long subsist without the confidence of the people," and this required "drawing the most numerous branch of the legislature directly from the people." Popular elections for the House were approved: six states were in favor, two opposed.

But though popular rule was to be one element of the new government, it was not to be the only one. State legislatures, not the people, would choose the senators; electors, not the people directly, would choose the president. As we have seen, without these arrangements, there would have been no Constitution at all, for the small states adamantly opposed any proposal that would have given undue power to the large ones. And direct popular election of the president would clearly have made the populous states the dominant ones. In short the Framers wished to observe the principle of majority rule, but they felt that, on the most important questions, two kinds of majorities were essential—a majority of the voters and a majority of the states.

The power of the Supreme Court to declare an act of Congress unconstitutional—**judicial review**—is also a way of limiting the power of popular majorities. It is not clear whether the Framers intended that there be judicial review, but there is little doubt that in the Framers' minds the fundamental law, the Constitution, had to be safeguarded against popular passions. They made the process for amending the Constitution easier than it had been under the Articles but still relatively difficult.

An amendment can be proposed either by a two-thirds vote of both houses of Congress *or* by a national convention called by Congress at the request of two-thirds of the states.* Once proposed, an amendment must be ratified by three-fourths of the states, either through their legislatures or through special ratifying conventions in each state. Twenty-seven amendments have survived this process, all of them proposed by Congress and all but one (the Twenty-first Amendment) ratified by state legislatures rather than state conventions.

In short the answer to the question of whether the Constitution brought into being a democratic government is yes, if by *democracy* one means a system of representative government based on popular consent. The degree of that consent has changed since 1787, and the institutions embodying that consent can take different forms. One form, rejected in 1787, gives all political authority to one set of representatives, directly elected by the people. (That is the case, for example, in most parliamentary regimes, such as Great Britain, and in some city governments in the United States.) The other form of democracy is one in which different sets of officials, chosen directly or indirectly by different groups of people, share politcal power. (That is the case with the United States and a few other nations where the separation of powers is intended to operate.)

Key Principles

The American version of representative democracy was based on two major principles, the separation of powers and federalism. In America political power was to be shared by three separate branches of gov-

---

*There have been many attempts to get a new constitutional convention. In the 1960s thirty-three states, one short of the required number, requested a convention to consider the reapportionment of state legislatures. In the 1980s efforts were made to call a convention to consider amendments to ban abortions and to require a balanced federal budget.

Checks and Balances

The Constitution creates a system of *separate* institutions that *share* powers. Because the three branches of government share powers, each can (partially) check the powers of the others. This is the system of **checks and balances**. The major checks possessed by each branch are listed below.

Congress

1. Can check the president in these ways:
   a. By refusing to pass a bill the president wants
   b. By passing a law over the president's veto
   c. By using the impeachment powers to remove the president from office
   d. By refusing to approve a presidential appointment (Senate only)
   e. By refusing to ratify a treaty the president has signed (Senate only)
2. Can check the federal courts in these ways:
   a. By changing the number and jurisdiction of the lower courts
   b. By using the impeachment powers to remove a judge from office
   c. By refusing to approve a person nominated to be a judge (Senate only)

The President

1. Can check Congress by vetoing a bill it has passed
2. Can check the federal courts by nominating judges

The Courts

1. Can check Congress by declaring a law unconstitutional
2. Can check the president by declaring actions by him or his subordinates to be unconstitutional or not authorized by law

In addition to these checks specifically provided for in the Constitution, each branch has informal ways of checking the others. For example, the president can try to withhold information from Congress (on the grounds of "executive privilege"), and Congress can try to get information by mounting an investigation.

The exact meaning of the various checks is explained in Chapter 11 on Congress, Chapter 12 on the presidency, and Chapter 14 on the courts.

---

ernment; in parliamentary democracies that power was concentrated in a single, supreme legislature. In America political authority was divided between a national government and several state governments—**federalism**—whereas in most European systems authority was centralized in the national government. Neither of these principles was especially controversial at Philadelphia. The delegates began their work in broad agreement that separated powers and some measure of federalism were necessary, and both the Virginia and New Jersey plans contained a version of each. How much federalism should be written into the Constitution was quite controversial, however.

Government and Human Nature

The desirability of separating powers and leaving the states equipped with a broad array of rights and responsibilities was not controversial at the Philadelphia convention because the Framers' experiences with British rule and state government under the Articles had shaped their view of human nature.

These experiences had taught most of the Framers that people would seek their own advantage in and out of politics; this pursuit of self-interest, unchecked, would lead some people to exploit others. Human nature was good enough to make it possible to have a decent government that was based on popular consent, but it was not good enough to make it inevitable. One solution to this problem would be to improve human nature. Ancient political philosophers such as Aristotle believed that the first task of any government was to cultivate virtue among the governed.

Many Americans were of the same mind. To them Americans would first have to become good people before they could have a good government. Samuel Adams, a leader of the Boston Tea Party, said that the new nation must become a "Christian Sparta." Others spoke of the need to cultivate frugality, industry, temperance, and simplicity.

But to James Madison and the other architects of the Constitution, the deliberate cultivation of virtue would require a government too strong and thus too dangerous to liberty, at least at the national level. Self-interest, freely pursued within reasonable limits, was a more practical and durable solution to the problem of government than any effort to improve the virtue of the citizenry. He wanted, he said, to make republican government possible "even in the absence of political virtue."

Madison argued that the very self-interest that leads people toward factionalism and tyranny might, if properly harnessed by appropriate constitutional arrangements, provide a source of unity and a guarantee of liberty. This harnessing was to be accomplished by dividing the offices of the new government among many people and giving to the holder of each office the "necessary means and personal motives to resist encroachments of the others." In this way "ambition must be made to counteract ambition" so that "the private interest of every individual may be a sentinel over the public rights."[11] If men were angels, all this would be unnecessary. But Madison and the other delegates pragmatically insisted on taking human nature pretty much as it was, and therefore they adopted "this policy of supplying, by opposite and rival interests, the defect of better motives."[12] The **separation of powers** would work, not in spite of the imperfections of human nature, but because of them.

So also with federalism. By dividing power between the states and the national government, one level of government can serve as a check on the other. This should provide a "double security" to the rights of the people: "The different governments will control each other, at the same time that each will be controlled by itself."[13] This was especially likely to happen in America, Madison thought, because it was a large country filled with diverse interests— rich and poor, Protestant and Catholic, northerner and southerner, farmer and merchant, creditor and debtor. Each of these interests would constitute a **faction** that would seek its own advantage. One faction might come to dominate government, or a part of government, in one place, and a different and rival faction might dominate it in another. The

pulling and hauling among these factions would prevent any single government—say, that of New York—from dominating all of government. The division of powers among several governments would give to virtually every faction an opportunity to gain some—but not full—power.

The Constitution and Liberty

A more difficult question is whether the Constitution created a system of government that would respect personal liberties. And that in fact is the question that was debated in the states when the document was presented for ratification. The proponents of the Constitution called themselves the **Federalists** (though they might more accurately have been called "nationalists"). The opponents came to be known as the **Antifederalists** (though they might more accurately have been called "states' righters").* To be put into effect, the Constitution had to be approved at ratifying conventions in at least nine states. This was perhaps the most democratic feature of the Constitution: it had to be accepted, not by the existing Congress (still limping along under the Articles of Confederation), nor by the state legislatures, but by special conventions elected by the people.

Though democratic, the process established by the Framers for ratifying the Constitution was technically illegal. The Articles of Confederation, which still governed, could be amended only with the approval of all thirteen state legislatures. The Framers wanted to bypass these legislatures because they feared that, for reasons of ideology or out of a desire to retain their powers, the legislators would oppose the Constitution. The Framers wanted ratification with less than the consent of all thirteen states because they knew that such unanimity could not be attained. And indeed the conventions in North Carolina and Rhode Island did initially reject the Constitution.

---

*To the delegates a truly "federal" system was one, like the New Jersey Plan, that allowed for very strong states and a weak national government. When the New Jersey Plan lost, the delegates who defeated it began using the word *federal* to describe their plan even though it called for a stronger national government. Thus men who began as "Federalists" at the convention ultimately became known as "Antifederalists" during the struggle over ratification.

The Antifederalist View

The great issue before the state conventions was liberty, not democracy. The opponents of the new Constitution, the Antifederalists, had a variety of objections but were in general united by the belief that liberty could be secure only in a small republic in which the rulers were physically close to—and closely checked by—the ruled. Their central objection was stated by a group of Antifederalists at the ratifying convention in an essay published just after they had lost: "a very extensive territory cannot be governed on the principles of freedom, otherwise than by a confederation of republics."[14]

These dissenters argued that a strong national government would be distant from the people and would use its powers to annihilate or absorb the functions that properly belonged to the states. Congress would tax heavily, the Supreme Court would overrule state courts, and the president would come to head a large standing army. (Since all these things have occurred, we cannot dismiss the Antifederalists as cranky obstructionists who opposed without justification the plans of the Framers.) These critics argued that the nation needed, at best, a loose confederation of states, with most of the powers of government kept firmly in the hands of state legislatures and state courts.

But if a stronger national government was to be created, the Antifederalists argued, it should be hedged about with many more restrictions than those in the constitution then under consideration. They proposed several such limitations, including narrowing the jurisdiction of the Supreme Court, checking the president's power by creating a council that would review his actions, leaving military affairs in the hands of the state militias, increasing the size of the House of Representatives so that it would reflect a greater variety of popular interests, and reducing or eliminating the power of Congress to levy taxes. And some of them insisted that a *bill of rights* be added to the Constitution.

James Madison gave his answer to these criticisms in *Federalist* No. 10 and No. 51 (reprinted in the Appendix). It was a bold answer, for it flew squarely in the face of widespread popular sentiment and much philosophical writing. Following the great French political philosopher Montesquieu, many Americans believed that liberty was safe only in small societies governed either by direct democracy

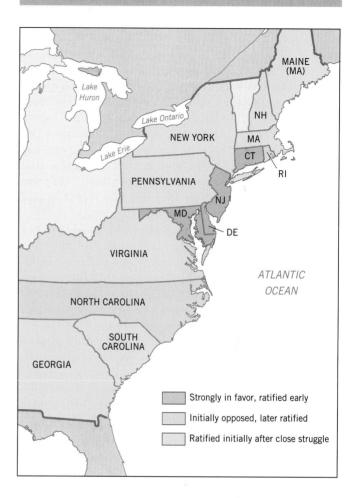

Ratification of the Federal Constitution by State Conventions, 1787–1790

Strongly in favor, ratified early

Initially opposed, later ratified

Ratified initially after close struggle

or by large legislatures with small districts and frequent turnover among members.

Madison argued quite the opposite—that liberty is safest in *large* (or as he put it, "extended") republics. In a small community, he said, there will be relatively few differences in opinion or interest; people will tend to see the world in much the same way. If anyone dissents or pursues an individual interest, he or she will be confronted by a massive majority and will have few, if any, allies. But in a large republic there will be many opinions and interests; as a result it will be hard for a tyrannical majority to form or organize, and anyone with an unpopular view will find it easier to acquire allies. If Madison's argument seems strange or abstract, ask yourself the following

The *Federalist* Papers

In 1787, to help win ratification of the new Constitution in the New York state convention, Alexander Hamilton decided to publish a series of articles defending and explaining the document in the New York City newspapers. He recruited John Jay and James Madison to help him, and the three of them, under the pen name "Publius," wrote eighty-five articles that appeared from late 1787 through 1788. The identity of the authors was kept secret at the time, but we now know that Hamilton wrote fifty-one of them, Madison twenty-six, and Jay five, and that Hamilton and Madison jointly authored three.

The ***Federalist* papers** probably played only a small role in securing ratification. Like most legislative battles, this one was not decisively influenced by philosophical writings. But these essays have had a lasting value as an authoritative and profound explanation of the Constitution. Though written for political purposes, the *Federalist* has become the single most important piece of American political philosophy ever produced. Ironically Hamilton and Madison were later to become political enemies; even at the Philadelphia convention they had different views of the kind of government that should be created. But in 1787–1788 they were united in the belief that the new constitution was the best that could have been obtained under the circumstances.

Although Hamilton wrote most of the *Federalist* papers, Madison wrote the two most famous articles—Nos. 10 and 51, reprinted here in the Appendix. After you have finished this chapter, turn to the Appendix and try to read them. On your first reading of the papers you may find Madison's language difficult to understand and his ideas overly complex. The following pointers will help you decipher his meaning.

In *Federalist* No. 10 Madison begins by stating that "a well constructed Union" can "break and control the violence of faction." He goes on to define a "faction" as any group of citizens who attempt to advance their ideas or economic interests at the expense of other citizens, or in ways that

James Madison

John Jay

Alexander Hamilton

conflict with "the permanent and aggregate interests of the community" or "public good." Thus what Madison terms "factions" are what we today call "special interests."

One way to defeat factions, according to Madison, is to remove whatever causes them to arise in the first place. This can be attempted in two ways. First, government can deprive people of the liberty they need to organize: "Liberty is to faction what air is to fire." But that is surely a cure "worse than the disease." Second, measures can be taken to make all citizens share the same ideas, feelings, and economic interests. However, as Madison observes, some people are smarter or more hard working than others, and this "diversity in the faculties" of citizens is bound to result

For the Independent Journal.

The FŒDERALIST. No. X.

To the People of the State of New-York.

AMONG the numerous advantages promised by a well constructed Union, none deserves to be more accurately developped than its tendency to break and control the violence of faction. The friend of popular governments, never finds himself so much alarmed for their character and fate, as when he contemplates their propensity to this dangerous vice. He will not fail therefore to set a due value on any plan which, without violating the principles to which he is attached, provides a proper cure for it. The instability, injustice and confusion introduced into the public councils, have in truth been the mortal diseases under which popular governments have every where perished; as they continue to be the favorite and fruitful topics from which the adversaries to liberty derive their most specious declamations. The valuable improvements made by the American Constitutions on the popular models, both ancient and modern, cannot certainly be too much admired; but it would be an unwarrantable partiality, to contend that they have as effectually obviated the danger on this side as was wished and expected. Complaints are every where heard from our most considerate and virtuous citizens, equally the friends of public and private faith, and of public and personal liberty; that our governments are too unstable; that the public good is disregarded in the conflicts of rival parties; and that measures are too often decided, not according to the rules of justice, and the rights of the minor party; but by the superior force of an interested and over-bearing majority. However anxiously we may

Madison thus proposes a second and, he thinks, more practical and desirable way of defeating faction. The way to cure "the mischiefs of faction" is not by removing its causes but by "controlling its effects." Factions will always exist, so the trick is to establish a form of government that is likely to serve the public good through the even-handed "regulation of these various and interfering interests." Wise and public-spirited leaders can "adjust these clashing interests and render them all subservient to the public good," but, he cautions, "enlightened statesmen will not always be at the helm." (Madison implies that "enlightened statesmen"—such as himself, Washington, and Jefferson—were at the "helm" of government in 1787.)

Madison's proposed cure for the evils of factions is in fact nothing other than a republican form of government. Use the following questions to guide your own analysis of Madison's ideas. Why does Madison think the problem of a "minority" faction is easy to handle? Conversely, why is he so troubled by the potential of a majority faction? How does he distinguish direct democracy from republican government? What is he getting at when he terms elected representatives "proper guardians of the public weal," and why does he think that "extensive republics" are more likely to produce such representatives than small ones?

When you are finished with *Federalist* No. 10, try your hand at *Federalist* No. 51. You will find that the ideas in the former paper anticipate many of those in the latter. And you will find many points on which you may or may not agree with Madison. For example, do you agree with his assumption that people—even your best friends or college roommates—are factious by nature? Likewise, do you agree with his view that government is "the greatest of all reflections on human nature"?

By attempting to meet the mind of James Madison, you can sharpen your own mind and deepen your understanding of American government.

in different economic interests as some people acquire more property than others. Consequently, protecting property rights, not equalizing property ownership, "is the first object of government." Even if everyone shared the same basic economic interests, they would still find reasons "to vex and oppress each other" rather than cooperate "for their common good." Religious differences, loyalties to different leaders, even "frivolous and fanciful distinctions" (not liking how other people dress or their taste in music) can be fertile soil for factions. In Madison's view people are factious by nature; the "causes of faction" are "sown" into their very being.

question: if I have an unpopular opinion, an exotic lifestyle, or an unconventional interest, will I find greater security living in a small town or a big city?

By favoring a large republic Madison was not trying to stifle democracy. Rather he was attempting to show how democratic government really works, and what can make it work better. To rule, different interests must come together and form a **coalition**—that is, an alliance. In *Federalist* No. 51 he argued that the coalitions that formed in a large republic would be more moderate than those that formed in a small one because the bigger the republic, the greater the variety of interests, and thus the more a coalition of the majority would have to accommodate a diversity of interests and opinions if it hoped to succeed. He concluded that in a nation the size of the United States, with its enormous variety of interests, "a coalition of a majority of the whole society could seldom take place on any other principles than those of justice and the general good." Whether he was right in that prediction is a matter to which we shall return repeatedly.

The implication of Madison's arguments was daring, for he was suggesting that the national government should be at some distance from the people and insulated from their momentary passions, because the people did not always want to do the right thing. Liberty was threatened as much (or even more) by public passions and popularly based factions as by strong governments. Now the Antifederalists themselves had no very lofty view of human nature, as is evidenced by the deep suspicion with which they viewed "power-seeking" officeholders. What Madison did was take this view to its logical conclusion, arguing that if people could be corrupted by office, they could also be corrupted by factional self-interest. Thus the government had to be designed to prevent both the politicians and the people from using it for ill-considered or unjust purposes.

To argue in 1787 against the virtues of small democracies was like arguing against motherhood, but the argument prevailed, probably because many citizens were convinced that a reasonably strong national government was essential if the nation were to stand united against foreign enemies, facilitate commerce among the states, guard against domestic insurrections, and keep one faction from oppressing another. The political realities of the moment and the recent bitter experiences with the Articles probably counted for more in ratifying the Constitution than did Madison's arguments. His

cause was helped by the fact that, for all their legitimate concerns and their uncanny instinct for what the future might bring, the Antifederalists could offer no agreed-upon alternative to the new Constitution. In politics, then as now, you cannot beat something with nothing.

But this does not explain why the Framers failed to add a bill of rights to the Constitution. If they were so preoccupied with liberty, why didn't they take this most obvious step toward protecting liberty, especially since the Antifederalists were demanding it? Some historians have suggested that this omission was evidence that liberty was not as important to the Framers as they claimed. In fact when one delegate suggested that a bill of rights be drawn up, the state delegations at the convention unanimously voted the idea down. There were several reasons for this.

First, the Constitution, as written, *did* contain a number of specific guarantees of individual liberty, including the right of trial by jury in criminal cases and the privilege of the writ of habeas corpus. The liberties guaranteed in the Constitution (before the Bill of Rights was added) are listed below.

- **Writ of habeas corpus*** may not be suspended (except during invasion or rebellion).
- No **bill of attainder** may be passed by Congress or the states.
- No **ex post facto law** may be passed by Congress or the states.
- Right of trial by jury in criminal cases is guaranteed.
- The citizens of each state are entitled to the privileges and immunities of the citizens of every other state.
- No religious test or qualification for holding federal office is imposed.
- No law impairing the obligation of contracts may be passed by the states.

Second, most states in 1787 had bills of rights. When Elbridge Gerry proposed to the convention that a federal bill of rights be drafted, Roger Sherman rose to observe that it was unnecessary because the state bills of rights were sufficient.[15]

But third, and perhaps most important, the Framers thought they were creating a government

---

*For a definition of this and the following terms used in connection with certain rights, see the Glossary.

The Bill of Rights

The First Ten Amendments to the Constitution Grouped by Topic and Purpose

Protections Afforded Citizens to Participate in the Political Process

Amendment 1: Freedom of religion, speech, press, and assembly; the right to petition the government.

Protections Against Arbitrary Police and Court Action

Amendment 4: No unreasonable searches or seizures.

Amendment 5: Grand jury indictment required to prosecute a person for a serious crime.

No "double jeopardy" (being tried twice for the same offense).

Forcing a person to testify against himself or herself prohibited.

No loss of life, liberty, or property without due process.

Amendment 6: Right to speedy, public, impartial trial with defense counsel and right to cross-examine witnesses.

Amendment 7: Jury trials in civil suits where value exceeds $20.

Amendment 8: No excessive bail or fines, no cruel and unusual punishments.

Protections of States' Rights and Unnamed Rights of People

Amendment 9: Unlisted rights are not necessarily denied.

Amendment 10: Powers not delegated to the United States or denied to states are reserved to the states.

Other Amendments

Amendment 2: Right to bear arms.

Amendment 3: Troops may not be quartered in homes in peacetime.

---

with specific, limited powers. It could do, they thought, only what the Constitution gave it the power to do, and nowhere in that document was there permission to infringe on freedom of speech or of the press or to impose cruel and unusual punishments. Some delegates probably feared that if any serious effort were made to list the rights that were guaranteed, later officials might assume that they had the power to do anything not explicitly forbidden.

Need for a Bill of Rights

Whatever their reasons, the Framers made at least a tactical and perhaps a fundamental mistake. It quickly became clear that without at least the promise of a **bill of rights,** the Constitution would not be ratified. Though the small states, pleased by their equal representation in the Senate, quickly ratified (in Delaware, New Jersey, and Georgia, the vote in the conventions was unanimous), the battle in the large states was intense and the outcome uncertain. In Pennsylvania Federalist supporters dragged boy-cotting Antifederalists to the legislature in order to ensure that a quorum was present so that a convention could be called. There were rumors of other rough tactics.

In Massachusetts the Constitution was approved by a narrow majority, but only after key leaders promised to obtain a bill of rights. In Virginia James Madison fought against the fiery Patrick Henry, whose climactic speech against ratification was dramatically punctuated by a noisy thunderstorm outside. The Federalists won by ten votes. In New York Alexander Hamilton argued the case for six weeks against the determined opposition of most of the state's key political leaders; he carried the day, but only by three votes, and then only after New York City threatened to secede from the state if it did not ratify. By June 21, 1788, the ninth state—New Hampshire—had ratified, and the Constitution was law.

Despite the bitterness of the ratification struggle, the new government that took office in 1789–1790, headed by President Washington, was greeted enthusiastically. By the spring of 1790 all thirteen states had ratified. There remained, however, the task of fulfilling the promise of a bill of rights. To that end James Madison introduced into the first session of the First Congress a set of proposals, many based on the existing Virginia bill of rights. Twelve were approved by Congress; ten of these were ratified by the states and went into effect in 1791. These amendments did not limit the power of state governments over citizens, only the power of the federal government. Later the Fourteenth Amendment, as interpreted by the Supreme Court, extended many of the guarantees of the Bill of Rights to cover state governmental action.

The Constitution and Slavery

Though black slaves amounted to one-third of the population of the five southern states, nowhere in the Constitution can one find the word *slave* or *slavery*. There are three provisions bearing on the matter, all designed to placate the slaveowning states. The apportionment of seats in the House of Representatives was to be made by counting all free persons and three-fifths of all "other persons." This meant giving a few extra seats in the House to those states that had a lot of "other persons"—that is, slaves. Congress was forbidden to prohibit the "importation" of "persons" (that is, slaves) before the year 1808. And if any "person held to service or labour" (that is, any slave) were to escape from a slaveowning state and get to a free state, that person would not become free but would have to be returned to his or her master.

To some the failure of the Constitution to address the question of slavery was a great betrayal of the promise of the Declaration of Independence that "all men are created equal."[16] For the Constitution to be silent on the subject of slavery, and thereby to allow that odious practice to continue, was to convert, by implication, the wording of the Declaration to "all white men are created equal."

It is easy to accuse the signers of the Declaration and the Constitution of hypocrisy. They knew of slavery, many of them owned slaves, and yet they were silent. Indeed, British opponents of the independence movement took special delight in taunting the colonists about their complaints of being "enslaved" to the British Empire while ignoring the slavery in their very midst. Increasingly, revolutionary leaders during this period spoke to this issue.

Thomas Jefferson had tried to get a clause opposing the slave trade put into the Declaration of Independence. James Otis of Boston had attacked slavery and argued that black as well as white men should be free. As revolutionary fervor mounted, so did northern criticism of slavery. The Massachusetts legislature and then the Continental Congress voted to end the slave trade; Delaware prohibited the importation of slaves; Pennsylvania voted to tax it out of existence; and Connecticut and Rhode Island decided that all slaves brought into those states would automatically become free.

Slavery continued unabated in the South, defended by some whites because they thought it right, by others because they found it useful. But even in the South there were opponents, though rarely conspicuous ones. George Mason, a large Virginia slaveholder and a delegate to the convention, warned prophetically that "by an inevitable chain of causes and effects, providence punishes national sins [slavery] by national calamities."[17]

The blunt fact, however, was that any effort to use the Constitution to end slavery would have meant the end of the Constitution. The southern states would never have signed a document that seriously interfered with slavery. Without the southern states there would have been a continuation of the Articles of Confederation, which would have left each state entirely sovereign and thus entirely free of any prospective challenge to slavery.

The Constitution was silent on slavery, and so buying and selling slaves continued for many years.

Thus the Framers compromised with slavery; political scientist Theodore Lowi calls this their Greatest Compromise.[18] Slavery is dealt with in three places in the Constitution, though never by name. In determining the representation each state was to have in the House, "three-fifths of all other persons" (that is, of slaves) are to be added to "the whole number of free persons."[19] The South originally wanted slaves to count fully even though, of course, none would be elected to the House; they settled for counting 60 percent of them. The convention also agreed not to allow the new government by law or even constitutional amendment to prohibit the importation of slaves until the year 1808.[20] The South thus had twenty years in which it could acquire more slaves from abroad; after that Congress was free (but not required) to end the importation. Finally, the Constitution guaranteed that if a slave were to escape his or her master and flee to a nonslave state, the slave would be returned by that state to "the party to whom . . . service or labour may be due."[21]

The unresolved issue of slavery was to prove the most explosive question of all. Allowing slavery to continue was a fateful decision, one that led to the worst social and political catastrophe in the nation's history—the Civil War. The Framers chose to sidestep the issue in order to create a union that, they hoped, would eventually be strong enough to deal with the problem when it could no longer be postponed. The legacy of that choice continues to this day.

The Motives of the Framers

The Framers were not saints or demigods. They were men with political opinions who also had economic interests and human failings. It would be a mistake to conclude that everything they did in 1787 was motivated by a disinterested commitment to the public good. But it would be an equally great mistake to think that what they did was nothing but an effort to line their pockets by producing a government that would serve their own narrow interests. As in almost all human endeavors, the Framers acted out of a mixture of motives. What is truly astonishing is that economic interests played only a modest role in their deliberations.

Economic Interests at the Convention

Some of the Framers were wealthy; some were not. Some owned slaves; some had none. Some were creditors (having loaned money to the Continental Congress or to private parties); some were deeply in debt. For nearly a century scholars have argued over just how important these personal interests were in shaping the provisions of the Constitution.

In 1913 Charles Beard, a historian, published a book—*An Economic Interpretation of the Constitution*—arguing that the better-off urban and commercial classes, especially those members who held the IOUs issued by the government to pay for the

Revolutionary War, favored the new Constitution because they stood to benefit from it.[22] But in the 1950s that view was challenged by historians who, after looking carefully at what the Framers owned or owed, concluded that one could not explain the Constitution exclusively or even largely in terms of the economic interests of those who wrote it.[23] Some of the richest delegates, such as Elbridge Gerry of Massachusetts and George Mason of Virginia, refused to sign the document, while many of its key backers—James Madison and James Wilson, for example—were men of modest means or heavy debts.

In the 1980s a new group of scholars, primarily economists applying more advanced statistical techniques, found evidence that some economic considerations influenced how the Framers voted on some issues during the Philadelphia convention. Interestingly, however, the economic position of the *states* from which they came had a greater effect on their votes than did their *own* monetary condition.[24]

We have already seen how delegates from small states fought to reduce the power of large states and how those from slaveowning states made certain that the Constitution would contain no provision that would threaten slavery.

But contrary to what Beard asserted, the individual interests of the Framers themselves did not dominate the convention except in a few cases where a constitutional provision would have affected them directly. As you might expect, all slaveowning delegates, even those who did not live in states where slavery was commonplace (and several northern delegates owned slaves), tended to vote for provisions that would have kept the national government's power over slavery as weak as possible. However, the effects of other personal business interests were surprisingly weak. Some delegates owned a lot of public debt that they had purchased for low prices. A strong national government of the sort envisaged by the Constitution was more likely than the weak Continental Congress to pay off this debt at face value, thus making the delegates who owned it much richer. Despite this, the ownership of public debt had no significant effect on how the Framers voted in Philadelphia. For example, five men who among them owned one-third of all the public securities

Elbridge Gerry (left, 1744–1814) was a wealthy Massachusetts merchant and politician who participated in the convention but refused to sign the Constitution. James Wilson (right, 1742–1798) of Pennsylvania, a brilliant lawyer and terrible businessman, was the principal champion of the popular election of the House. Near the end of his life he was jailed repeatedly for debts incurred as a result of his business speculations.

held by all the delegates voted against the Constitution. Nor did the big land speculators vote their interests. Some, such as George Washington and Robert Morris, favored the Constitution, while others, such as George Mason and William Blount, opposed it.[25]

In sum the Framers tended to represent their states' interests on important matters. Since they were picked by the states to do so, this is exactly what one would expect. If they had not met in secret, perhaps they would have voted even more often as their constituents wanted. But except with respect to slavery, they usually did not vote their own economic interests. They were reasonably but not wholly disinterested delegates who were probably influenced as much by personal beliefs as by economics.

Economic Interests and Ratification

At the popularly elected state ratifying conventions, economic factors played a larger role. Delegates who were merchants, who lived in cities, who owned large amounts of western land, who held government IOUs, and who did not own slaves were more likely to vote to ratify the new Constitution than were delegates who were farmers, who did not own public debt, and who did own slaves.[26] There were plenty of exceptions, however. Small farmers dominated the conventions in some states where the vote to ratify was unanimous.

Though interests made a difference, they were not simply elite interests. In most states the great majority of adult white males could vote for delegates to the ratifying conventions. This means that women and blacks were excluded from the debates, but by the standards of the time—standards that did not change for over a century—the ratification process was remarkably democratic.

The Constitution and Equality

Ideas counted for as much as interests. At stake were two views of the public good. One, espoused by the Federalists, was that a reasonable balance of liberty, order, and progress required a strong national government. The other, defended by the Antifederalists, was that liberty would not be secure in the hands of a powerful, distant government; freedom required decentralization.

Today that debate has a new focus. The defect of the Constitution, to some contemporary critics, is not that the government it created is too strong but that it is too weak. In particular the national government is too weak to resist the pressures of special interests that reflect and perpetuate social inequality.

This criticism reveals how our understanding of the relationship between liberty and equality has changed since the Founding. To Jefferson and Madison citizens naturally differed in their talents and qualities. What had to be guarded against was the use of governmental power to create *un*natural and undesirable inequalities. This might happen, for example, if political power was concentrated in the hands of a few people (who could use that power to give themselves special privileges) or if it was used in ways that allowed some private parties to acquire exclusive charters and monopolies. To prevent the inequality that might result from having too strong a government, its powers must be kept strictly limited.

Today some people think of inequality quite differently. To them it is the natural social order—the marketplace and the acquisitive talents of people operating in that marketplace—that leads to undesirable inequalities, especially in economic power. The government should be powerful enough to restrain these natural tendencies and produce, by law, a greater degree of equality than society allows when left alone.

To the Framers liberty and (political) equality were not in conflict; to some people today these two principles are deeply in conflict. To the Framers the task was to keep government so limited as to prevent it from creating the worst inequality—political privilege. To some modern observers the task is to make government strong enough to reduce what they believe is the worst inequality—differences in wealth.

Constitutional Reform: Modern Views

Almost from the day it was ratified, the Constitution has been the object of debate over ways in which it might be improved. These debates have rarely involved the average citizen, who tends to revere the document even if he or she cannot recall all its details. Because of this deep and broad popular support, scholars and politicians have been wary of attacking the Constitution or suggesting many wholesale changes. But such attacks have occurred. During the 1980s—the decade

Were Women Left Out of the Constitution?

In one sense, yes: Women were nowhere mentioned in the Constitution when it was written in 1787. Moreover, Article I, which set forth the provisions for electing members of the House of Representatives, granted the vote to those people who were allowed to vote for members of the lower house of the legislature in the states in which they resided. In no state at the time could women participate in those elections. In no state could they vote in any elections or hold any offices. Furthermore, wherever the Constitution uses a pronoun, it uses the masculine form—*he* or *him*.

In another sense, no: Wherever the Constitution or the Bill of Rights defines a right that people are to have, it either grants that right to "persons" or "citizens," not to "men," or it makes no mention at all of people or gender. For example:

- "The *citizens* of each State shall be entitled to all privileges and immunities of citizens of the several States." [Art. I, sec. 9]
- "No *person* shall be convicted of treason unless on the testimony of two witnesses to the same overt act, or on confession in open court." [Art. III, sec. 3]
- "No bill of attainder or ex post facto law shall be passed." [Art. I, sec. 9]
- "The right of the *people* to be secure in their persons, houses, papers, and effects, against unreasonable searches and seizures, shall not be violated." [Amend. IV]
- "No *person* shall be held to answer for a capital, or otherwise infamous crime, unless on presentment or indictment of a grand jury . . . nor shall any *person* be subject for the same offense to be twice put in jeopardy of life or limb; . . . nor be deprived of life, liberty, or property, without due process of law." [Amend. V]
- "In all criminal prosecutions the *accused* shall enjoy the right to a speedy and public trial, by an impartial jury." [Amend. VI]

Moreover, when the qualifications for elective office are stated, the word *person*, not *man*, is used.

- "No *person* shall be a Representative who shall not have attained to the age of twenty-five years." [Art. I, sec. 2]
- "No *person* shall be a Senator who shall not have attained to the age of thirty years." [Art. I, sec. 3]
- "No *person* except a natural born citizen . . . shall be eligible to the office of President; neither shall any *person* be eligible to that office who shall not have attained to the age of thirty-five years." [Art. II, sec. 1]

In places the Constitution and the Bill of Rights used the pronoun *he*, but always in the context of referring back to a *person* or *citizen*. At the time, and until quite recently, the male pronoun was often used in legal documents to refer generically to both men and women.

Thus, though the Constitution did not give women the right to vote until the Nineteenth Amendment was ratified in 1920, it did use language that extended fundamental rights, and access to office, to women and men equally.

Of course what the Constitution permitted did not necessarily occur. State and local laws denied to women rights that in principle they ought to have enjoyed. Except for a brief period in New Jersey, no women voted in statewide elections until, in 1869, they were given the right to cast ballots in territorial elections in Wyoming.

When women were first elected to Congress, there was no need to change the Constitution; nothing in it restricted officeholding to men.

When women were given the right to vote by constitutional amendment, it was not necessary to amend any existing language in the Constitution, because nothing in the Constitution itself denied women the right to vote; the amendment simply added a new right:

- "The right of citizens of the United States to vote shall not be denied or abridged by the United States or any state on account of sex." [Amend. XIX]

Source: Adapted from Robert Goldwin, "Why Blacks, Women and Jews Are Not Mentioned in the Constitution," *Commentary* (May 1987): 28–33.

Ways of Amending the Constitution

Under Article V there are two ways to *propose amendments* to the Constitution and two ways to *ratify* them.

To Propose an Amendment

1. Two-thirds of both houses of Congress vote to propose an amendment, *or*
2. Two-thirds of the state legislatures ask Congress to call a national convention to propose amendments.

To Ratify an Amendment

1. Three-fourths of the state legislatures approve it, *or*
2. Ratifying conventions in three-fourths of the states approve it.

Some Key Facts

- Only the first method of proposing an amendment has been used.
- The second method of ratification has been used only once, to ratify the Twenty-first Amendment (repealing Prohibition).
- Congress may limit the time within which a proposed amendment must be ratified. The usual limitation has been seven years.
- Thousands of proposals have been made, but only thirty-three have obtained the necessary two-thirds vote in Congress.
- Twenty-seven amendments have been ratified.
- The first ten amendments, ratified on December 15, 1791, are known as the Bill of Rights.

---

in which we celebrated the bicentennial of its adoption—we heard a variety of suggestions for improving the Constitution, ranging from particular amendments to wholesale revisions. In general there are today, as in the eighteenth century, two kinds of critics: those who think the federal government is too weak and those who think it is too strong.

Reducing the Separation of Powers

To the first kind of critic the chief difficulty with the Constitution is the separation of powers. By making every decision the uncertain outcome of the pulling and hauling between the president and Congress, the Constitution precludes the emergence—except perhaps in times of crisis—of the kind of effective national leadership the country needs. In this view our nation today faces a number of challenges that require prompt, decisive, and comprehensive action. Our problem is gridlock. Our position of international leadership, the dangerous and unprecedented proliferation of nuclear weapons among the nations of the globe, and the need to find ways of stimulating economic growth while reducing our deficit and conserving our environment—all these situations require that the president be able to formulate and carry out policies free of some of the pressures and delays from interest groups and members of Congress tied to local interests.

Not only would this increase in presidential authority make for better policies, these critics argue, it would also help the voters hold the president and his party accountable for their actions. As matters now stand, nobody in government can be held responsible for policies: everybody takes the credit for successes and nobody takes the blame for failures. Typically the president, who tends to be the major source of new programs, cannot get his policies adopted by Congress without long delays and much bargaining, the result of which often is some watered-down compromise that neither the president nor Congress really likes but that each must settle for if anything is to be done at all.

Finally, critics of the separation of powers complain that the government agencies responsible for implementing a program are exposed to undue interference from legislators and special interests. In this view the president is supposed to be in charge of the bureaucracy but in fact must share this authority with countless members of Congress and congressional committees.

Not all critics of the separation of powers agree with all these points, nor do they all agree on what should be done about the problems. But they all have in common a fear that the separation of powers makes the president too weak and insufficiently accountable. Their proposals for reducing the separation of powers include the following:

- Allow the president to appoint members of Congress to serve in the cabinet (the Constitution forbids members of Congress from holding any federal appointive office while in Congress).
- Allow the president to dissolve Congress and call for a special election (elections now can be held only on the schedule determined by the calendar).
- Allow Congress to require a president who has lost its confidence to face the country in a special election before his term would normally end.
- Require the presidential and congressional candidates to run as a team in each congressional district; thus a presidential candidate who carries a given district could be sure that the congressional candidate of his party would also win in that district.
- Have the president serve a single six-year term instead of being eligible for up to two four-year terms; this would presumably free the president to lead without having to worry about reelection.
- Lengthen the terms of members of the House of Representatives from two to four years so that the entire House would stand for reelection at the same time as the president.[27]

Some of these proposals are offered by critics out of a desire to make the American system of government work more like the British parliamentary system, in which, as we shall see in Chapters 11 and 12, the prime minister is the undisputed leader of the majority in the British Parliament. The parliamentary system is the major alternative in the world today to the American separation-of-powers system.

Both the diagnosis and the remedies proposed by these critics of the separation of powers have been challenged. Many defenders of our present constitutional system believe that nations, such as Great Britain, with a different, more unified political system have done no better than the United States in dealing with the problems of economic growth, national security, and environmental protection. Moreover, they argue, close congressional scrutiny

of presidential proposals has improved these policies more often than it has weakened them. Finally, congressional "interference" in the work of government agencies is a good way of ensuring that the average citizen can fight back against the bureaucracy; without that so-called interference, citizens and interest groups might be helpless before big and powerful agencies.

Each of the specific proposals, defenders of the present constitutional system argue, would either make matters worse or have, at best, uncertain effects. Adding a few members of Congress to the president's cabinet would not provide much help in getting his program through Congress; there are 535 senators and representatives, and probably only about half a dozen would be in the cabinet. Giving either the president or Congress the power to call a special election in between the regular elections (every two or four years) would cause needless confusion and great expense; the country would live under the threat of being in a perpetual political campaign with even weaker political parties. Linking the fate of the president and congressional candidates by having them run as a team in each district would reduce the stabilizing and moderating effect of having them elected separately. A Republican presidential candidate who wins in the new system would have a Republican majority in the House; a Democratic candidate winner would have a Democratic majority. We might as a result expect dramatic changes in policy as the political pendulum swung back and forth. Giving presidents a single six-year term would indeed free them from the need to worry about reelection, but it is precisely that worry that keeps presidents reasonably concerned about what the American people want.

Making the System Less Democratic

The second kind of critic of the Constitution thinks the government does too much, not too little. Though the separation of powers at one time may have slowed the growth of government and moderated the policies it adopted, in the last few decades government has grown helter-skelter. The problem, these critics argue, is not that democracy is a bad idea but that democracy can produce bad, or at least unintended, results if the government caters to the special-interest claims of the citizens rather than to their long-term values.

To see how these unintended results might occur, imagine a situation in which every citizen thinks the

government grows too big, taxes too heavily, and spends too much. Each citizen wants the government made smaller by reducing the benefits other people get—but not by reducing the benefits he or she gets. In fact such citizens may even be willing to see their own benefits cut, provided everybody else's are cut as well, and by a like amount.

But the political system attends to individual wants, not general preferences. It gives aid to farmers, contracts to industry, grants to professors, pensions to the elderly, and loans to students. As someone once said, the government is like an adding machine: during elections candidates campaign by promising to do more for whatever group is dissatisfied with what the incumbents are doing for it. As a result most elections bring to office men and women who are committed to doing more for somebody. The grand total of all these additions is more for everybody. Few politicians have an incentive to do less for anybody.

To remedy this state of affairs, these critics suggest various mechanisms, but principally a constitutional amendment that would either set a limit on the amount of money the government could collect in taxes each year or require that each year the government have a balanced budget (that is, not spend more than it takes in in taxes), or both. In some versions of these plans an extraordinary majority (say, 60 percent) of Congress could override these limits, and the limits would not apply in wartime.

The effect of such amendments, the proponents claim, would be to force Congress and the president to look at the big picture—the grand total of what they are spending—rather than just to operate the adding machine by pushing the "add" button over and over again. If they could spend only so much during a given year, they would have to allocate what they spend among all rival claimants. For example, if more money were to be spent on the poor, less could then be spent on the military, or vice versa.

Some critics of an overly powerful federal government think these amendments will not be passed or may prove unworkable; instead they favor enhancing the president's power to block spending by giving him a **line-item veto.** Most state governors can veto a particular part of a bill and approve the rest using a line-item veto. The theory is that such a veto would better equip the

president to stop unwarranted spending without vetoing the other provisions of a bill. In 1996 President Clinton signed the Line Item Veto Act, passed by the 104th Congress. But despite its name, the new law did not give the president full line-item veto power (only a change in the Constitution could confer that power). Instead the law gave the president authority to selectively eliminate individual items in large appropriations bills, expansions in certain income-transfer programs, and tax breaks (giving the president what budget experts call *enhanced rescission authority*). But it also left Congress free to craft bills in ways that would give the president few opportunities to veto (or *rescind*) favored items. For example, Congress could still force the president to accept or reject an entire appropriations bill simply by tagging on this sentence: "Appropriations provided under this act (or title or section) shall not be subject to the provisions of the Line Item Veto Act." In *Clinton et al. v. New York et al.* (1998), the Supreme Court struck down the 1996 law, holding 6 to 3 that the Constitution does not allow the president to cancel specific items in tax and spending legislation.

Finally, some of these critics of a powerful government feel that the real problem arises not from an excess of "adding-machine" democracy but from the growth in the power of the federal courts, as described in Chapter 14. What these critics would like to do is devise a set of laws or constitutional amendments that would narrow the authority of federal courts.

The opponents of these suggestions argue that constitutional amendments to restrict the level of taxes or to require a balanced budget are unworkable, even assuming—which they do not—that a smaller government is desirable. There is no precise, agreed-upon way to measure how much the government spends or to predict in advance how much it will receive in taxes during the year; thus defining and enforcing a "balanced budget" is no easy matter. Since the government can always borrow money, it might easily evade any spending limits. It has also shown great ingenuity in spending money in ways that never appear as part of the regular budget.

The line-item veto may or may not be a good idea. Unless the Constitution is amended to permit it, future presidents will have to do without it. The states, where some governors have long had the

House Backs Amendment to Give President New Veto Power

June 27
WASHINGTON

Yesterday the House of Representatives, by a 315-to-120 vote, proposed an amendment to the U.S. Constitution that would give future presidents the power to veto a particular part of a bill and approve the rest. The Senate will debate the bill next week . . .

MEMORANDUM

To: Senator Marty Lieb
From: Joseph Miceli, general counsel
Subject: Line-Item Veto Amendment

In 1996 you voted in favor of the Line Item Veto Act, which authorized the president to selectively eliminate items in certain appropriations bills subject to such exemptions as Congress might make. Despite its narrow application, the Supreme Court has declared the law unconstitutional. The amendment being debated next week would confer full line-item veto power on the president.

Arguments for:
1. Forty-three state constitutions, most of them explicitly modeled on the U.S. Constitution, confer line-item veto power on governors.
2. The line-item veto has equipped many governors to stop unwarranted spending without stopping the sensible provisions of a bill.
3. Most people favor giving the president this authority and holding him accountable.

Arguments against:
1. The national government is different. The Founding Fathers considered many veto alternatives and limited the president's "qualified negative" power to rejecting a bill in its entirety, subject to an override by a two-thirds vote of Congress.
2. There is no clear evidence that the line-item veto restrains state spending or that the aforementioned 1996 law restrained federal spending.
3. Popular support for the line-item veto dwindles when people are reminded about our system's separation of powers and checks and balances.

Your decision:
Favor amendment _____
Oppose amendment _____

veto, are quite different from the federal government in power and responsibilities. Whether a line-item veto would work as well in Washington, D.C., as it does in many state capitals is something that we may simply never know.

Finally, proposals to curtail judicial power are thinly veiled attacks, the opponents argue, on the ability of the courts to protect essential citizen rights. If Congress and the people do not like the way the Supreme Court has interpreted the Constitution, they can always amend the Constitution to change a specific ruling; there is no need to adopt some across-the-board limitation on court powers.

Who Is Right?

Some of the arguments of these two sets of critics of the Constitution may strike you as plausible or even entirely convincing. Whatever you may ultimately decide, decide nothing for now. One cannot make or remake a constitution based entirely on abstract reasoning or unproven factual arguments. Even when the Constitution was first written in 1787, it was not an exercise in abstract philosophy but rather an effort to solve pressing, practical problems in the light of a theory of human nature, the lessons of past experience, and a close consideration of how governments in other countries and at other times had worked.

Just because the Constitution is over two hundred years old does not mean that it is out-of-date. The crucial questions are these: How well has it worked over the long sweep of American history? How well has it worked compared to the constitutions of other democratic nations?

The only way to answer those questions is to study American government closely—with special attention to its historical evolution and to the practices of other nations. That is what this book is about. Of course, even after close study, people will still disagree about whether our system should be changed. People want different things and evaluate human experience according to different beliefs. But if we first understand how, in fact, the government works and why it has produced the policies it has, we can then argue more intelligently about how best to achieve our wants and give expression to our beliefs.

Summary

The Framers of the Constitution sought to create a government capable of protecting both liberty and order. The solution they chose—one without precedent at that time—was a government that was based on a written constitution that combined the principles of popular consent, the separation of powers, and federalism.

Popular consent was embodied in the procedure for choosing the House of Representatives but limited by the indirect election of senators and the electoral college system for selecting the president. Political authority was to be shared by three branches of government in a manner deliberately intended to produce conflict among these branches. This conflict, motivated by the self-interest of the people occupying each branch, would, it was hoped, prevent tyranny, even by a popular majority.

Federalism came to mean a system in which both the national and state governments had independent authority. Allocating powers between the two levels of government and devising means to ensure that neither large nor small states would dominate the national government required the most delicate compromises at the Philadelphia convention. The decision to do nothing about slavery was another such compromise.

In the drafting of the Constitution and the struggle over its ratification in the states, the positions people took were chiefly determined not by their economic interests but by a variety of factors. Among these were profound differences of opinion over whether the state governments or the national government would be the best protector of personal liberty.

Reconsidering the Enduring Questions

1. *What view of human nature is embodied in the Constitution?*

   The Constitution reflects a mixed view: people are self-interested, but they also have enough virtue to make representative democracy possible. Such key constitutional concepts as the separation of powers and federalism are predicated on the belief that humans are capable of virtue but prone to vice. As James Madison argues in *Federalist* No. 10, because people tend to "vex and oppress" one another, freedom begets factions. Because "enlightened statesmen will not always be at the helm," the Constitution structures government so that the "public good" may be achieved even when those in public office are neither especially wise nor especially good. As Madison himself summarized the answer in *Federalist* No. 51, "As there is a degree of depravity in mankind which requires a certain degree of circumspection and distrust, so there are other qualities in human nature, which justify a certain portion of esteem and confidence."

2. *Is representative democracy possible without political compromise?*

   On most issues, the answer is no. When the nation faces a crisis, or nobody notices the proposed policy, there may not be any need for compromise. But the American republic was born through political compromise, and contemporary government would grind to a halt without it. Delegates to the Constitutional Convention fought for weeks over the Virginia Plan and the New Jersey Plan, but settled for the Great (or Connecticut) Compromise, which permitted the small states to predominate in the Senate and the large states to predominate in the House. James Madison entered the convention demanding a strong national government that could veto state laws, but he left it defending a constitution that would protect states' rights and create a federal republic. Many Federalists opposed having a bill of rights, but they promised to add one to the Constitution in order to win enough votes in enough states to get the Constitution ratified. Of course, what is necessary politically is not thereby defensible morally. Witness the most con-

sequential political compromise in American history, namely, the so-called three-fifths compromise over slavery, which led to the worst social and political catastrophe in the nation's history—the Civil War. Today, many Americans say they favor politicians who are slow to compromise their principles, yet they are frustrated by how politicians always seem to be fighting with each other rather than getting things done. We cannot have it both ways: in a representative democracy, politicians fight more when they compromise less.

3. *Has the system of separate institutions sharing powers protected liberty and promoted equality as the Framers envisioned it would?*

   Up to a point, yes, but at least several caveats are in order. The Founders did not mean by "equality" what many Americans today mean by it. To the Framers the task was to keep government so limited as to prevent it from creating what they viewed as the worst inequality, namely, political privilege, not differences in wealth. Those who contend that the system has not, in fact, delivered on the Framers' promises do not all share the same diagnosis of what went wrong. For example, some argue that the failure resides in the fact that the national government has grown too strong, while others agree that the system has failed but insist that it has done so because the national government has become (or has always been) too weak. Likewise, some critics say liberty and equality have suffered because the system is now too democratic, while others maintain that the system is not now, and never has been, democratic enough. Contemporary constitutional reform proposals have been made to remedy each of these real or perceived defects, but so far none have been enacted. The best way to answer this question is one constitutional feature at a time. For example, the Federalists claimed that the division of powers between the national government and the states would leave most citizens free to grasp economic opportunity, protect the political rights of local minorities, and frustrate the formation of tyrannical national majorities. Has federalism fulfilled this promise? The next chapter should help you decide.

World Wide Web Resources

To find historical and legal documents:
- FedLaw's constitutional and early government documents: www.legal.gsa.gov/legal9.htm
- Emory University Law School: www.law.emory.edu/FEDERAL/conpict.html
- National Constitution Center: www.constitutioncenter.org
- Congress: www.thomas.loc.gov/ (choose Historical Documents)

To look at court cases about the Constitution:
- Yale University Law School: www.yale.edu/lawweb/avalon/avalon.htm
- Washington, D.C., newspapers:
   Washington Post: www.washingtonpost.com
   Washington Times: www. washtimes.com

Key Terms

unalienable *p. 19*
Articles of Confederation *p. 21*
Constitutional Convention *p. 22*
Shays's Rebellion *p. 23*
Great Compromise *p. 27*
republic *p. 28*
judicial review *p. 28*

checks and balances *p. 29*
federalism *p. 29*
separation of powers *p. 30*
faction *p. 30*
Federalists *p. 30*
Antifederalists *p. 30*
Federalist papers *p. 32*

coalition *p. 34*
writ of habeas corpus *p. 34*
bill of attainder *p. 34*
ex post facto law *p. 34*
bill of rights *p. 35*
amendments *p. 41*
line-item veto *p. 43*

Suggested Readings

Bailyn, Bernard. *The Ideological Origins of the American Revolution.* Cambridge: Harvard University Press, 1967. A brilliant account of how the American colonists formed and justified the idea of independence.

Becker, Carl L. *The Declaration of Independence.* New York: Vintage, 1942. The classic account of the meaning of the Declaration.

Farrand, Max. *The Framing of the Constitution of the United States.* New Haven, Conn.: Yale University Press, 1913. A good, brief account of the Philadelphia convention by the editor of Madison's notes on the convention.

Federalist papers. By Alexander Hamilton, James Madison, and John Jay. The definitive edition, edited by Jacob E. Cooke, was published in Middletown, Conn., in 1961, by the Wesleyan University Press.

Goldwin, Robert A., and William A. Schambra, eds. *How Capitalistic Is the Constitution?* Washington, D.C.: American Enterprise Institute, 1982. Essays from different viewpoints discussing the relationship between the Constitution and the economic order.

———. *How Democratic Is the Constitution?* Washington, D.C.: American Enterprise Institute, 1980. Collection of essays offering different interpretations of the political meaning of the Constitution.

McDonald, Forrest. *Novus Ordo Seclorum.* Lawrence: University of Kansas Press, 1985. A careful study of the intellectual origins of the Constitution. The Latin title means "New World Order," which is what the Framers hoped they were creating.

Robinson, Donald L., ed. *Reforming American Government.* Boulder, Colo.: Westview Press, 1985. Collection of essays advocating constitutional reform.

Sheldon, Garrett W. *The Political Philosophy of James Madison.* Baltimore: Johns Hopkins University Press, 2001. Masterful account of Madison's political thought and its roots in classical republicanism and Christianity.

Storing, Herbert J. *What the Anti-Federalists Were For.* Chicago: University of Chicago Press, 1981. Close analysis of the political views of those opposed to the ratification of the Constitution.

Wood, Gordon S. *The Creation of the American Republic.* Chapel Hill: University of North Carolina Press, 1969. A detailed study of American political thought before the Philadelphia convention.

———. *The Radicalism of the American Revolution.* New York: Knopf, 1992. Magisterial study of the nature and effects of the American Revolution and the relationship between the socially radical Revolution and the Constitution.

Federalism

Enduring Questions

1. Where is sovereignty located in the American political system?

2. How is power divided between the national government and the states under the Constitution?

3. How has America's federal system changed since the first days of the Republic?

Since the adoption of the Constitution in 1787, the single most persistent source of political conflict has been the relations between the national and state governments. The political conflict over slavery, for example, was intensified because some state governments condoned or supported slavery, while others took action to discourage it. The proponents and opponents of slavery were thus given territorial power centers from which to carry on the dispute. Other issues, such as the regulation of business and the provision of social welfare programs, were in large part fought out, for well over a century, in terms of "national interests" versus "states' rights." While other nations, such as Great Britain, were debating the question of whether the national government *ought* to provide old-age pensions or regulate the railroads, the United States debated a different question—whether the national government *had the right* to do these things. Even after these debates had ended—almost invariably with a decision favorable to the national government—the administration and financing of the programs that resulted have usually involved a large role for the states.

Today an effort is under way to scale back the size and activities of the national government and to shift responsibility for a wide range of domestic programs from Washington to the states. In recent years the effort to devolve onto the states the national government's functions in areas such as welfare, health care, and job training has become known as **devolution.** In the 104th Congress (1994–1996) Republican majorities in the House and Senate made proposals, several of them enacted into law, to accelerate the devolution of national power. Many of these proposals involved giving the states **block grants**—money from the national government for programs in certain general areas that the states can use at their discretion within broad guidelines set by Congress.

In 1908 Woodrow Wilson observed that how we structure the relationship between the national government and the states "is the cardinal question of our constitutional system," a question that cannot be settled by "one generation, because it is a question of growth, and every successive stage of our political and economic development gives it a new aspect, makes it a new question."[1]

Today, in the twenty-first century, is the American political system in the early stages of a "devolution revolution" that will make the states, not the national government, the dominant force in domestic affairs? Do most Americans support devolution? Have recent court decisions returned power to the states? What, if any, differences will devolution reforms make in who governs and to what ends? Before one can begin to address these questions, it is important to master the basic concepts and understand the political history of federalism.

Governmental Structure

Federalism refers to a political system in which there are local (territorial, regional, provincial, state, or municipal) units of government, as well as a national government, that can make final decisions with respect to at least some governmental activities and whose existence is specially protected.[2] Almost every nation in the world has local units of government of some kind, if for no other reason than to decentralize the administrative burdens of governing. But these governments are not federal unless the local units exist independent of the preferences of the national government and can make decisions on at least some matters without regard to those preferences.

The United States, Canada, Australia, India, Germany, and Switzerland are federal systems, as are a few other nations. France, Great Britain, Italy, and Sweden are not: they are unitary systems, because such local governments as they possess can be altered or even abolished by the national government and cannot plausibly claim to have final authority over any significant governmental activities.

The special protection that subnational governments enjoy in a federal system derives in part from the constitution of the country but also from the habits, preferences, and dispositions of the citizens and the actual distribution of political power in society. The constitution of the former Soviet Union in theory created a federal system, as claimed by that country's full name—the Union of Soviet Socialist Republics—but for most of their history, none of these "socialist republics" were in the slightest degree independent of the central government. Were the American Constitution the only guarantee of the independence of the American states, they would long since have become mere administrative subunits of the government in Washington. Their independence results in large measure from the commitment of Americans to the idea of local self-government and from the fact that Congress consists of people who are selected by and responsive to local constituencies.

"The basic political fact of federalism," writes David B. Truman, "is that it creates separate, self-sustaining centers of power, prestige, and profit."[3] Political power is locally acquired by people whose careers depend for the most part on satisfying local interests. As a result, though the national government has come to have vast powers, it exercises many of those powers through state governments. What many of us forget when we think about "the government in Washington" is that it spends much of its money and enforces most of its rules not on citizens directly but on other, local units of government. A large part of the welfare system, all of the interstate highway system, virtually every aspect of programs to improve cities, the largest part of the effort to supply jobs to the unemployed, the entire program to clean up our water, and even much of our military manpower (in the form of the National Guard) are enterprises in which the national government does not govern so much as it seeks, by regulation, grant, plan, argument, and cajolery, to get the states to govern in accordance with nationally defined (though often vaguely defined) goals.

In France welfare, highways, education, the police, and the use of land are all matters that are directed nationally. In the United States highways and some welfare programs are largely state functions (though they make use of federal money), while education, policing, and land-use controls are primarily local (city, county, or special-district) functions.

Federalism: Good or Bad?

A measure of the importance of federalism is the controversy that surrounds it. To some, federalism means allowing states to block action, prevent progress, upset national plans, protect powerful local interests, and cater to the self-interest of hack politicians. Harold Laski, a British observer, described American states as "parasitic and poisonous,"[4] and William H. Riker, an American political scientist, argued that "the main effect of federalism since the Civil War has been to perpetuate racism."[5] By contrast, another political scientist, Daniel J. Elazar, believes that the "virtue of the federal system lies in its ability to develop and maintain mechanisms vital to the perpetuation of the unique combination of governmental strength, political flexibility, and individual liberty, which has been the central concern of American politics."[6]

So diametrically opposed are the Riker and Elazar views that one wonders whether they are talking about the same subject. They are, of course, but they are stressing different aspects of the same phenomenon. Whenever the opportunity to exercise political power is widely available (as among the fifty states, three thousand counties, and many thousands of municipalities in the United States), it is obvious that in different places different people will make use of that power for different purposes. There is no question that allowing states and cities to make autonomous, binding political decisions will allow some people in some places to make those decisions in ways that maintain racial segregation, protect vested interests, and facilitate corruption. It is equally true, however, that this arrangement also enables other people in other places to pass laws that attack segregation, regulate harmful economic practices, and purify politics, often long before these ideas gain national support or become national policy.

★ **POLITICALLY SPEAKING** ★

Sovereignty, Federalism, and the Constitution

Sovereignty means supreme or ultimate political authority: A sovereign government is one that is legally and politically independent of any other government.

A **unitary system** is one in which sovereignty is wholly in the hands of the national government, so that the states and localities are dependent on its will.

A **confederation or confederal system** is one in which the states are sovereign and the national government is allowed to do only that which the states permit.

A **federal system** is one in which sovereignty is shared, so that in some matters the national government is supreme and in other matters the states are supreme.

The Founding Fathers often took *confederal* and *federal* to mean much the same thing. Rather than establishing a government in which there was a clear division of sovereign authority between the national and state governments, they saw themselves as creating a government that combined some characteristics of a unitary regime with some of a confederal one. Or, as James Madison expressed the idea in *Federalist* No. 39, the Constitution "is, in strictness, neither a national nor a federal Constitution, but a composition of both." Where sovereignty is located in this system is a matter that the Founders did not clearly answer.

In this text, a **federal regime** is defined in the simplest possible terms—as one in which local units of government have a specially protected existence and can make some final decisions over some governmental activities.

For example, in a unitary political system, such as that of France, a small but intensely motivated group could not have blocked civil rights legislation for as long as some southern senators blocked it in this country. But by the same token it would have been equally difficult for another small but intensely motivated group to block plans to operate a nuclear power plant in their neighborhood, as citizens have done in this country but not in France.

Federalism has permitted experimentation. Women were able to vote in the Wyoming Territory in 1888, long before they could do so in most states.

The existence of independent state and local governments means that different political groups pursuing different political purposes will come to power in different places. The smaller the political unit, the more likely it is to be dominated by a single political faction. James Madison understood this fact perfectly and used it to argue (in *Federalist* No. 10) that it would be in a large (or "extended") republic, such as the United States as a whole, that one would find the greatest opportunity for all relevant interests to be heard. When William Riker condemns federalism, he is thinking of the fact that in some places the ruling factions in cities and states have opposed granting equal rights to African Americans. When Daniel Elazar praises federalism, he is recalling that, in other states and cities, the ruling factions have taken the lead (long in advance of the federal government) in developing measures to protect the environment, extend civil rights, and improve social conditions. If you live in California, whether you like federalism

depends in part on whether you like the fact that California has, independent of the federal government, cut property taxes, strictly controlled coastal land use, heavily regulated electric utilities, and increased (at one time) and decreased (at another time) its welfare rolls.

Increased Political Activity

Federalism has many effects, but its most obvious effect has been to facilitate the mobilization of political activity. Unlike Don Quixote, the average citizen does not tilt at windmills. He or she is more likely to become involved in organized political activity if he or she feels there is a reasonable chance of having a practical effect. The chances of having such an effect are greater where there are many elected officials and independent governmental bodies, each with a relatively small constituency, than where there are few elected officials, most of whom have the nation as a whole for a constituency. In short a federal system, by virtue of the decentralization of authority, lowers the cost of organized political activity; a unitary system, because of the centralization of authority, raises the cost. We may disagree about the purposes of organized political activity, but the fact of widespread organized activity can scarcely be doubted—or if it can be doubted, it is only because you have not yet read Chapters 6 and 9.

It is impossible to say whether the Founders, when they wrote the Constitution, planned to produce such widespread opportunities for political participation. Unfortunately they were not very clear (at least in writing) about how the federal system was supposed to work, and thus most of the interesting questions about the jurisdiction and powers of our national and state governments had to be settled by a century and a half of protracted, often bitter, conflict.

The Founding

The goal of the Founders seems clear: federalism was one device whereby personal liberty was to be protected. (The separation of powers was another.) They feared that placing final political authority in any one set of hands, even in the hands of persons popularly elected, would so concentrate power as to risk tyranny. But they had seen what happened when independent states tried to form a compact, as under the Articles of Confederation; what the states put together, they could also take apart. The alliance among the states that existed from 1776 to 1787 was a confederation: that is, a system of government in which the people create state governments, which, in turn, create and operate a national government (see Figure 3.1). Since the national government in a confederation derives its powers from the states, it is dependent on their continued cooperation for its survival. By 1786 that cooperation was barely forthcoming.

A Bold, New Plan

A federation—or a "federal republic," as the Founders called it—derives its powers directly from the people, as do the state governments. As the Founders envisioned it, both levels of government, the national and the state, would have certain powers, but neither would have supreme authority over the other. Madison, writing in *Federalist* No. 46, said that both the state and federal governments "are in fact but different agents and trustees of the people, constituted with different powers." In *Federalist* No. 28 Hamilton explained how he thought the system would work: The people could shift their support between state and federal levels of government as needed to keep the two in balance. "If their rights are invaded by either, they can make use of the other as the instrument of redress."

It was an entirely new plan, for which no historical precedent existed. Nobody came to the Philadelphia convention with a clear idea of what a federal (as opposed to a unitary or a confederal) system would look like, and there was not much discussion at Philadelphia of how the system would work in practice. Few delegates then used the word *federalism* in the sense in which we now employ it (it was originally used as a synonym for *confederation* and only later came to stand for something different).[7] The Constitution does not spell out the powers that the states are to have, and until the Tenth Amendment was added at the insistence of various states, there was not even a clause in it saying (as did the amendment) that "the powers not delegated to the United States by the Constitution, nor prohibited by it to the states, are reserved to the states respectively, or to the people." The Founders assumed from the outset that the federal government would have only those powers given to it by the Constitution; the Tenth Amendment was an afterthought, added to make that assumption explicit and allay fears that something else was intended.[8]

| Figure 3.1 | Lines of Power in Three Systems of Government |

UNITARY SYSTEM

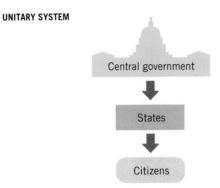

Power centralized.
State or regional governments derive authority from central government.
Examples: United Kingdom, France.

FEDERAL SYSTEM

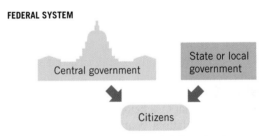

Power divided between central and state or local governments.
Both the government and constituent governments act directly upon the citizens.
Both must agree to constitutional change.
Examples: Canada, United States since adoption of Constitution.

CONFEDERAL SYSTEM (or CONFEDERATION)

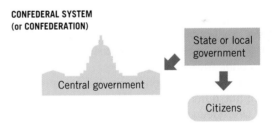

Power held by independent states.
Central government is a creature of the constituent governments.
Example: United States under the Articles of Confederation.

The Tenth Amendment has rarely had much practical significance, however. From time to time the Supreme Court has tried to interpret that amendment as putting certain state activities beyond the reach of the federal government, but invariably the Court has later changed its mind and allowed Washington to regulate such matters as the hours that employees of a city-owned mass-transit system may work. The Court did not find that running such a transportation system was one of the powers "reserved to the states."[9] But, as we explain later in this chapter, the Court has begun to give new life to the Tenth Amendment and the doctrine of state sovereignty.

Elastic Language

The need to reconcile the competing interests of large and small states and of northern and southern states, especially as they affected the organization of Congress, was sufficiently difficult without trying to spell out exactly what relationship ought to exist between the national and state systems. For example, Congress was given the power to regulate commerce "among the several states." The Philadelphia convention would have gone on for four years rather than four months if the Founders had decided that it was necessary to describe, in clear language, how one was to tell where commerce *among* the states ended and commerce wholly *within* a single state began. The Supreme Court, as we shall see, devoted over a century to that task before giving up.

Though some clauses bearing on federal-state relations were reasonably clear (see the box on page 55), other clauses were quite vague. The Founders knew, correctly, that they could not make an exact and exhaustive list of everything the federal government was empowered to do—circumstances would change, new exigencies would arise. Thus they added the following elastic language to Article I: Congress shall have the power to "make all laws which shall be necessary and proper for carrying into execution the foregoing powers."

The Founders themselves carried away from Philadelphia different views of what federalism meant. One view was championed by Hamilton. Since the people had created the national government, since the laws and treaties made pursuant to the Constitution were "the supreme law of the land" (Article VI), and since the most pressing needs were the development of a national economy and the conduct of foreign affairs, Hamilton thought that the national government was the superior and leading force in political affairs and that its powers ought to be broadly defined and liberally construed.

The other view, championed by Jefferson, was that the federal government, though important, was the product of an agreement among the states; and though "the people" were the ultimate sovereigns, the principal threat to their liberties was likely to come from the national government. (Madison, a strong supporter of national supremacy at the convention, later became a champion of states' rights.) Thus the powers of the federal government should be narrowly construed and strictly limited. As Madison put it in *Federalist* No. 45, in language that probably made Hamilton wince, "The powers delegated by the proposed Constitution to the federal government are few and defined. Those which are to remain in the State governments are numerous and indefinite."

Hamilton argued for national supremacy, Jefferson for states' rights. Though their differences were greater in theory than in practice (as we shall see in Chapter 12, Jefferson while president sometimes acted in a positively Hamiltonian manner), the differing interpretations they offered of the Constitution were to shape political debate in this country until well into the 1960s.

Thomas Jefferson (1743–1826) was not at the Constitutional Convention. His doubts about the new national government led him to oppose the Federalist administration of John Adams and to become an ardent champion of states' rights.

The States and the Constitution

The Framers made some attempt to define the relations between the states and the federal government and how the states were to relate to one another. The following points were made in the original Constitution—before the Bill of Rights was added.

Restrictions on Powers of the States
States may not make treaties with foreign nations, coin money, issue paper currency, grant titles of nobility, pass a bill of attainder or an ex post facto law,* or, without the consent of Congress, levy any taxes on imports or exports, keep troops and ships in time of peace, or enter into an agreement with another state or with a foreign power.
[Art. I, sec. 10]

Guarantees by the Federal Government to the States
The national government guarantees to every state a "republican form of government" and protection against foreign invasion and (provided the states request it) protection against domestic insurrection.
[Art. IV, sec. 4]
An existing state will not be broken up into two or more states or merged with all or part of another state without that state's consent.
[Art. IV, sec. 3]

*For definitions of *bill of attainder* and *ex post facto law,* see the Glossary.

Congress may admit new states into the Union.
[Art. IV, sec. 3]
Taxes levied by Congress must be uniform throughout the United States: they may not be levied on some states but not others.
[Art. I, sec. 8]
The Constitution may not be amended to give states unequal representation in the Senate.
[Art. V]

Rules Governing How States Deal with Each Other
"Full faith and credit" shall be given by each state to the laws, records, and court decisions of other states. (For example, a civil case settled in the courts of one state cannot be retried in the courts of another.)
[Art. IV, sec. 1]
The citizens of each state shall have the "privileges and immunities" of the citizens of every other state. (No one is quite sure what this is supposed to mean.)
[Art. IV, sec. 2]
If a person charged with a crime by one state flees to another, he or she is subjected to extradition—that is, the governor of the state that finds the fugitive is supposed to return the person to the governor of the state that wants him or her.
[Art. IV, sec. 2]

The Debate on the Meaning of Federalism

The Civil War was fought, in part, over the issue of national supremacy versus states' rights, but it settled only one part of that argument—namely, that the national government was supreme, its sovereignty derived directly from the people, and thus the states could not lawfully secede from the Union. Virtually every other aspect of the national-supremacy issue continued to animate political and legal debate for another century.

The Supreme Court Speaks

As arbiter of what the Constitution means, the Supreme Court became the focal point of that debate. In Chapter 14 we shall see in some detail how the Court made its decisions. For now it is enough to know that during the formative years of the new Republic, the Supreme Court was led by a staunch and brilliant advocate of Hamilton's position, Chief Justice John Marshall. In a series of decisions he and the Court powerfully defended the national-supremacy view of the newly formed federal government.

The most important decision was in a case, seemingly trivial in its origins, that arose when James McCulloch, the cashier of the Baltimore branch of the Bank of the United States, which had been created by Congress, refused to pay a tax levied on that bank by the state of Maryland. He was hauled into state court and convicted of failing to pay a tax. In

1819 McCulloch appealed all the way to the Supreme Court in a case known as *McCulloch v. Maryland.* The Court, in a unanimous opinion, answered two questions in ways that expanded the powers of Congress and confirmed the supremacy of the federal government in the exercise of those powers.

The first question was whether Congress had the right to set up a bank, or any other corporation, since such a right is nowhere explicitly mentioned in the Constitution. Marshall said that, though the federal government possessed only those powers enumerated in the Constitution, the "extent"—that is, the meaning—of those powers required interpretation. Though the word *bank* is not in that document, one finds there the power to manage money: to lay and collect taxes, issue a currency, and borrow funds. To carry out these powers Congress may reasonably decide that chartering a national bank is "necessary and proper." Marshall's words were carefully chosen to endow the **"necessary and proper" clause** with the widest possible sweep:

> Let the end be legitimate, let it be within the scope of the Constitution, and all means which are appropriate, which are plainly adapted to that end, which are not prohibited, but consistent with the letter and spirit of the Constitution, are constitutional.[10]

The second question was whether a federal bank could lawfully be taxed by a state. To answer it, Marshall went back to first principles. The government of the United States was not established by the states, but by the people, and thus the federal government was supreme in the exercise of those powers conferred upon it. Having already concluded that chartering a bank was within the powers of Congress, Marshall then argued that the only way for such powers to be supreme was for their use to be immune from state challenge and for the products of their use to be protected against state destruction. Since "the power to tax involves the power to destroy," and since the power to destroy a federal agency would confer upon the states using it supremacy over the federal government, the states may not tax any federal instrument. Hence the Maryland law was unconstitutional.

McCulloch won, and so did the federal government. Half a century later the Court decided that what was sauce for the goose was sauce for the gander. It held that just as state governments could not tax federal bonds, the federal government could not tax the interest people earn on state and municipal bonds. In 1988 the Supreme Court changed its mind and decided that Congress was now free, if it wished, to tax the interest on such state and local bonds.[11] Municipal bonds, which for nearly a century were a tax-exempt investment protected, so their holders thought, by the Constitution, were now protected only by politics. So far Congress hasn't wanted to tax them.

Nullification

The Supreme Court can decide a case without settling the issue. The struggle over states' rights versus national supremacy continued to rage in Congress, during presidential elections, and ultimately on the battlefield. The issue came to center on the doctrine of **nullification.** When Congress passed laws (in 1798) to punish newspaper editors who published stories critical of the federal government, James Madison and Thomas Jefferson opposed the laws, suggesting (in statements known as the Virginia and Kentucky Resolutions) that the states had the right to "nullify" (that is, declare null and void) a federal law that, in the states' opinion, violated the Constitution. The laws expired before the claim of nullification could be settled in the courts.

Later the doctrine of nullification was revived by John C. Calhoun of South Carolina, first in opposition to a tariff enacted by the federal government and later in opposition to federal efforts to restrict

At one time the states could issue their own paper money, such as this New York currency worth twenty-five cents in 1776. Under the Constitution this power was reserved to Congress.

public debt stayed more or less constant, or even declined, in the second half of the nineteenth century. By the mid-twentieth century people no longer worried about the national debt so much, or at least they worried about it for reasons other than the fear of being in debt. Thus the federal government came to accept, as a matter of policy, the proposition that when it needed money, it would print it. States could not do this: if they borrowed (and many could not), they had to pay it all back, in full.

These three economic reasons for the attractiveness of federal grants were probably not as important as a fourth reason: politics. Federal money seemed to a state official to be "free" money. If Alabama could get Washington to put up the money for improving navigation on the Tombigbee River, the citizens of the entire nation, not just those of Alabama, would pay for it. Of course if Alabama gets money for that purpose, every state will want it (and will get it). Even so, it was still an attractive political proposition: the governor of Alabama did not have to propose, collect, or take responsibility for federal taxes. Indeed, the governor could denounce the federal government for being profligate in its use of the people's money. Meanwhile he would cut the ribbon opening the new dam on the Tombigbee.

That every state had an incentive to ask for federal money to pay for local programs meant, of course, that it would be very difficult for one state to get money for a given program without every state's getting it. The senator from Alabama who votes for the project to improve navigation on the Tombigbee will have to vote in favor of projects improving navigation on every other river in the country if the senator expects his or her Senate colleagues to support such a request. Federalism as practiced in the United States means that when Washington wants to send money to one state or congressional district, it must send money to many states and districts.

In 1966, for example, President Lyndon Johnson proposed a "Model Cities" plan, under which federal funds would be spent on experimental programs in a small number of large cities that had especially acute problems. When the bill went to Congress, it quickly became clear that no such plan could be passed unless the number of cities to benefit was increased. Senator Edmund Muskie of Maine, whose support was crucial, would not vote for a bill that did not make Augusta, Bangor, and Portland eligible for aid originally intended to help New York, Chicago, and Philadelphia.[28]

> **Figure 3.2   The Changing Purpose of Federal Grants to State and Local Governments**

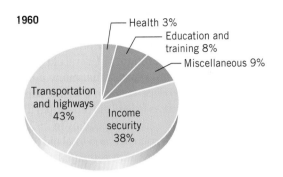

1960

Health 3%
Education and training 8%
Miscellaneous 9%
Transportation and highways 43%
Income security 38%

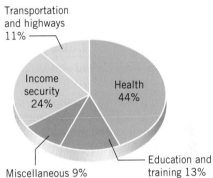

2001

Transportation and highways 11%
Income security 24%
Health 44%
Miscellaneous 9%
Education and training 13%

Note: Totals may not add up to 100 percent because of rounding.
Source: Budget of the U.S. Government, Fiscal Year 2001, table 12.2.

Meeting National Needs

Until the 1960s most federal grants-in-aid were conceived by or in cooperation with the states and were designed to serve essentially state purposes. Large blocs of voters and a variety of organized interests would press for grants to help farmers, build highways, or support vocational education. During the 1960s, however, an important change occurred: the federal government began devising grant programs based less on what states were demanding and more on what federal officials perceived to be important *national* needs (see Figure 3.2). Federal officials, not state and local ones, were the principal proponents of grant programs to aid the urban poor, combat crime, reduce pollution, and deal with drug abuse. Some of these programs even attempted to bypass the states, providing money directly to cities or even to local citizen groups. These were worrisome developments for governors, who were accustomed to being the conduit for money on its way from Washington to local communities.

The rise in federal activism in setting goals and the efforts, on occasion, to bypass state officials occurred at a time when the total amount of federal aid to states and localities had become so vast that many jurisdictions were completely dependent on it for the support of vital services. Whereas federal aid amounted to less than 2 percent of state and local spending in 1927, by 1980 it amounted to 26 percent, and total aid to state and local governments was 15.4 percent of the federal budget. After stabilizing and dipping slightly in the 1980s, Washington's grants to state and local governments increased in the 1990s and reached new highs after 2000 (see Figure 3.3).

The Intergovernmental Lobby

State and local officials, both elected and appointed, began to form an important new lobby—the "intergovernmental lobby," made up of mayors, governors, superintendents of schools, state directors of public health, county highway commissioners, local police chiefs, and others who had come to count on federal funds.[29] The four largest of these lobbies employed, in 1998, nearly four hundred people and spent about $62 million, about 10 percent of which came from the federal government. Even this has proved insufficient. After all, national organizations of governors or mayors can press for more federal money but not for increased funding for any particular state or city. Thus over thirty-one individual states, more than two dozen counties, and over one hundred cities have opened their own offices in Washington. Some are small, some share staff with other communities, but a few are quite large. Texas alone employs two dozen people in Washington to look after its interests.

The purpose of this intergovernmental lobby was the same as that of any private lobby—to obtain more federal money with fewer strings attached. For a while the cities and states did in fact get more money, but by 1980 federal grants had stopped growing.

Categorical Grants Versus Revenue Sharing

The effort to loosen the strings took the form of shifting, as much as possible, the federal aid from **categorical grants** to block grants or to **revenue sharing.** A categorical grant is one for a specific purpose defined by federal law: to build an airport or a college dormitory, for example, or to make welfare payments to low-income mothers. Such grants usually require that the state or locality put up money to "match" some part of the federal grant, though the amount of matching funds can be quite small. (In the federal highway program Washington pays about 90 percent of the construction costs and the states only about 10 percent.) Governors and mayors complained about these categorical grants because their purposes were often so narrow that it was impossible for a state to adapt federal grants to local needs. A mayor seeking federal money to build parks might have discovered that the city could get money only if it launched an urban-renewal program that entailed bulldozing several blocks of housing or small businesses.

One response to this problem was to consolidate several categorical or project grant programs into a single block grant devoted to some general purpose and with fewer restrictions on its use. Block grants (sometimes called *special revenue sharing* or *broad-based aid*) began in the mid-1960s, when such a grant was created in the health field. Though many block grants were proposed between 1966 and 1980, only five were enacted. Of the three largest, one consolidated various categorical grant programs aimed at cities (Community Development Block Grants), another created a program to aid local law enforcement (Law Enforcement Assistance Act), and a third authorized new kinds of locally managed programs for the unemployed (CETA, or the Comprehensive Employment and Training Act). Between 1980 and 1995 the number of block grants in effect rose from five to sixteen.

Revenue sharing (sometimes called *general revenue sharing*, or GRS) was even more permissive. Adopted in 1972 with the passage of the State and Local Fiscal Assistance Act, GRS provided for the distribution of about $6 billion a year in federal funds to states and localities, with no requirement as to matching funds and freedom to spend the money on almost any governmental purpose. Distribution of the money was determined by a statistical formula that took into account population, local tax effort, and the wealth of the state in a way intended to send more money to poorer, heavily taxed states and less to richer, lightly taxed ones. In 1986 the program was ended after having distributed about $85 billion over a fourteen-year period.

Figure 3.3 Federal Grants to State and Local Governments, 1983–2003

Total federal grants to state and local governments, in billions of constant 1996 dollars, and the aid as a percentage of total federal spending on all grants, for each fiscal year.

■ Total grants (scale at left)

■ Percentage of federal spending

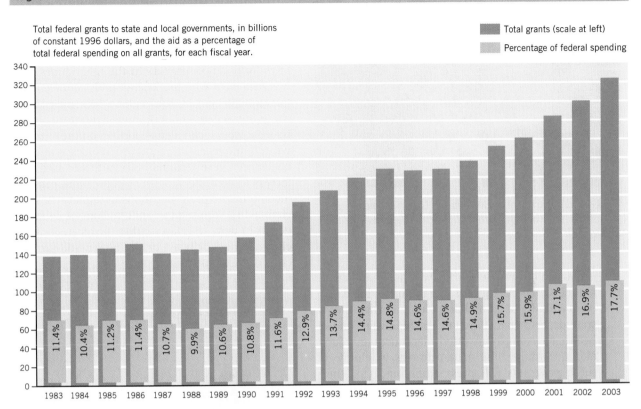

Note: Data for the years 2002–2003 are estimated.
Source: Budget of the U.S. Government, Fiscal Year 2002, Historical Tables, Composition of Outlays, table 6.1.

In theory block grants and revenue sharing were supposed to give the states and cities considerable freedom in deciding how to spend the money while helping to relieve their tax burdens. To some extent they did. However, neither the goal of "no strings" nor the one of fiscal relief was really attained. First, the amount of money available from block grants and revenue sharing did not grow as fast as the states had hoped nor as quickly as did the money available through categorical grants. Second, the federal government steadily increased the number of strings attached to the spending of this supposedly "unrestricted" money. Thus between 1993 and 1995 the number of federal grants to state and local governments increased from 599 to 633. The entire growth was in categorical grants (from 578 to 618); no new block grants were established.

Block grants grew more slowly than categorical grants because of the different kinds of political coalitions supporting each. Congress and the federal bureaucracy liked categorical grants for the same reason the states disliked them—the specificity of these programs enhanced federal control over how the money was to be used. Federal officials, joined by liberal interest groups and organized labor, tended to distrust state governments. Whenever Congress wanted to address some national problem, its natural inclination was to create a categorical grant program so that it, and not the states, would decide how the money would be spent.

Moreover, even though governors and mayors like block grants and revenue sharing, these programs cover such a broad range of activities that no single interest group has a vital stake in pressing for their enlargement. Revenue sharing, for example, provided a little money to many city agencies but rarely provided all or even most of the money for any single agency. Thus no single agency acted as if the

The Federal Department of Housing and Urban Development works with state housing authorities to create affordable places to live, such as this new mixed-income community in Atlanta.

expansion of revenue sharing were a life-and-death matter. Categorical grants, on the other hand, are often a matter of life and death for many agencies— state departments of welfare, of highways, and of health, for example, are utterly dependent on federal aid. Accordingly, the administrators in charge of these programs will press strenuously for their expansion. Moreover, categorical programs are supervised by special committees of Congress, and as we shall see in Chapter 11, many of these committees have an interest in seeing their programs grow.

Rivalry Among the States

The more important that federal money becomes to the states, the more likely they are to compete among themselves for the largest share of it. For a century or better the growth of the United States— in population, business, and income—was concentrated in the industrial Northeast. In recent decades, however, that growth—at least in population and employment, if not in income—has shifted to the South, Southwest, and Far West. This change has precipitated an intense debate over whether the federal government, by the way it distributes its funds and awards its contracts, is unfairly helping some regions and states at the expense of others. Journalists and politicians have dubbed the struggle as one between Snowbelt (or Frostbelt) and Sunbelt states.

Whether in fact there is anything worth arguing about is far from clear: the federal government has had great difficulty in figuring out where it ulti-

mately spends what funds for what purposes. For example, a $1 billion defense contract may go to a company with headquarters in California, but much of the money may actually be spent in Connecticut or New York, as the prime contractor in California buys from subcontractors in the other states. It is even less clear whether federal funds actually affect the growth rate of the regions. The uncertainty about the facts has not prevented a debate about the issue, however. That debate focuses on the formulas written into federal laws by which block grants are allocated. These formulas take into account such factors as a county's or city's population, personal income in the area, and housing quality. A slight change in a formula can shift millions of dollars in grants in ways that favor either the older, declining cities of the Northeast or the newer, still-growing cities of the Southwest.

The federal government helps shape the character of cities by giving money to build parts of the federal highway system.

With the advent of grants based on distributional formulas (as opposed to grants for a particular project), the results of the census, taken every ten years, assume monumental importance. A city or state shown to be losing population may, as a result, forfeit millions of dollars in federal aid. There are over one hundred programs (out of some five hundred federal grant programs in all) that distribute money on the basis of population. When the director of the census in 1960 announced figures showing that many big cities had lost population, he was generally ignored. When he made the same announcement in 1980, after the explosion in federal grants, he was roundly denounced by the mayors of those cities.

Senators and representatives now have access to computers that can tell them instantly the effect on their states and districts of even minor changes in a formula by which federal aid is distributed. These formulas rely on objective measures, but the exact measure is selected with an eye to its political consequences. There is nothing wrong with this in principle, since any political system must provide some benefits for everybody if it is to stay together. Given the competition among states in a federal system, however, the struggle over allocation formulas becomes especially acute. The results are sometimes plausible, as when Congress decides to distribute money intended to help disadvantaged local school systems in large part on the basis of the proportion of poor children in each school district. But sometimes the results are a bit strange, as when the formula by which federal aid for mass transit is determined gives New York, a city utterly dependent on mass transit, a federal subsidy of two cents per transit passenger but gives Grand Rapids, a city that relies chiefly on the automobile, a subsidy of forty-five cents per passenger.[30]

Federal Aid and Federal Control

So important has federal aid become for state and local governments that mayors and governors, along with others, began to fear that Washington was well on its way to controlling other levels of government. "He who pays the piper calls the tune," they muttered. In this view the constitutional protection of state government to be found in the Tenth Amendment was in jeopardy as a result of the strings being attached to the grants-in-aid on which the states were increasingly dependent.

Block grants and revenue sharing were efforts to reverse this trend by allowing the states and localities freedom (considerable in the case of block grants; almost unlimited in the case of revenue sharing) to spend money as they wished. But as we have seen, these new devices did not in fact reverse the trend. Categorical grants—those with strings attached—continued to grow even faster.

There are two kinds of federal controls on state governmental activities. The traditional control tells the state government what it must do if it wants to get some grant money. These strings are often called **conditions of aid.** The newer form of control tells the state government what it must do, period. These rules are called **mandates.** Sometimes the mandates must be observed only if the state takes any federal grants, but sometimes the mandates have nothing to do with federal aid—they apply to all state governments whether or not they accept grants.

Mandates

Most mandates concern civil rights and environmental protection. States may not discriminate in the operation of their programs, no matter who pays for them. Initially the antidiscrimination rules applied chiefly to distinctions based on race, sex, age, and ethnicity, but of late they have been broadened to include physical and mental disabilities as well. Various pollution control laws require the states to comply with federal standards for clean air, pure drinking water, and sewage treatment.[31]

Stated in general terms, these mandates seem reasonable enough. It is hard to imagine anyone arguing that state governments should be free to discriminate against people because of their race or national origin. In practice, however, some mandates create administrative and financial problems, especially when the mandates are written in vague language, thereby giving federal administrative agencies the power to decide for themselves what state and local governments are supposed to do.

In 1980 there were thirty-six mandates affecting state and local governments, twenty-two of them enacted in the 1970s. Both the Reagan administration and the administration of Bush the elder opposed the growth of mandates. Nevertheless, between 1981 and 1986 some 140 regulations, representing nearly six thousand new requirements on state and local government, were added to eighteen existing mandates. And between 1982 and 1991 Congress passed twenty-seven additional mandates (see Table 3.1).

All mandates are not created equal. Some mandates take the form of regulatory statutes and amendments that expand on previous legislation; the 1982 Voting Rights Act Amendments were based on federal civil rights laws dating back to the 1960s. Other mandates represent new areas of federal involvement. For example, the 1986 Handicapped Children's Protection Act introduced federal regulations intended to improve the life prospects of disabled youngsters. Some mandates are easy to understand, simple to administer, and relatively inexpensive—for example, the 1988 Ocean Dumping Ban Act, which prohibits any additional dumping of municipal sewage sludge in ocean waters. However, many mandates are hard to interpret, difficult to administer, and have high or uncertain costs. The 1990 Americans with Disabilities Act (ADA), which required businesses and state and local governments to provide the disabled with equal access to services, employment, buildings, and transportation systems, was one of twenty mandates signed into law by President Bush the elder in 1990. Unfortunately, the ADA was enacted with no clear-cut definition of "equal access," no unambiguous blueprint of how it was to be administered, and no reliable estimates of how much it would cost to implement.

Mandates are not the only way in which the federal government imposes costs on state and local governments. Certain federal tax and regulatory policies make it difficult or expensive for state and local governments to raise revenues, borrow funds, or privatize public functions. Other federal laws expose state and local governments to financial liability, and numerous federal court decisions and administrative regulations require state and local governments to do or not do various things, either by statute or through an implied constitutional obligation.[32]

It is clear that the federal courts have helped fuel the growth of mandates. As interpreted in this century by the U.S. Supreme Court, the Tenth Amendment provides state and local officials no protection against the march of mandates. Indeed, many of the more controversial mandates result not from congressional action but from court decisions. For example, many state prison systems have been, at one time or another, under the control of federal judges who required major changes in prison construction and management in order to meet standards the judges derived from their reading of the Constitution.

School-desegregation plans are of course the best-known example of federal mandates. Those involving busing—an unpopular policy—have typically been the result of court orders rather than of federal law or regulation.

Judges—usually, but not always, in federal courts—ordered Massachusetts to change the way it hires fire fighters, required Philadelphia to institute new procedures to handle complaints of police brutality, and altered the location in which Chicago was planning to build housing projects. Note that in most of these cases nobody in Washington was plac-

Table 3.1	Major Mandate Enactments Regulating State and Local Governments

Year	
1982	Surface Transportation Assistance Act
	Voting Rights Act Amendments
1983	Social Security Amendments
1984	Child Abuse Amendments
	Hazardous and Solid Waste Amendments
	Highway Safety Amendments
	Voting Accessibility for the Elderly and Handicapped Act
1985	Consolidated Omnibus Budget Reconciliation Act
1986	Age Discrimination in Employment Act Amendments
	Asbestos Hazard Emergency Response Act
	Commercial Motor Vehicle Safety Act
	Education of the Handicapped Act Amendments
	Emergency Planning and Community Right-to-Know Act
	Handicapped Children's Protection Act
	Safe Drinking Water Act Amendments
1987	Civil Rights Restoration Act
	Water Quality Act
1988	Drug-Free Workplace Act
	Fair Housing Act Amendments
	Lead Contamination Control Act
	Ocean Dumping Ban Act
1990	Americans with Disabilities Act
	Cash Management Improvement Act
	Clean Air Act Amendments
	Education of the Handicapped Act Amendments
	Older Workers Benefit Protection Act
1991	Social Security Fiscal Budget Reconciliation Act

Source: Adapted from Timothy J. Conlan and David R. Beam, "Federal Mandates: The Record of Reform and Future Prospects," *Intergovernmental Perspective* (Fall 1992): 8.

ing a mandate on a local government; rather a local citizen was using the federal courts to change a local practice.

The Supreme Court has made it much easier of late for citizens to control the behavior of local officials. A federal law, passed in the 1870s to protect newly freed slaves, makes it possible for a citizen to sue any state or local official who deprives that citizen of any "rights, privileges, or immunities secured by the Constitution and laws" of the United States. In 1980 the Court decided that this law permitted a citizen to sue a local official if the official deprived the citizen of *anything* to which the citizen was entitled under federal law (and not just those federal laws protecting civil rights). For example, a citizen can now use the federal courts to obtain from a state welfare office a payment to which he or she may be entitled under federal law. No one yet knows how this development will affect the way local government operates.

Conditions of Aid

By far the most important federal restrictions on state action are the conditions attached to the grants the states receive. In theory accepting these conditions is voluntary—if you don't want the strings, don't take the money. But when the typical state depends for a quarter or more of its budget on federal grants, many

of which it has received for years and on which many of its citizens depend for their livelihoods, it is not clear exactly how "voluntary" such acceptance is. During the 1960s some strings were added, the most important of which had to do with civil rights. But beginning in the 1970s the number of conditions began to proliferate and have expanded in each subsequent decade down to the present.

Some conditions are specific to particular programs, but most are not. For instance, if a state builds something with federal money, it must first conduct an environmental impact study, it must pay construction workers the "prevailing wage" in the area, it often must provide an opportunity for citizen participation in some aspects of the design or location of the project, and it must ensure that the contractors who build the project have nondiscriminatory hiring policies.

The states and the federal government, not surprisingly, disagree about the costs and benefits of such rules. Members of Congress and federal officials feel they have an obligation to develop uniform national policies with respect to important matters and to prevent states and cities from misspending federal tax dollars. State officials, on the other hand, feel these national rules fail to take into account diverse local conditions, require the states to do

Federal aid pays for training programs for the unemployed, as with this student of furniture refinishing.

things that the states must then pay for, and create serious inefficiencies.

What state and local officials discovered, in short, was that "free" federal money was not quite free after all. In the 1960s federal aid seemed to be entirely beneficial; what mayor or governor would not want such money? But just as local officials found it attractive to do things that another level of government then paid for, in time federal officials learned the same thing. Passing laws to meet the concerns of national constituencies—leaving the cities and states to pay the bills and manage the problems—began to seem attractive to Congress.

Because they face different demands, federal and local officials find themselves in a bargaining situation in which each side is trying to get some benefit (solving a problem, satisfying a pressure group) while passing on to the other side most of the costs (taxes, administrative problems).

The bargains struck in this process used to favor the local officials, because members of Congress were essentially servants of local interests: they were elected by local political parties, they were part of local political organizations, and they supported local autonomy. Beginning in the 1960s, however, changes in American politics that will be described in later chapters—especially the weakening of political parties, the growth of public-interest lobbies in Washington, and the increased activism of the courts—shifted the orientation of many in Congress toward favoring Washington's needs over local needs.

In 1981 President Reagan tried to reverse this trend. He asked Congress to consolidate eighty-three categorical grants into six large block grants, none of which would seriously restrict how the states could spend the money. Congress went along in name only—it consolidated fifty-seven programs into nine small block grants, each of which had many restrictions attached.

In general the states did not respond to Reagan-era block grants and budget cuts simply by slashing programs. A state-by-state study found that "state and local government responses to the 1981 federal aid cuts—through replacement funding, through a wide variety of financial coping and delaying measures, and through administrative reforms"—actually produced "higher service levels than otherwise would have been the case."[33] Likewise, another study concluded that on balance the Reagan block grants

had promoted greater state flexibility in program design, reduced administrative costs, and necessitated little reduction in services despite the fact that states had to operate with about 13 percent fewer federal dollars.[34]

In fact it appears that the Reagan-era cutbacks in the amount of federal money, and the threat of more to come, led many governors and mayors to find new ways of delivering old services. Many cities turned over trash collection and other tasks to private firms, often realizing financial savings. Many states experimented with ways of inducing welfare recipients to take jobs, thereby saving on welfare payments. During the prosperous 1980s the cutback in federal aid was made easier to bear because the economy brought in more tax money to the states without their having to raise new taxes. In tough times, such as the early 1990s, the states struggled to make ends meet. By the mid-1990s, however, the economy was back on track, and the effort begun by the Reagan administration to devolve federal power to the states got a powerful new push by the 104th Congress.

A Devolution Revolution?

With the election of Republican majorities in the House and Senate in 1994, a renewed effort was led by Congress to shift important functions back to the states. The key first issue was welfare—that is, Aid to Families with Dependent Children (AFDC). Since 1935 there had been a federal guarantee of cash assistance to states that offered support to low-income, unmarried mothers and their children. AFDC had become bitterly controversial as the number of women using it and the proportion of births out of wedlock rose dramatically. President Clinton vetoed the first two bills to cut it back but signed the third. It ended any federal guarantee of support and, subject to certain rules, turned the management of the program entirely over to the states, aided by federal block grants. The rules said that every aided woman should begin working within two years and no woman could receive benefits for more than five years.

These and other Republican initiatives were part of a new effort called devolution, which aimed to pass on to the states many federal functions. It is an old idea but one that acquired new vitality because Congress, rather than the president, was leading the effort. Traditionally members of Congress liked voting for federal programs and categorical grants; that way members could take credit for what they were doing for particular constituencies. Under its new conservative leadership, Congress, and especially the House, was looking for ways to scale back the size and activities of the national government. Even Clinton seemed to agree when, in his 1996 State of the Union address, he said that the era of big national government was over. But whatever politicians say, no one really knows how best to divide the responsibility between Washington and the states.

Block Grants for Entitlements

Consider what happened with block grants. Basically, there are three types of block grants: *operational grants,* for purposes such as running state child-care programs; *capital grants,* for purposes such as building local wastewater treatment plants; and *entitlement grants,* for transferring income to families and individuals. From 1966 to 1994 a total of twenty-three block grants were enacted, and fifteen were still in place when the 104th Congress came to power. But all of these block grants, including all nine of the Reagan-era block grants, were for operating and capital purposes; none were for major entitlement programs.

The federal government's two biggest grant-in-aid programs—the now defunct AFDC, often referred to simply as "welfare," which provided cash assistance to the poor, and Medicaid, which finances the majority of medical and long-term care services for low-income and disabled adults and children—were not created as block grant programs. Together AFDC and Medicaid accounted for half of all federal grant-in-aid spending. Both AFDC and Medicaid were operated as entitlement programs. Each state was entitled to federal dollars for AFDC and Medicaid based on the amount of money it paid to poor families and individuals. In turn each state determined the level and range of benefits eligible individuals received, within a framework defined by federal laws and regulations.

Republicans in the 104th Congress made a flurry of proposals for making *both* AFDC and Medicaid into block grant programs, as well as federal job training, vocational education, employment, childcare, foster care, school nutrition, and food programs. All told these proposals, had they been enacted, would have increased federal block grants to

about $183 billion and catapulted the amount of block grant funds in income-transfer programs from only 4 percent to nearly 79 percent.

In the end the devolution revolutionaries of the 104th Congress did not succeed in turning Medicaid into a block grant program. But they did succeed with AFDC and a number of related programs. And they did put the devolution of Medicaid and other important federal programs squarely on the national political agenda, possibly to stay.

There is also some early evidence that the devolution of federal welfare programs has triggered **second-order devolution,** a flow of power and responsibility from the states to local governments, and **third-order devolution,** the increased role of nonprofit organizations and private groups in policy implementation. For example, until the 1996 federal welfare reform law took effect, few states administered their welfare systems in close working partnerships with city or county governments. By 2000, however, fifteen states, including two of the biggest (California and New York), were using so-called county-administered systems. Subject to state direction, scores of local governments are now designing and administering welfare programs (job placement, job training, childcare, and others) through for-profit firms and a wide variety of nonprofit organizations, including local religious congregations.

The total number of people on welfare in America fell from 12.2 million in August 1996 (when the new federal welfare law was signed) to 5.3 million in September 2001, a 56 percent decline. Between 1994 and 1998 the welfare rolls in thirty of the largest cities declined by 35 percent.[35] Observers disagree about how much the devolution of welfare policy (independent of good economic times and other factors) had to do with these drops. But one thing is clear: With fewer people on welfare rolls receiving cash assistance, states amassed billions of dollars in unspent federal welfare funds. In the late 1990s, these so-called welfare surpluses, together with booming economic conditions in many places, permitted most states to increase spending. But the good times were short-lived. By January 2002, growth in state Medicaid costs fueled in part by new federal laws making the program more generous and covering more people, a shortfall in revenues states were projected to receive in tobacco-settlement payments from big cigarette companies (the payments were keyed to the companies' sales, which have been

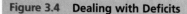

Figure 3.4   Dealing with Deficits

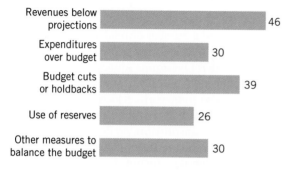

Key fiscal developments by number
of states, as of January 2002:

Revenues below projections — 46
Expenditures over budget — 30
Budget cuts or holdbacks — 39
Use of reserves — 26
Other measures to balance the budget — 30

Source: From "Dealing With Deficit," Council of State Governments, National Conference of State Legislatures, as reported in *Governing*, May 2002, p. 22. Reprinted with permission.

falling), and a sudden surge in funding for state police and other post–September 11 homeland security measures, among other factors, found most states dealing with budget deficits and raiding fiscal reserves (see Figure 3.4).

What's Driving Devolution?

The drive for devolution has complex roots, but three forces stand out: the beliefs of devolution's proponents, the realities of deficit politics, and the views of most citizens. According to R. Kent Weaver, the House Republicans who spearheaded the devolution effort harbored a "deep-seated ideological mistrust of the federal government reinforced by the belief that governments closer to the people were more responsive to popular sentiment, and more likely to constrain the growth of programs that were wasteful and redistributive."[36] At the same time, by 1994 many governors of both parties were convinced that the time had come to let state capitals take the lead in figuring out how best to address social problems and administer public health and welfare programs.

But deficit politics also played a role. Congressional Republicans sought not only to fund entitlement programs with block grants instead of categorical grants but also to make major cuts in entitlement spending. For example, one of their bills would have reduced Medicaid spending by $163 billion and various welfare entitlements by $175 billion over seven years.

As Figure 3.5 suggests, many Americans favor devolution, at least in theory. But it remains unclear how deep public sentiment in favor of devolution runs when "shifting responsibility to the states" also means cutting specific program benefits. For example, when asked in 1995 which federal programs "should be cut back in order to reduce the federal budget deficit," most Americans opposed cuts in Medicaid (73 percent), environmental spending (67 percent), unemployment insurance (64 percent), and many other programs. The one main exception was AFDC (only 35 percent opposed cutting it).[37]

Congress and Federalism

Just as it remains to be seen whether the Supreme Court will continue to revive the doctrine of state sovereignty, so it is not yet clear whether the devolution movement will gain momentum, stall, or be reversed. But whatever the movement's fate, the United States will not become a wholly centralized nation. There remains more political and policy diversity in America than one is likely to find in any other large industrialized nation. The reason is not only that state and local governments have retained certain constitutional protections but also that members of Congress continue to think of themselves as the representatives of localities *to* Washington and not as the representatives *of* Washington to the localities. As we shall see in Chapter 11, American politics, even at the national level, remains local in its orientation.

But if this is true, why do these same members of Congress pass laws that create so many problems for, and stimulate so many complaints from, mayors and governors? One reason is that members of Congress represent different constituencies from the same localities. For example, one member of Congress from Los Angeles may think of the city as a collection of businesspeople, homeowners, and taxpayers, while another may think of it as a group of African Americans, Hispanics, and nature lovers. If Washington wants to simply send money to Los Angeles, these two representatives could be expected to vote together. But if Washington wants to impose mandates or restrictions on the city, they might very well vote on opposite sides, each voting as his or her constituents would most likely prefer.

Another reason is that the organizations that once linked members of Congress to local groups have

Figure 3.5   The Politics of Devolution

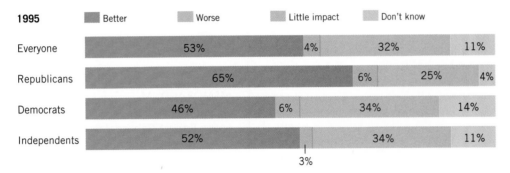

QUESTION

What if some of the tax dollars that go to the federal government now went to your state government instead? Generally speaking, do you think that would result in better government services, or in worse government services, or wouldn't it have much impact on the quality of government services?

1995   ▮ Better   ▮ Worse   ▮ Little impact   ▮ Don't know

Everyone	53%	4%	32%	11%
Republicans	65%	6%	25%	4%
Democrats	46%	6%	34%	14%
Independents	52%	3%	34%	11%

Source: Survey by the *Los Angeles Times,* January 19–22, 1995, as published in *The Public Perspective* (Storrs: Roper Center for Public Opinion Research, University of Connecticut), April/May 1995): 28. © The Public Perspective. Reprinted by permission.

eroded. As we shall see in Chapter 7, the political parties, which once allowed many localities to speak with a single voice in Washington, have decayed to the point where most members of Congress now operate as free agents, judging local needs and national moods independently. In the 1960s these needs and moods seemed to require creating new grant programs; in the 1970s they seemed to require voting for new mandates; in the 1980s and 1990s they seemed to require letting the cities and states alone to experiment with new ways of meeting their needs; and today some say they require rethinking devolution before it goes "too far."

There are exceptions. In some states the parties continue to be strong, to dominate decision-making in the state legislatures, and to significantly affect the way their congressional delegations behave. Democratic members of Congress from Chicago, for example, typically have a common background in party politics and share at least some allegiance to important party leaders.

But these exceptions are becoming fewer and fewer. As a result, when somebody tries to speak "for" a city or state in Washington, that person has little claim to any real authority. The mayor of Philadelphia may favor one program, the governor of Pennsylvania may favor another, and individual local and state officials—school superintendents, the insurance commissioner, public health administrators—may favor still others. In bidding for federal aid, those parts of the state or city that are best-organized often do the best, and increasingly the best-organized groups are not the political parties but rather specialized occupational groups such as doctors or schoolteachers. If one is to ask, therefore, why a member of Congress does not listen to his or her state anymore, the answer is, "What do you mean by *the state?* Which official, which occupational group, which party leader speaks for the state?"

Finally, Americans differ in the extent to which we like federal as opposed to local decisions. When people are asked which level of government gives them the most for their money, relatively poor citizens are likely to mention the federal government first, whereas relatively well-to-do citizens are more likely to mention local government. If we add to income other measures of social diversity—race, religion, and region—there emerge even sharper differences of opinion about which level of government works best. It is this social diversity, and the fact that it is represented not only by state and local leaders but also by members of Congress, that keeps federalism alive and makes it so important. Americans simply do not agree on enough things, or even on which level of government ought to decide on those things, to make possible a unitary system.

Out-of-Towner with Twins to Sue State for Failing to Fund Abortion

January 4
PIERRE, SD

An abortion rights group has filed a multimillion-dollar federal lawsuit against the South Dakota Department of Human Services. The suit is brought on behalf of a welfare-dependent Minnesota woman who was denied public funding for an abortion. In Minnesota, public funding for abortions is available to adult welfare recipients in all or most circumstances, but in South Dakota it is available only in cases of life endangerment. The woman claimed that while her life was not endangered, the abortion that she sought was "medically necessary" because she had previously been diagnosed as suffering from chronic fatigue syndrome. Agency doctors disagreed and denied her the procedure. While in the state seeking work, she went into premature labor and gave birth to twins . . .

MEMORANDUM
To: Judge Grace Viola
From: Robert George, law clerk
Subject: State abortion-funding policies

As requested, I have researched state abortion-funding policies. The main finding is that the laws vary greatly.
The first question before you is whether to accept the case for review.

Arguments for:

1. Three states provide public financing for abortion only in cases of life endangerment. Sixteen states provide it in all or most circumstances.
2. About two hundred thousand women nationwide receive government-funded abortions each year.
3. Advocates argue that just as the federal courts have narrowed state discretion in domains such as state prisoners' appeal rights, the courts should set and enforce national standards for women's abortion rights. Who gets what should not depend on who lives where.

Arguments against:

1. Twenty-six states provide public financing for abortions only in cases of rape, incest, or life endangerment. Only five provide it under those and other health circumstances.
2. About 85 percent of all abortions are privately funded, and federal courts have consistently upheld the right of states to restrict abortions and withhold public funding.
3. Opponents argue that just as the Supreme Court has begun to restore state sovereignty and revive the Eleventh Amendment, it would be a mistake, especially on such a morally controversial issue as abortion, to prevent the citizens of each state from setting and enforcing policies that are in accord with their preferences. Who gets what should sometimes depend on who lives where.

Your decision:
Accept case _____
Reject case _____

Summary

States participate actively both in determining national policy and in administering national programs. Moreover, they reserve to themselves or the localities within them important powers over public services, such as schooling and law enforcement, and public decisions, such as land-use control, that in unitary systems are dominated by the national government.

How one evaluates federalism depends in large part on the value one attaches to the competing criteria of equality and participation. Federalism means that citizens living in different parts of the country will be treated differently, not only in spending programs, such as welfare, but in legal systems that assign in different places different penalties to similar offenses or that differentially enforce civil rights laws. But federalism also means that there are more opportunities for participation in making decisions—in influencing what is taught in the schools and in deciding where highways and government projects are to be built. Indeed, differences in public policy—that is, unequal treatment—are in large part the result of participation in decision-making. It is difficult, perhaps impossible, to have more of one of these values without having less of the other.

Reconsidering the Enduring Questions

1. ***Where is sovereignty located in the American political system?***

   Strictly speaking, the answer is "nowhere." Sovereignty means supreme or ultimate political authority. A sovereign government is one that is legally and politically independent of any other government. No government in America, including the national government headquartered in Washington, D.C., meets that definition. In the American political system, federal and state governments share sovereignty in complicated and ever-changing ways. Both constitutional tradition (the doctrine of dual sovereignty) and everyday politicking (fights over federal grants, mandates, and conditions of aid) render the national government supreme in some matters (national defense, for example) and the states supreme in others (education, for instance). Try posing the sovereignty question in a somewhat different way: who has the ultimate political authority to make and administer public laws, and to tax and spend public monies? In the unitary French republic, the answer is always going to be the national government seated in Paris. But in the federal American republic, the answer will almost always depend on which public law domain are you talking about (crime? economic policy? military affairs?) and over what period of history (the 1780s? the 1860s? the 1960s? today?). For better or worse, this is very much as the Framers intended. In the late eighteenth century, as many European leaders argued in favor of instituting swift, strong, and sovereign national governments, James Madison and other American leaders defended political precepts such as the separation of powers, checks and balances, and federalism.

2. ***How is power divided between the national government and the states under the Constitution?***

   Early in American history, local governments and the states had most of it. In the twentieth century, the national government gained power. In the last two decades the states have won back some of their power because of Supreme Court decisions and legislative efforts to devolve certain federal programs to the states. But the distribution of power between the national government and the states is never as simple or as settled as it may appear to be. Recently, many federal courts have reasserted states' rights, but Supreme Court justices still disagree, often fundamentally, on where the national government's power ends and the states' begins. Likewise, the so-called devolution revolution in federal social policy that began in the 1980s and accelerated in the mid-1990s may already have run its course.

3. How has America's federal system changed since the first days of the Republic?

Washington has gained power and the states have lost it, but this did not happen overnight, and the federal character of the system remains strong. The Civil War increased the national government's powers. Before the New Deal, Washington and the state and local governments had fewer functions, spent less money, and mixed less with each other than they do today. In the 1960s and 1970s, the national government adopted many new policies and spent more freely, but it did not grow alone. Instead, state and local governments received federal grants to administer programs that national policymakers had adopted. By the 1990s, state and local governments were performing even their own traditional functions (for example, crime control and education) subject to regulations and mandates imposed by Congress and enforced by federal courts. Nevertheless, the system would still be instantly recognizable to the Framers. They adopted a federal system that divides power between two governments, both of which act directly upon citizens, and both of which must agree to any constitutional change. The system works much differently today than it did even a quarter-century ago, and the national government has gained power, but America remains every inch a federal republic.

World Wide Web Resources

- State news: www.stateline.org
- Council of State Governments: www.csg.org
- National Governors' Association: www.nga.org
- Supreme Court decisions: www.findlaw.com/casecode/supreme.html

Key Terms

devolution *p. 50*
block grants *p. 50*
federalism *p. 50*
sovereignty *p. 51*
unitary system *p. 51*
confederation or confederal system *p. 51*
federal system *p. 51*
federal regime *p. 51*
"necessary and proper" clause *p. 56*
nullification *p. 56*

dual federalism *p. 57*
city *p. 57*
municipal corporation or municipality *p. 57*
special-act charter *p. 57*
general-act charter *p. 57*
Dillon's rule *p. 57*
home-rule charter *p. 57*
ordinances *p. 57*
counties *p. 57*
special-district governments or authorities *p. 57*

school districts *p. 57*
police power *p. 59*
initiative *p. 59*
referendum *p. 59*
recall *p. 59*
grants-in-aid *p. 59*
categorical grants *p. 62*
revenue sharing *p. 62*
conditions of aid *p. 65*
mandates *p. 65*
second-order devolution *p. 69*
third-order devolution *p. 69*

Suggested Readings

Beer, Samuel H. *To Make a Nation: The Rediscovery of American Federalism*. Cambridge: Harvard University Press, 1993. The definitive study of the philosophical bases of American federalism.

Conlan, Timothy. *From New Federalism to Devolution*. Washington, D.C.: Brookings Institution, 1998. A masterful overview of the politics of federalism from Richard Nixon to Bill Clinton.

Derthick, Martha N. *Keeping the Compound Republic*. Washington, D.C.: Brookings Institution, 2001. A masterful analysis of trends in American federalism from the Founding to the present.

Diamond, Martin. "The Federalist's View of Federalism." In *Essays in Federalism*, edited by George C.S. Benson. Claremont, Calif.: Institute for Studies in Federalism of Claremont Men's College, 1961, 21–64. A profound analysis of what the Founders meant by federalism.

Grodzins, Morton. *The American System*. Chicago: Rand McNally, 1966. Argues that American federalism has always involved extensive sharing of functions between national and state governments.

Melnick, R. Shep. *Between the Lines: Interpreting Welfare Rights*. Washington, D.C.: Brookings Institution, 1994. An examination of how trends in statutory interpretation have affected broader policy developments, including the expansion of the agenda of national government, the persistence of divided government, and the resurgence and decentralization of Congress.

Riker, William H. *Federalism: Origin, Operation, Significance*. Boston: Little, Brown, 1964. A classic explanation and critical analysis of federalism here and abroad.

Thompson, Frank, and John J. DiIulio, Jr., eds. *Medicaid and Devolution: A View from the States*. Washington, D.C.: Brookings Institution, 1998. Essays on the devolution of the largest federal-state social welfare program for the poor.

4

American Political Culture

Enduring Questions

1. What distinctive set of beliefs is fundamental to how most Americans, past and present, think about politics and government?

2. How has American political culture changed over the past hundred years?

3. To what extent have Americans come to mistrust government, and what difference does it make?

If the Republic, created in 1787, had depended for its survival entirely on the constitutional machinery designed by the Founders, it probably would not have endured. That machinery has been copied by many other nations, notably those of Latin America, but in virtually no other country have devices such as federalism, an elected president, a bicameral legislature, and the separation of powers produced a political system capable of both effective government and the protection of liberty. In many nations (such as Argentina, Brazil, and the Philippines) that adopted the American model, there have been, at best, brief periods of democratic rule interrupted by military takeovers, the rise to power of demagogues, or the spread of wholesale corruption. The Constitution of the United States, like an old wine, has rarely survived an ocean crossing.

Alexis de Tocqueville, the perceptive French observer of American politics, noticed this as early as the 1830s. One reason a democratic republic took root in the United States but not in other countries that copied its constitution was that this country offered more abundant and fertile soil in which the roots could grow.[1] The vast territory of the United States created innumerable opportunities for people

Alexis de Tocqueville (1805–1859) was a young French aristocrat who came to the United States to study the American prison system. He wrote the brilliant Democracy in America *(2 vols., 1835–1840), a profound analysis of our political culture.*

to acquire land and make a living. No feudal aristocracy monopolized the land, the government imposed only minimal taxes, and few legal restraints existed. As one place after another filled up, people kept pushing west to find new opportunities. A nation of small, independent farmers, unlike the traditional European one of landless peasants and indentured servants, could make democracy work.

But other nations that were similarly favored did not achieve the same result. As Tocqueville noted, much of South America contains fertile land and rich resources, but democracy has not flourished there.[2] Had he returned to the United States fifty years later, when the frontier was no longer expanding and Americans were crowding into big cities, he would have found that democratic government was still more or less intact.

The Constitution and the physical advantages of the land cannot by themselves explain the persist-ence of the nation's democratic institutions. In addition we must consider the customs of the people—what Tocqueville called their "moral and intellectual characteristics"[3] and what modern social scientists call our political culture.

Political Culture

If you travel abroad, you will quickly become aware that other people often behave differently from Americans. Spaniards may eat dinner at 10:00 P.M., whereas Americans eat at 6:00 or 7:00 P.M. Italians may close their shops for three hours in the middle of the day, while American shops are open continuously from 9:00 to 5:00. Germans address people more formally than Americans, using last names when we would use first names. Japanese business executives attach a lot of importance to working together as a group, while their American counterparts often are more individualistic. In these and countless other ways we can observe cultural differences among people.

Such differences are not limited to eating, shopkeeping, or manners. They include differences in political culture as well. A **political culture** is a distinctive and patterned way of thinking about how political and economic life ought to be carried out (see the box on page 79). Beliefs about economic life are part of the political culture because politics affects economics.

Americans do not judge their political and economic systems in the same way. As we shall see, this difference makes them somewhat unique, for in many other nations people apply the same standards to both systems. For example, Americans think it very important that everybody should be equal politically, but they do not think it important that everybody should be equal economically. By contrast, people in some other nations believe that the principle of equality should be applied to both economic and political life.

The Political System

There are at least five important elements in the American view of the political system:

- *Liberty:* Americans are preoccupied with their rights. They believe they should be free to do pretty much as they please, with some exceptions, so long as they don't hurt other people.

- *Equality:* Americans believe everybody should have an equal vote and an equal chance to participate and succeed.
- *Democracy:* Americans think government officials should be accountable to the people.
- *Civic duty:* Americans generally feel people ought to take community affairs seriously and help out when they can.[4]
- *Individual responsibility:* A characteristically American view is that, barring some disability, individuals are responsible for their own actions and well-being.

By vast majorities Americans believe that every citizen should have an equal chance to influence government policy and to hold public office, and they oppose the idea of letting people have titles such as "Lord" or "Duke," as in England. By somewhat smaller majorities they believe that people should be allowed to vote even if they can't read or write or vote intelligently.[5] Though Americans recognize that people differ in their abilities, they overwhelmingly agree with the statement that "teaching children that all people are really equal recognizes that all people are equally worthy and deserve equal treatment."[6]

At least three questions can be raised about this political culture. First, how do we know that the American people share these beliefs? For most of our history there were no public opinion polls, and even after they became commonplace, they were rather crude tools for measuring the existence and meaning of complex, abstract ideas. There is in fact no way to prove that values such as those listed above are important to Americans. But neither is there good reason for dismissing the list out of hand. One can infer, as have many scholars, the existence of certain values by a close study of the kinds of books Americans read, the speeches they hear, the slogans to which they respond, and the political choices they make, as well as by noting the observations of insightful foreign visitors. Personality tests as well as opinion polls, particularly those asking similar questions in different countries, also supply useful evidence, some of which will be reviewed in the following paragraphs.

Second, if these values are important to Americans, how can we explain the existence in our society of behavior that is obviously inconsistent with them? For example, if white Americans believe in equality of opportunity, why did so many of them for so long deny that equality to African Americans?

★ POLITICALLY SPEAKING ★

Political Culture/Political Ideology

A political culture is a patterned set of ways of thinking about how politics and government ought to be carried out. It consists of a people's fundamental assumptions about how the political process should operate. For instance, Americans assume that a person who loses an election should not try to prevent the winner from taking office, and we eschew political violence: "ballots, not bullets," should decide who holds office. Likewise, Americans believe that nobody should have a greater claim to political authority simply because he or she comes from a rich or aristocratic family. In many societies these are not widely shared assumptions, and in some societies the opposite is believed. Most nations, however, are made up of distinctive regions, religions, and ethnic groups. Each of these may have a distinctive **political subculture**. For example, the American South has a political subculture that differs in important ways from that of the Northeast.

A **political ideology** is not the same as a political culture. Political ideology refers to more or less consistent sets of views concerning the policies government ought to pursue. A doctrinaire liberal or conservative has an ideology. Up to a point people can disagree on ideology (a viewpoint on what government should do) but still share a common political culture (basic beliefs about how government ought to operate). Some ideologies, however, are so critical of existing government policies and practices that they require a fundamental change in the way politics is carried on and thus embody a different political culture as well. The concept of political ideology is explained in Chapter 5.

That people act contrary to their professed beliefs is an everyday fact of life: people believe in honesty, yet they steal from their employers and sometimes underreport their taxable income. Besides values, self-interest and social circumstances also shape behavior. Gunnar Myrdal, a Swedish observer of American society, described race relations in this country as "an American dilemma" resulting from the conflict between the "American creed" (a belief in equality of opportunity) and American behavior

At the height of immigration to this country there was a striking emphasis on creating a shared political culture. Schoolchildren, whatever their national origin, were taught to salute this country's flag.

(denying African Americans full citizenship).[7] But the creed remains important because it is a source of change: as more and more people become aware of the inconsistency between their values and their behavior, that behavior slowly changes.[8] Race relations in this country would take a very different course if instead of an abstract but widespread belief in equality there were an equally widespread belief that one race is inherently inferior to another. (No doubt some Americans believe that, but most do not.)

Third, if there is agreement among Americans on certain political values, why has there been so much political conflict in our history? How could a people who agree on such fundamentals fight a bloody civil war, engage in violent labor-management disputes, take to the streets in riots and demonstrations, and sue each other in countless court battles? Conflict, even violent struggles, can occur over specific policies even among those who share, at some level of abstraction, common beliefs. Many political values may be irrelevant to specific controversies: there is no abstract value, for example, that would settle the question of whether steelworkers ought to organize unions. More important, much of our conflict has occurred precisely because we have strong beliefs that happen, as each of us interprets them, to be in conflict. Equality of opportunity seems an attractive idea,

but sometimes it can be pursued only by curtailing personal liberty, another attractive idea. The states went to war in 1861 over one aspect of that conflict— the rights of slaves versus the rights of slaveowners.

Indeed, the Civil War illustrates the way certain fundamental beliefs about how a democratic regime ought to be organized have persisted despite bitter conflict over the policies adopted by particular governments. When the southern states seceded from the Union, they formed not a wholly different government but one modeled, despite some important differences, on the U.S. Constitution. Even some of the language of the Constitution was duplicated, suggesting that the southern states believed not that a new form of government or a different political culture ought to be created but that the South was the true repository of the existing constitutional and cultural order.[9]

Perhaps the most frequently encountered evidence that Americans believe themselves bound by common values and common hopes has been the persistence of the word *Americanism* in our political vocabulary. Throughout the nineteenth and most of the twentieth centuries *Americanism* and *American way of life* were familiar terms not only in Fourth of July speeches but also in everyday discourse. For many years the House of Representatives had a committee called the House Un-American Activities Committee. There is hardly any example to be found abroad of such a way of thinking: There is no "Britishism" or "Frenchism," and when Britons and French people become worried about subversion, they call it a problem of internal security, not a manifestation of "un-British" or "un-French" activities.

The Economic System

Americans judge the economic system using many of the same standards by which they judge the political system, albeit with some very important differences. As it is in American politics, liberty is important in the U.S. economy. Thus Americans support the idea of a free-enterprise economic system, calling the nation's economy "generally fair and efficient" and denying that it "survives by keeping the poor down."[10] However, there are limits to how much freedom they think should exist in the marketplace. People support government regulation of business in order to keep some firms from becoming too powerful and to correct specific abuses.[11]

Americans are more willing to tolerate economic inequality than political inequality. They believe in maintaining "equality of opportunity" in the economy but not "equality of results." If everyone has an equal opportunity to get ahead, then it is all right for people with more ability to earn higher salaries and for wages to be set based on how hard people work rather than on their economic needs.[12] Although Americans are quite willing to support education and training programs to help disadvantaged people get ahead, they are strongly opposed to anything that looks like preferential treatment (for example, hiring quotas) in the workplace.[13]

The leaders of very liberal political groups, such as civil rights and feminist organizations, are more willing than the average American to support preferential treatment in the hiring and promoting of minorities and women. They do so because, unlike most citizens, they believe that whatever disadvantages minorities and women face are the result of failures of the economic system rather than the fault of individuals.[14] Even so, these leaders strongly support the idea that earnings should be based on ability and oppose the idea of having any top limit on what people can earn.[15]

This popular commitment to economic individualism and personal responsibility may help explain how Americans think about particular public poli-

In the 1950s Senator Joseph McCarthy of Wisconsin was the inspiration for the word "McCarthyism" after his highly publicized attacks on alleged Communists working in the federal government.

cies, such as welfare and civil rights. Polls show that Americans are willing to help people "truly in need" (this includes the elderly and the disabled) but not those deemed "able to take care of themselves" (this includes, in the public's mind, people "on welfare"). Also, Americans dislike preferential hiring programs and the use of quotas to deal with racial inequality.

At the core of these policy attitudes is a widely (but not universally) shared commitment to economic individualism and personal responsibility. Some scholars, among them Donald Kinder and David Sears, interpret these individualistic values as "symbolic racism"—a kind of plausible camouflage for antiblack attitudes.[16] But other scholars, such as Paul M. Sniderman and Michael Gray Hagen, argue that these views are not a smoke screen for bigotry or insensitivity but a genuine commitment to the ethic of self-reliance.[17] Since there are many Americans on both sides of this issue, debates about welfare and civil rights tend to be especially intense. What is striking about the American political culture is that in this country the individualist view of social policy is by far the most popular.[18]

Views about specific economic policies change. Americans now are much more inclined than they once were to believe that the government should help the needy and regulate business. But the commitment to certain underlying principles has been

Table 4.1 **Responsibility for Success or Failure**		
	Percentage of High School Students Agreeing	
Statement	**1924**	**1977**
It is entirely the fault of the man himself if he cannot succeed.	47%	47%
The fact that some men [in 1977: people] have so much more money than others shows there is an unjust condition in this country that ought to be changed.	30	34

Source: Theodore Caplow and Howard M. Bahr, "Half a Century of Change in Adolescent Attitudes: A Replication of a Middletown Survey by the Lynds," *Public Opinion Quarterly* 43 (Spring 1979): 1–17, table 1. Copyright © 1979, reprinted by permission of University of Chicago Press.

remarkably enduring. In 1924 almost half of the high school students in Muncie, Indiana, said that "it is entirely the fault of the man himself if he cannot succeed" and disagreed with the view that differences in wealth showed that the system was unjust. In 1977, over half a century later, the students in this same high school were asked the same questions again, with the same results (see Table 4.1).[19]

Comparing America with Other Nations

The best way to learn what is distinctive about the American political culture is to compare it with that of other nations. This comparison shows that Americans have somewhat different beliefs about the political system, the economic system, and religion.

The Political System

Sweden has a well-developed democratic government, with a constitution, free speech, an elected legislature, competing political parties, and a reasonably honest and nonpartisan bureaucracy. But the Swedish political culture is significantly different from ours; it is more deferential than participatory. Though almost all adult Swedes vote in national elections, few participate in politics in any other way.

They defer to the decisions of experts and specialists who work for the government, rarely challenge governmental decisions in court, believe leaders and legislators ought to decide issues on the basis of "what is best" more than on "what the people want," and value equality as much as (or more than) liberty.[20] Whereas Americans are contentious, Swedes value harmony; while Americans tend to assert their rights, Swedes tend to observe their obligations.

The contrast in political cultures is even greater when one looks at a nation, such as Japan, with a wholly different history and set of traditions. One study compared the values expressed by a small number of upper-status Japanese with those of some similarly situated Americans. Whereas the Americans emphasized the virtues of individualism, competition, and equality in their political, economic, and social relations, the Japanese attached greater value to maintaining good relations with colleagues, having decisions made by groups, preserving social harmony, and displaying respect for hierarchy. The Americans were more concerned than the Japanese with rules and with treating others fairly but impersonally, with due regard for their rights. The Japanese, on the other hand, stressed the importance of being sensitive to the personal needs of others, avoiding conflict, and reaching decisions through discussion rather than the application of rules.[21] These cultural differences affect in profound but hard-to-measure ways the workings of the political and economic systems of the two countries, making them function quite differently despite the fact that both are industrialized, capitalist nations.

It is easy to become carried away by the more obvious differences among national cultures and to overgeneralize from them. Thinking in stereotypes about the typical American, the typical Swede, or the typical Japanese is as risky as thinking of the typical white or the typical black American. This can be especially misleading in nations, such as the United States and Canada, that have been settled by a variety of ethnic and religious groups (English-speaking versus French-speaking Canadians, for example, or Jewish, Protestant, and Catholic Americans). But it is equally misleading to suppose that the operation of a political system can be understood entirely from the nation's objective features—its laws, economy, or physical terrain.

In 1959–1960 Gabriel Almond and Sidney Verba published a study of political culture in five nations.

In general they found that Americans, and to a lesser degree citizens of Great Britain, had a stronger sense of **civic duty** (a belief that one has an obligation to participate in civic and political affairs) and a stronger sense of **civic competence** (a belief that one can affect government policies) than did the citizens of Germany, Italy, or Mexico. Over half of all Americans and a third of all Britons believed that the average citizen ought to "be active in one's community," compared to only a tenth in Italy and a fifth in Germany. Moreover, many more Americans and Britons than Germans, Italians, or Mexicans believed that they could "do something" about an unjust national law or local regulation.[22] Since 1960 nobody has asked people in these five countries the same questions, and hence we do not know whether these views have changed in recent years. But in a 1995 study of citizen participation in politics, Verba and others reported that while America lagged behind Austria, the Netherlands, West Germany, and the United Kingdom in voter participation, when it came to campaigning, attending political meetings, becoming active in the local community, and contacting government officials, Americans were as active—or substantially more active—than citizens elsewhere.[23]

Today the American people have less trust in government than they once did. But even so, popular confidence in political institutions remains higher here than in many places abroad. In cross-national surveys conducted in the 1990s in the United States and sixteen other democracies, Americans expressed more confidence in public institutions (Congress/Parliament, the police, the armed forces, the legal system, and the civil service) than did the citizens of all but four other countries (Denmark, Ireland, Northern Ireland, and Norway), and

Though Japan is a democracy, one group, the Liberal Democratic Party, has ruled the country since the end of the Second World War.

greater confidence in private institutions (the church, major companies, the press, trade unions) than did the citizens of any other nation.[24] In other cross-national surveys conducted in the 1990s, Americans were more likely than the French or Germans to say they were "very patriotic" (see Table 4.2). Of course, Americans know that their country has a lot of faults. But even the most disaffected voters believe the United States needs to change only certain policies, not its system of government.[25]

The Economic System

The political culture of Sweden is not only more deferential than ours but also more inclined to favor equality of results over equality of opportunity. In 1985 Sidney Verba and Gary Orren compared the views of Swedish and American trade union and political party leaders on a variety of economic

Table 4.2	**Patriotism in America, France, and Germany**		
	Percentage Agreeing		
Statement	**U.S.**	**France**	**Germany**
I am very patriotic.	51%	27%	26%
I am proud to be (American, etc.).	74	25	23
We should be willing to fight for our country whether it is right or wrong.	22	17	5

Source: Adapted from *The Public Perspective* (April/May 1999): 23.

Table 4.3   Commitment to Income Equity in Sweden and the United States

	Political Party Leaders		Blue-Collar Union Leaders	
	Sweden (Social Democrats)	U.S. (Democrats)	Sweden	U.S.
Favor equality of results (%)	21%	9%	14%	4%
Favor equal pay (%)	58	12	68	11
Favor top limit on income (%)	44	17	51	13
Fair income ratio of executive to menial worker*	2:1	15:1	2:1	11:1

*In Sweden menial worker was a dishwasher; in U.S. menial worker was an elevator operator.

Source: Reprinted by permission of the publisher from *Equality in America: The View from the Top* by Sidney Verba and Gary R. Orren, Cambridge: Harvard University Press, Copyright © 1985 by the Presidents and Fellows of Harvard College.

issues. In both countries the leaders were chosen from either blue-collar unions or the major liberal political party (the Democrats in the United States, the Social Democrats in Sweden).

The results (see Table 4.3) are quite striking. By margins of four or five to one the Swedish leaders were more likely to believe in giving workers equal pay than were their American counterparts. Moreover, by margins of at least three to one, the Swedes were more likely than the Americans to favor putting a top limit on incomes.[26]

Just what these differences in beliefs mean in dollars-and-cents terms was revealed by the answers to another question. Each group was asked what should be the ratio between the income of an executive and that of a menial worker (a dishwasher in Sweden, an elevator operator in the United States). The Swedish leaders said the ratio should be a little over two to one. That is, if the dishwasher earned $200 a week, the executive should earn no more than $440 to $480 a week. But the American lead-

ers were ready to let the executive earn between $2,260 and $3,040 per week when the elevator operator was earning $200.

Americans, compared to people in many other countries, are more likely to think that freedom is more important than equality and less likely to think that hard work goes unrewarded or that the government should guarantee citizens a basic standard of living (see Table 4.4). These cultural differences make a difference in politics. In fact there is less income inequality in Sweden than in the United States—the government sees to that.

The Civic Role of Religion

In the 1830s Tocqueville was amazed at how religious Americans were in comparison to his fellow Europeans. From the first days of the new Republic right down to the present, America has been among the most religious countries in the world.[27] The average American is more likely than the average European to believe in God, to pray on a daily basis,

Table 4.4   Attitudes Toward Economic Equality in America and Europe

	Percentage Agreeing				
Statement	U.S.	Great Britain	Germany	Italy	France
It is government's responsibility to take care of the very poor who can't take care of themselves.	23%	62%	50%	66%	62%
Hard work guarantees success.	63	46	38	51	46
Government should *not* guarantee every citizen food and basic shelter.	34	9	13	14	10

Source: Adapted from *The Public Perspective* (November/December 1991): 5, 7. © *The Public Perspective,* a publication of the Roper Center for Public Opinion Research, University of Connecticut, Storrs. Reprinted with permission.

Table 4.5   Religious Belief in America and Europe

Statement	Percentage Agreeing				
	U.S.	**Great Britain**	**Germany**	**Italy**	**France**
I never doubt the existence of God.	60%	31%	20%	56%	29%
Prayer is an important part of my daily life.	77	37	44	69	32
There are clear guidelines about what is good and evil.	79	65	54	56	64

Source: Adapted from *The Public Perspective* (November/December 1991): 5, 8. Reprinted by permission of *The Public Perspective,* a publication of the Roper Center for Public Opinion Research, University of Connecticut.

Table 4.6   Religion in America Today

	Percentage of Adult Americans
Believe in God	96%
Say they have a personal relationship with God	80
Never doubt God's existence	79
Say they are seeking to grow in religious faith	76
Pray at least daily	75
Are a member of a church, synagogue, mosque, or other organized religious group	64
Say religion can solve all or most of today's problems	61
Attend worship services more than once a month	54

Source: Adapted from George Gallup, Jr., and Timothy Jones, *The Next American Spirituality* (Colorado Springs, Colo: Cook, 2000), ch. 1, appendices 1 and 2.

and to acknowledge clear standards of right and wrong (see Table 4.5).

There is some evidence that Americans are becoming more religious. It is doubtful that this is true for American elites (see Chapter 5) but it seems clear that mass religiosity has increased somewhat over the last two decades. For example, the percentage of Americans who "completely agree" that "God really exists" rose from 68 percent in 1987 to 79 percent in 1997, and, over the same period, the percentage who "completely agree" that "prayer is an important part of my daily life" rose from 41 percent to 53 percent.[28] It is clear that America remains a highly religious nation, both in absolute terms and relative to most European countries (see Tables 4.6 and 4.7).

Many present-day Americans, however, are attracted to religion as much for its civic as for its spiritual significance. Churches, synagogues, mosques, and other religious organizations are the country's major source of volunteer and community services: Half of their members do unpaid community work

each year; nine in ten give money to charity; and eight in ten give goods, clothing, or other property to

Religion plays a larger role in the lives of Americans than it does for citizens in most other Western democracies.

Table 4.7 Religion in Industrial Nations, 1990–1993								
	Percentage Answering Yes							
Statement	U.S.	Sweden	France	W. Germany	Britain	Spain	Canada	Mexico
Would you say you are. . .								
A religious person?	82%	29%	48%	54%	55%	64%	69%	72%
Not a religious person?	15	56	36	27	37	27	26	22
A convinced atheist?	1	7	11	2	4	4	3	2
Not sure	2	9	5	17	4	5	2	4

Source: Adapted from *The Public Perspective,* reporting data from surveys conducted from 1990 to 1993 by the Inter-University Consortium for Political and Social Research. *The Public Perspective* (Storrs: Roper Center for Public Opinion Research, University of Connecticut, April/May 1995): 2. © The Public Perspective. Reprinted by permission.

charity.[29] In many urban communities all across the country, religious organizations are major or sole providers of myriad social and health care services to low-income children, youth, and families.[30]

Still, how significant is religion as a civic force in America today? Perhaps the best answer can be found in research by Harvard University political scientist Robert D. Putnam. In the mid-1990s, Putnam published studies suggesting that fewer and fewer Americans were joining clubs, associations, churches, and other groups that promote civic trust and cooperation, or what some call "social capital." As a metaphor for the broader decline of civic participation that concerned him, he highlighted the fact that, between 1980 and 1994, league bowling had dropped by 40 percent. Americans, once a nation of joiners, were now "bowling alone."[31]

Putnam's "bowling alone" thesis attracted a tremendous amount of media attention. But some academic critics found the evidence that civic participation in America was in deep and steady decline to be more mixed than Putnam had initially allowed.[32] For example, more people were bowling alone, but more were also joining the country's over 260,000 teams registered in softball leagues, up from only 19,000 teams in 1967.[33]

Likewise, Putnam had argued that Americans were also now praying alone. Between 1974 and 1994, church attendance rates had fallen by about 25 percent, he stressed. True, but over the same period, the fraction of Americans who claimed membership in a church or synagogue remained between 65 and 75 percent, and about 60 percent still attended worship services once a month or more.[34] Moreover, as Putnam himself and other researchers have

acknowledged, churches, synagogues, mosques, and other houses of worship supply enormous amounts of social services to their communities and remain major seedbeds of volunteering and philanthropy.[35]

Religion and Politics

Religious beliefs have always played a significant role in American politics. The religious revivalist movement of the late 1730s and early 1740s (known as the First Great Awakening) transformed the political life of the American colonies. Religious ideas fueled the break with England, which, in the words of the Declaration of Independence, had violated "the laws of nature and nature's God." Religious leaders were central to the struggle over slavery in the nineteenth century and the temperance movement of the early twentieth century.

Both liberals and conservatives have used the pulpit to promote political change. The civil rights movement of the 1950s and 1960s was led mainly by black religious leaders, most prominently Martin Luther King, Jr. In the 1980s a conservative religious group known as the Moral Majority advocated constitutional amendments that would allow prayer in public schools and ban abortion. In the 1990s another conservative religious group, the Christian Coalition, attracted an enormous amount of media attention and became a prominent force in many national, state, and local elections.

Candidates for national office in most contemporary democracies mention religion rarely if they mention it at all. Not so in America. During the 2000 presidential campaign, for example, both Democratic candidate Al Gore and Republican candidate George W. Bush the younger gave major speeches extolling

the virtues of religion and advocating the right of religious organizations that deliver social services to receive government funding on the same basis as all other nonprofit organizations. Both Bush and Gore were responding in part to public support for so-called faith-based approaches to solving social ills. In 2000, three-quarters of all Americans favored allowing churches, synagogues, mosques, and other houses of worship to apply for government funding to provide social services such as homeless shelters, job training, or drug treatment counseling to people who need them. [36] When asked, in general, who can do the best job of providing social services to those in need, 40 percent of Americans said faith-based organizations, 28 percent chose federal and state government agencies, and 25 percent opted for secular community groups. [37]

Certain important constituencies in each political party favor government funding for faith-based social programs; for example, over 80 percent of both black Democrats and white Republican evangelical Christians support the idea. [38] Most people, however, express both reasons for supporting these programs, and concerns about doing so (see Table

4.8). But the general feeling about religion became apparent when a federal appeals court in 2002 tried to ban the Pledge of Allegiance because it contained the phrase "under God." There was an overwhelming and bipartisan condemnation of the ruling. To a degree that would be almost unthinkable in many other democracies, religious beliefs will probably continue to shape political culture in America for many generations to come.

The Sources of Political Culture

That Americans bring a distinctive way of thinking to their political life is easier to demonstrate than to explain. But even a brief, and necessarily superficial, effort to understand the sources of our political culture can help make its significance clearer.

The American Revolution, as we discussed in Chapter 2, was essentially a war fought over liberty: an assertion by the colonists of what they took to be their rights. Though the Constitution, produced eleven years after the Revolution, had to deal with

---

Table 4.8 American Beliefs About Faith-Based Programs

Important Reasons for Backing Faith-Based Programs			
Statement	Important Reason %	Not an Important Reason %	Don't Know %
People should have a variety of options.	77	20	3
Service providers more caring and compassionate.	72	25	3
Power of religion can change people's lives.	62	35	3
Faith-based programs more efficient.	60	36	4

Important Concerns About Funding for Faith-Based Programs			
Statement	Important Concern %	Not an Important Concern %	Don't Know %
Government too involved with religious organizations.	68	30	2
People forced to take part in religious practices.	60	38	2
Would interfere with church-state separation.	52	45	3
Might increase religious divisions.	46	48	4

Source: From *American Views on Religion, Politics, and Public Policy* (Washington, D.C.: Pew Forum on Religion and Public Life, April 2001) pp. 15–16. Reprinted with permission.

other issues as well, its animating spirit reflected the effort to reconcile personal liberty with the needs of social control. These founding experiences, and the political disputes that followed, have given to American political thought and culture a preoccupation with the assertion and maintenance of rights. This tradition has imbued the daily conduct of U.S. politics with a kind of adversarial spirit quite foreign to the political life of countries that did not undergo a libertarian revolution or that were formed out of an interest in other goals, such as social equality, national independence, or ethnic supremacy.

The adversarial spirit of the American political culture reflects not only our preoccupation with rights but also our long-standing distrust of authority and of people wielding power. The colonies' experiences with British rule was one source of that distrust. But another, older source was the religious belief of many Americans, which saw human nature as fundamentally depraved. To the colonists all of mankind suffered from original sin, symbolized by Adam and Eve eating the forbidden fruit in the Garden of Eden. Since no one was born innocent, no one could be trusted with power. Thus the Constitution had to be designed in such a way as to curb the darker side of human nature. Otherwise everyone's rights would be in jeopardy.

The contentiousness of a people animated by a suspicion of government and devoted to individualism could easily have made democratic politics so tumultuous as to be impossible. After all one must be willing to trust others with power if there is to be any kind of democratic government, and sometimes those others will be people not of one's own choosing. The first great test case took place around 1800 in a battle between the Federalists, led by John Adams and Alexander Hamilton, and the Democratic-Republicans, led by Thomas Jefferson and James Madison. The two factions deeply distrusted each other: The Federalists had passed laws designed to suppress Jeffersonian journalists; Jefferson suspected the Federalists were out to subvert the Constitution; and the Federalists believed Jefferson intended to sell out the country to France. But as we shall see in Chapter 7, the threat of civil war never materialized, and the Jeffersonians came to power peacefully. Within a few years the role of an opposition party became legitimate, and people abandoned the idea of making serious efforts to suppress their opponents.

By happy circumstance people came to accept that liberty and orderly political change could coexist.

The Constitution, by creating a federal system and dividing political authority among competing institutions, provided ample opportunity for widespread—though hardly universal—participation in politics. The election of Jefferson in 1800 produced no political catastrophe, and those who had predicted one were, to a degree, discredited. But other, more fundamental features of American life contributed to the same end. One of the most important of these was religious diversity.

The absence of an established or official religion for the nation as a whole, reinforced by a constitutional prohibition of such an establishment and by the migration to this country of people with different religious backgrounds, meant that religious diversity was inevitable. Since there could be no orthodox or official religion, it became difficult for a corresponding political orthodoxy to emerge. Moreover, the conflict between the Puritan tradition, with its emphasis on faith and hard work, and the Catholic Church, with its devotion to the sacraments and priestly authority, provided a recurrent source of cleavage in American public life. The differences in values between these two groups showed up not only in their religious practices but also in areas involving the regulation of manners and morals, and even in people's choice of political party. For more than a century candidates for state and national office were deeply divided over whether the sale of liquor should be prohibited, a question that arose ultimately out of competing religious doctrines.

Even though there was no established church, there was certainly a dominant religious tradition—Protestantism, and especially Puritanism. The Protestant churches provided people with both a set of beliefs and an organizational experience that had profound effects on American political culture. Those beliefs encouraged, or even required, a life of personal achievement as well as religious conviction: a believer had an obligation to work, save money, obey the secular law, and do good works. Max Weber explained the rise of capitalism in part by what he called the Protestant ethic—what we now sometimes call the **work ethic**.[39] Such values had political consequences, as people holding them were motivated to engage in civic and communal action.

Churches offered ready opportunities for developing and practicing civic and political skills. Since

most Protestant churches were organized along congregational lines—that is, the church was controlled by its members, who put up the building, hired the preacher, and supervised the finances—they were, in effect, miniature political systems, with leaders and committees, conflict and consensus. Developing a participatory political culture was undoubtedly made easier by the existence of a participatory religious culture. Even some Catholic churches in early America were under a degree of lay control. Parishioners owned the church property, negotiated with priests, and conducted church business.

All aspects of culture, including the political, are preserved and transmitted to new generations primarily by the family. Though some believe that the weakening of the family unit has eroded the extent to which it transmits anything, particularly culture, and has enlarged the power of other sources of values—the mass media and the world of friends and fashion, leisure and entertainment—there is still little doubt that the ways in which we think about the world are largely acquired within the family. In Chapter 5 we shall see that the family is the primary source of one kind of political attitude—identification with one or another political party. Even more important, the family shapes in subtle ways how we think and act on political matters. Erik Erikson, the psychologist, noted certain traits that are more characteristic of American than of European families—the greater freedom enjoyed by children, for example, and the larger measure of equality among family members. These familial characteristics promote a belief, carried through life, that every person has rights deserving protection and that a variety of interests have a legitimate claim to consideration when decisions are made.[40]

The combined effect of religious and ethnic diversity, an individualistic philosophy, fragmented political authority, and the relatively egalitarian American family can be seen in the absence of a high degree of **class consciousness** among Americans. Class consciousness means thinking of oneself as a worker whose interests are in opposition to those of management, or vice versa. In this country most people, whatever their jobs, think of themselves as "middle class."

Though the writings of Horatio Alger are no longer popular, Americans still seem to believe in the message of those stories—that the opportunity for success is available to people who work hard. This may help explain why the United States is the only large industrial democracy without a significant socialist party and why the nation has been slow to adopt certain welfare programs.

The Culture War

Almost all Americans share some elements of a common political culture. Why, then, is there so much cultural conflict in American politics? For many years, the most explosive political issues have included abortion, gay rights, drug use, school prayer, and pornography. Viewed from a Marxist perspective, politics in the United States is utterly baffling: Instead of two economic classes engaged in a bitter struggle over wealth, we have two cultural classes locked in a war over values.

To say that there are two cultural classes is, of course, an oversimplification, but to say that there is a culture war is not an exaggeration.[41] Groups supporting and opposing the right to abortion have had many angry confrontations in recent years. The latter have been arrested while attempting to block access to abortion clinics; some clinics have been fire-bombed; and at least seven physicians have been killed. A controversy over what schoolchildren should be taught about homosexuals was responsible, in part, for the firing of the head of the New York City school system; in other states there have been fierce arguments in state legislatures and before the courts over whether gay and lesbian couples should be allowed to adopt children. Although most Americans want to keep heroin, cocaine, and other drugs illegal, a significant number of people want to legalize (or at least decriminalize) their use. The Supreme Court has ruled that children cannot pray in public schools, but this has not stopped many parents and school authorities from trying to reinstate school prayer, or at least prayerlike moments of silence. The discovery that a federal agency, the National Endowment for the Arts, had given money to support exhibitions and performances that many people thought were obscene led to a furious congressional struggle over the future of the agency.

The culture war differs from other political disputes (over such matters as taxes, business regulations, and foreign policy) in several ways: Money is not at stake, compromises are almost impossible to arrange, and the conflict is more profound. It is animated by deep differences in people's beliefs about private and public morality—that is, about the standards that ought to govern individual behavior

and social arrangements. It is about what kind of country we ought to live in, not just about what kinds of policies our government ought to adopt.

To simplify, there are two opposed camps, the **orthodox** and the **progressive.** On the orthodox side are people who believe that morality is as important as, or more important than, self-expression and that moral rules derive from the commands of God or the laws of nature—commands and laws that are relatively clear, unchanging, and independent of individual preferences. On the progressive side are people who think that personal freedom is as important as, or more important than, certain traditional moral rules and that those rules must be evaluated in light of the circumstances of modern life—circumstances that are quite complex, changeable, and dependent on individual preferences.

Most conspicuous among the orthodox are fundamentalist Protestants and evangelical Christians, and so critics who dislike orthodox views often dismiss them as the fanatical expressions of "the Religious Right." But many people who hold orthodox views are not fanatical or deeply religious or right-wing on most issues; they simply have strong views about drugs, pornography, and sexual morality. Similarly, the progressive side often includes members of liberal Protestant denominations (for example, Episcopalians and Unitarians) and people with no strong religious beliefs, and so their critics often denounce them as immoral, anti-Christian radicals who have embraced the ideology of secular humanism, the belief that moral standards do not require religious justification. But in all likelihood few progressives are immoral or anti-Christian, and most do not regard secular humanism as their defining ideology.

Moreover, the culture war is occurring not just between different religious denominations but also within them. Catholic, Protestant, and Jewish leaders with an orthodox perspective tend to assign great importance to two-parent families, condemn pornography, denounce homosexuality, and think the United States is in general a force for good in the world. Leaders of the same faiths who have a progressive outlook are more likely to say that many legitimate alternatives to the traditional two-parent family exist, that pornography and homosexuality are private matters protected by individual rights, and that the United States has been at best a neutral and at worst a bad force in world affairs.[42] This conflict between the orthodox and progressive view of American culture is similar to, and has many of the same causes, as the cleavage (described in Chapter 5) between the traditional middle class and the new middle class.

American history has always had conflicts of this sort, but they have acquired special importance today as a result of two major changes in American society. The first is the great increase in the proportion of people who consider themselves progressive. Once almost everyone was religiously orthodox, even if politically liberal; today fewer are. The second factor is the rise of media (such as television, direct-mail advertising, and the Internet) that make it easy to wage a cultural war on a large scale. In the past preachers, writers, and lecturers could reach at most a few hundred people at a time; today television evangelists, radio talk-show hosts, and the authors of direct-mail messages or web sites can wage a furious war of words reaching tens of millions of people and recruiting hundreds of thousands of followers. A cultural war that once enlisted only a few activists can now mobilize mass armies.

The tensions generated by the culture war affect our views as to how well our government works, how much influence ordinary people can have over it, and how large a measure of freedom we ought to grant to our opponents. Trust in government, a sense of political efficacy, and tolerance for views we dislike are fragile under the best of circumstances. Have the cultural tensions of recent decades made matters worse? In the rest of this chapter we shall try to answer these questions.

Mistrust of Government

There is one aspect of public opinion that worries many people. Since the late 1950s, there has been a more or less steady decline in the proportion of Americans who say they trust the government in Washington to do the right thing. In the past, polls showed that about three-quarters of Americans said they trusted Washington most of the time or just about always, but by 1980 that proportion had declined sharply to about one-quarter. The level of trust briefly rose during the Reagan administration but sank back down about the time he left office. Another measure pollsters use shows pretty much the same thing. Between 1952 and 1992 the fraction of Americans who said public officials did not care what the public thought doubled from one-third to two-thirds (see Figure 4.1 on page 92).[43]

Before we get too upset about this, we should remember that people are talking about government officials, not the system of government. Americans are much more supportive of the country and its institutions than Europeans are of theirs. Even so, the decline in confidence in officials is striking. There are all sorts of explanations for why it has happened. In the 1960s there was our unhappy war in Vietnam, in the 1970s President Nixon had to resign because of his involvement in the Watergate scandal, and in the 1990s President Clinton went through scandals that led to his being impeached by the House of Representatives (but not convicted of that charge by the Senate).

But there is another way of looking at the matter. Maybe in the 1950s we had an abnormally *high* level of confidence in government, one that could never be expected to last no matter what any president did. After all, when President Eisenhower took office in 1952, we had won a war against fascism, overcome the Depression of the 1930s, possessed a near monopoly of the atom bomb, had a currency that was the envy of the world, and dominated international trade. Moreover, in those days not much was expected out of Washington. Hardly anybody thought that there should be important federal laws about civil rights, crime, illegal drugs, the environment, the role of women, highway safety, or almost anything else one now finds on the national agenda.

Since nobody expected much out of Washington, nobody was upset that they didn't get much out of it.

The 1960s and 1970s changed all of that. Domestic turmoil, urban riots, a civil rights revolution, the war in Vietnam, economic inflation, and a new concern for the environment dramatically increased what we expected Washington to do. And since these problems are very difficult ones to solve, a lot of people became convinced that our politicians couldn't do much.

Those events also pushed the feelings Americans had about their country—that is, their patriotism—into the background. We liked the country, but there weren't many occasions when expressing that approval seemed to make much sense. But on September 11, 2001, when hijacked airliners were crashed by terrorists into the World Trade Center in New York City and the Pentagon in Washington, all of that changed. There was an extraordinary outburst of patriotic fervor, with flags displayed everywhere, fire and police heroes widely celebrated, and strong national support for our going to war in Afghanistan to find the key terrorist, Osama bin Laden, and destroy the tyrannical Taliban regime that he supported. By November of that year about half of all Americans of both political parties said that they trusted Washington officials to do what is right most of the time, the highest level in many years.

Those who had hoped or predicted that this new level of support would last, not ebb and flow, have

Protests and demonstrations are a common feature of American politics, as with this attack in Seattle on American membership in the World Trade Organization in November 2001. Yet, despite disagreements Americans are a patriotic people, as seen in this photo of baseball fans waving flags and singing "God Bless America," taken a few days after 9/11.

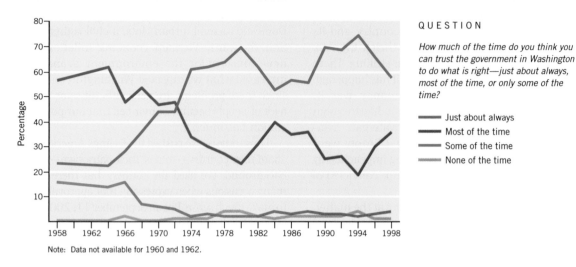

Figure 4.1   Trust in the Federal Government, 1958–1998

QUESTION

How much of the time do you think you can trust the government in Washington to do what is right—just about always, most of the time, or only some of the time?

—— Just about always
—— Most of the time
—— Some of the time
—— None of the time

Note: Data not available for 1960 and 1962.

Source: University of Michigan, *The National Election Studies* (September 1999), table 5A.1, updated by *Los Angeles Times*, poll taken November 10–13, 2001.

been disappointed. In October 2001, 57 percent of Americans (up from just 29 percent in July 2001) said they trusted the federal government to do what is right just about always or most of the time. But by May 2002, only 40 percent expresssed such trust in the federal government, and 57 percent said they trusted Washington only some of the time or never.[44] Still, it is premature to conclude that we have seen the last of post–September 11 surges in support for the federal government. Much will depend on how citizens will evaluate overall government performance, whether Washington will be widely credited with foiling terrorist attacks in the future, and how people will understand and respond to specific proposals.

As Table 4.9 suggests, Americans have lost confidence in many institutions. In addition, certain

Table 4.9   Public Confidence in Institutions, 1973–2001

Institution	Percentage Saying They Have a "Great Deal" or "Quite a Lot" of Confidence in Various Institutions							
	1973	1979	1985	1991	1997	1998	1999	2001
Church/organized religion	66%	65%	66%	59%	56%	59%	58%	60%
U.S. Supreme Court	44	45	56	48	50	50	49	50
Public schools	58	53	48	44	40	37	36	38
Newspapers	39	51	35	32	35	33	33	36
Big business	26	32	31	26	28	30	30	28
Small business	—	—	—	—	63	56	—	—
Congress	42	34	39	30	22	28	26	26
State government	63[a]	—	—	—	68	—	—	—
Local government	63[a]	—	—	—	69	—	—	—
Criminal justice system	—	—	—	—	19	24	23	—

[a]Data for 1972.

Source: The Gallup Organization, *Poll Releases: Confidence in Institutions,* June 10, 2001.

Figure 4.2   Changes in the Sense of Political Efficacy, 1952–2000

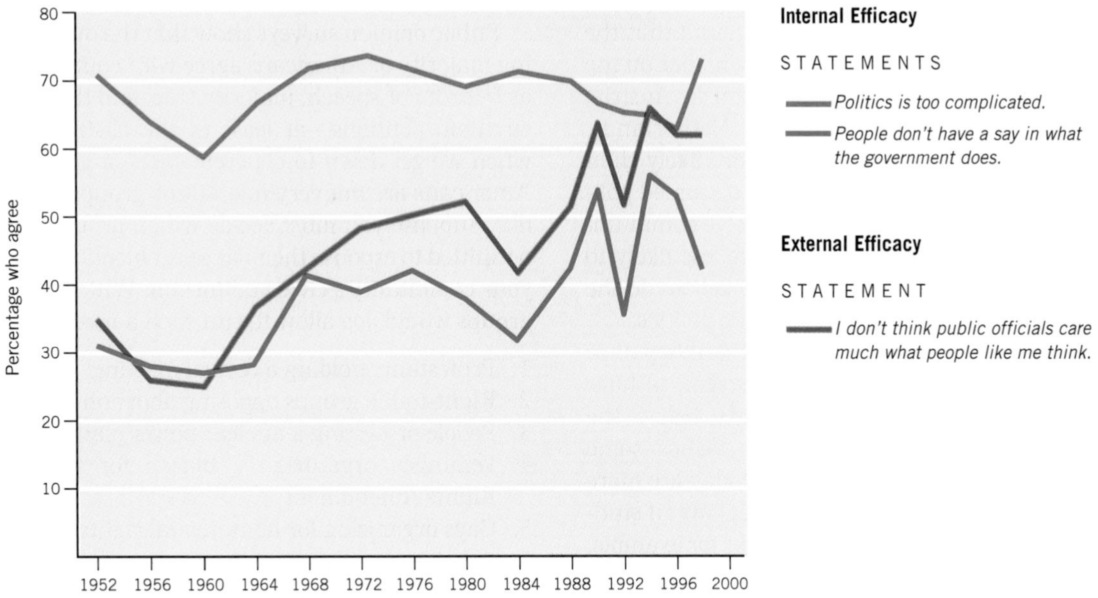

Internal Efficacy

STATEMENTS

——— Politics is too complicated.

——— People don't have a say in what the government does.

External Efficacy

STATEMENT

——— I don't think public officials care much what people like me think.

Source: University of Michigan, *The National Election Studies,* 1952–2000.

group differences in confidence have diminished. African Americans, for example, have more confidence in organized religion and less confidence in the criminal justice system than do white Americans.[45] But both blacks and whites have far more confidence in churches than they do in criminal courts, three-quarters of both say that they are "proud to live under our political system," and 95 percent of both say that there are no "countries better than the United States."[46] In sum, without regard to race or other factors, most Americans no longer give to political leaders and their policies the kind of support they gave in the 1950s, but they have never lost confidence in either the political system or each other.

Political Efficacy

Perhaps the most worrisome aspect of recent changes in the American political culture is the decline in the extent to which citizens feel that the political system will respond to their needs and beliefs. These changes are in what scholars call a citizen's sense of **political efficacy,** by which they mean a citizen's capacity to understand and influence political events.

This sense of efficacy has two parts—**internal efficacy** (the ability to understand and take part in political affairs) and **external efficacy** (the ability to make the system respond to the citizenry). Since the mid-1960s there has been a fairly sharp drop in the sense of external efficacy (or system responsiveness) but not much change in the sense of internal efficacy (personal competence).

As we can see in Figure 4.2, people today are not much different from people in 1952 with respect to whether they can understand what is going on in government (most find it too complicated to fathom) and whether they have much say in what the government does. But there has been a big change in how responsive people think the government is to their interests.

Unlike the increase in the mistrust of government, the increase in the feeling that government is unresponsive has not been shaped by any particular events; the sense of external efficacy dropped more or less steadily throughout the 1960s and 1970s. What seems to have happened is that Americans gradually have come to the view that government has become too big and pervasive for it to be sensitive to citizen preferences.

Though Americans may feel less effective as citizens than they once did, their sense of efficacy remains much higher than it is among Europeans. In 1974 a poll taken in five nations found that the average American scored significantly higher on the efficacy scale than the average person in Austria, Germany, Great Britain, or the Netherlands. Moreover, Americans were much more likely than Europeans to say that they regularly discussed politics, signed petitions, and worked to solve community problems.[47] Though Americans are less likely to vote than Europeans, they are more likely to do the harder chores that make up democratic politics.

Because Americans are less likely than they once were to hold their leaders in high esteem, to have confidence in government policies, and to believe the system will be responsive to popular wishes, some observers like to say that Americans today are more "alienated" from politics. Perhaps, but careful studies of the subject have not yet been able, for example, to demonstrate any relationship between overall levels of public trust in government or confidence in leaders, on the one hand, and the rates at which people come out to vote, on the other. There is, however, some evidence that the less voters trust political institutions and leaders, the more likely they are to support candidates from the nonincumbent major party (in two-candidate races) and third-party candidates.[48] If this is so, it helps to explain why the incumbent party has lost, and third parties have strongly contested, five of the last nine presidential elections (1968–2000).

Political Tolerance

Democratic politics depends crucially on citizens' being reasonably tolerant of the opinions and actions of others. If unpopular speakers were always shouted down, if government efforts to censor newspapers were usually met with popular support or even public indifference, if peaceful demonstrations were regularly broken up by hostile mobs, if the losing candidates in an election refused to allow their victorious opponents to take office, then the essential elements of a democratic political culture would be missing, and democracy would fail. Democracy does not require perfect tolerance; if it did, the passions of human nature would make democracy forever impossible. But at a minimum citizens must

have a political culture that allows the discussion of ideas and the selection of rulers in an atmosphere reasonably free of oppression.

Public opinion surveys show that the overwhelming majority of Americans agree with concepts such as freedom of speech, majority rule, and the right to circulate petitions—at least in the abstract.[49] But when we get down to concrete cases, a good many Americans are not very tolerant of groups they dislike. Suppose you must decide which groups will be permitted to espouse their causes at meetings held in your community's civic auditorium. Which of these groups would *you* allow to run such a meeting?

1. Protestants holding a revival meeting
2. Right-to-life groups opposing abortion
3. People protesting a nuclear power plant
4. Feminists organizing a march for the Equal Rights Amendment
5. Gays organizing for homosexual rights
6. Atheists preaching against God
7. Students organizing a sit-in to shut down city hall

In a national opinion poll conducted by Herbert McClosky and Alida Brill in 1978–1979, a majority of Americans would have allowed the first four groups to hold their meetings but would have refused to allow the last three. (Similar findings from another opinion survey are shown in Figure 4.3.) Leaders in the communities where this survey was performed would have allowed the first five groups to meet. Lawyers and judges in these communities would have allowed all seven to meet.[50]

Clearly community leaders, and especially lawyers and judges, are more tolerant of specific political activities than are most citizens. But three things need to be said on behalf of the average citizen.

First, one person's civic intolerance can be another person's heartfelt display of civic concern. As is suggested by Figure 4.4, most Americans believe that serious civic problems are rooted in a breakdown of moral values. Correctly or not, most citizens worry that the nation is becoming too tolerant of behaviors that harm society, and they favor defending common moral standards over protecting individual rights.

Second, Americans are willing to allow many people with whom they disagree to do a great deal politically. In the McClosky-Brill study, for example, the general public supported the right of the movie industry to make movies on any subjects it chooses, upheld the

Figure 4.3   Public Tolerance for Advocates of Unpopular Ideas, 1954–1998

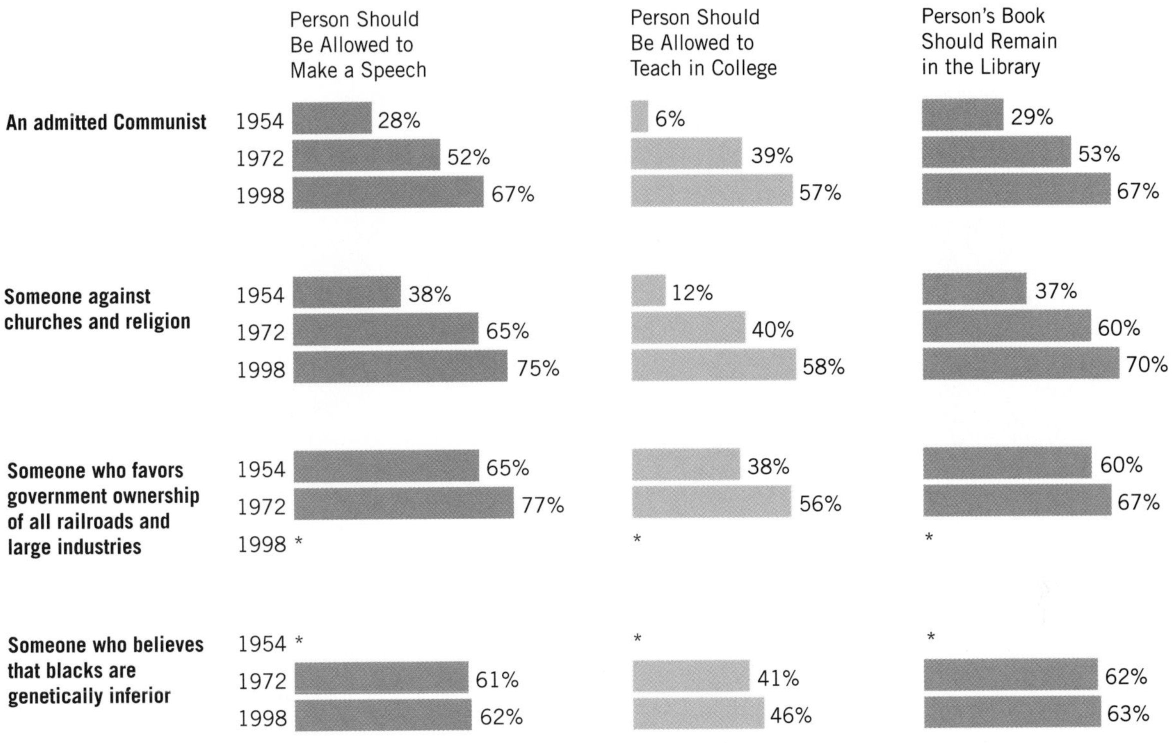

	Person Should Be Allowed to Make a Speech	Person Should Be Allowed to Teach in College	Person's Book Should Remain in the Library
An admitted Communist			
1954	28%	6%	29%
1972	52%	39%	53%
1998	67%	57%	67%
Someone against churches and religion			
1954	38%	12%	37%
1972	65%	40%	60%
1998	75%	58%	70%
Someone who favors government ownership of all railroads and large industries			
1954	65%	38%	60%
1972	77%	56%	67%
1998	*	*	*
Someone who believes that blacks are genetically inferior			
1954	*	*	*
1972	61%	41%	62%
1998	62%	46%	63%

*Question not asked

Source: Adapted from Robert S. Erickson and Kent L. Tedin, *American Public Opinion,* 6th ed. Copyright © 2001 by Longman. Reprinted by permission.

right of reporters to keep confidential their sources of information, defended the right of newspapers and television stations to hire "radical reporters," said that college officials should allow nonviolent protest demonstrations by students, and supported freedom of worship even for extremist religious groups.[51]

Third, Americans have become more tolerant over the years. For instance, in the 1990s people were much more willing to allow communists, socialists, and atheists to meet and disseminate their views than they were in the early 1950s, even though Americans in the 1990s were probably no more sympathetic to these causes than they were in the 1950s.[52] Similarly, there has been a general increase in the willingness of citizens to say that they would vote for a Catholic, Jew, black, or woman for president (see Figure 4.5 on page 98).

Nonetheless, this majority tolerance for many causes should not blind us to the fact that for most of us there is some group or cause from which we are willing to withhold political liberties—even though we endorse those liberties in the abstract.

If most people dislike one or another group strongly enough to deny it certain political rights that we usually take for granted, how is it that such groups (and such rights) survive? The answer, in part, is that most of us don't act on our beliefs. We rarely take the trouble—or have the chance—to block another person from making a speech or teaching school. Some scholars have argued that among people who are in a position to deny other people rights—officeholders and political activists, for example—the level of political tolerance is somewhat greater than among the public at large but that claim has been strongly disputed.[53]

Figure 4.4   Views of Toleration and Morality

QUESTION

Which worries you more, that the country will become too tolerant of behaviors that are bad for sociey, or that the country will become too intolerant of behaviors that don't do any real harm to society?

1998

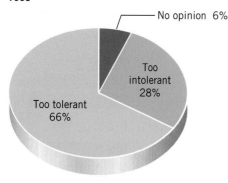

QUESTION

Is it more important to defend standards of right and wrong, to protect the rights of individuals, or are both equally important?

1998

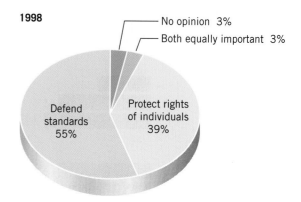

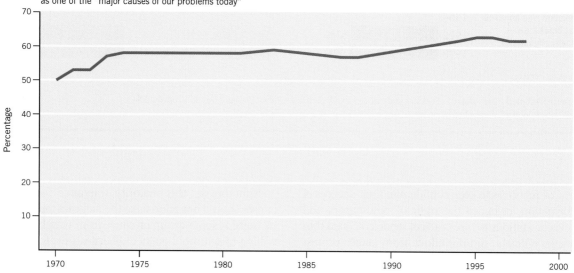

Source: The American Enterprise (January/February 1999): 37, reporting data from Roper, *Washington Post,* Harvard, and Kaiser Family Foundation polls.

But another reason may be just as important. Most of us are ready to deny *some* group its rights, but we usually can't agree on which group that should be. Sometimes we can agree, and then the disliked group may be in for real trouble. There have been times (1919–1920, and again in the early 1950s) when socialists or communists were disliked by most people in the United States. The government on each occasion took strong actions against them. Today fewer people agree that these left-wing groups are a major domestic threat, and so their rights are now more secure.

Religious Leaders Rally to Expand Federal Funding for "Charitable Choice"

August 28
WASHINGTON

Yesterday an interfaith coalition of religious leaders conducted an all-day prayer vigil on Capitol Hill and called for increased federal funding for antipoverty programs run by local religious congregations . . .

MEMORANDUM

To: Representative Heidi Unruh
From: Ron Sider, chief of staff
Subject: Charitable Choice Expansion Act

Section 104 of the 1996 federal welfare reform law encouraged states to utilize "faith-based organizations" as providers of federal welfare services. Known as Charitable Choice, the law prohibits participating organizations from discriminating against beneficiaries on the basis of religion but permits them to control "the definition, development, practice, and expression" of their religious convictions. The proposed act would expand Charitable Choice to crime prevention and other areas.

Arguments for:

1. Over 90 percent of Americans believe in God, and 80 percent favor government funding for faith-based social programs.
2. Local religious groups are the main nongovernmental providers of social services in poor urban neighborhoods. The primary beneficiaries of faith-based programs are needy neighborhood children who are not affiliated with any congregation.
3. So long as the religious organizations serve civic purposes and do not proselytize, the law is constitutional.

Arguments against:

1. Americans are a richly religious people precisely because we have never mixed church and state in this way.
2. Community-serving religious groups succeed because over 97 percent of their funding is private and they can flexibly respond to people's needs without government or other interference.
3. Constitutional or not, the law threatens to undermine both church and state: Children will have religion slid (if not jammed) down their throats, and religious leaders will be tempted to compromise their convictions.

Your decision:
Favor expansion _____
Oppose expansion _____

Figure 4.5   Changes in Levels of Political Tolerance, 1930–1999

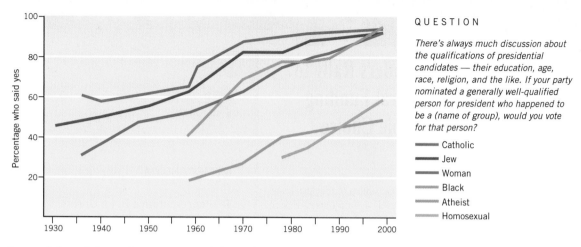

QUESTION

There's always much discussion about the qualifications of presidential candidates — their education, age, race, religion, and the like. If your party nominated a generally well-qualified person for president who happened to be a (name of group), would you vote for that person?

— Catholic
— Jew
— Woman
— Black
— Atheist
— Homosexual

Sources: Gallup poll data, various years, as compiled by Professor John Zaller, Department of Political Science, UCLA; The Gallup Organization, *Poll Releases* (March 29, 1999), 2–6.

Finally, the courts are sufficiently insulated from public opinion that they can act against majority sentiments and enforce constitutional protections (see Chapter 14). Most of us are not willing to give all rights to all groups, but most of us are not judges.

These facts should be a sober reminder that political liberty cannot be taken for granted. Men and women are not, it would seem, born with an inclination to live and let live, at least politically, and many—possibly most—never acquire that inclination. Liberty must be learned and protected. Happily the United States dur-

ing much of its recent history has not been consumed by a revulsion for any one group that has been strong enough to place the group's rights in jeopardy.

Nor should any part of society pretend that it is always more tolerant than another. In the 1950s, for example, ultraconservatives outside the universities were attacking the rights of professors to say and teach certain things. In the 1960s and 1970s ultraliberal students and professors inside the universities were attacking the rights of other students and professors to say certain things.

Summary

The American system of government is supported by a political culture that fosters a sense of civic duty, takes pride in the nation's constitutional arrangements, and provides support for the exercise of essential civil liberties (albeit out of indifference or diversity more than principle at times). In recent decades mistrust of government officials (though not of the system itself) has increased, and confidence in their responsiveness to popular feelings has declined.

Although Americans value liberty in both the political system and the economy, they believe equality is important in the political realm. In economic

affairs they wish to see equality of opportunity but accept inequality of results.

Not only is our culture generally supportive of democratic rule, it also has certain distinctive features that make our way of governing different from what one finds in other democracies. Americans are preoccupied with their rights, and this fact, combined with a political system that (as we shall see) encourages the vigorous exercise of rights and claims, gives to our political life an *adversarial* style. Unlike Swedes or Japanese, we do not generally reach political decisions by consensus, and we often do not defer to the authority of administrative agencies. American politics, more than that of many other nations, is shot through at every stage with protracted conflict.

But as we shall learn in the next chapter, that conflict is not easily described as always pitting liberals against conservatives. Not only do we have a lot of conflict, it is often messy conflict, a kind of political Tower of Babel. Foreign observers sometimes ask how we stand the confusion. The answer, of course, is that we have been doing it for over two hundred years. Maybe our Constitution is two centuries old not in spite of this confusion but because of it. We shall see.

Reconsidering the Enduring Questions

1. ***What distinctive set of beliefs is fundamental to how most Americans, past and present, think about politics and government?***

   Political culture is a patterned way of thinking about how politics and government ought to be carried out. At least five ideas are fundamental to American political culture: liberty, equality, democracy, civic duty, and individual responsibility. By vast majorities Americans believe that every citizen should have an equal chance to influence government policy and to hold public office. By somewhat smaller majorities they believe that people should be allowed to vote even if they can't read or write. But political consensus on basic beliefs does not preclude political conflict over specific issues. Also, we can sometimes have more of one shared value only at the cost of having less of another. For example, most Americans hold equality of opportunity dear, but sometimes we can achieve it only by curtailing personal liberty, another shared value.

2. ***How has American political culture changed over the past hundred years?***

   Because we lack opinion polls and other relevant data going back a century, it is difficult to chart how, and how much, American political culture has changed. Many things seem to have changed little if at all. For example, throughout the nineteenth and most of the twentieth centuries "Americanism" and "American way of life" were familiar and frequently used terms. Americans remain a highly religious people. But certain things clearly have changed. For example, over the last half-century, there has been a decline in the extent to which citizens feel that the political system will respond to their needs and beliefs. Accompanying this decline in citizens' sense of political efficacy has been an increase in their mistrust of government. Also, there is growing evidence that American political culture is divided between two opposed camps, the orthodox and the progressive. The orthodox believe that morality is as important as, or more important than, self-expression. The progressives believe that personal freedom is as important as, or more important than, traditional moral rules.

3. ***To what extent have Americans come to mistrust government, and what difference does it make?***

   Since the late 1950s, there has been a sharp decline in the proportion of Americans who say they trust the government in Washington to do the right thing. But the evidence for this worry is mixed and needs to be put in context. Americans trust government and its officials less, but they still are more supportive of the country and its political institutions than Europeans are of theirs. Trust in government peaked in the 1950s after America had just won a war against fascism, overcome the Depression of the 1930s, possessed a near monopoly on the atom bomb, had a currency that was the envy of the world, and dominated international trade. In the 1960s and 1970s, the country experienced urban riots, a civil rights revolution, the war in Vietnam, economic inflation, and other problems that government seemed powerless to solve, and that some insisted government itself had caused or made worse. Moreover, mass public mistrust of government is not so deep that it cannot be moved, if only momentarily, in a more positive direction. For example, eight months after the September 11, 2001, terrorist attacks on the United States, in May 2002, 40 percent of Americans said they trusted Washington to do what is right always or most of the time, down from the 57 percent who expressed such trust in October 2001, but still above the 29 percent who did so in July 2001.

World Wide Web Resources

- Polling organizations that frequently measure aspects of political culture:
    www.roper.com
    www.gallup.com
- U.S. Census Bureau: www.census.gov

Key Terms

political culture *p. 78*

political subculture *p. 79*

political ideology *p. 79*

civic duty *p. 83*

civic competence *p. 83*

work ethic *p. 88*

class consciousness *p. 89*

orthodox *p. 90*

progressive *p. 90*

political efficacy *p. 93*

internal efficacy *p. 93*

external efficacy *p. 93*

Suggested Readings

Almond, Gabriel, and Sidney Verba. *The Civic Culture*. Princeton, N.J.: Princeton University Press, 1963. A survey of the political cultures of five nations—the United States, Germany, Great Britain, Italy, and Mexico—as they were in 1959.

Gallup, George, Jr., and D. Michael Lindsay. *Surveying the Religious Landscape: Trends in U.S. Beliefs*. Harrisburg, Pa.: Morehouse Publishing, 1999. Masterful summary of polling data on religion and American life in the second half of the twentieth century.

Hartz, Louis. *The Liberal Tradition in America*. New York: Harcourt Brace Jovanovich, 1955. A stimulating interpretation of American political thought since the Founding, emphasizing the notion of a liberal consensus.

Lipset, Seymour Martin. *The First New Nation*. Rev. ed. New York: Norton, 1979. How the origins of American society gave rise to the partially competing values of equality and achievement and the ways in which these values shape political institutions.

McClosky, Herbert, and Alida Brill. *Dimensions of Tolerance: What Americans Believe About Civil Liberties*. New York: Russell Sage Foundation, 1983. How—and whether—different kinds of Americans learn political tolerance.

McClosky, Herbert, and John Zaller. *The American Ethos: Public Attitudes Toward Capitalism and Democracy*. Cambridge: Harvard University Press, 1984. Study of the ways in which Americans evaluate political and economic arrangements.

Nye, Joseph S., Philip D. Zelikow, and David C. King. *Why People Don't Trust Government*. Cambridge: Harvard University Press, 1997. An effort to explain distrust.

Putnam, Robert D. *Bowling Alone: The Collapse and Revival of American Community*. New York: Simon & Schuster, 2000. An important argument that American political culture has been harmed by the decline in membership in organizations that bring people together for communal activities.

Tocqueville, Alexis de. *Democracy in America*. Edited by Phillips Bradley. 2 vols. New York: Knopf, 1951. First published in 1835–1840, this was and remains the greatest single interpretation of American political culture.

Verba, Sidney, and Gary R. Orren. *Equality in America: The View from the Top*. Cambridge: Harvard University Press, 1985. Elite views on political and economic equality.

PART II

Opinions, Interests, and Organizations

The latent causes of faction are thus sown in the nature of man; and we see them everywhere brought into different degrees of activity, according to the different circumstances of civil society.

FEDERALIST NO. 10

Public Opinion

Enduring Questions

1. According to the Framers of the Constitution, what, if any, part should public opinion play in America's representative democracy?

2. How, if at all, does public opinion in America today vary by race, religion, region, and other differences?

3. What is political ideology, and to what extent are ideological differences reflected in political behavior?

In the Gettysburg Address Abraham Lincoln said that the United States has a government "of the people, by the people, and for the people." That suggests that the government should do what the people want. If that is the case, it is puzzling that:

- The federal government has often had a large budget deficit, but the people want a balanced budget.
- Courts have ordered that children be bused in order to balance the schools racially, but the people opposed busing.
- The Equal Rights Amendment to the Constitution was not ratified, but polls showed that most people supported it.
- The House of Representatives voted to impeach President Bill Clinton even though most Americans opposed this.
- Most people believe that there should be a limit on the number of terms to which U.S. senators and members of the U.S. House of Representatives can be elected, but Congress has not approved term limits.

103

Elderly Americans express—vocally—their opinions about Medicare benefits.

Some people, reflecting on the many gaps between what the government does and what the people want, may become cynical and think our system is democratic in name only. That would be a mistake. There are several very good reasons why government policy will often appear to be at odds with public opinion.

First, the Framers of the Constitution did not try to create a government that would do from day to day "what the people want." They created a government for the purpose of achieving certain substantive goals. The preamble to the Constitution lists six of these: "to form a more perfect Union, establish Justice, ensure domestic Tranquility, provide for the common defence, promote the general Welfare, and secure the Blessings of Liberty."

One means of achieving these goals was popular rule, as provided for by the right of the people to vote for members of the House of Representatives (and later for senators and presidential electors). But other means were provided as well: representative government, federalism, the separation of powers, a Bill of Rights, and an independent judiciary. These were all intended to be checks on public opinion. In addition the Framers knew that in a nation as large

and diverse as the United States there would rarely be any such thing as "public opinion"; rather there would be many "publics" (that is, factions) holding many opinions. The Framers hoped that the struggle among these many publics would protect liberty (no one "public" would dominate) while at the same time permitting the adoption of reasonable policies that commanded the support of many factions.

Second, it is not as easy as one may suppose to know what the public thinks. We are so inundated these days with public opinion polls that we may imagine that they tell us what the public believes. That may be true on a few rather simple, clear-cut, and widely discussed issues, but it is not true with respect to most matters on which the government must act. The best pollsters know the limits of their methods, and the citizen should know them as well.

Third, the more people are active in and knowledgeable about politics, the more weight their opinions carry in governmental circles. For most of us, politics ranks way down on the list of things to think about, well below our families, jobs, health, sweethearts, entertainment, and sports. Some people, however, are political activists, and so come to know as much about politics as the rest of us know about batting averages, soap operas, and car repair. Not only do these activists, or political elites, *know more* about politics than the rest of us, they *think differently* about it—they have different views and beliefs. The government attends more to the elite views than to popular views, at least on many matters.

In this chapter we take a close look at what "public opinion" is, how it is formed, the major cleavages in public opinion, and, especially, how political elites differ from ordinary citizens. In later chapters we examine the workings of political parties, interest groups, and government institutions and consider what impact they have on whether public opinion affects government policy.

What Is Public Opinion?

In 1984 some researchers at the University of Cincinnati asked twelve hundred local residents whether they favored passage of the Monetary Control Bill of 1983. About 21 percent said that they favored the bill, 25 percent said that they opposed it, and the rest said that they hadn't thought much about the matter or didn't know.

The members of Congress from Cincinnati would have been surprised to learn of this expression of public opinion from their constituents, for there was no such thing as the Monetary Control Bill. The researchers had made it up. Nor is there anything unusual about people in Cincinnati. A few years earlier about 26 percent of the people questioned in a national survey also expressed opinions on the same nonexistent piece of legislation.[1] Given this information, how much confidence should we place in polls that presumably tell us "what the American people think" about legislation and other issues?

Even if people have heard of a given person or issue, how a pollster words a question can dramatically affect the answer he or she gets. Suppose we want to know whether the public believes that the federal government should provide housing for people. One poll asked that question in three different ways. In the first example people were asked whether they agreed or disagreed with a one-sided statement ("The federal government should see to it that all people have adequate housing"). A majority agreed. In the second example people were given a choice between two statements, one favoring a federal housing policy (mentioned first) and the other favoring individual responsibility ("each person should provide for his own housing"). Given this choice, a small majority opposed federal housing programs. In the third example the question was repeated, but this time with the individual responsibility option mentioned first. Now over 70 percent of the respondents opposed federal housing programs. Simply altering the order in which people were presented with options affected which option they chose and changed "public opinion" on housing programs.

Many polls ask voters to think only about the benefits of a program and not about the costs. When Americans are asked whether the government should "spend more" on health, education, and crime reduction, big majorities say "yes." (And they say it even though these same voters want low taxes and balanced budgets.) But these programs all cost money. One poll asked people whether the size of public school classes should be reduced to fifteen. Huge majorities were in favor. But when a scholar asked people how much they were willing to pay to reduce class sizes to fifteen, support for the idea just about vanished.[2]

Moreover, opinions on public issues may not be stable—that is, they may not be firmly held. In a study

---

★ POLITICALLY SPEAKING ★

John Q. Public, Middle America, and the Silent Majority

John Q. Public is the average man or woman on the street, often portrayed by cartoonists as bespectacled and befuddled. The "little guy," the "common man" (or woman), John Doe or Jane Doe. John Q. Public is sometimes confused with James Q. Wilson, to whom he is only distantly related.

Middle America is a phrase coined by the late Joseph Kraft in 1968 to refer to Americans who have moved out of poverty but are not yet affluent and who cherish the traditional middle-class values.

The **silent majority** consists of those people, whatever their economic status, who uphold traditional values, especially against the counterculture of the 1960s.

Source: Adapted from *Safire's Political Dictionary* by William Safire. Copyright © 1968, 1972, 1978 by William Safire. Reprinted by permission of Random House, Inc. and the author.

---

conducted in 1980, the same people were asked the same questions in January and again in June of the same year. The first had to do with how tough we should be in dealing with the Soviet Union, the second with whether spending should be cut on things like health and education programs. Many people gave one opinion in January and then a different one in June. Of those who said in January that we should cooperate more with the Soviets, only one-quarter said in June that we should get together with them. Of those who said in January that the government should cut the services it provides, more than one-quarter said in June that they wanted to keep those services at the same level or expressed a middle-of-the-road position.

In sum, public opinion on many matters suffers from ignorance, instability, and sensitivity to the way questions are worded in polls. This does not mean that the American people are ignorant, unstable, or gullible, only that most Americans do not find it worth their while to spend the amount of time thinking about politics that they spend on their jobs, families, and friends. Moreover, just because people do not think much about politics does not mean that democracy is impossible, only that it can work best when people are given relatively simple, clear-cut choices—like the choice between Democrats and Republicans or between one presidential candidate and another.

Furthermore, our specific attitudes about particular matters may be much less important for the health of society than our underlying political culture—our commitment, discussed in Chapter 4, to liberty, equality, individualism, and civic duty. As we shall see, different people give different weight to the various parts of this culture, producing what can be described as a political ideology.

The Origins of Political Attitudes

Because our attitudes are often unstable or uninformed, some critics of American society have argued that we are brainwashed—duped by television or demagogic leaders into thinking one way or another. Often we are told that presidential candidates are "sold," as if they were boxes of soap flakes. Naturally these critics never say that *they* are brainwashed, only the rest of us.

However shallow their analysis, the argument is a serious one. If the government (or the media) were able to manipulate our political attitudes, then democracy would be a joke. It is akin to what would happen in the marketplace if automobile dealers were able to "brainwash" us into buying Chevrolets, Fords, Chryslers, or Toyotas. The car manufacturers would no longer have to strive to achieve greater efficiency and produce better products; they would only have to "persuade" us what to like. We would be happy not because we owned a good car but because Madison Avenue *told* us we owned a good car.

Of course advertising does affect our choice of candidates and policies, just as it affects our choice of automobiles. Otherwise why would companies and politicians spend so much money on advertising? But there are real and important limits to the impact of that advertising. Those limits exist because we have learned, independent of government and the market, some things that help us make our own choices.

The Role of the Family

The best-studied (though not necessarily the most important) case of opinion formation is that of party identification. The majority of young people identify with their parents' political party. A study of high school seniors showed that, of these young men and women, almost all (91 percent) knew accurately the presidential preference of their parents, the great majority (71 percent) knew accurately their parents' party identification, and most shared that identification (only 9 percent identified with the party opposite to that of their parents). This process begins fairly early in life: by the time they are in the fifth grade (age eleven), over half of all schoolchildren identify with one party or the other, and another fifth claim to be independents.[3]

Naturally, as people grow older, they become more independent of their parents in many ways, including politically, but there nonetheless remains a great deal of continuity between youthful partisanship, learned from one's parents, and adult partisanship. One study of adults found that around 60 percent still had the party identification—Democrat, Republican, or independent—of their parents. Of those who differed with their parents, the overwhelming majority did so not by identifying with the opposite party but by describing themselves as "independents."[4]

The ability of the family to inculcate a strong sense of party identification has declined in recent years. The proportion of citizens who say they consider themselves to be Democrats or Republicans has become steadily smaller since the early 1950s. This drop has been greatest among those who *strongly* identify with one party or another. In 1952 fully 22 percent of voters said they were strong Democrats and 13 percent said they were strong Republicans; by 1976 only 15 percent claimed to be strong Democrats and 9 percent to be strong Republicans. Accompanying this decline in partisanship has been

"Yes, son, we're Republicans."

Drawing by Richter; © The New Yorker *Magazine, Inc.*

a sharp rise in the proportion of citizens describing themselves as independents.

Part of this change results from the fact that young voters have always had a weaker sense of partisanship than older ones. But the youthfulness of the population cannot explain all the changes, for the decline in partisanship has occurred at all age levels. Moreover, those who reached voting age in the1960s were less apt than those who matured in the 1950s to keep the party identification of their parents.[5]

Though we still tend to acquire some measure of partisanship from our parents, the meaning of that identification is far from clear. There are, after all, liberal and conservative Democrats, as well as liberal and conservative Republicans. So far the evidence suggests that children are more independent of their parents in policy preferences than in party identification. The correlation of children's attitudes with parental attitudes on issues involving civil liberties and racial questions is much lower than the correlation in their party identification. This may be because issues change from one generation to the next, because children are more idealistic than their parents, or because most parents do not communicate to their children clear, consistent positions on a range of political issues. The family dinner table is not a seminar in political philosophy but a place where people discuss jobs, school, dates, and chores.

In some families, however, the dinner table is a political classroom. Fairly clear political ideologies (a term we shall define in a later section) seem to be communicated to that small proportion of children raised in families where politics is a dominant topic of conversation and political views are strongly held. Studies of the participants in various student radical movements in the 1960s suggested that college radicals were often the sons and daughters of people who had themselves been young radicals; some commentators dubbed them the "red-diaper babies." Presumably, deeply conservative people come disproportionately from families that were also deeply conservative. This transfer of political beliefs from one generation to the next does not appear in large national studies, because such a small proportion of the population is at either the far left or the far right of the political spectrum.

Religion

One way in which the family forms and transmits political beliefs is by its religious tradition. In general Catholic families are somewhat more liberal on economic issues than white Protestant ones, while Jewish families are much more liberal on both economic and social issues than families of either Catholics or Protestants.[6]

There are two theories as to why this should be so. The first has to do with the **social status** of religious groups in America. When they immigrated to this country, Catholics and Jews were often poor and the object of discrimination. As a result they often affiliated themselves with whichever party and social doctrine seemed most sympathetic to their plight. In many places the Democratic party and a liberal social doctrine seemed to offer the most support. Today Catholics and Jews enjoy greater economic prosperity and face much less discrimination, and so their support for Democrats and liberal candidates has weakened.

The status explanation cannot be the whole story, for if it were simply a matter of low status and discrimination, evangelical Christians, many of whom are poor, would be liberal Democrats. The second theory emphasizes the content of the **religious tradition** more than the social status of its adherents. In this view the Jewish religion has always emphasized social justice as much as personal rectitude. By contrast, evangelical Protestant denominations emphasize personal salvation (becoming "born again") more than questions of social policy. This difference in teachings has led Jews to be disproportionately liberal and fundamentalist Protestants to be disproportionately conservative on many social issues.

Religion is so important in America that every major political leader engages it, as President Bush does on the National Day of Prayer and Remembrance shortly after 9/11.

Whatever the reason, religious differences make for political differences. In Table 5.1 we can see how the religious beliefs of white voters affected their policy preferences in 1996. Fundamentalists believe that the Bible is God's word and literally true. They are more likely than those who doubt that the Bible is inspired by God to oppose cuts in defense spending, to oppose abortions, and to favor prayer in schools. (These differences remain essentially the same even after you divide the respondents between those who have a lot of political information and those who have rather little.)

Interestingly there are no significant differences in how people holding differing views of the Bible feel about economic issues, as opposed to social or foreign policy issues. Fundamentalists and nonfundamentalists have about the same opinion on government job guarantees and spending on government services. This suggests that both social status and religious tradition help explain the effect of religion on politics: the poor status of many fundamentalists inclines them to back liberal government economic policies, but the religious tradition of this group leads them to take a conservative position on social and foreign policy matters.

In the early 1990s a broad-based political movement arose to represent the views of conservative evangelical Christians. The movement was spearheaded by the Christian Coalition, an activist organization founded by Pat Robertson and led by Ralph Reed. Unlike the older Moral Majority, the Christian Coalition took seriously the task of entering politics at the grassroots and recognized the need to build working alliances with mainstream politicians. Within a short time people allied with the Christian Coalition won power in many local Republican party organizations, and its national conferences became important places for Republican presidential candidates to appear. Although the Christian Coalition was strongest in the South, Midwest, and West, it was unmistakably a national force in American politics. During the 1994 elections, for example, it distributed some 30 million voter guides nationwide, and affiliated local organizations may have distributed

Table 5.1 Religious Orientation of White Voters, 1996			
Political Opinion	**Secular (36%)**	**In Between (39%)**	**Fundamentalist (25%)**
Increase domestic spending	61%	76%	76%
For national health insurance	38	39	20
Guarantee good standard of living	23	24	11
Spend less on welfare	61	61	77
Always permit abortions	57	29	8
Allow gays in military	72	61	35
Punish criminals to cut crime	47	60	65
Favor gun control	44	46	29
Spend more on defense	48	69	76
Percentage Democratic (of party identifiers)	50	40	23
Percentage liberal (of ideological identifiers)	36	12	6
Percentage voted for Clinton (of 1996 two-party vote)	49	40	20

Source: From Robert S. Erikson and Kent L. Tedin, *American Public Opinion,* 6th ed., p. 196. Copyright © 2001 by Longman. Reprinted with permission.

several million more. Since 1960 evangelical Christians have become more attached to Republican presidential candidates (except in 1976, when Jimmy Carter ran), while Jews and those without a religious orientation have been consistently supportive of the Democratic party. After 2000, the Christian Coalition disbanded, having suffered financial difficulties. But its influence lived on in the work of its former leader and in other conservative Christian groups that have emerged in the last few years.

The Gender Gap

Journalists often point out that women have "deserted" Republican candidates to favor Democratic ones. In some cases that is true. But it would be more correct to say that men have "deserted" Democratic candidates for Republican ones. The **gender gap** is the difference in political views between men and women. That gap has existed for a long time, and it is a problem for both political parties.

Men have become increasingly Republican since the mid-1960s, while the voting behavior of women has remained unchanged. In 1952 men and women identified with the Democratic party at about the same level, around 58 or 59 percent. In 1996 women still identified with the Democrats at about the same level, while men had abandoned the Democratic party and identified more with the Republicans.[7] In the 2000 presidential election, women voted for Democrat Al Gore by a margin of 55 percent to 43 percent, while men voted for Republican George W. Bush the younger by a margin of 54 percent to 43 percent.[8]

The biggest reason for this gap seems to involve attitudes about the size of government, gun control, spending programs aimed at the poor, and gay rights. Men have always been more conservative than women in their views on these social issues, but by the late 1960s and early 1970s men had changed their party loyalty to match their policy preferences. As Table 5.2 shows, in 1996 men and women were similar in their views on abortion but quite different in their opinions about welfare, spending money to help the homeless or to increase military defense, and sexual harassment in the workplace. In the 1996 election women were much more likely than men to vote for Clinton even though he had been involved in extramarital affairs. In 1998 women were much more inclined than men to vote for female Senate candidates. Part of that difference was because most of the women candidates were Democrats; in fact,

in one race where the woman candidate was a Republican, the male (Democratic) candidate got a bigger share of the female vote than of the male vote.

Schooling and Information

Studies going back over half a century seem to show that attending college has a big impact on political attitudes, usually making them more liberal. College students are more liberal than the population generally, and students at the most prestigious or selective colleges are the most liberal of all.[9] For example, the undergraduates at Harvard College in 1984 preferred Mondale to Reagan 61 percent to 28 percent, while the country at large favored Reagan over Mondale 59 percent to 41 percent.[10] Moreover, the longer students stay in college, the more liberal they are, with seniors more liberal than freshmen and graduate students more liberal than undergraduates.[11] Harvard seniors were more supportive of Mondale than were Harvard freshmen. Students studying the social sciences tend to be more liberal than those studying engineering or the physical sciences.[12] As we shall see in the next chapter, having gone to college increases the rate at which people participate in politics.

Table 5.2	The Gender Gap: Differences in Political Views of Men and Women		
Issue		**Men**	**Women**
Federal spending for welfare programs should be increased.		8%	14%
Abortion should be permitted by law.		57	60
Sexual harassment is a very serious problem in the workplace.		24	38
This country would be better off if we just stayed home and did not concern ourselves with problems in other parts of the world.		24	29
I voted for Clinton in 1996.		45	59
Generally speaking, I think of myself as a Democrat.		32	44
The United States should increase defense spending.		37	26
The United States should increase spending on solving the problems of the homeless.		51	63
Ban all handguns except for the police.		33	58

Source: ICPSR American National Election Survey, 1996. Pre- and Post-Election Surveys.

Students tend to become more liberal as they go through college.

Why schooling should have this effect on attitudes is not clear. One possibility is that it has nothing to do with schooling but rather with the individual traits typically possessed by people who go to college and beyond. Some combination of temperament, intelligence, and family background may lead to greater liberalism, with the contents of a college education playing no role at all.

A second possibility is that college and postgraduate schooling expose people to more information about politics from all sources. College graduates, compared to high school graduates, read more newspapers and periodicals, join more organizations and social movements, and participate in more election campaigns and lobbying efforts. Their political beliefs may be shaped by these experiences as much as, or more than, by what they learn in the college classroom. In addition, evidence collected by John Zaller shows that the level of political information one has is the best single predictor of being liberal on some kinds of issues, such as civil liberties and civil rights.[13] Information on these matters, he suggests, is today produced by a predominantly liberal cultural elite (see Chapter 10). The longer you stay in school, the more you are exposed to the views of that elite.

The third possibility is that college somehow teaches liberalism. We know that professors are more liberal than members of other occupations, that professors at the most prestigious schools are more liberal than those at the less-celebrated ones, that professors in the social sciences are more liberal than those in engineering or business, and that younger faculty members are more liberal than older ones.[14]

The political disposition of professors is in part the result of the kinds of people who become college teachers, but it is also the result of the nature of intellectual work. Intellectuals require freedom to explore new or unpopular ideas and thus tend to be strong supporters of civil liberties. Intellectuals work with words and numbers to develop general or abstract ideas; frequently they do not take personal responsibility for practical matters. Thus they are often critical of people who do take such responsibility and who, in the management of complex human affairs, inevitably make compromises. Intellectuals are by training and profession skeptical of common opinions, and thus they are often critical of accepted values and existing institutions. They are interested in ideas and the ideal and thus are sometimes disdainful of the interests and institutions of society.

At one time the liberalizing effect of college had only a small impact on national politics, because so few persons were college graduates. In 1900 only 6 percent of Americans seventeen years of age had even graduated from high school, and less than 1 percent of twenty-three-year-olds were college graduates. By 1999, however, 83 percent of all Americans age twenty-five and over were high school graduates, and 25 percent of the same group were college graduates.[15] College, or the exposure to ideas and movements that one encounters there, has become, along with the family, an important source of political opinion for the American electorate.

Some people believe that college students today are more conservative than students were ten or twenty years ago. That is partly true and partly false. As indicated in Table 5.3, college freshmen in 1993 were less likely than freshmen in the 1970s to favor legalizing marijuana or abortion and less willing to support increased military spending. Their opinions about government-sponsored consumer protection changed slightly.

How long the liberalizing effect of college persists depends on a number of factors. One study found that former college students still described themselves as more liberal than their parents seven years after graduation.[16] Another study found that students who changed in college from being conservative to being liberal tended to maintain that liberalism for at least twenty years if they acquired, after graduation, liberal friends and spouses.[17] College graduates who go on to get a postgraduate degree—say, a law degree or a Ph.D.—tend to become decidedly more liberal than those who stop with just a B.A. degree.[18] A scholar who tracked students graduating from college in 1969 found that those who had taken part in protests remained very liberal well into the 1980s, while nonprotesters became somewhat more conservative over the years.[19]

Cleavages in Public Opinion

The way in which political opinions are formed helps explain the cleavages that exist among these opinions and why these cleavages do not follow any single political principle but instead overlap and crosscut in bewildering complexity. If, for example, the United States lacked regional differences and was composed almost entirely of white Protestants who had never attended college, there would still be plenty of political conflict—the rich would have different views from the poor; workers would have different views from farmers—but that conflict would be much simpler to describe and explain. It might even lead to political parties that were more clearly aligned with competing political philosophies than those we now have. In fact some democratic nations in the world today do have a population very much like the one we have asked you to imagine, and the United States itself, during the first half of the nineteenth century, was overwhelmingly white, Protestant, and without much formal schooling.

Today, however, there are crosscutting cleavages based on race, ethnicity, religion, region, and education, in addition to those created by income and occupation. To the extent that politics is sensitive to public opinion, it is sensitive to a variety of different and even competing publics. Not all these publics have influence proportionate to their numbers or even to their numbers adjusted for the intensity of their feelings. As will be described later, a filtering process occurs that makes the opinions of some publics more influential than those of others.

Table 5.3 **The Changing College Student**		
Since the 1970s college freshmen have become more conservative on some issues and more liberal on others.		
		Percentage Agreeing
Issue	**1970s[*]**	**1993**
Abolish death penalty	33%	22%
Legalize abortion	83	62
Legalize marijuana	47	28
Increase military spending	39	23
Criminals have too many rights	52	68
Government not doing enough to:		
Control pollution	91	84
Protect consumers	77	72

Note: We have no comparable figures for college seniors. Freshmen may change their opinions on these matters while in school.

[*]Exact year the question was asked in 1970s varies between 1970 and 1976, depending on the question.

Sources: Richard C. Braungart and Margaret M. Braungart, "Black Colleges: Freshmen Attitudes," *Public Opinion* (May/June 1989): 14. Reprinted with the permission of the American Enterprise Institute for Public Policy Research, Washington, D.C. Updated to 1993 from Alexander W. Astin, William S. Korn, and Ellyne R. Riggs, *The American Freshman* (Los Angeles: UCLA Graduate School of Education, 1993), 25.

Whatever this state of affairs may mean for democracy, it creates a messy situation for political scientists. It would be so much easier if everyone's opinion on political affairs reflected some single feature of his or her life, such as income, occupation, age, race, or sex. Of course some writers have argued that political opinion is a reflection of one such feature, social class, usually defined in terms of income or occupation, but that view, though containing some truth, is beset with inconsistencies: poor blacks and poor whites disagree sharply on many issues involving race; well-to-do Jews and well-to-do Protestants often have opposing opinions on social welfare policy; and low-income elderly people are much more worried about crime than are low-income graduate students. Plumbers and professors may have similar incomes, but they rarely have similar views, and business people in New York City often take a very different view of government than business people in Houston or Birmingham.

In some other democracies a single factor such as class may explain more of the differences in political attitudes than it does in the more socially heterogeneous United States. Most blue-collar workers in America think of themselves as being "middle-class," whereas most such workers in Britain and France describe themselves as "working-class." In England the working class prefers the Labour party by a margin of three to one, while in the United States workers prefer the Democratic party by less than two to one, and in 1980 and 1984 they gave most of their votes to the Republican Ronald Reagan.[20]

Social Class

Americans speak of "social class" with embarrassment. The norm of equality tugs at our consciences, urging us to judge people as individuals, not as parts of some social group (such as "the lower class"). Social scientists speak of "class" with confusion. They know it exists but quarrel constantly about how to define it: by income? occupation? wealth? schooling? prestige? personality?

Let's face up to the embarrassment and skip over the confusion. Truck drivers and investment bankers look different, talk differently, and vote differently. There is nothing wrong with saying that the first group consists of "working-class" (or "blue-collar") people and the latter of "upper-class" (or "management") people. Moreover, though different definitions of class produce slightly different groupings of

Traditional labor unions have lost members, but they still are a force in politics.

people, most definitions overlap to such an extent that it does not matter too much which we use.

However defined, public opinion and voting have been less determined by class in the United States than in Europe, and the extent of class cleavage has declined in the last few decades in both the United States and Europe. In the 1950s V. O. Key, Jr., found that differences in political opinion were closely associated with occupation. He noted that people holding managerial or professional jobs had distinctly more conservative views on social welfare policy and more internationalist views on foreign policy than did manual workers.[21]

During the next decade this pattern changed greatly. Opinion surveys done in the late 1960s showed that business and professional people had views quite similar to those of manual workers on matters such as the poverty program, health insurance, American policy in Vietnam, and government efforts to create jobs.[22]

The voting patterns of different social classes have also become somewhat more similar. Class voting has declined sharply since the late 1940s in the United States, France, Great Britain, and West Germany and declined moderately in Sweden.

Class differences remain, of course. Unskilled workers are more likely than affluent white-collar workers to be Democrats and to have liberal views on economic policy. And when economic issues pinch—for example, when farmers are hurting or steelworkers are being laid off—the importance of economic interests in differentiating the opinions of various groups rises sharply. Moreover, there is some evidence that during the Reagan administration, income once again began to make a large difference in the party affiliation of voters.

Why should social class, defined along income lines, have become less important over the long term? One reason has to do largely with schooling. At one time the income of people did not depend so heavily as it now does on having educational credentials. Most people had only a high school education, whatever their job might be, and only a small minority had a college or postgraduate degree. Today access to higher-paying jobs (outside of sports and entertainment) is increasingly restricted to people with extensive schooling. Since, as we have seen, college and (especially) postgraduate education tends to make people more liberal than they would otherwise be, the arrival of millions of college graduates, lawyers, and Ph.D.'s into the ranks of the financially affluent has brought into the upper classes a more liberal political outlook than once was the case. This development probably favors Democrats. For example, an analysis of voting in a hundred of America's richest communities found that the Democratic share of the vote increased steadily, from 25 percent in 1980 to 41 percent in 1996, a gain of 16 points.[23]

Still, many of the issues that now lead us to choose which party to support and that determine whether we think of ourselves as liberals or conservatives are noneconomic issues. In recent years our political posture has been shaped by the positions we take on race relations, abortion, school prayer, arms control, and environmentalism, issues that do not clearly affect the rich differently than the poor (or at least do not affect them as differently as do the union movement, the minimum wage, and unemployment). Moral, symbolic, and foreign policy matters do not divide rich and poor in the same way as economic ones. Thus we have many well-off people who think of themselves as liberals because they take liberal positions on these noneconomic matters, and many not-so-well-off people who think of themselves as conservatives because that is the position they take on these issues.

Race and Ethnicity

Social class clearly has become a less clear-cut source of political cleavage, but it is harder to know what to make of race and ethnicity. In some ways racial differences are of central importance. African Americans are overwhelming Democrats while whites are much more likely to be Republicans. African Americans thought that O. J. Simpson was innocent of killing his wife, but white Americans thought that he was guilty. Blacks believe that the criminal justice system is biased against them; whites disagree. Blacks favor a stronger affirmative action program; whites are opposed to it (see Table 5.4).

But in other respects the opinions of whites and blacks are similar. Majorities of both groups oppose the use of racial quotas, want the courts to get tougher on criminals, oppose making abortion legal in all cases, and nearly identical percentages wish that the Census Bureau would stop collecting data on race and ethnicity. Huge majorities in both groups think that too much is made of racial differences and would be willing to vote for an African American presidential candidate.

There is some evidence that the differences between white and black Americans may be narrowing. About 26 percent of African Americans ages twenty-six to thirty-five (as opposed to only 3 percent of those ages fifty-one to sixty-four) identify themselves as Republicans.[24] Likewise, African American teenagers are only half as likely as African American adults to think that the social and economic differences between whites and blacks are mainly due to racial discrimination.[25] Some hints of these differences can be seen in Table 5.5, which shows that between 1974 and 1996 African Americans became less convinced that the government should help them and more convinced that they should help themselves. A 2001 study examined gaps in opinion

Table 5.4 **African American and White Opinion**

	African American	White
Favor expanding affirmative action programs[a]	53%	22%
Believe the justice system is racially biased against blacks[a]	72	44
Favor harsher treatment of criminals by the courts[b]	78	76
Favor more spending on national defense[c]	13	18
Favor national health insurance by government[c]	39	23
Believe the U.S. Census Bureau should stop collecting information on race and ethnicity[d]	48	47
Believe abortion should be legal in all cases[e]	24	28
Approve of black/white marriages[a]	77	61
Willing to vote for a black person for president[a]	93	91
Believe that too much is made of the differences between blacks and whites and not enough of what they have in common[f]	89	92

Sources: (a) *Black/White Perspectives in the United States* (Princeton, N.J.: The Gallup Organization, June 1997), 14, 16, 23, 24; (b) Gallup Polls, 1993 and 1994; (c) American National Election Survey, 1996; (d) "The Newsweek Poll," *Newsweek* (February 13, 1995): 65; (e) *The Public Perspective* (May 1995): 19; (f) *The American Enterprise* (November/December 1998): 92, reporting results of a March–April 1998 Public Agenda survey of white and black parents or guardians of children in kindergarten through twelfth grade.

between younger and older blacks with regard to criminal justice, education, the environment, voting, and other issues.[26] Among other significant differences, black young adults (ages eighteen to twenty-five) were far more likely than those ages fifty-one to sixty-four to say that it is okay not to vote if you do not like any of the candidates and were far more receptive than their elders to arguments in favor of school vouchers. It remains to be seen, however, whether this generation gap between younger and older African Americans will persist or have any important political effects.

In the meantime, however, it is clear that there is a big opinion gap between the leaders of African American organizations and African Americans in general. A 1985 survey of more than a hundred African American leaders and six hundred African American citizens found that the leaders were much more likely than the rank and file to favor abortions, school busing, and affirmative action. Most African American leaders deny that blacks are making progress, while most African American citizens think that they are.[27] This cleavage should not surprise us; as we shall see, there is a similar cleavage between white leaders and white citizens.

America is now home to over 30 million Latinos. But the literature on Latino public opinion has been called "small, disproportionately oriented toward immigration, and relatively silent on the influence of gender" and other possible intragroup opinion cleavages.[28] Likewise, despite the country's growing Asian population, there is as yet also virtually no literature

Table 5.5 **Changes in Racial Opinion**

	Whites		African Americans	
	1974	1996	1974	1996
Government should help blacks	25%	16%	63%	40%
Blacks should help themselves	50	61	12	40

Source: Robert S. Erikson and Kent L. Tedin, *American Public Opinion*, 5th ed. Copyright © 1995 by Allyn and Bacon. Reprinted by permission. Updated for 1996 with National Election Survey figures.

on Asian public opinion. However, an early survey of ethnic groups in California, a state where fully one-third of all recent immigrants to this country live, gives us some hint of how Latinos and Asian Americans feel about political parties and issues. Latinos identify themselves as Democrats, but much less so than do blacks, and Asian Americans are even more identified with the Republican party than Anglo whites. On issues such as spending on the military and welfare programs, prayer in public schools, and the imposition of the death penalty for murder, Asian American views are much more like those of Anglo whites than those of either blacks or Hispanics. Latinos are somewhat more liberal than Anglos or Asian Americans, but much less liberal than blacks, except with respect to bilingual education programs.[29]

These figures conceal important differences within these ethnic groups. For example, Japanese Americans are among the more conservative Asian Americans, whereas Korean Americans (perhaps because they are among the most recent immigrants) are more liberal. Similarly, Latinos, the fastest-growing ethnic group in the United States, are a diverse mix of Cuban Americans, Mexican Americans, Central Americans, and Puerto Ricans, each with distinct political views. A study of Latino voting in the 1988 presidential election found that Mexican Americans were the most Democratic, Cuban Americans were the most Republican, and Puerto Ricans were in between the other two groups.[30] But no group of Latino voters has become predictably partisan. In 1998, 78 percent of California's Latino (predominantly Mexican American) vote went to Democrat Gray Davis in the governor's race, but in Texas half of the Latino (also predominantly Mexican American) vote went to reelect Republican governor George W. Bush.[31]

Region

It is widely believed that geographic region affects political attitudes and in particular that southerners and northerners disagree significantly on many policy questions. As we will see, southern members of Congress tend to vote differently—and more conservatively—than northern ones, and it should stand to reason that this is because their constituents, southern voters, expect them to vote differently. At one time white southerners were conspicuously less liberal than easterners, midwesterners, or westerners on questions such as aid to minorities, legalizing

marijuana, school busing, and enlarging the rights of those accused of crimes. Although more conservative on these issues, they held views on economic issues similar to those of whites in other regions of the country. This helps to explain why the South was for so long a part of the Democratic party coalition: on national economic and social welfare policies, southerners expressed views not very different from those of northerners. That coalition was always threatened, however, by the divisiveness produced by issues of race and liberty.

Today the political views of white southerners are less distinct from those of whites living in other parts of the country. The proportion of white Protestants in the South who gave liberal answers to questions regarding both civil liberties/civil rights issues and economic/welfare issues in 1992 was only somewhat different from that of white Protestants in other regions.[32]

The southern lifestyle is in fact different from that of other regions of the country. The South has, on the whole, been more accommodating to business enterprise and less so to organized labor than, for example, the Northeast; it gave greater support to the third-party candidacy of George Wallace in 1968, which was a protest against big government and the growth of national political power as well as against civil rights; and it was in the South that the greatest opposition arose to income-redistribution plans such as the Family Assistance Plan of 1969. Moreover, there is some evidence that white southerners became by the 1970s more conservative than they had been in the 1950s, at least when compared to white northerners.[33] Finally, white southerners have become less attached to the Democratic party: whereas over three-fourths described themselves as Democrats in 1952, only a third did by 1996 (see Figure 5.1 on page 118).

These changes in the South can have great significance, as we shall see in the next three chapters when we consider how elections are fought. It is enough for now to remember that, without the votes of the southern states, no Democrat except Lyndon Johnson in 1964 would have been elected president from 1940 through 1976. (Without the South Roosevelt would have lost in 1944, Truman in 1948, Kennedy in 1960, and Carter in 1976. And even though Carter carried the South, he did not win a majority of white southern votes.) Clinton won in 1992 and 1996 without carrying the South, but those were three-man races.

The Art of Public Opinion Polling

A survey of public opinion—popularly called a **poll**—can provide us with a reasonably accurate measure of how people think, provided certain conditions are met. There are five key criteria that must be met in designing and interpreting surveys.

1. **The persons interviewed must be a random sample of the entire population.** In a **random sample** poll any given person, or any given voter or adult, has an equal chance of being interviewed. Most national surveys draw a sample of between a thousand and fifteen hundred persons by a process called stratified or multistage area sampling. The pollster makes a list of all the geographical units in the country (say, all the counties) and groups (or "stratifies") them by the size of their population. The pollster then selects at random units from each group or stratum in proportion to its total population. For example, if one stratum's total population is 10 percent of the national population, then 10 percent of the counties in the sample will be drawn from this stratum. Within each selected county smaller and smaller geographical units (cities, towns, census tracts, blocks) are chosen, and then, within the smallest unit, individuals are selected at random (by, for example, choosing the occupant of every fifth house). The key is to stick to the sample and not let people volunteer to be interviewed—volunteers often have views different from those who do not volunteer.

2. **The questions must be comprehensible.** The questions must ask people about things they have some knowledge of and some basis for forming an opinion about. Most people know, at least at election time, whom they would prefer as president; most people also have views about what they think the most important national problems are. But relatively few voters will have any opinion about our policy toward El Salvador (if indeed they have even heard of it) or about the investment tax credit. If everybody refused to answer questions about which they are poorly informed, no problem would arise, but unfortunately many of us like to pretend that we know things that in fact we don't or to be "helpful" to interviewers by inventing opinions on the spur of the moment.

3. **The questions must be asked fairly.** They should be worded in clear language, without the use of "loaded" or "emotional" words. They must give no indication of what the "right" answer is but offer a reasonable explanation, where necessary, of the consequences of each possible answer. For example, in 1971 a Gallup poll asked people whether they favored a proposal "to bring home all U.S. troops [from Vietnam] before the end of the year." Two-thirds of the public agreed with that. Then the question was asked in a different way: Do you agree or disagree with a proposal to withdraw all U.S. troops by the end of the year "regardless of what happens there [in Vietnam] after U.S. troops leave"? In this form substantially less than half the public agreed.

4. **The answer categories offered to a person must be carefully considered.** This is no problem when

Political Ideology

Up to now the words **liberal** and **conservative** have been used here as if everyone agreed on what they meant and as if they accurately described general sets of political beliefs held by large segments of the population. Neither of these assumptions is correct. Like many useful words—*love, justice, happiness*—they are as vague as they are indispensable.

When we refer to people as liberals, conservatives, socialists, or radicals, we are implying that they have a patterned set of beliefs about how government and other important institutions in fact operate and how they ought to operate, and in particular about what kinds of policies government ought to pursue. They are said to display to some degree a **political ideology**—that is, a coherent and consistent set of beliefs about who ought to rule, what principles rulers ought to obey, and what policies rulers ought to pursue. Political scientists measure the extent to which people have a political ideology in two ways: first, by seeing how frequently people use broad political cat-

there are only two candidates for office—say, Al Gore and George W. Bush the younger—and you want only to know which one the voters prefer. But it can be a big problem when you want more complex information. For example, if you ask people (as does George Gallup) whether they "approve" or "disapprove" of how the president is handling his job, you will get one kind of answer—let us say that 55 percent approve and 45 percent disapprove. On the other hand, if you ask them (as does Louis Harris) how they rate the job the president is doing, "excellent, pretty good, only fair, or poor," you will get very different results. It is quite possible that only 46 percent will pick such positive answers as "excellent" or "pretty good," and the rest will pick the more negative answers, "only fair" and "poor." If you are president, you can choose to believe Mr. Gallup (and feel pleased) or Mr. Harris (and be worried). The differences in the two polls do not arise from the competence of the two pollsters but entirely from the choice of answers that they include with their questions.

5. **Not every difference in answers is a significant difference.** A survey is based on a sample of people. Select another sample, by equally randomized methods, and you might get slightly different results. This difference is called a **sampling error,** and its likely size can be computed mathematically. In general the bigger the sample and the bigger the differences between the percentage of people giving one answer and the

percentage giving another, the smaller the sampling error. If a poll of about one thousand voters reveals that 47 percent favor Bill Clinton, we can be 95 percent certain that the actual proportion of all voters favoring Clinton is within three percentage points of this figure—that is, it lies somewhere between 44 and 50 percent. In a close race an error of this size could be quite important. It could be reduced by using a bigger sample, but the cost of interviewing a sample big enough to make the error much smaller is huge.

As a result of sampling error and for other reasons, it is very hard for pollsters to predict the winner in a close election. For any population over 500,000, at least 1,065 respondents are necessary to provide a 95 percent confidence level with a 3 percent plus or minus margin. Pollsters need to make about 15,000 telephone calls to reach that many people, and that is expensive. Some national news organizations still rely on polls with 600 or fewer respondents. Pollsters need to interview the people who will actually cast a ballot on election day, but these people are hard to identify in advance. Even a large sample of likely voters does not make polling precise. Note, for instance, that in a two-person race, the margin of error applies to *each* candidate, meaning that the actual level of support with a plus or minus 3 percent margin of error is 6 percent wide for *each* candidate. Still, since 1952 every major poll has in fact picked the winner of the presidential election. Polling is not an exact science, but done right, it is a highly skilled art.

egories (such as "liberal," "conservative," "radical") to describe their own views or to justify their preferences for various candidates and policies, and second, by seeing to what extent the policy preferences of a citizen are consistent over time or are based at any one time on consistent principles.

This second method involves a simple mathematical procedure: measuring how accurately one can predict a person's view on a subject at one time based on his or her view on that subject at an earlier time, or measuring how accurately one can predict a

person's view on one issue based on his or her view on a different issue. The higher the accuracy of such predictions (or correlations), the more we say a person's political opinions display "constraint," or ideology. Despite annual fluctuations, ideological self-identification surveys typically find that moderates are the largest group among American voters, conservatives the second largest, and liberals the smallest (see Figure 5.2 on page 119). This pattern held throughout the 1990s. In 1998 one-fifth of voters described themselves as liberal, one-third described

---

Figure 5.1   Whites in the South Leaving the Democrats

Percentage of southern white registered voters who identified with each party.

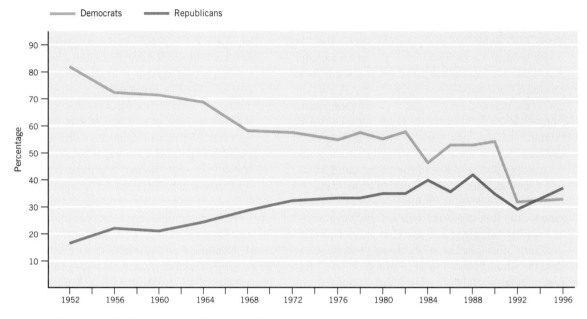

Source: ICPSR National Election Studies, Cumulative Data File, 1952–1996.

---

themselves as conservative, and a plurality called themselves moderate.[34]

Except when asked by pollsters, most Americans do not actually employ the words *liberal* or *conservative* in explaining or justifying their preferences for candidates or policies, and not many more than half can give plausible definitions of these terms. Furthermore, there are relatively low correlations among the answers to similar questions asked by pollsters at different times and to comparable questions asked at the same time. From this, many scholars have concluded that the great majority of Americans do not think about politics in an ideological or even in a very coherent manner and that they make little use of such concepts, so dear to political commentators and professors alike, as "liberal" and "conservative."[35]

Consistent Attitudes

This does not settle the question entirely, however. Critics of the view that Americans are nonideological have argued that people can have general, and strongly felt, political predispositions even though

they are not able to use terms such as *liberal* correctly. Moreover, public opinion polls must of necessity ask rather simple questions, and the apparent "inconsistency" in the answers people give at different times may mean only that the nature of the problem and the wording of the question have changed in ways not obvious to the people analyzing the surveys.[36]

People can have an ideology without using the words *liberal* or *conservative* and without having beliefs that line up neatly along the conventional liberal-versus-conservative dimension. We saw in Chapter 4 that most Americans share a distinctive political culture—a belief in freedom, equality (of political condition and economic opportunity), and civic duty. They also attach a great deal of importance to "Americanism." Though these words may be vague, they are not trivial—at some level they are an ideology.

Scholars regularly discover that people have what some would consider "inconsistent" opinions. For example, a voter may want the government to spend more on education and the environment and at the

Figure 5.2 Ideological Self-Identification, 1976–1999

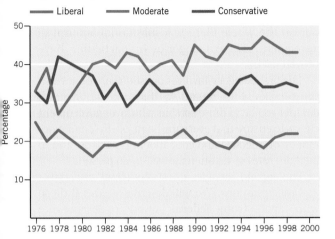

QUESTION
How would you describe your views on most political matters? Generally, do you think of yourself as a liberal, moderate, or conservative?

Source: The American Enterprise (March/April 1993): 84, Robert S. Ericson and Kent L. Tedin, *American Public Opinion* (New York: Longman, 2001), 101, citing surveys by CBS/*New York Times.*

same time favor a bigger military budget and a tough posture toward unfriendly nations. These views are "inconsistent" only in the sense that they violate a political rule of thumb, common in the media and in national policy debates, that expects people who favor a bigger welfare state to favor a smaller military establishment as well. That is the conventional "liberal" view. Similarly, the rule of thumb in the media is that people who support a strong military posture are also going to favor prayer in the schools and oppose abortion on demand. That is the conventional "conservative" position. But of course many citizens violate these rules of thumb, picking and choosing their positions without regard to the conventional definitions of liberalism and conservatism.

What Do Liberalism and Conservatism Mean?

Just because most people are not consistent liberals or consistent conservatives does not prove that these terms are meaningless. As we shall see, they are very meaningful for political elites. And they even have meaning for ordinary citizens, but this meaning is a complicated one that requires careful analysis.

The definition of these words has changed since they first came into use in the early nineteenth century. At that time a liberal was a person who favored personal and economic liberty—that is, freedom from the controls and powers of the state. An economic liberal, for example, supported the free market and opposed government regulation of trade. A conservative was originally a person who opposed the excesses of the French Revolution and its emphasis on personal freedom and favored instead a restoration of the power of the state, the church, and the aristocracy.

Beginning around the time of Franklin Roosevelt and the New Deal, the meaning of these terms began to change. Roosevelt used the term *liberal* to refer to his political program—one that called for an active national government that would intervene in the economy, create social welfare programs, and help certain groups (such as organized labor) acquire greater bargaining power. In time the opponents of an activist national government began using the term *conservative* to describe themselves. (Barry Goldwater, in 1964, was the first major U.S. politician to proclaim himself a conservative.) In general a conservative favored a free market rather than a regulated one, states' rights over national supremacy, and greater reliance on individual choice in economic affairs.

Though the meaning of these terms changed, it did not in the process become more precise. Two persons may describe themselves as liberals even though the first favors both the welfare state and a strong national defense and the second favors the welfare state but wants a sharp reduction in military spending. Similarly, one conservative may favor enforcement of laws against drug abuse, and another may believe that the government should let people decide for themselves what drugs to take. Once liberals favored laws guaranteeing equality of opportunity among the races; now some liberals favor "affirmative action" plans involving racial quotas or goals. Once conservatives opposed American intervention abroad; today many conservatives believe the United States should play an active role in foreign affairs.

In view of this confusion one is tempted to throw up one's hands in disgust and consign words like *liberal* and *conservative* to the garbage can. While understandable, such a reaction would be a mistake, because in spite of their ambiguities, these words

★ POLITICALLY SPEAKING ★

Ideology: You Versus Your Enemies

A political ideology is a coherent set of political rules for explaining how the world works and prescribing how it ought to work.

Liberals describe

- *themselves* as "caring," "committed," "an activist," or "progressive";
- *their enemies* as "reactionary," "right-wing," and "extremist"

Conservatives describe

- *themselves* as "moderate," "responsible," "prudent," or "mainstream";
- *their enemies* as "crackpot," "knee-jerk," "left-wing," or "bleeding-heart."

An easy way to tell whether a politician, newspaper, or magazine is liberal or conservative is to see whether, in describing liberals or conservatives, it uses terms from the "nice" (themselves) list or the "hostile" (their enemies) list.

Various Categories

We can imagine certain broad categories of opinion to which different people subscribe. These categories are found by analyzing the answers people give to dozens of questions about political issues. Different analysts come up with slightly different categories, but on the whole there is a substantial amount of agreement. Three categories in particular have proved useful.

The first category involves questions about government policy with regard to the *economy.* We will describe as liberal those persons who favor government efforts to ensure that everyone has a job, to spend more money on medical and educational programs, and to increase rates of taxation for well-to-do persons.

The second involves questions about *civil rights* and race relations. We will describe as liberal those who favor strong federal action to desegregate schools, to increase hiring opportunities for minorities, to provide compensatory programs for minorities, and to enforce civil rights laws strictly.

The third involves questions about public and political *conduct.* We will describe as liberal those who are tolerant of protest demonstrations, who favor legalizing marijuana and in other ways wish to "decriminalize" so-called victimless crimes, who emphasize protecting the rights of the accused over punishing criminals, and who see the solution to crime in eliminating its causes rather than in getting tough with offenders.

Analyzing Consistency

Now it is obvious that people can take a liberal position on one of these issues and a conservative position on another without feeling in the slightest degree "inconsistent." Several studies, such as those by Seymour Martin Lipset and Earl Raab and by Herbert McClosky and John Zaller, show that this is exactly what most people do.[37]

This fact does not mean that people are unideological but that we need more than two labels to describe their ideology. If we considered all possible combinations of the three sets of views described above, we would have nine categories of opinion; if people always stuck with whichever category they were in, we would need nine different ideological labels to describe those people.

To invent those labels and describe the people who have those views would take countless pages

remain in general use, convey some significant meaning, and point to real differences between, for example, the liberal and conservative wings of the Democratic and Republican parties. Our task is to clarify these differences by showing the particular meanings these words have. One way to do this is by considering how self-described liberals and conservatives differ in their opinions on prominent issues, such as those listed in Table 5.6.

Table 5.6 How Liberals and Conservatives Differ		
Belief	Support Among Self-Declared Liberals	Support Among Self-Declared Conservatives
The government should provide "more services even if it means an increase in spending."	73%	32%
The government should guarantee "that every person has a job and a good standard of living."	55	21
Favor "government insurance plan which would cover all medical and hospital expenses for everyone."	82	27
The government "should make every effort to improve the social and economic position of blacks."	55	18
The U.S. "should spend less on defense."	85	65
"Aid to [Russia] should be increased."	36	32
"Women should have an equal role in running business, industry, and government."	96	81
The United States should always permit abortion "as a matter of personal choice."	72	36
"Homosexuals should be allowed to serve in U.S. Armed Forces."	70	45
"Oppose death penalty for persons convicted of murder."	35	15

Source: Robert S. Erikson and Kent L. Tedin, *American Public Opinion,* 5th ed. (Boston: Allyn and Bacon, 1995), 69. Copyright © 1995 by Addison-Wesley-Longman. Reprinted with permission.

and bore readers to tears. To avoid all that pain and suffering, let's use just two sets of views—those on economic policy and those on personal conduct—and describe the kinds of people who have each of the four combinations (liberal or conservative on each set). The data are from a study by William S. Maddox and Stuart A. Lilie.[38]

1. *Pure liberals*[39]   These people are liberal on both economic policy and personal conduct. They want the government to reduce economic inequality, regulate business, tax the rich heavily, cure the (presumably) economic causes of crime, allow abortions, protect the rights of the accused, and guarantee the broadest possible freedoms of speech and press.
   Number: In 1994 about 17 percent of the population were pure liberals.
   Traits: Pure liberals are more likely than the average citizen to be young, college-educated, and either Jewish or nonreligious. They voted heavily against Ronald Reagan.

2. *Pure conservatives*   These people are conservative on both economic and conduct issues. They want the government to cut back on the welfare state, allow the market to allocate goods and services, keep taxes low, lock up criminals, and

curb forms of conduct they regard as antisocial.
   Number: In 1994 about 28 percent of the population were pure conservatives.
   Traits: Pure conservatives are more likely than the average citizen to be older, to have higher incomes, to be white, and to live in the Midwest. They voted overwhelmingly for Ronald Reagan.

3. *Libertarians*   These people are conservative on economic matters and liberal on social ones. The common theme is that they want a small, weak government—one that has little control over either the economy or the personal lives of citizens.
   Number: In 1994 about 21 percent of the population were libertarians.
   Traits: **Libertarians** are more likely than the average citizen to be young, college-educated, and white, to have higher incomes and no religion, and to live in the West. They voted for Ronald Reagan, but many also supported the third-party ticket of John Anderson.

4. *Populists*   These people are liberal on economic matters and conservative on social ones. They want a government that will reduce economic inequality and control business, but they also want it to regulate personal conduct, lock up criminals, and permit school prayer.

Number: In 1994 about 24 percent of the population were populists.

Traits: **Populists** are more likely than the average citizen to be older, poorly educated, low-income, religious, and female and to live in the South or Midwest. In 1980 they voted for Jimmy Carter, but in 1984 they voted for Reagan.

Obviously this classification is an oversimplification. There are many exceptions, and the number of people in each category changes from time to time. Moreover, this categorization leaves out about one-seventh of the population—their views do not fit any of these categories. Nonetheless, it is a useful way to explain how complex are the political ideologies in this country and why terms such as *liberal* and *conservative,* in their "pure" form, describe the views of relatively few people.

Political Elites

There is one group that can be classified as liberals or conservatives in a pure sense, and it is made up of people who are in the **political elite.** By "elite" we do not mean people who are "better" than others. *Elite* is a technical term used by social scientists to refer to people who have a disproportionate amount of some valued resource—money, schooling, prestige, athletic ability, political power, or whatever. Every society, capitalist or communist, has an elite, because in every society government officials will have more power than ordinary folk, some persons will make more money than others, and some people will be more popular than others. (In the former Soviet Union they even had an official name for the political elite—the *nomenklatura.*)

In this country we often refer to the political elite as "activists"—people who hold office, run for office, work in campaigns or on newspapers, lead interest groups and social movements, and speak out on public issues. Being an activist is not an all-or-nothing proposition; people display differing degrees of activism, from full-time politicians to persons who occasionally get involved in a campaign (see Chapter 6). But the more a person is an activist, the more

Activists tend to take political ideology more seriously than do most voters.

likely it is that he or she will display ideological consistency on the conventional liberal-conservative spectrum.

The reasons for this greater consistency seem to be information and peers. First, information: in general, the better informed people are about politics and the more interest they take in politics, the more likely they are to have consistently liberal or conservative views.[40] This higher level of information and interest may lead them to find relationships among issues that others don't see and to learn from the media and elsewhere what are the "right" things to believe. This does not mean that there are no differences within liberal elites (or within conservative ones), only that the differences occur within a liberal (or conservative) consensus that is more well defined, more consistent, and more important to those who share it than would be the case among ordinary citizens.

Second, peers: politics does not make strange bedfellows. On the contrary, politics is a process of likes attracting likes. The more active you are in politics, the more you will associate with people who agree with you on some issues; and the more time you spend with those people, the more your other views will shift to match theirs.

The greater ideological consistency of political elites can be seen in Congress. As we shall note in Chapter 11, Democratic members of Congress tend to be consistently liberal, and Republican members of Congress tend to be consistently conservative—*far more* consistently than Democratic voters and Republican voters. By the same token we shall see in Chapter 7 that the delegates to presidential nominating conventions are far more ideological (liberal in the Democratic convention, conservative in the Republican one) than is true of voters who identify with the Democratic or Republican party.

Still, on a large number of issues, the policy preferences of average Republican and Democratic voters do differ significantly from one another (see Table 5.7). Some political scientists argue that Republican and Democratic leaders in Congress are more polarized because voters are more polarized. For example, in 1970 only 30 percent of voters who opposed abortion under all circumstances identified themselves as Republicans; by 1998, 71 percent did so.[41] Since the 1980s partisan voting has become more common while the share of those who are independent has shrunk.[42]

Other political scientists, however, analyze the available polling and election data differently. They find that ideological changes among voters have been "marginal at best," while public opinion among Democrats voting in districts represented by Democrats and among Republicans voting in districts represented by Republicans has been remarkably stable.[43] Which side is right? We have no data that will allow us to compare in each district what voters think and how their representatives behave. To amass such data would require polls of perhaps five hundred voters in each congressional district taken several years apart. Nobody thinks it is worth spending millions of dollars to interview over ten thousand voters at different times just to answer this one academic puzzle.

Is There a "New Class"?

Some writers have speculated that political elites now represent a "new class" in American politics. The old classes were those who owned the means of production (the capitalists) and those who were employed by those owners (the workers). The "new class" consists of people who possess certain advantages conferred not by the power, resources, and growth of business but by the power, resources, and growth of government.[44]

Table 5.7 Policy Preferences of Democratic and Republican Voters

Issue	Preferences	
	Democrats	Republicans
Should allow people to invest part of Social Security taxes on their own.	44%	61%
For murder, penalty should be death.	46	55
Unfavorable opinion of National Rifle Association.	44	20
Abortion should be available to those who want it.	48	25
Must protect environment even if jobs are lost.	72	57
Parents should get tax-paid vouchers to help pay for children attending private schools.	41	53

Source: Adapted from *New York Times*/CBS News poll, *New York Times*, (August 14, 2000), A17. Copyright © 2000 *The New York Times*.

Politicians, bureaucrats, members of the media, interest group leaders—these people and others like them have, it is claimed, a stake in the growth of government. Because of that, they often have liberal (that is, progovernment) views even though they also have high incomes. The emergence of the new class helps explain, in this theory, why affluent people are not as consistently conservative as they were in the 1940s and 1950s.

It is true, as we have already seen, that many well-off people are liberals. That these people benefit from big government may be one explanation for this fact. But there is another explanation: the spread of higher education.

High levels of schooling, especially at the postgraduate level, tend to make people more liberal. This was not always the case. For example, in the 1940s and 1950s a clear majority of Harvard students, and probably of most college students, preferred Republican candidates for president.[45] For whatever reason, things are different now. Some people with law degrees and Ph.D.'s may favor government because they get grants and jobs from it, but most people probably favor it because they have acquired an ideology that is consistent with a more activist government.

In any event, it is striking how strongly postgraduate education affects political preferences. John McAdams has analyzed the voting results for several presidential, gubernatorial, and senatorial elections and for various state referenda elections on issues such as the death penalty, school busing, nuclear energy, gun control, environmental protection, and the Equal Rights Amendment. In each and every case he discovered that those with a postgraduate education were much more likely to take a liberal position, even after holding constant age, race, and income.[46]

On the basis of his findings, McAdams suggests that the middle class in the United States has been split in two—one part he calls the "traditional middle class," and the other he calls the "new class" (though it might more appropriately be called the "liberal middle class").[47] The traditional middle class consists of people who often have gone to college but not graduate school and who live in the suburbs, go to church, are well disposed toward business, have conservative views on social issues, and usually vote Republican. The liberal middle class is more likely to consist of people who have a postgraduate educa-

tion, live in or near big cities, are critical of business, have liberal views on social issues, and usually vote Democratic. The cleavage between the traditional and the liberal middle class has many of the same causes as the growing rift between orthodox and progressive ideologies discussed in Chapter 4.

As we shall see in Chapter 7, the strain within the middle class has been particularly felt by the Democratic party. That strain has made it harder to hold together the coalition (often called the New Deal coalition) that once made that party so strong, a coalition among blue-collar workers, southerners, African Americans, and intellectuals. Increasingly the workers and white southerners have displayed conservatism on social issues, while members of the liberal middle class have displayed liberalism on these issues. Each side has a label for the other: the workers in the Democratic party call the members of the liberal middle class the "cheese and white wine set," while the people in the liberal middle class call the workers "Joe Six-Pack."

Political Elites, Public Opinion, and Public Policy

Though the elites and the public see politics in very different ways, and though there are often intense antagonisms between the two groups, the elites influence public opinion in at least two important ways.

First, elites, especially those in or having access to the media (see Chapter 10), raise and frame political issues. At one time environmentalism was not on the political agenda; at a later time not only was it on the agenda, it was up near the top of government concerns. At some times the government had little interest in what it should do in South Africa or Central America; at other times the government was preoccupied with these matters. Though world events help shape the political agenda, so also do political elites. A path-breaking study by John Zaller shows in fact that elite views shape mass views by influencing both what issues capture the public's attention and how those issues are debated and decided.[48] Contrary to the myth of the pandering politician, recent evidence suggests that what scholars of the subject call opinion-policy congruence (essentially the rate at which governments adopt crime, health, trade, and other policies supported by majorities in polls) has been declining, not rising,

The media help shape public opinion about some issues, as when these photographers record the Israeli siege around Bethlehem's Church of the Holy Sepulchre.

since 1980, a trend that may reflect greater elite influence over how policy options are presented to the public.[49]

Second, elites state the norms by which issues should be settled. (A **norm** is a standard of right or proper conduct.) By doing this they help determine the range of acceptable and unacceptable policy options. For example, elites have for a long time emphasized that racism is wrong. Of late they have emphasized that sexism is wrong. Over a long period the steady repetition of views condemning racism and sexism will at least intimidate, and perhaps convince, those of us who are racist and sexist.

A recent example of this process has been the public discussion of AIDS and its relationship to homosexuality. The initial public reaction to AIDS was one of fear and loathing. But efforts to quarantine people infected with AIDS were met with firm resistance from the medical community and from other policy elites. The elites even managed to persuade some legislatures to bar insurance companies from testing insurance applicants for the disease.

There are limits to how much influence elites can have on the public. For instance, elites do not define

economic problems—people can see for themselves that there is or is not unemployment, that there is or is not raging inflation, that there are or are not high interest rates. Elite opinion may shape the policies, but it does not define the problem. Similarly, elite opinion has little influence on whether we think there is a crime or drug problem; it is, after all, *our* purses being snatched, cars being stolen, and children being drugged. On the other hand, elite opinion does define the problem as well as the policy options with respect to most aspects of foreign affairs; the public has little firsthand experience with which to judge what is going on in Panama or Iraq.

Because elites affect how we see some issues and determine how other issues get resolved, it is important to study the differences between elite and public opinion. But it is wrong to suppose that there is one elite, unified in its interests and opinions. Just as there are many publics, and hence many public opinions, there are many elites, and hence many different elite opinions. Whether there is enough variety of opinion and influence among elites to justify calling our politics "pluralist" is one of the central issues confronting any student of government.

U.S. Senate to Debate New Curbs on Legal Immigration

May 22

WASHINGTON

Legal immigration to the United States has reached record highs. From 1991 to 2000 more than 9 million people, or about 300,000 more than entered the country during the first decade of the twentieth century, came to America. Next week the Senate begins debate on several bills that would slow or stop the flow of legal immigrants . . .

MEMORANDUM

To: Senator Rebecca Kowal
From: Lia Fantuzzo, legislative intern
Subject: Reducing legal immigration

Your constituents are evenly divided over restrictions. Having declared yourself "neutral pending further study and debate," you are nonetheless being urged by valued colleagues on both sides of the issue and by the press to take a position on cutting legal immigration.

Arguments for:

1. Since Congress liberalized U.S. immigration laws in 1965, nearly 25 million legal immigrants have settled in America, and the percentage of foreign-born U.S. residents has risen to 10 percent. At this rate, by 2050 the total U.S. population will rise by about 125 million, to nearly 400 million. Two-thirds of the increase will be due to legal immigration.
2. For every ten legal immigrants, about three undocumented aliens enter the country. Together they take jobs away from native-born Americans.
3. Most immigrants settle in one of four states (California, Florida, New York, and Texas), placing an undue burden on those states to pay for services such as health care and welfare for immigrants.

Arguments against:

1. From 1860 to 1930 over 10 percent of U.S. residents were foreign born. Without immigration the U.S. population will reach 310 million by 2035 and then decline. Immigrants not only consume public services but also pay taxes and provide a younger, more vital labor pool.
2. All told only about 5 million noncitizens are living unlawfully in the United States. Legal immigrants include people with advanced degrees and highly marketable skills. Low-skilled immigrants often take menial jobs that nobody else wants.
3. Immigrants have always tended to settle in a few areas. In the first half of the twentieth century, most settled in a half dozen big cities. Today the federal government provides funds to the states to pay for at least some of the costs of social services for residents, including immigrants.

Your decision:
Favor curbs _____
Oppose curbs _____

Summary

"Public opinion" is a slippery notion, partly because there are many publics, with many different opinions, and partly because opinion on all but relatively simple matters tends to be uninformed, unstable, and sensitive to different ways of asking poll questions.

Americans are divided by their political ideologies but not along a single liberal-conservative dimension. There are several kinds of issues on which people may take "liberal" or "conservative" positions, and they often do not take the same position on all issues. Just using two kinds of issues—economic and social—it is possible to define four kinds of ideologies: pure liberal, pure conservative, libertarian, and populist.

Political elites are much more likely to display a consistently liberal or consistently conservative ideology. Elites are important because they have a disproportionate influence on public policy and even an influence on mass opinion (through the dissemination of information and the evocation of political norms).

Reconsidering the Enduring Questions

1. *According to the Framers of the Constitution, what, if any, part should public opinion play in America's representative democracy?*

   Students of American political thought differ on this question, but the consensus is that the Framers believed temporary or transient popular majorities should carry little if any weight with representatives, but persistent popular majorities—for example, ones that persist over the staggered terms of members of the House and Senate and over more than a single presidential term—should be heard and in many cases heeded. For example, turn to the Appendix and read *Federalist* No. 10 by James Madison. In it, Madison makes plain his view that the public interest is not always, or even often, the same as what most people demand from the government. Instead members of Congress are to be "proper guardians of the public weal," representatives who serve "the great and aggregate interests" of the country. He holds that "the regulation of these various and interfering interests" is the "principal task" of representatives.

2. *How, if at all, does public opinion in America today vary by race, religion, region, and other differences?*

   There are cleavages in American public opinion, but they change over time, and it is hard to generalize meaningfully about how they affect politics and government. For example, in the 1950s pollsters found that people in managerial or professional jobs had distinctly more conservative views on social welfare than manual laborers did. But opinion surveys done in the late 1960s found that business and professional people had views quite similar to those of manual laborers on matters such as the poverty program. Likewise, on some issues, the opinions of whites and blacks are similar or narrowing, but on other issues, wide opinion gaps remain between whites and blacks. Surprisingly, little major research exists on the opinions and partisan preferences of the country's over 30 million Latinos. People who attend worship services regularly are more conservative and far more likely to vote Republican in presidential elections than people who attend worship services rarely if ever. Women are far more sympathetic to liberal causes and Democratic candidates than men, but these so-called gender gaps in opinion and voting behavior are more pronounced in some elections than in others.

3. *What is political ideology, and to what extent are ideological differences reflected in political behavior?*

   Political ideology is a coherent and consistent set of beliefs about who ought to rule, what principles rulers ought to obey, and what policies rulers ought to pursue. Political scientists measure the extent to which people have a political ideology by seeing how frequently people use broad political categories (such as "liberal" and "conservative") to describe their own views or to justify their preferences for candidates and policies. They also measure it by seeing to what extent the policy preferences of a citizen are consistent over time or are based at any one time on consistent principles. Many scholars believe that most Americans are, both in absolute terms and relative to Europeans, nonideological. But there is some evidence to suggest that present-day Americans are becoming more ideological. On many issues, for example, the policy preferences of average Republican and Democratic voters now differ significantly from one another. There is clear evidence that political elites are more ideological today than they were just a generation or two ago. For example, Democratic leaders and activists are more liberal, and Republican leaders and activists are more conservative, than they were in the 1950s.

World Wide Web Resources

- CBS News poll: cbsnews.cbs.com
- Gallup opinion poll: www.gallup.com
- *Los Angeles Times* poll: www.latimes.com/ HOME/NEWS/POLITICS/POLLS

Key Terms

John Q. Public *p. 105*
Middle America *p. 105*
silent majority *p. 105*
social status *p. 107*
religious tradition *p. 107*
gender gap *p. 109*
poll *p. 116*
random sample *p. 116*

liberal *p. 116*
conservative *p. 116*
political ideology *p. 116*
sampling error *p. 117*
libertarians *p. 121*
populists *p. 122*
political elite *p. 122*
norm *p. 125*

Suggested Readings

Converse, Philip E. "The Nature of Belief Systems in Mass Publics." In *Ideology and Discontent*, edited by David Apter. Glencoe, Ill.: Free Press, 1964. The classic discussion of inconsistencies in public opinion.

Dionne, E. J. *Why Americans Hate Politics*. New York: Simon and Schuster, 1991. Misnamed, this book actually describes the emergence of various elite ideologies since the 1960s and why, in the author's view, none is relevant to actually solving problems.

Erikson, Robert S., and Kent L. Tedin. *American Public Opinion*. 5th ed. Boston: Allyn and Bacon, 1995. An excellent summary of how opinion is measured, what it shows, and how it affects politics.

Jennings, M. Kent, and Richard G. Niemi. *Generations and Politics*. Princeton, N.J.: Princeton University Press, 1981. A study of persistence and change in the political views of young adults and their parents.

————.*The Political Character of Adolescence: The Influence of Families and Schools*. Princeton, N.J.: Princeton University Press, 1974. A study of political attitudes among high school students.

Key, V. O., Jr. *The Responsible Electorate*. Cambridge: Harvard University Press, 1966. An argument, with evidence, that American voters are not fools.

Lipset, Seymour Martin. *Political Man: The Social Bases of Politics*. Garden City, N.Y.: Doubleday, 1959. An exploration of the relationship between society, opinion, and democracy in America and abroad.

Nie, Norman H., Sidney Verba, and John R. Petrocik. *The Changing American Voter*. Cambridge: Harvard University Press, 1976. Traces shifts in American voter attitudes since 1960.

Zaller, John. *The Nature and Origins of Mass Opinion*. Cambridge: Cambridge University Press, 1992. A path-breaking study of how the public forms an opinion, illustrating the ways in which elite views help shape mass views.

Political Participation

Enduring Questions

1. What role did the Framers of the Constitution believe average citizens should play in America's representative democracy?

2. Who votes, who doesn't?

3. Why do some people participate in politics at higher rates than others?

Americans are often embarrassed by their low rate of participation in national elections. Data such as those shown in Table 6.1 are frequently used to make the point: whereas well over 80 percent of the people vote in many European elections, only about half of the people vote in American presidential elections (and a much smaller percentage vote in congressional contests). Many observers blame this low turnout on voter apathy and urge the government and private groups to mount campaigns to get out the vote.

There are only three things wrong with this view. First, it is a misleading description of the problem; second, it is an incorrect explanation of the problem; and third, it proposes a remedy that won't work.

A Closer Look at Nonvoting

First, let's look at how best to describe the problem. The conventional data on voter turnout here and abroad are misleading because they compute participation rates by two different measures. In this country only two-thirds of the voting-age population is registered to vote. To understand what this means,

131

Table 6.1	Two Ways of Calculating Voter Turnout, 1996–2001 Elections, Selected Countries

A Turnout as Percentage of Voting-Age Population		B Turnout as Percentage of Registered Voters	
Belgium	83.2%	Australia	95.2%
Denmark	83.1	Belgium	90.6
Australia	81.8	Denmark	86.0
Sweden	77.7	New Zealand	83.1
Finland	76.8	Germany	82.2
Germany	75.3	Sweden	81.4
New Zealand	74.6	Austria	80.4
Norway	73.0	France	79.7
Austria	72.6	Finland	76.8
France	72.3	Norway	75.0
Netherlands	70.1	Netherlands	73.2
Japan	59.0	UNITED STATES	63.4
United Kingdom	57.6	Japan	62.0
Canada	54.6	Canada	61.2
UNITED STATES	47.2	United Kingdom	59.4
Switzerland	34.9	Switzerland	43.2

Source: From the International Institute for Democracy and Electoral Assistance (IDEA), *Voter Turnout: A Global Survey* (Stockholm, Sweden, 2001). Reprinted with the permission of Cambridge University Press.

look at Table 6.1. In column A are several countries ranked in terms of the percentage of the **voting-age population** that voted in 1996–2001 national elections. As you can see, the United States, where 47.2 percent voted, ranked near the bottom; only Switzerland was lower. Now look at column B, where the same countries are ranked in terms of the percentage of **registered voters** who participated in these national elections. The United States, where 63.4 percent of registered voters turned out at the polls, is now fifth from the bottom.[1]

Second, let's consider a better explanation for the problem. Apathy on election day is clearly not the source of the problem. Of those who are registered, the overwhelming majority vote. The real source of the participation problem in the United States is that a relatively low percentage of the adult population is registered to vote.

Third, let's look at how to cure the problem. Mounting a get-out-the-vote drive wouldn't make much difference. What might make a difference is a plan that would get more people to register to vote. But doing that does not necessarily involve overcoming the "apathy" of unregistered voters. Some people may not register because they don't care about poli-

tics or their duty as citizens. But there are other explanations for being unregistered. In this country the entire burden of registering to vote falls on the individual voters. They must learn how and when and where to register; they must take the time and trouble to go someplace and fill out a registration form; and they must reregister in a new county or state if they happen to move. In most European nations registration is done for you, automatically, by the government. Since it is costly to register in this country and costless to register in other countries, it should not be surprising that fewer people are registered here than abroad.

In 1993 Congress passed a law designed to make it easier to register to vote. Known as the **motor-voter law,** the law requires states to allow people to register to vote when applying for driver's licenses and to provide registration through the mail and at some state offices that serve the disabled or provide public assistance (such as welfare checks). The motor-voter law took effect in 1995. In just two months, 630,000 new voters signed up in twenty-seven states. Even so, the results of the law so far have been mixed.

Only 49 percent of eligible voters went to the polls in 1996, and in North Dakota, where voters are not required to register, turnout was still only 56 percent.[2] In 1998 only 17.6 percent of the eligible electorate voted in primary elections, and a record-low 36.1 percent of the voting-age population cast ballots in the midterm congressional elections.[3] On the other hand, registration among the voting-age population rose to 70.1 percent in 1998, the highest in a nonpresidential year since 1970, and turnout was less depressed in states that had fully implemented the motor-voter law or instituted universal election-day registration programs.[4] Contrary to the fears of congressional Republicans (90 percent of whom opposed the motor-voter law) and the hopes of congressional Democrats (95 percent of whom supported it), the adoption of motor-voter programs has not changed the two-party balance of registrants, but it has increased independent registrations.[5] The motor-voter law has allowed a lot of people to register that way. In 1999–2000, 17.4 million voter registration applications were filed at motor vehicle offices, representing over a third of all such applications filed during that period (see Figure 6.1).

Still, there is scant evidence that the motor-voter law has had much of an impact on either voter

Figure 6.1 Sources of Voter Registration Applications, 1999–2000

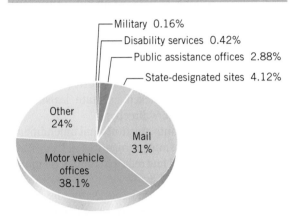

Military 0.16%
Disability services 0.42%
Public assistance offices 2.88%
State-designated sites 4.12%

Other 24%

Mail 31%

Motor vehicle offices 38.1%

Source: Federal Election Commission, *Executive Summary— Report to the Congress,* 2000.

turnout or election outcomes. A 2001 study found that turnout of motor voter registrants was lower than that of other new registrants, and concluded

"that those who register when the process is costless are less likely to vote."[6]

A final point: voting is only one way of participating in politics. It is important (we could hardly be considered a democracy if nobody voted), but it is not all-important. Joining civic associations, supporting social movements, writing to legislators, fighting city hall—all these and other activities are ways of participating in politics. It is possible that, by these measures, Americans participate in politics *more* than most Europeans—or anybody else, for that matter. Moreover, it is possible that low rates of registration indicate that people are reasonably well satisfied with how the country is governed. If 100 percent of all adult Americans registered and voted (especially under a system that makes registering relatively difficult), it could mean that people were deeply upset about how things were run. In short it is not at all clear whether low voter turnout is a symptom of political disease or a sign of political good health.

The important question about participation is not how much participation there is but how different kinds of participation affect the kind of government we get. This question cannot be answered just by

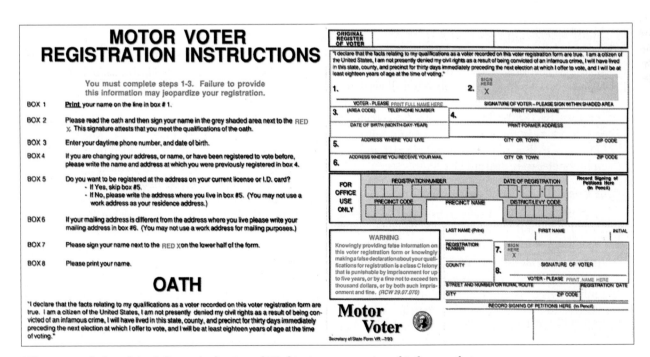

When you apply for a driver's license in the state of Washington, you are given this form so that you can register to vote at the same time. This "motor-voter" idea became the basis of a federal law passed in 1993.

looking at voter turnout, the subject of this chapter; it also requires us to look at the composition and activities of political parties, interest groups, and the media (the subjects of later chapters).

Nonetheless, voting is important. To understand why participation in American elections takes the form that it does, we must first understand how laws have determined who shall vote and under what circumstances.

The Rise of the American Electorate

It is ironic that relatively few citizens vote in American elections, since it was in this country that the mass of people first became eligible to vote. At the time the Constitution was ratified, the vote was limited to property owners or taxpayers, but by the administration of Andrew Jackson (1829–1837) it had been broadened to include virtually all white male adults. Only in a few states did property restrictions persist: they were not abolished in New Jersey until 1844 or in North Carolina until 1856. And, of course, African American males could not vote in many states, in the North as well as the South, even if they were not slaves. Women could not vote in most states until the twentieth century; Chinese Americans were widely denied the vote; and being in prison is grounds for losing the franchise even today. Aliens, on the other hand, were often allowed to vote if they had at least begun the process of becoming citizens. By 1880 only an estimated 14 percent of all adult males in the United States could not vote; in England in the same period about 40 percent of adult males were disfranchised.[7]

From State to Federal Control

Initially it was left entirely to the states to decide who could vote and for what offices. The Constitution gave Congress the right to pick the day on which presidential electors would gather and to alter state regulations regarding congressional elections. The only provision of the Constitution requiring a popular election was the clause in Article I stating that members of the House of Representatives be chosen by the "people of the several states."

Because of this permissiveness, early federal elections varied greatly. Several states picked their members of the House at large (that is, statewide) rather than by district; others used districts but elected more than one representative from each. Still others had their elections in odd-numbered years, and some even required that a congressional candidate win a majority, rather than simply a plurality, of votes to be elected (when that requirement was in effect, runoff elections—in one case as many as twelve—were necessary). Furthermore, presidential electors were at first picked by state legislatures rather than by the voters directly.

Congress, by law and constitutional amendment, has steadily reduced state prerogatives in these matters. In 1842 a federal law required that all members of the House be elected by districts; other laws over the years required that all federal elections be held in even-numbered years on the Tuesday following the first Monday in November.

The most important changes in elections have been those that extended the suffrage to women, African Americans, and eighteen-year-olds and made mandatory the direct popular election of U.S. senators. The Fifteenth Amendment, adopted in 1870, said that the "right of citizens of the United States to vote shall not be denied or abridged by the United States or by any state on account of race, color, or previous condition of servitude." Reading those words today, one would assume that they gave African Americans the right to vote. That is not what the Supreme Court during the 1870s thought they meant. By a series of decisions, it held that the Fifteenth Amendment did not necessarily confer the right to vote on anybody; it merely asserted that if someone was denied that right, the denial could not be explicitly on the grounds of race. And the burden of proving that it was race that led to the denial fell on the black who was turned away at the polls.[8]

This interpretation opened the door to all manner of state stratagems to keep blacks from voting. One was a **literacy test** (a large proportion of former slaves were illiterate); another was a requirement that a **poll tax** be paid (most former slaves were poor); a third was the practice of keeping blacks from voting in primary elections (in the one-party South the only meaningful election was the Democratic primary). To allow whites who were illiterate or poor to vote, a **grandfather clause** was added to the law, saying that a person could vote, even if he did not meet the legal requirements, if he or his ancestors voted before 1867 (blacks, of course, could not vote before 1867). When all else

WHITE SUPREMACY!

Attention, White Men!

Grand Torch-Light Procession

At JACKSON,

On the Night of the

Fourth of January, 1890.

**The Final Settlement of Democratic Rule
and White Supremacy in Mississippi.**

GRAND PYROTECHNIC DISPLAY!
Transparencies and Torches Free for all.

**All in Sympathy with the Grand Cause
are Cordially and Earnestly Invited to be
on hand, to aid in the Final Overthrow of
Radical Rule in our State.**

Come on foot or on horse-back; come any way, but
be sure to get there.
Brass Bands, Cannon, Flambeau Torches, Transparencies, Sky-rockets, Etc.

A GRAND DISPLAY FOR A GRAND CAUSE.

*After Reconstruction ended in 1876, black voting shrank
under the attack of white supremacists.*

*After the Civil War, while Union forces were still in control,
African Americans began to vote in the South, as shown here in
Richmond, Virginia, in 1871.*

failed, blacks were intimidated, threatened, or
harassed if they showed up at the polls.

There began a long, slow legal process of challenging in court each of these restrictions in turn.
One by one the Supreme Court set most of them
aside. The grandfather clause was declared unconstitutional in 1915,[9] and the **white primary** finally
fell in 1944.[10] Some of the more blatantly discriminatory literacy tests were also overturned.[11] The
practical result of these rulings was slight: only a
small proportion of voting-age blacks were able to
register and vote in the South, and they were found
mostly in the larger cities. A dramatic change did not
begin until 1965, with the passage of the Voting
Rights Act. This act suspended the use of literacy
tests and authorized the appointment of federal
examiners who could order the registration of
blacks in states and counties (mostly in the South)

where fewer than 50 percent of the voting-age population were registered or had voted in the last presidential election. It also provided criminal penalties
for interfering with the right to vote.

Though implementation in some places was slow,
the number of African Americans voting rose sharply
throughout the South. For example, in Mississippi the
proportion of voting-age blacks who registered rose
from 5 percent to over 70 percent in just ten years (see
Table 6.2). These changes had a profound effect on the
behavior of many white southern politicians:
Governor George Wallace stopped making prosegrega-
tion speeches and began courting the black vote.

Women were kept from the polls by law more than
by intimidation, and when the laws changed, women
almost immediately began to vote in large numbers.
By 1915 several states, mostly in the West, had
begun to permit women to vote. But it was not until
the Nineteenth Amendment to the Constitution was
ratified in 1920, after a struggle lasting many
decades, that women generally were allowed to vote.
At one stroke the size of the eligible voting population
almost doubled. Contrary to the hopes of some and
the fears of others, no dramatic changes occurred in
the conduct of elections, the identity of the winners,

Table 6.2 Voter Registration in the South

		Percentage of Voting-Age Population That Is Registered											
		Ala.	Ark.	Fla.	Ga.	La.	Miss.	N.C.	S.C.	Tenn.	Tex.	Va.	Total
1960	White	63.6%	60.9%	69.3%	56.8%	76.9%	63.9%	92.1%	57.1%	73.0%	42.5%	46.1%	61.1%
	Black*	13.7	38.0	39.4	29.3	31.1	5.2	39.1	13.7	59.1	35.5	23.1	29.1
1970	White	85.0	74.1	65.5	71.7	77.0	82.1	68.1	62.3	78.5	62.0	64.5	62.9
	Black	66.0	82.3	55.3	57.2	57.4	71.0	51.3	56.1	71.6	72.6	57.0	62.0
1986	White	77.5	67.2	66.9	62.3	67.8	91.6	67.4	53.4	70.0	79.0	60.3	69.9
	Black	68.9	57.9	58.2	52.8	60.6	70.8	58.4	52.5	65.3	68.0	56.2	60.8
1996	White	75.8	64.5	63.7	67.8	74.5	75.0	70.4	69.7	66.3	62.7	68.4	69.0
	Black	69.2	65.8	53.1	64.6	71.9	67.4	65.5	64.3	65.7	63.2	64.0	65.0

*Includes other minority races.

Source: Voter Education Project, Inc., of Atlanta, Georgia, as reported in *Statistical Abstract of the United States, 1990 and 1996.*

or the substance of public policy. Initially, at least, women voted more or less in the same manner as men, though not quite as frequently.

The political impact of the youth vote was also less than expected. The Voting Rights Act of 1970 gave eighteen-year-olds the right to vote in federal elections beginning January 1, 1971. It also contained a provision lowering the voting age to eighteen in state elections, but the Supreme Court declared this unconstitutional. As a result a constitutional amendment, the Twenty-sixth, was proposed by Congress and ratified by the states in 1971. The 1972 elections became the first in which all people between the ages of eighteen and twenty-one could cast ballots (before then, four states had allowed those under twenty-one to vote). About 25 million people suddenly became eligible to participate in elections, but their turnout (42 percent) was lower than for the population as a whole, and they did not flock to any particular party or candidate. George McGovern, the Democratic candidate for president in 1972, counted heavily on attracting the youth vote but did not succeed. Most young voters supported Richard Nixon (though college students favored McGovern).[12]

In the midterm congressional elections of 1994, only one-fifth of those between the ages of eighteen and twenty-four cast ballots, and in 1996 only 30 percent of young adults went to the polls.[13] At the same time, however, young Americans' rates of participation in civic activities such as community service rose to nearly 70 percent.[14] Senator Paul Wellstone of Minnesota, a liberal Democrat who taught political science and who was a campus political protester during the 1970s and 1980s, believed that among young people today, "community service is viewed as good, and political service is viewed as disreputable."[15] Systematic studies of the subject are few, but the senator was probably right.

National standards now govern almost every aspect of voter eligibility. All persons eighteen years of age and older may vote; there may be no literacy test or poll tax; states may not require residency of more than thirty days in that state before a person may vote; areas with significant numbers of citizens not speaking English must give those people ballots written in their own language; and federal voter registrars and poll watchers may be sent into areas where less than 50 percent of the voting-age population participates in a presidential election. Before 1961 residents of the District of Columbia could not vote in presidential elections; the Twenty-third Amendment to the Constitution gave them this right.

Voter Turnout

Given all these legal safeguards, one might expect that participation in elections would have risen sharply. In fact the proportion of the voting-age population that has gone to the polls in presidential elections has remained about the same—between 50 and 60 percent of those eligible—at least since 1928 and appears today to be much smaller than it was in the latter part of the nineteenth century (see Figure 6.2). In every presidential election between 1860 and 1900, at least 70 percent of the eligible population apparently went to the polls, and in some years (1860 and 1876) almost 80 percent seem to have voted. Since 1900 not a single presidential election turnout has reached 70 percent, and on two occasions (1920 and 1924) it did not even reach 50 percent.[16] Even outside the South, where efforts to disfranchise African Americans make data on voter turnout especially hard to interpret, turnout seems to have declined: over 84 percent of the voting-age population participated in presidential elections in nonsouthern states between 1884 and 1900, but only 68 percent participated between 1936 and 1960, and even fewer have done so since 1960.[17]

Scholars have vigorously debated the meaning of these figures. One view is that this decline in turnout, even allowing for the shaky data on which the estimates are based, has been real and is the result of a decline of popular interest in elections and a weakening of the competitiveness of the two major parties. During the nineteenth century, according to this theory, the parties fought hard, worked strenuously to get as many voters as possible to the polls, afforded the mass of voters a chance to participate in party politics through caucuses and

The campaign to win the vote for women nationwide succeeded with the adoption of the Nineteenth Amendment in 1920.

conventions, kept the legal barriers to participation (such as complex registration procedures) low, and looked forward to close, exciting elections. After 1896, by which time the South had become a one-party Democratic region and the North heavily

Figure 6.2   Voter Participation in Presidential Elections, 1860–2000

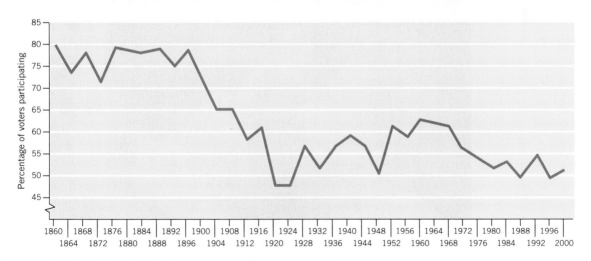

Note: Several southern states did not participate in the 1864 and 1868 elections.
Sources: For 1860–1928: Bureau of the Census, *Historical Statistics of the United States, Colonial Times to 1970,* part 2, 1071; 1932–1944: *Statistical Abstract of the United States, 1992,* 517; 1948–2000: Michael P. McDonald and Samuel L. Popkin, "The Myth of the Vanishing Voter," *American Political Science Review* 95 (December 2001): table 1, 966.

Republican, both parties became more conservative, national elections usually resulted in lopsided victories for the Republicans, and citizens began to lose interest in politics because it no longer seemed relevant to their needs. The parties ceased functioning as organizations to mobilize the mass of voters and fell under the control of leaders, mostly conservative, who resisted mass participation.[18]

There is another view, however. It argues that the decline in voter turnout has been more apparent than real. Though elections were certainly more of a popular sport in the nineteenth century than they are today, the parties were no more democratic then than now, and voters then may have been more easily manipulated. Until around the beginning of the twentieth century, voting fraud was commonplace, because it was easy to pull off. The political parties, not the government, printed the ballots; they were often cast in public, not private, voting booths; there were few serious efforts to decide who was eligible to vote, and the rules that did operate were easily evaded.

Under these circumstances it was easy for a person to vote more than once, and the party machines made heavy use of these "floaters," or repeaters. "Vote early and often" was not a joke but a fact. The parties often controlled the counting of votes, padding the totals whenever they feared losing. As a result of these machinations, the number of votes counted was often larger than the number cast, and the number cast was in turn often larger than the number of individuals eligible to vote.

Around 1890 the states began adopting the **Australian ballot**. This was a government-printed ballot of uniform size and shape that was cast in secret, created to replace the old party-printed ballots cast in public. By 1910 only three states were without the Australian ballot. Its use cut back on (but certainly did not eliminate) vote buying and fraudulent vote counts.

In short, if votes had been legally cast and honestly counted in the nineteenth century, the statistics on election turnout might well be much lower than the inflated figures we now have.[19] To the

In Florida, the closely contested 2000 presidential election required vote canvassers to study ballots to see if they had any "chads"—that is, dangling bits of cardboard from punched holes.

extent that this is true, we may not have had a decline in voter participation as great as some have suggested. Nevertheless, most scholars believe that turnout probably did actually decline somewhat after the 1890s. One reason was that voter-registration regulations became more burdensome: there were longer residency requirements; aliens who had begun but not completed the process of becoming citizens could no longer vote in most states; it became harder for African Americans to vote; educational qualifications for voting were adopted by several states; and voters had to register long in advance of the elections. These changes, designed to purify the electoral process, were aspects of the progressive reform impulse (described in Chapter 7) and served to cut back on the number of people who could participate in elections.

Strict voter-registration procedures tended, like most reforms in American politics, to have unintended as well as intended consequences. These changes not only reduced fraudulent voting but also reduced voting generally, because they made it more difficult for certain groups of perfectly honest voters—those with little education, for example, or those who had recently moved—to register and vote. This was not the first time, and it will not be the last, that a reform designed to cure one problem created another.

Following the controversy over Florida's vote count in the 2000 presidential election, many proposals were made to overhaul the nation's voting system. In 2002, Congress passed a measure that for the first time requires each state to have in place a system for counting the disputed ballots of voters whose names were left off official registration lists. In addition, the law provides federal funds for upgrading voting equipment and procedures and for training election officials. But it stops short of creating a uniform national voting system. Paper ballots, lever machines, and punch-card voting systems will still be used in some places, while optical scan and direct recording electronic equipment will still be used in others.

Even after all the legal changes are taken into account, there has still been a decline in citizen participation in elections. Between 1960 and 1980 the proportion of voting-age people casting a ballot in presidential elections fell by about 10 percentage points, a drop that cannot be explained by how ballots were printed or how registration rules were rewritten. Nor can these factors explain why 1996 witnessed not only the lowest level of turnout (49 percent) in a presidential election since 1924 but also the single steepest four-year decline (from 55 percent in 1992) since 1920.

There is, however, one intriguing explanation: voter turnout has not, in fact, been going down. As we saw earlier in this chapter (refer back to Figure 6.1), there are different ways of calculating voter turnout. Turnout means the percentage of the voting-age population that votes; an accurate measure of turnout means having an accurate count of both how many people voted and how many people could have voted. In fact, we do not have very good measures of either number. Eligible voters are derived from census reports that tell us what the voting-age population (VAP) is—that is, how many people exist who are age eighteen and over (or before younger people were allowed to vote, the number age twenty-one and over). But within the VAP are a lot of people who cannot vote, such as prisoners, felons, and aliens.

Political scientists Michael P. McDonald and Samuel L. Popkin have adjusted the VAP to take into account these differences.[20] They call their alternate measure of turnout the voting eligible population (VEP). Tables 6.3 and 6.4 show how turnout percentages differ depending on which measure, VAP or VEP, is used. Calculated by the VEP, national voter turnout in presidential elections has *not* fallen since the early 1970s. Calculated by the VAP, California's turnout rate in the 2000 presidential election was 44 percent, but calculated by the VEP, it was nearly 56 percent. Whichever measure one uses, however, two things are the same: the days when turnout routinely exceeded 60 percent (1952–1968) in presidential elections are gone, and post-1970 turnout in midterm congressional elections has been anemic, averaging only 38 to 40 percent, however it is calculated.[21]

Actual trends in turnout aside, what if they gave an election and everyone came? Would universal turnout change national election outcomes and the content of public policy? It has long been argued that because the poor, less educated, and minorities are overrepresented among nonvoters, universal turnout would strongly benefit Democratic candidates and liberal causes. But a careful study of this question found that the "party of nonvoters" largely mirrors the demographically diverse and

Table 6.3	Two Methods of Calculating Turnout in Presidential Elections, 1948–2000	
Year	**Voting Age Population (VAP)**	**Voting Eligible Population (VEP)**
1948	51.1%	52.2%
1952	61.6	62.3
1956	59.3	60.2
1960	62.8	63.8
1964	61.9	62.8
1968	60.9	61.5
1972	55.2	56.2
1976	53.5	54.8
1980	52.8	54.7
1984	53.3	57.2
1988	50.3	54.2
1992	55.0	60.6
1996	48.9	52.6
2000	51.2	55.6

Source: Adapted from Michael P. McDonald and Samuel L. Popkin, "The Myth of the Vanishing Voter," *American Political Science Review* 95 (December 2001): table 1, 966. Reprinted with permission of Cambridge University Press.

ideologically divided population that goes to the polls.[22] In 1992 and 1996, for example, the two most common demographic features of nonvoters were residential mobility and youth: "fully 43 percent of nonvoters had moved within two years of the election and one third were under the age of thirty."[23] If everyone who was eligible had voted in those elec-

Table 6.4	Two Methods of Calculating Voter Turnout in Selected States, 2000	
State	**Voting Age Population (VAP)**	**Voting Eligible Population (VEP)**
California	44.09%	55.78%
Florida	50.65	59.75
New York	49.42	57.72
Texas	43.14	50.33
New Jersey	51.04	58.24
Connecticut	58.35	64.25
Arizona	42.26	48.48
Nevada	43.81	49.86
Oregon	60.50	66.60
D.C.	48.99	54.61

Source: Data from Michael McDonald as reported in Louis Jacobson, "Recalibrating Voter Turnout Gauges," *National Journal* (January 1, 2002).

tions, Bill Clinton's winning margin over George Bush the elder and Bob Dole, respectively, would have been a bit wider, but there would have been "no Mother Lode of votes for Democratic candidates or pressure for liberal causes."[24]

Who Participates in Politics?

To understand better why voter turnout declined and what, if anything, that decline may mean, we must first look at who participates in politics.

Forms of Participation

Voting is by far the most common form of political participation, while giving money to a candidate and being a member of a political organization are the least common. Many Americans exaggerate how frequently they vote or how active they are in politics. In a study by Sidney Verba and Norman Nie, 72 percent of those interviewed said that they voted "regularly" in presidential elections.[25] Yet we know that since 1960, on average only 56 percent of the voting-age population has actually cast presidential ballots. Careful studies of this discrepancy suggest that 8 to 10 percent of Americans interviewed misreport their voting habits: they claim to have voted when in fact they have not. Young, low-income, less-educated, and nonwhite people are more likely to misreport than others.[26] If people misreport their voting behavior, it is likely that they also misreport—that is, exaggerate—the extent to which they participate in other ways.

Indeed, most research shows that "politics is not at the heart of the day-to-day life of the American people."[27] Work, family, church, and other voluntary activities come first, both in terms of how Americans spend their time and in terms of the money they donate. For example, a study by Verba and others found that a higher proportion of citizens take part in nonpolitical than political activities: "More citizens reported giving time to church-related or charitable activities than indicated contacting a government official or working informally on a community problem, two of the most frequent forms of political participation beyond the vote"[28] (see Figure 6.3).

In an earlier study Verba and Nie analyzed the ways in which people participate in politics and came up with six forms of participation that are

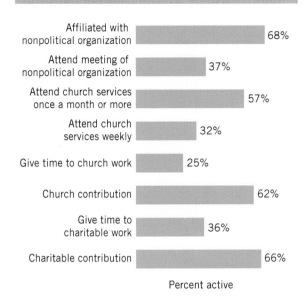

Figure 6.3 Nonpolitical Voluntary Activity Among Citizens

- Affiliated with nonpolitical organization — 68%
- Attend meeting of nonpolitical organization — 37%
- Attend church services once a month or more — 57%
- Attend church services weekly — 32%
- Give time to church work — 25%
- Church contribution — 62%
- Give time to charitable work — 36%
- Charitable contribution — 66%

Percent active

Source: Sidney Verba et al., *Voice and Equality: Civic Voluntarism in American Politics* (Cambridge: Harvard University Press, 1995), 77–79.

characteristic of six different kinds of U.S. citizens. About one-fifth (22 percent) of the population is completely inactive: they rarely vote, they do not get involved in organizations, and they probably do not even talk about politics very much. These inactives typically have little education and low incomes and are relatively young. Many of them are African American. At the opposite extreme are the complete **activists,** constituting about one-ninth of the population (11 percent). These people are highly educated, have high incomes, and tend to be middle-aged rather than young or old. They tend to participate in all forms of politics.

Between these extremes are four categories of limited forms of participation. The *voting specialists* are people who vote but do little else; they tend not to have much schooling or income and to be substantially older than the average person. *Campaigners* not only vote but also like to get involved in campaign activities. They are better educated than the average voter, but what seems to distinguish them most is their interest in the conflicts, passions, and struggle of politics; their clear identification with a political

party; and their willingness to take strong positions. *Communalists* are much like campaigners in social background but have a very different temperament: they do not like the conflict and tension of partisan campaigns. They tend to reserve their energy for community activities of a more nonpartisan nature—forming and joining organizations to deal with local problems and contacting local officials about these problems. Finally, there are some *parochial participants,* who do not vote and stay out of election campaigns and civic associations but are willing to contact local officials about specific, often personal, problems.[29]

The Causes of Participation

Whether participation takes the form of voting or being a complete activist, it is higher among people who have gone to college than among those who have not and higher among people who are over forty-four years of age than among those who are under thirty-five. (The differences in voting rates for these groups are shown in Figure 6.4.) Even after controlling for differences in income and occupation, the more schooling one has, the more likely one is to vote. Of course it may not be schooling itself that causes participation but something that is strongly correlated with schooling, such as high levels of political information.[30]

In fact the differences in participation that are associated with schooling (or its correlates) are probably even greater than reported in this figure, since we have already seen that less-educated people exaggerate how frequently they vote. An excellent study of turnout concludes that people are more likely to vote when they have those personal qualities that "make learning about politics easier and more gratifying."[31]

Religious involvement also increases political participation. If you are a regular churchgoer who takes your faith seriously, the chances are that you will be more likely to vote and otherwise take part in politics than if you are a person of the same age, sex, income, and educational level who does not go to church. Church involvement leads to social connectedness, teaches organizational skills, increases one's awareness of larger issues, and puts one in contact with like-minded people.[32]

Men and women vote at about the same rate, but blacks and whites do not. Although at one time that difference was largely the result of discrimination,

Figure 6.4   Voter Turnout in Presidential Elections, by Age, Schooling, and Race, 1964–1996

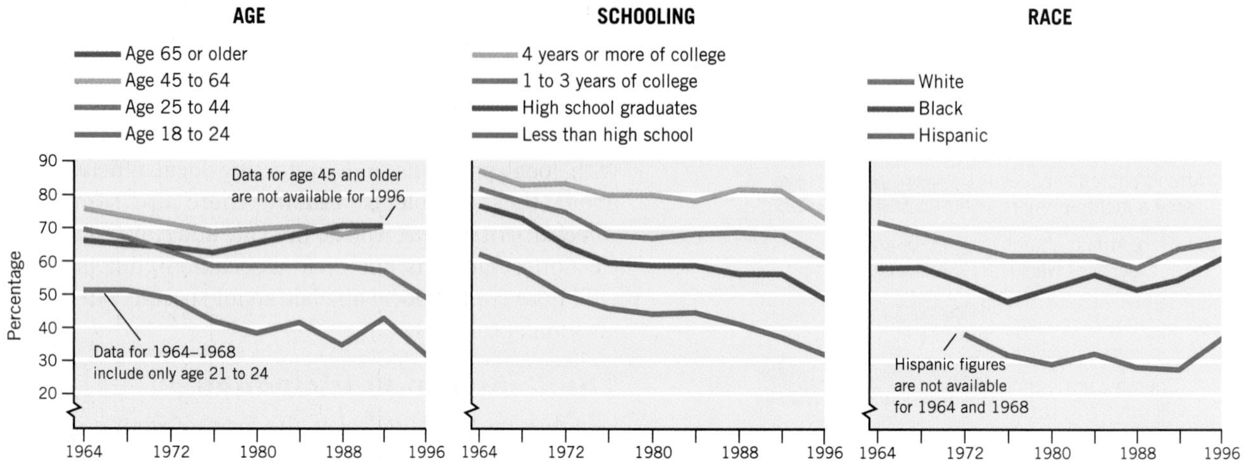

Sources: Updated from Gary R. Orren, "The Linkage of Policy to Participation," in *Presidential Selection,* ed. Alexander Heard and Michael Nelson (Durham, N.C.: Duke University Press, 1987). Data for 1996 are from *Statistical Abstract of the United States 1998,* 296, as supplied by Christopher Blunt.

today it can be explained mostly by differences in social class—blacks are poorer and have less schooling, on average, than whites. However, among people of the same socioeconomic status—that is, having roughly the same level of income and schooling—blacks tend to participate *more* than whites.[33]

Because the population has become younger (due to the baby boom of the 1960s and 1970s) and because blacks have increased in numbers faster than whites, one might suppose that these demographic changes would explain why the turnout in presidential elections has gone down a bit since the early 1960s. And they do—up to a point. But there is another factor that ought to make turnout go *up*—schooling. Since college graduates are much more likely to vote than those with less educational experience, and since the college-graduate proportion of the population has gone up sharply, turnout should have risen. But it has not. What is going on here?

Perhaps turnout has declined despite the higher levels of schooling because of the rising level of distrust of government. We saw in Chapter 4 that, well into the 1990s, more and more people were telling pollsters that they lacked confidence in political leaders. Rising distrust seems a plausible explanation for declining turnout, until one looks at the facts. The data show that there is *no correlation* between expressing distrust of political leaders and

not voting.[34] People who are cynical about our leaders are just as likely to vote as people who are not.

As we have seen, turnout is powerfully affected by the number of people who have registered to vote; perhaps in recent years it has become harder to register. But in fact exactly the opposite is true. Since 1970 federal law has prohibited residency requirements longer than thirty days for presidential elections, and a Supreme Court decision in 1972 held that requirements much in excess of this were invalid for state and local elections.[35] By 1982 twenty-one states and the District of Columbia, containing about half the nation's population, had adopted laws permitting voters to register by mail. In four states—Maine, Minnesota, Oregon, and Wisconsin—voters can register and vote on the same day, all at once.

What is left? Several small things. First, the greater youthfulness of the population, together with the presence of growing numbers of African Americans and other minorities, has pushed down the percentage of voters who are registered and vote.

Second, political parties today are no longer as effective as they once were in mobilizing voters, ensuring that they are registered, and getting them to the polls. As we shall see in Chapter 7, the parties once were grassroots organizations with which many people strongly identified. Today the parties are somewhat distant, national bureaucracies with which most of us do not identify very strongly.

Third, the remaining impediments to registration exert some influence. One study estimated that if every state had registration requirements as easy as the most permissive states, turnout in a presidential election would be about 9 percent higher.[36] The experience of the four states where you can register and vote on the same day is consistent with this: in 1976, when same-day registration first went into effect, three of the four states that had it saw their turnout go up by 3 or 4 percent, while those states that did not have it saw their turnout go down.[37] If an even bolder plan were adopted, such as the Canadian system of universal enrollment, whereby the government automatically puts on the voter list every eligible citizen, there would probably be some additional gain in turnout.[38]

Fourth, if *not* voting is costless, then there will be more nonvoting. Several nations with higher turnouts than ours make voting compulsory. For example, in Italy a person who does not vote has his or her government identification papers stamped *"DID NOT VOTE."*[39] In Australia and other countries fines can be levied on nonvoters. As a practical matter such fines are rarely imposed, but just the threat of them probably induces more people to register and vote.

Finally, voting (and before that, registering) will go down if people do not feel that elections matter much. There has been a decline in the proportion of people who feel that elections matter a lot, corresponding to the decrease in those who do participate in elections.

In short there are a number of reasons why we register and vote less frequently in the United States than do citizens of other countries. Two careful studies of all these factors found that almost all of the differences in turnout among twenty-four democratic nations, including the United States, could be explained by party strength, automatic registration, and compulsory voting laws.[40]

The presence of these reasons does not necessarily mean that somebody ought to do something about them. We could make registration automatic—but that might open the way to voter fraud, since people move around and change names often enough to enable some of them, if they wanted to, to vote more than once. We could make voting compulsory, but Americans have an aversion to government compul-

sion in any form and probably would object strenuously to any plan for making citizens carry identification papers that the government would stamp.

Democrats and Republicans fight over various measures designed to increase registration and voting because one party (usually the Democrats) thinks that higher turnout will help them and the other (usually the Republicans) fears that higher turnout will hurt them. In fact no one really knows whether either party would be helped or hurt by higher voter turnout.

Nonvoters are more likely than voters to be poor, black or Hispanic, or uneducated. However, the proportion of nonvoters with some college education rose from 7 percent in 1960 to 39 percent in 1996. In addition the percentage of nonvoters who held white-collar jobs rose from 33 percent to 50 percent

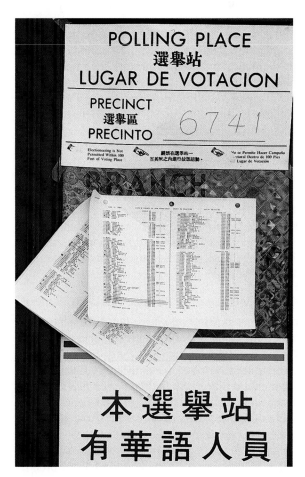

In San Fransisco, voting instructions are printed in English, Spanish, and Chinese.

Demonstrations are almost as important as elections in shaping public policy.

in the same period. Many of these better-off nonvoters might well have voted Republican had they gone to the polls. And even if the turnout rates only of blacks and Hispanics had increased, there would not have been enough votes added to the Democratic column to affect the outcome of the 1984 or 1988 presidential elections.[41]

Both political parties try to get a larger turnout among voters likely to be sympathetic to them, but it is hard to be sure that these efforts will produce real gains. If one party works hard to get its nonvoters to the polls, the other party will work just as hard to get its people there. For example, when Jesse Jackson ran for the presidency in 1984, registration of southern blacks increased, but registration of southern whites increased even more.

The Meaning of Participation Rates

Americans may be voting less, but there is evidence that they are participating more. As Table 6.5 shows, between 1967 and 1987 the percentage of Americans who voted regularly in presidential and local elections dropped, but the percentage who participated in ten out of twelve other political activities increased, steeply in some cases. Thus, although Americans are going to the polls less, they are campaigning, contacting government officials, and working on community issues more. And while the proportion of the population that votes is lower in the United States than in many other democracies, the percent-

age of Americans who engage in one or more political activities beyond voting is higher (see Table 6.6).

Public demonstrations such as sit-ins and protest marches have become much more common in recent decades than they once were. By one count there were only 6 demonstrations per year between 1950 and 1959 but over 140 per year between 1960 and 1967. Though the demonstrations of the 1960s began with civil rights and antiwar activists, public protests were later employed by farmers demanding government aid, truckers denouncing the national speed limit, people with disabilities seeking to dramatize their needs, parents objecting to busing to achieve racial balance in the schools, conservationists hoping to block nuclear power plants, and construction workers urging that nuclear power *not* be blocked.[42]

Although we vote at lower rates here than people do abroad, the meaning of our voting is different. For one thing we elect far more public officials than do the citizens of any other nation. One scholar has estimated that there are 521,000 elective offices in the United States and that almost every week of the year there is an election going on somewhere in this country.[43]

A citizen of Massachusetts, for example, votes not only for the U.S. president but also for two senators, the state governor, the member of the House of Representatives for his or her district, a state representative, a state senator, the state attorney general, the state auditor, the state treasurer, the secretary of state, a county commissioner, a sheriff, and clerks of various courts, as well as (in the cities) for the mayor, the city councillor, and school committee members and (in towns) for selectmen, town-meeting members, a town moderator, library trustees, health board members, assessors, water commissioners, the town clerk, housing authority members, the tree warden, and the commissioner of the public burial ground. (There are probably others that we have forgotten.)

In many European nations, by contrast, the voters get to make just one choice once every four or five years: they can vote for or against a member of parliament. When there is only one election for one office every several years, that election is bound to assume more importance to voters than many elections for scores of offices. But one election for one office probably has less effect on how the nation is governed than many elections for thousands of offices. Americans may not vote at high rates, but

Table 6.5 How Citizens Participate			
	Percentage Engaging in Fourteen Acts of Participation, 1967 and 1987		
Specific Activity	**1967**	**1987**	**Absolute Change**
Voting			
Regularly vote in presidential elections	66%	58%	–8%
Always vote in local elections	47	35	–12
Campaigning			
Persuade others how to vote	28	32	+4
Actively work for party or candidate	26	27	+1
Attend political meetings or rallies	19	19	0
Contribute money to a party or candidate	13	23	+10
Participate in a political club	8	4	–4
Contacting Government			
Contact local officials: issue-based	14	24	+10
Contact state or national officials: issue-based	11	22	+11
Contact local officials: particularized	7	10	+3
Contact state or national officials: particularized	6	7	+1
Taking Action in the Community			
Work with others on a local problem	30	34	+4
Actively participate in community problem-solving organization	31	34	+3
Form group to help solve local problem	14	17	+3

Source: Reprinted by permission of the publisher from *Voice and Equality: Civic Voluntarism in American Politics* by Sidney Verba, Kay Lehman Scholzman, and Henry A. Brady, Cambridge, Mass.: Harvard University Press, Copyright © 1995 by the Presidents and Fellows of Harvard College. Data from p. 72.

voting affects a far greater part of the political system here than abroad.

The kinds of people who vote here are also different from those who vote abroad. Since almost everybody votes in many other democracies, the votes cast there mirror almost exactly the social composition of those nations. Since only slightly over half of the voting-age population turns out even for presidential elections here, the votes cast in the United States may not truly reflect the country.

That is in fact the case. The proportion of each major occupational group—or if you prefer, social class—that usually votes in Japan, Sweden, and the United States votes at about the same rate in Japan and Sweden. But in the United States the turnout is heavily skewed toward higher-status persons: those in professional, managerial, and other white-collar occupations are overrepresented among the voters.[44]

Table 6.6 Participation Beyond Voting in Fourteen Democracies			
Percentage of adult population who engaged in some form of political participation beyond voting in 1990.			
Britain	77%	Italy	56%
Sweden	74	Iceland	55
Norway	68	Netherlands	54
UNITED STATES	66	Belgium	51
Denmark	59	Ireland	46
France	57	Finland	38
West Germany	57	Spain	32

Sources: U.S. percentage calculated from Sidney Verba et al., *Voice and Equality: Civic Voluntarism in American Politics* (Cambridge: Harvard University Press, 1995), 83; other percentages calculated from Max Kaase and Kenneth Newton, *Beliefs in Government*, vol. 5 (New York: Oxford University Press, 1995), 51.

Figure 6.5   Electoral and Nonelectoral Political Participation Among Anglo Whites, African Americans, and Latinos

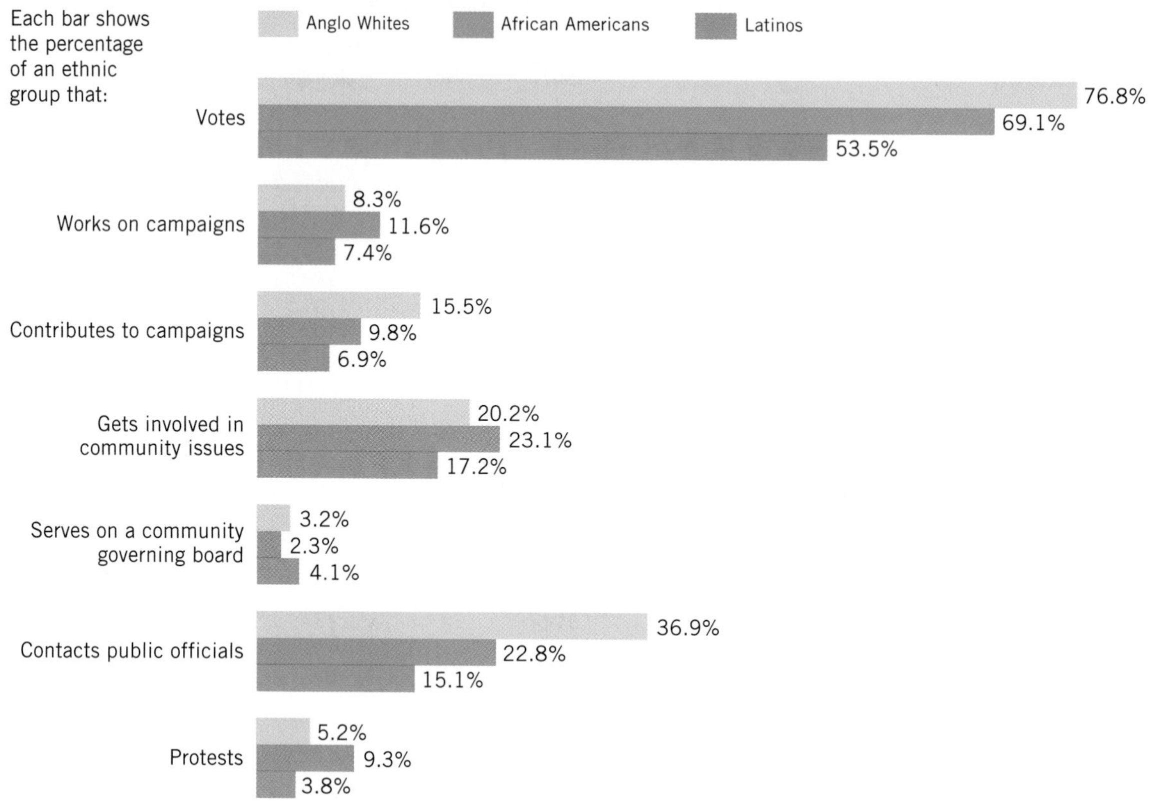

Each bar shows the percentage of an ethnic group that:

Anglo Whites   African Americans   Latinos

Votes
76.8%
69.1%
53.5%

Works on campaigns
8.3%
11.6%
7.4%

Contributes to campaigns
15.5%
9.8%
6.9%

Gets involved in community issues
20.2%
23.1%
17.2%

Serves on a community governing board
3.2%
2.3%
4.1%

Contacts public officials
36.9%
22.8%
15.1%

Protests
5.2%
9.3%
3.8%

Source: Adapted from Sidney Verba, Kay Lehman Scholzman, Henry Brady, and Norman H. Nie, *Voice and Equality: Civic Voluntarism in American Politics,* (Cambridge: Harvard University Press, 1995).

Although nonwhites and Latinos are the fastest-growing segment of the U.S. population, they tend to be the most underrepresented groups among American voters. Little is known about the relationship between political participation and variables such as command of the language and involvement in nonpolitical institutions that provide information or impart skills relevant to politics (such as workplaces and voluntary associations). However, such factors could be quite important in explaining differences in political participation rates among poor and minority citizens. As we can see in Figure 6.5, blacks, though less involved than whites, participate in voting and political activities at higher rates than do Latinos. One excellent study suggests that these differences are due in part to the fact that blacks are more likely than Latinos to be members of churches

that stimulate political interest, activity, and mobilization.[45] Language barriers also make it harder for many Latinos to get in touch with a public official, serve on local governing boards, and engage in other forms of political participation in which command of English is an asset. The lower participation rates of minority citizens are likely compounded by their being disproportionately of low socioeconomic status compared to white Americans.

Exactly what these differences in participation mean in terms of how the government is run is not entirely clear. But since we know from evidence presented in the last chapter that upper-status persons are more likely to have an ideological view of politics, it may suggest that governance here is a bit more sensitive not only to the interests of upper-status white people but also to their (conflicting) ideologies.

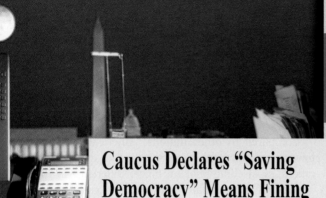

What Would You Do?

Caucus Declares "Saving Democracy" Means Fining Nonvoters

May 30
SACRAMENTO, CA

Voting has never been America's favorite pastime, but a report issued by the state senate's Democracy Caucus declares that "nonvoting is now a civic epidemic" that "can best be cured by fining nonvoters as they do in some other democracies"...

MEMORANDUM

To: Sheria Sellers-Crawley, state senator
From: Chuck Brutsche, legislative analyst
Subject: Caucus proposal to fine nonvoters

In the 1990s barely half of the electorate voted for president, and only a third or so cast ballots for the U.S. House of Representatives. In a few recent presidential primaries and statewide special elections, turnout has run 10 percent or below. In the mid-1960s, 47 percent of people who did not finish high school and one-third of people in their early twenties voted in the most recent election, but by the mid-1990s only one-quarter of the former group and one-fifth of the latter group did so. Does fining nonvoters make good sense, and would it work?

Arguments for:

1. Australia instituted compulsory voting after its turnout rate fell below 60 percent in 1922. Italy did the same after World War II. Since the early 1920s Australia's turnout has never fallen below 90 percent, and since the early 1950s Italy's has averaged between 85 and 90 percent.
2. The usual fine for nonvoting in these countries is under fifty dollars. Judges or other officials excuse people who are too sick to vote or have other valid excuses.
3. The law sends a moral message that voting is a civic duty in a democracy. More citizens will feel morally obliged to vote if all citizens are legally obliged to vote.

Arguments against:

1. Americans vote in more elections and participate in more political activities beyond voting than other democratic peoples do. Other reforms—streamlining voter registration requirements, holding elections on weekends, making election day a national holiday, increasing get-out-the-vote public service ads—are worth trying instead.
2. Most Americans would probably assert that they have a right not to vote, and many would simply refuse to pay even a small fine for not voting. What then, jail them?
3. Compelling people with limited or no political knowledge to vote leads to what Australians aptly call the "donkey vote." It is both unwise and undemocratic to legally oblige people to vote.

Your decision:
Favor proposal _____
Oppose proposal _____

Summary

The popular view that Americans don't vote as a result of apathy is not quite right. It is nearer to the truth to say that we don't all register to vote and don't always vote even when registered. There are many factors having nothing to do with apathy that shape our participation rates—age, race, party organization, the barriers to registration, and popular views about the significance of elections.

Compared to other nations, Americans vote at lower rates but more frequently and for many more offices, so elections make a bigger difference in the conduct of public affairs here than abroad. We also engage somewhat more frequently than do people abroad in various nonelectoral forms of participation.

Reconsidering the Enduring Questions

1. What role did the Framers of the Constitution believe average citizens should play in America's representative democracy?

The Framers believed that citizens should play an important but not the decisive role in the American Republic. They elect the House, but until the Constitution was amended in 1913, they did not elect the Senate; the president and senators, not ordinary people, select federal judges; and the president is chosen by electors. Over time the system has become much more responsive to public opinion. Voters now help pick party candidates through party primaries, and their views are regularly solicited by opinion polls.

2. Who votes, who doesn't?

The most powerful determinants of voting are age (older people vote more than younger people) and education (college graduates vote more than high

school graduates). Race makes a difference, but black participation rates approximate white rates once you control for socioeconomic status.

3. Why do some people participate in politics at higher rates than others?

Older people and college graduates have learned to have a greater interest in politics, in part because they see ways in which government policies will affect them, in part because they may have acquired a political ideology that makes politics intrinsically interesting. As we have seen, Americans vote less than people in most other democratic nations. That gap is in part the result of the failure of many Americans to register to vote; efforts to increase registration, such as the motor-voter law, have got more names onto the voting rolls, but these new additions often do not vote as often as do other registered voters.

World Wide Web Resources

- Information for voters
  Democracy Network: http://www.dnet.org/
  League of Women Voters: http://www.lwv.org/
  Voter Information Services: http://www.vis.org/
  Women's Voting Guide:
  http://www.womenvote.org/
- National Mail Voter Registration Form:
  http://www.fec.gov/votregis/vr.htm

- The Vanishing Voter:
  http://www.vanishingvoter.org/
- Voter turnout statistics:
  http://clerkhouse.gov/index.php
  http://www.fec.gov/elections.html

Key Terms

voting-age population *p. 132*

registered voters *p. 132*

motor-voter law *p. 132*

literacy test *p. 134*

poll tax *p. 134*

grandfather clause *p. 134*

white primary *p. 135*

Australian ballot *p. 138*

activists *p. 141*

Suggested Readings

Burnham, Walter Dean. *Critical Elections and the Mainsprings of American Politics.* New York: Norton, 1970. An argument about the decline of voter participation, linking it to changes in the economic system.

Conway, M. Margaret. *Political Participation in the United States.* 2d ed. Washington, D.C.: Congressional Quarterly Press, 1991. Good brief summary of what we need to know about who participates in politics and why.

Orren, Gary R. "The Linkage of Policy to Participation." In *Presidential Selection,* edited by Alexander Heard and Michael Nelson. Durham, N.C.: Duke University Press, 1987. Carefully evaluates various proposals for increasing electoral turnout in the United States.

Teixera, Ruy. *Why Americans Don't Vote.* Westport, Conn.: Greenwood Press, 1987. Good summary of what we know about nonvoting.

Verba, Sidney, et al. *Voice and Equality: Civic Voluntarism in American Politics.* Cambridge: Harvard University Press, 1995.

Verba, Sidney, Norman H. Nie, and Jae-on Kim. *Participation and Political Equality.* Cambridge: Cambridge University Press, 1978. Comparative study of political participation in seven nations.

Wolfinger, Raymond E., and Steven R. Rosenstone. *Who Votes?* New Haven, Conn.: Yale University Press, 1980. Excellent analysis of what factors determine turnout.

Political Parties

Enduring Questions

1. What did the Founding Fathers believe about political parties?

2. How has America's two-party system changed over the past century and a half? How does it differ today from the party systems of other representative democracies?

3. To what extent has the decline of mass attachment to the two major parties affected how Americans vote?

One of the reasons why voter turnout is higher abroad than in this country is that political parties in other democratic nations are more effective at mobilizing voters than are those here. The sense of being a party member and the inclination to vote the party ticket are greater in France, Italy, and Sweden than in the United States. From this fact you might suppose that political parties here are recent inventions with little experience at organizing and no history of attracting voter identification.

Quite the contrary. American political parties are the oldest in the world, and at one time being a Democrat or a Republican was a serious commitment that people did not make lightly or abandon easily. In those days it would have been hard to find anything in Europe that could match the vote-getting power of such party organizations as those in Chicago, New York, and Philadelphia.

Parties in the United States are relatively weak today, not because they are old but because the laws and rules under which they operate have taken away much of their power at the same time that many voters have lost their sense of commitment to party identification. This weakening has proceeded

151

unevenly, however, because our constitutional system has produced a decentralized party system just as it has produced a decentralized governmental system, with the result that parties in some places are strong and in other places almost nonexistent.

Parties—Here and Abroad

A **political party** is a group that seeks to elect candidates to public office by supplying them with a label—a "party identification"—by which they are known to the electorate.[1] This definition is purposefully broad so that it will include both familiar parties (Democratic, Republican) and unfamiliar ones (Whig, Libertarian, Socialist Workers) and will cover periods in which a party is very strong (having an elaborate and well-disciplined organization that provides money and workers to its candidates) as well as periods in which it is quite weak (supplying nothing but the label to candidates). The label by which a candidate is known may or may not actually be printed on the ballot opposite the candidate's name: in the United States it does appear on the ballot in all national elections but in only a minority of municipal ones; in Australia and Israel (and in Great Britain before 1969) it never appears on the ballot at all.

This definition suggests the three political arenas within which parties may be found. A party exists as a *label* in the minds of the voters, as an *organization* that recruits and campaigns for candidates, and as a *set of leaders* who try to organize and control the legislative and executive branches of government. A powerful party is one whose label has a strong appeal for the voters, whose organization can decide who will be candidates and how their campaigns will be managed, and whose leaders can dominate one or all branches of government.

American parties have become weaker in all three arenas. As a *label* with which voters identify, the parties are probably much weaker than they were in the nineteenth century but only somewhat weaker than they were forty years ago (see Figure 7.1). In 1952, a total of 36 percent of the electorate identified strongly as Democrats (22 percent) or Republicans (14 percent), while a total of 23 percent of the electorate identified as independents. By 2000, total strong party identifiers had dropped to 31 percent of the electorate, while all independents had risen to 40 percent of the electorate. But the best evidence of weakening party identification is what voters *do*. As we shall see in the next chapter, they have been increasingly voting split tickets—that is, supporting a president from one party and members of Congress from the other.

| Figure 7.1 | Decline in Party Identification, 1952–2000 |

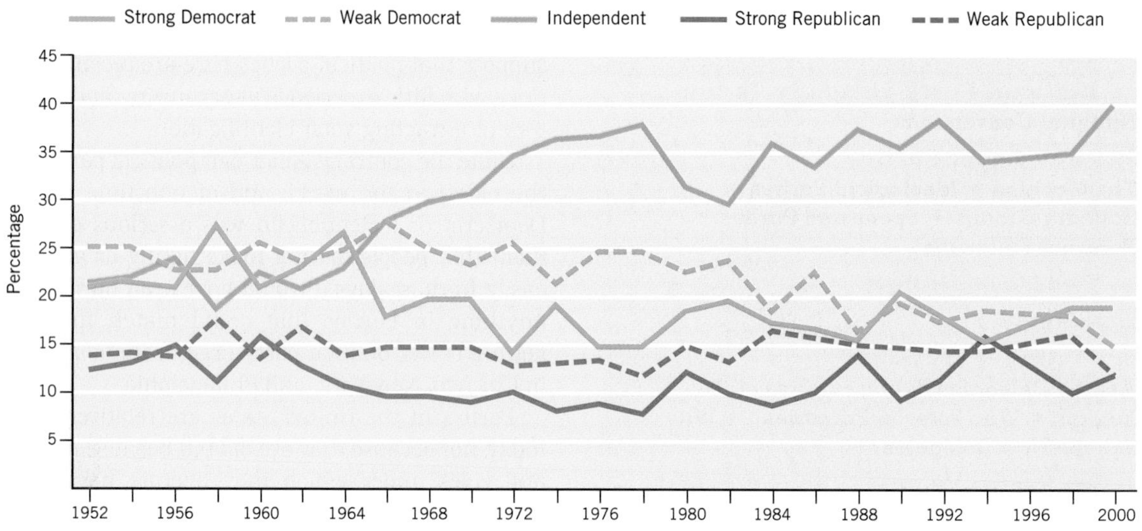

Source: National Election Studies, *The NES Guide to Public Opinion and Electoral Behavior, 1952–2000,* table 20.1.

As a *set of leaders* who organize government, especially Congress, political parties remain somewhat strong in ways that will be described in Chapter 11. As *organizations* that nominate and elect candidates, parties have become dramatically weaker since the 1960s. In most states parties have very little control over who gets nominated to office. The causes and consequences of that change are the subject of this chapter.

In Europe things are very different. Almost the only way a person can become a candidate for elective office is to be nominated by party leaders. Campaigns are run by the party, using party funds and workers, not by the candidate. Once in office the elected officials are expected to vote and act together with other members of their party. The principal criterion by which voters choose among candidates is their party identification or label. This has been changing somewhat of late: European parties, like American ones, have not been able to count as heavily as in the past on party loyalty among the voters.

Several factors explain the striking differences between American and European political parties. First, the federal system of government in the United States decentralizes political authority and thus decentralizes political party organizations. For nearly two centuries most of the important governmental decisions were made at the state and local levels— decisions regarding education, land use, business regulation, and public welfare—and thus it was at the state and local levels that the important struggles over power and policy occurred. Moreover, most people with political jobs—either elective or appointive— worked for state and local government, and thus a party's interest in obtaining these jobs for its followers meant that it had to focus attention on who controlled city hall, the county courthouse, and the state capitol. Federalism, in short, meant that political parties would acquire jobs and money from local sources and fight local contests. This, in turn, meant that the national political parties would be coalitions of local parties, and though these coalitions would have a keen interest in capturing the presidency (with it, after all, went control of large numbers of federal jobs), the national party leaders rarely had as much power as the local ones. The Republican leader of Cuyahoga County, Ohio, for example, could often ignore the decisions of the Republican national chairman and even of the Ohio state chairman.

Political authority in the United States has of late come to be far more centralized: the federal govern-

There are usually many more political parties in parliamentary regimes than in the United States. Here, a Ukranian voter looks at ads for thirty-two parties in 2002.

ment now makes decisions affecting almost all aspects of our lives, including those—such as schooling and welfare—once left entirely in local hands. Yet the political parties have not become more centralized as a result. If anything, they have become even weaker and more decentralized. One reason for this apparent paradox is that in the United States, unlike in most other democratic nations, political parties are closely regulated by state and federal laws, and these regulations have had the effect of weakening the power of parties substantially. Perhaps the most important of these regulations are those that prescribe how a party's candidates are to be selected.

In the great majority of American states, the party leaders do not select people to run for office; by law those people are chosen by the voters in primary elections. Though sometimes the party can influence who will win a primary contest, in general people running for state or national office in this country owe little to party leaders. In Europe, by contrast, there is no such thing as a primary election—the only way to become a candidate for office is to persuade party leaders to put your name on the ballot. In a later section of this chapter, the impact of the direct primary will be discussed in more detail; for now, it is enough to note that its use removes from the hands of the party leadership its most important source of power over officeholders.

Furthermore, if an American political party wins control of Congress, it does not—as in most European nations with a parliamentary system of government— also win the right to select the chief executive of the government. The American president, as we have seen, is independently elected, and this means that he will choose his principal subordinates not from among members of Congress but from among persons out of Congress. Should he pick a representative or senator for his cabinet, the Constitution requires that person to resign from Congress in order to accept the job. Thus an opportunity to be a cabinet secretary is not an important reward for members of Congress, and so the president cannot use the prospect of that reward as a way of controlling congressional action. All this weakens the significance and power of parties in terms of organizing the government and conducting its business.

Political Culture

The attitudes and traditions of American voters reinforce the institutional and legal factors that make American parties relatively weak. Political parties in this country have rarely played an important part in the life of the average citizen; indeed, one does not usually "join" a party here except by voting for its candidates. In many European nations, on the other hand, large numbers of citizens will join a party, pay dues, and attend regular meetings. Furthermore, in countries such as France, Austria, and Italy, the political parties sponsor a wide range of activities and dominate a variety of associations to which a person may belong—labor unions, youth groups, educational programs, even chess clubs.

In the United States we tend to keep parties separate from other aspects of our lives. As Democrats or Republicans, we may become excited by a presidential campaign, and a few of us may even participate in helping elect a member of Congress or state senator. Our social, business, working, and cultural lives, however, are almost entirely nonpartisan. Indeed, most Americans, unlike many Europeans, would resent partisanship's becoming a conspicuous feature of other organizations to which they belong. All this is a way of saying that American parties play a segmental, rather than a comprehensive, role in our lives and that even this role is diminishing as more and more of us proclaim ourselves to be "independents."

The Rise and Decline of the Political Party

Our nation began without parties, and today's parties, though far from extinct, are about as weak as at any time in our history. In between the Founding and the present, however, parties arose and became powerful. We can see this process in four broad periods of party history: when political parties were created (roughly from the Founding to the 1820s); when the more or less stable two-party system emerged (roughly from the time of President Jackson to the Civil War); when parties developed a comprehensive organizational form and appeal (roughly from the Civil War to the 1930s); and finally when party "reform" began to alter the party system (beginning in the early 1900s but taking effect chiefly since the New Deal).

The Founding

The Founders disliked parties, thinking of them as "factions" motivated by ambition and self-interest. George Washington, dismayed by the quarreling between Hamilton and Jefferson in his cabinet, devoted much of his Farewell Address to condemning parties. This hostility toward parties was understandable: the legitimacy and success of the newly created federal government were still very much in doubt. When Jefferson organized his followers to oppose Hamilton's policies, it seemed to Hamilton and *his* followers that Jefferson was opposing not just a policy or a leader but also the very concept of a national government. Jefferson, for his part, thought that Hamilton was not simply pursuing bad policies but was subverting the Constitution itself. Before political parties could become legitimate, it was necessary for people to be able to separate in their minds quarrels over policies and elections from disputes over the legitimacy of the new government itself. The ability to make that distinction was slow in coming, and thus parties were objects of profound suspicion, defended, at first, only as temporary expedients.

The first organized political party in American history was made up of the followers of Jefferson, who, beginning in the 1790s, called themselves *Republicans* (hoping to suggest thereby that their opponents were secret monarchists).* The followers of Hamilton kept the label *Federalist*, which once had been used to refer to all supporters of the new Constitution (hoping to imply that their oppo-

---

*The Jeffersonian Republicans were not the party that today we call Republican. In fact, present-day Democrats consider Jefferson to be the founder of their party.

When Andrew Jackson ran for president in 1828, over a million votes were cast for the first time in American history. This poster, from the 1832 election, was part of the emergence of truly mass political participation.

nents were "Antifederalists," or enemies of the Constitution).

These parties were loose caucuses of political notables in various localities, with New England being strongly Federalist and much of the South passionately Republican. Jefferson and his ally James Madison thought that their Republican party was a temporary arrangement designed to defeat John Adams, a Federalist, in his bid to succeed Washington in 1796. (Adams narrowly defeated Jefferson, who, under the system then in effect, became vice president because he had the second most electoral votes.) In 1800 Adams's bid to succeed himself intensified party activity even more, but this time Jefferson won and the Republicans assumed office. The Federalists feared that Jefferson would dismantle the Constitution, but Jefferson adopted a conciliatory posture, saying in his inaugural address that "we are all Republicans, we are all Federalists."[2] It was not true, of course: the Federalists detested Jefferson, and some were planning to have New England secede from the Union.

But it was good politics, expressive of the need that every president has to persuade the public that, despite partisan politics, the presidency exists to serve all the people.

So successful were the Republicans that the Federalists virtually ceased to exist as a party. Jefferson was reelected in 1804 with almost no opposition; Madison easily won two terms; James Monroe carried sixteen out of nineteen states in 1816 and was reelected without opposition in 1820. Political parties had seemingly disappeared, just as Jefferson had hoped. The weakness of this so-called first party system can be explained by the fact that it was the first: nobody had been born a Federalist or a Republican; there was no ancestral party loyalty to defend; the earliest political leaders did not think of themselves as professional politicians; and the Federalist party had such a limited sectional and class base that it could not compete effectively in national elections. The parties that existed in these early years were essentially small groups of local notables. Political participation was limited, and nominations for most local offices were arranged rather casually.

Even in this early period, the parties, though they had very different views on economic policy and somewhat different class bases, did not represent clear, homogeneous economic interests. Farmers in Virginia were Republicans, but farmers in Delaware were Federalists; the commercial interests of Boston were firmly Federalist, but commercial leaders in urban Connecticut were most likely to be Republican.

From the beginning to the present elections have created heterogeneous coalitions, as Madison anticipated.

The Jacksonians

What is often called the second party system emerged around 1824 with Andrew Jackson's first run for the presidency and lasted until the Civil War became inevitable. Its distinctive feature was that political participation became a mass phenomenon. For one thing, the number of voters to be reached had become quite large. Only about 365,000 popular votes were cast in 1824. But as a result of laws that enlarged the number of people eligible to vote and of an increase in the population, by 1828 well over a million votes were tallied. By 1840 the figure was well over 2 million. (In England at this time there were only 650,000 eligible voters.) In

★ POLITICALLY SPEAKING ★

The Donkey and the Elephant

Since 1874, when Thomas Nast published political cartoons using these figures, the elephant has been the symbol of the Republican party and the donkey (originally the jackass) the symbol of the Democratic party.

The association of the Democrats with donkeys may have begun with a remark by Ignatius Donnelly, a Republican in the Minnesota legislature, who said that the "Democratic party is like a mule—without pride of ancestry or hope of posterity." An equally uncharitable explanation for the link between Republicans and elephants was offered by Democratic presidential candidate Adlai Stevenson, who in the 1950s made the observation that "the elephant has a thick skin, a head full of ivory, and as everyone who has seen a circus parade knows, proceeds best by grasping the tail of its predecessor."

Source: Adapted from *Safire's Political Dictionary* by William Safire. Copyright © 1968, 1972, 1978 by William Safire. Reprinted by permission of Random House, Inc. and the author.

The party system of the Jacksonian era was built from the bottom up rather than—as during the period of the Founding—from the top down. No change better illustrates this transformation than the abandonment of the system of having caucuses composed of members of Congress nominate presidential candidates. The caucus system was an effort to unite the legislative and executive branches by giving the former some degree of control over who would have a chance to capture the latter. The caucus system became unpopular when the caucus candidate for president in 1824 ran third in a field of four in the general election, and it was completely discredited that same year when Congress denied the presidency to Jackson, the candidate with the greatest share of the popular vote.

To replace the caucus, the party convention was invented. The first convention in American history was that of the Anti-Masonic party in 1831; the first convention of a major political party was that of the anti-Jackson Republicans later that year (it nominated Henry Clay for president). The Democrats held a convention in 1832 that ratified Jackson's nomination for reelection and picked Martin Van Buren as his running mate. The first convention to select a man who would be elected president and who was not already the incumbent president was held by the Democrats in 1836; it chose Van Buren.

Considering the many efforts made in recent years to curtail or even abolish the national nominating convention, it is worth remembering that the convention system was first developed in part as a reform—a way of allowing for some measure of local control over the nominating process. Virtually no other nation adopted this method, just as no other nation was later to adopt the direct primary after the convention system became the object of criticism. It is interesting, but perhaps futile, to speculate on how American government would have evolved if the legislative caucus had remained the method for nominating presidents.

The Civil War and Sectionalism

Though the party system created in the Jacksonian period was the first truly national system, with Democrats (followers of Jackson) and Whigs (opponents of Jackson) fairly evenly balanced in most regions, it could not withstand the deep split in opinion created by the agitation over slavery. Both parties tried, naturally, to straddle the issue, since neither

addition, by 1832 presidential electors were selected by popular vote in virtually every state. (As late as 1816 electors were chosen by the state legislatures, rather than by the people, in about half the states.) Presidential politics had become a truly national, genuinely popular activity; indeed, in many communities election campaigns had become the principal public spectacle.

wanted to divide its followers and thus lose the election to its rival. But slavery and sectionalism were issues that could not be straddled. The old parties divided and new ones emerged. The modern Republican party (not the old Democratic-Republican party of Thomas Jefferson) began as a third party. As a result of the Civil War it came to be a major party (the only third party ever to gain major-party status) and to dominate national politics, with only occasional interruptions, for three-quarters of a century.

Republican control of the White House, and to a lesser extent of Congress, was in large measure the result of two events that gave to Republicans a marked advantage in the competition for the loyalties of voters. The first of these was the Civil War. This bitter, searing crisis deeply polarized popular attitudes. Those who supported the Union side became, for generations, Republicans; those who supported the Confederacy, or who had opposed the war, became Democrats.

As it turned out, this partisan division was, for a while, nearly even: though the Republicans usually won the presidency and the Senate, they often lost control of the House. There were many northern Democrats. In 1896, however, another event—the presidential candidacy of William Jennings Bryan—further strengthened the Republican party. Bryan, a Democrat, alienated many voters in the populous northeastern states while attracting voters in the South and Midwest. The result was to confirm and deepen the split in the country, especially North versus South, begun by the Civil War. From 1896 to the 1930s, with rare exceptions northern states were solidly Republican, southern ones solidly Democratic.

This split had a profound effect on the organization of political parties, for it meant that most states were now one-party states. As a result, competition for office at the state level had to go on *within* a single dominant party (the Republican party in Massachusetts, New York, Pennsylvania, Wisconsin, and elsewhere; the Democratic party in Georgia, Mississippi, South Carolina, and elsewhere). Consequently there emerged two major factions within each party, but especially within the Republican party. One was composed of the party regulars—the professional politicians, the "stalwarts," the Old Guard. They were preoccupied with building up the party machinery, developing party loyalty, and acquiring and dispensing patronage—jobs and other favors—for themselves and their faithful followers. Their great skills were in organization, negotiation, bargaining, and compromise; their great interest was in winning.

The other faction, variously called **mugwumps** or **progressives** (or "reformers"), was opposed to the heavy emphasis on patronage; disliked the party machinery, because it permitted only bland candidates to rise to the top; was fearful of the heavy influx of immigrants into American cities and of the ability of the party regulars to organize them into "machines"; and wanted to see the party take unpopular positions on certain issues (such as free trade). Their great skills lay in the areas of advocacy and articulation; their great interest was in principle.

At first the mugwumps tried to play a balance-of-power role, sometimes siding with the Republican party of which they were members, at other times defecting to the Democrats (as when they bolted the Republican party to support Grover Cleveland, the Democratic nominee, in 1884). But later, as the Republican strength in the nation grew, progressives within that party became less and less able to play a balance-of-power role, especially at the state level. Wisconsin, Michigan, Ohio, and Iowa were solidly Republican; Georgia, the Carolinas, and the rest of the Old South had by 1880 become so heavily Democratic that the Republican party in many areas had virtually ceased to exist. If the progressives were to have any power, it would require, they came to believe, an attack on the very concept of partisanship itself.

The Era of Reform

Progressives began to espouse measures to curtail or even abolish political parties. They favored primary elections to replace nominating conventions, because the latter were viewed as being manipulated by party bosses; they favored nonpartisan elections at the city level and in some cases at the state level as well; they argued against corrupt alliances between parties and businesses. They wanted strict voter-registration requirements that would reduce voting fraud (but would also, as it turned out, keep ordinary citizens who found the requirements cumbersome from voting); they pressed for civil service reform to eliminate patronage; and they made heavy use of the mass media as a way of attacking the abuses of partisanship and of promoting their own ideas and candidacies.

The Election of 1828

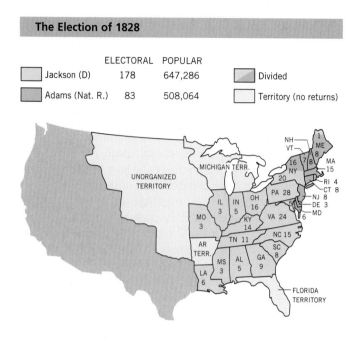

	ELECTORAL	POPULAR	
Jackson (D)	178	647,286	Divided
Adams (Nat. R.)	83	508,064	Territory (no returns)

The Election of 1860

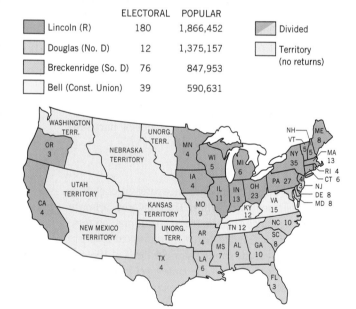

	ELECTORAL	POPULAR	
Lincoln (R)	180	1,866,452	Divided
Douglas (No. D)	12	1,375,157	Territory (no returns)
Breckenridge (So. D)	76	847,953	
Bell (Const. Union)	39	590,631	

The progressives were more successful in some places than in others. In California, for example, progressives led by Governor Hiram Johnson in 1910–1911 were able to institute the direct primary and to adopt procedures—called the *initiative* and the *referendum*—so that citizens could vote directly on proposed legislation, thereby bypassing the state legislature. Governor Robert La Follette brought about similar changes in Wisconsin.

The effect of these changes was to reduce substantially the worst forms of political corruption and ultimately to make boss rule in politics difficult if not impossible. But they also had the effect of making political parties, whether led by bosses or by statesmen, weaker, less able to hold officeholders accountable, and less able to assemble the power necessary for governing the fragmented political institutions created by the Constitution. In Congress party lines began to grow fainter, as did the power of congressional leadership. Above all, the progressives did not have an answer to the problem first faced by Jefferson: if there is not a strong political party, by what other means will candidates for office be found, recruited, and supported?

Party Realignments

There have clearly been important turning points in the strength of the major parties, especially in the twentieth century, when for long periods we have not so much had close competition between two parties as we have had an alternation of dominance by one party and then the other. To help explain these major shifts in the tides of politics, scholars have developed the theory of **critical** or **realigning periods.** During such periods a sharp, lasting shift occurs in the popular coalition supporting one or both parties. The issues that separate the two parties change, and so the kinds of voters supporting each party change. This shift may occur at the time of the election or just after, as the new administration draws in new supporters.[3] There seem to have been five realignments so far, during or just after these elections: 1800 (when the Jeffersonian Republicans defeated the Federalists), 1828 (when the Jacksonian Democrats came to power), 1860 (when the Whig party collapsed and the Republicans under Lincoln came to power), 1896 (when the Republicans defeated William Jennings Bryan), and 1932 (when the Democrats under Roosevelt came into office). Some observers, noting that these realignments have occurred with marked regularity every twenty-eight to thirty-six years, have speculated on whether they are the result of inevitable cycles in American political life.

Such speculations need not concern us, for what is more important is to understand why a realignment occurs at all. That is not entirely clear. For one thing, there are at least two kinds of realignments—one in which a major party is so badly defeated that it disappears and a new party emerges to take its place (this happened to the Federalists in 1800 and to the Whigs in 1856–1860), and another in which the two existing parties continue but voters shift their support from one to the other (this happened in 1896 and 1932). Furthermore, not all critical elections have been carefully studied.

The three clearest cases seem to be 1860, 1896, and 1932. By 1860 the existing parties could no longer straddle the fence on the slavery issue. The Republican party was formed in 1856 on the basis of clear-cut opposition to slavery; the Democratic party split in half in 1860, with one part (led by Stephen A. Douglas and based in the North) trying to waffle on the issue and the other (led by John C. Breckinridge and drawing its support from the South) categorically denying that any government had any right to outlaw slavery. The remnants of the Whig party, renamed the Constitutional Union party, tried to unite the nation by writing no platform at all, thus remaining silent on slavery. Lincoln and the antislavery Republicans won in 1860; Breckinridge and the proslavery Southern Democrats came in second. From that moment on, the two major political parties acquired different sources of support and stood (at least for a decade) for different principles. The parties that had tried to straddle the fence were eliminated. The Civil War fixed these new party loyalties deep in the popular mind, and the structure of party competition was set for nearly forty years.

In 1896 a different kind of realignment occurred. Economics rather than slavery was at issue. A series of depressions during the 1880s and 1890s fell especially hard on farmers in the Midwest and parts of the South. The prices paid to farmers for their commodities had been falling more or less steadily since the Civil War, making it increasingly difficult for them to pay their bills. A bitter reaction against the two major parties, which were straddling this issue as they had straddled slavery, spread like a prairie fire, leading to the formation of parties of economic protest—the Greenbackers and the Populists. Reinforcing the economic cleavages were cultural ones: Populists tended to be fundamentalist Protestants; urban voters were increasingly Catholic. Matters came to a head in 1896 when William

The Election of 1896

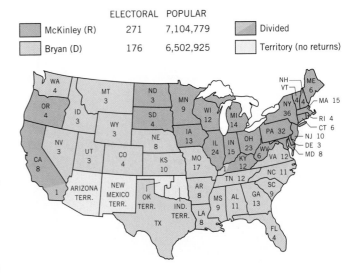

	ELECTORAL	POPULAR
McKinley (R)	271	7,104,779
Bryan (D)	176	6,502,925
Divided		
Territory (no returns)		

The Election of 1932

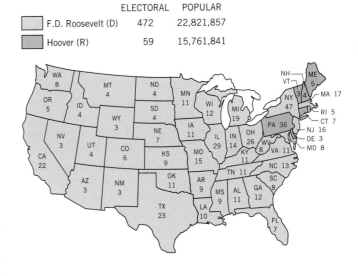

	ELECTORAL	POPULAR
F.D. Roosevelt (D)	472	22,821,857
Hoover (R)	59	15,761,841

Jennings Bryan captured the Democratic nomination for president and saw to it that the party adopted a Populist platform. The existing Populist party endorsed the Bryan candidacy. In the election anti-Bryan Democrats deserted the party in droves to support the Republican candidate, William McKinley. Once again a real issue divided the two parties: the Republicans stood for industry, business, hard

The 1896 election was a watershed in American politics—a "realigning election" that brought together new party coalitions. It pitted William McKinley, the Republican defender of the gold standard (left), against William Jennings Bryan, a fiery midwestern champion of strict religion and easy money (right).

money, protective tariffs, and urban interests; the Democrats for farmers, small towns, low tariffs, and rural interests. The Republicans won, carrying the cities, workers and businesspeople alike; the Democrats lost, carrying most of the southern and midwestern farm states. The old split between North and South that resulted from the Civil War was now replaced in part by an East versus West, city versus farm split.[4] It was not, however, only an economic cleavage—the Republicans had been able to appeal to Catholics and Lutherans, who disliked fundamentalism and its hostility toward liquor and immigrants.

This alignment persisted until 1932. Again change was triggered by an economic depression; again more than economic issues were involved. The New Deal coalition that emerged was based on bringing together into the Democratic party urban workers, northern blacks, southern whites, and Jewish voters. Unlike in 1860 and 1896, it was not preceded by any third-party movement; it occurred suddenly (though some groups had begun to shift their allegiance in 1928) and gathered momentum

throughout the 1930s. The Democrats, isolated since 1896 as a southern and midwestern sectional party, had now become the majority party by finding a candidate and a cause that could lure urban workers, blacks, and Jews away from the Republican party, where they had been for decades. It was obviously a delicate coalition—blacks and southern whites disagreed on practically everything except their liking for Roosevelt; Jews and the Irish bosses of the big-city machines also had little in common. But the federal government under Roosevelt was able to supply enough benefits to each of these disparate groups to keep them loyal members of the coalition and to provide a new basis for party identification.

These critical elections may have involved not converting existing voters to new party loyalties but recruiting into the dominant party new voters— young people just coming of voting age, immigrants just receiving their citizenship papers, and blacks just receiving, in some places, the right to vote. But there were also genuine conversions—northern blacks, for example, had been heavily Republican before Roosevelt but became heavily Democratic after his election.

In short an electoral realignment occurs when a new issue of utmost importance to the voters (slavery, the economy) cuts across existing party divisions and replaces old issues that were formerly the basis of party identification. Some observers have speculated that we are due for a new party realignment as the tensions within the New Deal coalition become more evident. As the memory of Roosevelt and the Great Depression fades and as new voters come of age, the ability of the Democrats to hold on to both people who are liberal and those who are conservative on social issues may decline.

Some people wondered whether the election of 1980, since it brought into power the most conservative administration in half a century, signaled a new realignment. Many of President Reagan's supporters began talking of their having a "mandate" to adopt major new policies in keeping with the views of the "new majority." But Reagan won in 1980 less because of what he stood for than because he was not Jimmy Carter, and he was reelected in 1984 primarily because people were satisfied with how the country was doing, especially economically.[5]

Just because we have had periods of one-party dominance in the past does not mean that we will have them in the future. Reagan's election could not have been a traditional realignment, because it left Congress in the hands of the Democratic party. Moreover, some scholars are beginning to question the theory of critical elections, or at least the theory that they occur with some regularity.

Nevertheless, one major change has occurred of late—the shift in the presidential voting patterns of the South. From 1972 through 1996 the South was more Republican than the nation as a whole. The proportion of white southerners describing themselves to pollsters as "strongly Democratic" fell from more than one-third in 1952 to about one-seventh in 1984. There has been a corresponding increase in "independents." As it turns out, southern white independents have voted overwhelmingly Republican in recent presidential elections.[6] If you lump independents together with the parties for which they actually vote, the party alignment among white southerners has gone from six-to-one Democratic in 1952 to about fifty-fifty Democrats and Republicans. If this continues, it will constitute a major realignment in a region of the country that is growing rapidly in population and political clout.

Franklin Roosevelt greets George Washington Carver at Tuskegee Institute in Alabama. Blacks had long voted Republican; during the New Deal they shifted to the Democratic party. This change was part of the political realignment that occurred in the elections of 1932 and 1936.

In general, however, the kind of dramatic realignment that occurred in the 1860s or after 1932 may not occur again, because party labels have lost their meaning for a growing number of voters. For these people politics may *de*align rather than *re*align.

Party Decline

The evidence that the parties are decaying, not realigning, is of several sorts. We have already noted that the proportion of people identifying with one or the other party declined between 1960 and 1980. Simultaneously, the proportion of those voting a **split ticket** (as opposed to a **straight ticket**) increased. Figure 7.2, for example, shows the steep increase in the percentage of congressional districts carried by one party for the presidency and by the other for Congress. Whereas in the 1940s one party would carry a given district for both its presidential and congressional candidates, today about a quarter of the districts split their votes between one party's presidential candidate and the other's congressional candidate.

In 1988 more than *half* of all House Democrats were elected in districts that voted for Republican George Bush as president. This ticket splitting was greatest in the South, but it was common everywhere. If every district that voted for Bush had also elected a Republican to Congress, the Republican party would have held a two-to-one majority in the

Figure 7.2 **Trends in Split-Ticket Voting for President and Congress, 1920–1996**

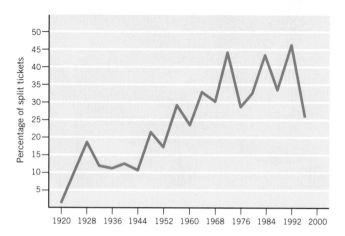

Note: The figure is the percentage of congressional districts carried by presidential and congressional candidates of different parties in each election year.

House of Representatives. Ticket splitting creates divided government—the White House and Congress are controlled by different parties (see Chapter 12). Ticket splitting helped the Democrats keep control of the House of Representatives from 1954 to 1994.

Ticket splitting was almost unheard-of in the nineteenth century, and for a very good reason. In those days the voter was either given a ballot by the party of his choice and he dropped it, intact, into the ballot box (thereby voting for everybody listed on the ballot), or he was given a government-printed ballot that listed in columns all the candidates of each party. All the voter had to do was mark the top of one column in order to vote for every candidate in that column. (When voting machines came along, they provided a single lever that, when pulled, cast votes for all the candidates of a particular party.) Progressives around the turn of the century began to persuade states to adopt the **office-bloc** (or "Massachusetts") **ballot** in place of the **party-column** (or "Indiana") **ballot.** The office-bloc ballot lists all candidates by office; there is no way to vote a straight party ticket by making one mark. Not surprisingly, states using the office-bloc ballot show much more ticket splitting than those without it.[7]

The National Party Structure Today

It would be a mistake, however, to conclude that parties have declined simply because many voters now split tickets in national elections. Despite many changes and challenges (see Figure 7.3), America's two-party system remains strong. In most elections—national, state, and local—voters registered as Democrats still vote for Democratic candidates, and voters registered as Republicans still vote for Republican candidates. In Congress, state legislatures, and city councils, members still normally vote along party lines. Local political machines have died, but, as we shall now explain, national party structures remain alive and well.

Since political parties exist at the national, state, and local levels, you might suppose that they are arranged like a big corporation, with a national board of directors giving orders to state managers, who in turn direct the activities of rank-and-file workers at the county and city level.

Nothing could be further from the truth. At each level a separate and almost entirely independent organization exists that does pretty much what it wants, and in many counties and cities there is virtually no organization at all.

On paper the national Democratic and Republican parties look quite similar. In both parties ultimate authority is in the hands of the **national convention** that meets every four years to nominate a presidential candidate. Between these conventions party affairs are managed by a **national committee,** made up of delegates from each state and territory. In Congress each party has a **congressional campaign committee** that helps members of Congress who are running for reelection or would-be members running for an open seat or challenging a candidate from the opposition party. The day-to-day work of the party is managed by a full-time, paid **national chairman,** who is elected by the committee.

For a long time the two national parties were alike in behavior as well as description. The national chairman, if his party held the White House, would help decide who among the party faithful would get federal jobs. Otherwise the parties did very little.

But beginning in the late 1960s and early 1970s the Republicans began to convert their national party into a well-financed, highly staffed organization devoted to finding and electing Republican candidates, especially to Congress. At about the same time, the Democrats began changing the rules governing how presidential candidates are nominated in ways that profoundly altered the distribution of power within the party. As a consequence the Republicans became a bureaucratized party and the Democrats became a factionalized one. After the Republicans won four out of five presidential elections from 1968 to 1984 and briefly took control of the Senate, the Democrats began to suspect that maybe an efficient bureaucracy was better than a collection of warring factions, and so they made an effort to emulate the Republicans.

What the Republicans had done was to take advantage of a new bit of technology—computerized mailings. They built up a huge file of names of people who had given or might give money to the party, usually in small amounts, and used that list to raise a big budget for the national party. In 1983 the Republican National Committee (RNC) raised $35 million from over 1.7 million individual donors; by the time of the 1994 election, the Republican party committees—the National Committee, the Senatorial Committee, and the Congressional Committee—had raised $246 million from 2.8 million donors. By the time of the 1999 election, the national Republican party had raised $132 million.

The RNC used this money to run, in effect, a national political consulting firm. Money went to recruit and train Republican candidates, give them legal and financial advice, study issues and analyze voting trends, and conduct national advertising campaigns on behalf of the party as a whole. No one can be sure how much political success this money bought (after all, the Republicans lost control of the Senate in 1986), but many observers believed that Republican losses in Congress in 1982 and 1986 would have been even greater if the RNC had not worked so vigorously on behalf of its candidates.

When the Democratic National Committee (DNC) decided to play catch-up, it followed the RNC strategy. Using the same computerized direct-mail techniques, the Democratic party committees—the National Committee, Senatorial Committee, and Congressional Committee—raised $131 million from 2.2 million contributors, about half of what the Republican equivalents had raised. This was a great improvement over what it had managed to do

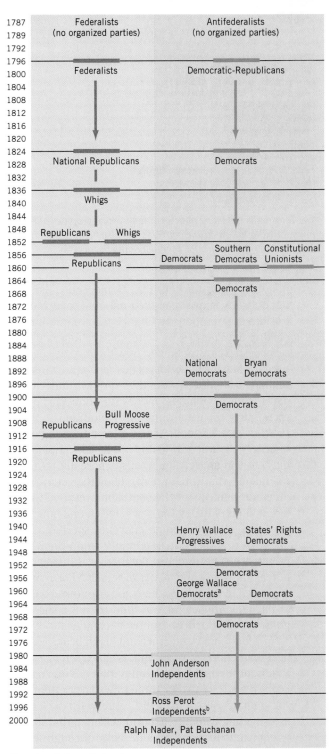

Figure 7.3 Cleavages and Continuity in the Two-Party System

[a]American Independent party.

[b]United We Stand America or Reform Party.

The Internet is the latest means through which people are becoming politically informed and active. It has also become an important way to raise money for candidates and parties.

just ten years earlier. The Democrats, like the Republicans, ship a lot of their national party money to state organizations to finance television ads supporting their parties. By doing this the national parties sidestep a restriction on how their money can be used. By law the national parties can spend only $12 million each directly on their presidential candidates. But by sending money to state parties to spend, they can get around this limitation.

A lot of RNC money goes to commission public opinion polls, not only to find out which candidate is likely to win an election but also, more importantly, to find out what issues are troubling the voters, how different segments of the population respond to different kinds of issues and news stories, and how people react to the campaign efforts of specific candidates. During the Reagan administration the RNC's principal pollster, Richard Wirthlin, was taking polls at least monthly and sometimes daily.[8] For reasons explained in Chapter 5, these polls can take you just so far; they are helpful, but they are not a sure-fire guide to public opinion or how to change it.

In 1996 both Democrats and Republicans redoubled their efforts to raise what is called *soft money*—that is, funds to aid parties (and their ads and polls). Both totals were two or three times larger than the soft money raised in 1992. Afterward a Senate investigating committee found evidence that illegal foreign contributions were funneled through intermediaries into both parties, that President Clinton

and Vice President Gore made many White House phone calls to raise funds, and that big donors were invited to spend the night in the White House's Lincoln Bedroom.

National Conventions

The national committee selects the time and place of the next national convention and issues a "call" for the convention that sets forth the number of delegates each state and territory is to have and also the rules under which delegates must be chosen. The number of delegates and their manner of selection can significantly influence the chances of various presidential candidates, and considerable attention is thus devoted to these matters. In the Democratic party, for example, a long struggle took place between those who wished to see southern states receive a large share of delegates to the convention, in recognition of their firm support of Democratic candidates in presidential elections, and those who preferred to see a larger share of delegates allotted to northern and western states, which, though less solidly Democratic, were larger or more liberal. A similar conflict within the Republican party has pitted conservative Republican leaders in the Midwest against liberal ones in the East.

A compromise formula is usually chosen; nevertheless, over the years these formulas have gradually changed, shifting voting strength in the Democratic convention away from the South and toward the North and West and in the Republican convention away from the East and toward the South and Southwest. These delegate allocation formulas are but one sign (others will be mentioned later in this chapter) of the tendency of the two parties' conventions to move in opposite ideological directions—Democrats more to the left, Republicans more to the right.

The exact formula for apportioning delegates is extremely complex. For the Democrats it takes into account the vote each state cast for Democratic candidates in past elections and the number of electoral votes of each state; for the Republicans it takes into account the number of representatives in Congress and whether the state in past elections cast its electoral votes for the Republican presidential candidate and elected Republicans to the Senate, the House, and the governorship. Thus the Democrats give extra delegates to large states while the Republicans give extra ones to loyal states.

No longer functioning as deliberate bodies, party conventions have become arenas for made-for-television hoopla.

The way in which delegates are chosen can be even more important than their allocation. The Democrats, beginning in 1972, have developed an elaborate set of rules designed to weaken the control over delegates by local party leaders and to increase the proportion of women, young people, African Americans, and Native Americans attending the convention. These rules were first drafted by a party commission chaired by Senator George McGovern (who was later to make skillful use of these new procedures in his successful bid for the Democratic presidential nomination). They were revised in 1974 by another commission, chaired by Barbara Mikulski, whose decisions were ratified by the 1974 midterm convention. After the 1976 election yet a third commission, chaired by Morley Winograd, produced still another revision of the rules, which took effect in 1980. Then a fourth commission, chaired by North Carolina governor James B. Hunt, recommended in 1981 yet another set of rules, which became effective with the 1984 convention.

The general thrust of the work of the first three rules commissions was to broaden the antiparty changes started by the progressives at the beginning of this century. Whereas the earlier reformers had tried to minimize the role of parties in the election process, those of the 1970s sought to weaken the influence of leaders within the party. In short the newer reforms were aimed at creating *intra*party democracy as well as *inter*party democracy. This was done by rules that, for the 1980 convention, required:

- Equal division of delegates between men and women
- Establishment of "goals" for the representation of African Americans, Hispanics, and other groups in proportion to their presence in a state's Democratic electorate
- Open delegate selection procedures, with advance publicity and written rules
- Selection of 75 percent of the delegates at the level of the congressional district or lower

T·R·I·V·I·A

Political Parties

First national political convention	Anti-Masonic party, 1831, in Baltimore
First time incumbent governors were nominated for president	Rutherford B. Hayes of Ohio, by Republicans in 1876 Samuel J. Tilden of New York, by Democrats in 1876
First African American to receive a vote at a national party convention	Frederick Douglass, at Republican convention in 1888
First year in which women attended conventions as delegates	1900 (one woman at both Democratic and Republican conventions)
Most ballots needed to choose a presidential nominee	103, by Democrats in 1924 to select John W. Davis
Closest vote in convention history	$543\frac{3}{20}$ to $542\frac{7}{20}$, defeating a motion to condemn the Ku Klux Klan at 1924 Democratic convention
First Catholic nominated for president by a major party	Al Smith, by Democrats in 1928
Only person nominated for president four times by a major political party	Franklin D. Roosevelt, by Democrats in 1932, 1936, 1940, and 1944
First presidential nominee to make an acceptance speech at the party convention	Franklin D. Roosevelt

- No "unit rule" that would require all delegates to vote with the majority of their state delegation
- Restrictions on the number of party leaders and elected officials who could vote at the convention
- A requirement that all delegates pledged to a candidate vote for that candidate

In 1981 the Hunt Commission changed some of these rules—in particular, the last two—in order to increase the influence of elected officials and to make the convention a somewhat more deliberative body. The commission reserved about 14 percent of the delegate seats for party leaders and elected offi-cials, who would not have to commit themselves in advance to a presidential candidate, and it repealed the rule requiring that delegates pledged to a candidate vote for that candidate.

Rules have consequences. Whereas in 1980 only one-seventh of the Democratic senators and represen-tatives got to be delegates to the national convention, in 1984 more than half were delegates. In the 1984 presidential primaries, Walter Mondale was the chief beneficiary of the delegate selection rules. He won the support of the overwhelming majority of elected offi-cials—the so-called **superdelegates**—and he did especially well in those states that held winner-take-all primaries. Had different rules been in effect (if, for example, the delegates had been allocated strictly in proportion to the primary votes that the candidates won), Mondale probably would not have entered the Democratic convention with an assured majority.

But the "reform" of the parties, especially the Democratic party, has had far more profound conse-quences than merely helping one candidate or another. Before 1968 the Republican party repre-sented, essentially, white-collar voters and the Democratic party represented blue-collar ones. After a decade of "reform" the Republican and the Democratic parties each represented two ideologi-cally different sets of upper-middle-class voters (see Table 7.1). In the terminology of Chapter 5, the Republicans came to represent the more conserva-tive wing of the traditional middle class and the Democrats the more leftist wing of the liberal middle class (or the "new class").

This was more troubling to the Democrats than to the Republicans, because the traditional middle class is somewhat closer to the opinions of most citi-zens than is the liberal middle class (and thus the Republican national convention more closely reflected public opinion than did the Democratic national convention). And for whatever reason, the Republicans won five out of six presidential races between 1968 and 1988.

Before the 1988 convention the Democrats took a long, hard look at their party procedures. Under the leadership of DNC chairman Paul Kirk, they decided against making any major changes, especially ones that would increase the power of grassroots activists at the expense of elected officials and party leaders. The number of such officials (or superdelegates) to be given delegate seats was increased. For example, 80 percent of the Democratic members of Congress

Table 7.1 Who Are the Party Delegates?

Characteristics of delegates to Democratic and Republican national conventions in 2000.

	Democrats	Republicans
Sex and Race		
Women	48%	35%
Blacks	19	4
Religion		
Protestant	47	63
Catholic	31	27
Jewish	8	2
Education		
College degree and beyond	74	77
Post graduate	49	46
Family Income		
Under $50,000	18	10
$100,000 and over	36	41
Belong to union	31	4
Born-again Christian	12	27
Gun owner in household	35	57

Source: New York Times (August 14, 2000): A17.

and all Democratic governors were automatically made convention delegates in 1988. The official status of some special-interest caucuses (such as those organized to represent African Americans, homosexuals, and various ethnic groups) was reduced in order to lessen the perception that the Democrats were simply a party of factions.

The surface harmony was a bit misleading, however, as some activists, notably supporters of Jesse Jackson, protested that the rules made it harder for candidates like Jackson to win delegates in proportion to their share of the primary vote. (In 1984 Jackson got 18 percent of the primary vote but only 12 percent of the delegates.) The DNC responded by changing the rules for the 1992 campaign. Former DNC chairman Ronald H. Brown (later President Clinton's secretary of commerce) won approval for three important requirements:

• The winner-reward systems of delegate distribution, which gave the winner of a primary or caucus extra delegates, were banned. (In 1988 fifteen states used winner-reward systems, including such vote-rich states as Florida, Illinois, New Jersey, and Pennsylvania.)

• The proportional representation system was put into use. This system divides a state's publicly elected delegates among candidates who receive at least 15 percent of the vote.

• States that violate the rules are now penalized with the loss of 25 percent of their national convention delegates.

Even though the Democrats have retreated a bit from the reforms of the 1960s and 1970s, the conventions of both parties have changed fundamentally, and probably permanently. Delegates once selected by party leaders are now chosen by primary elections and grassroots caucuses. As a result the national party conventions are no longer places where party leaders meet to bargain over the selection of their presidential candidates; they are instead places where delegates come together to ratify choices already made by party activists and primary voters.

Most Americans dislike bosses, deals, and manipulation and prefer democracy, reform, and openness. These are commendable instincts. But such instincts, unless carefully tested against practice, may mislead us into supposing that anything carried out in the name of reform is a good idea. Rules must be judged by their practical results as well as by their conformity to some principle of fairness. Rules affect the distribution of power: they help some people win and others lose. Later in this chapter we shall try to assess delegate selection rules by looking more closely at how they affect who attends conventions and which presidential candidates are selected there.

State and Local Parties

While the national party structures have changed, the grassroots organizations have withered. In between, state party systems have struggled to redefine their roles.

In every state there is a Democratic and a Republican state party organized under state law. Typically each consists of a state central committee, below which are found county committees and sometimes city, town, or even precinct committees. The members of these committees are chosen in a variety of ways—sometimes in primary elections, sometimes by conventions, sometimes by a building-block process whereby people elected to serve on precinct or town committees choose the members of county committees, who in turn choose state committee members.

Knowing these formal arrangements is much less helpful than knowing the actual distribution of power in each state party. In a few places strong party bosses handpick the members of these committees; in other places powerful elected officials—key state legislators, county sheriffs, or judges—control the committees. And in many places no one is in charge, so that either the party structure is largely meaningless or it is made up of the representatives of various local factions.

To understand how power is distributed in a party, we must first know what *incentives* motivate people in a particular state or locality to become active in a party organization. Different incentives lead to different ways of organizing parties.

The Machine

A **political machine** is a party organization that recruits its members by the use of tangible incentives—money, political jobs, an opportunity to get favors from government—and that is characterized by a high degree of leadership control over member activity. At one time many local party organizations were machines, and the struggle over political jobs—patronage—was the chief concern of their members. Though Tammany Hall in New York City began as a caucus of well-to-do notables in the local Democratic party, by the late nineteenth century it had become a machine organized on the basis of political clubs in each assembly district. These clubs were composed of party workers whose job it was to get out the straight party vote in their election districts and who hoped for a tangible reward if they were successful.

And there were abundant rewards to hope for. During the 1870s it was estimated that one out of every eight voters in New York City had a federal, state, or city job.[9] The federal bureaucracy was one important source of those jobs. The New York Customhouse alone employed thousands of people, virtually all of whom were replaced if their party lost the presidential election. The postal system was another source, and it was frankly recognized as such. When James N. Tyner became postmaster general in 1876, he was "appointed not to see that the mails were carried, but to see that Indiana was carried."[10] Elections and conventions were so frequent and the intensity of party competition so great that

being a party worker was for many a full-time paid occupation.

Well before the arrival of vast numbers of poor immigrants from Ireland, Italy, and elsewhere, old-stock Americans had perfected the machine, run up the cost of government, and systematized voting fraud. Kickbacks on contracts, payments extracted from officeholders, and funds raised from business-people made some politicians rich but also paid the huge bills of the elaborate party organization. When the immigrants began flooding the eastern cities, the party machines were there to provide them with all manner of services in exchange for their support at the polls: the machines were a vast welfare organization operating before the creation of the welfare state.

The abuses of the machine were well known and gradually curtailed. Stricter voter registration laws reduced fraud, civil service reforms cut down the number of patronage jobs, and competitive-bidding laws made it harder to award overpriced contracts to favored businesses. The Hatch Act (passed by Congress in 1939) made it illegal for federal civil service employees to take an active part in political management or political campaigns by serving as party officers, soliciting campaign funds, running for partisan office, working in a partisan campaign, endorsing partisan candidates, taking voters to the polls, counting ballots, circulating nominating petitions, or being delegates to a party convention. (They may still vote and make campaign contributions.)

These restrictions gradually took federal employees out of machine politics, but they did not end the machines. In many cities—Chicago, Philadelphia, and Albany—ways were found to maintain the machines even though city employees were technically under the civil service. Far more important than the various progressive reforms that weakened the machines were changes among voters. As voters grew in education, income, and sophistication, they depended less and less on the advice and leadership of local party officials. And as the federal government created a bureaucratic welfare system, the parties' welfare systems declined in value.

It is easy either to scorn the political party machine as a venal and self-serving organization or to romanticize it as an informal welfare system. In truth it was a little of both. Above all it was a frank recognition of the fact that politics requires organization; the machine was the supreme expression of the value of organization. Even allowing for voting

Ex-senator George Washington Plunkitt of Tammany Hall explains machine politics from atop the bootblack stand in front of the New York County Courthouse around 1905.

fraud, in elections where party machines were active, voter turnout was huge: more people participated in politics when mobilized by a party machine than when appealed to by television or good-government associations.[11] Moreover, because the party machines were interested in winning, they would subordinate any other consideration to that end. This has meant that the machines were usually willing to support the presidential candidate with the best chance of winning, regardless of his policy views (provided, of course, that he was not determined to wreck the machines once in office). Republican machines helped elect Abraham Lincoln as well as Warren G. Harding; Democratic machines were of crucial importance in electing Franklin D. Roosevelt and John F. Kennedy.

The old-style machine is almost extinct, though important examples still can be found in the Democratic organization in Cook County (Chicago) and the Republican organization in Nassau County (New York). But a new-style machine has emerged in a few places. It is a machine in the sense that it uses money to knit together many politicians, but it is new in that the money comes not from patronage and contracts but from campaign contributions supplied by wealthy individuals and the proceeds of direct-mail campaigns.

The political organization headed by Democratic congressmen Henry A. Waxman and Howard L. Berman on the west side of Los Angeles is one such new-style machine. By the astute use of campaign funds, the "Waxman-Berman organization" builds loyalties to it among a variety of elected officials at all levels of government. Moreover, this new-style machine, unlike the old ones, has a strong interest in issues, especially at the national level. In this sense it is not a machine at all, but a cross between a machine and an ideological party.

Ideological Parties

At the opposite extreme from the machine is the **ideological party.** Where the machine values winning above all else, the ideological party values principle above all else. Where the former depends on money incentives, the latter spurns them. Where the former is hierarchical and disciplined, the latter is usually contentious and factionalized.

The most firmly ideological parties have been independent "third parties," such as the Socialist, Socialist Workers, Libertarian, and Right-to-Life parties. But there have been ideological factions within the Democratic and Republican parties as well, and in some places these ideological groups have taken over the regular parties.

In the 1950s and 1960s these ideological groups were "reform clubs" within local Democratic and Republican parties. In Los Angeles, New York, and many parts of Wisconsin and Minnesota issue-oriented activists fought to take over the party from election-oriented regulars. Democratic reform clubs managed to defeat the head of Tammany Hall in Manhattan; similar activist groups became the dominant force in California state politics.[12] Democratic club leaders were more liberal than rank-and-file Democrats, and Republican club leaders were often more conservative than rank-and-file Republicans.

The 1960s and 1970s saw these "reform" movements replaced by more focused social movements. The "reform" movement was based on a generalized sense of liberalism (among Democrats) or conservatism (among Republicans). With the advent of social movements concerned with civil rights, peace, feminism, environmentalism, libertarianism, and abortion, the generalized ideology of the clubs was replaced by the specific ideological demands of single-issue activists.

The result is that in many places the party has become a collection of people drawn from various social movements. For a candidate to win the party's support, he or she often has to satisfy the "litmus test" demands of the ideological activists in the party. Democratic senator Barbara Mikulski put it this way: "The social movements are now our farm clubs."

With social movements as their farm clubs, the big-league teams—the Democrats and Republicans at the state level—behave very differently than they did when political machines were the farm clubs. Internal factionalism is more intense, and the freedom of action of the party leader (say, the chairperson of the state committee) has been greatly reduced. A leader who demands too little or gives up too much, or who says the wrong thing on a key issue, is quickly accused of having "sold out." Under these circumstances many "leaders" are that in name only.

Solidary Groups

Many people who participate in state and local politics do so not in order to earn money or vindicate some cause, but simply because they find it fun. They enjoy the game, they meet interesting people, and they like the sense of being "in the know" and rubbing shoulders with the powerful. When people get together out of gregarious or game-loving instincts, we say that they are responding to **solidary incentives;** if they form an organization, it is a solidary association.

Some of these associations were once machines. When a machine loses its patronage, some of its members—especially the older ones—may continue to serve in the organization out of a desire for camaraderie. In other cases precinct, ward, and district committees are built up on the basis of friendship networks. One study of political activists in Detroit found that most of them mentioned friendships and a liking for politics, rather than an interest in issues, as their reasons for joining the party organization.[13] Members of ward and town organizations in St. Louis County gave the same answers when asked why they joined.[14] Since patronage has declined in value and since the appeals of ideology are limited to a minority of citizens, the motivations for participating in politics have become very much like those for joining a bowling league or a bridge club.

The advantage of such groups is that they are neither corrupt nor inflexible; the disadvantage is that they often do not work very hard. Knocking on doors on a rainy November evening to try to talk people into voting for your candidate is a chore under the best of circumstances; it is especially unappealing if you joined the party primarily because you like to attend meetings or drink coffee with your friends.[15]

Sponsored Parties

Sometimes a relatively strong party organization can be created among volunteers without heavy reliance on money or ideology and without depending entirely on people's finding the work fun. This type of **sponsored party** occurs when another organization exists in the community that can create, or at least sponsor, a local party structure. The clearest example of this is the Democratic party in and around Detroit, which has been developed, led, and to a degree financed by the political-action arm of the United Auto Workers union. The UAW has had a long tradition of rank-and-file activism, stemming from its formative struggles in the 1930s, and since the city is virtually a one-industry town, it was not hard to transfer some of this activism from union organizing to voter organizing.

By the mid-1950s union members and leaders made up over three-fourths of all the Democratic

The personal following of former President George Bush was passed on to his sons, George W. (left) and Jeb (right), both of whom became governors of large states, and the former of whom is now president.

party district leaders within the city.[16] On election day union funds were available for paying workers to canvass voters; between elections political work on an unpaid basis was expected of union leaders. Though the UAW-Democratic party alliance in Detroit has not always been successful in city elections (the city is nonpartisan), it has been quite successful in carrying the city for the Democratic party in state and national elections.

Not many areas have organizations as effective or as dominant as the UAW that can bolster, sponsor, or even take over the weak formal party structure. Thus sponsored local parties are not common in the United States.

Personal Following

Because most candidates can no longer count on the backing of a machine, because sponsored parties are limited to a few unionized areas, and because solidary groups are not always productive, a person wanting to get elected will often try to form a **personal following** that will work for him or her during a campaign and then disband until the next election rolls around. Sometimes a candidate tries to meld a personal following with an ideological group, especially during the primary election campaign, when candidates need the kind of financial backing and hard work that only highly motivated activists are likely to supply.

To form a personal following, the candidate must have an appealing personality, a lot of friends, or a

big bank account. The Kennedy family has all three, and the electoral success of the personal followings of John F. Kennedy, Edward M. Kennedy, Robert Kennedy, and Joseph P. Kennedy II are legendary. President George Bush also established such a following. After he left office, one son (Jeb) became governor of Florida and another one (George W.) became governor of Texas and forty-third president of the United States.

Southern politicians who have to operate in one-party states with few, if any, machines have become grand masters at building personal followings, such as those of the Talmadge family in Georgia, the Long family in Louisiana, and the Byrd family in Virginia. But the strategy is increasingly followed wherever party organization is weak. The key asset is to have a known political name. That has helped the electoral victories of the son of Hubert Humphrey in Minnesota, the son and daughter of Pat Brown in California, the son of Birch Bayh in Indiana, the son of George Wallace in Alabama, and the son and grandson of Robert La Follette in Wisconsin.

The traditional party organization—one that is hierarchical, lasting, based on material incentives, and capable of influencing who gets nominated for office—exists today, according to political scientist David Mayhew, in only about eight states, mostly the older states of the Northeast. Another five states, he feels, have faction-ridden versions of the traditional party organization.[17] The states in the rest of the country display the weak party system of solidary clubs, personal followings, ideological groups, and sponsored parties. What that means can be seen in the composition of Democratic national conventions. More than half of the delegates have been drawn from the ranks of the AFL-CIO, the National Education Association, and the National Organization for Women.[18]

The Two-Party System

With so many different varieties of local party organizations (or nonorganizations), and with such a great range of opinion found within each party, it is remarkable that we have had only two major political parties for most of our history. In the world at large a **two-party system** is a rarity; by one estimate only fifteen nations have one.[19] Most European democracies are multiparty systems. We have only two parties with any chance of winning nationally, and these parties have been, over time, rather evenly balanced—between 1888 and 2000, the Republicans won sixteen presidential elections and the Democrats thirteen. Furthermore, whenever one party has achieved a temporary ascendancy and its rival has been pronounced dead (as were the Democrats in the first third of this century and the Republicans during the 1930s and the 1960s), the "dead" party has displayed remarkable powers of recuperation, coming back to win important victories.

At the state and congressional district levels, however, the parties are not evenly balanced. For a long time the South was so heavily Democratic at all levels of government as to be a one-party area, while upper New England and the Dakotas were strongly Republican. All regions are more competitive today than once was the case, but even now one party tends to enjoy a substantial advantage in at least half the states and in perhaps two-thirds of the congressional districts. Nevertheless, though the parties are not as competitive in state elections as they are in presidential ones, states have rarely had, at least for any extended period, political parties other than the Democratic and Republican (see Table 7.2).

Scholars do not entirely agree on why the two-party system should be so permanent a feature of American political life, but two explanations are of major importance. The first has to do with the system of elections, the second with the distribution of public opinion.

Table 7.2   The Rise of Republican Politics in the South, 1956–2002

Year	Number of Representatives		Number of Senators		Number of Governors		Number of States Voting for Presidential Nominee	
	Dem.	Rep.	Dem.	Rep.	Dem.	Rep.	Dem.	Rep.
1956	99	7	22	0	11	0	6	5
1958	99	7	22	0	11	0	—	—
1960	99	7	22	0	11	0	8[a]	2
1962	95	11	21	1	11	0	—	—
1964	89	17	21	1	11	0	6	5
1966	83	23	19	3	9	2	—	—
1968	80	26	18	4	9	2	1	5[b]
1970	79	27	16 (1)[c]	5	9	2	—	—
1972	74	34	14 (1)[c]	7	8	3	0	11
1974	81	27	15 (1)[c]	6	8	3	—	—
1976	82	26	16 (1)[c]	5	9	2	10	1
1978	77	31	15 (1)[c]	6	8	3	—	—
1980	55	53	11 (1)[c]	10	6	5	1	10
1982	80	33	11	11	11	0	—	—
1984	72	41	11	11	10	1	0	11
1986	77	39	16	6	6	5	—	—
1988	80	36	15	7	6	5	0	11
1990	77	39	15	7	8	3	—	—
1992	82	43	14	8	8	3	4	7
1994	61	64	9	13	5	6	—	—
1996	54	71	9	13	4	7	4	7
1998	54	71	8	14	4	7	—	—
2000	54	71	7	15	6	5	0	11
2002	86(1)[d]	64	8	14	6	5	—	—

[a]Eight Mississippi electors voted for Harry Byrd.

[b]George Wallace won five states on the American Independent ticket.

[c]Harry Byrd, Jr., was elected in Virginia in 1970 and 1976 as an independent.

[d]Virgil H. Goode, Jr., was elected in Virginia in 1996 as an independent.

Elections at every level of government are based on the plurality, winner-take-all method. The **plurality system** means that in all elections for representative, senator, governor, or president, and in almost all elections for state legislator, mayor, or city councillor, the winner is that person who gets the *most* votes, even if he or she does not get a *majority* of all votes cast. We are so familiar with this system that we sometimes forget that there are other ways of running an election. For example, one could require that the winner get a majority of the votes, thus producing runoff elections if nobody got a majority on the first try. France does this in choosing its national legislature. In the first election candidates for parliament who win an absolute majority of the votes cast are declared elected. A week later remaining candidates who received at least one-eighth but less than one-half of the vote go into a runoff election; those who then win an absolute majority are also declared elected.

The French method encourages many political parties to form, each hoping to win at least one-eighth of the vote in the first election and then to enter into an alliance with its ideologically nearest rival in order to win the runoff. In the United States the plurality system means that a party must make all the alliances it can before the first election—there is no second chance. Hence every party must be as broadly based as possible; a narrow, minor party has no hope of winning.

The winner-take-all feature of American elections has the same effect. Only one member of Congress is elected from each district. In many European countries the elections are based on proportional representation. Each party submits a list of candidates for parliament, ranked in order of preference by the party leaders. The nation votes. A party winning 37 percent of the vote gets 37 percent of the seats in parliament; a party winning 2 percent of the vote gets 2 percent of the seats. Since even the smallest parties have a chance of winning something, minor parties have an incentive to organize.

The most dramatic example of the winner-take-all principle is the electoral college (see Chapter 12, page 334). In every state but Maine and Nebraska, the candidate who wins the most popular votes in a state wins *all* of that state's electoral votes. In 1992, for example, Bill Clinton won only 45 percent of the popular vote in Missouri, but he got all of Missouri's eleven electoral votes because his two rivals (George Bush and Ross Perot) each got fewer popular votes. Minor parties cannot compete under this system. Voters are often reluctant to "waste" their votes on a minor-party candidate who cannot win.

The United States has experimented with other electoral systems. Proportional representation was used for municipal elections in New York City at one time and is still in use for that purpose in Cambridge, Massachusetts. Many states have elected more than one state legislator from each district. In Illinois, for example, three legislators have been elected from each district, with each voter allowed to cast two votes, thus virtually guaranteeing that the minority party will be able to win one of the three seats. But none of these experiments has altered the national two-party system, probably because of the existence of a directly elected president chosen by a winner-take-all electoral college.

The presidency is the great prize of American politics; to win it you must form a party with as broad appeal as possible. As a practical matter that means there will be, in most cases, only two serious parties—one made up of those who support the party already in power, and the other made up of everybody else. Only one third party ever won the presidency—the Republicans in 1860—and it had by then pretty much supplanted the Whig party. No third party is likely to win, or even come close to winning, the presidency anytime soon. Despite the decline in mass party attachment, among Americans who actually vote in presidential elections, party voting is almost as strong today as it was in the early 1950s. As Table 7.3 shows, in the presidential elections of 1984 through 2000, the vast majority of Democrats voted for the Democrat, and the vast majority of Republicans voted for the Republican. Meanwhile, most independents voted for the winning Republican in 1984, 1988, and 2000, and pluralities of independents voted for the winning Democrat in 1992 and 1996.

The second explanation for the persistence of the two-party system is to be found in the opinions of the voters. There remains a kind of rough parity between the two parties regarding which of them most citizens think is likely to govern best on given issues. For example, in public opinion surveys conducted in 1997 and 1998, respondents favored the Republicans over the Democrats on national defense and crime, favored the Democrats over the Republicans on poverty and the environment, and

Table 7.3   Party Voting in Presidential Elections

Party Affiliation of Voter	1984 Dem.	1984 Rep.	1988 Dem.	1988 Rep.	1992 Dem.	1992 Rep.	1992 Ind.	1996 Dem.	1996 Rep.	1996 Ind.	2000 Dem.	2000 Rep.	2000 Ind.
Democrat	79%	21%	85%	15%	82%	8%	10%	84%	10%	5%	85%	10%	3%
Republican	4	96	7	93	7	77	16	13	80	6	7	91	1
Independent	33	67	43	57	39	30	31	43	35	17	37	42	9

Source: Gallup poll, as reported in Harold W. Stanley and Richard G. Niemi, *Vital Statistics on American Politics,* 6th ed. (Washington, D.C.:Congressional Quarterly Press, 1998), 128; and data for 2000 compiled by Lia Fantuzzo.

were split evenly between the two parties on taxes and economic prosperity (see Table 7.4).

Though there have been periods of bitter dissent, most of the time most citizens have agreed enough to permit them to come together into two broad coalitions. There has not been a massive and persistent body of opinion that has rejected the prevailing economic system (and thus we have not had a Marxist party with mass appeal); there has not been

Table 7.4   The Public Rates the Two Parties

Question
Do you think the Republican party or the Democratic party would do a better job of dealing with each of the following issues and problems?

	Democrats	Republicans
Advantage Republicans		
National defense*	37%	53%
Foreign trade	35	48
Crime	36	43
Campaign finance reform	31	37
Split Between the Parties		
Economic prosperity	44	42
Taxes	43	42
Advantage Democrats		
Poverty*	61	27
Environment	54	31
Health care	51	34
Social Security	46	35

*Question on this item asked as "Which party, the Democrats or the Republicans, do you trust to do a better job on . . . ?"

Source: The Public Perspective (April/May 1998): 13, reporting the results of a survey by the Gallup Organization for CNN/*USA Today,* October 27–28, 1997, and a survey by ABC News/*Washington Post,* January 15–19, 1998.

in our history an aristocracy or monarchy (and thus there has been no party that has sought to restore aristocrats or monarchs to power). Churches and religion have almost always been regarded as matters of private choice that lie outside politics (and thus there has not been a party seeking to create or abolish special government privileges for one church or another). In some European nations the organization of the economy, the prerogatives of the monarchy, and the role of the church have been major issues with long and bloody histories. So divisive have these issues been that they have helped prevent the formation of broad coalition parties.

But Americans have had other deep divisions—between white and black, for example, and between North and South—and yet the two-party system has endured. This suggests that our electoral procedures are of great importance—the winner-take-all, plurality election rules have made it useless for anyone to attempt to create an all-white or an all-black national party except as an act of momentary defiance or in the hope of taking enough votes away from the two major parties to force the presidential election into the House of Representatives. (That may have been George Wallace's strategy in 1968.)

For many years there was an additional reason for the two-party system: the laws of many states made it difficult, if not impossible, for third parties to get on the ballot. In 1968, for example, the American Independent party of George Wallace found that it would have to collect 433,000 signatures (15 percent of the votes cast in the last statewide election) in order to get on the presidential ballot in Ohio. Wallace took the issue to the Supreme Court, which ruled, six to three, that such a restriction was an unconstitutional violation of the equal-protection clause of the Fourteenth Amendment.[20]

Types of Minor Parties

Ideological parties: Parties professing a comprehensive view of American society and government that is radically different from that of the established parties. Most have been Marxist in outlook, but some are quite the opposite, such as the Libertarian party.

Examples:
Socialist party (1901 to 1960s)
Socialist Labor party (1888 to present)
Socialist Workers party (1938 to present)
Communist party (1920s to present)
Libertarian party (1972 to present)
Green party (1984 to present)

One-issue parties: Parties seeking a single policy, usually revealed by their names, and avoiding other issues.

Examples:
Free-Soil party—to prevent the spread of slavery (1848–1852)
American or "Know-Nothing" party—to oppose immigration and Catholics (1856)
Prohibition party—to ban the sale of liquor (1869 to present)
Woman's party—to obtain the right to vote for women (1913–1920)

Economic-protest parties: Parties, usually based in a particular region, especially involving farmers, that protest against depressed economic conditions. These tend to disappear as conditions improve.

Examples:
Greenback party (1876–1884)
Populist party (1892–1908)

Factional parties: Parties that are created by a split in a major party, usually over the identity and philosophy of the major party's presidential candidate.

Examples:
Split off from the Republican party:
   "Bull Moose" Progressive party (1912)
   La Follette Progressive party (1924)
Split off from the Democratic party:
   States' Rights ("Dixiecrat") party (1948)
   Henry Wallace Progressive party (1948)
   American Independent (George Wallace) party (1968)
Split off from both Democrats and Republicans:
   Reform party (Ross Perot)

Wallace got on the ballot. In 1980 John Anderson, running as an independent, was able to get on the ballot in all fifty states; in 1992 Ross Perot did the same. But for the reasons already indicated, the two-party system will probably persist even without the aid of legal restrictions.

Minor Parties

The electoral system may prevent minor parties from winning, but it does not prevent them from forming. Minor parties—usually called, erroneously, "third parties"—have been a permanent feature of American political life. Four major kinds of minor parties, with examples of each, are described in the box above.

The minor parties that have endured have been the ideological ones. Their members feel themselves to be outside the mainstream of American political life and sometimes, as in the case of various Marxist parties, look forward to a time when a revolution or some other dramatic change in the political system will vindicate them. They are usually not interested in immediate electoral success and thus persist despite their poor showing at the polls. One such party, however, the Socialist party of Eugene Debs, won nearly 6 percent of the popular vote in the 1912 presidential election and during its heyday elected some twelve hundred candidates to local offices, including seventy-nine mayors. Part of the Socialist appeal arose from its opposition to municipal corruption, part from its opposition to American entry into World War I, and part from its critique of

The Socialist party and the Progressive party were both minor parties, but their origins were different. The Socialist party was an ideological party; the "Bull Moose" Progressive party split off from the Republicans to support Theodore Roosevelt.

American society. No ideological party has ever carried a state in a presidential election.

Apart from the Republicans, who quickly became a major party, the only minor parties to carry states and thus win electoral votes were one party of economic protest (the Populists, who carried five states in 1892) and several factional parties (most recently, the States' Rights Democrats in 1948 and the American Independent party of George Wallace in 1968). Though factional parties may hope to cause the defeat of the party from which they split, they have not always been able to achieve this. Harry Truman was elected in 1948 despite the defections of both the leftist progressives, led by Henry Wallace, and the right-wing Dixiecrats, led by J. Strom Thurmond. In 1968 it seems likely that Hubert Humphrey would have lost even if George Wallace had not been in the race (Wallace voters would probably have switched to Nixon rather than to Humphrey, though of course one cannot be certain). It is quite possible, on the other hand, that a Republican might have beaten Woodrow Wilson in 1912 if the Republican party had not split in two (the regulars supporting William Howard Taft, the progressives supporting Theodore Roosevelt).

What is striking is not that we have had so many minor parties but that we have not had more. There have been several major political movements that did not produce a significant third party: the civil rights movement of the 1960s, the antiwar movement of the same decade, and, most important, the labor movement of the twentieth century. African Americans were part of the Republican party after the Civil War and part of the Democratic party after the New Deal (even though the southern wing of that party for a long time kept them from voting). The antiwar movement found candidates with whom it could identify within the Democratic party (Eugene McCarthy, Robert F. Kennedy, George McGovern), even though it was a Democratic president, Lyndon

B. Johnson, who was chiefly responsible for the U.S. commitment in Vietnam. After Johnson only narrowly won the 1968 New Hampshire primary, he withdrew from the race. Unions have not tried to create a labor party—indeed, they were for a long time opposed to almost any kind of national political activity. Since labor became a major political force in the 1930s, the largest industrial unions have been content to operate as a part (a very large part) of the Democratic party.

One reason why some potential sources of minor parties never formed such parties, in addition to the dim chance of success, is that the direct primary and the national convention have made it possible for dissident elements of a major party, unless they become completely disaffected, to remain in the party and influence the choice of candidates and policies. The antiwar movement had a profound effect on the Democratic conventions of 1968 and 1972; African Americans have played a growing role in the Democratic party, especially with the candidacy of Jesse Jackson in 1984 and 1988; only in 1972 did the unions feel that the Democrats nominated a presidential candidate (McGovern) unacceptable to them.

The impact of minor parties on American politics is hard to judge. One bit of conventional wisdom holds that minor parties develop ideas that the major parties later come to adopt. The Socialist party, for example, is supposed to have called for major social and economic policies that the Democrats under Roosevelt later embraced and termed the New Deal. It is possible that the Democrats did steal the thunder of the Socialists, but it hardly seems likely that they did it because the Socialists had proposed these things or proved them popular. (In 1932 the Socialists got only 2 percent of the vote and in 1936 less than one-half of 1 percent.) Roosevelt probably adopted the policies he did in part because he thought them correct and in part because dissident elements within his *own* party—leaders such as Huey Long of Louisiana—were threatening to bolt the Democratic party if it did not move to the left. Even Prohibition was adopted more as a result of the efforts of interest groups such as the Anti-Saloon League than as the consequence of its endorsement by the Prohibition party.

The minor parties that have probably had the greatest influence on public policy have been the factional parties. Mugwumps and liberal Republicans, by bolting the regular party, may have made that party more sensitive to the issue of civil service

Ralph Nader campaigned in 2000 as a candidate of the Green party.

reform; the Bull Moose and La Follette Progressive parties probably helped encourage the major parties to pay more attention to issues of business regulation and party reform; the Dixiecrat and Wallace movements probably strengthened the hands of those who wished to go slow on desegregation. The threat of a factional split is a risk that both major parties must face, and it is in the efforts that each makes to avoid such splits that one finds the greatest impact, at least in this century, of minor parties.

In 1992 and again in 1996, Ross Perot led the most successful recent third-party movement. It began as United We Stand America and was later renamed the Reform party. Perot's appeal seemed to reflect a growing American dissatisfaction with the existing political parties and a heightened demand for bringing in a leader who would "run the government without politics." Of course it is no more possible to take politics out of governing than it is to take churches out of religion. Though unrealistic, people seem to want policies without bargaining.

Nominating a President

The major parties face, as we have seen, two contrary forces: one, generated by the desire to win the presidency, pushes them in the direction of nominating a candidate who can appeal to the majority of voters and who will thus have essentially middle-of-the-road views. The other, produced by the need to keep dissident elements in the party from bolting and forming a third party, leads them to compromise with dissidents or extremists in ways that may damage the party's standing with the voters.

The Democrats and Republicans have always faced these conflicting pressures, but of late they have become especially acute. When the presidential nomination was made by a party convention that was heavily influenced, if not controlled, by party leaders and elected officials, it was relatively easy to ignore dissident factions and pick candidates on the basis of who could win. The *electoral* objectives of the party were predominant. The result was that often a faction left the party and ran a separate ticket—as in 1912, 1924, 1948, 1968, and 1980. Today the power of party leaders and elected officials within the parties is greatly diminished, with most delegates now selected by primary elections. A larger proportion of the delegates is likely to be more interested in issues and to be less amenable to compromise over those issues than formerly. In these circumstances the *policy* interests of the party activists are likely to be important.

Are the Delegates Representative of the Voters?

There would be no conflict between the electoral and policy interests of a political party if the delegates to its nominating convention had the same policy views as most voters, or at least as most party supporters. In fact this is not the case: in parties, as in many organizations, the activists and leaders tend to have views different from those of the rank and file.[21] In American political parties in recent years this difference has become very great.

In 1964 the Republican party nominated the highly conservative Barry Goldwater for president. We have no opinion data for delegates to that convention as detailed and comprehensive as those available for subsequent conventions, but it seems clear that the Republican delegates selected as their nominee a person who was not the most popular candidate among voters at large and thus not the candidate most likely to win.

At every Democratic national convention since 1972 the delegates have had views on a variety of important issues that were vastly different from those of rank-and-file Democrats. On welfare, military policy, school desegregation, crime, and abortion, Democratic delegates expressed opinions almost diametrically opposed to those of most Democrats. The delegates to the 1980, 1984, and (to a lesser extent) 1988, 1992, and 1996 conventions were ideological-

ly very different from the voters at large. The Democratic delegates were more liberal than the Democratic voters, and the Republican delegates were more conservative than the Republican voters (see Table 7.5).[22]

What accounts for the sharp disparity between delegate opinion (and often delegate candidate preference) and voter attitudes? Some blame the discrepancy on the rules, described earlier in this chapter, under which Democratic delegates are chosen, especially those that require increased representation for women, minorities, and the young. Close examination suggests that this is not a complete explanation. For one thing, it does not explain why the Republicans nominated Goldwater in 1964 (and almost nominated Ronald Reagan instead of Gerald Ford in 1976). For another, women, minorities, and youth have among them all shades of opinions: there are many middle-of-the-road women and young people, as well as very liberal or very conservative ones. (There are not many very conservative African Americans, at least on race issues, but there are certainly plenty who are moderate on race and conservative on other issues.) The question is why only *certain* elements of these groups are heavily represented at the conventions.

Who Votes in Primaries?

Maybe delegates are unrepresentative of the party rank and file because they are chosen in caucuses and primary elections whose participants are unrepresentative. Before 1972 most delegates were picked by party leaders; primaries were relatively unimportant, and voter caucuses were almost unheard-of.

Table 7.5   How Party Delegates and Party Voters Differ in Liberal Ideology

Liberal Ideology	1984	1988	1992	1996
Democrats				
Delegates	66%	39%	47%	43%
Voters	31	25	28	27
Republicans				
Delegates	2	1	1	0
Voters	15	12	12	7

Sources: For 1984: *Los Angeles Times* (August 19, 1984); for 1988: *New York Times*/CBS News poll, in *New York Times* (August 14, 1988); for 1992: *New York Times* (July 13 and August 17, 1992) and unpublished CBS News poll, "The 1992 Republican Convention Delegates"; for 1996: *New York Times* (August 12 and 26, 1996).

Adlai Stevenson in 1952 and Hubert Humphrey in 1968 won the Democratic presidential nominations without even entering a primary. Harry Truman once described primaries as "eyewash."[23]

After 1972 they were no longer eyewash. The vast majority of delegates were selected in primaries and caucuses. In 1992 forty states and territories held primaries, and twenty held caucuses (some places had both primaries and caucuses).

Only about half as many people vote in primaries as in general elections. If these primary voters have more extreme political views than do the rank-and-file party followers, then they might support presidential delegates who also have extreme views. However, there is not much evidence that such is the case. Studies comparing the ideological orientations of primary voters with those of rank-and-file party voters show few strong differences.[24]

When it comes to presidential primaries, a good fight draws a crowd. For example, in twelve of the first eighteen Republican presidential primaries in 2000, voter turnout hit record highs as Governor George W. Bush battled state by state to stay ahead of Senator John McCain. But the "crowd" represented only 13.6 percent of the voting-age population, up 4.3 percent from the 1996 turnout, and the highest since Senator Barry Goldwater's campaign for the nomination divided Republicans in 1964.[25] In the states that voted after Bush had the nomination all but won, turnout was considerably lower. Likewise, the contest between Vice President Al Gore and Senator Bill Bradley resulted in the second-lowest Democratic presidential primary turnout since 1960.

Primaries differ from caucuses. A **caucus** is a meeting of party followers, often lasting for hours and held in the dead of winter in a schoolhouse miles from home, in which party delegates are picked. Only the most dedicated partisans attend. For the Democrats these have been liberals; for the Republicans conservatives. In 1988 the most liberal Democratic candidate, Jesse Jackson, got more delegates in the Alaska, Delaware, Michigan, and Vermont caucuses than did Michael Dukakis, the eventual nominee. Republican evangelist Pat Robertson did not win any primary, but he won the caucuses in Alaska, Hawaii, and Washington.

Who Are the New Delegates?

However delegates are chosen, they are a different breed today than they once were. Whether picked by caucuses or primaries, and whatever their sex and race, a far larger proportion of convention delegates, both Republican and Democratic, are issue-oriented activists—people with an "amateur" or "purist" view of politics. Far fewer delegates are in it for the money (there is no longer much patronage to pass around) or to help their own reelection prospects. For example, in 1980 only 14 percent of the Democratic senators and 15 percent of the Democratic members of the House were delegates to the national convention. In 1956, by contrast, 90 percent of the senators and 33 percent of the representatives were delegates.[26] Party activists, especially those who work without pay and who are in politics out of an interest in issues, are not likely to resemble the average citizen, for whom politics is merely an object of observation, discussion, and occasional voting.

The changing incentives for participation in party work, in addition to the effects of the primary system, have contributed to the development of a national presidential nominating system different from that which once existed. The advantage of the new system is that it increases the opportunity for those with strong policy preferences to play a role in the party and thus reduces the chance that they will bolt the party and form a factional minor party. The disadvantage of the system is that it increases the chances that one or both parties may nominate presidential candidates who are not appealing to the average voter or even to a party's rank and file.

In sum, presidential nominating conventions are now heavily influenced by ideologically motivated activists. Democratic conventions have heavy representation from organized feminists, unionized schoolteachers, and abortion rights activists; Republican conventions have large numbers of antiabortion activists, Christian conservatives, and small-government libertarians. As a result the presidential nominating system is now fundamentally different from what it was as late as the mid-1960s.

Parties Versus Voters

Since 1968 the Democratic party has had no trouble winning congressional elections but great difficulty winning presidential contests. Except for 1980–1986 and since 1994, the Democrats have controlled both houses of Congress; except for 1976, 1992, and 1996, they have lost every presidential election. The

Republican party has had the opposite problem: though it won five out of seven presidential elections between 1968 and 1992, it did not control Congress for the forty years preceding its big win in 1994.

There are many reasons for this odd state of affairs, most of which will be discussed later. But one requires attention here. The difficulty the Democrats have had in competing for the presidency is in part because their candidates for the presidency have had, on certain issues—chiefly social and taxation issues—views very different from those of the average voter. That disparity to a large degree mirrors (and may be caused by) the gulf that separates the opinions of delegates to Democratic nominating conventions from the opinions of most citizens.

The Republicans have not been immune to this problem. In 1964 they nominated a candidate, Barry Goldwater, whose beliefs placed him well to the right of most voters. Not surprisingly, he lost. And the delegates to recent Republican conventions have held opinions on some matters that continue to be very different from most people's. Still, the problem has been more acute for the Democrats.

The problem can be seen in Table 7.6. A lot of information is shown there; to understand it, study the table step by step. First, look at the middle column, which summarizes the views of voters in 2000. (Because there are about the same number of Democratic and Republican voters, the opinion of the average voter is about halfway between those of the followers of the two parties.) Now look at the columns on the far left and the far right. These show the views of delegates to the 2000 Democratic and Republican conventions. On almost every issue the delegates are in sharp disagreement. There were hardly any conservatives at the Democratic convention or liberals at the Republican convention. On every social issue and every tax or spending issue, the delegates were at opposite ends of the spectrum.

Still, either party can win if its delegates nominate a candidate whose views put him or her closer to the average citizen than to the average delegate or if the campaign is fought out over issues on which the delegates and the voters agree. For example, if the election turned on what to do about an economic recession, the delegates, the voters, and the candidate would probably all agree: do whatever is necessary to end the recession. Exactly that happened in 1992, and the Democrats won.

Of course, even without a scandal, recession, or some other unifying issue, the need to win an election will lead all candidates to move toward the middle of the road. That is where the votes are. But this creates a dilemma for a candidate of either party. The stance one takes to win support from party activists in the caucuses and primaries will often be quite different from the stance one should take to win votes from the general public. In the next chapter we shall look more closely at how politicians try to cope with that dilemma.

Table 7.6   Political Opinions of Delegates and Voters, 2000

	Democratic Delegates	Voters	Republican Delegates
Who They Are			
Male	52%	46%	65%
Female	48	54	35
African American	19	10	4
Income over $75,000	57	19	57
What They Think			
Government should do more to solve national problems.	73	33	4
Favor affirmative action.	83	51	29
Should ban soft money (unregulated gifts to political parties).	47	64	24
Support vouchers for private religious schools.	10	47	71

Source: New York Times/CBS News polls as reported in Adam Nagourney with Janet Elder, "The Republicans: Poll of Delegates Shows Convention Solidly on Right," New York Times, July 31, 2000; and Adam Clymer with Marjorie Connelly, "The Democrats: Poll Finds Delegates to the Left of Both Public and Party," New York Times, August 14, 2000.

Pro-Life Group Threatens to Bolt GOP

February 1
HARRISBURG, PA

At a televised press conference last week several top Republican officials called for "moderating" their party's pro-life platform. Yesterday a leading antiabortion political action committee responded by running full-page newspaper ads calling for "independent candidates and a third party to represent the views of pro-life Republicans and Democrats alike" . . .

MEMORANDUM

To: Harry Bower, president of Republicans for Life
From: Patricia Nucanon, political consultant
Subject: Forming a third party

Without regard to your organization's particular cause or issue, I have been employed to brief you on the general pros and cons of backing independent candidates and forming a third party.

Arguments for:

1. Independent and third-party candidates can garner votes and even win. In 1992 independent candidate Ross Perot won nearly a fifth of the vote for president. In 1998 the Reform party candidate Jesse Ventura became governor of Minnesota.
2. Even losing independent candidates (Eugene Debs, Robert La Follette, and George Wallace, to name just three) have made real marks on American politics. "Unsuccessful" third parties were the first to advocate policy positions later championed by the two main parties: abolishing slavery (Free-Soil party), giving women the vote (Woman's party), the direct election of senators (Progressive party), and many others.
3. Splitting off from a major party courts public attention and eventually gets policy results.

Arguments against:

1. The two-party system is supported by more than 150 years of political tradition featuring winner-take-all, single-member election districts. Since the 1850s more than 100 third parties and thousands of independent candidates have come, gone, and been forgotten by all except historians.
2. Usually the two main parties adapt and co-opt, not adopt, third-party ideas and positions. In the 1930s the Democrats watered down the Socialist party's plan and gave birth to the Social Security system. In the 1980s the Republican position on tax relief was but a faint echo of the Libertarian party's.
3. Splitting off from a major party courts political oblivion and reduces the chances that the issue or cause will be raised or represented even halfheartedly by either main party.

Your decision:
Favor a third party _____
Oppose third party _____

Summary

Apolitical party exists in three arenas: among the voters who psychologically identify with it, as a grassroots organization staffed and led by activists, and as a group of elected officials who follow its lead in lawmaking. In this chapter we have looked at the party primarily as an organization and seen the various forms it takes at the local level—the machine, the ideological party, the solidary group, the sponsored party, and the personal following.

The spread of the direct primary has made it harder for parties to control who is nominated for elective office, thus making it harder for the parties to influence the behavior of these people once elected. Delegate selection rules, especially in the Democratic party, have helped shift the center of power in the national nominating convention. Because of the changes in rules, power has moved away from office-holders and party regulars and toward the more ideological wings of the parties.

Minor parties have arisen from time to time, but the only ones that have affected the outcome of presidential elections have been those that represented a splinter group within one of the major parties (such as the Bull Moose Progressives). The two-party system is maintained, and minor parties are discouraged, by an election system (winner-take-all, plurality elections) that makes voters reluctant to waste a vote on a minor party and by the ability of potential minor parties to wield influence within a major party by means of the primary system.

In the next chapter we shall look at the role of parties in shaping voter attitudes, and in Chapter 11 we shall look at the role of parties in Congress. In each of these areas we will find more evidence of party decay.

Reconsidering the Enduring Questions

1. **What did the Founding Fathers believe about political parties?**

   The nation's founders did not think much of political parties—for a while. George Washington denounced "factions," but as soon as it was time to select his replacement, political leaders realized they had to organize their followers in order to win the election, and so parties were born.

2. **How has America's two-party system changed over the past century and a half? How does it differ today from the party systems of other representative democracies?**

   American parties during the nineteenth and the first half of the twentieth centuries were strong organizations that picked their candidates for office.

   Parties in European democracies still do that, but America has changed. Now, candidates are usually picked by direct primary elections as the American voters' loyalty to parties has weakened.

3. **To what extent has the decline of mass attachment to the two major parties affected how Americans vote?**

   The declining attachment of voters to parties and their weakness as organizations have led candidates to run more as individuals than as party members. They try to develop personal followings; among presidential candidates this has been quite successful, as we can see with the Kennedy and Bush families. We will see this in greater detail in the next chapter.

World Wide Web Resources

- Democratic National Committee: www.democrats.org
- Republican National Committee: www.rnc.org
- Green party: www.greens.org
- Libertarian party: www.lp.org
- Reform party: www.reformparty.org

Key Terms

political party *p. 152*
mugwumps or progressives *p. 157*
critical or realigning periods *p. 158*
split ticket *p. 161*
straight ticket *p. 161*
office-bloc ballot *p. 162*
party-column ballot *p. 162*
national convention *p. 162*
national committee *p. 162*
congressional campaign committee *p. 162*

national chairman *p. 162*
superdelegates *p. 166*
political machine *p. 168*
ideological party *p. 169*
solidary incentives *p. 170*
sponsored party *p. 170*
personal following *p. 171*
two-party system *p. 171*
plurality system *p. 173*
caucus *p. 179*

Suggested Readings

Chambers, William Nisbet, and Walter Dean Burnham, eds. *The American Party Systems: Stages of Political Development.* 2nd ed. New York: Oxford University Press, 1975. Essays tracing the rise of the party system since the Founding.

Goldwin, Robert A., ed. *Political Parties in the Eighties.* Washington, D.C.: American Enterprise Institute, 1980. Essays evaluating parties and efforts at reform.

Kayden, Xandra, and Eddie Mahe, Jr. *The Party Goes On.* New York: Basic Books, 1985. How the two major parties have adjusted to new political conditions.

Key, V. O., Jr. *Southern Politics.* New York: Knopf, 1949. A classic account of the one-party South.

Mayhew, David R. *Placing Parties in American Politics.* Princeton, N.J.: Princeton University Press, 1986. A state-by-state description of state party organizations.

Polsby, Nelson W. *Consequences of Party Reform.* New York: Oxford University Press, 1983. Fine analysis of how changed party rules have affected the parties and the government.

Ranney, Austin. *Curing the Mischiefs of Faction: Party Reform in America.* Berkeley: University of California Press, 1975. History and analysis of party "reforms," with special attention to the 1972 changes in the Democratic party rules.

Riordan, William L. *Plunkitt of Tammany Hall.* New York: Knopf, 1948. (First published in 1905.) Insightful account of how an old-style party boss operated.

Schattschneider, E. E. *Party Government.* New York: Holt, Rinehart and Winston, 1942. An argument for a more disciplined and centralized two-party system.

Shafer, Byron E. *Quiet Revolution: The Struggle for the Democratic Party and the Shaping of Post-Reform Politics.* New York: Russell Sage Foundation, 1983. Detailed, insightful history of how the Democratic party came to be reformed.

Sundquist, James L. *Dynamics of the Party System.* Rev. ed. Washington, D.C.: Brookings Institution, 1983. History of the party system, emphasizing the impact of issues on voting.

Wilson, James Q. *The Amateur Democrat.* Chicago: University of Chicago Press, 1962. Analysis of the issue-oriented political clubs that rose in the 1950s and 1960s.

Elections and Campaigns

Enduring Questions

1. How have primaries and general-election campaigns changed over the past century and a half?

2. What matters most in deciding who wins presidential and congressional elections?

3. Do elections really make a difference in what laws get passed?

If you want to be elected to Congress or to the presidency, you must develop a game plan that is in tune with the unique legal, political, and financial realities of American politics. A plan that will work here would be useless in almost any other democratic nation; one that would work abroad would be useless here.

Elections have two crucial phases—getting nominated and getting elected. Getting nominated means getting your name on the ballot. In the great majority of states winning your party's nomination for either the presidency or Congress requires an *individual* effort—*you* decide to run, *you* raise money, *you* and your friends collect signatures to get your name on the ballot, and *you* appeal to voters in primary elections on the basis of your personality and your definition of the issues. In most European nations winning your party's nomination for parliament involves an *organizational* decision—*the party* looks you over, *the party* decides whether to allow you to run, and *the party* puts your name on its list of candidates.

American political parties do play a role in determining the outcome of the final election, but even that role involves parties more as labels in the voters'

minds than as organizations that get out the vote. By contrast, many other democratic nations conduct campaigns that are almost entirely a contest between parties as organizations. In Israel and the Netherlands the names of the candidates for the legislature do not even appear on the ballot; only the party names are listed there. And even where candidate names are listed, as in Great Britain, the voters tend to vote "Conservative" or "Labour" more than they vote for Smith or Jones. European nations (except France) do not have a directly elected president; instead the head of the government—the prime minister—is selected by the party that has won the most seats in parliament.

At one time parties played a much larger role in elections in the United States than they do now. Until well into this century they determined, or powerfully influenced, who got nominated. In the early nineteenth century the members of Congress from a given party would meet in a caucus to pick their presidential candidate. After these caucuses were replaced by national nominating conventions, the real power over presidential nominations was wielded by local party leaders, who came together (sometimes in the legendary "smoke-filled rooms") to choose the candidate, whom the rest of the delegates would then endorse.

Congressional candidates were often handpicked by powerful local party bosses. In the past people were much more likely to vote a straight party ticket than they are today.

Chapter 7 described the factors that weakened the parties' ability to control nominations. There is little chance that they will ever regain that control. Thus candidates are now pretty much on their own. So if you want to be a candidate, what do you do?

Presidential Versus Congressional Campaigns

Presidential and congressional races differ in important ways. The most obvious, of course, is size: more voters participate in the former than the latter contests, and so presidential candidates must work harder and spend more. But there are some less obvious differences that are equally important.

First, presidential races are more competitive than those for the House of Representatives. In the thirty-five elections from 1932 to 2000 the Republicans won control of the House only six times

(17 percent of the time); in the eighteen presidential elections during the same period the Republicans won the White House on eight occasions (44.5 percent of the time). In the typical presidential race the winner gets less than 55 percent of the two-party vote; in the typical House race, the **incumbent** wins with over 60 percent of the vote.

Second, a much smaller proportion of people vote in congressional races during off years (that is, when there is no presidential contest) than vote for president. This lower turnout (around 36 percent of the voting-age population) means that candidates in congressional races must be appealing to the more motivated and partisan voter.

Third, members of Congress can do things for their constituents that a president cannot. They take credit—sometimes deserved, sometimes not—for every grant, contract, bridge, canal, and highway that the federal government provides the district or state. They send letters (at the government's expense) to large fractions of their constituents and visit their districts every weekend. Presidents get little credit for district improvements and must rely on the mass media to communicate with voters.

Fourth, a candidate for Congress can deny that he or she is responsible for "the mess in Washington," even when the candidate is an incumbent. Incumbents tend to run as individuals, even to the point of denouncing the very Congress of which they are a part. An incumbent president can't get away with this; rightly or wrongly, he is often held responsible for whatever has gone wrong, not only in the government but in the nation as a whole.

These last three factors—low voter turnout, services to constituents, and the ability to duck responsibility—probably help explain why so high a percentage of congressional incumbents get reelected.

But they do not enjoy a completely free ride. Members of Congress who belong to the same party as the president often feel voters' anger about national affairs, particularly economic conditions. When the economy turns sour and a Republican is in the White House, Republican congressional candidates lose votes; if a Democrat is in the White House, Democratic congressional candidates lose votes.

At one time the **coattails** of a popular presidential candidate could help congressional candidates in his own party. But there has been a sharp decline in the value of presidential coattails; indeed, some scholars doubt that they still exist.

The net effect of all these factors is that, to a substantial degree, congressional elections have become independent of presidential ones. Though economic factors may still link the fate of a president and some members of his party, by and large the incumbent members of Congress enjoy enough of a cushion to protect them against whatever political storms engulf an unpopular president. This fact further reduces the meaning of party—members of Congress can get reelected even though their party's "leader" in the White House has lost popular support, and nonincumbent candidates for Congress may lose despite the fact that a very popular president from their party is in the White House.

Running for President

The first task facing anyone who wishes to be president is to get "mentioned" as someone who is of "presidential caliber." No one is quite sure why some people are mentioned and others are not. The journalist David Broder has suggested that somewhere there is "The Great Mentioner," who announces from time to time who is of presidential caliber (and only The Great Mentioner knows how big that caliber is).

But if The Great Mentioner turns out to be as unreal as the Easter Bunny, you have to figure out for yourself how to get mentioned. One way is to let it be known to reporters, "off the record," that you are thinking about running for president. Another is to travel around the country making speeches (Ronald Reagan, while working for General Electric, made a dozen or more speeches *a day* to audiences all over the country). Another way is to already have a famous name (John Glenn, the former astronaut, was in the public eye long before he declared for the presidency in 1984). Another way to get mentioned is to be identified with a major piece of legislation. Former Senator Bill Bradley of New Jersey was known as an architect of the Tax Reform Act of 1986; Representative Richard Gephardt of Missouri was known as an author of a bill designed to reduce foreign imports. Still another way is to be the governor of a big state. Former New York governors, such as Mario Cuomo, are often viewed as presidential prospects, partly because New York City is the headquarters of the television and publishing industries.

Once you are mentioned, it is wise to set aside a lot of time to run, especially if you are only "mentioned" as opposed to being really well known. Ronald Reagan devoted the better part of six years to running; Walter

★ POLITICALLY SPEAKING ★

Coattails

Today the word is used in the sense of riding into office on the coattails of a better-known or more popular candidate. The political carrying power of coattails depends on the voters' casting a straight-ticket ballot so that their support for a popular presidential candidate is translated into support for lesser candidates on the same party ticket. Scholars are skeptical that such an effect exists today.

The word first came into popular usage in 1848, when Abraham Lincoln defended the Whig party's effort to take shelter under the military coattails of that party's presidential candidate, General Zachary Taylor. Lincoln argued that in the past the Democrats had run under the coattails of General Andrew Jackson.

Later the military connotation of **coattails** fell by the wayside, and the term came to mean any effort to obtain straight-ticket voting.

Source: Adapted from *Safire's Political Dictionary* by William Safire. Copyright © 1968, 1972, 1978 by William Safire. Reprinted by permission of Random House, Inc. and the author.

Mondale spent four years campaigning; Howard Baker resigned from the Senate in 1984 to prepare to run in 1988 (he finally dropped out of the race). However, most post-1988 candidates—senators Bob Dole, Tom Harkin, Bob Kerrey, and Paul Simon; governors Michael Dukakis, Bill Clinton, and George W. Bush; vice presidents George Bush and Al Gore; and House members Richard Gephardt and Jack Kemp—made the run while holding elective office.

Political campaigns are hard work, even when you get to fly on the vice president's airplane.

■ **Money**   One reason why running takes so much time is that it takes so long to raise the necessary money and build up an organization of personal followers. As we shall see later in this chapter, federal law restricts the amount that any single individual can give a candidate to $2,000 in each election. (A **political action committee,** or PAC, which is a committee set up by and representing a corporation, labor union, or other special-interest group, can give up to $5,000.) Moreover, to be eligible for federal matching grants to pay for your primary campaign, you must first raise at least $5,000, in individual contributions of $250 or less, in each of twenty states.

■ **Organization**   Raising and accounting for this money requires a staff of fund-raisers, lawyers, and accountants. You also need a press secretary, a travel scheduler, an advertising specialist, a direct-mail company, and a pollster, all of whom must be paid, plus a large number of volunteers in at least those states that hold early primary elections or party caucuses. These volunteers will brief you on the facts of each state, try to line up endorsements from local politicians and celebrities, and put together a group of people who will knock on doors, make telephone calls, organize receptions and meetings, and try to keep you from mispronouncing the name of the town in which you are speaking. Finally, you have to assemble advisers on the issues. These advisers will write "position papers" for you on all sorts of things that you are supposed to know about (but probably don't). Because a campaign is usually waged around a few broad themes, these position papers rarely get used or even read. The papers exist so that you can show important interest groups that you have taken "sound" positions, so that you can be prepared to answer tough questions, and so that journalists can look up your views on matters that may become topical.

■ **Strategy and Themes**   Every candidate picks a strategy for the campaign. In choosing one, much depends on whether you are the incumbent. Incumbents must defend their records, like it or not. (An incumbent ran for president in 1964, 1972, 1976, 1980, 1984, 1992, and 1996.) The challenger attacks the incumbent. When there is no incumbent (as in 1960, 1968, 1988, and 2000), both candidates can announce their own programs; however, the candidate from the party that holds the White House must take, whether he thinks he deserves it or not, some of the blame for whatever has gone wrong in the preceding four years. Within these limits a strategy consists of the answers to questions about tone, theme, timing, and targets:

• What *tone* should the campaign have? Should it be a positive (build-me-up) or negative (attack-the-opponent) campaign? In 1988 George Bush began with a negative campaign; Michael Dukakis followed suit.

• What *theme* can I develop? A theme is a simple, appealing idea that can be repeated over and over again. For Jimmy Carter in 1976 it was "trust"; for Ronald Reagan in 1980 it was "competence" and in 1984 it was "it's morning again in America"; for Bush in 1988 it was "stay the course;" for Clinton in 1992 it was "we need to change;" for George W. Bush in 2000 it was "compassionate conservatism."

• What should be the *timing* of the campaign? If you are relatively unknown, you will have to put everything into the early primaries and caucuses, try to emerge a front-runner, and then hope for the best. If you are already the front-runner, you may either go for broke early (and try to drive out all your opponents) or hold back some reserves for a long fight.

• Whom should you *target?* Only a small percentage of voters change their vote from one election to the next. Who is likely to change this time—unemployed steelworkers? Unhappy farmers? People upset by inflation?

Getting Elected to Congress

A president cannot serve more than two terms, so at least once every eight years you have a chance of running against a nonincumbent; members of Congress can serve for an unlimited number of terms, and so chances are you will run against an incumbent. If you decide to run for the House, the odds are very much against you. Since 1962, over 90 percent of the House incumbents who sought reelection won it. In 2000, 394 reelection-seeking incumbents won, and only 9 lost.

But the incredible incumbency advantage enjoyed by modern-day House members is hardly the whole story of getting elected to Congress. Who serves in Congress, and what interests are represented there, is affected by how its members are elected. Each state is entitled to two senators, who serve six-year terms, and at least one representative, who serves a two-year term. How many more representatives a state has depends on its population; what local groups these representatives speak for depends in part on how the district lines are drawn.

The Constitution says very little about how representatives will be selected except to require that they be inhabitants of the states from which they are chosen. It says nothing about districts and originally left it up to the states to decide who would be eligible to vote for representatives. The size of the first House was set by the Constitution at sixty-five members, and the apportionment of the seats among the states was spelled out in Article I, section 2. From that point on it has been up to Congress to decide how many representatives each state would have (provided that each had at least one).

Initially some states did not create congressional districts; all their representatives were elected at large. In other states representatives were elected from multimember as well as single-member districts. In time all states with more than one representative elected each from a single-member district. How those district boundaries were drawn, however, could profoundly affect the outcomes of elections. There were two problems. One was **malapportionment,** which results from having districts of very unequal size. If one district is twice as populous as another, twice as many votes are needed in the larger district to elect a representative. Thus a citizen's vote in the smaller district is worth twice as much as a vote in the larger.

The original Gerrymander: Elbridge Gerry had this Massachusetts district drawn to ensure the election of a Republican. Cartoonist Elkanah Tinsdale in 1812 compared the district to a salamander and termed it a "Gerry-Mander."

The other problem was **gerrymandering,** which means drawing a district boundary in some bizarre or unusual shape to make it easy for the candidate of one party to win election in that district. In a state entitled to ten representatives, where half the voters are Democrats and half are Republicans, district lines could be drawn so that eight districts would have a slight majority of citizens from one party and two districts would have lopsided majorities from the other. Thus it can be made easy for one party to win eight of the ten seats.

Malapportionment and gerrymandering have been conspicuous features of American congressional politics. In 1962, for example, one district in Texas had nearly a million residents, while another had less than a quarter million. In California Democrats in control of the state legislature drew district lines in the early 1960s so that two pockets of Republican strength in Los Angeles separated by many miles were connected by a thin strip of coastline. In this way most Republican voters were

thrown into one district, while Democratic voters were spread more evenly over several.

Hence there are four problems to solve in deciding who gets represented in the House:

1. Establishing the total size of the House
2. Allocating seats in the House among the states
3. Determining the size of congressional districts within states
4. Determining the shape of those districts

By and large Congress has decided the first two questions, and the states have decided the last two—but under some rather strict Supreme Court rules.

In 1911 Congress decided that the House had become large enough and voted to fix its size at 435 members. There it has remained ever since (except for a brief period when it had 437 members owing to the admission of Alaska and Hawaii to the Union in 1959). Once the size was decided upon, it was necessary to find a formula for performing the painful task of apportioning seats among the states as they gained and lost population. The Constitution requires such reapportionment every ten years. A more or less automatic method was selected in 1929 based on a complex statistical system that has withstood decades of political and scientific testing. Under this system, since 1990 eighteen states have lost representation in the House and eleven have gained it. Florida and California posted the biggest gains, while New York and Pennsylvania suffered the largest losses (see Table 8.1).

The states did little about malapportionment and gerrymandering until ordered to do so by the Supreme Court. In 1964 the Court ruled that the Constitution requires that districts be drawn so that, as nearly as possible, one person's vote would be worth as much as another's.[1] The Court rule, "one person, one vote," seems clear but in fact leaves a host of questions unanswered. How much deviation from equal size is allowable? Should other factors be considered besides population? (For example, a state legislature might want to draw district lines to make it easier for African Americans, Italian Americans, farmers, or some other group with a distinct interest to elect a representative; the requirement of exactly equal districts might make this impossible.) And the gerrymandering problem remains: districts of the same size can be drawn to favor one party or another. The courts have struggled to find answers to these questions, but they remain far from settled.

Table 8.1	Changes in State Representation in the House of Representatives			
	Number of Seats			
States	Before 1990 Census	After 1990 Census	After 2000 Census	Change
Gained Seats				
After Both 1990 and 2000 Census				
Arizona	6	8	10	+4
California	45	52	53	+8
Florida	15	23	25	+10
Georgia	10	11	13	+3
North Carolina	11	12	13	+2
Texas	27	30	32	+5
Lost Seats				
After Both 1990 and 2000 Census				
Illinois	22	20	19	−3
Michigan	18	16	15	−3
New York	34	31	29	−5
Ohio	21	19	18	−3
Pennsylvania	23	21	19	−4

Source: U.S. Bureau of the Census.

■ **Winning the Primary** However the district lines are drawn, getting elected to Congress first requires getting one's name on the ballot. At one time the political parties nominated candidates and even printed ballots with the party slates listed on them. All the voter had to do was take the ballot of the preferred party and put it in the ballot box. Today, with rare exceptions, a candidate wins a party's nomination by gathering enough voter signatures to get on the ballot in a primary election, the outcome of which is often beyond the ability of political parties to influence. Candidates tend to form organizations of personal followings and win "their party's" nomination simply by getting more primary votes than the next candidate. It is quite unusual for an incumbent to lose a primary: from 1946 to 1988 only 6 percent of incumbent senators and fewer than 2 percent of incumbent representatives seeking reelection failed to win renomination in primaries. These statistics suggest how little opportunity parties have to control or punish their congressional members.

Most newly elected members become strong in their districts very quickly; this is called the **sophomore surge.** It is the difference between the votes

candidates get the first time they are elected (and thus become freshman members) and the votes they get when they run for reelection (in hopes of becoming sophomore members). Before the 1960s House candidates did not do much better the second time they ran than the first. Beginning then, however, the sophomore surge kicked in, so that today freshman candidates running for reelection will get 8 to 10 percent more votes than when they were first elected. Senate candidates also benefit now from a sophomore surge, though to a lesser degree.

The reason for this surge is that members of Congress have figured out how to use their offices to run *personal* rather than party campaigns. They make use of free ("franked") mail, frequent trips home, radio and television broadcasts, and the distribution of services to their districts to develop among their constituents a good opinion of themselves, not their party. They also cater to their constituents' distrust of the federal government by promising to "clean things up" if reelected. They run *for* Congress by running *against* it.[2]

To the extent that they succeed, they enjoy great freedom in voting on particular issues and have less need to explain away votes that their constituents might not like. If, however, any single-issue groups are actively working in their districts for or against abortion, gun control, nuclear energy, or tax cuts, muting the candidates' voting record may not be possible.

■ **Staying in Office**   The way people get elected to Congress has two important effects. First, it produces legislators who are closely tied to local concerns (their districts, their states), and second, it ensures that party leaders will have relatively weak influence over them (because those leaders cannot determine who gets nominated for office).

The local orientation of legislators has some important effects on how policy is made. For example:

- Every member of Congress organizes his or her office to do as much as possible for people back home.
- If your representative serves on the House Transportation and Infrastructure Committee, your state has a much better chance of getting a new bridge or canal than if you do not have a representative on this committee.[3]
- If your representative serves on the House Appropriations Committee, your district is more like-

T·R·I·V·I·A

Congress

First woman in Congress	Jeannette Rankin (Mont., 1916)
First African American in Congress	Joseph H. Rainey (S.C., 1870)
Longest session of Congress	366 days (75th Congress, meeting from Jan. 3, 1940, to Jan. 3, 1941)
Shortest time for states to ratify a constitutional amendment	3 months, 7 days—26th Amendment
Longest time to ratify an amendment	203 years—27th Amendment
Longest service in Congress by one member	57 years, Carl Hayden of Arizona (15 years in House, 42 years in Senate), 1912–1969
First member of the House to be elected president	James Madison
First member of the Senate to be elected president	James Monroe
The only woman to serve in the House at the same time as her son	Frances Bolton, whose son was Oliver Bolton (served together 1953–1957, 1963–1965)
Longest speech ever made in the Senate	24 hours 18 minutes, made on August 28–29, 1957, by Senator J. Strom Thurmond (D-S.C.), seeking to block a civil rights bill
First woman elected to the Senate for a full term who was not preceded in office by her husband	Nancy Landon Kassebaum, elected in 1978 from Kansas

ly to get approval for a federal grant to improve your water and sewage-treatment programs than if your representative does not serve on that committee.[4]

Former House Speaker Thomas P. "Tip" O'Neill had this in mind when he said, "All politics is local." Some people think that this localism is wrong; in their view members of Congress should do what is best for "the nation as a whole." This argument is

Qualifications for Entering Congress and Privileges of Being in Congress

Qualifications

Representative

- Must be twenty-five years of age (when seated, not when elected)
- Must have been a citizen of the United States for seven years
- Must be an inhabitant of the state from which elected (*Note*: Custom, but *not* the Constitution, requires that a representative live in the district that he or she represents.)

Senator

- Must be thirty years of age (when seated, not when elected)
- Must have been a citizen of the United States for nine years
- Must be an inhabitant of the state from which elected

Judging Qualifications

Each house is the judge of the "elections, returns, and qualifications" of its members. Thus Congress alone can decide disputed congressional elections. On occasion it has excluded a person from taking a seat on the grounds that the election was improper.

Either house can punish a member—by reprimand, for example—or, by a two-thirds vote, expel a member.

Privileges

Members of Congress have certain privileges, the most important of which, conferred by the Constitution, is that "for any speech or debate in either house they shall not be questioned in any other place." This doctrine of "privileged speech" has been interpreted by the Supreme Court to mean that members of Congress cannot be sued or prosecuted for anything that they say or write in connection with their legislative duties.

When Senator Mike Gravel read the Pentagon Papers—some then-secret government documents about the Vietnam War—into the *Congressional Record* in defiance of a court order restraining their publication, the Court held that this was "privileged speech" and beyond challenge [*Gravel v. United States*, 408 U.S. 606 (1972)]. But when Senator William Proxmire issued a press release critical of a scientist doing research on monkeys, the Court decided that the scientist could sue him for libel because a press release was not part of the legislative process [*Hutchinson v. Proxmire*, 443, U.S. 111 (1979)].

---

about the role of legislators: are they supposed to be *delegates* who do what their district wants or *trustees* who use their best judgment on issues without regard to the preferences of their district?

Naturally most members are some combination of delegate and trustee, with the exact mix depending on the nature of the issue. But some, as we shall see, definitely lean one way or the other. All members want to be reelected, but "delegates" tend to value this over every other consideration and so seek out committee assignments and projects that will produce benefits for their districts. On the other hand, "trustees" will seek out committee assignments that give them a chance to address large questions, such as foreign affairs, that may have no implications at all for their districts.

Primary Versus General Campaigns

If you are running for president, you are (you hope) entering two elections, not just one. The first consists of primary elections and caucuses, which select the nominees; the second is the general election, which decides who wins the office. Each election attracts a different mix of voters, workers, and media attention. What works in the primary election may not work in the general one, and vice versa.

To win the nomination you must mobilize political activists who will give money, do volunteer work, and attend local caucuses. As we saw in Chapters 5

The Road to the Nomination

A campaign for the presidential nomination must begin early. Among the key steps are these.

Create an organization: A campaign manager, fund-raiser, pollster, and several lawyers and accountants must be hired early—two or even three years before the election. Money cannot legally be raised until an organization exists to receive and account for it.

Start raising money: To be eligible for federal matching dollars for your primary-election campaign, you must raise $250 from each of at least twenty donors in each of twenty states. You cannot receive more than $2,000 from any individual or $5,000 from any PAC. There are national and state-by-state limits on what you can spend.

Prepare for the early primaries and caucuses: To show that you are a serious contender and have "momentum," you should enter the early primaries and caucuses. In 1996 some key early ones were:

- February 12: Iowa caucus
- February 20: New Hampshire primary
- March 12: "Super Tuesday" (primaries in six states, mostly in the South)
- March 19: "Big 10 Tuesday" (primaries in the Midwest)

To win a primary you must campaign hard and often; to win a caucus you must have an organization that can get your supporters to attend and vote at the local caucus.

Pick a strategy: If you are relatively unknown, you must campaign heavily in the early primaries (this is called a "front-loaded" campaign). But then you risk running out of money before the later primaries in the big states. If you are the front-runner, you are in better shape, but then you must worry about losing even one primary (as did Dole to Buchanan in New Hampshire in 1996), thereby tarnishing your "unbeatable" image.

Control the convention: If you win the most delegates in the primaries and caucuses, you will be nominated. (From 1956 through 2000 the winning candidate was nominated on the first ballot at the Democratic and Republican conventions.) Then your problem is to control everything else that goes on at the convention—the platform, the speeches, the vice-presidential nomination—so nothing happens that will embarrass you.

---

and 6, activists are more ideologically stringent than the voters at large. To motivate these activists you must be more liberal (if you are a Democrat) in your tone and theme than are rank-and-file Democrats, or more conservative (if you are a Republican) than are rank-and-file Republicans.

Consider the caucuses held in Iowa in early February of a presidential election year. This is the first real test of the candidates vying for the nomination. Anyone who does poorly here is at a disadvantage, in terms of media attention and contributor interest, for the rest of the campaign.

The several thousand Iowans who participate in their parties' caucuses are not representative of the followers of their party in the state, much less nationally. In 1988 Senator Robert Dole came in first and

evangelist Pat Robertson came in second in the Iowa Republican caucus, with Vice President George Bush finishing third. As it turned out, there was little support for Dole or Robertson in the rest of the country.

Democrats who participate in the Iowa caucus tend to be more liberal than Democrats generally.[5] Moreover, the way the caucuses are run is a far cry from how most elections are held. To vote in the Republican caucus, you need not prove you are a Republican or even a voter. The Democratic caucus is not an election at all; instead a person supporting a certain candidate stands in one corner of the room with people who also support him, while those supporting other candidates stand in other corners with other groups. There is a lot of calling back and forth, intended to persuade people to leave one group and

★ POLITICALLY SPEAKING ★

Clothespin Vote

The vote cast by a person who does not like either candidate and so votes for the less objectionable of the two, putting a clothespin over his or her nose to keep out the unpleasant stench.

join another. No group with fewer than 15 percent of the people in attendance gets to choose any delegates, so people in these small groups then go to other, larger ones. It is a cross between musical chairs and fraternity pledge week.

Suppose you are a Democrat running for president and you do well in the Iowa caucus. Suppose you go on to win your party's nomination. Now you have to go back to Iowa to campaign for votes in the general election. Since 1940 Iowa has voted Republican in every presidential election but five (1948, 1964, 1988, 1996, and 2000). Your Republican opponent is not going to let you forget all of the liberal slogans you uttered nine months before. The Republican candidate faces the mirror image of this problem—sounding very conservative to get support from Republican activists in states such as Massachusetts and New York and then having to defend those speeches when running against his Democratic opponent in those states.

The problem is not limited to Iowa but exists in every state where activists are more ideologically polarized than the average voter. To get activist support for the nomination, candidates move to the ideological extremes; to win the general election, they try to move back to the ideological center. The typical voter looks at the results and often decides that nei-

ther candidate appeals to him or her very much, and so casts a "clothespin vote" (see the box on this page).

Occasionally even the voters in the primary elections will be more extreme ideologically than are the general-election voters. This certainly happened in 1972. George McGovern won the Democratic nomination with the support of voters who were well to the left of the public at large (and even of rank-and-file Democratic voters) on issues such as U.S. policy in Vietnam, amnesty for draft resisters, decriminalizing marijuana, and helping minorities.[6] His general-election opponent, Richard Nixon, was able to take advantage of this by portraying McGovern as a leftist. But even when primary voters are not too different from general-election voters, the activists who contribute the time, money, and effort to mount a campaign are very different from the voters—in both parties.

Two Kinds of Campaign Issues

In election campaigns there are two different kinds of issues.[7] A **position issue** is one in which the rival candidates have opposing views on a question that also divides the voters. For example, in the 2000 election George W. Bush wanted to let people put some of their Social Security money into private savings accounts; Al Gore opposed this.

Since 1860 many of the great party realignments have been based on differing position issues. After the Civil War the question was whether African Americans should be slaves or free. In the 1890s it was whether tariffs should be high or low and whether the dollar should be made cheaper. In the 1960s it was whether broad new civil rights legislation was needed.

But sometimes voters are not divided on important issues. Instead the question is whether a candidate fully supports the public's view on a matter about which nearly everyone agrees. These are called **valence issues.** For example, everybody wants a strong economy and low crime rates, and so no candidate favors high unemployment or more crime. What voters look for on valence issues is which candidate seems most closely linked to a universally shared view.

Valence issues are quite common. In 1968 Richard Nixon seemed to be more supportive of anticrime measures than his rival; in 1976 Jimmy Carter seemed more likely to favor honesty in government than his opponent; in 1984 Ronald Reagan seemed more closely identified with a strong economy than his opponent; in 1988 George Bush seemed more closely linked to patriotism than his opponent. Notice that we have said "seemed." This is how voters perceived the winners; it does not mean that the opponents favored crime, corruption, unemployment, or anti-Americanism.

In 1992 Bill Clinton was beset with charges that he was guilty of dodging the draft, marital infidelity, and smoking pot. But his strategists decided to focus the campaign on the valence issue of the economy, and they went about rescuing Clinton from the other criticisms. One observer later reported, "Retooling the image of a couple who had already been in the public eye for five battering months required a campaign of behavior modification and media manipulation so elaborate that its outline ran to fourteen single-spaced pages."[8] Bill Clinton and his wife, Hillary, made joint appearances on television during which they demonstrated their affection for each other. The plan even called for staging an event where Bill Clinton and his daughter would surprise Hillary Clinton on Mother's Day.[9]

The 1996 campaign was run almost entirely in valence terms. Clinton took credit for improving the economy and putting more police on the street. He took swipes at Bob Dole's advanced age and criticized him as an "extremist" who would abolish Medicare. Clinton won easily.

Likewise, the 2000 campaign relied on valence issues, but some position issues also became important. George W. Bush and Al Gore disagreed about the need for across-the-board cuts in the federal income tax, on the value of a national missile defense system, and on whether parents could use public money to send their children to whichever schools they chose.

Campaigns have usually combined both position and valence questions, but the latter have increased in importance in recent years. This has happened in part because presidential campaigns are now conducted largely on television, where it is important to project popular symbols and manipulate widely admired images. Candidates try to show that they are likable, and they rely on televised portraits of their similarity to ordinary people.

Television, Debates, and Direct Mail

Once campaigns mostly involved parades, big rallies, "whistle-stop" train tours, and shaking hands outside factory gates and near shopping centers. All of this still goes on, but increasingly presidential and senatorial candidates (and those House candidates with television stations in their districts) use broadcasting.

T·R·I·V·I·A

Elections

Only two men to have been elected president by the House of Representatives after failing to win a majority in the electoral college	Thomas Jefferson (1800) and John Quincy Adams (1824)
Only Democratic senator to be the running mate of a Republican presidential candidate	Andrew Johnson (1864)
Candidates for president who received more popular votes than their opponents but were not elected	Grover Cleveland and Al Gore got more popular votes but fewer electoral votes than their opponents
President who won the largest percentage of the popular vote	Lyndon B. Johnson, 61.7 percent (1964)
Only person to serve as vice president and president without having been elected to either post	Gerald Ford (1973–1976)
President who won the most electoral votes	Ronald Reagan (525 in 1984)
First woman to run for national office on a major-party ticket	Geraldine Ferraro (Democratic candidate for vice president, 1984)

There are two ways to use television—by running paid advertisements and by getting on the nightly news broadcasts. In the language of campaigners, short television ads are called *spots*, and a campaign activity that appears on a news broadcast is called a *visual*. Much has been written about the preparation of spots, usually under titles such as "the selling of the president" or "packaging the candidate" (and mostly by advertising executives, who are not especially known for underestimating their own influence). No doubt spots can have an important effect in some cases. A little-known candidate can increase his or her visibility by frequent use of spots (this is what Jimmy Carter did in the 1976 presidential primaries). Sometimes a complete unknown can

Kinds of Elections

There are two kinds of elections in the United States: general and primary. A **general election** is used to fill an elective office. A **primary election** is used to select a party's candidates for an elective office, though in fact those who vote in a primary election may not consider themselves party members. Some primaries are closed. In a **closed primary** you must declare in advance (sometimes several weeks in advance) that you are a registered member of the political party in whose primary you wish to vote. About forty states have closed primaries.

Other primaries are open. In an **open primary** you can decide when you enter the voting booth which party's primary you wish to participate in. You are given every party's ballot; you may vote on one. Idaho, Michigan, Minnesota, Montana, North Dakota, Utah, Vermont, and Wisconsin have open primaries. A variant on the open primary is the **blanket** (or "free love") **primary**—in the voting booth you mark a ballot that lists the candidates of all the parties, and thus you can help select the Democratic candidate for one office and the Republican candidate for another. Alaska and Washington have blanket primaries.

The differences among these kinds of primaries should not be exaggerated, for even the closed primary does not create any great barrier for a voter who wishes to vote in the Democratic primary in one election and the Republican in another. Some states also have a **runoff primary:** if no candidate gets a majority of the votes, there is a runoff between the two with the most votes. Runoff primaries are common in the South.

A special kind of primary, a **presidential primary,** is that used to pick delegates to the presidential nominating conventions of the major parties. Presidential primaries come in a bewildering variety. A simplified list looks like this:

- **Delegate selection only** Only the names of prospective delegates to the convention appear on the ballot. They may or may not indicate their presidential preferences.
- **Delegate selection with advisory presidential preference** Voters pick delegates and indicate their preferences among presidential candidates. The delegates are not legally bound to observe these preferences.
- **Binding presidential preference** Voters indicate their preferred presidential candidates. Delegates must observe these preferences, at least for a certain number of convention ballots. The delegates may be chosen in the primary or by a party convention.

In 1981 the Supreme Court ruled that political parties, not state legislatures, have the right to decide how delegates to national conventions are selected. Thus Wisconsin could not retain an open primary if the national Democratic party objected (*Democratic Party v. La Follette,* 101 Sup. Ct. 1010, 1981). Now the parties can insist that only voters who declare themselves Democrats or Republicans can vote in presidential primaries. The Supreme Court's ruling may have relatively little practical effect, however, since the "declaration" might occur only an hour or a day before the election.

win a primary by clever use of television, as allegedly happened when Mike Gravel became the Democratic nominee for senator from Alaska in 1968 and Milton Shapp became the Democratic nominee for governor of Pennsylvania in 1966.

The effect of television advertising on general elections is probably a good deal less than its effect on primaries; indeed, as we shall see in Chapter 10, most scientific studies of television's influence on voting decisions have shown that either it has no effect or the

effect is subtle and hard to detect. Nor is it surprising that this should be the case. In a general election, especially one for a high-visibility office (such as president or governor), the average voter has many sources of information—his or her own party or ideological preference, various kinds of advertising, the opinions of friends and family, and newspaper and magazine stories. Furthermore, both sides will use TV spots; if well done, they are likely to cancel each other out. In short it is not yet clear that a gullible public is being sold a bill of goods by slick Madison Avenue advertisers, whether the goods are automobiles or politicians.

Visuals are a vital part of any major campaign effort because, unlike spots, they cost the campaign little and, as "news," they may have greater credibility with the viewer. A visual is a brief filmed episode showing the candidate doing something that a reporter thinks is newsworthy. Simply making a speech, unless the speech contains important new facts or charges, is often thought by TV editors to be uninteresting: television viewers are not attracted by pictures of "talking heads," and in the highly competitive world of TV, audience reactions are all-important determinants of what gets on the air. Knowing this, campaign managers will strive to have their candidates do something visually interesting every day, no later than 3:00 P.M. (if the visual is to be on the 6:00 P.M. news)—talk to elderly folks in a nursing home, shake hands with people waiting in an unemployment line, or sniff the waters of a polluted lake. Obviously all these efforts are for naught if a TV camera crew is not around; great pains are therefore taken to schedule these visuals at times and in places that make it easy for the photographers to be present.

Ironically, visuals—and television newscasts generally—may give the viewer less information than commercial spots. This, of course, is the exact opposite of what many people believe. It is commonplace to deplore political advertising, especially the short spot, on the grounds that it is either devoid of information or manipulative, and to praise television news programs, especially longer debates and interviews, because they are informative and balanced. In fact the best research we have so far suggests that the reverse is true: news programs covering elections tend to convey very little information (they often show scenes of crowds cheering or candidates shouting slogans) and make little or no impression on viewers, if indeed they are watched at all. Paid commercials, on the other hand, especially the shorter spots, often contain a good deal of information that is seen, remembered, and evaluated by a public that is quite capable of distinguishing between fact and humbug.[10]

A special kind of television campaigning is the campaign debate. Incumbents or well-known candidates have little incentive to debate their opponents; by so doing, they only give more publicity to lesser-known rivals. Despite the general rule among politicians never to help an opponent, Vice President Nixon debated the

Republican candidate George W. Bush emphasized "compassionate conservatism" in his campaign and illustrated it by talking to schoolchildren.

less-well-known John Kennedy in 1960, and President Gerald Ford debated the less-well-known Jimmy Carter in 1976. Nixon and Ford lost. Lyndon Johnson would not debate Barry Goldwater in 1964, nor would Nixon debate Humphrey in 1968 or McGovern in 1972. Johnson and Nixon won. Carter debated the equally well-known Reagan in 1980 (but refused to join in a three-way debate with Reagan and John Anderson). Carter lost. It is hard to know what effect TV debates have on election outcomes, but poll data suggest that in 1980 voters who watched the debates were reassured by Reagan's performance; after the second debate with Carter, he took a lead in the polls that he never relinquished.[11] In 1984 most people thought that Mondale did better than Reagan in the first debate, but there is little evidence that the debate affected the outcome of the election. In 1992 and 1996 Clinton was probably the better debater, but he most likely would have won even if he had stumbled.

In 1988 the televised debate became a major activity during—and even before—the primary elections. The half dozen or so contenders for both the Democratic and the Republican presidential nominations participated in so many debates that one journalist was led to compare the campaign to a political version of the television program "The Dating Game," with the candidates, like bachelors trying to impress a woman, describing over and over again all their good qualities. Other than providing free television exposure (and probably boring the candidates to tears), it is hard to see what this accomplished.

In the 1888 presidential campaign, supporters of Benjamin Harrison rolled a huge ball covered with campaign slogans across the country. The gimmick, first used in 1840, gave rise to the phrase "keep the ball rolling."

Though TV visuals and debates are free, they are also risky. The risk is the slip of the tongue. You may have spent thirty years of your life in unblemished public service, you may have thought through your position on the issues with great care, you may have rehearsed your speeches until your dog starts to howl, but just make one verbal blunder and suddenly the whole campaign focuses on your misstep. In 1976 President Ford erroneously implied that Poland was not part of the Soviet bloc. For days the press dwelt on this slip. His opponent, Jimmy Carter, admitted in a *Playboy* interview that he had sometimes had lust in his heart. It is hard to imagine anyone who has not, but apparently presidents are supposed to be above that sort of thing. In 1980 Ronald Reagan said that trees cause pollution—oops, here we go again.

Because of the fear of a slip, because the voters do not want to hear long, fact-filled speeches about complex issues, and because general-election campaigns are fights to attract the centrist voter, the candidates will rely on a stock speech that sets out the campaign theme as well as on their ability to string together several proven applause-getting lines. For reporters covering the candidate every day, it can be a mind-numbing experience. Nelson Rockefeller spoke so

Candidates first made phonographic recordings of their speeches in 1908. Warren G. Harding is shown here recording a speech during the 1920 campaign.

The first televised presidential campaign debate took place in 1960 between John F. Kennedy and Richard M. Nixon.

often of the "brotherhood of man and the fatherhood of God" that the reporters started referring to it as his BOMFOG speech. Occasionally this pattern is interrupted by a "major" address—that is, a carefully composed talk on some critical issue, usually delivered before a live audience and designed to provide issue-related stories for the reporters to write.

If you dislike campaign oratory, put yourself in the candidate's shoes for a moment. Every word you say will be scrutinized, especially for slips of the tongue. Interest group leaders and party activists will react sharply to any phrase that departs from their preferred policies. Your opponent stands ready to pounce on any error of fact or judgment. You must give countless speeches every day. The rational reaction to this state of affairs is to avoid controversy, stick to prepared texts and tested phrases, and shun anything that sounds original (and hence untested). You therefore wind up trying to sell yourself as much as or more than your ideas. Voters may *say* that they admire a blunt, outspoken person, but in a tough political campaign they would probably find such bluntness a little unnerving.

Television is the most visible example of modern technology's effect on campaigns. Since 1960 presidential elections have been contested largely through television. Without television the campaign

waged in 1992 by independent candidate Ross Perot might not have happened at all. Perot launched his candidacy with successive appearances on Cable News Network's call-in program "Larry King Live," and he bought several half-hour chunks of television time to air his views on the federal budget deficit. In early October, before the first of three televised debates featuring Perot, Republican incumbent George Bush, and Democratic challenger Bill Clinton, most national polls showed Perot with only 10 percent of the vote. But after the debates Perot's support in the polls doubled, and he ended up with about 19 percent of the votes cast on election day.

In 1996 the big television networks agreed to make some free television time available to the major presidential candidates. The Federal Communications Commission approved the plan to limit the free TV to "major" candidates, thus denying it to minor third-party nominees.

Less visible than television but perhaps just as important is the computer. The computer makes possible sophisticated direct-mail campaigning, and this in turn makes it possible for a candidate to address specific appeals to particular voters easily and rapidly solicit campaign contributions. In the 2000 presidential campaign, Republican John McCain and

Democrat Bill Bradley raised substantial money via the Internet. Both lost their primary challenge, but fund-raising via the Internet is surely here to stay.

Whereas television is heard by everybody—and thus leads the candidate using it to speak in generalities to avoid offending anyone—direct mail is aimed at particular groups (college students, Native Americans, bankers, autoworkers), to whom specific views can be expressed with much less risk of offending someone. So important are the lists of names of potential contributors to whom a computer may send appeals that a prized resource of any candidate, guarded as if it were a military secret, is "The List." Novices in politics must slowly develop their own lists or beg sympathetic incumbents for a peek at theirs.

The chief consequence of the new style of campaigning is not, as some think, that it is more manipulative than old-style campaigning (picnics with free beer and $5 bills handed to voters can be just as manipulative as TV ads); rather it is that running campaigns has become divorced from the process of governing. Previously the party leaders who ran the campaigns would take part in the government once it was elected, and since they were *party* leaders, they had to worry about getting their candidate *re*elected. Modern political consultants take no

responsibility for governing, and by the time the next election rolls around, they may be working for someone else.

Money

All these consultants, TV ads, and computerized mailings cost money—lots of it. A powerful California politician once observed that "money is the mother's milk of politics," and many people think that our democracy is drowning in it. In 1998 winning House and Senate candidates spent a combined total of $448 million (see Figure 8.1). When that kind of money is spent, many people will cynically conclude that elections are being bought and sold. Clever television producers are being paid huge sums, so the theory goes, to put on TV ads that sell candidates as if they were boxes of soap.

But matters are a good deal more complicated and less sinister than the popular theory supposes. Money is important in politics as in everything else, but it is not obvious that the candidates with the most money always win or that the donors of the money buy big favors in exchange for their big bucks. In Chapter 9 we will consider what, if anything, interest groups get for the money they give to politicians, and in Chapter 10 we shall summarize what we know about the effects of television advertising on elections. Here let us try to answer four questions: Where does campaign money come from? What rules govern how it is raised and spent? What has been the effect of campaign finance reform? What does campaign spending buy?

The Sources of Campaign Money

Presidential candidates get part of their money from private donors and part from the federal government; congressional candidates get all of their money from private sources. In the presidential primaries candidates raise money from private citizens and interest groups. The federal government will provide matching funds, dollar for dollar, for all monies raised from individual donors who contribute no more than $250. Since every candidate wants as much of this "free" federal money as possible, each has an incentive to raise money from small, individual givers. (To prove they are serious candidates, they must first raise $5,000 in each of twenty states from such small contributors.) The government also gives a lump-sum grant to each political party to help pay the costs of its nominating convention. In the general election the government

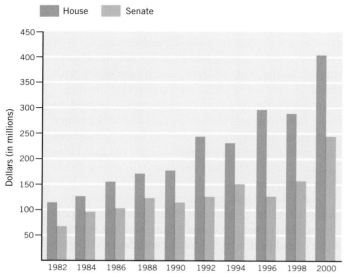

Figure 8.1   The Cost of Winning

House   Senate

Dollars (in millions)

450
400
350
300
250
200
150
100
50

1982 1984 1986 1988 1990 1992 1994 1996 1998 2000

Source: Federal Election Commission Report, May 15, 2001.

pays all the costs of each candidate, up to a limit set by law (in 1996 that limit was $61.8 million for each major candidate and $29 million for Perot).

Congressional candidates get no government funds; all their money must come out of their own pockets or be raised from individuals, interest groups (PACs), or the political parties. Contrary to what many people think, most of that money comes—and has always come—from individual donors (see Table 8.2). Because the rules sharply limit how much any individual can give, these donors tend not to be fat cats but people of modest means who contribute $100 or $200 per person.

Since the typical individual contribution is very small (and in no case larger than $2,000), some candidates have turned to rock bands and movie stars to put on benefit performances. If five thousand people will each pay $75 for a performance by U2, a lot of money can be raised in a hurry.

The most a PAC can give a candidate in any election is $5,000, but the typical PAC does not donate anything approaching the maximum amount; usually it gives a few hundred dollars to each candidate it supports.

These figures conceal some important differences among kinds of candidates, however. As Table 8.2 shows, incumbent members of Congress running for reelection get over a third of their money from PACs and spend next to nothing out of their own pockets. Their challengers, by contrast, spend only half as much and are able to get only one-tenth of that from

PACs. Challengers have to put up much more of their own money. As we shall see in the next section, these money problems weaken the ability of challengers to mount effective campaigns. Three states, Arizona, Maine, and Vermont, now fund campaigns with public money, but there is as yet no solid evidence about what difference it makes, or how.

Campaign Finance Rules

During the 1972 presidential election men hired by President Nixon's campaign staff broke into the headquarters of the Democratic National Committee in the Watergate office building. They were caught by an alert security guard. The subsequent investigation disclosed that the Nixon people had engaged in dubious or illegal money-raising schemes, including taking large sums from wealthy contributors in exchange for appointing them to ambassadorships. Many individuals and corporations were indicted for making illegal donations (since 1925 it had been against the law for corporations or labor unions to contribute money to candidates, but the law had been unenforceable). Some of the accused had given money to Democratic candidates as well as to Nixon.

When the break-in was discovered, the Watergate scandal unfolded. It had two political results: President Nixon was forced to resign, and a new campaign finance law was passed.

Under the new law, individuals could not contribute more than $1,000 to a candidate during any single election. Corporations and labor unions had for

Table 8.2	Sources of Campaign Funds: All House and Senate Candidates in 1997–1998, by Incumbents, Challengers, and Open					
	Incumbents		Challengers		Open	
	Sum (millions)	Percent	Sum	Percent	Sum	Percent
Individuals	$292.4	57.5%	$109.1	51.9%	$71.2	50.7%
PACs	158.3	37.6	21.4	10.2	26.9	19.2
Candidates	0.07	0.02	4.1	2.0	2.5	1.8
Loans	5.6	1.3	62.6	29.8	33.7	24.0
Parties	14.9	3.5	12.9	6.1	6.1	4.3
Total	$421.3		$210.1		$140.4	

Note: The data on candidates, loans, and parties are especially messy. "Candidates" includes only direct personal contributions by the office seekers. "Loans" includes money lent to the campaigns by the candidates as well as other loans. Loans from incumbents are almost always repaid by campaign committees. "Parties" includes both direct party contributions and a variety of "party-coordinated expenditures."

Source: Federal Election Commission Report, April 28, 1999.

many decades been prohibited from spending money on campaigns, but the new law created a substitute: political action committees (PACs). A PAC must have at least fifty members (all of whom enroll voluntarily), give to at least five federal candidates, and must not give more than $5,000 to any candidate in any election or more than $15,000 per year to any political party.

Since most candidates must go through both a primary and a general campaign in any election year, the spending limits per candidate were in fact $2,000 for an individual and $10,000 for a PAC.

In addition, the law made federal tax money available to help pay for presidential primary campaigns and for paying all of the campaign costs of a major-party candidate and a fraction of the costs of a minor-party candidate in a presidential general election.

The new law helped increase the amount of money spent on elections and, in time, changed the way money was spent. There are now more than four thousand PACs (see Figure 8.2). In 1998 they gave over $207 million to congressional candidates. But PACs are not a dominant influence on candidates because, though they can give up to $10,000, they in fact give rather little (often no more than $500). PACs in 1998 produced about 27 percent of the money congressional candidates spent. A small

contribution is enough to ensure that a phone call to a member of Congress from a PAC sponsor will be returned but not enough, in most cases, to guarantee that the member will act as the PAC wishes.

Moreover, most money for congressional candidates still comes from individuals. But since the limit until 2002 was $1,000 per election (a limit set in the early 1970s), candidates had to devise clever ways of reaching a lot of individuals in order to raise the amount of money they needed. This usually meant direct mail and telephone solicitations. If you are bothered by constant appeals for campaign funds, remember—that's what the new law requires.

By contrast, when George McGovern ran against Richard Nixon in 1972, he was chiefly supported by the large contributions of one wealthy donor, and when Eugene McCarthy ran against Lyndon Johnson in 1968, he benefited from a few big donations and did not have to rely on massive fund-raising appeals.

Presidential candidates are treated differently than congressional candidates. The former get money directly from the federal government. In the primary campaign, candidates can receive *matching funds.* Any candidate who raises at least $5,000 in individual contributions of $250 or less from people living in twenty states is eligible for matching funds. Once eligible, a candidate gets federal money to

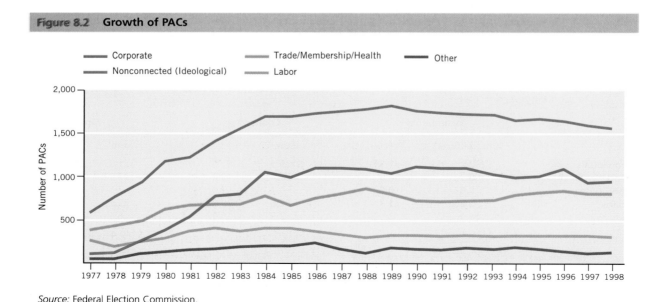

Figure 8.2   Growth of PACs

Legend: Corporate; Nonconnected (Ideological); Trade/Membership/Health; Labor; Other

Source: Federal Election Commission.

Major Federal Campaign Finance Rules

General

- All federal election contributions and expenditures are reported to a Federal Election Commission.
- All contributions over $100 must be disclosed, with name, address, and occupation of contributor.
- No *cash* contributions over $100 or foreign contributions.
- No ceiling on how much candidates may spend out of their own money (unless they accept federal funding for a presidential race).

Individual Contributions

- An individual may not give more than $2,000 to any candidate in any election.
- An individual may not make federal political gifts exceeding $95,000 every two years, of which only $37,500 may go to candidates.

Political Action Committees (PACs)

- Each corporation, union, or association may establish one.
- A PAC must register six months in advance, have at least fifty contributors, and give to at least five candidates.
- PAC contributions may not exceed $5,000 per candidate per election, or $15,000 to a national political party.

Ban on Soft Money

- No corporation or union may give money from its own treasury to any national political party.

Independent Expenditures

- Corporations, unions, and associations may not use their own money to fund "electioneering communications" that refer to clearly identified candidates sixty days before a general election or thirty days before a primary contest.
- PACs may fund electioneering communications up to their expenditure limits.

Presidential Primaries

- Federal matching funds can be given to match individual contributions of $250 or less.
- To be eligible, a candidate must raise $5,000 in each of twenty states in contributions of $250 or less.

Presidential Election

- The federal government will pay all campaign costs (up to a legal limit) of major-party candidates and part of the cost of minor-party candidates (those winning between 5 and 25 percent of the vote).

---

match, dollar for dollar, what he or she has raised in contributions of $250 or less. After the parties have chosen their nominees, the federal government pays the entire cost of the campaign up to a limit set by law. (In 1996 Bill Clinton and Bob Dole each received about $62 million). But a candidate can forego federal funding and run using money he has raised as George W. Bush did in 2000.

If you are a minor-party candidate, you can get some support from the federal government provided you have won at least 5 percent of the vote in the last election. In 2000, both Pat Buchanan (Reform party) and Ralph Nader (Green party) got partial support from Washington because their parties had won more than 5 percent of the vote in 1996. But this time out, neither party won that much, and so neither will get federal support in 2004.

The amount we spend on elections has shot up (in 2000, congressional candidates spent over $1 billion), but that explosion in spending has not been a major political problem. The real political problems arose from two changes in how the money was spent.

The first was **independent expenditures.** A PAC, or a corporation or a labor union, could spend whatever it wanted on advertising supporting or opposing a candidate, so long as this spending was

The 2000 Election

The presidential race in 2000 was a cliffhanger, producing the narrowest margin between the winner and loser in this century. It all came down to Florida, where the vote was so close that recounts had to be ordered. After five weeks and a Supreme Court decision that ended the recounts, George W. Bush won Florida and the election, 271 electoral votes to 267.

But even more astonishing than this razor-thin race was why Vice President Al Gore did not win with a landslide. The country was at peace, the economy was booming, unemployment was less than 4 percent, inflation scarcely existed, and the stock market was near its record high, yet going into the election Gore trailed in most public-opinion polls, and in the election his popular vote was only slightly ahead of that of Governor Bush.

This is not supposed to have happened. In general, a good economy helps the party that controls the White House. Take a look at Figure 8.3 on page 213. It shows that the better the economy, the better the candidate of that party does in the presidential race. Never in this century has the economy been stronger than it was in 2000, yet Gore rarely led in the polls (he should have been ahead by eight points) and was in a squeaker of an election. What went wrong for him?

No one is quite sure, but here are some guesses. First, Gore had to run in the face of President Clinton's sexual and fund-raising scandals in the White House. Though Americans liked the job Clinton did as president, Gore believed they didn't think he was a good man. Gore, as the vice president, believed he had to confront a lot of anti-Clinton hostility. Gore did what he could to deal with this problem by choosing as his vice-presidential nominee Senator Joe Lieberman, one of the first Democrats to speak out against Clinton, and by not letting Clinton campaign for him except in a few carefully chosen places. Maybe this was not enough.

Second, Gore ran a more liberal campaign than Bush did, in a country where liberals are a minority. He denounced large corporations and opposed giving tax breaks to "the rich." His campaign, designed in part to get his hard-core followers to the polls, may have irritated many more moderate voters.

Third, the economy in 2000 had been so good for so long that the voters may no longer have credited it to the Clinton-Gore administration. There is no doubt that the economy does affect most elections, but in the past that effect has occurred when a good economy has suddenly gone sour or a bleak one has suddenly gotten better. When Franklin Roosevelt beat Herbert Hoover in 1932 and when Ronald Reagan beat Jimmy Carter in 1980, the victors both took advantage of a sudden economic downturn. When George Bush the elder beat Michael Dukakis in 1988, the elder Bush took advantage of an upturn in economic news. In 2000 there was no recent change on which to capitalize.

Long before the election, several political scientists predicted its outcome, using economic models to estimate that Gore would win between 53 and 60 percent of the vote. All were wrong.

The Vice President

Gore, in picking Lieberman, chose to emphasize a moderate Democrat who was an Orthodox Jew and had been critical of Clinton. Bush, in picking former Secretary of Defense Dick Cheney, chose to emphasize long Washington experience and a deep familiarity with military and foreign-policy issues. The Lieberman choice was especially interesting, not

"independent," that is, not coordinated with or made at the direction of the candidate's wishes. Simply put, independent expenditures are ordinary advertising that is directed at or against candidates.

The second was **soft money.** Under the law, individuals, corporations, labor unions, and other groups could give unlimited amounts of money to political parties provided the money was not used to back candidates by name. But the money could be used in ways that helped candidates by financing voter-registration and get-out-the-vote drives. Over $270 million in soft money was spent during the 1996 presidential campaign.

Campaign Finance Reform

Reform is a tricky word. We think it means fixing something that has gone wrong, and so we are disposed to support things called "reforms." But some

only because he was the first Jew to be on a major-party ticket for national office, but because he did not hesitate to discuss the importance of religion in public affairs, a subject that many politicians avoid because they fear that people will criticize them for relaxing a barrier that is supposed to exist, in the eyes of some people, between church and state.

The Campaign

The campaign was concentrated in a few key states that held the balance of power. Everyone knew that Bush would do well in the South and much of the Midwest; everyone knew that Gore would do well in New York, most of New England, and California. That meant that the battleground would be in states like Michigan, Missouri, Ohio, and Pennsylvania.

Nationally, Gore won more popular votes than Bush, but failed to carry a key state: Florida. Bush carried the state by only about 500 votes, a victory that gave him the presidency. The Gore campaign persuaded several Florida counties to recount questionable ballots, a process that continued for some time until the Supreme Court stopped the recounts just days before the final results had to be sent to Congress. Some Democrats complained that Bush, aided by the Supreme Court majority, had "stolen" the victory. But a careful nonpartisan study of the disputed ballots (see "The Florida Vote-Count Controversy" on page 206) showed that Bush would have won the election even if the Supreme Court had not stopped the recounts.

Gore did well but he failed to carry his own state (Tennessee) or Clinton's (Arkansas).

The Role of Third Parties

Ross Perot led the Reform Party to a major showing in 1992, when he got 19 percent of the vote, and in 1996, when he won 9 percent. But in 2000, Pat Buchanan, a conservative Republican, left his own party and won the Reform nomination. This enabled him to get access to the federal election money available to parties that have won at least 5 percent of the vote (in this case, around $12 million), but Buchanan wound up with nothing to show for it, getting less than 1 percent of the vote. The Reform party will have no federal money in 2004, and so it may not be long for this world.

The major third-party effort was led by Ralph Nader, who became the nominee of the Green Party, an ultra-liberal group. Nader campaigned hard on a slim budget, hoping to win at least 5 percent of the vote and thus become eligible for federal funds. But he won only 2 percent, meaning he will have no federal money in 2004. But he did frighten the Gore campaign: the polls showed that most of his backers would have supported Gore if Nader had not run. Nader may have kept Gore from winning Florida and the presidency.

Congress

The Republicans managed to keep control of the House, but with a reduced majority of five seats. Usually the party that wins the White House picks up House seats, but that did not happen in 2000 (or with Clinton in 1992 or the older Bush in 1988). In early 2001, the Republicans also had 50 Senate seats, enough (with the tie-breaking votes that could be cast by Vice President Cheney) to give them control. But in Spring 2001, Senator James Jeffords abandoned the Republican party and became an independent, giving control of the Senate to the Democrats, 51 to 49.

reforms can make matters worse. For example, the campaign finance reforms enacted in the early 1970s helped matters in some ways by ensuring that all campaign contributors would be identified by name. But they made things worse in other ways by, for example, requiring candidates to raise small sums from many donors. This made it harder for challengers to run (incumbents are much better known and raise more money) and easier for wealthy candidates to run because, under the law as interpreted by the Supreme Court, candidates can spend as much of their own money as they want.

After the 2000 campaign, a strong movement developed in Congress to reform the reforms of the 1970s. The result was the Bipartisan Campaign Finance Reform Act of 2002, which passed easily in

The Florida Vote-Count Controversy

The presidential election of 2000 was decided in favor of George W. Bush on December 12, 2000, when the U.S. Supreme Court suspended the counting of disputed ballots in Florida as ordered by the Florida Supreme Court. When the recounting was halted, Bush was ahead by 537 votes. But would Bush have won Florida and the election anyway?

According to an exhaustive nine-month analysis of 175,010 Florida ballots conducted by eight media organizations in 2001 with the help of the National Opinion Research Center (NORC) at the University of Chicago, the answer is yes. The analysis suggested that if the U.S. Supreme Court had allowed the vote counting ordered by the Florida Supreme Court to continue, Bush still would have won Florida by 493 votes, rather than by 537 votes. Likewise, the analysis suggested that if Al Gore had won his original request for hand counts in just four heavily Democratic Florida counties, Bush would have won by 225 votes.

But the controversy was hardly settled by these results. For one thing, the NORC study also suggested that a majority of Florida voters who went to the polls on November 7, 2000, went intending to vote for Gore, but thousands more Gore than Bush voters failed to cast their ballots for their favorite candidate because of mistakes engendered by confusing ballots. For another, the NORC study's findings further indicated that, had the ballots been recounted using the exacting "equal protection" standard that the U.S. Supreme Court ruled was constitutionally necessary but that was impossible to complete given legal time limits, Gore probably would have won.

The U.S. Supreme Court's five-to-four decision in *Bush v. Gore* was hotly debated at the time it was announced, and it has only grown more controversial since. Even some conservative Republicans who wanted Bush to win have criticized not only the Florida Supreme Court for extending the recounts, but the U.S. Supreme Court's majority for deciding the issue as it did. They would have preferred the Florida Supreme Court to do nothing except uphold the state's vote recount law and, failing that, the U.S. Supreme Court to allow Congress to decide the matter as the Constitution seems to require.

Sources: Jackie Calmes and Edward P. Foldessy, "Florida Revisited: Bush Wins Without Supreme Court Help," *Wall Street Journal* (November 2001); E.J. Dionne and William J. Kristol, eds., *Bush v. Gore* (Washington, D.C.: Brookings Institution, 2001).

the House and Senate and was signed by President Bush.

The law made three important changes. First, it banned "soft money" contributions to national political parties from corporations and unions. After the federal elections in 2002, no national party or party committee can accept soft money. Any money the national parties get must come from "hard money"—that is, individual donations or PAC contributions as limited by federal law.

Second, the limit on individual contributions was raised from $1,000 per candidate per election to $2,000.

Third, "independent expenditures" by corporations, labor unions, trade associations, and (under certain circumstances) nonprofit organizations are sharply restricted. Now none of these organizations can use their own money to refer to a clearly identi-

fied federal candidate in any advertisement during the sixty days preceding a general election or the thirty days preceding a primary contest. (PACs can still refer to candidates in their ads, but of course PACs are restricted to "hard money"—that is, the amount they can spend under federal law.)

Immediately after the law was signed, critics filed suit in federal court claiming that it was unconstitutional. The suit brought together a number of organizations that rarely work together, such as the American Civil Liberties Union and the National Right to Life Committee.

The suit's central arguments are that the ban on independent spending that "refers to" clearly identified candidates sixty days before an election is unconstitutional because it is an abridgement of the right of free speech. Under the law, an organization need not even endorse or oppose a candidate; it is enough that it mention a politician. This means that an organization, sixty days before an election, cannot say that it "supports (or opposes) a bill proposed by Congressman Hastert."

Newspapers, magazines, and radio and television stations are not affected by the law, so that they can say whatever they want for or against a candidate. One way of evaluating the law is to observe that it shifts influence away from businesses and unions and toward the media.

Groups defending the law argue that its restrictions are constitutionally sound. As of the summer of 2002, no court decision had been announced.

Money and Winning

In the general election for president money does not make much difference, because both major-party candidates have the same amount, contributed by the federal government. During peacetime presidential elections are usually decided by three things: political party affiliation, the state of the economy, and the character of the candidates.

For all the talk about voting for "the person, not the party," history teaches that at least 80 percent of the presidential vote will go to the candidates of the two main parties. This means that a presidential election will normally be decided by the 20 percent of voters who cannot be counted on to vote either Democratic or Republican.

In good economic times the party holding the White House normally does well; in poor times it does badly. This is sometimes called the "pocketbook vote." But it is not clear whose pocketbook determines how a person will vote. Many people who are doing well financially will vote against the party in power if the country as a whole is not doing well. A person who is doing well may have friends or family members who are doing poorly. Or the well-off voter may think that if the country is doing poorly, he or she will soon feel the pinch by losing a job or losing customers.

Voters also care about character, and so some money from presidential campaign coffers goes to fund "character ads." *Character* here means several things: Is the candidate honest and reliable? Does the candidate think as the voter thinks about social issues such as crime, abortion, and school prayer? Does the candidate act presidential? Acting presidential seems to mean being an effective speaker, displaying dignity and compassion, sounding like someone who can take charge and get things done, and com-

ing across consistently as a reasonable, likable person. Rash, disagreeable extremists need not apply.

Since both major candidates get the same amount of federal money for the general-election campaign, money does not make much of a difference in determining the winner. Other factors that also do not make much of a difference include the following:

- *Vice-presidential nominee:* There has rarely been an election in which his or her identity has made a difference.
- *Political reporting:* It may make a difference in some elections, but not in presidential ones.
- *Religion:* Being a Catholic was once a barrier, but since John F. Kennedy was elected president in 1960, this is no longer true.
- *Abortion:* This probably affects who gets a party's nomination, but in the general election ardent supporters and ardent opponents are about evenly balanced.
- *New voting groups:* Political scientists have shown that, whatever reporters may say, "angry white males" did not elect the Republican Congress in 1994 and "soccer moms" did not elect Bill Clinton in 1996.[12]

In congressional races, however, in general it seems that money does make a decisive difference. Scholars are not entirely agreed on the facts, but there is strong evidence that how much the challenger spends is most important, because the challenger usually must become known to the public. Buying name recognition is expensive. Gary Jacobson has shown that, other things being equal, in every congressional election from 1972 to the mid-1980s, challengers who spent more money did better than those who spent less.[13] Jacobson also suggested that how much the incumbents spent was not very important, presumably because they already had all the name recognition they needed (as well as the other benefits of holding office, such as free mail and travel). Other scholars, applying different statistical methods to the same facts, have come to different conclusions. It now seems that, other things being equal, high-spending incumbents do better than low-spending ones.[14] It also now seems that ever higher spending by incumbents, both in absolute dollars and relative to what challengers spend, has become the congressional campaign norm. As Table 8.3 shows, in 1978 average incumbent spending in congressional races was $284,577, average challenger spending was $202,863, and the

Table 8.3   **The Incumbency Advantage in Congressional Campaign Spending (constant 1992 dollars)**

Year	Average Incumbent Spending	Average Challenger Spending	Number of Races	Incumbent-to-Challenger Spending Ratio	Median Ratio
1978	$284,577	$202,863	235*	1.40	1.93
1980	$298,510	$174,031	338	1.72	3.82
1982	$400,630	$202,689	315	1.98	3.24
1984	$417,815	$192,433	338	2.17	4.47
1986	$488,447	$175,418	319	2.78	5.39
1988	$496,894	$148,723	328	3.34	7.08
1990	$479,969	$124,899	321	3.84	10.02
1992	$609,060	$172,802	307	3.52	5.35
1994	$573,374	$223,664	328	2.56	4.68
1996	$630,852	$254,964	357	2.47	5.11
Total	$473,421	$187,587	3,186	2.52	4.66

*Number of cases is small due to nonfilers.

Source: Stephen Ansolabehere and James Snyder, "The Sources of the Incumbency Advantage in Congressional Campaign Finance," Department of Political Science, Massachusetts Institute of Technology, June 1997, 29.

incumbent-to-challenger spending ratio was 1.40. By 1996 the average for incumbents had soared to $630,852, the average for challengers had grown to $254,964, and the incumbency spending advantage was 2.47.

That money makes a difference does not mean it makes the only difference. In 1986 and 1988 Republican challengers for Senate seats spent more money than the Democratic incumbents to whom they lost. Political party, incumbency, and issues also affect the outcomes of congressional elections.

Incumbents find it easier to raise money than do challengers; incumbents provide services to their districts that challengers cannot; incumbents regularly send free ("franked") mail to their constituents, while challengers must pay for their mailings; incumbents can get free publicity by sponsoring legislation or conducting an investigation. Thus it is hardly surprising that incumbents who run for reelection win in the overwhelming majority of races.

What Decides the Election?

To the voter it all seems quite simple—he or she votes for "the best person" or maybe "the least-bad person." To scholars it is all a bit mysterious. How do voters decide who the best person is? What does "best" mean, anyway?

Party

One answer to these questions is party identification. People may say that they are voting for the "best person," but for many people the best person is always a Democrat or a Republican. Moreover, we have seen in Chapter 5 that many people know rather little about the details of political issues. They may not even know what position their favored candidate has taken on issues that the voters care about. Given these facts many scholars have argued that party identification is the principal determinant of how people vote.[15]

If it were only a matter of party identification, though, the Democrats would always win the presidency, since more people identify with the Democratic than the Republican party (that gap narrowed, however, in the early 1980s). But we know that the Democrats lost six of the nine presidential elections between 1968 and 2000. Here are three reasons for this.

First, those people who consider themselves Democrats are less firmly wedded to their party than are Republicans. Table 8.4 shows how people identifying themselves as Democrats, Republicans, or independents voted in presidential elections from 1960 to 2000. In every election except 1992, at least 80 percent of Republican voters supported the Republican candidate in each election. By contrast, there have been more defections among Democratic voters—in 1972 a third of Democrats supported Nixon, and in 1984 some 26 percent supported Reagan.

The second reason, also clear from Table 8.3, is that the Republicans do much better than the Democrats among the self-described "independent" voters. In every election since 1960 (except 1964, 1992, and 1996), the Republican candidate has won a larger percentage of the independent vote than the Democratic nominee; in fact the Republicans usually got a majority of the independents, who tend to be younger whites.

Finally, a higher percentage of Republicans than Democrats vote in elections. In every presidential contest in the past thirty years, those describing themselves as "strongly Republican" have been much more likely to vote than those describing themselves as "strongly Democratic."

Issues, Especially the Economy

Even though voters may not know a lot about the issues, that does not mean that issues play no role in elections or that voters respond irrationally to them. For example, V. O. Key, Jr., looked at those voters who switched from one party to another between elections and found that most of them switched in a direction consistent with their own interests. As Key put it, the voters are not fools.[16]

Moreover, voters may know a lot more than we suppose about issues that really matter to them. They may have hazy, even erroneous, views about monetary policy, Central America, and the trade deficit, but they are likely to have a very good idea about whether unemployment is up or down, prices

Table 8.4	Percentage of Popular Vote by Groups in Presidential Elections, 1960–2000				
		National	Republicans	Democrats	Independents
1960	Kennedy	50%	5%	84%	43%
	Nixon	50	95	16	57
1964	Johnson	61	20	87	56
	Goldwater	39	80	13	44
1968	Humphrey	43	9	74	31
	Nixon	43	86	12	44
	Wallace	14	5	14	25
1972	McGovern	38	5	67	31
	Nixon	62	95	33	69
1976	Carter	51	11	80	48
	Ford	49	89	20	52
1980[a]	Carter	41	11	66	30
	Reagan	51	84	26	54
	Anderson	7	4	6	12
1984	Mondale	41	7	73	35
	Reagan	59	92	26	63
1988	Dukakis	46	8	82	43
	Bush	54	91	17	55
1992	Clinton	43	10	77	38
	Bush	38	73	10	32
	Perot	19	17	13	30
1996	Clinton	49	13	84	43
	Dole	41	80	10	35
	Perot	8	6	5	17
2000	Gore	49	8	86	45
	Bush	48	91	11	47

[a]The figures for 1980, 1984, 1988, and 1996 fail to add up to 100 percent because of missing data.

Sources: Gallup poll data, compiled by Robert D. Cantor, *Voting Behavior and Presidential Elections* (Itasca, Ill.: F. E. Peacock, 1975), 35; Gerald M. Pomper, *The Election of 1976* (New York: David McKay, 1977), 61; Gerald M. Pomper et al., *The Election of 1980* (Chatham, N.J.: Chatham House, 1981), 71; *New York Times*/CBS Poll, November 5, 1992.

The Congressional Election of 2002

Suddenly the president's coattails grew longer. After decades in which the president's party lost strength in Congress during the off-year election, the Republicans, led by President George W. Bush, gained strength.

The Republicans picked up two Senate seats, thus returning that chamber to Republican control (51 Republicans, 48 Democrats, 1 Independent, and 1 seat still undecided), and they expanded their control of the House by about eight seats (Republicans 229, Democrats 205, and 1 Independent).

At the state level, Republicans lost some governorships so that in 2003 the parties were almost evenly split, 26 Republicans and 24 Democrats. Despite losing a few governorships, the Republicans increased their strength in state legislatures so that they and the Democrats have almost the same number of seats, with the Republicans controlling both state houses in more states than do the Democrats.

How did this happen? Not since the direct election of senators became possible in 1913 has the party of an incumbent president been able, during an off-year election, to regain control of the Senate from its opponents. Not since 1934, when Franklin Roosevelt was president, has the president's party increased its control of both the House and the Senate in an off-year election.

There seem to be three reasons: Bush was personally very popular, he campaigned hard in the key states, and voters were worried about terrorism and a possible war with Iraq and trusted him to manage those issues well. In the closely fought contests, voter turnout went up despite predictions that it would go down.

There are at least three lessons from this experience. First, presidential popularity remains important, especially in times of international tension. Second, the country is deeply divided between the two major parties. Third, it is increasingly difficult to predict election results since fewer and fewer people are responding to polls.

---

at the supermarket are stable or rising, or crime is a problem in their neighborhoods. And on some issues—such as abortion, school prayer, and race relations—they are likely to have some strong principles that they want to see politicians obey.

Contrary to what we learn in our civics classes, representative government does not require voters to be well informed on the issues. If it were our duty as citizens to have accurate facts and sensible ideas about how best to negotiate with foreign adversaries, stabilize the value of the dollar, revitalize failing industries, and keep farmers prosperous, we might as well forget about citizenship and head for the beach. It would be a full-time job, and then some, to be a citizen. Politics would take on far more importance in our lives than most of us would want, given our need to earn a living and our belief in the virtues of limited government.

To see why our system can function without well-informed citizens, we must understand the differences between two ways in which issues can affect elections.

■ **Prospective Voting**   *Prospective* means "forward-looking"; we vote prospectively when we examine the views that the rival candidates have on the issues of the day and then cast our ballots for the person we think has the best ideas for handling these matters. **Prospective voting** requires a lot of information about issues and candidates. Some of us do vote prospectively. Those who do tend to be political junkies. They are either willing to spend a lot of time learning about issues or are so concerned about some big issue (abortion, school busing, nuclear energy) that all they care about is how a candidate stands on that question.

Prospective voting is more common among people who are political activists, have a political ideology that governs their voting decision, or are involved in interest groups with a big stake in the election. They are a minority of all voters, but (as we saw in Chapters 5 and 6) they are more influential than their numbers would suggest. Some prospective voters (by no means all) are organized into single-issue groups, to be discussed in the next section.

■ **Retrospective Voting**   *Retrospective* means "backward-looking"; **retrospective voting** involves looking at how things have gone in the recent past and then voting for the party that controls the White House if we like what has happened and voting against that party if we don't like what has happened. Retrospective voting does not require us to have a lot

Forecasting Presidential Election Outcomes

In August 2000, a panel of political scientists offered forecasts for the 2000 presidential election. Although they differed in many particulars, most of the forecasters' models emphasized three factors: rates of economic growth, trends in the incumbent president's public approval ratings, and opinion polls concerning which candidate will best promote peace and prosperity in the future. At that time, the economy was booming. President Bill Clinton, the two-term incumbent Democrat, enjoyed high approval ratings, and surveyed voters were generally split concerning which, if any, candidate could command future conditions.

The consensus prediction was that Clinton's vice president, Democratic candidate Al Gore, would beat then-Governor of Texas George W. Bush, his Republican opponent, by six points or more. The most widely cited forecast model had Gore winning 56.2 percent of the two-party vote and beating Bush by over ten percentage points. Gore did get a majority of the popular vote, but only 50.2 percent, a virtual dead heat. Following the Florida vote-count controversy (see box on page 206), Bush was awarded a majority of votes in the electoral college (see Chapter 12, page 334) and became president.

Many journalists, and not a few political scientists themselves, have concluded that the forecasters' failure in 2000 demonstrates that such fundamentals as economic conditions matter less, while unique circumstances and campaign tactics matter more, than has generally been believed, and that these idiosyncratic factors matter in ways that cannot be meaningfully captured by even the most sophisticated statistical models. For example, according to one expert, Gore lost because he "didn't run a campaign consistent with the models": he did not stress the good economy, he did not embrace the popular incumbent president of his own party, and he was too wooden as a public personality to woo most voters into thinking that he could guarantee them peace and prosperity in the future.

Other experts, however, argue instead that while no one statistical model accurately predicted the presidential race of 2000, a sort of supermodel based on a new statistical technique would have predicted it almost exactly right. For example, when political scientists Larry M. Bartels and John Zaller combined certain key features of forty-eight different models, they were thereby able to "forecast" the 2000 presidential election within a percentage point or two of the actual results.

The real issue, however, is not whether these models can predict close elections but whether they call our attention to the main factors that influence elections. And the main factors are, indeed, economic conditions and high approval ratings. But "main factors" are not enough. Campaigns and subtle voter judgments also matter. No statistical model can capture these factors.

Predictions based on statistical models tell us what we know. But we don't know, and probably never will know, enough to call a close election.

---

of information—all we need to know is whether things have, in our view, gotten better or worse.

Elections are decided by retrospective voters.[17] In 1980 they decided to vote against Jimmy Carter because inflation was rampant, interest rates were high, and we seemed to be getting the worst of things overseas. The evidence suggests rather clearly that they did not vote *for* Ronald Reagan; they voted for *an alternative to* Jimmy Carter. (Some people did vote for Reagan and his philosophy; they were voting prospectively, but they were in the minority.) In 1984 people voted for Ronald Reagan because unemployment, inflation, and interest rates were down and because we no longer seemed to be getting pushed around overseas. In 1980 retrospective voters wanted change; in 1984 they wanted continuity. In 1988 there was no incumbent running, but George Bush portrayed himself as the candidate who would continue the policies that had led to prosperity and depicted Michael Dukakis as a "closet liberal" who would change those policies. In 1992 the economy had once again turned sour, and so voters turned away from Bush and toward his rivals, Bill Clinton and Ross Perot.

Though most incumbent members of Congress get reelected, those who lose do so, it appears, largely because they are the victims of retrospective voting.

The Hispanic Vote

Some people call the Hispanic vote the "sleeping giant." In 1998 there were an estimated 30 million people of Hispanic origin in the United States, making them a potentially powerful voting bloc. But two things reduce this power considerably.

First, only about 2 million Hispanics voted in the 1980 and 1984 presidential elections. And in 1998, although they were about 10 percent of the population, they cast only 5 percent of the votes. The main reason for this low turnout is that many Hispanic citizens are not registered to vote. In addition, about one-third of all Hispanics are resident aliens and hence not entitled to register.

Second, the Hispanic vote is not homogeneous. Cuban Americans, many of them concentrated in the Miami area, tend to be strongly Republican, while Mexican Americans are strongly Democratic. But Mexican Americans outnumber Cuban Americans, and the Hispanic vote nationally has favored Democrats in every election since 1980, albeit more strongly in recent presidential elections than in midterm congressional elections. In 2000, George W. Bush did reasonably well among Hispanics.

Because the Hispanic vote is chiefly located in a few key states—California, Texas, and New York—any presidential candidate who can succeed in get-

The Hispanic vote has picked up as more and more of these voters have worked for Latino candidates.

ting Hispanic voters to the polls could enjoy a big advantage. These three states have almost half of the total number of electoral votes needed to win the presidency. In nearly two dozen congressional districts in these states the Hispanic vote has already become crucial to winning election to Congress; it remains to be seen how or when the Hispanic vote will take on the same importance on the national level.

Source: New York Times (November 9, 1998): A20.

After Reagan was first elected, the economy went into a recession in 1981–1982. As a result Republican members of Congress were penalized by the voters, and Democratic challengers were helped. But it is not just the economy that can hurt congressional candidates. Since 1860 every midterm election but one (1934) has witnessed a loss of congressional seats by the party holding the White House. Just why this should be is not entirely clear, but it probably has something to do with the tendency of some voters to change their opinions of the presidential party once that party has had a chance to govern—which is to say, a chance to make some mistakes, disappoint some supporters, and irritate some interests.

Some scholars believe that retrospective voting is based largely on economic conditions. Figure 8.3 certainly provides support for this view. Each dot represents a presidential election (fourteen of them,

from 1948 to 2000). The horizontal axis is the percentage increase or decrease in per capita disposable income (adjusted for inflation) during the election year. The vertical axis is the percentage of the two-party vote won by the party already occupying the White House. You can see that, as per capita income goes up (as you move to the right on the horizontal axis), the incumbent political party tends to win a bigger share of the vote.

Other scholars feel that matters are more complicated than this. As a result a small industry has grown up consisting of people who use different techniques to forecast the outcome of elections. If you know how the president stands in the opinion polls several months before the election and how well the economy is performing, you can make a pretty good guess as to who is going to win the presidency. For congressional races predicting is a lot tougher, because so many local factors affect these contests. Election forecasting remains an inexact science. As one study of the performance of presidential election forecasting models and the 1992 election concluded, "Models may be no improvement over pundits."[18]

The Campaign

If party loyalty and national economic conditions play so large a role in elections, is the campaign just sound and fury, signifying nothing?

No. Campaigns can make a difference in three ways. First, they reawaken the partisan loyalties of voters. Right after a party's nominating convention selects a presidential candidate, that person's standing with voters of both parties goes way up in the polls. The reason is that the just-nominated candidate has received a lot of media attention during the summer months, when not much else is happening. When the campaign gets under way, however, both candidates get publicity, and voters return to their normal Democratic or Republican affiliations.[19]

Second, campaigns give voters a chance to watch how the candidates handle pressure, and they give candidates a chance to apply that pressure. The two rivals, after promising to conduct a campaign "on the issues" without mudslinging, immediately start searching each other's personal histories and records to find acts, statements, or congressional votes that can be shown in the worst possible light in newspaper or television ads. In 1988 George Bush asserted that as governor, Michael Dukakis had vetoed a bill to make the Pledge of Allegiance mandatory in the Massachusetts schools; Dukakis retaliated by saying that Bush had to accept responsibility for some of the scandals of the Reagan administration, because "a fish rots from the head." Many voters don't like these "negative ads"—but they work. Careful statistical studies based on actual campaigns (as opposed to voter surveys or laboratory-like focus group studies) suggest that negative ads work by stimulating voter turnout.[20] As a result every politician constantly worries about how an opponent might portray his or her record, a fact that helps explain why so many politicians never do or say anything that can't be explained in a thirty-second television spot.

Third, campaigns allow voters an opportunity to judge the character and core values of the candidates. Most voters don't study in detail a candidate's positions on issues; even if they had the time, they know that you can't predict how politicians will

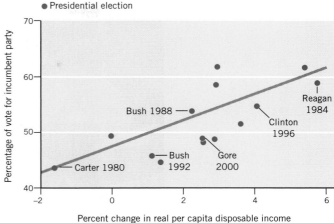

Figure 8.3 **Economic Performance and Vote for the Incumbent President's Party**

Note: Each dot represents a presidential election, showing the popular vote received by the incumbent president's party; 1992 data do not include votes for independent candidate H. Ross Perot.

Source: From Robert S. Erikson and Kent L. Tedin, *American Public Opinion,* 5th ed., p. 271. Copyright © 1995 by Allyn & Bacon/Longman. Reprinted by permission of Pearson Education, Inc.

behave just from knowing what a campaign manager has written in a position paper. The voters want some guidance as to how a candidate will behave once elected. They get that guidance by listening not to the details of what a candidate says but to the themes and tone of those statements. Is the candidate tough on crime and drugs? Are his or her statements about the environment sincere or perfunctory? Does the candidate favor having a strong military? Does the candidate care more about not raising taxes or more about helping the homeless?

The desire of voters to discern character, combined with the mechanics of modern campaigning—short radio and television ads and computer-targeted direct mail—lend themselves to an emphasis on themes at the expense of details. This tendency is reinforced by the expectations of ideological party activists and single-issue groups.

Thematic campaigning, negative ads, and the demands of single-issue groups are not new; they are as old as the republic. In the nineteenth century the theme was slavery and the single-issue groups were abolitionists and their opponents; their negative ads

Union members were once heavily Democratic, but since Ronald Reagan began winning white union votes in 1980, these votes have been up for grabs.

make the ones we have today sound like Sunday school sermons. At the turn of the century the themes were temperance and the vote for women; both issues led to no-holds-barred, rough-and-tumble campaigning. In the 1970s and 1980s new themes were advanced by fundamentalist Christians and by pro- and antiabortion groups.

What has changed is not the tone of campaigning but the advent of primary elections. Once, political parties picked candidates out of a desire to win elections. Today activists and single-issue groups influence the selection of candidates, sometimes out of a belief that it is better to lose with the "right" candidate than to win with the wrong one. In a five-candidate primary, only 21 percent of the voters can pick the winner. Single-issue groups can make a big difference under these conditions, even though they may not have much influence in the general election.

Finding a Winning Coalition

Putting together a winning electoral coalition means holding on to your base among committed partisans and attracting the swing voters who cast their ballots in response to issues (retrospectively or prospectively) and personalities.

There are two ways to examine the nature of the parties' voting coalitions. One is to ask what percentage of various identifiable groups in the population supported the Democratic or Republican candidate for president. The other is to ask what proportion of a party's total vote came from each of these groups. The answer to the first question tells us how *loyal* African Americans, farmers, union members, and others are to the Democratic or Republican party or candidate; the answer to the second question tells us how *important* each group is to a candidate or party.

For the Democratic coalition African Americans are the most loyal voters. In every election but one since 1952, two-thirds or more of all African Americans voted Democratic; since 1964 four-fifths have gone Democratic. Usually, Jewish voters are almost as solidly Democratic. Most Hispanics have been Democrats, though the label "Hispanic" conceals differences among Cuban Americans (who often vote Republican) and Mexican Americans and Puerto Ricans (who are strongly Democratic). The turnout among most Hispanic groups has been quite low (many are not yet citizens), so their political power is not equivalent to their numbers (see the box on page 212).

The Democrats have lost their once strong hold on Catholics, southerners, and union members. In 1960 Catholics supported John F. Kennedy (a Democrat and fellow Catholic), but they also voted for Eisenhower, Nixon, and Reagan, all Republicans. Union members deserted the Democrats in 1968 and 1972, came back in 1980 and 1988, and divided about evenly between the two parties in 1952, 1956, and 1980. White southerners have voted Republican in national elections but Democratic in many local ones (see Table 8.5).

The Republican party is often described as the party of business and professional people. The loyalty of these groups to Republicans is in fact strong: only in 1964 did they desert the Republican candidate to support Lyndon Johnson. Farmers have usually been Republican, but they are a volatile group, highly sensitive to the level of farm prices—and thus quick to change parties. They abandoned the Republicans in 1948 and 1964. Contrary to popular wisdom, the Republican party usually wins a majority of the votes of poor people (defined as those earning less than roughly $5,000 a year). Only in 1964 did most poor people support the Democratic candidate. This can be explained by the fact that the poor include quite different elements—low-income blacks

Table 8.5 Who Likes the Democrats?

Percentage of various groups saying that they voted for the Democratic presidential candidate, 1964–2000.

	1964	1968[a]	1972	1976	1980[c]	1984	1988	1992[d]	1996	2000
Sex										
Men	60%	41%	37%	53%	37%	37%	41%	41%	43%	42%
Women	62	45	38	48	45	42	49	46	54	54
Race										
White	59	38	32	46	36	34	40	39	43	42
Nonwhite	94	85	87	85	82	90	86	82	84	90
Education										
College	52	37	37	42	35	40	43	44	47	45
Grad school	66	52	49	58	43	49	56	55	52	52
Occupation										
Professional and business	54	34	31	42	33	37	40	NA	NA	NA
Blue-collar	71	50	43	58	46	46	50	NA	NA	NA
Age										
Under 30	64	47	48	53	43	41	47	44	53	48
50 and over	59	41	36	52	41[e]	39	49	50	48[g]	48
Religion										
Protestant	55	35	30	46	NA	NA	33[f]	33	36	42
Catholic	76	59	48	57	40	44	47	44	53	50
Jewish[b]	89	85	66	68	45	66	64	78	78	79
Southerners	52	31	29	54	47	36	41	42	46	NA

[a]1968 election had three major candidates (Humphrey, Nixon, and Wallace). [b]Jewish vote estimated from various sources; since the number of Jewish persons interviewed is often less than 100, the error in this figure, as well as that for nonwhites, may be large. [c]1980 election had three major candidates (Carter, Reagan, and Anderson). [d]1992 election had three major candidates (Clinton, Bush, and Perot). [e]For 1980–1992, refers to age 60 and over. [f]For 1988, white Protestants only. [g]For 1996, refers to age 45 and over.

Sources: For 1964–1976: Gallup poll data, as tabulated in Jeane J. Kirkpatrick, "Changing Patterns of Electoral Competition," in *The New American Political System,* ed. Anthony King (Washington, D.C.: American Enterprise Institute, 1978), 264–256. For 1980–1992: Data from *New York Times/CBS News* exit polls. For 1996: *Congressional Quarterly Weekly Report,* 1997, p. 188; For 2000: Exit polls supplied by ABC news.

(who are Democrats) and many elderly, retired persons (who usually vote Republican).

In sum, the loyalty of most identifiable groups of voters to either party is not overwhelming. Only African Americans, businesspeople, and Jews usually give two-thirds or more of their votes to one party or the other; other groups display tendencies, but none that cannot be overcome.

The contribution that each of these groups makes to the party coalitions is a different matter. Though African Americans are overwhelmingly and persistently Democratic, they make up so small a portion of the total electorate that they have never accounted for more than a quarter of the total Democratic vote (see Table 8.6). The groups that make up the largest part of the Democratic vote—Catholics, union members, southerners—are also the least dependable parts of that coalition.[21]

When representatives of various segments of society make demands on party leaders and presidential candidates, they usually stress their numbers or their loyalty, but rarely both. African American leaders, for example, sometimes describe the black vote as being of decisive importance to Democrats and thus deserving of special consideration from a Democratic president. But African Americans are so loyal that a Democratic candidate can almost take their votes for granted, and in any event they are not as numerous as other groups. Union leaders emphasize how many union voters there are, but a president will know that union leaders cannot "deliver" the union vote and

that this vote may go to the president's opponent, whatever the leaders say. For any presidential candidate a winning coalition must be put together anew for each election. Only a few voters can be taken for granted or written off as a lost cause.

The Effects of Elections on Policy

To the candidates, and perhaps to the voters, the only interesting outcome of an election is who won. To a political scientist the interesting outcomes are the broad trends in winning and losing and what they imply about the attitudes of voters, the operation of the electoral system, the fate of political parties, and the direction of public policy.

Figure 8.4 shows the trend in the popular vote for president since before the Civil War. From 1876 to 1896 the Democrats and Republicans were hotly competitive. The Republicans won three times, the Democrats twice in close contests. Beginning in 1896 the Republicans became the dominant party, and except for 1912 and 1916, when Woodrow Wilson, a Democrat, was able to win owing to a split in the Republican party, the Republicans carried every presidential election until 1932. Then Franklin Roosevelt put together what has since become known as the "New Deal coalition," and the Democrats became the dominant party. They won every election until 1952, when Eisenhower, a

Table 8.6	The Contribution Made to Democratic Vote Totals by Various Groups, 1956–1996[a]										
	1956	**1960**	**1964**	**1968**	**1972**	**1976**	**1980**	**1984**	**1988**	**1992**	**1996**
Poor (income under $3,000 before 1980, $5,000 in 1990)	19%	16%	15%	12%	10%	7%	5%	8%	5%	5%	5%
Black (and nonwhite)	5	7	12	19	22	16	22	24	15	23	25
Union member (or union member in family)	36	31	32	28	32	33	32	32	27	21	23
Catholic (and other non-Protestant)	38	47	36	40	34	35	32	47	43	46	44
South (including border states)	23	27	21	24	25	36	39	29	24	33	31
Central cities (12 largest metropolitan areas)	19	19	15	14	14	11	12	12	14	NA	6

[a]The figures shown represent the percentage of the party's vote in any specific election attributable to the group in question.

Source: Extracted from figures presented by Robert Axelrod, "Communications," *American Political Science Review* (June 1981). Updated by Daron Shaw; ICPSR American National Election Study, 1992, Pre- and Post-Election Surveys. 1996 estimates based on analyses of NES data by Daron R. Shaw.

Figure 8.4 Partisan Division of the Presidential Vote in the Nation, 1856–2000

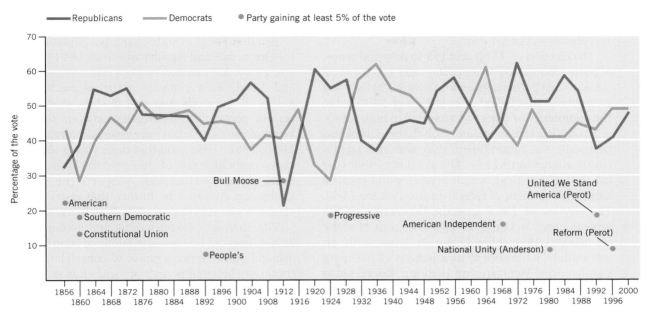

Sources: Updated from Historical Data Archive, Inter-University Consortium for Political Research, as reported in William H. Flanigan and Nancy H. Zingale, *Political Behavior of the American Electorate*, 3rd ed., 32.

Republican and a popular military hero, was elected for the first of his two terms. In the dozen presidential elections since 1952, power has switched hands between the parties six times.

Still, cynics complain that elections are meaningless: no matter who wins, crooks, incompetents, or self-serving politicians still hold office. The more charitable argue that elected officials are usually decent enough but that public policy remains more or less the same no matter which official or party is in office.

There is no brief and simple response to this latter view. Much depends on which office or policy you examine. One reason it is so hard to generalize about the policy effects of elections is that the offices to be filled by the voters are so numerous and the ability of the political parties to unite these officeholders behind a common policy is so weak that any policy proposal must run a gauntlet of potential opponents. Though we have but two major parties, and though only one party can win the presidency, each party is a weak coalition of diverse elements that reflect the many divisions in public opinion. The

proponents of a new law must put together a majority coalition almost from scratch, and a winning coalition on one issue tends to be somewhat different—quite often dramatically different—from a winning coalition on another issue.

In a parliamentary system with strong parties, such as that in Great Britain, an election can often have a major effect on public policy. When the Labour party won office in 1945, it put several major industries under public ownership and launched a comprehensive set of social services, including a nationalized health care plan. Its ambitious and controversial campaign platform was converted, almost item by item, into law. When the Conservative party returned to power in 1951, it accepted some of these changes but rejected others (for example, it denationalized the steel industry).

American elections, unless accompanied by a national crisis such as a war or a depression, rarely produce changes of the magnitude of those that occurred in Britain in 1945. The constitutional system within which our elections take place was designed to moderate the pace of change—to make it neither easy nor impossible to adopt radical proposals. But the fact that the system is intended to moderate the rate of change does not mean that it will always work that way.

The election of 1860 brought to national power a party committed to opposing the extension of slavery and southern secession; it took a bloody war to vindicate that policy. The election of 1896 led to the dominance of a party committed to high tariffs, a strong currency, urban growth, and business prosperity—a commitment that was not significantly altered until 1932. The election of that year led to the New Deal, which produced the greatest single enlargement of federal authority since 1860. The election of 1964 gave the Democrats such a large majority in Congress (as well as control of the presidency) that there began to issue forth an extraordinary number of new policies of sweeping significance—Medicare and Medicaid, federal aid to education and to local law enforcement, two dozen environmental and consumer protection laws, the Voting Rights Act of 1965, a revision of the immigration laws, and a new cabinet-level Department of Housing and Urban Development.

The election of 1980 brought into office an administration determined to reverse the direction of policy over the preceding half century. Reagan's administration succeeded in obtaining large tax cuts, significant reductions in spending (or in the rate of increase of spending) on some domestic programs, and changes in the policies of some regulatory agencies. The election of 1982, in which the Democrats made gains in the House of Representatives, stiffened congressional resistance to further spending cuts and stimulated renewed interest in tax increases as a way of reducing the deficit. Following the election of 1984 a major tax reform plan was passed. After the 1996 election Clinton and Republican congressional leaders agreed on a plan to balance the budget.

In view of all these developments it is hard to argue that the pace of change in our government is always slow or that elections never make a difference. Studies by scholars confirm that elections are often significant, despite the difficulty of getting

laws passed. One analysis of about fourteen hundred promises made between 1944 and 1964 in the platforms of the two major parties revealed that 72 percent were put into effect.[22]

Another study examined the party platforms of the Democrats and Republicans from 1844 to 1968 and all the laws passed by Congress between 1789 and 1968. By a complex statistical method, the author of the study was able to show that during certain periods the differences between the platforms of the two parties were especially large (1856, 1880, 1896, 1932) and that there was at about the same time a high rate of change in the kinds of laws being passed.[23] This study supports the general impression conveyed by history that elections can often be central to important policy changes.

Why then do we so often think that elections make little difference? It is because public opinion and the political parties enter a phase of consolidation and continuity between periods of rapid change. During this phase the changes are, so to speak, digested, and party leaders adjust to the new popular consensus, which may (or may not) evolve around the merits of these changes. During the 1870s and 1880s Democratic politicians had to come to terms with the failure of the southern secessionist movement and the abolition of slavery; during the 1900s the Democrats had to adjust again, this time to the fact that national economic policy was going to support industrialization and urbanization, not farming; during the 1940s and 1950s the Republicans had to learn to accept the popularity of the New Deal.

Elections in ordinary times are not "critical"— they do not produce any major party realignment, they are not fought out over a dominant issue, and they provide the winners with no clear mandate. In most cases an election is little more than a retrospective judgment on the record of the incumbent president and the existing congressional majority. If times are good, incumbents win easily; if times are bad, incumbents may lose even though their opponents may have no clear plans for change. But even a "normal" election can produce dramatic results if the winner is a person such as Ronald Reagan, who helped give his party a distinctive political philosophy.

U.S. Senate Challenger Launches Blistering Media Attack

TV and Radio Ads Call Incumbent "Callous" Puppet of Big Money

October 20
PHOENIX, AZ

Until last week every statewide poll showed U.S. senator Joseph P. Tierney coasting to a comfortable reelection victory. Today, however, the Tierney campaign is reeling. Polls show the race tightening fast, thanks to thirty-second negative ads depicting the senator's votes against certain gun control bills and prescription drug price control plans as evidence of his "heartless approach to public safety and callous disregard for the lives of the medically needy." The ads call Tierney's votes "political payoffs to the gun makers and big drug companies who have owned him" for years . . .

MEMORANDUM

To: Senator Joseph P. Tierney
From: Gary Walker, campaign manager
Subject: Responding to negative ads

Never in your political career have you been attacked so viciously. The fact is that your lead is now in the single digits, and we think it is because of the negative ads. With only a few weeks left until election day, you need to decide whether you want us to fight fire with fire.

Arguments for:

1. Negative ads work. In particular some studies, and lots of political lore, suggest that "going negative" helps lesser-known, less-well-financed challengers against better-known, better-financed incumbents who fail to respond in kind and in time.
2. In the age of the political sound bite, it is much easier to dish dirt on an opponent's personal history and official record than it is to explain the complexities behind one's own past votes or to put one's past public statements back into context.
3. If you don't sling the mud back, it will stick to you, and people will question not only your integrity but also your toughness.

Arguments against:

1. Negative ads can backfire. People don't like them, esecially when the charges are harshly personal or otherwise over the top.
2. A tit-for-tat sound bite volley can be positive: "I am a person of integrity. I vote my conscience. I live to serve."
3. If you stay positive and "wrap yourself in the flag," the mud will melt away and people will question your opponent's decency and character.

Your decision:
Go negative _____
Stay positive _____

Summary

Today's political candidates face the problem of creating a temporary organization that can raise money from large numbers of small donors, mobilize enthusiastic supporters, and win a nomination in a way that will not harm their ability to appeal to a broader, more diverse constituency in the general election. Campaigning has an uncertain effect on election outcomes, but election outcomes can have important effects on public policy, especially at those times—during critical or "realigning" elections—when new voters are coming into the electorate in large numbers, old party loyalties are weakening, or a major issue is splitting the majority party. Most people vote retrospectively rather than prospectively.

Reconsidering the Enduring Questions

1. *How have primaries and general-election campaigns changed over the past century and a half?*

   Elections have changed in this country because political parties have become weaker. Political campaigns have increasingly become personalized, with little or no connection to formal party organizations, as a result of the decay of parties, the rise of the direct primary and the electronic media, and campaign finance laws.

2. *What matters most in deciding who wins presidential and congressional elections?*

   We don't have a theory of elections that will accurately predict the results (political scientists made huge mistakes in 2000), but we do know what factors make the biggest difference. The better the economy and the more popular the candidate, the greater the chance he or she will win. And party loyalty (or its counterpart, political ideology) still makes a big difference even though voters will tell you that they vote "for the candidate, not the party." In congressional races, district lines drawn to help incumbents keep the number of really competitive districts rather small. In elections, most people vote retrospectively; that is, they ask whether the nation was well off or poorly off under the party that is now in control.

3. *Do elections really make a difference in what laws get passed?*

   Elections often make a bigger difference in European democracies because there the winner has more complete control of the government, at least for a while. Here the president must contend all of the time with rivals, including those in his own party.

World Wide Web Resources

- Federal Election Commission: www.fec.gov
- Project Vote Smart: www.vote-smart.org
- Election history: clerkweb.house.gov
- Electoral college: www.avagara.com/e_c
- Campaign finance: www.opensecrets.org

Key Terms

incumbent *p. 186*
coattails *p. 186*
political action committee (PAC) *p. 188*
malapportionment *p. 189*
gerrymandering *p. 189*
sophomore surge *p. 190*

position issue *p. 194*
valence issue *p. 194*
general election *p. 196*
primary election *p. 196*
closed primary *p. 196*
open primary *p. 196*
blanket primary *p. 196*

runoff primary *p. 196*
presidential primary *p. 196*
independent expenditure *p. 203*
soft money *p. 204*
prospective voting *p. 210*
retrospective voting *p. 210*

Suggested Readings

Asher, Herbert. *Presidential Elections and American Politics*. 5th ed. Pacific Grove, Calif.: Brooks/Cole, 1992. A useful, brief analysis of how Americans have voted.

Burnham, Walter Dean. *Critical Elections and the Mainsprings of American Politics*. New York: Norton, 1970. An argument about the decline in voting participation and the significance of the realigning election of 1896.

Jacobson, Gary C. *The Politics of Congressional Elections*. 2d ed. Boston: Little, Brown, 1987. Careful analysis of how people get elected to Congress.

Kayden, Xandra. *Campaign Organization*. Lexington, Mass.: D. C. Heath, 1978. A close look at how political campaigns are organized, staffed, and led at the state level.

Malbin, Michael J., ed. *Money and Politics in the United States: Financing Elections in the 1980s*. Chatham, N.J.: Chatham House, 1984. Articles on the sources and uses of campaign money, with special attention to political parties and political action committees.

Page, Benjamin I. *Choices and Echoes in Presidential Elections*. Chicago: University of Chicago Press, 1978. Analyzes the interaction between the behavior of candidates and of voters in American elections.

Sorauf, Frank. *Money in American Elections*. Glenview, Ill.: Scott Foresman, 1988. The best summary of what we know about the sources and effects of campaign spending.

Sundquist, James L. *Dynamics of the Party System: Alignment and Realignment of Political Parties in the United States*. Rev. ed. Washington, D.C.: Brookings Institution, 1983. Historical analysis of realigning elections from 1860 to the nonrealignment of 1980.

Interest Groups

Enduring Questions

1. Why do people join interest groups?
2. With so many interest groups active, has America succeeded in "curing the mischiefs of faction"?
3. Are there any ways, both feasible and desirable, of regulating interest groups?

Almost every tourist arriving in Washington visits the White House and the Capitol. Many look at the Supreme Court building. But hardly any walk down K Street, where much of the political life of the country occurs.

K Street? From the sidewalk it is just a row of office buildings, no different from what one might find in downtown Seattle or Kansas City. What's to see? But in these buildings, and in similar ones lining nearby streets, are the offices of the nearly seven thousand organizations that are represented in Washington.

It is doubtful whether there is any other nation in which so many organizations are represented in its capital. They are there to participate in politics. They are interest groups, or, if you prefer, lobbies.

Explaining Proliferation

There are at least three reasons why interest groups are so common in this country. First, the more cleavages there are in a society, the greater the variety of

★ **POLITICALLY SPEAKING** ★

Lobby

To **lobby** means to attempt to influence governmental decisions, especially legislation. A lobby is a group organized for this purpose, and a **lobbyist** is an individual who engages in lobbying.

The term came into vogue in the mid-seventeenth century to refer to a large anteroom near the English House of Commons, wherein members of Parliament could be approached by people pleading their cases.

In the United States lobbyists were people who met members of Congress just outside the chambers of the House or Senate to argue their cause. In the nineteenth century *lobbyist* became synonymous with *vote buyer*, because of the widespread belief that lobbyists were using money to corrupt legislators.

Today lobbying is no longer regarded as an inevitably corrupt activity, and lobbyists in Washington are no longer embarrassed to refer to themselves by this term.

Source: Adapted from *Safire's Political Dictionary* by William Safire. Copyright © 1968, 1972, 1978 by William Safire. Reprinted by permission of Random House, Inc. and the author.

Federalist No. 10, "The latent causes of faction are thus sown in the nature of man."

Second, the American constitutional system contributes to the number of interest groups by multiplying the points at which such groups can gain access to the government. In a nation such as Great Britain, where most political authority is lodged in a single official such as the prime minister, there are only a few places where important decisions are made—and thus only a few opportunities for affecting those decisions. But when political authority is shared by the president, the courts, and Congress (and within Congress among two houses and countless committees and subcommittees), there are plenty of places where one can argue one's case. And the more chances there are to influence policy, the more organizations there will be that seek to exercise that influence.

This fact helps explain why in Great Britain there is often only one organization representing a given interest, whereas in the United States there are several. In London only one major association represents farmers, one represents industry, one represents veterans, and one represents doctors. In the United States, by contrast, at least three organizations represent farmers (the American Farm Bureau Federation, the National Farmers' Union, and the Grange), and each of these is made up of state and county branches, many of which act quite independently of national headquarters. Though there is one major American labor organization, the AFL-CIO, it is in fact a loose coalition of independent unions (plumbers, steelworkers, coal miners), and some large unions, such as the Teamsters, were for many years not part of the AFL-CIO at all.

Third, the weakness of political parties in this country may help explain the number and strength of our interest groups. Where parties are strong, interests work through the parties; where parties are weak, interests operate directly on the government. That at least is the theory. Though scholars are not certain of its validity, it is a plausible theory and can be illustrated by differences among American cities. In cities such as Chicago where a party (in this case, the Democrats) has historically been very strong, labor unions, business associations, and citizens groups have had to work with the party and on its terms. But in cities such as Boston and Los Angeles where the parties are very weak, interest groups proliferate and play a large role in making policy.[1]

interests that will exist. In addition to divisions along lines of income and occupation found in any society, America is a nation of countless immigrants and many races. There are at least seventy-two religions that claim sixty-five thousand members or more. Americans are scattered over a vast land made up of many regions with distinctive traditions and cultures. These social facts make for a great variety of interests and opinions. As James Madison said in

In Austria, France, and Italy many if not most interest groups are closely linked to one or another political party. In Italy, for example, each party—Socialist, Communist, and Christian Democrat—has a cluster of labor unions, professional associations, and social clubs allied with it.[2] Though American interest groups often support one party (the AFL-CIO, for example, almost always backs Democratic candidates for office), the relationship between party and interest group here is not as close as it is in Europe.

The Birth of Interest Groups

The number of interest groups has grown rapidly since 1960. A study of Washington-based political associations revealed that roughly 70 percent of them established their Washington offices after 1960, and nearly half opened their doors after 1970.[3]

The 1960s and 1970s were boom years for interest groups, but there have been other periods in our history when political associations were created in especially large numbers. During the 1770s many groups arose to agitate for American independence; during the 1830s and 1840s the number of religious associations increased sharply, and the antislavery movement began. In the 1860s trade unions based on crafts emerged in significant numbers, farmers formed the Grange, and various fraternal organizations were born. In the 1880s and 1890s business associations proliferated. The great era of organization building, however, was in the first two decades of the twentieth century. Within this twenty-year period many of the best-known and largest associations with an interest in national politics were formed: the Chamber of Commerce, the National Association of Manufacturers, the American Medical Association, the National Association for the Advancement of Colored People (NAACP), the Urban League, the American Farm Bureau Federation, the Farmers' Union, the National Catholic Welfare Conference, the American Jewish Committee, and the Anti-Defamation League. The wave of interest group formation that occurred in the 1960s led to the emergence of environmental, consumer, and political reform organizations such as those sponsored by consumer activist Ralph Nader.

The fact that associations in general, and political interest groups in particular, are created more rapidly in some periods than in others suggests that these groups do not arise inevitably out of natural social processes. There have always been farmers in this country, but there were no national farm organizations until the latter part of the nineteenth century. Blacks had been victimized by various white-

The greater the activity of government—for example, in regulating the timber industry—the greater the number of interest groups.

supremacy policies from the end of the Civil War on, but the NAACP did not emerge until 1910. Men and women worked in factories for decades before industrial unions were formed.

At least four factors help explain the rise of interest groups. The first consists of broad economic developments that create new interests and redefine old ones. Farmers had little reason to become organized for political activity so long as most of them consumed what they produced. The importance of regular political activity became evident only after most farmers began to produce cash crops for sale in markets that were unstable or affected by forces (the weather, the railroads, foreign competition) that farmers could not control. Similarly, for many decades most workers were craftspeople working alone or in small groups. Such unions as existed were little more than craft guilds interested in protecting members' jobs and in training apprentices. The reason for large, mass-membership unions did not exist until there arose mass-production industry operated by large corporations.

Second, government policy itself helped create interest groups. Wars create veterans, who in turn demand pensions and other benefits. The first large veterans organization, the Grand Army of the Republic, was made up of Union veterans of the Civil War. By the 1920s these men were receiving about a quarter of a billion dollars a year from the government, and naturally they created organizations to watch over the distribution of this money. The federal government encouraged the formation of the American Farm Bureau Federation (AFBF) by paying for county agents who would serve the needs of farmers under the supervision of local farm organizations; these county bureaus eventually came together as the AFBF. The Chamber of Commerce was launched at a conference attended by President William Howard Taft.

Professional societies, such as those made up of lawyers and doctors, became important in part because state governments gave to such groups the authority to decide who was qualified to become a lawyer or a doctor. Workers had a difficult time organizing so long as the government, by the use of injunctions enforced by the police and the army, prevented strikes. Unions, especially those in mass-production industries, began to flourish after Congress passed laws in the 1930s that prohibited the use of injunctions in private labor disputes, that required employers to bargain with unions, and that allowed a union representing a majority of the workers in a plant to require all workers to join it.[4]

Third, political organizations do not emerge automatically, even when government policy permits them and social circumstances seem to require them. Somebody must exercise leadership, often at substantial personal cost. These organizational entrepreneurs are found in greater numbers at certain times than at others. They are often young, caught up in a social movement, drawn to the need for change, and inspired by some political or religious doctrine. Antislavery organizations were created in the 1830s and 1840s by enthusiastic young people influenced by a religious revival then sweeping the country. The period from 1890 to 1920, when so many national organizations were created, was a time when the college-educated middle class was growing rapidly. (The number of men and women who received college degrees each year tripled between 1890 and 1920.)[5] During this era natural science and fundamentalist Christianity were locked in a bitter contest, with the Gospels and Darwinism offering competing ideas about personal salvation and social progress. The 1960s, when many new organizations were born, was a decade in which young people were powerfully influenced by the civil rights and antiwar movements and when college enrollments more than doubled.

Finally, the more activities government undertakes, the more organized groups there will be that are interested in those activities. As can be seen from Table 9.1, most Washington offices representing corporations, labor unions, and trade and professional associations were established before 1960—in some cases many decades before—because it was during the 1930s or even earlier that the government began making policies important to business and labor. The great majority of "public-interest" lobbies (those concerned with the environment or consumer protection), social welfare associations, and organizations concerned with civil rights, the elderly, and the handicapped established offices in Washington after 1960. Policies of interest to these groups, such as the major civil rights and environmental laws, were adopted after that date. In fact over half the public-interest lobbies opened their doors after 1970.

Kinds of Organizations

An **interest group** is any organization that seeks to influence public policy. When we think of an organization, we usually think of something like the Boy Scouts or the League of Women Voters—a group consisting of individual members. In Washington, however, many organizations do not have individual members at all but are offices—corporations, law firms, public relations firms, or "letterhead" organizations that get most of their money from foundations or from the government—out of which a staff operates. It is important to understand the differences between the two kinds of interest groups—institutional and membership interests.[6]

Institutional Interests

Institutional interests are individuals or organizations representing other organizations. General Motors, for example, has a Washington representative. Over five hundred firms have such representatives in the capital, most of whom have opened their offices since 1970.[7] Firms that do not want to place their own full-time representative in Washington can hire a Washington lawyer or public relations expert on a part-time basis. Between 1970 and 1980 the number of lawyers in Washington more than tripled; Washington now has more lawyers (over 38,000) than Los Angeles, a city three times its size.[8] Another kind of institutional interest is the trade or governmental association, such as the National Independent Retail Jewelers or the National Association of Counties.

Individuals or organizations that represent other organizations tend to be interested in bread-and-butter issues of vital concern to their clients. Some of the people who specialize in this work can earn very large fees. Top public relations experts and Washington lawyers can charge $400 an hour or more for their time. Since they earn a lot, they are expected to deliver a lot.

Just what they are expected to deliver, however, varies with the diversity of the groups making up the organization. The American Cotton Manufacturers Institute represents southern textile mills. Those mills are few enough in number and similar enough in outlook to allow the institute to carry out clear policies squarely based on the business interests of its clients. For example, the institute works hard to get the federal government to adopt laws and rules that will keep foreign-made textiles from competing too

easily with American-made goods. Sometimes the institute is successful, sometimes not, but it is never hard to explain what it is doing.

By contrast, the U.S. Chamber of Commerce represents thousands of different businesses in hundreds of different communities. Its membership is so large and diverse that the Chamber in Washington can speak out clearly and forcefully on only those relatively few matters in which all, or most, businesses take the same position. Since all businesses would like lower taxes, the Chamber favors that. On the other hand, since some businesses (those that import goods) want low tariffs and other businesses (those that face competition from imported goods) want higher tariffs, the Chamber says little or nothing about tariffs.

Institutional interests do not just represent business firms; they also represent governments, foundations, and universities. For example, the American Council on Education claims to speak for most institutions of higher education, the American Public Transit Association represents local mass-transit systems, and the National Association of Counties argues on behalf of county governments.

Membership Interests

It is often said that Americans are a nation of joiners, and so we take for granted the many organizations around us supported by the activities and contributions of individual citizens. But we should not take this multiplicity of organizations for granted; in fact their existence is something of a puzzle.

Table 9.1   Dates of Founding of Organizations Having Washington Offices

Organization	Percentage Founded	
	After 1960	After 1970
Corporations	14%	6%
Unions	21	14
Professional	30	14
Trade	38	23
Civil rights	56	46
Women/elderly/disabled	56	46
"Public interest"	76	57
Social welfare	79	51

Source: Kay Lehman Schlozman and John T. Tierney, *Organized Interests and American Democracy* (New York: Harper & Row, 1986), 76. Copyright © 1986 by Kay Lehman Schlozman and John T. Tierney. Reprinted by permission of Addison-Wesley Educational Publishers, Inc.

Americans join only certain kinds of organizations more frequently than do citizens of other democratic countries. We are no more likely than the British, for example, to join social, business, professional, veterans, or charitable organizations, and we are *less* likely to join labor unions. Our reputation as a nation of joiners arises chiefly out of our unusually high tendency to join religious and civic or political associations. About three times as many Americans as Britons say that they are members of a civic or political organization.[9]

This proclivity of Americans to get together with other citizens to engage in civic or political action reflects, apparently, a greater sense of political efficacy and a stronger sense of civic duty in this country. When Gabriel Almond and Sidney Verba asked citizens of five nations what they would do to protest an unjust local regulation, 56 percent of the Americans—but only 34 percent of the British and 13 percent of the Germans—said that they would try to organize their neighbors to write letters, sign petitions, or otherwise act in concert.[10] Americans are also more likely than Europeans to think that organized activity is an effective way to influence the national government, remote as that institution may seem. And this willingness to form civic or political groups is not a product of higher levels of education in this country; Americans of every level of schooling are political joiners.[11]

But explaining the American willingness to join politically active groups by saying that Americans feel a "sense of political efficacy" is not much of an explanation; we might as well say that people vote because they think that their vote makes a difference. But one vote clearly makes no difference at all in almost any election; similarly, one member, more or less, in the Sierra Club, the Christian Coalition, or the NAACP clearly will make no difference in the success of those organizations.

And in fact most people who are sympathetic to the aims of a mass-membership interest group do not join it. The NAACP, for example, enrolls as members only a tiny fraction of all African Americans. This is not because people are selfish or apathetic but because they are rational and numerous. A single African American, for example, knows that he or she can make no difference in the success of the NAACP, just as a single nature enthusiast knows that he or she cannot enhance the power of the Sierra Club. Moreover, if the NAACP or the Sierra Club succeeds, African Americans and nature lovers will benefit even if they are not members. Therefore rational people who value their time and money would no more join such organizations than they would attempt to empty a lake with a cup—unless they got something out of joining.

Incentives to Join

To get people to join mass-membership organizations, they must be offered an **incentive**—something of value they cannot get without joining. There are three kinds of incentives.

Solidary incentives are the sense of pleasure, status, or companionship that arises out of meeting together in small groups. Such rewards are extremely important, but because they tend to be available only from face-to-face contact, national interest groups offering them often have to organize themselves as coalitions of small local units. For example, the League of Women Voters, the Parent Teacher Association (PTA), the NAACP, the Rotary Club, and the American Legion all consist of small local chapters that support a national staff. It is the task of the local chapters to lure members and obtain funds from them; the state or national staff can then pursue political objectives by using these funds. Forming organizations made up of small local chapters is probably easier in the United States than in Europe because of the great importance of local government in our federal system. There is plenty for a PTA, an NAACP, or a League of Women Voters to do in its own community, and so its members can be

W.E.B. Du Bois (center) was one of the founders of the NAACP in 1910 and the editor of its magazine, The Crisis.

kept busy with local affairs while the national staff pursues larger goals.

A second kind of incentive consists of **material incentives**—that is, money, or things and services readily valued in monetary terms. Farm organizations have recruited many members by offering a wide range of services. The Illinois Farm Bureau, for example, offers to its members—and *only* to its members—a chance to buy farm supplies at discount prices, to market their products through cooperatives, and to purchase low-cost insurance. These material incentives help explain why the Illinois Farm Bureau has been able to enroll nearly every farmer in the state as well as many nonfarmers who also value these rewards.[12]

Similarly, the American Association of Retired Persons (AARP) has recruited over 30 million members by supplying them with everything from low-cost life insurance and mail-order discount drugs to tax advice and group travel plans. About 45 percent of the nation's population that is fifty and older—one out of every four registered voters—belongs to the AARP. With an annual operating budget of over $200 million and a cash flow estimated at a whopping $10 billion, the AARP seeks to influence public policy in many areas, from health and housing to taxes and transportation.

The third—and most difficult—kind of incentive is the *purpose* of the organization. Many associations rely chiefly on this **purposive incentive**—the appeal of their stated goals—to recruit members. If the attainment of those goals will also benefit people who do not join, individuals who do join will have to be those who feel passionately about the goal, who have a strong sense of duty (or who cannot say no to a friend who asks them to join), or for whom the cost of joining is so small that they are indifferent to joining or not. Organizations that attract members by appealing to their interest in a coherent set of (usually) controversial principles are sometimes called **ideological interest groups.**

When the purpose of the organization, if attained, will principally benefit nonmembers, it is customary to call the group a **public-interest lobby.** (Whether the public at large will really benefit, of course, is a matter of opinion, but at least the group members think that they are working selflessly for the common good.)

Though some public-interest lobbies may pursue relatively noncontroversial goals (for example, persuading people to vote or raising money to house orphans), the most visible of these organizations are highly controversial. It is precisely the controversy that attracts the members, or at least those members who support one side of the issue. Many of these groups can be described as markedly liberal or decidedly conservative in outlook.

Perhaps the best known of the liberal public-interest groups are those founded by or associated with Ralph Nader. Nader became a popular figure in the mid-1960s after General Motors made a clumsy attempt to investigate and discredit his background at a time when he was testifying in favor of an auto-safety bill. Nader won a large out-of-court settlement against General Motors, his books began to earn royalties, and he was able to command substantial lecture fees. Most of this money was turned

The largest interest group in America is the AARP, the American Association of Retired Persons.

small contributors and sought foundation grants. Finally, he helped create Public Interest Research Groups (PIRGs) in a number of states, supported by donations from college students (voluntary at some colleges, a compulsory assessment levied on all students at others) and concerned with organizing student activists to work on local projects.

Recently cracks have begun to appear in the Nader movement. When Hawaii and California considered plans to develop no-fault automobile insurance, some former allies of Nader led the effort to reduce auto insurance prices by adopting a no-fault system. Nader denounced this effort and urged Hawaii's governor to veto the no-fault bill. Each side criticized the other.

Conservatives, though slow to get started, have also adopted the public-interest organizational strategy. As with such associations run by liberals, they are of two kinds: those that engage in research and lobbying and those that bring lawsuits designed to advance their cause. The boxes on pages 231 and 232 list some examples of public-interest organizations that support liberal or conservative causes.

Membership organizations that rely on purposive incentives, especially appeals to deeply controversial purposes, tend to be shaped by the mood of the times. When an issue is hot—in the media or with the public—such organizations can grow rapidly. When the spotlight fades, the organization may lose support. Thus such organizations have a powerful motive to stay in the public eye. To remain visible public-interest lobbies devote a lot of attention to generating publicity by developing good contacts with the media and issuing dramatic press releases about crises and scandals.

Because of their need to take advantage of a crisis atmosphere, public-interest lobbies often do best when the government is in the hands of an administration that is *hostile*, not sympathetic, to their views. Environmentalist organizations could mobilize more resources when James Watt, an opponent of much of the environmental movement, was secretary of the interior than they could when Cecil D. Andrus, his proenvironment predecessor, was in office. By the same token many conservative interest groups were able to raise more money with the relatively liberal Jimmy Carter or Bill Clinton in the White House than with the conservative Ronald Reagan.

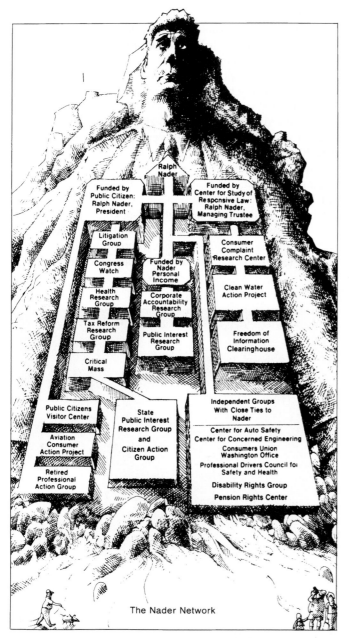

The Nader Network

Since the mid-1960s consumer activist Ralph Nader has spawned more than a dozen interest groups. In 2000 Nader ran for president as a Green party candidate.

over to various organizations he created that dealt with matters of interest to consumers. In addition he founded a group called Public Citizen that raised money by direct-mail solicitation from thousands of

Public-Interest Law Firms

A special kind of public-interest lobby is an organization that advances its cause by bringing lawsuits to challenge existing practices or proposed regulations. A public-interest law firm will act in one of two ways: First, it will find someone who has been harmed by some public or private policy and bring suit on his or her behalf. Second, it will file a brief with a court supporting somebody else's lawsuit (this is called an amicus curiae brief; it is explained in Chapter 14).

Here are some examples of liberal and conservative public-interest law firms:

Liberal	*Conservative*
American Civil Liberties Union	Atlantic Legal Foundation
Asian American Legal Defense Fund	The Center for Individual Rights
Lawyers' Committee for Civil Rights	Criminal Justice Legal Foundation
Mexican American Legal Defense Fund	Landmark Legal Foundation
NAACP Legal Defense and Education Fund	Mountain States Legal Foundation
Natural Resources Defense Council	Pacific Legal Foundation
Women's Legal Defense Fund	Washington Legal Foundation

The Influence of the Staff

We often make the mistake of assuming that what an interest group does politically is simply to exert influence on behalf of its members. That is indeed the case when all the members have a clear and similar stake in an issue. But many issues affect different members differently. In fact, if the members joined to obtain solidary or material benefits, they may not care at all about many of the issues with which the organization gets involved. In such cases what the interest group does may reflect more what the staff wants than what the members believe.

For example, a survey of the white members of a large labor union showed that one-third of them believed that the desegregation of schools, housing, and job opportunities had gone too fast; only one-fifth thought that it had gone too slowly. But among the staff members of the union, *none* thought that desegregation had gone too fast, and over two-thirds thought that it had gone too slowly.[13] As a result the union staff aggressively lobbied Congress for the passage of tougher civil rights laws, even though most of the union's members did not feel that they were needed. The members stayed in the union for reasons unrelated to civil rights, giving the staff the freedom to pursue its own goals.

The National Council of Churches (NCC), an organization of various Protestant denomina-

tions claiming several million members, has spoken out frequently on political questions, generally by taking a strongly liberal position. But opinion surveys show that most white Protestants are relatively conservative, especially those in the South. Thus it is quite likely that the staff of the NCC does not, on many political questions, actually represent the majority of the churchgoers for whom it claims to speak.[14] It can ignore them because people join churches, by and large, for reasons other than how staff members in New York or Washington think.

Interest Groups and Social Movements

Because it is difficult to attract people with purposive incentives, interest groups employing them tend to arise out of social movements. A **social movement** is a widely shared demand for change in some aspect of the social or political order. The civil rights movement of the 1960s was such an event, as was the environmentalist movement of the 1970s. A social movement need not have liberal goals. In the nineteenth century, for example, there were various nativist movements that sought to reduce immigration to this country or to keep Catholics or Masons

Think Tanks in Washington

Think tanks are public-interest organizations that do research on policy questions and disseminate their findings in books, articles, conferences, op-ed essays for newspapers, and (occasionally) testimony before Congress. Some are nonpartisan and ideologically more or less neutral, but others—and many of the most important ones—are aligned with liberal or conservative causes. Here are some examples of each:

Liberal	*Conservative*
Center on Budget and Policy Priorities	American Enterprise Institute
Center for Defense Information	Cato Institute
Children's Defense Fund	Center for Strategic and
Economic Policy Institute	International Studies
Institute for Policy Studies	Competitive Enterprise Institute
Joint Center for Political and	Ethics and Public Policy Center
Economic Studies	Free Congress Foundation
Progressive Policy Institute	Heritage Foundation

Note that the labels "liberal" and "conservative," while generally accurate, conceal important differences among the think tanks in each list.

out of public office. Broad-based religious revivals are social movements.

No one is quite certain why social movements arise. At one moment people are largely indifferent to some issue; at another moment many of these same people care passionately about religion, civil rights, immigration, or conservation. A social movement may be triggered by a scandal (an oil spill on the Santa Barbara beaches helped launch the environmental movement), the dramatic and widely publicized activities of a few leaders (lunch counter sit-ins helped stimulate the civil rights movement), or the coming of age of a new generation that takes up a cause advocated by eloquent writers, teachers, or evangelists.

The Environmental Movement

Whatever its origin, the effect of a social movement is to increase the value some people attach to purposive incentives. As a consequence new interest groups are formed that rely on these incentives. In the 1890s, as a result of the emergence of conservation as a major issue, the Sierra Club was organized. In the 1930s conservation once again became popular, and the Wilderness Society and the National Wildlife Federation took form. In the 1960s and 1970s environmental issues again came to the fore, and we saw the emergence of the Environmental Defense Fund and Environmental Action.

The smallest of these organizations (Environmental Action and the Environmental Defense Fund) tend to have the most liberal members. This is often the case with social movements. A movement will spawn many organizations. The most passionately aroused people will be the fewest in number, and they will gravitate toward the organizations that take the most extreme positions; as a result these organizations are small but vociferous. The more numerous and less passionate people will gravitate toward more moderate, less vociferous organizations, which will tend to be larger.

The Feminist Movement

There have been several feminist social movements in this country's history—in the 1830s, in the 1890s, in the 1920s, and in the 1960s. Each period has brought into being new organizations, some of which have endured to the present. For example, the League of Women Voters was founded in 1920 to educate and organize women for the purpose of using effectively their newly won right to vote.

Though a strong sense of purpose may lead to the creation of organizations, each will strive to find some incentive that will sustain it over the long haul. These permanent incentives will affect how the organization participates in politics.

There are at least three kinds of feminist organizations. First, there are those that rely chiefly on solidary incentives, enroll middle-class women with relatively high levels of schooling, and tend to support those causes that command the widest support among women generally. The League of Women Voters and the Federation of Business and Professional Women are examples. Both supported the campaign to ratify the Equal Rights Amendment (ERA), but as Jane Mansbridge has observed in her history of the ERA, they were uneasy with the kind of intense, partisan fighting displayed by some other women's organizations and with the tendency of more militant groups to link the ERA to other issues, such as abortion. The reason for their uneasiness is clear: to the extent they relied on solidary incentives, they had a stake in avoiding issues and tactics that would divide their membership or reduce the extent to which membership provided camaraderie and professional contacts.[15]

Second, there are women's organizations that attract members with purposive incentives. The National Organization for Women (NOW) and the National Abortion Rights Action League (NARAL) are two of the largest such groups, though there are many smaller ones. Because they rely on purposes, these organizations must take strong positions, tackle divisive issues, and employ militant tactics. Anything less would turn off the committed feminists who make up the rank and file and contribute the funds. But because these groups take controversial stands, they are constantly embroiled in internal quarrels between those who think that they have gone too far and those who think that they have not gone far enough, between women who want NOW or NARAL to join with lesbian and socialist organizations and those who want them to steer clear. Moreover, as Mansbridge showed, purposive organizations often cannot make their decisions stick on the local level (local chapters will do pretty much as they please).[16]

The third kind of women's organization is the caucus that takes on specific issues that have some material benefit to women. The Women's Equity Action League (WEAL) is one such group. Rather than relying on membership dues for financial support, it obtains grants from foundations and government agencies. Freed of the necessity of satisfying a large rank-and-file membership, WEAL has concentrated its efforts on bringing lawsuits aimed at enforcing or enlarging the legal rights of women in higher education and other institutions. In electoral politics

A march in Los Angeles campaigns for gun control.

the National Women's Political Caucus (officially nonpartisan, but generally liberal and Democratic) and the National Federation of Republican Women (openly supportive of the Republican party) work to get more women active in politics and more women elected or appointed to office.

The feminist movement has, of course, spawned an antifeminist movement, and thus feminist organizations have their antifeminist counterparts. The campaign by NOW for the ERA was attacked by a women's group called STOP ERA; the proabortion position of NARAL has been challenged by the various organizations associated with the right-to-life movement. These opposition groups have their own tactical problems, which arise in large part from their reliance on different kinds of incentives. In the chapter on civil rights we shall see how the conflict between these opposing groups shaped the debate over the ERA.

The Union Movement

When social movements run out of steam, they leave behind organizations that continue the fight. But with the movement dead or dormant, the organizations often must struggle to stay alive. This has happened to labor unions.

The major union movement in this country occurred in the 1930s, when the Great Depression, popular support, and a sympathetic administration in Washington led to a rapid growth in union membership. In 1945 union membership peaked; at that time nearly 36 percent of all nonfarm workers were union members.

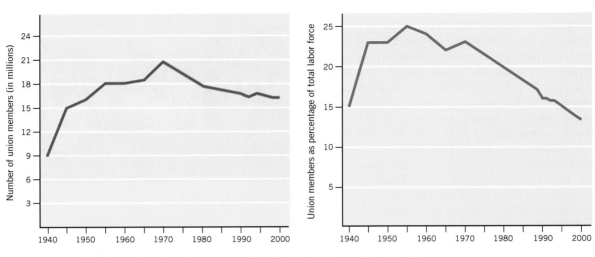

Figure 9.1 The Decline in Union Membership

Sources: *Historical Statistics of the United States,* vol. 1, 178; *Statistical Abstract of the United States, 1998,* 444; U.S. Census Bureau.

Since then union membership has fallen more or less steadily, so that by 2000 only 13.5 percent of all workers were unionized (see Figure 9.1). This decline has been caused by several factors. There has been a shift in the nation's economic life away from industrial production (where unions have traditionally been concentrated) and toward service delivery (where unions have usually been weak). But accompanying this decline, and perhaps contributing to it, has been a decline in popular approval of unions.

Approval has moved down side by side with a decline in membership and declines in union victories in elections held to see whether workers in a plant want to join a union. The social movement that supported unionism has faded.

But unions will persist, because most can rely on incentives other than purposive ones to keep them going. In many industries they can require workers to join if they wish to keep their jobs, and in other industries workers believe that they get sufficient

Table 9.2 The Rise in Four Government Employee Unions

Union	Number of Members			
	1979	1983	1993	2000
National Association of Letter Carriers	151,000	201,000	210,000	220,000
Postal Workers	245,000	213,999	249,000	366,000
American Federation of Teachers	423,000	544,000	574,000	1 million*
American Federation of State and County Municipal Employees	889,000	1 million	1.16 million	1.3 million
	Four-Union Total 1979: 1.71 million			
	Four-Union Total 2000: 2.89 million			
	Percent Change, 1979–2000: +69%			

*Data for 1999.

Sources: *Statistical Abstract of the United States, 1994,* table 696, 443; post-1998 press releases and fact sheets by each organization.

benefits from the union to make even voluntary membership worthwhile. And in a few industries, such as teaching and government, there has been a growth in membership, as some white-collar workers have turned to unions to advance their interests.

Unions composed of government workers are becoming the most important part of the union movement. They are almost the only part that is growing in size. For example, from 1983 to 1999 the number of private sector union members fell from 11.9 million to 9.4 million, a 21 percent drop. Over the same period, however, the number of public sector union members rose from 5.7 million to 7 million, a 22 percent increase.[17] Especially significant has been the membership growth in certain government employee unions affiliated with the AFL-CIO (see Table 9.2). These unions have gained new members and political clout at a time when almost every industrial union was losing both.

Funds for Interest Groups

All interest groups have some trouble raising money, but membership organizations have more trouble than most, especially membership organizations relying on appeals to purpose—to accomplishing stated goals. As a result the Washington office of a public-interest lobbying group is likely to be small, stark, and crowded, whereas that of an institutional lobby, such as the AFL-CIO or the American Council on Education, will be rather lavish.

To raise more money than members supply in dues, lobbying organizations have turned to three sources that have become important in recent years: foundation grants, government grants, and direct-mail solicitation.

Foundation Grants

One study of eighty-three (primarily liberal) public-interest lobbying groups found that one-third of them received half or more of all their funds from foundation grants; one-tenth received over 90 percent from such sources.[18] Between 1970 and 1980 the Ford Foundation alone contributed about $21 million to liberal public-interest groups. Many of these organizations were law firms that, other than the staff lawyers, really had no members at all. The Environmental Defense Fund is supported almost entirely by grants from foundations such as the Rockefeller Family Fund. The more conservative Scaife foundations gave $1.8 million to a conservative public-interest group, the National Legal Center for the Public Interest.[19]

Federal Grants and Contracts

The expansion of federal grants during the 1960s and 1970s benefited interest groups as well as cities and states; the cutbacks in those grants during the early 1980s hurt interest groups even more than they hurt local governments. Of course the federal government usually does not give the money to support lobbying itself; it is given instead to support some project that the organization has undertaken. For example, the National Alliance of Business received $20 million in 1980 from Washington, much of it for summer youth job programs and the like. But money for a project helps support the organization as a whole and thus enables the organization to press Congress for policies it favors (including, of course, policies that will supply it with more grants and contracts).

Before running for president in 1984, the Reverend Jesse Jackson had been heavily supported for several years by federal grants to his community-development organization, PUSH. Between 1978 and 1982 PUSH received in excess of $5 million from various federal agencies.

Since most public-interest groups pursue liberal policies, the Reagan administration became interested in saving money by reducing grants to interest groups and was particularly interested in cutting back on money being spent to lobby for liberal causes. Some writers called this an effort to "de-fund the left."

Direct Mail

If there is any one technique that is unique to the modern interest group, it is the sophistication with which mailings are used both to raise money and to mobilize supporters. By using computers, membership interest groups can mail directly to specialized audiences identified from lists developed by the staff or purchased from other organizations. Letters can be tailor-made, for example, to appeal to upper-income residents of Oregon who belong to the Sierra Club, live near the Columbia River, own four-wheel-drive vehicles, and thus might be interested in maintaining a local wilderness area.

A classic example of an interest group that was created and maintained by direct-mail solicitation is Common Cause, a liberal organization founded in

1970. Its creator, John Gardner, sent letters to tens of thousands of people selected from mailing lists it had acquired, urging them to join the organization and to send in money. Over two hundred thousand members were obtained in this way, each of whom mailed in dues (initially $15 a year) in return for nothing more than the satisfaction of belonging.

But raising money by mail costs money—lots of money. To bring in more money than it spends, the interest group must write a letter that will galvanize enough readers to send in a check. "Enough" usually amounts to at least 2 percent of the names on the list. Techniques include the following:

- Put a "teaser" on the outside of the envelope so that it won't be thrown out as "junk mail." If the letter is going to African Americans, put a picture of Reverend Martin Luther King, Jr. on the envelope.
- Arouse emotions, preferably by portraying the threat posed by some "devil." To environmentalists, a typical devil would be former secretary of the interior James Watt; to civil libertarians, former Moral Majority leader Jerry Falwell; to conservatives, Senator Ted Kennedy.
- Have the endorsement of a famous name. For liberals it is often Senator Kennedy; for conservatives it may be Senator Jesse Helms.
- Personalize the letter by instructing the computer to insert the recipient's name into the text of the letter to create the impression that it was written personally to him or her.

The Problem of Bias

Many observers believe that the interest groups active in Washington reflect an upper-class bias. There are two reasons for this belief: first, well-off people are more likely than poor people to join and be active in interest groups, and second, interest groups representing business and the professions are much more numerous and better financed than organizations representing minorities, consumers, or the disadvantaged.

Doubtless both these facts are true. Many scholars have shown that people with higher incomes, those whose schooling went through college or beyond, and those in professional or technical jobs were much more likely to belong to a voluntary association than people with the opposite characteristics. Just as we would expect, higher-income people can afford more organizational memberships than lower-income ones; people in business and the professions find it both easier to attend meetings (they have more control over their own work schedules) and more necessary to do so than people in blue-collar jobs; and people with college degrees often have a wider range of interests than those without.

Of the nearly seven thousand groups that were represented in Washington in 1976, over half were corporations, and another third were professional and trade associations. Only 4 percent were public-interest groups; fewer than 2 percent were civil rights or minority groups.[20] About 170 organizations represented in Washington were concerned just with the oil industry.

But the question of an upper-class bias cannot be settled by these two facts taken alone. In the first place, they describe only certain *inputs* into the political system; they say nothing about the *outputs*— that is, who wins and who loses on particular issues. Even if 170 interest groups are trying to protect the oil industry, this is important only if the oil industry in fact gets protected. Sometimes it does; sometimes it does not. At one time, when oil prices were low, oil companies were able to get Congress to pass a law that sharply restricted the importation of foreign oil. A few years later, after oil prices had risen and people were worried about energy issues, these restrictions were ended.

In the second place, business-oriented interest groups are often divided among themselves. Take one kind of business: farming. Once, farm organizations seemed so powerful in Washington that scholars spoke of an irresistible "farm bloc" in Congress that could get its way on almost anything. Today dozens of agricultural organizations operate in the capital, with some (such as the Farm Bureau) attempting to speak for all farmers and others (such as the Tobacco Institute and Mid-America Dairymen) representing particular commodities and regions.

Farmers still have a great deal of influence, especially when it comes to blocking a bill that they oppose. But it is proving difficult for them to get Congress to approve a bill that they want passed. In part this political weakness reflects the decline in the number of farmers and thus in the number of legislators who must take their interests into account. (Only 2.5 percent of all Americans live on farms—just one-sixth of the number who lived there thirty

How Political Mail Piles Up

One day Daniel Aaron Schlozman of Massachusetts joined eight interest groups, four liberal and four conservative.

Over the next eighteen months, he received 248 pieces of mail, weighing a total of *eighteen pounds.* Included were 135 separate appeals for money.

Of the total, 63 pieces of mail were from organizations that he had not joined but that, apparently, had bought or borrowed mailing lists from organizations that he had joined. The conservative organizations allowed their mailing lists to be used by other conservatives; the liberal organizations by other liberals.

For example, by joining the National Conservative Caucus, he found himself on the mailing lists of Young Americans for Freedom, the Committee for the Survival of a Free Congress, the National Tax Limitation Committee, and the Senator Orrin Hatch Election Committee.

By joining Common Cause, he found himself on the mailing lists of the NAACP, the League of Women Voters, the National Organization for Women, the Campaign to Save the Massachusetts Bottle Bill, and the Union of Concerned Scientists.

But it didn't do any of these organizations much good. Daniel Schlozman was only four months old. His mother, Professor Kay Schlozman, a political scientist at Boston College, had enrolled him just to find out who shares mailing lists.

Source: Adapted from Kay Lehman Schlozman and John T. Tierney, *Organized Interests and American Democracy* (New York: Harper & Row, 1986), 94–95.

---

years ago.) In part their political weakness reflects splits among the farmers themselves, with southern cotton growers often seeing things differently from midwestern wheat growers or New England dairy farmers. And to some extent it reflects the context within which interest group politics must operate. In the 1950s few people thought that providing subsidies for farmers was too expensive—if indeed they knew of such programs at all. But by the 1980s consumers were acutely aware of food prices, and their legislators were keenly aware of the cost of farm-support programs.[21]

Whenever American politics is described as having an upper-class bias, it is important to ask exactly what this bias is. Most of the major conflicts in American politics—over foreign policy, economic affairs, environmental protection, or equal rights for women—are conflicts *within* the upper middle class; they are conflicts, that is, among politically active elites. As we saw in Chapter 5, there are profound cleavages of opinion among these elites. Interest group activity reflects these cleavages.

Nonetheless, it would be a mistake to ignore the overrepresentation of business in Washington. A student of politics should always take differences in the availability of political resources as an important clue to possible differences in the outcomes of political conflicts. But they are only clues, not conclusions.

The Activities of Interest Groups

Size and wealth are no longer entirely accurate measures of an interest group's influence—if indeed they ever were. Depending on the issue, the key to political influence may be the ability to generate a dramatic newspaper headline, mobilize a big letter-writing campaign, stage a protest demonstration, file a suit in federal court to block (or compel) some government action, or quietly supply information to key legislators. All of these things require organization, but only some of them require big or expensive organizations.

Information

Of all these tactics, the single most important one—in the eyes of virtually every lobbyist and every academic student of lobbying—is supplying credible information. The reason why information is so valuable is that, to busy legislators and bureaucrats, information is in short supply. Legislators in particular must take positions on a staggering number of issues about which they cannot possibly become experts.

Though there are nonpolitical sources of information, such as encyclopedias, they often do not provide the kind of detailed, specific, up-to-date information that politicians need. This kind of information will ordinarily be gathered only by a group

Farmers once had great influence in Congress and could get their way with a few telephone calls. Today they often must use mass protest methods.

that has a strong interest in some issue. Lobbyists, for the most part, are not flamboyant, party-giving arm-twisters; they are specialists who gather information (favorable to their clients, naturally) and present it in as organized, persuasive, and factual a manner as possible. All lobbyists no doubt exaggerate, but few can afford to misrepresent the facts or mislead a legislator, and for a very simple reason: almost every lobbyist must develop and maintain the confidence of a legislator over the long term, with an eye on tomorrow's issues as well as today's. Misrepresentation or bad advice can embarrass a legislator who accepts it or repel one who detects it, leading to distrust of the lobbyist. Maintaining contacts and channels of communication is vital; to that end, maintaining trust is essential.

The value of the information provided by a lobbyist is often greatest when the issue is fairly narrow, involving only a few interest groups or a complex economic or technical problem. The value of information, and thus the power of the lobbyist, is likely to be least when the issue is one of broad and highly visible national policy.

Sometimes the nature of an issue or the governmental process by which an issue is resolved gives a great advantage to the suppliers of certain information and imposes a great burden on would-be suppliers of contrary information. This is an example of what is called "client politics." For example, the Civil Aeronautics Board (CAB) once set airline fares and decided what airlines would fly to what cities. Historically the only organizations with any incentive to appear before the CAB and supply the necessary information were, naturally, the airlines. Until the CAB began to deregulate civil aviation, CAB decisions often tended to favor the established airlines.

For a long time only radio and television broadcasters had any incentive (or could afford) to appear before the Federal Communications Commission (FCC), which decides which broadcasters shall be licensed and on what terms. Owing to changes in the industry (such as the rise of cable and satellite television) and to the growth of consumer groups, FCC hearings are now often hotly contested. When the Federal Energy Administration (FEA) was trying to allocate scarce oil and gasoline supplies among competing users, it discovered that the information it needed was possessed only by the oil companies. (It later took steps to develop its own sources of data.)

Public officials not only want technical information; they also want political cues. A **political cue** is a signal telling the official what values are at stake in an issue—who is for, who against a proposal—and how that issue fits into his or her own set of political beliefs. Some legislators feel comfortable when they are on the liberal side of an issue, and others feel comfortable when they are on the conservative side, especially when they are not familiar with the details of the issue. A liberal legislator will look to see whether the AFL-CIO, the NAACP, the Americans for Democratic Action, the Farmers' Union, and various consumer organizations favor a proposal; if so, that is often all he or she has to know. If these liberal groups are split, then the legislator will worry about the matter and try to look into it more closely. Similarly, a conservative legislator will feel comfortable taking a stand on an issue if the Chamber of Commerce, the Christian Coalition, the American Medical Association, various business associations, and Americans for Constitutional Action are in agreement about it; he or she will feel less comfortable if such conservative groups are divided. As a result of this process lobbyists often work together in informal coalitions based on general political ideology.

One important way in which these cues are made known is by **ratings** that interest groups make of legislators. These are regularly compiled by the AFL-CIO (on who is prolabor), by the Americans for Democratic Action (on who is liberal), by the Americans for Constitutional Action (on who is conservative), by the Consumer Federation of America (on who is proconsumer), and by the League of Conservation Voters (on who is pro-environment). These ratings are designed to generate public support for (or opposition to) various legislators. They can be helpful sources of information, but they are sometimes biased by the arbitrary determination of what constitutes a liberal, proconsumer, or conservative vote.

Both political information and political cues now arrive in the offices of politicians at a faster rate than ever before, thanks to fax machines and the Internet. Many interest groups and political activists have banks of computer-operated fax machines that can get a short, snappy document into the hands of every legislator within minutes. William Kristol, a Republican activist, used this technique to good effect in 1993 when he bombarded Republican members of Congress with arguments concerning why they should oppose President Clinton's health care plan. Many credit him with having played a major role in the defeat of that plan.

Public Support: The Rise of the New Politics

Once upon a time, when the government was small, Congress was less individualistic, and television was nonexistent, lobbyists mainly used an *insider strategy:* they worked closely with a few key members of Congress, meeting them privately to exchange information and (sometimes) favors. Matters of mutual interest could be discussed at a leisurely pace, over dinner or while playing golf. Public opinion was important on some highly visible issues, but there were not many of these.

Following an insider strategy is still valuable, but increasingly interest groups have turned to an *outsider strategy.* The newly individualistic nature of Congress has made this tactic useful, and modern technology has made it possible. Radio, fax machines, and the Internet can now get news out almost immediately. Satellite television can be used to link interested citizens in various locations across the country. Toll-free phone numbers can be publicized, enabling voters to call the offices of their members of Congress without charge. Public opinion polls can be done by telephone, virtually overnight, to measure (and help generate) support for or opposition to proposed legislation. Mail can be directed by computers to people already known to have an interest in a particular matter.

This kind of *grassroots lobbying* is central to the outsider strategy. It is designed to generate public pressure directly on government officials. The "public" that exerts this pressure is not every voter or even most voters; it is that part of the public (sometimes called an *issue public*) that is directly affected by or deeply concerned with a government policy. What modern technology has made possible is the overnight mobilization of specific issue publics.

Not every issue lends itself to an outsider strategy: it is hard to get many people excited about, for example, complex tax legislation affecting only a few firms. But as the government does more and more, its policies affect more and more people, and so more and more will join in grassroots lobbying efforts over matters such as abortion, Medicare, Social Security, environmental protection, and affirmative action.

Undoubtedly the new politics creates new conflicts. Since conflict is the essence of politics, it may seem strange that politicians dislike controversy. But they do, and for perfectly human reasons: no one enjoys dealing with people who are upset or who find one's viewpoint objectionable or unworthy. Consequently, most legislators tend to hear what they want to hear and to deal with interest groups that agree with them.[22] Two senators from the same state may choose to listen to very different constituencies in that state and to take very different policy positions. Neither senator may feel "pressured" or "lobbied," because each has heard mostly from groups or persons who share his or her views. (Politicians define "pressure" as arguments and inducements supplied by somebody with whom they disagree.)

Members of an interest group will also tend to work primarily with legislators with whom they agree; lobbyists do not like to argue with people who are suspicious of them or who are unlikely to change their minds no matter what is said. For the lobbyist the key target is the undecided or wavering legislator or bureaucrat. Sometimes lobbyists will make a major effort to persuade an undecided legislator that public opinion is strongly inclined in one direction. A lobbyist will do this by commissioning public opinion polls, stimulating local citizens to write letters or send telegrams, arranging for constituents to pay personal visits to the legislator, or getting newspapers to run editorials supporting the lobbyist's position.

Though most lobbying organizations cultivate the goodwill of government officials, there are important exceptions. Some groups, especially those that use an ideological appeal to attract supporters or that depend for their maintenance and influence on media publicity, will deliberately attack actual or potential allies in government in order to embarrass them. Ralph Nader is as likely to denounce as to praise those officials who tend to agree with him, if their agreement is not sufficiently close or public. He did this with Senator Edmund Muskie, the author of the Clean Air Act, and with William Haddon, Jr., an early administrator of the National Highway Traffic Safety Administration. The head of the Fund for Animals is not reluctant to attack those officials in the Forest Service and the Interior Department on whose cooperation the fund must rely if it is to achieve its goals.[23] Sometimes, as we shall see later in this chapter, the use of threats instead of rewards extends to physical confrontations.

It is not clear how often public pressure works. Members of Congress are skilled at recognizing and

discounting organized mail campaigns and feel that they can occasionally afford to go against even legitimate expressions of hostile public opinion. Only a few issues of great symbolic significance and high visibility are so important that a member of Congress would think that to ignore public opinion would mean losing the next election. In 1978 the proposed Panama Canal treaties were one such case; since the 1980s abortion has been another. Issues such as these can make or break a member of Congress.

Of late, interest groups have placed great emphasis on developing grassroots support. Sometimes it is impossible to develop such support, as when a complicated tax regulation of interest to only a few firms is being changed. But sometimes a proposed bill touches a public nerve such that even businesses can help generate an outpouring of mail: when the Food and Drug Administration announced it was going to ban saccharin on the grounds that it caused cancer in laboratory animals, the Calorie Control Council (closely tied to the Coca-Cola Company, a big user of saccharin in soft drinks such as Tab) ran newspaper ads denouncing the policy. The public, worried about losing access to an artificial sweetener important to dieters, responded with an avalanche of mail to Congress, which promptly passed a law reversing the ban.

Usually, however, the public at large doesn't care that much about an issue, and so interest groups will try by direct-mail campaigns to arouse a small but passionate group to write letters or vote (or not vote) for specified candidates. Beginning in 1970 Environmental Action designated certain members of the House of Representatives as the "Dirty Dozen" because of their votes against bills that the lobbying group claimed were necessary to protect the environment. Of the thirty-one members of Congress so listed in various elections, only seven survived in office. Many members of Congress believe that the "Dirty Dozen" label hurts them with pro-environment voters in their districts, and though they are angry over what they feel is the unfair use of that label, they strive to avoid it if at all possible.

The press sometimes depicts certain large, well-funded interest groups as all-powerful, but few are. Take, for example, the National Rifle Association (NRA). Founded in 1871 as a group dedicated to shooting instruction, the NRA in the 1960s and 1970s became a lobby opposing policies that would restrict citizens' rights to own and use firearms for sporting and other legal purposes. By the 1980s the NRA's dues-paying membership had increased from one million to nearly three million. Its members receive magazines, decals, and other direct benefits. From 1983 to 1992 the NRA spent $8 million on congressional races both in direct contributions to their favored candidates and in independent expenditures supporting or opposing various candidates. Still, in the mid-1990s the NRA lost a major battle to repeal New Jersey's ban on certain types of semi-automatic weapons and lost similar battles in Connecticut, Virginia, and other states. In 1993, over fierce opposition from the NRA, Congress passed the Brady bill, a major piece of gun control legislation named after Jim Brady, the press secretary who was shot and permanently disabled during an attempt to assassinate President Reagan. By the late 1990s the NRA had a negative image even among most gun owners, and the organization found itself constantly in the political cross hairs of small but media-savvy pro–gun control lobbies such as Handgun Control, Inc. As the NRA's recent history teaches, in American politics no interest group, no matter how big its budget or mammoth its membership, is a lobby that cannot be beat.

Money and PACs

Contrary to popular suspicions, money is probably one of the less effective ways by which interest groups advance their causes. That was not always the case. Only a few decades ago powerful interests used their bulging wallets to buy influence in Congress. The passage of the campaign finance reform law in 1973 changed that. The law had two effects. First, it sharply restricted the amount that any interest could give to a candidate for federal office (see Chapter 8). Second, it made it legal for corporations and labor unions to form political action committees (PACs) that could make political contributions.

The effect of the second change was to encourage the rapid growth of PACs. By 1993 some 4,200 PACs existed, over six times the number that existed in 1975. In 1999–2000 they gave nearly $260 million to congressional candidates. Some people worry that the existence of all this political money has resulted in our having, as Senator Edward Kennedy put it, "the finest Congress that money can buy." More likely the increase in the number of PACs has had just the opposite effect. The reason is simple:

with PACs so numerous and so easy to form, it is now probable that there will be money available on every side of almost every conceivable issue. As a result members of Congress can take money and still decide for themselves how to vote. As we shall see, there is not much scholarly evidence that money buys votes in Congress.

Indeed, some members of Congress tell PACs what to do rather than take orders from them. Members will frequently inform PACs that they "expect" money from them; grumbling PAC officials feel that they have no choice but to contribute for fear of alienating the members. Moreover, some members have created their *own* PACs—organizations set up to raise money from individual donors that is then given to favored political allies in and out of Congress or used to advance the members' own political ambitions. When Charles Rangel, congressman from New York, was hoping to be elected whip of the Democratic party in the House, he set up a PAC that made campaign contributions to fellow representatives in hopes that they might vote for him as whip. There are many other examples from both sides of the aisle. An ironic consequence of this is that a conservative Republican may give money to a PAC set up by a moderate Democrat, who then gives the money to a liberal Democrat (or vice versa), with the result that the original donor winds up having his or her money go to somebody that he or she profoundly dislikes.

Almost any kind of organization—corporation, labor union, trade association, public-interest lobby, citizens group—can form a PAC. Over half of all PACs are sponsored by corporations, about a tenth by labor unions, and the rest by various groups, including ideological ones.

The rise of ideological PACs has been the most remarkable development in interest group activity in recent years. They have increased in number at a faster rate than business or labor PACs, and in the 1980 and 1982 elections they raised more money than either business or labor. In the 1992 election there were more than one thousand ideological PACs; about one-third were liberal, about two-thirds conservative.[24]

Though the ideological PACs raised more money than business or labor ones, they spent less on campaigns and gave less to candidates. The reason for this anomaly is that an ideological PAC usually has to raise its money by means of massive direct-mail solicitations, expensive efforts that can consume all the money raised, and more. By contrast, a typical business or labor PAC solicits money from within a single corporation or union. Even a well-run ideological PAC must spend fifty cents to raise a dollar; some spend much more than that.[25]

As Table 9.3 shows, of the ten PACs that gave the most money to candidates in the 2000 election, most were labor unions, business organizations, and groups that represented doctors, lawyers, realtors, and government employees. Except for Democratic Republican Independent Voter Education, none was an ideological PAC.

Table 9.4 shows that, as we learned in Chapter 8, incumbents received more PAC money than challengers and that, whereas labor PACs gave almost exclusively to Democrats, business PACs favored Republicans.

Both parties have become dependent on PAC money. Still, the popular image of rich PACs stuffing huge sums into political campaigns and thereby buying the attention and possibly the favors of the grateful candidates is a bit overdrawn. For one thing, the typical PAC contribution is rather small. The average PAC donation to a House candidate is only a few hundred dollars and accounts for less than 1 percent of the candidate's total receipts. Most PACs spread small sums of money over many candidates, and despite their great growth in numbers and expenditures, PACs still provide only about one-third of all the money spent by candidates for the House.[26]

Moreover, scholars have yet to find systematic evidence that PAC contributions generally affect how members of Congress vote. On most issues how legislators vote can be explained primarily by their general ideological outlooks and the characteristics of

Table 9.3	Spending by Political Action Committees (PACs), 2000
Committee	**Contribution**
Realtors Political Action Committee	$3,423,441
Association of Trial Lawyers	2,656,000
American Federation of State and County Municipal Employees –PEOPLE Qualified	2,590,074
Dealers Election Action Committee of the National Automobile Dealers Association (NADA)	2,498,700
Democratic Republican Independent Voter Education	2,494,450
International Brotherhood of Electrical Workers Committee on Political Education	2,244,325
Machinists Non-Partisan Political League	2,181,113
UAW-V-CAP (UAW Voluntary Community Action Program)	1,942,623
American Medical Association Political Action Committee	1,887,649
Service Employees International Union Political Campaign Committee	1,887,649

Source: Federal Election Commission.

their constituents; how much PAC money they have received turns out to be a small factor. On the other hand, when an issue arises in which most of their constituents have no interest and ideology provides little guidance, there is a slight statistical correlation between PAC contributions and votes. But even here the correlation may be misleading. The same groups that give money also wage intensive lobbying campaigns, flooding representatives with information,

Table 9.4	How PACs Spent Their Money in 2000 (in millions of dollars)									
	House					**Senate**				
PAC Sponsor	**Dem.**	**Rep.**	**Incumbent**	**Challenger**	**Open**	**Dem.**	**Rep.**	**Incumbent**	**Challenger**	**Open**
Corporate	$22.0	$39.9	$54.3	$2.2	$5.3	$5.1	$16.9	$19.3	$1.5	$4.5
Trade/professional	22.3	32.6	45.6	3.5	5.7	3.8	9.4	9.3	1.2	2.8
Labor	39.9	3.5	30.1	7.9	5.2	6.2	0.4	2.3	2.8	1.4
Nonconnected	11.4	15.6	15.1	5.7	6.3	3.0	5.5	4.9	1.4	2.2

Source: Federal Election Commission.

Conflict of Interest

In 1978 a new federal law, the Ethics in Government Act, codified and broadened the rules governing possible conflicts of interest among senior members of the executive branch. The key provisions were as follows.

The president, vice president, and top-ranking (GS-16 and above) executive branch employees must each year file a public financial disclosure report that lists:

- The source and amount of all earned income as well as income from stocks, bonds, and property; the worth of any investments or large debts; and the source of a spouse's income, if any
- Any position held in business, labor, or certain nonprofit organizations

Employment after government service is restricted. Former executive branch employees may *not:*

- Represent anyone before their former agencies in connection with any matter that the former employees had been involved in before leaving the government
- Appear before an agency, for two years after leaving government service, on matters that came within the former employees' official sphere of responsibility, even if they were not personally involved in the matter

- Represent anyone on any matter before their former agencies, for one year after leaving them, even if the former employees had no connection with the matter while in the government

In addition, another law prohibits bribery. It is illegal to ask for, solicit, or receive anything of value in return for being influenced in the performance of one's duties.

Finally, an executive order forbids outside employment. An official may not hold a job or take a fee, even for lecturing or writing, if such employment or income might create a conflict of interest or an apparent conflict of interest.

Sources: National Journal (November 19, 1977): 1796–1803; *Congressional Quarterly Weekly Report* (October 28, 1978): 3121–3127.

press releases, and letters from interested constituents. What these studies may be measuring is the effect of persuasive arguments, not dollars; no one can be certain.[27]

It is possible that money affects legislative behavior in ways that will never appear in studies of roll-call votes in Congress. Members of Congress may be more willing to set aside time in their busy schedules for a group that has given money than for a group that has not. What the money has bought is access: it has helped open the door. Or contributions might influence how legislators behave on the committees on which they serve, subtly shaping the way in which they respond to arguments and the facts on which they rely. No one knows, because the research has not been done.

In any event, if interest group money makes a difference at all, it probably makes it on certain kinds of issues more than others. In the chapter on policymaking we define the kind of issues—we call them "client politics"—on which a given interest group is likely to be especially influential, whether by means of arguments, money, or both. After reading that chapter and considering the examples given there, it will be easier to put the present discussion of PAC money into context.

The "Revolving Door"

Every year, hundreds of people leave important jobs in the federal government to take more lucrative positions in private industry. Some go to work as lobbyists, others as consultants to business, still others

Law suits, such as this one arguing that Massachusetts allow marriages among gay and lesbian couples, are often more effective than protest demonstrations in changing policies.

as key executives in corporations, foundations, and universities. Many people worry that this "revolving door" may give private interests a way of improperly influencing government decisions. If a federal official uses his or her government position to do something for a corporation in exchange for a cushy job after leaving government, or if a person who has left government uses his or her personal contacts in Washington to get favors for private parties, then the public interest may suffer.

From time to time there are incidents that seem to confirm these fears. Michael K. Deaver, once the deputy chief of staff in the Reagan White House, was convicted of perjury in connection with a grand jury investigation of his having used his former government contacts to help the clients of his public relations firm. Lyn Nofziger, a former Reagan White House aide, was convicted of violating the Ethics in Government Act by lobbying the White House, soon after he left it, on behalf of various businesses and labor unions.

In 1988 federal investigators revealed evidence of corrupt dealings between some Defense Department officials and industry executives. Contractors and their consultants, many of whom were former Pentagon personnel, obtained favors from procurement officials, gaining an edge on their competitors.

How systematic is this pattern of abuse? We don't know. Studies of the revolving door in federal regulatory agencies have found no clear pattern of officials' tilting their decisions in hopes of landing a lucrative business job.[28]

Agencies differ in their vulnerability to outside influences. If the Food and Drug Administration is not vigilant, people in that agency who help decide whether a new drug should be placed on the market may have their judgment affected somewhat by the possibility that, if they approve the drug, the pharmaceutical company that makes it will later offer them a lucrative position.

On the other hand, lawyers in the Federal Trade Commission who prosecute businesses that violate the antitrust laws may decide that their chances for getting a good job with a private law firm later on will increase if they are particularly vigorous and effective prosecutors. The firm, after all, wants to hire competent people, and winning a case is a good test of competence.[29]

Trouble

Public displays and disruptive tactics—protest marches, sit-ins, picketing, and violence—have always been a part of American politics. Indeed, they were among the favorite tactics of the American colonists seeking independence in 1776.

Both ends of the political spectrum have used display, disruption, and violence. On the left feminists, antislavery agitators, coal miners, autoworkers, welfare mothers, African Americans, anti–nuclear power groups, public housing tenants, the American Indian Movement, the Students for a Democratic Society, and the Weather Underground have created "trouble" ranging from peaceful sit-ins at segregated lunch counters to bombings and shootings. On the right the Ku Klux Klan has used terror, intimidation, and murder; parents opposed to forced busing of schoolchildren have demonstrated; business firms have used strong-arm squads against workers; right-to-life groups have blockaded abortion clinics; and an endless array of "anti-" groups (anti-Catholics, anti-Masons, anti-Jews, anti-immigrants, antisaloons, antiblacks, antiprotesters, and probably even anti-antis) have taken their disruptive turns on stage. These various activities are not morally the same—a sit-in demonstration is quite different from a lynching—but politically they constitute a similar problem for a government official.

An explanation of why and under what circumstances disruption occurs is beyond the scope of this book. To understand interest group politics, however, it is important to remember that making trouble has, since the 1960s, become a quite conventional political resource and is no longer simply the last resort of extremist groups. Making trouble is now an accepted political tactic of ordinary middle-class citizens as well as the disadvantaged or disreputable.

There is of course a long history of the use of disruptive methods by "proper" people. In a movement that began in England at the turn of the century and then spread here, feminists would chain themselves to lampposts or engage in what we now call "sit-ins" as part of a campaign to win the vote for women. The object then was much the same as the object of similar tactics today: to disrupt the working of some institution so that it is forced to negotiate with you, or, failing that, to enlist the sympathies of third parties (the media, other interest groups) who will come to your aid and press your target to negotiate with

you, or, failing that, to goad the police into making attacks and arrests so that martyrs are created.

The civil rights and antiwar movements of the 1960s gave experience in these methods to thousands of young people and persuaded others of the effectiveness of such methods under certain conditions. Though these movements have abated or disappeared, their veterans and emulators have put such tactics to new uses—trying to block the construction of a nuclear power plant, for example, or occupying the office of a cabinet secretary to obtain concessions for a particular group.

Government officials dread this kind of trouble. They usually find themselves in a no-win situation. If they ignore the disruption, they are accused of being "insensitive," "unresponsive," or "arrogant." If they give in to the demonstrators, they encourage more demonstrations by proving that this is a useful tactic. If they call the police, they run the risk of violence and injuries, followed not only by bad publicity but by lawsuits.

Regulating Interest Groups

Interest group activity is a form of political speech protected by the First Amendment to the Constitution: it cannot lawfully be abolished or even much curtailed. In 1946 Congress passed the Federal Regulation of Lobbying Act, which requires groups and individuals seeking to influence legislation to register with the secretary of the Senate and the clerk of the House and to file quarterly financial reports. The Supreme Court upheld the law but restricted its application to lobbying efforts involving direct contacts with members of Congress.[30] More general "grassroots" interest group activity may not be restricted by the government. The 1946 law had little practical effect. Not all lobbyists took the trouble to register, and there was no guarantee that the financial statements were accurate. There was no staff in charge of enforcing the law.

After years of growing popular dissatisfaction with Congress, prompted in large measure by the (exaggerated) view that legislators were the pawns of powerful special interests, Congress in late 1995 unanimously passed a bill that tightened up the registration and disclosure requirements. Signed by the president, the law restates the obligation of lobbyists to register with the House and Senate, but it broadens the definition of a lobbyist to include the following:

- People who spend at least 20 percent of their time lobbying
- People who are paid at least $5,000 in any six-month period to lobby
- Corporations and other groups that spend more than $20,000 in any six-month period on their own lobbying staffs

The law covers people and groups who lobby the executive branch and congressional staffers as well as elected members of Congress, and it includes law firms that represent clients before the government. Twice a year, all registered lobbyists must report the following:

- The names of their clients
- Their income and expenditures
- The issues on which they worked

The registration and reporting requirements do not, however, extend to so-called grassroots organizations—that is, campaigns (sometimes led by volunteers, sometimes by hired professionals) to mobilize citizens to write or call the government about some issue. Nor was any new enforcement organization created, although congressional officials may refer violations to the Justice Department for investigation. Fines for breaking the law could amount to $50,000. In addition, the law bars tax-exempt, nonprofit advocacy groups that lobby from getting federal grants, a provision aimed at organizations such as the American Association of Retired Persons (AARP).

The most significant legal constraints on interest groups come not from the current federal lobbying law (though that may change) but from the tax code and the campaign finance laws. A nonprofit organization—which includes not only charitable groups but almost all voluntary associations that have an interest in politics—need not pay income taxes, and financial contributions to it can be deducted on the donor's income tax return, provided that the organization does not devote a "substantial part" of its activities to "attempting to influence legislation."[31] Many tax-exempt organizations do take public positions on political questions and testify before congressional committees. If the organization does any serious lobbying, however, it will lose its tax-exempt status (and thus find it harder to solicit donations and more expensive to operate). Exactly this happened to the Sierra Club in 1968 when the Internal Revenue Service revoked its tax-exempt status because of its extensive lobbying activities. Some voluntary associations try to deal with this problem by setting up separate organizations to collect tax-exempt money—for example, the NAACP, which lobbies, must pay taxes, but the NAACP Legal Defense and Education Fund, which does not lobby, is tax-exempt.

Finally, the campaign finance laws, described in detail in Chapter 8, limit to $5,000 the amount any political action committee can spend on a given candidate in a given election. These laws have sharply curtailed the extent to which any *single* group can give money, though they have increased the *total* amount that different groups are providing.

Beyond making bribery or other manifestly corrupt forms of behavior illegal and restricting the sums that campaign contributors can donate, there is probably no system for controlling interest groups that would both make a useful difference and leave important constitutional and political rights unimpaired. Ultimately the only remedy for imbalances or inadequacies in interest group representation is to devise and sustain a political system that gives all affected parties a reasonable chance to be heard on matters of public policy. That, of course, is exactly what the Founders thought they were doing. Whether they succeeded or not is a question to which we shall return at the end of this book.

What Would You Do?

U.S. Senator Wants Feds to Foot the Bill for Political Campaigns

September 4
WASHINGTON

Calling the country's campaign finance system "corrupt and complicated beyond comprehension," an ex-presidential contender and sitting senator is corralling congressional cosponsors for a new law that would have the federal government pay the entire cost of presidential races and lead to full federal funding for congressional campaigns as well . . .

MEMORANDUM

To: Senator Rita McCord
From: Jack Smith, chief of staff
Subject: Federal finance of campaigns

Every presidential election since 1976 has been financed in part by federal funds, but the proposal in question would start by limiting major presidential candidates to federal financing.

Arguments for:

1. The legal precedents are promising. Federal matching funds already go to presidential-primary candidates who have raised at least a total of $5,000, in contributions of $250 or less, in each of twenty states, and each major party nominee is already eligible for federal grants if he or she agrees to spend no more than the grant amount (about $62 million in 1996).
2. The sums required would be trivial. The hard money spent on the 1996 presidential campaigns (about $400 million) plus the soft money spent on them (about $260 million) totaled less than $700 million—hardly a fiscal drain were it paid out of a nearly $2 trillion annual federal budget.
3. The effects would be pervasive. Candidates and party leaders would stop covertly courting soft-money suppliers, stop compromising themselves with big-money donors (phone calls, luncheons, personal visits), and start focusing on the needs of average citizens.

Arguments against:

1. The constitutional precedents are prohibitive. The Supreme Court's *Buckley v. Valeo* (1976) decision upheld legal limits on campaign contributions but defined spending money for political purposes as a form of political expression protected by the First Amendment.
2. The sums spent would soon spiral. The federal government would be unable to restrict spending by individuals or organizations working independently, and federal funds would supplement, not supplant, new private money.
3. The effects would be perverse. Candidates would rely less on party leaders, which would further weaken the political parties. Many average citizens (most of whom have not opted to help pay for campaigns through voluntary federal income tax checkoffs) and nonvoters would feel as if they were being bullied into bankrolling a process that serves the politicians, not the people.

Your decision:
Favor proposal _____
Oppose proposal _____

Summary

Interest groups in the United States are more numerous and more fragmented than those in nations such as Great Britain, where the political system is more centralized. The goals and tactics of interest groups reflect not only the interests of their members but also the size of the groups, the incentives with which they attract supporters, and the role of their professional staffs. The chief source of interest group influence is information; public support, money, and the ability to create "trouble" are also important. The right to lobby is protected by the Constitution, but the tax and campaign finance laws impose significant restrictions on how money may be used.

Reconsidering the Enduring Questions

1. *Why do people join interest groups?*

   Every organization must induce people to join. Interest groups and other political organizations are no exception. There are three kinds of incentives. Solidary incentives are the sense of pleasure, status, or companionship that arises out of meeting together in small groups. Material incentives include money or things and services readily valued in monetary terms. Purposive incentives concern the appeal of the organization's stated purpose or goals. Organizations that attract members by appealing to their beliefs in a coherent set of principles are sometimes called ideological interest groups. Organizations that principally benefit nonmembers are sometimes called public-interest lobbies.

2. *With so many groups active, has America succeeded in "curing the mischiefs of faction"?*

   In *Federalist* No. 10, James Madison defined a "faction" as "a number of citizens, whether amounting to a majority or minority of the whole, who are united by some common impulse of passion, or of interest, adverse to the rights of other citizens, or to the permanent and aggregate interests of the community." Madison recognized that freedom begat factions, but he hoped that the government proposed under the Constitution would succeed in the "regulation of these various and interfering interests" in ways that served the "public good." Thus the mere proliferation of interest groups—for example, the fact that since the 1970s America has become home to thousands of political action committees, or PACs—would not in and of itself justify a negative answer to this question. Rather, one would also have to believe that the legislative process is dominated by groups that seek to serve their members with little or no regard for the well-being and rights of other citizens. But such groups, though they do exist, are almost always quite marginal to the legislative process and exercise little if any real influence over public policy. Still, one citizen's special-interest group is often another citizen's public-interest lobby. To some pro-choice voters, certain pro-life groups may appear as factions, and to some pro-life citizens, certain pro-choice groups may appear as factions.

3. *Are there any ways, both feasible and desirable, of regulating interest groups?*

   Congress has enacted, amended, and reamended literally scores of laws attempting to regulate interest groups. Lobbyists must register with the government and disclose as public information their client lists, incomes, expenditures, and issues on which they work. There are legal limits on how much money political action committees can spend on campaigns and the conditions under which they can spend it. There are complicated batteries of rules governing possible conflicts of interest among senior members of the executive branch, including regulations prohibiting former executive branch employees from representing anyone before their former agencies in connection with any matter that the former executive employee had been involved in before leaving the government. People differ over whether these laws and rules have been effective in balancing two competing values: on the one side, ensuring that citizens can seek to influence government in accordance with their policy preferences and constitutional rights and, on the other side, ensuring that government and its officials are not corrupted into using public offices for private gains.

World Wide Web Resources

- Index of interest groups
  www.policy.com/community/advoc.html
- Conservative interest groups
  American Conservative Union:
    www.conservative.org
  Christian Coalition: www.cc.org
- Liberal interest groups
  American Civil Liberties Union: www.aclu.org
  Americans for Democratic Action:
    www.adaction.org

- Environmental groups
  Environmental Defense Fund: www.edf.org
  National Resources Defense Council:
    www.nrdc.org
- Civil rights groups
  NAACP: www.naacp.org
  Center for Equal Opportunity: www.ceousa.org
- Feminist group
  National Organization for Women:
    www.now.org

Key Terms

lobby *p. 224*
lobbyist *p. 224*
interest group *p. 227*
incentive *p. 228*

solidary incentives *p. 228*
material incentives *p. 229*
purposive incentive *p. 229*
ideological interest groups *p. 229*

public-interest lobby *p. 229*
social movement *p. 231*
political cue *p. 239*
ratings *p. 239*

Suggested Readings

Bauer, Raymond A., Ithiel de Sola Pool, and Lewis A. Dexter. *American Business and Public Policy*. New York: Atherton, 1963. A classic study of how business groups tried to shape foreign-trade legislation, set in a broad analysis of pressure groups and Congress.

Berry, Jeffrey M. *Lobbying for the People*. Princeton, N.J.: Princeton University Press, 1977. Analyzes more than eighty "public-interest" lobbies, with a detailed discussion of two.

Cigler, Allan J., and Burdett A. Loomis, eds. *Interest Group Politics*. 3d ed. Washington, D.C.: Congressional Quarterly Press, 1991. Essays on several interest groups active in Washington.

Lowi, Theodore J. *The End of Liberalism*. New York: Norton, 1969. A critique of the role of interest groups in American government.

Malbin, Michael J., ed. *Money and Politics in the United States*. Chatham, N.J.: Chatham House, 1984. Excellent studies of PACs and of the influence of money in elections.

Mansbridge, Jane J. *Why We Lost the ERA*. Chicago: University of Chicago Press, 1986. Insightful analysis of the relationship between organizational incentives and tactics in the ERA campaign.

Olson, Mancur. *The Logic of Collective Action*. Cambridge: Harvard University Press, 1965. An economic analysis of interest groups, especially the "free-rider" problem.

Sabato, Larry. *PAC Power*. New York: Norton, 1985. A full discussion of the nature and activities of political action committees.

Schlozman, Kay Lehman, and John T. Tierney. *Organized Interests and American Democracy*. New York: Harper and Row, 1985. Comprehensive treatise on interest groups based on original research.

Truman, David B. *The Governmental Process*. 2d ed. New York: Knopf, 1971. First published in 1951, this was the classic analysis—and defense—of interest group pluralism.

Wilson, James Q. *Political Organizations*. Rev. ed. Princeton, N.J.: Princeton University Press, 1995. A theory of interest groups emphasizing the incentives they use to attract members.

The Media

Enduring Questions

1. Why do politicians worry so much about the media?

2. Can we trust the media to be fair?

3. Should people care more about getting political information?

All public officials have a love-hate relationship with newspapers, television, and the other media of mass communication. They depend on the media for the advancement of their careers and policies but fear the media's power to criticize, expose, and destroy. As political parties have declined—especially, strong local party organizations—politicians have become increasingly dependent on the media. Their efforts to woo the press have become ever greater, and their expressions of rage and dismay when that courtship is spurned, ever stronger. At the same time, the media have been changing, especially in regard to the kinds of people who have been attracted to leading positions in journalism and the attitudes they have brought with them. There has always been an adversarial relationship between those who govern and those who write, but events of recent decades have, as we shall see, made that conflict especially keen.

The relationships between government and the media in this country are shaped by laws and understandings that accord the media a degree of freedom greater than that found in almost any other nation.

251

Though many public officials secretly might like to control the media, and though no medium of communication in the United States or elsewhere is totally free of government influence, the press in this country is among the freest in the world. A study of ninety-four countries found only sixteen in which the press enjoyed a high degree of freedom; the United States was one of these.[1] Some democratic nations, such as France and Great Britain, place more restrictions on the communications media than are found here. The laws governing libel in England are so strict that public figures frequently sue newspapers for printing statements that tend to defame or ridicule them—and they collect. In the United States, as will be explained, the law of libel is loose enough to permit intense and even inaccurate criticism of anybody in the public eye. England also has an Official Secrets Act that can be used to punish any present or past public official who divulges to the press private government business.[2] In this country, by contrast, the Freedom of Information Act, together with a long tradition of leaking inside stories and writing memoirs of one's public service, virtually guarantees that very little can be kept secret for very long.

Almost all American radio and television stations are privately owned, though they require government licenses (issued for seven- and five-year terms, respectively) to operate. In France broadcasting is operated by a government agency (Radio-Diffusion-Télévision Française) under the control of the minister of information, who is not averse to using that control to protect the government's image. Until recently the French government had the power to ban the showing of any motion picture that was thought likely to "disturb the public order" or for other "reasons of state."[3] A French newspaper editor was heavily fined by a court for having written an article critical of the president of France.[4] While the federal government does impose rules on American broadcasters, it does not have the power to censor or dictate the contents of particular stories. As we shall see, though, its power to license broadcasters has been used, on occasion, to harass station owners who were out of favor with the White House.

The freedom from government control that comes with the private ownership of the media of mass communication has a price, of course: newspapers, magazines, and broadcast stations are businesses that must earn a profit. Some critics believe that the need for profit leads publishers and station owners to distort the news coverage of politics to satisfy the desires of advertisers, the pecuniary interests of stockholders, or the private ideology of the managers. This is much too simple a view, however. Every owner of a communications medium must satisfy the often competing interests of a number of distinct constituencies—advertisers, readers or viewers, editors and reporters, and organized external pressure groups. How each newspaper or broadcaster balances the preferences of these groups varies from case to case. Moreover, the relative strength of these groups has changed over time. In general the history of American journalism, at least among newspapers, has been the history of the growing power and autonomy of editors and reporters.

Journalism in American Political History

Important changes in the nature of American politics have gone hand in hand with major changes in the organization and technology of the press. It is the nature of politics, being essentially a form of communication, to respond to changes in how communications are carried on. This can be seen by considering four important periods in journalistic history.

The Party Press

In the early years of the Republic, politicians of various factions and parties created, sponsored, and controlled newspapers to further their interests. This was possible because circulation was of necessity small (newspapers could not easily be distributed to large audiences, owing to poor transportation) and newspapers were expensive (the type was set by hand and the presses printed copies slowly). Furthermore, there were few large advertisers to pay the bills. These newspapers circulated chiefly among the political and commercial elites, who could afford the high subscription prices. Even with high prices, the newspapers, to exist, often required subsidies. That money frequently came from the government or from a political party.

During the Washington administration the Federalists, led by Alexander Hamilton, created the *Gazette of the United States.* The Republicans, led by

The National Gazette, *edited by Philip Freneau, supported the Thomas Jefferson faction in national politics. Jefferson, as secretary of state, helped Freneau by giving him a job in the State Department. The* Gazette of the United States, *published by John Fenno, supported Jefferson's rival, Alexander Hamilton.*

Thomas Jefferson, retaliated by creating the *National Gazette* and made its editor, Philip Freneau, "clerk for foreign languages" in the State Department at $250 a year to help support him. After Jefferson became president, he induced another publisher, Samuel Harrison Smith, to start the *National Intelligencer,* subsidizing him by giving him a contract to print government documents. Andrew Jackson, when he became president, aided in the creation of the *Washington Globe.* By some estimates there were over fifty journalists on the government payroll during this era.[5] Naturally these newspapers were relentlessly partisan in their views. Citizens could choose among different party papers, but only rarely could they find a paper that presented both sides of an issue.

The Popular Press

Changes in society and technology made possible the rise of a self-supporting, mass-readership daily newspaper. The development of the high-speed rotary press enabled publishers to print thousands of copies of a newspaper cheaply and quickly. The invention of the telegraph in the 1840s meant that news from Washington could be flashed almost immediately to New York, Boston, Philadelphia, and Charleston, thus providing local papers with access to information that once only the Washington papers enjoyed. The creation in 1848 of the Associated Press allowed telegraphic dissemination of information to newspaper editors on a systematic basis. Since the AP provided stories that had to be

Muckraker

A **muckraker** is a journalist who searches through the activities of public officials and organizations, especially business firms, seeking to expose conduct contrary to the public interest.

Anyone who has been around stables knows that *muck* means "manure"; by extension it can refer to anything that is filthy or disgusting.

The word was first used in a political sense by President Theodore Roosevelt, who warned in a 1906 speech that antibusiness journalism could go too far. He said that "the men with the muckrakes are often indispensable to the well-being of society; but only if they know when to stop raking the muck, and to look upward to the celestial crown above them, to the crown of worthy endeavor."

Roosevelt was referring to a character named the Man with the Muck Rake in John Bunyan's book *Pilgrim's Progress*; this fellow was so preoccupied with raking the muck on the stable floor that he could never look any way but down.

Source: Adapted from *Safire's Political Dictionary* by William Safire. Copyright © 1968, 1972, 1978 by William Safire. Reprinted by permission of Random House, Inc. and the author.

paying only a penny per copy and by patronizing merchants who advertised in its pages. Newspapers no longer needed political patronage to prosper, and soon such subsidies began to dry up. In 1860 the Government Printing Office was established, thereby putting an end to most of the printing contracts that Washington newspapers had once enjoyed.

The mass-readership newspaper was scarcely nonpartisan, but the partisanship it displayed arose from the convictions of its publishers and editors rather than from the influence of its party sponsors. And these convictions blended political beliefs with economic interest. The way to attract a large readership was with sensationalism: violence, romance, and patriotism, coupled with exposés of government, politics, business, and society. As practiced by Joseph Pulitzer and William Randolph Hearst, founders of large newspaper empires, this editorial policy had great appeal for the average citizen and especially for the immigrants flooding into the large cities.

Strong-willed publishers could often become powerful political forces. Hearst used his papers to agitate for war with Spain when the Cubans rebelled against Spanish rule. Conservative Republican political leaders were opposed to the war, but a steady diet of newspaper stories about real and imagined Spanish brutalities whipped up public opinion in favor of intervention. At one point Hearst sent the noted artist Frederic Remington to Cuba to supply paintings of the conflict. Remington cabled back: "Everything is quiet.... There will be no war." Hearst supposedly replied: "Please remain. You furnish the pictures and I'll furnish the war."[6] When the battleship USS *Maine* blew up in Havana harbor, President William McKinley felt helpless to resist popular pressure, and war was declared in 1898.

For all their excesses, the mass-readership newspapers began to create a common national culture, to establish the feasibility of a press free of government control or subsidy, and to demonstrate how exciting (and profitable) could be the criticism of public policy and the revelation of public scandal.

Magazines of Opinion

The growing middle class was often repelled by what it called "yellow journalism" and was developing, around the turn of the century, a taste for political reform and a belief in the doctrines of the progres-

brief and that went to newspapers of every political hue, it could not afford to be partisan or biased; to attract as many subscribers as possible, it had to present the facts objectively. Meanwhile the nation was becoming more urbanized, with large numbers of people brought together in densely settled areas. These people could support a daily newspaper by

sive movement. To satisfy this market, a variety of national magazines appeared that, unlike those devoted to manners and literature, discussed issues of public policy. Among the first of these were the *Nation,* the *Atlantic Monthly,* and *Harper's,* founded in the 1850s and 1860s; later there came the more broadly based mass-circulation magazines such as *McClure's, Scribner's,* and *Cosmopolitan.* They provided the means for developing a national constituency for certain issues, such as regulating business (or in the language of the times, "trustbusting"), purifying municipal politics, and reforming the civil service system. Lincoln Steffens and other so-called muckrakers were frequent contributors to the magazines, setting a pattern for what we now call "investigative reporting."

The national magazines of opinion provided an opportunity for individual writers to gain a nationwide following. The popular press, though initially under the heavy influence of founder-publishers, made the names of certain reporters and columnists household words. In time the great circulation wars between the big-city daily newspapers started to wane, as the more successful papers bought up or otherwise eliminated their competition. This reduced the need for the more extreme forms of sensationalism, a change that was reinforced by the growing sophistication and education of America's readers. And the founding publishers were gradually replaced by less flamboyant managers. All of these changes—in circulation needs, in audience interests, in managerial style, in the emergence of nationally known writers—helped increase the power of editors and reporters and make them a force to be reckoned with.

Although politics dominated the pages of most national magazines in the late nineteenth century, today national magazines that focus mainly on politics and government affairs account for only a small and declining portion of the national magazine market. Among all magazines in circulation today, only a fraction focus on politics—the majority of today's magazines focus on popular entertainment and leisure activities.

Electronic Journalism

Radio came on the national scene in the 1920s, television in the late 1940s. They represented a major change in the way news was gathered and disseminated, though few politicians at first understood the importance of this change. A broadcast permits public officials to speak directly to audiences without their remarks being filtered through editors and reporters. This was obviously an advantage to politicians, provided they were skilled enough to use it: they could in theory reach the voters directly on a national scale without the services of political parties, interest groups, or friendly editors.

But there was an offsetting disadvantage—people could easily ignore a speech broadcast on a radio or television station, either by not listening at all or by tuning to a different station. By contrast, the views of at least some public figures would receive prominent and often unavoidable display in newspapers, and in a growing number of cities there was only one daily paper. Moreover, space in a newspaper is cheap compared to time on a television broadcast. Adding one more story, or one more name to an existing story, costs the newspaper little. By contrast, less news can be carried on radio or television, and each news segment must be quite brief to avoid boring the audience. As a result, the number of political personalities that can be covered by radio and television news is much smaller than is the case with newspapers, and the cost (to the station) of making a news item or broadcast longer is often prohibitively large.

Thus, to obtain the advantages of electronic media coverage, public officials must do something sufficiently bold or colorful to gain free access to radio and television news—or they must find the money to purchase radio and television time. The president of the United States, of course, is routinely covered by radio and television and can ordinarily get free time to speak to the nation on matters of importance. All other officials must struggle for access to the electronic media by making controversial statements, acquiring a national reputation, or purchasing expensive time.

The rise of the talk show as a political forum has increased politicians' access to the electronic media, as has the televised "town meeting." But such developments need to be understood as part of a larger story.

Until the 1990s, the "big three" television networks (ABC, CBS, and NBC) together claimed 80 percent or more of all viewers (see Table 10.1). Their evening newscasts dominated electronic media cov-

In 1933 White House press conferences were informal affairs, as when reporters gathered around Franklin Roosevelt's desk in the Oval Office. Today they are huge gatherings held in a special conference room, as on the right.

erage of politics and government affairs. When it came to presidential campaigns, for example, the three networks were the only television games in town—they reported on the primaries, broadcast the party conventions, and covered the general election campaigns, including any presidential debates. But over the last few decades, the networks' evening newscasts have changed in ways that have made it harder for candidates to use them to get their messages across. For instance, the average **sound bite**—a video clip of a presidential contender speaking—dropped from about forty-two seconds in 1968 to 7.3 seconds in 2000.[7]

Today politicians have sources other than the network news for sustained and personalized television exposure. Cable television, early-morning news and entertainment programs, and prime-time "newsmagazine" shows have greatly increased and diversified politicians' access to the electronic media. One of the most memorable moments of the 1992 presidential campaign—Ross Perot's declaring his willingness to run for president on CNN's "Larry King Live"—occurred on cable television. And while the networks' evening news programs feature only small sound bites, their early-morning programs and newsmagazine shows feature lengthy interviews with candidates.

Naturally many politicians favor the call-in format, town-meeting setups, lengthy human interest interviews, and casual appearances on entertainment shows to televised confrontations on policy issues with seasoned network journalists who push, probe, and criticize. And naturally they favor being a part of visually interesting programs rather than traditional "talking heads" news shows. But what is preferable to candidates is not necessarily helpful to the selection process that voters must go through in choosing a candidate. No one has yet systematically

Table 10.1	Decline in Viewership of the Television Networks

"Big Three" Networks: Average Shares of Prime-Time Viewing Audience

Year	Share
1961	94%
1971	91
1981	83
1991	41
1997	33
2002	29

Source: Updated from *The Public Perspective* (September/October 1992): 6, reporting data provided by Nielsen Media Research and NBC. Used by permission of *The Public Perspective,* a publication of the Roper Center for Public Opinion Research, University of Connecticut; Cabletelevision Advertising Bureau analysis of Nielsen data, April 25, 2002–May 21, 2002.

analyzed what, if any, positive or negative consequences these recent changes in politicians' access to the electronic media hold for campaigns, elections, or governance. Nor, for that matter, is there yet any significant research on the broader societal consequences of so-called narrowcasting—the proliferation of television and radio stations that target highly segmented listening and viewing audiences, and the relative decline of electronic and print media that reach large and heterogeneous populations.

One thing is clear: most politicians crave the media spotlight, both on the campaign trail and in office. The efforts made by political candidates to get "visuals"—filmed stories—on television continue after they are elected. Since the president is always news, a politician wishing to make news is well advised to attack the president. Even better, attack him with the aid of a photogenic prop: when the late Senator John Heinz III of Pennsylvania wanted to criticize a president's bridge-repair program, Heinz had himself filmed making the attack not in his office but standing on a bridge.

The Internet

The newest electronic source of news is the Internet and the World Wide Web. In a 1998 survey more than forty million people, especially young people, said that they had used the Internet within the past thirty days. The political news that is found there ranges from summaries of news stories from newspapers and magazines to political rumors and hot (but often unverified) news tips. Users can get gossip before it is printed or broadcast, learn about (or even join) political organizations, and participate in chat rooms with people who have similar political views. The Internet is the ultimate free market in political news: no one can ban, control, or regulate it, and no one can keep either facts or nonsense off of it.

During the discussion of the sexual liaison between former White House intern Monica Lewinsky and President Bill Clinton, the Internet was a source of facts, gossip, and news leads. In the 2000 presidential campaign every major candidate had a web site both to promote his or her views and to raise money. When Senator John McCain won the Republican primary in New Hampshire, the number of people going to his web site, and the money he raised through it, shot up.

The rise of the Internet has completed a remarkable transformation in American journalism. In the days of the party press only a few people read newspapers. When mass-circulation newspapers arose, there also arose mass politics. When magazines of opinion developed, there also developed interest groups. When radio and television became dominant, politicians could build their own bridges to voters without party or interest group influence. And now, with the Internet, voters and political activists can talk to each other.

The Structure of the Media

The relationship between journalism and politics is a two-way street: though politicians take advantage as best they can of the communications media available to them, these media in turn attempt to use politics and politicians as a way of both entertaining and informing their audiences. The mass media, whatever their disclaimers, are not simply a mirror held up to reality or a messenger that carries the news. There is inevitably a process of selection, of editing, and of emphasis, and this process reflects, to some degree, the way in which the media are organized, the kinds of audiences they seek to serve, and the preferences and opinions of the members of the media.

Degree of Competition

There has been a significant decline in the number of daily newspapers in this country, as well as in the number of cities in which there are competing daily papers. There were competing newspapers in 60 percent of American cities in 1900 but in only 4 percent by 1972. The largest cities—New York, Chicago, Detroit, Philadelphia, Los Angeles, Washington, Atlanta, Boston—have at least two central-city newspapers, but most other cities have just one. This is partially offset by the fact that in many metropolitan areas, two or more neighboring cities will each have a newspaper whose readership overlaps. Residents of Manchester, New Hampshire, for example, can easily obtain the *Manchester Union Leader,* the *Boston Globe,* and the *Boston Herald.* But newspaper circulation overall has fallen since 1967. People now get most of their news from television. Young people especially have turned away from political news (see Figure 10.1).

Radio and television, by contrast, are intensely competitive and becoming more so. Almost every

Figure 10.1   Young People Have Become Less Interested in Political News

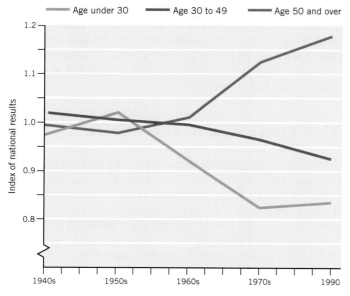

Legend: Age under 30 — Age 30 to 49 — Age 50 and over

The three lines show how attentive people of different ages were to news stories during the 1940s, 1950s, 1960s, and 1990. The tan line represents those under age 30, the blue line those 30–49, and the red line those 50 and older.

Source: Los Angeles Times, *Times Mirror Center for the People and the Press (June 28, 1990).*

American home has a radio and a television set. Though there are only five major television networks, there are over one thousand television stations, each of which has its own news programs. Local stations affiliated with a network are free to accept or reject network programs. There are more than eleven thousand cable TV systems, serving over fifty million people (and a typical cable can carry dozens of channels). In addition there are nearly ten thousand radio stations; some broadcast nothing but news, and others develop a specialized following among blacks, Hispanics, or other minorities. Magazines exist for every conceivable interest. The number of news sources available to an American is vast—more than even dedicated readers and viewers can keep up with.

To a degree that would astonish most foreigners, the American press—radio, television, and newspapers—is made up of locally owned and managed enterprises. In Britain, France, Germany, Japan, Sweden, and elsewhere, the media are owned and operated with a national audience in mind. The *Times* of London may be published in that city, but it is read throughout Great Britain, as are the *Guardian,* the *Daily Telegraph,* and the *Daily Mirror.* Radio and television broadcasts are centrally planned and nationally aired.

The American newspaper, however, is primarily oriented to its local market and local audience, and there is typically more local than national news in it. Radio and television stations accept network programming, but the early- and late-evening news programs provide a heavy diet of local political, social, and sports news. Government regulations developed by the Federal Communications Commission (FCC) are in part responsible for this. Until the mid-1990s, no one could own and operate more than one newspaper, one AM radio station, one FM radio station, or one television station in a given market. The networks still today may not compel a local affiliate to accept any particular broadcast. (In fact almost all network news programs are carried by the affiliates.) The result has been the development of a decentralized broadcast industry.

The National Media

The local orientation of much of the American communications media is partially offset, however, by the emergence of certain publications and broadcast services that constitute a kind of national press. The wire services—the Associated Press and United Press International—supply most of the national news that local papers publish. Certain newsmagazines—*Time, Newsweek, U.S. News & World Report*—have a national readership. The network evening news broadcasts produced by ABC, CBS, and NBC are carried by most television stations with a network affiliation. CNN—the Cable News Network—broadcasts national news around the clock. There are only three truly national newspapers, the *Wall Street Journal,* the *Christian Science Monitor,* and *USA Today,* but the *New York Times* and the *Washington Post* have acquired national influence because they are read daily by virtually every important official in Washington (and thus have become an important channel by which these officials keep track of one another) and because the television networks and many local newspapers use the stories that the *Times* and the *Post* print. In fact one study found that the front page of the morning

Times significantly shapes the contents of each network's evening news broadcasts.[8]

The existence of a national press is important for two reasons: First, government officials in Washington pay great attention to what these media say about them and their programs. They pay much less attention to what local papers and broadcasters say (if, indeed, they even know about their comments). Politicians read and worry about newspaper editorials, something the average citizen rarely does. Second, reporters and editors for the national press tend to differ from those who work for the local press. They are usually better paid than most other journalists, they have often graduated from the most prestigious colleges and universities, and in general they have more liberal political views.[9] Above all they seek—and frequently obtain—the opportunity to write stories that are not accounts of a particular news event but "background," investigative, or interpretive stories about issues and policies.[10]

The national press plays the role of gatekeeper, scorekeeper, and watchdog for the federal government.

■ **Gatekeeper**   As gatekeeper it can influence what subjects become national political issues and for how long. Automobile safety, water pollution, and the quality of prescription drugs were not major political issues before the national press began giving substantial attention to these matters and thus helped place them on the political agenda. When crime rates rose in the early 1960s, the subject was given little political attention in Washington, in part because the media did not cover it extensively. Media attention to crime increased in the late 1960s and early 1970s, slackened in the late 1970s, and rose again in the 1980s and early 1990s. Throughout most of these years crime went up. In short *reality* did not change during this time; only the focus of media and political attention shifted. Elite opinion about the war in Vietnam also changed significantly as the attitude toward the war expressed by the national media changed.

■ **Scorekeeper**   As scorekeepers the national media keep track of and help make political reputations, note who is being "mentioned" as a presidential candidate, and help decide who is winning and losing in Washington politics. When Jimmy Carter, a virtually unknown former governor of Georgia, was planning his campaign to get the Democratic nomination for president, he understood clearly the

To help reach voters directly without going through reporters, political leaders, such as Vice President Dick Cheney, appear on television programs such as Meet the Press.

importance of being "mentioned." So successful was he in cultivating members of the national press that between November 1975 and February 1976, before the first primary election was held, he was the subject of more stories in the *New York Times*, the *Washington Post*, and the *Columbus Dispatch* than any other potential Democratic presidential candidate, even though the others (Henry Jackson, Hubert Humphrey, and George Wallace) were much better known. He did almost as well in getting mentioned on the three television networks.

The scorekeeper role of the media often leads the press to cover presidential elections as if they were horse races rather than choices among policies. Consider the enormous attention the media give to the Iowa caucus and the New Hampshire primary election, despite the fact that these states produce only a tiny fraction of the delegates to either party's nominating convention and that neither state is representative of the nation as a whole. The results of the Iowa caucus, the first in the nation, are given great importance by the press. Consequently the coverage received by a candidate who does well in Iowa constitutes a tremendous amount of free publicity that can help him or her in the New Hampshire primary election. Doing well in that primary results in even more media attention, thus boosting the candidate for the next primaries, and so on.

For example, in 2000 John McCain won the Republican primary in New Hampshire. Even though New Hampshire is a small state and lots of candidates who win its primary fail to win the presidency, McCain became a major political figure, just as Gary Hart did in 1984. The media were already fascinated by McCain, but their coverage of him increased greatly, and he became the key rival to George W. Bush. The horse race—once involving six candidates—was then a two-horse contest.

This is not the only time that the press has decided that New Hampshire is important. In 1972 George McGovern became part of the horse race after he lost the primary to Edmund Muskie, and in 1968 Eugene McCarthy won what the press called a "moral victory" after he lost to Lyndon Johnson.

■ **Watchdog** Once the scorekeepers decide that you are the person to watch, they adopt their watchdog role. Before his New Hampshire victory in 1984, Hart's background went largely unexamined; after he had been declared a "front-runner," stories began appearing about how he had changed his name and altered his birth date by a year. In 1987, when Hart was already the front-runner for the 1988 Democratic presidential nomination, the press played its watchdog role right from the start. When rumors circulated that he was unfaithful to his wife, the *Miami Herald* staked out his apartment in Washington, D.C., and discovered that he had spent several evening hours there with an attractive young woman, Donna Rice. Soon there appeared other stories about his having taken Ms. Rice on a boat trip to Bimini. Not long thereafter Hart dropped out of the presidential race, accusing the press of unfair treatment. Then, in late 1987, Hart reentered the race only to drop out again after getting little popular support.

This close scrutiny is natural. The media have an instinctive—and profitable—desire to investigate personalities and expose scandals. To some degree all reporters probably share H. L. Mencken's belief that the role of the press is to "comfort the afflicted and afflict the comfortable." They tend to be tolerant of underdogs, tough on front-runners. Though some reporters develop close relations with powerful personages, many—especially younger ones—find the discovery of wrongdoing both more absorbing and more lucrative. Bob Woodward and Carl Bernstein, who wrote most of the Watergate stories for the *Washington Post*, simultaneously performed an important public service, received the accolades of their colleagues, and earned a lot of money.

Newspapers and television stations play these three roles in somewhat different ways. A newspaper can cover more stories in greater depth than a TV station and faces less competition from other papers than TV stations face from other broadcasters. A TV station faces brutal competition, must select its programs in part for their visual impact, and must keep its stories short and punchy. As a result newspaper reporters have more freedom to develop their own stories, but they earn less money than television news broadcasters. The latter have little freedom (the fear of losing their audience is keen), but they can make a lot of money (if they are attractive personalities who photograph well).

Rules Governing the Media

Ironically, the least competitive media outlets—the big-city newspapers—are almost entirely free from government regulation, while the most competitive ones—radio and television stations—must have a government license to operate and must adhere to a variety of government regulations.

Newspapers and magazines need no license to publish, their freedom to publish may not be restrained in advance, and they are liable for punishment for what they do publish only under certain highly restricted circumstances. The First Amendment to the Constitution has been interpreted as meaning that no government, federal or state, can place "prior restraints" (that is, censorship) on the press except under very narrowly defined circumstances.[11] When the federal government sought to prevent the *New York Times* from publishing the Pentagon Papers, a set of secret government documents stolen by an antiwar activist, the Court held that the paper was free to publish them.[12]

Once something is published, a newspaper or magazine may be sued or prosecuted if the material is libelous or obscene or if it incites someone to commit an illegal act. But these are usually not very serious restrictions, because the courts have defined *libelous*, *obscene*, and *incitement* so narrowly as to make it more difficult here than in any other nation to find the press guilty of such conduct. For example, for a paper to be found guilty of libeling a public official or other prominent person, the person must not only show that what was printed was wrong and damaging but must also show, with "clear and convincing evidence," that it was printed maliciously—that is, with "reckless disregard" for its truth or falsity.[13] When in 1984 Israeli General Ariel Sharon sued *Time* magazine for libel, the jury decided that the story that *Time* had printed was false and defamatory but that *Time* had not published it as the result of malice, and so Sharon did not collect any damages.

There are also laws intended to protect the privacy of citizens, but they do not really inhibit newspapers. In general, your name and picture can be printed without your consent if they are part of a news story of some conceivable public interest. And if a paper attacks you in print, the paper has no legal obligation to give you space for a reply.[14]

It is illegal to use printed words to advocate the violent overthrow of the government if by your advocacy you incite others to action, but this rule has been applied to newspapers only rarely.[15]

Confidentiality of Sources

Reporters believe that they should have the right to keep confidential the sources of their stories. Some states agree and have passed laws to that effect. Most states and the federal government do not agree, so the courts must decide in each case whether the need of a journalist to protect confidential sources does or does not outweigh the interest of the government in gathering evidence in a criminal investigation. In general the Supreme Court has upheld the right of the government to compel reporters to divulge information as part of a properly conducted criminal investigation, if it bears on the commission of a crime.[16]

This conflict arises not only between reporters and law enforcement agencies but also between reporters and persons accused of committing a crime. Myron Farber, a reporter for the *New York Times*, wrote a series of stories that led to the indictment and trial of a physician on charges that he had murdered five patients. The judge ordered Farber to show him his notes to determine whether they should be given to the defense lawyers. Farber refused, arguing that revealing his notes would infringe upon the confidentiality that he had promised to his sources. Farber was sent to jail for contempt of court. On appeal the New Jersey Supreme Court and the U.S. Supreme Court decided against

Farber, holding that the accused person's right to a fair trial includes the right to compel the production of evidence, even from reporters.

In another case the Supreme Court upheld the right of the police to search newspaper offices, so long as they have a warrant. But Congress then passed a law forbidding such searches (except in special cases), requiring instead that the police subpoena the desired documents.[17]

Regulating Broadcasting

Although newspapers and magazines by and large are not regulated, broadcasting is regulated by the government. No one may operate a radio or television station without a license from the Federal Communications Commission, renewable every seven years for radio and every five for television stations. An application for renewal is rarely refused, but until recently the FCC required the broadcaster to submit detailed information about its programming and how it planned to serve "community needs" in order to get a renewal. Based on this information or on the complaints of some group, the FCC could use its powers of renewal to influence what the station put on the air. For example, it could induce stations to reduce the amount of violence shown, increase the proportion of "public service" programs on the air, or alter the way it portrayed various ethnic groups.

Of late a movement has arisen to deregulate broadcasting, on the grounds that so many stations are now on the air that competition should be allowed to determine how each station defines and serves community needs. In this view citizens can choose what they want to hear or see without the government's shaping the content of each station's programming. For example, since the early 1980s a station can simply submit a postcard requesting that its license be renewed, a request automatically granted unless some group formally opposes the renewal. In that case the FCC holds a hearing. As a result some of the old rules—for instance, that each hour on TV could contain only sixteen minutes of commercials—are no longer rigidly enforced.

Radio broadcasting has been deregulated the most. Before 1992 one company could own one AM and one FM station in each market. In 1992 this number was doubled. And in 1996 the Telecommunications Act allowed one company to own as many as eight stations in large markets (five in smaller ones) and as many as it wished nationally. This trend has had two results. First, a few large companies now own most of the big-market radio stations. Second, the looser editorial restrictions that accompanied deregulation mean that a greater variety of opinions and shows can be found on radio. There are many more radio talk shows than would have been heard when content was more tightly controlled.

The content of radio and television is still regulated in ways that newspapers and magazines are not. These include the following:

- **Equal time rule:** If a station sells time to one candidate for office, it must be willing to sell equal time to opposing candidates.
- **Right-of-reply rule:** If a person is attacked on a broadcast (other than in a regular news program), that person has the right to reply over that same station.
- **Political editorializing rule:** If a broadcaster endorses a candidate, the opposing candidate has a right to reply.

For many years there was also in place the **fairness doctrine,** which required broadcasters to give time to opposing views if they broadcast a program giving one side of a controversial issue. In 1987 the FCC, believing that the doctrine inhibited the free discussion of issues, abolished it; Congress has tried to pass a law to reinstate it (so far without success). Most broadcasters still follow the rule voluntarily.

Spanish-speaking voters have become so important that candidates (such as George W. Bush here) run Spanish-language websites.

Campaigning

When candidates wish to campaign on radio or television, the equal time rule applies. A broadcaster must provide equal access to candidates for office and charge them rates no higher than the cheapest rate applicable to commercial advertisers for comparable time.

At one time this rule meant that a station or network could not broadcast a debate between the Democratic and Republican candidates for an office without inviting all other candidates as well—Libertarian, Prohibitionist, or whatever. Thus a presidential debate in 1980 could be limited to the major candidates, Reagan and Carter (or Reagan and Anderson), only by having the League of Women Voters sponsor it and then allowing radio and TV to cover it as a "news event." Now stations and networks can themselves sponsor debates limited to major candidates.

Though laws guarantee that candidates can buy time at favorable rates on television, not all candidates take advantage of this. The reason is that television is not always an efficient way to reach voters. A television message is literally "broad cast"—spread out to a mass audience without regard to the boundaries of the district in which a candidate is running. Presidential candidates, of course, always use television, because their constituency is the whole nation. Candidates for senator or representative, however, may or may not use television, depending on whether the boundaries of their state or district conform well to the boundaries of a television market.

A **market** is an area easily reached by a television signal; there are about two hundred such markets in the country. Congressman Tim Roemer comes from a district in Indiana centered on the city of South Bend, which is also the hub of a distinct TV market. Roemer can use television effectively and relatively cheaply (in terms of dollars per viewer reached). By contrast, when Adam K. Levin ran for a congressional seat in New Jersey in 1982, he spent large sums on television ads on the only stations—those in New York City—that reach his district. But just 4 percent of the viewers of those stations lived in Levin's district, and so most of the money was wasted. As a more experienced politician commented, he "might as well give the money away at a bus station." Because of these factors, a far higher proportion of Senate than of House candidates buy television ads.[18]

How to Read a Newspaper

Newspapers don't simply report the news; they report somebody's idea of what is news, written in language intended to *persuade* as well as inform. To read a newspaper intelligently, look for three things: what is covered, who are the sources, and how language is used.

Coverage   Every newspaper will cover a big story, such as a flood, fire, or presidential trip, but newspapers can pick and choose among lesser stories. One paper will select stories about the environment, business fraud, and civil rights; another will prefer stories about crime, drug dealers, and "welfare cheats." What do these choices tell you about the beliefs of the editors and reporters working for these two papers? What do these people want you to believe are the important issues?

Sources   For some stories, the source is obvious: "The Supreme Court decided . . . ," "Congress voted . . . ," or "The president said. . . ." For others, the source is not so obvious. There are two kinds of sources you should beware of. The first is an anonymous source. When you read phrases such as "a high official said today . . . " or "White House sources revealed that . . . " always ask yourself this question: Why does the source want me to know this? The answer usually will be this: because if I believe what he or she said, it will advance his or her interests. This can happen in one of three ways. First, the source may support a policy or appointment and want to test public reaction to it. This is called floating a **trial balloon.** Second, the source may oppose a policy or appointment and hope that by leaking word of it, the idea will be killed. Third, the source may want to take credit for something good that happened or shift blame onto somebody else for something bad that happened. When you read a story that is based on anonymous sources, ask yourself these questions: Judging from the tone of the story, is this leak designed to support or kill an idea? Is it designed to take credit or shift blame? In whose interest is it to accomplish these things? By asking these questions, you often can make a pretty good guess as to the identity of the anonymous source.

Some stories depend on the reader's believing a key fact, previously unknown. For example: "The world's climate is getting hotter because of man-made pollution," "drug abuse is soaring," "the death penalty will prevent murder," "husbands are more likely to beat up on their wives on Super Bowl Sunday." Each of these "facts" is either wrong, grossly exaggerated, or stated with excessive confidence. But each comes from an advocate organization that wants you to believe it, because if you do, you will take that organization's solution more seriously. Be skeptical of key facts if they come from an advocacy source. Don't be misled by the tendency of many advocacy organizations to take neutral or scholarly names like "Center for the Public Interest" or "Institute for Policy Research." Some of these really are neutral or scholarly, but many aren't.

Language   Everybody uses words to persuade people of something without actually making a clear argument for it. This is called using **loaded language.** For example: if you like a politician, call him "Senator Smith"; if you don't like him, refer to him as "right-wing (or left-wing) senators such as Smith." If you like an idea proposed by a professor, call her "respected"; if you don't like the idea, call her "controversial." If you favor abortion, call somebody who agrees with you "pro-choice" ("choice" is valued by most people); if you oppose abortion, call those who agree with you "pro-life" ("life," like "choice," is a good thing). Recognizing loaded language in a newspaper article can give you important clues to the writer's own point of view.

The Effects of the Media on Politics

Everyone believes that the media have a profound effect, for better or for worse, on politics. A small but growing body of research indicates that what appears in print or on the air probably does have an effect on how citizens think and what they think about—what they cite as "important problems," how they attribute responsibility for problems, what policy preferences they hold—and what policymakers

The Maxims of Media Relations

The importance of the national media to politicians has given rise to some shared understandings among officeholders about how one deals with the media. Some of these are caught in the following maxims:

- All secrets become public knowledge. The more important the secret, the sooner it becomes known.

- All stories written about me are inaccurate; all stories written about you are entirely accurate.

- The rosier the news, the higher ranking the official who announces it.

- Always release bad news on Saturday night. Fewer people notice it.

- Never argue with a person who buys ink by the barrel.

do.[19] But there is as of yet relatively little scholarly evidence that enables us to know precisely how large that effect is or under what conditions it exists. The reason for this gap between what everyone knows and what no one can prove is probably that until recently scholars have chiefly tried to measure the effect of the media on election outcomes. But as we have seen (Chapter 8), elections—especially those for important, highly visible offices—are occasions when the voter is bombarded with all manner of cues from friends, family, interest groups, candidates, memories, and loyalties, as well as radio, television, and newspapers. It would be surprising if the effect of the media were very strong, or at least very apparent, under these circumstances.

Efforts to determine whether voters who watch a lot of television or who see candidates on television frequently vote differently from those who do not watch television at all (or who watch only nonpolitical messages) have generally proved unavailing.[20] This is quite consistent with studies of political propaganda generally. At least in the short run, television

and radio suffer from processes called **selective attention** (the citizen sees and hears only what he or she wants) and mental tune-out (the citizen simply ignores or gets irritated by messages that are not in accord with existing beliefs). Radio and television may tend to reinforce existing beliefs, but it is not clear that they change them.[21]

But if this is true, why do companies spend millions of dollars advertising deodorants and frozen pizza? And if advertising can sell these products, why can't it sell candidates? The answer is quite simple: citizens are not idiots. They can tell the difference between a deodorant and a Democrat, between a pizza and a Republican. If an ad persuades them to try a deodorant or a pizza, they will do so, knowing that not much is at stake, the costs are small, and if they do not like it, they can change brands in an instant. But they know that government is a more serious business, that one is stuck with the winning candidate for two, four, or even six years, and that as citizens they have accumulated a lot of information about the past behavior of the two major parties and their principal figures.

Local newspapers have generally endorsed Republican candidates for president throughout this century. Indeed, only in 1964 did more newspapers endorse the Democrat (Johnson) than the Republican (Goldwater). Since the Democrats won eight of the fourteen presidential elections between 1932 and 1984, you might think that newspaper endorsements are worthless. They may have some value, however. A careful study of the effect of such endorsements on the 1964 presidential election found that, at least in the North, a newspaper endorsement may have added about five percentage points to what the Democratic candidate would otherwise have obtained.[22]

There are some elections, however, in which voters have few sources of information beyond what the media provide. Primary elections involving political unknowns and general elections for low-visibility offices (for example, tax assessor or superior court judge) may make voters dependent on newspaper and broadcast ads for information. Skillful ads may have a big effect on the results of these contests.

The major effects of the media, however, probably have much less to do with how people vote in an election and much more to do with how politics is conducted, how candidates are perceived, and how policies are formulated. National nominating con-

Senator Estes Kefauver pioneered the televised Senate investigation with hearings into organized crime and (pictured here) teenage drug addiction.

ventions have been changed to fit the needs of television broadcasters. Some candidates have found it possible to win their party's nomination for senator or governor with expensive advertising campaigns that bypass the parties and ultimately weaken them. Unknown politicians can acquire a national reputation overnight by being shrewd enough—or lucky enough—to be at the center of an event heavily covered by the press.

In 1950 Estes Kefauver was a little-known senator from Tennessee. Then he chaired a special Senate investigating committee that brought before it various figures in organized crime. When these dramatic hearings were televised to audiences numbering in the millions, Kefauver became a household word, and in 1952 he became a leading contender for the Democratic nomination for president. He was a strong vote getter in the primaries and actually led on the first ballot at the Chicago convention, only to lose to Adlai Stevenson.

The lesson was not lost on other politicians. From that time on, developing through the media a recognized name and a national constituency became important to many senators. It also became a strate-

gy whereby a variety of issues could be placed on the national agenda and pressed on Congress. Environmental and consumer issues benefited especially from the attention given them by the national press.

A survey of public opinion in North Carolina found that the issues that citizens believed to be important politically were very similar to the issues that newspapers and television newscasts had featured. Experiments conducted in New Haven, Connecticut, also showed that watching television news programs affected the importance people attached to various issues. TV influenced the political agenda.[23] On the other hand, people are much less likely to take their cues from the media on matters that affect them personally. Everybody who is unemployed, the victim of crime, or worried about high food prices will identify these matters as issues whether or not the media emphasize them.[24] In short the media help set the political agenda on matters with which citizens have little personal experience, but they have much less influence over how people react to things that touch their lives directly.

When President Theodore Roosevelt cultivated the media, reporters were usually unknown and poorly paid.

The media also affect how we perceive certain issues and candidates. A study of the differences between voters who get their news primarily from television and those who get it chiefly from newspapers found that the two groups did not view political matters the same way. On a variety of issues, newspaper readers thought that Gerald Ford was more conservative and Jimmy Carter more liberal than did television viewers. This difference persisted even after taking into account the fact that newspaper readers tend to have more schooling than do television viewers. Put another way, newspaper readers saw bigger differences between the 1976 presidential candidates than did television viewers.[25]

Another study found that television news stories affect the popularity of presidents and that television "commentary"—that is, the expression by newscasters of their personal opinions—tends to have a large effect, at least in the short run.[26] This will not come as a surprise to White House officials, who spend almost every waking minute trying to get the television networks to say something nice about the president. The data support much anecdotal evidence on this score, such as Lyndon Johnson's belief that his war policy in Vietnam was doomed when Walter Cronkite, in his heavily watched CBS News programs, turned against the war.

Government and the News

Every government agency, every public official, spends a great deal of time trying to shape public opinion. From time to time somebody publishes an exposé of the efforts of the Pentagon, the White House, or some bureau to "sell" itself to the people, but in a government of separated powers, weak parties, and a decentralized legislature, any government agency that fails to cultivate public opinion will sooner or later find itself weak, without allies, and in trouble.

Prominence of the President

Theodore Roosevelt was the first president to raise the systematic cultivation of the press to an art form. From the day he took office, he made it clear that he would give inside stories to friendly reporters and withhold them from hostile ones. He made sure that scarcely a day passed without his doing something newsworthy. In 1902 he built the West Wing of the White House and included in it, for the first time, a special room for reporters near his office, and he invited the press to become fascinated by the antics of his children. In return the reporters adored him. Teddy's nephew Franklin Roosevelt institutionalized this system by making his press secretary (a job created by

Herbert Hoover) a major instrument for cultivating and managing, as well as informing, the press.[27]

Today the press secretary heads a large staff that meets with reporters, briefs the president on questions he is likely to be asked, attempts to control the flow of news from cabinet departments to the press, and arranges briefings for out-of-town editors (to bypass what many presidents think are the biases of the White House press corps).

All this effort is directed primarily at the White House press corps, a group of men and women who have a lounge in the White House itself where they wait for a story to break, attend the daily press briefing, or take advantage of a "photo op"—an opportunity to photograph the president with some newsworthy person.

No other nation in the world has brought the press into such close physical proximity to the head of its government. The result is that the actions of our government are personalized to a degree not found in most other democracies. Whether the president rides a horse, comes down with a cold, greets a Boy Scout, or takes a trip in his airplane, the press is there. The prime minister of Great Britain does not share his home with the press or expect to have his every sneeze recorded for posterity.

Coverage of Congress

Congress has watched all this with irritation and envy. It resents the attention given the president, but it is not certain how it can compete. The 435 members of the House are so numerous and play such specialized roles that they do not get much individualized press attention. In the past the House was quite restrictive about television or radio coverage of its proceedings. Until 1978 it prohibited television cameras on the floor except on purely ceremonial occasions (such as the annual State of the Union message delivered by the president). From 1952 to 1970 the House would not even allow electronic coverage of its committee hearings (except for a few occasions during those periods when the Republicans were in the majority). Significant live coverage of committee hearings began in 1974 when the House Judiciary Committee was discussing the possible impeachment of President Nixon.[28] Since 1979 cable TV (C-SPAN) has provided gavel-to-gavel coverage of speeches on the House floor.

The Senate has used television much more fully, heightening the already substantial advantage that senators have over representatives in getting the public eye. Although radio and television coverage of the Senate floor was not allowed until 1978 (when the debates on the Panama Canal treaties were broadcast live), Senate committee hearings have frequently been televised for either news films or live broadcasts ever since Estes Kefauver demonstrated the power of this medium in 1950. Since 1986 the Senate has allowed live C-SPAN coverage of its sessions.

Senatorial use of televised committee hearings has helped turn the Senate into the incubator for presidential candidates. At least in most states, if you are a governor, you are located far from network television news cameras; the best you can hope for is that some disaster—a flood or a blizzard—will bring the cameras to you and focus them on your leadership. But senators all work in Washington, a city filled with cameras. No disaster is necessary to get on the air; only an investigation, a scandal, a major political conflict, or an articulate and telegenic personality is needed.

Interpreting Political News

News stories, especially those about events of which we have no firsthand knowledge, are apt to be accepted without question. This may be particularly true of television news stories, since they enable us to judge not only what is said but how it is said.

Americans tell pollsters that they get most of their news from television, not newspapers, and that they regard TV as more reliable than the printed press. Though in general the public has a favorable view of the media, between 1985 and 1989 there was a sharp increase in the proportion of Americans who thought the media tended to favor one side of a story—from 53 percent in 1985 to 68 percent in 1989. Between 1985 and 1998, there was also a sharp increase in the percentage who thought stories were inaccurate (see Figure 10.2). This is in sharp contrast to how the press sees itself. Two-thirds of all journalists think that the press deals fairly with all sides of political and social questions. Among the biggest losers in public confidence were Dan Rather and Ted Koppel; the biggest gainer was CNN (Cable News Network).

Bias is difficult to define and harder to measure, but in general the popular worry is that editors and reporters allow their personal political beliefs to influence the stories that they choose to run and to color the way in which they report them.

Figure 10.2 Public Perception of Accuracy in the Media

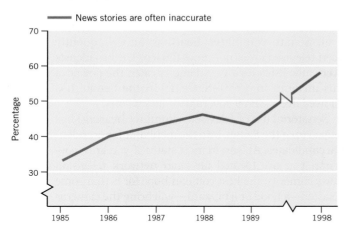

Source: Pew Research Center, "The People and the Press" (February 1999), 13.

Table 10.2 Journalist Opinion Versus Public Opinion

	Journalists	The Public
Self-described ideology:		
Liberal	55%	23%
Conservative	17	29
Favor government regulation of business	49	22
U.S. should withdraw investments from South Africa	62	31
Allow women to have abortions	82	49
Allow prayer in public schools	25	74
Favor "affirmative action"	81	56
Favor death penalty for murder	47	75
Want stricter controls on handguns	78	50
Increase defense budget	15	38
Favor hiring homosexuals	89	55

Sources: Los Angeles Times poll of about 3,000 citizens and 2,700 journalists nationwide, as reported in William Schneider and I. A. Lewis, "Views on the News," *Public Opinion* (August/September 1985): 7. Reprinted with permission of American Enterprise Institute for Public Policy Research.

Table 10.3 The Political Attitudes of the Media Elite

	Percentage Agree
People with ability should earn more.	86%
Less regulation of business is good for the United States.	63
Government should reduce the income gap.	68
There should be a strong affirmative-action program for blacks.	80
A woman has a right to decide on an abortion.	90
Homosexuality is wrong.	25
The United States exploits the Third World and causes poverty.	56
U.S. use of resources is immoral.	57
The CIA should sometimes undermine hostile governments.	45

Sources: Survey of 240 journalists and broadcasters employed by the national media, reported in S. Robert Lichter and Stanley Rothman, "Media and Business Elites," *Public Opinion* (October/November 1981): 44.

Once people worried that the press was slanted because newspaper editorial pages usually endorsed Republicans. In 1948, 85 percent of all newspapers endorsed a presidential candidate, and of those 77 percent endorsed the Republican. (He lost.) In 1996 only 30 percent of the papers made an endorsement, and of those 63 percent endorsed the Republican. (He lost.)

In a presidential election it is unlikely that editorial endorsements make any difference (which is one reason papers have stopped issuing them). The question today is whether the liberal views of reporters bias the news. According to polls, journalists are much more liberal than the public at large, and those in the national media are the most liberal of all. In Table 10.2 we can see how the beliefs of some 2,700 journalists from around the country compared with those of about three thousand ordinary citizens in the 1980s. On most issues the journalists were more liberal. In Table 10.3 we see the views of the members of the "elite" or "national" media, also in the 1980s. Unfortunately, this survey did not ask the same questions of the public as it did of the journalists. Nonetheless, on such questions as abortion and affirmative action there is little doubt that the media elite were significantly to the left of the public. This has been confirmed by a comparison of their voting patterns. In 1972, for example, when 61 percent of the American people voted for Richard Nixon, only 19 percent of persons in the national media voted for him.[29] Likewise, in 1992 over 80 percent of media leaders in Washington, D.C., versus 43 percent of the public, voted for Bill Clinton.[30] And as can be seen in Table 10.4, in the 1990s members of the media, especially those who worked in television, were more likely than members of many other professions to identify themselves as politically liberal.

Are News Stories Slanted?

The fact that reporters tend to have liberal views does not mean that their stories will inevitably have a liberal slant. Other factors influence how stories are written, including the need to meet an urgent deadline, the desire to attract an audience, a professional obligation to be fair and to tell the truth, and the need to develop sources among people holding different views. For example, whatever their views, the national media gave, according to a careful study, quite evenhanded treatment to both the Republican and Democratic presidential candidates during the 1980 campaign, although they gave quite decidedly anti-Reagan coverage during the 1984 campaign and appeared to have been consistently tougher on George Bush than on his 1992 campaign rivals, especially in the primaries.[31]

Still, it would be astonishing if strongly held beliefs had *no* effect on what is written or broadcast. To understand the circumstances under which a reporter's or editor's opinion is more or less likely to affect a story—and thus to be able to interpret intelligently what we read and hear—we must distinguish among these three *kinds* of stories:

1. **Routine stories:** These are public events regularly covered by reporters and involving relatively simple, easily described acts or statements. For example, the president takes a trip, a bill passes Congress, the Supreme Court rules on an important case.
2. **Feature stories:** These are public events knowable to any reporter who cares to inquire but involving acts and statements not routinely covered by a group of reporters. Thus a reporter must take the initiative and select a particular event as newsworthy, decide to write about it, and persuade an editor to run it. Examples: an obscure agency issues a controversial ruling, an unknown member of Congress conducts an investigation, an interest group works for the passage of a bill.
3. **Insider stories:** Information not usually made public becomes public because someone with inside knowledge tells a reporter. The reporter may have worked hard to learn these facts, in which case we say it is "investigative reporting," or some official may have wanted a story to get out, in which case we call it a "leak."

Routine stories are covered in almost exactly the same way by almost all the media, differing only in their length, the kinds of headlines written, and the position the story occupies on the pages or the evening news. The wire services—AP and Reuters—supply routine stories immediately to practically every daily newspaper in America. (The headlines and placement, however, can make a big difference in how the same story is perceived.) The political opinions of journalists have the least effect on these stories, especially if several competing journalists are covering the same story over a protracted period of time.

Even a routine news story can be incorrectly reported, however, if something dramatic or unique occurs. For example, toward the end of the Vietnam War the North Vietnamese army launched a massive, all-out attack on cities held by the South Vietnamese and their American allies. The attack failed—it was repulsed, and there were heavy North Vietnamese casualties. But the news stories reported exactly the opposite: the North Vietnamese could

Table 10.4	Self-Identified Ideology Among American Elites		
	Percentages		
	Liberal	**Conservative**	**Moderate**
Television	75	14	12
Labor	73	6	20
Bureaucrats	56	27	17
Media	55	17	28
Judges	54	23	22
Lawyers	47	32	22
Business	14	63	17
Military	14	75	12

Source: From Robert Lerner et al., *American Elites* (New Haven, Conn.: Yale University Press, 1996), 50, table 3.2. Reprinted by permission.

move and fight at will, and the Americans were helpless to defend the cities or even their own fortified positions. Peter Braestrup, who later analyzed the Tet Offensive and its journalistic coverage, painstakingly described the errors and omissions that led to the misleading versions published. He did not conclude that the political views of reporters explained the mistakes, and surely it would be difficult for any reporters, however fair, to grasp quickly and accurately an event as complex, dramatic, and violent as a major military struggle. But it is also probably the case that the antiwar attitudes of most reporters reinforced the interpretation of Tet that they wrote.[32]

Feature and insider stories must be selected, and thus someone must do the selecting. The grounds on which the selections are made include not only the intrinsic interest of a story but also the reporter's or editor's beliefs about what *ought* to be interesting. Among these beliefs are the political ideologies of the journalists. A liberal paper may well select for coverage stories about white-collar crime, consumerism, the problems of minorities, and environmentalism; a conservative paper might instead select stories about street crime, the decline of a city's central business district, and the need for family values.

Nor are selected stories rare. In order to compete with television, newspapers increasingly print feature stories, thereby becoming more like a magazine, with something for everybody. As a result, a large part of a newspaper consists of precisely the kinds of stories that are most likely to be influenced by the ideological attitudes of reporters.

In one of the few studies of the effect of journalistic opinions on news stories, the authors found that in two examples of selected stories—articles concerning nuclear power and stories on the use of busing to integrate schools—the coverage provided by the national press reflected more the views of the press than those of experts or the public. But different segments of the media differed in how much slant they gave to their stories.

On nuclear power plants the vast majority of the stories in the *New York Times* gave a balanced view of the issue; the national newsmagazines (especially *Time* and *Newsweek*) and network television news programs, however, gave a predominately antinuclear slant to their stories. Moreover, though the great majority of scientists and engineers working in the field favor the rapid development of nuclear power plants, very few of the experts quoted on this subject by the national press favored nuclear power.[33] On school busing the majority of the stories run by the *New York Times*, the *Washington Post*, *Time*, and CBS News had a probusing slant.

If a nonroutine story is a major, complex, somewhat unusual event, such as the congressional investigation of Irangate in 1987, all the media will cover it, but each will choose what themes to emphasize and what questions to raise. Almost inevitably the media will put some "spin" on the story. (For example, was the star witness, Lieutenant Colonel Oliver North, a "hero," a "loose cannon," or a "Rambo"? It depended on whom you read or listened to.) If it is an offbeat story, it will be covered by one newspaper or TV station but not others; the very act of selection usually involves some political perspective. In evaluating feature and insider stories, every reader or viewer should keep these questions in mind:

- What beliefs or opinions led the editors to run this story?
- How representative of expert and popular opinion are the views of the people quoted in the story?
- What adjectives are being used to color the story?

Insider stories raise the most difficult questions of all—those of motive. When somebody inside government with private or confidential information gives a story to a reporter, that somebody must have a reason for doing so. But the motives of those who leak information are almost never reported. Sometimes the reporter does not know the motives. More often, one suspects, the reporter is dependent on his or her "highly placed source" and is reluctant to compromise it.

The reliance on the insider leak is as old as the Republic. At one time reporters were grateful for "background briefings" at which top government officials tried to put themselves in the best possible light while explaining the inner meaning of American policy. In the aftermath of Vietnam and Watergate, which weakened the credibility of "the Establishment," many reporters became even more interested in the leaks from insiders critical of top officials. In neither case were the motives of the sources discussed, leaving the reader or viewer to accept at face value whatever remarks are attributed to unnamed "highly placed sources" or "well-informed observers."

Why Do We Have So Many News Leaks?

American government is the leakiest in the world. The bureaucracy, members of Congress, and the White House staff regularly leak stories favorable to their interests. Of late the leaks have become geysers, gushing forth torrents of insider stories. Many people in and out of government find it depressing that our government seems unable to keep anything secret for long. Others think that the public has a right to know even more and that there are still too many secrets.

However you view leaks, you should understand why we have so many. The answer is found in the Constitution. Because we have separate institutions that must share power, each branch of government competes with the others to get power. One way to compete is to try to use the press to advance your pet projects and to make the other side look bad. There are far fewer leaks in other democratic nations in part because power is centralized in the hands of a prime minister, who does not need to leak in order to get the upper hand over the legislature, and because the legislature has too little information to be a good source of leaks. In addition we have no Official Secrets Act of the kind that exists in England; except for a few matters, it is not against the law for the press to receive and print government secrets.

Even if the press and the politicians loved each other, the competition between the various branches of government would guarantee plenty of news leaks. But since the Vietnam War, the Watergate scandal, and the Iran-contra affair, the press and the politicians have come to distrust one another. As a result, journalists today are far less willing to accept at face value the statements of elected officials and are far more likely to try to find somebody who will leak "the real story." We have come, in short, to have an **adversarial press**—that is, one that (at least at the national level) is suspicious of officialdom and eager to break an embarrassing story that will win for its author honor, prestige, and (in some cases) a lot of money.

This cynicism and distrust of government and elected officials have led to an era of attack journalism—seizing upon any bit of information or rumor that might call into question the qualifications or character of a public official. Media coverage of gaffes—misspoken words, misstated ideas, clumsy moves—has become a staple of political journalism.

At one time, such "events" as President Ford slipping down some stairs, Governor Dukakis dropping the ball while playing catch with a Boston Red Sox player, or Vice President Quayle misspelling the word *potato* would have been ignored, but now they are hot news items. Attacking public figures has become a professional norm, where once it was a professional taboo.

During the 1992 election, most of the national press clearly supported Bill Clinton. The love affair between Clinton and reporters lasted for several months after his inauguration. But when stories began to appear about Whitewater (an Arkansas real estate deal in which the Clintons were once involved), Clinton's alleged sexual escapades while governor, and Hillary Rodham Clinton's profits in commodities trading, the press went into a feeding frenzy. The Clintons learned the hard way the truth of an old adage: if you want a friend in Washington, buy a dog.

Many people do not like this type of journalism, and the media's rising cynicism about the government is mirrored by the public's increasing cynicism about the media. As Figure 10.3 shows, most Americans had less confidence in the news media in 1993 than they did when they first began paying attention to the news. Most people surveyed also believed that the press slanted its coverage, had too much influence over events, and abused its constitutional protections. In a national survey of registered voters conducted shortly before the 2000 presidential election, 89 percent of respondents agreed that the media's "political views influence coverage" often (57 percent) or sometimes (32 percent); 47 percent believed that "most journalists" were "pulling for" Gore to win; and 23 percent believed that most journalists were partial to Bush.[34] Most Americans really dislike biased journalism (or journalism they perceive as biased): 53 percent say they would require a license to practice journalism, and 70 percent favor court-imposed fines for inaccurate or biased reporting.[35]

Furthermore, the public's confidence in big business has eroded along with its confidence in government, and the media are increasingly big business. As noted earlier in this chapter, network television has become a highly competitive industry. Under these circumstances, every contribution to "market share" is vitally important, and the newsroom is no exception. In a highly competitive environment that is rich

Figure 10.3   Decline in Public Trust of the Media

QUESTION

Do you have more or less or about the same amount of confidence in the news media today as you did when you first began paying attention to news and current events?

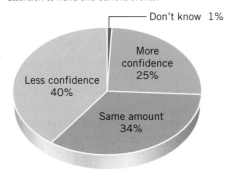

QUESTION

Do you agree or disagree with this statement: "The news media give more coverage to stories that support their own point of view than to those that don't"?

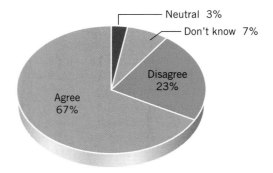

QUESTION

Generally speaking, do you feel that the news media have too much or too little or the right amount of influence over what happens today?

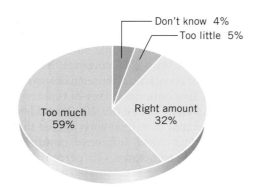

QUESTION

The Bill of Rights of the U.S. Constitution guarantees freedom of the press so that the news media can be a watchdog over the government and other powerful institutions. And the courts have ruled that the news media should be protected even in some cases when they have been unfair or inaccurate. Do you think the news media are careful to use this power responsibly?

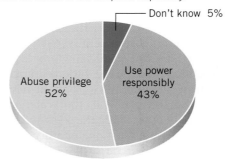

Source: David Shaw, "Trust in Media Is on Decline," *Los Angeles Times* (March 31, 1993): A16, reporting data a Times poll conducted March 6–9,1993. Copyright © 1993, Los Angeles Times. Reprinted by permission.

in information, those who aspire to reach a mass market must find a mass theme into which they can tap with visually dramatic, quick-tempo messages. In politics the theme is obvious: politics is a corrupt, self-serving enterprise. Many people include the profit-driven press in their antipolitical sentiments.

Given their experiences with Watergate and Irangate, given the highly competitive nature of national newsgathering, and given their political ideol-

ogy (which tends to put them to the left of the administration in power), American editors and reporters, at least at the national level, are likely to have an adversarial relationship with government for a long time to come. Given our constitutional system, there will always be plenty of people in government eager to help them with leaks hostile to one faction or another.

One side effect of the increasingly adversarial nature of the press is the increased prevalence of negative campaign advertising—that is, of ads that lambaste opponents and attack them on a personal level. Adversarial media coverage has helped make these types of ads more socially acceptable. The reason candidates use attack ads is simple: they work. A good negative ad will change the preferences of some voters. But this change is purchased at a price. Research shows that a negative ad not only changes voter preferences, it reduces voter turnout. Negative advertising may help a candidate win, but only by turning other people against elections.

Sensationalism in the Media

Back in the 1930s newspaper reporters knew that President Franklin Roosevelt had a romantic affair with a woman other than his wife. They did not report it. In the early 1960s many reporters knew that President John Kennedy had many sexual affairs outside his marriage. They did not report this. In 1964 the director of the Federal Bureau of Investigation played for reporters secret tape recordings of the Reverend Martin Luther King, Jr., having sex with women other than his wife. They did not report it.

By the 1980s sex and politics were extensively covered. When presidential candidate Gary Hart was caught in adultery and when President Bill Clinton was accused of adultery by Gennifer Flowers, of asking for sexual favors by Paula Jones, and of having sex with Monica Lewinsky in the Oval Office, these were headline news stories.

What had changed? Not politics: all of the people whom the press protected or reported on were Democrats. The big change was in the economics of journalism and the ideas of reporters.

Until the 1970s Americans gathered their political news from one of three networks—ABC, CBS, or NBC. For a long time these networks had only one half-hour news show a day. Today, however, viewers have the same three networks plus three cable news networks, two sports networks, ten weekly newsmagazine shows, countless radio talk shows, and the Internet. Many of the cable networks, such as CNN, carry news 24 hours a day. The result of this intense competition is that each radio or television network has a small share of the audience. Today less than half the public watches the evening network news shows. Dozens of news programs are trying to reach a shrinking audience, with the result that the audience share of each program is small. To attract any audience at all, each program has a big incentive to rely on sensational news stories—sex, violence, and intrigue. Reinforcing this desire to go with sensationalism is the fact that covering such stories is cheaper than investigating foreign policy or analyzing the tax code. During its first month, the Lewinsky story consumed more than one-third of the on-air time of the news networks—more than the U.S. showdown with Iran, the Winter Olympics, the pope's visit to Cuba, and the El Niño weather pattern combined.

Since the days of Vietnam and Watergate, journalists have become adversaries of the government. They instinctively distrust people in government. But to that attitude change can be added an economic one: in their desperate effort to reclaim market share, journalists are much more likely to rely on unnamed sources than once was the case. When the *Washington Post* broke the Watergate story in the 1970s, it required the reporters to have at least two sources for their stories. Now many reporters break stories that have only one unnamed source, and often not a source at all but a rumor posted on the Internet.

As a result, reporters are more easily manipulated by sources than once was the case. Spokesmen for President Clinton tried to "spin" the news about his affairs, usually by attacking his critics. Gennifer Flowers, Paula Jones, and Monica Lewinsky were portrayed as bimbos, liars, or stalkers. Much of the press used the spin. To see how successful spin can be, compare independent counsel Lawrence Walsh's investigation of aides to President Ronald Reagan over the sale of arms to Iran with independent counsel Kenneth Starr's investigation of the Clinton administration. Walsh's inquiry got full press support, while Starr was regularly attacked by the press.

Since the terrorist attack on the United States on September 11, 2001, there has been scattered evidence to suggest that sensationalism in the media has declined a bit, while public interest in national news and trust of news organizations have increased somewhat. The big stories of the preceding years were the sexual conduct of President Clinton and the connection between California representative Gary Condit and a missing young woman. After September 11, the press focused on a more important matter—defeating terrorism at home and abroad. By early 2002, surveys indicated that the number of people

★ POLITICALLY SPEAKING ★

On Background

When politicians talk to the press, they set certain ground rules that the press usually observes. These rules specify who, if anyone, is quoted as the source of the story.

On the record. The official is quoted by name. For example: "I say that water runs downhill, and you can quote me on that."

Off the record. What the official says cannot be printed. For example: "Off the record, the head of my party is a complete wacko."

On background. What the official says can be printed, but it may not be attributed to him or her by name. For example: "A well-placed source said today that the sun will continue to rise in the east."

On deep background. What the official says can be printed, but it cannot be attributed to anybody. The reporter must say it on his or her own authority. For example: "In my opinion this administration secretly believes that two plus two equals five."

ber who rated the media's coverage of the war on terrorism as good or excellent never fell below three-quarters.[36] But the television networks do not seem to be gaining any viewers back as a result of the crisis: fully 53 percent cited cable as their primary source for news on terrorism, versus 18 percent for local television and 17 percent for national networks.[37]

Government Constraints on Journalists

An important factor works against the influence of ideology and antiofficial attitudes on reporters—the need every reporter has for access to key officials. A reporter is only as good as his or her sources, and it is difficult to cultivate good sources if you regularly antagonize them. Thus Washington reporters must constantly strike a balance between expressing their own views (and risk losing a valuable source) and keeping a source (and risk becoming its mouthpiece).

The great increase in the number of congressional staff members has made striking this balance easier than it once was. Since it is almost impossible to keep anything secret from Congress, the existence of fifteen thousand to twenty thousand congressional staffers means that there is a potential source for every conceivable issue and cause. Congress has become a gold mine for reporters. If a story annoys one congressional source, another source can easily be found.

The government is not without means to fight back. The number of press officers on the payroll of the White House, Congress, and the executive agencies has grown sharply in recent decades. Obviously these people have a stake in putting out news stories that reflect favorably on their elected superiors. They can try to do this with press releases, but adversarial journalists are suspicious of "canned news" (although they use it nonetheless). Or the press officers can try to win journalistic friends by offering leaks and supplying background stories to favored reporters. (A **background story** is one that purportedly explains current policy and is given on condition that the source not be identified by name.) Finally, the press officers can try to bypass the national press and directly reach the local press—the hometown newspapers and radio stations. Members of the local press are less likely to feel an adversarial attitude toward official Washington and perhaps are more likely to have a political ideology akin to that of the national administration.

who said they followed national news closely had increased slightly from 48 percent to 53 percent; the number who said the media usually get the facts straight rose from 35 percent to 46 percent (the best public grade for accuracy in a decade); and the num-

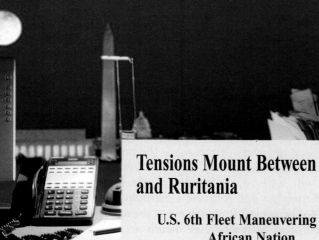

Tensions Mount Between U.S. and Ruritania

U.S. 6th Fleet Maneuvering near African Nation

February 23
WASHINGTON

The State Department today denied Ruritanian claims that the United States is planning military action against Ruritania in the wake of Ruritanian-sponsored terrorist actions . . .

MEMORANDUM

To: Editor in chief, Washington Post
From: Foreign news editor
Subject: Ruritania

One of our best reporters has information that the United States plans to invade Ruritania three days from now. His source is a top military official who has been reliable in the past. As of now we do not think that any other newspaper has this story. As you know, opinion in the government is deeply divided over the wisdom of any action against Ruritania. So far all official sources in the White House and the State Department have denied that anything is afoot. But we all know that the president is deeply upset by the continuation of Ruritanian-sponsored terrorism against U.S. personnel overseas. Your options are:

1. Print the story in tomorrow's edition.

Advantages: (a) This is important news, and we have an obligation to publish news. (b) We get a major scoop that no other newspaper can match. (c) In our editorials we have said that we think an invasion of Ruritania would be a mistake. This story, if printed now, may lead to a cancellation of the military action.

Disadvantages: (a) There is a small chance that we could be wrong and no invasion is planned. (b) We will be criticized for leaking military secrets. (c) If the invasion takes place despite our story, the United States may lose the element of surprise, and this may affect the outcome and cause additional casualties.

2. Do not print the story.

Advantages: (a) We avoid charges that we are leaking military secrets. (b) If an invasion occurs, we will not have alerted the enemy.

Disadvantages: (a) There is the possibility that another newspaper may learn of this story in the next two days; if we don't publish now, they may publish later and we will look foolish. (b) We will be failing in our duty to inform the people about the activities of their government. (c) The Ruritanians may already know of the planned invasion, and so our story will not have alerted them.

Your decision:
Option 1 _____
Option 2 _____

"Those are the headlines, and we'll be back in a moment to blow them out of proportion."

The ultimate weapon in the government's effort to shape the press to its liking is the president's rewarding of reporters and editors who treat him well and his punishing of those who treat him badly. President Kennedy regularly called in offending reporters for brutal tongue-lashings and favored friendly reporters with tips and inside stories. Johnson did the same, with special attention to television reporters. Nixon made the mistake of attacking the press publicly, thereby allowing it to defend itself with appeals to the First Amendment. (Kennedy's and Johnson's manipulative skills were used privately.) Probably every president tries to use the press with whatever means are at his disposal, but in the long run it is the press, not the president, who wins. Johnson decided not to run again in 1968 in part because of press hostility to him; Nixon was exposed by the press; Carter came to be disliked by national reporters. The press and the president need but do not trust one another; it is inevitably a stormy relationship.

Summary

Changes in the nature of American politics have been accompanied by—and influenced by—changes in the nature of the mass media. The rise of strong national political party organizations was facilitated by the emergence of mass-circulation daily newspapers. Political reform movements depended in part on the development of national magazines catering to middle-class opinion. The weakening of political parties was accelerated by the ability of candidates to speak directly to constituents by radio and television.

The role of journalists in a democratic society poses an inevitable dilemma: if they are to serve well their functions as information gatherer, gatekeeper, scorekeeper, and watchdog, they must be free of government controls. But to the extent that they are free of such controls, they are also free to act in their own interests, whether political or economic. In the United States a competitive press largely free of government controls (except in the area of broadcast licenses) has produced both a substantial diversity of opinion and a general (though not unanimous) commitment to the goal of fairness in news reporting. The national media are in general more liberal than the local media, but the extent to which a reporter's beliefs affect reporting varies greatly with the kind of story—routine, feature, or insider.

Reconsidering the Enduring Questions

1. Why do politicians worry so much about the media?
They worry so much about the media because the media are now so important to virtually everything that happens in American politics and government. Politicians generally need the media to mobilize supporters, combat challengers, reach constituents, conduct campaigns, communicate information, and enact (or block) legislation. Even in the first days of the Republic, the media mat-

tered mightily to many politicians. The *Federalist* papers themselves were a series of opinion-editorial essays written in defense of the proposed Constitution and published in a leading New York newspaper. *Media* is a plural noun, and today's electronic media include talk radio stations, major television networks, hundreds of cable television outlets, and the Internet. No politicians worry more about the press than presidents. For example, continuing a practice perfected by the Clinton White House, when President George W. Bush's senior staff meets each morning at 7:30 A.M., their first item of business is to prepare for that day's press coverage and to decide how to handle any negative news items that are out or appear to be brewing.

2. *Can we trust the media to be fair?*

Most Americans think not. The mass public believes that press stories are often slanted and that journalists' own political views, policy preferences, and ideological dispositions bias their coverage of campaigns and elections. The decline in public trust of the media was halted somewhat by the media's coverage of the war on terrorism, but most citizens still think that the media normally fail to get their facts straight and that the press is partisan. It is true that, compared to the general public, journalists are more likely to identify them-

selves as liberals and to vote as Democrats. Press bias is probably at its worst when the reporting concerns nonroutine and insider stories.

3. *Should people care more about getting political information?*

College professors (like us) who teach political science courses always seem to think so. If you believe that the media are biased, you could decide not to care about getting political news (why bother if it is inaccurate or slanted anyhow?), or you could get tons more of it and get it from multiple sources (the better to sift the truth for yourself). If you believe that more citizens should get out and vote, then you might want people to care more about getting political information (on the assumption that having it would stimulate civic interest and voting), or you might not (on the assumption that having it would only breed political cynicism and dampen the desire to vote). In Chapter 8, we distinguished between valence issues and position issues, and between retrospective voters and prospective voters. If you believe that most citizens should vote prospectively on position issues, then people getting more political information is a must. But if you believe that most citizens are or ought to be retrospective valence-issue voters, then people getting more political information might be nice but is not a must.

World Wide Web Resources

- To search many newspapers: www.ipl.org
- CNN/*Time* news: www.allpolitics.com
- *New York Times:* www.nytimes.com
- Washington, D.C., newspapers
  Washington Post: www.washingtonpost.com
  Washington Times: www. washtimes.com

Key Terms

Suggested Readings

Braestrup, Peter. *Big Story: How the American Press and Television Reported and Interpreted the Crises of Tet 1968 in Vietnam and Washington.* 2 vols. Boulder, Colo.: Westview Press, 1977. A massive, detailed account of how the press reported one critical event; the factual accuracy or inaccuracy of each story is carefully checked.

Crouse, Timothy. *The Boys on the Bus.* New York: Random House, 1973. A lively, irreverent account by a participant of how reporters cover a presidential campaign.

Epstein, Edward J. *Between Fact and Fiction: The Problem of Journalism.* New York: Random House, 1975. Essays by a perceptive student of the press on media coverage of Watergate, the Pentagon Papers, the deaths of Black Panthers, and other major stories.

———. *News from Nowhere.* New York: Random House, 1973. Analysis of how television network news programs are produced and shaped.

Garment, Suzanne. *Scandal.* New York: Random House, 1991. A careful look at the role of the media (and others) in fostering the "culture of mistrust."

Graber, Doris A. *Mass Media and American Politics.* 3d ed. Washington, D.C.: Congressional Quarterly Press, 1989. A good summary of what we know about the press and politics.

Iyengar, Shanto, and Donald R. Kinder. *News That Matters.* Chicago: University of Chicago Press, 1987. The report of experiments testing the effect of television news on public perceptions of politics.

Kurtz, Howard. *Spin Cycle: Inside the Clinton Propaganda Machine.* New York: Free Press, 1998. A journalistic account of how one president's staff tried to influence the media.

Lichter, S. Robert, Stanley Rothman, and Linda S. Lichter. *The Media Elite.* Bethesda, Md.: Adler and Adler, 1986. A study of the political beliefs of "elite" journalists and how those beliefs influence what we read and hear.

McGowan, William. *Coloring the News.* San Francisco: Encounter Books, 2001. An argument about the harmful effects of affirmative action and "identity politics" on news coverage.

Patterson, Thomas W. *The Mass Media Election.* New York: Praeger, 1980. Analyzes what effect, if any, the media had on the 1976 election.

Robinson, Michael J., and Margaret A. Sheehan. *Over the Wire and on TV.* New York: Russell Sage Foundation, 1983. Analyzes how CBS News and United Press International covered the 1980 election.

Sabato, Larry J. *Feeding Frenzy.* New York: Free Press, 1991. Explains the press focus on political misconduct.

PART III

Institutions of Government

*But the great security against a gradual concentration
of the several powers in the same department consists
in giving to those who administer each department the
necessary constitutional means and personal motives to
resist encroachments of the others.*

FEDERALIST NO. 51

Congress

Enduring Questions

1. Are the members of Congress representative of the American people?
2. Should Congress run under strong leadership, or should it allow its members a lot of freedom?
3. Why does it take so long for Congress to act?

oth in the minds of the Federalists (see Chapter 2) and in terms of its present-day constitutional powers and prerogatives, Congress was and remains the "first branch" of American national government. As we shall explain, it has the ultimate power of the purse, can pass a law even if the president vetoes it, and can alter, profoundly at times, how existing laws are administered through its oversight of executive agencies. Congress can likewise expand or contract the appellate jurisdiction of the U.S. Supreme Court. It may use these powers only rarely, but it has them, and myriad others, in reserve.

However, Congress is now considered by many to be the system's broken branch, badly in need of fixing. It has probably been the object of more mass public mistrust and more elite reform proposals than either the presidency or the federal judiciary combined. This is true even though most incumbent members of Congress who seek reelection win it, and even though Congress as a whole has pretty consistently expanded the programs and adopted the reforms that most citizens favor.

Once you master its basics, Congress is full of supremely interesting political puzzles. Its diverse membership, its daily workings, and its legislative decisions arguably reveal more about America's representative democracy, past and present, warts and all, than is revealed by any other institution. It would be only a slight exaggeration to say that he or she who really knows Congress knows more about American politics than he or she who knows virtually everything else about the system but not much about Congress. There is no one key to understanding who governs and to what ends in America, but if we had to nominate a single candidate, we would nominate Congress.

Former senator Daniel Patrick Moynihan of New York once remarked that the United States is the only democratic government that has a legislative branch. Of course lots of democracies have parliaments that can pass laws. What he meant is that among the large democracies of the world, only the U.S. Congress has great powers that it can exercise independently of the executive branch. To see why this is so, we must understand the difference between a congress and a parliament.

The work of Congress takes place in committees with members of both parties—here Senators Orrin Hatch (R-Utah) and Patrick Leahy (D-Vt.).

Congress Versus Parliament

The United States (along with many Latin American nations) has a congress; Great Britain (along with most Western European nations) has a parliament. A hint as to the difference between the two kinds of legislatures can be found in the original meanings of the words: *Congress* derives from a Latin term that means "a coming together," a meeting, as of representatives from various places. *Parliament* comes from a French word, *parler,* that means "to talk."

There is of course plenty of talking—some critics say that there is nothing *but* talking—in the U.S. Congress, and certainly members of a parliament represent to a degree their local districts. But the differences implied by the names of the lawmaking groups are real ones, with profound significance for how laws are made and how the government is run. These differences affect two important aspects of lawmaking bodies: how one becomes a member and what one does as a member.

Ordinarily a person becomes a member of a parliament (such as the British House of Commons) by persuading a political party to put his or her name on the ballot. Though usually a local party committee selects a person to be its candidate, that committee often takes suggestions from national party headquarters. In any case the local group selects as its candidate someone willing to support the national party program and leadership. In the election voters in the district choose not between two or three personalities running for office, but between two or three national parties.

By contrast, a person becomes a candidate for representative or senator in the U.S. Congress by running in a primary election. Except in a very few places, political parties exercise little control over the choice of who is nominated to run for congressional office. (This is the case even though the person who wins the primary will describe himself or herself in the general election as a Democrat or a Republican.) Voters select candidates in the primaries because of their personalities, positions on issues, or overall reputation. Even in the general election, where the party label affects who votes for whom, many citizens vote "for the man" (or for the woman), not for the party. As a result of these different systems a parliament tends to be made up of people loyal to the national party leadership who meet to debate and vote on party issues. A congress, on the other hand, tends to be made up of people who think of themselves as independent representatives of their districts or states and who, while willing to support their party on many matters, expect to vote as their (or their constituents') beliefs and interests require.

Once they are in the legislature, members of a parliament discover that they can make only one important decision—whether or not to support the government. The government in a parliamentary system such as Britain's consists of a prime minister and various cabinet officers selected from the party that has the most seats in parliament. As long as the members of that party vote together, that government will remain in power (until the next election). Should members of a party in power in parliament decide to vote against their leaders, the leaders lose office, and a new government must be formed. With so much at stake, the leaders of a party in parliament have a powerful incentive to keep their followers in line. They insist that all members of the party vote together on almost all issues. If someone refuses, the penalty is often drastic: the party does not renominate the offending member in the next election.

Members of the U.S. Congress do not select the head of the executive branch of government—that is done by the voters when they choose a president. Far from making members of Congress less powerful, this makes them more powerful. Representatives and senators can vote on proposed laws without worrying that their votes will cause the government to collapse and without fearing that a failure to support their party will lead to their removal from the ballot in the next election. Congress has independent powers, defined by the Constitution, that it can exercise without regard to presidential preferences. Political parties do not control nominations for office, and thus they cannot discipline members of Congress who fail to support the party leadership. Because Congress is constitutionally independent of the president, and because its members are not tightly disciplined by a party leadership, individual members of Congress are free to express their views and vote as they wish. They are also free to become involved in the most minute details of lawmaking, budget making, and supervision of the administration of laws. They do this through an elaborate set of committees and subcommittees.

A real parliament, such as that in Britain, is an assembly of party representatives who choose a government and discuss major national issues. The principal daily work of a parliament is debate. A congress, such as that in the United States, is a meeting place of the representatives of local constituencies—districts and states. Members of the U.S. Congress can initiate, modify, approve, or reject laws, and they share with the president supervision of the administrative agencies of the government. The principal work of a congress is representation and action, most of which takes place in committees.

What this means in practical terms to the typical legislator is easy to see. Since members of the British House of Commons have little independent power, they get rather little in return. They are poorly paid, may have no offices of their own and virtually no staff, are allowed only small sums to buy stationery, and can make a few free local telephone calls. Each is given a desk, a filing cabinet, and a telephone, but not always in the same place.

By contrast, a member of the U.S. House of Representatives, even a junior one, has power and is rewarded accordingly. For example, in 2002 each member earned a substantial salary ($150,000) and was entitled to a large office (or "clerk-hire") allowance, to pay for as many as twenty-two staffers. Each member also received individual allowances for travel, computer services, and the like. In addition each member could mail newsletters and certain other documents to constituents for free using the "franking privilege." Senators, and representatives with seniority, received even larger benefits. Each senator was entitled

When an anthrax scare forced Diane Feinstein to vacate her senate offices, she remained surrounded by her staffers.

The Powers of Congress

The powers of Congress are found in Article I, section 8, of the Constitution.

- To lay and collect taxes, duties, imposts, and excises
- To borrow money
- To regulate commerce with foreign nations and among the states
- To establish rules for naturalization (that is, becoming a citizen) and bankruptcy
- To coin money, set its value, and punish counterfeiting
- To fix the standard of weights and measures
- To establish a post office and post roads
- To issue patents and copyrights by inventors and authors
- To create courts inferior to (that is, below) the Supreme Court
- To define and punish piracies, felonies on the high seas, and crimes against the law of nations

- To declare war
- To raise and support an army and navy and make rules for their governance
- To provide for a militia (reserving to the states the right to appoint militia officers and to train the militia under congressional rules)
- To exercise exclusive legislative powers over the seat of government (that is, the District of Columbia) and other places purchased to be federal facilities (forts, arsenals, dockyards, and "other needful buildings")
- To "make all laws which shall be necessary and proper for carrying into execution the foregoing powers, and all other powers vested by this Constitution in the government of the United States" (*Note*: This "necessary and proper," or "elastic," clause has been generously interpreted by the Supreme Court, as explained in Chapter 14.)

to a generous office budget and legislative assistance allowance and was free to hire as many staff members as he or she wished with the money. These examples are not given to suggest that members of Congress are overrewarded, but only that their importance, as individuals, in our political system can be inferred from the resources that they command.

Because the United States has a congress made up of people chosen to represent their states and districts, rather than a parliament made up to represent competing political parties, no one should be surprised to learn that members of the U.S. Congress are more concerned with their own constituencies and careers than with the interests of any organized party or program of action. And since Congress does not choose the president, members of Congress know that worrying about the voters they represent is much more important than worrying about whether the president succeeds with his programs. These two factors taken together mean that Congress tends to be a decentralized institution, with each member more interested in his or her own views and those of his or her voters than with the programs proposed by the president.

Indeed, Congress was designed by the Founders in ways that almost inevitably make it unpopular with voters. Americans want government to take action, follow a clear course of action, and respond to strong leaders. Americans dislike political arguments, the activities of special-interest groups, and the endless pulling and hauling that often precede any congressional decision. But the people who feel this way are deeply divided about what government should do: Be liberal? Be conservative? Spend money? Cut taxes? Support abortions? Stop abortions? Since they are divided, and since members of Congress must worry about how voters feel, it is inevitable that on controversial issues Congress will engage in endless arguments, worry about what interest groups (who represent different groups of voters) think, and work out compromise decisions. When it does those things, however, many people feel let down and say that they have a low opinion of Congress.

Of course a member of Congress might explain all these constitutional facts to the people, but not many members are eager to tell their voters that they do not really understand how Congress was created and organized. Instead they run for reelection by promising voters that they will go back to Washington and "clean up that mess."

The Evolution of Congress

The Framers chose to place legislative powers in the hands of a congress rather than a parliament for philosophical and practical reasons. They did not want to have all powers concentrated in a single governmental institution, even one that was popularly elected, because they feared that such a concentration could lead to rule by an oppressive or impassioned majority. At the same time, they knew that the states were jealous of their independence and would never consent to a national constitution if it did not protect their interests and strike a reasonable balance between large and small states. Hence they created a **bicameral** (two-chamber) **legislature**— with a House of Representatives, to be elected directly by the people, and a Senate, consisting of two members from each state, to be chosen by the legislatures of each state. Though "all legislative powers" were to be vested in Congress, those powers would be shared with the president (who could veto acts of Congress), limited to powers explicitly conferred on the federal government, and, as it turned out, subject to the power of the Supreme Court to declare acts of Congress unconstitutional.

For decades critics of Congress have complained that the body cannot plan or act quickly. They are right, but two competing values are at stake: centralization versus decentralization. If Congress were to act quickly and decisively as a body, then there would have to be strong central leadership, restrictions on debate, few opportunities for stalling tactics, and minimal committee interference. If, on the other hand, the interests of individual members—and the constituencies that they represent—were to be protected or enhanced, then there would have to be weak leadership, rules allowing for delay and discussion, and many opportunities for committee activity.

Though there have been periods of strong central leadership in Congress, the general trend, especially in this century, has been toward decentralizing decision-making and enhancing the power of the

Three powerful Speakers of the House: Thomas B. Reed (1889–1891, 1895–1899) (left), Joseph G. Cannon (1903–1911) (center), and Sam Rayburn (1941–1947, 1949–1953, 1955–1961) (right). Reed put an end to a filibuster in the House by refusing to allow dilatory motions and by counting as "present"—for purposes of a quorum—members in the House even though they were not voting. Cannon further enlarged the Speaker's power by refusing to recognize members who wished to speak without Cannon's approval and by increasing the power of the Rules Committee, over which he presided. Cannon was stripped of much of his power in 1910. Rayburn's influence rested more on his ability to persuade than on his formal powers.

House History: Six Phases

One of the most powerful Speakers of the House, Henry Clay, is shown here addressing the U.S. Senate around 1850.

Phase One: The Powerful House

During the first three administrations—of George Washington, John Adams, and Thomas Jefferson—leadership in Congress was often supplied by the president or his cabinet officers. Rather quickly, however, Congress began to assert its independence. The House of Representatives was the preeminent institution, overshadowing the Senate.

Phase Two: The Divided House

In the late 1820s the preeminence of the House began to wane. Andrew Jackson asserted the power of the presidency by vetoing legislation that he did not like. The party unity necessary for a Speaker, or any leader, to control the House was shattered by the issue of slavery. Of course representatives from the South did not attend during the Civil War, and their seats remained vacant for several years after it ended. A group called the Radical Republicans, led by men such as Thaddeus Stevens of Pennsylvania, produced strong majorities for measures aimed at punishing the defeated South. But as time passed, the hot passions the war had generated began to cool, and it became clear that the leadership of the House remained weak.

Phase Three: The Speaker Rules

Toward the end of the nineteenth century the Speaker of the House gained power. When Thomas B. Reed of Maine became Speaker in 1889, he obtained by vote of the Republican majority more authority than any of his predecessors, including the right to select the chairmen and members of all committees. He chaired the Rules Committee and

individual member at the expense of the congressional leadership. This decentralization may not have been inevitable. Most American states have constitutional systems quite similar to the federal one, yet in many state legislatures, such as those in New York, Massachusetts, and Indiana, the leadership is quite powerful. In part the position of these strong state legislative leaders may be the result of the greater strength of political parties in some states than in the nation as a whole. In large measure, however, it is a consequence of permitting state legislative leaders to decide who shall chair what committee and who shall receive what favors.

The House of Representatives, though always powerful, has often changed the way in which it is organized and led. In some periods it has given its leader, the Speaker, a lot of power; in other periods it has given much of that power to the chairmen of the House committees; and in still other periods it has allowed individual members to acquire great influence. In the 1990s it seemed for a while that the Speaker would permanently reclaim powers previously given away to individual members, but it is too early to tell whether that change will endure. To simplify a complicated story, the box above outlines six different periods in the history of the House.

The House faces fundamental problems: it wants to be both big (it has 435 members) and powerful, and its members want to be powerful both as individuals and as a group. But being big makes it hard for the House to be powerful unless some small group is given the authority to run it. If a group runs the place, however, the individual members lack much power. Individuals can gain power, but only at the price of making the House harder to run and thus reducing its collective power in government.

decided what business would come up for a vote, what the limitations on debate would be, and who would be allowed to speak and who would not. In 1903, Joseph G. Cannon of Illinois became Speaker. He tried to maintain Reed's tradition, but he had many enemies within his Republican ranks.

Phase Four: The House Revolts

In 1910–1911 the House revolted against "Czar" Cannon, voting to strip the Speaker of his right to appoint committee chairmen and to remove him from the Rules Committee. The powers lost by the Speaker flowed to the party caucus, the Rules Committee, and the chairmen of the standing committees. It was not, however, until the 1960s and 1970s that House members struck out against all forms of leadership.

Phase Five: The Members Rule

Newly elected Democrats could not get the House to vote on a meaningful civil rights bill until 1965 because powerful committee chairmen, most of them from the South, kept such legislation bottled up. In response, Democrats changed their rules so that chairmen lost much of their authority. Beginning in the 1970s committee chairmen would no longer be selected simply on the basis of seniority: they had to be elected by the members of the majority party. Chairmen could no longer

refuse to call committee meetings, and most meetings had to be public. Committees without subcommittees had to create them and allow their members to choose subcommittee chairmen. Individual members' staffs were greatly enlarged, and half of all majority-party members were chairmen of at least one committee or subcommittee.

Phase Six: The Leadership Returns

Since every member had power, it was harder for the House to get anything done. By slow steps, culminating in some sweeping changes made in 1995, there were efforts to restore some of the power the Speaker had once had. The number of committees and subcommittees was reduced. Republican Speaker Newt Gingrich dominated the choice of committee chairmen, often passing over more senior members for more agreeable junior ones. But Gingrich's demise was as quick as his rise. His decision not to pass some appropriations bills forced many government offices to close for a short period, he had to pay a fine for using tax-exempt funds for political purposes, and then the Republicans lost a number of seats in the 1998 election. Gingrich resigned as Speaker and as a member of the House and was replaced by a more moderate Speaker, Dennis Hastert of Illinois, with a penchant for accommodating his colleagues.

There is no lasting solution to these dilemmas, and so the House will always be undergoing changes.

The Senate does not face any of these problems. It is small enough (100 members) that it can be run without giving much authority to any small group of leaders. In addition it has escaped some of the problems the House once faced. During the period leading up to the Civil War it was carefully balanced so that the number of senators from slaveowning states exactly equaled the number from free states. Hence fights over slavery rarely arose in the Senate.

From the first the Senate was small enough that no time limits had to be placed on how long a senator could speak. This meant that there never was anything like a Rules Committee that controlled the amount of debate.

Finally, senators were not elected by the voters until this century. Prior to that they were picked instead by

state legislatures. Thus senators were often the leaders of local party organizations, with an interest in funneling jobs and contracts back to their states.

The big changes in the Senate came not from any fight about how to run it (nobody ever really ran it) but from a dispute over how its members should be chosen. For more than a century after the Founding members of the Senate were chosen by state legislatures. Though often these legislatures picked popular local figures to be senators, just as often there was intense political maneuvering among the leaders of various factions, each struggling to win (and sometimes buy) the votes necessary to become senator. By the end of the nineteenth century the Senate was known as the Millionaires' Club because of the number of wealthy party leaders and businessmen in it. There arose a demand for the direct, popular election of senators.

★ POLITICALLY SPEAKING ★

Filibuster

A filibuster is a technique by which a small number of senators attempt to defeat a measure by talking it to death—that is, by speaking continuously and at such length as to induce the supporters of the measure to drop it in order to get on with the Senate's business.

The right to filibuster is governed by the Senate's Rule 22, which allows for unlimited debate unless at least sixty senators agree to a motion to cut it off.

Originally *filibusterers* were sixteenth-century English and French pirates and buccaneers who raided Spanish treasure ships. The term came from a Dutch word, *vrijbuiter*, meaning "freebooter," which was converted into the English word *filibuster*.

The word came into use in America as a term for "continuous talking" in the mid-nineteenth century. One of its first appearances was in 1854, when a group of senators tried to talk to death the Kansas-Nebraska Act.

Source: From *Safire's Political Dictionary* by William Safire. Copyright © 1968, 1972, 1978 by William Safire. Reprinted by permission of Random House, Inc. and the author.

---

many state legislatures devised ways to ensure that the senators they picked would already have won a popular election. The Senate finally agreed to a constitutional amendment that required the popular election of its members, and in 1913 the Seventeenth Amendment was approved by the necessary three-fourths of the states. Ironically, given the intensity of the struggle over this question, no great change in the composition of the Senate resulted; most of those members who had first been chosen by state legislatures managed to win reelection by popular vote.

The other major issue in the development of the Senate was the filibuster. A **filibuster** is a prolonged speech, or series of speeches, made to delay action in a legislative assembly. It had become a common—and unpopular—feature of Senate life by the end of the nineteenth century. It was used by liberals and conservatives alike and for lofty as well as self-serving purposes. The first serious effort to restrict the filibuster came in 1917, after an important foreign policy measure submitted by President Wilson had been talked to death by, as Wilson put it, "eleven willful men." Rule 22 was adopted by a Senate fear-

THE WAY WE BECOME SENATOR NOWADAYS.

A cartoon from Puck *in 1890 expressed popular resentment over the "Millionaires' Club," as the Senate had become known.*

Naturally the Senate resisted, and without its approval the necessary constitutional amendment could not pass Congress. When some states threatened to demand a new constitutional convention, the Senate feared that such a convention would change more than just the way in which senators were chosen. A protracted struggle ensued, during which

Table 11.1   Blacks, Hispanics, and Women in Congress, 1971–2002

Congress	Senate			House		
	Blacks	Hispanics	Women	Blacks	Hispanics	Women
108th (2003–2004)	0	0	13	39	23	62
107th	0	0	13	36	19	59
106th	0	0	9	39	19	58
105th	1	1	9	37	18	51
104th	1	0	8	38	18	48
103rd	1	0	6	38	17	47
102nd	0	0	2	26	10	29
101st	0	0	2	24	11	25
100th	0	0	2	23	11	23
99th	0	0	2	20	11	22
98th	0	0	2	21	10	22
97th	0	0	2	17	6	19
96th	0	0	1	16	6	16
95th	1	0	2	16	5	18
94th	1	1	0	15	5	19
93rd	1	1	0	15	5	14
92nd (1971–1972)	1	1	2	12	5	13

Source: Congressional Quarterly Almanac, various years.

ful of tying a president's hands during a wartime crisis. The rule provided that debate could be cut off if two-thirds of the senators present and voting agreed to a "cloture" motion (it has since been revised to allow sixty senators to cut off debate). Two years later it was first invoked successfully when the Senate voted cloture to end, after fifty-five days, the debate over the Treaty of Versailles. Despite the existence of Rule 22, the tradition of unlimited debate remains strong in the Senate.

Who Is in Congress?

With power so decentralized in Congress, the kind of person elected to it is especially important. Since each member exercises some influence, the beliefs and interests of each individual affect policy. Viewed simplistically, most members of Congress seem the same: the typical representative or senator is a middle-aged white Protestant male lawyer. If all such persons usually thought and voted alike, that would be an interesting fact, but they do not, and so it is necessary to explore the great diversity of views among seemingly similar people.

Sex and Race

Congress has gradually become less male and less white. Between 1950 and 2002 the number of women in the House increased from nine to fifty-nine and the number of African Americans from two to thirty-six. There are also nineteen Hispanic members.

Until recently the Senate changed much more slowly (see Table 11.1). Before the 1992 election there were no African Americans and only two women in the Senate. But in 1992 four more women, including one black woman, Carol Mosely Braun of Illinois, were elected. Two more were elected in 1994, when a Native American, Ben Nighthorse Campbell of Colorado, also became a senator. By 2002, there were no African Americans and thirteen women in the Senate.

The relatively small number of African Americans and Hispanics in the House understates their influence, at least when the Democrats are in the majority. In 1994 four House committees were chaired by blacks and three by Hispanics. In the same year, however, no woman chaired a committee. The reason for this difference in power is that the former tend to come from safe districts (see page 291) and thus to have more seniority than the latter. Since 1995, Republican control of the House has reduced minority influence.

Incumbency

The most important change that has occurred in the composition of Congress has been so gradual that most people have not noticed it. In the nineteenth century a large fraction—often a majority—of congressmen served only one term. In 1869, for example, more than half the members of the House were serving their first term in Congress. Being a congressman in those days was not regarded as a career. This was in part because the federal government was not very important (most of the interesting political decisions were made by the states); in part because travel to Washington, D.C., was difficult and the city was not a pleasant place in which to live; and in part because being a congressman did not pay well. Furthermore, many congressional districts were highly competitive, with the two political parties fairly evenly balanced in each.

By the 1950s, however, serving in Congress had become a career. Between 1863 and 1969 the proportion of first-termers in the House fell from 58 percent to 8 percent (see Figure 11.1).[1] As the public

took note of this shift, people began to complain about "professional politicians" being "out of touch with the people." A movement to impose term limits was started. In 1995 the House approved a constitutional amendment to do just that, but it died in the Senate. Then the Supreme Court struck down an effort by a state to impose term limits on its own members of Congress.

As it turned out, natural political forces were already doing what the term limits amendment was supposed to do. The 1992 and 1994 elections brought scores of new members to the House, with the result that by 1995 the proportion of members who were serving their first or second terms had risen sharply. Three things were responsible for this change. First, when congressional district lines were redrawn after the 1990 census, a lot of incumbents found themselves running in new districts that they

---

Figure 11.1   Changing Percentage of First-Term Members in Congress

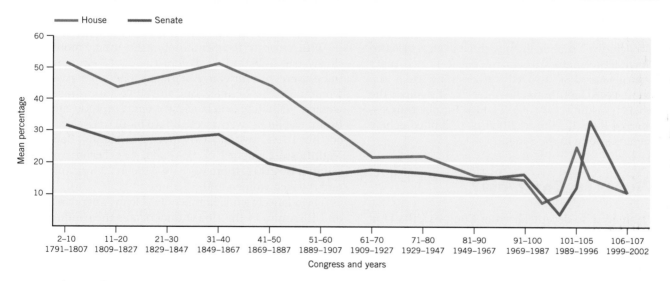

Notes: The 1989 freshman class in the House was the smallest in history. The 1993 freshman class in the House was the largest since 1949.

Sources: Data for 90th through 103rd congresses are from *Congressional Quarterly Weekly Reports*. Data for 69th through 89th congresses are adapted from Nelson W. Polsby, "The Institutionalization of the U.S. House of Representatives," *American Political Science Review* (March 1968): 146. Data for 1st through 68th congresses are from Stuart A. Rice, *Quantitative Methods in Politics* (New York: Knopf, 1928), 296–297, as reported in Polsby, 146. Data for Senate are from N. J. Ornstein, T. J. Mann, and M. J. Malbin, *Vital Statistics on Congress, 1989–1990* (Washington, D.C.: Congressional Quarterly Press, 1990), 56–57, 59–60; and Stanley Harold and Richard Niemi, *Vital Statistics on American Politics* (Washington, D.C.: Congressional Quarterly Press, 2001).

couldn't carry. Second, voter disgust at a variety of Washington political scandals made them receptive to appeals from candidates who could describe themselves as "outsiders." And third, the Republican victory in 1994—made possible in part by the conversion of the South from a Democratic bastion to a Republican stronghold—brought a lot of new faces to the Capitol.

This influx of freshman members should not obscure the fact that incumbents still enjoy enormous advantages in congressional elections.[2] Even in 1994, when thirty-five incumbent Democrats lost to Republicans, over 90 percent of all House members who ran for reelection were reelected. In the Senate 92 percent of incumbents who ran again were reelected. In 2000, one of the most hotly contested elections in recent history, only six of the 339 House incumbents who ran for reelection lost.

The arrival of scores of new faces in the 1990s should not obscure the fact that most House members still win big in their districts. Political scientists call districts that have close elections (when the winner gets less than 55 percent of the vote) **marginal districts** and districts where incumbents win by wide margins (55 percent or more) **safe districts.** The proportion of House incumbents who have won reelection with at least 60 percent of the vote increased from about three-fifths in the 1950s and early 1960s to three-quarters in the 1970s and almost nine-tenths in the late 1980s (see Figure 11.2). Even as this trend began to change in 1990, most House districts remained safe. Senators remained less secure: the rule, to which the period 1980–1990 and the year 1998 are the exceptions, is that fewer than half of Senate incumbents win with as much as 60 percent of the vote (see Table 11.2).

Why congressional seats have become less marginal—that is, safer—is a matter on which scholars do not agree. Some feel that it is the result of television and other media. But challengers can go on television, too, so why should this benefit incumbents? Another possibility is that voters are becoming less and less likely to automatically support whatever candidate wins the nomination of their own party. They are more likely, in short, to vote for the person rather than the party. And they are more likely to have heard of a person who is an incumbent: incumbents can deluge the voter with free mailings, they can travel frequently (and at public expense) to meet constituents, and they can get their names in the newspaper by sponsoring bills or conducting investigations. Simply having a familiar name is important in getting elected, and incumbents find it easier than challengers to make their names known.

Finally, some scholars argue that incumbents can use their power to get programs passed or funds spent to benefit their districts—and thereby to benefit themselves. They can help keep an army base open, support the building of a new highway (or block the building of an unpopular one), take credit for federal grants to local schools and hospitals, make certain that a particular industry or labor union is protected by tariffs against foreign competition, and so on.[3]

Probably all of these factors make some difference. Whatever the explanation, the tendency of voters to return incumbents to office means that in ordinary times no one should expect any dramatic changes in the composition of Congress.

Party

From 1933 to 1998 thirty-three Congresses convened (a new Congress convenes every two years). The Democrats controlled both houses in twenty-five of these Congresses and at least one house in twenty-eight of them. Scholars differ in their explanations of why the Democrats have so thoroughly

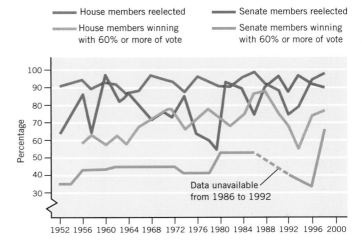

Figure 11.2   Percentage of Incumbents Reelected to Congress

Source: Harold W. Stanley and Richard G. Niemi, *Vital Statistics on American Politics, 1999–2000* (Washington, D.C.: Congressional Quarterly Press, 2000), table 1-18.

Table 11.2 Incumbents in Congress Reelected by 60 Percent or More

House, 1956–2002

Year	Number of Incumbents Running in General Election	Percentage of Incumbents Reelected with at Least 60 Percent of the Vote
1956	403	59.1%
1958	390	63.1
1960	400	58.9
1962	376	63.6
1964	388	58.5
1966	401	67.7
1968	397	72.2
1970	389	77.3
1972	373	77.8
1974	383	66.4
1976	381	71.9
1978	377	78.0
1980	392	72.9
1982	383	68.9
1984	406	74.6
1986	391	86.4
1988	407	88.5
1990	406	76.4
1992	349	65.6
1994	383	64.5
1996	383	73.6
1998	400	77.2
2000	403	81.1
2002	394	83.5

Senate, 1944–2002

Election Period	Number of Incumbents Running in General Election	Percentage of Incumbents Reelected with at Least 60 Percent of the Vote
1944–1948	61	39.3%
1950–1954	76	35.5
1956–1960	84	42.9
1962–1966	86	44.2
1968–1972	74	44.6
1974–1978	70	41.4
1980–1984	84	54.1
1986–1990	87	57.5
1992–1994	53	43.4
1996–1998	49	57.1
1998–2000	29	65.5
2000–2002	29	69.0
2002–2004	27	55.6

Source: Harold W. Stanley and Richard G. Niemi, *Vital Statistics on American Politics, 2001–2002* (Washington, D.C.: Congressional Quarterly Press, 2001), table 1-18.

Table 11.3 Republican Vote-Seat Gap, 1968–2002

Year	Percentage of Popular Vote for Republican House Candidates	Percentage of House Seats Held by Republicans
1968	48.2%	44.1%
1970	44.5	41.4
1972	46.4	44.2
1974	40.5	33.1
1976	42.1	32.9
1978	44.7	36.3
1980	48.0	44.1
1982	43.3	38.2
1984	47.0	41.8
1986	44.6	40.7
1988	45.5	40.2
1990	45.0	38.4
1992	45.6	40.5
1994	52.4	52.9
1996	48.9	52.2
1998	48.7	51.3
2000	48.7	50.8
2002	53.4	52.4

Source: Harold W. Stanley and Richard G. Niemi, *Vital Statistics on American Politics, 2001–2002* (Washington, D.C.: Congressional Quarterly Press, 2001), table 1–12.

As Table 11.3 shows, in every election from 1968 to 1992 the percentage of the popular vote for Republican candidates to the House was higher than the percentage of House seats that actually went to Republicans. For example, in 1976 the Republicans won 42.1 percent of the vote but received only 32.9 percent of the seats. Some have argued that this gap between votes and seats has occurred because Democratic-controlled state legislatures have redrawn congressional district maps in ways that make it hard for Republicans to win House seats. There is some striking anecdotal evidence to support this conclusion. For example, following the 1990 census, the Democratic-controlled Texas legislature crafted a new congressional district map clearly designed to benefit Democrats. In 1992 Republicans won 48 percent of the House vote in Texas but received only 30 percent of the seats. Similarly, in 1984 Democrats in California won nine more congressional seats than did Republicans, even though the latter received about one hundred thousand more votes statewide. After 1990 California's congressional map was redrawn by a state court, and in 1992 Republican House candidates won 41 percent of the statewide vote and 42 percent of the seats.[4]

dominated Congress. Most of the research on the subject has focused on the reasons for Democratic control of the House.

Only in 1994, with the historic election of the first Republican majorities in Congress in four decades, did the gap close and begin to work slightly in Republicans' favor.

Partisan tinkering with district maps and other structural features of House elections is not a sufficient explanation of why Democrats dominated the House until 1994. As one study concluded, "Virtually all the political science evidence to date indicates that the electoral system has little or no partisan bias, and that the net gains nationally from redistricting for one party over another are very small."[5] To control the redistricting process, one party must control both houses of the legislature, the governor's office, and, where necessary, the state courts. These conditions simply do not exist in most states. And even if district lines were consistently drawn with scrupulous fairness, the Democrats would still win control of the House, because they win more votes. The Republican vote-seat gap is accounted for in part by the fact that the Democrats tend to do exceptionally well in low-turnout districts such as minority-dominated inner cities, while the Republicans tend to do well in high-turnout districts such as affluent white suburbs (see Figure 11.3).

In 1994, however, the year the gap closed, Republican candidates for the House ran especially strong in the roughly half of all districts that have predominantly suburban constituencies. Thus even though only 19 percent of eligible voters cast a vote for a Republican, it was enough to best the Democrats, who won the votes of only 16.6 percent of all eligible voters.

Congressional incumbents have come to enjoy certain built-in electoral advantages over challengers, and the Democrats were in the majority as the advantages of incumbency grew. Studies suggest that the incumbency advantage was worth about two percentage points prior to the 1960s but has grown to six to eight points today.

But as political scientist Gary C. Jacobson has observed, the historical Democratic dominance of the House cannot be explained simply by reference to incumbency advantages. Instead Jacobson argues that "Democrats' continued dominance of the House (as well as of other lower offices) despite a string of Republican presidential victories is a consequence of electoral politics."[6] In comparison with the Republicans, the Democrats, he finds, generally have fielded better, more experienced congressional candidates, have more closely reflected district-level

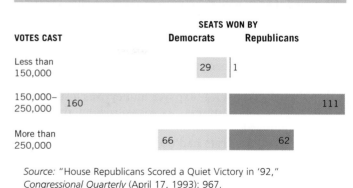

Figure 11.3   Results of 1992 House Election by Turnout

| VOTES CAST | SEATS WON BY | |
	Democrats	Republicans
Less than 150,000	29	1
150,000–250,000	160	111
More than 250,000	66	62

Source: "House Republicans Scored a Quiet Victory in '92," *Congressional Quarterly* (April 17, 1993): 967.

voters' policy preferences, and have been able to fashion winning, district-level coalitions from among national Democratic constituencies such as organized labor, civil rights activists, feminists, and environmentalists. This implies that more than mere changes in the structural features of House elections (incumbency advantages, partisan redistricting) would be necessary to keep the GOP's vote-seat gap closed.

It is important to remember that from time to time major electoral convulsions do alter the membership patterns in Congress. For example, in the election of 1938 the Democrats lost seventy seats in the House; in 1942 they lost fifty; in 1950 they lost twenty-nine; and in 1966 they lost forty-eight. Despite these big losses, the Democrats retained a majority in the House in each of these years. Not so, however, in 1994, when the Democrats lost fifty-two House seats (the largest loss by either party since the Republicans lost seventy-five seats in 1948), and Republicans gained majorities in both the House and the Senate.

Just as it is not easy to explain why Democrats dominated Congress for half a century, so it is not easy to explain why that domination ended when and as it did. Several reasons, however, stand out. By the 1990s the advantages of incumbency had turned into disadvantages: voters increasingly came to dislike "professional politicians," whom they held responsible for "the mess in Washington." Just what "the mess" was varied according to which voter you asked, but it included chronic budget deficits, the congressional habit of exempting itself from laws that affected everybody else, constant bickering between Congress and the White House, and various congressional scandals. During the 1980s about forty members of Congress were charged with misconduct ranging from having sex with minors to accepting illegal gifts. When it was disclosed that the House had its own bank that would cash checks even for members who (temporarily) had no funds in their accounts, public indignation exploded, even though almost no taxpayer money was lost. Public respect for Congress, as measured by the polls, plummeted.

The Democrats had the misfortune of being the majority party in Congress when all of this happened. The anti-incumbent mood, coupled with the effects of redistricting after the 1990 census and the shift of the South to the Republican party, brought the Republicans into power in the House and Senate in the 1994 elections.

In the past the Democratic party was more deeply divided than the Republicans, because of the presence in Congress of conservative Democrats from the South. Often these southern Democrats would vote with the Republicans in the House or Senate, thereby forming what came to be called the **conservative coalition.** During the 1960s and 1970s that coalition came together in about one-fifth of all roll-call votes. When it did, it usually won, defeating northern Democrats. But since the 1980s, and especially since the watershed election of 1994, the conservative coalition has become much less important. The reason is simple: many southern Democrats in Congress have been replaced by southern Republicans, and the southern Democrats who remain (many of them African Americans) are as liberal as northern Democrats. The effect of this change is to make Congress, and especially the House, more ideologically partisan—Democrats are liberals, Republicans are conservatives—and this in turn helps explain why there is more party unity in voting.

Do Members Represent Their Voters?

In a decentralized, individualistic institution such as Congress, it is not obvious how its members will behave. They could be devoted to doing whatever their constituents want or, since most voters are not aware of what their representatives do, act in accor-

dance with their own beliefs, the demands of pressure groups, or the expectations of congressional leaders. You may think it would be easy to figure out whether members are devoted to their constituents by analyzing how they vote, but that is not quite right. Members can influence legislation in many ways other than by voting: they can conduct hearings, help mark up bills in committee meetings, and offer amendments to the bills proposed by others. A member's final vote on a bill may conceal as much as it reveals: some members may vote for a bill that contains many things they dislike because it also contains a few things they value.

There are at least three theories about how members of Congress behave: representational, organizational, and attitudinal.

The *representational* explanation is based on the reasonable assumption that members want to get reelected, and therefore they vote to please their constituents. The *organizational* explanation is based on the equally reasonable assumption that since most constituents do not know how their legislator has voted, it is not essential to please them. But it is important to please fellow members of Congress, whose goodwill is valuable in getting things done and in acquiring status and power in Congress. The *attitudinal* explanation is based on the assumption that there are so many conflicting pressures on members of Congress that they cancel one another out, leaving them virtually free to vote on the basis of their own beliefs.

Political scientists have studied, tested, and argued about these (and other) explanations for decades, and nothing like a consensus has emerged. Some facts have been established, however.

Representational View

The representational view has some merit under certain circumstances—namely, when constituents have a clear view on some issue and a legislator's vote on that issue is likely to attract their attention. Such is often the case for civil rights laws: representatives with significant numbers of black voters in their districts are not likely to oppose civil rights bills; representatives with few African Americans in their districts are comparatively free to oppose such bills. (Until the late 1960s many southern representatives were able to oppose civil rights measures because the African Americans in their districts were prevented from voting. On the other hand, many representatives without black constituents have supported civil rights bills, partly out of personal belief and partly, perhaps, because certain white groups in their districts—organized liberals, for example—have insisted on such support.)

One study of congressional roll-call votes and constituency opinion showed that the correlation between the two was quite strong on civil rights bills. There was also a positive (though not as strong) correlation between roll-call votes and constituency opinion on social welfare measures. Scarcely any correlation, however, was found between congressional votes and hometown opinion on foreign policy measures.[7] Foreign policy is generally remote from the daily interests of most Americans, and public opinion about such matters can change rapidly. It is not surprising, therefore, that congressional votes and constituent opinion should be different on such questions.

From time to time an issue arouses deep passions among the voters, and legislators cannot escape the need either to vote as their constituents want, whatever their personal views, or to anguish at length about which side of a divided constituency to support. Gun control has been one such question, the use of federal money to pay for abortions has been another, and the effort to impeach President Clinton was a third. Some fortunate members of Congress get unambiguous cues from their constituents on these matters, and no hard decision is necessary. Others get conflicting views, and they know that whichever way they vote, it may cost them dearly in the next election. Occasionally members of Congress in this fix will try to be out of town when the matter comes up for a vote. One careful study found that constituency influences were an important factor in Senate votes,[8] but no comparable study has been done for the House.

You might think that members of Congress who won a close race in the last election—who come from a "marginal" district—would be especially eager to vote the way that their constituents want. Research so far has shown that is not generally the case. There seem to be about as many independent-minded members of Congress from marginal as from safe districts. Perhaps it is because opinion is so divided in a marginal seat that one cannot please everybody; as a result the representative votes on other grounds.

Political issues may be national, but campaigning for office is intensely local, as when Dennis Hastert talks to factory employees in his Illinois district.

In general the problem with the representational explanation is that public opinion is not strong and clear on most measures on which Congress must vote. Many representatives and senators face constituencies that are divided on key issues. Some constituents go to special pains to make their views known (these interest groups were discussed in Chapter 9). But as we indicated, the power of interest groups to affect congressional votes depends, among other things, on whether a legislator sees them as united and powerful or as disorganized and marginal.

This does not mean that constituents rarely have a direct influence on voting. The influence that they have probably comes from the fact that legislators risk defeat should they steadfastly vote in ways that can be held against them by a rival in the next election. Though most congressional votes are not known to most citizens, blunders (real or alleged) quickly become known when an electoral opponent exploits them.

Still, any member of Congress can choose the positions that he or she takes on most roll-call votes (and on all voice or standing votes, where names are not recorded). And even a series of recorded votes that are against constituency opinion need not be fatal: a member of Congress can win votes in other ways—for example, by doing services for constituents or by appealing to the party loyalty of the voters.

Organizational View

When voting on matters where constituency interests or opinions are not vitally at stake, members of Congress respond primarily to cues provided by their colleagues. This is the organizational explanation of their votes. The principal cue is party; as already noted, what party a member of Congress belongs to explains more about his or her voting record than any other single factor. Additional organizational cues come from the opinions of colleagues with whom the member of Congress feels a close ideological affinity: for liberals in the House it is the Democratic Study Group; for conservatives it has often been the Republican Study Committee or the Wednesday Club. But party and other organizations do not have clear positions on all matters. For the scores of votes that do not involve the "big questions," a representative or senator is especially likely to be influenced by the members of his or her party on the sponsoring committee.

It is easy to understand why. Suppose you are a Democratic representative from Michigan who is summoned to the floor of the House to vote on a bill to authorize a new weapons system. You haven't the faintest idea what issues might be at stake. There is no obvious liberal or conservative position on this matter. How do you vote? Simple. You take your cue from several Democrats on the House Armed Services Committee that handled the bill. Some are liberal; others are conservative. If both liberals and conservatives support the bill, you vote for it unhesitatingly. If they disagree, you vote with whichever Democrat is generally closest to your own political ideology. If the matter is one that affects your state, you can take your cue from members of your state's delegation to Congress.

Attitudinal View

Finally, there is evidence that the ideology of a member of Congress affects how he or she votes. We have seen that Democratic and Republican legislators differ sharply on a liberal-versus-conservative scale. On both domestic and foreign policy issues many tend to be consistently liberal or conservative.[9]

This consistency isn't surprising. As we saw in Chapter 5, political elites think more ideologically than the public generally.

On many issues the average member of the House has opinions close to those of the average voter. Senators, by contrast, are often less in tune with public opinion. In the 1970s they were much more liberal than voters; in the early 1980s more conservative. Two senators from the same state often mobilize quite different bases of support. The result is that many states, such as California, Delaware, and New York, have been represented by senators with almost diametrically opposed views.

Of late the Senate has gone through three phases. In the first, during the 1950s and early 1960s, it was a cautious, conservative institution dominated by southern senators and displaying many of the features of a "club" that welcomed members into its inner circle only after they had displayed loyalty to its gentlemanly (and, in effect, conservative) customs. This was the era when the Senate was the graveyard of civil rights bills.

The second period began in the mid-1960s as liberal senators rose steadily in number, seniority, and influence, helped along by the Johnson reforms, which made it easier for junior senators to gain chairmanships. The decentralization of the Senate gave more power to individual senators, including liberals. In 1972 there were about twenty-four liberal senators, but among them they held forty subcommittee chairmanships.[10]

The third period began in the late 1970s and became most visible after the 1980 elections, when many liberals lost their seats to conservative Republicans. The conservatism of the present Senate is based more on ideology than on the rules of the southern "club" that characterized it in the 1950s.

The Democratic party is more deeply divided than the Republican. There are only a few liberal Republicans, but there have been many more conservative Democrats from the South and West. Southern Democrats often teamed up with Republicans to form a conservative coalition. In a typical year a majority of Republicans and southern Democrats would vote together against a majority of northern Democrats about 20 to 25 percent of the time. When the conservative coalition did form, it usually won: between 1970 and 1982 it won about two-thirds of the votes on which it held together. After the Reagan victory and the Republican gain of thirty seats in the House in 1981, the conservative coalition became even more effective, dominating key votes on the Reagan budget and tax plans.

But the conservative coalition was important only when there were a lot of conservative southern Democrats. Many of these have now been replaced with southern Republicans. As a result almost all of the conservatives are now in the Republican party, so there is not much of a coalition left to form. In 1998 this coalition—that is, a majority of Republicans and southern Democrats voting against a majority of northern Democrats—existed in only 6 percent of all congressional votes. In the 1970s, by contrast, it appeared in about one-quarter of all votes.

Ideology and Civility in Congress

Congress has become an increasingly ideological organization. By that we mean its members are more sharply divided by political ideology than they once were and certainly more divided than are American voters. In short the attitudinal explanation of how members vote has increased in importance, while the organizational explanation has declined. All of Congress's most liberal members are Democrats, and all of its most conservative ones are Republicans. That is not what you would find among ordinary voters. A lot of us split our tickets, voting for one party's presidential nominee and a different party's congressional candidate.

This higher level of congressional ideology does not mean that its existing members have changed how they think. Rather it means that new kinds of members have been elected, bringing to Congress a more ideological perspective.[11] In 1974 (the election right after Watergate) a large number of more ideological Democrats entered Congress. In 1994 there was a large influx of more ideological Republicans.

Congress has become more polarized than voters in terms of political beliefs. Among voters the average Democrat and the average Republican, though they surely disagree, nonetheless have views that put them close to the center of the political spectrum. But among members of Congress the average Democrat is very liberal and the average Republican very conservative, a fact that keeps them far from the political center. There are, of course, some conservative Democrats and some liberal Republicans, but their numbers have been getting smaller and smaller.

One result of this polarization is that members of Congress, especially those in the House, do not get along as well as they once did with members who disagree with them, and they are more likely to challenge, investigate, and denounce one another. Two Speakers of the House, Jim Wright and Newt Gingrich, were

investigated and resigned. Many presidential nominees have been subjected to withering investigations, some based on ideological differences and some on charges of ethical violations, many of which were dubious. President Clinton was impeached on a nearly party-line vote. Members regularly accuse one another of misconduct. When they run for reelection, they often use negative ads of the sort discussed in Chapter 5. The mass media feed on and aggravate this tendency because of their interest in scandal.

The result is that the public—already puzzled by the constitutional need members have to discuss policy matters for long periods, listen to interest groups, and reach compromise settlements—are now put off even more by the political disposition members have to attack one another. At one time the constitutional need to negotiate was facilitated by reasonably good relationships between Democrats and Republicans, most of whom treated one another with politeness and socialized together after hours. This congenial social relationship no longer exists in most cases, and the public has noticed.

The Organization of Congress: Parties and Caucuses

Congress is not a single organization; it is a vast and complex collection of organizations by which the business of the legislative branch is carried on and through which its members form alliances. If we were to look inside the British House of Commons, we would find only one kind of organization of any importance—the political party. Though party organization is important in the U.S. Congress, it is only one of many important elements. In fact other organizations have grown in number as the influence of the parties has declined.

The Democrats and Republicans in the House and the Senate are organized by party leaders. The key leaders in turn are elected by the full party membership within the House and Senate. The description that follows is confined to the essential positions.

Party Organization of the Senate

The majority party chooses one of its members—usually the person with the greatest seniority—to be president pro tempore of the Senate. It is largely an honorific position, required by the Constitution so that the Senate will have a presiding officer in the absence of

★ POLITICALLY SPEAKING ★

Whip

A whip is a party leader who makes certain that party members are present for a vote and vote the way the party wishes. In the British House of Commons the whips produce strong party votes; in the U.S. Congress whips are a lot less successful.

The word comes from *whipper-in*, a term from fox hunting denoting the person whose job it is to keep the hounds from straying off the trail. It became a political term in England in the eighteenth century, and from there came to the United States.

Source: From *Safire's Political Dictionary* by William Safire. Copyright © 1968, 1972, 1978 by William Safire. Reprinted by permission of Random House, Inc. and the author.

the vice president of the United States (who is also, according to the Constitution, the president of the Senate). In fact presiding over the Senate is a tedious chore that neither the vice president nor the president pro tem relishes, and so the actual task of presiding is usually assigned to some junior senator.

The real leadership is in the hands of the **majority leader** (chosen by the senators of the majority party) and the **minority leader** (chosen by the senators of the other party). In addition the senators of each party elect a whip. The principal task of the majority leader is to schedule the business of the Senate, usually in consultation with the minority leader. The majority leader has the right to be recognized first in any floor debate. A majority leader with a strong personality who is skilled at political bar-

gaining may do much more. Lyndon Johnson, who was Senate majority leader for the Democrats during much of the 1950s, used his prodigious ability to serve the needs of fellow senators. He helped them with everything from obtaining extra office space to getting choice committee assignments, and in this way he acquired substantial influence over the substance as well as the schedule of Senate business. Johnson's successor, Mike Mansfield, was a less assertive majority leader and had less influence.

The **whip** is a senator who helps the party leader stay informed about what party members are thinking, rounds up members when important votes are to be taken, and attempts to keep a nose count on how the voting on a controversial issue is likely to go. The whip has several senators who assist him or her in this task.

Each party in the Senate also chooses a Policy Committee composed of a dozen or so senators who help the party leader schedule Senate business, choosing what bills are to be given major attention and in what order.

From the point of view of individual senators, however, the key party organization is the group that assigns senators to the standing committees of the Senate. The Democrats have a Steering Committee that does this; the Republicans have a Committee on Committees. These assignments are especially important for newly elected senators: their political careers, their opportunities for favorable publicity, and their chances for helping their states and their supporters depend in great part on the committees to which they are assigned.

Party control of the Senate has changed frequently. When George W. Bush took office in 2001, the Republicans briefly retained control by having 50 seats plus a tie-breaking vote cast by Vice President Cheney. But then Senator James Jeffords, a Republican, became an independent and voted to let the Democrats control it, 51 to 49. But that ended when the Republicans won enough seats in the 2002 election to regain control. Having a tiny majority in the Senate does not affect most important votes since the other side can filibuster, but having your own party control the chairmanships is very important because it helps determine what issues will get to the floor for a vote.

The key—and delicate—aspect of selecting party leaders, of making up the important party committees, and of assigning freshman senators to Senate committees is achieving ideological and regional

Minority leader Nancy Pelosi, the first woman to hold a party leadership role in Congress.

balance. Liberals and conservatives in each party will fight over the choice of majority and minority leader, but factors in addition to ideology play a part in the choice. These include personal popularity, the ability of the leader to make an effective television appearance, and who owes whom what favors.

Party Structure in the House

Though the titles of various posts are different, the party structure is essentially the same in the House as in the Senate. Leadership carries more power in the House than in the Senate because of the House rules. Being so large (435 members), the House must restrict debate and schedule its business with great care; thus leaders who do the scheduling and who determine how the rules shall be applied usually have substantial influence.

The Speaker is the most important person in the House. He is elected by whichever party has a major-

ity, and he presides over all House meetings. Unlike the president pro tem of the Senate, however, his position is anything but honorific. He is the principal leader of the majority party as well as the presiding officer of the entire House. Though Speakers-as-presiders are expected to be fair, Speakers-as-party-leaders are expected to use their powers to help pass legislation favored by their party.

In helping his party, the Speaker has some important formal powers at his disposal: he decides who shall be recognized to speak on the floor of the House; he rules whether a motion is relevant and germane to the business at hand; and he decides (subject to certain rules) the committees to which new bills shall be assigned. He influences what bills are brought up for a vote and appoints the members of special and select committees (to be explained on pages 304–306). Since 1975 the Speaker has been able to nominate the majority-party members of the Rules Committee. He also has some informal powers: he controls some patronage jobs in the Capitol building and the assignment of extra office space. Even though he is far less powerful than in the days of Clay, Reed, and Cannon, the Speaker is still an important person to have on one's side. Sam Rayburn of Texas exercised great influence as Speaker, and Tip O'Neill, Jim Wright, Tom Foley, and Newt Gingrich tried to do the same.

In the House, as in the Senate, the majority party elects a floor leader, called the majority leader. The other party also chooses a leader—the minority leader. Traditionally the majority leader becomes Speaker when the person in that position dies or retires—provided, of course, that the departing Speaker's party is still in the majority. Each party also has a whip, with several assistant whips in charge of rounding up votes from various state delegations. Committee assignments are made and the scheduling of legislation is discussed, by the Democrats, in a Steering and Policy Committee, chaired by the Speaker. The Republicans have divided committee assignments and policy discussions, with the former task assigned to a Committee on Committees and the latter to a Policy Committee. Each party also has a congressional campaign committee to provide funds and other assistance to party members running for election or reelection to the House.

The Strength of Party Structures

One important measure of the strength of the parties in Congress is the ability of party leaders to get their

Party Leadership Structure

SENATE

President Pro Tempore Selected by majority party

Democrats

Majority Leader Leads the party

Majority Whip Assists the leader, rounds up votes, heads group of deputy whips

Chairman of the Conference Presides over meetings of all Senate Democrats

Policy Committee Schedules legislation

Steering Committee Assigns Democratic senators to committees

Democratic Senatorial Campaign Committee Provides funds, assistance to Democratic candidates for the Senate

Republicans

Minority Leader Leads the party

Assistant Minority Leader Assists the leader, rounds up votes

Chairman of the Conference Presides over meetings of all Senate Republicans

Policy Committee Makes recommendations on party policy

Committee on Committees Assigns Republican senators to committees

Republican Senatorial Committee Provides funds, advice to Republican candidates for the Senate

HOUSE

Speaker of the House Selected by majority party

Democrats

Majority Leader Leads the party

Majority Whip Assists the leader, rounds up votes, heads group of deputy and assistant whips

Chairman of the Caucus Presides over meetings of all House Democrats

Steering and Policy Committee Schedules legislation, assigns Democratic representatives to committees

Democratic Congressional Campaign Committee Provides funds, advice to Democratic candidates for the House

Republicans

Minority Leader Leads the party

Minority Whip Assists the leader, rounds up votes, heads large group of deputy and assistant whips

Chairman of the Conference Presides over meetings of all House Republicans

Committee on Committees Assigns Republican representatives to committees

Policy Committee Advises on party policy

National Republican Congressional Committee Provides funds, advice to Republican candidates for the House

Research Committee On request, provides information about issues

members to vote together on the rules and structure of Congress. When Newt Gingrich became Speaker of the Republican-controlled House in 1995, he proposed sweeping changes in House rules, many not popular with some Republican members. For example, he wanted no one to serve as a committee chairman for more than six years, for three committees to be abolished, and for other committees to lose either functions or members. He also wanted to pass over some senior members in picking committee chairmen. Though these moves adversely affected some Republican representatives, they all voted in favor of the new rules.[12] Of course Gingrich would not have made these proposals unless he was certain he could

get them adopted. But it was a measure of his influence and support among newly elected Republicans that even major changes in congressional procedures would get unanimous party support.[13] Getting support on proposed legislation is a harder task.

The Senate is another matter. As Barbara Sinclair has argued, in the last few decades the Senate has been transformed by changes in norms (informal understandings governing how members ought to behave toward their colleagues), without any far-reaching changes in the written Senate rules.[14] Compared to the Senate of the 1950s and 1960s, today's Senate is less party-centered, less leader-oriented, more hospitable to freshmen (who no longer have to "pay their dues"

The U.S. Congress

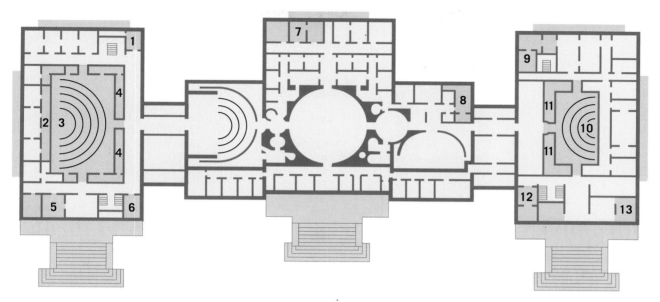

HOUSE OF REPRESENTATIVES
1. House Minority Whip
2. Lobby
3. House chamber
4. Cloakrooms
5. Speaker of the House
6. Ways and Means Committee
7. House Minority Leader

SENATE
8. Senate Minority Leader
9. Office of the Secretary
10. Senate chamber
11. Cloakrooms
12. Senate Majority Leader
13. Vice President

The House and Senate meet at opposite ends of the Capitol building. When there is a joint session of Congress—for example, to hear the president's State of the Union address—the senators sit with the representatives in the House chamber. Though the most important work of Congress goes on in committee meetings, which are held in office buildings behind the Capitol, some important political negotiations occur in the offices surrounding the chambers—especially in the cloakrooms (actually, lounges) and the offices of the majority and minority leaders, the Speaker and the vice president, and the secretary of the Senate.

before assuming major roles as legislators), more heavily staffed, and more subcommittee-oriented.

Party Unity

The strength of Congress's elaborate party machinery can also be measured by the extent to which members of a party vote together in the House and Senate. **Party polarization** is defined as a vote in which a majority of voting Democrats oppose a majority of voting Republicans. In seven of the thirteen years from 1953 to 1965, at least half of all House votes pitted a majority of voting Democrats against a majority of voting Republicans (see Table 11.4). But in 1966 the number dropped to 41 percent, and it was not until 1983 that voting in the

House once again took on a distinctively partisan cast. By the 1990s party unity voting was the norm in both the House and the Senate. A kindred measure of party strength is the cohesion of the parties on votes that elicit a party split. By this measure, between 1991 and 1994 over 80 percent of all House and Senate Democrats voted with a majority of their party on party unity votes, as did over 80 percent of House and Senate Republicans.

As these recent trends make plain, party unity in Congress is hardly a thing of the past. Specific issues can trigger an extraordinary degree of party cohesion. For example, in 1993 every single Republican in both the House and Senate voted against the Clinton budget plan, the first budget offered by a Democratic

Table 11.4 **Party Polarization in Congressional Voting, 1953–2000 (percentage of all votes)**

Year	House	Senate	Year	House	Senate
1953	52%	N.A.	1977	42%	42%
1954	38	47%	1978	33	45
1955	41	30	1979	47	47
1956	44	53	1980	38	46
1957	59	36	1981	37	48
1958	40	44	1982	36	43
1959	55	48	1983	56	44
1960	53	37	1984	47	40
1961	50	62	1985	61	50
1962	46	41	1986	57	52
1963	49	47	1987	64	41
1964	55	36	1988	47	42
1965	52	42	1989	55	35
1966	41	50	1990	49	54
1967	36	35	1991	55	49
1968	35	32	1992	64	53
1969	31	36	1993	65	67
1970	27	35	1994	62	52
1971	38	42	1995	73	69
1972	27	36	1996	56	62
1973	42	40	1997	50	50
1974	29	44	1998	56	56
1975	48	48	1999	47	63
1976	36	37	2000	43	49

Source: Harold W. Stanley and Richard G. Niemi, *Vital Statistics on American Politics, 2001–2002* (Washington, D.C.: Congressional Quarterly Press, 2001), table 5.7.

president since Jimmy Carter left office in 1980. This may be an extreme example, but it reflects the increasingly adversarial relationship between Democrats and Republicans, especially in the House.

Still, it is worth remembering that even today's Congress is less divided along party lines than many of its predecessors were. During the years 1890–1910, for example, two-thirds of all votes evoked a party split, and in several sessions more than half the roll calls found 90 percent of each party's members opposing the other party.[15] Whereas the party splits of the past often reflected the routine operations of highly disciplined parties interested mainly in winning elections, dispensing patronage, and keeping power, today's party splits often reflect sharp ideological differences between the parties (or at least between their respective leaders).

The sharp increase in party votes among members of Congress since 1970 is remarkable, since it is not obvious that the Americans who vote for these members are as deeply divided by party. When social scientists describe a trait among people—say, their height—they usually note that there are a few very short ones and a few very tall ones, but that most people are in the middle. They call this distribution "unimodal." But when one describes voting in Congress, except on matters of national urgency, the votes are "bimodal"—that is, almost all of the Democrats vote one way and almost all of the Republicans vote a different way.

For example, when President Clinton was impeached, 98 percent of the House Republicans voted for at least one of the four impeachment articles and 98 percent of the House Democrats voted against all four, and this happened despite the fact that most Americans did not want to have the president impeached. In fact, the Republican vote did not even match how people felt who lived in districts represented by Republicans. On abortion, most Americans favor it but with some important limitations, but in Congress Democrats almost always support it with no restrictions and Republicans usually want to put on lots of restrictions. Votes on less emotional matters, like the tax bills, often show the same pattern of Democrats and Republicans at loggerheads.

How could these things happen in a democratic nation? If the American people are usually in the center on political issues, why are congressional Democrats almost always liberal and congressional Republicans almost always conservative?

There is no simple or agreed-upon answer to this question. Some scholars have argued that in the last thirty years or so voters have in fact become more partisan. "More partisan" means that they see important differences between the two parties, they identify themselves as either conservatives or liberals, and they favor parties that share their ideological preferences.[16]

One reason this has happened has been the way congressional districts are drawn for House members. The vast majority are drawn so as to protect one party or the other. This means that if you are a Republican living in a pro-Democratic district (or a Democrat living in a pro-Republican one), your votes don't make much difference in an election. Most House districts are not competitive, meaning that in them the only election that counts is the primary used to pick a candidate. In primaries voter turnout is lower, so that the most motivated (and thus most ideological) voters play a disproportionate role in choosing candidates.

A second possibility is that the voters have become more partisan as a result of Congress having become more partisan. When House Democrats vote liberal and House Republicans vote conservative, a lot of voters follow this cue and take positions based on a similar ideology.[17] People who don't see the world this way have either become less numerous or vote less often.

And a third is the role of seniority. Even though the so-called seniority rule is no longer strictly followed, the chairmen of committees are typically the members who have been on those committees the longest, and they will, of course, be ones from the safest districts. Since the chairmen have a lot of influence over how bills are written, their views—which have been shaped by a lifetime of dedication to Democratic or Republican causes—will be very important. If the Democrats had won control of the House in 2002, something that would only have required their winning six more seats, the chairmanship of several committees would have changed from very conservative to very liberal members.*

In short party *does* make a difference in Congress—not as much as it once did, and not nearly as much as

it does in a parliamentary system, but enough so that party affiliation is still the most important thing to know about a member of Congress. Knowing whether a member is a Democrat or a Republican will not tell you everything about the member, but it will tell you more than any other single fact.

Caucuses

Congressional caucuses are a growing rival to the parties as a source of policy leadership. A **caucus** is an association of members of Congress created to advocate a political ideology or a regional or economic interest. In 1959 there were only four caucuses; by the late 1980s there were over one hundred.

As Congress expert Susan Webb Hammond has observed, "The pace of caucus formation accelerated rapidly during the 1970s as members, operating with increased and more equitably distributed resources within a decentralized institution, sought to respond to increased external demands. . . . Members derive benefits—gaining information, being identified as a 'leader,' symbolically showing that they care about an issue of importance to constituents—from caucus activities."[18] In January 1995, at the beginning of the Republican-led 104th Congress, it was widely reported that the House of Representatives would "abolish" congressional caucuses. Yet as of January 1996 there were 129 congressional caucuses—111 from the 103rd Congress and 18 new ones established by the 104th. What the Republicans did do was to adopt a rule making the operation of caucuses more difficult. All aides working on caucus matters must be housed in members' offices. Therefore aides are often scattered among several offices, and coordination becomes more difficult. Some caucuses responded by spinning off informational functions to new outside groups. Clearly the death of the caucuses was greatly exaggerated.

The caucuses are alive, well, and changing. Hammond has identified six types, four of which are constituency-based (see Table 11.5). Intraparty caucuses are formed by groups whose members share a similar ideology; for example, the Democratic Study Group was established by liberal Democrats. Personal-interest caucuses form around a common interest in an issue—for example, the environment, the arts, or

---

*The chairmanship of Government Reform and Oversight would have gone from Dan Burton to Henry Waxman, of Judiciary from Henry Hyde to John Conyers, and of Ways and Means from Bill Archer to Charles Rangel.

The Congressional Black Caucus.

human rights. Constituency caucuses are established to represent certain groups (African Americans, women, Vietnam veterans), regions (New England, the western states), or both (in states or congressional districts with diffuse constituents, such as different ethnic populations or family and corporate farms).

One long-established national constituency caucus is the Congressional Black Caucus (CBC). Founded in 1970, its membership increased from nine members that year to forty in the 104th Congress. Most CBC members have been liberal House Democrats. J. C. Watts, a black Republican from Oklahoma, was elected in 1994 but refused to join the CBC. In the Democratic-controlled 103rd Congress, CBC members chaired three standing committees and eighteen subcommittees.

But in the Republican-controlled 104th Congress, CBC committee leaders became ranking minority members, and some caucus Democrats lost their seats on major House committees— Appropriations, Ways and Means, and Rules. Moreover, the CBC grew less unified as liberal Democratic members from northern districts were forced to share power with more centrist members representing southern rural and suburban districts.

By contrast, other caucuses (and not only Republican ones), have fared better in recent years.

For example, an intraparty caucus of "Blue Dog Democrats" known as the Coalition was born in February 1995. The Coalition's two dozen moderate-to-conservative members favor "middle-of-the-road" policies, especially on welfare and budget issues. For example, in 1995 the Coalition introduced its own welfare and budget bills, and although neither proposal was enacted, certain provisions of each strongly influenced final House deliberations. As Hammond has concluded, although the political fortunes of the CBC, the Coalition, and other caucuses may change from year to year, caucuses will continue and thrive as congressional institutions "because they help members to achieve personal goals of policy, representation, or power."[19]

The Organization of Congress: Committees

The most important organizational feature of Congress is the set of legislative committees of the House and Senate. It is there that the real work of Congress is done, and it is in the chairmanships of these committees and their subcommittees that most of the power in Congress is found. The number and jurisdiction of these committees are of the

Table 11.5	Congressional Caucuses
Type	**Typical Examples**
Intraparty	Class Clubs The Coalition Conservative Opportunity Society Democratic Study Group Tuesday Lunch Bunch Wednesday Groups
Personal interest	Arts Caucuses Constitutional Caucus Constitutional Forum Congressional Family Caucus Human Rights Caucuses Military Reform Caucus Population and Development Coalition Senate Children's Caucus
Constituency concerns, national	Congressional Black Caucus Congressional Caucus for Women's Issues Congressional Hispanic Caucus Vietnam Veterans Caucus
Constituency concerns, regional	Congressional Border Caucus Congressional Sunbelt Council Northeast-Midwest Congressional Coalition Tennessee Valley Authority Caucus Western Caucus Western States Senate Coalition

Constituency concerns, state/district	Congressional Caucus on
	  American Issues
	Export Caucus
	Irish Caucuses
	Rural Caucus
	Suburban Caucus
	Task Force on Industrial
	  Innovation and Productivity

Constituency concerns, industry	Automotive Caucus Boating Caucus Depot Caucus Steel Caucuses Textile Caucus Travel and Tourism Caucus

Source: Lawrence C. Dodd and Bruce I. Oppenheimer, eds., *Congress Reconsidered*, 6th ed. Washington, D.C.: Congressional Quarterly Press, 1997), table 12-1 by Susan Hammond.

greatest interest to members of Congress, since decisions on these subjects determine what group of members, with what political views, will pass on legislative proposals, oversee the workings of agencies in the executive branch, and conduct investigations.

There are three kinds of committees: **standing committees** (more or less permanent bodies with specified legislative responsibilities), **select committees** (groups appointed for a limited purpose and usually lasting for only a few congresses), and **joint committees** (those on which both representatives and senators serve). An especially important kind of joint committee is the **conference committee,** made up of representatives and senators appointed to resolve differences in the Senate and House versions of the same piece of legislation before final passage.

In the 104th Congress (1995–1996) the new Republican majority reduced the number of committees as part of its larger plan to reform House operations. Similar efforts were made in the Senate. When the dust settled on Capitol Hill, the total number of House and Senate committees had fallen from 252 in the previous Congress to 198, a smaller total even than the 242 committees of the 84th Congress (1955–1956). The House went from 22 to 19 standing committees and from 115 to 84 subcommittees of standing committees. The Senate maintained 17 committees but reduced the number of subcommittees of standing committees from 86 to 68.

Though members of the majority party could, in theory, occupy all of the seats on all of the committees, in practice they take the majority of seats on each committee, name the chairman, and allow the minority party to have the other seats. Usually the ratio of Democrats to Republicans on a committee roughly corresponds to their ratio in that house of Congress, but on occasion the majority party will try to take extra seats on some key panels, such as the House Appropriations or Ways and Means Committees. Then the minority party complains, as the Republicans did in 1981 and the Democrats did in 1999, usually with little effect. In 2001, with the Senate evenly divided between Democrats and Republicans, each committee had the same number of members from each party with Republicans serving as chairmen.

Standing committees are the important ones, because, with a few exceptions, they are the only ones that can propose legislation by reporting a bill out to the full House or Senate. Each member of the House usually serves on two standing committees, unless he or she is on an "exclusive" committee—Appropriations, Rules, or Ways and Means. In such a case the representative is limited to one. Each senator may serve on two "major" committees and one "minor" committee.

When party leaders were strong, as under Speakers Reed and Cannon, committee chairmen

★ **POLITICALLY SPEAKING** ★

Caucus

A *caucus* is a closed meeting of the members of a political party either to select a candidate for office or to agree on a legislative position.

The term is from an American Indian word meaning "elder" or "counsellor." It quickly entered political usage in the United States, there being a Caucus Club in Boston as early as 1763.

The first national political caucuses were in Congress, where legislators would gather to select their party's candidate for president. Persons who did not get a caucus endorsement soon began denouncing the entire procedure, referring contemptuously to the "decrees of King Caucus." Popular resentment led in the 1830s to the creation of the nominating convention as a way of choosing presidential candidates.

Today congressional caucuses are organizations of legislators from a single party (Democrats or Republicans), with a common background (for example, women, African Americans, Hispanics), sharing a particular ideology (liberals or conservatives), or having an interest in a single issue (such as mushrooms, steel mills, or the environment).

Source: From *Safire's Political Dictionary* by William Safire. Copyright © 1968, 1972, 1978 by William Safire. Reprinted by permission of Random House, Inc. and the author.

then through 1991 they used that procedure to remove six committee chairmen. When the Republicans took control of the House in 1995, they could have returned to the strict seniority rule, but they did not. House Speaker Gingrich passed over three senior representatives in favor of more junior ones as committee chairmen. The Republicans imposed six-year term limits on House chairmen, so in 2001, when they organized the House, many veteran chairmen were replaced with new leaders. For example, Henry Hyde was replaced as chairman of the Judiciary Committee by James Sensenbrenner.

Traditionally the committees of Congress were dominated by the chairmen. They often did their most important work behind closed doors (though their hearings and reports were almost always published in full). In the early 1970s Congress further decentralized and democratized its operations by a series of changes that some members regarded as a "bill of rights" for representatives and senators, especially those with relatively little seniority. These changes were by and large made by the Democratic Caucus, but since the Democrats were in the majority, the changes, in effect, became the rules of Congress. The more important ones were as follows.

■ House

- Committee chairmen to be elected by secret ballot in party caucus
- No member to chair more than one committee
- All committees with more than twenty members to have at least four subcommittees (at the time, Ways and Means had no subcommittees)
- Committee and personal staffs to be increased in size
- Committee meetings to be public unless members vote to close them

■ Senate

- Committee meetings to be public unless members vote to close them
- Committee chairmen to be selected by secret ballot at the request of one-fifth of the party caucus
- Committees to have larger staffs
- No senator to chair more than one committee

The effect of these changes, especially in the House, was to give greater power to individual members and to lessen the power of party leaders and committee chairmen. The decentralization of the House

were picked on the basis of loyalty to the leader. Now that this leadership has been weakened, seniority on the committee governs the selection of chairmen. Of late, however, even seniority has been under attack. In 1971 House Democrats decided in their caucus to elect committee chairmen by secret ballot. From

Standing Committees of the Senate

Major Committees
No senator is supposed to serve on more than two (but some do).

Agriculture, Nutrition, and Forestry
Appropriations
Armed Services
Banking, Housing, and Urban Affairs
Budget
Commerce, Science, and Transportation
Energy and Natural Resources
Environment and Public Works
Finance
Foreign Relations
Governmental Affairs
Health, Education, Labor, and Pensions
Judiciary

Minor Committees
No senator is supposed to serve on more than one (but some do).

Rules and Administration
Small Business
Veterans' Affairs

Select Committees
Aging
Ethics
Indian Affairs
Intelligence

---

meant that it was much harder for chairmen to block legislation they did not like or to discourage junior members from playing a large role. House members were quick to take advantage of these enlarged opportunities. In the 1980s they proposed three times as many amendments to bills as they had in the 1950s.[20]

There was a cost to be paid, however, for this empowerment of the membership. The 435 members of the House could not get much done if they all talked as much as they liked and introduced as many amendments as they wished. And with the big increase in the number of subcommittees, many subcommittee meetings were attended by (and thus controlled by) only one person, the chairman. To deal with this, the Democratic leaders began reclaiming some of their lost power. They made greater use of restrictive rules that sharply limited debate and the introduction of amendments. Committee chairmen began casting proxy votes. (A proxy is a written authorization to cast another person's vote.) In this way a chairman could control the results of committee deliberations by casting the proxies of absent members.

Republican House members were angered by all of this. They suspected that restrictive rules and proxy voting were designed to keep them from having any voice in House affairs. When they took control of the House in 1995, they announced some changes:

- They banned proxy voting.
- They limited committee and subcommittee chairmen's tenures to three terms (six years) and the Speaker's to four terms (eight years).
- They allowed more frequent floor debate under open rules.
- They reduced the number of committees and subcommittees.
- They authorized committee chairmen to hire subcommittee staffs.

The endless arguments about rules illustrate a fundamental problem that the House faces. Closed rules, proxy voting, powerful committee chairmen, and strong Speakers make it easier for business to get done; they put the House in a good bargaining position with the president and the Senate; and they make it easier to reduce the number of special-interest groups with legislative power. But this system also keeps individual members weak. The opposite arrangements—open rules, weak chairmen, many subcommittees, meetings open to the public—help individual members be heard and increase the amount of daylight shining on congressional processes. But if everyone is heard, no one is heard, because the noise is deafening and the speeches endless. And though open meetings and easy amending processes

---

Standing Committees of the House

Exclusive Committees
Members may not serve on any other committee except Budget.

Appropriations
Rules
Ways and Means

Major Committees
Members may serve on only one major committee.

Agriculture
Armed Services
Education and the Workforce
Energy and Commerce
Financial Services
International Relations
Judiciary
Transportation and Infrastructure

Nonmajor Committees
Members may serve on one major and one nonmajor committee, or on two nonmajor committees.

Budget
Government Reform
House Administration
Resources
Science
Small Business
Standards of Official Conduct
Veterans' Affairs

Note: In 1995 the House Republican majority abolished three committees—District of Columbia, Post Office and Civil Service, and Merchant Marine and Fisheries—and gave their duties to other standing committees.

---

may be intended to open up the system to "the people," the real beneficiaries are the lobbyists.

The House Republican rules of 1995 gave back some power to the chairmen (for example, by letting them pick all staff members) but further reduced it

Committee hearings are an important means of defining issues, as when the Senate Commerce Committee investigated the financial failure of Enron.

in other ways (for example, by imposing term limits and banning proxy voting). The commitment to public meetings remained.

In the Senate there have been fewer changes, in part because individual members of the Senate have always had more power than their counterparts in the House. Two important changes were made by the Republicans in 1995:

- A six-year term limit on all committee chairmen (no limit on the majority leader's term)
- A requirement that committee members select their chairmen by secret ballot

Despite these new rules, the committees remain the place where the real work of Congress is done. The different types of committees tend to attract different kinds of members. Some, such as the committees that draft tax legislation (the Senate Finance Committee and the House Ways and Means Committee) or that oversee foreign affairs (the Senate Foreign Relations Committee and the House International Relations Committee) are attractive to members who want to shape public policy, become experts on important issues, or have influence with their colleagues. Others, such as the House and Senate committees dealing with public lands, small business, and veterans' affairs, are attractive to members who want to serve particular constituents.[21]

The Organization of Congress: Staffs and Specialized Offices

In 1900 representatives had no personal staffs, and senators averaged fewer than one staff member each. As recently as 1935 the typical representative had but two aides. In 1998 the average representative had seventeen assistants and the average senator over forty. To the more than ten thousand individuals who served on the personal staffs of members of the 103rd Congress must be added three thousand more who worked for congressional committees and yet another three thousand employed by various congressional research agencies. Until the 1990s Congress had the most rapidly growing bureaucracy in Washington—the personal staffs of legislators increased more than fivefold from 1947 to 1991, then leveled off and declined slightly (see Figure 11.4). Though some staffers perform routine chores, many help draft legislation, handle constituents, and otherwise shape policy and politics.

Tasks of Staff Members

Staff members assigned to a senator or representative spend most of their time servicing requests from constituents—answering mail, handling problems, sending out newsletters, and meeting with voters. In short a major function of a member of Congress's staff is to help constituents solve problems and thereby help that member get reelected. Indeed, over the last two decades a larger and larger portion of congressional staffs—now about one-third—work in the local (district or state) office of the member of Congress rather than in Washington. Almost all members of Congress have such offices on a full-time basis; about half maintain two or more offices in their constituencies. Some scholars believe that this growth in constituency-serving staffs helps explain why it is so hard to defeat an incumbent representative or senator.

The legislative function of congressional staff members is also important. With each senator serving on an average of more than two committees and seven subcommittees and each representative serving on an

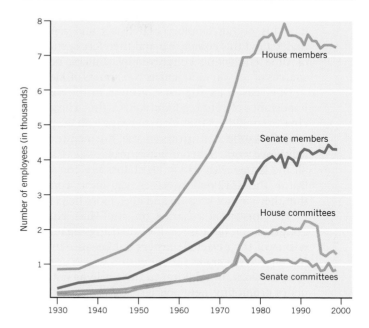

Figure 11.4   The Growth in Staffs of Members and Committees in Congress, 1930–2000

Source: From Harold Stanley and Richard Niemi, *Vital Statistics on American Politics 2001–2002* (Washington, D.C.: Congressional Quarterly Press, 2001). Reprinted with permission.

average of six committees and subcommittees, it is virtually impossible for members of Congress to become familiar in detail with all the proposals that come before them or to write all the bills that they feel ought to be introduced. As the workload of Congress has grown (over six thousand bills are introduced, about six hundred public laws are passed, and uncounted hearings and meetings are held during a typical Congress), the role of staff members in devising proposals, negotiating agreements, organizing hearings, writing questions for members of Congress to ask of witnesses, drafting reports, and meeting with lobbyists and administrators has grown correspondingly.

Those who work for individual members of Congress, as opposed to committees, see themselves entirely as advocates for their bosses. As the mass media have supplanted political parties as ways of communicating with voters, the advocacy role of staff members has led them to find and promote legislation for which a representative or senator can take credit.

This is the entrepreneurial function of the staff. While it is sometimes performed under the close supervision of the member of Congress, just as often a staff member takes the initiative, finds a policy, and then "sells" it to his or her employer. Lobbyists and reporters understand this completely and therefore spend a lot of time cultivating congressional staffers, both as sources of information and as consumers of ideas.

One reason for the rapid growth in the size and importance of congressional staffs is that a large staff creates conditions that seem to require an even larger staff. As the staff grows in size, it generates more legislative work. Subcommittees proliferate to handle all the issues with which legislators are concerned. But as the workload increases, legislators complain that they cannot keep up and need more help.

The increased reliance on staff has changed Congress, not because staffers do things against the wishes of their elected masters but because the staff has altered the environment within which Congress does its work. In addition to their role as entrepreneurs promoting new policies, staffers act as negotiators. As a result members of Congress are more likely to deal with one another through staff intermediaries than personally. Congress has thereby become less collegial, more individualistic, and less of a deliberative body.[22]

Staff Agencies

In addition to increasing the number of staff members, Congress has also created a set of staff agencies that work for Congress as a whole. These staff agencies have come into being in large part to give Congress specialized knowledge equivalent to what the president has by virtue of his position as chief of the executive branch.

■ **Congressional Research Service (CRS)** Formerly the Legislative Reference Service, the CRS is part of the Library of Congress. Since 1914 it has responded to congressional requests for information and now employs nearly nine hundred people, many with advanced academic training, to respond to more than a quarter of a million questions each year. As a politically neutral body, it does not recommend policy, but it will look up facts and indicate the arguments for and against a proposed policy. CRS also keeps track of the status of every major bill before Congress and produces a summary of each bill introduced. This information is instantly available to legislators via computer terminals located in almost all Senate and most House offices.

■ **General Accounting Office (GAO)** Created in 1921, this agency once performed primarily routine financial audits of the money spent by executive-branch departments. Today it also investigates agencies and policies and makes recommendations on almost every aspect of government—defense contracting, drug enforcement policies, the domestic security investigations of the FBI, Medicare and Medicaid programs, water pollution programs, and so forth. Though the head of the GAO—the comptroller general—is appointed by the president (with the consent of the Senate), he or she serves for a fifteen-year term and is very much the servant of Congress rather than of the president. The GAO employs about five thousand people, many of whom are permanently assigned to work with various congressional committees.

■ **Office of Technology Assessment (OTA)** Established in 1972 to study and evaluate policies and programs with a significant use of or impact on technology, the OTA had a staff of more than one hundred. Staff members looked into matters such as a plan to build a pipeline to transport coal slurry. The agency had little impact and was abolished in 1995.

■ **Congressional Budget Office (CBO)** Created in 1974, the CBO advises Congress on the likely economic effects of different spending programs and provides information on the costs of proposed policies. This latter task has been more useful to Congress than the more difficult job of estimating future economic trends. The CBO prepares analyses of the president's budget and economic projections that often come to conclusions different from those of the administration, thus giving members of Congress arguments to use in the budget debates.

How a Bill Becomes Law

Some bills zip through Congress; others make their way slowly and painfully. Congress, an English observer once remarked, is like a crowd, moving either sluggishly or with great speed.

Bills that have sped through on the fast track include ones to reduce drug abuse, reform Defense Department procurement procedures, end the mandatory retirement age, and help the disabled. Those that have plodded through on the slow track include ones dealing with health care, tax laws, energy conservation, and foreign trade, as well as several appropriations bills.

Why the difference? Studying the list above gives some clues. Bills to spend a lot of money move slowly, especially during times (such as the 1980s and early 1990s) when the government is running up big deficits. Bills to tax or regulate businesses move slowly because so many different interests have to be heard and accommodated. On the other hand, bills that seem to embody a clear, appealing idea ("stop drugs," "help old folks," "end scandal") gather momentum quickly, especially if the government doesn't have to spend a lot of its money (as opposed to requiring other people to spend their money) on the idea.

In the following account of how a bill becomes law, keep in mind the central fact that the complexity of these procedures ordinarily gives a powerful advantage to the opposition. There are many points at which action can be blocked. This does not mean that nothing gets done but that, to get something done, a member of Congress must *either* assemble a majority coalition slowly and painstakingly *or* take advantage of temporary enthusiasm for some new cause that sweeps away the normal obstacles.

Introducing a Bill

Any member of Congress may introduce a bill—in the House simply by handing it to a clerk or dropping it in a box (the "hopper"), in the Senate by being recognized by the presiding officer and announcing the bill's introduction. Bills are numbered and sent to the printer: a House bill bears the prefix *H.R.,* a Senate bill the prefix S. A bill can be either a **public bill** (pertaining to public affairs generally) or a **private bill** (pertaining to a particular individual, such as a person pressing a financial claim against the government or seeking special permission to become a naturalized citizen). Private bills were once very numerous; today many such matters have been delegated to administrative agencies or the courts. If a bill is not passed by both houses and signed by the president within the life of one Congress, it is dead and must be reintroduced during the next Congress. Pending legislation does not carry over from one Congress to the next. (A new Congress is organized every two years.)

We often hear that legislation is initiated by the president and enacted by Congress—the former proposes, the latter disposes. The reality is more complicated. Congress frequently initiates legislation; in fact most of the consumer and environmental protection legislation passed since 1966 began in Congress, not in the executive branch. And even laws formally proposed by the president often represent presidential versions of proposals that have incubated in Congress. This was the case, for example, with some civil rights laws and with the proposal that eventually became Medicare. Even when the president is the principal author of a bill, he usually submits it (if he is prudent) only after careful consultation with key congressional leaders. In any case the president cannot himself introduce legislation; he must get a member of Congress to do it for him.

One study showed that of ninety major laws passed between 1880 and 1945, seventy-seven were introduced without presidential sponsorship. In shaping the final contents, congressional influence dominated in thirty-five cases, presidential influence dominated in nineteen, and influence was mixed in the remaining thirty-six. Another study, covering the period 1940 to 1967, found that Congress was the major contributor to the contents of about half of all laws passed.[23]

In addition to bills, Congress can pass resolutions. A **simple resolution** (passed by either the House or the Senate) is used for matters such as establishing the rules under which each body will operate. A **concurrent resolution** settles housekeeping and procedural matters that affect both houses. Simple and concurrent resolutions are not signed by the president and do not have the force of law. A **joint resolution** requires the approval of both houses and the signature of the president; it is essentially the same as a law. A joint resolution is also used to propose a constitutional amendment; in this case it must be approved by a two-thirds vote of both houses, but it does not require the signature of the president.

Study by Committees

A bill is referred to a committee for consideration by either the Speaker of the House or the presiding officer of the Senate. Rules govern which committee will get which bill, but sometimes a choice is possible. In the House the right of the Speaker to make such choices is an important component of his powers. (His decisions can be appealed to the full House.) In

How a Bill Becomes Law

INTRODUCTION

Draft and Introduce You do not need to be a member of Congress to draft a bill; lobbyists, congressional staff, and others draft legislation all the time. But you do need to be a member of Congress to introduce legislation. The bill or resolution gets a number preceded by *H.R.* for House bills and *S.* for Senate bills.

Refer to Committee Numbered bills get referred to standing committees depending on their content and in accordance with detailed rules and procedures that differ somewhat between the House and the Senate. Once referred, the bill gets on the committee's calendar for review by a subcommittee or by the full committee.

COMMITTEE ACTION

Get Committee Action Not every bill on the calendar gets action. Many bills get referred to subcommittees for staff analysis and hearings held in public. But getting a hearing is not the same thing as getting action. Even after study, hearings, and other consideration of the bill, if the committee fails to act, the bill is dead.

Go to Mark Up If, however, the committee so chooses, the bill then goes to "mark up," a process that normally works by subcommittee members and staff editing or amending the bill, often extensively. But even after "the mark," the subcommittee may decide not to recommend the bill to the full committee, and the bill dies there.

Order the Bill Once the full committee gets the bill, it may or may not conduct more analysis and hold more hearings on the legislation, consider amendments thereto, and vote its recommendation to the House or Senate (a procedure called "ordering the bill" or "ordering the bill reported"). If the bill is ordered, it still has a chance; if not, it is dead.

Publish a Report The committee chairman orders a public report on the bill. Most such reports are prepared by committee staff and describe the nature and purpose of the bill; what various experts have said or testified concerning it; what, if any, position

the president has taken on it; what, if any, public comments the relevant cabinet agencies or other executive branch units have offered on it; and what dissenting members of the committee have to say about it.

FLOOR ACTION AND CONFERENCE ACTION

Get a Date The bill goes back to the chamber that originated it and is scheduled for floor debate and a vote. The House has many different scheduling procedures or "calendars," while the Senate has but one. Even having come this far, the bill might or might not get a date, or come up in an order that makes it likely to keep going.

Win Two Chambers The debate over the bill and any amendments having concluded, the members vote. If the bill is defeated, it is dead. If the bill is approved, it next goes to the other chamber, which begins the process again, starting with the bill being referred to committee. Anything can happen. The second chamber can accept the bill as is, change it, or never even consider it. The bill can go back to the first chamber with few or no changes, go to a "conference committee" to reconcile any significant differences between the two versions of the bill, or go nowhere. If the two chambers agree, a conference report on the final bill is prepared. Only if the two chambers approve exactly the same final bill with identical language does the bill get sent to the president for consideration.

PRESIDENT

Get President's Signature If the president signs the bill, it becomes law. If the president takes no action for ten days after receiving the bill, and Congress is still in session, the bill becomes law. If the president takes no action after the Congress has adjourned, the bill dies from his "pocket veto." Or, the president can veto the bill outright, in which case it goes back to Congress.

Override President's Veto If the president vetoes a bill, Congress can still turn it into law, but that requires a two-thirds vote of the members, and there must be enough members present to form a quorum.

HOW THINGS WORK

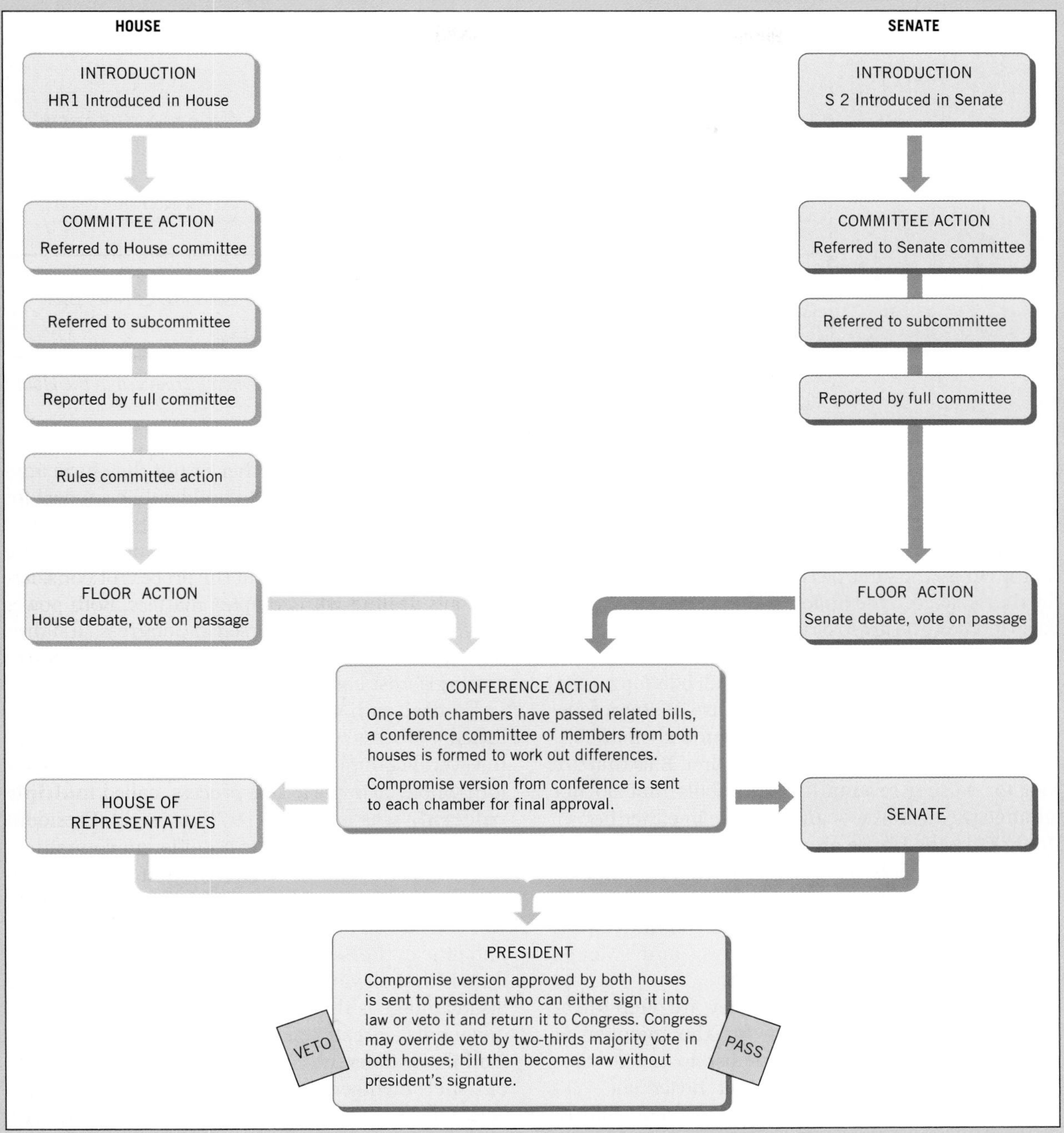

HOUSE

INTRODUCTION
HR1 Introduced in House

COMMITTEE ACTION
Referred to House committee

Referred to subcommittee

Reported by full committee

Rules committee action

FLOOR ACTION
House debate, vote on passage

SENATE

INTRODUCTION
S 2 Introduced in Senate

COMMITTEE ACTION
Referred to Senate committee

Referred to subcommittee

Reported by full committee

FLOOR ACTION
Senate debate, vote on passage

CONFERENCE ACTION

Once both chambers have passed related bills, a conference committee of members from both houses is formed to work out differences.

Compromise version from conference is sent to each chamber for final approval.

HOUSE OF REPRESENTATIVES

SENATE

PRESIDENT

Compromise version approved by both houses is sent to president who can either sign it into law or veto it and return it to Congress. Congress may override veto by two-thirds majority vote in both houses; bill then becomes law without president's signature.

VETO

PASS

H.R.1661

Children's Health Insurance Accountability Act of 1999 (Introduced in the House)

HR 1661 IH

106th CONGRESS

1st Session

H. R. 1661

To amend title XXVII of the Public Health Service Act and part 7 of subtitle B of title 1 of the Employee Retirement Income Security Act of 1974 to establish standards for the health quality improvement of children in managed care plans and other health plans.

IN THE HOUSE OF REPRESENTATIVES

May 4, 1999

Mrs. MORELLA (for herself, Mr. BALDACCI, Mr. SAWYER, and Mr. HILLIARD) introduced the following bill; which was referred to the Committee on Commerce, and in addition to the Committee on Education and the Workforce, for a period to be subsequently determined by the Speaker, in each case for consideration of such provisions as fall within the jurisdiction of the committee concerned

---

A BILL

To amend title XXVII of the Public Health Service Act and part 7 of subtitle B of title I of the Employee Retirement Income Security Act of 1974 to establish standards for the health quality improvement of children in managed care plans and other health plans.

Be it enacted by the Senate and House of Representatives of the United States of America in Congress assembled,

---

A bill (H.R. 1661) as it looks when introduced in the House.

1963 a civil rights bill was referred by the presiding officer of the Senate to the Commerce Committee in order to keep it out of the hands of the chairman of the Judiciary Committee, who was hostile to the bill. In the House the same piece of legislation was referred by the Speaker to the Judiciary Committee in order to keep it out of the grasp of the hostile chairman of the Interstate and Foreign Commerce Committee.

The Constitution requires that "all bills for raising revenue shall originate in the House of Representatives." The Senate can and does amend such bills, but only after the House has acted first. Bills that are not for raising revenue—that is, bills that do not change the tax laws—can originate in either house. In practice the House also originates appropriations bills—that is, bills directing how money shall be spent. Because of the House's special position in relation to revenue legislation, the committee that handles those bills—the Ways and Means Committee—is particularly powerful.

Most bills die in committee. They are often introduced only to get publicity for the member of Congress or to enable the member to say to constituents or pressure groups that he or she "did something" on a matter concerning them. Bills of general interest—many of which are drafted in the executive branch but introduced by a member of Congress—are assigned to a subcommittee for a hearing, where witnesses appear, evidence is taken, and questions are asked. These hearings are used to inform members of Congress, to permit interest groups to speak out (whether or not they have anything helpful to say), and to build public support for a measure favored by the majority of the committee.

Though committee hearings are necessary and valuable, they also fragment the process of considering bills dealing with complex matters. Both power and information are dispersed in Congress, and thus it is difficult to take a comprehensive view of matters cutting across committee boundaries.

To deal with this problem Congress has established a process whereby a bill may now be referred to several committees that simultaneously consider it in whole or in part. This process, called **multiple referral,** was used in 1977 to send President Carter's energy proposals to six different committees in both the House and Senate. An even bigger multiple referral was used for the 1988 trade bill, which was considered by fourteen committees in the House and nine in the Senate. The advantage of this procedure is that all views have a chance to be heard; the disadvantage is that it takes a lot of time and gives opponents a greater chance to kill or modify the bill. And if the different committees disagree about the bill, their members have to come together in a gargantuan joint meeting to iron out their differences. In these cases the advantages of the committee system—providing expert knowledge and careful deliberation—are often lost. Before the practice was abolished in 1995, about a quarter of all House bills and resolutions went through multiple referrals. Under the new rules, the Speaker is allowed to send a bill to

Congressional Calendars

House

Union Calendar   Bills to raise revenue or spend money
   Example: an appropriations bill
House Calendar   Nonmoney bills of major
   importance
   Example: a civil rights bill
Private Calendar   Private bills
   Example: a bill to waive the immigration laws so
   that a Philadelphia woman could be joined by
   her Italian husband

Consent Calendar   Noncontroversial bills
   Example: a resolution creating National
   Stenographers Week
Discharge Calendar   Discharge petitions

Senate

Executive Calendar   Presidential nominations,
   proposed treaties
Calendar of Business   All legislation

---

a second committee after the first is finished acting, or he may refer parts of a bill to separate committees. This process, called **sequential referral,** did not noticeably slow down the pace of legislative activity in the 104th Congress.

After the hearings the committee or subcommittee will "mark up" the bill—that is, make revisions and additions, some of which are extensive. These changes do not become part of the bill unless they are approved by the house of which the committee is a part. If a majority of the committee votes to report a bill out to the House or Senate, it goes forward. It is accompanied by a report that explains why the committee favors the bill and why it wishes to see its amendments, if any, adopted. Committee members who oppose the bill have an opportunity to include their dissenting opinions in the report.

If the committee does not report the bill out favorably, that ordinarily kills it. There is a procedure whereby the full House or Senate can get a bill that is stalled in committee out and onto the floor, but it is rarely used. In the House a **discharge petition** must be signed by 218 members; if the petition is approved by a vote of the House, the bill comes before it directly. In the Senate a member can move to discharge a committee of any bill, and if the motion passes, the bill comes before the Senate. During the last century there have been over eight hundred efforts in the House to use discharge petitions; only two dozen have succeeded. Discharge is rarely tried in the Senate, in part because Senate rules permit almost any proposal to get to the floor as an amendment to another bill.

For a bill to come before either house, it must first be placed on a calendar. There are five such calendars in the House and two in the Senate (see the box above).

Though the bill goes onto a calendar, it is not necessarily considered in chronological order or even considered at all. In the House the Rules Committee reviews most bills and adopts a rule that governs the procedures under which they will be considered by the House. A **closed rule** sets a strict time limit on debate and forbids the introduction of any amendments from the floor, or forbids amendments except those offered by the sponsoring committee. Obviously such a rule can make it very difficult for opponents to do anything but vote yes or no on the measure. An **open rule** permits amendments from the floor. A **restrictive rule** permits some amendments but not others.

In the early 1970s most bills were debated under open rules. In the 1980s the Rules Committee—which is controlled by the Speaker—increasingly introduced bills for consideration under closed or restrictive rules in an effort to reduce the number of amendments from the floor (and, the Republicans argued, to reduce Republican influence). By the end of the 1980s roughly half of all bills, and nearly three-fourths of all important ones, were debated under restrictive or closed rules. In 1992 only one-third of all bills were considered under an open rule.[24] In 1995 the Republicans allowed more debate under open rules.

The House has at least three ways of bypassing the Rules Committee: (1) a member can move that the rules be suspended, which requires a two-thirds

Riders and Christmas Trees

A **rider** is a provision added to a piece of legislation that is not germane to the bill's purpose. The goal is usually to achieve one of two outcomes: either to get the president (or governor) to sign an otherwise objectionable bill by attaching to it, as an amendment, a provision that the chief executive desperately wants to see enacted, or to get the president to veto a bill that he would otherwise sign by attaching to it, as an amendment, a provision that the chief executive strongly dislikes.

A rider is a convenient way for a legislator to get a pet project approved that might not be approved if it had to be voted on by itself. The term can be traced back to seventeenth-century England.

When a bill has lots of riders, it becomes a **Christmas tree bill.** In 1966, for example, the Foreign Investors Act, a bill designed to solve the balance-of-payments problem, had added to it riders giving assistance to hearse owners, the mineral ore business, importers of scotch whiskey, and presidential candidates.

Source: From *Safire's Political Dictionary* by William Safire. Copyright © 1968, 1972, 1978 by William Safire. Reprinted by permission of Random House, Inc. and the author.

In theory few such barriers to floor consideration exist in the Senate. There bills may be considered in any order at any time whenever a majority of the Senate chooses. The majority leader, in consultation with the minority leader, schedules bills for consideration. In practice, however, getting proposals to the Senate floor is far more complicated. Whereas the House normally plows through its legislative schedule, ignoring individual members' complaints in favor of getting its work done, the Senate majority leader must accommodate the interests of individual senators before proceeding with the Senate's business.

Floor Debate—The House

Once on the floor, the bills are debated. In the House all revenue and most other bills are discussed by the "Committee of the Whole," which is nothing more than whoever happens to be on the floor at the time. The **quorum,** or minimum number of members who must be present for business to be conducted, is only 100 members for the Committee of the Whole. Obviously this number is easier to assemble than a quorum for the House itself, which the Constitution specifies as a majority, or 218 members. The Speaker does not preside but chooses another person to wield the gavel. The Committee of the Whole debates, amends, and generally decides the final shape of the bill, but technically cannot pass it. To do that the Committee of the Whole reports the bill back to the House (that is, to itself), which takes final action. During the debate in the Committee of the Whole, the committee sponsoring the bill guides the discussion, divides the time equally between proponents and opponents, and decides how long each member will be permitted to speak. If amendments are allowed under the rule, they must be germane to the purpose of the bill—extraneous matters (riders) are not allowed—and no one may speak for more than five minutes on an amendment. During this process people wishing to take time out to huddle about strategy or to delay action can demand a **quorum call—**

vote; (2) a discharge petition, as explained above, can be filed; or (3) the House can use the "Calendar Wednesday" procedure.* These methods are not used very often, but they are available if the Rules Committee departs too far from the sentiments of the House.

---

*On Wednesdays the list of committees of the House is called more or less in alphabetical order, and any committee can bring up for action a bill of its own already on a calendar. Action on a bill brought to the floor on Calendar Wednesday must be completed that day, or the bill goes back to committee. Since major bills rarely can be voted on in one day, this procedure is not often used.

a calling of the roll to find out whether the necessary minimum number of members are present. If a quorum is not present, the House must either adjourn or dispatch the sergeant at arms to round up missing members. The sponsoring committee almost always wins; its bill, as amended by it, usually is the version that the House passes.

Floor Debate—The Senate

Things are a good deal more casual in the Senate. Short of cloture (discussed below), there is no rule limiting debate, and members can speak for as long as they can stay on their feet. A senator's remarks need not be relevant to the matter under consideration (some senators have read aloud from the Washington telephone directory), and anyone can offer an amendment at any time. There is no Committee of the Whole. Amendments need not be germane to the purpose of the bill, and thus the Senate often attaches riders to bills.

In fact the opportunity to offer nongermane amendments gives a senator a chance to get a bill onto the floor without regard to the calendar or the schedule of the majority leader: he or she need only offer a pet bill as an "amendment" to a bill already under discussion. (This cannot be done to an appropriations bill.) Indeed, the entire committee hearing process can be bypassed in the Senate if the House has already passed the bill. In that case a senator can get the House-passed measure put directly onto the Senate calendar without committee action. In 1957 and again in 1964 this was done with House-passed civil rights bills to make certain that they would not be bottled up in the conservative Senate Judiciary Committee.

A Senate filibuster is difficult to break. The current **cloture rule** requires that sixteen senators sign a petition to move cloture. The motion is voted on two days after the petition is introduced; to pass, three-fifths of the entire Senate membership (sixty senators if there are no vacancies) must vote for it. If it passes, each senator is thereafter limited to one hour of debate on the bill under consideration. The total debate, including roll calls and the introduction of amendments, cannot exceed one hundred hours.

In recent years both filibusters and cloture votes have become more common. The filibuster occurs more frequently because it is now easier to stage one. Often it consists not of a senator's making a long speech but of endless requests for the clerk to call the roll. More filibusters means more cloture votes, which are now easier to win since the 1975 change lowering the required number of supporters from two-thirds to three-fifths of all senators. During the 100th Congress (1987–1988) there were almost as many cloture votes—forty-three—as there had been in the half century after the procedure was invented. Since 1975 about 40 percent of all cloture votes have succeeded in cutting off debate.

Conservatives have used the filibuster to try to block civil rights laws; liberals have used it to try to block decontrol of gas prices. Since both factions have found the filibuster useful, it seems most unlikely that it will ever be abolished, though it has been somewhat curtailed. One way to keep the Senate going during a filibuster is through **double-tracking,** whereby the disputed bill is shelved temporarily so that the Senate can get on with other business. Because double-tracking permits the Senate to discuss and vote on matters other than the bill that is being filibustered, it is less costly to individual senators to stage a filibuster. In the past, before double-tracking, a senator and his allies had to keep talking around the clock to keep their filibuster alive. If they stopped talking, the Senate was free to take up other business. Opponents of the filibuster would bring cots and blankets to the Senate so that they could sleep and eat there, ready to take the floor the moment the filibuster faltered. But with double-tracking other business can go on while the stalled bill is temporarily set aside. As a result the number of filibusters has skyrocketed. In the words of two expert Senate watchers, the "Senate has become increasingly unmanageable as filibusters have become virtually commonplace on both major and minor pieces of legislation, raising the standard for passage of even routine bills from fifty to sixty votes and resulting in frequent delays in scheduling, stop-and-go patterns of floor debate," and the use of other procedures "that make the institution hostage to the whims of individual senators."[25]

What the threat of a filibuster means in practice is this: neither political party can control the Senate unless it has at least sixty votes. Neither party has had that many Senate seats since 1979, and so for the Senate to act there must be a bipartisan majority.

Methods of Voting

Some observers of Congress make the mistake of deciding who was for and who was against a bill by the final vote. This can be misleading—often a member of Congress will vote for final passage of a bill after

House-Senate Differences: A Summary

House	Senate
435 members serve two-year terms.	100 members serve rotating six-year terms.
House members have only one major committee assignment, thus tend to be policy specialists.	Senators have two or more major committee assignments, thus tend to be policy generalists.
Speaker's referral of bills to committee is hard to challenge.	Referral decisions are easy to challenge.
Committees almost always consider legislation first.	Committee consideration is easily bypassed.
Scheduling and rules are controlled by the majority party.	Scheduling and rules are generally agreed to by majority and minority leaders.
Rules Committee is powerful; controls time of debate, admissibility of amendments.	Rules Committee is weak; few limits on debate or amendments.
Debate is usually limited to one hour.	Debate is unlimited unless shortened by unanimous consent or by invoking cloture.
Nongermane amendments may not be introduced from the floor.	Nongermane amendments may be introduced.

having supported amendments that, if they had passed, would have made the bill totally different. To keep track of various members' voting records, therefore, it is often more important to know how they voted on key amendments than to know how they voted on the bill itself.

Finding that out is not always easy, though it has become more so in recent years. There are four procedures for voting in the House. A **voice vote** consists of the members' shouting "yea" or "nay"; a **division** (or standing) **vote** involves the members' standing and being counted. In neither a voice nor a standing vote are the names of members recorded as having voted one way or the other.

To learn how an individual votes there must be either a recorded teller vote or a roll call. In a **teller vote** the members pass between two tellers, the yeas first and then the nays. Since 1971 a teller vote can be "recorded," which means that, at the request of twenty members, clerks write down the names of those favoring or opposing a bill as they pass the tellers. Since teller votes but not roll calls may be taken in the Committee of the Whole, the use of a recorded teller vote enables observers to find out how members voted in those important deliberations.

A **roll-call vote,** of course, consists of people answering "yea" or "nay" to their names. It can be done at the request of one-fifth of the representatives present in the House. When roll calls were handled orally, it was a time-consuming process, since the clerk had to drone though 435 names. Since 1973 an electronic voting system has been in operation that permits each member, by inserting a plastic card into a slot, to record his or her own vote and to learn the total automatically. Owing to the use of recorded teller votes and the advent of electronic roll-call votes, the number of recorded votes has gone up sharply in the House. There were only seventy-three House roll calls in 1955; twenty years later there were over eight times that many. Voting in the Senate is much the same, only simpler: there is no such thing as a teller vote, and no electronic counters are used.

If a bill passes the House and Senate in different forms, the differences must be reconciled if the bill is to become law. If they are minor, the last house to act may simply refer the bill back to the other house, which then accepts the alterations. If the differences are major, it is often necessary to appoint a conference committee to iron them out. Only a minority of bills require a conference. Each house must vote to form such a committee. The members are picked by the chairmen of the House and Senate standing committees that have been handling the legislation, with representation given to

Should We Have a Bigger Congress?

November 15
WASHINGTON

A powerful citizens organization has demanded that the House of Representatives be made larger so that voters can feel closer to their members. Each representative now speaks for about 600,000 people—far too many, the group argues, to make it possible for all points of view to be heard. In its petition . . .

MEMORANDUM

To: Representative Peter Skerry
From: Martha Bayles, legislative aide
Subject: The Size of the House of Representatives

The House can decide how big it wishes to be. When it was created, there was one representative for every 30,000 people. Now there is one for every 600,000. In most other democracies each member of parliament represents far fewer than 600,000 people. Doubling the size of the House may be a way of avoiding term limits.

Arguments for:

1. Doubling the size of the House would reduce the huge demand for constituent services each member now faces.
2. A bigger House would represent more shades of opinion more fairly.
3. Each member could raise less campaign money because his or her campaign would be smaller.

Arguments against:

1. A bigger House would be twice as hard to manage, and it would take even longer to pass legislation.
2. Campaigns in districts of 300,000 people would cost as much as ones in districts with 600,000 people.
3. Interest groups do a better job of representing public opinion than would a House with more members.

Your decision:
Increase size of House _____
Do not increase size of House _____

the minority as well as the majority party. There are usually between three and fifteen members from each house. No decision can be made unless approved by a majority of both delegations.

Bargaining is long and hard; in the past it was also secret. Now some conference sessions are open to the public. Often—as with President Carter's energy bill—the legislation is substantially rewritten in conference. Complex bills can lead to enormous conference committees. The 1988 trade bill went before a conference committee of two hundred members. Theoretically the conferees are not supposed to change anything already agreed to by both the House and Senate, but in the inevitable give-and-take even matters already approved may be changed.

In most cases the conference reports tend to favor, slightly, the Senate version of the bill. Several studies have suggested that the Senate wins in 57 to 65 percent of cases.[26] Whoever wins (and both sides always claim that they got everything out of the bargaining that they possibly could have), conferees report their agreement back to their respective houses, which usually consider the report immediately. The report can be accepted or rejected; it cannot be amended. In the great majority of cases it is accepted: the alternative is to have no bill at all, at least for that Congress. The bill, now in final form, goes to the president for signature or veto. If a veto is cast, the bill returns to the house of origin. There an effort can be made to override the veto. This requires that two-thirds of those present (provided that there is a quorum) must vote to override; this vote must be a roll call. If both houses override in this manner, the bill becomes law without the president's approval.

Reducing Power and Perks

While most citizens are only vaguely familiar with the rules and procedures under which Congress operates, they do care whether Congress as an institution serves the public interest and fulfills its mission as a democratic body. Over the last several decades, many proposals have been made to reform and improve Congress—term limitations, new ethics and campaign finance laws, and organizational changes intended to reduce the power and perks of members while making it easier for Congress to pass needed legislation in a timely fashion. Some of these proposals—for example, campaign finance reforms (see Chapter 8)—have recently become law.

Many would-be reformers share the view that Congress is overstaffed and self-indulgent. It is, they complain, quick to impose new laws on states, cities, businesses, and average citizens but slow to apply those same laws to itself and its members. It is quick to pass **pork-barrel legislation**—bills that give tangible benefits (highways, dams, post offices) to constituents in the hope of winning their votes in return—but slow to tackle complex and controversial questions of national policy. The reformers' image of Congress is unflattering, but is it wholly unwarranted?

No perk is more treasured by members of Congress than the frank. Members of Congress are allowed by law to send material through the mail free of charge by substituting their facsimile signature *(frank)* for postage. But rather than using this **franking privilege** to keep their constituents informed about the government, most members use franked newsletters and questionnaires as campaign literature. That is why use of the frank soars in the months before an election. For example, more than 30 million newsletters were sent out in March 1992, the last month in which members facing June primaries could send franked mailings.[27]

Thus the frank amounts to a taxpayer subsidy of members' campaigns, a perk that bolsters the electoral fortunes of incumbents. Some reformers do not believe that it is possible to fence in congressional use of the frank for public education or other legitimate purposes, and so they propose abolishing it outright. Other reformers argue that the frank can be fenced in by prohibiting mailings just before primaries and general elections (to dilute any electoral impact) and by placing a prominent notice, "Paid For at Taxpayer Expense," on the front of every franked piece of mail.[28] Such measures could well discourage members from abusing their franking privilege.

For years Congress routinely exempted itself from many of the laws it passed. In defense of this practice members said that if members of Congress were subject to, for example, the minimum wage laws, the executive branch, charged with enforcing these laws, would acquire excessive power over Congress. This would violate the separation of powers. But as public criticism of Congress grew and confidence in government declined, more and more people demanded that Congress subject itself to the laws that applied to everybody else. In 1995 the 104th Congress did this by passing a bill that obliges Congress to obey eleven important laws governing things such as civil rights, occupational safety, fair labor standards, and family leave.

The bipartisan Congressional Accountability Act of 1995 had to solve a key problem: under the constitutional doctrine of separated powers, it would have been unwise and perhaps unconstitutional for the executive branch to enforce congressional compliance with executive-branch regulations. So Congress created the independent Office of Compliance and an employee grievance procedure to deal with implementation. Now Congress, too, must obey laws such as the Civil Rights Act, the Equal Pay Act, the Age Discrimination Act, and the Family and Medical Care Leave Act.

As already mentioned, bills containing money for local dams, bridges, roads, and monuments are referred to disparagingly as pork-barrel legislation. Reformers complain that when members act to "bring home the bacon," Congress misallocates tax dollars by supporting projects with trivial social benefits in order to bolster their reelection prospects.

No one can doubt the value of trimming unnecessary spending, but pork is not necessarily the villain it is made out to be. For example, the main cause of the budget deficit was the increase in spending on entitlement programs (like health care and interest on the national debt) without a corresponding increase in taxes. Spending on pork is a small fraction of spending on entitlements, and most categories of pork spending have decreased in the last ten or fifteen years. Furthermore, one person's pork is another person's necessity. No doubt some congressional districts get an unnecessary bridge or highway, but others get bridges and highways that are long overdue. The notion that every bridge or road a member of Congress gets for his or her district is wasteful pork is tantamount to saying that no member attaches any importance to merit.

Even if all pork were bad, it would still be necessary. Congress is an independent branch of government,

★ POLITICALLY SPEAKING ★

Pork Barrel

Before the Civil War it was the custom to take salt pork from barrels and distribute it to the slaves. Often the eagerness of the slaves to get the food would result in a rush on the barrels, with each slave trying to get as much as possible.

By the 1870s members of Congress were using the term *pork* to refer to benefits for their districts and *pork barrel* to mean the piece of legislation containing those benefits.

Today the classic example of pork-barrel legislation is the rivers and harbors bill, which provides appropriations for countless dams, bridges, and canals to be built in congressional districts all over the country.

Source: From *Safire's Political Dictionary* by William Safire. Copyright © 1968, 1972, 1978 by William Safire. Reprinted by permission of Random House, Inc. and the author.

and each member is, by constitutional design, the advocate of his or her district or state. No member's vote can be won by coercion, and few can be had by mere appeals to party loyalty or presidential needs. Pork is a way of obtaining consent. The only alternative is bribery, but bribery, besides being wrong, would benefit only the member, whereas pork usually benefits voters in the member's district. If you want to eliminate pork, you must eliminate Congress, by converting it into a parliament under the control of a powerful party leader or prime minister. In a tightly controlled parliament no votes need be bought; they can be commanded. But members of such a parliament can do little to help their constituents cope with government or

Rules on Congressional Ethics

Senate

Gifts: No gifts (in money, meals, or things) totaling $100 or more from anyone except a spouse or personal friend.

Lobbyists may not pay for gifts, official travel, legal defense funds, or charitable contributions to groups controlled by senators.

Fees: No fees for lectures or writing ("honoraria"), except that fees of up to $2,000 may go to a senator-designated charity.

Outside earned income may not exceed 15 percent of a senator's salary.

Ex-senators may not try to influence members of Congress for one year after leaving the Senate.

Mass mailings: No senator may receive more than $50,000 from the Senate to send out a mailing to constituents.

House

Gifts: No gifts (in money, meals, or things) totaling $100 or more from anyone except a spouse or personal friend.

Lobbyists may not offer gifts or pay for travel, even if lobbyist is a spouse or personal friend.

Travel: House members may travel at the expense of others if travel is for officially connected meetings.

Fees: No honoraria for House members.

Ex–House members may not lobby Congress for one year after leaving office.

to defend them against bureaucratic abuses, nor can they investigate the conduct of the executive branch. The price of a citizen-oriented Congress is a pork-oriented Congress.

Ethics and Congress

Most contemporary proposals to reform Congress are motivated at least in part by a belief that "congressional ethics" has become an oxymoron.* The Framers of the Constitution hoped that members of Congress would be virtuous citizens, but they feared that some would not. They had, as stated earlier, a rather sober view of human nature and designed the system of checks and balances in part to minimize the chance that anybody, by gaining undue influence over one part of the government, would be able to tyrannize over the other parts.

It could be argued that this very separation of power made corruption more, rather than less, likely. If power were concentrated in one set of hands—say, those of a prime minister—nobody would have any incentive to bribe or even influence any other political figure; there is little that subordinate officials could do for that person. And though a favor seeker

might try to influence the prime minister, few could pay the price of bribing someone with so much power. When bits and pieces of power are placed in many different hands, as in the United States, there are many opportunities to exercise influence: lots of officials have something that they could sell, and at a price that many favor seekers could afford.

For example, the appointive power is shared by the president and the Senate. Since the Senate will not confirm anybody for appointment to federal office who is personally obnoxious to either senator from the candidate's state (the rule of "senatorial courtesy"), the opportunity exists for an office seeker to try to influence a senator to get the desired appointment. The stage is also set for a senator, who may want the president to nominate a certain person, to delay some piece of presidential legislation until the nomination is made, or for the president to try to get a piece of legislation passed by offering to appoint the senator's campaign manager, brother-in-law, or law partner to a lucrative federal post.

---

*An oxymoron is a phrase that combines contradictory terms ("deafening silence").

How Congress Raises Its Pay

For over two hundred years Congress has tried to find a politically painless way to raise its own pay. It has managed to vote itself a pay increase twenty-three times in those two centuries, but usually at the price of a hostile public reaction. Twice during the nineteenth century a pay raise led to a massacre of incumbents in the next election.

Knowing this, Congress has invented various ways to get a raise without actually appearing to vote for it. These have included the following:

- Voting for a tax deduction for expenses incurred as a result of living in Washington
- Creating a citizens commission that could recommend a pay increase that would take effect automatically provided Congress did not vote *against* it
- Linking increases in pay to decreases in honoraria (that is, speaking fees)

In 1989 a commission recommended a congressional pay raise of over 50 percent (from $89,500 to $135,000) and a ban on honoraria. The House planned to let it take effect automatically. But the public wouldn't have it, demanding that Congress vote on the raise—and vote it down. It did.

Embarrassed by its maneuvering, Congress retreated. At the end of 1989 it voted itself (as well as most top executive and judicial branch members) a small pay increase (7.9 percent for representatives, 9.9 percent for senators) that also provided for automatic cost-of-living adjustments (up to 5 percent a year) in the future. But the automatic adjustments in congressional pay have been rejected every year in recorded roll-call votes. Apparently nobody in Congress wants to be accused of "getting rich" at the taxpayers' expense.

Some of these attempts at influence may involve money; some may not. The point is that divided power means divided responsibility, and divided responsibility creates the possibility for evaded responsibility. It also creates the need to use influence to assemble enough power to get anything done. What the Constitution has separated, individuals must pull together; sometimes the pulling together involves mere persuasion, sometimes an exchange of favors, occasionally the payment of money.

Though the moral climate of American politics has improved in the last century, scandals continue. From 1941 to 1989 nearly fifty members of Congress faced criminal charges; most were convicted. From 1978 to 1992 Congress considered charges involving sixty-three members; thirty-one were sanctioned or convicted, and sixteen resigned or announced their intention to retire.[29] Charges of congressional misconduct included misuse of funds, having sex with minors, failing to disclose income, and accepting illegal gifts. In 2002, Rep. James Traficant of Ohio was forced to resign after he was convicted in court.

Ethics codes and related reforms enacted in 1978, 1989, and 1995 have placed members of Congress under tight rules governing financial disclosure, accepting gifts, and other practices that were already regulated, while also prohibiting numerous practices (such as the use of office accounts for campaign purposes) that had been unregulated.

Each successive wave of ethics laws has been predicated on the assumption that improper influence is associated with financial transactions, yet obviously that is not always the case. Many members of Congress who in the past earned substantial incomes from speaking and writing did not have their votes corrupted by such activities; other members of Congress who rarely take such fees may be heavily influenced, perhaps unduly so, by personal friendships and political alliances that have no direct monetary value at all. And no ethics code can address the bargaining among members of Congress, or between members of Congress and the president, involving the exchange of favors and votes.

We would do well to remember that the Framers' object was not to create a simon-pure Congress but to create one that was powerful, one that would be composed of representatives who (at least in the lower house) could be closely checked by the voters, and one that would offer manifold opportunities for competing interests and opinions to check one another. Their goal was liberty more than morality, though they knew that in the long run the latter was essential to the former.

Nonpartisan Panel Proposes Letting Party Chiefs Pick Committee Chairs

February 14
WASHINGTON

Traditionally, there has been only one way to become a congressional committee chair: outlast everyone else. The so-called seniority system let the person with the longest tenure on a committee chair it. This eliminated fights over selection, and made it easier for legislators with unpopular views and for African Americans with tenure to become chairs. But, critics claim, it also sometimes landed incompetent people atop important committees, and made it harder for party leaders to move major legislation. Yesterday, a nonpartisan group of experts called for giving the seniority system "a decent but deep burial" and letting party leaders appoint committee chairs . . .

MEMORANDUM

To: Representative Sally Brook
From: Joe Tell, chief of staff
Subject: Proposal for Appointment by Party Leaders

You are on record as opposing the seniority system, but you have hitherto expressed no views in public about other methods by which committee chairs can be selected. One is election by party caucus. Letting party members elect committee chairs has some advantages: autocratic chairs can be ousted and committee chairs are likely to reflect the views of most party members. But it also has several disadvantages: it invites bruising fights for chairships that can divide party members and produce committee chairs who are not loyal to party leaders. Another method, now being debated around town and about which you might be asked at tomorrow's press briefing, is appointment by party leaders.

Arguments for:

1. Having the speaker, majority leader, or minority leader choose chairs would increase party discipline and accountability.
2. Appointment by party leaders would make it easier for party programs to be enacted.

Arguments against:

1. Concentrating so much power in the hands of party leaders could corrupt even the best or most public-spirited of them.
2. Chairships could be denied to qualified and worthy members just because they are out of favor with party leaders.

Your decision:
Favor proposal _____
Oppose proposal _____

Summary

Over the last half century or so Congress, especially the House, has evolved through three stages.

During the first stage, lasting from the end of World War I until the early 1960s, the House was dominated by powerful committee chairmen who controlled the agenda, decided which members would get what services for their constituents, and tended to follow the leadership of the Speaker. Newer members were expected to be seen but not heard; power and prominence came only after a long apprenticeship. Congressional staffs were small, and so members dealt with each other face to face.

The second stage emerged in the early 1970s, in part as the result of trends already under way (for example, the steady growth in the number of staffers assigned to each member) and in part as a result of changes in procedures and organization brought about by younger, especially northern, members. Dissatisfied with southern resistance to civil rights bills and emboldened by a sharp increase in the number of liberals who had been elected in the Johnson landslide of 1964, the House Democratic caucus adopted rules that allowed the caucus to select committee chairmen without regard to seniority, dramatically increased the number and staffs of subcommittees (for the first time, the Ways and Means Committee was required to have subcommittees), authorized individual committee members (instead of the chairman) to choose the chairmen of these subcommittees, ended the ability of chairmen to refuse to call meetings, and made it much harder for those meetings to be closed to the public. The installation of electronic voting made it easier to require recorded votes, and so the number of times each member had to go on record rose sharply. The Rules Committee was instructed to issue more rules that would allow floor amendments.

At the same time, the number of southern Democrats in leadership positions began to decline, and the conservatism of the remaining ones began to lessen. (In 1990 southerners held only a quarter of committee chairmanships in the House and none of the major party leadership posts.) Moreover, northern and southern Democrats began to vote together a bit more frequently (though the conservative Boll Weevils remained a significant—and often swing—group).

These changes created a House ideally suited to serve the reelection needs of its members. Each representative could be an individual political entrepreneur, seeking publicity, claiming credit, introducing bills, holding subcommittee hearings, and assigning staffers to work on constituents' problems. There was no need to defer to powerful party leaders or committee chairmen. But because representatives in each party were becoming more alike ideologically, there was a rise in party voting. Congress became a career attractive to men and women skilled in these techniques, and these people entered Congress in large numbers. Their skill was manifest in the growth of the sophomore surge—the increase in their winning percentage during their first reelection campaign.

Even junior members could now make their mark on legislation. In the House more floor amendments were offered and passed; in the Senate filibusters became more commonplace. Owing to multiple referrals and overlapping subcommittee jurisdictions, more members could participate in writing bills and overseeing government agencies.

But lurking within the changes that defined the second stage were others, less noticed at the time, that created the beginnings of a new phase. The third stage was an effort in the House to strengthen and centralize party leadership. The Speaker acquired the power to appoint a majority of the members of the Rules Committee. That body, worried by the flood of floor amendments, began issuing more restrictive rules. By the mid-1980s this had reached the point where Republicans were complaining that they were being gagged. The Speaker also got control of the Democratic Steering and Policy Committee (it assigns new members to committees) and was given the power to refer bills to several committees simultaneously.

The evolution of the House remains an incomplete story; it is not yet clear whether it will remain in stage two or find some way of moving decisively into stage three. For now it has elements of both.

Meanwhile the Senate remains as individualistic and decentralized as ever—a place where it has always been difficult to exercise strong leadership.

Though its members may complain that Congress is collectively weak, to any visitor from abroad it seems extraordinarily powerful, probably the most powerful legislative body in the world. Congress has always been jealous of its constitutional independence and authority. Three compelling events led to Congress's reasserting its authority: the increasingly unpopular war in Vietnam; the Watergate scandals, which revealed a White House meddling illegally in the electoral process; and the advent of divided governments—with one party in control of the presidency and the other in control of Congress.

Claims that Congress became weak as the president grew stronger are a bit overdrawn. As we shall see in the next chapter, the view from the White House is quite different. Recent presidents have complained bitterly of their inability to get Congress even to act on, much less approve, many of their key proposals and have resented what they regard as congressional interference in the management of executive-branch agencies and the conduct of foreign affairs.

Reconsidering the Enduring Questions

1. *Are the members of Congress representative of the American people?*

   Demographically, no: most Americans are not middle-aged white males with law degrees or past political careers. Some groups (for example, women) are much less prevalent in Congress than they are in the nation as a whole, while other groups (for example, Catholics) constitute about the same fraction of Congress as they do of the American people. Ideologically, Republican members of Congress are more conservative than average Americans, and Democratic members of Congress are more liberal than average Americans. On most issues most of the time, Congress is in step with the public. But on some issues, most representatives' opinions are generally out of sync with mass public preferences. For example, most Americans have long favored protectionist trade policies, but most members of Congress have consistently voted for free trade policies. Likewise, most citizens are less solicitous of laws that reinforce civil liberties than the Congress has traditionally been. This, however, is much as the Framers of the Constitution had hoped and expected. They believed that representatives should refine, not reflect, public wishes, and mediate, not mirror, public views.

2. *Should Congress run under strong leadership, or should it allow its members a lot of freedom?*

   Congress has tried it both ways. Sometimes the House has had a strong Speaker, sometimes a weak one; sometimes committee chairmen were selected by seniority, sometimes by the Speaker, and sometimes by party vote. If we want a Congress that can act quickly and decisively as a body, then we should desire strong leadership, place restrictions on debate, provide few opportunities for stalling tactics, and brook only minimal committee interference. But if we want a Congress in which the interests of individual members and the people they represent are routinely protected or enhanced, then we must reject strong leadership, proliferate rules allowing for delay and discussion, and permit many opportunities for committee activity. Unfortunately, the public often wants both systems to operate, the first for some issues and the second for others.

3. *Why does it take so long for Congress to act?*

   The Framers of the Constitution knew that Congress would normally proceed slowly and err in favor of deliberative, not decisive, action. Congress was intended to check and balance strong leaders in the executive branch, not automatically cede its authority to them, not even during a war or other national crisis. Today, the increased ideological and partisan polarization among members has arguably made Congress even less capable than it traditionally has been of planning ahead or swiftly adopting coherent changes in national policies. There is, however, only conflicting evidence concerning whether so-called policy gridlock has become more common than in decades past. Within months following the September 11, 2001, terrorist attacks on the United States, Congress passed a host of new laws intended to enhance America's homeland security. But Congress took its time with several major proposals to reorganize the government around homeland security priorities. Some cite this as but the latest, and potentially the gravest, example of what's wrong with Congress. But others cite it as a salutary reminder that a Congress that could move swiftly to enact wise homeland security or other policies could also move swiftly to adopt unwise ones.

World Wide Web Resources

- House of Representatives: www.house.gov
- Senate: www.senate.gov
- Library of Congress
  thomas.loc.gov
  lcweb.loc.gov/global/legislative/congress

- For news about Congress
  Roll Call magazine: www.rollcall.com
  C-SPAN: www.c-span.org

Key Terms

bicameral legislature *p. 285*
filibuster *p. 288*
marginal districts *p. 291*
safe districts *p. 291*
conservative coalition *p. 294*
majority leader *p. 298*
minority leader *p. 298*
whip *p. 298*
party polarization *p. 301*
caucus (congressional) *p. 303*
standing committees *p. 305*
select committees *p. 305*
joint committees *p. 305*

conference committee *p. 305*
public bill *p. 311*
private bill *p. 311*
simple resolution *p. 311*
concurrent resolution *p. 311*
joint resolution *p. 311*
multiple referral *p. 314*
sequential referral *p. 315*
discharge petition *p. 315*
closed rule *p. 315*
open rule *p. 315*
restrictive rule *p. 315*
rider *p. 316*

Christmas tree bill *p. 316*
quorum *p. 316*
quorum call *p. 316*
cloture rule *p. 317*
double-tracking *p. 317*
voice vote *p. 318*
division vote *p. 318*
teller vote *p. 318*
roll-call vote *p. 318*
pork-barrel legislation *p. 320*
franking privilege *p. 320*

Suggested Readings

Davidson, Roger H., and Walter J. Oleszek. *Congress and Its Members.* 7th ed. Washington, D.C.: Congressional Quarterly Press, 2000. Complete and authoritative account of who is in Congress and how it operates.

Dodd, Lawrence C., and Bruce I. Oppenheimer, eds. *Congress Reconsidered.* 6th ed. Washington, D.C.: Congressional Quarterly Press, 1997. Recent studies of congressional politics.

Fenno, Richard F., Jr. *Congressmen in Committees.* Boston: Little, Brown, 1973. Study of the styles of twelve standing committees.

Fiorina, Morris P. *Congress: Keystone of the Washington Establishment.* 2d ed. New Haven, Conn.: Yale University Press, 1989. Argues that congressional behavior is aimed at guaranteeing their chances for reelection.

Jacobson, Gary. *The Politics of Congressional Elections.* 4th ed. New York: Longman, 1997. Authoritative study of how members of Congress are elected.

Maass, Arthur. *Congress and the Common Good.* New York: Basic Books, 1983. Insightful account of congressional operations, especially those involving legislative-executive relations. Disputes Fiorina's argument that reelection needs explain congressional behavior.

Malbin, Michael J. *Unelected Representatives.* New York: Basic Books, 1980. Study of the influence of congressional staff members.

Mann, Thomas E., and Norman J. Ornstein. *Renewing Congress.* 2 vols. Washington, D.C.: Brookings Institution and American Enterprise Institute, 1993. Superb, up-to-date overview of what's really wrong with Congress and how to fix it.

Smith, Steven S., and Christopher J. Deering. *Committees in Congress.* Washington, D.C.: Congressional Quarterly, 1984. Analysis of how different kinds of congressional committees operate.

Sundquist, James L. *The Decline and Resurgence of Congress.* Washington, D.C.: Brookings Institution, 1981. A history of the fall and, after 1973, the rise of congressional power vis-à-vis the president.

The Presidency

Enduring Questions

1. Did the Founding Fathers want the president to be stronger or weaker than Congress?

2. Does the personal character of a president make a difference in how he does his job?

3. Should we abolish the electoral college?

P rofessor Jones speaks to his political science class:
"The president of the United States occupies one
of the most powerful offices in the world. Presidents
Kennedy and Johnson sent American troops to
Vietnam, President Bush sent them to Saudi Arabia,
and President Clinton sent them to Kosovo, all without war being declared by Congress. President Nixon
imposed wage and price controls on the country.
Between them, Presidents Carter and Reagan selected most of the federal judges now on the bench; thus
the political philosophies of these two men were
stamped on the courts. No wonder people talk about
our having an 'imperial presidency.' "

A few doors down the hall, Professor Smith
speaks to her class: "The president, compared to the
prime ministers of other democratic nations, is one
of the weakest chief executives anywhere. President
Carter signed an arms-limitation treaty with the
Soviets, but the Senate wouldn't ratify it. President
Reagan was not allowed even to test antisatellite
weapons, and in 1986 Congress rejected his budget
before the ink was dry. President Clinton's health
care plan was ignored, and the House voted to

The first cabinet: left to right, Secretary of War Henry Knox, Secretary of State Thomas Jefferson, Attorney General Edmund Randolph, Secretary of the Treasury Alexander Hamilton, and President George Washington.

impeach him. Regularly, subordinates who are supposed to be loyal to the president leak his views to the press and undercut his programs before Congress. No wonder people call the U.S. president a 'pitiful, helpless giant.' "

Can Professors Jones and Smith be talking about the same office? Who is right? In fact they are both right. The American presidency is a unique office, with elements of great strength *and* profound weakness built into it by its constitutional origins.

Presidents and Prime Ministers

The popularly elected president is an American invention. Of the roughly five dozen countries in which there is some degree of party competition and thus, presumably, some measure of free choice for the voters, only sixteen have a directly elected president, and thirteen of these are nations of North and South America. The democratic alternative is for the chief executive to be a prime minister, chosen by and responsible to the parliament. This system prevails in most Western European countries as well as in Israel and Japan. There is no nation with a purely presidential political system in Europe; France combines a directly elected president with a prime minister and parliament.[1]

In a parliamentary system the prime minister is the chief executive. The prime minister is chosen not by the voters but by the legislature, and he or she in turn selects the other ministers from the members of parliament. If the parliament has only two major parties, the ministers will usually be chosen from the majority party; if there are many parties (as in Italy), several parties may participate in a coalition cabinet. The prime minister remains in power as long as his or her party has a majority of the seats in the legislature or as long as the coalition he or she has assembled holds together. The voters choose who is to be a member of parliament—usually by voting for one or another party—but cannot choose who is to be the chief executive officer.

Whether a nation has a presidential or a parliamentary system makes a big difference in the identity and powers of the chief executive.

■ **Presidents Are Often Outsiders** People become president by winning elections, and sometimes winning is easier if you can show the voters that you are not part of "the mess in Washington." Prime ministers are selected from among people already in parliament, and so they are always insiders.

Jimmy Carter, Ronald Reagan, and Bill Clinton did not hold national office before becoming president. Franklin Roosevelt had been assistant secretary of the navy, but his real political experience was as governor of New York. Dwight Eisenhower was a general, not a politician. John F. Kennedy, Lyndon Johnson, and Richard Nixon had been in Congress, but only Nixon had had top-level experience in the executive branch (he had been vice president). George Bush had had a great deal of executive experience in Washington—as vice president, director of the CIA, and representative to China, whereas Bill Clinton and George W. Bush both served as governors.

■ **Presidents Choose Cabinet Members from Outside Congress** Under the Constitution, no sitting member of Congress can hold office in the executive branch. The persons chosen by a prime minister to be in the cabinet are almost always members of parliament.

Of the fourteen heads of the cabinet-level government departments in the first Clinton administration, only three had been members of Congress. The rest, as is customary with most presidents, were close personal friends or campaign aides, representatives of important constituencies (for example, farmers, blacks, or women), experts on various policy issues, or some combination of all three.

The prime minister of Great Britain, by contrast, picks all of his or her cabinet ministers from among members of Parliament. This is one way by which the prime minister exercises control over the legislature. If you were an ambitious member of Parliament, eager to become prime minister yourself someday, and if you knew that your main chance of realizing that ambition was to be appointed to a series of ever-more-important cabinet posts, then you would not be likely to antagonize the person doing the appointing.

■ **Presidents Have No Guaranteed Majority in the Legislature** A prime minister's party (or coalition) always has a majority in parliament; if it did not, somebody else would be prime minister. A president's party often does not have a congressional majority; instead, Congress is often controlled by the opposite party, creating a divided government. Divided government means that cooperation between the two branches, hard to achieve under the best of circumstances, is often further reduced by partisan bickering.

Even when one party controls both the White House and Congress, the two branches often work at cross-purposes. The U.S. Constitution created a system of separate branches sharing powers. The authors of the document expected that there would be conflict between the branches, and they have not been disappointed.

When Kennedy was president, his party, the Democrats, held a big majority in the House and the Senate. Yet Kennedy was frustrated by his inability to get Congress to approve proposals to enlarge civil rights, supply federal aid for school construction, create a Department of Urban Affairs and Housing, or establish a program of subsidized medical care for the elderly. During his last year in office, Congress

passed only about one-fourth of his proposals. Carter did not fare much better; even though the Democrats controlled Congress, many of his most important proposals were defeated or greatly modified. Only Franklin Roosevelt (1933–1945) and Lyndon Johnson (1963–1969) had even brief success in leading Congress, and for Roosevelt most of that success was confined to his first term or to wartime.

Divided Government

In the forty-eight years between 1952 and 2000, there were twenty-four congressional or presidential elections. Sixteen of the twenty-four produced **divided government**—that is, a government in which one party controls the White House and a different party controls one or both houses of Congress. When George W. Bush became president in 2001, it was only the third time since 1969 that the same party controlled the White House and Congress, creating a **unified government.** And it was only the first time since 1953 when the Republicans were in charge. But not long after the Senate convened, one Republican, James Jeffords of Vermont, left his party,

British prime minister Tony Blair, unlike the president of the United States, knows that almost any bill he submits to his legislature will be approved.

announced that he was an independent, and started voting for the Democrats. Divided government had returned.

Americans say they don't like divided government. They, or at least the pundits who claim to speak for them, think divided government produces partisan bickering, political paralysis, and policy gridlock. During the 1990 battle between President Bush and a Democratic Congress, one magazine compared it to a movie featuring the Keystone Kops, characters from the silent movies who wildly chased each other around while accomplishing nothing.[2] In the 1992 campaign, Bush, Clinton, and Ross Perot bemoaned the "stalemate" that had developed in Washington. When Clinton was sworn in as president, many commentators spoke approvingly of the "end of gridlock."

There are two things wrong with these complaints. First, it is not clear that divided government produces a gridlock that is any worse than that which exists with unified government. Second, it is not clear that, even if gridlock does exist, it is always, or even usually, a bad thing for the country.

Does Gridlock Matter?

Despite the well-publicized stories about presidential budget proposals being ignored by Congress (Democrats used to describe Reagan's and Bush's budgets as being "dead on arrival"), it is not easy to tell whether divided governments produce fewer or worse policies than unified ones. The scholars who have looked closely at the matter have, in general, concluded that divided governments do about as well as unified ones in passing important laws, conducting important investigations, and ratifying significant treaties.[3] Political scientist David Mayhew studied 267 important laws that were enacted between 1946 and 1990. These laws were as likely to be passed when different parties controlled the White House and Congress as when the same party controlled both branches.[4] For example, divided governments produced the 1946 Marshall Plan to rebuild war-torn Europe and the 1986 Tax Reform Act.

Why do divided governments produce about as much important legislation as unified ones? The main reason is that "unified government" is something of a myth. Just because the Democrats control both the presidency and Congress does not mean that the Democratic president and the Democratic

senators and representatives will see things the same way. For one thing, Democrats are themselves divided between conservatives (mainly from the South) and liberals (mainly from the Northeast and the West). They disagree about policy almost as much as Republicans and Democrats disagree. For another thing, the Constitution ensures that the president and Congress will be rivals for power and thus rivals in policy-making. That's what the separation of powers and checks and balances are all about.

As a result, periods of unified government often turn out not to be so unified. Democratic president Lyndon Johnson could not get many Democratic members of Congress to support his war policy in Vietnam. Democratic president Jimmy Carter could not get the Democratic-controlled Senate to ratify his strategic arms limitation treaty. Democratic president Bill Clinton could not get the Democratic Congress to go along with his policy on gays in the military or his health proposals; and when the heavily revised Clinton budget did pass in 1993, it was by just one vote.

The only time there really is a unified government is when not just the same party but the same *ideological wing* of that party is in effective control of both branches of government. This was true in 1933 when Franklin Roosevelt was president and change-oriented Democrats controlled Congress, and it was true again in 1965 when Lyndon Johnson and liberal Democrats dominated Congress. Both were periods when many major policy initiatives became law: Social Security, business regulations, Medicare, and civil rights legislation. But these periods of ideologically unified government are very rare.

Is Policy Gridlock Bad?

An American president has less ability to decide what laws get passed than does a British prime minister. If you think that the job of a president is to "lead the country," that weakness will worry you. The only cure for that weakness is either to change the Constitution so that our government resembles the parliamentary system in effect in Great Britain or always to vote into office members of Congress who not only are of the same party as the president but also agree with him on policy issues.

We suspect that even Americans who hate gridlock and want more leadership aren't ready to make sweeping constitutional changes or to stop voting for presidents and members of Congress from different parties. This unwillingness suggests that they like the idea of somebody being able to block a policy they don't like. Since all of us don't like something, we all have an interest in some degree of gridlock.

And we seem to protect that interest. In a typical presidential election, about one-fourth of all voters will vote for one party's candidate for president and the other party's candidate for Congress. As a result, about one-third of all congressional districts will be represented in the House by a person who does not belong to the party of the president who carried that district. Some scholars believe that voters split tickets deliberately in order to create divided government and thus magnify the effects of the checks and balances built into our system, but the evidence supporting this belief is not conclusive.

Gridlock, to the extent that it exists, is a necessary consequence of a system of **representative democracy.** Such a system causes delays, intensifies deliberations, forces compromises, and requires the creation of broad-based coalitions to support most new policies. This system is the opposite of **direct democracy.** If you believe in direct democracy, you believe that what the people want on some issue should become law with as little fuss and bother as possible. Political gridlocks are like traffic gridlocks—people get overheated, things boil over, nothing moves, and nobody wins except journalists who write about the mess and lobbyists who charge big fees to steer their clients around the tie-up. In a direct democracy, the president would be a traffic cop with broad powers to decide in what direction the traffic should move and to make sure that it moves that way.

But if unified governments are not really unified—if in fact they are split by ideological differences within each party and by the institutional rivalries between the president and Congress—then this change is less important than it may seem. What *is* important is the relative power of the president and Congress. That has changed greatly.

The Evolution of the Presidency

In 1787 few issues inspired as much debate or concern among the Framers as the problem of defining the chief executive. The delegates feared anarchy and monarchy in about equal measure. When the Constitutional Convention met, the existing state constitutions gave most, if not all, power to the legislatures. In eight states the governor was actually chosen by the legislature, and in ten states the governor could not serve more than one year. Only in New York, Massachusetts, and Connecticut did governors have much power or serve for any length of time.

Some of the Framers proposed a plural national executive (that is, several people would each hold the executive power in different areas, or they would exercise the power as a committee). Others wanted the executive power checked, as it was in Massachusetts, by a council that would have to approve many of the chief executive's actions. Alexander Hamilton strongly urged the exact opposite: in a five-hour speech he called for something very much like an elective monarchy, patterned in some respects after the British kind. No one paid much attention to this plan or even, at first, to the more modest (and ultimately successful) suggestion of James Wilson for a single, elected president.

In time those who won out believed that the governing of a large nation, especially one threatened by foreign enemies, required a single president with significant powers. Their cause was aided, no doubt, by the fact that everybody assumed that George Washington would be the first president, and confidence in him—and in his sense of self-restraint—was widely shared. Even so, several delegates feared that the presidency would become, in the words of Edmund Randolph of Virginia, "the foetus of monarchy."

Concerns of the Founders

The delegates in Philadelphia, and later the critics of the new Constitution during the debate over its ratification, worried about aspects of the presidency that were quite different from those that concern us today. In 1787–1789 some Americans suspected that the president, by being able to command the state militia, would use the militia to overpower state governments. Others were worried that if the president were allowed to share treaty-making power with the Senate, he would be "directed by minions and favorites" and become a "tool of the Senate."

But the most frequent concern was over the possibility of presidential reelection: Americans in the late eighteenth century were sufficiently suspicious of human nature and sufficiently experienced in the arts of mischievous government to believe that a president, once elected, would arrange to stay in office in perpetuity by resorting to bribery, intrigue, and force. This might happen, for example, every time the presidential election was thrown into the House of Representatives because no candidate had received a majority of the votes in the electoral college, a situation that most people expected to happen frequently.

In retrospect these concerns seem misplaced, even foolish. The power over the militia has had little significance; the election has gone to the House only twice (1800 and 1824); and though the Senate dominated the presidency off and on during the second half of the nineteenth century, it has not done so recently. The real sources of the expansion of presidential power—the president's role in foreign affairs, his ability to shape public opinion, his position as head of the executive branch, and his claims to have certain "inherent" powers by virtue of his office—were hardly predictable in 1787. And not surprisingly. There was nowhere in the world at that time, nor had there been at any time in history, an example of an American-style presidency. It was a unique and unprecedented institution, and the Framers and their critics can easily be forgiven for not predicting accurately how it would evolve. At a more general level, however, they understood the issue quite clearly. Gouverneur Morris of Pennsylvania put the problem of the presidency this way: "Make him too weak: the Legislature will usurp his powers. Make him too strong: he will usurp on the Legislature."

The Framers knew very well that the relations between the president and Congress and the manner in which the president is elected were of profound importance, and they debated both at great length. The first plan was for Congress to elect the president—in short, for the system to be quasi-parliamentary. But if that were done, some delegates pointed out, Congress could dominate an honest or lazy president, while a corrupt or scheming president might dominate Congress.

After much discussion it was decided that the president should be chosen directly by voters. But by which voters? The emerging nation was large and diverse. It seemed unlikely that every citizen would be familiar enough with the candidates to cast an informed vote for a president directly. Worse, a direct popular election would give inordinate weight to the large, populous states, and no plan with that outcome had any chance of adoption by the smaller states.

The Electoral College

Thus the electoral college was invented, whereby each of the states would select electors in whatever manner it wished. The electors would then meet in each state capital and vote for president and vice president. Many Framers expected that this procedure would lead to each state's electors' voting for a favorite son, and thus no candidate would win a majority of the popular vote. In this event, it was decided, the House of Representatives should make the choice, with each state delegation casting one vote.

The plan seemed to meet every test: large states would have their say, but small states would be protected by having a minimum of three electoral votes no matter how tiny their population. The small states together could wield considerable influence in the House, where, it was widely expected, most presidential elections would ultimately be decided. Of course it did not work out quite this way: the Framers did not foresee the role that political parties would play in producing nationwide support for a slate of national candidates.

Once the manner of electing the president was settled, the question of his powers was much easier to decide. After all, if you believe that the procedures are fair and balanced, then you are more confident in assigning larger powers to the president within this system. Accordingly, the right to make treaties and the right to appoint lesser officials, originally reserved for the Senate, were given to the president "with the advice and consent of the Senate."

The President's Term of Office

Another issue was put to rest soon thereafter. George Washington, the unanimous choice of the electoral college to be the first president, firmly limited himself to two terms in office (1789–1797), and no president until Franklin D. Roosevelt (1933–1945) dared to run for more (though Ulysses S. Grant tried). In 1951 the Twenty-second Amendment to the Constitution was ratified, formally limiting all subsequent presidents to two terms. The remaining issues concerning the nature of the presidency, and especially the relations between the president and Congress, have been the subject of continuing dispute. The pattern of relationships that we see today is the result of an evolutionary process that has extended over more than two centuries.

The first problem was to establish the legitimacy of the presidency itself: that is, to ensure, if possible, public acceptance of the office, its incumbent, and its powers and to establish an orderly transfer of power from one incumbent to the next.

Today we take this for granted. When Bill Clinton was inaugurated in January 1993 as our forty-second president, George Bush, the forty-first president, quietly left the White House and went home. In the world today such an uneventful succession is unusual. In many nations a new chief executive comes to power with the aid of military force or as a result of political intrigue; his predecessor often leaves office disgraced, exiled, or dead. At the time that the Constitution was written, the Founders could only hope that an orderly transfer of power from one president to the next would occur. France had just undergone a bloody revolution; England in the not-too-distant past had beheaded a king; and in Poland the ruler was elected by a process so manifestly corrupt and so open to intrigue that Thomas Jefferson, in what may be the first example of ethnic humor in American politics, was led to refer to the proposed American presidency as a "bad edition of a Polish king."

Yet by the time Abraham Lincoln found himself at the helm of a nation plunged into a bitter, bloody civil war, fifteen presidents had been elected, served their time, and left office without a hint of force being used to facilitate the process and with the people accepting the process—if not admiring all the presidents. This orderly transfer of authority occurred despite passionate opposition and deeply divisive elections (such as that which brought Jefferson to power). And it did not happen by accident.

The First Presidents

Those who first served as president were among the most prominent men in the new nation, all active either in the movement for independence or in the Founding or in both. Of the first five presidents, four (all but John Adams) served two full terms. Washington and Monroe were not even opposed. The first administration had at the highest levels the leading spokesmen for all of the major viewpoints: Alexander Hamilton was Washington's secretary of the treasury (and was sympathetic to the urban commercial interests), and Thomas Jefferson was secretary of state (and more inclined toward rural, small-town, and farming views). Washington spoke out strongly against political parties, and though parties

America has witnessed peaceful transfers of power not only between leaders of different parties (such as Woodrow Wilson and William Howard Taft in 1913) but also after a popular leader has been assassinated (Lyndon Johnson is sworn in after John F. Kennedy's death).

The Electoral College

Until November 2000, it was almost impossible to get a student interested in the electoral college. But in the 2000 presidential election Florida's electoral vote hung in the balance for weeks, with Bush finally winning it and (though he had fewer popular votes than Al Gore) the presidency.

Here are the essential facts: Each state gets electoral votes equal to the number of its senators and representatives (the District of Columbia also gets 3 even though it has no representatives in Congress). There are 538 electoral votes. To win, a candidate must receive at least half, or 270.

In all but two states, the candidate who wins the most popular votes wins all of the state's electoral votes. Maine and Nebraska have a different system. They allow electoral votes to be split by awarding some votes on the basis of a candidate's statewide total and some on the basis of how the candidate did in each congressional district.

The winning slates of electors assemble in their state capitals about six weeks after the election to cast their ballots. Ordinarily this is a pure formality. Occasionally, however, an elector will vote for a presidential candidate other than the one who carried the state. Such "faithless electors" have appeared in nine elections since 1796. The state electoral ballots are opened and counted before a joint session of Congress during the first week of January. The candidate with a majority is declared elected.

If no candidate wins a majority, the House of Representatives chooses the president from among the three leading candidates, with each state casting one vote. By House rules, each state's vote is allotted to the candidate preferred by a majority of the state's House delegation. If there is a tie within a delegation, that state's vote is not counted.

The House has had to decide two presidential contests. In 1800 Thomas Jefferson and Aaron Burr tied in the electoral college because of a defect in the language of the Constitution—each state cast two electoral votes, without indicating which was for president and which for vice president. (Burr was supposed to be vice president, and after much maneuvering he was.) This problem was corrected by the Twelfth Amendment, ratified in 1804. The only House decision under the modern system was in 1824, when it chose John Quincy Adams over Andrew Jackson and William H. Crawford, even though Jackson had more electoral votes (and probably more popular votes) than his rivals.

Today, the winner-take-all system in effect in forty-eight states makes it possible for a candidate to win at least 270 electoral votes without winning a majority of the popular votes. This happened in 2000, 1888, and 1876, and almost happened in 1960 and 1884. Today a candidate who carries the eleven largest states wins 230 electoral votes, only 40 short of a presidential victory.

This means that the candidates have a strong incentive to campaign hard in big states they have a chance of winning. In 2000, Gore worked hard in California, New York, and Pennsylvania but pretty much ignored Texas, where Bush was a shoo-in. Bush campaigned hard in Florida, Illinois, and Ohio, but not so much in New York, where Gore was an easy winner.

But the electoral college can also help small states. South Dakota, for example, has 3 electoral votes (about 0.5 percent of the total) even though it casts only about 0.3 percent of the popular vote. South Dakota and other small states are thus overrepresented in the electoral college.

Most Americans would like to abolish the electoral college. But doing away with it entirely would have some unforeseen effects. If we relied just on the popular vote, there would have to be a runoff election among the two leading candidates if neither got a

soon emerged, there was a stigma attached to them: many people believed that it was wrong to take advantage of divisions in the country, to organize deliberately to acquire political office, or to make legislation depend upon party advantage. As it turned out, this hostility to party (or "faction," as it was more commonly called) was unrealistic: parties are as natural to democracy as churches are to religion.

Establishing the legitimacy of the presidency in the early years was made easier by the fact that the national government had relatively little to do. It had, of course, to establish a sound currency and to settle

Electoral Votes per State

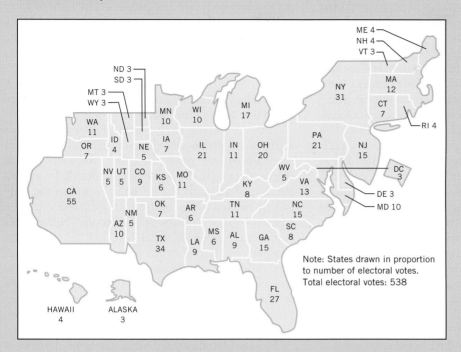

ME 4
NH 4
VT 3
ND 3
SD 3
MT 3
WY 3
WA 11
OR 7
ID 4
NE 5
MN 10
WI 10
MI 17
NY 31
MA 12
CT 7
RI 4
NV 5
UT 5
CO 9
KS 6
MO 11
IA 7
IL 21
IN 11
OH 20
PA 21
NJ 15
DC 3
CA 55
OK 7
AR 6
KY 8
WV 5
VA 13
DE 3
MD 10
NM 5
AZ 10
TX 34
LA 9
MS 6
AL 9
GA 15
TN 11
NC 15
SC 8
HAWAII 4
ALASKA 3
FL 27

Note: States drawn in proportion to number of electoral votes. Total electoral votes: 538

majority because third-party candidates won a lot of votes. This would encourage the formation of third parties (we might have a Jesse Jackson party, a Pat Buchanan party, a Pat Robertson party, and a Ralph Nader party). Each third party would then be in a position to negotiate with one of the two major parties between the first election and the runoff about favors it wanted in return for its support. American presidential politics might come to look like the multiparty systems in France and Italy.

There are other changes that could be made. The states could adopt a system of allocating their electoral votes in proportion to their popular votes. But no major change in the electoral college is likely because too many states benefit from it and so their representatives would not vote for the necessary constitutional amendment. The majority leader in the Senate (as of 2002), Tom Daschle, comes from South Dakota. It is not clear why he would vote for a plan that would reduce his state's influence in the presidential election.

And the electoral college serves a larger purpose: it makes candidates worry about carrying states as well as popular votes, and so heightens the influence of states in national politics.

the debt accrued during the Revolutionary War. The Treasury Department inevitably became the principal federal office, especially under the strong leadership of Hamilton. Relations with England and France were important—and difficult—but otherwise government took little time and few resources.

In appointing people to federal office, a general rule of "fitness" emerged: those appointed should have some standing in their communities and be well thought of by their neighbors. Appointments based on partisanship soon arose, but community stature could not be neglected.

The presidency was kept modest. Washington clearly had not sought the office and did not relish the exercise of its then modest powers. He traveled widely so that as many people as possible could see their new president. His efforts to establish a semiregal court etiquette were quickly rebuffed; the presidency was to be kept simple. Congress decided that not until after a president was dead might his likeness appear on a coin or on currency; no president until Eisenhower was given a pension on his retirement.

The president's relations with Congress were correct but not close. Washington appeared before the Senate to ask its advice on a proposed treaty with some Indian tribes. He got none and instead was politely told that the Senate would like to consider the matter in private. He declared that he would be "damned if he ever went there again," and he never did. Thus ended the responsibility of the Senate to "advise" the president. Vetoes were sometimes cast by the president, but sparingly, and only when the president believed that the law was not simply unwise but unconstitutional. Washington cast only two vetoes; Jefferson and Adams cast none.

The Jacksonians

At a time roughly corresponding to the presidency of Andrew Jackson (1829–1837), broad changes began to occur in American politics. These changes,

President Andrew Jackson thought of himself as the "Tribune of the People," and he symbolized this by throwing a White House party that anyone could attend. Hundreds of people showed up and ate or carried away most of a 1,400-pound block of cheese.

together with the personality of Jackson himself, altered the relations between president and Congress and the nature of presidential leadership. As so often happens, few people at the time Jackson took office had much sense of what his presidency would be like. Though he had been a member of the House of Representatives and of the Senate, he was elected as a military hero—and an apparently doddering one at that. Sixty-one years old and seemingly frail, he nonetheless used the powers of his office as no one before him had.

Jackson vetoed twelve acts of Congress, more than all his predecessors combined and more than any subsequent president until Andrew Johnson thirty years later. His vetoes were not simply on constitutional grounds but on policy ones: as the only official elected by the entire voting citizenry, he saw himself as the "Tribune of the People." None of his vetoes were overridden. He did not initiate many new policies, but he struck out against the ones that he did not like. He did so at a time when the size of the electorate was increasing rapidly, and new states, especially in the West, had entered the Union. (There were then twenty-four states in the Union, nearly twice the original number.)

Jackson demonstrated what could be done by a popular president. He did not shrink from conflict with Congress, and the tension between the two branches of government that was intended by the Framers became intensified by the personalities of those in government: Jackson in the White House, and Henry Clay, Daniel Webster, and John Calhoun in Congress. These powerful figures walked the political stage at a time when bitter sectional conflicts—over slavery and commercial policies—were beginning to split the country. Jackson, though he was opposed to a large and powerful federal government and wished to return somehow to the agrarian simplicities of Jefferson's time, was nonetheless a believer in a strong and independent presidency. This view, though obscured by nearly a century of subsequent congressional dominance of national politics, was ultimately to triumph—for better or for worse.

The Reemergence of Congress

With the end of Jackson's second term, Congress quickly reestablished its power, and except for the wartime presidency of Lincoln and brief flashes of presidential power under James Polk (1845–1849) and Grover Cleveland (1885–1889, 1893–1897), the presidency for a hundred years was the subordinate branch of the national government. Of the eight presidents who succeeded Jackson, two (William H. Harrison and Zachary Taylor) died in office, and none of the others served more than one term. Schoolchildren, trying to memorize the list of American presidents, always stumble in this era of the "no-name" presidents. This is hardly a coincidence: Congress was the leading institution, struggling, unsuccessfully, with slavery and sectionalism.

It was also an intensely partisan era, a legacy of Jackson that lasted well into the twentieth century. Public opinion was closely divided. In nine of the seventeen presidential elections between the end of Jackson's term in 1837 and Theodore Roosevelt's election in 1904, the winning candidate received less than half the popular vote. Only two candidates (Lincoln in 1864 and Ulysses S. Grant in 1872) received more than 55 percent of the popular vote.

During this long period of congressional—and usually senatorial—dominance of national government, only Lincoln broke new ground for presidential power. Lincoln's expansive use of that power, like Jackson's, was totally unexpected. He was first elected in 1860 as a minority president, receiving less than 40 percent of the popular vote in a field of four candidates. Though a member of the new Republican party, he had been a member of the Whig party, a group that had stood for limiting presidential power. He had opposed America's entry into the Mexican War and had been critical of Jackson's use of executive authority. But as president during the Civil War, he made unprecedented use of the vague gift of powers in Article II of the Constitution, especially those that he felt were "implied" or "inherent" in the phrase "take care that the laws be faithfully executed" and in the express authorization for him to act as commander in chief. Lincoln raised an army, spent money, blockaded southern ports, temporarily suspended the writ of habeas corpus, and issued the Emancipation Proclamation to free the slaves—all without prior congressional approval. He justified this, as most Americans probably would have, by the emergency conditions created by civil war. In this he acted little differently from Thomas Jefferson, who while president waged undeclared war against various North African pirates.

After Lincoln, Congress reasserted its power and became, during Reconstruction and for many decades thereafter, the principal federal institution. But it had become abundantly clear that a national emergency could equip the president with great powers and that a popular and strong-willed president could expand his powers even without an emergency.

Except for the administrations of Theodore Roosevelt (1901–1909) and Woodrow Wilson (1913–1921), the president was, until the New Deal, at best a negative force—a source of opposition to Congress, not a source of initiative and leadership for it. Grover Cleveland was a strong personality, but for all his efforts he was able to do little more than veto bills that he did not like. He cast 414 vetoes—more than any other president until Franklin Roosevelt. A frequent target of his vetoes were bills to confer special pensions on Civil War veterans.

Today we are accustomed to thinking that the president formulates a legislative program to which Congress then responds, but until the 1930s the opposite was more the case. Congress ignored the initiatives of such presidents as Grover Cleveland, Rutherford Hayes, Chester Arthur, and Calvin Coolidge. Woodrow Wilson in 1913 was the first president since John Adams to deliver personally the State of the Union address, and he was one of the first to develop and argue for a presidential legislative program.

Our popular conception of the president as the central figure of national government, devising a legislative program and commanding a large staff of advisers, is very much a product of the modern era and of the enlarged role of government. In the past the presidency became powerful only during a national crisis (the Civil War, World War I) or because of an extraordinary personality (Andrew Jackson, Theodore Roosevelt, Woodrow Wilson). Since the 1930s, however, the presidency has been powerful no matter who occupied the office and whether or not there was a crisis. Because government now plays such an active role in our national life, the president is the natural focus of attention and the titular head of a huge federal administrative system (whether he is the real boss is another matter).

But the popular conception of the president as the central figure of national government belies the realities of present-day legislative-executive relations. In a thorough analysis of national policy-making from the Eisenhower years through the Reagan administration, Mark A. Peterson demonstrated that Congress, not the president, often took the lead in setting the legislative agenda.[5] For example, the 1990 Clean Air Act, like the 1970 Clean Air Act before it, was born and bred mainly by congressional, not presidential, action. Indeed, administration officials played almost no role in the legislative process that culminated in these laws.[6] When President Bush signed the 1990 Clean Air Act or President Clinton signed the 1996 Welfare Reform Act, each took credit for it, but in fact both bills were designed by members of Congress, not by the president.[7] Likewise, although presidents dominated budget policy-making from the 1920s into the early 1970s, they no longer do. Instead, the "imperatives of the budgetary process have pushed congressional leaders to center stage."[8] Thus, as often as not, Congress proposes, the president disposes, and legislative-executive relations involve hard bargaining and struggle between these two branches of government.

The Powers of the President

Though the president, unlike a prime minister, cannot command an automatic majority in the legislature, he does have some formidable, albeit vaguely defined, powers. These are mostly set forth in Article II of the Constitution and are of two sorts: those he can exercise in his own right without formal legislative approval, and those that require the consent of the Senate or of Congress as a whole.

■ Powers of the President Alone

- Serve as commander in chief of the armed forces
- Commission officers of the armed forces
- Grant reprieves and pardons for federal offenses (except impeachment)
- Convene Congress in special sessions
- Receive ambassadors
- Take care that the laws be faithfully executed
- Wield the "executive power"
- Appoint officials to lesser offices

■ Powers of the President That Are Shared with the Senate

- Make treaties
- Appoint ambassadors, judges, and high officials

■ Powers of the President That Are Shared with Congress as a Whole

- Approve legislation

Taken alone and interpreted narrowly, this list of powers is not very impressive. Obviously the presi-

dent's authority as commander in chief is important, but literally construed, most of the other constitutional grants seem to provide for little more than a president who is chief clerk of the country. A hundred years after the Founding, that is about how matters appeared to even the most astute observers. In 1884 Woodrow Wilson wrote a book about American politics titled *Congressional Government*, in which he described the business of the president as "usually not much above routine," mostly "*mere administration.*" The president might as well be an officer of the civil service. To succeed, he need only obey Congress and stay alive.[9]

But even as Wilson wrote, he was overlooking some examples of enormously powerful presidents, such as Lincoln, and was not sufficiently attentive to the potential for presidential power to be found in

A military officer carrying "the football," the briefcase containing the secret codes the president can use to launch a nuclear attack.

The President: Qualifications and Benefits

Qualifications

- A natural-born citizen (can be born abroad of parents who are American citizens)
- Thirty-five years of age
- A resident of the United States for at least fourteen years (but not necessarily the fourteen years just preceding the election)

Benefits

- A nice house
- A salary of $400,000 per year (taxable)
- An expense account of $50,000 per year (tax-free)
- Travel expenses of $100,000 per year (tax-free)
- A pension, on retirement, equal to the pay of a cabinet member (taxable)
- Staff support and Secret Service protection on leaving the presidency
- A White House staff of 400 to 500 persons
- A place in the country—Camp David
- A personal airplane—Air Force One
- A fine chef

the more ambiguous clauses of the Constitution as well as in the political realities of American life. The president's authority as commander in chief has grown—especially, but not only, in wartime—to encompass not simply the direction of the military forces but also the management of the economy and the direction of foreign affairs as well. A quietly dramatic reminder of the awesome implications of the president's military powers occurs at the precise instant that a new president assumes office. An army officer carrying a locked briefcase moves from the side of the outgoing president to the side of the new one. In the briefcase are the secret codes and orders that permit the president to authorize the launching of American nuclear weapons.

The president's duty to "take care that the laws be faithfully executed" has become one of the most elastic phrases in the Constitution. By interpreting this broadly, Grover Cleveland was able to use federal troops to break a labor strike in the 1890s, and Dwight Eisenhower was able to send troops to help integrate a public school in Little Rock, Arkansas, in 1957.

The greatest source of presidential power, however, is not found in the Constitution at all but in politics and public opinion. Increasingly since the 1930s, Congress has passed laws that confer on the executive branch broad grants of authority to achieve some general goals, leaving it up to the president and his deputies to define the regulations and programs that will actually be put into effect. In Chapter 13 we shall see how this delegation of legislative power to the president has contributed to the growth of the bureaucracy. Moreover, the American people—always in times of crisis, but increasingly as an everyday matter—look to the president for leadership and hold him responsible for a large and growing portion of our national affairs. The public thinks, wrongly, that the presidency is the "first branch" of government.

The Office of the President

It was not until 1857 that the president was allowed to have a private secretary paid for with public funds, and it was not until after the assassination of President McKinley in 1901 that the president was given a Secret Service bodyguard. He was not able to submit a single presidential budget until after 1921, when the Budget and Accounting Act was passed and the Bureau of the Budget (now called the Office of Management and Budget) was created. Grover Cleveland personally answered the White House telephone, and Abraham Lincoln often answered his own mail.

Today, of course, the president has hundreds of people assisting him, and the trappings of power—helicopters, guards, limousines—are plainly visible. The White House staff has grown enormously. (Just how big the staff is, no one knows. Presidents like to

Figure 12.1   Growth of the White House Office, 1935–1985

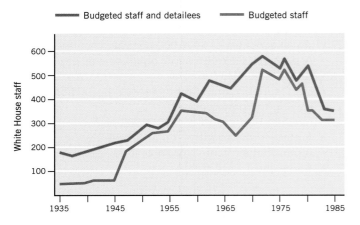

Note: Detailees are people who are employed by and paid by another federal agency but are assigned to work in the White House. Number of detailees for 1981 unavailable.

Sources: For 1935–1977: *Congressional Record* (April 13, 1978), 10111; for 1979–1985: annual reports filed by the White House with the House of Representatives Committee on Post Office and Civil Service, titled "Aggregate Report on Personnel; Pursuant to Title 3, United States Code, Section 113"; and *Budget of the United States Government.* From Samuel Kernell and Samuel Popkin, eds., *Chief of Staff* (Berkeley: University of California Press, 1986), 201.

pretend that the White House is not the large bureaucracy that it in fact has become.) Add to this the opportunities for presidential appointments to the cabinet, the courts, and various agencies, and the resources at the disposal of the president would appear to be awesome. That conclusion is partly true and partly false, or at least misleading, and for a simple reason. If the president was once helpless for lack of assistance, he now confronts an army of assistants so large that it constitutes a bureaucracy that he has difficulty controlling (see Figure 12.1). Note that Figure 12.1 ends in 1985. Recent presidents have made it very hard to find out how many people work for them and, as a result, we cannot tell you how many employees Presidents Reagan, Bush, and Clinton have had.

The ability of a presidential assistant to affect the president is governed by the rule of propinquity: in general power is wielded by people who are in the room when a decision is made. Presidential appointments can thus be classified in terms of their proximity, physical and political, to the president. There are three degrees of propinquity: the White House Office, the Executive Office, and the cabinet.

The White House Office

The president's closest assistants have offices in the White House, usually in the West Wing of that building. Their titles often do not reveal the functions that they actually perform: "counsel," "counselor," "assistant to the president," "special assistant," "special consultant," and so forth. The actual titles vary from one administration to another, but in general the men and women who hold them oversee the political and policy interests of the president. As part of the president's personal staff, these aides do not have to be confirmed by the Senate; the president can hire and fire them at will. In 2000 the Bush White House had four hundred staff members and a budget of $35.4 million.

There are essentially three ways in which a president can organize his personal staff—through the "pyramid," "circular," and "ad hoc" methods. In a **pyramid structure,** used by Eisenhower, Nixon, Reagan, Bush, and (after a while) Clinton, most assistants report through a hierarchy to a chief of staff, who then deals directly with the president. In a **circular structure,** used by Carter, cabinet secretaries and assistants report directly to the president. In an **ad hoc structure,** used for a while by President Clinton, task forces, committees, and informal groups of friends and advisers deal directly with the president. For example, the Clinton administration's health care policy planning was spearheaded not by Health and Human Services secretary Donna E. Shalala but by First Lady Hillary Rodham Clinton and a White House adviser, Ira Magaziner. Likewise, its initiative to reform the federal bureaucracy (the National Performance Review) was led not by Office of Management and Budget director Leon E. Panetta but by an adviser to Vice President Gore, Elaine Kamarck.[10]

It is common for presidents to mix methods; for example, Franklin Roosevelt alternated between the circular and ad hoc methods in the conduct of his domestic policy and sometimes employed a pyramid structure when dealing with foreign affairs and military policy. Taken individually, each method of organization has advantages and disadvantages. A pyramid structure provides for an orderly flow of information and decisions but does so at the risk of isolating or misinforming the president. The circular method has the virtue of giving the president a great deal of infor-

The Myth and Reality of the White House Office

The Myth

The White House Office was created in the 1930s following recommendations made by the President's Commission on Administrative Management. The principles underlying those recommendations have been endorsed by almost every presidential chief of staff since then. The key ones are:

1. *Small is beautiful.* The presidential staff should be small. At first there were only six assistants.
2. *A passion for anonymity.* The president's personal assistants should stay out of the limelight.
3. *Honest brokers.* The presidential staff should not make decisions for the president; it should only coordinate the flow of information to the president.

The Reality

Increasingly the operations of the White House Office seem to reflect almost the exact opposite of these principles.

1. *Big is better.* The White House staff has grown enormously in size. Hundreds now work there.
2. *Get out front.* Key White House staffers have become household words—Henry Kissinger (under Nixon and Ford), H. R. Haldeman (under Nixon), Hamilton Jordan (under Carter), Donald Regan and Howard Baker (under Reagan), George Stephanopoulos (under Clinton).
3. *Be in charge.* Cabinet officers regularly complain that White House staffers are shutting them out and making all the important decisions. Congressional investigations have revealed the power of such White House aides as Haldeman, John Poindexter, and Lieutenant Colonel Oliver North.

Why the Gap Between Myth and Reality?

The answer is—the people and the government. The people expect much more from presidents today; no president can afford to say, "We're too busy here to worry about that." The government is much more complex, and so leadership requires more resources. Even conservatives such as Ronald Reagan have been activist presidents.

Source: Adapted from Samuel Kernell and Samuel L. Popkin, eds., *Chief of Staff* (Berkeley: University of California Press, 1986), 193–232.

---

mation, but at the price of confusion and conflict among cabinet secretaries and assistants. An ad hoc structure allows great flexibility, minimizes bureaucratic inertia, and generates ideas and information from disparate channels, but it risks cutting the president off from the government officials who are ultimately responsible for translating presidential decisions into policy proposals and administrative action.

All presidents claim that they are open to many sources of advice, and some presidents try to guarantee that openness by using the circular method of staff organization. President Carter liked to describe his office as a wheel with himself as the hub and his several assistants as spokes. But most presidents discover, as did Carter, that the difficulty of managing the large White House bureaucracy and of conserving their own limited supply of time and energy makes it necessary for them to rely heavily on one or two key subordinates. Carter, in July 1979, dramatically altered the White House staff organization by elevating Hamilton Jordan to the post of chief of staff, with the job of coordinating the work of the other staff assistants.

At first President Reagan adopted a compromise between the circle and the pyramid, putting the White House under the direction of three key aides. At the beginning of his second term in 1985, however, the president shifted to a pyramid, placing all his assistants under a single chief of staff. Clinton began with an ad hoc system and then changed to one more like a pyramid. Each assistant has, of course, others working for him or her, sometimes a large number. There are, at a slightly lower level of status, "special assistants to the president" for various purposes. (Being "special" means, paradoxically, being less important.)

Perks

Perks is the short form of *perquisites*, meaning "the fringe benefits of office." Among the perks of political office for high-ranking officials are limousines, expense accounts, free air travel, fancy offices, and staff assistants.

The word comes to us from Great Britain, probably in the 1960s, and was first applied to the fringe benefits given to top executives in business firms.

Among the kinds of perks are:

- Freebies (small gifts)
- Annie Oaklies (free tickets or passes to theatrical or sporting events)
- Junkets (free trips abroad)

Source: From *Safire's Political Dictionary* by William Safire. Copyright © 1968, 1972, 1978 by William Safire. Reprinted by permission of Random House, Inc. and the author.

Typically senior White House staff members are drawn from the ranks of the president's campaign staff—longtime associates in whom he has confidence. A few members, however, will be experts brought in after the campaign: such was the case, for example, with Henry Kissinger, a former Harvard professor who became President Nixon's assistant for national security affairs. The offices that these men and women occupy are often small and crowded (Kissinger's was not much bigger than the one that he had while a professor at Harvard), but their occupants willingly put up with any discomfort in exchange for the privilege (and the power) of being

in the White House. The arrangement of offices—their size, and especially their proximity to the president's Oval Office—is a good measure of the relative influence of the people in them.

To an outsider, the amount of jockeying among the top staff for access to the president may seem comical or even perverse. The staff attaches enormous significance to whose office is closest to the president's, who can see him on a daily as opposed to a weekly basis, who can get an appointment with the president and who cannot, and who has a right to see documents and memoranda just before they go to the Oval Office. To be sure, there is ample grist here for Washington political novels. But there is also something important at stake: it is not simply a question of power plays and ego trips. Who can see the president and who sees and "signs off" on memoranda going to the president affect in important ways who influences policy and thus whose goals and beliefs become embedded in policy.

For example, if a memo from a secretary of the treasury who believes in free trade can go directly to the president, the president may be more likely to support free trade (low tariffs). On the other hand, if that memo must be routed through the office of the assistant to the president for political affairs, who is worried about the adverse effects of foreign competition on jobs in the American steel industry because the votes of steelworkers are important to the president's reelection campaign, then the president may be led to support higher tariffs.

The Executive Office of the President

Agencies in the Executive Office report directly to the president and perform staff services for him but are not located in the White House itself. Their members may or may not enjoy intimate contact with him; some agencies are rather large bureaucracies. The top positions in these organizations are filled by presidential appointment, but unlike the White House staff positions, these appointments must be confirmed by the Senate.

The principal agencies in the Executive Office are:

- Office of Management and Budget (OMB)
- Central Intelligence Agency (CIA)
- Council of Economic Advisers (CEA)
- Office of Personnel Management (OPM)
- Office of the U.S. Trade Representative

Of all the agencies in the Executive Office of the President, perhaps the most important in terms of the president's need for assistance in administering the federal government is the Office of Management and Budget. First called the Bureau of the Budget when it was created in 1921, it became OMB in 1970 to reflect its broader responsibilities. Today it does considerably more than assemble and analyze the figures that go each year into the national budget that the president submits to Congress. It also studies the organization and operations of the executive branch, devises plans for reorganizing various departments and agencies, develops ways of getting better information about government programs, and reviews proposals that cabinet departments want included in the president's legislative program.

OMB has a staff of over five hundred people, almost all career civil servants, many of high professional skill and substantial experience. Traditionally OMB has been a nonpartisan agency—experts serving all presidents, without regard to party or ideology. In recent administrations, however, OMB has played a major role in advocating policies rather than merely analyzing them. David Stockman, President Reagan's OMB director, was the primary architect of the 1981 and 1985 budget cuts that were proposed by the president and enacted by Congress. Stockman's proposals were often adopted over the objections of the affected department heads.

The Cabinet

The **cabinet** is a product of tradition and hope. At one time the heads of the federal departments met regularly with the president to discuss matters, and some people, especially those critical of strong presidents, would like to see this kind of collegial decision-making reestablished. But in fact this role of the cabinet is largely a fiction. Indeed, the Constitution does not even mention the cabinet (though the Twenty-fifth Amendment implicitly defines it as consisting of "the principal offices of the executive departments"). When Washington tried to get his cabinet members to work together, its two strongest members—Alexander Hamilton and Thomas Jefferson—spent most of their time feuding. The cabinet, as a presidential committee, did not work any better for John Adams or Abraham Lincoln, for Franklin Roosevelt or John Kennedy. Dwight Eisenhower is almost the only modern president who came close to making the cabinet a truly deliberative

Table 12.1   The Cabinet Departments

Department	Created	Approximate Employment (2000)
State	1789	27,000
Treasury	1789	142,700
Defense[a]	1947	673,500
Justice	1789	126,300
Interior	1849	68,000
Agriculture[b]	1889	99,300
Commerce	1913	45,000
Labor	1913	16,100
Health and Human Services[c]	1953	62,700
Housing and Urban Development	1965	10,300
Transportation	1966	63,900
Energy	1977	15,700
Education	1979	4,700
Veterans Affairs	1989	220,200

[a]Formerly the War Department, created in 1789. Figures are for civilians only.

[b]Agriculture Department created in 1862; made part of cabinet in 1889.

[c]Originally Health, Education and Welfare; reorganized in 1979.

Source: Harold Stanley and Richard Niemi, *Vital Statistics on American Politics, 2001–2002* (Washington, D.C.: Congressional Quarterly Press, 2001).

body: he gave it a large staff, held regular meetings, and listened to opinions expressed there. But even under Eisenhower, the cabinet did not have much influence over presidential decisions, nor did it help him gain more power over the government.

By custom, cabinet officers are the heads of the fourteen major executive departments. These departments, together with the dates of their creation and the approximate number of their employees, are given in Table 12.1. The order of their creation is unimportant except in terms of protocol: where one sits at cabinet meetings is determined by the age of the department that one heads. Thus the secretary of state sits next to the president on one side and the secretary of the treasury next to him on the other. Down at the foot of the table are found the heads of the newer departments.

The president appoints or directly controls vastly more members of his cabinet departments than does the British prime minister (see Table 12.2). The reason is simple: the president must struggle with

Table 12.2	Number of Political Appointments in Cabinet Departments	
Department		**Political Appointees***
Agriculture		412
Commerce		221
Defense		601
Education		205
Energy		441
Health and Human Services		333
Housing and Urban Development		142
Interior		228
Justice		459
State		453
Transportation		248
Treasury		204
Veterans Affairs		319

*All noncompetitive appointments, including personnel appointed by the president with or without Senate confirmation, Senior Executive Service positions, Schedule C positions, and statutory excepted positions.

Source: Committee on Governmental Affairs, United States Senate, *Policy and Supporting Positions*, November 8, 2000.

Congress for control of these agencies, while the prime minister has no rival branch of government that seeks this power. Presidents get more appointments than do prime ministers to make up for what the separation of powers denies them.

This abundance of political appointments, however, does not give the president ample power over the departments. The secretary of Health and Human Services (HHS) reports to the president and has a few hundred political appointees to assist him or her in responding to the president's wishes. But the secretary of HHS heads an agency with over 65,000 employees, 11 operating divisions, hundreds of grant-making programs, and a budget of more than $460 billion. Likewise, the secretary of Housing and Urban Development (HUD) spends most of his or her time on departmental business and vastly less on talking to the president. It is hardly surprising that the secretary is largely a representative of HUD to the president than his representative to HUD. And no one should be surprised that the secretary of HUD rarely finds much to talk about with the secretary of defense at cabinet meetings.

Having the power to make these appointments does give the president one great advantage: he has a lot of opportunities to reward friends and political supporters. In the Education Department, for example, President Clinton found jobs for onetime mayors, senators, state legislators, and campaign aides.

Independent Agencies, Commissions, and Judgeships

The president also appoints people to four dozen or so agencies and commissions that are not considered part of the cabinet and that by law often have a quasi-independent status. The difference between an "executive" and an "independent" agency is not precise. In general it means that the heads of executive agencies serve at the pleasure of the president and can be removed at his discretion. On the other hand, the heads of many independent agencies serve for fixed terms of office and can be removed only "for cause."

The president can also appoint federal judges, subject to the consent of the Senate. Judges serve for life unless they are removed by impeachment and conviction. The reason for the special barriers to the removal of judges is that they represent an independent branch of government as defined by the Constitution, and limits on presidential removal powers are necessary to preserve that independence.

One new feature of appointing top government officials is the increasing use of "acting" appointments. An acting appointee holds office until the Senate acts on his or her nomination. In 1998 acting officials held one-fifth of all of the Clinton administration's cabinet-level (or subcabinet-level)* jobs. Some were in office for many months. Many senators feel that this violates their right to consent to appointments and in particular violates the Vacancies Act passed in 1868. That law limits acting appointees to 120 days in office. If the Senate takes no action during those 120 days, the acting official may stay in office until he or she, or someone else, is confirmed for the post. Administration officials defend the practice as necessary given the slow pace of confirmations; senators attack it as an opportunity for a president to fill up his administration with unconfirmed officials.

---

*Subcabinet refers to under secretary, deputy secretary, and assistant secretaries in each cabinet department.

Federal Agencies

The following agencies are classified by whether the president has unlimited or limited right of removal.

"Executive" Agencies
Head can be removed at any time.

Action
Arms Control and Disarmament Agency
Commission on Civil Rights
Energy Research and Development Agency
Environmental Protection Agency
Federal Mediation and Conciliation Service
General Services Administration
National Aeronautics and Space Administration
Postal Service
Small Business Administration
All cabinet departments
Executive Office of the President

"Independent" or "Quasi-Independent" Agencies
Members serve for a fixed term.

Federal Reserve Board (14 years)
Consumer Product Safety Commission (6 years)
Equal Employment Opportunity Commission (5 years)
Federal Communications Commission (7 years)
Federal Deposit Insurance Corporation (6 years)
Federal Energy Regulatory Commission (5 years)
Federal Maritime Commission (5 years)
Federal Trade Commission (7 years)
National Labor Relations Board (5 years)
National Science Foundation (6 years)
Securities and Exchange Commission (5 years)
Tennessee Valley Authority (9 years)

Who Gets Appointed

As we have seen, a president can make a lot of appointments but he rarely knows more than a few of the people whom he does appoint.

Unlike cabinet members in a parliamentary system, the president's cabinet officers and their principal deputies usually have not served with the chief executive in the legislature. Instead they come from private business, universities, "think tanks," foundations, law firms, labor unions, and the ranks of former and present members of Congress as well as past state and local government officials. A president is fortunate if most cabinet members turn out to agree with him on major policy questions. President Reagan made a special effort to ensure that his cabinet members were ideologically in tune with him, but even so Secretary of State Alexander Haig soon got into a series of quarrels with senior members of the White House staff and had to resign.

The men and women appointed to the cabinet and to the subcabinet will usually have had some prior federal experience. One study of over a thousand such appointments made by five presidents (Franklin Roosevelt through Lyndon Johnson) found that about 85 percent of the cabinet, subcabinet,

and independent-agency appointees had some prior federal experience. In fact most were in government service (at the federal, state, or local levels) just before they received their cabinet or subcabinet appointment.[11] Clearly the executive branch is not, in general, run by novices.

Many of these appointees are what Richard Neustadt has called "in-and-outers": people who alternate between jobs in the federal government and ones in the private sector, especially in law firms and in universities. Donald Rumsfeld, before becoming secretary of defense to President George W. Bush, had been secretary of defense and chief of staff under President Ford and before that a member of Congress. Between his Ford and Bush services, he was an executive in a large pharmaceutical company. This pattern is quite different from that of parliamentary systems, where all the cabinet officers come from the legislature and are typically full-time career politicians.

At one time the cabinet had in it many people with strong political followings of their own—former senators and governors and powerful local party leaders. Under Franklin Roosevelt, Truman, and Kennedy, the postmaster general was the president's campaign manager. George Washington, Abraham Lincoln, and other presidents had to contend with

Secretary of Labor Frances Perkins (left), appointed by President Franklin Roosevelt, was the first woman cabinet member. When Colin Powell (second from left) was made secretary of state by President Bush (second from right), he became the first African American to hold that key post.

cabinet members who were powerful figures in their own right: Alexander Hamilton and Thomas Jefferson worked with Washington; Simon Cameron (a Pennsylvania political boss) and Salmon P. Chase (formerly governor of Ohio) worked for—and against—Lincoln. Before 1824 the post of secretary of state was regarded as a steppingstone to the presidency; and after that at least ten persons ran for president who had been either secretary of state or ambassador to a foreign country.[12]

Of late, however, a tendency has developed for presidents to place in their cabinets people known for their expertise or administrative experience rather than for their political following. This is in part because political parties are now so weak that party leaders can no longer demand a place in the cabinet and in part because presidents want (or think they want) "experts." A remarkable illustration of this is the number of people with Ph.D.'s who have entered the cabinet. President Nixon, who supposedly did not like Harvard professors, appointed two—Henry Kissinger and Daniel Patrick Moynihan—to important posts; Gerald Ford added a third, John Dunlop.

A president's desire to appoint experts who do not have independent political power is modified—but not supplanted—by his need to recognize various politically important groups, regions, and organizations. Since Robert Weaver became the first African American to serve in the cabinet (as secretary of HUD under President Johnson), it is clear that it would be quite costly for a president *not* to have one or more blacks in his cabinet. The secretary of labor must be acceptable to the AFL-CIO, the secretary of agriculture to at least some organized farmers. President George W. Bush, like President Clinton, appointed many women and minorities to his cabinet. Colin Powell became Bush's secretary of state and Condoleezza Rice, also an African American, his national security adviser.

Because political considerations must be taken into account in making cabinet and agency appointments and because any head of a large organization will tend to adopt the perspective of that organization, there is an inevitable tension—even a rivalry— between the White House staff and the department heads. Staff members see themselves as extensions of the president's personality and policies; department heads see themselves as repositories of expert knowledge (often knowledge of why something will not work as the president hopes). White House staffers, many of them young men and women in their twenties or early thirties with little executive experience,

HOW THINGS WORK

The Presidential (Non)Appointment Process

During President George W. Bush's first year in office, every morning around 8:00 A.M. Clay Johnson, a senior aide to the president, reported to the entire White House senior staff on the status of presidential appointments. But often Mr. Johnson had nothing to report, because it now takes months or even years to get the president's appointees approved by the Senate and on the job. Even after President Bill Clinton had been in office for five years, fifteen important countries had no U.S. ambassador; nearly 250 of the federal government's 726 most senior jobs (more than a third) were unfilled; and one out of every eight federal judgeships was vacant. The Food and Drug Administration had no commissioner for eighteen months. The country went for a year without a surgeon general.

It was not always this way. On average, President John F. Kennedy's appointees were on the job 2.4 months after he selected them, whereas President Clinton's took 8.5 months to get in position. The problem has been caused to some extent by increased senatorial polarization (see Chapter 11) and by an expansion in the power of federal judges (see Chapter 14). In addition, at least three features of the system are clearly implicated.

Feature One: The Long Ordeal

All presidential appointees, even those who do not need to be confirmed by the Senate, must fill out hundreds and hundreds of pages of forms covering every aspect of their personal and professional life. In addition, the Federal Bureau of Investigation (FBI) conducts a thorough background check that may involve visits to their home, contacts with former boyfriends or girlfriends, research into rumors about their personal character or business conduct, and so on. The FBI is busy, and for manpower reasons alone, its investigation may drag on for months.

Feature Two: The Rapid Turnover

Federal judges tend to stay put once they wear the robes, but most presidential appointees serve only a few years. One study found that for Executive Schedule positions (see Chapter 13) the median length of service was only 2.1 years. In 14 years the Federal Housing Administration had thirteen commissioners, and in 24 years the General Services Administration (the government's own personnel agency) had eighteen commissioners.

Feature Three: The Senate Game

A game of tit for tat has become the norm. It goes something like this. Senator X, a Republican, used a filibuster to block the last Democratic president's nominee as ambassador, irritating Senator Y, who was the nominee's chief sponsor in the Senate and from the nominee's home state. Now Senator X is sponsoring the new Republican president's nominee to head a federal agency, and Senator Y (even though he knows and likes the nominee personally) holds up the works in order to repay the favor and extract other concessions on unrelated matters both from Senator X and from the White House. When Senators X and Y consider presidential appointments to the federal bench, especially any that are controversial, and any at all to the U.S. Supreme Court, they can often only agree to disagree. As a result, it takes months before the nominee comes before the Senate for a vote.

Sources: G. Galvin Mackenzie, "Nasty and Brutish Without Being Short: The State of the Presidential Appointment Process," *Brookings Review* (Spring 2001) 4–7; and John J. Dilulio, Jr., notes for "Cross Pressures: A Top Academic Insider's Political Analysis of President George W. Bush's First 180 Days in Office," paper prepared for the annual meeting of the American Political Science Association, Boston, Massachusetts, August 2002.

will call department heads, often persons in their fifties with substantial executive experience, and tell them that "the president wants" this or that or that "the president asked me to tell you" one thing or another. Department heads try to conceal their irritation and then maneuver for some delay so that they can develop their own counterproposals. On the other hand, when department heads call a White House staff person and ask to see the president, unless they are one of the privileged few in whom the

T·R·I·V·I·A

Presidents

Only divorced president	Ronald Reagan
Only bachelor president	James Buchanan
Three presidents who died on the Fourth of July	Thomas Jefferson (1826) John Adams (1826) James Monroe (1831)
The shortest presidential term	William Henry Harrison (1 month)
The longest presidential term	Franklin D. Roosevelt (12 years and 1 month)
The youngest president when inaugurated	Theodore Roosevelt (42)
The oldest president when inaugurated	Ronald Reagan (69)
First president born in a hospital	Jimmy Carter
First presidential automobile	Owned by William Howard Taft
Only former presidents elected to Congress	John Quincy Adams (to House) and Andrew Johnson (to Senate)
Only president who never attended school	Andrew Johnson

president has special confidence, they are often told that "the president can't be bothered with that" or "the president doesn't have time to see you."

Presidential Character

Every president brings to the White House a distinctive personality; the way the White House is organized and run will reflect that personality. Moreover, the public will judge the president not only in terms of what he accomplished but also in terms of its perception of his character. Thus personality plays a more important role in explaining the presidency than it does in explaining Congress.

DWIGHT EISENHOWER brought an orderly, military style to the White House. He was accustomed to delegating authority and to having careful and complete staff work done for him by trained specialists.

Though critics often accused him of having a bumbling, incoherent manner of speaking, in fact much of that was a public disguise—a strategy for avoiding being pinned down in public on matters where he wished to retain freedom of action. His private papers reveal a very different Eisenhower—sharp, precise, deliberate.

JOHN KENNEDY brought a very different style to the presidency. He projected the image of a bold, articulate, and amusing leader who liked to surround himself with talented amateurs. Instead of clear, hierarchical lines of authority, there was a pattern of personal rule and an atmosphere of improvisation. Kennedy did not hesitate to call very junior subordinates directly and tell them what to do, bypassing the chain of command.

LYNDON JOHNSON was a master legislative strategist who had risen to be majority leader of the Senate on the strength of his ability to persuade other politicians in face-to-face encounters. He was a consummate deal maker who, having been in Washington for thirty years before becoming president, knew everybody and everything. As a result he tried to make every decision himself. But the style that served him well in political negotiations did not serve him well in speaking to the country at large, especially when trying to retain public support for the war in Vietnam.

RICHARD NIXON was a highly intelligent man with a deep knowledge of and interest in foreign policy, coupled with a deep suspicion of the media, his political rivals, and the federal bureaucracy. In contrast to Johnson, he disliked personal confrontations and tended to shield himself behind an elaborate staff system. Distrustful of the cabinet agencies, he tried first to centralize power in the White House and then to put into key cabinet posts former White House aides loyal to him. Like Johnson, his personality made it difficult for him to mobilize popular support. Eventually he was forced to resign under the threat of impeachment arising out of his role in the Watergate scandal.

GERALD FORD, before being appointed vice president, had spent his political life in Congress and was at home with the give-and-take, discussion-oriented procedures of that body. He was also a genial man who liked talking to people. Thus he preferred the circular to the pyramid system of White House organization. But this meant that many decisions were made in a disorganized fashion in which key people—and sometimes key problems—were not taken into account.

JIMMY CARTER was an outsider to Washington and boasted of it. A former Georgia governor, he was determined not to be "captured" by Washington insiders. He also was a voracious reader with a wide range of interests and an appetite for detail. These dispositions led him to try to do many things and to do them personally. Like Ford, he began with a circular structure; unlike Ford, he based his decisions on reading countless memos and asking detailed questions. His advisers finally decided that he was trying to do too much in too great detail, and toward the end of his term he shifted to a pyramid structure.

RONALD REAGAN was also an outsider, a former governor of California. But unlike Carter, he wanted to set the broad directions of his administration and leave the details to others. He gave wide latitude to subordinates and to cabinet officers, within the framework of an emphasis on lower taxes, less domestic spending, a military buildup, and a tough line with the Soviet Union. He was a superb leader of public opinion, earning the nickname "The Great Communicator."

GEORGE BUSH lacked Reagan's speaking skills and was much more of a hands-on manager. Drawing on his extensive experience in the federal government (he had been vice president, director of the CIA, ambassador to the United Nations, representative to China, and a member of the House), Bush made decisions on the basis of personal contacts with key foreign leaders and Washington officials.

BILL CLINTON, like Carter, paid a lot of attention to public policy and preferred informal, ad hoc arrangements for running his office. Unlike Carter, he was an effective speaker who could make almost any idea sound plausible. He was elected as a centrist Democrat but immediately pursued liberal policies such as comprehensive health insurance. When those failed and the Republicans won control of Congress in 1994, Clinton became a centrist again. His sexual affairs became the object of major investigations, and he was impeached by the House but acquitted by the Senate.

GEORGE W. BUSH, the forty-third president, entered office as an outsider from Texas, but he was an outsider with a difference: his father had served as the forty-first president of the United States, his late paternal grandfather had served as a United States senator from Connecticut, and he won the presidency only after the U.S. Supreme Court halted a recount of ballots in Florida, where his brother was governor. During the campaign, he focused almost

Three presidents—George Bush, Bill Clinton, and Jimmy Carter—at a summit to encourage volunteer activity.

entirely on domestic issues, especially cutting taxes and reforming education. A deeply religious man, he talked openly about how he had stopped excessive drinking only after he had found God. He ran as a "compassionate conservative" concerned about America's needy children and families. Bush, who had earned an advanced degree in business administration from Harvard, ran a very tight White House ship, insisting that meetings run on time and that press contacts be strictly controlled. He turned back public doubts about his intellect through self-deprecating humor. Following the terrorist attack on America on September 11, 2001, his agenda shifted almost entirely to foreign and military affairs, the "war on terror," and the issue of homeland security.

The Power to Persuade

The sketchy constitutional powers given the president, combined with the lack of an assured legislative majority, mean that he must rely heavily on persuasion if he is to accomplish much. Here the Constitution gives him some advantages: he and the vice president are the only officials elected by the whole nation, and he is the ceremonial head of state as well as the chief executive of the government. The president can use his national constituency and ceremonial duties to enlarge his power, but he must do so quickly: the second half of his first term in office will be devoted to running for reelection, especially if he faces opposition for his own party's nomination (as was the case with Carter and Ford).

The Three Audiences

The president's persuasive powers are aimed at three audiences. The first, and often the most important, is his Washington, D.C., audience of fellow politicians and leaders. As Richard Neustadt points out in his book *Presidential Power*, a president's reputation among his Washington colleagues is of great importance in affecting how much deference his views receive and thus how much power he can wield.[13] If a president is thought to be "smart," "sure of himself," "cool," "on top of things," or "shrewd," and thus "effective," he *will* be effective. Franklin Roosevelt had that reputation, and so did Lyndon Johnson, at least for his first few years in office. Truman, Ford, and Carter often did not have that reputation, and they lost ground accordingly. Power, like beauty, exists largely in the eye of the beholder.

A second audience is composed of party activists and officeholders outside Washington—the partisan grassroots. These persons want the president to exemplify their principles, trumpet their slogans, appeal to their fears and hopes, and help them get reelected. Since, as we explained in Chapter 7, partisan activists increasingly have an ideological orientation toward national politics, these people will expect "their" president to make fire-and-brimstone speeches that confirm in them a shared sense of purpose and, incidentally, help them raise money from contributors to state and local campaigns.

The third audience is "the public." But of course that audience is really many publics, each with a different view or set of interests. A president on the campaign trail speaks boldly of what he will accomplish; a president in office speaks quietly of the problems that must be overcome. Citizens are often irritated at the apparent tendency of officeholders, including the president, to sound mealy-mouthed and equivocal. But it is easy to criticize the cooking when you haven't been the cook. A president learns quickly that his every utterance will be scrutinized closely by the media and by organized groups here and abroad, and his errors of fact, judgment, timing, or even inflection will be immediately and forcefully pointed out. Given the risks of saying too much, it is a wonder that presidents say anything at all.

Presidents have made fewer and fewer impromptu remarks in the years since Franklin Roosevelt held office and have instead relied more and more on prepared speeches from which political errors can be removed in advance. Hoover and Roosevelt held six or seven press conferences each month, but every president from Nixon through Clinton has held barely one a month. Instead modern presidents make formal speeches. These speeches help them wage media politics by saying things, using phrases, and displaying attitudes that opinion polls tell them are politically useful.

Popularity and Influence

The object of all this talk is to convert personal popularity into congressional support for the president's legislative programs (and improved chances for reelection). It is not obvious, of course, why Congress should care about a president's popularity. After all, as we saw in Chapter 11, most members of Congress are secure in their seats, and few need fear any "party bosses" who might deny them renomination. Moreover, the president cannot ordinarily provide credible electoral rewards or penalties to members of Congress. By working for their defeat in the 1938 congressional election, President Roosevelt attempted to "purge" members of Congress who opposed his program, but he failed. Nor does presidential support help a particular member of Congress: most representatives win reelection anyway, and the few who are in trouble are rarely saved by presidential intervention. When President Reagan campaigned hard for Republican senatorial candidates in 1986, he, too, failed to have much impact.

For a while scholars thought that congressional candidates might benefit from the president's coattails: they might ride into office on the strength of the popularity of a president of their own party. It is true, as can be seen from Table 12.3, that a winning president will find that his party's strength in Congress increases.

| Table 12.3 | Partisan Gains or Losses in Congress in Presidential Election Years | | | | |

			Gains or Losses of President's Party In:	
Year	President	Party	House	Senate
1932	Roosevelt	Dem.	+90	+9
1936	Roosevelt	Dem.	+12	+7
1940	Roosevelt	Dem.	+7	−3
1944	Roosevelt	Dem.	+24	−2
1948	Truman	Dem.	+75	+9
1952	Eisenhower	Rep.	+22	+1
1956	Eisenhower	Rep.	−3	−1
1960	Kennedy	Dem.	−20	+1
1964	Johnson	Dem.	+37	+1
1968	Nixon	Rep.	+5	+7
1972	Nixon	Rep.	+12	−2
1976	Carter	Dem.	+1	+1
1980	Reagan	Rep.	+33	+12
1984	Reagan	Rep.	+16	−2
1988	Bush	Rep.	−3	−1
1992	Clinton	Dem.	−9	+1
1996	Clinton	Dem.	+9	−2
2000	Bush	Rep.	−3	−4

Sources: Updated from Congressional Quarterly, *Guide to U.S. Elections,* 928; and *Congress and the Nation,* vol. 4 (1973–1976), 28.

But there are good reasons to doubt whether the pattern observed in Table 12.3 is the result of presidential coattails. For one thing, there are some exceptions. Eisenhower won 57.4 percent of the vote in 1956, but the Republicans lost seats in the House and Senate. Kennedy won in 1960, but the Democrats lost seats in the House and gained but one in the Senate. When Nixon was reelected in 1972 with one of the largest majorities in history, the Republicans lost seats in the Senate.

Careful studies of voter attitudes and of how presidential and congressional candidates fare in the same districts suggest that, whatever may once have been the influence of coattails, their effect has declined in recent years and is quite small today. The weakening of party loyalty and of party organizations, combined with the enhanced ability of members of Congress to build secure relations with their constituents, has tended to insulate congressional elections from presidential ones. When voters choose as members of Congress people of the same party as an incoming president, they probably do so out of desire for a general change and as an adverse judgment about the outgoing party's performance as a whole, not because they want to supply the new president with members of Congress favorable to him.[14] The big increase in Republican senators and representatives that accompanied the election of Ronald Reagan in 1980 was probably as much a result of the unpopularity of the outgoing president and the circumstances of various local races as it was of Reagan's coattails.

Nonetheless, a president's personal popularity may have a significant effect on how much of his program Congress passes, even if it does not affect the reelection chances of those members of Congress. Though they do not fear a president who threatens to campaign against them (or cherish one who promises to support them), members of Congress do have a sense that it is risky to oppose too adamantly the policies of a popular president. Politicians share a sense of a common fate: they tend to rise or fall together. Statistically a president's popularity, as measured by the Gallup poll (see Figure 12.2), is associated with the proportion of his legislative proposals that are approved by Congress (see Figure 12.3). Other things being equal, the more popular the president, the higher the proportion of his bills that Congress will pass.

But use these figures with caution. How successful a president is with Congress depends not just on the numbers reported here but on a lot of other factors as well. First, he can be "successful" on a big bill or on a trivial one. If he is successful on a lot of small matters and never on a big one, the measure of presidential victories does not tell us much. Second, a president can keep his victory score high by not taking a position on any controversial measure. (President Carter made his views known on only 22 percent of the House votes, while President Eisenhower made his views known on 56 percent of those votes.) Third, a president can appear successful if a few bills he likes are passed but most of his legislative program is bottled up in Congress and never comes to a vote. Given these problems, "presidential victories" are hard to measure accurately.

A fourth general caution: presidential popularity is hard to predict and can be greatly influenced by factors over which nobody, including the president, has much control. For example, when he took office in 2001, President George W. Bush's approval rating was 57 percent, nearly identical to what President

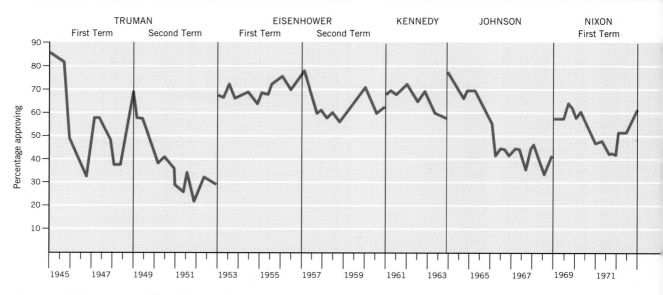

Figure 12.2   **Presidential Popularity**

Note: Popularity was measured by asking every few months, "Do you approve of the way _____ is handling his job as president?"

Source: Thomas E. Cronin, *The State of the Presidency* (Boston: Little, Brown, 1975), 110–111. Copyright © 1975 by Little, Brown and Company, Inc. Reprinted by permission. Updated with Gallup poll data, 1976–1993. Reprinted by permission of the Gallup Poll News Service.

Bill Clinton received in his initial rating (58 percent) in 1993. But Bush also had the highest initial *disapproval* rating (25 percent) of any president since polling began. This was undoubtedly partly due to his becoming president on the heels of the Florida vote-count controversy (see Chapter 8). Bush's approval ratings through his first six months were fairly typical for post-1960 presidents. But from the terrorist attack on the United States on September 11, 2001 through mid-2002, his approval ratings never dipped below 70 percent, and the approval ratings he received shortly after the attack (hovering around 90 percent) were the highest ever recorded.

The Decline in Popularity

Though presidential popularity is an asset, its value tends inexorably to decline. As can be seen from Figure 12.2, every president except Eisenhower, Reagan, and Clinton lost popular support between his inauguration and the time that he left office, except when his reelection gave him a brief burst of renewed popularity. Truman was hurt by impropri-

eties among his subordinates and by the protracted Korean War; Johnson was crippled by the increasing unpopularity of the Vietnam War; Nixon was severely damaged by the Watergate scandal; Ford was hurt by having pardoned Nixon for his part in Watergate; Carter was weakened by continuing inflation, staff irregularities, and the Iranian kidnapping of American hostages; Bush was harmed by a protracted economic recession. Remarkably, Clinton's approval rating was not greatly harmed by his affair with Monica Lewinsky and his impeachment.

Because a president's popularity tends to be highest right after an election, political commentators like to speak of a "honeymoon," during which, presumably, the president's love affair with the people and with Congress can be consummated. Certainly Roosevelt enjoyed such a honeymoon. In the legendary "first hundred days" of his presidency, from March to June 1933, FDR obtained from a willing Congress a vast array of new laws creating new agencies and authorizing new powers. But those were extraordinary times: the most serious economic

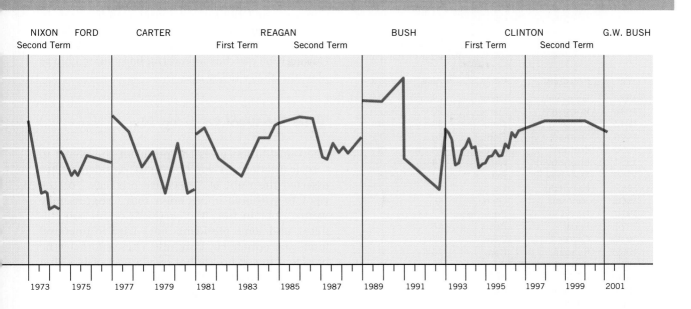

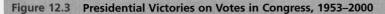

Figure 12.3   Presidential Victories on Votes in Congress, 1953–2000

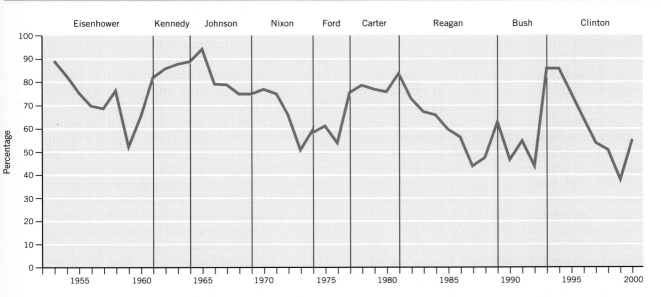

Note: Percentages indicate number of congressional votes supporting the president divided by the total number of votes on which the president has taken a position.
Source: From Harold Stanley and Richard Niemi, *Vital Statistics on American Politics,* 2001–2002 (Washington, D.C.: Congressional Quarterly Press, 2001); and Gallup News Service, February 6, 2001. Reprinted with permission.

Table 12.4	Partisan Gains or Losses in Congress in Off-Year Elections			
			Gains or Losses of President's Party In:	
Year	President	Party	House	Senate
1934	Roosevelt	Dem.	+9	+9
1938	Roosevelt	Dem.	−70	−7
1942	Roosevelt	Dem.	−50	−8
1946	Truman	Dem.	−54	−11
1950	Truman	Dem.	−29	−5
1954	Eisenhower	Rep.	−18	−1
1958	Eisenhower	Rep.	−47	−13
1962	Kennedy	Dem.	−5	+2
1966	Johnson	Dem.	−48	−4
1970	Nixon	Rep.	−12	+1
1974	Ford	Rep.	−48	−5
1978	Carter	Dem.	−12	−3
1982	Reagan	Rep.	−26	0
1986	Reagan	Rep.	−5	−8
1990	Bush	Rep.	−9	−1
1994	Clinton	Dem.	−52	−9
1998	Clinton	Dem.	+5	0
2002	Bush	Rep.	+8	+2

Source: Updated from Harold W. Stanley and Richard G. Niemi, *Vital Statistics on American Politics, 2001–2002* (Washington, D.C.: Congressional Quarterly, 2001), table 1–15.

depression of this century had put millions out of work, closed banks, impoverished farmers, and ruined the stock market. It would have been political suicide for Congress to have blocked, or even delayed, action on measures that appeared designed to help the nation out of the crisis.

Other presidents, serving in more normal times, have not enjoyed such a honeymoon. Truman had little success with what he proposed; Eisenhower proposed little. Kennedy, Nixon, Ford, and Carter had some victories in their first year in office, but nothing that could be called a honeymoon. Only Lyndon Johnson enjoyed a highly productive relationship with Congress; until the Vietnam War sapped his strength, he rarely lost. Reagan began his administration with important victories in his effort to cut expenditures and taxes, but in his second year in office he ran into trouble.

The decay in the reputation of the president and his party in midterm is evident in Table 12.4. Since 1934, in every off-year election but one, the president's party has lost seats in one or both houses of Congress. In 1998 the Democrats won five seats in the House and lost none in the Senate. The ability of the president to persuade is important but limited. However, he also has a powerful bargaining chip to play: the ability to say no.

The Power to Say No

The Constitution gives the president the power to veto legislation. In addition most presidents have asserted the right of "executive privilege," or the right to withhold information that Congress may want to obtain from the president or his subordinates, and some presidents have tried to impound funds appropriated by Congress. These efforts by the president to say no are not only a way of blocking action but also a way of forcing Congress to bargain with him over the substance of policies.

Veto

If a president disapproves of a bill passed by both houses of Congress, he may veto it in one of two ways. One is by a **veto message.** This is a statement that the president sends to Congress accompanying the bill, within ten days (not counting Sundays) after the bill has been passed. In it he sets forth his reasons for not signing the bill. The other is the **pocket veto.** If the president does not sign the bill within ten days *and* Congress has adjourned within that time, then the bill will not become law. Obviously a pocket veto can be used only during a certain time of the year—just before Congress adjourns at the end of its second session. At times, however, presidents have pocket-vetoed a bill just before Congress recessed for a summer vacation or to permit its members to campaign during an off-year election. In 1972 Senator Edward M. Kennedy of Massachusetts protested that this was unconstitutional, since a recess is not the same thing as an adjournment. In a case brought to federal court, Kennedy was upheld, and it is now understood that the pocket veto can be used only just before the life of a given Congress expires.

A bill that is not signed or vetoed within ten days while Congress is still in session becomes law automatically, without the president's approval. A bill that has been returned to Congress with a veto mes-

Table 12.5	**Presidential Vetoes, 1789–2000**			
	Regular Vetoes	Pocket Vetoes	Total Vetoes	Vetoes Overridden
Washington	2	—	2	—
Madison	5	2	7	—
Monroe	1	—	1	—
Jackson	5	7	12	—
Tyler	6	3	9	1
Polk	2	1	3	—
Pierce	9	—	9	5
Buchanan	4	3	7	—
Lincoln	2	4	6	—
A. Johnson	21	8	29	15
Grant	45	49	94	4
Hayes	12	1	13	1
Arthur	4	8	12	1
Cleveland	304	109	413	2
Harrison	19	25	44	1
Cleveland	43	127	170	5
McKinley	6	36	42	—
T. Roosevelt	42	40	82	1
Taft	30	9	39	1
Wilson	33	11	44	6
Harding	5	1	6	—
Coolidge	20	30	50	4
Hoover	21	16	37	3
F. Roosevelt	372	263	635	9
Truman	180	70	250	12
Eisenhower	73	108	181	2
Kennedy	12	9	21	—
L. Johnson	16	14	30	—
Nixon	26	17	43	7
Ford	48	18	66	12
Carter	13	18	31	2
Reagan	39	39	78	9
Bush	29	15	44	1
Clinton	36	1	37	2

Source: Harold W. Stanley and Richard G. Niemi, *Vital Statistics on American Politics, 2001–2002* (Washington, D.C.: Congressional Quarterly, 2001), table 6-9.

sage can be passed over the president's objections if at least two-thirds of each house votes to override the veto. A bill that has received a pocket veto cannot be brought back to life by Congress (since Congress has adjourned), nor does such a bill carry over to the next session of Congress. If Congress wants to press the matter, it will have to start all over again by passing the bill anew in its next session, and then hope that the president will sign it or, if he does not, that they can override his veto.

Until 1996 the president had to either accept or reject the entire bill. Presidents did not have the power, possessed by most governors, to exercise a **line-item veto,** with which the chief executive can approve some provisions of a bill and disapprove others. Congress could take advantage of this by putting items the president did not like into a bill he otherwise favored, forcing him to approve those provisions along with the rest of the bill or reject the whole thing. But in 1996 Congress passed a bill, which the president signed into law, that gives the president the power of "enhanced rescission." This means the president could cancel parts of a spending bill passed by Congress without vetoing the entire bill. The president had five days after signing a bill to send a message to Congress rescinding some parts of what he had signed. These rescissions would take effect unless Congress, by a two-thirds vote, overturned them. Congress could choose which parts of the president's cancellations it wanted to overturn. But the Supreme Court has decided that this law is unconstitutional. The Constitution gives the president no such power to carve up a bill: he must either sign the whole bill, veto the whole bill, or allow it to become law without his signature.[15]

Nevertheless, the veto power is a substantial one, because Congress rarely has the votes to override it. From George Washington to Bill Clinton, over 2,500 presidential vetoes were cast; about 4 percent were overridden (see Table 12.5). Cleveland, Franklin Roosevelt, Truman, and Eisenhower made the most extensive use of vetoes, accounting for 65 percent of all vetoes ever cast. Often the vetoed legislation is revised by Congress and passed in a form suitable to the president. There is no tally of how often this happens, but it is frequent enough so that both branches of government recognize that the veto, or even the threat of it, is part of an elaborate process of political negotiation in which the president has substantial powers.

Executive Privilege

The Constitution says nothing about whether the president is obliged to divulge private communications between himself and his principal advisers, but presidents have acted as if they do have that privilege of confidentiality. The presidential claim is based on two grounds. First, the doctrine of the separation of powers means that one branch of government does not have the right to inquire into the internal workings of another branch headed by constitutionally named officers. Second, the principles of statecraft and of prudent administration require that the president have the right to obtain confidential and candid advice from subordinates; such advice could not be obtained if it would quickly be exposed to public scrutiny.

For almost two hundred years there was no serious challenge to the claim of presidential confidentiality. The Supreme Court did not require the disclosure of confidential communications to or from the president.[16] Congress was never happy with this claim but until 1973 did not seriously dispute it. Indeed, in 1962 a Senate committee explicitly accepted a claim by President Kennedy that his secretary of defense, Robert S. McNamara, was not obliged to divulge the identity of Defense Department officials who had censored certain speeches by generals and admirals.

In 1973 the Supreme Court for the first time met the issue directly. A federal special prosecutor sought tape recordings of White House conversations between President Nixon and his advisers as part of his investigation of the Watergate scandal. In the case of *United States v. Nixon,* the Supreme Court, by a vote of eight to zero, held that while there may be a sound basis for the claim of executive privilege, especially where sensitive military or diplomatic matters are involved, there is no "absolute unqualified Presidential privilege of immunity from judicial process under all circumstances."[17] To admit otherwise would be to block the constitutionally defined function of the federal courts to decide criminal cases.

Thus Nixon was ordered to hand over the disputed tapes and papers to a federal judge so that the judge could decide which were relevant to the case at hand and allow those to be introduced into evidence. In the future another president may well persuade the Court that a different set of records or papers is so sensitive as to require protection, especially if there is no allegation of criminal misconduct requiring the production of evidence in court. As a practical matter it seems likely that presidential advisers will be able, except in unusual cases such as Watergate, to continue to give private advice to the president.

In 1997 and 1998 President Clinton was sued while in office by a private person, Paula Jones, who claimed that he had solicited sex from her in ways that hurt her reputation. In defending himself against that and other matters, his lawyers attempted to claim executive privilege for Secret Service officers and government-paid lawyers who worked with him, but federal courts held that not only could a president be sued, but these other officials could not claim executive privilege.[18] One unhappy consequence of this episode is that the courts have greatly weakened the number of officials with whom the president can speak in confidence. It is not easy to run an organization when the courts can later compel your associates to testify about everything you said.

Impoundment of Funds

From time to time presidents have refused to spend money appropriated by Congress. Truman did not spend all that Congress wanted spent on the armed forces, and Johnson did not spend all that Congress made available for highway construction. Kennedy refused to spend money appropriated for new weapons systems that he did not like. Indeed, the precedent for impounding funds goes back at least to the administration of Thomas Jefferson.

But what has precedent is not thereby constitutional. The Constitution is silent on whether the president *must* spend the money that Congress appropriates; all it says is that the president cannot spend money that Congress has *not* appropriated. The major test of presidential power in this respect occurred during the Nixon administration. Nixon wished to reduce federal spending. He proposed in 1972 that Congress give him the power to reduce federal spending so that it would not exceed $250 billion for the coming year. Congress, under Democratic control, refused. Nixon responded by pocket-vetoing twelve spending bills and then impounding funds appropriated under other laws that he had not vetoed.

Congress in turn responded by passing the Budget Reform Act of 1974, which, among other things, requires the president to spend all appropriated funds unless he first tells Congress what funds he wishes not to spend and Congress, within forty-five days, agrees to delete the items. If he wishes simply to delay spending the money, he need only inform Congress, but Congress then can refuse the delay by passing a resolution requiring the immediate release of the money. Federal courts have upheld the rule that the president must spend, without delay for policy reasons, money that Congress has appropriated.

The President's Program

Imagine that you have just spent three or four years running for president, during which time you have given essentially the same speech over and over again. You have had no time to study the issues in any depth. To reach a large television audience, you have couched your ideas largely in rather simple—if not simple-minded—slogans. Your principal advisers are political aides, not legislative specialists.

You win. You are inaugurated. Now you must *be* a president instead of just talking about it. You must fill hundreds of appointive posts, but you know personally only a handful of the candidates. You must deliver a State of the Union message to Congress only two or three weeks after you are sworn in. It is quite possible that you have never read, much less written, such a message before. You must submit a new budget; the old one is hundreds of pages long, much of it comprehensible only to experts. Foreign governments, as well as the stock market, hang on your every word, interpreting many of your remarks in ways that totally surprise you. What will you do?

The Constitution is not much help. It directs you to report on the state of the union and to recommend "such measures" as you shall judge "necessary and expedient." Beyond that you are charged to "take care that the laws be faithfully executed."

At one time, of course, the demands placed on a newly elected president were not very great, because the president was not expected to do very much. The president, on assuming office, might speak of the tariff, or relations with England, or the value of veterans' pensions, or the need for civil service reform, but he was not expected to have something to say (and offer) to everybody. Today he is.

Putting Together a Program

To develop policies on short notice, a president will draw on several sources, each with particular strengths and weaknesses:

- **Interest groups**
  Strength: Will have specific plans and ideas.
  Weakness: Will have narrow view of the public interest.
- **Aides and campaign advisers**
  Strength: Will test new ideas for their political soundness.
  Weakness: Will not have many ideas to test, being inexperienced in government.

- **Federal bureaus and agencies**
  Strength: Will know what is feasible in terms of governmental realities.
  Weakness: Will propose plans that promote own agencies and will not have good information on whether plans will work.
- **Outside, academic, and other specialists and experts**
  Strength: Will have many general ideas and criticisms of existing programs.
  Weakness: Will not know the details of policy or have good judgment as to what is feasible.

There are essentially two ways for a president to develop a program. One, exemplified by Presidents Carter and Clinton, is to have a policy on almost everything. To do this they worked endless hours and studied countless documents, trying to learn something about, and then state their positions on, a large number of issues. The other method, illustrated by President Reagan, is to concentrate on three or four major initiatives or themes and leave everything else to subordinates.

But even when a president has a governing philosophy, as did Reagan, he cannot risk plunging ahead on his own. He must judge public and congressional reaction to this program before he commits himself fully to it. Therefore he will often allow parts of his program to be "leaked" to the press, or to be "floated" as a trial balloon. Reagan's commitment to a 30 percent tax cut and larger military expenditures was so well known that it required no leaking, but he did have to float his ideas on Social Security and certain budget cuts to test popular reaction. His opponents in the bureaucracy did exactly the same thing, hoping for the opposite effect. They leaked controversial parts of the program in an effort to discredit the whole policy. This process of testing the winds by a president and his critics helps explain why so many news stories coming from Washington mention no person by name but only an anonymous "highly placed source."

In addition to the risks of adverse reaction, the president faces three other constraints on his ability to plan a program. One is the sheer limit of his time and attention span. Every president works harder than he has ever worked before. A ninety-hour week is typical. Even so, he has great difficulty keeping up with all the things that he is supposed to know and make decisions about. For example, Congress during an average year passes between four hundred and six hundred bills, each of which the president must sign, veto, or allow to take effect without his signature. Scores of people wish to see him. Hundreds of phone calls must be made to members of Congress and others in order to ask for help, to smooth ruffled feathers, or to get information. He must receive all newly appointed ambassadors and visiting heads of state and in addition have his picture taken with countless people, from a Nobel Prize winner to a child whose likeness will appear on the Easter Seal.

The second constraint is the unexpected crisis. Franklin Roosevelt obviously had to respond to a depression and to the mounting risks of world war. But most presidents get their crises when they least expect them. Consider these crises:

Kennedy

- Failure of Bay of Pigs invasion of Cuba
- Soviets put missiles in Cuba
- China invades India
- Federal troops sent to the South to protect blacks

Johnson

- Vietnam War
- Black riots in major cities
- War between India and Pakistan
- Civil war in Dominican Republic
- Arab-Israeli war
- Civil rights workers murdered in South

Nixon

- Watergate scandal
- Arab-Israeli war
- Value of dollar falls in foreign trade
- Arabs raise the price of oil

Carter

- OMB director Bert Lance accused of improprieties
- Lengthy coal strike
- Seizure of American hostages in Iran
- Soviet invasion of Afghanistan

Reagan

- Poland suppresses Solidarity movement
- U.S. troops sent to Lebanon
- U.S. hostages held in Lebanon
- Civil war in Nicaragua
- Iran-contra crisis

Bush (the elder)

- Soviet Union dissolves
- Iraq invades Kuwait

Clinton

- Civil war continues in Bosnia and other parts of the former Yugoslavia
- Investigation of possible wrongdoing of President and Mrs. Clinton in Whitewater real estate development
- Clinton impeached

Bush (the younger)

- Terrorist attacks on World Trade Center and Pentagon kill close to 3,000 people
- U.S.-led war against terrorists in Afghanistan

The third constraint is the fact that the federal government and most federal programs, as well as the federal budget, can only be changed marginally, except in special circumstances. The vast bulk of federal expenditures are beyond control in any given year: the money must be spent whether the president likes it or not. Many federal programs have such strong congressional or public support that they must be left intact or modified only slightly. And this means that most federal employees can count on being secure in their jobs, whatever a president's views on reducing the bureaucracy.

The result of these constraints is that the president, at least in ordinary times, has to be selective about what he wants. He can be thought of as having a stock of influence and prestige the way that he might have a supply of money. If he wants to get the most "return" on his resources, he must "invest" that influence and prestige carefully in enterprises that promise substantial gains—in public benefits and political support—at reasonable costs. Each president tends to speak in terms of changing everything at once, calling his approach a "New Deal," a "New Frontier," a "Great Society," or the "New Federalism." But beneath the rhetoric he must identify a few specific proposals on which he wishes to bet his resources, mindful of the need to leave a substantial stock of resources in reserve to handle the inevitable crises and emergencies. In recent decades events have required every president to devote much of his time and resources to two key issues: the state of the economy and foreign affairs. What he manages to do beyond this will depend on his personal views and his sense of what the nation, as well as his reelection, requires.

And it will depend on one other thing: opinion polls. The last president who never used polls was Herbert Hoover. Franklin Roosevelt began making heavy use of them, and every president since has relied on them. Bill Clinton had voters polled about almost everything— where he should go on vacation (the West) and how to deal with Bosnia (no ground troops).

Once, when polls did not exist, politicians often believed that they should do what they thought the public interest required. Now that polls are commonplace, some politicians act on the basis of what their constituents want. Scholars call the first view the **trustee approach:** do what the public good requires, even if the voters are skeptical. The second view is the **delegate model:** do what your constituents want you to do.

But there is another way of looking at polls. They may be a device not for picking a policy but for deciding what language to use in explaining that policy. Choose a policy that helps you get reelected or that satisfies an interest group, but then explain it with poll-tested words. President Clinton wanted to keep affirmative action (described in the chapter titled "Civil Rights") but knew that most voters disliked it. So he used a poll-tested phrase—"mend it but don't end it"—and then did nothing to mend it.

Finally, a president's program can be radically altered by a dramatic event or prolonged crisis. George W. Bush ran as a candidate interested in domestic issues and with little background in foreign affairs, but the terrorist attack of September 11, 2001, on the World Trade Center and the Pentagon dramatically changed his presidency into one preoccupied with foreign and military policy. He quickly launched a military attack on the Taliban regime in Afghanistan and assembled an international coalition to support it. His approval ratings rose to the highest level yet recorded.

Attempts to Reorganize

One item on the presidential agenda has been the same for almost every president since Herbert Hoover: reorganizing the executive branch of government. In the wake of the terrorist attack on the United States on September 11, 2001, the president, by executive order, created a new White House Office of Homeland Security, headed by his friend and former Pennsylvania governor, Tom Ridge. In the

months that followed, it became clear to all, including the president, that he had given Ridge an impossible job. For one thing, despite its obvious importance, Ridge's office, like most units with the Executive Office of the President, had only a dozen or so full-time staff, little budgetary authority, and virtually no ability to make and enforce decisions regarding how cabinet agencies operated. Nobody could meaningfully coordinate the literally dozens of administrative units that the administration's new homeland security blueprint required Ridge's office to somehow manage.

To address this problem, President Bush called for a reorganization that would create the third-largest cabinet department encompassing twenty-two federal agencies, nearly 170,000 employees, and an annual budget of close to $40 billion. Among the federal agencies that will be placed under the new department of homeland security are the Coast Guard, the Customs Service, the Federal Emergency Management Agency, and the Immigration and Naturalization Service. A law authorizing a new department of homeland security was enacted in November 2002, but it will take years and much effort for the new agency to become fully operational.

Important as it is, the ongoing attempt to reorganize the federal government around homeland security goals is neither the first, nor even the largest, reorganization effort made by a sitting president. With few exceptions every president since 1928 has tried to change the structure of the staff, departments, and agencies that are theoretically subordinate to him. Every president has been appalled by the number of agencies that report to him and by the apparently helter-skelter manner in which they have grown up. But this is only one— and often not the most important—reason for wanting to reorganize. If a president wants to get something done, put new people in charge of a program, or recapture political support for a policy, it is often easier to do so by creating a new agency or reorganizing an old one than by abolishing a program, firing a subordinate, or passing a new law. Reorganization serves many objectives and thus is a recurring theme.

Legally the president can reorganize his personal White House staff anytime that he wishes. To reorganize in any important way the larger Executive Office of the President or any of the executive departments or agencies, however, Congress must

"15% LIKE YOU AS A CONSERVATIVE, 15% LIKE YOU LIBERAL, AND 70% DON'T CARE ... SO MY ADVICE IS TO REINVENT YOURSELF AS THE 'I DON'T CARE' CANDIDATE."

Polling dominates not only politics but also government, since some presidents rely on polls to decide how to discuss issues.

first be consulted. For over forty years this consultation usually took the form of submitting to Congress a reorganization plan that would take effect provided that neither the House nor the Senate passed, within sixty days, a concurrent resolution disapproving the plan (such a resolution was called a **legislative veto**). This procedure, first authorized by the Reorganization Act of 1939, could be used to change, but not create or abolish, an executive agency. In 1981 authority under that act expired, and Congress did not renew it. Two years later the Supreme Court declared that all legislative vetoes were unconstitutional (see Chapter 13), and so today any presidential reorganization plan would have to take the form of a regular law, passed by Congress and signed by the president.

What has been said so far may well give the reader the impression that the president is virtually helpless. That is not the case. The *actual* power of the president can only be measured in terms of what he can accomplish. What this chapter has described so far is the office as the president finds it—the burdens, restraints, demands, complexities, and resources that he encounters on entering the Oval Office for the first time. Every president since Truman has commented feelingly on how limited the powers of the president seem from the inside compared to what they appear to be from the outside. Franklin Roosevelt compared his struggles with the bureaucracy to punching a feather bed; Truman wrote that the power of the president was chiefly the power to persuade people to do what they ought to

do anyway. After being in office a year or so, Kennedy spoke to interviewers about how much more complex the world appeared than he had first supposed. Johnson and Nixon were broken by the office and the events that happened there.

Yet Franklin Roosevelt helped create the modern presidency, with its vast organizational reach, and directed a massive war effort. Truman ordered two atomic bombs dropped on Japanese cities. Eisenhower sent American troops to Lebanon; Kennedy supported an effort to invade Cuba. Johnson sent troops to the Dominican Republic and to Vietnam; Nixon ordered an invasion of Cambodia; Reagan launched an invasion of Grenada and sponsored an antigovernment insurgent group in Nicaragua; Bush invaded Panama and sent troops to the Persian Gulf to fight Iraq; Clinton sent troops to Haiti and Bosnia. George W. Bush ordered a U.S. military operation in Afghanistan. Obviously Europeans, Russians, Vietnamese, Cambodians, Dominicans, Panamanians, and Iraqis do not think of the American president as "helpless."

Presidential Transition

No president but Franklin Roosevelt has ever served more than two terms, and since the ratification of the Twenty-second Amendment in 1951, no president will ever again have the chance. But more than tradition or the Constitution escorts presidents from office. Only about one-third of the forty-two presidents since George Washington have been elected to a second term. Of the twenty-seven not reelected, four died in office during their first term. But the remainder either did not seek or (more usually) could not obtain reelection.

Of the eight presidents who died in office, four were assassinated: Lincoln, Garfield, McKinley, and Kennedy. At least six other presidents were the objects of unsuccessful assassination attempts: Jackson, Theodore Roosevelt, Franklin Roosevelt, Truman, Ford, and Reagan. (There may have been attempts on other presidents that never came to public notice; the attempts mentioned here involved public efforts to fire weapons at presidents.)

The presidents who served two or more terms fall into certain periods, such as the Founding (Washington, Jefferson, Madison, Monroe) or wartime (Lincoln, Wilson, Roosevelt), or they happened to be in office during especially tranquil times

(Monroe, McKinley, Eisenhower, Clinton), or some combination of the above. When the country was deeply divided, as during the years just before the Civil War and during the period of Reconstruction after it, it was the rare president who was reelected.

The Vice President

Eight times a vice president has become president because of the death of his predecessor. It first happened to John Tyler, who became president in 1841 when William Henry Harrison died peacefully after only one month in office. The question for Tyler and for the country was substantial: was Tyler simply to be the acting president and a kind of caretaker until a new president was elected, or was he to be *president* in every sense of the word? Despite criticism and despite what might have been the contrary intention of the Framers of the Constitution, Tyler decided on the latter course and was confirmed in that opinion by a decision of Congress. Ever since, the vice president has automatically become president, in title and in powers, when the occupant of the White House has died or resigned.

But if vice presidents frequently acquire office because of death, they rarely acquire it by election. Since the earliest period of the Founding, when John Adams and Thomas Jefferson were each elected president after having first served as vice president under their predecessors, there have only been three occasions when a vice president was later able to win the presidency without his president's having died in office. One was in 1836, when Martin Van Buren was elected president after having served as Andrew Jackson's vice president; the second was in 1968, when Richard Nixon became president after having served as Dwight Eisenhower's vice president eight years earlier; the third was in 1988, when George Bush succeeded Ronald Reagan. Many vice presidents who entered the Oval Office because their predecessors died were subsequently elected to terms in their own right—Theodore Roosevelt, Calvin Coolidge, Harry Truman, and Lyndon Johnson. But no one who wishes to become president should assume that to become vice president first is the best way to get there.

The vice-presidency is just what so many vice presidents have complained about its being: a rather empty job. John Adams described it as "the most insignificant office that ever the invention of man contrived or his imagination conceived," and most of his successors would have agreed. Thomas Jefferson, almost alone, had a good word to say for it: "The second office of the government is honorable and easy, the first is but a splendid misery."[19] Daniel Webster rejected a vice-presidential nomination in 1848 with the phrase, "I do not choose to be buried until I am really dead."[20] (Had he taken the job, he would have become president after Zachary Taylor died in office, thereby achieving a remarkable secular resurrection.) For all the good and bad jokes about the vice-presidency, however, candidates still struggle mightily for it. John Nance Garner gave up the speakership of the House to become Franklin Roosevelt's vice president (a job he valued as "not worth a pitcher of warm spit"*), and Lyndon Johnson gave up the majority leadership of the Senate to become Kennedy's. Truman, Nixon, Humphrey, Mondale, and Gore all left reasonably secure Senate seats for the vice-presidency.

The only official task of the vice president is to preside over the Senate and to vote in case of a tie. Even this is scarcely time-consuming, as the Senate chooses from among its members a president pro tempore, as required by the Constitution, who (along with others) presides in the absence of the vice president. The vice president's leadership powers in the Senate are weak, especially when the vice president is of a different party from the majority of the senators. But on occasion the vice president can become very important. Right after the terrorists attacked the United States in 2001, President Bush was in his airplane while his advisers worried that he might be attacked next. Vice President Cheney was quickly hidden away in a secret, secure location so he could run the government if anything happened to President Bush. And for many months thereafter, Cheney stayed in this location in case he suddenly became president. But absent a crisis, the vice president is, at best, only an adviser to the president.

Problems of Succession

If the president should die in office, the right of the vice president to assume that office has been clear since the time of John Tyler. But two questions remain: What if the president falls seriously ill but does not die? And if the vice president steps up, who then becomes the new vice president?

The first problem has arisen on a number of occasions. After President James A. Garfield was shot in 1881, he lingered through the summer before he died. President Woodrow Wilson collapsed from a stroke and was a virtual recluse for seven

---

*The word he actually used was a good deal stronger than *spit,* but historians are decorous.

President Reagan, moments before he was shot on March 30, 1981, by a would-be assassin. The Twenty-fifth Amendment solves the problem of presidential disability by providing for an orderly transfer of power to the vice president.

months in 1919 and an invalid for the rest of his term. Eisenhower had three serious illnesses while in office; Reagan was shot during his first term and hospitalized during his second.

The second problem has arisen on eight occasions when the vice president became president owing to the death of the incumbent. In these cases no elected person was available to succeed the new president should he die in office. For many decades the problem was handled by law. The Succession Act of 1886, for example, designated the secretary of state as next in line for the presidency should the vice president die, followed by the other cabinet officers in order of seniority. But this meant that a vice president who became president could pick his own successor by choosing his own secretary of state. In 1947 the law was changed to make the Speaker of the House and then the president pro tempore of the Senate next in line for the presidency. But that created still other problems: a Speaker or a president pro tempore is

likely to be chosen because of seniority, not executive skill, and in any event might well be of the party opposite to that occupying the White House.

Both problems were addressed in 1967 by the Twenty-fifth Amendment to the Constitution. It deals with the disability problem by allowing the vice president to serve as "acting president" whenever the president declares that he is unable to discharge the powers and duties of his office or whenever the vice president and a majority of the cabinet declare that the president is incapacitated. If the president disagrees with the opinion of his vice president and a majority of the cabinet, then Congress decides the issue. A two-thirds majority is necessary to confirm that the president is unable to serve.

The amendment deals with the succession problem by requiring a vice president who assumes the presidency (after a vacancy is created by death or resignation) to nominate a new vice president. This person takes office if the nomination is confirmed by a majority vote of both houses of Congress. When there is no vice president, then the 1947 law governs: next in line are the Speaker, the Senate president, and the fourteen cabinet officers, beginning with the secretary of state.

The disability problem has not arisen since the adoption of the amendment, but the succession problem has. In 1973 Vice President Spiro Agnew resigned, having pleaded no contest to criminal charges. President Nixon nominated Gerald Ford as vice president, and after extensive hearings he was confirmed by both houses of Congress and sworn in. Then on August 9, 1974, Nixon resigned the presidency—the first man to do so—and Ford became president. He nominated as his vice president Nelson Rockefeller, who was confirmed by both houses of Congress—again, after extensive hearings—and was sworn in on December 19, 1974. For the first time in history, the nation had as its two principal executive officers men who had not been elected to either the presidency or the vice-presidency. It is a measure of the legitimacy of the Constitution that this arrangement caused no crisis in public opinion.

Impeachment

There is one other way—besides death, disability, or resignation—by which a president can leave office before his term expires, and that is by impeachment. Not only the president and vice president but also all "civil officers of the United States" can be removed by being impeached and convicted. As a practical matter civil officers—cabinet secretaries, bureau chiefs, and the like—are not subject to impeachment, because the president can remove them at any time and usually will if their behavior makes them a serious political liability. Federal judges, who serve during "good behavior"* and who are constitutionally independent of the president and Congress, have been the most frequent objects of impeachment.

An **impeachment** is like an indictment in a criminal trial: a set of charges against somebody, voted by (in this case) the House of Representatives. To be removed from office, the impeached officer must be convicted by a two-thirds vote of the Senate,

---

*"Good behavior" means a judge can stay in office until he retires or dies, unless he or she is impeached and convicted.

President George W. Bush and Vice President Dick Cheney. Because in 2001–2002 the Senate was evenly divided between Democrats and Republicans, Vice President Cheney's role as the tie-breaker meant that Republicans controlled the chamber.

which sits as a court, hears the evidence, and makes its decision under whatever rules it wishes to adopt. Sixteen persons have been impeached by the House, and seven have been convicted by the Senate. The last conviction was in 1989, when two federal judges were removed from office.

Only two presidents have ever been impeached—Andrew Johnson in 1868 and Bill Clinton in 1998. Richard Nixon would surely have been impeached in 1974 had he not resigned after the House Judiciary Committee voted to recommend impeachment.

The Senate did not convict either Johnson or Clinton by the necessary two-thirds vote. The case against Johnson was entirely political—Radical Republicans, who wished to punish the South after the Civil War, were angry at Johnson, a southerner,

Lame Duck

A **lame duck** is a politician whose power has diminished because he or she is about to leave office as a result of electoral defeat or statutory limitation (for example, the president can serve no more than two terms).

The expression was first used in eighteenth-century England, where it meant a "bankrupt businessman." Soon it was used to refer to "bankrupt" politicians. Perhaps they were called "lame ducks" because they had been shot on the wing and, though still alive, could no longer fly.

A lame duck is not to be confused with a "sitting duck" (somebody who is an easy target).

Source: From *Safire's Political Dictionary* by William Safire. Copyright © 1968, 1972, 1978 by William Safire. Reprinted by permission of Random House, Inc. and the author.

who had a soft policy toward the South. The argument against him was flimsy.

The case against Clinton was more serious. The House Judiciary Committee, relying on the report of independent counsel Kenneth Starr, charged Clinton with perjury (lying under oath about his sexual affair with Monica Lewinsky), obstruction of justice (trying to block the Starr investigation), and abuse of power (making false written statements to the Judiciary Committee). The vote to impeach was passed by the House along party lines. A majority, but not two-thirds, of the Senate voted to convict.

Why did Clinton survive? There were many factors. The public disliked his private behavior but did not think it amounted to an impeachable offense. (In fact right after Lewinsky revealed her sexual affair with him, his standing in opinion polls went up.) The economy was strong, and the nation was at peace. Clinton was a centrist Democrat who did not offend most voters.

The one casualty of the entire episode was the death of the law creating the office of the Independent Counsel. Passed in 1978 by a Congress that was upset by the Watergate crisis, the law directed the attorney general to ask a three-judge panel to appoint an independent counsel whenever a high official is charged with serious misconduct. (In 1993, when the 1978 law expired, President Clinton asked that it be passed again. It was.) Eighteen people were investigated by various independent counsels from 1978 to 1999. In about half the cases, no charges were brought to court.

For a long time Republicans disliked the law because the counsels were investigating them. After Clinton came to office, the counsels started investigating him and his associates, and so the Democrats began to oppose it. In 1999, when the law expired, it was not renewed.

A problem remains, however. How will any high official, including the president, be investigated when the attorney general, who does most investigations, is part of the president's team? One answer is to let Congress do it, but Congress may be controlled by the president's party. No one has yet solved this puzzle.

Some Founders may have thought that impeachment would be used frequently against presidents, but as a practical matter it is so complex and serious an undertaking that we can probably expect it to be reserved in the future only for the gravest forms of presidential misconduct. No one quite knows what a high crime or misdemeanor is, but most scholars agree that the charge must involve something illegal or unconstitutional, not just unpopular. Unless a president or vice president is first impeached and convicted, many experts believe that he is not liable to prosecution as would be an ordinary citizen. (No one is certain, because the question has never arisen.) President Ford's pardon of Richard Nixon meant that he could not be prosecuted under federal law for things that he may have done while in office.

Students may find the occasions of misconduct or disability remote and the details of succession or impeachment tedious. But the problem is not remote—succession has occurred nine times and

Six-Year Term for President

Delegates Divided on Big Issue

October 15
EUDORA, KS

Here at the convention called to propose amendments to the United States Constitution, the major issue facing the delegates is the proposal to limit the president to a single six-year term. Proponents of the measure claim . . .

MEMORANDUM

To: Delegate James Nagle
From: Robert Gilbert, legal staff
Subject: Six-year presidential term

The proposal to give the president a single six-year term is perhaps the most popular amendment now before the convention. Polls suggest that it is supported by a sizable percentage of the American people.

Arguments for:

1. Today a president no sooner learns the ropes after being elected for the first time than he or she has to start preparing for the next election. A six-year term will give the president a chance to govern for several years after learning how to be president. This will lessen the extent to which political pressures dictate what the president does.
2. Limited to a single term, the president need not cater to special-interest groups or the media in deciding on policy. He or she can concentrate on what is good for the country.
3. Many states have limited their governors to a single term.

Arguments against:

1. It is the need to win reelection that keeps the president (like any politician) attentive to what the people want. A president unable to succeed himself or herself will be tempted to ignore public opinion.
2. Limiting a president to a single term will not free him or her from the need to play to the media or special-interest groups, since the formal powers of the presidency are too weak to permit the incumbent to govern without the aid of Congress and the press.
3. There is no evidence that presidents (such as Dwight Eisenhower) who served a second term knowing that they could not run for reelection did a better or less "political" job in the second term than in the first.

Your decision:
Favor amendment _____
Oppose amendment _____

disability at least twice—and what may appear tedious goes, in fact, to the heart of the presidency. The first and fundamental problem is to make the office legitimate. That was the great task George Washington set himself, and that was the substantial accomplishment of his successors. Despite bitter and sometimes violent partisan and sectional strife, beginning almost immediately after Washington stepped down, presidential succession has always occurred peacefully, without a military coup or a political plot. For centuries, in the bygone times of kings as well as in the present times of dictators and juntas, peaceful succession has been a rare event among the nations of the world. Many of the critics of the Constitution believed in 1787 that peaceful succession would not happen in the United States either: somehow the president would connive to hold office for life or to handpick his successor. Their predictions were wrong, though their fears are understandable.

How Powerful Is the President?

Just as members of Congress bemoan their loss of power, so presidents bemoan theirs. Can both be right?

In fact they can. If Congress is less able to control events than it once was, it does not mean that the president is thereby more able to exercise control. The federal government *as a whole* has become more constrained, so it is less able to act decisively. The chief source of this constraint is the greater complexity of the issues with which Washington must deal.

It was one thing to pass the Social Security Act in 1935; it is quite another thing to keep the Social Security system adequately funded. It was one thing for the nation to defend itself when attacked in 1941; it is quite another to maintain a constant military preparedness while simultaneously exploring possibilities for arms control. It was not hard to give pensions to veterans; it seems almost impossible today to find the cure for drug abuse or juvenile crime.

In the face of modern problems, all branches of government, including the presidency, seem both big and ineffectual. Add to this the much closer and more critical scrutiny of the media and the proliferation of interest groups, and it is small wonder that both presidents and members of Congress feel that they have lost power.

Presidents have come to acquire certain rules of thumb for dealing with their political problems. Among them are these:

- *Move it or lose it.* A president who wants to get something done should do it early in his term, before his political influence erodes.
- *Avoid details.* President Carter's lieutenants regret having tried to do too much. Better to have three or four top priorities and forget the rest.
- *Cabinets don't get much accomplished; people do.* Find capable White House subordinates and give them well-defined responsibility; then watch them closely.[21]

Summary

A U.S. president, chosen by the people and with powers derived from a written constitution, has less power than does a British prime minister, even though the latter depends entirely on the support of his or her party in Parliament. The separation of powers between the executive and legislative branches, the distinguishing feature of the American system, means that the president must deal with a competitor—Congress—in setting policy and even in managing executive agencies.

Presidential power, though still sharply limited, has grown from its constitutional origins as a result of congressional delegation, the increased importance of foreign affairs, and public expectations. But if the president today has more power, more is also demanded of him. As a result how effective he is depends not on any general grant of authority but on the nature of the issue that he confronts and the extent to which he can mobilize informal sources of power (public opinion, congressional support).

Though the president seemingly controls a vast executive-branch apparatus, in fact he appoints but a small portion of the officials, and the behavior of even these is often beyond his easy control. Moreover, public support, high at the beginning of any new presidency, usually declines as the term proceeds. Consequently each president must conserve his power (and his energy and time), concentrating these scarce resources to deal with a few matters of major importance. Virtually every president since Franklin Roosevelt has tried to enlarge his ability to manage the executive branch—by reorganization, by appointing White House aides, by creating specialized staff agencies—but no president has been satisfied with the results.

The extent to which a president will be weak or powerful will vary with the kind of issue and the circumstances of the moment. It is a mistake to speak of an "imperial presidency" or of an ineffectual one. A president's power is better assessed by considering how he behaves in regard to specific issues.

Reconsidering the Enduring Questions

1. *Did the Founding Fathers want the president to be stronger or weaker than Congress?*

   The Framers of the Constitution wanted a president, not a prime minister, and they vested Congress, not the executive, with the government's lawmaking authority. While they desired ample "energy in the executive," and while they often spoke and wrote of three "co-equal" branches, Congress was intended by them to be the "first branch" of American national government, capable of checking the president's power, passing laws over a presidential veto, and limiting the Supreme Court's appellate jurisdiction. At the same time, however, the Framers were determined that, at least in foreign affairs, the president would normally be first among equals. During times of war and other national crises, presidents have wielded extraordinary powers, almost always with little resistance (at least at first) from Congress. In normal times, America's system of separated institutions sharing powers has sometimes favored presidents over Congress, but usually only after Congress itself assented to an expansion in presidential powers. For example, virtually every one of the major budgetary powers and functions presently exercised by the White House was initiated and legislated into being by Congress, beginning with laws passed in the 1920s. But when, as it did in the mid-1970s, Congress decides to take back some of its budgetary and other powers, there is little that even popular presidents can do about it except complain.

2. *Does the personal character of a president make a difference in how he does his job?*

   Naturally, it does, but personal character is but one of several factors affecting how, and how well, a president fares politically and discharges constitutional duties. For example, President Eisenhower, a lifelong military man in his sixties when he became president in 1952, organized the White House into highly structured units. His successor, President Kennedy, a man with military experience but a senator in his forties when he became president in 1960, favored having senior staff relate to him and to each other through collegial groupings more reminiscent of university than of military life. President Nixon was a so-so public speaker with a brooding personality. He disliked the media and was disliked in turn by many reporters. President Reagan was a gifted public speaker with a sunny personality. Many in the media who disagreed strongly with his policy views liked him nonetheless. President Johnson was a master legislative strategist who loved brokering deals with members of Congress. President Carter was a highly intelligent man who clearly never much enjoyed inside-the-beltway politics. But the differences in how these presidents governed and with what success are hardly all due to differences in presidential character. For example, President Johnson moved massive amounts of new domestic legislation through Congress. His personality was definitely part of that story, but so were the fact that he had won office by a landslide, his party had overwhelming majorities in both congressional chambers, and he could (and often did) invoke the memory of his immediate predecessor, the fallen President Kennedy, to muster media sympathy and mass support for controversial measures.

3. Should we abolish the electoral college?

Most Americans think we should, and soon. But, then again, most Americans, even after the 2000 presidential election controversy, do not really know how the system presently works. First, the system is a bulwark of American federalism and heightens the influence of states in national politics. Because of its winner-take-all feature (in effect in all but two states), candidates have a strong incentive to campaign hard in big states they have a chance of winning. Second, if we relied just on the popular vote, there would have to be a runoff election among the two leading candidates if neither got a majority because third-party candidates won a lot of votes. This would encourage the formation of third parties, and American presidential politics might come to resemble the multiparty systems we find in France and Italy. If that is what we want, then we should abolish the electoral college. But if not, then we should preserve the system or reform it in more minor ways.

World Wide Web Resources

- www.whitehouse.gov
- www.ipl.org/ref/POTUS/
- lcweb.loc.gov/global/executive/fed.html
- www.interlink-cafe.com/uspresidents

Key Terms

divided government *p. 331*
unified government *p. 331*
representative democracy *p. 333*
direct democracy *p. 333*
pyramid structure *p. 342*
circular structure *p. 342*
ad hoc structure *p. 342*
perks *p. 344*
cabinet *p. 345*

veto message *p. 356*
pocket veto *p. 356*
line-item veto *p. 357*
trustee approach *p. 361*
delegate model *p. 361*
legislative veto *p. 362*
impeachment *p. 365*
lame duck *p. 366*

Suggested Readings

General

Barber, James David. *The Presidential Character*. 3d ed. Englewood Cliffs, N.J.: Prentice-Hall, 1985. How a president's personality evolves and shapes his conduct in office.

Corwin, Edward S. *The President: Office and Powers*. 5th ed. New York: New York University Press, 1985. Historical, constitutional, and legal development of the office.

Jones, Charles O. *Passage to the Presidency* (Washington, D.C.: Brookings Institution, 1998). Insightful account of how four presidents—Nixon, Carter, Reagan, and Clinton—moved from the campaign to the presidency.

Neustadt, Richard E. *Presidential Power: The Politics of Leadership*. Rev. ed. New York: Wiley, 1976. How presidents try to acquire and hold political power in the competitive world of official Washington, by a man who has been both a scholar and an insider.

Peterson, Mark A. *Legislating Together: The White House and Congress from Eisenhower to Reagan*. Cambridge: Harvard University Press, 1990. Challenges the conventional view that "the president proposes, Congress disposes." Contains many excellent examples of bargaining and cooperation between Congress and the executive branch.

On Franklin D. Roosevelt

Leuchtenberg, William E. *Franklin D. Roosevelt and the New Deal, 1932–1940*. New York: Harper & Row, 1963.

Maney, Richard J. *The Roosevelt Presence*. New York: Twayne, 1992.

On Harry S Truman

Hamby, A. L. *Beyond the New Deal: Harry S Truman and American Liberalism*. New York: Columbia University Press, 1973.

McCullough, David. *Truman*. New York: Simon and Schuster, 1984.

On Dwight D. Eisenhower

Ambrose, Stephen E. *Eisenhower*. New York: Simon and Schuster, 1984.

Greenstein, Fred I. *The Hidden-Hand Presidency: Eisenhower as Leader*. New York: Basic Books, 1982.

On John F. Kennedy

Paper, Lewis J. *The Promise and the Performance: The Leadership of John F. Kennedy*. New York: Crown, 1975.

Parmet, Herbert C. *Jack*. New York: Dial Press, 1980.

On Lyndon B. Johnson

Dallek, Robert. *Lone Star Rising and Flawed Giant*. New York: Oxford University Press, 1991 and 1996.

Kearns, Doris. *Lyndon Johnson and the American Dream*. New York: Harper and Row, 1976.

On Richard M. Nixon

Ambrose, Stephen E. ———. *Nixon*. 3 vols. New York: Simon and Schuster, 1987, 1989, 1991.

On Jimmy Carter

Bourne, Peter G. *Jimmy Carter*. New York: Scribner, 1997.

On Ronald Reagan

Cannon, Lou. *President Reagan*. New York: Simon and Schuster, 1991.

On George Bush

Parmet, Herbert C. *George Bush*. New York: Scribner, 1997.

The Bureaucracy

Enduring Questions

1. What happened to make the bureaucracy a "fourth branch" of American national government?

2. What are the actual size and scope of the federal bureaucracy?

3. What has been done to improve bureaucratic performance?

There is probably not a man or woman in the United States who has not, at some time or other, complained about "the bureaucracy." Your letter was slow in getting to Aunt Minnie? The Internal Revenue Service took months to send you your tax refund? The Defense Department paid $400 for a hammer? The Occupational Safety and Health Administration told you that you installed the wrong kind of portable toilet for your farm workers? The "bureaucracy" is to blame.

For most people and politicians *bureaucracy* is a pejorative word implying waste, confusion, red tape, and rigidity. But for scholars—and for bureaucrats themselves—*bureaucracy* is a word with a neutral, technical meaning. A **bureaucracy** is a large, complex organization composed of appointed officials. By *complex* we mean that authority is divided among several managers; no one person is able to make all the decisions. A large corporation is a bureaucracy; so also are a big university and a government agency. With its sizable staff, even Congress has become, to some degree, a bureaucracy.

What is it about complex organizations in general, and government agencies in particular, that leads so many people to complain about them? In part the answer is to be found in their very size and complexity.

373

But in large measure the answer is to be found in the political context within which such agencies must operate. If we examine that context carefully, we will discover that many of the problems that we blame on "the bureaucracy" are in fact the result of what Congress, the courts, and the president do.

Distinctiveness of the American Bureaucracy

Bureaucratic government has become an obvious feature of all modern societies, democratic and nondemocratic. In the United States, however, three aspects of our constitutional system and political traditions give to the bureaucracy a distinctive character. First, political authority over the bureaucracy is not in one set of hands but is shared among several institutions. In a parliamentary regime, such as in Great Britain, the appointed officials of the national government work for the cabinet ministers, who are in turn dominated by the prime minister. In theory, and to a considerable extent in practice, British bureaucrats report to and take orders from the ministers in charge of their departments, do not deal directly with Parliament, and rarely give interviews to the press. In the United States the Constitution permits both the president and Congress to exercise authority over the bureaucracy. Every senior appointed official has at least two masters: one in the executive branch and the other in the legislative. Often there are many more than two: Congress, after all, is not a single organization but a collection of committees, subcommittees, and individuals. This divided authority encourages bureaucrats to play one branch of government off against the other and to make heavy use of the media.

Second, most of the agencies of the federal government share their functions with related agencies in state and local government. Though some federal agencies deal directly with American citizens—the Internal Revenue Service collects taxes from them, the Federal Bureau of Investigation looks into crimes for them, the Postal Service delivers mail to them—many agencies work with other organizations at other levels of government. For example, the Department of Education gives money to local school systems; the Health Care Financing Administration in the Department of Health and Human Services reimburses states for money spent on health care for the poor; the Department of Housing and Urban Development gives grants to cities for community development; and the Employment and Training Administration in the Department of Labor supplies funds to local governments so that they can run job-training programs. In France, by contrast, government programs dealing with education, health, housing, and employment are centrally run, with little or no control exercised by local governments.

Third, the institutions and traditions of American life have contributed to the growth of what some writers have described as an "adversary culture," in which the definition and expansion of personal rights, and the defense of rights and claims through lawsuits as well as political action, are given central importance. A government agency in this country operates under closer public scrutiny and with a greater prospect of court challenges to its authority than in almost any other nation. Virtually every important decision of the Occupational Safety and Health Administration or of the Environmental Protection Agency is likely to be challenged in the courts or attacked by an affected party; in Sweden the decisions of similar agencies go largely uncontested.

The scope as well as the style of bureaucratic government differs. In most Western European nations the government owns and operates large parts of the economy: the French government operates the railroads and owns companies that make automobiles and cigarettes, and the Italian government owns many similar enterprises and also the nation's oil refineries. In just about every large nation except the United States, the telephone system is owned by the government. Publicly operated enterprises account for about 12 percent of all employment in France but less than 3 percent in the United States.[1] The U.S. government regulates privately owned enterprises to a degree not found in many other countries, however. Why we should have preferred regulation to ownership as the proper government role is an interesting question to which we shall return.

The Growth of the Bureaucracy

The Constitution made scarcely any provision for an administrative system other than to allow the president to appoint, with the advice and consent of the Senate, "ambassadors, other public ministers and consuls, judges of the Supreme Court, and all other officers of the United States whose appointments are not herein otherwise provided for, and which shall be established by law."[2] Departments and bureaus were not mentioned.

In the first Congress, in 1789, James Madison introduced a bill to create a Department of State to assist the new secretary of state, Thomas Jefferson, in carrying out his duties. People appointed to this department were to be nominated by the president and approved by the Senate, but they were "to be removable by the president" alone. These six words, which would confer the right to fire government officials, occasioned six days of debate in the House. At stake was the locus of power over what was to become the bureaucracy. Madison's opponents argued that the Senate should consent to the removal of officials as well as their appointment. Madison responded that, without the unfettered right of removal, the president would not be able to control his subordinates, and without this control he would not be able to discharge his constitutional obligation to "take care that the laws be faithfully executed."[3] Madison won, twenty-nine votes to twenty-two. When the issue went to the Senate, another debate resulted in a tie vote, broken in favor of the president by Vice President John Adams. The Department of State, and all cabinet departments subsequently created, would be run by people removable only by the president.

That decision did not resolve the question of who would really control the bureaucracy, however. Congress retained the right to appropriate money, to investigate the administration, and to shape the laws that would be executed by that administration—more than ample power to challenge any president who claimed to have sole authority over his subordinates. And many members of Congress expected that the cabinet departments, even though headed by people removable by the president, would report to Congress.

The government in Washington was at first minuscule. The State Department started with only nine employees; the War Department did not have eighty civilian employees until 1801. Only the Treasury Department, concerned with collecting taxes and finding ways to pay the public debt, had much power, and only the Post Office Department provided any significant service.

The Appointment of Officials

Small as the bureaucracy was, people struggled, often bitterly, over who would be appointed to it. From George Washington's day to modern times, presidents have found appointment to be one of their most important and difficult tasks. The officials that they select affect how the laws are interpreted (thus the political ideology of the job holders is important), what tone the administration will display (thus personal character is important), how effectively the public business is discharged (thus competence is important), and how strong the political party or faction in power will be (thus party affiliation is important). Presidents trying to balance the competing needs of ideology, character, fitness, and partisanship have rarely pleased most people. As John Adams remarked, every appointment creates one ingrate and ten enemies.

Because Congress, during most of the nineteenth and twentieth centuries, was the dominant branch of government, congressional preferences often controlled the appointment of officials. And since Congress was, in turn, a collection of people who represented local interests, appointments were made with an eye to rewarding the local supporters of members of Congress or building up local party organizations. These appointments made on the basis of political considerations—patronage—were later to become a major issue. They galvanized various reform efforts that sought to purify politics and to raise the level of competence of the public service. Many of the abuses that the reformers complained about were real enough, but patronage served some useful purposes as well. It gave the president a way to ensure that his subordinates were reasonably supportive of his policies; it provided a reward that the president could use to induce recalcitrant members of Congress to vote for his programs; and it enabled party organizations to be built up to perform the necessary functions of nominating candidates and getting out the vote.

Though at first there were not many jobs to fight over, by the middle of the nineteenth century there were a lot. From 1816 to 1861 the number of federal employees increased eightfold. This expansion was not, however, the result of the government's taking on new functions but simply a result of the increased demands on its traditional functions. The Post Office alone accounted for 86 percent of this growth.[4]

The Civil War was a great watershed in bureaucratic development. Fighting the war led, naturally, to hiring many new officials and creating many new offices. Just as important, the Civil War revealed the administrative weakness of the federal government and led to demands by the civil service reform movement for an improvement in the quality and

★ POLITICALLY SPEAKING ★

Spoils System

The **spoils system** is another phrase for *political patronage*—that is, the practice of giving the fruits of a party's victory, such as jobs and contracts, to the loyal members of that party.

Spoils became a famous word when it was used in 1832 by Senator William Marcy of New York in a speech that he made defending the decision of President Andrew Jackson to appoint one of his supporters, Martin Van Buren, as ambassador to Great Britain. New York politicians, he said, "boldly preach what they practice. . . . If they are successful, they claim, as a matter of right, the advantages of success. They see nothing wrong in the rule, that to the victor belong the spoils of the enemy."

In fact both the word and the practice are much older than Marcy and Jackson. Thomas Jefferson had appointed his partisans to office when he won the presidency from John Adams. Though Jackson is remembered as a heavy user of spoils, in fact he only replaced about 20 percent of all the officeholders that he inherited from his predecessor.

By the late nineteenth century the spoils system was both more extensively used and sharply criticized. Ending the system and replacing it with appointments based on merit was a major goal of the progressive movement around the turn of the century.

Today most federal appointments are based on merit, but in many state governments there continues to be a heavy reliance on patronage.

Source: From *Safire's Political Dictionary* by William Safire. Copyright © 1968, 1972, 1978 by William Safire. Reprinted by permission of Random House, Inc. and the author.

organization of federal employees. And finally, the war was followed by a period of rapid industrialization and the emergence of a national economy. The effects of these developments could no longer be managed by state governments acting alone. With the creation of a nationwide network of railroads, commerce among the states became increasingly important. The constitutional powers of the federal government to regulate interstate commerce, long dormant for want of much commerce to regulate, now became an important source of controversy.

A Service Role

From 1861 to 1901 new agencies were created, many to deal with particular sectors of society and the economy. Over two hundred thousand new federal employees were added, with only about half of this increase in the Post Office. The rapidly growing Pension Office began paying benefits to Civil War veterans; the Department of Agriculture was created in 1862 to help farmers; the Department of Labor was founded in 1882 to serve workers; and the Department of Commerce was organized in 1903 to assist businesspeople. Many more specialized agencies, such as the National Bureau of Standards, also came into being.

These agencies had one thing in common: their role was primarily to serve, not to regulate. Most did research, gathered statistics, dispensed federal lands, or passed out benefits. Not until the Interstate Commerce Commission (ICC) was created in 1887 did the federal government begin to regulate the economy (other than by managing the currency) in any large way. Even the ICC had, at first, relatively few powers.

There were several reasons why federal officials primarily performed a service role. The values that had shaped the Constitution were still strong: these included a belief in limited government, the importance of states' rights, and the fear of concentrated discretionary power. The proper role of government in the economy was to promote, not to regulate, and a commitment to **laissez-faire**—a freely competitive economy—was strongly held. But just as important, the Constitution said nothing about giving any regulatory powers to bureaucrats. It gave to *Congress* the power to regulate commerce among the states. Now obviously Congress could not make the necessary day-to-day decisions to regulate, for example, the rates that interstate railroads charged to farmers and other shippers. Some agency or commission composed of appointed officials and experts would have to be created to do

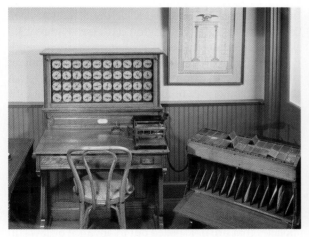

The Hollerith machine (left), invented by Herman Hollerith, helped the government calculate census data in the early part of the twentieth century. Today, high-speed computers, such as these in Phoenix, do the job at great speed.

that. For a long time, however, the prevailing interpretation of the Constitution was that no such agency could exercise such regulatory powers unless Congress first set down clear standards that would govern the agency's decisions. As late as 1935 the Supreme Court held that a regulatory agency could not make rules on its own; it could only apply the standards enacted by Congress.[5] The Court's view was that the legislature may not delegate its powers to the president or to an administrative agency.[6]

These restrictions on what administrators could do were set aside in wartime. During World War I, for example, President Woodrow Wilson was authorized by Congress to fix prices, operate the railroads, manage the communications system, and even control the distribution of food.[7] This kind of extraordinary grant of power usually ended with the war.

Some changes in the bureaucracy did not end with the war. During the Civil War, World War I, World War II, the Korean War, and the war in Vietnam, the number of civilian (as well as military) employees of the government rose sharply. These increases were not simply in the number of civilians needed to help serve the war effort; many of the additional people were hired by agencies, such as the Treasury Department, not obviously connected with the war. Furthermore, the number of federal officials did not return to prewar levels after each war. Though there was some reduction, each war left the number of federal employees larger than before.[8]

It is not hard to understand how this happens. During wartime almost every government agency argues that its activities have *some* relation to the war effort, and few legislators want to be caught voting against something that may help that effort. Hence in 1944 the Reindeer Service in Alaska, an agency of the Interior Department, asked for more employees because reindeer are "a valued asset in military planning."

A Change in Role

Today's bureaucracy is largely a product of two events: the depression of the 1930s (and the concomitant New Deal program of President Roosevelt) and World War II. Though many agencies have been added since then, the basic features of the bureaucracy were set mainly as a result of changes in public attitudes and in constitutional interpretation that occurred during these periods. The government was now expected to play an active role in dealing with economic and social problems. In the late 1930s the Supreme Court reversed its earlier decisions (see Chapter 14) on the question of delegating legislative powers to administrative agencies and upheld laws by which Congress merely instructs agencies to make decisions that serve "the public interest" in some area.[9] As a result it was possible for President Nixon to set up in 1971 a system of price and wage controls based on a statute that simply authorized the president "to issue such orders and regulations as he may deem appropriate to stabilize prices, rents, wages, and salaries."[10] The Cost of Living Council and other agencies that Nixon established to carry out this order were run by appointed officials who had the legal authority to make sweeping decisions based on general statutory language.

World War II was the first occasion during which the government made heavy use of federal income taxes—on individuals and corporations—to finance its activities. Between 1940 and 1945 total federal tax collections increased from about $5 billion to nearly $44 billion. The end of the war brought no substantial tax reduction: the country believed that a high level of military preparedness continued to be necessary and that various social programs begun before the war should enjoy the heavy funding made possible by wartime taxes. Tax receipts continued, by and large, to grow. Before 1913, when the Sixteenth Amendment to the Constitution was passed, the federal government could not collect income taxes at all (it financed itself largely from customs duties and excise taxes). From 1913 to 1940 income taxes were small (in 1940 the average American paid only $7 in federal income taxes). World War II created the first great financial boom for the government, permitting the sustained expansion of a wide variety of programs and thus entrenching a large number of administrators in Washington.[11]

The Federal Bureaucracy Today

No president wants to admit that he has increased the size of the bureaucracy. He can avoid saying this by pointing out that the number of civilians working for the federal government, excluding postal workers, has not increased significantly in recent years and is about the same today (2 million persons) as it was in 1960, and less than it was during World War II. This explanation is true but misleading, for it neglects the roughly 13 million people who work *indirectly* for Washington as employees of private firms and state or local agencies that are largely, if not entirely, supported by federal funds. As Figure 13.1 shows, there are nearly three persons earning their living indirectly from the federal government for every one earning it directly. While federal employment has remained quite stable, employment among federal contractors and consultants and in state and local governments has mushroomed. Indeed, most federal bureaucrats, like

most other people who work for the federal government, live outside Washington, D.C. (see Figure 13.3 later in this chapter).

The power of the federal bureaucracy cannot be measured by the number of employees, however. A bureaucracy of five million persons would have little power if each employee did nothing but type letters or file documents, whereas a bureaucracy of only one hundred persons would have awesome power if each member were able to make arbitrary life-and-death decisions affecting the rest of us. The power of the bureaucracy depends on the extent to which appointed officials have **discretionary authority**—that is, the ability to choose courses of action and to make policies that are not spelled out in advance by laws. In Figure 13.2 we see how the volume of regulations issued and the amount of money spent have risen much faster than the number of federal employees who write the regulations and spend the money.

By this test the power of the federal bureaucracy has grown enormously. Congress has delegated substantial authority to administrative agencies in three areas: (1) paying subsidies to particular groups and organizations in society (farmers, veterans, scientists, schools, universities, hospitals); (2) transferring money from the federal government to state and local governments (the grant-in-aid programs described in Chapter 3); and (3) devising and enforcing regulations for various sectors of society and the economy. Some of

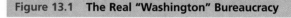

Figure 13.1   The Real "Washington" Bureaucracy

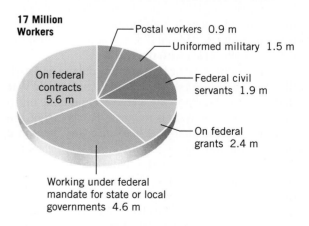

Source: Paul C. Light, *The True Size of Government* (Washington, D.C.: Brookings Institution, 1999). Data for 1996.

these administrative functions, such as grants-in-aid to states, are closely monitored by Congress; others, such as the regulatory programs, usually operate with a greater degree of independence. These delegations of power, especially in the areas of paying subsidies and regulating the economy, did not become commonplace until the 1930s, and then only after the Supreme Court decided that such delegations were constitutional. Today, by contrast, appointed officials can decide, within rather broad limits, who shall own a television station, what safety features automobiles shall have, what kinds of scientific research shall be specially encouraged, what drugs shall appear on the market, which dissident groups shall be investigated, what fumes an industrial smokestack may emit, which corporate mergers shall be allowed, what use shall be made of national forests, and what prices crop and dairy farmers shall receive for their products.

If appointed officials have this kind of power, then how they use it is of paramount importance in understanding modern government. There are, broadly, four factors that may explain the behavior of these officials:

1. The manner in which they are recruited and rewarded
2. Their personal attributes, such as their socioeconomic backgrounds and their political attitudes
3. The nature of their jobs
4. The constraints that outside forces—political superiors, legislators, interest groups, journalists—impose on their agencies

Recruitment and Retention

The federal civil service system was designed to recruit qualified people on the basis of merit, not political patronage, and to retain and promote employees on the basis of performance, not political favoritism. Many appointed federal officials belong to the **competitive service.** This means that they are appointed only after they have passed a written examination administered by the Office of Personnel Management (OPM) or met certain selection criteria (such as training, educational attainments, or prior experience) devised by the hiring agency and approved by the OPM. Where competition for a job exists and candidates can be ranked by their scores or records, the agency must usually appoint one of the three top-ranking candidates.

In recent years the competitive service system has become decentralized, so that each agency now hires

Figure 13.2 Federal Government: Money, People, and Regulations

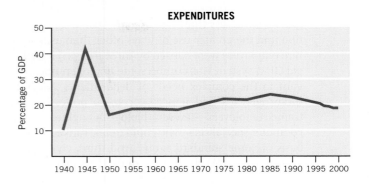

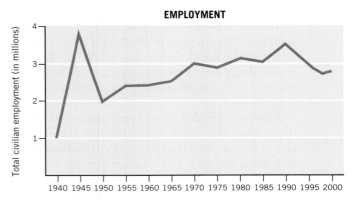

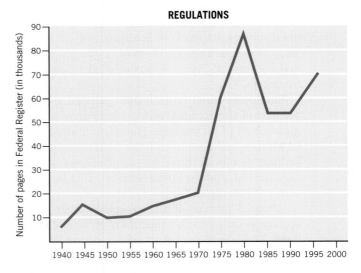

Sources: Expenditures and employment: *Statistical Abstract of the United States, 2000*, Nos. 483 and 582; regulations: Harold W. Stanley and Richard G. Niemi, *Vital Statistics on American Politics* (Washington, D.C.: Congressional Quarterly Press, 1998), tables 6-12, 6-14.

its own people without an OPM referral, and examinations have become less common. In 1952 more than 86 percent of all federal employees were civil servants hired by the competitive service; by 1996 that figure had fallen to less than 54 percent. This decentralization and the greater use of ways other than exams to hire employees were caused by three things. First, the old OPM system was cumbersome and often not relevant to the complex needs of departments. Second, these agencies had a need for more professionally trained employees—lawyers, biologists, engineers, and computer specialists—who could not be ranked on the basis of some standard exam. And third, civil rights groups pressed Washington to make the racial composition of the federal bureaucracy look more like the racial composition of the nation.

Thus it is wrong to suppose that a standardized, centralized system governs the federal service. As one recent study concluded, today much of the "real responsibility for recruiting, testing, and hiring has shifted to the agencies from OPM and its central system."[12]

Moreover, the kinds of workers being recruited into the federal civil service have changed. For example, blue-collar employment fell from 26 percent of the federal work force in 1973 to 16 percent in 1993. Meanwhile, the federal government's white-collar work force has become more diverse occupationally. As one writer on civil service reform has noted, the "need to recruit and retain physicists, biologists, oceanographers, nurses, statisticians, botanists, and epidemiologists, as well as large numbers of engineers, lawyers, and accountants, now preoccupies federal personnel managers."[13]

Employees hired outside the competitive service are part of the excepted service. They now make up almost half of all workers. Though not hired by the OPM, they still are typically hired in a nonpartisan fashion. Some are hired by agencies—such as the CIA, the FBI, and the Postal Service—that have their own selection procedures.

About 3 percent of the excepted employees are appointed on grounds other than or in addition to merit. These legal exceptions exist to permit the president to select, for policy-making and politically sensitive posts, people who are in agreement with his policy views. Such appointments are generally of three kinds:

1. Presidential appointments authorized by statute (cabinet and subcabinet officers, judges, U.S. mar-

Federal employees aren't just paper shufflers; many, such as this biologist, perform skilled professional tasks.

shals and U.S. attorneys, ambassadors, and members of various boards and commissions).
2. "Schedule C" appointments to jobs that are described as having a "confidential or policy-determining character" below the level of cabinet or subcabinet posts (including executive assistants, special aides, and confidential secretaries).
3. Noncareer executive assignments (NEAs) given to high-ranking members of the regular competitive civil service or to persons brought into the civil service at these high levels. These people are deeply involved in the advocacy of presidential programs or participate in policy-making.

These three groups of excepted appointments constitute the patronage available to a president and his administration. When President Kennedy took office in 1961, he had 451 political jobs to fill. When President Clinton took office in 1993, he had more

A Day in the Life of a Bureaucrat

Here is how the commissioner of the Social Security Administration (SSA), a high-level bureaucrat, spent a typical day:

5:45 A.M.	Arise.
6:50 A.M.	Leave for the office.
7:30 A.M.	Read newspapers.
8:00 A.M.	Meet with deputy commissioner.
8:30 A.M.	Brief cabinet secretary on Social Security data.*
9:45 A.M.	Decide how to respond to press criticisms.
10:05 A.M.	Leave for meeting in another building.
11:30 A.M.	Meet with top staff.
1:00 P.M.	Meet with bureau chiefs on half a dozen issues.
2:45 P.M.	Meet with a deputy to discuss next year's budget.
3:30 P.M.	Meet with business executive about use of computers in SSA.
4:30 P.M.	Meet with deputy in charge of Medicare to discuss plan for national health insurance.
5:10 P.M.	Catch up on phone calls; meet with committee concerned with drug abuse.
6:10 P.M.	Leave for home. Get out of attending a dinner meeting in Washington.

As is obvious, high-level bureaucrats spend most of their time discussing things in meetings. It is in such meetings that government policy is made.

*SSA was part of the Department of Health and Human Services but no longer is.

Source: Adapted from "A Day in the Life of a Government Executive," in *Inside the System,* ed. Charles Peters and Nicholas Leamann, 4th ed. (New York: Holt, Rinehart and Winston, 1979), 205–213.

than four times that number, including nearly four times the number of top cabinet posts (see Table 13.1 on page 382). Scholars disagree over whether this proliferation of political appointees has improved or worsened Washington's performance, but one thing is clear: widespread presidential patronage is hardly unprecedented. In the nineteenth century practically every federal job was a patronage job. For example, when Grover Cleveland, a Democrat, became president in 1885, he replaced some forty thousand Republican postal employees with Democrats.

Ironically, two years earlier, in 1883, the passage of the Pendleton Act had begun a slow but steady transfer of federal jobs from the patronage to the merit system. It may seem strange that a political party in power (the Republicans) would be willing to relinquish its patronage in favor of a merit-based appointment system. Two factors made it possible for the Republicans to pass the Pendleton Act: (1) public outrage over the abuses of the spoils system, highlighted by the assassination of President James Garfield by a man always described in the history books as a "disappointed office seeker" (*lunatic* would be a more accurate term); and (2) the fear that if the Democrats came to power on a wave of antispoils sentiment, existing Republican officeholders would be fired. (The Democrats won anyway.)

The merit system spread to encompass most of the federal bureaucracy, generally with presidential support. Though presidents may have liked in theory the idea of hiring and firing subordinates at will, most felt that the demands for patronage were impossible either to satisfy or to ignore. Furthermore, by increasing the coverage of the merit system a president could "blanket in" patronage appointees already holding office, thus making it difficult or impossible for the next administration to fire them.

■ **The Buddy System**   The actual recruitment of civil servants, especially in middle- and upper-level jobs, is somewhat more complicated, and slightly more political, than the laws and rules might suggest. Though many people enter the federal bureaucracy by learning of a job, filling out an application, perhaps taking a test, and being hired, many also enter on a "name-request" basis. A **name-request job** is one that is filled by a person whom an agency has already identified. In this respect the federal government is not so different from private business. A person learns of a job from somebody who already has one, or the head of a bureau decides in advance whom he or she wishes to hire. The agency must still send a form describing the job to the OPM, but it also names the person whom the agency wants to appoint. Sometimes the job is even described in such a way that the person named is the

Table 13.1	The Rise in Top Political Jobs	
	Administration	
	Kennedy	Clinton
Top cabinet posts		
Secretary	10	14
Deputy secretary	6	21
Undersecretary	14	32
Assistant secretary	81	212
Deputy assistant secretary	77	507
Deputy administrator	52	190
Total top cabinet posts	240	976
Total top political jobs	451	2,393

Source: Paul C. Light, *Thickening Government* (Washington, D.C.: Brookings Institution, 1995).

ical supporter taken care of; more often it is made available because the bureaucracy itself knows whom it wishes to hire and wants to circumvent an elaborate search. This is the "buddy system."

The buddy system does not necessarily produce poor employees. Indeed, it is frequently a way of hiring people known to the agency as being capable of handling the position. It also opens up the possibility of hiring people whose policy views are congenial to those already in office. Such networking is based on shared policy views, not (as once was the case) on narrow partisan affiliations. For example, bureaucrats in consumer protection agencies recruit new staff from private groups with an interest in consumer protection, such as the various organizations associated with Ralph Nader, or from academics who have a proconsumer inclination.

There has always been an informal "old boys' network" among those who move in and out of high-level government posts; with the increasing appointment of women to these jobs, there has begun to

only one who can qualify for it. Occasionally this tailor-made, name-request job is offered to a person at the insistence of a member of Congress who wants a polit-

One barrier to improving presidential control of the federal bureaucracy is that even the White House has become a large bureaucracy.

Firing a Bureaucrat

To fire or demote a member of the competitive civil service, these procedures must be followed:

1. The employee must be given written notice at least thirty days in advance that he or she is to be fired or demoted for incompetence or misconduct.
2. The written notice must contain a statement of reasons, including specific examples of unacceptable performance.
3. The employee has the right to an attorney and to reply, orally or in writing, to the charges.
4. The employee has the right to appeal any adverse action to the Merit Systems Protection Board (MSPB), a three-person, bipartisan body appointed by the president with the consent of the Senate.
5. The MSPB must grant the employee a hearing, at which the employee has the right to have an attorney present.
6. The employee has the right to appeal the MSPB decision to a U.S. court of appeals, which can hold new hearings.

---

emerge an old girls' network as well.[14] In a later section we will consider whether, or in what ways, these recruitment patterns make a difference.

■ **Firing a Bureaucrat** The great majority of bureaucrats who are part of the civil service and who do not hold presidential appointments have jobs that are, for all practical purposes, beyond reach. An executive must go through elaborate steps to fire, demote, or suspend a civil servant. Realistically this means that no one is fired or demoted unless his or her superior is prepared to invest a great deal of time and effort in the attempt. In 1987 about 2,600 employees who had completed their probationary period were fired for misconduct or poor performance. That is about one-tenth of 1 percent of all federal employees. It is hard to believe that a large private company would fire only one-tenth of 1 percent of its workers in a given year. It's also impossible to believe that, as is often the case in Washington, it would take a year to fire anyone. To cope with this problem, federal executives have devised a number of stratagems for bypassing or forcing out civil servants with whom they cannot work—denying them promotions, transferring them to undesirable locations, or assigning them to meaningless work.

With the passage of the Civil Service Reform Act of 1978 Congress recognized that many high-level positions in the civil service have important policy-making responsibilities and that the president and his cabinet officers ought to have more flexibility in recruiting, assigning, and paying such people.

Accordingly, the act created the Senior Executive Service (SES), about eight thousand top federal managers who can (in theory) be hired, fired, and transferred more easily than ordinary civil servants. Moreover, the act stipulated that members of the SES would be eligible for substantial cash bonuses if they performed their duties well. (To protect the rights of SES members, anyone who is removed from the SES is guaranteed a job elsewhere in the government.)

Things did not work out quite as the sponsors of the SES had hoped. Though most eligible civil servants joined it, there was only a modest increase in the proportion of higher-ranking positions in agencies that were filled by transfer from another agency; the cash bonuses did not prove to be an important incentive (perhaps because the base salaries of top bureaucrats did not keep up with inflation); and hardly any member of the SES was actually fired. Two years after the SES was created, less than one-half of 1 percent of its members had received an unsatisfactory rating, and none had been fired. Nor does the SES give the president a large opportunity to make political appointments: only 10 percent of the SES can be selected from outside the existing civil service. And no SES member can be transferred involuntarily.

■ **The Agency's Point of View** When one realizes that most agencies are staffed by people who were recruited by those agencies, sometimes on a name-request basis, and who are virtually immune from dismissal, it becomes clear that the recruitment and retention policies of the civil service work to ensure that most bureaucrats will have an "agency" point of view. Even with the encouragement for transfers created by the SES, most government agencies are dominated by people who have not served in any other agency and who have been in government service most of their lives. This fact has some advantages: it means that most top-tier bureaucrats are experts in the procedures and policies of their agencies and that there will be a substantial degree of continuity in agency behavior no matter which political party happens to be in power.

But the agency point of view has its costs as well. A political executive entering an agency with responsibility for shaping its direction will discover that he or she must carefully win the support of career subordinates. A subordinate has an infinite capacity for discreet sabotage and can make life miserable for a political superior by delaying action, withholding information, following the rule book with literal exactness, or making an "end run" around a superior to mobilize members of Congress who are sympathetic to the bureaucrat's point of view. For instance, when one political executive wanted to downgrade a bureau in his department, he found, naturally, that the bureau chief was opposed. The bureau chief spoke to some friendly lobbyists and a key member of Congress. When the political executive asked the congressman whether he had any problem with the contemplated reorganization, the congressman replied, "No, you have the problem, because if you touch that bureau, I'll cut your job out of the budget."[15]

Personal Attributes

A second factor that might shape the way bureaucrats use their power is their personal attributes. These include their social class, education, and personal political beliefs. The federal civil service as a whole looks very much like a cross section of American society in the education, sex, race, and social origins of its members (see Figure 13.3). But as with many other employers, African Americans and other minorities are most likely to be heavily represented in the lowest grade levels and tend to be underrepresented at the executive level (see Table 13.2). At the higher-ranking levels, where the most power is found—say, in the supergrade ranks of GS 16 through GS 18—the typical civil servant is a middle-aged white male with a college degree whose father was somewhat more advantaged than the average citizen. In the great majority of

cases this individual is in fact very different from the typical American in both background and personal beliefs.

Because political appointees and career bureaucrats are unrepresentative of the average American, and because of their supposed occupational self-interest, some critics have speculated that the people holding these jobs think about politics and government in ways very different from the public at large. The results of a 1998 survey would seem to prove them right: 57 percent of average citizens, versus 76 percent of career bureaucrats and 88 percent of Clinton administration appointees, described themselves as progovernment; 60 percent of all Americans, compared to just 4 percent of all career bureaucrats and Clinton appointees, agreed that most popular criticisms of the federal government were justified; about a third of the public, but under a fifth of the career and appointed public servants, described themselves as conservative; and only 13 or 14 percent of those in government agreed that the public knew enough about the issues to form wise opinions on policy.[16]

It is important, however, not to overgeneralize from such differences. For example, whereas Clinton appointees (virtually all of them strong Democrats) were more liberal than average citizens, Reagan appointees (virtually all of them loyal Republicans) were undoubtedly more conservative than average citizens. Likewise, career civil servants are more progovernment than the public at large, but on most specific policy questions, federal bureaucrats do not have extreme positions. They don't, for example,

Table 13.2	**Minority Employment in the Federal Bureaucracy by Rank, 2000**			
			Percentage of Total	
Grade	**Black**	**Hispanic**	**Black**	**Hispanic**
GS 1–4	26,895	8,526	29.7%	9.4%
GS 5–8	99,937	31,703	27.0	8.6
GS 9–12	82,809	36,813	16.0	7.0
GS 13–15	31,494	12,869	10.3	4.2
SES	1,180	547	7.3	3.4
Total	298,701	115,247	17.0	6.7

Note: GS stands for "General Service." The higher the number, the higher the rank of people with that number.

Source: Statistical Abstract of the United States, 2001, 482.

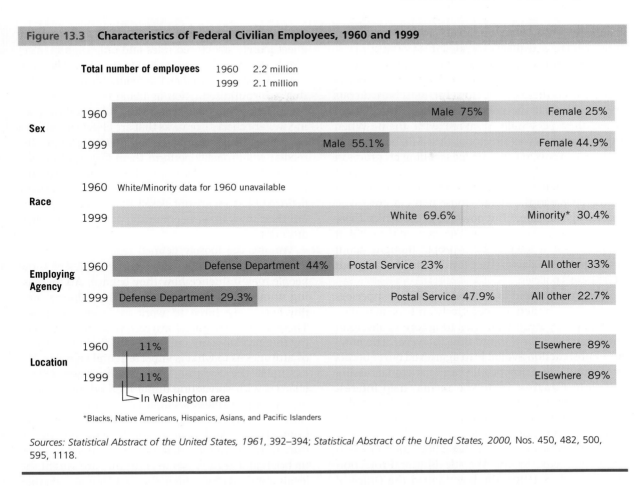

Figure 13.3 Characteristics of Federal Civilian Employees, 1960 and 1999

Total number of employees   1960   2.2 million
                            1999   2.1 million

Sex
1960 — Male 75% | Female 25%
1999 — Male 55.1% | Female 44.9%

Race
1960 — White/Minority data for 1960 unavailable
1999 — White 69.6% | Minority* 30.4%

Employing Agency
1960 — Defense Department 44% | Postal Service 23% | All other 33%
1999 — Defense Department 29.3% | Postal Service 47.9% | All other 22.7%

Location
1960 — 11% | Elsewhere 89%
1999 — 11% | Elsewhere 89%
In Washington area

*Blacks, Native Americans, Hispanics, Asians, and Pacific Islanders

Sources: Statistical Abstract of the United States, 1961, 392–394; *Statistical Abstract of the United States, 2000,* Nos. 450, 482, 500, 595, 1118.

think that the government should take over the big corporations, they support some amount of business deregulation, and a majority (by a slim margin) don't think that the goal of U.S. foreign policy has been to protect business.[17]

We can also see, however, that the kind of agency for which a bureaucrat works makes a difference. Those employed in "activist" agencies, such as the Federal Trade Commission, Environmental Protection Agency, and Food and Drug Administration, have much more liberal views than those who work for the more "traditional" agencies, such as the departments of Agriculture, Commerce, and the Treasury.

This association between attitudes and kind of agency has been confirmed by other studies. Even when the bureaucrats come from roughly the same social backgrounds, their policy views seem to reflect the type of government work that they do. For example, people holding foreign service jobs in the State Department tended to be more liberal than those com-

ing from similar family backgrounds and performing similar tasks (such as working on foreign affairs) in the Defense Department.[18] It is not clear whether these differences in attitudes were produced by the jobs that they held or whether certain jobs attract people with certain beliefs. Probably both forces were at work.

Whatever the mechanism involved, there seems little doubt that different agencies display different political ideologies. A study done in 1976 revealed that Democrats and people with liberal views tended to be overrepresented in social service agencies, whereas Republicans and people with conservative views tend to be overrepresented in defense agencies.[19]

Do Bureaucrats Sabotage Their Political Bosses?

Because it is so hard to fire career bureaucrats, it is often said that these people will sabotage any actions by their political superiors with which they disagree. And since civil servants tend to have liberal views, it has been conservative presidents and cabinet secretaries who have usually expressed this worry.

There is no doubt that some bureaucrats will drag their heels if they don't like their bosses, and a few will block actions they oppose. However, most bureaucrats try to carry out the policies of their superiors even when they personally disagree with them. When David Stockman was director of the OMB, he set out to make sharp cuts in government spending programs in accordance with the wishes of his boss, President Reagan. He later published a book complaining about all the people in the White House and Congress who worked against him.[20] But nowhere in the book is there any major criticism of the civil servants at the OMB. It appears that whatever these people thought about Stockman and Reagan, they loyally tried to carry out Stockman's policies.

Bureaucrats tend to be loyal to political superiors who deal with them cooperatively and constructively. An agency head who tries to ignore or discredit them can be in for a tough time, however. The powers of obstruction available to aggrieved bureaucrats are formidable. Such people can leak embarrassing stories to Congress or to the media, help interest groups mobilize against the agency head, and discover a thousand procedural reasons why a new course of action won't work.

The exercise of some of those bureaucratic powers is protected by the Whistle Blower Protection Act. Passed in 1989, the law created the Office of Special Counsel, charged with investigating complaints from bureaucrats that they were punished after reporting to Congress about waste, fraud, or abuse in their agencies.

It may seem odd that bureaucrats, who have great job security, would not always act in accordance with their personal beliefs instead of in accordance with the wishes of their bosses. Bureaucratic sabotage, in this view, ought to be very common. But bureaucratic cooperation with superiors is not odd, once you take into account the nature of a bureaucrat's job.

If you are a voter at the polls, your beliefs will clearly affect how you vote (see Chapter 5). But if you are the second baseman for the Boston Red Sox, your political beliefs, social background, and education will have nothing to do with how you field ground balls. Sociologists like to call the different things that people do in their lives "roles" and to distinguish between roles that are loosely structured (such as the role of voter) and those that are highly structured (such as

that of second baseman). Personal attitudes greatly affect loosely structured roles and only slightly affect highly structured ones. Applied to the federal bureaucracy, this suggests that civil servants performing tasks that are routinized (such as filling out forms), tasks that are closely defined by laws and rules (such as issuing welfare checks), or tasks that are closely monitored by others (supervisors, special-interest groups, the media) will probably perform them in ways that can only partially be explained, if at all, by their personal attitudes. Civil servants performing complex, loosely defined tasks that are not closely monitored may carry out their work in ways powerfully influenced by their attitudes.

Among the loosely defined tasks are those performed by professionals, and so the values of these people may influence how they behave. An increasing number of lawyers, economists, engineers, and physicians are hired to work in federal agencies. These men and women have received extensive training that produces not only a set of skills but also a set of attitudes as to what is important and valuable. For example, the Federal Trade Commission (FTC), charged with preventing unfair methods of competition among businesses, employs two kinds of professionals—lawyers, organized into a Bureau of Competition, and economists, organized into a Bureau of Economics. Lawyers are trained to draw up briefs and argue cases in court and are taught the legal standards by which they will know whether they have a chance of winning a case or not. Economists are trained to analyze how a competitive economy works and what costs consumers must bear if the goods and services are produced by a monopoly (one firm controlling the market) or an oligopoly (a small number of firms dominating the market).

Because of their training and attitudes, lawyers in the FTC prefer to bring cases against a business firm that has done something clearly illegal, such as attending secret meetings with competitors to rig the prices that will be charged to a purchaser. These cases appeal to lawyers because there is usually a victim (the purchaser or a rival company) who complains to the government, the illegal behavior can be proved in a court of law, and the case can be completed rather quickly.

Economists, on the other hand, are trained to measure the value of a case not by how quickly it can be proved in court but by whether the illegal practice imposes large or small costs on the consumer. FTC economists often dislike the cases that appeal to lawyers. The economists feel that the amount of money that such cases save the consumer is often small and that the cases are a distraction from the major issues—such as whether IBM unfairly dominates the computer business or whether General Motors is too large to be efficient. Lawyers, in turn, are leery of big cases, because the facts are hard to prove and they may take forever to decide (one blockbuster case can drag through the courts for ten years). In many federal agencies divergent professional values such as these help explain how power is used.

Culture and Careers

Unlike the lawyers and economists working in the FTC, the government bureaucrats in a typical agency don't have a lot of freedom to choose a course of action. Their jobs are spelled out not only by the laws, rules, and routines of their agency but also by the informal understandings among fellow employees as to how they are supposed to act. These understandings are the *culture* of the agency.[21]

If you belong to the air force, you can do a lot of things, but only one thing really counts: flying airplanes, especially advanced jet fighters and bombers. The culture of the air force is a pilots' culture. If you belong to the navy, you have more choices: fly jet aircraft or operate nuclear submarines. Both jobs provide status and a chance for promotion to the highest ranks. By contrast, sailing minesweepers or transport ships (or worse, having a desk job and not sailing anything at all) is not a very rewarding job. The culture of the CIA emphasizes working overseas as a clandestine agent; staying in Washington as a report writer is not as good for your career. The culture of the State Department rewards skill in political negotiations; being an expert on international economics or embassy security is much less rewarding.

You can usually tell what kind of culture an agency has by asking an employee, "If you want to get ahead here, what sort of jobs should you take?" The jobs that are career enhancing are part of the culture; the jobs that are not career enhancing (NCE in bureaucratic lingo) are not part of it.

Being part of a strong culture is good—up to a point. It motivates employees to work hard in order to win the respect of their coworkers as well as the approval of their bosses. But a strong culture also makes it hard to change an agency. FBI agents for many years resisted getting involved in civil rights or

T·R·I·V·I·A

Famous Bureaucrats

The federal government has employed as bureaucrats people who were later to become famous in other careers.

Clara Barton, founder of the American Red Cross	Clerk in the U.S. Patent Office, 1854–1861
Alexander Graham Bell, inventor of the telephone	Special agent of the U.S. Census Bureau, 1890
Nathaniel Hawthorne, author	Weigher in the Boston Custom House, 1839–1841, and surveyor of the Port of Salem, Massachusetts, 1845–1849
Washington Irving, author	U.S. foreign service
Abraham Lincoln, president	Postmaster of New Salem, Illinois, 1833–1836
Knute Rockne, football coach	Clerk in Chicago Post Office, 1907–1910
James Thurber, humorist	Code clerk in State Department
James Whistler, painter	Draftsman, U.S. Coast Survey, 1854–1855
Walt Whitman, poet	Clerk, U.S. Department of the Interior, 1865

organized crime cases, and diplomats in the State Department didn't pay much attention to embassy security. These important jobs were not a career-enhancing part of the culture.

Constraints

The biggest difference between a government agency and a private organization is the vastly greater number of constraints on the agency. Unlike a business firm, the typical government bureau cannot hire, fire, build, or sell without going through procedures set down in laws. How much money it pays its members is determined by statute, not by the market. Not only the goals of an agency but often its exact procedures are spelled out by Congress.

At one time the Soil Conservation Service was required by law to employ at least 14,177 full-time workers. The State Department is forbidden by law

The "Rules" of Politics

How to Get Rid of a Career Civil Servant Without Going Through the System

The frontal assault   Tell him that he is no longer wanted and that if he quits, he will get a nice letter of recommendation and a farewell luncheon. If he won't quit but later wants to leave for a better job, he will get a nasty letter of recommendation.

The transfer technique   Find out where in the country the civil servant does *not* want to live and threaten to transfer her there. Send Bostonians to Texas and Texans to Maine.

The special-assignment technique   Useful for a family person who does not like to travel. Tell him that to keep his job he must inspect all the agency's offices in cities with a population under twenty thousand and stay in bad motels. Even if he doesn't quit, at least you will have him out of the office.

The layering technique   Put loyal subordinates in charge of disloyal ones, or put the objectionable civil servant into an out-of-the-way post where you can ignore her.

Source: Adapted from "Federal Political Personnel Manual," printed in "Presidential Campaign Activities of 1972," Hearings Before the Select Committee on Presidential Campaign Activities, Ninety-third Congress, 2nd Session, vol. 19 (1974). This manual was produced by members of the Nixon administration, but in some version its principles have been applied by all administrations.

Some of the more general constraints include the following:

- Administrative Procedure Act (1946). Before adopting a new rule or policy, an agency must give notice, solicit comments, and (often) hold hearings.
- Freedom of Information Act (1966). Citizens have the right to inspect all government records except those containing military, intelligence, or trade secrets or revealing private personnel actions.
- National Environmental Policy Act (1969). Before undertaking any major action affecting the environment, an agency must issue an environmental impact statement.
- Privacy Act (1974). Government files about individuals, such as Social Security and tax records, must be kept confidential.
- Open Meeting Law (1976). Every part of every agency meeting must be open to the public unless certain matters (for example, military or trade secrets) are being discussed.

One of the biggest constraints on bureaucratic action is that Congress rarely gives any job to a single agency. Stopping drug trafficking is the task of the Customs Service, the FBI, the Drug Enforcement Administration, the Border Patrol, and the Defense Department (among others). Disposing of the assets of failed savings-and-loan associations is the job of the Resolution Funding Corporation, Resolution Trust Corporation, Federal Housing Finance Board, Office of Thrift Supervision in the Treasury Department, Federal Deposit Insurance Corporation, Federal Reserve Board, and Justice Department (among others).

The effects of these constraints on agency behavior are not surprising.

- The government will often act slowly. (The more constraints that must be satisfied, the longer it will take to get anything done.)
- The government will sometimes act inconsistently. (What is done to meet one constraint—for example, freedom of information—may endanger another constraint—for example, privacy.)
- It will be easier to block action than to take action. (The constraints ensure that lots of voices will be heard; the more voices that are heard, the more they may cancel each other out.)
- Lower-ranking employees will be reluctant to make decisions on their own. (Having many constraints means having many ways to get into

from opening a diplomatic post in Antigua or Barbuda but forbidden from closing a post anywhere else. The Agency for International Development (which administers our foreign-aid program) has been given by Congress 33 objectives and 75 priorities and must send to Congress 288 reports each year. When it buys military supplies, the Defense Department must give a "fair proportion" of its contracts to small businesses, especially those operated by "socially and economically disadvantaged individuals," and must buy from American firms even if, in some cases, buying abroad would be cheaper.

Learning Bureaucratese

A few simple rules, if remembered, will enable you to speak and write in the style of a government official.

- **Use nouns as if they were verbs.** Don't say, "We must set priorities"; say instead, "We must prioritize."

- **Use adjectives as if they were verbs.** Don't say, "We put the report in final form"; say instead, "We finalized the report."

- **Use several words where one word would do.** Don't say, "now"; say instead, "at this point in time."

- **Never use ordinary words where unusual ones can be found.** Don't say that you "made a choice"; say that you "selected an option."

- **No matter what subject you are discussing, employ the language of sports and war.** Never say, "progress"; say, "breakthrough." Never speak of a "compromise"; instead consider "adopting a fallback position."

- **Avoid active verbs.** Never say, "Study the problem"; say instead, "It is felt that the problem should be subjected to further study."

trouble; to avoid trouble, let your boss make the decision.)
- Citizens will complain of red tape. (The more constraints to serve, the more forms to fill out.)

These constraints do not mean that government bureaucracy is powerless, only that, however great its power, it tends to be clumsy. That clumsiness arises not from the fact that the people who work for agencies are dull or incompetent but from the complicated political environment in which that work must be done.

The moral of the story: the next time you get mad at a bureaucrat, ask yourself, Why would a rational, intelligent person behave that way? Chances are you will discover that there are good reasons for that action. You would probably behave the same way if you were working for the same organization.

■ **Why So Many Constraints?**   Government agencies behave as they do in large part because of the many different goals they must pursue and the complex rules they must follow. Where does all this red tape come from?

From us. From us, the people.

Every goal, every constraint, every bit of red tape, was put in place by Congress, the courts, the White House, or the agency itself responding to the demands of some influential faction. Civil rights groups want every agency to hire and buy from women and minorities. Environmental groups want every agency to file environmental impact statements. Industries being regulated want every new agency policy to be formulated only after a lengthy public hearing with lots of lawyers present. Labor unions also want those hearings so that they can argue against industry lawyers.

The "Rules" of Politics

"Laws" of Bureaucratic Procedure

Acheson's Rule A memorandum is written not to inform the reader but to protect the writer.

Boren's Laws
When in doubt, mumble.
When in trouble, delegate.
When in charge, ponder.

Chapman's Rules of Committees
Never arrive on time, or you will be stamped a beginner.
Don't say anything until the meeting is half over; this stamps you as being wise.
Be as vague as possible; this prevents irritating others.
When in doubt, suggest that a subcommittee be appointed.

Meskimen's Law There's never time to do it right but always time to do it over.

Murphy's Law If anything can go wrong, it will.

O'Toole's Corollary to Murphy's Law Murphy was an optimist.

Parkinson's First Law Work expands to fill the time available for its completion.

Parkinson's Second Law Expenditure rises to meet income.

Peter Principle In every hierarchy, each employee tends to rise to his level of incompetence; thus, every post tends to be filled by an incompetent employee.

Robertson's Rule The more directives you issue to solve a problem, the worse it gets.

Smith's Principle Never do anything for the first time.

Everybody who sells something to the government wants a "fair chance" to make the sale, and so everybody insists that government contracts be awarded only after complex procedures are followed. A lot of people don't trust the government, and so they insist

that everything it does be done in the sunshine—no secrets, no closed meetings, no hidden files.

If we wanted agencies to pursue their main goal with more vigor and less encumbering red tape, we would have to ask Congress, the courts, or the White House to repeal some of these constraints. In other words, we would have to be willing to give up something we want in order to get something else we want even more. But politics does not encourage people to make these trade-offs; instead it encourages us to expect to get everything—efficiency, fairness, help for minorities—all at once.

Agency Allies

Despite these constraints, government bureaucracies are not powerless. In fact some of them actively seek certain constraints. They do so because it is a way of cementing a useful relationship with a congressional committee or an interest group.

At one time scholars described the relationship between an agency, a committee, and an interest group as an **iron triangle.** For example, the Department of Veterans Affairs, the House and Senate committees on veterans' affairs, and veterans' organizations (such as the American Legion) would form a tight, mutually advantageous alliance. The department would do what the committees wanted and in return get political support and budget appropriations; the committee members would do what the veterans' groups wanted and in return get votes and campaign contributions. Iron triangles are examples of what are called *client politics*.

Many agencies still have important allies in Congress and the private sector, especially those bureaus that serve the needs of specific sectors of the economy or regions of the country. The Department of Agriculture works closely with farm organizations, the Department of the Interior with groups interested in obtaining low-cost irrigation or grazing rights, and the Department of Housing and Urban Development with mayors and real-estate developers.

Sometimes these allies are so strong that they can defeat a popular president. For years President Reagan tried to abolish the Small Business Administration (SBA), arguing that its program of loans to small firms was wasteful and ridden with favoritism. But Congress, reacting to pressures from small-business groups, rallied to the SBA's defense. As a result Reagan had to oversee an agency that he didn't want.

But iron triangles are much less common today than once was the case. Politics of late has become far more complicated. For one thing, the number and variety of interest groups have increased so much in recent years that there is scarcely any agency that is not subject to pressures from several competing interests instead of only from one powerful interest. For another, the growth of subcommittees in Congress has meant that most agencies are subject to control by many different legislative groups, often with very different concerns. Finally, the courts have made it much easier for all kinds of individuals and interests to intervene in agency affairs.

As a result, nowadays government agencies face a bewildering variety of competing groups and legislative subcommittees that constitute not a loyal group of allies but a fiercely contentious collection of critics. The Environmental Protection Agency is caught between the demands of environmentalists and those of industry organizations, the Occupational Safety and Health Administration between the pressures of labor and those of business, and the Federal Communications Commission between the desires of broadcasters and those of cable television companies. Even the Department of Agriculture faces not a unified group of farmers but many different farmers split into rival groups, depending on the crops they raise, the regions in which they live, and the attitudes they have toward the relative merits of farm subsidies or free markets.

Political scientist Hugh Heclo has described the typical government agency today as being embedded not in an iron triangle but in an **issue network**.[22] These issue networks consist of people in Washington-based interest groups, on congressional staffs, in universities and think tanks, and in the mass media, who regularly debate government policy on a certain subject—say, health care or auto safety. The networks are contentious, split along political, ideological, and economic lines. When a president takes office, he often recruits key agency officials from those members of the issue network who are most sympathetic to his views.

When Jimmy Carter, a Democrat, became president, he appointed to key posts in consumer agencies people who were from that part of the consumer issue network associated with Ralph Nader. Ronald Reagan, a conservative Republican, filled these same jobs with people who were from that part of the issue network holding free market or antiregulation views. When George Bush the elder, a more centrist Republican,

The real federal bureaucracy is bigger than just who works for the national government. Because defense contractors depend on government contracts, the bureaucracy includes people who work in these private firms.

took office, he filled these posts with more centrist members of the issue network. Bill Clinton brought back the consumer activists.

Congressional Oversight

The main reason why some interest groups are important to agencies is that they are important to Congress. Not every interest group in the country has substantial access to Congress, but those that do and that are taken seriously by the relevant committees or subcommittees must also be taken seriously by the agency. Furthermore, even apart from interest groups, members of Congress have constitutional powers over agencies and policy interests in how agencies function.

Congressional supervision of the bureaucracy takes several forms. First, no agency may exist (except for a few presidential offices and commissions) without congressional approval. Congress influences—and sometimes determines precisely—agency behavior by the statutes it enacts.

Second, no money may be spent unless it has first been authorized by Congress. **Authorization legislation** originates in a legislative committee (such as Agriculture, Education and Labor, or Public Works) and states the maximum amount of money that an agency may spend on a given program. This authorization may be permanent, it may be for a fixed number of years, or it may be annual (that is, it must be

Congressional Oversight and Homeland Security

Shortly after the September 11, 2001 terrorist attack on the United States, Senator Joseph Lieberman called for the creation of a new "Department of Homeland Defense." What Lieberman had in mind was a large new cabinet department that would bring many federal agencies under one administrative roof. The director of the new department, he argued, should be a cabinet official subject to Senate confirmation.

Instead, by executive order, President George W. Bush created a new Office of Homeland Security within the Executive Office of the President. He appointed his friend, former Republican governor of Pennsylvania Tom Ridge, to head the office as an assistant to the president. Within a few months, Ridge's office released a homeland security blueprint specifying the critical tasks necessary to secure the safety of the United States.

But who, in which federal, state, or local public agencies, was to perform these critical tasks, with what government monies, and under whose ultimate administrative authority? By spring 2002, the new homeland security office was plagued by two issues. First, congressional leaders insisted that Ridge testify before Congress about the Bush administration's homeland security strategy. The Bush administration refused, citing Ridge's status as an assistant to the president, not a Senate-confirmed appointee. Second, to administer its strategy, Ridge's office would need to coordinate personnel and budgets across scores of agencies (see Figure 13.4 on page 393).

On June 6, 2002, the Bush administration proposed the creation of a Department of Homeland Security that would consolidate twenty-two federal agencies into one umbrella cabinet-level bureaucracy with nearly 170,000 federal employees (third behind Defense and Veterans Affairs) and a total of about $40 billion in budgets (fourth behind Defense, Health and Human Services, and Education). The plan called for organizing the new department into four divisions: border and transportation security; emergency preparedness and response; chemical, biological, radiological, and nuclear counter-measures; and information analysis and infrastructure protection (see Figure 13.4). The secretary of the new department would require Senate approval. Ridge's EOP unit, with about 100 White House employees, would continue to exist as an advisory body to the president.

Regardless of how the new Department of Homeland Security is organized, one thing is certain: Congress will need to restructure itself to make the new bureaucracy work. Because of committee-centered congressional decision-making, over the last several decades the federal bureaucracy has evolved through agency-by-agency, procedure-by-procedure, program-by-program responses to problems as they appeared. Thus, excluding the Department of Defense, the State Department, the Federal Bureau of Investigation (FBI), and the Central Intelligence Agency (CIA), some seventy separate federal agencies are authorized by Congress to spend money on counterterrorist activities.

A law creating the new Department of Homeland Security was passed late in 2002, but how Congress will oversee it will take years to learn. The day after the Bush plan was announced, congressional committee chairmen in both parties issued public statements strongly supporting the idea of creating a new homeland security department, *but* opposing any efforts to "tamper" with their respective committees' or subcommittees' jurisdiction over given federal agencies or "strip" them of oversight of those agencies.

History also counsels against assuming that Congress will streamline itself as it creates and oversees a new homeland security department. Over the past half-century, Congress has created many big new agencies. Never, however, has Congress recast its own structures or procedures to ensure that a new

renewed each year, or the program or agency goes out of business).

Third, even funds that have been authorized by Congress cannot be spent unless (in most cases) they are also appropriated. Appropriations are usually made annually, and they originate not with the legislative committees but with the House Appropriations Committee and its various (and influential) subcommittees. An **appropriation** (money formally set aside for a specific use) may be, and often is, for less than the amount authorized. The Appropriations Committee's action thus tends

Figure 13.4   Department of Homeland Security as Proposed by President George W. Bush, June 6, 2002

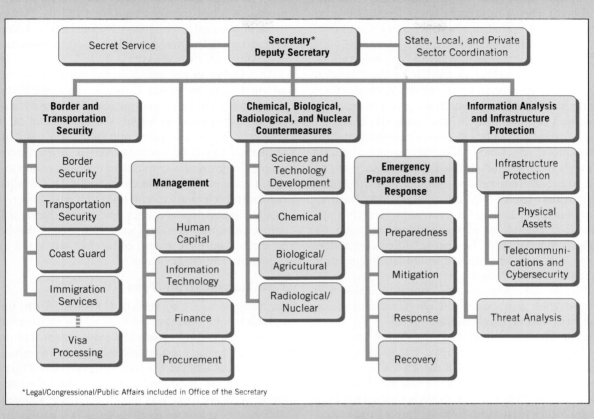

*Legal/Congressional/Public Affairs included in Office of the Secretary

Source: White House Office of Homeland Security.

bureaucracy functions well or that its leaders are not required to spend much of their time giving the same testimony and answering the same questions before multiple committees or subcommittees. Whether congressional oversight of homeland security will prove an exception remains to be seen.

Sources: Ivo H. Daalder, Statement before the Committee on Governmental Affairs, United States Senate, October 12, 2001;

John J. Dilulio, Jr., "Homeland Insecurity," *The Weekly Standard* (April 22, 2002) 15–17; Joseph Curl, "Bush Wants New Cabinet Post," *The Washington Times,* (June 7, 2002): A1; Adriel Bettelheim and Jill Barshay, "Bush's Swift, Sweeping Plan Is Work Order for Congress," *Congressional Quarterly Weekly* (June 8, 2002): 1498–1504; Adriel Bettelheim, "Security Plan Gets Solid Backing But No Rubber Stamps on Hill," *Congressional Quarterly Weekly* (June 15, 2002): 1577–1580; Bob Williams and David Nather, "Homeland Security Debate: Balancing Swift and Sure," *Congressional Quarterly Weekly* (June 22, 2002): 1642–1647.

to have a budget-cutting effect. There are some funds that can be spent without an appropriation, but in virtually every part of the bureaucracy each agency is keenly sensitive to congressional concerns at the time that the annual appropriations process is going on.

The Appropriations Committee and Legislative Committees

The fact that an agency budget must be both authorized and appropriated means that each agency serves not one congressional master but several, and that these masters may be in conflict. The real power over an agency's budget is exercised by the Appropriations Committee; the legislative committees are especially important when a substantive law is first passed or an agency is first created, or when an agency is subject to annual authorization.

In the past the power of the Appropriations Committee was rarely challenged: from 1947 through 1962, fully 90 percent of the House Appropriations Committee's recommendations on expenditures were approved by the full House without change.[23] Furthermore, the Appropriations Committee tends to recommend less money than an agency requests (though some specially favored agencies, such as the FBI, the Soil Conservation Service, and the Forest Service, have tended to get almost everything that they have asked for). Finally, the process of "marking up" (revising, amending, and approving) an agency's budget request gives to the Appropriations Committee, or one of its subcommittees, substantial influence over the policies that the agency follows.

Of late the appropriations committees have lost some of their great power over government agencies. This has happened in three ways:

First, Congress has created trust funds to pay for the benefits many people receive. The Social Security trust fund is the largest of these. In 1990 it took in about $260 billion in Social Security taxes and paid out about $220 billion in old-age benefits. There are several other trust funds as well. **Trust funds** operate outside the regular government budget, and the appropriations committees have no control over these expenditures. They are automatic.

Second, Congress has changed the authorization of many programs from permanent or multiyear to **annual authorizations.** This means that every year the legislative committees, as part of the reauthorization process, get to set limits on what these agencies can spend. This limits the ability of the appropriations committees to determine the spending limits. Before 1959 most authorizations were permanent or multiyear. Now a long list of agencies must be reauthorized every year—the State Department, NASA, military procurement programs of the Defense Department, the Justice Department, the Energy Department, and parts or all of many other agencies.

Third, the existence of huge budget deficits during the 1980s and early 1990s has meant that much of Congress's time has been taken up with trying (usually not very successfully) to keep spending down. As a result there has rarely been much time to discuss the merits of various programs or how much ought to be spent on them; instead attention has been focused on meeting a target spending limit. In 1981 the budget resolution passed by Congress mandated cuts in several programs before the appropriations committees had even completed their work.[24]

In addition to the power of the purse, there are informal ways by which Congress can control the bureaucracy. An individual member of Congress can call an agency head on behalf of a constituent. Most such calls merely seek information, but some result in, or attempt to second, special privileges for particular people. Congressional committees may also obtain the right to pass on certain agency decisions. This is called **committee clearance,** and though it is usually not legally binding on the agency, few agency heads will ignore the expressed wish of a committee chair that he or she be consulted before certain actions (such as transferring funds) are taken.

The Legislative Veto

For many decades Congress made frequent use of the legislative veto to control bureaucratic or presidential actions. A **legislative veto** is a requirement that an executive decision must lie before Congress for a specified period (usually thirty or ninety days) before it takes effect. Congress could then veto the decision if a resolution of disapproval was passed by either house (a "one-house veto") or both houses (a "two-house veto"). Unlike laws, such resolutions were not signed by the president. Between 1932 and 1980 about two hundred laws were passed providing for a legislative veto, many of them involving presidential proposals to sell arms abroad.

But in June 1983 the Supreme Court declared the legislative veto to be unconstitutional. In the *Chadha* case the Court held that the Constitution clearly requires in Article I that "every order, resolution, or vote to which the concurrence of the Senate and House of Representatives may be necessary" (with certain minor exceptions) "shall be presented to the President of the United States," who must either approve it or return it with his veto attached. In short Congress cannot take any action that has the force of law unless the president concurs in that action.[25] At a stroke of the pen parts of some two hundred laws suddenly became invalid.

At least that happened in theory. In fact since the *Chadha* decision Congress has passed a number of laws that contain legislative vetoes, despite the Supreme Court's having ruled against them! (Someone will have to go to court to test the constitutionality of these new provisions.)

Opponents of the legislative veto hope that future Congresses will have to pass laws that state much more clearly than before what an agency may or may not do. But it is just as likely that Congress will continue to pass laws stated in general terms and require that agencies implementing those laws report their plans to Congress so that it will have a chance to enact and send to the president a regular bill disapproving the proposed action. Or Congress may rely on informal (but scarcely weak) means of persuasion, including threats to reduce the appropriations of an agency that does not abide by congressional preferences.

Congressional Investigations

Perhaps the most visible and dramatic form of congressional supervision of an agency is the investigation. Since 1792, when Congress investigated an army defeat by a Native American tribe, congressional investigations of the bureaucracy have been a regular feature—sometimes constructive, sometimes destructive—of legislative-executive relations. The investigative power is not mentioned in the Constitution but has been inferred from the power to legislate. The Supreme Court has consistently upheld this interpretation, though it has also said that such investigations should not be solely for the purpose of exposing the purely personal affairs of private individuals and must not operate to deprive citizens of their basic rights.[26] Congress may compel a person to attend an investigation by issuing a subpoena; anyone who ignores the subpoena may be punished for contempt. Congress can vote to send the person to jail or can refer the matter to a court for further action. As explained in Chapter 12, the president and his principal subordinates have refused to answer certain congressional inquiries on grounds of "executive privilege."

Although many areas of congressional oversight— budgetary review, personnel controls, investigations— are designed to control the exercise of bureaucratic discretion, other areas are intended to ensure the freedom of certain agencies from effective control, especially by the president. In dozens of cases Congress has authorized department heads and bureau chiefs to operate independent of presidential preferences. Congress has resisted, for example, presidential efforts to ensure that policies to regulate pollution do not impose excessive costs on the economy, and interest groups have brought suit to prevent presidential coordination of various regulatory agencies. If the bureaucracy sometimes works at cross-purposes, it is usually because Congress—or competing committees in Congress—wants it that way.

Bureaucratic "Pathologies"

Everyone complains about bureaucracy in general (though rarely about bureaucratic agencies that everyone believes are desirable). This chapter should persuade you that it is difficult to say anything about bureaucracy "in general"; there are too many different kinds of agencies, kinds of bureaucrats, and kinds of programs to label the entire enterprise with some single adjective. Nevertheless, many people who recognize the enormous variety among government agencies still believe that they all have some general features in common and suffer from certain shared problems or pathologies.

This is true enough, but the reasons for it—and the solutions, if any—are not often understood. There are five major (or at least frequently mentioned) problems with bureaucracies: red tape, conflict, duplication, imperialism, and waste. **Red tape** refers to the complex rules and procedures that must be followed to get something done. *Conflict* exists because some agencies seem to be working at cross-purposes with other agencies. (For example, the Agricultural Research Service tells farmers how to grow crops more efficiently, while the Agricultural Stabilization and Conservation Service pays farmers to grow fewer crops or to produce less.) *Duplication* (usually called "wasteful duplication") occurs when two government agencies seem to be doing the same thing, as when the Customs Service and the Drug Enforcement Administration both attempt to intercept illegal drugs being smuggled into the country. *Imperialism* refers to the tendency of agencies to grow without regard to the benefits that their programs confer or the costs that they entail. *Waste* means spending more than is necessary to buy some product or service.

These problems all exist, but they do not necessarily exist because bureaucrats are incompetent or power-hungry. Most exist because of the very nature of government itself. Take red tape: partly we encounter cumbersome rules and procedures

These long lines of cars at the border between the United States and Mexico may be a symbol of "bureaucratic red tape" to some travelers, but they are a sign of "effective law enforcement" to people who want to cut off the flow of drugs and illegal immigrants.

because any large organization, governmental or not, must have some way of ensuring that one part of the organization does not operate out of step with another. Business corporations have red tape also; it is to a certain extent a consequence of bigness. But a great amount of governmental red tape is also the result of the need to satisfy legal and political requirements. Government agencies must hire on the basis of "merit," must observe strict accounting rules, must supply Congress with detailed information on their programs, and must allow for citizen access in countless ways. Meeting each need requires rules; enforcing the rules requires forms.

Or take conflict and duplication: they do not occur because bureaucrats enjoy conflict or duplication. (Quite the contrary!) They exist because Congress, in setting up agencies and programs, often wants to achieve a number of different, partially inconsistent goals or finds that it cannot decide which goal it values the most. Congress has 535 members and little strong leadership; it should not be surprising that 535 people will want different things and will sometimes succeed in getting them.

Imperialism results in large measure from government agencies' seeking goals that are so vague and so difficult to measure that it is hard to tell when they have been attained. When Congress is unclear as to exactly what an agency is supposed to do, the agency will often convert that legislative vagueness into bureaucratic imperialism by taking the largest possible view of its powers. It may do this on its own; more often it does so because interest groups and judges rush in to fill the vacuum left by Congress. As we saw in Chapter 3, the 1973 Rehabilitation Act was passed with a provision barring discrimination against people with disabilities in any program receiving federal aid. Under pressure from people with disabilities, that lofty but vague goal was converted by the Department of Transportation into a requirement that virtually every big-city bus have a device installed to lift people in wheelchairs on board.

Waste is probably the biggest criticism that people have of the bureaucracy. Everybody has heard stories of the Pentagon's paying $91 for screws that cost 3 cents in the hardware store. President Reagan's "Private Sector Survey on Cost Control," generally known as the Grace Commission (after its chairman, J. Peter Grace), publicized these and other tales in a 1984 report.

No doubt there is waste in government. After all, unlike a business firm worried about maximizing profits, in a government agency there are only weak incentives to keep costs down. If a business employee cuts costs, he or she often receives a bonus or raise, and the firm gets to add the savings to its profits. If a government official cuts costs, he or she receives no reward, and the agency cannot keep the savings—they go back to the Treasury.

But many of the horror stories are either exaggerations or unusual occurrences.[27] Most of the screws, hammers, and light bulbs purchased by the government are obtained at low cost by means of competitive bidding among several suppliers. When the government does pay outlandish amounts, the reason typically is that it is purchasing a new or one-of-a-kind item not available at your neighborhood hardware store—for example, a new bomber or missile.

Even when the government is not overcharged, it still may spend more money than a private firm in buying what it needs. The reason is red tape—the rules and procedures designed to ensure that when the government buys something, it will do so in a way that serves the interests of many groups. For example, it must often buy from American rather than foreign suppliers, even if the latter charge a lower price; it must make use of contractors that employ minorities; it must hire only union laborers and pay them the "prevailing" (that is, the highest) wage; it must allow public inspection of its records; it frequently is required to choose contractors favored by influential members of Congress; and so on. Private firms do not have to comply with all these rules and thus can buy for less.

From this discussion it should be easy to see why these five basic bureaucratic problems are so hard to correct. To end conflicts and duplication Congress would have to make some policy choices and set some clear priorities, but with all the competing demands that it faces, Congress finds it difficult to do that. You make more friends by helping people than by hurting them, and so Congress is more inclined to add new programs than to cut old ones, whether or not the new programs are in conflict with existing ones. To check imperialism some way would have to be found to measure the benefits of government, but that is often impossible; government exists in part to achieve precisely those goals—such as national defense—that are least measurable. Furthermore, what might be done to remedy some problems would make other problems worse: if you simplify rules and procedures to cut red tape, you are also likely to reduce the coordination among agencies and thus to increase the extent to which there is duplication or conflict. If you want to reduce waste, you will have to have more rules and inspectors—in short, more red tape. The problem of bureaucracy is inseparable from the problem of government generally.

Just as people are likely to say that they dislike Congress but like their own member of Congress, they are inclined to express hostility toward "the bureaucracy" but goodwill for that part of the bureaucracy with which they have dealt personally. In 1973 a survey of Americans found that over half had had some contact with one or more kinds of government agencies, most of which were either run directly or funded indirectly by the federal government. The great majority of people were satisfied with these contacts and felt that they had been treated fairly and given useful assistance. When these people were asked their feelings about government officials in general, however, they expressed much less favorable attitudes. Whereas about 80 percent liked the officials with whom they had dealt, only 42 percent liked officials in general.[28] This finding helps explain why government agencies are rarely reduced in size or budget: whatever the popular feelings about the bureaucracy, any given agency tends to have many friends.

★ POLITICALLY SPEAKING ★

Red Tape

As early as the seventh century, legal and government documents in England were bound together with a tape of pinkish red color. In the 1850s historian Thomas Carlyle described a British politician as "little other than a red tape Talking Machine," and later the American writer Washington Irving said of an American figure that "his brain was little better than red tape and parchment."

Since then *red tape* has come to mean "bureaucratic delay or confusion," especially that accompanied by unnecessary paperwork.

Source: From *Safire's Political Dictionary* by William Safire. Copyright © 1968, 1972, 1978 by William Safire. Reprinted by permission of Random House, Inc. and the author.

Reforming the Bureaucracy

The history of American bureaucracy has been punctuated with countless efforts to make it work better and cost less. There were eleven major attempts in the twentieth century alone. The latest was the National Performance Review (NPR)—popularly called the plan to "reinvent government"—led by Vice President Al Gore. The results of the review were published in 1993.

The NPR differed from many of the preceding reform efforts in one important way. Most of the earlier ones suggested ways of increasing central (that is, presidential) control of government agencies: the Brownlow Commission (1936–1937) recommended giving the president more assistants, the First Hoover

Commission (1947–1949) suggested ways of improving top-level management, and the Ash Council (1969–1971) called for consolidating existing agencies into a few big "super departments." The intent was to make it easier for the president and his cabinet secretaries to run the bureaucracy. The key ideas were efficiency, accountability, and consistent policies.

The NPR, by contrast, emphasized customer satisfaction (the "customers" in this case being the citizens who come into contact with federal agencies). To the authors of the NPR report, the main problem with the bureaucracy was that it had become too centralized, too rule-bound, too little concerned with making programs work, and too much concerned with avoiding scandal. The NPR report contained many horror stories about useless red tape, excessive regulations, and cumbersome procurement systems that make it next to impossible for agencies to do what they were created to do. (For example, before it could buy an ashtray, the General Services Administration issued a nine-page document that described an ashtray and specified how many pieces it must break into should it be hit with a hammer.)[29] To solve these problems the NPR called for less centralized management and more employee initiative, fewer detailed rules and more emphasis on customer satisfaction. It sought to create a new kind of organizational culture in government agencies, one more like that found in the more innovative, quality-conscious American corporations. The NPR was reinforced legislatively by the Government Performance and Results Act (GPRA) of 1993, which required agencies "to set goals, measure performance, and report on the results."

But making these changes is easier said than done. Most of the rules and red tape that make it hard for agency heads to do a good job are the result either of the struggle between the White House and Congress for control over the agencies or of the agencies' desire to avoid irritating influential voters. Silly as the rules for ashtrays may sound, they were written so that the government could say it had an "objective" standard for buying ashtrays. If it simply went out and bought ashtrays at a department store the way ordinary people do, it would risk being accused by the Acme Ashtray Company of buying trays from its competitor, the A-1 Ashtray Company, because of political favoritism.

The rivalry between the president and Congress for control of the bureaucracy makes bureaucrats nervous about irritating either branch, and so they issue rules designed to avoid getting into trouble, even if these rules make it hard to do their job. Matters become even worse during periods of divided government when different parties control the White House and Congress. As we saw in Chapter 12, divided government may not have much effect on *making* policy, but it can have a big effect on *implementing* it. Presidents of one party have tried to increase political control over the bureaucracy ("executive micromanagement"), and Congresses of another party have responded by increasing the number of investigations and detailed rule-making ("legislative micromanagement"). Divided government intensifies the cross-fire between the executive and legislative branches, making bureaucrats dig into even deeper layers of red tape to avoid getting hurt.

This does not mean that reform is impossible, only that it is very difficult. For example, despite a lack of clear-cut successes in other areas, the NPR's procurement reforms stuck: government agencies can now buy things costing as much as $100,000 without following any complex regulations.

It might be easier to make desirable changes if the bureaucracy were accountable to only one master—say, the president—instead of to several. But that situation, which exists in many parliamentary democracies, creates its own problems. When the bureaucracy has but one master, it often ends up having none: it becomes so powerful that it controls the prime minister and no longer listens to citizen complaints. A weak, divided bureaucracy, such as exists in the United States, may strike us as inefficient, but that very inefficiency may help protect our liberties.

Most bureaucrats are people we like, such as the letter carriers in the Postal Service.

What Would You Do?

New Administration Struggling to Fill Top Posts

Cabinet Secretaries Say "The President Needs Help!"

May 20
WASHINGTON

Four months into the new administration, hundreds of assistant secretary and deputy assistant secretary positions remain unfilled. In 1960 the total number of presidential political appointees was just 450. Today the total is over 2,400, but sheer growth is not the whole story. Rather, say experts on federal bureaucracy, plum public service posts go unfilled because the jobs have become so unrewarding, even punishing . . .

MEMORANDUM

To: Dr. Robert Smith, president of Cybersystems Engineering
From: James Logan, secretary of defense
Subject: Becoming an assistant secretary of defense

As both secretary and a dear old college buddy of yours, I write again to express my hope that you will accept the president's call to service. We all desperately want you aboard. Yes, conflict-of-interest laws will require you to sell your stock in your present company and drop out of its generous pension plan. No, the government won't even pay moving costs. And once you leave office, you will be barred for life from lobbying the executive branch on matters in which you were directly involved while in office, and you will be barred for two years from lobbying on matters that were under your general official authority. Your other concerns have teeth, too, but let me help you weigh your options.

Arguments for:

1. I hate to preach, but it is one's duty to serve one's country when called. Your sacrifice would honor your family and benefit your fellow Americans for years to come.
2. As an accomplished professional and the head of a company that has done business with the government, you could help the president succeed in reforming the department so that it works better and costs less.
3. Despite the restrictions, you could resume your career once your public service was complete.

Arguments against:

1. Since you will have to be confirmed by the Senate, your life will be put under a microscope, and everything (even some of our old college mischief together) will be fair game for congressional staffers and reporters.
2. You will face hundreds of rules telling you what you can't do and scores of congressmen telling you what you should do. Old friends will get mad at you for not doing them favors. The president will demand loyalty. The press will pounce on your every mistake, real or imagined.
3. Given the federal limits on whom in the government you can deal with after you leave office, your job at Cybersystems may well suffer.

Your decision:
Accept position _____ Reject position _____

Summary

Bureaucracy is characteristic of almost all aspects of modern life, not simply the government. Government bureaucracies, however, pose special problems because they are subject to competing sources of political authority, must function in a constitutional system of divided powers and federalism, have vague goals, and lack incentive systems that will encourage efficiency. The power of a bureaucracy should be measured by its discretionary authority, not by the number of its employees or the size of its budget.

War and depression have been the principal sources of bureaucratic growth, aided by important changes in constitutional interpretation in the 1930s that permitted Congress to delegate broad grants of authority to administrative agencies. With only partial success Congress seeks to check or recover those grants by controlling budgets, personnel, and policy decisions and by the exercise of legislative vetoes. The uses to which bureaucrats put their authority can be explained in part by their recruitment and security (they have an agency orientation), their personal political views, and the nature of the tasks that their agencies are performing.

Many of the popular solutions for the problems of bureaucratic rule—red tape, duplication, conflict, agency imperialism, and waste—fail to take into account that these problems are to a degree inherent in any government that serves competing goals and is supervised by rival elected officials. Nevertheless, some reform efforts have succeeded in making government work better and cost less to operate.

Reconsidering the Enduring Questions

1. What happened to make bureaucracy a "fourth branch" of American national government?

The Constitution made no provision for an administrative system other than to allow the president to appoint, with the advice and consent of the Senate, ambassadors, Supreme Court judges, and "all other officers . . . which shall be provided by law." By the early twentieth century, however, Washington's role in making, administering, and funding public policies had already grown far beyond what the Framers had contemplated. Two world wars, the New Deal, and the Great Society each left the government with expanded powers and requiring new batteries of administrative agencies to exercise them. Today, the federal bureaucracy is as vast as most people's expectations about Washington's responsibility for every public concern one can name. It is the appointed officials—the bureaucrats—not the elected officials or policymakers, who command the troops, deliver the mail, audit the tax returns, run the federal prisons, decide who qualifies for public assistance, and do countless other tasks. Unavoidably, many bureaucrats exercise discretion in deciding what public laws and regulations mean and how to apply them. Still, the president, cabinet secretaries, and thousands of political appointees are ultimately their bosses. Congress and the courts have ample, if imperfect, means of checking and balancing even the biggest bureaucracy, old or new.

2. What are the actual size and scope of the federal bureaucracy?

A few million civil servants work directly for the federal government, but over five times as many people work indirectly for Washington as employees of business firms or of nonprofit organizations that receive federal grants or contracts, or as state and local government employees working under federal mandates. For example, the U.S. Department of Health and Human Services (HHS) has about 65,000 employees, runs over 300 different programs, and makes over 60,000 grants a year. But millions more people work indirectly for the HHS—as state and local government employees whose entire jobs involve the administration of one or more HHS programs (for example Medicaid), and as people who work for community-serving nonprofit organizations that receive HHS grants to administer social services.

3. What has been done to improve bureaucratic performance?

There have been numerous efforts to make the bureaucracy work better and cost less, including eleven presidential or other major commissions in the twentieth century. The latest was the National Performance Review (NPR), popularly called the plan to "reinvent government." Vice President Gore led the NPR during the two terms of the Clinton administration. The NPR was predicated on the view that bureaucracy had become too centralized, too rule-bound, too little concerned with program results, and too much concerned with avoiding scandal. In the end, the NPR produced certain money-saving changes in the federal procurement process (how government purchases goods and services from private contractors), and it also streamlined parts of the federal personnel process (how Washington hires career employees). Most experts, however, gave the NPR mixed grades and concluded that it had fallen far short of its ambitious goals of improving government performance.

World Wide Web Resources

- For addresses and reports of various cabinet departments
  Web addresses: www.whitehouse.gov/
  Documents and bulletin boards:
  www.fedworld.gov
  National Performance Review: www.npr.gov

- A few specific web sites of federal agencies
  Department of Defense: www.defenselink.mil
  Department of Education: www.ed.gov
  Department of Health and Human Services:
  www.dhhs.gov
  Department of State: www.state.gov
  Federal Bureau of Investigation: www.fbi.gov
  Department of Labor: www.dol.gov

Key Terms

bureaucracy *p. 373*
spoils system *p. 376*
laissez-faire *p. 376*
discretionary authority *p. 378*
competitive service *p. 379*

name-request job *p. 381*
iron triangle *p. 390*
issue network *p. 391*
authorization legislation *p. 391*
appropriation *p. 392*

trust funds *p. 394*
annual authorizations *p. 394*
committee clearance *p. 394*
legislative veto *p. 394*
red tape *p. 395*

Suggested Readings

Burke, John P. *Bureaucratic Responsibility*. Baltimore: Johns Hopkins University Press, 1986. Examines the problem of individual responsibility—for example, when to be a whistle blower—in government agencies.

DiIulio, John J., Gerald Garvey, and Donald F. Kettl. *Improving Government Performance: An Owner's Manual*. Washington, D.C.: Brookings Institution, 1993. A concise overview of the history of federal bureaucracy and ideas about how to reform it.

Downs, Anthony. *Inside Bureaucracy*. Boston: Little, Brown, 1967. An economist's explanation of why bureaucrats and bureaus behave as they do.

Halperin, Morton H. *Bureaucratic Politics and Foreign Policy*. Washington, D.C.: Brookings Institution, 1974. Insightful account of the strategies by which diplomatic and military bureaucracies defend their interests.

Heclo, Hugh. *A Government of Strangers*. Washington, D.C.: Brookings Institution, 1977. Analyzes how political appointees attempt to gain control of the Washington bureaucracy and how bureaucrats resist those efforts.

Johnson, Ronald L., and Gary Libecap. *The Federal Civil Service System and the Problem of Bureaucracy*. Chicago: University of Chicago Press, 1994. Two economists analyze how federal bureaucrats acquire positions and salaries.

Light, Paul C. *The True Size of Government*. Washington, D.C.: Brookings Institution, 1999. A revealing explanation of why the federal government is a lot bigger than is suggested by simply counting employees.

Moore, Mark H. *Creating Public Value: Strategic Management in Government*. Cambridge: Harvard University Press, 1995. A thoughtful account of how wise bureaucrats can make government work better.

Parkinson, C. Northcote. *Parkinson's Law*. Boston: Houghton Mifflin, 1957. Half-serious, half-joking explanation of why government agencies tend to grow.

Wilson, James Q. *Bureaucracy: What Government Agencies Do and Why They Do It*. New York: Basic Books, 1989. A comprehensive review of what we know about bureaucratic behavior in the United States.

The Judiciary

Enduring Questions

1. Should judges be limited to interpreting what the law says?

2. Why should federal courts have the right to declare an act of Congress unconstitutional?

President Bush nominated Clarence Thomas to the Supreme Court on July 1, 1991. He was confirmed by a Senate vote of 52 to 48 on October 15. Thomas's margin of confirmation was the closest in more than one hundred years, and the second closest in U.S. history. His hearings were dominated by allegations of sexual harassment lodged against him by Anita F. Hill, a former subordinate during his tenure at the Equal Employment Opportunity Commission and later a University of Oklahoma law professor. Apart from the sexual harassment allegations, which both sides estimated cost him about ten votes, opponents of his confirmation claimed that his judicial philosophy was outside the mainstream, while supporters claimed that he would be sensitive to the rights of the disadvantaged, having himself risen from childhood poverty.

Only in the United States would the selection of a judge produce so dramatic and bitter a conflict. The reason is simple: only in the United States do judges play so large a role in making public policy.

One aspect of this power is **judicial review**—the right of the federal courts to declare laws of

Congress and acts of the executive branch void and unenforceable if they are judged to be in conflict with the Constitution. Since 1789 the Supreme Court has declared over one hundred sixty federal laws to be unconstitutional. In Britain, by contrast, Parliament is supreme, and no court may strike down a law that it passes. As the second earl of Pembroke is supposed to have said, "A parliament can do anything but make a man a woman and a woman a man." All that prevents Parliament from acting contrary to the (unwritten) constitution of Britain are the consciences of its members and the opinions of the citizens. About sixty nations do have something resembling judicial review, but in only a few cases does this power mean much in practice. Where it means something—in Australia, Canada, Germany, India, and some other nations—one finds a stable, federal system of government with a strong tradition of an independent judiciary.[1] (Some other nations—France, for example—have special councils, rather than courts, that can under certain circumstances decide that a law is not authorized by the constitution.)

Judicial review is the federal courts' chief weapon in the system of checks and balances on which the American government is based. Today few people would deny to the courts the right to decide that a legislative or executive act is unconstitutional, though once that right was controversial. What

Chief Justice William H. Rehnquist presiding over the Clinton impeachment trial

remains controversial is the method by which such review is conducted.

There are two competing views, each ardently pressed during the fight to confirm Clarence Thomas. The first holds that judges should only judge—that is, they should confine themselves to applying those rules that are stated in or clearly implied by the language of the Constitution. This is often called the **strict-constructionist approach.** The other argues that judges should discover the general principles underlying the Constitution and its often vague language, amplify those principles on the basis of some moral or economic philosophy, and apply them to cases. This is sometimes called the **activist approach.**

Note that the difference between activist and strict-constructionist judges is not necessarily the same as the difference between liberals and conservatives. Judges can be political liberals and still believe that they are bound by the language of the Constitution. A liberal justice, Hugo Black, once voted to uphold a state law banning birth control because nothing in the Constitution prohibited such a law. Or judges can be conservative and still think

Table 14.1	**Chief Justices of the United States**	
Chief Justice	**Appointed By**	**Years of Service**
John Jay	Washington	1789–1795
Oliver Ellsworth	Washington	1796–1800
John Marshall	Adams	1801–1835
Roger B. Taney	Jackson	1836–1864
Salmon P. Chase	Lincoln	1864–1873
Morrison R. Waite	Grant	1874–1888
Melville W. Fuller	Cleveland	1888–1910
Edward D. White	Taft	1910–1921
William Howard Taft	Harding	1921–1930
Charles Evans Hughes	Hoover	1930–1941
Harlan Fiske Stone	F. Roosevelt	1941–1946
Fred M. Vinson	Truman	1946–1953
Earl Warren	Eisenhower	1953–1969
Warren E. Burger	Nixon	1969–1986
William H. Rehnquist	Reagan	1986–present

Note: Omitted is John Rutledge, who served for only a few months in 1795 and who was not confirmed by the Senate.

that they have a duty to use their best judgment in deciding what is good public policy. Rufus Peckham, one such conservative, voted to overturn a state law setting maximum hours of work because he believed that the Fourteenth Amendment guaranteed something called "freedom of contract," even though those words are not in the amendment.

Fifty years ago judicial activists tended to be conservatives and strict-constructionist judges tended to be liberals; today the opposite is usually the case.

The Development of the Federal Courts

Most of the Founders probably expected the Supreme Court to have the power of judicial review (though they did not say that in so many words in the Constitution), but they did not expect federal courts to play so large a role in making public policy. The traditional view of civil courts was that they judged disputes between people who had direct dealings with each other—they had entered into a contract, for example, or one had dropped a load of bricks on the other's toe—and decided which of the two parties was right. The court then supplied relief to the wronged party, usually by requiring the other person to pay him or her money ("damages").

This traditional understanding was based on the belief that judges would find and apply existing law. The purpose of a court case was not to learn what the judge believes but what the law requires. The later rise of judicial activism occurred when judges questioned this traditional view and argued instead that judges do not merely find the law, they make the law.

The view that judges interpret the law and do not make policy made it easy for the Founders to justify the power of judicial review and led them to predict that the courts would play a relatively neutral, even passive, role in public affairs. Alexander Hamilton, writing in *Federalist* No. 78, described the judiciary as the branch "least dangerous" to political rights. The president is commander in chief and thus holds the "sword of the community"; Congress appropriates money and thus "commands the purse" as well as decides what laws shall govern. But the judiciary "has no influence over either the sword or the purse" and "can take no active resolution whatever." It has "neither force nor will but merely judgment," and thus is "beyond comparison the weakest of the three

departments of power." As a result "liberty can have nothing to fear from the judiciary alone." Hamilton went on to state clearly that the Constitution intended to give to the courts the right to decide whether a law is contrary to the Constitution. But this authority, he explained, was designed not to enlarge the power of the courts but to confine that of the legislature.

Obviously things have changed since Hamilton's time. The evolution of the federal courts, especially the Supreme Court, toward the present level of activism and influence has been shaped by the political, economic, and ideological forces of three historical eras. From 1787 to 1865 nation building, the legitimacy of the federal government, and slavery were the great issues; from 1865 to 1937 the dominant issue was the relationship between the government and the economy; from 1938 to the present the major issues confronting the Court have involved personal liberty and social equality and the potential conflict between the two. In the first period the Court asserted the supremacy of the federal government; in the second it placed important restrictions on the powers of that government; and in the third it enlarged the scope of personal freedom and narrowed that of economic freedom.

National Supremacy and Slavery

"From 1789 until the Civil War, the dominant interest of the Supreme Court was in that greatest of all the questions left unresolved by the Founders—the nation-state relationship."[2] The answer that the Court gave, under the leadership of Chief Justice John Marshall, was that national law was in all instances the dominant law, with state law having to give way, and that the Supreme Court had the power to decide what the Constitution meant. In two cases of enormous importance—*Marbury v. Madison* in 1803 and *McCulloch v. Maryland* in 1819—the Court, in decisions written by Marshall, held that the Supreme Court could declare an act of Congress unconstitutional; that the power granted by the Constitution to the federal government flows from the people and thus should be generously construed (and thus any federal laws that are "necessary and proper" to the attainment of constitutional ends are permissible); and that federal law is supreme over state law, even to the point that a state may not tax an enterprise (such as a bank) created by the federal government.[3]

Marbury v. Madison

The story of *Marbury v. Madison* is often told, but it deserves another telling because it illustrates so many features of the role of the Supreme Court—how apparently small cases can have large results, how the power of the Court depends not simply on its constitutional authority but also on its acting in ways that avoid a clear confrontation with other branches of government, and how the climate of opinion affects how the Court goes about its task.

When President John Adams lost his bid for reelection to Thomas Jefferson in 1800, he—and all members of his party, the Federalists—feared that Jefferson and the Republicans would weaken the federal government and turn its powers to what the Federalists believed were wrong ends (states' rights, an alliance with the French, hostility to business). Feverishly, as his hours in office came to an end, Adams worked to pack the judiciary with fifty-nine loyal Federalists by giving them so-called midnight appointments before Jefferson took office.

John Marshall, as Adams's secretary of state, had the task of certifying and delivering these new judicial commissions. In the press of business he delivered all but seventeen; these he left on his desk for the incoming secretary of state, James Madison, to send out. Jefferson and Madison, however, were furious at Adams's behavior and refused to deliver the seventeen. William Marbury and three other Federalists who had been promised these commissions hired a lawyer and brought suit against Madison to force him to produce the documents. The suit requested the Supreme Court to issue a writ of mandamus (from the Latin, "we command") ordering Madison to do his duty. The right to issue such writs had been given to the Court by the Judiciary Act of 1789.

Marshall, the man who had failed to deliver the commissions to Marbury and his friends in the first place, had become the chief justice and was now in a position to decide the case. These days a justice who had been involved in an issue before it came to the Court would probably disqualify himself or herself, but Marshall had no intention of letting others decide this question. He faced, however, not simply a partisan dispute over jobs but what was nearly a constitutional crisis. If he ordered the commission delivered, Madison might still refuse, and the Court had no way—if Madison was determined to resist—to compel him. The Court had no police force, whereas Madison had the support of the president of the

---

The supremacy of the federal government was reaffirmed by other decisions as well. In 1816 the Supreme Court rejected the claim of the Virginia courts that the Supreme Court could not review the decisions of state courts. The Virginia courts were ready to acknowledge the supremacy of the U.S. Constitution but believed that they had as much right as the U.S. Supreme Court to decide what the Constitution meant. The Supreme Court felt otherwise, and in this case and another like it the Court asserted its own broad powers to review any state court decision if that decision seemed to violate federal law or the federal Constitution.[4]

The power of the federal government to regulate commerce among the states was also established. When New York gave to Robert Fulton, the inventor of the steamboat, the monopoly right to operate his steamboats on the rivers of that state, the Marshall Court overturned the license because the rivers connected New York and New Jersey and thus trade on those rivers would involve *inter*state commerce, and federal law in that area was supreme. Since there was a conflicting federal law on the books, the state law was void.[5]

All of this may sound rather obvious to us today, when the supremacy of the federal government is largely unquestioned. In the early nineteenth century, however, these were almost revolutionary decisions. The Jeffersonian Republicans were in power and had become increasingly devoted to states' rights; they were aghast at the Marshall decisions. President Andrew Jackson attacked the Court bitterly for defending the right of the federal government to create a national bank and for siding with the Cherokee Indians in a dispute with Georgia. In speaking of the latter case, Jackson is supposed to have remarked, "John Marshall has made his decision; now let him enforce it!"[6]

Though Marshall seemed to have secured the supremacy of the federal government over the state

United States. And if the order were given, whether or not Madison complied, the Jeffersonian Republicans in Congress would probably try to impeach Marshall. On the other hand, if Marshall allowed Madison to do as he wished, the power of the Supreme Court would be seriously reduced.

Marshall's solution was ingenious. Speaking for a unanimous Court, he announced that Madison was wrong to withhold the commissions, that courts could issue writs to compel public officials to do their prescribed duty—*but* that the Supreme Court had no power to issue such writs in this case because the law (the Judiciary Act of 1789) giving it that power was unconstitutional. The law said that the Supreme Court could issue such writs as part of its "original jurisdiction"—that is, persons seeking such writs could go *directly* to the Supreme Court with their request (rather than go first to a lower federal court and then, if dissatisfied, appeal to the Supreme Court). Article III of the Constitution, Marshall pointed out, spelled out precisely the Supreme Court's original jurisdiction; it did not mention issuing writs of this sort and plainly indicated that on all matters not mentioned in the Constitution, the Court would have only appellate jurisdiction. Congress may

John Adams   James Madison

not change what the Constitution says; hence the part of the Judiciary Act attempting to do this was null and void.

The result was that a showdown with the Jeffersonians was avoided—Madison was not ordered to deliver the commissions—but the power of the Supreme Court was unmistakably clarified and enlarged. As Marshall wrote, "It is emphatically the province and duty of the judicial department to say what the law is." Furthermore, "a law repugnant to the Constitution is void."

governments, another even more divisive issue had arisen; that, of course, was slavery. Roger B. Taney succeeded Marshall as chief justice in 1836. He was deliberately chosen by President Jackson because he was an advocate of states' rights, and he began to chip away at federal supremacy, upholding state claims that Marshall would have set aside. But the decision for which he is famous—or infamous— came in 1857, when in the *Dred Scott* case he wrote perhaps the most disastrous judicial opinion ever issued. A slave, Dred Scott, had been taken by his owner to a territory (near what is now St. Paul, Minnesota) where slavery was illegal under federal law. Scott claimed that since he had resided in a free territory, he was now a free man. Taney held that Negroes were not citizens of the United States and could not become so, and that the federal law—the Missouri Compromise—prohibiting slavery in northern territories was unconstitutional.[7] The public outcry against this view was enormous, and the Court

and Taney were discredited in the North, at least. The Civil War was ultimately fought over what the Court mistakenly had assumed was a purely legal question.

Government and the Economy

The supremacy of the federal government may have been established by John Marshall and the Civil War, but the scope of the powers of that government or even of the state governments was still to be defined. During the period from the end of the Civil War to the early years of the New Deal, the dominant issue the Supreme Court faced was deciding when the economy would be regulated by the states and when by the nation.

The Court revealed a strong though not inflexible attachment to private property. In fact that attachment had always been there: the Founders thought that political and property rights were inextricably linked, and Marshall certainly supported the sanctity of contracts. But now, with the muting of the federal

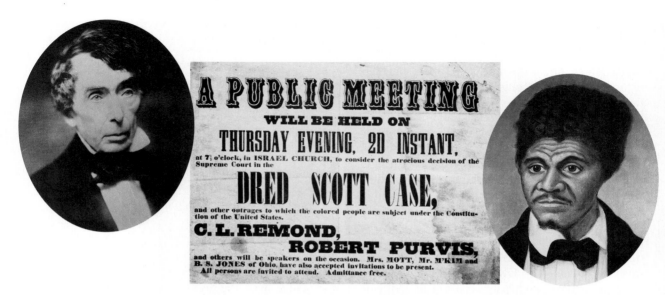

Roger B. Taney, chief justice from 1836 to 1864, wrote the Dred Scott *decision, which asserted that blacks were not citizens of the United States. Dred Scott claimed that when his master brought him north to a free state, he ceased to be a slave. The public outcry against the decision was intense, at least in the North, as is evident from this poster announcing a mass meeting "to consider the atrocious decision."*

supremacy issue and the rise of a national economy with important unanticipated effects, the property question became the dominant one. In general the Court developed the view that the Fourteenth Amendment, adopted in 1868 primarily to protect African American claims to citizenship from hostile state action, also protected private property and the corporation from unreasonable state action. The crucial phrase was this: no state shall "deprive any person of life, liberty, or property, without due process of law." Once it became clear that a "person" could be a firm or a corporation as well as an individual, business and industry began to flood the courts with cases challenging various government regulations.

The Court quickly found itself in a thicket: it began ruling on the constitutionality of virtually every effort by any government to regulate any aspect of business or labor, and its workload rose sharply. Judicial activism was born in the 1880s and 1890s as the Court set itself up as the arbiter of what kind of regulation was permissible. In the first seventy-five years of this country's history, only 2 federal laws were held to be unconstitutional; in the next seventy-five years, 71 were.[8] Of the roughly 1,300 state laws held to be in conflict with the federal Constitution since 1789, about 1,200 were overturned after

1870. In one decade alone—the 1880s—5 federal and 48 state laws were declared unconstitutional.

Many of these decisions provided clear evidence of the Court's desire to protect private property: it upheld the use of injunctions to prevent labor strikes,[9] struck down the federal income tax,[10] sharply limited the reach of the antitrust law,[11] restricted the powers of the Interstate Commerce Commission to set railroad rates,[12] prohibited the federal government from eliminating child labor,[13] and prevented the states from setting maximum hours of work.[14] In 184 cases between 1899 and 1937, the Supreme Court struck down state laws for violating the Fourteenth Amendment, usually by economic regulation.[15]

But the Court also rendered decisions that authorized various kinds of regulation. It allowed states to regulate businesses "affected with a public interest,"[16] changed its mind about the Interstate Commerce Commission and allowed it to regulate railroad rates,[17] upheld rules requiring railroads to improve their safety,[18] approved state antiliquor laws,[19] approved state mine safety laws,[20] supported state workers' compensation laws,[21] allowed states to regulate fire-insurance rates,[22] and in time upheld a number of state laws regulating wages and hours.

Indeed, between 1887 and 1910, in 558 cases involving the Fourteenth Amendment, the Supreme Court upheld state regulations over 80 percent of the time.[23]

To characterize the Court as probusiness or antiregulation is both simplistic and inexact. More accurate, perhaps, is to characterize it as supportive of the rights of private property but unsure how to draw the lines that distinguish "reasonable" from "unreasonable" regulation. Nothing in the Constitution clearly differentiates reasonable from unreasonable regulation, and the Court has been able to invent no consistent principle of its own to make this determination. For example, what kinds of businesses are "affected with a public interest"? Grain elevators and railroads are, but are bakeries? Sugar refiners? Saloons? And how much of commerce is "interstate"—anything that moves? Or only something that actually crosses a state line? The Court found itself trying to make detailed judgments that it was not always competent to make and to invent legal rules where no clear legal rules were possible.

In one area, however, the Supreme Court's judgments were clear: the Fourteenth and Fifteenth Amendments were construed so narrowly as to give African Americans only the most limited benefits of their provisions. In a long series of decisions the Court upheld segregation in schools and on railroad cars and permitted blacks to be excluded from voting in many states.

Government and Political Liberty

After 1936 the Supreme Court stopped imposing any serious restrictions on state or federal power to regulate the economy, leaving such matters in the hands of the legislatures. From 1937 to 1974 the Supreme Court did not overturn a single federal law designed to regulate business but did overturn thirty-six congressional enactments that violated personal political liberties. It voided as unconstitutional laws that restricted freedom of speech,[24] denied passports to communists,[25] permitted the government to revoke a person's citizenship,[26] withheld a person's mail,[27] or restricted the availability of government benefits.[28]

This new direction began when one justice changed his mind, and it continued as the composition of the Court changed. At the outset of the New Deal the Court was, by a narrow margin, dominated by justices who opposed the welfare state and federal regulation based on broad grants of discretionary authority to administrative agencies. President Franklin Roosevelt, who was determined to get just such legislation implemented, found himself powerless to alter the composition of the Court during his first term (1933–1937): because no justice died retired, he had no vacancies to fill. After his

The "nine old men": The Supreme Court in 1937, not long after President Franklin D. Roosevelt tried, unsuccessfully, to "pack" it by appointing six additional justices who would have supported his New Deal legislation. Justice Owen J. Roberts (standing, second from the left) changed his vote on these matters, and the Court ceased to be a barrier to the delegation of power to the bureaucracy.

U.S. District and Appellate Courts

Note: Washington, D.C., is in a separate court. Puerto Rico is in the first circuit; the Virgin Islands are in the third; Guam and the Northern Mariana Islands are in the ninth.
Source: Administrative Office of the United States Courts (January 1983).

overwhelming reelection in 1936, he moved to remedy this problem by "packing" the Court.

Roosevelt proposed a bill that would have allowed him to appoint one new justice for each one over the age of seventy who refused to retire, up to a total membership of fifteen. Since there were six men in this category then on the Supreme Court, he would have been able to appoint six new justices, enough to ensure a comfortable majority supportive of his economic policies. A bitter controversy ensued, but before the bill could be voted on, the Supreme Court, perhaps reacting to Roosevelt's big win in the 1936 election, changed its mind. Whereas it had been striking down several New Deal measures by votes of five to four, now it started approving them by the same vote. One justice, Owen Roberts, had switched his position. This was called the "switch in time that saved nine," but in fact Roberts had changed his mind *before* the FDR plan was announced.

The "Court-packing" bill was not passed, but it was no longer necessary. Justice Roberts had yielded before public opinion in a way that Chief Justice Taney a century earlier had not, thus forestalling an assault on the Court by the other branches of government. Shortly thereafter several justices stepped down, and Roosevelt was able to make his own appointments (he filled seven seats during his four terms in office). From then on the Court turned its attention to new issues—political liberties and, in time, civil rights.

With the arrival in office of Chief Justice Earl Warren in 1953, the Court began its most active period yet. Activism now arose to redefine the relationship of citizens to the government and especially to protect the rights and liberties of citizens from governmental trespass. Although the Court has always seen itself as protecting citizens from arbitrary government, before 1937 that protection was of a sort that conservatives preferred; after 1937 it was of a kind that liberals preferred.

The Revival of State Sovereignty

For many decades the Supreme Court allowed Congress to pass almost any law authorized by the Constitution, no matter how it affected the states. As we saw in Chapter 3, the Court had long held that Congress could regulate almost any activity if it affected interstate commerce, and in the Court's opinion virtually every activity did affect it. The states were left with few rights to challenge federal power. But since around 1992 the Court has backed away from this view. By narrow majorities it has begun to restore the view that states have the right to resist some forms of federal action.

When Congress passed a bill that forbade anyone from carrying a gun near a school, the Court held that carrying guns did not affect interstate commerce, and so the law was invalid.[29] One year later it struck down a law that allowed Indian tribes to sue the states in federal courts, arguing that Congress lacks the power to ignore the "sovereign immunity" of states—that is, the right, protected by the Eleventh Amendment, not to be sued in federal court. (It has since upheld that view in two more cases.) And the next year it held that the Brady gun control law could not be used to require local law enforcement officers to do background checks on people trying to buy weapons.[30] These cases are all hints that there are some real limits to the supremacy of the federal government created by the existence and powers of the several states.

The Structure of the Federal Courts

The only federal court that the Constitution requires is the Supreme Court, as specified in Article III. All other federal courts and their jurisdictions are creations of Congress. Nor does the Constitution indicate how many justices shall be on the Supreme Court (there were originally six, now there are nine) or what its appellate jurisdiction shall be.

Congress has created two kinds of lower federal courts to handle cases that need not be decided by the Supreme Court: constitutional and legislative courts. A **constitutional court** is one exercising the judicial powers found in Article III of the Constitution, and therefore its judges are given constitutional protection: they may not be fired (they serve during "good behavior"), nor may their salaries be reduced while they are in office. The most important of the constitutional courts are the **district courts** (a total of ninety-four, with at least one in each state, the District of Columbia, and the commonwealth of Puerto Rico) and the **courts of appeals** (one in each of eleven regions, or circuits, plus one in the District of Columbia). There are also certain specialized courts having constitutional status, such as the Court of International Trade, but we shall not be concerned with them.

A **legislative court** is one set up by Congress for some specialized purpose and staffed with people who have fixed terms of office and can be removed or have their salaries reduced. Legislative courts include the Court of Military Appeals and the territorial courts.

Selecting Judges

Since the judges on the constitutional courts serve for life and have the power of judicial review, how they are selected and what attitudes they bring to the bench are obviously important. All are nominated by the president and confirmed by the Senate. Almost invariably the president nominates a member of his own political party.

Party background does have some effect on how judges behave. A study by Robert A. Carp and C. K. Rowland of over twenty-seven thousand district court cases decided between 1933 and 1977 revealed that Democratic judges took somewhat more liberal positions than Republican ones (see Table 14.2). The biggest differences were in cases alleging discrimination based on race or sex and in those involving the rights of the accused in criminal prosecutions. In these matters Democratic judges reached a "liberal" decision 13 to 18 percent more frequently than Republican ones. Comparable findings have come from studies of appeals court and Supreme Court justices.[31] This is consistent with what we have already learned about public opinion: within political elites partisanship is associated with ideology, and this affects behavior.

But ideology does not determine behavior. So many other things shape court decisions—the facts of the case, prior rulings by other courts, the arguments presented by lawyers—that there is no reliable way of

Table 14.2   How Partisanship Affects Judicial Attitudes

In 1984 over one hundred federal judges were interviewed to learn about their background and attitudes. There were about equal numbers of Democrats and Republicans, and they were quite similar in social background. The overwhelming majority were white males; their average age was sixty. Most had attended a prestigious college. Despite these similarities, they expressed quite different political views and applied quite different judicial philosophies.

	Judges Appointed By:	
Attitudes	**Democrats**	**Republicans**
Political Ideology		
Liberal	75%	28%
Conservative	11	37
Policy Positions		
Favor less government regulation of business	54	85
Government should reduce income gap between rich and poor	78	44
Special preference should be given to blacks in hiring	62	41
Special preference should be given to women in hiring	47	22
A woman has right to decide on abortion	81	80
Judicial Philosophy		
Courts show too much concern for criminals	16	44
Judges should just apply the law, leave the rest to legislators	51	69
Judges need to supervise public bureaucracies	81	64

Source: Althea K. Nagai, Stanley Rothman, and S. Robert Lichter, "The Verdict of Federal Judges," *Public Opinion* (November/December 1987): 52–56. Reprinted with the permission of the American Enterprise Institute for Public Policy Research, Washington, D.C.

predicting how judges will behave in all matters. Presidents often make the mistake of thinking that they know how their appointees will behave, only to be surprised by the facts. Theodore Roosevelt appointed Oliver Wendell Holmes to the Supreme Court, only to remark later, after Holmes had voted in a way that Roosevelt did not like, that "I could carve out of a banana a judge with more backbone than that!" Holmes, who had plenty of backbone, said that he did not "give a damn" what Roosevelt thought. Richard Nixon, an ardent foe of court-ordered school busing, appointed Warren Burger to be chief justice. Burger promptly sat down and wrote the opinion upholding busing. Another Nixon appointee, Harry Blackmun, wrote the opinion declaring the right to an abortion to be constitutionally protected.

In addition, getting judges confirmed by the Senate has become quite a long process. As discussed in Chapter 12 (see page 346), the presidential appointment process now works very slowly. Thus in

2002 the sixth circuit had eight judges at work and eight vacancies; nationally, some ninety federal judgeships were not filled.

■ **Senatorial Courtesy**   In theory the president nominates a "qualified" person to be a judge, and the Senate approves or rejects the nomination based on those "qualifications." In fact the tradition of *senatorial courtesy* gives heavy weight to the preferences of the senators from the state where a federal district judge is to serve. Ordinarily the Senate will not confirm a district court judge if the senior senator from the state where the district is located objects (if he is of the president's party). The senator can exercise this veto power by means of the "blue slip"—a blue piece of paper on which the senator is asked to record his or her views on the nominee. A negative opinion, or even failure to return the blue slip, usually kills the nomination. This means that as a practical matter the president nominates only persons recommended to him by that key senator. Someone once suggested that, at least with respect to district judges, the Constitution has been turned on its head. To reflect reality, he said, Article II, section 2, ought to read: "The senators shall nominate, and by and with the consent of the President, shall appoint" federal judges.

■ **The "Litmus Test"** Of late, presidents have tried to exercise more influence on the selection of federal district and appellate court judges by getting the Justice Department to find candidates that not only are supported by their party's senators but also reflect the political and judicial philosophy of the president. Presidents Carter and Clinton sought out liberal, activist judges; President Reagan sought out conservative, strict-constructionist ones. The party membership of federal judges makes a difference in how they vote. A review of eighty-four studies shows that Democratic judges are more liberal than Republican ones.[32]

Because different courts of appeals have different combinations of judges, some will be more liberal than others. For example, there are more liberal judges in the court of appeals for the ninth circuit (which includes most of the far western states) and more conservative ones in the fifth circuit (Texas, Louisiana, and Mississippi). The ninth circuit takes liberal positions, the fifth more conservative ones. Since the Supreme Court does not have time to settle every disagreement among appeals courts, different interpretations of the law may exist in different circuits. In the fifth and eleventh circuits, for instance, it is unconstitutional for state universities to have affirmative action programs.

These differences make some people worry about the use of a political **litmus test**—a test of ideological purity—in selecting judges. When conservatives are out of power, they complain about how liberal presidents use such a test; when liberals are out power, they complain about how conservative presidents use it. Many people would like to see judges picked on the basis of professional qualifications, without reference to ideology, but the courts are now so deeply involved in political issues that it is hard to imagine what an ideologically neutral set of professional qualifications might be.

The litmus test has grown in importance. During the Clinton administration it was hard for the president to get his candidates for judgeships approved by the Senate. This was not just a result of his being a Democrat and the Senate being under Republican control. That has happened before, but without producing

Figure 14.1 Female and Minority Judicial Appointments, 1963–2000

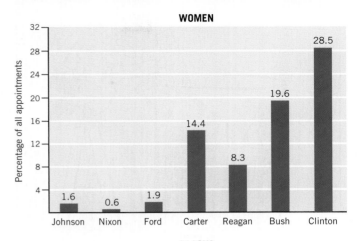

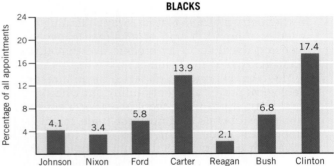

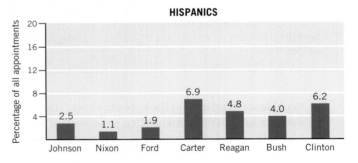

Source: Harold W. Stanley and Richard G. Niemi, *Vital Statistics on American Politics, 2001–2002* (Washington, D.C.: Congressional Quarterly, 2001), table 7.5.

a logjam. The real problem is the litmus test: Democrats want judges that support abortion, look favorably on affirmative action, and oppose giving public money to students who attend private schools.

Litmus Test

In chemistry a litmus test is a way of finding out whether a liquid is acid or alkaline. It involves exposing the fluid to an organic dye that turns red in acids, blue in alkalines.

The term is used in politics to mean a test of ideological purity, a way of finding out whether a person is a dyed-in-the-wool liberal or a conservative. For liberals a litmus test issue might be support for abortion or opposition to school prayer; for conservatives it might be holding the opposite of these views, or perhaps favoring tax cuts.

Source: From *Safire's Political Dictionary* by William Safire. Copyright © 1968, 1972, 1978 by William Safire. Reprinted by permission of Random House, Inc. and the author.

Republicans tend to have the opposite views. These differences in opinion would not be so important if the courts did not play an active role in making decisions on these matters. At one time they did not. But now the courts are settling these issues, and so politicians increasingly want them to be decided the "right way." With divided government, the litmus test has become much more important.

The litmus test issue is of greatest importance in selecting Supreme Court justices. Here there is no tradition of senatorial courtesy. The president takes a keen personal interest in the choices and, of late, has sought to find nominees who share his philosophy. In the Reagan administration there were bruising fights in the Senate over the nomination of William Rehnquist to be chief justice (he won) and Robert Bork to be an associate justice (he lost), with liberals pitted against conservatives. When President Bush nominated David Souter, there were lengthy hearings as liberal senators tried to pin down Souter's views on issues such as abortion. Souter refused to discuss matters on which he might later have to judge, however. Clarence Thomas, another Bush nominee, also tried to avoid the litmus test by saying that he had not formed an opinion on prominent abortion cases. In his case, however, the litmus test issue was overshadowed by sensational allegations from a former employee, Anita Hill, that Thomas had sexually harassed her.

Of the 145 Supreme Court nominees presented to it, the Senate has rejected 29. Only 5 of these were in the twentieth century. The reasons for rejecting a Supreme Court nominee are complex—each senator may have a different reason—but have involved such matters as the nominee's alleged hostility to civil rights, questionable personal financial dealings, a poor record as a lower-court judge, and Senate opposition to the nominee's political or legal philosophy. Nominations of district court judges are rarely defeated, because typically no nomination is made unless the key senators approve in advance.

The Jurisdiction of the Federal Courts

We have a dual court system—one state, one federal—and this complicates enormously the task of describing what kinds of cases federal courts may hear and how cases beginning in the state courts may end up before the Supreme Court. The Constitution lists the kinds of cases over which federal courts have jurisdiction (in Article III and the Eleventh Amendment); by implication all other matters are left to state courts. Federal courts (see Figure 14.2) can hear all cases "arising under the Constitution, the laws of the United States, and treaties" (these are **federal-question cases**), and cases involving citizens of different states (called **diversity cases**).

Some kinds of cases can be heard in either federal or state courts. For example, if citizens of different states wish to sue one another and the matter involves more than $75,000, they can do so in either a federal or a state court. Similarly, if someone robs a federally insured bank, he or she has broken both state and

Figure 14.2   The Jurisdiction of the Federal Courts

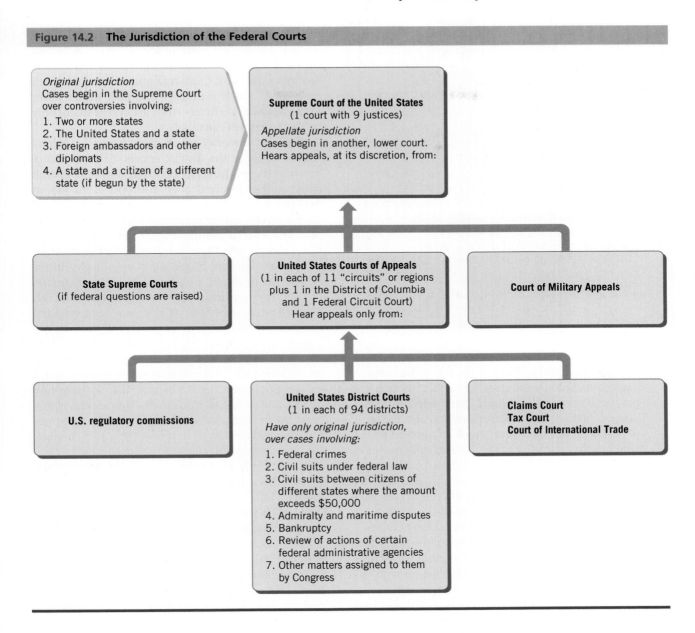

Original jurisdiction
Cases begin in the Supreme Court over controversies involving:

1. Two or more states
2. The United States and a state
3. Foreign ambassadors and other diplomats
4. A state and a citizen of a different state (if begun by the state)

Supreme Court of the United States
(1 court with 9 justices)
Appellate jurisdiction
Cases begin in another, lower court.
Hears appeals, at its discretion, from:

State Supreme Courts
(if federal questions are raised)

United States Courts of Appeals
(1 in each of 11 "circuits" or regions plus 1 in the District of Columbia and 1 Federal Circuit Court)
Hear appeals only from:

Court of Military Appeals

U.S. regulatory commissions

United States District Courts
(1 in each of 94 districts)
Have only original jurisdiction, over cases involving:

1. Federal crimes
2. Civil suits under federal law
3. Civil suits between citizens of different states where the amount exceeds $50,000
4. Admiralty and maritime disputes
5. Bankruptcy
6. Review of actions of certain federal administrative agencies
7. Other matters assigned to them by Congress

Claims Court
Tax Court
Court of International Trade

---

federal law and thus can be prosecuted in state or federal courts, or both. Lawyers have become quite sophisticated in deciding whether, in a given civil case, their clients will get better treatment in a state or federal court. Prosecutors often send a person who has broken both federal and state law to whichever court system is likelier to give the toughest penalty.

Sometimes defendants may be tried in both state and federal courts for the same offense. In 1992 four Los Angeles police officers accused of beating Rodney King were tried in a California state court and acquitted of assault charges. They were then prosecuted in federal court for violating King's civil rights. This time two of the four were convicted. Under the dual sovereignty doctrine, state and federal authorities can prosecute the same person for the same conduct. The Supreme Court has upheld this doctrine on two grounds: First, each level of government has the right to enact laws serving its own purposes.[33] As a result federal civil rights charges could have been

★ **POLITICALLY SPEAKING** ★

Kinds of Law

The differences between *civil* and *criminal* law are not precise. Generally speaking:

- **Civil law** is the body of rules defining relationships among private citizens. It consists of both statutes and the accumulated customary law embodied in judicial decisions (the "common law").
- **Criminal law** is the body of rules defining offenses that, though they harm an individual (such as murder, rape, and robbery), are considered to be offenses against society as a whole and thus warrant punishment by and in the name of society.

You can go to prison if convicted of a crime but not if you lose a civil suit.

brought against the officers even if they had already been convicted of assault in state court (though as a practical matter this would have been unlikely). Second, neither level of government wants the other to be able to block prosecution of an accused person who has the sympathy of the authorities at one level. For example, when certain southern state courts were in sympathy with whites who had lynched blacks, the absence of the dual sovereignty doctrine would have meant that a trumped-up acquittal in state court would have barred federal prosecution.

Furthermore, a matter that is exclusively within the province of a state court—for example, a criminal case in which the defendant is charged with violating only a state law—can be appealed to the U.S. Supreme Court under certain circumstances (described below). Thus federal judges can overturn state court rulings even when they had no jurisdiction over the original matter. Under what circumstances this should occur has been the subject of long-standing controversy between the state and federal courts.

Some matters, however, are exclusively under the jurisdiction of federal courts. When a federal criminal law is broken—but not a state one—the case is heard in federal district court. If you wish to appeal the decision of a federal regulatory agency, such as the Federal Communications Commission, you can

do so only before a federal court of appeals. And if you wish to declare bankruptcy, you do so in federal court. If there is a controversy between two state governments—say, California and Arizona sue each other over which state is to use how much water from the Colorado River—the case can be heard only by the Supreme Court.

The vast majority of all cases heard by federal courts begin in the district courts. The volume of business there is huge. In 2000 the 650 or so district court judges received over 300,000 cases (about 500 per judge). Most of the cases heard in federal courts involve rather straightforward applications of law; few lead to the making of new public policy. Cases that do affect how the law or the Constitution is interpreted can begin with seemingly minor events. For example, a major broadening of the Bill of Rights—requiring for the first time that all accused persons in *state* as well as federal criminal trials be supplied with a lawyer, free if necessary—began when impoverished Clarence Earl Gideon, imprisoned in Florida, wrote an appeal in pencil on prison stationery and sent it to the Supreme Court.[34]

The Supreme Court does not have to hear any appeal it does not want to hear. At one time it was required to listen to certain appeals, but Congress has changed the law so that now the Court can pick the cases it wants to consider.

It does this by issuing a **writ of certiorari.** *Certiorari* is a Latin word meaning, roughly, "made more certain"; lawyers and judges have abbreviated it to *cert.* It works this way: The Court considers all the petitions it receives to review lower-court decisions. If four justices agree to hear a case, cert is issued and the case is scheduled for a hearing.

In deciding whether to grant certiorari, the Court tries to reserve its time for cases decided by lower federal courts or by the highest state courts in which a significant federal or constitutional question has been raised. For example, the Court will often grant certiorari when one or both of the following is true:

- Two or more federal circuit courts of appeals have decided the same issue in different ways.
- The highest court in a state has held a federal or state law to be in violation of the Constitution or has upheld a state law against the claim that it is in violation of the Constitution.

In a typical year the Court may consider over seven thousand petitions asking it to review deci-

Clarence Earl Gideon studied law books while in prison so that he could write an appeal to the Supreme Court. His handwritten appeal asked that his conviction be set aside because he had not been provided with an attorney. His appeal was granted.

sions of lower or state courts. It rarely accepts more than about one hundred of them for full review.

In exercising its discretion in granting certiorari, the Supreme Court is on the horns of a dilemma. If it grants it frequently, it will be inundated with cases. As it is, the Court's workload has quintupled in the last fifty years. If, on the other hand, the Court grants certiorari only rarely, then the federal courts of appeals have the last word on the interpretation of the Constitution and federal laws, and since there are twelve of these, staffed by about 167 judges, they may well be in disagreement. In fact this has already happened: because the Supreme Court reviews only about 1 or 2 percent of appeals court cases, applicable federal law may be different in different parts of the country.[35] One proposal to deal with this dilemma is to devote the Supreme Court's time entirely to major questions of constitutional interpretation and to create a national court of appeals that would ensure that the twelve circuit courts of appeals are producing uniform decisions.[36]

Because the Supreme Court has a heavy workload, the influence wielded by law clerks has grown. These clerks—recent graduates of law schools hired by the justices—play a big role in deciding which cases should be heard under a writ of certiorari. Indeed, some of the opinions written by the justices are drafted by the clerks. Since the reasons for a decision may be as important as the decision itself, and since these reasons are sometimes created by the clerks, the power of the clerks can be significant.

Getting to Court

In theory the courts are the great equalizer in the federal government. To use the courts to settle a question, or even to alter fundamentally the accepted interpretation of the Constitution, one need not be elected to any office, have access to the mass media, be a member of an interest group, or be otherwise powerful or rich. Once the contending parties are before the courts, they are legally equal.

It is too easy to believe this theory uncritically or to dismiss it cynically. In fact it is hard to get before the Supreme Court: it rejects over 96 percent of the applications for certiorari that it receives. And the costs involved in getting to the Court can be high. To apply for certiorari costs only $300 (plus forty copies of the petition), but if certiorari is granted and the case is heard, the costs—for lawyers and for copies of the lower-court records in the case—can be very high. And by then one has already paid for the cost of the first hearing in the district court and probably one appeal to the circuit court of appeals. Furthermore, the time it takes to settle a matter in federal court can be quite long.

But there are ways to make these costs lower. If you are indigent—without funds—you can file and be heard as a pauper for nothing; about half the petitions arriving before the Supreme Court are **in forma pauperis** (such as the one from Gideon, described earlier). If your case began as a criminal trial in the district courts and you are poor, the government will supply you with a lawyer at no charge. If the matter is not a criminal case and you cannot afford to hire a lawyer, interest groups representing a wide spectrum of opinion sometimes are willing to take up the cause if the issue in the case seems sufficiently important. The American Civil Liberties Union (ACLU), a liberal group, represents some people who believe that their freedom of speech has been abridged or that their constitutional rights in criminal proceedings have been violated. The Center for Individual Rights, a conservative group, represents some people who feel that they have been victimized by racial quotas.

But interest groups do much more than just help people pay their bills. Many of the most important cases decided by the Court got there because an interest group organized the case, found the plaintiffs, chose the legal strategy, and mobilized legal allies. The NAACP has brought many key civil rights cases on behalf of individuals. Although in the past most such cases were brought by liberal interest groups, of late conservative interest groups have entered the courtroom on behalf of individuals. One helped sue CBS for televising a program that allegedly libeled General William Westmoreland, once the American commander in Vietnam. (Westmoreland lost the case.) And many important issues are raised by attorneys representing state and local governments. Several price-fixing cases have been won by state attorneys general on behalf of consumers in their states.

Fee Shifting

Unlike what happens in most of Europe, each party to a lawsuit in this country must pay its own way. (In England, by contrast, if you sue someone and lose, you pay the winner's costs as well as your own.) But various laws have made it easier to get someone else to pay. **Fee shifting** enables the **plaintiff** (the party that initiates the suit) to collect its costs from the defendant if the defendant loses, at least in certain kinds of cases. For example, if a corporation is found to have violated the antitrust laws, it must pay the legal fees of the winner. If an environmentalist group sues the Environmental Protection Agency, it can get the EPA to pay the group's legal costs. Even more important to individuals, Section 1983 of Chapter 42 of the *United States Code* allows a citizen to sue a state or local government official—say, a police officer or a school superintendent—who has deprived the citizen of some constitutional right or withheld some benefit to which the citizen is entitled. If the citizen wins, he or she can collect money damages and lawyers' fees from the government. Citizens, more aware of their legal rights, have become more litigious, and a flood of such "Section 1983" suits has burdened the courts. The Supreme Court has restricted fee shifting to cases authorized by statute,[37] but it is clear that the drift of policy has made it cheaper to go to court—at least for some cases.

Standing

There is, in addition, a nonfinancial restriction on getting into federal court. To sue, one must have **standing,** a legal concept that refers to who is entitled to bring a case. It is especially important in determining who can challenge the laws or actions of the government itself. A complex and changing set of rules governs standings; some of the more important ones are these:

- There must be an actual controversy between real adversaries. (You cannot bring a "friendly" suit against someone, hoping to lose in order to prove your friend right. You cannot ask a federal court for an opinion on a hypothetical or imaginary case or ask it to render an advisory opinion.)
- You must show that you have been harmed by the law or practice about which you are complaining. (It is not enough to dislike what the government or a corporation or a labor union does; you must show that you were actually harmed by that action.)
- Merely being a taxpayer does not ordinarily entitle you to challenge the constitutionality of a federal governmental action. (You may not want your tax money to be spent in certain ways, but your remedy is to vote against the politicians doing the spending; the federal courts will generally require that you show some other personal harm before you can sue.)

Congress and the courts have recently made it easier to acquire standing. It has always been the rule that a citizen could ask the courts to order federal officials to carry out some act that they were under a legal obligation to perform or to refrain from some action that was contrary to law. A citizen can also sue a government official personally in order to collect damages if the official acted contrary to law. For example, it was for long the case that if an FBI agent broke into your office without a search warrant, you could sue the agent and, if you won, collect money. However, you cannot sue the government itself without its consent. This is the doctrine of **sovereign immunity.** For instance, if the army accidentally kills your cow while testing a new cannon, you cannot sue the government to recover the cost of the cow unless the government agrees to be sued. (Since testing cannons is legal, you cannot sue the army officer who fired the cannon.) By statute Congress has given its consent for the government to be sued in many cases involving a dispute over a contract or damage done as a result of negligence (for example, the dead cow). Over the years these statutes have made it easier to take the government into court as a defendant.

Even some of the oldest rules defining standing have been liberalized. The rule that merely being a taxpayer does not entitle you to challenge in court a government decision has been relaxed where the citizen claims that a right guaranteed under the First Amendment is being violated. The Supreme Court allowed a taxpayer to challenge a federal law that would have given financial aid to parochial (or church-related) schools on the grounds that this aid violated the constitutional requirement of separation between church and state. On the other hand, another taxpayer suit to force the CIA to make public its budget failed because the Court decided that the taxpayer did not have standing in matters of this sort.[38]

Class-Action Suits

Under certain circumstances a citizen can benefit directly from a court decision, even though the citizen himself or herself has not gone into court. This can happen by means of a **class-action suit:** a case brought into court by a person on behalf not only of himself or herself but of all other persons in similar circumstances. Among the most famous of these was the 1954 case in which the Supreme Court found that Linda Brown, a black girl attending the fifth grade in the Topeka, Kansas, public schools, was denied the equal protection of the laws (guaranteed under the Fourteenth Amendment) because the schools in Topeka were segregated. The Court did not limit its decision to Linda Brown's right to attend an unsegregated school but extended it—as Brown's lawyers from the NAACP had asked—to cover all "others similarly situated."[39] It was not easy to design a court order that would eliminate segregation in the schools, but the principle was clearly established in this class action.

Since the *Brown* case, many other groups have been quick to take advantage of the opportunity created by class-action suits. By this means the courts could be used to give relief not simply to a particular person but to all those represented in the suit. A landmark class-action case was that which challenged the malapportionment of state legislative districts (see Chapter 11).[40] There are thousands of class-action suits in the federal courts involving civil rights, the rights of prisoners, antitrust suits against corporations, and other matters. These suits

became more common partly because people were beginning to have new concerns that were not being met by Congress and partly because some class-action suits became quite profitable. The NAACP got no money from Linda Brown or from the Topeka Board of Education in compensation for its long and expensive labors, but beginning in the 1960s court rules were changed to make it financially attractive for lawyers to bring certain kinds of class-action suits.

Suppose, for example, that you think your telephone company overcharged you by $75. You could try to hire a lawyer to get a refund, but not many lawyers would take the case, because there would be no money in it. Even if you were to win, the lawyer would stand to earn no more than perhaps one-third of the settlement, or $25. Now suppose that you bring a class action against the company on behalf of everybody who was overcharged. Millions of

Linda Brown was refused admission to a white elementary school in Topeka, Kansas. On her behalf the NAACP brought a class-action suit that resulted in the 1954 landmark Supreme Court decision Brown v. Board of Education.

Table 14.3 **Supreme Court Justices in Order of Seniority, 1999**			
Name (Birth Date)	**Home State**	**Prior Experience**	**Appointed By (Year)**
William H. Rehnquist, Chief Justice (1924)	Arizona	Justice; assistant attorney general	Reagan (1986) as chief; Nixon (1971) as justice
John Paul Stevens (1916)	Illinois	Federal judge	Ford (1975)
Sandra Day O'Connor (1930)	Arizona	State judge	Reagan (1981)
Antonin Scalia (1936)	New York	Federal judge	Reagan (1986)
Anthony Kennedy (1936)	California	Federal judge	Reagan (1988)
David Souter (1939)	New Hampshire	State judge	Bush (1990)
Clarence Thomas (1948)	Georgia	Federal judge	Bush (1991)
Ruth Bader Ginsburg (1933)	New York	Federal judge	Clinton (1993)
Stephen Breyer (1938)	Massachusetts	Federal judge	Clinton (1994)

dollars might be at stake; lawyers would line up eagerly to take the case, because their share of the settlement, if they won, would be huge. The opportunity to win profitable class-action suits, combined with the possibility of having the loser pay the attorneys' fees, led to a proliferation of such cases.

In response to the increase in its workload, the Supreme Court decided in 1974 to tighten drastically the rules governing these suits. It held that it would no longer hear (except in certain cases defined by Congress, such as civil rights matters) class-action suits seeking monetary damages unless each and every ascertainable member of the class was individually notified of the case. To do this is often prohibitively expensive (imagine trying to find and send a letter to every customer that may have been overcharged by the telephone company!), and so the number of such cases declined and the number of lawyers seeking them out dropped.[41]

But it remains easy to bring a class-action suit in most state courts. State Farm automobile insurance company was told by a state judge in a small Illinois town that it must pay over $1 billion in damages on behalf of a "national" class, even though no one in this class had been notified. Big class-action suits powerfully affect how courts make public policy. Such suits have forced into bankruptcy companies making asbestos and silicone breast implants and have threatened to put out of business tobacco companies and gun manufacturers. (Ironically, in some of these cases, such as the one involving breast implants, there was no scientific evidence showing that the product was harmful.) Some class-action suits, such as the one ending school segregation, are good, but others are frivolous efforts to get companies to pay large fees to the lawyers who file the suits.

In sum, getting into court depends on having standing and having resources. The rules governing standing are complex and changing, but generally they have been broadened to make it easier to enter the federal courts, especially for the purpose of challenging the actions of the government. Obtaining the resources is not easy but has become easier because laws in some cases now provide for fee shifting, private interest groups are willing to finance cases, and it is sometimes possible to bring a class-action suit that lawyers find lucrative.

The Supreme Court in Action

If your case should find its way to the Supreme Court—and of course the odds are that it will not—you will be able to participate in one of the more impressive, sometimes dramatic ceremonies of American public life. The Court is in session in its white marble building for thirty-six weeks out of each year, from early October until the end of June. The nine justices read briefs in their individual offices, hear oral arguments in the stately courtroom, and discuss their decisions with one another in a conference room where no outsider is ever allowed.

Most cases, as we have seen, come to the Court on a writ of certiorari. The lawyers for each side may then submit their briefs. A **brief** is a document that sets forth the facts of the case, summarizes the lower-court decision, gives the arguments for the side represented by the lawyer who wrote the brief, and discusses the other cases that the Court has decided bear on the issue. Then the lawyers are allowed to present their oral arguments in open court. They usually summarize their briefs or

This photo of the Supreme Court in session on February 8, 1932, may be the only one ever taken while the justices were actually hearing a case.

emphasize particular points in them, and they are strictly limited in time—usually to no more than a half hour. (The lawyer speaks from a lectern that has two lights on it. When the white light goes on, the attorney has five minutes remaining; when the red flashes, he or she must stop—instantly.) The oral arguments give the justices a chance to question the lawyers, sometimes searchingly.

Since the federal government is a party—as either plaintiff or defendant—to about half the cases that the Supreme Court hears, the government's top trial lawyer, the solicitor general of the United States, appears frequently before the Court. The solicitor general is the third-ranking officer of the Department of Justice, right after the attorney general and deputy attorney general. The solicitor general decides what cases the government will appeal from lower courts and personally approves every case the government presents to the Supreme Court. In recent years the solicitor general has often been selected from the ranks of distinguished law school professors.

In addition to the arguments made by lawyers for the two sides in a case, written briefs and even oral arguments may also be offered by "a friend of the court," or **amicus curiae.** An amicus brief is from an interested party not directly involved in the suit. For example, when Allan Bakke complained that he had

been the victim of "reverse discrimination" when he was denied admission to a University of California medical school, fifty-eight amicus briefs were filed supporting or opposing his position. Before such briefs can be filed, both parties must agree or the Court must grant permission. Though these briefs sometimes offer new arguments, they are really a kind of polite lobbying of the Court that declare which interest groups are on which side. The ACLU, the NAACP, the AFL-CIO, and the U.S. government itself have been among the leading sources of such briefs.

These briefs are not the only source of influence on the justices' views. Legal periodicals such as the *Harvard Law Review* and the *Yale Law Journal* are frequently consulted, and citations to them often appear in the Court's decisions. Thus the outside world of lawyers and law professors can help shape, or at least supply arguments for, the conclusions of the justices.

The justices retire every Friday to their conference room, where in complete secrecy they debate the cases they have heard. The chief justice speaks first, followed by the other justices in order of seniority. After the arguments they vote, traditionally in reverse order of seniority: the newest justice votes first, the chief justice last. By this process an able chief justice can exercise considerable influence—in guiding or limiting debate, in setting forth the issues,

The members of the U.S. Supreme Court: from left to right, Antonin Scalia, Ruth Bader Ginsburg, John Paul Stevens, David Souter, William Rehnquist, Clarence Thomas, Sandra Day O'Connor, Stephen Breyer, Anthony Kennedy.

and in handling sometimes temperamental personalities. In deciding a case, a majority of the justices must be in agreement: if there is a tie, the lower-court decision is left standing. (There can be a tie among nine justices if one is ill or disqualifies himself or herself because of prior involvement in the case.)

Though the vote is what counts, by tradition the Court usually issues a written opinion explaining its decision. Sometimes the opinion is brief and unsigned (called a **per curiam opinion**); sometimes it is quite long and signed by the justices agreeing with it. If the chief justice is in the majority, he will either write the opinion or assign the task to a justice who agrees with him. If he is in the minority, the senior justice on the winning side will decide who writes the Court's opinion. There are three kinds of opinions—an **opinion of the Court** (reflecting the majority's view), a **concurring opinion** (an opinion by one or more justices who agree with the majority's conclusion but for different reasons that they wish to express), and a **dissenting opinion** (the opinion of the justices on the

losing side). Each justice has three or four law clerks to help him or her review the many petitions the Court receives, study cases, and write opinions.

People like to think of the courts as expressing "liberal" or "conservative" opinions, and in many cases they seem to do just that. But that is far from the whole story. In many cases, perhaps two-fifths of those decided by the Supreme Court, the decisions are unanimous. Even two justices as different as Antonin Scalia and Ruth Bader Ginsburg vote the same way much of the time. The most important thing to remember is not the decision but the reasons behind the decision. Many times judges will vote for a position that they don't personally like but feel obliged to support because that is how the law reads.

The Power of the Federal Courts

The great majority of the cases heard in the federal courts have little or nothing to do with changes in

"Strategic Retirements" from the U.S. Supreme Court

Between 1789 and 2002, 101 justices departed from the U.S. Supreme Court. Overall. voluntary departures (retirements) and departures due to death have been about the same: 52 percent of the justices have retired; 48 percent have died while still members of the Court. But when University of Pennsylvania political science major Patrick Marecki studied these numbers more closely, he discovered an important fact: there has been a sharp increase in the rate of retirements. For example, two-thirds of the first fifty Court vacancies were due to deaths, 34 percent due to retirements. But of the last fifty-one vacancies, 71 percent were due to retirements, 29 percent due to deaths. Moreover, since 1954, nineteen Court members have departed, all due to retirements rather than to deaths.

Before 1891, Supreme Court justices were required to travel to the district courts within their assigned circuits to hear cases. In those days, medical technologies were primitive, roads were bumpy,

indoor plumbing was not yet universal, and central heating and air-conditioning were unknown. As Marecki's historical research revealed, the "physical requirements of circuit riding were onerous" and "adversely affected the health" of many justices, "especially as they grew older."

These conditions do not exist today. Still, why in recent decades have healthy and well-paid judges quit the most prestigious bench in the land at such high rates? The answer, in a word, is politics. Through a clever statistical analysis, Marecki found "a very strong correlation between shared political party identification and the mode of departure from the Supreme Court." A justice's "strategic retirement" occurs when he or she picks "a retirement date during the administration of a president that shares his or her political philosophy . . . ."

Source: Patrick Marecki, "Strategic Retirements in the U.S. Supreme Court," *Sound Politicks: University of Pennsylvania Political Science Journal 8* (Spring 2002): 3–10.

---

public policy: people accused of bank robbery are tried, disputes over contracts are settled, personal-injury cases are heard, and the patent law is applied. In most instances the courts are simply applying a relatively settled body of law to a specific controversy.

The Power to Make Policy

The courts make policy whenever they reinterpret the law or the Constitution in significant ways, extend the reach of existing laws to cover matters not previously thought to be covered by them, or design remedies for problems that involve the judges' acting in administrative or legislative ways. By any of these tests the courts have become exceptionally powerful.

One measure of that power is the fact that more than 160 federal laws have been declared unconstitutional, although since 1937 relatively few of these have had broad national significance. And as we shall see, on matters where Congress feels strongly, it can often get its way by passing slightly revised versions of a voided law.

Another measure, and perhaps a more revealing one, is the frequency with which the Supreme Court

changes its mind. An informal rule of judicial decision-making has been **stare decisis,** meaning "let the decision stand." It is the principle of precedent: a court case today should be settled in accordance with prior decisions on similar cases. (What constitutes a similar case is not always clear; lawyers are especially gifted at finding ways of showing that two cases are different in some relevant way.) There are two reasons why precedent is important. The practical reason should be obvious: if the meaning of the law continually changes, if the decisions of judges become wholly unpredictable, then human affairs affected by those laws and decisions become chaotic. A contract signed today might be invalid tomorrow. The other reason is at least as important: if the principle of equal justice means anything, it means that similar cases should be decided in a similar manner. On the other hand, times change, and the Court can make mistakes. As Justice Felix Frankfurter once said, "Wisdom too often never comes, and so one ought not to reject it merely because it comes late."[42]

However compelling the arguments for flexibility, the pace of change can become dizzying. By one count the Court has overruled its own previous decisions in over 260 cases since 1810.[43] In fact it may have done it more often, because sometimes the Court does not say that it is abandoning a precedent, claiming instead that it is merely distinguishing the present case from a previous one.

A third measure of judicial power is the degree to which courts are willing to handle matters once left to the legislature. For example, the Court refused for a long time to hear a case about the size of congressional districts, no matter how unequal their populations.[44] The determination of congressional district boundaries was regarded as a **political question**—that is, as a matter that the Constitution left entirely to another branch of government (in this case, Congress) to decide for itself. Then in 1962 the Court decided that it was competent after all to handle this matter, and the notion of a "political question" became a much less important (but by no means absent) barrier to judicial power.[45]

By all odds the most powerful indicator of judicial power can be found in the kinds of remedies that the courts will impose. A **remedy** is a judicial order setting forth what must be done to correct a situation that a judge believes to be wrong. In ordinary cases, such as when one person sues another, the remedy is straightforward: the loser must pay the winner for some injury that he or she has caused, the loser must agree to abide by the terms of a contract he or she has broken, or the loser must promise not to do some unpleasant thing (such as dumping garbage on a neighbor's lawn). Today, however, judges design remedies that go far beyond what is required to do justice to the individual parties who actually appear in court. The remedies now imposed often apply to large groups and affect the circumstances under which thousands or even millions of people work, study, or live. For example, when a federal district judge in Alabama heard a case brought by a prison inmate in that state, he issued an order not simply to improve the lot of that prisoner but to revamp the administration of the entire prison system. The result was an improvement in the living conditions of many prisoners, at a cost to the state of an estimated $40 million a year. Similarly, a person who feels entitled to welfare payments that have been denied him or her may sue in court to get the money, and the court order will in all likelihood affect all welfare recipients. In one case certain court orders made an additional one hundred thousand people eligible for welfare.[46]

The basis for sweeping court orders can sometimes be found in the Constitution; the Alabama prison decision, for example, was based on the judge's interpretation of the Eighth Amendment, which prohibits "cruel and unusual punishments."[47] Others are based on court interpretations of federal laws. The Civil Rights Act of 1964 forbids discrimination on grounds of "race, color, or national origin" in any program receiving federal financial assistance. The Supreme Court interpreted that as meaning that the San Francisco school system was obliged to teach English to Chinese students unable to speak it.[48] Since a Supreme Court decision is the law of the land, the impact of that ruling was not limited to San Francisco. Local courts and legislatures elsewhere decided that that decision meant that classes must be taught in Spanish for Hispanic children. What Congress meant by the Civil Rights Act is not clear; it may or may not have believed that teaching Hispanic children in English rather than Spanish was a form of discrimination. What is important is that it was the Court, not Congress, that decided what Congress meant.

Views of Judicial Activism

Judicial activism has, of course, been controversial. Those who support it argue that the federal courts must correct injustices when the other branches of the federal government, or the states, refuse to do so. The courts are the institution of last resort for those without the votes or the influence to obtain new laws, and especially for the poor and powerless. After all, Congress and the state legislatures tolerated segregated public schools for decades. If the Supreme Court had not declared segregation unconstitutional in 1954, it might still be law today.

Those who criticize judicial activism rejoin that judges usually have no special expertise in matters of school administration, prison management, environmental protection, and so on; they are lawyers, expert in defining rights and duties but not in designing and managing complex institutions. Furthermore, however desirable court-declared rights and principles may be, implementing those principles means balancing the conflicting needs of various interest groups, raising and spending tax monies, and assessing the costs and benefits of complicated alternatives. Finally, federal judges are not elected; they are appointed and are thus immune to popular control. As a result, if they depart from their traditional role of making careful and cautious

Supreme Court to Decide Constitutionality of Capital Punishment

March 20
WASHINGTON

The Supreme Court has been asked to decide whether the death penalty is constitutional. A decision in this important case is expected by June . . .

MEMORANDUM

To: Justice Robert Gilbert
From: David Wilson, law clerk

Before I draft your opinion, I want to know how you feel about declaring the death penalty unconstitutional.

Arguments for:

1. As enforced, the death penalty tends to be discriminatory. Black convicts are, in some cases, more likely to be executed than white ones.
2. The death penalty is irrevocable. If an innocent man is executed, he cannot be brought back to life when his innocence becomes known.
3. The death penalty is "cruel and unusual punishment" that is banned by the Constitution.

Arguments against:

1. The Constitution does not ban the death penalty.
2. The death penalty existed when the Constitution and Bill of Rights were written. Their authors meant by "cruel and unusual punishment" the use of torture.
3. When a legislature decides to punish murder by death, its views are entitled to deference.
4. There is no strong evidence that the death penalty is imposed in a discriminatory manner.

Your decision:
Ban death penalty _____
Do not ban death penalty _____

interpretations of what a law or the Constitution means and instead begin formulating wholly new policies, they become unelected legislators.

Some people think that we have activist courts because we have so many lawyers. The more we take matters to courts for resolution, the more likely it is that the courts will become powerful. It is true that we have more lawyers in proportion to our population than most other nations. There is one lawyer for every 325 Americans but only one for every 970 Britons, every 1,220 Germans, and every 8,333 Japanese.[49] But that may well be a symptom, not a cause, of court activity. As we suggested in Chapter 4, we have an adversary culture based on an emphasis on individual rights and an implicit antagonism between the people and the government. Generally speaking, lawyers do not create cases; contending interests do, thereby gen-

erating a demand for lawyers.[50] Furthermore, we had more lawyers in relation to our population in 1900 than in 1970, yet the courts at the turn of the twentieth century were far less active in public affairs. In fact, in 1932 there were more court cases per 100,000 people than there were in 1972.

A more plausible reason for activist courts has been the developments discussed earlier in this chapter that have made it easier for people to get standing in the courts, to pay for the costs of litigation, and to bring class-action suits. The courts and Congress have gone a long way toward allowing private citizens to become "private attorneys general." Making it easier to get into court increases the number of cases being heard. For example, in 1961 civil rights cases, prisoners' rights cases, and cases under the Social Security laws were relatively uncommon in federal court. Between 1961 and 1990 the increase in the number of such matters was phenomenal: civil rights cases rose over sixtyfold and prisoners' petitions over fortyfold. Such matters are the fastest-growing portion of the courts' civil workload.

Legislation and the Courts

An increase in cases will not by itself lead to sweeping remedies. For that to occur, the law must be sufficiently vague to permit judges wide latitude in interpreting it, and the judges must want to exercise that opportunity fully. The Constitution is filled with words of seemingly ambiguous meaning—"due process of law," the "equal protection of the laws," the "privileges or immunities of citizens." Such phrases may have been clear to the Framers, but to the Supreme Court they have become equivocal or elastic. How the Court has chosen to interpret such phrases has changed greatly over the last two centuries in ways that can be explained in part by the personal political beliefs of the justices.

Increasingly Congress has passed laws that also contain vague language, thereby adding immeasurably to the courts' opportunities for designing remedies. Various civil rights acts outlaw discrimination but do not say how one is to know whether discrimination has occurred or what should be done to correct it if it does occur. That is left to the courts and the bureaucracy. Various regulatory laws empower administrative agencies to do what the "public interest" requires but say little about how the public interest is to be defined. Laws intended to alleviate poverty or rebuild neighborhoods speak of "citizen

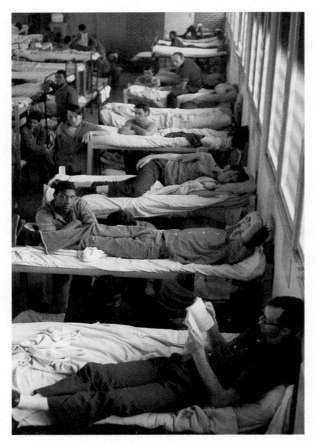

The activism of federal courts is exemplified by the sweeping orders they have issued to correct such problems as overcrowded prisons.

participation" or "maximum feasible participation" but do not explain who the citizens are that should participate, or how much power they should have.

In addition to laws that require interpretation, other laws induce litigation. Almost every agency that regulates business will make decisions that cause the agency to be challenged in court—by business firms if the regulations go too far, by consumer or labor organizations if they do not go far enough. One study showed that the federal courts of appeals heard over three thousand cases in which they had to review the decision of a regulatory agency. In two-thirds of them the agency's position was supported; in the other third the agency was overruled.[51] Perhaps one-fifth of these cases arose out of agencies or programs that did not even exist in 1960. The federal government today is much more likely to be on the defensive in court than it was twenty or thirty years ago.

Finally, the attitudes of the judges powerfully affect what they will do, especially when the law gives them wide latitude. There have been very few studies of the attitudes of federal judges, but their decisions and opinions have been extensively analyzed—well enough, at least, to know that different judges often decide the same case in different ways. Conservative southern federal judges in the 1950s, for example, often resisted plans to desegregate public schools while judges with a different background authorized bold plans.[52] Some of the greatest disparities in judicial behavior can be found in the area of sentencing criminals.[53]

Checks on Judicial Power

No institution of government, including the courts, operates without restraint. The fact that judges are not elected does not make them immune to public opinion or to the views of the other branches of government. How important these restraints are varies from case to case, but in the broad course of history they have been significant.

One restraint exists because of the very nature of courts. A judge has no police force or army; decisions that he or she makes can sometimes be resisted or ignored, *if* the person or organization resisting is not highly visible and is willing to run the risk of being caught and charged with contempt of court. For example, long after the Supreme Court had decided that praying and Bible reading could not take place in public schools,[54] schools all over the country were still allowing prayers and Bible reading.[55] Years after the Court declared segregated schools to be unconstitutional, scores of school systems remained segregated. On the other hand, when a failure to comply is easily detected and punished, the courts' power is usually unchallenged. When the Supreme Court declared the income tax to be unconstitutional in 1895, income tax collections promptly ceased. When the Court in 1952 declared illegal President Truman's effort to seize the steel mills in order to stop a strike, the management of the mills was immediately returned to their owners.

Congress and the Courts

Congress has a number of ways of checking the judiciary. It can gradually alter the composition of the judiciary by the kinds of appointments that the Senate is willing to confirm, or it can impeach judges that it does not like. Fifteen federal judges have been the object of impeachment proceedings in our history, and nine others have resigned when such proceedings seemed likely. Of the fifteen who were impeached, seven were acquitted, four were convicted, and one resigned. The most recent convictions were those of Alcee Hastings of Florida and Walter Nixon of Mississippi, both in 1989.[56] In practice, however, confirmation and impeachment proceedings do not make much of an impact on the federal courts because simple policy disagreements are not generally regarded as adequate grounds for voting against a judicial nominee or for starting an impeachment effort.

Congress can alter the number of judges, though, and by increasing the number sharply, it can give a president a chance to appoint judges to his liking. As described above, a "Court-packing" plan was proposed (unsuccessfully) by Franklin Roosevelt in 1937 specifically to change the political persuasion of the Supreme Court. In 1978 Congress passed a bill creating 152 new federal district and appellate judges to help ease the workload of the federal judiciary. This bill gave President Carter a chance to appoint over 40 percent of the federal bench. In 1984 an additional eighty-four judgeships were created; by 1988 President Reagan had appointed about half of all federal judges. In 1990 an additional seventy-two judges were authorized.

During and after the Civil War, Congress may have been trying to influence Supreme Court

T·R·I·V·I·A

The Supreme Court

Supreme Court justice who served the longest	William O. Douglas: 36 years (1939–1975)
Only Supreme Court justice to run for president	Charles Evans Hughes (resigned from Court in 1916 to seek presidency; lost to Woodrow Wilson)
Only president to become Supreme Court justice	William Howard Taft (president, 1909–1913; chief justice, 1921–1930)
First Catholic Supreme Court justice	Roger B. Taney (1836–1864)
First Jewish Supreme Court justice	Louis Brandeis (1916–1939)
First black Supreme Court justice	Thurgood Marshall (1967–1991)
First woman Supreme Court justice	Sandra Day O'Connor (1981 to present)
Only Supreme Court justice to be impeached	Samuel Chase (impeached by House in 1804; acquitted by Senate)
Only Supreme Court justice whose grandson also served on the Court	John Harlan (1877–1911), whose grandson John Harlan served from 1954 to 1971

decisions when it changed the size of the Court three times in six years (raising it from nine to ten in 1863, lowering it again from ten to seven in 1866, and raising it again from seven to nine in 1869).

Congress and the states can also undo a Supreme Court decision interpreting the Constitution by amending that document. This happens, but rarely: the Eleventh Amendment was ratified to prevent a citizen from suing a state in federal court; the Thirteenth, Fourteenth, and Fifteenth were ratified to undo the *Dred Scott* decision regarding slavery; the Sixteenth was added to make it constitutional for Congress to pass an income tax; and the Twenty-sixth was added to give the vote to eighteen-year-olds in state elections.

On over thirty occasions Congress has merely repassed a law that the Court has declared unconsti-

tutional. In one case a bill to aid farmers, voided in 1936, was accepted by the Court in slightly revised form three years later.[57] (In the meantime, of course, the Court had changed its collective mind about the New Deal.)

One of the most powerful potential sources of control over the federal courts, however, is the authority of Congress, given by the Constitution, to decide what the entire jurisdiction of the lower courts and the appellate jurisdiction of the Supreme Court shall be. In theory Congress could prevent matters on which it did not want federal courts to act from ever coming before the courts. This happened in 1868. A Mississippi newspaper editor named McCardle was jailed by federal military authorities who occupied the defeated South. McCardle asked the federal district court for a writ of habeas corpus to get him out of custody; when the district court rejected his plea, he appealed to the Supreme Court. Congress at that time was fearful that the Court might find the laws on which its Reconstruction policy was based (and under which McCardle was in jail) unconstitutional. To prevent that from happening, it passed a bill withdrawing from the Supreme Court appellate jurisdiction in cases of this sort. The Court conceded that Congress could do this and thus dismissed the case because it no longer had jurisdiction.[58]

Congress has threatened to withdraw jurisdiction on other occasions, and the mere existence of the threat may have influenced the nature of Court decisions. In the 1950s, for example, congressional opinion was hostile to Court decisions in the field of civil liberties and civil rights, and legislation was proposed that would have curtailed the Court's jurisdiction in these areas. It did not pass, but the Court may have allowed the threat to temper its decisions.[59] On the other hand, as congressional resistance to the Roosevelt Court-packing plan shows, the Supreme Court enjoys a good deal of prestige in the nation, even among people who disagree with some of its decisions, and so passing laws that would frontally attack it would not be easy except perhaps in times of national crisis.

Furthermore, laws narrowing jurisdiction or restricting the kinds of remedies that a court can impose are often blunt instruments that might not achieve the purposes of their proponents. Suppose that you, as a member of Congress, would like to prevent the federal courts from ordering schoolchildren to be bused for the purpose of achieving

Judicial Review in Canada and Europe

Courts outside the United States can declare laws to be unconstitutional, but most can do so in ways that are very different from that in the United States.

Canada: The highest court can declare a law unconstitutional, but not if the legislature has passed it with a special provision that says the law will survive judicial scrutiny notwithstanding the country's Charter of Rights. Such laws must be renewed every five years.

Europe: The European Court of Human Rights in Strasbourg can decide human rights cases that begin in any of fifteen nations that make up the European Community.

France: Its Constitutional Council can declare a law unconstitutional, but only if asked to do so by government officials and only before (not after) the law goes into effect.

Germany: The Federal Constitutional Court can declare in an advisory opinion, before a case has emerged, that a law is unconstitutional, and it can judge the constitutionality of laws when asked to do so by a lower court (which itself cannot rule a law unconstitutional). The Federal Constitutional Court may hold an administrative or judicial action to be unjustified when a citizen, having exhausted all other remedies, files a petition.

---

racial balance in the schools. If you denied the Supreme Court appellate jurisdiction in this matter, you would leave the lower federal courts and all state courts free to do as they wished, and many of them would go on ordering busing. If you wanted to attack that problem, you could propose a law that would deny to all federal courts the right to order busing as a remedy for racial imbalance. But the courts would still be free to order busing (and of course a lot of busing goes on even without court orders), provided that they did not say that it was for the purpose of achieving racial balance. (It could be for the purpose of "facilitating desegregation" or making possible "redistricting.") Naturally you could always make it illegal for children to enter a school bus for any reason, but then many children would not be able to get to school at all. Finally, the Supreme Court might well decide that if busing were essential to achieve a constitutional right, then any congressional law prohibiting such busing would itself be unconstitutional. Trying to think through how *that* dilemma would be resolved is like trying to visualize two kangaroos simultaneously jumping into each other's pouches.

Public Opinion and the Courts

Though they are not elected, judges read the same newspapers as members of Congress, and thus they, too, are aware of public opinion, especially elite opinion. Though it may be going too far to say that the Supreme Court follows the election returns, it is nonetheless true that the Court is sensitive to certain bodies of opinion, especially of those elites—liberal or conservative—to which its members happen to be attuned. The justices will keep in mind historical cases in which their predecessors, by blatantly disregarding public opinion, very nearly destroyed the legitimacy of the Court itself. This was the case with the *Dred Scott* decision, which infuriated the North and was widely disobeyed. No such crisis exists today, but it is altogether possible that changing political moods affect the kinds of remedies that judges will think appropriate.

Opinion not only restrains the courts; it may also energize them. The most activist periods in Supreme Court history have coincided with times when the political system was undergoing profound and lasting changes. The assertion by the Supreme Court, under John Marshall's leadership, of the principles of national supremacy and judicial review occurred at the time when the Jeffersonian Republicans were coming to power and their opponents, the Federalists, were collapsing as an organized party. The proslavery decisions of the Taney Court came when the nation was so divided along sectional and ideological lines as to make almost any Court decision on this matter unpopular. Supreme Court review of economic regulation in the 1890s and 1900s came at a time when the political parties were realigning and the Republicans were acquiring dominance that would last for several decades. The Court decisions of the 1930s corresponded to another period of partisan realignment. (The meaning of a realigning election was discussed in Chapter 8.)

| Figure 14.3 | Patterns of Public Confidence in the Court, 1974–1998 |

Source: Updated from *The Gallup Poll: Public Opinion 1991* (Wilmington, Del.: Scholarly Resources, Inc., 1992), 213.

Pollsters have been measuring how much confidence the public has in the Supreme Court. The results are shown in Figure 14.3. The percentage of people saying that they had a "great deal of confidence" in the Court rose sharply from 1971 to 1974, fell again until 1976, seesawed up and down until 1989, took a sharp dip and then recovered from 1989 to 1991, and again seesawed before rising in 1996. These movements seem to reflect the public's reaction not only to what the Court does but also to what the government as a whole is doing. The upturn in the early 1970s was probably caused by the Watergate scandal, an episode that simultaneously discredited the presidency and boosted the stock of those institutions (such as the courts) that seemed to be checking the abuses of the White House. The gradual upturn in the 1980s may have reflected a general restoration of public confidence in government during that decade.[60]

Though popular support is now relatively low for the Supreme Court, this decline has so far not resulted in any legal checks being placed on it. In the 1970s and 1980s several bills were introduced in Congress that would have restricted the jurisdiction of federal courts over busing for purposes of racial integration or altered the Supreme Court's decisions regarding school prayer and abortion. None passed.

The changes that have occurred in the Court have been caused by changes in its personnel. Presidents Nixon and Reagan attempted to produce a less activist Court by appointing justices who were more inclined to be strict constructionists and conservatives. To some extent they succeeded: Justices Kennedy, O'Connor, Rehnquist, and Scalia were certainly less inclined than Justice Thurgood Marshall to find new rights in the Constitution or to overturn the decisions of state legislatures. But as of yet there has been no wholesale retreat from the positions staked out by the Warren Court. As noted above, a Nixon appointee, Justice Blackmun, wrote the decision-making antiabortion laws unconstitutional; and another Nixon appointee, Chief Justice Burger, wrote the opinion upholding court-ordered school busing to achieve racial integration. A Reagan appointee, Justice O'Connor, voted to uphold a right to an abortion. The Supreme Court has become somewhat less willing to impose restraints on police practices, and it has not blocked the use of the death penalty. But in general the major features of Court activism and liberalism during the Warren years—school integration, sharper limits on police practice, greater freedom of expression—have remained intact.

The reasons for the growth in court activism are clear. One is the sheer growth in the size and scope of the government as a whole. The courts have come to play a larger role in our lives because Congress, the bureaucracy, and the president have come to play larger ones. In 1890 hardly anybody would have thought of asking Congress—much less the courts—to make rules governing the participation of women in college sports or the district boundaries of state legislatures. Today such rules are commonplace, and the courts are inevitably drawn into interpreting them.

The other reason for increased activism is the acceptance by a large number of judges, conservative as well as liberal, of the activist view of the function of the courts. If courts once existed solely to "settle disputes," today they also exist in the eyes of their members to "solve problems."

Summary

An independent judiciary with the power of judicial review—the right to decide the constitutionality of acts of Congress, the executive branch, and state governments—can be a potent political force in American life. That influence has been realized from the earliest days of the nation, when Marshall and Taney put the Supreme Court at the center of the most important issues of the time. From 1787 to 1865 the Supreme Court was preoccupied with the establishment of national supremacy. From 1865 to 1937 it struggled with defining the scope of political power over the economy. In the present era it has sought to expand personal liberties.

The scope of the courts' political influence has increasingly widened as various groups and interests have acquired access to the courts, as the judges serving on them have developed a more activist stance, and as Congress has passed more laws containing vague or equivocal language. Whereas in other political arenas (the electorate, Congress, the bureaucracy) the influence of contending groups is largely dependent on their size, intensity, prestige, and political resources, the influence of contending groups before the courts depends chiefly on their arguments and the attitudes of the judges.

Though the Supreme Court is the pinnacle of the federal judiciary, most decisions, including many important ones, are made by the twelve courts of appeals and the ninety-four district courts. The Supreme Court can control its own workload by deciding when to grant certiorari. It has become easier for citizens and groups to gain access to the federal courts (through class-action suits, by amicus curiae briefs, by laws that require government agencies to pay legal fees, and because of the activities of private groups such as the NAACP and the ACLU).

At the same time, the courts have widened the reach of their decisions by issuing orders that cover whole classes of citizens or affect the management of major public and private institutions. However, the courts can overstep the bounds of their authority and bring upon themselves a counterattack from both the public and Congress. Congress has the right to control much of the courts' jurisdiction, but it rarely does so. As a result the ability of judges to make law is only infrequently challenged directly.

Reconsidering the Enduring Questions

1. ***Should judges be limited to interpreting what the law says?***

   The main function of judges is to apply the laws and the Constitution as they were written. But there is a problem: sometimes the provisions of the laws and Constitution are vague, with no clear meaning. What does the Constitution mean by "due process of law," "respecting an establishment of religion," or the "equal protection of the law"?

   Occasionally an answer can be found in what the authors of these provisions said when they wrote such phrases, but just as often their views are incomplete or contradictory. The task of judges is to try to understand the philosophy that shaped these views and apply them to new circumstances. For example, the Constitution's ban on unreasonable searches and seizures was written long before telephone taps were invented, but judges today have to apply the spirit of that phrase to new technologies. On the other hand, when laws or the Constitution are really unclear, the best way to settle the matter is to revise the laws or amend the Constitution.

2. Why should federal courts have the right to declare an act of Congress unconstitutional?

The Constitution does not explicitly give to federal judges that authority, but it can be implied from the phrase that the Constitution shall be the "supreme law of the land." If it is supreme, some-one must be able to overturn presidential and congressional acts that deny its supremacy, and we cannot allow the president and Congress to do it themselves without making them judges in their own cases. Moreover, their judgments might differ. This leaves federal courts as the only branch of government that, in principle, does not make laws and therefore is in a position to judge the constitutionality of the laws others produce. To help them remain independent, the Constitution gives them lifetime tenure (unless they are impeached).

World Wide Web Resources

- Federal Judicial Center: www.fjc.gov
- Federal courts: www.uscourts.gov
- Supreme Court decisions: www.law.cornell.edu
- Finding laws and reports: www.findlaw.com

Key Terms

judicial review *p. 403*
strict-constructionist approach *p. 404*
activist approach *p. 404*
constitutional court *p. 411*
district courts *p. 411*
courts of appeals *p. 411*
legislative court *p. 411*
litmus test *p. 413*
federal-question cases *p. 414*

diversity cases *p. 414*
civil law *p. 416*
criminal law *p. 416*
writ of certiorari *p. 416*
in forma pauperis *p. 417*
fee shifting *p. 418*
plaintiff *p. 418*
standing *p. 418*
sovereign immunity *p. 418*
class-action suit *p. 419*

brief *p. 420*
amicus curiae *p. 421*
per curiam opinion *p. 422*
opinion of the Court *p. 422*
concurring opinion *p. 422*
dissenting opinion *p. 422*
stare decisis *p. 423*
political question *p. 424*
remedy *p. 424*

Suggested Readings

Abraham, Henry J. *The Judicial Process.* 6th ed. New York: Oxford University Press, 1993. An excellent, comprehensive survey of how the federal courts are organized and function.

Cardozo, Benjamin N. *The Nature of the Judicial Process.* New Haven, Conn.: Yale University Press, 1921. Important statement of how judges make decisions, by a former Supreme Court justice.

Carp, Robert A., and Ronald Stidham. *The Federal Courts.* Washington, D.C.: Congressional Quarterly Press, 1985. Excellent summary of the workings of the lower federal courts.

Ely, John Hart. *Democracy and Distrust.* Cambridge: Harvard University Press, 1980. Effort to create a theory of judicial review that is neither strict-constructionist nor activist.

Hall, Kermit L., ed. *The Oxford Companion to the Supreme Court of the United States.* New York: Oxford University Press, 1992. Everything you ever wanted to know about the Supreme Court, its justices, and its major decisions, arranged in more than one thousand alphabetical entries.

Lasser, William. *The Limits of Judicial Power.* Chapel Hill: University of North Carolina Press, 1988. Shows how the Court through history has withstood the political storms created by its more controversial decisions.

Lazarus, Edward. *Closed Chamber.* New York: Times Books, 1998. An eyewitness account of how the Supreme Court operates. Written by a former law clerk, it is filled with both interesting facts and personal opinions.

McCloskey, Robert G. *The American Supreme Court.* 2d ed. Edited by Sanford Levinson. Chicago: University of Chicago Press, 1994. Superb brief history of the Supreme Court, updated by one of McCloskey's former students who now teaches law at the University of Texas.

Rabkin, Jeremy. *Judicial Compulsions.* New York: Basic Books, 1989. Explains (and argues against) the extensive Court intervention in the work of administrative agencies.

Wolfe, Christopher. *The Rise of Modern Judicial Review.* New York: Basic Books, 1986. An excellent history of judicial review from 1787 to the present.

PART IV

The Politics of Public Policy

In the extended republic of the United States, and among the great variety of interests, parties, and sects which it embraces, a coalition of a majority of the whole society could seldom take place on any other principles than those of justice and the general good.

FEDERALIST NO. 51

15

The Policy-Making Process

Enduring Questions

1. Do interest groups have too much power in making government policy?

2. Is it true that ordinary citizens can't tell the government what to do?

If our political system handled all issues in the same way, this study of American government would be at an end. Now that we have seen how Congress, the presidency, the courts, the parties, the mass media, and other interest groups operate, we should be able to explain how policies get made (or not made). Some observers do argue that the system always operates more or less the same way—to serve corporate interests (the Marxist view), to manage conflict among organized groups (the pluralist view), to sustain the dominance of a pervasive bureaucracy (the Weberian view), and so on. In this part we shall look at how policies are actually made to see whether any of these generalizations are correct.

Consider some outcomes that need to be explained if we are to understand the political influence wielded by just one kind of institution—the business corporation. Certain oil companies were once able to persuade the government to restrict sharply the amount of foreign oil imported into the United States, to give them preferential tax treatment, and to permit them to drill for new oil just about anywhere they liked. Today the restrictions on

435

foreign oil imports have ended, the tax breaks the oil companies enjoy have been reduced considerably (though they still exist), and their freedom to drill in certain places, particularly offshore locations, has been restricted.

Automobile manufacturers once faced virtually no federal controls on the products they manufactured; now they face many. In the past some corporations have been regulated in ways that have increased their profitability (the airlines), reduced it (the railroads), or had no appreciable effect one way or the other (electric utilities). These outcomes of government action or inaction are complicated. To understand why they happen, we need some theory of policy-making. This chapter will provide one; subsequent chapters will apply it.

Setting the Agenda

The most important decision that affects policy-making is also the least noticed one: deciding what to make policy *about*, or in the language of political science, deciding what belongs on the **political agenda.** We take for granted that politics is about certain familiar issues such as taxes, energy, welfare, and civil rights. We forget that there is nothing inevitable about having these issues—rather than some other ones—on the nation's agenda. At one time it was unconstitutional for the federal government to levy income taxes; energy was a nonissue because everybody (or at least everybody who could chop down trees for a fireplace) had enough; welfare was something for cities and towns to handle; and civil rights were supposed to be a matter of private choice rather than government action. Until the 1930s the national political agenda was quite short, and even in the 1950s many people would have been astonished or upset to be told that the federal government was supposed to worry about the environment, consumerism, or civil rights.

"He who decides what politics is about runs the country."[1] This is a statement of profound significance, though it exaggerates the extent to which somebody—some person—actually "decides" what politics is all about. The statement correctly suggests that at any given time certain shared beliefs determine what is legitimate (proper, right) for the government to do. This legitimacy is affected by several forces:

- Shared political values—for example, if many people believe that poverty is the result of individual failure rather than social forces, then there is no reason for a government program to combat poverty.
- The weight of custom and tradition—people will usually accept what the government has customarily done, even if they are leery of what it proposes to do.
- The impact of events—wars, depressions, and the like alter our sense of the proper role of government.
- Changes in the way political elites think and talk about politics.

The Legitimate Scope of Government Action

Because many people believe that whatever the government now does it ought to continue doing, and because changes in attitudes and the impact of events tend to increase the number of things that government does, the scope of legitimate government action is always getting larger. As a result the scope of what is illegitimate for the government to do steadily gets smaller. This means that today we hear far fewer debates about the legitimacy of a proposed government policy than we heard in the 1920s or the 1930s. The existence of "big government" is sustained by these expanded beliefs about legitimacy and is not the consequence of some sinister power grab by politicians or bureaucrats. When President Gerald Ford, a Republican, ran for election in 1976, a favorite slogan of his was that a government big enough to give you everything you want is also big enough to take away everything you have. No doubt he thought that he was criticizing liberal Democrats. But it was his immediate predecessor, President Nixon, also a Republican, who had imposed peacetime wage and price controls and proposed a guaranteed annual income for every family, working or not working. It was another Republican president, Dwight Eisenhower, who had sent federal troops to Little Rock, Arkansas, to enforce a school-desegregation order. And it was yet another Republican president, Ronald Reagan, who was in office when federal payments to farmers grew to be six times larger than they had been in the 1970s. For better or worse, the expansion of government has been the result, fundamentally, of a nonpartisan process.

September 11, 2001, known ever after as 9/11, had a powerful effect on the agenda of American politics. This photo was taken one year after the disaster.

Popular views on the legitimate scope of government action, and thus on the kinds of issues that ought to be on the political agenda, are changed by the impact of events. During wartime or after a terrorist attack on this country, the people expect the government to do whatever is necessary to win, whether or not such actions are clearly authorized by the Constitution. (As we saw in Chapter 13, the federal bureaucracy enjoys its most rapid growth in wartime.) A depression, such as the one that began in 1929, also leads people to expect the government to do something. As we shall see in Chapter 17, public opinion favored federal action to deal with the problems of the unemployed, the elderly, and the poor well in advance of the actual decisions of the government to take action. A coal mine disaster leads to an enlarged role for the government in promoting mine safety. A series of airplane hijackings leads to a change in public opinion so great that what once would have been unthinkable—requiring all passengers at airports to be searched before boarding their flights—becomes routine.

But sometimes the government enlarges its agenda of policy issues, often dramatically, without any crisis or widespread public demand. This may happen even at a time when the conditions at which a policy is directed are improving. There was no public demand for government action to make automobiles safer before 1966, when a law was passed imposing safety standards on cars. Though the number of auto fatalities (per 100 million miles driven) had gone up slightly just before the law was passed, the long-term trend in highway deaths had been more or less steadily downward. The Occupational Safety and Health Act was passed in 1970 at a time when the number of industrial deaths (per 100,000 workers) had been steadily dropping for almost twenty years.[2] Programs to combat urban poverty and unemployment were adopted in the mid-1960s at a time when the number of persons, black as well as white, living below the poverty line was declining and when the adult unemployment rate—for blacks as well as whites—was lower than it had been at any time in the preceding ten years.[3] Affirmative action programs were introduced to increase the flow of minorities into jobs and colleges at a time when minorities were already making rapid progress.

It is not easy to explain why the government adds new issues to its agenda and adopts new programs when there is little public demand and when, in fact, there has been an improvement in the conditions to which the policies are addressed. In general the explanation may be found in the behavior of groups, the workings of institutions, and the opinions of political elites.

■ **Groups**   Many policies are the result of small groups of people enlarging the scope of government by their demands. Sometimes these are organized interests (for example, corporations or unions); sometimes they are intense but unorganized groups (urban minorities). The organized groups often work quietly, behind the scenes; the intense, unorganized ones may take their causes to the streets.

Organized labor favored a tough federal safety law governing factories and other workplaces not because it was unaware that factory conditions had been improving but because the standards by which union leaders and members judged working conditions had risen even faster. As people became better off, conditions that once were thought normal suddenly became intolerable. When Alexis de Tocqueville sought to explain the French Revolution, he observed that citizens are most restless and easily aroused not when they are living in abject poverty or under grinding repression but when they have started to become better off.[4] Social scientists sometimes refer to this as a sense of "relative deprivation."

On occasion a group expresses in violent ways its dissatisfaction with what it judges to be intolerable conditions. The black riots in American cities during the mid-1960s had a variety of causes, and people participated out of a variety of motives. For many, rioting was a way of expressing pent-up anger at what they regarded as an unresponsive and unfair society. This sense of relative deprivation—of being worse off than one thinks one *ought* to be—helps explain why so large a proportion of the rioters were not uneducated, unemployed recent migrants to the city, but rather young men and women born in the North, educated in its schools, and employed in its factories.[5] Life under these conditions turned out to be not what they had come to expect or what they were prepared to tolerate.

The new demands of such groups need not result in an enlarged political agenda, and they do not when society and its governing institutions are confident of the rightness of the existing state of affairs. Unions could have been voted down on the occupational safety bill; rioting blacks could have been jailed

and ignored. At one time exactly this would have happened. But society itself had changed: many people who were not workers sympathized with the plight of the injured worker and distrusted the good intentions of business in this matter. Many whites felt that a constructive as well as a punitive response to the urban riots was required and thus urged the formation of commissions to study—and the passage of laws to deal with—the problems of inner-city life. Such changes in the values and beliefs of people generally—or at least of people in key government positions—are an essential part of any explanation of why policies not demanded by public opinion nonetheless become part of the political agenda.

■ **Institutions**   Among the institutions whose influence on agenda-setting has become especially important are the courts, the bureaucracy, and the Senate.

The courts can make decisions that force the hand of the other branches of government. When in 1954 the Supreme Court ordered schools desegregated, Congress and the White House could no longer ignore the issue. Local resistance to implementing the order led President Eisenhower to send troops to Little Rock, Arkansas, despite his dislike for using force against local governments. When the Supreme Court ruled in 1973 that the states could not ban abortions during the first trimester of pregnancy, abortion suddenly became a national political issue. Right-to-life activists campaigned to reverse the Court decision or, failing that, to prevent federal funds from being used to pay for abortions. Pro-choice activists fought to prevent the Court from changing its mind and to get federal funding for abortions. In these and many other cases the courts act like tripwires: when activated, they set off a chain reaction of events that alters the political agenda and creates a new constellation of political forces.

Indeed, they are more than tripwires. As the government agenda has expanded, the courts have become the favorite method for doing things for which there is no popular majority. There may be no electoral support for allowing abortion on demand, eliminating school prayer, creating affirmative action, ordering school busing, or attacking tobacco companies, but in the courts elections do not matter. The courts are the preferred vehicles for the advocates of unpopular causes.

The bureaucracy has acquired a new significance in American politics not simply because of its size or power but also because it is now a source of political innovation. At one time the federal government *reacted* to events in society and to demands from segments of society; ordinarily it did not itself propose changes and new ideas. Today the bureaucracy is so large, and includes within it so great a variety of experts and advocates, that it has become a *source* of policy proposals as well as an implementer of those that become law. Daniel Patrick Moynihan called this the "professionalization of reform," by which he meant, in part, that the government bureaucracy had begun to think up problems for government to solve rather than simply to respond to the problems identified by others.[6] In the 1930s many of the key elements of the New Deal—Social Security, unemployment compensation, public housing, old-age benefits—were ideas devised by nongovernment experts and intellectuals here and abroad and then, as the crisis of the depression deepened, taken up by the federal government. In the 1960s, by contrast, most of the measures that became known as part of Lyndon Johnson's "Great Society"—federal aid to education, manpower development and training, Medicare and Medicaid, the "War on Poverty," the "safe-streets" act providing federal aid to local law enforcement agencies—were developed, designed, and advocated by government officials, bureaucrats, and their political allies.

Chief among these political allies are U.S. senators and their staffs. Once the Senate was best described as a club that moved slowly, debated endlessly, and resisted, under the leadership of conservative southern Democrats, the plans of liberal presidents. With the collapse of the one-party South and the increase in the number of liberal activist senators, the Senate became in the 1960s an incubator for developing new policies and building national constituencies.[7] As the Senate became more conservative in the 1980s, it retained the initiative, but now on behalf of reversing some of the changes wrought earlier. The Senate has thus become one of the sources of political change rather than, as the Founders intended, a balance wheel designed to moderate change.[8] That senators are tempted to run for president magnifies this tendency. When senators such as Edward M. Kennedy, George McGovern, Robert Dole, Gary Hart, Edmund Muskie, Joseph Biden, Albert Gore, Paul Simon, and John McCain decide to try for the presidency, they have an incentive to seek out new issues and raise new proposals as a way of attracting attention.

■ **Media**   Finally, the national press can either help place new matters on the agenda or publicize those matters placed there by others. There was a close correlation between the political attention given in the Senate to proposals for new safety standards for industry, coal mines, and automobiles and the amount of space devoted to these questions in the pages of the *New York Times*. Newspaper interest in the matter, low before the issue was placed on the agenda, peaked at about the time that the bill was passed.[9] It is hard, of course, to decide which is cause and which effect. The press may have stimulated congressional interest in the matter or merely reported on what Congress had already decided to pursue. Nonetheless, the press must choose which of thousands of proposals it will cover. The beliefs of editors and reporters led it to select the safety issue. In later chapters we shall discuss the kinds of issues for which the national press is important.

In short, the political agenda can change because of changes in popular attitudes, elite interest, critical events, or government actions. An overly simple but essentially correct generalization might be this: popular attitudes usually change slowly, often in response to critical events; elite attitudes and government actions are more volatile and interdependent and thus change more quickly, often in response to each other.

Making a Decision

Once an issue is on the political agenda, its nature affects the kind of politicking that ensues. Some issues provoke intense interest group conflict; others allow one group to prevail almost unchallenged. Some issues involve ideological appeals to broad national constituencies; other involve quiet bargaining in congressional offices. We all know that private groups try to influence government policies; we often forget that the nature of the issues with which government is dealing influences the kinds of groups that become politically active.

One way to understand how an issue affects the distribution of political power among groups and institutions is to examine what appear to be the costs and benefits of the proposed policy. The **cost** is any burden, monetary or nonmonetary, that some people must bear, or think that they must bear, if the policy is adopted. The costs of a government

Highway safety was always a problem, but it became a national issue after policy entrepreneurs, such as Mothers Against Drunk Driving (MADD), emphasized it.

spending program are the taxes that it entails; the cost of a foreign policy initiative may be the increased chance of having the nation drawn into war. The **benefit** is any satisfaction, monetary or nonmonetary, that people believe they will enjoy if the policy is adopted. The benefits of a government spending program are the payments, subsidies, or contracts received by some people; the benefits of a foreign policy initiative may include the enhanced security of the nation, the protection of a valued ally, or the vindication of some important principle such as human rights.

Two aspects of these costs and benefits should be borne in mind. First, it is the *perception* of costs and benefits that affects politics. People may think that the cost of an auto emissions control system is paid by the manufacturer, when it is actually passed on to the consumer in the form of higher prices and reduced performance. Political conflict over pollution control will take one form when people think that Ford and GM pay the costs and another form when they think that the consumers pay.

Second, people take into account not only who benefits but also whether it is *legitimate* for that group to benefit. When programs providing financial assistance to women with dependent children were first developed in the early part of this century, they were relatively noncontroversial because people saw the money

as going to widows and orphans who deserved such aid. Later on giving aid to mothers with dependent children became controversial because some people now perceived the recipients not as deserving widows but as sexually loose women who had never married. Whatever the truth of the matter, the program had lost some of its legitimacy because the beneficiaries were no longer seen as "deserving." By the same token, groups once thought undeserving, such as men out of work, were later thought to be entitled to aid, and thus the unemployment compensation program acquired a legitimacy that it once lacked.

Politics is in large measure a process of raising and settling disputes over who *will* benefit or pay for a program and who *ought* to benefit or pay. Since beliefs about the results of a program and the rightness of those results are matters of opinion, it is evident that ideas are at least as important as interests in shaping politics. In recent years ideas have become especially important with the rise of issues whose consequences are largely intangible, such as abortion, school prayer, and racial integration.

Though perceptions about costs and benefits change, most people most of the time prefer government programs that provide substantial benefits to them at low cost. This rather obvious fact can have important implications for how politics is carried out.

In a political system based on some measure of popular rule, public officials have a strong incentive to offer programs that confer—or appear to confer—benefits on people with costs that are either small in amount, remote in time, or borne by "somebody else." Policies that seem to impose high, immediate costs in return for small or remote benefits will be avoided, enacted with a minimum of publicity, or proposed only in response to a real or apparent crisis.

Ordinarily no president would propose a policy that would immediately raise the cost of fuel, even if he were convinced that future supplies of oil and gasoline were likely to be exhausted unless higher prices reduced current consumption. But when a crisis occurs, such as the Arab oil cartel's price increases beginning in 1973, it becomes possible for the president to offer such proposals—as did Nixon, Ford, and Carter in varying ways. Even then, however, people are reluctant to bear increased costs, and thus many are led to dispute the president's claim that an emergency actually exists.

These entirely human responses to the perceived costs and benefits of proposed policies can be organized into a simple theory of politics.[10] It is based on the observation that the costs and benefits of a policy may be *widely distributed* (spread over many, most, or even all citizens) or *narrowly concentrated* (limited to a relatively small number of citizens or to some identifiable, organized group). For instance, a widely distributed cost would include an income tax, a Social Security tax, or a high rate of crime; a widely distributed benefit might include retirement benefits for all citizens, clean air, national security, or low crime rates. Examples of narrowly concentrated costs include the expenditures by a factory to reduce its pollution, government regulations imposed on doctors and hospitals participating in the Medicare program, or restrictions on freedom of speech imposed on a dissident political group. Examples of narrowly concentrated benefits include subsidies to farmers or merchant ship companies, the enlarged freedom to speak and protest afforded a dissident group, or protection against competition given to an industry because of favorable government regulation.

The perceived distribution of costs and benefits shapes the *kinds of political coalitions that will form*—but it will not necessarily determine *who wins*. A given popular majority, interest group, client, or entrepreneur may win or lose depending on its influence and the temper of the times.

In the remainder of this chapter we shall describe the politics of four kinds of policies and then illustrate each kind with examples drawn from government efforts to regulate business.

Majoritarian Politics: Distributed Benefits, Distributed Costs

Some policies promise benefits to large numbers of people at a cost that large numbers of people will have to bear (see Figure 15.1). For example, almost everybody will sooner or later receive Social Security benefits, and almost everybody who works has to pay Social Security taxes. Similarly, defending the nation against military attack benefits everyone, and every taxpayer contributes to its cost. If government-sponsored research to find cures for cancer and heart disease is successful, a large proportion of the citizenry will benefit from a program that all taxpayers have been obliged to support.

Such **majoritarian politics** are usually not dominated by pulling and hauling among rival interest groups; instead they involve making appeals to large blocs of voters and their representatives in hopes of finding a majority. The reason why interest groups are not so important in majoritarian politics is that, as we saw in Chapter 9, citizens rarely will have much incentive to join an interest group if the policy that such a group supports will benefit everybody, whether or not they are members of the group. This is the "free-rider" problem. Why join the Committee to Increase (or Decrease) the Defense Budget when what you personally contribute to that committee makes little difference in the outcome and when you will enjoy the benefits of more (or less) national defense even if you have stayed on the sidelines?

Majoritarian politics may be controversial, but the controversy is usually over matters of cost or ideology, not between rival interest groups. When Congress passed three laws to reduce drug use, this was a majoritarian issue (that is, there were no interest groups active on behalf of drug dealers). The arguments were over matters such as the desirability of the death penalty for big traffickers. The military budget went up during the early 1980s, down in the late 1980s, and up again after 2001; the changes reflected different views on how much

Figure 15.1	A Way of Classifying and Explaining the Politics of Different Policy Issues

PERCEIVED COSTS

		Distributed	Concentrated
PERCEIVED BENEFITS	**Distributed**	Majoritarian Politics	Entrepreneurial Politics
	Concentrated	Client Politics	Interest Group Politics

we should spend and the relationship between military spending and arms-control negotiations.

Interest Group Politics: Concentrated Benefits, Concentrated Costs

In **interest group politics,** a proposed policy will confer benefits on some relatively small, identifiable group and impose costs on another small, equally

Majoritarian politics: Widespread bank failures in the 1930s helped pave the way for laws regulating and insuring financial institutions.

identifiable group. For example, when Congress passed a bill requiring companies to give sixty days' notice of a plant closing or a large-scale layoff, labor unions (whose members would benefit) backed the bill, and many business firms (which would pay the costs) opposed it.

Issues of this kind tend to be fought out by organized interest groups. Each side will be so powerfully affected by the outcome that it has a strong incentive to mobilize: union members who worry about layoffs will have a personal stake in favoring the notice bill; business leaders who fear government control of investment decisions will have an economic stake in opposing it.

Interest group politics often produces decisions about which the public is uninformed. The bitter debates between television broadcasters and cable companies over who may send what kind of signals to which homes hardly draws any public notice—until after a law is passed and people can see what their cable charges will be. Similarly, the long struggle to give banks the right to sell insurance involved not the public, but banks and insurance companies. In time the public will discover whether they like the results.

Though many issues of this type involve monetary costs and benefits, they can also involve intangible considerations. If the American Nazi party wants to march through a predominantly Jewish neighborhood carrying flags with swastikas on them, the community may organize itself to resist out of revulsion against the disgraceful treatment of

Jews by Nazi Germany. Each side may hire lawyers to debate the issue before the city council and in the courts.

Client Politics: Concentrated Benefits, Distributed Costs

With **client politics** some identifiable, often small group will benefit, but everybody—or at least a large part of society—will pay the costs. Because the benefits are concentrated, the group that is to receive those benefits has an incentive to organize and work to get them. But because the costs are widely distributed, affecting many people only slightly, those who pay the costs may be either unaware of any costs or indifferent to them, because per capita they are so small.

This situation gives rise to client politics (sometimes called clientele politics); the beneficiary of the policy is the "client" of the government. For example, many farmers benefit substantially from agricultural price supports, but the far more numerous food consumers have no idea what these price supports cost them in taxes and higher food prices. In the same way, airlines for a long time benefited from the higher prices that they were able to charge on certain routes as a result of government regulations that restricted competition over prices. But the average passenger was either unaware that his or her costs were higher or did not think that the higher prices were worth making a fuss about.

Not all clients are economic interests. Localities can also benefit as clients when, for example, a city or county obtains a new dam, a better harbor, or an improved irrigation system. Some of these projects may be worthwhile, others may not; by custom, however, they are referred to as **pork-barrel projects.** Usually several pieces of "pork" are put into one barrel—that is, several projects are approved in a single piece of legislation, such as the "rivers and harbors" bill that Congress passes almost every year. Trading votes in this way attracts the support of members of Congress from each affected area; with enough projects a majority coalition is formed. This process is called **logrolling.**

Not every group that wants something from government at little cost to the average citizen will get it. Welfare recipients cost the typical taxpayer a small amount each year, yet there was great resistance to increasing these benefits. The homeless have not

Logrolling

Among settlers in the American wilderness it was often necessary to cooperate in order to move logs off a piece of property that was to be farmed.

By the early nineteenth century *logrolling* had come to mean mutual aid among politicians, whereby one legislator supported another's pet project in return for the latter's support of his. Congressman B. F. Butler put it this way in 1870: "If you will vote for my interest, I will vote for yours. That is how these low tariffs are log rolled through."

Logrolling is the equivalent of the saying "You scratch my back and I'll scratch yours."

Source: From *Safire's Political Dictionary* by William Safire. Copyright © 1968, 1972, 1978 by William Safire. Reprinted by permission of Random House, Inc. and the author.

organized themselves to get benefits; indeed, most do not even vote. Yet benefits are being provided (albeit in modest amounts so far). These examples illustrate the importance of popular views concerning the legitimacy of client claims as a factor in determining the success of client demands. As we shall see in Chapter 17, welfare recipients have never enjoyed much legitimacy in the public's eye, and so programs to increase their benefits were hard to sell to Congress. The plight of the homeless, on the other hand, has aroused a good deal of sympathy and produced bipartisan agreement on a bill providing emergency aid. Moreover, that agreement seems to have persisted.

Senior citizens rallying to get prescription drugs included in Medicare.

By the same token, groups can lose legitimacy that they once had. People who grow tobacco once were supported simply because they were farmers, and were thus seen as both "deserving" and politically important. But when people began worrying about the health risks associated with using tobacco, farmers who produce tobacco lost some legitimacy compared to those who produce corn or cotton. As a result it became harder to get votes for maintaining tobacco price supports and easier to slap higher taxes on cigarettes.

Entrepreneurial Politics: Distributed Benefits, Concentrated Costs

In **entrepreneurial politics** society as a whole or some large part of it benefits from a policy that imposes substantial costs on some small, identifiable segment of society. The antipollution and safety requirements for automobiles were proposed as ways of improving the health and well-being of all people at the expense (at least initially) of automobile manufacturers. Similarly, Congress enacted the Brady bill, which requires a background check on gun buyers before they can purchase a firearm.

It is remarkable that policies of this sort are ever adopted, and in fact many are not. After all, the American political system creates many opportunities for checking and blocking the actions of others. The Founders deliberately arranged things so that it would be difficult to pass a new law; a determined minority therefore has an excellent chance of blocking a new policy. And any organized group that fears the loss of some privilege or the imposition of some burden will become a very determined minority indeed. The opponent has every incentive to work hard; the large group of prospective beneficiaries may be unconvinced of the benefit or regard it as too small to be worth fighting for.

Nonetheless, policies with distributed benefits and concentrated costs are in fact adopted, and in recent decades they have been adopted with increasing frequency. A key element in the adoption of such policies has been the work of people who act on behalf of the unorganized or indifferent majority. Such people, called **policy entrepreneurs,** are those both in and out of government who find ways of pulling together a legislative majority on behalf of interests that are not well represented in the government.

These policy entrepreneurs may or may not represent the interests and wishes of the public at large, but they do have the ability to dramatize an issue in a convincing manner. Ralph Nader is perhaps the best-known example of a policy entrepreneur, or as he might describe himself, a "consumer advocate." But there are other examples from both ends of the political spectrum, conservative as well as liberal.

Entrepreneurial politics can occur without the leadership of a policy entrepreneur if voters or legislators in large numbers suddenly become disgruntled by the high cost of some benefit that a group is receiving (or become convinced of the urgent need for a new policy to impose such costs). For example, voters may not care about government programs that benefit the oil industry when gasoline costs only one dollar a gallon, but they might care very much when the price rises to two dollars a gallon, even if the government benefits had nothing to do with the price increase. By the same token, legislators may not worry much about the effects of smog in the air until a lot of people develop burning eyes and runny noses during an especially severe smog attack.

Likewise, most legislators did not worry very much about toxic or hazardous wastes until 1977, when the Love Canal dump site near Buffalo, New York, spilled some of its toxic waste into the backyards of an adjacent residential neighborhood and people were forced to leave their homes. Five years later anyone who had forgotten about Love Canal was reminded of it when the town of Times Beach,

Missouri, had to be permanently evacuated because it had become contaminated with the chemical dioxin. Only then did it become widely known that there were more than thirty thousand toxic waste sites nationwide that posed public safety risks. Although researchers have yet to find any conclusive evidence of health damage at either site, the Superfund program was born in 1980 of the political pressure that developed in the wake of these and other highly publicized tales of toxic waste dangers. Superfund was intended to force industries to clean up their own toxic waste sites. It also authorized the Environmental Protection Agency (EPA) to act speedily, with or without cooperation from industries, in identifying and cleaning up any sites that posed a large or imminent danger.

Superfund has suffered a number of political and administrative problems, and only a few of the 1,300 sites initially targeted by the EPA have actually been cleaned up since the program went into effect.[11] However, Superfund is a good illustration of entrepreneurial politics in action. Special taxes on once largely unregulated oil and chemical companies have funded the program. Previously these companies enjoyed special tax privileges as beneficiaries of client politics; today they face special tax burdens as the targets of entrepreneurial politics.

A car is crashed to test how well it will withstand an accident.

For many reasons—including the enlarged political role of the media, the decentralization of Congress, and a change in the attitudes of many citizens—entrepreneurial politics has become more common and policy entrepreneurs more visible in recent decades.

The Case of Business Regulation

Efforts by government to regulate business not only illustrate these four kinds of policy-making processes but also shed light on an issue that many people think is central to the study of politics—namely, the relationship between wealth and power.

To some observers the very existence of large corporations is a threat to popular rule. Economic power will dominate political power, they believe, for one or more of three reasons: first, because wealth can be used to buy influence; second, because politicians and business leaders have similar class backgrounds and thus similar beliefs about public policy; and third, because elected officials must defer to the preferences of business so as to induce corporations to keep the economy healthy and growing. Karl Marx, of course, proposed the most sweeping version of the view that economics controls politics; for him the state in a capitalist society was nothing more than the executive committee of the propertied classes.[12] But there are other non-Marxist or neo-Marxist versions of the same concern.[13]

To other observers politics, far from being subordinate to economic power, is a threat to the very existence of a market economy and the values—economic growth, private property, personal freedom—that they believe such an economy protects. In this view politicians will find it in their interest, in their struggle for votes, to take the side of the nonbusiness majority against that of the business minority. The heads of large corporations, few in number but great in wealth, fear that they will be portrayed as a sinister elite on whom politicians can blame war, inflation, unemployment, and pollution. Defenders of business worry that corporations will be taxed excessively to pay for social programs that in turn will produce more votes for politicians. Just as bad, in this view, is the tendency of universities (on which corporations must rely for technical experts) to inculcate antibusiness values in their students.[14]

The theory of the policy-making process presented earlier in this chapter should suggest that neither of these two extreme views of business-government relations is entirely correct. These relations depend on many things, including the *kind* of policy being proposed. Instead of clenching our fists and shouting probusiness or antibusiness slogans at each other, we should be able, after applying this theory to the available facts, to make more careful and exact statements of the following sort: "If certain conditions exist, then business-government relations will take certain forms."

Majoritarian Politics

Not all efforts to regulate business pit one group against another. From time to time laws are passed that reflect the views of a majority of voters that is neither imposing its will on a hostile business community nor acceding to the desires of a privileged industry.

Much of the antitrust legislation passed in this country, including the Sherman Act (1890) and parts of the Federal Trade Commission Act (1914) and the Clayton Act (1914), has been the result of majoritarian politics. Toward the end of the nineteenth century there arose a broadly based criticism of business monopolies (then called trusts) and, to a lesser extent, of large corporations, whether or not they monopolized trade. The Grange, an organization of farmers, was especially outspoken in its criticism, and popular opinion generally—insofar as we can know it in an era without pollsters—seems to have been indignant about trusts and in favor of "trustbusting." Newspaper editorials and magazine articles frequently dwelt on the problem.[15]

But though antitrust feeling was strong, it was also relatively unfocused: no single industry was the special target of this criticism (the oil industry, and especially the Standard Oil Company, came as close as any), and no specific regulation was proposed. In fact there was no general agreement about how to define the problem: for some it was monopoly; for others sheer bigness; and for still others the legal basis of the modern corporation. The bill proposed by Senator John Sherman did not clarify matters much: while it made it a crime to "restrain" or "monopolize" trade, it did not define these terms, nor did it create any new regulatory agency charged with enforcing the law.[16]

No doubt some large corporations worried about what all this would mean for them, but few felt sufficiently threatened to try very hard to defeat the bill. It passed the Senate by a voice vote and the House by a vote of 242 to 0.

Laws are not self-executing, and vague laws are especially likely to lie dormant unless political leaders work hard at bringing them to life. For the first decade or so after 1890, only one or two antitrust cases a year were filed in the courts. In 1904 President Theodore Roosevelt persuaded Congress to provide enough money to hire five full-time lawyers, and soon the number of prosecutions increased to about seven a year. Then in 1938 President Franklin Roosevelt appointed as head of the Antitrust Division of the Justice Department a vigorous lawyer named Thurman Arnold, who began bringing an average of fifty cases a year.[17] Today over four hundred lawyers in the division sift through complaints alleging monopolistic or other unfair business practices. Though controversy exists over the kinds of cases that should be brought, there is no serious effort among either politicians or business leaders to abandon the commitment to a firm antitrust policy, the strongest such policy to be found in any industrial nation.

The antitrust laws were strengthened in 1914 by bills that created the Federal Trade Commission and made (via the Clayton Act) certain specific practices, such as price discrimination, illegal. As with the earlier Sherman Act, the advocates of these measures had a variety of motives. Some proponents favored these laws because they would presumably help consumers (by preventing unfair business practices); other proponents supported them because they might help business (by protecting firms against certain tactics that competitors might employ).

President Woodrow Wilson endorsed both of these bills and helped create a broad coalition on behalf of the legislation; the Federal Trade Commission Act and the Clayton Act passed Congress by lopsided majorities.[18]

As with the Sherman Act, there has been continual controversy about how these laws should be administered. But this controversy, like the debate over the initial passage of the laws, has not been dominated by interest groups.[19] The reason for the relative absence of interest group activity is that these laws do not divide society into permanent and identifiable blocs of proponents and opponents. Any given business firm can be either helped or hurt by

The Grange sought to warn farmers of the dangers of a railroad monopoly.

the enforcement of the antitrust laws. One year the XYZ Widget Company may be sued by the government to prevent it from unfairly advertising its widgets, and the next year the same XYZ Company may ask the government to prosecute its competitor for trying to drive XYZ out of business by selling widgets at prices below cost.

The amount of money that the federal government devotes to antitrust enforcement and the direction that those enforcement efforts take are determined more by the political ideology and personal convictions of the administration in power than by interest group pressures. For example, the Reagan administration decided that the benefits of trying to break up IBM were not worth the costs, and thus it ended its antitrust prosecution of the giant computer firm. At the same time, however, it decided that it was desirable to break up American Telephone and Telegraph (AT&T), making the local phone companies independent of AT&T and forcing AT&T to compete with other long-distance service providers. In the 1990s the Clinton administration brought an antitrust suit against computer software giant Microsoft.

Boycott

In 1880 an Irish landowner, Captain Boycott, was the target of an effort by the Irish Land League to get people to refuse to do business with him.

Today the term **boycott** refers to any concerted effort to get people to stop buying goods and services from a merchant or farmer in order to punish that person or to coerce him or her into changing policies.

The boycott has become a favored tool of interest group politics. The Reverend Jesse Jackson has, in recent years, tried to get African Americans to boycott certain businesses that have not, in his judgment, hired a sufficient number of black employees.

In sum, as with most majoritarian policies, antitrust regulation tends to reflect broad philosophies of governance more than interest group activity.

Interest Group Politics

Organized interest groups are very powerful, however, when the regulatory policies confer benefits on a particular group and costs on another, equally distinct group.

In 1935 labor unions sought government protection for their right to organize, to bargain collectively with industry, and to compel workers in unionized industries to join the unions. Business firms opposed these plans. The struggle was fought out in Congress, where the unions won. The Wagner Act, passed that year, created the National Labor Relations Board (NLRB) to regulate the conduct of union organizing drives and to hear complaints of unfair labor practices brought by workers against management.

But the struggle was far from over. In 1947 management sought to reverse some of the gains won by unions by pressing for a law (the Taft-Hartley Act) that would make illegal certain union practices (such as the closed shop and secondary boycotts) and would authorize the president to obtain a court order blocking for up to eighty days any strike that imperiled the "national health or safety." Business won.

Business and labor fought round three in 1959 over a bill (the Landrum-Griffin Act) intended to prevent corruption in unions, to change the way in which organizing drives were carried out, and to prohibit certain kinds of strikes and picketing. Business won.

In each of these cases the struggle was highly publicized. The winners and losers were determined by the partisan composition of Congress (Republicans and southern Democrats tended to support business, northern Democrats to support labor) and by the existence of economic conditions (a depression in 1935, revelations of labor racketeering in 1959) that affected public opinion on the issue.

But the interest group struggle did not end with the passage of the laws; it continued throughout their administration. The National Labor Relations Board, composed of five members appointed by the president, had to adjudicate countless disputes between labor and management over the interpretation of these laws. The losing party often appealed the NLRB decision in the courts, where the issue was fought out again. Moreover, each president has sought to tilt the NLRB in one direction or another by means of whom he appoints to it. Democratic presidents favor labor and thus tend to appoint prounion board members; Republican presidents favor business and thus tend to appoint promanagement members. Since NLRB members serve five-year terms, a new president cannot immediately appoint all of the board's members; thus there is often a split on the board between two factions.

A similar pattern of interest group influence is revealed by the history of the Occupational Safety and Health Act, passed in 1970. Labor unions wanted a strict bill with tough standards set by a single administrator; business organizations wanted a more flexible bill with standards set by a commission that would include some business representatives. After a long struggle labor won, and the Occupational Safety and Health Administration

(OSHA), headed by a single administrator, was set up inside the Department of Labor.

As with the NLRB, conflict did not end with the passage of the law, and OSHA decisions were frequently appealed to the courts. The politics swirling about OSHA were all the more contentious because of the vast mandate of the agency: it is supposed to determine the safe limits for worker exposure to hundreds of chemicals and to inspect tens of thousands of workplaces to see whether they should be cited for violating any standards. During the Carter administration an OSHA administrator was appointed who was sympathetic to the labor view and thus set many standards and issued many citations; during the Reagan administration an administrator was selected who was admired by business because he set fewer standards and issued fewer citations.

Client Politics

Many people suppose that when government sets out to regulate business, the firms that are supposed to be regulated will in fact "capture" the agency that is supposed to do the regulating. But as we have already seen, certain kinds of policies—those that give rise to majoritarian and interest group politics—do not usually lead to capture, because the agency either faces no well-organized, enduring opponent (as with majoritarian politics) or is caught in a crossfire of competing forces (as with interest group politics).

But when a policy confers a benefit on one group at the expense of many other people, client politics arises, and so agency "capture" is likely. More precisely, nothing needs to be captured at all, since the agency will have been created from the outset to serve the interests of the favored group. We sometimes think that regulations are always resisted. But a regulation need not be a burden; it can be a great benefit.

How this works can be seen close to home. State and city laws regulate the practice of law and medicine as well as a host of other occupations—barbers, beauticians, plumbers, dry cleaners, taxi drivers, and undertakers. These regulations are sometimes designed and always defended as ways of preventing fraud, malpractice, and safety hazards. But they also have the effect of restricting entry into the regulated occupation, thereby enabling its members to charge higher prices than they otherwise might.[20] Ordinarily citizens do not object to this, in part because they believe, rightly or wrongly, that the regulations in fact protect them, and in part because

the higher prices are spread over so many customers as to be unnoticed.

Much the same thing can be found at the national level. In the early 1930s the American dairy industry was suffering from rapidly declining prices for milk. As the farmers' incomes fell, many could no longer pay their bills and were forced out of business. Congress responded with the Agricultural Adjustment Act, which authorized an agency of the Department of Agriculture to regulate the milk industry. This agency, the Dairy Division of the Agricultural Marketing Service, would issue "market orders" that had the effect of preventing price competition among dairy farmers and thus kept the price of milk up. If this guaranteed minimum price leads to the production of more milk than people want to drink, then another part of the Agriculture Department—the Commodity Credit Corporation—stands ready to buy up the surplus with tax dollars.[21]

Consumers wind up paying more for milk than they otherwise would, but they have no way of knowing the difference between the regulated and unregulated price of milk (economists estimate that it amounts to between five and twenty-one cents per gallon).[22] Consumers have little incentive to organize politically to do much about it. The total cost, however, can be very high. Although consumers are not helped by high prices, not every dairy farmer is helped either. More milk is produced than people will buy, and so many dairy farmers have gone out of business.

A similar system works with sugar. Sugar produced abroad, in countries such as Brazil and the Philippines, costs much less than sugar produced here, in states such as Louisiana. To keep the incomes of U.S. sugar producers high, Congress decided to restrict the importation of cheap foreign sugar by imposing quotas. This costs the consumer money—maybe as much as $3 billion a year—but the extra cost per pound of sugar is not noticeable.[23]

From time to time various officials attempt to change the regulations that benefit a client group. But they must confront some sobering political facts. Dairy farmers are found scattered through scores of congressional districts; sugar beet growers are concentrated in southern states that are important in any presidential election. Efforts have been made in Congress to cut milk subsidies and sugar quotas, but with only limited success.

In 1996 Congress passed and President Clinton signed a bill that began, at least for wheat and corn

Client politics: To operate a New York taxi, the owner must have a medallion bolted to the hood. The number of medallions (and thus of taxis) is limited. This keeps competition down and prices up.

crops, to phase out the practice of paying farmers the difference between what they can sell their crops for and what the government thinks the crops ought to be worth. It replaced these crop subsidies with direct cash payments to farmers that they can use for anything, including not farming.

But the 1996 plan to lure farmers into a free-market economy did not last. Between 1996 and 2001, the subsidies they got increased rather than decreased. In 2002 President Bush signed a new farm bill that did away with the 1996 law and authorized paying farmers $171 billion in new subsidies by 2012. Though defended as a way of protecting "the little farmer," most of the money will go to big farmers who produce wheat, corn, rice, cotton, and soybeans (but not to those who produce cattle, hogs, poultry, fruits, or vegetables).

Farm subsidies are justified by the fact that the prices farmers earn swing wildly, but subsidies don't go to people who make computer chips or raise cattle even though they also experience big swings in the prices they can charge. The existence of farm subsidies is the result of history (a legacy of the time, during the Great Depression, when the government wanted to help nearly one-fourth of all employed Americans who then worked on farms) and politics (farmers are key and changeable voters in many important states).

Client politics has become harder to practice in this country unless a group is widely thought to be a "deserving" client. Dairy farmers, sugar producers, and tobacco growers struggle (sometimes successfully, sometimes unsuccessfully) to keep their benefits, but the struggle relies on "insider politics"—that is, on dealing with key Washington decision-makers and not on building widespread public support. By contrast, when a devastating flood, tornado, earthquake, or hurricane strikes a community, the victims are thought to be eminently deserving of help. After all, people say, it was not their fault that their homes were destroyed. (In fact in some cases it was, because they built homes in areas they knew were at high risk for hurricanes or floods.) They receive client benefits.

Although client politics for "special interests" seems to be on the decline, that is true mostly for programs that actually send certain groups money. Pietro Nivola reminds us of a different form of client politics: using regulations instead of cash to help groups. For example, regulations encourage the use of ethanol (a kind of alcohol made from corn) in gasoline, which benefits corn farmers and ethanol manufacturers. Clients that might not be thought legitimate increasingly get their way by means of regulations rather than subsidies.[24]

But regulation that starts out by trying to serve a client can end up hurting it. Radio broadcasters supported the creation of the Federal Communications Commission (FCC), which would, broadcasters and telephone companies thought, bring order and stability to their industries. It did. But then it started doing a bit more than the industries had hoped for. It began reviewing efforts by companies to merge. When one telephone company tried to merge with another, the FCC said that it would have to review the consolidation even though the law did not give it the power to do so. After long (and secret) negotiations, it extracted concessions from the companies as a condition of their merger. Because there was no law requiring such concessions, the firms accepted them "voluntarily." But if they had not agreed, they would have been in deep trouble with the FCC in the future.

Regulatory agencies created to help clients can become burdens to those clients when the laws the agencies enforce are sufficiently vague so as to provide freedom of action for the people who run them. For a long time most of these laws were hopelessly vague. The FCC, for example, was told to award licenses as "the public interest, convenience, and necessity" required. In time such language can give an agency wide, undefined powers.

Entrepreneurial Politics

During the 1960s and 1970s some two dozen consumer- and environmental-protection laws were passed, including laws that regulated the automobile industry, oil companies, toy manufacturers, poultry producers, the chemical industry, and pharmaceutical companies.*

When measures such as these become law, it is often because a policy entrepreneur has dramatized an issue, galvanized public opinion, and mobilized congressional support. Sometimes that entrepreneur is in the government (a senator or an outspoken bureaucrat); sometimes that entrepreneur is a private person (the best known, of course, is Ralph Nader). The motives of such entrepreneurs can be either self-serving or public-spirited; the policies that they embrace may be either good or bad. (Just because someone succeeds in regulating business does not mean that the public will necessarily benefit; by the same token, just because business claims that a new regulation will be excessively costly does not mean that business will in fact have to pay those costs.)

An early example of a policy entrepreneur inside the government was Dr. Harvey Wiley, a chemist in the Department of Agriculture, who actively campaigned for what was to become the Pure Food and Drug Act of 1906. Later Senator Estes Kefauver held hearings that built support for the 1962 drug laws (and incidentally for his presi-

dential bid), and Senator Edmund Muskie called attention to the need for air and water pollution control legislation (and incidentally to his own 1972 presidential aspirations).

When a policy entrepreneur is outside the government, he or she will need a sympathetic ear within it. Occasionally the policy needs of the entrepreneur and the political needs of an elected official coincide. When Ralph Nader was walking the corridors of the Capitol looking for someone interested in auto safety, he found Senators Abraham Ribicoff and Warren Magnuson, who themselves were looking for an issue with which they could be identified.

The task of the policy entrepreneur is made easier when a crisis or scandal focuses public attention on a problem. Upton Sinclair's book *The Jungle*[25] dramatized the frightful conditions in meatpacking plants at the turn of the century and helped pave the way for the Meat Inspection Act of 1906. The stock market collapse of 1929 helped develop support for the Securities and Exchange Act. When some people who had taken a patent medicine (elixir of sulfanilamide) died as a result, the passage of the 1938 drug laws became easier. Oil spilled on the beaches of Santa Barbara, California, drew attention to problems addressed by the Water Quality Improvement Act of 1970.

The dramatic event need not be an actual crisis; in some cases a political scandal will do. Highway fatalities were not a matter of great concern to most citizens when Congress began considering the auto-safety act in 1965–1966, but support for the bill grew when it was revealed that General Motors had hired a private detective who made a clumsy effort to collect (or manufacture) gossip harmful to Ralph Nader, whose book *Unsafe at Any Speed* had criticized the safety of certain GM cars.

In some cases no dramatic event at all is required for entrepreneurial politics to succeed. Most of the air and water pollution control bills were passed despite the absence of any environmental catastrophe.[26] Support for such measures was developed by holding carefully planned committee hearings that were closely followed by the media. For example, by drawing attention to the profits of the pharmaceutical companies, Senator Kefauver was able to convince many people that these firms were insensitive to public needs. By drawing on information made available to him by environmentalists, Senator Muskie was able to capitalize on and help further a

---

*The Motor Vehicle Air Pollution Control Act of 1965, the National Traffic and Motor Vehicle Safety Act of 1966, the Clean Air Act of 1970, the Water Quality Improvement Act of 1970, the Children's Protection and Toy Safety Act of 1969, the Wholesome Poultry Act of 1968, the Toxic Substances Control Act of 1976, and the 1962 amendments to the Pure Food and Drug Act.

Entrepreneurial politics: Upton Sinclair's book The Jungle, *published in 1906, shocked readers with its description of conditions in the meatpacking industry and helped bring about passage of the Meat Inspection Act of 1906.*

growing perception in the country during the early 1970s that nature was in danger.

Because political resistance must be overcome without the aid of a powerful economic interest group, policy entrepreneurs seeking to regulate an industry often adopt a moralistic tone, with their opponents portrayed as devils, their allies viewed with suspicion, and compromises fiercely resisted. When Senator Muskie was drafting an air pollution bill, Ralph Nader issued a highly publicized report *attacking* Muskie, his nominal ally, for not being tough enough. This strategy forced Muskie—who wanted acclaim, not criticism, for his efforts—to revise the bill so that it imposed even more stringent standards.[27] Other allies of Nader, such as Dr. William Haddon, Jr., and Joan Claybrook, got the same treatment when they later became administrators of the National Highway Traffic Safety Administration. They came under attack not only from the auto industry, for designing rules that the companies thought were too strict, but also from Nader, for devising rules that he thought were not strict enough.

Once a policy entrepreneur manages to defeat an industry that is resisting regulation, he or she creates—at least for a while—a strong impetus for additional legislation of the same kind. A successful inno-

vator produces imitators, in politics as in rock music. After the auto safety law was passed in 1966, it became easier to pass a coal mine safety bill in 1969 and an occupational safety and health bill in 1970.

The great risk faced by policy entrepreneurs is not that their hard-won legislative victories will later be reversed but that the agency created to do the regulating will be captured by the industry that it is supposed to regulate. The Food and Drug Administration (FDA), which regulates the pharmaceutical industry, has fallen victim during much of its history to precisely this kind of capture. Once the enthusiasm of its founders had waned and public attention had turned elsewhere, the FDA seemed to develop a cozy and rather uncritical attitude toward the drug companies. (In 1958 the head of the FDA received an award from the Pharmaceutical Manufacturers' Association.)[28] In the mid-1960s, under the spur of renewed congressional and White House attention, the agency was revitalized. During the Reagan administration environmentalists worried that the leadership of the Environmental Protection Agency had been turned over to persons who were unduly sympathetic to polluters.

There are at least five reasons, however, why the newer consumer and environmental protection agencies may not be as vulnerable to capture as some critics contend. First, these agencies often enforce laws that impose specific standards in accordance with strict timetables, and so they have relatively little discretion. (The Environmental Protection Agency, for example, is required by law to reduce certain pollutants by a fixed percentage within a stated number of years.) Second, the newer agencies, unlike the FDA, usually regulate many different industries and so do not confront a single, unified opponent. The Occupational Safety and Health Administration, for example, deals with virtually every industry. Third, the very existence of these agencies has helped strengthen the hand of the "public interest" lobbies that initially demanded their creation. Fourth, these lobbies can now call upon many sympathetic allies in the media who will attack agencies that are thought to have a probusiness bias.

Finally, as explained in Chapter 14, it has become easier for groups to use the federal courts to put pressure on the regulatory agencies. These groups do not have to be large or broadly representative of the public; all they need are the services of one or two able lawyers. If the Environmental Protection Agency

(EPA) issues a rule disliked by a chemical company, the company will promptly sue the EPA; if it issues a ruling that pleases the company, the Environmental Defense Fund will sue.

Perceptions, Beliefs, Interests, and Values

The politics of business regulation provides a good illustration of the theory of policy-making offered in this book, but the reader should not be misled by a discussion of costs and benefits into thinking that all or even most of politics is about getting or losing money or that it is an easy matter to classify the costs and benefits of a policy and thus put it into the correct pigeonhole.

For one thing, what constitutes a cost or a benefit is a matter of opinion, and opinions change. We have already said that it is the *perception* of costs and benefits that affects politics. If people think that laws requiring factories to install devices to remove from their smokestacks chemicals that contribute to acid rain can be implemented in ways that make the companies but not the consumers pay the bills, they will favor such measures, and the affected industries will oppose them. But if people believe that the cost of preventing acid rain will be borne by them—in the form of fewer jobs or higher prices—then these citizens may be less enthusiastic about such measures.

Some people favor having the government regulate the price of natural gas, and others oppose it. One reason for the conflict, obviously, is that people who use natural gas in their homes want to buy it cheaply, whereas people who work in the natural gas industry want gas prices to go up so that they can earn more. Interests are clearly in conflict.

Yet some users may oppose regulating the price of gas because they believe that keeping the price of gas artificially low now will discourage exploration for new gas fields, thereby creating shortages—and much higher prices—in the future. Thus *beliefs* are also in conflict; in this case some users believe that it is more important to take the long view and worry about gas shortages ten years from now, while others believe that what counts is how much you have to pay for natural gas today.

A political conflict is in large measure a struggle to make one definition of the costs and benefits of a pro-

Though many economists question the value of the Small Business Administration, it remains popular because it loans money to a lot of voters.

posal prevail over others; that is, it is a struggle to alter perceptions and beliefs. Material interests do play a part in all this: the more you stand to gain or lose in hard cash from a proposal, the harder it will be for someone else to change your mind about your position. But many, perhaps most, government proposals will not have an immediate, unambiguous impact on your pocketbook, and so your perceptions and beliefs about what will happen in the future become the prize for which political activists compete.

In that competition certain arguments enjoy a natural advantage over others. One might be called the *here-and-now* argument. What happens now or in the near future is more important to most people than what happens in the distant future. (Economists refer to this as the human tendency to "discount the future.") Thus most users of natural gas probably care more about present prices than future shortages, and so many will tend to favor price regulation today.

Another political tactic that enjoys a natural advantage might be called the *cost* argument. People seem to react more sharply to what they will lose if a policy is adopted than to what they may gain. Thus there will usually be strong opposition to putting a tax on imported oil, even if the benefit gained will be to reduce our dependence on foreign oil.

Politicians know the value of the here-and-now and the cost arguments and so try to present their proposals in ways that take advantage of these sentiments. Regulations aimed at new drugs, for example, will emphasize the harm that will be prevented now from keeping dangerous drugs off the market, not the harm that may come later if lifesaving drugs with some dangerous side effects are kept off the market. Plans to solve the problems of our Social Security system stress keeping intact the benefits now received by people already retired, postponing into the future the tax increases necessary to pay for these benefits.

Policies are affected not only by our perceptions and beliefs about where our interests lie but also by our *values*—that is, by our conceptions of what is good for the country or for our community. Many whites, for example, want to see opportunities increased for minorities, not because such opportunities will make whites better off but because they think that it is the right thing to do. Many citizens worry about political conditions in Central America, not because they fear having to fight a war there or because they work for a company that does business there but because they wish a better life for people who live in that region and want them to be free of both right-wing and Marxist dictatorships. Some citizens oppose restrictions on the sale of obscene magazines and others favor those restrictions; neither group stands to benefit—those who oppose censorship usually don't plan to read the publications, and those who favor it would not thereby have their own lives improved—yet both groups often advocate their opposing views with great passion.

All this may seem obvious, but the reader should recall how often he or she assumes that people are only "looking out for themselves" and so politics is only about "who gets what." We all have a tendency to be a bit cynical about government—that is, to impute self-seeking motives to whoever is involved. Since there is plenty of self-interest in politics, this assumption is often a pretty good one. But following it blindly can lead us to ignore those cases in which ideas—beliefs, perceptions, and values—are the decisive forces in political conflict.

There are many examples of the power of ideas, even in conflicts that involve money interests. Here

two examples are noted: the deregulation of certain industries and the ending of certain taxpayer-financed agricultural subsidies.

Deregulation

In the 1980s several industries were deregulated over the objections of those industries. Airline fares were once set by the Civil Aeronautics Board. The airlines liked it that way—it kept competition down and prices up. But today airline fares are set by the market, with the result that in some (but not all) areas fares are lower than they once were. Not only did most airlines fight tooth and nail to prevent this deregulation from occurring, but some couldn't adjust to the new era of competition and, like Eastern Airlines, went bankrupt.

Long-distance telephone services were once provided on a monopoly basis by AT&T; its prices were set by the Federal Communications Commission. Today there are several long-distance telephone systems—MCI, Sprint, AT&T—and prices are heavily influenced by competition. AT&T was not eager to have this happen, but it couldn't prevent it.

Once, the number of trucking companies and the prices they charged were set by the Interstate Commerce Commission (ICC). The trucking companies and the Teamsters Union favored this pattern of regulation—as with the airlines, the system kept competition down and prices up. But then Congress changed the law, and in January 1996 the ICC was abolished.

People who think that politics is simply the result of deals struck between certain favored industries and friendly or "captured" agencies would have a hard time explaining this period of deregulation. Client politics—the cozy relationship (or "iron triangle") between a private client, a government agency, and a supportive Congress—was ended. How did it happen?

Martha Derthick and Paul Quirk, two political scientists, answered the question in their book *The Politics of Deregulation.*[29] The key to that answer is the power of ideas. Academic economists were in agreement that regulating prices in industries that were competitive, or could easily be made so, was a bad idea; the regulations hurt consumers by keeping prices artificially high. But academic ideas by themselves are powerless. In the three cases described above, key political leaders—Presidents Carter, Ford, and Reagan, and Senators Edward Kennedy and Howard Cannon—accepted and acted on these ideas, albeit for very different reasons. The regulatory commissions—the Civil Aeronautics Board (CAB), the Federal Communications Commission (FCC), the ICC—were led by people who wanted to deregulate. In one case, the breakup of AT&T, a federal judge made many of the key decisions. The public did not support deregulation, but it was concerned about inflation, and deregulation could be defended as a way of bringing prices down. Finally, the industries that fought to save their client relationships with government—the airlines, the trucking companies, the phone company—were not wildly popular businesses; once they were subjected to political criticism, they found that they had relatively few allies.

Reducing Tobacco Subsidies

At one time the taxpayer shelled out a lot of money to help tobacco growers make money. Under that system, tobacco farmers who could not sell all the tobacco they were entitled to grow under a federal license could get a federal loan, using their unsold tobacco as collateral. If they did not pay back the loan, they got to keep the money, and the government was stuck with the bill.

Since tobacco farming is a key industry in certain states (such as Kentucky and North Carolina), the members of Congress from those states had a big stake in making certain that the subsidy program kept going. Since the program did not cost the average taxpayer too much (and since, in any case, the public had no idea of how much money went to pay for the program), most people had no incentive to organize to end the favored treatment of tobacco farmers.

They didn't, that is, until smoking became a well-publicized national health problem. Then many members of Congress from nontobacco states became upset about spending money to grow crops that contributed to cancer, heart disease, and emphysema. In 1982, when the tobacco-subsidy program was up for renewal, its congressional backers realized that they had to make concessions if the program was to survive. They did this by agreeing to a system in which the subsidies to the farmers would be paid for by the farmers themselves (in the form of mandatory contributions to a fund set up to pay for crop loans). The principle was to be "no net cost to the taxpayer" (except for administrative expenses).

Client politics was weakened when larger concerns (in this case, antismoking groups) were activated. Widely held beliefs ("smoking is bad for you") significantly reduced the influence of narrowly distributed benefits. The tobacco lobby lost again when the ban on smoking on all domestic airline flights was enacted in 1987 and once again when cigarette taxes were raised in the 1990s.

Under the threat of losing expensive lawsuits brought by state governments, the tobacco industry began negotiating with the attorneys general of these states to change tobacco marketing practices. The tobacco companies would make a big cash payment to the governments in return for a cap on the size of any future lawsuit settlements.

Since the mid-1970s every president has put in place machinery to bring government regulation of industry under more central review. President Ford in 1974 ordered all regulatory agencies to assess the inflationary impact of their decisions. President Carter in 1978 directed each agency to consider alternative ways of achieving the goals of regulation. President Reagan in 1981 created the Task Force on Regulatory Relief and instructed those agencies under his control not to issue a regulation if, in the judgment of the Office of Management and Budget, its potential benefits to society did not outweigh its costs.[30] President Bush the elder essentially continued the Reagan system.

Deregulation is opposed, of course, by groups that benefit from it. But it is controversial in at least two other ways. First, some members of the public do not like the results, especially if the world becomes more complicated as a result of relying on the market. Many people liked CAB control of the airlines, for example, because the higher prices kept the number of air travelers down, and so airports were less congested. Second, some people who favor deregulating *prices* oppose deregulating *processes*. **Process regulation** (sometimes called social regulation) includes rules aimed at improving consumer or worker safety and reducing environmental damage. There are good and bad ways of achieving these goals, and much of the dispute about regulation concerns the question of means, not ends. The intensity of that dispute shows how important perceptions and beliefs are even when economic interests are at stake.

The Limits of Ideas

Ideas can be powerful, but there are limits to their power. There are many forms of client politics that persist—some because people agree that the client deserves to benefit, others because the conditions do not exist for mounting an effective challenge to the client.

Tobacco subsidies no longer are paid for by taxpayers, but dairy, sugar, and other agricultural price supports still are. Regulations that increased above market levels the prices charged by airlines and trucking companies were successfully challenged; regulations that increased above market levels the prices charged by oceangoing freighters were not.

The wages paid to airline pilots and truck drivers are no longer protected by federal rules; the wages paid to merchant seamen and construction workers employed on federal projects still are.

It is not entirely clear why it is easier to challenge client politics in some industries and occupations than in others. We can say, however, why it is generally harder to maintain client politics free of challenge today than once was the case.

Summary

Policy-making involves two stages—placing an issue on the governmental agenda and deciding what to do about that issue once it is on the agenda. The agenda steadily expands as the result of historical crises, interest group activity, the competition for votes, and the operation of key institutions, especially the courts, the bureaucracy, and the mass media.

Decision-making requires that a majority coalition be formed. The kinds of coalitions that form will depend in large measure on the nature of the issue, especially the perceived distribution of costs and benefits. We have identified four kinds of coalitions, or distinctive political processes: majoritarian, client, interest group, and entrepreneurial.

Government regulation of business illustrates the relationship between these four kinds of policies and the sorts of coalitions that will form in each instance. These case studies make clear that there is no single, simple answer to the question of how much influence business has over government (or vice versa).

The outcome of these political struggles will depend not only on who gains and who loses but also on the perceptions, beliefs, and values of key political actors. The example of airline deregulation shows that changes in how people think can make a big difference even in the case of policies where money interests are at stake.

Reconsidering the Enduring Questions

1. *Do interest groups have too much power in making government policy?*

They obviously have power, but it makes little sense to say they have "too much" without answering two questions: First, on what kinds of issues will interest groups have a lot of power? (We have suggested that they will chiefly have power with respect to client politics when what one group wants is not opposed vigorously by a rival group.) Second, how do interest groups differ from ordinary American voters? (We have suggested that they don't differ very much, since practically everybody is a member, or could easily become a member, of groups representing their

views.) It is important to remember a simple rule: What you want out of politics you will describe as required by "the public interest." What your opponents want out of it you will describe as "special interest group demands." And your opponents will see matters in exactly the same way, except they will see *you* as part of a special interest group.

2. *Is it true that ordinary citizens can't tell the government what to do?*

Of course it is true, if you take people one citizen at a time. If one of us could tell the government what to do, that person would be a dictator. In reality, citizens influence policy in three ways: First, they vote. Since the parties differ in what they want, the winning party will make policies that are not what the losing party would make. Second, people join interest groups. Upper-status, better-educated people join more groups than lower-status, less-educated people, and so some groups have more members, and probably more influence, than others. But even among groups of well-educated people there is so much conflict and rivalry that it is rarely the case that one group, speaking for some political class, can determine policy. Third, citizens help define and sustain our political culture. We sometimes forget that politicians can rarely violate this culture with impunity. We insist on honest leaders, fairness in policy-making, ample scope for local and individual initiative, and a strong defense. These expectations set real limits on what policy-makers can do.

World Wide Web Resources

- Nonpartisan reviews of public policy issues:
  www.policy.com
  www.publicagenda.org

- For partisan discussion of issues, use the World Wide Web addresses of the Washington, D.C., think tanks listed in Chapter 9.

Key Terms

political agenda *p. 436*
cost *p. 439*
benefit *p. 440*
majoritarian politics *p. 441*

interest group politics *p. 442*
client politics *p. 443*
pork-barrel projects *p. 443*
logrolling *p. 443*

entrepreneurial politics *p. 444*
policy entrepreneurs *p. 444*
boycott *p. 448*
process regulation *p. 455*

Suggested Readings

Derthick, Martha. *Up in Smoke.* Washington D.C.: Congressional Quarterly Press, 2002. Fascinating account of how lawyers and tobacco companies created a private regulation of smoking.

Derthick, Martha, and Paul J. Quirk. *The Politics of Deregulation.* Washington, D.C.: Brookings Institution, 1985. A brilliant analysis of how three industries—airlines, trucking, and telecommunications—were deregulated, often in the teeth of industry opposition.

Kingdon, John W. *Agendas, Alternatives, and Public Policies.* Boston: Little, Brown, 1984. An insightful account of how issues, especially those involving health and transportation, get on (or drop off) the federal agenda.

Lowi, Theodore J. "American Business, Public Policy, Case Studies, and Political Theory." *World Politics* 16 (July 1964). A theory of policy-making somewhat different from that offered in this book.

Nadel, Mark V. *The Politics of Consumer Protection.* 2d ed. Indianapolis: Bobbs-Merrill, 1975. An analysis of the sources and uses of political influence in consumer legislation.

Polsby, Nelson W. *Political Innovation in America.* New Haven, Conn.: Yale University Press, 1984. Explains how eight policy innovations were adopted by the federal government.

Wilson, James Q., ed. *The Politics of Regulation.* New York: Basic Books, 1980. Analyzes regulatory politics in nine agencies and provides a more detailed statement of the theory presented in this text.

Economic Policy

Enduring Questions

1. Can the president make the country prosperous?
2. Why does the government ever have a budget deficit?

In 1999 and 2000, a financial miracle occurred in Washington: the federal government, for the first time since 1969, spent less money than it took in. The nation, by not having a deficit in those two years, did not add to the federal debt.

The average American has never liked the idea of the government spending more money than it receives and has repeatedly told politicians to stop allowing a deficit. The politicians, naturally, agreed with voters but did little about it. The reason was not that they did not care, but that they were split into two groups—those who thought the deficit could be eliminated by cutting spending and those who thought it could be eliminated by raising taxes. In general (though there are many exceptions) conservatives want to cut spending and liberals want to raise taxes.

In 1996 the arguments between these groups were so intense that the Republican Congress refused to pass President Clinton's spending plan and the president refused to sign Congress's spending bills. As a result the government (briefly) ran out of money, and many agencies had to close their doors for a while.

459

During the two years when we had no deficit, the politicians claimed that their policies had made it disappear. Some of their efforts no doubt helped. For example, Congress had adopted some important restrictions on any new spending plans by requiring that an increase in money for one program must be met by a similar decrease in spending on another. But the main reason the deficit disappeared was that the American economy had grown so rapidly and produced so much new personal income that Washington was flooded with tax money.

Then a new debate began: what should we do with all the extra money? One group, primarily Republicans, wanted to give the surplus back to the people by cutting taxes. Another group, primarily Democrats, wanted to use the surplus for new programs.

Both of these goals were served. As for the first, President Bush proposed and Congress passed the Economic Growth and Tax Relief Reconciliation Act of 2001, which, over a ten-year period, will do the following:

- Cut tax rates on all income groups*
- Increase the tax credit for children
- Make it easier to deduct expenses
- Eliminate the "marriage penalty"
- Make it easier to save for education
- Phase out the tax on estates of deceased persons

This law was one of only three large federal tax cuts since the Second World War. The others were introduced by President Kennedy and President Reagan. The second goal was achieved by requiring that these tax cuts would end on December 31, 2010, and by passing laws that increased spending on many federal programs.

Doing both things at once makes you wonder whether there will be enough money for both. We don't know and almost certainly can't know. Nobody can guess what our economy and laws will look like in 2010. The Office of Management and Budget (OMB), part of the White House, and the Congressional Budget Office (CBO), part of Congress, employ skilled economists who try to estimate what the money world will look like in the future, but just like economists in the private sector, they make big mistakes.

Between 1993 and 1997 the OMB and CBO predicted that we would have a bigger deficit than we actually had. In 1997 they thought that our deficit would be almost nine times greater than it really was (see Figure 16.1). In 1995 the CBO guessed that these deficits would continue until 2002, but by 1999 it had changed its mind: instead we would have big surpluses.[1] If they were wrong about more deficits, would they be right about new surpluses? In 1999 the CBO said that over the next ten years the government would take in $2.9 trillion more than it would spend. But just three years later, in 2002, the CBO said that we would have a deficit of $121 billion in 2003 and $51 billion in 2004.

It changed its mind for several reasons. Because of the terrorist attack on September 11, the government had to spend huge new sums on the damages, the ensuing war against the Taliban in Afghanistan required a lot of money, and the defense buildup to prevent future attacks cost many billions of dollars. Then the economy went into a recession, so that tax revenues were sharply reduced and social programs required more spending.

The Politics of Economic Prosperity

The health of the American economy creates majoritarian politics. Hardly anyone wants inflation or unemployment; everyone wants rapid increases in income and wealth. But this fact is a bit puzzling. You might think that people would care about their own jobs and worry only about avoiding their own unemployment. If that were the case, they would vote for politicians who promised to award contracts to firms that would hire them or who would create programs that would benefit them, regardless of how well other people were getting along. In fact, though, people see connections between their own well-being and that of the nation, and they tend to hold politicians responsible for the state of the country.

Everybody knows that just before an election politicians worry about the *pocketbook issue*. We have seen in Chapter 8 that economic conditions are strongly associated with how much success the incumbent party has in holding on to the White House and to the seats held by the White House's party in Congress. But whose pocketbook are voters worried about?

---

*The tax rates would fall as follows: from 28 to 25 percent, from 31 to 28 percent, from 36 to 33 percent, and from 39.5 to 35 percent.

In part, of course, it is their own. We know that low-income people are more likely to worry about unemployment and to vote Democratic, and higher-income people are more likely to worry about inflation and to vote Republican.[2] We also know that people who tell pollsters that their families' finances have gotten worse are more likely than other people to vote against the incumbent president.[3] In 1980 about two-thirds of those who said that they had become worse off economically voted for Ronald Reagan, the challenger, while over half of those who felt that they had become better off voted for Jimmy Carter, the incumbent.[4] In 1992 people who felt economically pinched were more likely to vote for Clinton than for Bush. Clinton campaign aides often reminded each other, "It's the economy, stupid!"

But people do not simply vote their own pocketbooks. In any recession the vast majority of people still have jobs; nevertheless, these people say that unemployment is the nation's biggest problem, and many of them vote accordingly—against the incumbent during whose watch unemployment went up.[5] Why should employed people worry about other people's unemployment?

By the same token younger voters, whose incomes tend to go up each year, often worry more about inflation than do retired people living on fixed incomes, the purchasing power of which goes down with inflation.[6] In presidential elections those people who think that national economic trends are bad are much more likely to vote against the incumbent, *even when* their own personal finances have not worsened.[7]

In technical language voting behavior and economic conditions are strongly correlated at the national level but not at the individual level, and this is true both in the United States and in Europe.[8] Such voters are behaving in an "other-regarding" or "sociotropic" way. In ordinary language voters seem to respond more to the condition of the national economy than to their own personal finances.

It is not hard to understand why this might be true. Part of the explanation is that people understand what government can and cannot be held accountable for. If you lose your job at the aircraft plant because the government has not renewed the plant's contract, you will be more likely to hold the government responsible than

---

Figure 16.1   Bad Economic Guesses

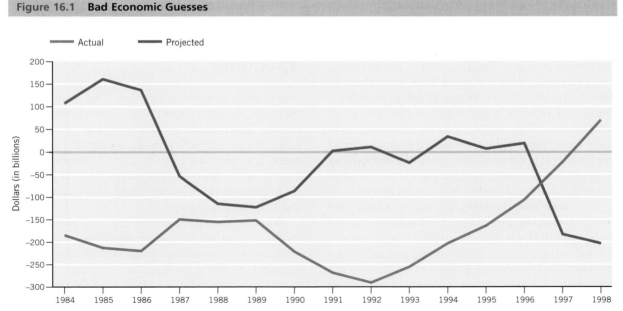

Note: The figure compares the actual budget deficit or surplus with the president's projection made five years earlier.
Source: National Journal (January 30, 1999), 251.

if you lose your job because you were always showing up drunk or because the plant moved out of town.

And part of the explanation is that people see general economic conditions as having indirect effects on them even when they are still doing pretty well. They may not be unemployed, but they may have friends who are, and they may worry that if unemployment grows worse, they will be the next to lose their jobs.

What Politicians Try to Do

Elected officials, who have to run for reelection every few years, are strongly tempted to take a short-run view of the economy and to adopt those policies that will best satisfy the self-regarding voter. They would dearly love to produce low unemployment rates and rising family incomes just before an election. Some scholars think that they do just this.

Since the nineteenth century the government has used money to affect elections. At first this mostly took the form of patronage passed out to the party faithful and money benefits given to important blocs of voters. The massive system of Civil War pensions for Union army veterans was run in a way that did no harm to the political fortunes of the Republican party. After the Social Security system was established, Congress voted to increase the benefits in virtually every year in which there was an election (see Chapter 17).

But it is by no means clear that the federal government can or will do whatever is necessary to reduce unemployment, cut inflation, lower interest rates, and increase incomes just to win an election. For one thing, the government does not know how to produce all these desirable outcomes. Moreover, doing one of these things may often be possible only at the cost of not doing another. For example, reducing inflation can, in many cases, require the government to raise interest rates, and this in turn can slow down the economy by making it harder to sell houses, automobiles, and other things that are purchased with borrowed money.

If it were easy to stimulate the economy just before an election, practically every president would serve two full terms. But because of the uncertainties and complexities of the economy, presidents can lose elections over economic issues that they do not manage to the satisfaction of voters. Ford lost in 1976, Carter in 1980, and Bush in 1992. In all cases economic conditions played a major role.

All this means that politicians must make choices about economic policy, choices that are affected by uncertainty and ignorance. Those choices are shaped significantly by the ideological differences between the two political parties over what ought to be the principal goal of economic policy. Democrats and Republicans alike would prefer to have both low unemployment and no inflation, but if they must choose (and choose they must), then the Democrats mainly attempt to reduce unemployment and the Republicans chiefly attempt to reduce inflation.[9] This is no hard-and-fast rule; some say that Jimmy Carter, a Democrat, tried so hard to cut inflation in 1980 that he lost the support of many liberal Democrats, such as Edward Kennedy, who thought that he should be worrying more about creating jobs. But the general tendency seems clear: the Democratic party worries more about unemployment, the Republican party about inflation.

This tendency mirrors to some degree what Democratic and Republican voters want their parties to do. Polls regularly show that those who think of themselves as Democrats are much more worried about unemployment than those who think of themselves as Republicans.[10] (There is not as much of a difference between Democratic and Republican voters in worrying about inflation.) Because of these beliefs, voters concerned about unemployment not only are more likely to vote against the incumbent but also are more likely to vote Democratic.

The Politics of Taxing and Spending

People want prosperity, but they also want no tax increases, no government deficit, and continued (or higher) government spending on the things they like, such as education, medical care, the environment, and retirement benefits. But it is obvious that voters cannot have all of these things: it is impossible to produce generous spending on programs with low taxes and no deficit.

What politicians confront are two inconsistent kinds of majoritarian politics: everybody wants general prosperity, and large majorities want more government spending on popular programs. But the more the government spends on popular programs, the more money it requires, and the more it takes in, the less that is left over for private investment that produces prosperity.

Most voters would like to have all three actions—lower taxes, less debt, and new programs. All three produce majoritarian politics. But the difficulty with this is that the policies being endorsed are inconsistent with one another. We cannot have lower taxes, no debt, and higher spending on politically popular programs such as health care, education, the environment, and retirement benefits. If we have more spending, we have to pay for it, either with higher taxes or with more borrowing.

Most politicians, trying to reconcile these competing political demands, have argued that some of the surplus should pay down the debt and the rest should be to used for either a big tax cut (with less for new programs) or a small tax cut (with more for new programs).

When there was a big annual deficit, there was no new money to pass out. People who wanted new programs had to either cut existing programs, let the government go deeper in debt, or raise taxes. But how do you raise taxes without alienating voters? The answer is that you raise taxes on *other people*.

The "other people" are always a minority of the voters. For example, if you want to put more money into medical research (something that everybody likes), you raise taxes on cigarettes (only a minority smoke them). If you want to pay for new education programs (most people like those), you increase taxes on inheritances (only a minority pass on inheritances large enough to be taxed). If you want a new environmental program, you raise taxes on affluent voters. In this way you can find a majority of voters who will support—or at least not oppose very strongly—tax increases on a small group of voters— cigarette smokers or high-income people.

Many politicians believe that lowering everyone's tax rate is a good idea. They say this because they don't think the government needs as much money as it now receives. Other politicians who want the government to have more money will not oppose a tax cut; instead they will insist that it be limited to ordinary people (and thus denied to affluent ones) and targeted for specific activities (such as education or childcare) that the government wants to encourage. Since there are fewer affluent people than average ones, lowering the top tax rate always has less political muscle behind it than keeping the top rate high. Legislators who like high rates say that "people who can afford it should pay a lot." Legislators who want low rates say that their opponents are trying to "soak the rich" by denying tax cuts to the people who now pay the biggest share of taxes.

A Project Head Start preschool class.

Because cutting taxes to any meaningful extent is politically difficult, politicians have a strong tendency to get reelected by spending public money on specific programs that are popular. Some of these programs may involve majoritarian politics (such as Social Security or highway construction); some may involve client politics (such as grants to businesses, universities, or other special interests). This means that increasing spending will tend to be more popular than cutting taxes.

Economic Theories and Political Needs

Since most tax issues are majoritarian issues, they involve the president. He takes a direct and visible lead in these matters. If everyone who advised him knew what effect a change in tax laws would have, it would probably be easier for him to make economic policy. But the economic health of a nation is an extraordinarily complex, poorly understood matter. Nations, such as the old Soviet Union, that have tried to manage their economies centrally have done poorly.

Presidents rely on economic advisers, but the advice they get varies dramatically depending on what kind of advisers they have. There are at least four major theories about how best to manage the economy. Each theory, if fully stated, would be quite complicated; moreover, many experts combine parts of one theory with parts of another. What follows is a highly simplified account of these theories that highlights their differences.

Monetarism

A monetarist, such as the economist Milton Friedman, believes that inflation occurs when there is too much money chasing too few goods. The federal government has the power to create money (in ways to be described on page 467); according to monetarists, inflation occurs when it prints too much money. When inflation becomes rampant and government tries to do something about it, it often cuts back sharply on the amount of money in circulation. Then a recession will occur, with slowed economic growth and an increase in unemployment. Since the government does not understand that economic problems result from its own start-and-stop habit of issuing new money, it will try to cure some of these problems with policies that make matters worse—such as having an unbalanced budget or creating new welfare programs. **Monetarism** suggests that the proper thing for government to do is to have a steady, predictable increase in the money supply at a rate about equal to the growth in the economy's productivity; beyond that it should leave matters alone and let the free market operate.

Keynesianism

John Maynard Keynes, an English economist who died in 1946, believed that the market will not automatically operate at a full-employment, low-inflation level. Its health depends on what fraction of people's incomes they save or spend. If they save too much, there will be too little demand, production will decline, and unemployment will rise. If they spend too much, demand will rise too fast, prices will go up, and shortages will develop. According to **Keynesianism,** the key is to create the right level of demand. This is the task of government. When demand is too little, the government should pump more money into the economy (by spending more than it takes in in taxes and by creating public-works programs). When demand is too great, the government should take money out of the economy (by increasing taxes or cutting federal expenditures). There is no need for the government's budget to be balanced on a year-to-year basis; what counts is the performance of the economy. Keynesians, unlike monetarists, tend to favor an activist government.

Planning

Some economists have too little faith in the workings of the free market to be pure Keynesians, much less monetarists. They believe that the government should plan, in varying ways, some part of the country's economic activity. One form of **economic planning** is **price and wage controls,** as advocated by John Kenneth Galbraith and others. In this view big corporations can raise prices because the forces of competition are too weak to restrain them, and labor unions can force up wages because management finds it easy to pass the increases along to consumers in the form of higher prices. Thus during inflationary times the government should regulate the maximum prices that can be charged and wages that can be paid, at least in the larger industries.

In the mid-1980s inflation was not the problem that it once had been, however; instead the automakers were cutting car prices and labor unions were accepting wage reductions. This shift drew attention to a different form of economic planning. Called an **industrial policy,** it reflected the public's concern for the declining health of certain basic industries such as steel and automobile manufacturing. People thought that these "smokestack" industries would not recover through market forces; what was needed instead was for the government somehow to direct or plan investments so that either these industries would recover or new and better industries would take their place. Advocates of this form of planning, such as Robert Reich (who became secretary of labor in the Clinton administration), often point to Japan as an example of a country in which the government directs industrial investments.

Supply-Side Tax Cuts

Exactly the opposite remedy for declining American productivity is suggested by people who call themselves supply-siders. The view of economists such as Arthur Laffer and Paul Craig Roberts is that the market, far from having failed, has not been given an adequate chance. According to **supply-side theory,** what is needed is not more planning but less government interference. In particular, sharply cutting taxes will increase people's incentive to work, save, and invest. Greater investments will then lead to more jobs, and if the earnings from these investments and jobs are taxed less, it will lessen the tendency of many individuals to shelter their earnings from the tax collector by taking advantage of various tax loopholes or cheating on their income tax returns. The greater productivity of the economy will produce more tax revenue for the government. Even though tax *rates* will be lower, the total national income to which these rates are applied will be higher.

Ideology and Theory

Each economic theory has clear political consequences, and so it is no accident that people embrace one theory or another in part because of their political beliefs. If you are a conservative, monetarism or supply-side tax cuts will appeal to you, because both imply that the government will be smaller and less intrusive. If you are a liberal, Keynesian economics will appeal to you, because it permits (or even requires) the federal government to carry on a wide range of social welfare programs. And if you are a socialist, economic planning will appeal to you, because it is an alternative to the free market and the private management of economic resources.

Of course there are many exceptions to these patterns. Many advocates of so-called industrial policy are not socialists; some liberals have become skeptical of Keynesian economics; and quite a few conservatives think that supply-side economics is unrealistic. But in general one's economic theory tends to be consistent with one's political convictions.

"Reaganomics"

When Ronald Reagan became president in 1981, he set in motion changes in federal economic policies that were soon called **Reaganomics.** These changes were not dictated by any single economic theory but by a combination of monetarism, supply-side tax cuts, and domestic budget cutting. The president wanted to achieve several goals simultaneously— reduce the size of the federal government, stimulate economic growth, and increase American military strength. As it turned out for him (as for most presidents), the things that he wanted were not entirely consistent.

Spending on some domestic programs was reduced. These reductions slowed the rate of growth of federal spending on these programs but did not actually decrease the spending. Military spending was sharply increased. The money supply was held under control in order to combat inflation (at the price of allowing interest rates to rise). Finally, and most important, there were sharp across-the-board cuts in personal income taxes, but for many people these cuts were more than offset by increases in Social Security taxes.

The effect of lowering taxes while increasing spending was to stimulate the economy (by pumping more money into it) and to create large deficits. The stimulated economy resulted in a drop in the unemployment rate and a rise in business activity. The large deficits increased dramatically the size of the national debt. The effects of the tax cuts on productivity and investment were hard to estimate and remain a matter of controversy.

John Maynard Keynes, had he been alive, would have been startled. A conservative president (aided, of course, by Congress) created a massive budget deficit that helped reduce unemployment—just as Keynes, a liberal, might have recommended.

Milton Friedman

John Maynard Keynes

John Kenneth Galbraith

Arthur B. Laffer

Defining Some Economic Terms

Fiscal policy An attempt to use taxes and expenditures to affect the economy. A **budget deficit** means that the government spends more than it takes in, thus pumping more money into the economy. A **budget surplus** means that the government takes in more than it spends, thus draining money out of the economy.

Monetary policy An attempt to use the amount of money and bank deposits and the price of money (the interest rate) to affect the economy.

Fiscal year (FY) October 1 to September 30, the period of time for which federal government appropriations are made and federal books are kept. A fiscal year is named after the year in which it *ends*—thus "fiscal 2000" (or "FY 00") means the twelve-month period ending September 30, 2000.

At one time every U.S. dollar could be exchanged for gold. Today the dollar is backed chiefly by public confidence rather than by a precious metal.

The Machinery of Economic Policy Making

Even if the president knew exactly the right thing to do, he would still have to find some way of doing it. In our government that is no easy task. The machinery for making decisions about economic matters is complex and not under the president's full control. Within the executive branch three people other than the president are of special importance. Sometimes called the troika,* these are the chairman of the Council of Economic Advisers (CEA), the director of the Office of Management and Budget (OMB), and the secretary of the treasury.

The CEA, composed of three professional economists plus a small staff, has existed since 1946. In theory it is an impartial group of experts responsible for forecasting economic trends, analyzing economic issues, and helping prepare the economic report that the president submits to Congress each year. Though quite professional in tone, the CEA is not exactly impartial in practice, since each president picks members sympathetic to his point of view. Kennedy picked Keynesians; Reagan picked supply-siders and monetarists. But whatever its philosophical tilt, the CEA is seen by other executive agencies as the advocate of the opinion of professional economists, who despite their differences generally tend to favor reliance on the market.

The OMB was originally the Bureau of the Budget, which was created in 1921 and made part of the executive office of the president in 1939; in 1970 it was renamed the Office of Management and Budget. Its chief function is to prepare estimates of the amount that will be spent by federal agencies, to negotiate with other departments over the size of their budgets, and to make certain (insofar as it can) that the legislative proposals of these other departments are in accord with the president's program. Of late it has acquired something of a split personality; it is in part an expert, nonpartisan agency that analyzes spending and budget patterns and in part an activist, partisan organization that tries to get the president's wishes carried out by the bureaucracy.

The secretary of the treasury is often close to or drawn from the world of business and finance and is

*From the Russian word for a carriage pulled by three horses.

The Federal Reserve Board

The Tools by Which the Fed Implements Its Monetary Policy

1. **Buying and selling federal government securities** (bonds, Treasury notes, and other pieces of paper that constitute government IOUs). When the Fed buys securities, it in effect puts more money into circulation and takes securities out of circulation. With more money around, interest rates tend to drop, and more money is borrowed and spent. When the Fed sells government securities, it in effect takes money out of circulation, causing interest rates to rise and making borrowing more difficult.

2. **Regulating the amount of money that a member bank must keep in hand as reserves** to back up the customer deposits it is holding. A bank lends out most of the money deposited with it. If the Fed says that it must keep in reserve a larger fraction of its deposits, then the amount that it can lend drops, loans become harder to obtain, and interest rates rise.

3. **Changing the interest charged banks** that want to borrow money from the Federal Reserve System. Banks borrow from the Fed to cover short-term needs. The interest that the Fed charges for this is called the *discount* rate. The Fed can raise or lower that rate; this will have an effect, though usually rather small, on how much money the banks will lend.

Federal Reserve Board (7 members)
- Determines how many government securities will be bought or sold by regional and member banks.
- Determines interest rates to be charged by regional banks and amount of money member banks must keep in reserve in regional banks.

Regional Federal Reserve Banks (12)
- Buy and sell government securities.
- Loan money to member banks.
- Keep percentage of holdings for member banks.

Member Banks (6,000)
- Buy and sell government securities.
- May borrow money from regional banks.
- Must keep percentage of holdings in regional banks.
- Interest rates paid to regional banks determine interest rates charged for business and personal loans and influence all bank interest rates.

expected to argue the point of view of the financial community. (Since its members do not always agree, this is not always easy.) The secretary provides estimates of the revenue that the government can expect from existing taxes and what will be the result of changing tax laws. He or she represents the United States in its dealings with the top bankers and finance ministers of other nations.

A good deal of pulling and hauling takes place among members of the troika, but if that were the extent of the problem, presidential leadership would be fairly easy. The problem is far more complex. One study found 132 separate government bureaus engaged in formulating economic policy. They regulate business, make loans, and supply subsidies. For example, as foreign trade becomes increasingly important to this country, the secretary of state (among many others) acquires an interest in economic policy. One-third of corporate profits come from overseas investments, and one-fourth of farm output is sold abroad.

The Fed

Among the most important of these other agencies is the board of governors of the Federal Reserve System (the "Fed"). Its seven members are appointed by the president, with the consent of the Senate, for fourteen-year, nonrenewable terms and may not be removed except for cause. (No member has been removed since it was created in 1913.) The chairman serves for four years. In theory, and to some degree in practice, the Fed is independent of both the president and Congress. Its most important function is to regulate, insofar as it can, the supply of money (both in circulation and in bank deposits) and the price of money (in the form of interest rates). The box above shows the means employed by the Fed to achieve this goal and the structure of the system over which it presides. During

Alan Greenspan, chairman of the Federal Reserve Board.

2001, the Fed cut the interest rates it charges banks eleven times to help minimize the recession.

Just how independent the Fed is can be a matter of dispute. During the 1980 election Fed policies helped keep interest rates at a high level, a circumstance that did not benefit President Carter's reelection bid. On the other hand, whenever a president is determined to change monetary policy, he usually can do so. For example, the term of Fed chairman Arthur F. Burns, appointed by President Nixon, came up for renewal in 1978. President Carter, seeking to influence Burns's decisions, held out the prospect of reappointing him chairman. When Burns balked, he was passed over, and G. William Miller was appointed in his stead. Presidents Truman, Johnson, and Nixon were all able to obtain changes in monetary policy. When Alan Greenspan, a conservative, became Fed chairman in 1987 under President Reagan, he was so successful in curbing inflation that he was reappointed by President Clinton, a Democrat.

Congress

The most important part of the economic policy making machinery, of course, is Congress. It must approve all taxes and almost all expenditures; there can be no wage or price controls without its consent; and it has the ability to alter the policy of the nominally independent Federal Reserve Board by threatening to pass laws that would reduce its powers. And Congress itself is fragmented, with great influence wielded by the members of key committees, especially the House and Senate Budget Committees, the House and Senate Appropriations Committees, the House Ways and Means Committee, and the Senate Finance Committee.

In sum, no matter what economic theory the president may have, if he is to put that theory into effect he needs the assistance of many agencies within the executive branch, such independent agencies as the Federal Reserve Board, and the various committees of Congress. Though members of the executive and legislative branches are united by their common desire to get reelected (and thus have a common interest in producing sound economic growth), each part of this system may also be influenced by different economic theories and will be motivated by the claims of interest groups.

The effect of these interest group claims is clearly shown in the debate over trade restriction. Usually the economic health of the nation affects everyone in pretty much the same way—we are all hurt by inflation or helped by stable prices; the incomes of all of us tend to grow (or remain stagnant) together. In these circumstances the politics of economic health is majoritarian.

Suppose, however, that most of us are doing pretty well but that the people in a few industries or occupations are suffering. That is sometimes the result of foreign competition. In many countries labor costs are much lower than they are in the United States. That means that these countries can ship to American buyers goods—such as shoes, textiles, and beef—that sell at much lower prices than American producers can afford to charge. By contrast, if the price of a product is based chiefly on having advanced technology rather than low labor costs, American manufacturers can beat almost any foreign competitor.

When Congress passes laws governing foreign trade, it is responding to interest group politics. Industries that find it easy to sell American products abroad want free trade—that is, they want no taxes or restrictions on international exchanges. Industries that find it hard to compete with foreign imports oppose free trade—that is, they want tariffs and other limitations on imports.

When the North American Free Trade Agreement (NAFTA) was passed by Congress in 1993, the free traders won, and tariffs on our commerce with Canada and Mexico were largely abolished. But when the government later suggested creating free trade with all of Latin America, the critics of free trade opposed the idea, and it died. This is a good example of how people who bear the costs of a policy are often much more effective in influencing the votes on it than are those who stand to benefit from it.

Not only has the United States not extended the NAFTA idea to other countries, but it has done things that reward certain economic interest groups. Even though Republicans tend to support free trade, President George W. Bush imposed sharp increases in the taxes that must be paid on imported steel. The reason is not hard to find. Steel is produced in certain states, such as Ohio and Pennsylvania, that the president would like to carry in 2004.

Spending Money

If only the economic health of the nation mattered, then majoritarian politics would dominate, and the president and Congress would both work to improve economic conditions. Although they still might work at cross-purposes because they held to different economic theories, the goal would be the same.

But the government must also respond to the demands of voters and interest groups. While these demands are no less legitimate than the voters' general interest in economic health, they produce not majoritarian but client and interest group politics.

The sources of this conflict can be seen in public opinion polls. Voters consistently say that they want a balanced budget and lower government spending. They believe that the government spends too much and that if it wanted to, it could cut spending. When the government runs a deficit, the reason in the voters' eyes is that it is spending too much, not that it is taxing too little. But these same polls show that the voters believe that the government should spend more on education, homelessness, childcare, and crime control.

The voters are not irrational, thinking that they can have more spending and less spending simultaneously. Nor are they hypocrites, pretending to want less spending overall but more spending for particular programs. They are simply expressing a variety of concerns. They want a limited government with no deficit; they also want good schools, cleaner air, better health care, and less crime. They believe that a frugal government could deliver what they want by cutting out waste. They may by wrong about that belief, but it is not obviously silly.

What this means for the government is easy to imagine. Politicians have an incentive to make two kinds of appeals: The first is, "Vote for me and I will keep government spending down and cut the deficit." The second is, "Vote for me and I will make certain that your favorite program gets more money." Some people will vote for the candidate because of the first appeal; some will vote for him or her because of the second. But acting on these two appeals is clearly going to lead to inconsistent policies. These inconsistencies become evident in the budget.

The Budget

A **budget** is a document that announces how much the government will collect in taxes and spend in revenues and how those expenditures will be allocated among various programs. In theory the federal budget should be based on *first* deciding how much money the government is going to spend and *then* allocating that money among different programs and agencies. That is the way a household makes up its budget: "We have this much in the paycheck, and so we will spend *X* dollars on rent, *Y* dollars on food, and *Z* dollars on clothing, and what's left over on entertainment. If the amount of the paycheck goes down, we will cut something out—probably entertainment."

In fact the federal budget is a list of everything the government is going to spend money on, with only slight regard (sometimes no regard at all) for how much money is available to be spent. Instead of being a way of *allocating* money to be spent on various purposes, it is a way of *adding up* what is being spent.

Indeed, there was no federal budget at all before 1921, and there was no unified presidential budget until the 1930s. Even after the president began submitting a single budget, the committees of Congress acted on it separately, adding to or subtracting from the amounts he proposed. (Usually they followed his lead, but they were certainly free to depart from it as they wished.) If one committee wanted to spend more on housing, no effort was made to take that amount away from the committee that was spending money on health (in fact, there was no machinery for making such an effort).

The Congressional Budget Act of 1974 changed this somewhat. Now after the president submits his budget in February, two budget committees—one in the House, one in the Senate—study his overall package and obtain an analysis of it from the Congressional Budget Office (CBO). Each committee then submits to its house a **budget resolution** that proposes a total budget ceiling and a ceiling for each of several spending areas (such as health or defense).

Figure 16.2   History of the National Debt

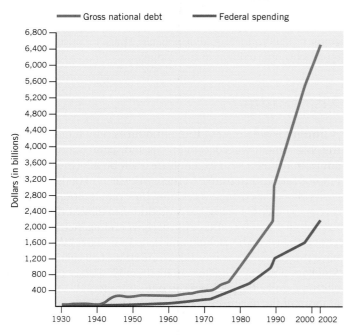

Source: Economic Reports of the President, various years.

about one-third of federal spending in any year.

There is a big loophole in the current budget process: nothing in the process requires Congress to tighten the government's financial belt. It can pass a budget resolution authorizing spending that is more or less than what the president has proposed. Nonetheless, the process has made a difference. Congress is now conscious of how its spending decisions match up with estimates of tax revenues.

When President Reagan took office, he and his allies in Congress took advantage of the Congressional Budget Act to start the controversial process of cutting federal spending. The House and Senate budget committees, with the president's support, used the first budget resolution in May 1981 not simply to set a budget ceiling that, as in the past, looked pretty much like the previous year's budget but to direct each committee of Congress to make *cuts*—sometimes deep cuts—in the programs for which it was responsible. These cuts were to be made in the authorization legislation (see Chapter 13) as well as in the appropriations.

The object was to get members of Congress to vote for a total package of cuts before they could vote on any particular cut. Republican control of the Senate and an alliance between Republicans and conservative southern Democrats in the House allowed this strategy to succeed. The first budget resolution ordered Senate and House committees to reduce federal spending during fiscal 1982 by about $36 billion—less than the president had first asked, but a large sum nonetheless. Then the individual committees set to work trying to find ways of making these cuts.

Note how the *procedures* used by Congress can affect the *policies* adopted by Congress. If the Reagan plan had been submitted in the old piecemeal way, it is unlikely that cuts of this size would have occurred in so short a time, or at all. The reason is not that Congress would have wanted to ignore the president but that, then as now, Congress reflects public opinion on economic policy. As stated at the beginning of the chapter, the public wants less total federal spending but more money spent on specific federal programs. Thus, if you allow the public or Congress to vote first on specific programs, spending is bound to rise. But if you require Congress to vote first on a budget ceiling, then (unless it changes its mind as it goes along) total spending will go down, and tough choices will have to be made about the component parts of the budget.

That, at least, is the theory. It worked once, in 1981, but it did not work very well thereafter. During the rest

Each May Congress is supposed to adopt, with some modifications, these budget resolutions, intending them to be targets to guide the work of each legislative committee as it decides what should be spent in its area. During the summer Congress then takes up the specific appropriations bills, informing its members as it goes along whether or not the spending proposed in these bills conforms to the May budget resolution. The object, obviously, is to impose some discipline on the various committees. After each committee approves its appropriations bill and Congress passes it, it goes to the president for his signature.

These appropriations bills, however, can rarely make big changes in government spending. About two-thirds of what the government spends is mandatory—that is, the money goes to people who are entitled to it. **Entitlements** include Social Security and Medicare payments, veterans' benefits, food stamps, and money the government owes investors who have bought Treasury bonds (that is, the interest on the national debt). In theory the government could change these entitlements by, for example, cutting Social Security payments, but that would be a political disaster. In reality the government can change only

of the Reagan years the budget process broke down in the warfare between the president and Congress. President Reagan represented the part of public opinion that wanted less government spending in general; most members of Congress represented the part of public opinion that wanted more spending on particular programs. The result was a stalemate. It continued with Presidents Clinton and both the elder and younger Bush. In 2002 no budget resolution was adopted by Congress, and so the money struggle was left to the appropriations committees.

Reducing Spending

Because the 1974 Congressional Budget Act did not automatically lead to spending cuts, people concerned about the growing federal deficit decided to find ways to put a cap on spending. The first such cap was the Balanced Budget Act of 1985, now called the Gramm-Rudman Act after two of its sponsors, Senators Phil Gramm (R-Tex.) and Warren Rudman (R-N.H.). The law required that each year from 1986 to 1991 the budget would automatically be cut until the federal deficit had disappeared. What made the cuts automatic, its authors hoped, was a provision in the bill, called a **sequester,** that required across-the-board percentage cuts in all federal programs (except for entitlements) if the president and Congress failed to agree on a total spending level that met the law's targets. No one liked this plan, but it seemed necessary. Senator Rudman called it a "bad idea whose time has come."

But the plan failed. By various devices that people began to call "smoke and mirrors," Congress and the president found ways to get new spending that was higher than the targeted amounts. By 1990 it was evident that a new strategy was needed if the government was going to help eliminate the deficit.

That strategy had two parts. First, Congress voted for a tax increase. Second, the Budget Enforcement Act of 1990 imposed a cap on discretionary (that is, nonentitlement) spending. As long as the president and Congress stay under that cap, they can change the amount of money they spend. The law does not limit mandatory spending, but it does impose a pay-as-you-go approach. If Congress increases spending in one program, it must either cut spending in another program or raise taxes. The combined effect of a spending cap and a pay-as-you-go policy helped restrain federal spending, and to that extent the government contributed to eliminating the deficit.

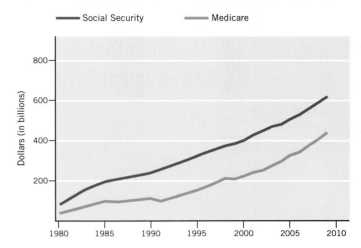

Figure 16.3 When Will the Crunch Come? Projections of the Growth in Federal Spending

Source: Congressional Budget Office, *The Economic and Budget Outlook: An Update* (July 1, 1999).

Levying Taxes

Tax policy reflects a mixture of majoritarian politics ("What is a 'fair' tax law?") and client politics ("How much is in it for me?"). In the United States a fair tax law has generally been viewed as one that keeps the overall tax burden rather low, requires everyone to pay something, and requires the better-off to pay at a higher rate than the less-well-off. The law, in short, was viewed as good if it imposed modest burdens, prevented cheating, and was mildly progressive.

Americans have had their first goal satisfied. The tax burden in the United States is lower than it is in most other democratic nations (see Figure 16.4). There is some evidence that they have also had their second goal met—there is reason to believe that Americans evade their income taxes less than do citizens of, say, France or Italy. (That is one reason why many nations rely more on sales taxes than we do— they are harder to evade.) Just how progressive our tax rates are is a matter of dispute; to determine whether the rich really pay at higher rates than the poor, one has to know not only the official rates but also the effect of deductions, exemptions, and exclusions (that is, of loopholes).

Keeping the burden low and the cheating at a minimum are examples of majoritarian politics:

Balanced Budget Amendment Debated

July 26
WASHINGTON
Congress began today a search for a more effective budget process, one that would keep a tighter check on federal spending and prevent future deficits. One idea . . .

MEMORANDUM

To: Representative Ellen Brown
From: Russel Burgos, legislative assistant

The most far-reaching proposal before the House is a constitutional amendment that would require Congress to pass a balanced budget every year (except in wartime or when three-fifths of the members believed that a deficit was needed). What is your view on this?

Arguments for:

1. A constitutional amendment is the only way to compel Congress to keep the budget in balance. Left to its own devices, Congress will adopt spending caps that are easy for it to evade.
2. A balanced budget amendment would allow for deficit spending when there was a compelling need.
3. Thirty-two states have called for such an amendment.

Arguments against:

1. A constitutional amendment would be ineffective. If Congress defied the amendment by passing an unbalanced budget, there would be no authority that could compel it to change its mind.
2. A constitutional amendment does not take into account that passing a balanced budget requires a guess about tax revenues in the coming year and what emergency spending bills (for example, to deal with hurricanes) might be needed.

Your decision:
Favor amendment _____
Oppose amendment _____

most people benefit, most people pay. The loopholes, however, are another matter—all manner of special interests can get some special benefit from the tax law that the rest of us must pay for but, given the complexity of the law, rarely notice. Loopholes are client politics par excellence.

Because of that, hardly any scholars believed that tax reform (dramatically reducing the loopholes) was politically possible. Every interest that benefited from a loophole—and these included not just corporations but universities, museums, states, cities, and investors—would lobby vigorously to protect it.

Nevertheless, in 1986 a sweeping tax reform act was passed. Many of the most cherished loopholes were closed or reduced. What happened? It is as if scientists who had proved that a bumblebee could not fly got stung by a flying bumblebee.

The Rise of the Income Tax

To understand what happened in 1986, one must first understand the political history of taxation in the United States. Until almost the end of the nineteenth century, there was no federal income tax (except for a brief period during the Civil War). The money that the government needed came mostly from tariffs (that is, taxes on goods imported into this country). And when Congress did enact a peacetime income tax, the Supreme Court in 1895 struck it down as unconstitutional.[11] To change this, Congress proposed, and in 1913 the states ratified, the Sixteenth Amendment, which authorized such a tax.

For the next forty years or so tax rates tended to go up during wartime and down during peacetime (see Figure 16.5). The rates were progressive—that is, the wealthiest individuals paid at a higher rate than the less affluent. For example, during World War II incomes in the highest bracket were taxed at a rate of 94 percent. (The key tax rate is called by economists the "marginal rate." This is the percentage of the last dollar that you earn that must be paid out in taxes.)

An income tax offers the opportunity for majoritarian politics to become class politics. The majority of the citizenry earn average incomes and control most of the votes. In theory there is nothing to prevent the mass of people from voting for legislators who will tax only the rich, who, as a minority, will always be outvoted. During the early decades of this century, that is exactly what the rich feared would happen. Since the highest marginal tax rate was 94 percent, you might think that that is in fact what did happen.

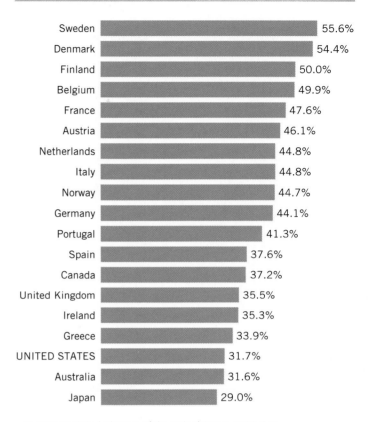

Figure 16.4   Tax Burdens in Nineteen Democratic Nations

Nation	Tax Burden
Sweden	55.6%
Denmark	54.4%
Finland	50.0%
Belgium	49.9%
France	47.6%
Austria	46.1%
Netherlands	44.8%
Italy	44.8%
Norway	44.7%
Germany	44.1%
Portugal	41.3%
Spain	37.6%
Canada	37.2%
United Kingdom	35.5%
Ireland	35.3%
Greece	33.9%
UNITED STATES	31.7%
Australia	31.6%
Japan	29.0%

Source: Statistical Abstract of the United States, 1998, 841.

You would be wrong. Offsetting the high rates were the deductions, exemptions, and exclusions by which people could shelter some of their income from taxation. These loopholes were available for everyone, but they particularly helped the well-off. In effect a political compromise was reached during the first half of the twentieth century. The terms were these: the well-off, generally represented by the Republican party, would drop their bitter opposition to high marginal rates provided that the less-well-off, generally represented by the Democratic party, would support a large number of loopholes. The Democrats (or more accurately, the liberals) were willing to accept this compromise because they feared that if they insisted on high rates with no loopholes, the economy would suffer as people and businesses lost their incentive to save and invest.

Figure 16.5   Federal Taxes on Income, Top Percentage Rates, 1913–2002

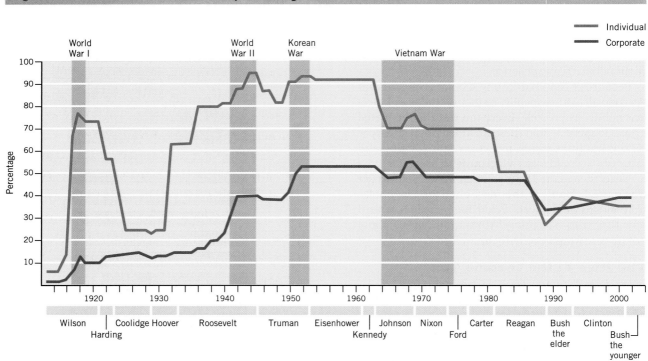

Source: Updated from *Congressional Quarterly Weekly Report* (September 18, 1993), 2488.

For at least thirty years after the adoption of the income tax in 1913, only a small number of high-income people paid any significant amount in federal income taxes. The average citizen paid very little in such taxes until World War II. After the war, taxes did not fall to their prewar levels.

Most people did not complain too much, because they, too, benefited greatly from the loopholes. They could deduct from their taxable income the interest they paid on their home mortgages, the state and local taxes they paid, much of what they paid in medical insurance premiums, and the interest they paid on consumer loans (such as those used to buy automobiles). On the eve of the Tax Reform Act of 1986, an opinion poll showed that more people favored small cuts in tax rates coupled with many large deductions than favored big cuts in tax rates coupled with fewer and smaller deductions.[12]

Interest groups organized around each loophole. Home builders organized to support the mortgage-interest deduction; universities supported the charitable-contribution deduction; insurance companies supported the deduction for medical insurance premiums; and automakers supported the deduction for interest on consumer loans.

In addition to these well-known loopholes there were countless others, not so well known and involving much less money, that were defended and enlarged through the efforts of other interest groups: for instance, oil companies supported the deduction for drilling costs, heavy industry supported the investment tax credit, and real estate developers supported special tax write-offs for apartment and office buildings.

Until 1986 the typical tax fight was less about rates than about deductions. Rates were important, but not as important as tax loopholes. "Loophole politics" was client politics. When client groups pressed for benefits, they could take advantage of the decentralized structure of Congress to find well-placed advocates who could advance these interests through low-visibility bargaining. In effect these groups were getting a subsidy from the federal government equal to the amount of the tax break. However, the tax break was even better than a subsidy, because it did not have to be voted

WHO GOVERNS? TO WHAT ENDS?

Terrorism and the Federal Budget

When George W. Bush took office in 2001, the federal government was taking in through taxes much more than it was spending. There were several reasons: American businesses and workers had become more productive, the Clinton tax increase had brought in more money, and tough budget restrictions had made it hard for the government to spend more money. By law, increased spending in many areas had to be offset either by cutting other spending or raising taxes. Since politicians hate to cut spending or raise taxes, there was not much room for adding new spending programs.

What should Washington do with the extra money?

Republicans, led by President Bush, said that a lot of the extra money should go back to the people by cutting taxes. In addition, the president wanted to change Social Security by finding a way to let people invest some of this money privately.

Democrats responded by saying that taxes should not be cut. The extra money could be used either to reduce the federal deficit, fund new programs, or guard against the possibility that the predicted surpluses would not materialize. And most were critical of doing anything to privatize Social

Security even though it was clear that in a few decades the program would run out of money.

The outcome was legislation that split the difference. It cut taxes over a ten-year period while spending more on some favorite domestic programs.

Then came the terrorist attacks. Immediately any talk of how to spend the budget surplus disappeared. Working together, the president and Congress rushed through bills that offered billions of dollars in aid to airlines that had been forced to cancel thousands of flights, to New York City for help with removal of the remains of the World Trade Center buildings, and to citizens who had directly suffered from the attacks. Help also went to the military, engaged in a struggle in Afghanistan to eliminate the radical Taliban regime and hunt down Osama Bin Laden, the leader of the network of terrorist cells responsible for the attacks.

The commission the president had appointed to find ways of privatizing a part of Social Security issued a report that offered no single plan and that most people ignored.

In short, the debate over how big the federal government should be gave way to a discussion of how to keep it big enough to accomplish all that was necessary.

on every year as part of an appropriations bill: once part of the tax code, it lasted for a long time, and given the length and complexity of that code, scarcely anyone would notice it was there.

Many of these loopholes could be justified by arguments about economic growth. Low tax rates on a certain kind of investment encouraged more investment of that kind. Deductions for mortgage interest and property taxes encouraged people to own their own homes and boosted the construction industry.

Then the Tax Reform Act of 1986 turned the decades-old compromise on its head: instead of high rates with big deductions, we got low rates with

much smaller deductions. The big gainers were individuals; the big losers were businesses.

But soon the old system began to reassert itself. Not long after the 1986 bill became law, tax rates started to go up again, this time with far fewer of the deductions that had once made it easy for affluent citizens to keep their rates low. In 1990 President Bush, after having campaigned on the slogan "Read my lips, no new taxes," signed a tax increase. The top rate was 31 percent. In 1993 President Clinton proposed another tax increase, one that would raise the top rate to over 39 percent (it had been 28 percent in 1986) and make most Social Security benefits

taxable for upper-income retirees. His bill narrowly passed by a vote of 218 to 216 in the House, a vote of 51 to 50 in the Senate, with Vice President Al Gore casting the deciding vote. Not a single Republican voted for it. It was the first time since 1945 that the majority party in Congress had passed a major bill without one vote from the minority party.

When President George W. Bush got his tax cut plan through Congress in 2002, many Democrats as well as most Republicans voted for it. The next issue is clear: should the tax cuts, now expiring at the end of 2010, be made permanent? There is no point in guessing what will happen; events more than personalities will determine the outcome.

Summary

There are three economic factors that make a difference to voters; the policies for each are formulated by a distinctive type of policy-making. The first is the economic health of the nation, the second the amount and kinds of government spending, and the third the level and distribution of taxes.

National economic health has powerful effects on the outcome of elections, as much through people's perception of national conditions as from their worries about their own finances. The politics of inflation, unemployment, and economic growth tend to be majoritarian. The president is held responsible for national conditions. But he must meet that responsibility by using imperfect economic theories to manage clumsy government tools controlled by divided political authorities.

When economic ill health occurs in some industries and places but not others (as a result of such forces as foreign competition), the politics of economic health are shaped by interest group politics. Firms that import foreign products or sell to foreign nations try to avoid trade restrictions, while firms and unions hurt by foreign competition try to impose such restrictions.

The amount of spending is theoretically determined by the budget, but in fact the nation has no meaningful budget. Instead the president and Congress struggle over particular spending bills whose amounts reflect interest group and client pressures. In the 1980s those pressures, coupled with a large tax cut, led to a sharp increase in the size of the federal debt.

The general shape of federal tax legislation is determined by majoritarian politics, but the specific provisions (especially the deductions, exemptions, and exclusions) are the result of client group politics. The Tax Reform Act of 1986 was a remarkable example of the reassertion of majoritarian politics over client group pressures made possible by policy entrepreneurs and political incentives.

Reconsidering the Enduring Questions

1. *Can the president make the country prosperous?*

Most of us would like to think so, but in fact there are real limits to what he can achieve. Much of what the economy produces and pays its workers is generated by internal processes over which the government has little control (unless it is determined to make a mess of things). As we have seen, the government can make a difference by setting tax rates, controlling the flow of new money into the economy, and spending less or more than it earns in taxes. It can also try to solve some problems by paying for unemployment insurance and keeping people's incomes above some minimum level. But even to do these things wisely, the president must be very smart, have the cooperation of Congress, and know how to keep all of his subordinates in line. This is not easy.

2. *Why does the government ever have a budget deficit?*

Hardly anybody likes a deficit, but it is hard not to have one and even harder to end one if you have it. We get a deficit because people tend to vote for a party that will give them things they want, whether it is a strong defense, better unemployment benefits, a prescription drug plan, or a cleaner environment. So the government is always under pressure to do more. Since people want these things without knowing what they will cost, the pressure often makes spending exceed income. And when a deficit occurs, there are two ways to end it: cutting spending or raising taxes. Politicians don't like to do either because voters don't like to endure either, and so the leaders run up a deficit. Voters don't like deficits, but they are less likely to vote against politicians that produce them than they are to vote against leaders who cut spending or raise taxes.

World Wide Web Resources

- Internal Revenue Service: www.irs.gov
- Tax Foundation: www.taxfoundation.org

Key Terms

monetarism *p. 464*
Keynesianism *p. 464*
economic planning *p. 464*
price and wage controls *p. 464*
industrial policy *p. 464*
supply-side theory *p. 464*

Reaganomics *p. 465*
fiscal policy *p. 466*
budget deficit *p. 466*
budget surplus *p. 466*
monetary policy *p. 466*
fiscal year (FY) *p. 466*

budget *p. 469*
budget resolution *p. 469*
entitlements *p. 470*
sequester *p. 471*

Suggested Readings

Birnbaum, Jeffrey H., and Alan S. Murray. *Showdown at Gucci Gulch.* New York: Random House, 1987. Lively journalistic account of the passage of the Tax Reform Act of 1986.

Kiewiet, D. Roderick. *Macroeconomics and Micropolitics.* Chicago: University of Chicago Press, 1983. Argues that citizens vote on the basis of their estimate of national economic conditions as well as their own financial circumstances.

Samuelson, Robert J. *The Good Life and Its Discontents.* New York: Times Books/Random House, 1995. A readable, intelligent account of American economic life since the Second World War.

Schick, Allen. *The Federal Budget.* Washington, D.C.: Brookings Institution, 1995. Excellent overview of how Washington allocates money.

Shlaes, Amity. *The Greedy Hand.* New York: Random House, 1999. Spirited attack on federal tax policy.

Stein, Herbert, and Murray Foss. *The New Illustrated Guide to the American Economy.* 2d ed. Washington, D.C.: American Enterprise Institute, 1995. A vivid collection of graphs, all clearly explained, that describes the American economy and government spending from the 1950s through the early 1990s.

Tufte, Edward R. *Political Control of the Economy.* Princeton, N.J.: Princeton University Press, 1978. Argues that there is a "political business cycle" caused by politicians' trying to stimulate the economy just before an election.

Social Welfare

Enduring Questions

1. What does the Constitution mean by "promote the general Welfare"?

2. How, if at all, have Americans' views of government's responsibility to help the "deserving poor" changed over time?

3. Why are some government social welfare programs politically protected while others are politically imperiled?

There are two kinds of welfare programs in the United States: those that benefit most or all of the people and those that help only a small number of them. In the first category are Social Security and Medicare, programs that provide retirement benefits or medical assistance to almost every citizen who has reached a certain age. In the second are programs such as Medicaid and Food Stamps that offer help only to people with low incomes.

Legally the difference between the two kinds of programs is that the first have no *means test* (that is, they are available to everyone without regard to income) while the second are *means tested* (that is, you must fall below a certain income level to enjoy them). Politically the programs differ in how they get money from the government. The first kind of welfare program represents **majoritarian politics:** nearly everyone benefits, nearly everyone pays. The second kind represents **client politics:** a (relatively) few number of people benefit, but almost everyone pays. The biggest problem facing majoritarian welfare programs is their cost: who will pay, and how much will they pay? The biggest problem facing

479

client-oriented programs is their legitimacy: who should benefit, and how should they be served?

This political difference between these programs has a huge impact on how the government acts in regard to them. Social Security and Medicare are sacrosanct. The thought of making any changes that might lower the benefits these programs pay is so politically risky that most politicians never even discuss them. When programs such as these run into trouble because of rising expenses (Medicare is in deep trouble today, and Social Security will be in even deeper trouble in a few decades), politicians scramble to look for ways of maintaining benefits while hiding the rising costs or postponing dealing with them. As we shall see later in this chapter, there has been a sharp growth in the proportion of people who are retired and are thus entitled to Social Security and Medicare. To keep benefits flowing to these individuals, people who are not retired will have to pay more and more in taxes. No politician wants to raise taxes or cut benefits, so they adopt a variety of halfhearted measures (like slowly increasing the age at which people can get these benefits) designed to postpone the tough decisions until they are out of office.

Client-based welfare programs—those that are means tested—are a very different matter. Like many other client-based programs, their political appeal changes as popular opinion about them changes. Take the old Aid to Families with Dependent Children (AFDC) program. When it was started in 1935, people thought of it as a way of helping poor women whose husbands had been killed in war or had died in mining accidents. The goal was to help these women support their children, who had been made fatherless by death or disaster. Most people thought of these women as the innocent victims of a tragedy. No one thought that they would take AFDC for very long. It was a program to help smooth things over for them until they could remarry.

About thirty years later, however, the public's opinion of AFDC had begun to change. People started to think that AFDC was paying money to women who had never married and had no intention of marrying. The government, according to this view, was subsidizing single-parent families, encouraging out-of-wedlock births, and creating social dependency. Moreover, some people thought that African Americans were taking undue advantage of the pro-

gram. (In fact, when this opinion emerged, African Americans were still a minority among AFDC recipients.) From the mid-1960s through the mid-1990s these views became stronger. AFDC had lost the legitimacy it needed, as a client program, to survive politically.

Whenever a client program loses political legitimacy, the program is in trouble. Client politics depends on the beneficiaries' being thought of as legitimate. Almost any means-tested program risks losing its political legitimacy, because some people will always wonder whether the program itself causes people to avoid working in order to claim the benefits. Some people think that about Food Stamps, the program that gives low-income people free stamps that they can exchange for food. There have been a few publicized cases of people using food stamps to buy luxury items. But no powerful opposition to the program has developed, because in general the only thing the beneficiaries have in common is that they have low incomes. Many Americans can imagine becoming poor, and so they probably are willing to allow such a program to operate as part of a government-supplied safety net that might, someday, help them.

But AFDC was a different matter. Having to accept AFDC was not something the typical taxpayer thought would ever happen to him or her. Moreover, the beneficiaries weren't just poor; some of them did things—such as having babies without getting married—that most Americans thought were simply wrong. The legitimacy of AFDC was thus in jeopardy, because it either made possible or actually encouraged behavior that most Americans found improper. As a result something happened to AFDC that almost never happens to decades-old government programs: it was abolished.

In this chapter we provide examples of both majoritarian and client welfare programs and describe how they have been reformed over the years. There are far too many social welfare programs to describe them all here; rather the main purpose of this chapter is to explain the key features of the two main kinds of programs.

Social Welfare in the United States

Before analyzing how these programs came into being, it is first necessary to understand that social

Social welfare programs, once limited to the poor and the unemployed, now may help handicapped persons as well.

welfare policy in the United States is shaped by three factors that make it different from what exists in many other nations. First, Americans have generally taken a more restrictive view of who is entitled to government assistance. Second, America has been slower than other countries to embrace the welfare state. And third, we have insisted that the states (and to a degree private enterprise) play a large role in running welfare programs.

The first distinctive feature of the American welfare state involves who benefits. To Americans, who benefits has been a question of who *deserves* to benefit. We have usually insisted that public support be given only to those who cannot help themselves. But what does it mean to say that a person cannot help himself or herself? Surely a disabled, blind, elderly woman deserted by her family cannot do much to help herself, but would she still be deserving of public aid were she merely disabled? Or merely elderly? And to what extent should we require that her family support her? As we shall see, American welfare policy since the 1930s has been fundamentally shaped by a slow but steady change in how we have separated the "deserving" from the "undeserving" poor.

That we have always thought this way may make us forget that there are other ways of thinking about welfare. The major alternative view is to ask not who deserves help but what each person's "fair share" of the national income is. Seen this way, the role of government is to take money from those who have a lot and give it to those who have only a little, until each person has, if not the same amount, then at least a fair share. But defining a "fair share" is even more difficult than defining the "deserving poor." Moreover, Americans have generally felt that giving money to people who are already working, or who could work if they chose to, is unfair. In some nations—Sweden is an example—government policy is aimed at redistributing income from better-off to not-so-well-off persons, without regard to who "deserves" the money.

Thus Americans base welfare policy on the concept of "help for the deserving poor" rather than "redistribution to produce fair shares."[1] They have done so, one suspects, because they believe that citizens should be encouraged to be self-reliant, that people who work hard will get what they deserve, and that giving money to people who could help themselves will produce a class of "welfare chiselers." If Americans believed that success at work was a matter of luck rather than effort or was dictated by forces over which they had no control, they might support a different concept of welfare.

Moreover, we have always been a bit uneasy about giving money to people. Though we recognize that many people through no fault of their own cannot buy groceries and thus need funds, we would prefer that, to the extent possible, people who deserve help be given *services* (education, training, medical care) rather than money. Throughout much of our history our welfare policies have reflected a general philosophical disposition in favor of providing services to deserving persons.

The second striking fact about American welfare policy is how late in our history it arrived (at least at the national level) compared to other nations. By 1935, when Congress passed the Social Security Act, at least twenty-two European nations already had similar programs, as did Australia and Japan.[2] Germany was the first to create a nationwide social security program when it developed sickness and maternity insurance in 1883. Six years later it added old-age insurance and in 1927 unemployment insurance.

England offers perhaps the clearest contrast with the United States. In 1908 a national system of old-age pensions was set up, followed three years later by a plan for nationwide health and unemployment insurance.[3] England had a parliamentary regime in which a political party with liberal sentiments and a large majority had come to power. With authority concentrated in the hands of the prime minister and his cabinet, there was virtually no obstacle to instituting measures, such as welfare programs, that commended themselves to party leaders on grounds of either principle or party advantage. Furthermore, the British Labour party was then beginning to emerge. Though the party was still small (it had only thirty seats in Parliament in 1908), its leaders included people who had been influential in formulating welfare programs that the leaders of the dominant Liberal party backed. And once these programs were approved, they were in almost all cases nationally run: there were no state governments to which authority had to be delegated or whose different experiences had to be accommodated.

Moreover, the British in 1908 were beginning to think in terms of social classes, to accept the notion of an activist government, and to make welfare the central political issue. Americans at that time also had an activist leader, Theodore Roosevelt; there was a progressive movement; and labor was well along in its organizing drives. But the issues were defined differently in the United States. Progressives, or at least most of them, emphasized the reform of the political process—by eliminating corruption, by weakening the parties, and by improving the civil service—and attacked bigness by breaking up industrial trusts. Though some progressives favored the creation of a welfare state, they were a distinct minority. They had few allies in organized labor (which was skeptical of public welfare programs) and could not overcome the general distrust of big government and the strong preference for leaving matters of welfare in state hands. In sum what ordinary politics brought to England in 1908–1911, only the crisis politics of 1935 would bring to the United States. But once started, the programs grew. By 1983 almost one-third of all Americans received benefits from one or more social welfare programs.

The third factor involves the degree to which federalism has shaped national welfare policy. Since the Constitution was silent on whether Congress had the power to spend money on welfare and since powers not delegated to Congress were reserved to the states, it was not until the constitutional reinterpretation of the 1930s (see Chapter 14) that it became clear that the federal government could do anything in the area of social policy. At the same time, federalism meant that any state so inclined could experiment with welfare programs. Between 1923 and 1933 thirty states enacted some form of an old-age pension. By 1935 all but two states had adopted a "mother's pension"—a program whereby a widow with children was given financial assistance, provided that she was a "fit mother" who ran a "suitable home." The poor were given small doles by local governments, helped by private charities, or placed in almshouses. Only one state, Wisconsin, had an unemployment insurance program.

Politically the state programs had a double-edged effect: they provided opponents of a federal welfare system with an argument (the states were already providing welfare assistance), but they also supplied a lobby for federal financial assistance (state authorities would campaign for national legislation to help them out). Some were later to say that the states were the laboratories for experimentation in welfare policy. When the federal government entered the field in 1935, it did so in part by spending money through the states, thereby encouraging the formation in the states of a strong welfare bureaucracy whose later claims would be difficult to ignore.

Majoritarian Welfare Programs: Social Security and Medicare

Today, tens of millions of Americans receive food, money, or medicine through programs funded largely by the federal government (see Figure 17.1).

At the time the Great Depression began, in 1929, the job of providing relief to needy people fell almost entirely to state and local governments or to private charities, and even these sources were primarily concerned with widows, orphans, and the elderly.[4] Hardly any state had a systematic program for supporting the unemployed, though many states provided some kind of help if it was clear that the person was out of work through no fault of his or her own. When the economy suddenly ground to a near standstill and the unemployment rate rose to include one-fourth of the work force, private charities and city relief programs nearly went bankrupt.

The election of 1932 produced an overwhelming congressional majority for the Democrats and placed

Major Social Welfare Programs

Insurance, or "Contributory," Programs

Old Age, Survivors, and Disability Insurance (OASDI) Monthly payments to retired or disabled people and to surviving members of their families. This program, popularly called Social Security, is paid for by a payroll tax on employers and employees. *No means test.*

Medicare Federal government pays for part of the cost of hospital care for retired or disabled people covered by Social Security. Paid for by payroll taxes on employees and employers. *No means test.*

Assistance, or "Noncontributory," Programs

Unemployment Insurance (UI) Weekly payments to workers who have been laid off and cannot find work. Benefits and requirements determined by states. Paid for by taxes on employers. *No means test.*

Temporary Assistance for Needy Families (TANF) Payments to needy families with children. Replaced the old AFDC program. Partially paid for by block grants from the federal government to the states. *Means test.*

Supplemental Security Income (SSI) Cash payments to aged, blind, or disabled people whose income is below a certain amount. Paid for from general federal revenues. *Means test.*

Food Stamps Vouchers, given to people whose income is below a certain level, that can be used to buy food at grocery stores. Paid for out of general federal revenues. *Means test.*

Medicaid Pays medical expenses of persons receiving TANF or SSI payments. *Means test.*

Earned Income Tax Credit Pays a cash subsidy (or tax credit) to poor working families. *Means test.*

Franklin D. Roosevelt in the White House. Almost immediately a number of emergency measures were adopted to cope with the depression by supplying federal cash to bail out state and local relief agencies and by creating public works jobs under federal auspices. These measures were recognized as temporary expedients, however, and were unsatisfactory to those who believed that the federal government had a permanent and major responsibility for welfare. Roosevelt created the Cabinet Committee on Economic Security to consider long-term policies. The committee drew heavily on the experience of European nations and on the ideas of various American scholars and social workers, but it understood that it would have to adapt these proposals to the realities of American politics. Chief among these was the widespread belief that any direct federal welfare program might be unconstitutional. The Constitution nowhere explicitly gave to Congress the authority to set up an unemployment compensation or old-age retirement program. And even if a welfare program were constitutional, many believed, it would be wrong because it violated the individualistic creed that people should help themselves unless they were physically unable to do so.

But failure by the Roosevelt administration to produce a comprehensive social security pro-

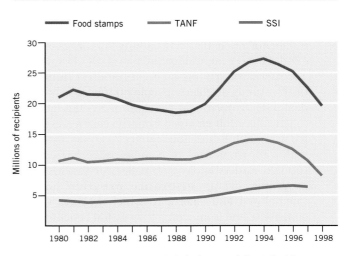

Figure 17.1 SSI, TANF, and Food Stamp Recipients, 1980–1998

Source: U.S. Census Bureau, *Statistical Abstract of the United States, 1999*, 382.

gram, his supporters felt, might make the president vulnerable in the 1936 election to the leaders of

The Great Depression: a bread line forms on a New York City street in December 1931.

President Roosevelt meets with members of the Civilian Conservation Corps, which put unemployed young men to work; he feared that Long might challenge him in the 1936 election.

various radical social movements. Huey Long of Louisiana was proposing a "Share Our Wealth" plan; Upton Sinclair was running for governor of California on a platform calling for programs to "End Poverty in California"; and Dr. Francis E. Townsend was leading an organization of hundreds of thousands of elderly people on whose behalf he demanded government pensions of $200 a month.

The plan that emerged from the cabinet committee was carefully designed to meet popular demands within the framework of popular beliefs and constitutional understandings. It called for two kinds of programs: (1) an **insurance program** for the unemployed and elderly, to which workers would contribute and from which they would benefit when they became unemployed or retired; and (2) an **assistance program** for the blind, dependent children, and the aged. (Giving assistance as well as providing "insurance" for the aged was necessary because for the first few years the insurance program would not pay out any benefits.) The federal government would use its power to tax to provide the funds, but all of the programs (except for old-age insurance) would be administered by the states.

Everybody, rich or poor, would be eligible for the insurance programs. Only the poor, as measured by a **means test** (a measure to determine that incomes are below a certain level), would be eligible for the assistance programs. Though bitterly opposed by some, the resulting Social Security Act passed swiftly and virtually unchanged through Congress. It was introduced in January 1935 and signed by President Roosevelt in August of that year.

The idea of having the government pay the medical and hospital bills of the elderly and the poor had been discussed in Washington since the drafting of the Social Security Act. President Roosevelt and his Committee on Economic Security sensed that medical care would be very controversial, and so health programs were left out of the 1935 bill in order not to jeopardize its chances of passage.[5]

The proponents of the idea did not abandon it, however. Working mostly within the executive branch, they continued to press, sometimes publicly, sometimes behind the scenes, for a national health care plan. Democratic presidents, including Truman, Kennedy, and Johnson, favored it; Republican president Eisenhower opposed it;

President Lyndon Johnson signs the Medicare Act in 1965 in the company of Vice President Hubert Humphrey (standing) and former president Harry S Truman (seated).

Congress was deeply divided on it. The American Medical Association attacked it as "socialized medicine." For thirty years key policy entrepreneurs, such as Wilbur Cohen, worked to find a formula that would produce a congressional majority.

The first and highest hurdle to overcome, however, was not Congress as a whole but the House Ways and Means Committee, especially its powerful chairman from 1958 to 1975, Wilbur Mills of Arkansas. A majority of the committee members opposed a national health care program. Some members believed it wrong in principle; others feared that adding a costly health component to the Social Security system would jeopardize the financial solvency and administrative integrity of one of the most popular government programs. By the early 1960s a majority of the House favored a health care plan, but without the approval of Ways and Means it would never reach the floor.

The 1964 elections changed all that. The Johnson landslide produced such large Democratic majorities in Congress that the composition of the committees changed. In particular the membership of the Ways and Means Committee was altered.

Whereas before it had three Democrats for every two Republicans, after 1964 it had two Democrats for every one Republican. The House leadership saw to it that the new Democrats on the committee were strongly committed to a health care program. Suddenly the committee had a majority favorable to such a plan, and Mills, realizing that a bill would pass and wanting to help shape its form, changed his position and became a supporter of what was to become Medicare.

The policy entrepreneurs in and out of the government who drafted the Medicare plan attempted to anticipate the major objections to it. First, the bill would apply only to the aged—those eligible for Social Security retirement benefits. This would reassure legislators worried about the cost of providing tax-supported health care for everybody. Second, the plan would cover only hospital expenses, not doctors' bills. Since doctors were not to be paid by the government, they would not be regulated by it; thus, presumably, the opposition of the American Medical Association would be blunted.

Unexpectedly, however, the Ways and Means Committee broadened the coverage of the plan beyond what the administration had thought was politically feasible. It added sections providing medical assistance, called Medicaid, for the poor (defined as those already getting public assistance payments) and payment of doctors' bills for the aged (a new part of Medicare). The new, much-enlarged bill passed both houses of Congress with ease. The key votes pitted a majority of the Democrats against a majority of the Republicans.

Reforming Majoritarian Welfare Programs

Both Social Security and Medicare are changing. What a majority of the people want will soon cost them more money than they can afford. But not every citizen is prepared to do what is necessary to fix this problem, and so the politicians are left in a bind: they must "save" Social Security and Medicare without changing Social Security and Medicare. It will not be easy.

The key problem for Social Security is that, as the population ages, soon there will not be enough people paying Social Security taxes to provide benefits for every retired person. By 2020 there will be fewer than four workers for every retiree, and the payroll taxes on these workers would have to double to pay that retiree's bills.

There are three ways to solve this problem. The first involves three moves: raise the retirement age to seventy, freeze the amount of retirement benefits, and raise Social Security taxes. The public opposes all of these strategies (see Table 17.1).

The second solution would be to privatize Social Security by requiring either citizens or some government agency to invest all or part of their Social Security taxes in the stock market. When people retired, they would live on these stock market gains. In theory the stock market would give people a greater return on their money than has Social Security. But there are risks to any investment, and this one may not pan out. In addition the government would still need money to pay the benefits of people already retired or about to retire.

The third solution would be to use the first two changes and in addition permit citizens to invest some of their Social Security taxes in carefully chosen mutual funds. A national advisory commission proposed this to President Clinton, but he did nothing. Another commission proposed three ways of doing this to President George W. Bush, but he

received the report just a few months after September 11, 2001. By that time the government and the country were absorbed by the war on terror, and so there was no political opportunity to consider the plan. But Bush appears to be committed to some such change, and so the matter will probably reappear on the policy agenda.

The key problem with Medicare is that it not only costs a huge amount of money, but it also is not a very efficient way of paying for health care. When Medicare was enacted in 1965, the government said that by 1990 it would cost $12 billion a year. When 1990 rolled around, Medicare actually cost $110 billion. As the population gets older and new (and expensive) life-prolonging technologies are developed, the cost of the program will rise even faster. Without major changes, the program may run out of money as early as 2008.

Medicare allows people to visit the doctor or go to the hospital whenever they feel they need to (see the box on page 488). The doctor or hospital is paid a fee for each visit. This creates three problems: (1) a lot of people use medical services when they don't really need them; (2) some doctors and hospitals overcharge the government for their services; and (3) doctors and hospitals are paid on the basis of a government-approved payment plan that can change whenever the government wants to save money.

In 1997 a bipartisan commission was formed to solve the problem of Medicare, but President Clinton, who had helped create it, repudiated its report. Few politicians are willing to propose cost-cutting measures for fear of being burned at the voting booth.

One possible cure is to get rid of Medicare and instead have doctors and hospitals work for the government. That is done in several countries, and as a result the citizens of these countries pay less for health care than do U.S. citizens (see Table 17.2 on page 488). But many critics claim that government-run health care provides fewer benefits and slower care and discourages aggressive new health care innovations.

A second solution to the problem is to let the elderly take their Medicare money and buy health insurance from private suppliers, including health maintenance organizations (HMOs). This may or may not be an affordable alternative for individuals.

Instead of either solution, a federal government budget surplus in 1999 led President Clinton to

Table 17.1　**Public Views on Reforming Social Security**

	Percent Who Agree
Program Solvency[a]	
Social Security can be counted on as a source of retirement income	
18–34-year-olds	6
35–49	10
50–64	35
65 and over	59
Program Benefits[a]	
Gradually raise the retirement age to 70	28
Reduce benefits	10
Individual Investment[b]	
Let workers shift some Social Security tax payments into personal retirement accounts that they would invest on their own	80
Let workers decide how some of their own Social Security contributions are invested	71
Let workers have individual accounts and make their own investments with a portion of their Social Security tax payments	64
Let workers invest a portion of their Social Security taxes in investments like the stock market, getting more money if investments do well, less if they do poorly	60
Let people invest some of their Social Security tax payments in stock market, with benefits higher or lower than expected depending on stock market's performance	48
Government Investment[b]	
Invest some Social Security revenues in stock market instead of putting them all in government bonds	50
Have government invest in private stock market a portion of Social Security reserve funds, currently invested in government bonds	38
Keep system intact, but government invests 40 percent of Social Security revenues in stock market	37
Invest a portion of Social Security tax funds in stock market	36
Let government invest part of money it holds in Social Security in stock market	29

Sources: (a) *The American Enterprise* (March/April 1999): 92–93, reporting data from two national surveys conducted in 1997; (b) Robert Blendon et al., "America in Denial," *The Brookings Review* (Summer 1998): 46, 48, reporting data from eight national surveys conducted in 1998.

propose spending $794 billion on prolonging Medicare's life while adding many new benefits, such as payment for some prescription drugs. Few politicians wanted to criticize this politically popular idea, even though many of them knew that spending more money on a broken system would only postpone the inevitable.

One day it will become clear that "the inevitabilities of disease and aging" cannot be avoided simply by spending more money or employing the latest technology.[6] For the foreseeable future, however, politicians will continue to propose all kinds of health care legislation. In late 2001, President George W. Bush and key members of Congress seemed to be approaching agreement on a patients' bill of rights, prescription drug benefits for the elder-

ly, and a half-dozen other new health care measures. By June 2002, however, no new health care measures had passed, and only 5 percent of the public ranked "poor hospital care/high cost of healthcare" as "the most important problem facing this country today," way behind "terrorism" at 33 percent and "economy in general" at 14 percent, and a far cry from the 28 percent who had ranked health as the country's number one problem in September 1993.[7] But the aging of the baby boom population, the continued growth in total government expenditures on health care, and political pressures exerted by powerful interest groups like the AARP (see Chapter 9), among other factors, make it certain that health care issues will remain high on the federal social welfare policy agenda for many years to come.

Medicare

Medicare has two parts: Part A (hospital insurance) and Part B (medical insurance). Everyone who is age sixty-five or older is entitled to Part A; to get Part B, you must enroll in the program (almost everybody age sixty-five or older does enroll).

Part A pays for inpatient visits to hospitals, covering most (but not all) of the services you receive there for up to ninety days during any benefit period. (A benefit period is a hospital stay that occurs at least sixty days after the patient was last released from a hospital.) When a patient uses Part A, he or she must pay the first $696 in hospital costs. Part A is financed by Medicare payroll taxes.

Part B pays for doctors' services and outpatient hospital care. There are no limits on the number of visits to the doctor, but the patient must pay an annual $100 deductible and 20 percent of the cost of each visit. The recipient pays a monthly premium (in mid-2000, about $45), which covers only a small part of the total cost of care; the rest of the money comes from the government's general revenues.

Client Welfare Programs: Aid to Families with Dependent Children

One part of the Social Security Act of 1935 created what came to be called Aid to Families with Dependent Children (AFDC). It was scarcely noticed at the time. The federal government, in response to the depression, promised to provide aid to states that were, in many cases, already running programs to help poor children who lacked a father.

Because AFDC involved giving federal aid to existing state programs, it allowed the states to define what constituted "need," to set benefit levels, and to administer the program. Washington did set—(and, over the years, continued to increase) a number of rules governing how the program would work, however. Washington told the states how to calculate applicants' incomes and required the states to give Medicaid to AFDC recipients. The states had to establish mandatory job-training programs for many AFDC recipients and to provide child-care programs for working AFDC parents. Washington also required that women on AFDC identify their children's fathers.

In addition to the growing list of requirements, Washington created new programs for which AFDC recipients were eligible, such as Food Stamps, the **Earned Income Tax Credit** (a cash grant to poor parents who were working), free school meals, various forms of housing assistance, and certain other benefits. But while all this was happening, public opinion moved against the AFDC program.

The combination of souring public opinion, increasing federal regulations, and a growing roster of benefits produced a program that irritated almost everyone. The states disliked having to conform to a growing list of federal regulations. The public disliked the program because they thought it was weakening the family by encouraging out-of-wedlock births (since AFDC recipients received additional benefits for each new child). The public worried that AFDC recipients were working covertly on the side; the data proved that this was true of at least half of them in

Table 17.2   Health Care Spending in the United States and Abroad, 1996

Country	Share of Gross Domestic Product
United States	14.0
Germany	10.5
France	9.7
Canada	9.6
Australia	8.5
United Kingdom	6.9

Source: Charles R. Morris, *Too Much of a Good Thing? Why Health Care Spending Won't Make Us Sick* (New York: Century Foundation, 2000), 56.

several large cities. AFDC recipients saw that the actual (that is, inflation-adjusted) value of their AFDC checks was going down. Critics countered that if you added together all the benefits they were receiving (food stamps, Medicaid, housing assistance, and so on), benefit levels were actually going up. Politicians complained that healthy parents were living off AFDC instead of working. The AFDC law was revised many times, but never in a way that satisfied all, or even most, of its critics. Though AFDC recipients were only a small fraction of all Americans, they had become a large political problem.

What made matters worse was that the composition of the people in the program had changed. In 1970 about half of the mothers on AFDC were there because their husbands had died or divorced them; only a quarter had never been married.[8] By 1994 the situation had changed dramatically: only about a quarter of AFDC mothers were widowed or divorced, and over half had never been married at all. And though most women on AFDC for the *first* time got off it after just a few years, almost two-thirds of the women on AFDC at any given moment had been on it for eight years or more.

These facts, combined with the increased proportion of out-of-wedlock births in the country as a whole, made it virtually impossible to sustain political support for what had begun as a noncontroversial client program. In 1996 the program was abolished.

Two Kinds of Welfare Politics

The programs just described illustrate two patterns of policy-making. The old-age pensions created by the Social Security Act of 1935 and the health care benefits created by the Medicare Act of 1965 are examples of majoritarian politics: almost everybody benefits, and almost everybody pays. The TANF program is an example of client politics: a relatively few people benefit, but everybody pays.

Majoritarian Politics

When both the benefits and the costs of a proposed program are widely distributed, the proposal will be adopted if the beneficiaries believe that their benefits will exceed their costs *and* if political elites believe that it is legitimate for the federal government to adopt the program.

Aid to Families with Dependent Children (AFDC) became controversial as Americans began to see it as a program that chiefly aided unmarried black mothers.

Initially the benefits people received from the retirement program greatly exceeded its costs to them. Older people were able to get an old-age pension or health care even though they had paid in taxes only a small fraction of what these benefits cost. Social Security and Medicare seemed initially like the nearest thing to a free lunch.

The big debate in 1935 and 1965 was not over whether the people wanted these programs—the polls showed that they did—but over whether it was legitimate for the federal government to provide them.[9] In 1935 conservatives argued that as desirable as Social Security might be, nothing in the Constitution authorized the federal government to spend money for this purpose; welfare, they said, was a policy area reserved to the states. Liberals rejoined that the federal government had an obligation to help people avoid poverty in their old age. Besides, they said, as an "insurance" program, retirement benefits were not really a federal expenditure at all: Washington was merely collecting payments and holding them in a trust fund until the people who paid them were ready to retire. In the midst of the Great Depression and at a time when liberals had large majorities in Congress, it was an easy argument to make, and so the Social Security bill readily crossed over the legitimacy barrier.

In 1965 the same issues were raised. Conservatives argued that medical care was a private, not a governmental, matter and that any federal involvement

WHO GOVERNS? TO WHAT ENDS?

Reforming Majoritarian Education Programs

America is home to about 50 million public school children. Most citizens, even the elderly and young adults with no children in public schools, tend to think of public education in majoritarian terms: everyone benefits, everyone pays.

Until recently, Democrats pretty much owned this majoritarian issue. With the exception of some Democratic mayors, most Democratic leaders have opposed plans to give parents school vouchers (public monies that can be used to pay for private or religious school tuitions). Meanwhile, most Republican leaders have favored vouchers. In 2000, voucher referenda were defeated soundly in California and Michigan.

Three days after taking office in January 2001, Republican president George W. Bush proposed an education reform plan that he then described as "the cornerstone of my administration." It contained voucher language and related provisions that would have effected sweeping changes in the Elementary and Secondary Education Act (ESEA). But just a few months into negotiations on the bill with Senate Democrats, virtually every aspect of the original Bush plan that could not be credibly couched in majoritarian terms, reconciled with existing ESEA programs, or otherwise justified as "recruiting high-quality teachers," "promoting informed parental choice," or

"improving the academic achievement of the disadvantaged" was abandoned.

On January 8, 2002, Congress easily passed the No Child Left Behind Act of 2001. The president's major ally in getting the 670-page education reform plan into law was Democratic senator Ted Kennedy of Massachusetts. Democrats applauded the act mainly for increasing federal education funding under the ESEA by 49 percent over 2000 levels, to over $22 billion a year. Republicans, led by House conservatives, complained about the increased ESEA spending and lamented that the new law did nothing to advance the cause of school vouchers. The public, however, gave the Bush administration high marks. Shortly after the president signed the bill into law, polls showed that, for the first time in many years, most citizens rated Republicans on a par with Democrats in dealing with education issues.

On June 27, 2002, the U.S. Supreme Court declared in the case of *Zelman v. Simmons-Harris* that school voucher programs that provide "true private choice" are constitutional. President Bush issued a public statement strongly supporting the Court's decision. It remains to be seen, however, whether either the Bush administration or other Republican leaders will identify themselves in the future with school reform proposals that are not obviously or strictly in accord with majoritarian sentiments on education policy.

would subject doctors and hospitals to endless red tape and harm the quality of the doctor-patient relationship. Liberals rejoined that the elderly had health needs that they could not meet without help and that only the federal government had the resources to provide that assistance. Because the 1964 elections, when Lyndon Johnson defeated Barry Goldwater, had swept into the House and Senate large majorities of

liberal Democrats, there was no chance that a conservative coalition of Republicans and southern Democrats could defeat Medicare, and so it passed.

As can be seen in Table 17.4, the votes in Congress on Social Security and Medicare followed party lines. Since the Democratic opponents of these bills were typically conservative southerners, the vote followed ideological lines even more closely.

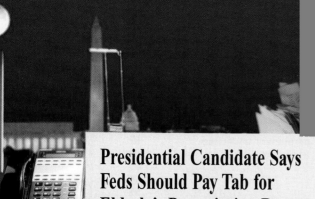

Presidential Candidate Says Feds Should Pay Tab for Elderly's Prescription Drugs

Rx for Budget Busting, Rivals Respond

July 9
WILMINGTON, DE

Speaking yesterday before representatives of the nation's largest association of elderly and retired persons, Delaware governor and presidential hopeful John Pergolini drew thunderous applause when he pledged to expand federal health care plans to cover prescription drug payments for needy persons age sixty-five or older . . .

MEMORANDUM

To: Governor John Pergolini
From: Richard A. Smith, presidential campaign manager
Subject: New federal health care program: Medipharmacy

According to the latest polls, your proposal that Washington pay more for prescription drugs for needy elderly persons is quite popular. The staff recommends that you next call for a new federal health care program, Medipharmacy, which would provide drug coverage through the Medicaid program to Medicare beneficiaries age seventy or older who make up to $15,000 a year and would expand drug coverage for all children on Medicaid.

Arguments for:

1. Medicare does not cover prescription drugs. Medicaid, with more than four million recipients age sixty-five or older and nearly twenty million child beneficiaries, varies from state to state and covers prescription drugs for some but not all beneficiaries.
2. Beginning in 2002 Medicaid will cover all children under the age of nineteen, but it will not cover all children age six or older who live in families that make even a penny a year above the official federal poverty line ($16,530 a year for a family of four in 1998).
3. Price-gouging drug companies could be blamed for spiraling costs and required to sell to Medipharmacy beneficiaries at deep discounts.

Arguments against:

1. In 2010 Americans age sixty-five or older will have an average life expectancy of 18.5 additional years. Starting coverage for the elderly at sixty-five would be prohibitively expensive. Starting it at age seventy would contain but not control costs.
2. Medipharmacy could crowd out already meager per capita federal health care spending on poor children, as some would say has already happened with Medicaid.
3. By increasing the demand for prescription drugs paid for by the government, Medipharmacy could further distort the market in ways that make medicine more expensive for everyone.

Your decision:
Propose Medipharmacy _____
Reject Medipharmacy _____

Table 17.3   Opinions on Welfare by Race

Percentage saying item is a "very serious" problem.	Blacks	Whites
People abuse the system by staying on too long and not trying hard enough to get off.	72%	72%
Welfare is passed on from generation to generation, creating a permanent underclass.	62	68
The system gives people benefits without requiring them to do work in return.	60	66
People cheat and commit fraud to get welfare benefits.	69	62
Welfare encourages teenagers to have kids out of wedlock.	59	61
The system costs taxpayers too much.	55	59
The system does not give people the skills and help they need to get off welfare.	66	53
The system gives out benefits too easily, without making sure applicants deserve them.	50	51

Source: Adapted from *The Values We Live By: What Americans Want From Welfare Reform* (New York: Public Agenda Foundation, 1996), 40. Reprinted with permission.

Client Politics

When the benefits of a proposal are to go to a relatively small group but the public at large pays, we have client politics. Proposals to benefit clients will pass if the cost to the public at large is not perceived to be great *and* if the client receiving the benefit is thought to be "deserving."

As noted previously, when AFDC was first enacted, it was relatively noncontroversial. Originally it seemed intended to help deserving people. In 1935 the typical welfare mother was perceived to be a woman living in a small town, whose husband had been killed in a mining accident. Who could object to giving some modest help to a person who was the victim of circumstances?

Right or wrong, American values on this subject changed. Today most Americans believe that able-bodied people on welfare should be made to work for their benefits, period. The work-based welfare provisions of TANF plainly reflect this belief. In 2002, during the largely consensual congressional debate over reauthorizing TANF, even many who had opposed these strategies in 1996 (when TANF replaced AFDC) now supported them. There remains, however, some popular sentiment for giving welfare recipients job training or even creating government jobs for them. This **service strategy** (providing training and education) is strongly preferred to an **income strategy** (giving people money)—unless, of course, the income can be called "insurance."[10]

Indeed, some critics of welfare, such as Charles Murray, have argued that AFDC actually increased the number of people living in poverty. Murray claimed that high welfare benefits made it more attractive for some people to go on welfare than to look for a job and more attractive for some women to have babies than to get married. This kept them poor. Other scholars have criticized Murray's thesis. They have argued that there is no direct evidence that welfare encourages family breakup and have suggested that the rise in the number of illegitimate children occurred during a period (the 1970s)

Table 17.4   Key Votes on Major Welfare Proposals in the House

Proposals	Democrats	Republicans
Social Security (1935)		
For	252	1
Against	45	95
Economic Opportunity (1964)		
For	204	22
Against	40	145
Medicare (1965)		
For	226	10
Against	63	128
Family Assistance Plan (1970)		
For	141	102
Against	83	72

when welfare benefits, in real (that is, inflation-adjusted) dollars, were going down.[11]

In short the clients of these programs never acquired in the public's mind the legitimacy necessary for their programs to prosper. As a result, whereas for forty years it was thought to be good politics to increase old-age benefits, it increasingly became considered bad politics to do anything but attack, investigate, and curtail "welfare" programs.

Summary

We can explain the politics of social welfare policy in America principally in terms of two factors: who benefits and who pays, and the beliefs citizens have about social justice. Neither factor is static: gainers and losers vary as the composition of society and the workings of the economy change, and beliefs about who deserves what are modified as attitudes toward work, the family, and the obligations of government change.

The congressional (as opposed to the parliamentary) system of government means that greater political effort and more time are required for the adoption of a new welfare policy. Federalism means that the states will play a large role in determining how any welfare program is administered and at what level benefits are set.

Reconsidering the Enduring Questions

1. **What does the Constitution mean by "promote the general Welfare"?**

   The Framers of the Constitution did not mean by this phrase that government has a duty to provide cash assistance or other benefits to citizens in economic need, or that the president or Congress has to manage the economy. Rather, they undoubtedly meant something closer to "protect private property and promote public safety and morals." It is difficult, however, to be sure about what they meant by those words. Without relying on any particular interpretation of that phrase from the Constitution's preamble, some present-day advocates for the poor have suggested that the federal government, by enacting laws intended to lift low-income citizens out of poverty, to provide health care at public expense, and to guarantee access to affordable housing, has thereby established a constitutional right to such social welfare programs, services, or supports. There is little constitutional case law to support that view, but the idea may be catching on.

2. **How, if at all, have Americans' views of government's responsibility to help the "deserving poor" changed over time?**

   Americans once insisted that public aid be given only to people who cannot help themselves. American welfare policy since the 1930s has undergone a slow but steady change in how it has separated the "deserving" from the "undeserving" poor. In essence, today we separate them less and are more willing to have people rely solely on the government for help. For example, even before the New Deal, most Americans would surely have counted a poor, disabled, blind, elderly woman deserted by her family as deserving of public aid. Today, however, many citizens would also favor giving her aid even if she were only disabled, without regard to her income or family situation. Likewise, whereas once most Americans were inclined to provide public aid only if the beneficiary's family helped too, today most citizens do not believe in strictly conditioning public aid on family support. Thus, in 2002, Washington policymakers were debating whether to provide prescription drug benefits to the elderly. They called for providing such benefits even to middle-income elderly citizens, without regard for whether grown children might also be able to help pay for their parents' medications.

3. *Why are some government social welfare programs politically protected while others are politically imperiled?*

Majoritarian programs (nearly everyone benefits, nearly everyone pays) like Social Security and Medicare are politically sacrosanct. Client-based programs (a relatively few number of people benefit, but almost everyone pays) like the now-defunct Aid to Families with Dependent Children (AFDC) are politically shaky. Debates about the former normally concern only how to keep the benefits flowing; debates about the latter often concern *whether* to keep the program ongoing. But certain client-based programs are less politically vulnerable than others—it all depends on who the clients are, or are widely perceived to be. For example, in the mid-1990s, Republican leaders in Congress declared that they wanted to slow the growth of Medicaid and abolish AFDC. In the end, Medicaid grew faster and AFDC was abolished. Medicaid was protected largely because its clients included middle-class retirees who received nursing home benefits and medically needy low-income children. AFDC was targeted because its clients were perceived by many to include able-bodied adults who chose to receive public aid rather than go to work.

World Wide Web Resources

- Social welfare programs
    Medicare: www.medicare.gov
    Social Security: www.ssa.gov
    TANF: www.acf.dhhs.gov/programs/ofa/
- Views on Social Security reform
    www.socialsecurityreform.org
    www.socialsecurity.org
    www.socsec.org

Key Terms

majoritarian politics *p. 479*
client politics *p. 479*
insurance program *p. 484*
assistance program *p. 484*
means test *p. 484*
Earned Income Tax Credit *p. 488*
service strategy *p. 492*
income strategy *p. 492*

Suggested Readings

Derthick, Martha. *Policymaking for Social Security*. Washington, D.C.: Brookings Institution, 1979. A detailed analysis of how the Social Security program grew.

Heclo, Hugh. *Modern Social Politics in Britain and Sweden*. New Haven, Conn.: Yale University Press, 1974. Comparative analysis of how social welfare programs came to Britain and Sweden.

Mead, Lawrence. *Beyond Entitlement: The Social Obligations of Citizenship*. New York: Free Press, 1986. Argument for "workfare," a requirement that able-bodied people work as a condition of receiving welfare.

Moynihan, Daniel Patrick. *Family and Nation*. New York: Harcourt Brace Jovanovich, 1986. Argument for the importance of federal policy to aid families. Disputes the Murray thesis.

Murray, Charles. *Losing Ground: American Social Policy, 1950–1980*. New York: Basic Books, 1984. An argument that federal spending on the poor actually increased poverty during the 1960s and 1970s.

Wilson, William J. *The Truly Disadvantaged*. Chicago: University of Chicago Press, 1987. Disputes Murray's explanation, arguing instead that ghetto poverty is the result of the movement of jobs out of cities.

Civil Liberties

Enduring Questions

1. Should it be all right for religious symbols to be displayed on government property?

2. If a person confesses that he committed a crime, is there any reason why the confession should not be used in court?

3. How much can the government do to fight terrorism?

Dogs trained to sniff out drugs go down your high school corridors and detect marijuana in some lockers. The school authorities open and search your locker without permission or a court order. You are expelled from school without any hearing. Have your liberties been violated?

Angry at what you consider unfair treatment, you decide to wear a cloth American flag sewn to the seat of your pants, and your fellow students decide to wear black armbands to class to protest how you were treated. The police arrest you for wearing a flag on your seat, and the school punishes your classmates for wearing armbands contrary to school regulations. Have your liberties, or theirs, been violated?

You go into federal court to find out. We cannot be certain how the court would decide the issues in this particular case, but in similar cases in the past the courts have held that school authorities can use dogs to detect drugs in schools and that these officials can conduct a "reasonable" search of you and your effects if they have a "reasonable suspicion" that you are violating a school rule. But they cannot punish your classmates for wearing black armbands, they cannot expel you without a hearing, and the state cannot make it illegal to treat the flag "contemptuously" (by sewing it to the seat of your pants, for example).[1]

Your claim that these actions violated your constitutional rights would have astonished the Framers of the Constitution. They thought that they had written a document that stated what the federal government *could* do, not one that specified what state governments (such as school systems) *could not* do. And they thought that they had created a national government of such limited powers that it was not even necessary to add a list—a bill of rights—stating what that government was forbidden from doing. It would be enough, for example, that the Constitution did not authorize the federal government to censor newspapers; an amendment prohibiting censorship would be superfluous.

The people who gathered in the state ratifying conventions weren't so optimistic. They suspected—rightly, as it turned out—that the federal government might well try to do things that it was not authorized to do, and so they insisted that the Bill of Rights be added to the Constitution. But even they never imagined that the Bill of Rights would affect what *state* governments could do. Each state would decide that for itself, in its own constitution. And if by chance the Bill of Rights did apply to the states, surely its guarantees of free speech and freedom from unreasonable searches and seizures would apply to big issues—the freedom to attack the government in a newspaper editorial, for example, or to keep the police from breaking down the door of your home without a warrant. The courts would not be deciding who could wear what kinds of armbands or under what circumstances a school could expel a student.

To understand the nature of civil liberties today, it is necessary to understand why the liberties mentioned in the Bill of Rights were thought to be important, how they came to apply to the states, and why they have grown in scope and meaning.

Politics, Culture, and Civil Liberties

The Bill of Rights is an important limitation on popular rule. It says that there are things that a government cannot do even if a majority wants them done. But why would the government, to say nothing of a popular majority, ever want to do these things? In our review of the politics of policy-making, we have repeatedly observed the ability of small but intensely motivated minorities to block actions that would impose heavy costs on them. Milk producers for a long time resisted efforts that would reduce government subsidies for their products, and ship owners and merchant seamen have been able to block efforts to introduce more competition (and presumably lower prices) into their industry. The political system has facilitated this kind of client politics.

If a largely indifferent public permits various economic, occupational, or professional minorities to safeguard their own interests, why should other kinds of minorities—religious or ideological ones—require special constitutional protection? Just as the average citizen bears only slight costs created by the advantages enjoyed by milk producers or truck drivers, presumably the average citizen bears only slight (if any) costs from the publication of a Communist party newspaper or from the refusal of a member of the Jehovah's Witnesses to recite the pledge of allegiance to the flag. If costs are small and widely distributed, then one would expect that political activity to reduce those costs would be infrequent and often ineffective. Moreover, some of these "costs"—such as the consequences of reading a Communist party newspaper—will occur in the distant future, if at all. Ordinarily people are not politically sensitive to such distant or hypothetical burdens.

So why do the liberties claimed by some people ever become a major issue? There are three reasons. In two of the three the politics surrounding civil liberties are similar to those around any other issue. First, there may be rights in conflict (in which case we have interest group politics). Second, passions may be inflamed by a skilled policy entrepreneur (in which case we have entrepreneurial politics). But the third reason makes the politics of civil liberties different from that of most issues: the political culture of the United States, described in Chapter 4, contains principles that are in conflict with one another. Most Americans accept that culture and thus accept the contradictions built into it. From time to time we tend to favor one part of that culture (say, a belief in "Americanism") over another part (say, a belief in personal freedom). When that happens, we find ourselves fighting over matters such as flag burning with an intensity that seems out of proportion to what is actually at stake.

Rights in Conflict

We often think of "civil liberties" as a set of principles that protect the freedoms of all of us all of the time. That is true—up to a point. But in fact the Constitution and the Bill of Rights contain a list of *competing* rights and duties. That competition becomes obvious when one person asserts one constitutional right or duty and another person asserts a different one. For example:

- Dr. Samuel H. Sheppard of Cleveland, Ohio, asserted his right to have a fair trial on the charge of having murdered his wife. Bob Considine and Walter Winchell, two radio commentators, as well as other reporters, asserted their right to broadcast whatever facts and rumors they heard about Dr. Sheppard and his love life. Two rights in conflict.
- The U.S. government has an obligation to "provide for the common defense" and, in pursuit of that duty, has claimed the right to keep secret certain military and diplomatic information. The *New York Times* claimed the right to publish such secrets as the "Pentagon Papers" without censorship, citing the Constitution's guarantee of freedom of the press. A duty and a right in conflict.
- Carl Jacob Kunz delivered inflammatory anti-Jewish speeches on the street corners of a Jewish neighborhood in New York City, suggesting, among other things, that Jews be "burnt in incinerators." The Jewish people living in that area were outraged. The New York police commissioner revoked Kunz's license to hold public meetings on the streets. When he continued to air his views on the public streets, Kunz was arrested for speaking without a permit. Freedom of speech versus the preservation of public order.

Even a disruptive high school student's right not to be a victim of arbitrary or unjustifiable expulsion is in partial conflict with the school's obligation to maintain an orderly environment in which learning can take place.

Political struggles over civil liberties follow much the same pattern as interest group politics involving economic issues, even though the claims in question are made by individuals. Indeed, there are formal, organized interest groups concerned with civil liberties. The Fraternal Order of the Police complains about restrictions on police powers, whereas the American Civil Liberties Union defends and seeks to enlarge those restrictions. Catholics have pressed for public support of parochial schools; Protestants and Jews have argued against it. Sometimes the opposed groups are entirely private; sometimes one or both are government agencies. Often their clashes end up in the courts. (When the Supreme Court decided the cases given earlier, Sheppard, the *New York Times,* and Kunz all won.[2])

Policy Entrepreneurs

Just as a skilled policy entrepreneur can sometimes arouse legislators to act against the normally undisputed claims of an interest group, so also can such an entrepreneur sometimes arouse people to take action against the rights and liberties claimed by political or religious dissidents. The success of entrepreneurial politics, whether involving money interests or civil liberties, often depends on the existence of a crisis.

War has usually been the crisis that has facilitated entrepreneurial politics aimed at restricting the liberty of some minority. For example:

- The Sedition Act was passed in 1798, making it a crime to write, utter, or publish "any false, scandalous, and malicious writing" with the intention of defaming the president, Congress, or the government or of exciting against the government "the hatred of the people." The occasion was a kind of half-war between the United States and

A 1919 cartoon expresses popular fears of "Reds" (that is, leftist radicals) threatening American institutions.

McCarthyism

In 1950 Senator Joseph R. McCarthy of Wisconsin began making a long series of charges, usually unsubstantiated, that people working for various government agencies were communists. Since then anyone making a charge that unfairly impugns the motives, attacks the patriotism, or violates the rights of individuals is often criticized for engaging in **McCarthyism.** The word has become a synonym for "character assassination." Senator McCarthy was a conservative, and so liberals today are often quick to denounce conservative attacks on them as "McCarthyism." But increasingly conservatives have used the term against liberals, usually by modifying it to read "McCarthyism of the left."

Source: From *Safire's Political Dictionary* by William Safire. Copyright © 1968, 1972, 1978 by William Safire. Reprinted by permission of Random House, Inc. and the author.

"advocating or urging treason, insurrection, or forcible resistance to any law of the United States," or to utter or write any disloyal, profane, scurrilous, or abusive language intended to incite resistance to the United States or to curtail war production. The occasion was World War I; the impetus was the fear that Germans in this country were spies and that radicals were seeking to overthrow the government. Under these laws more than two thousand persons were prosecuted (about half were convicted), and thousands of aliens were rounded up and deported. The policy entrepreneur leading this massive crackdown (the so-called Red Scare) was Attorney General A. Mitchell Palmer.

- The Smith Act was passed in 1940, the Internal Security Act in 1950, and the Communist Control Act in 1954. These laws made it illegal to advocate the overthrow of the U.S. government by force or violence (Smith Act), required members of the Communist Party to register with the government (Internal Security Act), and declared the Communist Party to be part of a conspiracy to overthrow the government (Communist Control Act). The occasion was World War II and the Korean War, which, like earlier wars, inspired fears that foreign agents (Nazi and Soviet) were trying to subvert the government. For the latter two laws the policy entrepreneur was Senator Joseph McCarthy, who attracted a great deal of attention with his repeated (and sometimes inaccurate) claims that Soviet agents were working inside the U.S. government.

These laws had in common an effort to protect the nation from threats, real and imagined, posed by people who claimed to be exercising their freedom to speak, publish, organize, and assemble. In each case a real threat (a war) led the government to narrow the limits of permissible speech and activity. Almost every time such restrictions were imposed, the Supreme Court was called upon to decide whether Congress (or sometimes state legislatures) had drawn those limits properly. In most instances the Court tended to uphold the legislatures. But as time passed and the war or crisis ended, popular passions abated and many of the laws proved to be unimportant.

Though it is uncommon, some use is still made of the sedition laws. In the 1980s various white

France, stimulated by fear in this country of the violence following the French Revolution of 1789. The policy entrepreneurs were Federalist politicians who believed that Thomas Jefferson and his followers were supporters of the French Revolution and would, if they came to power, encourage here the kind of anarchy that seemed to be occurring in France.

- The Espionage and Sedition Acts were passed in 1917–1918, making it a crime to utter false statements that would interfere with the American military, to send through the mails material

supremacists and Puerto Rican nationalists were charged with sedition. In each case the government alleged that the accused had not only spoken in favor of overthrowing the government but had actually engaged in violent actions such as bombings. Later in this chapter we shall see how the Court has increasingly restricted the power of Congress and state legislatures to outlaw political speech; to be found guilty of sedition now it is usually necessary to do something more serious than just talk about it.

Cultural Conflicts

In the main the United States was originally the creation of white European Protestants. Blacks were, in most cases, slaves, and American Indians were not citizens. Catholics and Jews in the colonies composed a small minority, and often a persecuted one. The early schools tended to be religious—that is,

Protestant—ones, many of them receiving state aid. It is not surprising that under these circumstances a view of America arose that equated "Americanism" with the values and habits of white Anglo-Saxon Protestants.

But immigration to this country brought a flood of new settlers, many of them coming from very different backgrounds (see Figure 18.1). In the mid-nineteenth century the potato famine led millions of Irish Catholics to migrate here. At the turn of the century religious persecution and economic disadvantage brought more millions of people, many Catholic or Jewish, from southern and eastern Europe.

In recent decades political conflict and economic want have led Hispanics (mostly from Mexico but increasingly from all parts of Latin America), Caribbeans, Africans, Middle Easterners, Southeast

Figure 18.1   Annual Immigration, 1840–1996

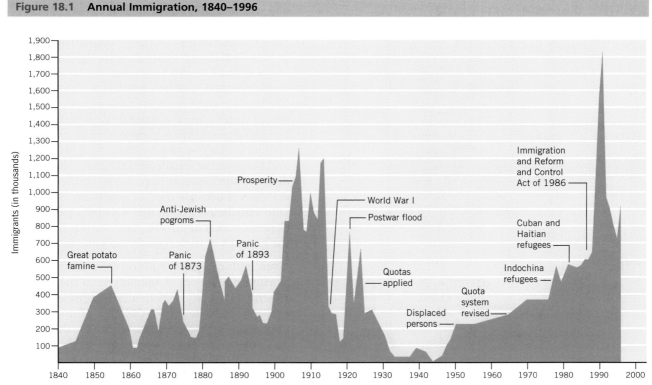

Note: Figures for 1989 and 1990 include persons who were granted permanent residence under the legalization program of the Immigration and Reform and Control Act of 1986.
Source: Statistical Abstract of the United States, 1998, 10.

Figure 18.2   Changing Composition of U.S. Immigration, 1901–1996

1901–1920

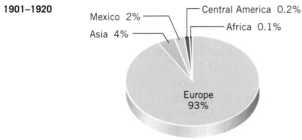

Central America 0.2%
Africa 0.1%
Mexico 2%
Asia 4%
Europe 93%

1921–1940

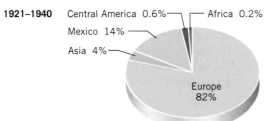

Central America 0.6%
Africa 0.2%
Mexico 14%
Asia 4%
Europe 82%

1941–1960

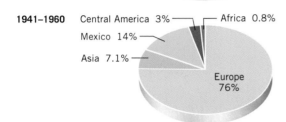

Central America 3%
Africa 0.8%
Mexico 14%
Asia 7.1%
Europe 76%

1961–1980

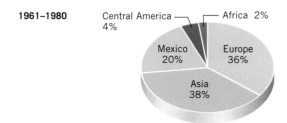

Central America 4%
Africa 2%
Mexico 20%
Europe 36%
Asia 38%

1981–1996

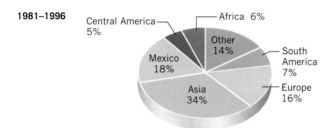

Central America 5%
Africa 6%
Mexico 18%
Other 14%
South America 7%
Asia 34%
Europe 16%

Sources: For 1901–1980: Associated Press, adapted from a *Boston Globe* graphic by Steven Nelson. Reprinted courtesy of the *Boston Globe*. For 1981–1996: *Statistical Abstract of the United States, 1998,* 11.

Asians, and Asians to cross our borders—some legally, some illegally (see Figure 18.2). Among them have been Buddhists, Catholics, Muslims, and members of many other religious and cultural groups.

Ethnic, religious, and cultural differences have given rise to different views as to the meaning and scope of certain constitutionally protected freedoms. For example:

- Many Jewish groups find it offensive for a crèche (that is, a scene depicting the birth of Christ in a manger) to be displayed in front of a government building such as city hall at Christmastime, while many Catholics and Protestants regard such displays as an important part of our cultural heritage. Does a religious display on public property violate the First Amendment requirement that the government pass no law "respecting an establishment of religion"?

- Many English-speaking people believe that the public schools ought to teach all students to speak and write English, because the language is part of our nation's cultural heritage. Some Hispanic groups argue that the schools should teach pupils in both English and Spanish, since Spanish is part of the Hispanic cultural heritage. Is bilingual education constitutionally required?

- The Boy Scouts of America refuses to allow homosexual men to become scout leaders even though federal law says that homosexuals may not be the victims of discrimination. Many civil libertarians and homosexuals challenged this policy because it discriminated against gays, while the Boy Scouts defended it because their organization was a private association free to make its own rules. (The Supreme Court in 2000 upheld the Boy Scouts on the grounds of their right to associate freely.)

Even within a given cultural tradition there are important differences of opinion as to the balance between community sensitivities and personal self-expression. To some people the sight of a store carrying pornographic books or a theater showing a pornographic movie is deeply offensive; to others pornography is offensive but such establishments ought to be tolerated to ensure that laws restricting them do not also restrict politically or artistically important forms of speech; to still others pornography itself is not especially offensive. What forms of expression are entitled to constitutional protection?

Interpreting and Applying the First Amendment

The First Amendment contains the language that has been at issue in most of the cases to which we have thus far referred. It has roughly two parts: one protecting **freedom of expression** ("Congress shall make no law . . . abridging the freedom of speech, or of the press, or the right of people peaceably to assemble, and to petition the government for a redress of grievances") and the other protecting **freedom of religion** ("Congress shall make no law respecting an establishment of religion; or abridging the free exercise thereof").

Speech and National Security

The traditional view of free speech and a free press was expressed by William Blackstone, the great English jurist, in his *Commentaries*, published in 1765. A free press is essential to a free state, he wrote, but the freedom that the press should enjoy is the freedom from **prior restraint**—that is, freedom from censorship, or rules telling a newspaper in advance what it can publish. Once a newspaper has published an article or a person has delivered a speech, that paper or speaker has to take the consequences if what was written or said proves to be "improper, mischievous, or illegal."[3]

The U.S. Sedition Act of 1798 was in keeping with traditional English law. Like it, the act imposed no prior restraint on publishers; it did, however, make them liable to punishment after the fact. The act was an improvement over the English law, however, because unlike the British model, it entrusted the decision to a jury, not a judge, and allowed the defendant to be acquitted if he or she could prove the truth of what had been published. Although several newspaper publishers were convicted under the act, none of these cases reached the Supreme Court. When Jefferson became president in 1801, he pardoned everyone who had been convicted under the Sedition Act. Though Jeffersonians objected vehemently to the law, their principal objection was not to the idea of holding newspapers accountable for what they published but to letting the *federal* government do this. Jefferson was perfectly prepared to have the *states* punish what he called the "overwhelming torrent of slander" by means of "a few prosecutions of the most prominent offenders."[4]

It would be another century before the federal government would attempt to define the limits of free

Women picketed in front of the White House, urging President Warren Harding to release political radicals arrested during his administration.

speech and writing. Perhaps recalling the widespread opposition to the sweep of the 1798 act, Congress in 1917–1918 placed restrictions not on publications that were critical of the government but only on those that advocated "treason, insurrection, or forcible resistance" to federal laws or attempted to foment disloyalty or mutiny in the armed services.

In 1919 this new law was examined by the Supreme Court when it heard the case of Charles T. Schenck, who had been convicted of violating the Espionage Act because he had mailed circulars to men eligible for the draft, urging them to resist. At issue was the constitutionality of the Espionage Act and, more broadly, the scope of Congress's power to control speech. One view held that the First Amendment prevented Congress from passing *any* law restricting speech; the other held that Congress could punish dangerous speech. For a unanimous Supreme Court, Justice Oliver Wendell Holmes announced a rule by which to settle the matter. It soon became known as the **clear-and-present-danger test:**

> The question in every case is whether the words used are used in such circumstances and are of such a nature as to create a clear and present danger that they will bring about

the substantive evils that Congress has a right to prevent.[5]

The Court held that Schenck's leaflets did create such a danger, and so his conviction was upheld. In explaining why, Holmes said that not even the Constitution protects a person who has been "falsely shouting fire in a theatre and causing a panic." In this case things that might safely be said in peacetime may be punished in wartime.

The clear-and-present-danger test may have clarified the law, but it kept no one out of jail. Schenck went, and so did the defendants in five other cases in the period 1919–1927, even though during this time Holmes, the author of the test, shifted his position and began writing dissenting opinions in which he urged that the test had not been met and so the defendant should go free.

During the same period the Court for the first time came to grips with the power of state governments to punish speech. As we saw in Chapter 2, the Bill of Rights was originally intended only to limit the powers of the *federal* government. The adoption in 1868 of the Fourteenth Amendment, however, brought into the Constitution language that for the first time created the possibility that some or all of the Bill of Rights might now restrict the states' actions. The key phrase was the **due-process clause:**

> No state shall . . . deprive any person of life, liberty or property, without due process of law.

For over half a century after 1868, the Supreme Court steadfastly denied that the due-process clause made the Bill of Rights applicable to the states. Therefore, state legislatures could pass sedition laws or antiobscenity laws without fear of having them overturned by the Supreme Court.

Then in 1925 Benjamin Gitlow was convicted of violating New York's sedition law—a law similar to the federal Sedition Act of 1918—by passing out some leaflets. The Supreme Court upheld his conviction but added a statement that changed constitutional history: freedom of speech and of the press were now among the "fundamental personal rights" protected by the due-process clause of the Fourteenth Amendment from infringements by *state* action.[6] Thereafter state laws involving speech, the press, and peaceful assembly were struck down by the Supreme Court for being in violation of the freedom-of-expression guarantees of the First Amendment, made applicable to the states by the Fourteenth Amendment.[7]

The clear-and-present-danger test was a way of balancing the competing demands of free expression and national security. As the memory of World War I and the ensuing Red Scare evaporated, the Court began to develop other tests, ones that shifted the balance more toward free expression. Some of these tests are listed in the box on page 507.

But when a crisis reappears, as it did in World War II and the Korean conflict, the Court has tended to defer, up to a point, to legislative judgments about the need to protect national security. For example, it upheld the conviction of eleven leaders of the Communist party for having advocated the violent overthrow of the U.S. government, a violation of the Smith Act of 1940.

This conviction once again raised the hard question of the circumstances under which words can be punished. Hardly anybody would deny that actually *trying* to overthrow the government is a crime; the question is whether *advocating* its overthrow is a crime. In the case of the eleven Communist leaders, the Court said that the government did not have to wait to protect itself until "the *putsch* [rebellion] is about to be executed, the plans have been laid and the signal is awaited." Even if the Communists were not likely to be successful in their effort, the Court held that specifically advocating violent overthrow could be punished. "In each case," the opinion read, the courts "must ask whether the gravity of the 'evil,' discounted by its improbability, justifies such invasion of free speech as is necessary to avoid the danger."[8]

But as the popular worries about communists began to subside and the membership of the Supreme Court changed, the Court began to tip the balance even farther toward free expression. By 1957 the Court made it clear that for advocacy to be punished, the government would have to show not just that a person believed in the overthrow of the government but also that he or she was using words "calculated to incite" that overthrow.[9]

By 1969 the pendulum had swung to the point where the speech would have to be judged likely to incite "imminent" unlawful action. In this case Clarence Brandenburg, a leader of the Ku Klux Klan in Ohio, staged a cross-burning rally during which he reviled blacks and Jews. The police told him to clear the street; as he left, he said, "We'll take the [expletive] street later." He was convicted of attempting to incite lawless mob action. The Supreme Court overturned the conviction, holding that any speech that does not call for illegal action is protected, and even speech that *does* call for illegal action is protected if the action is not "imminent" or there is reason to believe that the listeners will not take action.[10]

This means that no matter how offensive or provocative some forms of expression may be, this expression has powerful constitutional protections. In 1977 a group of American Nazis wanted to parade through the streets of Skokie, Illinois, a community with a large Jewish population. The residents, outraged, sought to ban the march. Many feared violence if it occurred. But the lower courts, under prodding from the Supreme Court, held that, noxious and provocative as the anti-Semitic slogans of the Nazis may be, the Nazi party had a constitutional right to speak and parade peacefully.[11]

Similar reasoning led the Supreme Court in 1992 to overturn a Minnesota statute that made it a crime to display symbols or objects, such as a Nazi swastika or a burning cross, that are likely to cause alarm or resentment among an ethnic or racial group, such as Jews or African Americans.[12] On the other hand, if you are convicted of actually hurting someone, you may be given a tougher sentence if it can be shown that you were motivated to assault them by racial or ethnic hatred.[13] To be punished for such a hate crime, your bigotry must result in some direct and physical harm and not just the display of an odious symbol.

Even hateful symbols, such as this burning cross lit by members of the Ku Klux Klan, enjoy constitutional protection.

What Is Speech?

If most political speaking or writing is permissible, save that which actually incites someone to take illegal actions, what *kinds* of speaking and writing qualify for this broad protection? Though the Constitution says that the legislature may make "no law" abridging freedom of speech or the press, and although some justices have argued that this means literally *no* law, the Court has held that there are at least four forms of speaking and writing that are not automatically granted full constitutional protection: libel, obscenity, symbolic speech, and false advertising.

Libel

A **libel** is a written statement that defames the character of another person. (If the statement is oral, it is called a slander.) In some countries, such as England, it is easy to sue another person for libel and to collect. In this country it is much harder. For one thing, you must show that the libelous statement was false. If it was true, you cannot collect no matter how badly it harmed you.

A beauty contest winner was awarded $14 million (later reduced on appeal) when she proved that *Penthouse* magazine had libeled her. The actress Carol Burnett collected a large sum from a libel suit brought against a gossip newspaper. But when Theodore Roosevelt sued a newspaper for falsely claiming that he was a drunk, the jury awarded him damages of only six cents.[14]

If you are a public figure, it is much harder to win a libel suit. A public figure such as an elected official, an army general, or a well-known celebrity must prove not only that the publication was false and damaging but also that the words were published with "actual malice"—that is, with reckless disregard for their truth or falsity or with knowledge that they were false.[15] As we saw in Chapter 10, that is not easily done. General Ariel Sharon was able to prove that the statements made about him by *Time* magazine were false and damaging but not that they were the result of "actual malice."

Obscenity

Obscenity is not protected by the First Amendment. The Court has always held that obscene materials, because they have no redeeming social value and are calculated chiefly to appeal to one's sexual rather than political or literary interests, can be regulated by the state. The problem, of course, arises with the meaning of *obscene*. In the eleven-year period from 1957 to 1968 the Court decided thirteen major cases involving the definition of obscenity, which resulted in fifty-five separate opinions.[16] Some justices, such as Hugo Black, believed that the First Amendment protected all publications, even wholly obscene ones. Others believed that obscenity deserved no protection and struggled heroically to define the term. Still others shared the view of former Justice Potter Stewart, who objected to "hardcore pornography" but admitted that the best definition he could offer was "I know it when I see it."[17]

It is unnecessary to review in detail the many attempts by the Court at defining obscenity. The justices have made it clear that nudity and sex are not, by definition, obscene and that they will provide First Amendment protection to anything that has political, literary, or artistic merit, allowing the government to punish only the distribution of "hardcore pornography." Their most recent (1973) definition of this is as follows: to be obscene, the work, taken as a whole, must be judged by "the average person applying contemporary community standards" to appeal to the "prurient interest" or to depict "in a patently offensive way, sexual conduct specifically defined by applicable state law" and to lack "serious literary, artistic, political, or scientific value."[18]

After Albany, Georgia, decided that the movie *Carnal Knowledge* was obscene by contemporary local standards, the Supreme Court overturned the distributor's conviction on the grounds that the authorities in Albany failed to show that the film depicted "patently offensive hard-core sexual conduct."[19]

It is easy to make sport of the problems the Court has faced in trying to decide obscenity cases (one conjures up images of black-robed justices leafing through the pages of *Hustler* magazine, taking notes), but these problems reveal, as do other civil liberties cases, the continuing problem of balancing competing claims. One part of the community wants to read or see whatever it wishes; another part wants to protect private acts from public degradation. The first part cherishes liberty above all; the second values decency above liberty. The former fears that *any* restriction on literature will lead to *pervasive* restrictions; the latter believes that reasonable people can distinguish (or reasonable laws can require them to distinguish) between patently offensive and artistically serious work.

Anyone strolling today through an "adult" bookstore must suppose that no restrictions at all exist on the distribution of pornographic works. This condition does not arise simply from the doctrines of the Court. Other factors operate as well, including the priorities of local law enforcement officials, the political climate of the community, the procedures that must be followed to bring a viable court case, the clarity and workability of state and local laws on the subject, and the difficulty of changing the behavior of many people by prosecuting one person. The current view of the Court is that localities can decide for themselves whether to tolerate hard-core pornography; but if they choose not to, they must meet some fairly strict constitutional tests.

The protections given by the Court to expressions of sexual or erotic interest have not been limited to books, magazines, or films. Almost any form of visual or auditory communication can be considered "speech" and thus protected by the First Amendment. In one case even nude dancing was given protection as a form of "speech,"[20] although in 1991 the Court held that nude dancing was only "marginally" within the purview of First Amendment protections, and so it upheld an Indiana statute that banned *totally* nude dancing.[21]

Of late some feminist organizations have attacked pornography on the grounds that it exploits and degrades women. They persuaded Indianapolis to pass an ordinance that defined pornography as portrayals of the "graphic, sexually explicit subordination of women" and allowed people to sue the producers of such material. Sexually explicit portrayals of women in positions of equality were not defined as pornography. The Court disagreed. In 1986 it

HOW THINGS WORK

Testing Restrictions on Expression

The Supreme Court has employed various standards and tests to decide whether a restriction on freedom of expression is constitutionally permissible.

1. **Preferred position** The right of free expression, though not absolute, occupies a higher, or more preferred, position than many other constitutional rights, such as property rights. This is still a controversial rule; nonetheless, the Court always approaches a restriction on expression skeptically.

2. **Prior restraint** With scarcely any exceptions, the Court will not tolerate a prior restraint on expression, such as censorship, even when it will allow subsequent punishment of improper expressions (such as libel).

3. **Imminent danger** Punishment for uttering inflammatory sentiments will be allowed only if there is an imminent danger that the utterances will incite an unlawful act.

4. **Neutrality** Any restriction on speech, such as a requirement that parades or demonstrations not disrupt other people in the exercise of their rights, must be neutral—that is, it must not favor one group more than another.

5. **Clarity** If you must obtain a permit to hold a parade, the law must set forth clear (as well as neutral) standards to guide administrators in issuing that permit. Similarly, a law punishing obscenity must contain a clear definition of obscenity.

6. **Least-restrictive means** If it is necessary to restrict the exercise of one right to protect the exercise of another, the restriction should employ the least-restrictive means to achieve its end. For example, if press coverage threatens a person's right to a fair trial, the judge may only do what is minimally necessary to that end, such as transferring the case to another town rather than issuing a "gag order."

Cases cited, by item: (1) *United States v. Carolene Products,* 304 U.S. 144 (1938). (2) *Near v. Minnesota,* 283 U.S. 697 (1931). (3) *Brandenburg v. Ohio,* 395 U.S. 444 (1969). (4) *Kunz v. New York,* 340 U.S. 290 (1951). (5) *Hynes v. Mayor and Council of Oradell,* 425 U.S. 610 (1976). (6) *Nebraska Press Association v. Stuart,* 427 U.S. 539 (1976).

affirmed a lower-court ruling that such an ordinance was a violation of the First Amendment because it represented a legislative preference for one form of expression (women in positions of equality) over another (women in positions of subordination).[22]

One constitutionally permissible way to limit the spread of pornographic materials has been to establish rules governing where in a city they can be sold. When one city adopted a zoning ordinance prohibiting an "adult" movie theater from locating within one thousand feet of any church, school, park, or residential area, the Court upheld the ordinance, noting that the purpose of the law was not to regulate speech but to regulate the use of land. And in any case the adult theaters still had much of the city's land area in which to find a location.[23]

With the advent of the Internet it has become more difficult for the government to regulate obscenity. The Internet spans the globe. It offers an amazing variety of materials—some educational, some entertaining, some sexually explicit. But it is difficult to apply the Supreme Court's standard for judging whether sexual material is obscene—the "average person" applying "contemporary community standards"—to the Internet, because there is no easy way to tell what "the community" is. Is it the place where the recipient lives or the place where the material originates? And since no one is in charge of the Internet, who can be held responsible for controlling offensive material? Since anybody can send anything to anybody else without knowing the age or location of the recipient, how can the Internet protect children? When Congress tried to ban obscene, indecent, or "patently offensive" materials from the Internet, the Supreme Court struck down the law as unconstitutional. The Court went even

WHO GOVERNS? TO WHAT ENDS?

Flag Burning

Texas passed a law that made burning the American flag a crime. In 1989 the U.S. Supreme Court declared, by a five-to-four vote, that the law was unconstitutional because it violated a citizen's right to free speech.* The public was outraged, thinking that flag burning was inexcusable. Within a few days the House passed by a vote of 380 to 38 a bill that would make flag burning a federal crime. Not long after, the Senate agreed by a vote of 91 to 9. Under the law a person could be sent to prison for up to one year if he or she "knowingly mutilates, defaces, physically defiles, burns, maintains on the floor or ground, or tramples upon" any U.S. flag.

The Supreme Court was not satisfied. In 1990 by a similar five-to-four vote, it struck down the new federal law as unconstitutional, repeating its view that flag burning was a form of constitutionally protected speech.† The public was still upset, but now it was clear that only a constitutional amendment could make flag burning a crime.

But the constitutional amendment, which would have required a two-thirds majority vote in both the House and the Senate, never passed. Why? A year earlier both houses of Congress had approved a similar law by margins well in excess of a two-thirds vote, and the public still wanted such a law. In fact many veterans' organizations argued vigorously in favor of an amendment.

Who governed? The answer, it seems, is those members of Congress who were reluctant to amend the Constitution even for a popular cause. The amendment that would have made flag burning illegal passed both houses, but without enough votes to meet the two-thirds requirement. The missing votes were cast by members who said that although flag burning was wrong, it was a mistake to limit the Bill of Rights to deal with this rare and unhappy form of "speech."

The congressional action cannot be explained by public opinion, interest groups, or electoral politics. More Republicans than Democrats favored the amendment, but there were members from both parties on both sides of the issue. In this case members of Congress voted to a large degree on the basis of their personal convictions.

*Texas v. Johnson, 491 U.S. 397 (1989).
†United States v. Eichman, 496 U.S. 310 (1990).

---

further with child pornography. Though it has long held that child pornography is illegal even if it is not obscene because of the government's interest in protecting children, it would not let Congress ban pornography involving computer-designed children. Under the 1996 law, it would be illegal to display computer simulations of children engaged in sex even if no real children were involved. The Court, in 2002, said "no." It held that Congress could not ban "virtual" child pornography without violating the First Amendment because, in its view, the law might bar even harmless depictions of children and sex (for example, in a book on child psychology).[24]

Symbolic Speech

You cannot ordinarily claim that an illegal act should be protected because that action is meant to convey a political message. For example, if you burn your draft card in protest against the foreign policy of the United States, you can be punished for the illegal act (burning the card), even if your intent was to communicate your beliefs. The Court reasoned that giving such **symbolic speech** the same protection as real speech would open the door to permitting all manner of illegal actions—murder, arson, rape—if the perpetrator meant thereby to send a message.[25]

On the other hand, a statute that makes it illegal to burn the American flag is an unconstitutional infringement of free speech.[26] Why is there a difference between a draft card and the flag? The Court argues that the government has a right to run a military draft and so can protect draft cards, even if this incidentally restricts speech. But the only motive that the government has in banning flag burning is to restrict this form of speech, and that would make such a restriction improper. In 1989–1990 Congress refused to endorse a proposed constitutional amendment that, if ratified, would have reversed this Court ruling. It did pass a bill making flag burning a crime, but the Supreme Court, consistent with its decision in an earlier Texas case, held that this law was an unconstitutional infringement of free speech.[27]

"Symbolic speech": when young men burned their draft cards during the 1960s to protest the Vietnam War, the Supreme Court ruled that it was an illegal act for which they could be punished.

Who Is a Person?

If people have a right to speak and publish, do corporations, interest groups, and children have the same right? By and large the answer is yes, though there are some exceptions.

When the attorney general of Massachusetts tried to prevent the First National Bank of Boston from spending money to influence votes in a local election, the Court stepped in and blocked him. The Court held that a corporation, like a person, has certain First Amendment rights. Similarly, when the federal government tried to limit the spending of a group called Massachusetts Citizens for Life (an antiabortion organization), the Court held that such organizations have First Amendment rights.[28] The Court has also told states that they cannot forbid liquor stores to advertise their prices and informed federal authorities that they cannot prohibit casinos from plugging gambling.[29]

When the California Public Utility Commission tried to compel one of the utilities that it regulates, the Pacific Gas and Electric Company, to enclose in its monthly bills to customers statements written by groups attacking the utility, the Supreme Court blocked the agency, saying that forcing it to disseminate political statements violated the firm's free speech rights. "The identity of the speaker is not decisive in determining whether speech is protected," the Court said. "Corporations and other associations, like individuals, contribute to the 'discussion, debate, and the dissemination of information and ideas' that the First Amendment seeks to foster." In this case the right to speak includes the choice of what *not* to say.[30]

Even though corporations have some First Amendment rights, the government can place more limits on commercial than on noncommercial speech. The legislature can place restrictions on advertisements for cigarettes, liquor, and gambling; it can even regulate advertising for some less harmful products provided that the regulations are narrowly tailored and serve a substantial public interest.[31] If the regulations are too broad or do not serve a clear interest, then ads are entitled to some constitutional protection. For example, the states cannot bar lawyers from advertising or accountants from personally soliciting clients.[32]

Under certain circumstances, young people may have less freedom of expression than adults. In 1988 the Supreme Court held that the principal of Hazelwood High School could censor articles appearing in the student-edited newspaper. The newspaper was published using school funds and was part of a journalism class. The principal ordered the deletion of stories dealing with student pregnancies and the impact of parental divorce on students. The student editors sued, claiming their First Amendment rights had been violated. The Court agreed that students do not "shed their constitutional rights to freedom of speech or expression at the schoolhouse gate" and that they cannot be punished for expressing on campus their personal views. But students do not have exactly the same rights as adults if the exercise of those rights impedes the educational mission of the school. Students may lawfully say things on campus, as individuals, that they cannot say if they are part of school-sponsored activities, such as plays or school-run newspapers, that are part of the curriculum. School-sponsored activities can be controlled so long as the controls are "reasonably related to legitimate pedagogical concerns."[33]

Church and State

Everybody knows, correctly, the language of the First Amendment that protects freedom of speech and the press, though most people are not aware of how complex the legal interpretations of these provisions have become. But many people also believe, wrongly, that the language of the First Amendment clearly requires the "separation of church and state." It does not.

What that amendment actually says is quite different and maddeningly unclear. It has two parts. The first, often referred to as the **free-exercise clause,** states that Congress shall make no law prohibiting the "free exercise" of religion. The second, which is called the **establishment clause,** states that Congress shall make no law "respecting an establishment of religion."

The Free-Exercise Clause

The free-exercise clause is the clearer of the two, though by no means is it lacking in ambiguity. It obviously means that Congress cannot pass a law prohibiting Catholics from celebrating Mass, requiring Baptists to become Episcopalians, or preventing Jews from holding a bar mitzvah. Since the First Amendment has been applied to the states via the due-process clause of the Fourteenth Amendment, it means that state governments cannot pass such laws either. In general the courts have treated religion like speech: you can pretty much do or say what you want so long as it does not cause some serious harm to others.

Even some laws that do not appear on their face to apply to churches may be unconstitutional if their enforcement imposes particular burdens on churches or greater burdens on some churches than others. For example, a state cannot apply a license fee on door-to-door solicitors when the solicitor is a Jehovah's Witness selling religious tracts.[34] By the same token, the courts ruled that the city of Hialeah,

Florida, cannot ban animal sacrifices by members of an Afro-Caribbean religion called Santeria. Since killing animals is generally not illegal (if it were, there could be no hamburgers or chicken sandwiches served in Hialeah's restaurants, and rat traps would be unlawful), the ban in this case was clearly directed against a specific religion and hence was unconstitutional.[35]

Having the right to exercise your religion freely does not mean, however, that you are exempt from laws binding other citizens, even when the law goes against your religious beliefs. A man cannot have more than one wife, even if (as once was the case with Mormons) polygamy is thought desirable on religious grounds.[36] For religious reasons you may oppose being vaccinated or having blood transfusions, but if the state passes a compulsory vaccination law or orders that a blood transfusion be given to a sick child, the courts will not block them on grounds of religious liberty.[37] Similarly, if you belong to an Indian tribe that uses a drug, peyote, in religious ceremonies, you cannot claim that your freedom was abridged if the state decides to ban the use of peyote, provided the law applies equally to all.[38] Since airports have a legitimate need for tight security measures, begging can be outlawed in them even if some of the people doing the begging are part of a religious group (in this case, the Hare Krishnas).[39]

Unfortunately some conflicts between religious belief and public policy are even more difficult to settle. What if you believe on religious grounds that war is immoral? The draft laws have always exempted a conscientious objector from military duty, and the Court has upheld such exemptions. But the Court has gone further: it has said that people cannot be drafted even if they do not believe in a Supreme Being or belong to any religious tradition, so long as their "consciences, spurred by deeply held moral, ethical, or religious beliefs, would give them no rest or peace if they allowed themselves to become part of an instrument of war."[40] Do exemptions on such grounds create an opportunity for some people to evade the draft because of their political preferences? In trying to answer such questions, the courts often have had to try to define a religion—no easy task.

And even when there is no question about your membership in a bona fide religion, the circumstances under which you may claim exemption from laws that apply to everybody else are not really clear. What if you, a member of the Seventh-Day Adventists, are fired by your employer for refusing on religious grounds to work on Saturday, and then it turns out that you cannot collect unemployment insurance because you refuse to take an available job—one that also requires you to work on Saturday? Or what if you are a member of the Amish sect, which refuses, contrary to state law, to send its children to public schools past the eighth grade? The Court has ruled that the state must pay you unemployment compensation and cannot require you to send your children to public schools beyond the eighth grade.[41]

These last two decisions, and others like them, show that even the "simple" principle of freedom of religion gets complicated in practice and can lead to the courts' giving, in effect, preference to members of one church over members of another.

The Establishment Clause

What in the world did the members of the First Congress mean when they wrote into the First Amendment language prohibiting Congress from making a law "respecting" an "establishment" of religion? The Supreme Court has more or less consistently interpreted this vague phrase to mean that the Constitution erects a "wall of separation" between church and state.

That phrase, so often quoted, is not in the Bill of Rights nor in the debates in the First Congress that drafted the Bill of Rights; it comes from the pen of Thomas Jefferson, who was opposed to having the Church of England as the established church of his native Virginia. (At the time of the Revolutionary War there were established churches—that is, official, state-supported churches—in at least eight of the thirteen former colonies.) But it is not clear that Jefferson's view was the majority view.

During much of the debate in Congress the wording of this part of the First Amendment was quite different and much plainer than what finally emerged. Up to the last minute the clause was intended to read "no religion shall be established by law" or "no national religion shall be established." The meaning of those words seems quite clear: whatever the states may do, the federal government cannot create an official, national religion or give support to one religion in preference to another.[42]

But Congress instead adopted an ambiguous phrase, and so the Supreme Court had to decide what it meant. It has declared that these words do not simply mean "no national religion" but mean as well no government involvement with religion at all, even on a nonpreferential basis. They mean, in short, erecting a "wall of separation" between church and state.[43] Though the interpretation of the establishment clause remains a topic of great controversy among judges and scholars, the Supreme Court has more or less consistently adopted this **wall-of-separation principle.**

Its first statement of this interpretation was in 1947. The case involved a New Jersey town that reimbursed parents for the costs of transporting their children to school, including parochial (in this case Catholic) schools. The Court decided that this reimbursement was constitutional, but it made it clear that the establishment clause of the First Amendment applied (via the Fourteenth Amendment) to the states and that it meant, among other things, that the government cannot require a person to profess a belief or disbelief in any religion; it cannot aid one religion, some religions, or all religions; and it cannot spend any tax money, however small the amount might be, in support of any religious activities or institutions.[44] The reader may wonder, in view of the Court's reasoning, why it allowed the town to pay for busing children to Catholic schools. The answer that it gave is that busing is a religiously neutral activity, akin to providing fire and police protection to Catholic schools. Busing, available to public- and private-school children alike, does not breach the wall of separation.

Students pray in front of a high school in Virginia. The Supreme Court will not let this happen inside a public school.

Since 1947 the Court has applied the wall-of-separation theory to strike down as unconstitutional every effort to have any form of prayer in public schools, even if it is nonsectarian,[45] voluntary,[46] or limited to reading a passage of the Bible.[47] Since 1992 it has even been unconstitutional for a public school to ask a rabbi or minister to offer a prayer—an invocation or a benediction—at the school's graduation ceremony, and since 2001 it has been unconstitutional for a student, elected by other students, to lead a voluntary prayer at the beginning of a high school football game.[48] Moreover, the Court has held that laws prohibiting teaching the theory of evolution or requiring giving equal time to "creationism" (the biblical doctrine that God created mankind) are religiously inspired and thus unconstitutional.[49] A public school may not allow its pupils to take time out from their regular classes for religious instruction if this occurs within the schools, though "released-time" instruction is all right if it is done outside the public school building.[50] The school prayer decisions in particular have provoked a storm of controversy, but efforts to get Congress to propose to the states a constitutional amendment authorizing such prayers have failed.

Almost as controversial have been Court-imposed restrictions on public aid to parochial schools, though here the wall-of-separation principle has not been used to forbid any and all forms of aid. For example, it is permissible for the federal government to provide aid for constructing buildings on denominational (as well as nondenominational) college campuses[51] and for state governments to loan free textbooks to parochial-school pupils,[52] grant tax-exempt status to parochial schools,[53] allow parents of parochial-school children to deduct their tuition payments on a state's income tax returns,[54] and pay for computers and a deaf child's sign language interpreter at private and religious schools.[55] But the government cannot pay a salary supplement to teachers who teach secular subjects in parochial schools,[56] reimburse parents for the cost of parochial-school tuition,[57] supply parochial schools with services such as counseling,[58] give money with which to purchase instructional materials, require that "creationism" be taught in public schools, or create a special school district for Hasidic Jews.[59]

The Court sometimes changes its mind on these matters. In 1985 it said that the states could not send teachers into parochial schools to teach remedial courses for needy children, but twelve years later it decided that they could. "We no longer presume," the Court wrote, "that public employees will inculcate religion simply because they happen to be in a sectarian environment."[60]

If you find it confusing to follow the twists and turns of Court policy in this area, you are not alone. The wall-of-separation principle has not been easy to apply, and with its membership undergoing change, the Court has begun to alter its position on church-state matters. (O'Connor, Rehnquist, Scalia, Kennedy, and Thomas have generally supported lowering—or perhaps perforating—the wall a bit.) The Court has tried to sort out the confusion by developing a three-part test to decide under what circumstances government involvement in religious activities is improper.[61] That involvement is constitutional if it meets these tests:

1. It has a secular purpose.
2. Its primary effect neither advances nor inhibits religion.
3. It does not foster an excessive government entanglement with religion.

No sooner had the test been developed than the Court decided that it was all right for the government of Pawtucket, Rhode Island, to erect a Nativity scene as part of a Christmas display in a local park. But five years later it said that Pittsburgh could not put a Nativity scene in front of the courthouse but could display a menorah (a Jewish symbol of Chanukah) next to a Christmas tree and a sign extolling liberty. The Court claimed that the crèche had to go (because, being too close to the courthouse, a government endorsement was implied) but the menorah could stay (because, being next to a Christmas tree, it would not lead people to think that Pittsburgh was endorsing Judaism).[62]

Confused? It gets worse. Though the Court has struck down prayer in public schools, it has upheld prayer in Congress (since 1789, the House and Senate open each session with a prayer).[63] A public school cannot have a chaplain, but the armed services can. The Court has said that the government cannot "advance" religion, but it has not objected to the printing of the phrase "In God We Trust" on the back of every dollar bill.

It is obvious that despite its efforts to set forth clear rules governing church-state relations, the Court's actual decisions are hard to summarize. It is deeply divided—some would say deeply confused—on these

How Would You Decide?

Suppose that you are on the Supreme Court. In each of the actual cases summarized below, you are asked to decide whether the First Amendment to the Constitution permits or prohibits a particular action. What would be your decision? (How the Supreme Court actually decided is given on page 516.)

Case 1: Jacksonville, Florida, passed a city ordinance prohibiting drive-in movies from showing films containing nudity if the screen was visible to passersby on the street. A movie theater manager protested, claiming that he had a First Amendment right to show such films, even if they could be seen from the street. Who is correct?

Case 2: Dr. Benjamin Spock wanted to enter Fort Dix Military Reservation in New Jersey to pass out campaign literature and discuss issues with service personnel. The military denied him access on grounds that regulations prohibit partisan campaigning on military bases. Who is correct?

Case 3: A town passed an ordinance forbidding the placing of "For Sale" or "Sold" signs in front of homes in racially changing neighborhoods. The purpose was to reduce "white flight" and panic selling. A realty firm protested, claiming that its freedom of speech was being abridged. Who is correct?

Case 4: A girl in Georgia was raped and died. A local television station broadcast the name of the girl, having obtained it from court records. Her father sued, claiming that his family's right to privacy had been violated, and pointed to a Georgia law that made it a crime to broadcast the name of a rape victim. The television station claimed that it had a right under the First Amendment to broadcast the name. Who is correct?

Case 5: Florida passed a law giving a political candidate the right to equal space in a newspaper that had published attacks on him. A newspaper claimed that this violated the freedom of the press to publish what it wants. Who is correct?

Case 6: Zacchini is a "human cannonball" whose entire fifteen-second act was filmed and broadcast by an Ohio television station. Zacchini sued the station, claiming that his earning power had been reduced by the film because the station showed for free what he charges people to see at county fairs. The station replied that it had a First Amendment right to broadcast such events. Who is correct?

matters, and so the efforts to define the "wall of separation" will continue to prove to be as difficult as the Court's earlier efforts to decide what is interstate and what is local commerce (see Chapter 3).

Crime and Due Process

Whereas the central problem in interpreting the religion clauses of the First Amendment has been to decide what they mean, the central problems in interpreting those parts of the Bill of Rights that affect people accused of a crime have been to decide not only what they mean but also how to put them into effect. It is not obvious what constitutes an "unreasonable search," but even if we settle that question, we still must decide how best to protect people against such searches in ways that do not unduly hinder criminal investigations.

There are at least two ways to provide that protection. One is to let the police introduce in court evidence relevant to the guilt or innocence of a person, no matter how it was obtained and then, after the case is settled, punish the police officer (or his or her superiors) if the evidence was gathered improperly (for example, by an unreasonable search). The other way is to exclude improperly gathered evidence from the trial in the first place, even if it is relevant to determining the guilt or innocence of the accused.

Most democratic nations, including England, use the first method; the United States uses the second. Because of this, many of the landmark cases decided by the Supreme Court have been bitterly controversial. Opponents of these decisions have argued that a guilty person should not go free just because the police officer blundered, especially if the mistake was minor. Supporters rejoin that there is no way to punish errant police officers effectively other than by

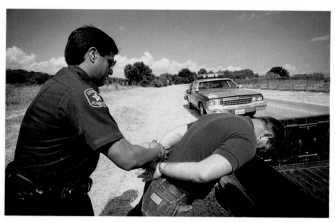

A man is arrested in Texas.

excluding tainted evidence; moreover, nobody should be convicted of a crime except by evidence that is above reproach.[64]

The Exclusionary Rule

The American method relies on what is called the **exclusionary rule.** That rule holds that evidence gathered in violation of the Constitution cannot be used in a trial. The rule has been used to implement two provisions of the Bill of Rights—the right to be free from unreasonable searches and seizures (Fourth Amendment) and the right not to be compelled to give evidence against oneself (Fifth Amendment).*

Not until 1949 did the Supreme Court consider whether to apply the exclusionary rule to the states. In a case decided that year the Court made it clear that the Fourth Amendment prohibited the police from carrying out unreasonable searches and obtaining improper confessions but held that it was not necessary to use the exclusionary rule to enforce those prohibitions. It noted that other nations did not require that evidence improperly gathered had to be excluded from a criminal trial. The Court said that the local police should not improperly gather

---

*We shall consider here only two constitutional limits— those bearing on searches and confessions. Thus we will omit many other important constitutional provisions affecting criminal cases, such as rules governing wiretapping, prisoner rights, the right to bail and to a jury trial, the bar on ex post facto laws, the right to be represented by a lawyer in court, the ban on "cruel and unusual" punishment, and the rule against double jeopardy.

and use evidence, but if they did, the remedy was to sue the police department or punish the officer.[65]

But in 1961 the Supreme Court changed its mind about the use of the exclusionary rule. It all began when the Cleveland police broke into the home of Dollree Mapp in search of drugs and, finding none, arrested her for possessing some obscene pictures that they found there. The Court held that this was an unreasonable search and seizure because the police had not obtained a search warrant, though they had had ample time to do so. Furthermore, such illegally gathered evidence could not be used in the trial of Mapp.[66] Beginning with this case—*Mapp v. Ohio*—the Supreme Court required the use of the exclusionary rule as a way of enforcing a variety of constitutional guarantees.

Search and Seizure

After the Court decided to exclude improperly gathered evidence, the next problem was to decide what evidence was improper. What happened to Dollree Mapp was an easy case: hardly anybody argued that it was reasonable for the police to break into someone's home without a warrant, ransack their belongings, and take whatever they could find that might be incriminating. But that left a lot of hard choices still to be made.

When can the police search you without its being unreasonable? Under two circumstances—when they have a search warrant and when they have lawfully arrested you. A **search warrant** is an order from a judge authorizing the search of a place; the order must describe what is to be searched and seized, and the judge can issue it only if he or she is persuaded by the police that good reason **(probable cause)** exists to believe that a crime has been committed and that the evidence bearing on that crime will be found at a certain location. (The police can also search a building if the occupant gives them permission.)

In addition, you can be searched if the search occurs when you are being lawfully arrested. When can you be arrested? You can be arrested if a judge has issued an arrest warrant for you, if you commit a crime in the presence of a police officer, or if the officer has probable cause to believe that you have committed a serious crime (usually a felony). If you are arrested and no search warrant has been issued, the police, and not a judge, decide what they can search. What rules should they follow?

In trying to answer that question, the courts have elaborated a set of rules that are complex, subject to

What Would You Do?

Congress Debates the Exclusionary Rule

October 15
WASHINGTON

Congress takes up tomorrow a proposed constitutional amendment that would ban the exclusionary rule from trials. The Supreme Court has required courts to exclude improperly gathered evidence from criminal cases . . .

MEMORANDUM

To: Senator Edward Cortez
From: Mary Briscoe, legislative assistant

Federal courts have been required to exclude improperly gathered evidence since 1886 and state courts since 1961. The rule is an effort to prevent unconstitutional searches and seizures. The constitutional amendment would ban the rule and create instead a procedure for punishing police officers who violate the Constitution.

Arguments for:

1. The rule makes it easy for defense attorneys to attack police evidence by having the judge declare it inadmissible. As a result a guilty person may go free because a police officer made a mistake.
2. The rule does not punish a police officer who violates the Constitution. Instead it benefits only accused persons.
3. No other democratic country uses the exclusionary rule.

Arguments against:

1. The rule protects the privacy of every individual by discouraging illegal searches.
2. There is no easy way to punish police officers who gather illegal evidence except by preventing them from using it in court.
3. There is no strong evidence that guilty people go free because of the rule.

Your decision:
Favor amendment _____
Oppose amendment _____

How the Court Decided

The United States Supreme Court answered the questions on page 513 in the following ways:

Case 1:   The drive-in movie won. The Supreme Court, 6–3, decided that the First Amendment protects the right to show nudity; it is up to the unwilling viewer on the public streets to avert his or her eyes.   *Erznoznik v. Jacksonville,*
422 U.S. 205 (1975)

Case 2:   The military won. The Supreme Court, 6–2, decided that military reservations are not like public streets or parks, and thus civilians can be excluded from them, especially if such exclusion prevents the military from appearing to be the handmaiden of various political causes.
Greer v. Spock,
424 U.S. 828 (1976)

Case 3:   The realty firm won. The Supreme Court, 8–0, decided that the First Amendment prohibits the banning of signs, even of a commercial nature, without a strong, legitimate state interest. Banning the signs would not obviously reduce "white flight," and the government has no right to withhold information from citizens for fear that they will act unwisely.
Linmark Associates, Inc. v. Willingboro,
431 U.S. 85 (1977)

Case 4:   The television station won. The Court, 8–1, decided that the First Amendment protects the right to broadcast the names of rape victims obtained from public (that is, court) records.
Cox Broadcasting Corp. v. Cohn,
420 U.S. 469 (1975)

Case 5:   The newspaper won. The Supreme Court decided unanimously that the First Amendment prohibits the state from intruding into the function of editors.
Miami Herald Publishing Co. v. Tornillo,
418 U.S. 241 (1974)

Case 6:   Zacchini, the human cannonball, won. The Supreme Court, 5–4, decided that broadcasting the entire act without the performer's consent jeopardized his means of livelihood, even though the First Amendment would guarantee the right of the station to broadcast newsworthy facts about the act.
Zacchini v. Scripps-Howard Broadcasting Co.,
433 U.S. 562 (1977)

---

frequent change, and quite controversial. In general the police, after arresting you, can search:

- You
- Things in plain view
- Things or places under your immediate control

As a practical matter, things "in plain view" or "under your immediate control" mean the room in which you are arrested but not other rooms of the house.[67] If the police want to search the rest of your house or a car parked in your driveway, they will first have to go to a judge to obtain a search warrant. But if the police arrest a college student on campus for drinking under age and then accompany that student back to his or her dormitory room so that the student can get proof that he or she was old enough to drink, the police can seize drugs that are in plain view in that room.[68] And if marijuana is growing in

plain view in an open field, the police can enter and search that field even though it is fenced off with a locked gate and a "No Trespassing" sign.[69]

But what if you are arrested while driving your car—how much of it can the police search? The answer to that question has changed almost yearly. In 1979 the Court ruled that the police could not search a suitcase taken from a car of an arrested person, and in 1981 it extended this protection to any "closed, opaque container" found in the car.[70] But the following year the Court decided that all parts of a car, closed or open, could be searched if the officers had probable cause to believe that they contained contraband (that is, goods illegally possessed). And recently the rules governing car searches have been relaxed even further. Officers who have probable cause to search a car can also search the things passengers are carrying in the car. And if the car is stopped to give the driver a traffic ticket, the car can be searched if the officer develops a "reasonable, articulable suspicion" that the car is involved in other illegal activity.[71]

In this confusing area of the law the Court is attempting to protect those places in which a person has a "reasonable expectation of privacy." Your body is one such place, and so the Court has held that the police cannot compel you to undergo surgery to remove a bullet that might be evidence of your guilt or innocence in a crime.[72] But the police can require you to take a Breathalyzer test to see whether you have been drinking while driving.[73] Your home is another place where you have an expectation of privacy, but a barn next to your home is not, nor is your backyard viewed from an airplane, nor is your home if it is a motor home that can be driven away, and so the police need not have a warrant to look into these places.[74]

If you work for the government, you have an expectation that your desk and files will be private; nonetheless, your supervisor may search the desk and files without a warrant, provided that he or she is looking for something related to your work.[75] But bear in mind that the Constitution protects you only against *the government*; a private employer has a great deal of freedom to search your desk and files.

Some people had hoped that the Court would develop a general right of privacy so that nothing done in your home among consenting adults would be subject to government regulation. Support for this hope was given by the Court's decisions forbidding states from prohibiting the sale of contraceptives. But when the Court was asked to pass on the constitutionality of a Georgia statute that made it illegal to engage in homosexual activities, it held, by a narrow five-to-four vote, that the right to privacy does not extend to such activities, and so the Georgia statute may stand.[76]

Confessions and Self-Incrimination

The constitutional ban on being forced to give evidence against oneself was originally intended to prevent the use of torture or "third-degree" police tactics to extract confessions. But it has since been extended to cover many kinds of statements uttered not out of fear of torture but from lack of awareness of one's rights, especially the right to remain silent, whether in the courtroom or in the police station.

For many decades the Supreme Court had held that involuntary confessions could not be used in federal criminal trials but had not ruled that they were barred from state trials. But in the early 1960s

it changed its mind in two landmark cases— *Escobedo* and *Miranda*.[77] The story of the latter and of the controversy that it provoked is worth telling.

Ernesto A. Miranda was convicted in Arizona of the rape and kidnapping of a young woman. The conviction was based on a written confession that Miranda signed after two hours of police questioning. (The victim also identified him.) Two years earlier the Court had decided that the rule against self-incrimination applied to state courts.[78] Now the question arose of what constitutes an "involuntary" confession. The Court decided that a confession should be presumed involuntary unless the person in custody had been fully and clearly informed of his or her right to be silent, to have an attorney present during any questioning, and to have an attorney provided free of charge if he or she could not afford one. The accused may waive these rights and offer to talk, but the waiver must be truly voluntary. Since Miranda did not have a lawyer present when he was questioned and had not knowingly waived his right to a lawyer, the confession was excluded from evidence in the trial and his conviction was overturned.[79]

Miranda was tried and convicted again, this time on the basis of evidence supplied by his girlfriend, who testified that he had admitted to her that he was guilty. Nine years later he was released from prison; four years after that he was killed in a barroom fight. When the Phoenix police arrested the prime suspect in Ernesto Miranda's murder, they read him his rights from a "Miranda card."

Everyone who watches cops-and-robbers shows on television probably knows the "Miranda warning" by heart (see the box on page 518). The police now read it routinely to people whom they arrest. It is not clear whether it has much impact on who does or does not confess or what effect, if any, it may have on the crime rate.

In time the Miranda rule was extended to mean that you have a right to a lawyer when you appear in a police lineup[80] and when you are questioned by a psychiatrist to determine whether you are competent to stand trial.[81] The Court threw out the conviction of a man who had killed a child, because the accused, without being given the right to have a lawyer present, had led the police to the victim's body.[82] You do not have a right to a Miranda warning, however, if while in jail you confess a crime to another inmate who turns out to be an undercover police officer.[83]

A recent case may change the meaning of the Miranda rule. The U.S. Court of Appeals for the

The Miranda Rule

The Supreme Court has interpreted the due-process clause to require that local police departments issue warnings of the sort shown below to people whom they are arresting.

PHILADELPHIA POLICE DEPARTMENT

STANDARD POLICE INTERROGATION CARD

WARNINGS TO BE GIVEN ACCUSED

We are questioning you concerning the crime of (state specific crime).

> We have a duty to explain to you and to warn you that you have the following legal rights:

A. You have a right to remain silent and do not have to say anything at all.

B. Anything you say can and will be used against you in Court.

C. You have a right to talk to a lawyer of your own choice before we ask you any questions, and also to have a lawyer here with you while we ask questions.

D. If you cannot afford to hire a lawyer, and you want one, we will see that you have one provided to you free of charge before we ask you any questions.

E. If you are willing to give us a statement, you have a right to stop any time you wish.

75-Misc.-3   (Over)

(6-24-70)

Ernesto A. Miranda was convicted in Arizona of rape and kidnapping. When the Supreme Court overturned the conviction, it issued a set of rules—the "Miranda rules"—governing how police must conduct an arrest and interrogation.

Fourth Circuit (a court that covers Atlantic coast states between Maryland and South Carolina) ruled that the Miranda warning is only one of several ways by which the right not to incriminate oneself might be protected. Congress, the court said, had passed a law that did not require a Miranda warning if the confession was made voluntarily.[84] But the Supreme Court disagreed, deciding that the Miranda rule was required by the Constitution and Congress could not alter it.[85]

Relaxing the Exclusionary Rule

Cases such as *Miranda* were highly controversial and led to efforts in Congress to modify or overrule the decisions by statute—without much coming of the attempts. But as the rules governing police conduct became increasingly more complex, pressure mounted to find an alternative. Some thought that any evidence should be admissible, with the question of police conduct left to lawsuits or other ways of punishing official misbehavior. Others felt that the exclusionary rule served a useful purpose but had simply become too technical to be an effective deterrent to police misconduct (the police cannot obey rules that they cannot understand). And still others felt that the exclusionary rule was a vital safeguard to essential liberties and should be kept intact. The Court has refused to let Congress abolish Miranda because it is a Constitutional rule.*

The courts themselves began to adopt the second position, deciding a number of cases in ways that retained the exclusionary rule but modified it by limiting its coverage (police were given greater freedom to question juveniles)[86] and by incorporating what was called a **good-faith exception.** For example, if the police obtain a search warrant that they believe is valid, the evidence that they gather will not be excluded if it later turns out that the warrant was defective for some reason (such as the judge's having used the wrong form).[87] And the Court decided that "overriding considerations of public safety" may justify questioning a person without first reading the person his or her rights.[88] Moreover, the Court changed its mind about the killer who led the police to the place where he had disposed of his victim's body. After the man was convicted a second time and again appealed, the Court in 1984 held that the body would have been discovered anyway; thus evidence will not be excluded if it can be shown that it would "inevitably" have been found.[89]

Dickerson v. United States, 120 S. Ct. 2326 (2000).

Terrorism and Civil Liberties

The attacks of September 11, 2001, raised important questions about how far the government can go in investigating and prosecuting individuals.

A little over one month after the attacks, Congress passed a new law, the USA Patriot Act, designed to increase federal powers to investigate terrorists.* Its main provisions are these:

- Telephone taps. The government may tap, if it has a court order, any telephone a suspect uses instead of having to get a separate order for each telephone.
- Internet taps. The government may tap, if it has a court order, Internet communications.
- Voice mail. The government, with a court order, may seize voice mail.
- Grand jury information. Investigators can now share with other government officials things learned in secret grand jury hearings.
- Immigration. The attorney general may hold any noncitizen who is thought to be a national security risk for up to seven days. If the alien cannot be charged with a crime or deported within that time, he or she may still be detained if he or she is certified to be a security risk.
- Money laundering. The government gets new powers to track the movement of money across U.S. borders and among banks.
- Crime. This provision eliminates the statute of limitation on terrorist crimes and increases the penalties.

About a month later, President Bush, by executive order, proclaimed a national emergency under which any noncitizen who is believed to be a terrorist or has harbored a terrorist will be tried by a military, rather than a civilian, court.

A military trial is carried on before a commission of military officers and not a civilian jury. The tribunal can operate in secret if classified information is used in evidence. Two-thirds of the commission must agree before the suspect can be convicted and sentenced. If convicted, the suspect can appeal to

*The name of the law is an acronym derived from the official title of the bill, drawn from the first letters of the following capitalized words: Uniting and Strengthening America by Providing Appropriate Tools Required to Intercept and Obstruct Terrorism (USA PATRIOT).

Osama bin Laden.

the secretary of defense and the president, but not to a civilian court.

These commissions may eventually be used to try some of the men captured by the U.S. military during its campaign in Afghanistan against the Taliban regime and the al Queda terrorist network that was created by Osama bin Laden. These detainees were held in a prison at our Guantanamo naval base in Cuba and are not regarded by the Defense Department as ordinary prisoners of war.

In addition to the USA Patriot Act and the presidential order about military tribunals, key federal agencies have intensified their investigations. The Justice Department has detained many immigrants, authorized federal investigators to listen in on conversations between some federal prisoners and their lawyers, promised to help in obtaining citizenship for immigrants who help the nation identify terrorists, and (with the State Department) intensified scrutiny of applications for visas filed by people from certain countries.

Many of these measures have been criticized by civil liberties organizations and may be challenged in court. To meet some of these arguments, Congress provided that certain provisions of the Patriot Act, such as seizing voice mail in pursuance of a court order, would automatically expire in 2005.

No one yet knows what may result from a court challenge, but typically the Supreme Court has granted exceptional powers to the federal government during wartime. For example, a military tribunal was used to try several Nazi spies who were smuggled into New York during the Second World War. When the procedure was challenged, the Supreme Court unanimously upheld the use of the tribunal, saying that these men, who, without wearing uniforms, came secretly into the country during a war for the purpose of committing hostile acts, were neither citizens nor prisoners of war but "unlawful combatants." [90]

Summary

Civil liberties questions are in some ways like and in some ways unlike ordinary policy debates. Like most issues, civil liberties problems often involve competing interests—in this case conflicting rights or conflicting rights and duties—and so we have groups mobilized on both sides of issues involving free speech and crime control. Like some other issues, civil liberties problems can also arise from the successful appeals of a policy entrepreneur, and so we have periodic reductions in liberty resulting from popular fears, usually aroused during or just after a war.

But civil liberties are unlike many other issues in at least one regard: more than struggles over welfare spending or defense or economic policy, debates about civil liberties reach down into our fundamental political beliefs and political culture, challenging us to define what we mean by religion, Americanism, and decency.

The most important of these challenges focuses on the meaning of the First Amendment: What is "speech"? How much of it should be free? How far can the state go in aiding religion? How do we strike a balance between national security and personal expression? The zigzag course followed by the courts in judging these matters has, on balance, tended to enlarge freedom of expression.

Almost as important has been the struggle to strike a balance between the right of society to protect itself from criminals and the right of people (including criminals) to be free from unreasonable searches and coerced confessions. As with free speech cases, the courts have generally broadened the rights at some expense to the power of the police. But in recent years the Supreme Court has pulled back from some of its more sweeping applications of the exclusionary rule.

The resolution of these issues by the courts is political in the sense that differing opinions about what is right or desirable compete, with one side or another prevailing (often by a small majority). In this competition of ideas federal judges, though not elected, are often sensitive to strong currents of popular opinion.

When entrepreneurial politics has produced new action against apparently threatening minorities, judges are inclined, at least for a while, to give serious consideration to popular fears and legislative majorities. And when no strong national mood is discernible, the opinions of elites influence judicial thinking (as described in Chapter 14).

At the same time, courts resolve political conflicts in a manner that differs in important respects from the resolution of conflicts by legislatures or executives. First, the very existence of the courts, and the relative ease with which one may enter them to advance a claim, facilitates challenges to accepted values. An unpopular political or religious group may have little or no access to a legislature, but it will have substantial access to the courts. Second, judges often settle controversies about rights not simply by deciding the case at hand but by formulating a general rule to cover like cases elsewhere. This has an advantage (the law tends to become more consistent and better known) but a disadvantage as well: a rule suitable for one case may be unworkable in another. Judges reason by analogy and sometimes assume that two cases are similar when in fact there are important differences. A definition of "obscenity" or of "fighting words" may suit one situation but be inadequate in another. Third, judges interpret the Constitution, whereas legislatures often consult popular preferences or personal convictions. However much their own beliefs influence what judges read into the Constitution, almost all of them are constrained by its language.

Taken together, the desire to find and announce rules, the language of the Constitution, and the personal beliefs of judges have led to a general expansion of civil liberties. As a result, even allowing for temporary reversals and frequent redefinitions, any value that is thought to hinder freedom of expression and the rights of the accused has generally lost ground to the claims of the First, Fourth, Fifth, and Sixth Amendments.

Reconsidering the Enduring Questions

1. *Should it be all right for religious symbols to be displayed on government property?*

   The Supreme Court says the answer is "no," but with some exceptions. We can print "In God We Trust" on our dollar bills and allow Congress to open its sessions with prayers. We can say the pledge of allegiance with the phrase "under God" in the language. But what we can't do is put up a nativity scene on the steps of a school or courthouse at Christmas time (unless, perhaps, we also put up scenes that represent Jewish and Muslim holidays). And we can't require public school students to pray in class. The public is deeply divided about this matter, with some saying that religion should play no role in governmental institutions and others saying that the country was founded and inhabited by people who believe in God.

2. *If a person confesses that he committed a crime, is there any reason why the confession should not be used in court?*

   If the confession was obtained lawfully, obviously it can be used in court. But what if it is obtained unlawfully? In most democratic countries, including England, a confession obtained even when the police misbehave can be used in court, with the police then punished separately. In the United States that confession cannot be used. People who support this view can say that it is hard to punish the police except by excluding their evidence and it is wrong to use a tainted confession to convict anyone. People who oppose our practice say that if a confession is true it is wrong to the victim and to society to exclude it.

3. *How much can the government do to fight terrorism?*

   We shall find out. After September 11, Congress passed tougher antiterrorism laws, but they have not yet been tested in court. If past practice is any guide, the Supreme Court will generally allow the government to have greater investigative powers during a time of national crisis.

World Wide Web Resources

- Court cases: www.law.cornell.edu
- Civil Rights Division of the Department of Justice: www.usdoj.gov
- American Civil Liberties Union: www.aclu.org

Key Terms

McCarthyism *p. 500*
freedom of expression *p. 503*
freedom of religion *p. 503*
prior restraint *p. 503*
clear-and-present-danger test
   p. 503

due-process clause *p. 504*
libel *p. 505*
symbolic speech *p. 508*
free-exercise clause *p. 510*
establishment clause *p. 510*
wall-of-separation principle *p. 511*

exclusionary rule *p. 514*
search warrant *p. 514*
probable cause *p. 514*
good-faith exception *p. 518*

Suggested Readings

Abraham, Henry J., and Barbara A. Perry, *Freedom and the Court.* 7th ed. New York: Oxford University Press, 1998. Analysis of leading Supreme Court cases on civil liberties and civil rights.

Amar, Akhil Reed. *The Constitution and Criminal Procedure: First Principles.* New Haven, Conn.: Yale University Press, 1997. A brilliant critique of how the Supreme Court has interpreted those parts of the Constitution bearing on search warrants, the exclusionary rule, and self-incrimination.

Berns, Walter. *The First Amendment and the Future of American Democracy.* New York: Basic Books, 1976. A look at what the Founders intended by the First Amendment that takes issue with contemporary Supreme Court interpretations of it.

Clor, Harry M. *Obscenity and Public Morality.* Chicago: University of Chicago Press, 1969. Argues for the legitimacy of legal restrictions on obscenity.

Levy, Leonard W. *Legacy of Suppression: Freedom of Speech and Press in Early American History.* Rev. ed. New York: Oxford University Press, 1985. Careful study of what the Founders and the early leaders meant by freedom of speech and press.

Civil Rights

Enduring Questions

1. Should numerical goals ever be used to ensure that students and workers are drawn from every racial group?

2. To what extent should the government be able to limit the opportunity to have an abortion?

In 1830 Congress passed a law requiring all Indians east of the Mississippi River to move to the Indian Territory west of the river, and the army set about implementing it. In the 1850s a major political fight broke out in Boston over whether the police department should be obliged to hire an Irish officer. Until 1920 women could not vote in most elections. In the 1930s the Cornell University Medical School had a strict quota limiting the number of Jewish students who could enroll. In the 1940s the army, at the direction of President Franklin D. Roosevelt, removed all Japanese Americans from their homes in California and placed them in relocation centers far from the coast.

In all such cases some group, usually defined along racial or ethnic lines, was denied access to facilities, opportunities, or services that were available to other groups. Such cases raise the issue of **civil rights.** The pertinent question regarding civil rights is not whether the government has the authority to treat different people differently; it is whether such differences in treatment are reasonable. All laws and policies make distinctions among

523

people—for example, the tax laws require higher-income people to pay taxes at a higher rate than lower-income ones—but not all such distinctions are defensible. The courts have long held that classifying people on the basis of their income and taxing them at different rates is quite permissible because such classifications are not arbitrary or unreasonable and are related to a legitimate public need (that is, raising revenue). Increasingly, however, the courts have said that classifying people on the basis of their race or ethnicity is unreasonable. These are **suspect classifications,** and while not every law making such classifications has been ruled unconstitutional, they have all become subject to especially strict scrutiny.[1]

Given the theory of policy-making described so far in this book, it may seem surprising that specific groups, particularly those that constitute only a small minority of the population, should require any special protection at all. We have seen how easy it is

for many small groups—businesses, occupations, unions—to practice client politics. They can obtain some special advantage (a grant, a license, a subsidy) or avoid some threatened regulation because, being small, they find it easy to organize and to escape general public notice. Yet Native Americans, African Americans, Japanese Americans, and Mexican Americans are also relatively small groups whose demands seemingly place little burden on the majority population. Despite this, they have been more often the victims than the clients of the policy-making process.

To explain the victimization of certain groups and the methods by which they have begun to overcome it, we shall consider chiefly the case of African Americans. Black-white relations have in large measure defined the problem of civil rights in this country; most of the landmark laws and court decisions have involved black claims. The strategies employed by or on behalf of African Americans have typically set the pattern for the strategies employed by other groups. At the end of this chapter we shall look at the related but somewhat different issues of women's rights and gay rights.

The Black Predicament

Though constituting more than 12 percent of the population, African Americans until fairly recently could not in many parts of the country vote, attend integrated schools, ride in the front seats of buses, or buy homes in white neighborhoods.

One reason is that the perceived costs of granting these rights to blacks were not widely distributed among the public at large but instead fell on some relatively small and readily organized group. Although today white citizens generally do not feel threatened when a black family moves into Cicero, Illinois, a black child goes to school at Little Rock Central High School, or a black group organizes voters in Neshoba County, Mississippi, at one time most whites in Cicero, Little Rock, and Neshoba County felt deeply threatened by these things (and some whites still do). In the language of this book, civil rights in these places was not a matter of client politics but of competitive or interest group politics. This was especially the case in those parts of the country, notably the Deep South, where blacks were often in the majority. There the politically dominant white

A segregated bus station in Durham, North Carolina, in 1940.

minority felt keenly the potential competition for jobs, land, public services, and living space posed by large numbers of people of another race. But even in the North, black gains often appeared to be at the expense of lower-income whites who lived or worked near them, not at the expense of upper-status whites who lived in suburbs.

The interest group component of racial politics put African Americans at a decided disadvantage: they were not allowed to vote at all in many areas; they could vote only with great difficulty in others; and even in those places where voting was easy, they often lacked the material and institutional support for effective political organization. If your opponent feels deeply threatened by your demands and in addition can deny you access to the political system that will decide the fate of those demands, you are, to put it mildly, at a disadvantage. Yet from the end of Reconstruction to the 1960s—for nearly a century— many blacks in the South found themselves in just such a position.

A second reason why the restrictions on African Americans continued for so long is that majoritarian politics worked to the disadvantage of blacks. Because of white attitudes, this was the case even when white and black interests were not directly in competition. To the dismay of those who prefer to explain political action in terms of economic motives, people often attach greater importance to the intangible costs and benefits of policies than to the tangible ones. Thus, even though the average black represented no threat to the average white, antiblack attitudes—racism—produced some appalling actions. Between 1882 and 1946, 4,715 people, about three-fourths of them African Americans, were lynched in the United States.[2] Some lynchings were carried out by small groups of vigilantes acting with much ceremony, but others were the actions of frenzied mobs. In the summer of 1911 a black man charged with murdering a white man in Livermore, Kentucky, was dragged by a mob to the local theater, where he was hanged. The audience, which had been charged admission, was invited to shoot the swaying body (those in the orchestra seats could empty their revolvers; those in the balcony were limited to a single shot).[3]

Though the public in other parts of the country was shocked by such events, little was done: lynching was a local, not a federal, crime. It obviously would not require many lynchings to convince

★ **POLITICALLY SPEAKING** ★

Jim Crow

Thomas D. ("Daddy") Rice, a white entertainer, began around 1828 to stage a vaudeville sketch in which he blacked his face with burned cork and sang a ditty that acquired the title "Wheel About and Turn About and Jump, Jim Crow." Thus was born what later became the immensely popular minstrel shows, a burlesque by whites of black songs and speech mannerisms. The term **Jim Crow**, from Rice's song, soon came to be a slang expression for blacks and was later applied to laws and practices that segregated blacks from whites.

African Americans in these localities that it would be foolhardy to try to vote or enroll in a white school. And even in those states where blacks did vote, popular attitudes were not conducive to blacks' buying homes or taking jobs on an equal basis with whites. Even among those professing to support equal rights, a substantial portion opposed African Americans' efforts to obtain them and federal action to secure them. In 1942 a national poll showed that only 30 percent of whites thought that black and white children should attend the same schools; in 1956 the proportion had risen, but only to 49 percent, still less than a majority. (In the South white support for school integration was even lower—14 percent favored it in 1956, about 31 percent in 1963.) As late as 1956 a majority of southern whites were opposed to integrated public transportation facilities. Even among whites who generally favored integration, there was in 1963 (*before* the ghetto riots) considerable opposition to the black civil rights movement: nearly half of the whites who were classified in a survey as moderate integrationists thought that demonstrations hurt the black cause; nearly two-thirds disapproved of actions taken by the civil rights movement; and over a third felt that civil rights should be left to the states.[4]

In short the political position in which African Americans found themselves until the 1960s made it difficult for them to advance their interests through a feasible legislative strategy; their opponents were aroused, organized, and powerful. Thus if black interests were to be championed in Congress or state legislatures, blacks would have to have white allies. Though some such allies could be found, they were too few to make a difference in a political system that gives a substantial advantage to strongly motivated opponents of any new policy. For that to change, one or both of two things would have to happen: additional allies would have to be recruited (a delicate problem, given that many white integrationists disapproved of aspects of the civil rights movement), or the struggle would have to be shifted to a policy-making arena in which the opposition enjoyed less of an advantage.

Partly by plan, partly by accident, black leaders followed both of these strategies simultaneously. By publicizing their grievances and organizing a civil rights movement that (at least in its early stages) concentrated on dramatizing the denial to blacks of essential and widely accepted liberties, African Americans were able to broaden their base of support both among political elites and among the general public and thereby to raise civil rights matters from a low to a high position on the political agenda. By waging a patient, prolonged, but carefully planned legal struggle, black leaders shifted decision-making power on key civil rights issues from Congress, where they had been stymied for generations, to the federal courts.

After this strategy had achieved some substantial successes—after blacks had become enfranchised and legal barriers to equal participation in political and economic affairs had been lowered—the politics of civil rights became more conventional. African Americans were able to assert their demands directly in the legislative and executive branches of government with reasonable (though scarcely certain) prospects of success. Civil rights became less a matter of gaining entry into the political system and more one of waging interest group politics within that system. At the same time, the goals of civil

rights politics were broadened. The struggle to gain entry into the system had focused on the denial of fundamental rights (to vote, to organize, to obtain equal access to schools and public facilities); later the dominant issues were manpower development, economic progress, and the improvement of housing and neighborhoods.

The Campaign in the Courts

The Fourteenth Amendment was both an opportunity and a problem for black activists. Adopted in 1868, it seemed to guarantee equal rights for all: "No state shall make or enforce any law which shall abridge the privileges or immunities of citizens of the United States; nor shall any state deprive any person of life, liberty, or property, without due process of law; nor deny to any person within its jurisdiction the equal protection of the laws."

The key phrase was "equal protection of the laws." Read broadly, it might mean that the Constitution should be regarded as color-blind: no state law could have the effect of treating whites and blacks differently. Thus a law segregating blacks and whites into separate schools or neighborhoods would be unconstitutional. Read narrowly, "equal protection" might mean only that blacks and whites had certain fundamental legal rights in common, among them the right to sign contracts, to serve on juries, or to buy and sell property, but otherwise they could be treated differently.

Historians have long debated which view Congress held when it proposed the Fourteenth Amendment. What forms of racial segregation, if any, were still permissible? Segregated trains? Hotels? Schools? Neighborhoods?

The Supreme Court took the narrow view. Though in 1880 it declared unconstitutional a West Virginia law requiring juries to be composed only of white males,[5] it decided in 1883 that it was unconstitutional for Congress to prohibit racial discrimination in public accommodations such as hotels.[6] The difference between the two cases seemed, in the eyes of the Court, to be this: serving on a jury was an essential right of citizenship that the state could not deny to any person on racial grounds without violating the Fourteenth Amendment, but registering at a hotel was a convenience controlled by a private person (the hotel owner), who could treat blacks and whites differently if he or she wished.

The major decision that was to determine the legal status of the Fourteenth Amendment for over half a century was *Plessy v. Ferguson.* Louisiana had passed a law requiring blacks and whites to occupy separate cars on railroad trains operating in that state. When Adolph Plessy, who was seven-eighths white and one-eighth black, refused to obey the law, he was arrested. He appealed his conviction to the Supreme Court, claiming that the law violated the Fourteenth Amendment. In 1896 the Court rejected his claim, holding that the law treated both races equally even though it required them to be separate. The equal-protection clause guaranteed political and legal but not social equality. "Separate-but-equal" facilities were constitutional because if "one race be inferior to the other socially, the Constitution of the United States cannot put them on the same plane."[7]

"Separate but Equal"

Thus began the **separate-but-equal doctrine.** Three years later the Court applied it to schools as well, declaring in *Cumming v. Richmond County Board of Education* that a decision in a Georgia community to close the black high school while keeping open the white high school was not a violation of the Fourteenth Amendment because blacks could always go to private schools. Here the Court seemed to be saying that not only could schools be separate, they could even be unequal.[8]

What the Court has made, the Court can unmake. But to get it to change its mind requires a long, costly, and uncertain legal battle. The National Association for the Advancement of Colored People (NAACP) was the main organization that waged that battle. Formed in 1909 by a group of whites and blacks in the aftermath of a race riot, the NAACP did many things—lobbying in Washington and publicizing black grievances, especially in the pages of *The Crisis,* a magazine edited by W.E.B. Du Bois—but its most influential role was played in the courtroom.

It was a rational strategy. Fighting legal battles does not require forming broad political alliances or changing public opinion, tasks that would have been very difficult for a small and unpopular organization. A court-based approach also enabled the organization to remain nonpartisan.

The cover of the first issue of The Crisis, *the magazine started by the NAACP in 1910 to raise African American consciousness and publicize racist acts.*

But it was a slow and difficult strategy. The Court had adopted a narrow interpretation of the Fourteenth Amendment. To get the Court to change its mind would require the NAACP to bring before it cases involving the strongest possible claims that a black had been unfairly treated—and under circumstances sufficiently different from those of earlier cases that the Court could find some grounds for changing its mind.

The steps in that strategy were these: First, persuade the Court to declare unconstitutional laws creating schools that were separate but obviously unequal. Second, persuade it to declare unconstitutional laws supporting schools that were separate but unequal in not-so-obvious ways. Third, persuade it to rule that racially separate schools were inherently unequal and hence unconstitutional.

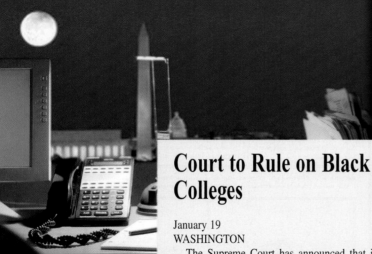

Court to Rule on Black Colleges

January 19
WASHINGTON

The Supreme Court has announced that it will decide whether all-black colleges in the South can receive state support if there are too few whites attending them. The case began in Mississippi, where . . .

MEMORANDUM

To: Justice Murray
From: Ella Fitzgerald, law clerk

Until school segregation ended, southern blacks could attend only all-black colleges. Now they are free to apply to previously all-white colleges, and these schools are integrated. But the traditional black colleges still exist, and very few whites apply to them. In 1992 the Supreme Court held that the state could not solve the problem by requiring a race-neutral admissions policy.* Now the Court must decide whether a predominantly black college can receive state support.

Arguments for all-black colleges:

1. These schools have a long tradition that ought to be preserved.
2. Many black students will learn better in an all-black environment.
3. African American organizations, in particular the United Negro College Fund, raise money for these schools.

Arguments against all-black colleges:

1. If the state once required single-race schools, it now has an obligation to dismantle them.
2. Race is a suspect classification, and no state program that chiefly serves one race can be allowed.

Your decision:
Allow all-black colleges _____
Ban all-black colleges _____

*United States v. Fordice, 505 U.S. 717 (1992).

Can Separate Schools Be Equal?

The first step was accomplished in a series of court cases stretching from 1938 to 1948. In 1938 the Court held that Lloyd Gaines had to be admitted to an all-white law school in Missouri because no black law school of equal quality existed in that state.[9] In 1948 the Court ordered the all-white University of Oklahoma Law School to admit Ada Lois Sipuel, a black, even though the state planned to build a black law school later. For education to be equal, it had to be equally available.[10] It still could be separate, however: the university admitted Ms. Sipuel but required her to attend classes in a section of the state capitol, roped off from other students, where she could meet with her law professors.

The second step was taken in two cases decided in 1950. Heman Sweatt, an African American, was treated by the University of Texas Law School much as Ada Sipuel had been treated in Oklahoma: "admitted" to the all-white school but relegated to a separate building. Another African American, George McLaurin, was allowed to study for his Ph.D. in a "colored section" of the all-white University of Oklahoma. The Supreme Court unanimously decided that these arrangements were unconstitutional because, by imposing racially based barriers on the black students' access to professors, libraries, and other students, they created unequal educational opportunities.[11]

The third step, the climax of the entire drama, began in Topeka, Kansas, where Linda Brown wanted to enroll in her neighborhood school but could not because she was black and the school was by law reserved exclusively for whites. When the NAACP took her case to the federal district court in Kansas, the judge decided that the black school that Linda could attend was substantially equal in quality to the white school that she could not attend. Thus denying her access to the white school was constitutional. To change that the lawyers would have to persuade the Supreme Court to overrule the district judge on the grounds that racially separate schools were unconstitutional even if they were equal. In other words, the separate-but-equal doctrine would have to be overturned by the Court.

It was a risky and controversial step to take. Many states, Kansas among them, were trying to make their all-black schools equal to those of whites by launching expensive building programs. If the NAACP succeeded in getting separate schools declared unconstitutional, the Court might well put a stop to the building of these new schools. Blacks could win a moral and legal victory but suffer a practical defeat—the loss of these new facilities. Despite these risks, the NAACP decided to go ahead with the appeal.

Brown v. Board of Education

On May 17, 1954, a unanimous Supreme Court, speaking through an opinion written and delivered by Chief Justice Earl Warren, found that "in the field of public education the doctrine of 'separate but equal' has no place" because "separate educational facilities are inherently unequal."[12] *Plessy v. Ferguson* was overruled, and "separate but equal" was dead.

The ruling was a landmark decision, but the reasons for it and the means chosen to implement it were as important and as controversial as the decision itself. There were at least three issues. First, how would the decision be implemented? Second, on what grounds were racially separate schools unconstitutional? Third, what test would a school system have to meet in order to be in conformity with the Constitution?

■ **Implementation** The *Brown* case involved a class-action suit; that is, it applied not only to Linda Brown but to all others similarly situated. This meant that black children everywhere now had the right to attend formerly all-white schools. This change would be one of the most far-reaching and conflict-provoking events in modern American history. It could not be effected overnight or by the stroke of a pen. In 1955 the Supreme Court decided that it would let local federal district courts oversee the end of segregation by giving them the power to approve or disapprove local desegregation plans. This was to be done "with all deliberate speed."[13]

In the South "all deliberate speed" turned out to be a snail's pace. Massive resistance to desegregation broke out in many states. Some communities simply defied the Court; some sought to evade its edict by closing their public schools. In 1956 over one hundred southern members of Congress signed a "Southern Manifesto" that condemned the *Brown* decision as an "abuse of judicial power" and pledged to "use all lawful means to bring about a reversal of the decision."

On September 25, 1957, troops of the 101st Airborne Division escorted nine black children into Little Rock (Arkansas) Central High School to begin its integration.

In the late 1950s and early 1960s the National Guard and regular army paratroopers were used to escort black students into formerly all-white schools and universities. It was not until the 1970s that resistance collapsed and most southern schools were integrated. The use of armed force convinced people that resistance was futile; the disruption of the politics and economy of the South convinced leaders that it was imprudent; and the voting power of blacks convinced politicians that it was suicidal. In addition, federal laws began providing financial aid to integrated schools and withholding it from segregated ones. By 1970 only 14 percent of southern black schoolchildren still attended all-black schools.[14]

■ **The Rationale**   As the struggle to implement the *Brown* decision continued, the importance of the rationale for that decision became apparent. The case was decided in a way that surprised many legal scholars. The Court could have said that the equal-protection clause of the Fourteenth Amendment makes the Constitution, and thus state laws, color-blind. Or it could have said that the authors of the Fourteenth Amendment meant to ban segregated schools. It did neither. Instead it said that segregated education is bad because it "has a detrimental effect upon the colored children" by generating "a feeling of inferiority as to their status in the community" that may "affect their hearts and minds in a way unlikely ever to be undone."[15] This conclusion was supported by a footnote reference to social science studies of the apparent impact of segregation on black children.

Why did the Court rely on social science as much as or more than the Constitution in supporting its decision? Apparently for two reasons. One was the justices' realization that the authors of the Fourteenth Amendment may *not* have intended to outlaw segregated schools. The schools in Washington, D.C., were segregated when the amendment was proposed, and when this fact was mentioned during the debate, it seems to have been made clear that the amendment was not designed to abolish this segregation. When Congress debated a civil rights act a few years later, it voted down provisions that would have ended segregation in schools.[16] The Court could not easily base its decision on a constitutional provision that had, at best, an uncertain application to schools. The other reason grew out of the first. On so important a matter the chief justice wanted to speak for a unanimous court. Some justices did not agree that the Fourteenth

Amendment made the Constitution color-blind. In the interests of harmony the Court found an ambiguous rationale for its decision.

■ Desegregation Versus Integration

That ambiguity led to the third issue. If separate schools were inherently unequal, what would "unseparate" schools look like? Since the Court had not said that race was irrelevant, an "unseparate" school could be either one that blacks and whites were free to attend if they chose or one that blacks and whites in fact attended whether they wanted to or not. The first might be called a desegregated school, the latter an integrated school. Think of the Topeka case. Was it enough that there was now no barrier to Linda Brown's attending the white school in her neighborhood? Or was it necessary that there be black children (if not Linda, then some others) actually going to that school together with white children?

As long as the main impact of the *Brown* decision lay in the South, where laws had prevented blacks from attending white schools, this question did not seem important. Segregation by law (***de jure* segregation**) was now clearly unconstitutional. But in the North laws had not kept blacks and whites apart; instead all-black and all-white schools were the result of residential segregation, preferred living patterns, informal social forces, and administrative practices (such as drawing school district lines so as to produce single-race schools). This was often called segregation in fact (***de facto* segregation**).

In 1968 the Supreme Court settled the matter. In New Kent County, Virginia, the school board had created a "freedom-of-choice" plan under which every pupil would be allowed without legal restriction to attend the school of his or her choice. As it turned out, all the white children chose to remain in the all-white school, and 85 percent of the black children remained in the all-black school. The Court rejected this plan as unconstitutional because it did not produce the "ultimate end," which was a "unitary, nonracial system of education."[17] In the opinion written by Justice William Brennan, the Court seemed to be saying that the Constitution required actual racial mixing in the schools, not just the repeal of laws requiring racial separation.

This impression was confirmed three years later when the Court considered a plan in North Carolina under which pupils in Mecklenburg County (which includes Charlotte) were assigned to the nearest

In 1963 Governor George Wallace of Alabama stood in the doorway of the University of Alabama to block the entry of black students. Facing him is U.S. Deputy Attorney General Nicholas Katzenbach.

neighborhood school without regard to race. As a result about half the black children now attended formerly all-white schools, with the other half attending all-black schools. The federal district court held that this was inadequate and ordered some children to be bused into more distant schools in order to achieve a greater degree of integration. The Supreme Court, now led by Chief Justice Warren Burger, upheld the district judge on the grounds that the court plan was necessary to achieve a "unitary school system."[18]

This case—*Swann v. Charlotte-Mecklenburg Board of Education*—pretty much set the guidelines for all subsequent cases involving school segregation. The essential features of those guidelines are as follows:

- To violate the Constitution, a school system, by law, practice, or regulation, must have engaged in discrimination. Put another way, a plaintiff must show an intent to discriminate on the part of the public schools.
- The existence of all-white or all-black schools in a district with a history of segregation creates a presumption of intent to discriminate.
- The remedy for past discrimination will not be limited to freedom of choice, or what the Court called

Antibusing protesters buried a school bus (unoccupied) to drama-tize their cause.

"the walk-in school." Remedies may include racial quotas in the assignment of teachers and pupils, redrawn district lines, and court-ordered busing.

- Not every school must reflect the social composition of the school system as a whole.

Relying on *Swann*, district courts have supervised redistricting and busing plans in localities all over the nation, often in the face of bitter opposition from the community. In Boston the control of the city schools by a federal judge, W. Arthur Garrity, lasted for more than a decade and involved him in every aspect of school administration.

One major issue not settled by *Swann* was whether busing and other remedies should cut across city and county lines. In some places the central-city schools had become virtually all black. Racial integration could be achieved only by bringing black pupils to white suburban schools or moving white pupils into central-city schools. In a series of split-vote decisions the Court ruled that court-ordered intercity busing could be authorized only if it could be demonstrated that the suburban areas as well as the central city had in fact practiced school segregation. Where that could not be shown, such intercity busing would not be required. The Court was not persuaded that intent had been proved in Atlanta, Detroit, Denver, Indianapolis, and Richmond, but it was persuaded that it had been proved in Louisville and Wilmington.[19]

The importance that the Court attaches to intent means that if a school system that was once integrated becomes all black as a result of whites' moving to the suburbs, the Court will not require that district lines constantly be redrawn or new busing plans adopted to adjust to the changing distribution of the population.[20] This in turn means that as long as blacks and whites live in different neighborhoods for whatever reason, there is a good chance that some schools in both areas will be heavily of one race. If mandatory busing or other integration measures cause whites to move out of a city at a faster rate than they otherwise would (a process often called "white flight"), then efforts to integrate the schools may in time create more single-race schools. Ultimately integrated schools will exist only in integrated neighborhoods or where the quality of education is so high that both blacks and whites want to enroll in the school even at some cost in terms of travel and inconvenience.

Mandatory busing to achieve racial integration has been a deeply controversial program and has generated considerable public opposition. Surveys show that a majority of people oppose it.[21] As recently as 1992 a poll showed that 48 percent of whites in the Northeast and 53 percent of southern whites felt that it was "not the business" of the federal government to ensure "that black and white children go to the same schools."[22] Presidents Nixon, Ford, and Reagan opposed busing; all three supported legislation to prevent or reduce it, and Reagan petitioned the courts to reconsider busing plans. The courts refused to reconsider, and Congress has passed only minor restrictions on busing.

The reason why Congress has not followed public opinion on this matter is complex. It has been torn between the desire to support civil rights and uphold

Chronology of Major Events in the Civil Rights Movement, 1955–1968

Dec. 5, 1955	Blacks in Montgomery, Alabama, begin yearlong boycott of bus company; the Reverend Martin Luther King, Jr., emerges as leader.
Feb. 1, 1960	First sit-in demonstration. Black students at North Carolina Agricultural and Technical College sit in at a dime-store lunch counter in Greensboro.
May 4, 1961	Freedom rides begin as blacks attempt to ride in white sections of interstate buses. Violence erupts, a bus is burned, U.S. marshals are dispatched to restore order.
Sept. 30, 1962	Violence greets effort of James Meredith, a black, to enroll in University of Mississippi.
April 3, 1963	Demonstrations by blacks begin in Birmingham, Alabama; police retaliate.
June 12, 1963	Medgar Evers, Mississippi state chairman of NAACP, murdered in Jackson.
Aug. 28, 1963	March on Washington by 250,000 whites and blacks.
Fall 1963	Blacks boycott schools in several northern cities to protest *de facto* segregation.
June 1964	Three civil rights workers killed in Neshoba County, Mississippi.
Summer 1964	First ghetto riots by blacks in northern cities, beginning in Harlem on July 18.
Jan. 2, 1965	King begins protest marches in Selma, Alabama; police attack marchers in February and March.
Aug. 11, 1965	Black riots in Watts section of Los Angeles and on West Side of Chicago.
June 6, 1966	James Meredith shot (but not killed) while on protest march in Mississippi.
Summer 1966	Black ghetto riots in Chicago, Cleveland, New York, and other cities; King leads protest marches in Chicago.
Summer 1967	Riots or violent demonstrations in 67 cities.
April 4, 1968	Martin Luther King, Jr., murdered in Memphis, Tennessee.

the courts and the desire to represent the views of its constituents. Because it faces a dilemma, Congress has taken both sides of the issue simultaneously.

During the 1970s the House of Representatives passed bills restricting busing, but the Senate amended them to allow busing ordered by a court. The result was no policy at all. In 1981 the Senate approved a bill forbidding federal judges from ordering busing except in very narrow circumstances, but it never became law. Although a House version of these bills was adopted in 1982, it, too, never became law. Throughout the 1980s Congress did enact laws forbidding the use of federal funds to bus schoolchildren for purposes of racial integration;

these laws had little effect, however, since a judge could still order states and cities to pay the costs. By the late 1980s busing was a dying issue in Congress, in part because no meaningful legislation seemed possible and in part because popular passion over busing had somewhat abated.

Then, in 1992, the Supreme Court made it easier for local school systems to reclaim control over their schools from the courts. In DeKalb County, Georgia (a suburb of Atlanta), the schools had been operating under court-ordered desegregation plans for many years. Despite this effort full integration had not been achieved, largely because the county's neighborhoods had increasingly become either all black or all white. The Court held that the local schools could not be held responsible for segregation caused solely by segregated living patterns and so the courts would have to relinquish their control over the schools.[23]

The Campaign in Congress

The campaign in the courts for desegregated schools, though slow and costly, was a carefully managed effort to alter the interpretation of a constitutional provision. But to get new civil rights laws out of Congress required a far more difficult and decentralized strategy, one that was aimed at mobilizing public opinion and overcoming the many congressional barriers to action.

The first problem was to get civil rights on the political agenda by convincing people that something had to be done. This could be achieved by dramatizing the problem in ways that tugged at the conscience of whites who were not racist but were ordinarily indifferent to black problems. Brutal lynchings of blacks had shocked these whites, but lynchings were becoming less frequent in the 1950s, and obviously black leaders had no desire to provoke more lynchings just to get sympathy for their cause.

Those leaders could, however, arrange for dramatic confrontations between blacks claiming some obvious right and the whites who denied it to them.

Beginning in the late 1950s these confrontations began to occur in the form of sit-ins at segregated lunch counters and "freedom rides" on segregated bus lines. At about the same time, efforts were made to get blacks registered to vote in counties where whites had used intimidation and harassment to prevent it.

The best-known campaign occurred in 1955–1956 in Montgomery, Alabama, where blacks, led by a young minister named Martin Luther King, Jr., boycotted the local bus system after it had a black woman, Rosa Parks, arrested because she refused to surrender her seat on a bus to a white man.

These early demonstrations were based on the philosophy of **nonviolent civil disobedience**—that is, peacefully violating a law, such as one requiring blacks to ride in a segregated section of a bus, and allowing oneself to be arrested as a result.

But the momentum of protest, once unleashed, could not be centrally directed or confined to nonviolent action. A rising tide of anger, especially among younger blacks, resulted in the formation of more militant organizations and the spontaneous eruption of violent demonstrations and riots in dozens of cities across the country. From 1964 to 1968 there were in the North as well as the South four "long, hot summers" of racial violence.

The demonstrations and rioting succeeded in getting civil rights on the national political agenda, but at a cost: many whites, opposed to the demonstrations or

In 1960 black students from North Carolina Agricultural and Technical College staged the first "sit-in" when they were refused service at a lunch counter in Greensboro (left). Twenty years later graduates of the college returned to the same lunch counter (right). Though prices had risen, the service had improved.

appalled by the riots, dug in their heels and fought against making any concessions to "lawbreakers," "troublemakers," and "rioters." In 1964 and again in 1968 over two-thirds of the whites interviewed in opinion polls said that the civil rights movement was pushing too fast, had hurt the black cause, and was too violent.[24]

In short there was a conflict between the agenda-setting and coalition-building aspects of the civil rights movement. This was especially a problem since conservative southern legislators still controlled many key congressional committees that had for years been the graveyard of civil rights legislation. The Senate Judiciary Committee was dominated by a coalition of southern Democrats and conservative Republicans, and the House Rules Committee was under the control of a chairman hostile to civil rights bills, Howard Smith of Virginia. Any bill that passed the House faced an almost certain filibuster in the Senate. Finally, President John F. Kennedy was reluctant to submit strong civil rights bills to Congress.

Four developments made it possible to break the deadlock. First, public opinion was changing. As Figure 19.1 shows, between 1959 and 1965 the proportion of whites who said that they were willing to

Rosa Parks was arrested for refusing to move to the black section at the back of a bus in Montgomery, Alabama.

Figure 19.1   Changing White Attitudes Toward Differing Levels of School Integration

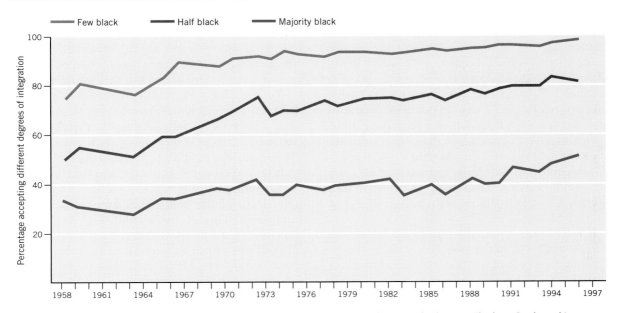

Source: Reprinted by permission of the publishing from *Racial Attitudes in America* by Howard Schuman, Charlotte Steeh, and Lawrence Bobo, p. 69, Cambridge, Mass.: Harvard University Press. Copyright © 1985, 1997, by the Presidents and Fellows of Harvard College.

have their children attend a school that was half black increased sharply (though the proportion of whites willing to have their children attend a school that was predominantly black increased by much less). About the same change could be found in attitudes toward allowing blacks equal access to hotels and buses.[25] Of course support in principle for these civil rights measures was not necessarily the same as support in practice; nonetheless, there clearly was occurring a major shift in popular approval of at least the principles of civil rights. At the leading edge of this change were young, college-educated people.[26]

Second, certain violent reactions by white segregationists to black demonstrators were vividly portrayed by the media, especially television, in ways that gave to the civil rights cause a powerful moral force. In May 1963 the head of the Birmingham police, Eugene "Bull" Connor, ordered his men to use attack dogs and high-pressure fire hoses to repulse a peaceful march by African Americans demanding desegregated public facilities and increased job opportunities. The pictures of that confrontation (such as the one on this page) created a national sensation and contributed greatly to the massive participation, by whites and blacks alike, in the "March on Washington" that summer. About a quarter of a million people gathered in front of the Lincoln Memorial to hear Martin Luther King, Jr., deliver a stirring and widely hailed address, often called the "I Have a Dream" speech. The following summer in Neshoba County, Mississippi, three young civil rights workers (two white and one black) were brutally murdered by Klansmen aided by the local sheriff. When the FBI identified the murderers, the effect on national public opinion was galvanic; no white southern leader could any longer offer persuasive opposition to federal laws protecting voting rights when white law enforcement officers had killed students working to protect those rights. And the next year a white woman, Viola Liuzzo, was shot and killed while driving a car used to transport civil rights workers. Her death was the subject of a presidential address.

Third, President John F. Kennedy was assassinated in Dallas, Texas, in November 1963. Many people originally (and wrongly) thought that he had been killed by a right-wing conspiracy. Even after the assassin had been caught and shown to have left-wing associations, the shock of the president's murder—in a southern city—helped build support for

This picture of a police dog lunging at a black man during a racial demonstration in Birmingham, Alabama, in May 1963 was one of the most influential news photographs ever published. It was widely reprinted throughout the world and was frequently referred to in congressional debates on the civil rights bill of 1964.

efforts by the new president, Lyndon B. Johnson (himself a Texan), to obtain passage of a strong civil rights bill as a memorial to the slain president.

Fourth, the 1964 elections not only returned Johnson to office with a landslide victory but also sent a huge Democratic majority to the House and retained the large Democratic margin in the Senate. This made it possible for northern Democrats to outvote or outmaneuver southerners in the House.

The cumulative effect of these forces led to the enactment of five civil rights laws between 1957 and 1968. Three (1957, 1960, and 1965) were chiefly directed at protecting the right to vote; one (1968) was aimed at preventing discrimination in housing; and one (1964), the most far-reaching of all, dealt with voting, employment, schooling, and public accommodations.

The passage of the 1964 act was the high point of the legislative struggle. Liberals in the House had

Key Provisions of Major Civil Rights Laws

1957   **Voting** Made it a federal crime to try to prevent a person from voting in a federal election. Created the Civil Rights Commission.

1960   **Voting** Authorized the attorney general to appoint federal referees to gather evidence and make findings about allegations that African Americans were being deprived of their right to vote. Made it a federal crime to use interstate commerce to threaten or carry out a bombing.

1964   **Voting** Made it more difficult to use devices such as literacy tests to bar African Americans from voting.

Public accommodations Barred discrimination on grounds of race, color, religion, or national origin in restaurants, hotels, lunch counters, gasoline stations, movie theaters, stadiums, arenas, and lodging houses with more than five rooms.

Schools Authorized the attorney general to bring suit to force the desegregation of public schools on behalf of citizens.

Employment Outlawed discrimination in hiring, firing, or paying employees on grounds of race, color, religion, national origin, or sex.

Federal funds Barred discrimination in any activity receiving federal assistance.

1965   **Voter registration** Authorized appointment by the Civil Service Commission of voting examiners who would require registration of all eligible voters in federal, state, and local elections, general or primary, in areas where discrimination was found to be practiced or where less than 50 percent of voting-age residents were registered to vote in the 1964 election. The law was to have expired in 1970, but Congress extended it; it will expire in 2007.

Literacy tests Suspended use of literacy tests or other devices to prevent African Americans from voting.

1968   **Housing** Banned, by stages, discrimination in sale or rental of most housing (excluding private owners who sell or rent their homes without the services of a real-estate broker).

Riots Made it a federal crime to use interstate commerce to organize or incite a riot.

1972   **Education** Prohibited sex discrimination in education programs receiving federal aid.

1988   **Discrimination** If any part of an organization receives federal aid, no part of that organization may discriminate on the basis of race, sex, age, or physical handicap.

1991   **Discrimination** Made it easier to sue over job discrimination and collect damages; overturned certain Supreme Court decisions. Made it illegal for the government to adjust, or "norm," test scores by race.

---

drafted a bipartisan bill, but it was now in the House Rules Committee, where such matters had often disappeared without a trace. In the wake of Kennedy's murder a discharge petition was filed, with President Johnson's support, to take the bill out of committee and bring it to the floor of the House. But the Rules Committee, without waiting for a vote on the petition (which it probably realized it would lose), sent the bill to the floor, where it passed overwhelmingly. In the Senate an agreement between Republican minority leader Everett Dirksen and President Johnson smoothed the way for passage in several important respects. The House bill was sent directly to the Senate floor, thereby bypassing the southern-dominated Judiciary Committee. Nineteen southern senators began an eight-week filibuster against the bill. On June 10, 1964, by a vote of seventy-one to twenty-nine, cloture was invoked and the filibuster ended—the first time in history that a filibuster aimed at blocking civil rights legislation had been broken.

President Lyndon Johnson signs the Civil Rights Act of 1965 in the company of the Reverend Martin Luther King, Jr. (right), and the Reverend Ralph Abernathy (center).

Figure 19.2   Growing Support Among Southern Democrats in Congress for Civil Rights Bills

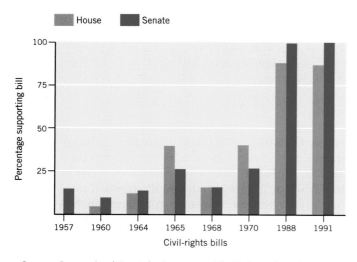

Sources: Congressional Quarterly, *Congress and the Nation,* vols. 1, 2, 3, 7, 8.

Since the 1960s congressional support for civil rights legislation has grown—so much so, indeed, that labeling a bill a civil rights measure, once the kiss of death, now almost guarantees its passage. For example, in 1984 the Supreme Court decided that the federal ban on discrimination in education applied only to the "program or activity" receiving federal aid and not to the entire school or university.[27] In 1988 Congress passed a bill to overturn this decision by making it clear that antidiscrimination rules applied to the entire educational institution and not just to that part (say, the physics lab) receiving federal money. When President Reagan vetoed the bill (because, in his view, it would diminish the freedom of church-affiliated schools), Congress overrode the veto. In the override vote every southern Democrat in the Senate and almost 90 percent of those in the House voted for the bill. This was a dramatic change from 1964, when over 80 percent of the southern Democrats in Congress voted against the Civil Rights Act (see Figure 19.2).

Table 19.1	Increase in Number of Black Elected Officials		
Office	**1970**	**1991**	**1993**
Congress and state legislatures	182	476	561
City and county offices	715	4,493	4,819
Judges and sheriffs	213	847	922
Boards of education	362	1,629	1,682
Total	1,472	7,445	7,984

Sources: Statistical Abstract of the United States, 1990, 260; Statistical Abstract of the United States, 1992, 267; Statistical Abstract of the United States, 1995, 287.

This change partly reflected the growing political strength of southern blacks. In 1960 less than one-third of voting-age blacks in the South were registered to vote; by 1971 more than half were, and by 1984 two-thirds were. In 1993 over nearly eight thousand blacks held elective office in the South (see Table 19.1). But this was only half of the story. Attitudes among white political elites and members of Congress had also changed. This was evident as early as 1968, when Congress passed a law barring discrimination in housing even though polls showed that only 35 percent of the public supported the measure.

Civil rights is not an issue easily confined to schools, housing, and jobs. Sometimes it is extended to crime. When crack cocaine became a popular drug, it was cheap and easily sold on street corners. When the public demanded that the police get tough on crack dealers, arrests followed. Since the great majority of arrested dealers were black, there was a sharp increase in black drug dealers going to prison. Some blacks claimed that they were being singled out by the police because of their race. The Supreme Court disagreed, holding that no evidence had been presented to show that drug dealers of other races had not been prosecuted.[28]

Racial Profiling

Many African Americans complain that they are stopped by the police for "driving while black," which means being stopped by the police because you belong to a certain race and for no other reason. The claim became a national issue in 1998 after the governor of New Jersey fired the head of the state police for saying that blacks were stopped more frequently because they broke the law more frequently.

Soon President Clinton, and after him President Bush, made statements condemning racial profiling, and bills were introduced in Congress to penalize it.

Stopping or arresting people because you dislike the color of their skin or the ethnic group of which they are members is obviously wrong. Many wholly innocent people are the victims of such stops. But the issue is complicated and is the subject of debate. Opponents of racial profiling argue that it is inherently discriminatory and therefore never the right thing to do. Proponents of profiling argue that if some racial groups are more likely than others to break the speed limit (which was possibly the case in New Jersey) or if airport inspectors think that ethnicity is a clue to being an airline terrorist, then it is justified.

It is important to consider what advantage, if any, profiling provides, and to weigh it against the costs. Does profiling by race improve the police's ability to find criminals by 1 percent, or 5 percent, or 20 percent? The terrorists who hijacked airplanes for the attacks on September 11, 2001, were all young male Middle Easterners; most, in fact, were from Saudi Arabia. Airport security people can screen everyone with magnetic detectors to see if they may be carrying weapons, but they select some people for a personal search. Should the screeners select people randomly for such searches (which most do now) or should they select young Middle Eastern males?

If police officers or airport screeners use race or ethnicity as a guide for their actions, it is inevitable that they will stop and question (or in airports, search) many innocent people. Race and ethnicity are only clues to, not determinants of, behavior. Unfortunately, racial profiling has become a major political issue without, as yet, being based on firm factual grounds. We still need to know how police make their judgements and which judgements would strike the right balance between safety and rights.

Women and Equal Rights

The political and legal efforts to secure civil rights for African Americans were accompanied by efforts to expand the rights of women. There was an important difference between the two movements, however: whereas African Americans were arguing against a legal tradition that explicitly aimed to keep them in a subservient status, women had to argue against a tradition that claimed to be protecting

Though many women have enlisted in the armed forces, the Supreme Court in 1981 held that Congress could exclude women from the draft.

them. For example, in 1908 the Supreme Court upheld an Oregon law that limited female laundry workers to a ten-hour workday against the claim that it violated the Fourteenth Amendment. The Court justified its decision with this language:

> The two sexes differ in structure of body, in the functions to be performed by each, in the amount of physical strength, in the capacity for long-continued labor, particularly when done standing. . . . the self-reliance which enables one to assert full rights, and in the capacity to maintain the struggle for subsistence. This difference justifies a difference in legislation and upholds that which is designed to compensate for some of the burdens which rest upon her.[29]

The feminist movement that resurfaced not long after the civil rights movement questioned the claim that women differed from men in ways that justified differences in legal status. Congress responded by passing laws that required equal pay for equal work, prohibited discrimination on the basis of sex in employment and among students in any school or university receiving federal funds, and banned discrimination against pregnant women on the job.[30]

At the same time, the Supreme Court was altering the way it interpreted the Constitution. The key passage was the Fourteenth Amendment, which prohibits any state from denying to "any person" the "equal protection of the laws." For a long time the traditional standard, as we saw in the 1908 case, was a kind of protective paternalism. By the early 1970s, however, the Court had changed its mind. In deciding whether the Constitution bars all, some, or no sexual discrimination, the Court had a choice between two standards. The first is the *reasonableness* standard. This says that when the government treats some classes of people differently from others—for example, applying statutory rape laws to men but not to women—the different treatment must be reasonable and not arbitrary. The second is the **strict scrutiny** standard. This says that some instances of drawing distinctions between different groups of people—for example, by treating whites and blacks differently—are inherently suspect; thus the Court will subject them to strict scrutiny to ensure that they are clearly necessary to attain a legitimate state goal.

When women complained that some laws treated them unfairly, the Court adopted a standard somewhere between the reasonableness and strict scrutiny tests. Thus a law that treats men and women differently must be more than merely reasonable, but the allowable differences need not meet the strict scrutiny test.

And so in 1971 the Court held that an Idaho statute was unconstitutional because it required that males be preferred over females when choosing people to administer the estates of deceased children. To satisfy the Constitution, a law treating men and women differently "must be reasonable, not arbitrary, and must rest on some ground of difference having a fair and substantial relation to the object of legislation so that all persons similarly circumstanced shall be treated alike."[31] In later decisions some members of the Court wanted to make classifications based on sex inherently suspect and subject to the strict scrutiny test, but no majority has yet embraced this position.[32]

But sexual classifications can also be judged by a different standard. The Civil Rights Act of 1964 prohibits sex discrimination in the hiring, firing, and compensation of employees. The 1972 Civil Rights Act bans sex discrimination in local education programs receiving federal aid. These laws apply to *private* and not just government action.

Over the years the Court has decided many cases involving sexual classification. The following lists provide several examples of illegal sexual discrimination (violating either the Constitution or a civil rights act) and legal sexual distinctions (violating neither).

■ Illegal Discrimination

- A state cannot set different ages at which men and women legally become adults.[33]
- A state cannot set different ages at which men and women are allowed to buy beer.[34]
- Women cannot be barred from jobs by arbitrary height and weight requirements.[35]
- Employers cannot require women to take mandatory pregnancy leaves.[36]
- Girls cannot be barred from Little League baseball teams.[37]
- Business and service clubs, such as the Junior Chamber of Commerce and Rotary Club, cannot exclude women from membership.[38]
- Though women as a group live longer than men, an employer must pay them monthly retirement benefits equal to those received by men.[39]
- High schools must pay the coaches of girls' sports the same as they pay the coaches of boys' sports.[40]

■ Decisions Allowing Differences Based on Sex

- A law that punishes males but not females for statutory rape is permissible; men and women are not "similarly situated" with respect to sexual relations.[41]
- All-boy and all-girl public schools are permitted if enrollment is voluntary and quality is equal.[42]
- States can give widows a property-tax exemption not given to widowers.[43]
- The navy may allow women to remain officers longer than men without being promoted.[44]

The lower federal courts have been especially busy in the area of sexual distinctions. They have said that public taverns may not cater to men only and that girls may not be prevented from competing against boys in noncontact high school sports; on the other hand, hospitals may bar fathers from the delivery room. Women may continue to use their maiden names after marriage.[45]

In 1996 the Supreme Court ruled that women must be admitted to the Virginia Military Institute, until then an all-male state-supported college that had for many decades supplied what it called an "adversative method" of training to instill physical and mental discipline in cadets. In practical terms this meant being very tough on students. The Court said that for a state to justify spending tax money on a single-sex school, it must supply an "exceedingly persuasive justification" for excluding the other gender. Virginia countered by offering to support an all-female training course at another college, but this was not enough.[46] This decision came close to imposing the strict scrutiny test, and so it has raised important questions about what could happen to all-female or traditionally black colleges that accept state money.

Perhaps the most far-reaching cases defining the rights of women have involved the draft and abortion. In 1981 the Court held in *Rostker v. Goldberg* that Congress may require men but not women to register for the draft without violating the due-process clause of the Fifth Amendment.[47] In the area of national defense the Court will give great deference to congressional policy (Congress had already decided to bar women from combat roles). For many years women could be pilots and sailors but not on combat aircraft or combat ships. In 1993 the secretary of defense opened air and sea combat positions to all persons regardless of gender; only ground-troop combat positions are still reserved for men. The issue played a role in preventing the ratification of the Equal Rights Amendment to the Constitution, because of fears that it would reverse *Rostker v. Goldberg*, and remains controversial.

Sexual Harassment

When Paula Corbin Jones accused President Clinton of sexual harassment, the judge threw the case out of court because she had not submitted enough evidence such that, if the jury believed her story, she would have made a legally adequate argument that she had been sexually harassed.

What, then, is sexual harassment? Drawing on rulings by the Equal Employment Opportunities Commission, the Supreme Court has held that harassment can take one of two forms. First, it is

---

The Constitutional Position of Abortion Laws

This is what a narrow majority of the Court held in decisions made in 1992 and 2000:

1. "It is a constitutional liberty of the woman to have some freedom to terminate her pregnancy. . . . No state may prohibit a woman from terminating her pregnancy" before the fetus becomes "viable."

2. After the fetus has become viable, a state may "regulate, and even proscribe, abortion except where it is necessary . . . for the preservation of the life and the health of the mother."

3. States may put restrictions on the right to an abortion, but these restrictions must not place an "undue burden" on the exercise of a woman's rights.

4. States may not ban partial birth abortions—that is, abortions performed by removing most of the fetus from the womb and then collapsing its skull—if they fail to allow an exception to preserve the "health" of the mother.

Sources: Planned Parenthood v. Casey, 505 U.S. 833 (1992); Stenberg v. Carhart, 530 U.S. 914 (2000).

---

illegal for someone to request sexual favors as a condition of employment or promotion. This is the "quid pro quo" rule. If a person does this, the employer is "strictly liable." Strict liability means that the employer can be found at fault even if he or she did not know that a subordinate was requesting sex in exchange for hiring or promotion.

Second, it is illegal for an employee to experience a work environment that has been made hostile or intimidating by a steady pattern of offensive sexual teasing, jokes, or obscenity. But employers are not strictly liable in this case; they can be found at fault only if

When the Supreme Court decided the abortion issue, it guaranteed endless protests, as here in front of its building.

they were "negligent"—that is, they knew about the hostile environment but did nothing about it.

In 1998 the Supreme Court decided three cases that made these rules either better or worse, depending on your point of view. In one it determined that a school system was not liable for the conduct of a teacher who seduced a female student because the student never reported the actions. In a second it held that a city was liable for a sexually hostile work environment confronting a female lifeguard even though she did not report this to her superiors. In the third it decided that a female employee who was not promoted after having rejected the sexual advances of her boss could recover financial damages from the firm. But, it added, the firm could have avoided paying this bill if it had put in place an "affirmative defense" against sexual exploitation, although the Court never said what such a policy might be.[48]

Sexual harassment is a serious matter, but because there are almost no federal laws governing it, we are left with somewhat vague and often inconsistent court and bureaucratic rules to guide us.

Abortion

Until 1973 it was up to the states to decide whether and under what circumstances a woman could obtain an abortion. For example, New York allowed abortion on demand during the first twenty-four weeks of pregnancy, but Texas banned abortion except when the mother's life was threatened.

By a seven-to-two vote in the 1973 case of *Roe v. Wade*, the Supreme Court struck down the Texas law (and all similar state laws).[49] The majority argued that the due-process clause of the Fourteenth Amendment implies a "right to privacy" that protects a woman's freedom to choose, during the first three months of pregnancy, whether to have an abortion. (During the second three months, or trimester, the states are allowed to regulate abortion procedures to protect the mother's health; during the final trimester, states might ban abortions.)

In reaching this decision, the Court denied that it was trying to decide when human life began—at the moment of conception, at the moment of birth, or somewhere in between. But that is not how critics of the decision saw things. To them life begins at conception, and so the human fetus is a "person" entitled to the equal protection of the laws guaranteed by the Fourteenth Amendment. People feeling this way began to use the slogans "right to life" and "pro-life." Supporters of the Court's action saw matters differently. In their view, no one can say for certain when human life begins; what one *can* say, however, is that a woman is entitled to choose whether or not to have a baby. These people took the slogans "right to choose" and "pro-choice."

Almost immediately the congressional allies of pro-life groups introduced constitutional amendments to overturn *Roe v. Wade*, but none passed Congress. Nevertheless, abortion foes did persuade Congress, beginning in 1976, to bar the use of federal funds to pay for abortions except when the life of the mother is at stake. This provision is known as the Hyde Amendment, after its sponsor, Representative Henry Hyde. The chief effect of the amendment has been to deny the use of Medicaid funds to pay for abortions for low-income women. (In 1980 the Supreme Court upheld the constitutionality of the Hyde amendment.)[50] During the Bush administration the government carried the spirit of this amendment one step further by barring the use of federal funds for family planning clinics that provided abortion counseling. Called a "gag rule" by some, this policy was repealed by the Clinton administration.

Despite pro-life opposition, the Supreme Court for sixteen years steadfastly reaffirmed and even broadened its decision in *Roe v. Wade*. It struck down laws requiring, before an abortion could be performed, a woman to have the consent of her husband, an "emancipated" but underage girl to have the con-

sent of her parents, or a woman to be advised by her doctor as to the facts about abortion.[51]

But in 1989, under the influence of justices appointed by President Reagan, it began in the *Webster* case to uphold some state restrictions on abortions. When that happened, many people predicted that in time *Roe v. Wade* would be overturned, especially if President Bush was able to appoint more justices. He appointed two (Souter and Thomas), but *Roe* survived. The key votes were cast by Justices O'Connor, Souter, and Kennedy. In 1992, in its *Casey* decision, the Court by a vote of five to four explicitly refused to overturn *Roe*, declaring that there was a right to abortion. At the same time, however, it upheld a variety of restrictions imposed by the state of Pennsylvania on women seeking abortions. These included a mandatory twenty-four-hour waiting period between the request for an abortion and the performance of it, the requirement that teenagers obtain the consent of one parent (or, in special circumstances, of a judge), and a requirement that women contemplating an abortion be given pamphlets about alternatives to it. Similar restrictions had been enacted in many other states, all of which looked to the Pennsylvania case for guidance as to whether they could be enforced. In allowing these restrictions, the Court overruled some of its own earlier decisions.[52] On the other hand, the Court did strike down a state law that would have required married women to obtain the consent of their husbands before having an abortion.

In 2000 the Court visited abortion again, and by another five-to-four vote refused to allow states to ban so-called partial birth abortions. This method is usually done to fetuses that are at least twenty weeks old. The key provisions of the *Casey* and *Stenberg* cases are summarized in the box on page 542.

With the right to an abortion again politically secure, the struggle over its implementation took a new turn. Antiabortion activists conducted demonstrations at many abortion clinics, and a few extremists wounded or killed some abortion doctors. This led to a demand for laws protecting the clinics. Laws were passed and court orders issued, designed to strike a balance between the activists' right to protest and the clinics' right to operate.

In 1997 the Supreme Court upheld legal orders that forbid acts of physical obstruction and that provide a "buffer zone" of fifteen feet around the entrance to a clinic within which demonstrations cannot occur.[53]

Affirmative Action

A common thread running through the politics of civil rights is the argument between equality of results and equality of opportunity.

Equality of Results

One view, expressed by most civil rights and feminist organizations, is that the burdens of racism and sexism can be overcome only by taking race or sex into account in designing remedies. It is not enough to give rights to people; they must be given benefits. If life is a race, everybody must be brought up to the same starting line (or possibly even to the same finish line). This means that the Constitution is not and should not be color-blind or sex-neutral. In education this implies that the races must actually be mixed in the schools, by busing if necessary. In hiring it means that **affirmative action**—preferential hiring practices—must be used to find and hire women, African Americans, and other minorities. Women should not simply be free to enter the labor force; they should be given the material necessities (for example, free daycare) that will help them enter it. On payday workers' checks should reflect not just the results of people's competing in the marketplace but the results of plans designed to ensure that people earn comparable amounts for comparable jobs. Of late, affirmative action has been defended in the name of diversity or multiculturalism—the view that every institution (firm, school, or agency) and every college curriculum should reflect the cultural (that is, ethnic) diversity of the nation.

Equality of Opportunity

The second view holds that if it is wrong to discriminate *against* African Americans and women, it is equally wrong to give them preferential treatment over other groups. To do so constitutes **reverse discrimination.** The Constitution and laws should be color-blind and sex-neutral.[54] In this view allowing children to attend the school of their choice is sufficient; busing them to attain a certain racial mixture is wrong. Eliminating barriers to job opportunities is right; using numerical "targets" and "goals" to place minorities and women in specific jobs is wrong. If people wish to compete in the market, they should be satisfied with the market verdict concerning the worth of their work.

These two views are intertwined with other deep philosophical differences. Supporters of **equality of opportunity** tend to have orthodox beliefs; they favor letting private groups behave the way that they want (and so may defend the right of a men's club to exclude women). Supporters of the opposite view are likely to be progressive in their beliefs and insist that private clubs meet the same standards as schools or business firms. Adherents to the equality-of-opportunity view often attach great importance to traditional models of the family and so are skeptical of daycare and federally funded abortions. Adherents to the equality-of-results view prefer greater freedom of choice in lifestyle questions and so take the opposite position on daycare and abortion.

Of course the debate is more complex than this simple contrast suggests. Take, for example, the question of affirmative action. Both the advocates of equality of opportunity and those of equality of results might agree that there is something odd about a factory or university that hires no African Americans or women, and both might press it to prove that its hiring policy is fair. Affirmative action in this case can mean *either* looking hard for qualified women and minorities and giving them a fair shot at jobs *or* setting a numerical goal for the number of women and minorities that should be hired and insisting that that goal be met. Persons who defend the second course of action call these goals "targets"; persons who criticize that course call them "quotas."

The issue has largely been fought out in the courts. Between 1978 and 1990 about a dozen major cases involving affirmative action were decided by the Supreme Court; in about half it was upheld, and in the other half it was overturned. The different outcomes reflect two things—the differences in the facts of the cases and the arrival on the Court of three justices (Kennedy, O'Connor, and Scalia) appointed by a president, Ronald Reagan, who was opposed to at least the broader interpretation of affirmative action. As a result of these decisions, the law governing affirmative action is now complex and confusing.

Consider one issue: should the government be allowed to use a quota system to select workers, enroll students, award contracts, or grant licenses? In the *Bakke* decision in 1978, the Court said that the medical school of the University of California at

Becoming a Citizen

For persons born in the United States, the rights of U.S. citizenship have been ensured, in constitutional theory if not in everyday practice, since the passage of the Fourteenth Amendment in 1868 and the civil rights laws of the 1960s. The Fourteenth Amendment conferred citizenship upon "all persons born in the United States . . . and subject to the jurisdiction thereof." Subsequent laws also gave citizenship to children born outside the United States to parents who are American citizens.

But immigrants, by definition, are not born with the rights of U.S. citizenship. Instead those seeking to become U.S. citizens must, in effect, assume certain responsibilities in order to become citizens. The statutory requirements for naturalization, as they have been broadly construed by the courts, are as follows:

- Five years' residency, or three years if married to a citizen.
- Continuous residency since filing of the naturalization petition.

- Good moral character, which is loosely interpreted to mean no evidence of criminal activity.
- Attachment to constitutional principles. This means that potential citizens have to answer basic factual questions about American government (e.g., "Who was the first president of the United States?") and publicly denounce any and all allegiance to their native country and its leaders (e.g., Italy and the king of Italy), but devotion to constitutional principles is now regarded as being implicit in the act of applying for naturalization.
- Being favorably disposed to "the good order and happiness of the United States."*

Today about 97 percent of aliens who seek citizenship are successful in meeting these requirements and becoming naturalized citizens of the United States.

*8 U.S.C. 1423, 1427 (1970); *Girouard v. United States*, 328 U.S. 61 (1946).

Source: *New York Times* (July 25, 1993), 33. Copyright © 1993 by the *New York Times*. Reprinted by permission.

Davis could not use an explicit numerical quota in admitting minority students but could "take race into account."[55] So no numerical quotas, right? Wrong. Two years later the Court upheld a federal rule that set aside 10 percent of all federal construction contracts for minority-owned firms.[56] All right, maybe quotas can't be used in medical schools, but they can be used in the construction industry. Not exactly. In 1989 the Court overturned a Richmond, Virginia, law that set aside 30 percent of its construction contracts for minority-owned firms.[57] Well, maybe the Court just changed its mind between 1980 and 1989. No. One year later it upheld a federal rule that gave preference to minority-owned firms in the awarding of broadcast licenses.[58] Then in 1993 it upheld the right of white contractors to challenge minority set-aside laws in Jacksonville, Florida.[59]

It is too early to try to make sense of these twists and turns, especially since a deeply divided Court is still wrestling with these issues and Congress (as with the Civil Rights Act of 1991) is modifying or

superseding some earlier Court decisions. But a few general standards seem to be emerging. In simplified form, they are as follows:

- The courts will subject any quota system created by state or local governments to "strict scrutiny" and will look for a "compelling" justification for it.
- Quotas or preference systems cannot be used by state or local governments without first showing that such rules are needed to correct an actual past or present pattern of discrimination.[60]
- In proving that there has been discrimination, it is not enough to show that African Americans (or other minorities) are statistically underrepresented among employees, contractors, or union members; you must identify the actual practices that have had this discriminatory impact.[61]
- Quotas or preference systems that are created by *federal* law will be given greater deference, in part because Section 5 of the Fourteenth Amendment gives to Congress powers not given to the states to

The Rights of Aliens

America is a nation of immigrants. Some have arrived legally, others illegally. An illegal, or undocumented, alien is subject to being deported. With the passage in 1986 of the Immigration Reform and Control Act, illegal aliens who have resided in this country continuously since before January 1, 1982, are entitled to amnesty—that is, they can become legal residents. However, the same legislation stipulated that employers (who once could hire undocumented aliens without fear of penalty) must now verify the legal status of all newly hired employees; if they knowingly hire an illegal alien, they face civil and criminal penalties.

Aliens—people residing in this country who are not citizens—cannot vote or run for office. Nevertheless, they must pay taxes just as if they were citizens. And they are entitled to many constitutional rights, even if they are in this country illegally. This is because most of the rights mentioned in the Constitution refer to "people" or "persons," not to "citizens." For example, the Fourteenth Amendment bars a state from depriving "*any person* of life, liberty, or property, without due process of law" or from denying "to *any person* within its jurisdiction the equal protection of the laws" [italics added]. As a result, the courts have held that:

- The children of illegal aliens cannot be excluded from the public school system.[1]
- Legally admitted aliens are entitled to welfare benefits.[2]
- Illegal aliens cannot be the object of reprisals if they attempt to form a labor union where they work.[3]

- The First Amendment rights of free speech, religion, press, and assembly and the Fourth Amendment protections against arbitrary arrest and prosecution extend to aliens as well as to citizens.[4]
- Aliens are entitled to own property.

The government can make rules that apply to aliens only, but they must justify the reasonableness of the rules. For example:

- The Immigration and Naturalization Service has broader powers to arrest and search illegal aliens than police departments have to arrest and search citizens.[5]
- States can limit certain jobs, such as police officer and schoolteacher, to citizens.[6]
- The president or Congress can bar the employment of aliens by the federal government.[7]
- States can bar aliens from serving on a jury.[8]
- Illegal aliens are not entitled to obtain a Social Security card.

[1]*Plyler v. Doe,* 457 U.S. 202 (1982).

[2]*Graham v. Richardson,* 403 U.S. 365 (1971).

[3]*Sure-Tan v. National Labor Relations Board,* 467 U.S. 883 (1984).

[4]*Chew v. Colding,* 344 U.S. 590 (1953).

[5]*U.S. v. Brignoni-Ponce,* 422 U.S. 873 (1975); *INS v. Delgado,* 466 U.S. 210 (1984); *INS v. Lopez-Mendoza,* 486 U.S. 1032 (1984).

[6]*Cabell v. Chavez-Salido,* 454 U.S. 432 (1982); *Foley v. Connelie,* 435 U.S. 291 (1978); *Amblach v. Norwick,* 441 U.S. 68 (1979).

[7]*Hampton v. Mow Sun Wong,* 436 U.S. 67 (1976).

[8]*Schneider v. New Jersey,* 308 U.S. 147 (1939).

---

correct the effects of racial discrimination.[62]
- It may be easier to justify in court a voluntary preference system (for example, one agreed to in a labor-management contract) than one that is required by law.[63]
- Even when you can justify special preferences in *hiring* workers, the Supreme Court is not likely to allow racial preferences to govern who gets *laid off.* A worker laid off to make room for a minority

worker loses more than does a worker not hired in preference to a minority applicant.[64]

Complex as they are, these rulings still generate a great deal of passion. Supporters of the decisions barring certain affirmative action plans hail these decisions as steps back from an emerging pattern of reverse discrimination. In contrast, civil rights organizations have denounced those decisions that

The Rights of the Disabled

In 1990 the federal government passed the Americans with Disabilities Act (ADA), a sweeping law that extended many of the protections enjoyed by women and racial minorities to disabled persons.

Who Is a Disabled Person?

Anyone who *has* a physical or mental impairment that substantially limits one or more major life activities (for example, holding a job), anyone who has a *record* of such impairment, or anyone who is *regarded* as having such an impairment is considered disabled.

What Rights Do Disabled Persons Have?

Employment Disabled persons may not be denied employment or promotion if, with "reasonable accommodation," they can perform the duties of that job. (Excluded from this protection are people who currently use illegal drugs, gamble compulsively, or are homosexual or bisexual.) Reasonable accommodation need not be made if this would cause "undue hardship" on the employer.

Government Programs and Transportation Disabled persons may not be denied access to government programs or benefits. New buses, taxis, and trains must be accessible to disabled persons, including those in wheelchairs.

Public Accommodations Disabled persons must enjoy "full and equal" access to hotels, restaurants, stores, schools, parks, museums, auditoriums, and the like. To achieve equal access, owners of existing facilities must alter them "to the maximum extent feasible"; builders of new facilities must ensure that they are readily accessible to disabled persons, unless this is structurally impossible.

Telephones The ADA directs the Federal Communications Commission to issue regulations to ensure that telecommunications devices for hearing- and speech-impaired people are available "to the extent possible and in the most efficient manner."

Congress The rights under this law apply to employees of Congress.

Rights Compared The ADA does not enforce the rights of disabled persons in the same way as the Civil Rights Act enforces the rights of African Americans and women. Racial or gender discrimination must end *regardless of cost*; denial of access to disabled persons must end unless "undue hardship" or excessive costs would result.

have overturned affirmative action programs. In 1990 their congressional allies introduced legislation that would reverse several decisions. In particular this legislation would put the burden of proof on the employer, not the employee, to show that the underrepresentation of minorities in the firm's work force was the result of legitimate and necessary business decisions and not the result of discrimination. If the employer could not prove this, the aggrieved employee would be able to collect large damage awards. (In the past, he or she could collect only back pay.) In 1991 the bill was passed and was signed by President Bush.

In thinking about these matters, most Americans distinguish between compensatory action and preferential treatment. They define **compensatory action** as "helping disadvantaged people catch up, usually by giving them extra education, training, or services." A majority of the public supports this. They define preferential treatment as "giving minorities preference in hiring, promotions, college admissions, and contracts." Large majorities oppose this.[65] These views reflect an enduring element in American political culture—a strong commitment to individualism ("nobody should get something without deserving it") coupled with support for help for the disadvantaged ("somebody who is suffering through no fault of his or her own deserves a helping hand").

Where does affirmative action fit into this culture? Polls suggest that if affirmative action is defined as "helping," people will support it, but if it is defined as "using quotas," they will oppose it. On this matter blacks and whites see things differently. Blacks think that they should receive preferences in employment to create a more diverse work force and

The federal government subsidizes some job training programs, as for these medical assistants.

to make up for past discrimination; whites oppose using goals to create diversity or to remedy past ills. In sum the controversy over affirmative action depends on what you mean by it and on what your racial identity is.[66]

The courts are likewise divided on this matter. In 1996 the federal appeals court for the fifth circuit (covering Louisiana, Mississippi, and Texas) decided that the University of Texas Law School's refusal to admit a white woman, Cheryl Hopwood, even though her academic record was much better than that of many black and Hispanic students who had been admitted, was unconstitutional. The school said it gave preference to racial minorities to achieve diversity among its students, but the appeals court held that diversity was not a sufficiently compelling state interest to justify racial preferences. When the school appealed the decision to the Supreme Court, it refused to hear the matter because, by then, the school had stopped using racial admissions criteria.[67] This means that no law school in Louisiana, Mississippi, and Texas can use race at all in making admissions decisions, but those in other states still can.

What may be the most important recent Supreme Court decision on affirmative action was made in 1995. A small construction company named Adarand tried to get a contract to build guardrails along a highway in Colorado. Though it was the low bidder, it lost the contract because of a government policy that favors small businesses owned by "socially and economically disadvan-taged individuals"—that is, by racial and ethnic minorities. In a five-to-four decision the Court agreed with Adarand and sent the case back to Colorado for a new trial.

The essence of its decision was that *any* discrimination based on race must be subject to strict scrutiny, even if its purpose is to help, not hurt, a racial minority. Strict scrutiny means two things:

- Any racial preference must serve a "compelling government interest."
- The preference must be "narrowly tailored" to serve that interest.[68]

To serve a compelling governmental interest, it is likely that any racial preference will have to remedy a clear pattern of past discrimination. No such pattern had been shown in Colorado.

This decision prompted a good deal of political debate about affirmative action. The Republicans introduced a bill in Congress to ban it, but they later withdrew the bill. In California, however, an initiative was put on the 1996 ballot to prevent state authorities from using "race, sex, color, ethnicity, or national origin as a criterion for either discriminating against, or granting preferential treatment to, any individual or group" in public employment, public education, or public contracting. When the votes were counted, it passed. Washington has also adopted a similar measure, and other states are debating it.

Gays and the Supreme Court

As conflicts over homosexuality have risen in political importance, the Supreme Court has had to confront the issue of gay rights more frequently. Because the nation is divided about it, it shouldn't be surprising that the Court is also.

When some Georgians protested that a state law barring homosexual actions between two consenting adults was unconstitutional, the Court voted five to four that there was no constitutional reason to prevent a state from passing such a law.[69] Homosexuality in that state remained illegal.

In many cities in Colorado ordinances were passed to ban discrimination against people because of their sexual orientation. Most voters did not approve of this, and so in response they adopted a state constitutional amendment that made it illegal to pass any law to protect persons based on their "homosexual, lesbian, or bisexual orientation." The amendment did not penalize gays and lesbians; instead it said that they could not become the object of specific legal protection of the sort that has traditionally been given to racial or ethnic minorities. The Court struck down this amendment on the grounds that it violated the equal protection clause of the Constitution by singling out as unworthy of protection one specific group of citizens.[70]

So now we have an odd condition: a state can pass a law banning homosexual activities, but it cannot pass a law preventing the cities within that state from reversing that ban. (The decision that overturned the Colorado amendment did not mention the decision sustaining the Georgia law.)

In 2000 the Court was asked whether the Boy Scouts could prevent gay boys and men from being members. The majority of the Court, in a five-to-four decision, said it was not opposing homosexuality but merely reaffirming the right of a private organization to define its own membership. The dissenters did not object to the claim that private organizations could choose their own members but argued that the Boy Scouts had not published a clear opposition to homosexuality.[71] The status of civil rights for homosexuals remains unclear. Complicating matters is the role of gays in the military. In 1993 the Clinton administration instituted the policy of "don't ask, don't tell" in the military, but the Court has yet to speak authoritatively about what this means in practice.

On one matter, however, the Court seems quite clear. When a private group of Irish Americans sponsored a St. Patrick's Day parade in Boston, an organization called the Irish-American Gay, Lesbian, and Bisexual Group asked for the right to march with the others. In protest the traditional sponsors of the march canceled it. The case went to the Supreme Court, which held, unanimously, that the sponsors of the march had a First Amendment right to deliver their message and that the state could not require it to alter that message by including among the marchers people with whom it disagreed.[72]

Summary

The civil rights movement in the courts and in Congress profoundly changed the nature of African American participation in politics by bringing southern blacks into the political system so that they could become an effective interest group. The decisive move was to enlist northern opinion in this cause, a job made easier by the northern perception that civil rights involved simply an unfair contest between two minorities—southern whites and southern blacks. That perception changed when it became evident that the court rulings and legislative decisions would apply to the North as well as the South, leading to the emergence of northern opposition to court-ordered busing and affirmative action programs.

By the time this reaction developed, the legal and political system had been changed sufficiently to make it difficult if not impossible to limit the application of civil rights laws to the special circumstances of the South or to alter by legislative means the decisions of federal courts. Though the courts can accomplish little when they have no political allies (as revealed by the massive resistance to early school-desegregation decisions), they can accomplish a great deal, even in the face of adverse public opinion, when they have some organized allies (as revealed by their ability to withstand antibusing moves).

The feminist movement has paralleled in organization and tactics many aspects of the black civil rights movement, but with important differences. Women sought to repeal or reverse laws and court rulings that in many cases were ostensibly designed to protect rather than subjugate them. The conflict between protection and liberation was sufficiently intense to defeat the effort to ratify the Equal Rights Amendment.

The most divisive civil rights issues in American politics are abortion and affirmative action. From 1973 to 1989 the Supreme Court seemed committed to giving constitutional protection to all abortions within the first trimester; since 1989 it has approved various state restrictions on the circumstances under which abortions can be obtained.

There has been a similar shift in the Court's view of affirmative action. Though it will still approve some quota plans, it now insists that they pass strict scrutiny to ensure that they are used only to correct a proven history of discrimination, that they place the burden of proof on the party alleging discrimination, and that they be limited to hiring and not extended to layoffs. Congress has modified some of these rulings with new civil rights legislation.

Reconsidering the Enduring Questions

1. Should numerical goals ever be used to ensure that students and workers are drawn from every racial group?

Critics of these goals call them "quotas"; supporters call them "targets." Either way they constitute affirmative action. The case for goals is this: Unless we count the racial, ethnic, or sexual identity of students and workers, we won't know whether some group is being excluded by discrimination. And if we find that discrimination exists, creating a goal is a way to remedy it. The case against goals is this: Most forms of discrimination should be illegal and any evidence that they exist should be grounds for punishment. But if a private business hires only pretty women as cocktail waitresses or a college admits only blacks or men, these actions express freedom of choice rather than unlawful discrimination. Provided realistic alternatives exist, changing these practices with goals would narrow the range of legitimate human activity.

2. To what extent should the government be able to limit the opportunity to have an abortion?

Political elites are more divided about this question than is the general public. Many Americans disapprove of abortion unless the woman is the victim of rape or incest or her physical health is threatened. But for liberal elites, abortion is "the right to choose"; for conservative elites, it is "the right to life." Since abortion laws are made by courts and not, generally speaking, by legislatures, elites have more influence than do citizens. An interesting test case is the effort to ban late-term or partial birth abortions. Some states have done this, but the courts have generally held that the laws are too broad in scope or do not take into account the mental (as opposed to physical) health of the mother. But the public at large is strongly opposed to such abortions. And there matters stand.

World Wide Web Resources

- Court cases: www.law.cornell.edu
- Department of Justice: www.usdoj.gov
- Civil rights organizations:
  National Association for the Advancement of
  Colored People: www.naacp.org
  National Organization for Women:
  www.now.org

National Gay and Lesbian Task Force:
www.ngltf.org
National Council of La Raza: www.nclr.org
American Arab Anti-Discrimination Committee:
www.adc.org
Anti-Defamation League: www.adl.org

Key Terms

civil rights *p. 523*
suspect classifications *p. 524*
Jim Crow *p. 525*
separate-but-equal doctrine *p. 527*
de jure segregation *p. 531*

de facto segregation *p. 531*
nonviolent civil disobedience *p. 534*
strict scrutiny *p. 540*
affirmative action *p. 544*
reverse discrimination *p. 544*

equality of opportunity *p. 544*
compensatory action *p. 547*

Suggested Readings

Branch, Taylor. *Parting the Waters: America in the King Years*. New York: Simon and Schuster, 1988. A vivid account of the civil rights struggle.

Flexner, Eleanor. *Century of Struggle: The Women's Rights Movement in the United States*. Rev. ed. Cambridge: Harvard University Press, 1975. A historical account of the feminist movement and its political strategies.

Foreman, Christopher A. *The African-American Predicament*. Washington, D.C.: Brookings Institution, 1999. Thoughtful essays on problems faced by African Americans today.

Franklin, John Hope. *From Slavery to Freedom*. 5th ed. New York: Knopf, 1980. A survey of black history in the United States.

Kluger, Richard. *Simple Justice*. New York: Random House/Vintage Books, 1977. Detailed and absorbing account of the school-desegregation issue, from the Fourteenth Amendment to the *Brown* case.

Kull, Andrew. *The Color-Blind Constitution*. Cambridge: Harvard University Press, 1992. A history of efforts, none yet successful, to make the Constitution color-blind.

Mansbridge, Jane J. *Why We Lost the ERA*. Chicago: University of Chicago Press, 1986. Explains why the Equal Rights Amendment did not become part of the Constitution.

Thernstrom, Stephan, and Abigail Thernstrom. *America in Black and White*. New York: Simon and Schuster, 1997. Detailed history and portrait of African Americans.

Wilhoit, Francis M. *The Politics of Massive Resistance*. New York: George Braziller, 1973. The methods—and ultimate collapse—of all-out southern resistance to school desegregation.

Woodward, C. Vann. *The Strange Career of Jim Crow*. New York: Oxford University Press, 1957. Brief, lucid account of the evolution of Jim Crow practices in the South.

Foreign and Military Policy

Enduring Questions

1. How can a democracy maintain enough secrecy to conduct a good foreign policy?

2. Should our foreign policy reflect what is in America's interests or should it be based on some conception of human rights?

The attacks on the World Trade Center and the Pentagon on September 11, 2001, gave foreign and military policy a new focus and a new set of problems. When this country experienced a large and ruthless example of foreign terrorist activity, its people for the first time confronted the need to curb terrorism around the world in order to protect this country from further sneak attacks.

The public response was impressive, as was evident in an outburst of patriotism and a heightened sense of confidence in the national government. Valuable as these reactions were, they left unanswered some fundamental questions:

- How can America wage war in remote nations that harbor terrorists?
- If terrorists are sheltered or supported by nations that are otherwise friendly to the United States, what do we do about these countries?
- Should the United States allow other nations (for example, Israel) to wage war against terrorists (for example, those in neighboring Palestine), or should we try to be mediators?

553

- How can the military, designed to fight big, conventional land wars in Europe, be redesigned to make it effective in small, long-lasting struggles against terrorists?

And terrorism is not our only foreign or military problem. It is a new and very important one added to a long list of other issues. Among them are two questions:

- Do we support any nation that goes along with us, or only those that are reasonably free and democratic?
- Are we the world's policeman? We did not intervene to prevent China from occupying Tibet, to end the massacre of thousands of Tutsis in Rwanda, or to help Bosnia when it was being attacked by Serbs. But we did intervene to try to end a dictatorship in Haiti, to help starving people in Somalia, to turn back an Iraqi invasion of Kuwait, and to punish Serbs who were attacking Kosovo.

These choices must be made in a democracy, and some observers think that democratic politics makes managing foreign and military policy harder. Tocqueville said that the conduct of foreign affairs requires precisely those qualities most lacking in a democratic nation: "A democracy can only with great difficulty regulate the details of an important undertaking, persevere in a fixed design, and work out its execution in spite of serious obstacles. It cannot combine its measures with secrecy or await their consequences with patience."[1] In plain language a democracy is forced to play foreign policy poker with its cards turned up. As a result aggressors, from Hitler to Saddam Hussein, can bluff or misjudge us.

Others find fault not with the system but with what they view as the reckless policies of American presidents. If Congress had been more involved, they say, we would not have gotten bogged down in Vietnam, tried to trade arms for hostages in Iran, or supported the rebels in Nicaragua.

Happily, most foreign policy issues are not matters of war or peace. But the same issues can be found in them all: How great are the powers of the president? What role should Congress play? How important is public opinion? When do interest groups make a difference? To answer those questions we must first distinguish among foreign policy issues that involve majoritarian, interest group, and client politics.

Kinds of Foreign Policy

The majoritarian component of foreign policy includes those decisions (and nondecisions) that are perceived to confer widely distributed benefits and impose widely distributed costs. The decision to go to war is an obvious example of this. So, too, are the establishment of military alliances with Western Europe, the negotiation of a nuclear test ban treaty or a strategic arms limitation agreement, the response to the crisis posed by the Soviet blockade of West Berlin or the placement of Soviet offensive missiles in Cuba, the decision to aid the contras in Nicaragua, and the opening up of diplomatic relations with the People's Republic of China. These may be good or bad policies, but such benefits and such costs as they have accrue to the nation generally. Some argue that the costs of many of these policies are in fact highly concentrated—for example, soldiers bear the burden of a military operation—but that turns out, on closer inspection, not to shape the positions that people take on issues of war and peace. Though soldiers and their immediate families may feel the costs of a war to an especially high degree, public opinion surveys taken during the Vietnam War showed that having a family member in the armed forces did not significantly affect how people evaluated the war.[2] There is a sense that, during wartime, we are all in this together.

Foreign policy decisions may also reflect interest group politics. Tariff decisions confer benefits on certain business firms and labor unions and impose costs on other firms and unions. If the price of Japanese steel imported into this country is increased by tariffs, quotas, or other devices, this helps the American steel industry and the United Steel workers of America. On the other hand, it hurts those firms (and associated unions) that had been purchasing the once-cheap Japanese steel.

Examples of client politics also occur in foreign affairs. Washington often provides aid to American corporations doing business abroad because the aid helps those firms directly without imposing any apparent costs on an equally distinct group in society. Our policy toward Israel has in part reflected the fact that Jews in this country feel strongly about the need to support a Jewish state abroad and are well organized to make those concerns felt. (Other factors also help explain our support of Israel; it is by no means a pure case of client politics.) Arab

The embargo with Cuba remains a divisive foreign policy issue. Former President Jimmy Carter paid a visit there in 2002, and was the first U.S. president to do so since Fidel Castro rose to power almost fifty years ago.

Americans have begun to organize and to press on the government concerns very different from the pro-Israel arguments. We may in fact be witnessing a change of our policy toward Israel from one chiefly influenced by client politics to one more subject to interest group politics.

Who has power in foreign policy depends very much on what kind of foreign policy we have in mind. Where it is of a majoritarian nature, the president is clearly the dominant figure, and much, if not everything, depends on his beliefs and skills and on those of his chief advisers. Public opinion will ordinarily support this presidential leadership, but it will not guide it. As we shall see, public opinion on majoritarian foreign policy issues usually reflects a disposition to trust the president. But woe to the president who by his actions forfeits that trust.

When interest group or client politics is involved, Congress plays a much larger role. Although Congress has a subsidiary role in the conduct of foreign diplomacy, the decision to send troops overseas, or the direction of intelligence operations, it has a large one in decisions involving foreign economic aid, the structure of the tariff system, the shipment of weapons to foreign allies, the creation of new weapons systems, and the support of Israel.

And Congress is the central political arena on those occasions when entrepreneurial politics shapes foreign policy. If a multinational corporation is caught in a scandal, congressional investigations shake the usual indifference of politicians to the foreign conduct of such corporations. If presidential policies abroad lead to reversals, as when in 1986 presidential aides sought to trade arms for U.S. hostages in Iran and then use some profits from the arms sales to support the anti-Marxist contras fighting in Nicaragua, Congress becomes the forum for investigations and criticism. At such moments Congress often seeks to expand its power over foreign affairs.

In this chapter we will be chiefly concerned with foreign policy insofar as it displays the characteristics of majoritarian politics. Limiting the discussion in this way permits us to focus on the grand issues of foreign affairs—war, peace, and global diplomacy. It allows us to see how choices are made in a situation in which public majorities support but do not direct policy, in which opinion tends to react to events, and in which interest groups are relatively unimportant.

The Constitutional and Legal Context

The Constitution defines the authority of the president and of Congress in foreign affairs in a way that, as Edward Corwin put it, is an "invitation to struggle."[3] The president is commander in chief of the armed forces, but Congress must authorize and appropriate money for those forces. The president appoints ambassadors, but they must be confirmed by the Senate. The president may negotiate treaties, but the Senate must ratify these by a two-thirds vote. Only Congress may regulate commerce with other nations and "declare" war. (In an early draft of the Constitution the Framers gave Congress the power to "make" war but changed this to "declare" so that the president, acting without Congress, could take military measures to repel a sudden attack.) Because power over foreign affairs is shared by the president and Congress, conflict between them is to be expected.

Yet almost every American thinks instinctively that the president is in charge of foreign affairs, and what popular opinion supposes, the historical record confirms. Presidents have asserted the right to send troops abroad on their own authority in more than 125 instances.[4] Only five of the thirteen major wars that this country has fought have followed a formal declaration of war by Congress.[5] The State Department, the Central Intelligence Agency, and the

Shifting Patterns of Leadership in Foreign Policy

Depending on the personalities, skills, and interests of those involved, leadership in making American foreign policy may be found centered in the White House (the president and his national security adviser) or in the State Department (the secretary of state).

Periods of White House Dominance

President	Secretary of State
Franklin D. Roosevelt	Cordell Hull (1933–1944)
John F. Kennedy (and National Security Adviser McGeorge Bundy)	Dean Rusk (1961–1969)
Richard M. Nixon (and National Security Adviser Henry A. Kissinger)	William P. Rogers (1969–1973)

Periods of Leadership by the Secretary of State

Secretary of State	President
George C. Marshall (1947–1949) and Dean Acheson (1949–1953)	Harry S Truman
John Foster Dulles (1953–1959)	Dwight D. Eisenhower
Henry A. Kissinger (1973–1977)	Gerald R. Ford
Warren Christopher (1993–1996)	Bill Clinton

Periods of Tension Between the White House and Secretary of State

President	Secretary of State
Jimmy Carter	Cyrus Vance (1977–1980)
Ronald Reagan	George Shultz (1982–1989)

National Security Agency are almost entirely "presidential" agencies, with only modest congressional control. The Defense Department, though keenly sensitive to congressional views on weapons procurement and the location of military bases, is very much under the control of the president on matters of military strategy. While the Senate has since 1789 ratified well over a thousand treaties signed by the president, the president during this period has also signed around seven thousand executive agreements with other countries that did not require Senate ratification and yet have the force of law.[6]

Presidential Box Score

When the president seeks congressional approval for foreign policy matters, he tends to win more often than when he asks for support on domestic matters. One student of the presidency, Aaron Wildavsky, concluded that the American political system has "two presidencies"—one in domestic affairs that is relatively weak and closely checked, and another in foreign affairs that is quite powerful.[7] As we shall see, this view considerably overstates presidential power in certain areas.

When it comes to international diplomacy and the use of American troops, the president is indeed strong, much stronger than the Framers may have intended and certainly stronger than many members of Congress would prefer. Examples abound:

- 1801: Thomas Jefferson sent the navy to deal with the Barbary pirates.
- 1845: James K. Polk sent troops into Mexico to defend newly acquired Texas.
- 1861: Abraham Lincoln blockaded southern ports and declared martial law.
- 1940: Franklin D. Roosevelt sent fifty destroyers to England to be used against Germany, with which we were then technically at peace.
- 1950: Harry Truman sent American troops into South Korea to help repulse a North Korean attack on that country.
- 1960s: John F. Kennedy and Lyndon Johnson sent American forces into South Vietnam without a declaration of war.
- 1983: Ronald Reagan sent troops to overthrow a pro-Castro regime in Grenada.

- 1987: Reagan sent the navy to protect oil tankers in the Persian Gulf.
- 1989: George H.W. Bush ordered the U.S. invasion of Panama to depose dictator Manuel Noriega.
- 1990: Bush ordered troops to Saudi Arabia in response to Iraq's invasion of Kuwait.
- 1999: Bill Clinton ordered the military to attack, with bombs and cruise missiles, Serbian forces that were trying to control Kosovo.
- 2001: George W. Bush sent U.S. troops to liberate Afghanistan from the Taliban, a regime supportive of Osama bin Laden, the architect of the September 11 terrorist attacks.

However, by the standards of other nations, even other democratic ones, the ability of an American president to act decisively often appears rather modest. England was dismayed at the inability of Woodrow Wilson in 1914–1915 and Franklin Roosevelt in 1939–1940 to enter into an alliance when England was engaged in a major war with Germany. Wilson was unable to bring this country into the League of Nations. Gerald Ford could not intervene covertly in Angola in support of an anti-Marxist faction. Ronald Reagan was heavily criticized in Congress for sending fifty-five military advisers to El Salvador and a few hundred Marines to Lebanon. After George Bush sent U.S. troops to the Persian Gulf in 1990, he began a long debate with Congress over whether he would need a formal declaration of war before the troops were sent into combat.

Furthermore, a treaty signed by the president is little more than his promise to try to get the Senate to go along. He can sign executive agreements without Senate consent, but most of these are authorized in advance by Congress.[8]

By contrast, the leaders of other democratic nations (to say nothing of totalitarian ones) are often able to act with much greater freedom. While Reagan was arguing with Congress over whether we should assign any military advisers to El Salvador, the president of France, François Mitterrand, ordered twenty-five hundred combat troops to Chad with scarcely a ripple of opposition. A predecessor of Mitterrand, Charles de Gaulle, brought France into the European Common Market over the explicit opposition of the French Assembly and granted independence to Algeria, then a French colony, without seriously consulting the Assembly.[9] The British prime minister brought his country into the Common Market despite popular opposition and can declare war without the consent of Parliament.[10]

Evaluating the Power of the President

Whether one thinks the president is too strong or too weak in foreign affairs depends not only on whether one holds a domestic or international point of view but also on whether one agrees or disagrees with his policies. Historian Arthur M. Schlesinger, Jr., thought that President Kennedy exercised commendable presidential vigor when he made a unilateral decision to impose a naval blockade on Cuba to induce the Soviets to remove missiles installed there. However, he viewed President Nixon's decision to extend U.S. military action in Vietnam into neighboring Cambodia as a deplorable example of the "imperial presidency."[11] To be sure, there were important differences between these two actions, but that is precisely the point: a president strong enough to do something that one thinks proper is also strong enough to do something that one finds wrong.

The Supreme Court has fairly consistently supported the view that the federal government has powers in the conduct of foreign and military policy beyond those specifically mentioned in the Constitution. The leading decision, rendered in 1936, holds that the right to carry out foreign policy is an inherent attribute of any sovereign nation:

> The power to declare and wage war, to conclude peace, to make treaties, to maintain diplomatic

In 1962 President Kennedy forced the Soviet Union to withdraw the missiles it had placed in Cuba after their presence was revealed by aerial photography.

Under military guard Japanese Americans await transportation from their homes on the West Coast to relocation camps in the interior, where they remained for the duration of World War II.

relations with other sovereignties, if they had never been mentioned in the Constitution, would have vested in the Federal Government as necessary concomitants of nationality.[12]

The individual states have few rights in foreign affairs.

Moreover, the Supreme Court has been most reluctant to intervene in disputes over the conduct of foreign affairs. When various members of Congress brought suit challenging the right of President Nixon to enlarge the war in Vietnam without congressional approval, the court of appeals handled the issue, as one scholar was later to describe it, with all the care of porcupines making love. The Court said that it was a matter for the president and Congress to decide and that if Congress was unwilling to cut off the money to pay for the war, it should not expect the courts to do the job for it.[13]

The Supreme Court upheld the extraordinary measures taken by President Lincoln during the Civil War and refused to interfere with the conduct of the Vietnam War by Presidents Johnson and Nixon.[14] After Iran seized American hostages in 1979,

President Carter froze Iranian assets in this country. To win the hostages' freedom the president later agreed to return some of these assets and to nullify claims on them by American companies. The Court upheld the nullification because it was necessary for the resolution of a foreign policy dispute.[15]

How great the deference to presidential power may be is vividly illustrated by the actions of President Franklin Roosevelt in ordering the army to move over one hundred thousand Japanese Americans—the great majority of them born in this country and citizens of the United States—from their homes on the West Coast to inland "relocation centers" for the duration of World War II. Though this action was a wholesale violation of the constitutional rights of U.S. citizens and was unprecedented in American history, the Supreme Court decided that with the West Coast vulnerable to attack by Japan, the president was within his rights to declare that people of Japanese ancestry might pose a threat to internal security; thus the relocation order was upheld.[16] (No Japanese American was ever found guilty of espionage or sabotage.) One of the few cases in which the Court denied the president broad wartime powers occurred in 1952, when by a five-to-four vote it reversed President Truman's seizure of the steel mills—a move that he had made in order to avert a strike that, in his view, would have imperiled the war effort in Korea.[17]

Checks on Presidential Power

If there is a check on the powers of the federal government or the president in foreign affairs, it is chiefly political rather than constitutional. The most important check is Congress's control of the purse strings. In addition, Congress has imposed three important kinds of restrictions on the president's freedom of action, all since Vietnam:

■ **Limitations on the President's Ability to Give Military or Economic Aid to Other Countries** For example, between 1974 and 1978 the president could not sell arms to Turkey because of a dispute between Turkey and Greece over control of the island of Cyprus. The pressure on Congress from groups supporting Greece was much stronger than that from groups supporting Turkey. In 1976 Congress prevented President Ford from giving aid to the pro-Western faction in the Angolan civil war. Until the method was declared unconstitutional, Congress for many years could use a legislative veto, a resolution

Rivalry Versus Cooperation: The President and the Senate

Because the Senate must ratify treaties and consent to the appointment of ambassadors and other high foreign policy officials, it has the opportunity to play a large role in the conduct of foreign affairs. The key figure in the Senate is usually the chairman of the Senate Foreign Relations Committee.

Depending on personalities and circumstances, the president and the chairman have sometimes been able to work together closely but at other times have been bitter, outspoken rivals. In general cooperation occurs when there is a widely shared foreign policy worldview; rivalry erupts when worldviews diverge.

Periods of Shared Worldviews and Political Cooperation

President	Chairman of Foreign Relations Committee
Franklin D. Roosevelt	Tom Connally (1941–1947, 1949–1953)
Harry S Truman	Arthur H. Vandenberg (1947–1949)

Periods of Competing Worldviews and Political Rivalry

President	Chairman of Foreign Relations Committee
Woodrow Wilson	Henry Cabot Lodge (1919–1924)
Lyndon B. Johnson	J. William Fulbright (1959–1975)
Richard M. Nixon	J. William Fulbright (1959–1975)
Bill Clinton	Jesse Helms (1995–1999)

---

disapproving of an executive decision (see Chapter 13), to block the sale by the president of arms worth more than $25 million to another country.

■ **The War Powers Act** Passed in 1973 over a presidential veto, this law placed the following restrictions on the president's ability to use military force:

- He must report in writing to Congress within forty-eight hours after he introduces U.S. troops into areas where hostilities have occurred or are imminent.
- Within sixty days after troops are sent into hostile situations, Congress must, by declaration of war or other specific statutory authorization, provide for the continuation of hostile action by U.S. troops.
- If Congress fails to provide such authorization, the president must withdraw the troops (unless Congress has been prevented from meeting as a result of an armed attack).

- If Congress passes a concurrent resolution (which the president may not veto) directing the removal of U.S. troops, the president must comply.

The War Powers Act has had very little influence on American military actions. Since its passage every president—Ford, Carter, Reagan, Bush, Clinton, and Bush the younger—has sent American forces abroad without any explicit congressional authorization. (Bush the elder asked for that support when he attacked Iraq and, by a narrow margin, received it.) No president has acknowledged that the War Powers Act is constitutional. In its 1983 decision in the *Chadha* case the Supreme Court struck down the legislative veto, which means that this section of the act is already in constitutional trouble.[18]

Even if the act is constitutional, politically it is all but impossible to use. Few members of Congress would challenge a president who carried out a successful military operation (for example, those in Grenada, Panama, and Afghanistan). More might challenge the president if, after a while, the military action were in trouble, but the easiest way to do that would be to cut off funding for the operation. But even during the Vietnam War, a conflict that preceded the War Powers Act, Congress, though it contained many critics of U.S. policy, never stopped military appropriations.

■ **Intelligence Oversight** Owing to the low political stock of President Nixon during the Watergate scandal and the revelations of illegal operations by the Central Intelligence Agency (CIA) within the United States, Congress required that the CIA notify appropriate congressional committees about any proposed covert action (between 1974 and 1980 it had to notify *eight* different committees). Today it must keep two groups, the House and the Senate Intelligence Committees, "fully and currently informed" of all intelligence activities, including covert actions. The committees do not have the authority to disapprove such actions.

However, from time to time Congress will pass a bill blocking particular covert actions. This happened when the Boland Amendment (named after its sponsor, Representative Edward Boland) was passed on several occasions between 1982 and 1985. Each version of the amendment prevented, for specifically stated periods, intelligence agencies from supplying military aid to the Nicaraguan contras. After the surprise terrorist attack on September 11, some key members of Congress demanded an investigation to find out why the CIA had not warned the country of this risk.

The Machinery of Foreign Policy

From the time that Thomas Jefferson took the job in Washington's first administration until well into the twentieth century, foreign policy was often made and almost always carried out by the secretary of state. No more. When America became a major world power during and after World War II, our commitments overseas expanded dramatically. With that expansion two things happened. First, the president began to put foreign policy at the top of his agenda and to play a larger role in directing it. Second, that policy was shaped by the scores of agencies (some brand-new) that had acquired overseas activities.

Today Washington, D.C., has not one State Department but many. The Defense Department has military bases and military advisers abroad. The Central Intelligence Agency has intelligence officers abroad, most of them assigned to "stations" that are part of the American embassy but not under the full control of the American ambassador there. The Departments of Agriculture, Commerce, and Labor have missions abroad. The Federal Bureau of Investigation and the Drug Enforcement Administration have agents abroad. The Agency for International Development has offices to dispense foreign aid in host countries. The United States Information Agency runs libraries, radio stations, and educational programs abroad.

Every new secretary of state bravely announces that he or she is going to "coordinate" and "direct" this enormous foreign policy establishment. He or she never does. The reason is partly that the job is too big for any one person and partly that most of these agencies owe no political or bureaucratic loyalty to the secretary of state. If anyone is to coordinate them, it will have to be the president. But the president cannot keep track of what all these organizations are doing in the more than 170 nations and 50 international organizations where we have representatives, or in the more than 800 international conferences that we attend each year.

So he has hired a staff to do the coordinating for him. That staff is part of the National Security Council (NSC), a committee created by statute and chaired by the president, whose members include by law the vice president and the secretaries of state and defense, by custom the director of the CIA and the chairman of the Joint Chiefs of Staff, and often the attorney general. Depending on the president, the NSC can be an important body in which to hammer out foreign policy. Attached to it is a staff headed by the national security adviser. That staff, which usually numbers a few dozen men and women, can be (again, depending on the president) an enormously powerful instrument for formulating and directing foreign policy.

Nominally that staff exists only to bring before the president a balanced account of the views of the heads of the major government agencies with a stake in foreign policy decisions, to help the president choose among the options that these advisers identify, and to oversee the implementation of the president's decisions. These decisions are usually in the form of a National Security Decision Directive, or NSDD, signed by the president.

Presidents Truman and Eisenhower made only limited use of the NSC staff, but beginning with President Kennedy it has grown greatly in influence. Its head, the national security adviser, has come to rival the secretary of state for foreign policy leadership, especially when the adviser is a powerful personality such as Henry Kissinger. President Reagan attempted to downgrade the importance of the national security adviser, but ironically it was one of his relatively low-visibility appointees, Admiral John Poindexter, and his subordinate, Lieutenant Colonel Oliver North, who precipitated the worst crisis of the Reagan presidency when, allegedly without informing the president, they tried to use cash realized from the secret sale of arms to Iran to finance guerrillas fighting against the Marxist government of Nicaragua. The sale and the diversion became known, North was fired, a congressional investigation ensued, criminal charges were filed against Poindexter and North, and the president's political position was weakened.

But even in ordinary times the NSC staff has been the rival of the secretary of state, except during that period in the Ford administration when Henry Kissinger held *both* jobs.

The way in which the machinery of foreign policy making operates has two major consequences for the substance of that policy. First, as former secretary of state George Shultz asserted, "It's never over." Foreign policy issues are endlessly agitated, rarely settled. The reason is that the rivalries *within* the executive branch intensify the rivalries *between* that branch and Congress. In ways already described, Congress has steadily increased its influence over the conduct of foreign policy. Anybody in the executive branch who loses out in a struggle over foreign policy can take his or her case (usually by means of a well-timed leak) to a sympathetic member of Congress, who then can make a speech, hold a hearing, or introduce a bill.

Second, the interests of the various organizations making up the foreign policy establishment profoundly affect the positions that they take. Because the State Department has a stake in diplomacy, it tends to resist bold or controversial new policies that might upset established relationships with other countries. Part of the CIA has a stake in gathering and analyzing information; that part tends to be skeptical of the claims of other agencies that their overseas operations are succeeding. Another part of the CIA conducts covert operations abroad; it tends to resent or ignore the skepticism of the intelligence analysts. The air force flies airplanes and so tends to be optimistic about what can be accomplished through the use of air power in particular and military power in general; the army, on the other hand, which must fight in the trenches, is often dubious about the prospects for military success.

Americans often worry that their government is keeping secrets from them. In fact there are no secrets in Washington—at least not for long.

Foreign Policy and Public Opinion

These organizational conflicts shape the details of foreign policy, but its broad outlines are shaped by public and elite opinion.

World War II was the great watershed event in American foreign policy. Before that time a clear majority of the American public opposed active involvement in world affairs. The public saw the costs of such involvement as being substantially in excess of the benefits, and only determined, skillful leaders were able, as was President Roosevelt during 1939–1940, to affect in even a limited fashion the diplomatic and military struggles then convulsing Europe and Asia.

Our participation in the war produced a dramatic shift in popular opinion that endured for three decades, supplying broad (though often ambiguous) public support for an internationalist foreign policy. World War II had this effect, alone among all wars that we have fought, for several reasons. First, it was almost the only universally popular war in which we have been engaged, one that produced few, if any, recriminations afterward. Second, the war seemed successful: an unmitigated evil (the Nazi regime) was utterly destroyed; an attack on our own land (by Japan at Pearl Harbor) was thoroughly avenged. Third, that war ended with the United States recognized as the dominant power on earth, owing to its sole possession of the atomic bomb and its enormous military and economic productivity.

In 1937, 94 percent of the American public preferred the policy of doing "everything possible to keep out of foreign wars" to the policy of doing "everything possible to prevent war, even if it means threatening to fight countries that fight wars." In 1939, after World War II had begun in Europe but before Pearl Harbor was attacked, only 13 percent of

WHO GOVERNS? TO WHAT ENDS?

The War Against Terrorism

In 2000, it would have been impossible to find any Americans who thought it would be a good idea if America fought a war in Afghanistan. After September 11, 2001, it was hard to find an American who did not think it a good idea.

We began to fight there after the terrorist attacks on New York City's World Trade Center and on the Pentagon. Terrorists from Middle Eastern countries hijacked three American airliners just after they took off and then crashed two into the Trade Center and one into the Pentagon, killing everyone on board and over three thousand innocent civilians. A fourth airliner was also hijacked and was directed toward Washington, D.C., for some unknown target, but it crashed in western Pennsylvania after some passengers struggled with the terrorists.

It soon became clear to American intelligence officers that these attacks had been planned by Osama bin Laden and his allies. Bin Laden is a Saudi Arabian who fought against the Soviet occupation of Afghanistan, succeeding—with American aid—in driving the Soviets out of that country. But during and after the American-led war against Saddam Hussein's invasion of Kuwait, bin Laden learned that American troops were stationed in Saudi Arabia. He regarded them as "infidels" who were "desecrating" a country that was the homeland of the Muslim religion and the site of its most important shrines. The Saudi government did not share

Osama bin Laden

this view and made clear to bin Laden that he would not be welcomed back to his birth place.

Bin Laden, a radical Muslim who detests Western culture, inherited a great deal of money from his

Americans polled thought that we should enter the war against Germany. Just a month before Pearl Harbor only 19 percent felt that the United States should take steps, at the risk of war, to prevent Japan from becoming too powerful.[19] Congress reflected the noninterventionist mood of the country: in the summer of 1941, with war breaking out almost everywhere, the proposal to continue the draft passed the House of Representatives by only one vote.

The Japanese attack on Pearl Harbor on December 7 changed all that. Not only was the American war effort supported almost unanimously, not only did Congress approve the declaration of war with only one dissenting vote, but World War II—unlike World War I—produced popular support for an active assumption of international responsibilities that continued after the war had ended.[20] Whereas after World War I a majority opposed U.S. entry into the

Secretary of Defense Donald Rumsfeld visiting soldiers in Afghanistan.

father. He used it to help another group of radicals, the Taliban,[1] to gain control of Afghanistan and to help pay for a network of terrorist organizations called Al Qaeda.[2] Much of this happened when the United States, after covertly helping drive the Soviets out of Afghanistan, lost interest in the country and stood by while a radical regime seized power there.

Bin Laden, though intensely anti-American, is at the same time a smart organizer who knows how to build up a well-trained network of terrorist cells and work out alliances with other radical organizations. The carefully planned destruction he visited on the United States in 2001 was preceded by his success at arranging the bombing of two American embassies in Africa and a U.S. destroyer based in the Middle East.

Once the United States knew that bin Laden's forces were behind the terrorist attacks, they had to strike back at his home base, Afghanistan, without alienating the Afghan people (most of whom detested the Taliban regime) and other Muslims (most of whom disapproved of bin Laden's extremism).

To do this, the United States forged a coalition of many other nations who were willing to share in military, intelligence, or economic work; announced that its struggle was not with Islam but with bin Laden and allied terrorist groups and the nations that harbored terrorists; and formed an agreement with dissident Afghan groups, such as the Northern Alliance. With the help of other nations, including Russia, it armed the dissidents and then provided air force attacks on the Taliban while the dissidents fought the ground war.

Many Americans thought we could not win such a battle in so remote a place, but the dissidents, with our help, did win. Under European and United Nations leadership, a new government for Afghanistan was organized.

As this edition of the book goes to press, no one knows whether the United States will extend its campaign by taking on other nations that harbor terrorists.

---

[1] "Taliban" means, roughly, "soldier monks" or "student monks" and refers to radical young men trained in schools found in Pakistan and other Near Eastern countries.

[2] "Al Qaeda" means, roughly, "the base." It is a terrorist network of small cells that includes alliances with other militant Muslim groups, such as the Islamic Jihad.

League of Nations, after World War II a clear majority favored our entry into the United Nations.[21]

This willingness to see the United States remain a world force persisted. Even during the Vietnam War the number of people thinking that we should "keep independent" in world affairs as opposed to "working closely with other nations" rose from 10 percent in 1963 to only 22 percent in 1969.[22] In 1967, after more than two years of war in Vietnam, 44 percent of Americans believed that this country had an obligation to "defend other Vietnams if they are threatened by communism."[23]

But the support for an internationalist American foreign policy was, and is, highly general and heavily dependent on the phrasing of poll questions, the opinions expressed by popular leaders, and the impact of world events. Public opinion, while more internationalist than once was the case, is both

Table 20.1	Popular Reactions to Foreign Policy Crises		
Percentage of public saying that they approve of the way the president is handling his job			
Foreign Policy Crisis		**Before**	**After**
1960	American U-2 spy plane shot down over Soviet Union	62%	68%
1961	Abortive landing at Bay of Pigs in Cuba	73	83
1962	Cuban missile crisis	61	74
1975	President Ford sends forces to rescue the American ship	40	51
1979	American embassy in Teheran seized by Iranians	32	61
1980	Failure of military effort to rescue hostages in Iran	39	43
1983	U.S. invasion of Grenada	43	53
1989	U.S. invasion of Panama	71	80
1990	U.S. troops to Persian Gulf	60	75
1995	U.S. troops to Bosnia	59	54
1999	U.S. troops to Kosovo	55	51
2001	U.S. combat in Afghanistan	51	86

Source: Updated from Theodore J. Lowi, *The End of Liberalism* (New York: Norton, 1969), 184. Poll data are from Gallup poll. Time lapse between "before" and "after" samplings of opinion was in no case more than one month.

mushy and volatile. Just prior to President Nixon's decision to send troops into Cambodia, only 7 percent of the people said that they supported such a move. After the troops were sent and Nixon made a speech explaining his move, 50 percent of the public said that they supported it.[24] Similarly, only 49 percent of the people favored halting the American bombing of North Vietnam before President Johnson ordered such a halt in 1968; afterward 60 percent of the people said that they supported such a policy.[25]

Backing the President

Much of this volatility in specific opinions (as opposed to general mood) reflects the already-mentioned deference to the "commander in chief" and a desire to support the United States when it confronts other nations. Table 20.1 shows the proportion of people who said that they approved of the way the president was doing his job before and after various major foreign policy events. Each foreign crisis increased the level of public approval of the president, often dramatically. The most vivid illustration of this was the Bay of Pigs fiasco: an American-supported, American-directed invasion of Cuba by anti-Castro Cuban émigrés was driven back into the sea. President Kennedy accepted responsibility for the aborted project. His popularity *rose*. (Comparable data for domestic crises tend to show no similar effect.)

This tendency to "rally round the flag" operates for some but not all foreign military crises.[26] The rally not only helped Kennedy after the Bay of Pigs, but it also helped Ronald Reagan when he invaded Grenada and George Bush the elder when he sent troops to fight Iraq. But it did not help Bill Clinton when he sent forces to Bosnia or launched bombing attacks on Iraq. If there is an attack on America, the president will do very well. Just before September 11, 2001, George Bush's favorability rating was 51 percent; just after the attack, it was 86 percent.

Sometimes people argue that whatever support a president gets during a military crisis will disappear once dead soldiers in body bags begin returning home. There are two things wrong with this statement. First, dead soldiers do not come home in body bags; they come home in coffins. Second, a close study of how casualty rates affect public opinion showed that although deaths tend to reduce how "favorable" people are toward a war, what they then support is not withdrawal but an *escalation* in the fighting so as to defeat the enemy more quickly. This was true during Korea, Vietnam, and the Persian Gulf War.[27]

In sum people tend to be leery of overseas military expeditions by the United States—until they start. Then they support them and want to win, even if it means more intense fighting. When Americans began to dislike our involvement in Korea and Vietnam,[28] they did not conclude that we should pull out; they concluded instead that we should do whatever was necessary to win.

If this is how the public thinks, you might think that a president would be well advised to start a war to boost his popularity. On occasion a president might launch some cruise missiles against alleged terrorist hideouts to look tough, but in general presidents do not act so cynically. There is too much at stake.

Mass Versus Elite Opinion

The public is poorly informed about foreign affairs. It probably has only a vague idea where Kosovo is, how far it is from Baghdad to Kuwait, or why the Palestinians and the Jews disagree about the future of Israel.[29] But that is to be expected. Foreign affairs are, well, foreign. They do not have much to do with the daily lives of American citizens, except during wartime.

But the public, since World War II, has consistently felt that the United States should play an important international role.[30] And if our troops go abroad, it is a foolish politician who will try to talk the public out of supporting them.

Political elites, however, have a different perspective. They are better informed about foreign policy issues, but their opinions are more likely to change rapidly. Initially, college-educated people gave *more* support to the war in Vietnam than those without college training; by the end of the war, however, that

support had decreased dramatically. Whereas the average citizen was upset when the United States seemed to be on the *defensive* in Vietnam, college-educated voters tended to be more upset when the United States was on the *offensive*.[31]

Though the average citizen did not want our military in Vietnam in the first place, he or she felt that we should support our troops once they were there. The average person also was deeply opposed to the antiwar protests taking place on college campuses. When the Chicago police roughed up antiwar demonstrators at the 1968 Democratic convention, public sentiment was overwhelmingly on the side of the police.[32] Contrary to myths much accepted at the time, younger people were *not* more opposed to the war than older ones. There was no "generation gap."

By contrast, college-educated citizens, thinking at first that troops should be involved, soon changed their minds, decided that the war was wrong, and grew increasingly upset when the United States seemed to be enlarging the war (by invading Cambodia, for example). College students protested against the war largely on moral grounds, and their protests received more support from college-educated adults than from other citizens.

Elite opinion changes more rapidly than public opinion. During the Vietnam War, upper-middle-class people who regularly read several magazines and newspapers underwent a dramatic change in opinion between 1964 (when they supported the war) and 1968 (when they opposed it). But the views of blue-collar workers scarcely changed at all.[33]

The cleavage between mass and elite opinion is even wider if you restrict the definition of *elite* to only those involved in making foreign policy rather than including all college-educated people. In Table 20.2 we see the differences in foreign policy views of a cross section of American citizens and a group of 379 leaders active in government, academia, the mass media, and various organizations concerned with foreign affairs.[34]

In general the leaders have a more liberal and internationalist outlook than the public: they are more likely to favor giving economic aid to other countries, defending our allies, reducing tariffs, and opposing oppressive regimes. The public, on the other hand, wants the United States to be less active overseas and worries about protecting the jobs of American workers. Accordingly, it wants the United States to keep tariffs high, protect American jobs from foreign competition, and give less economic aid to other nations.

Table 20.2   How the Public and the Elite See Foreign Policy, 1999

	Percentage Agreeing	
	Public	Leaders
Tariffs are necessary to protect American jobs	60%	36%
Oppose giving economic aid to foreign countries	49	10
Russia should solve its problems alone, without U.S. aid	42	18
Oppose U.S. troops helping South Korea if North Korea invades	66	25
Reducing illegal immigration is very important	57	21
Oppose an independent Palestinian state in Israel	42	19
Support assassinating terrorist leaders to combat terrorism	61	35

Source: John E. Rielly, *American Public Opinion and U.S. Foreign Policy, 1999* (Chicago: Chicago Council on Foreign Relations, 1999).

Iron Curtain and Cold War

The **iron curtain** was neither iron nor a curtain; it was the political barrier, maintained by the Soviet Union, to free travel and communication between Eastern and Western Europe. In 1989 the iron curtain began to collapse. The phrase was given its present meaning by Winston Churchill in a speech that he delivered at Westminster College in Fulton, Missouri, on March 5, 1946: "From Stettin in the Baltic to Trieste in the Adriatic, an iron curtain has descended across the continent. Behind that line lie all the capitals of the ancient states of central and eastern Europe."

The **cold war** referred to the nonmilitary struggle between the United States (and its allies) and the former Soviet Union (and its allies). (A *cold war* is distinguished from a *hot,* or *shooting,* war.) The phrase was coined by journalist Herbert Bayard Swope in 1946 and popularized by columnist Walter Lippmann.

Source: Adapted from *Safire's Political Dictionary* by William Safire. Copyright © 1968, 1972, 1978 by William Safire. Reprinted by permission of Random House, Inc. and the author.

Cleavages Among Foreign Policy Elites

As we have seen, public opinion on foreign policy is permissive and a bit mushy: it supports presidential action without giving it much direction. Elite opinion therefore acquires extraordinary importance. Of course events and world realities are also important, but since events have no meaning except as they are perceived and interpreted by people who must react to them, the attitudes and beliefs of those people in and out of government who are actively involved in shaping foreign policy often assume decisive importance. Contrary to the views of people who think that some shadowy, conspiratorial group of insiders runs our foreign policy, the foreign policy elite in this country is deeply divided.

That elite consists not only of those people with administrative positions in the foreign policy field—the senior officials of the State Department and the staff of the National Security Council—but also the members and staffs of the key congressional committees concerned with foreign affairs (chiefly the Senate Foreign Relations Committee and the House Foreign Affairs Committee) and various private organizations that help shape elite opinion, such as the members of the Council on Foreign Relations and the editors of two important publications, *Foreign Affairs* and *Foreign Policy.* To these must be added influential columnists and editorial writers whose work appears regularly in the national press. One could extend the list by adding ever-wider circles of people with some influence (lobbyists, professors, leaders of veterans' organizations); this would complicate without changing the central point: elite beliefs are probably more important in explaining foreign policy than in accounting for decisions in other policy areas.

How a Worldview Shapes Foreign Policy

These beliefs can be described in simplified terms as **worldviews** (or, as some social scientists put it, as paradigms)—more or less comprehensive mental pictures of the critical problems facing the United States in the world and of the appropriate and inappropriate ways of responding to these problems. The clearest, most concise, and perhaps most influential statement of one worldview that held sway for many years was in an article published in 1947 in *Foreign Affairs,* titled "The Sources of Soviet Conduct."[35] Written by a "Mr. X" (later revealed to be George F. Kennan, director of the Policy Planning Staff of the State Department and thereafter ambassador to Moscow), the article argued that the Russians were pursuing a policy of expansion that could only be met by the United States' applying "unalterable counterforce at every point where they show signs of encroaching upon the interests of a peaceful and stable world." This he called the strategy of "containment," and it became the governing principle of American foreign policy for at least two decades.

There were critics of the containment policy at the time—Walter Lippmann, in his book *The Cold War*, argued against it in 1947[36]—but the criticisms were less influential than the doctrine. A dominant worldview is important precisely because it prevails over alternative views. One reason why it prevails is that it is broadly consistent with the public's mood. In 1947, when Kennan wrote, popular attitudes toward the Soviet Union, favorable during World War II when Russia and America were allies, had turned quite hostile. In 1946 less than one-fourth of the American people believed that Russia could be trusted to cooperate with this country,[37] and by 1948 over three-fourths were convinced that the Soviet Union was trying not simply to defend itself but to become the dominant world power.[38]

Such a worldview was also influential because it was consistent with events at the time: Russia had occupied most of the previously independent countries of Eastern Europe and was turning them into puppet regimes. When governments independent of both the United States and the Soviet Union attempted to rule in Hungary and Czechoslovakia, they were overthrown by Soviet-backed coups. A worldview also becomes dominant when it is consistent with the prior experiences of the people holding it.

■ **Four Worldviews** Every generation of political leaders comes to power with a foreign policy worldview shaped, in large measure, by the real or apparent mistakes of the previous generation.[39] This pattern can be traced back, some have argued, to the very beginnings of the nation. Frank L. Klingberg traces the alteration since 1776 between two national "moods" that favored first "extroversion" (or an active, internationalist policy) and then "introversion" (a less active, even isolationist posture).[40]

Since the 1920s American elite opinion has moved through four dominant worldviews: isolationism, containment (or antiappeasement), disengagement, and human rights. **Isolationism** was the view adopted as a result of our unhappy experience in World War I. Our efforts to help European allies had turned

---

★ POLITICALLY SPEAKING ★

Domino Theory

In 1954 President Eisenhower said that "you have a row of dominoes set up; you knock over the first one, and what will happen to the last one is that it will go over very quickly." He used this analogy to justify giving economic aid to South Vietnam to prevent it, and thus its Southeast Asian neighbors, from being taken over by communists.

Supporters of aid to South Vietnam accepted this **domino theory**; opponents of that aid denied the theory, arguing (as did novelist Norman Mailer) that these countries were not dominoes but "sand castles" that were being engulfed by a "tide of nationalism."

In the 1980s the domino theory was part of the argument about whether we should help El Salvador and support the contras in Nicaragua as a way of keeping Central America from being dominated by Marxist governments.

For the record, after South Vietnam fell to communist North Vietnam, two other nearby dominoes—Cambodia and Laos—also went communist, but Thailand did not.

Source: Adapted from *Safire's Political Dictionary* by William Safire. Copyright © 1968, 1972, 1978 by William Safire. Reprinted by permission of Random House, Inc. and the author.

---

sour: thousands of American troops had been killed in a war that had seemed to accomplish little and certainly had not made the world, in Woodrow Wilson's words, "safe for democracy." As a result in the 1920s and 1930s elite opinion (and popular opinion) opposed getting involved in European wars.

A meeting that named an era: In Munich British prime minister Neville Chamberlain attempted to appease the territorial ambitions of Hitler. Chamberlain's failure brought World War II closer.

The battleship West Virginia *burns after being hit by Japanese warplanes at Pearl Harbor on December 7, 1941.*

The **containment (or antiappeasement)** paradigm was the result of World War II. Pearl Harbor was the death knell for isolationism. Senator Arthur H. Vandenberg of Michigan, a staunch isolationist before the attack, became an ardent internationalist not only during but after the war. He later wrote of the Japanese attack on Pearl Harbor on December 7, 1941, "that day ended isolationism for any realist."[41] At a conference in Munich, efforts of British and French leaders to satisfy Hitler's territorial demands in Europe had led not to "peace in our time," as Prime Minister Neville Chamberlain of Britain had claimed, but to evergreater territorial demands and ultimately to world war. This crisis brought to power men determined not to repeat their predecessors' mistakes: "Munich" became a synonym for weakness, and leaders such as Winston Churchill made antiappeasement the basis of their postwar policy of resisting Soviet expansionism. Churchill summed up the worldview that he had acquired from the Munich era in a famous speech delivered in 1946 in Fulton, Missouri, in which he coined the term *iron curtain* to describe Soviet policy in Eastern Europe.

The events leading up to World War II were the formative experiences of those leaders who came to power in the 1940s, 1950s, and 1960s. What they took to be the lessons of Pearl Harbor and Munich were applied repeatedly—in building a network of defensive alliances in Europe and Asia during the late 1940s and 1950s, in operating an airlift to aid West Berlin when road access to it was cut off by the Russians, in coming to the aid of South Korea, and finally in intervening in Vietnam. Most of these applications of the containment worldview were successful in the sense that they did not harm American interests, they proved welcome to allies, or they prevented a military conquest.

The **disengagement** (or "Vietnam") view resulted from the experience of the younger foreign policy elite that came to power in the 1970s. Unlike previous applications of the antiappeasement view, our entry into Vietnam had led to a military defeat and a domestic political disaster. There were three ways of interpreting that crisis: (1) we applied the correct worldview in the right place but did not try hard enough; (2) we had the correct worldview but tried to apply it in the wrong place under the wrong circumstances; (3) the worldview itself was wrong. By and large the critics of our Vietnam policy tended toward the third conclusion, and thus when they supplanted in office the architects of our Vietnam policy, they inclined toward a worldview based on the slogan "no more Vietnams." Critics of this view called it the "new isolationism," arguing that it would encourage Soviet expansion.

The language of Vietnam colored many discussions of foreign policy. Almost every military initiative since then has been debated in terms of whether it would lead us into "another Vietnam": sending the Marines to Lebanon, invading Grenada, dispatching military advisers to El Salvador, supporting the contras in Nicaragua, helping South American countries fight drug producers, sending troops to the Persian Gulf to force Iraq to abandon its invasion of Kuwait, sending troops to Somalia, and using American air power in Bosnia.

How elites thought about Vietnam affected their foreign policy views for many years. If they thought the war was "immoral," they were reluctant to see American military involvement elsewhere. They played a large role in the Carter administration but were replaced by rival elites—those more inclined to a containment view—during the Reagan presidency.[42] When Bush sought to expel Iraqi troops from Kuwait, the congressional debate pitted those committed to containment against those who believed in disengagement. The Senate vote on Bush's request for permission to use troops was narrowly carried by containment advocates.

When Clinton became president in 1992, he brought to office a lack of interest in foreign policy coupled with advisers who were drawn from the ranks of those who believed in disengagement. His strongest congressional supporters were those who had argued against the Gulf War. But then a remarkable change occurred. When Slobodan Milosevic, the Serbian leader, sent troops into neighboring Kosovo to suppress the ethnic Albanians living there, the strongest voices for American military intervention came from those who once advocated disengagement. Representative David Bonior, the minority whip in the House, who had voted against fighting Iraq's Saddam Hussein, now spoke out in favor of fighting Milosevic. During the Gulf War 47 Senate Democrats voted to oppose U.S. participation. A few years later 42 Senate Democrats voted to support our role in Kosovo.

★ **POLITICALLY SPEAKING** ★

Third World

Originally a French term (*tiers monde*) referring to nations neutral in the cold war between the United Nations and the Soviet Union, the **Third World** now means almost any underdeveloped nation in Africa, Asia, Latin America, or the Middle East.

When the oil-producing nations, such as Saudi Arabia, became wealthy after having succeeded in raising oil prices in the early 1970s, some observers began to use a new phrase, the **Fourth World,** to refer to underdeveloped nations that had no oil reserves and thus had to pay heavily for imported oil.

And some nations, such as Taiwan and the Republic of Korea, once thought to be part of the Third World because they were underdeveloped have made such startling economic progress that they are now referred to as the "newly industrialized nations" (NINs).

Source: Adapted from *Safire's Political Dictionary* by William Safire. Copyright © 1968, 1972, 1978 by William Safire. Reprinted by permission of Random House, Inc. and the author.

What had happened? The change was inspired by the view that helping the Albanians was required by the doctrine of **human rights.** Liberal supporters of U.S. air attacks on Serbian forces believed that we were helping Albanians escape mass killing. By contrast, many conservative members of Congress who had followed a containment policy in the Gulf War now felt that disengagement ought to be followed in Kosovo. Of course politics also mattered. Clinton was a Democratic president; Bush had been a Republican one.

U.S. Military Intervention in the Middle East

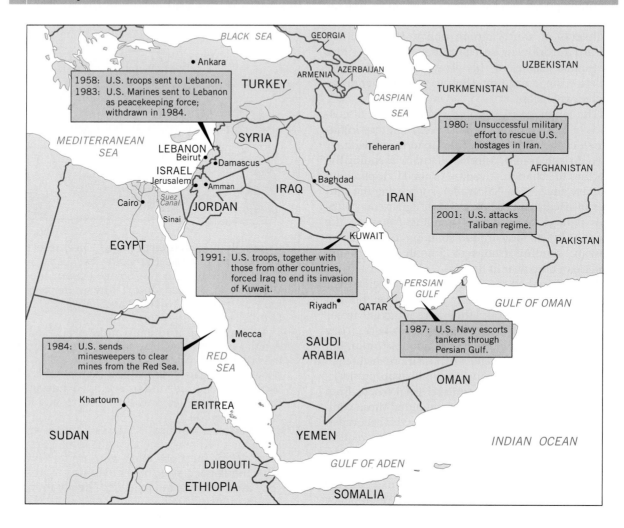

1958: U.S. troops sent to Lebanon.
1983: U.S. Marines sent to Lebanon as peacekeeping force; withdrawn in 1984.

1980: Unsuccessful military effort to rescue U.S. hostages in Iran.

2001: U.S. attacks Taliban regime.

1991: U.S. troops, together with those from other countries, forced Iraq to end its invasion of Kuwait.

1987: U.S. Navy escorts tankers through Persian Gulf.

1984: U.S. sends minesweepers to clear mines from the Red Sea.

But politics was not the whole story. American liberal elites had persuaded themselves that the attack in Kosovo resembled the genocide—that is, the mass murder of people because of their race or ethnicity—that the Jews had suffered in Nazi Germany. They held that we must "never again" permit a whole people to be killed.

There are some problems with this view. Hardly any human rights advocates had called for U.S. intervention in Rwanda, China, or the Soviet Union—all countries that massacred millions of their own citizens. In addition, the historical record suggests that the Serbs and the Albanians have been killing each other for centuries. Now that the Serbian army has withdrawn from Kosovo, Serbian civilians who stayed behind are being killed by the Albanians whom they once killed. The response that some human rights advocates would give to these criticisms is that America owes a special obligation to Europe and that even if Albanians kill Serbs, a Western military presence there will at least prevent organized military killing.

In the aftermath of 9/11, a new issue has arisen that may divide foreign policy elites in the future. Should the United States "go it alone" against its enemies abroad, or do so only on the basis of a broad coalition of supporting nations? President Bush the elder assembled just such a coalition to force Iraq out

U.S. Military Intervention in Central America and the Caribbean Since 1950

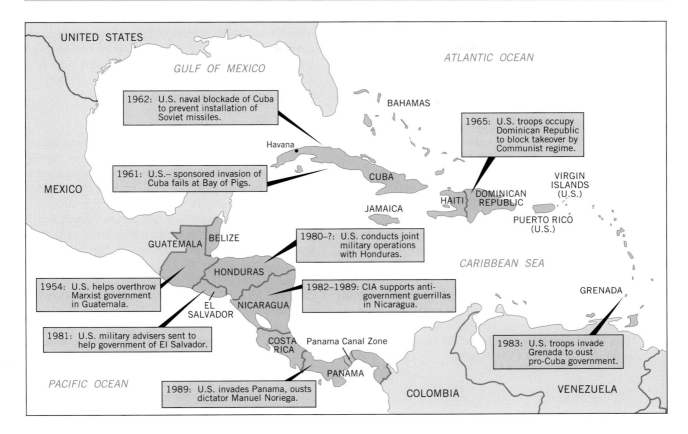

UNITED STATES

GULF OF MEXICO

ATLANTIC OCEAN

BAHAMAS

1962: U.S. naval blockade of Cuba to prevent installation of Soviet missiles.

1965: U.S. troops occupy Dominican Republic to block takeover by Communist regime.

Havana

1961: U.S.– sponsored invasion of Cuba fails at Bay of Pigs.

CUBA

VIRGIN ISLANDS (U.S.)

MEXICO

JAMAICA

HAITI   DOMINICAN REPUBLIC

PUERTO RICO (U.S.)

GUATEMALA   BELIZE

1980–?: U.S. conducts joint military operations with Honduras.

CARIBBEAN SEA

HONDURAS

1954: U.S. helps overthrow Marxist government in Guatemala.

1982–1989: CIA supports anti-government guerrillas in Nicaragua.

GRENADA

EL SALVADOR   NICARAGUA

1981: U.S. military advisers sent to help government of El Salvador.

COSTA RICA   Panama Canal Zone

1983: U.S. troops invade Grenada to oust pro-Cuba government.

PACIFIC OCEAN

1989: U.S. invades Panama, ousts dictator Manuel Noriega.

PANAMA

COLOMBIA   VENEZUELA

of Kuwait, but President Bush the younger acted almost alone in invading Afghanistan to destroy the Taliban, though he received crucial support from Great Britain, Australia, and Canada.

Many people believe the United States should attack Iraq in order to remove Saddam Hussein from power. As of late-2002, that had not happened, but if it does happen it will again raise the coalition issue. Can we do this alone or just with the British, or must we have hard-to-find European and Middle Eastern allies?

The Use of Military Force

Foreign policy takes many forms—discussions are held, treaties are signed, organizations are joined— but in many cases it depends on the ability to use military force. Troops, ships, and aircraft are not the only ways of influencing other countries; interna-

tional trade and foreign aid are also useful. But in modern times, as in the past, the nations of the world know the difference between a "great power" (that is, a heavily armed one) and a weak nation.

With the collapse of the Soviet Union and the end of the cold war, one might think that military power has become less important. But in fact it remains as important as ever. Since the Soviet Union was dissolved and the Berlin Wall came down in 1989, the United States has used military force to attack Iraq, maintain order in Bosnia, defend Kosovo, and go to war in Afghanistan. Various rogue nations, such as Iraq, Libya, and North Korea, have acquired or are about to acquire long-range rockets and weapons of mass destruction (that is, nuclear, chemical, and biological arms). Many nations that feel threatened by their neighbors, such as China, India, Pakistan, and Israel, have nuclear bombs. And Russia still has many of the nuclear weapons that the old Soviet Union built.

It would be foolish to assume that the end of the cold war means the end of war.

There are two views about the role of the military in American life. One is majoritarian: the military exists to defend the country or to help other nations defend themselves. When troops are used, almost all Americans benefit and almost all pay the bill. (Some Americans, such as those who lose a loved one in war, pay much more than the rest of us.) The president is the commander in chief, and Congress plays a largely supportive role.

Although the other view does not deny that the armed forces are useful, it focuses on the extent to which the military is a large and powerful client. The real beneficiaries of military spending are the generals and admirals, as well as the big corporations and members of Congress whose districts get fat defense contracts. Everyone pays, but these clients get most of the benefits. What we spend on defense is shaped by the **military-industrial complex,** a supposedly unified bloc of Defense Department leaders and military manufacturers. A good example of the waste this entails, people with this view allege, can be found in stories about the military buying $435 hammers.

The Defense Budget

To sort out these competing claims, one has to understand how America raises and spends its defense dollars. There are two important things to know: how much money we spend and how it is divided up. The first reflects majoritarian politics, the second interest group bargaining.

Total Spending

Throughout most of our history the United States has not maintained large military forces during peacetime. For instance, the percentage of the gross national product (GNP) spent on defense in 1935, on the eve of World War II, was about the same as it was in 1870, when we were on the eve of nothing in particular.[43] We armed when a war broke out, then we disarmed when the war ended. But all of that changed after World War II, when defense spending declined sharply but did not return to its prewar levels. And in 1950 our defense expenditures soared again.

In that year we rearmed to fight a war in Korea, but when it was over, we did not completely disarm. The reason was our containment policy toward the

The Pentagon, headquarters of the U.S. armed forces, after a terrorist attack.

Figure 20.1   Trends in Military Spending (in constant dollars)

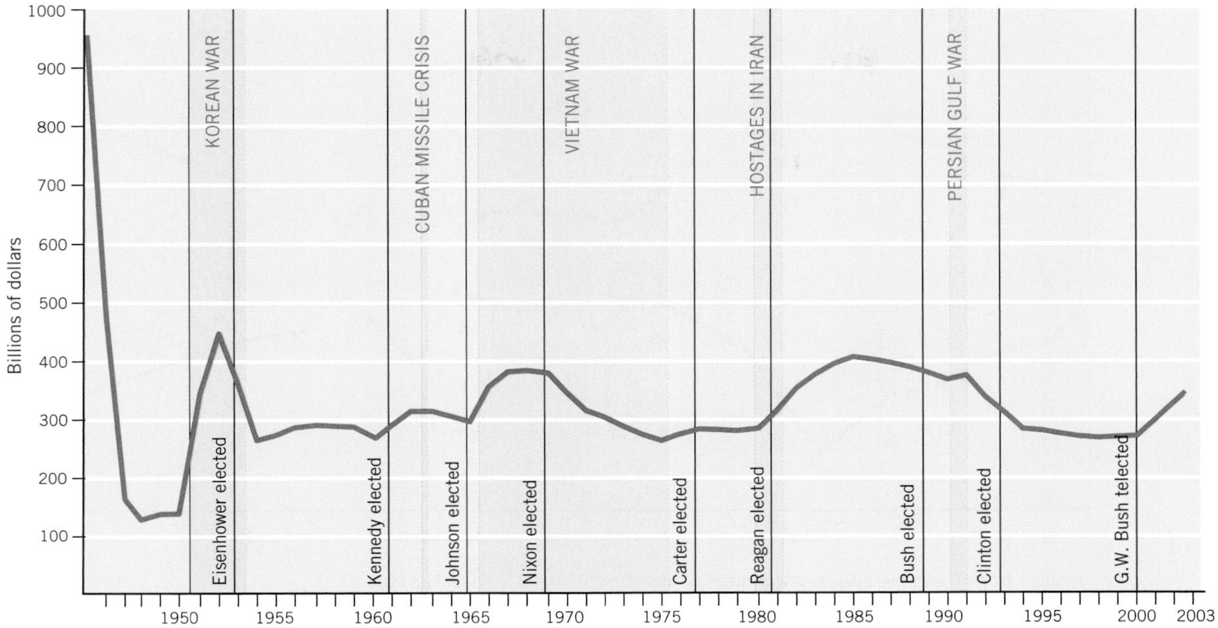

Source: Office of the Under Secretary of Defense (Comptroller), "National Defense Budget Estimates for FY 2003."

Soviet Union. For about forty years—from the outbreak of the Korean War in 1950 to the collapse of the Soviet Union in 1991—American military spending was driven by our desire to contain the Soviet Union and its allies. The Soviet Union had brought under its control most of Eastern Europe; would it also invade Western Europe? Russia had always wanted access to the oil and warm-water ports of the Middle East; would the Soviets someday invade or subvert Iran or Turkey? The Soviet Union was willing to help North Korea invade South Korea and North Vietnam to invade South Vietnam; would it next use an ally to threaten the United States? Soviet leaders supported "wars of national liberation" in Africa and Latin America; would they succeed in turning more and more nations against the United States?

To meet these threats the United States built up a military system that was designed to repel a Soviet invasion of Western Europe and at the same time help allies resist smaller-scale invasions or domestic uprisings. Figure 20.1 depicts the dramatic increase in military spending in 1950. It also shows that even after we decided to have a large military force, there were many ups and downs in the actual level of spending. After the Korean War was over, we spent less; when we became involved in Vietnam, we spent more; when the Soviet Union invaded Afghanistan, we spent more again. These changes in spending tended to reflect changes in public opinion about the defense budget.

As Figure 20.2 shows, a majority of Americans have said that we are spending the right amount or even too little on defense, and that percentage rose to very high levels in 1980 (when the Soviet Union invaded Afghanistan), in 1991 (when Iraq invaded Kuwait), and in 2001 after the terrorist attack on America.

Then, suddenly, the Soviet Union ceased to exist. The troops that once occupied Eastern Europe and Afghanistan withdrew to Russia; there were huge cuts in Russian military spending; and military and

Figure 20.2   Public Sentiment on Defense Spending, 1960–2002

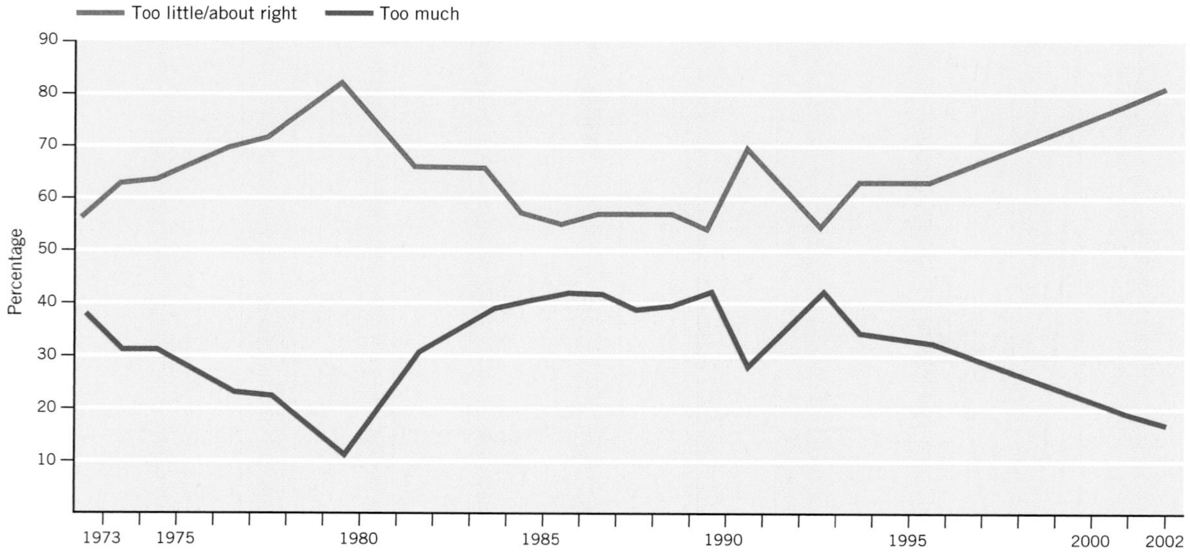

Source: Updated from *The Public Perspective* (August/September 1997), 19, and Gallup Poll.

economic aid to the Soviets' longtime ally, Cuba, was suspended. For the first time since 1950 American leaders were faced with defining the principles of our military policy (and thus the size of our defense budget) in the absence of a Soviet threat.

The debate that occurred, and is still continuing, largely reflected personal beliefs and political ideologies[44] (that is, *majoritarian* politics). Liberals demanded sharp cuts in defense spending, weapons procurement, and military personnel, arguing that with the Soviet threat ended, it was time to the collect our "peace dividend" and divert funds from the military to domestic social programs. Conservatives agreed that some military cuts were in order, but they argued that the world was still a dangerous place and therefore that a strong (and well-funded) military remained essential to the nation's defense. This disagreement reflected different predictions about what the future would be like. Many liberals (and some conservatives, such as Pat Buchanan, who believed that America should "stay at home") argued that we could not afford to be the "world's policeman." Many conservatives (and some liberals) responded by saying that Russia was still a military powerhouse that might once again fall under the

control of ruthless leaders and that many other nations hostile to the United States (such as Libya, North Korea, Iran, and Iraq) were becoming potential adversaries as they tried to build or acquire nuclear weapons and missile systems.

Saddam Hussein soon proved that international aggression had not ended with the collapse of the Soviet Union. In 1990 Iraq invaded Kuwait, a small oil-producing country on the Persian Gulf. The United States, aided by troops from several nations, landed in nearby Saudi Arabia. In January 1991 Operation Desert Storm began. Within days Iraq's forces were driven out of Kuwait.

In 1999 Serbian forces led by Slobodan Milosevic moved into Kosovo—a province that, like Serbia, had been part of Yugoslavia—to suppress the Albanians who lived there. The United States and its European allies launched a series of air attacks against Serbia. After several weeks the Serbian military withdrew.

These campaigns made clear that whether or not the United States was the "world's policeman," there was no escaping its need to use military force. The Kosovo campaign also made clear that the United States had reduced its armed forces so sharply since

Table 20.3	U.S. Military Forces Before and After the Breakup of the Soviet Union	
Service	Before 1991	End FY 1998
Army		
Active divisions	18	10
National Guard divisions	10	8
Navy		
Aircraft carriers	15	11
Training carriers	1	2
Ships	546	346
Air Force		
Active fighter wings	24	13
Reserve fighter wings	12	7
Marine Corps		
Active divisions	3	3
Reserve divisions	1	1
Strategic Nuclear Forces		
Ballistic missile submarines	31	18
Strategic bombers	324	182
ICBMs	1,000	550

Source: Statistical Abstract of the United States, 1998, 363.

■ **Personnel** Efforts to develop our military forces before World War II reflected the considerable American discomfort with a strong central government. The United States did not institute a peacetime draft until 1940, when the rest of the world was already at war, and the draft was renewed the following year (only a few months before Pearl Harbor) by only a one-vote margin in the House. Until 1973 the United States relied on the draft to obtain military personnel. Then, at the end of the Vietnam War, it replaced the draft with the all-volunteer force (AVF). After getting off to a rocky start, the AVF began to improve thanks to increases in military pay and rising civilian unemployment. Abolishing the draft had been politically popular: nobody likes being drafted, and even in congressional districts that otherwise are staunch supporters of a strong defense, the voters tell their representatives that they do not want to return to the draft.

There has been a steady increase in the percentage of women in the military (in 1999 they constituted 14 percent of the total). For a long time, however, women were barred by law from serving in combat roles. (What constitutes a "combat role" is a

Desert Storm (there were half a million fewer people in the military in 1996 than in 1991) that it was hard-pressed to carry out any sustained military campaign (see Table 20.3). When the national budget deficit was eliminated in 1999, both President Clinton and the Republican Congress called for more military spending.

But that increase did not pay for what the military had been authorized to buy, and did little to get us ready for the war in Afghanistan against Osama bin Laden. But once the battle began, the federal purse strings loosened and the defense budget grew.

What Do We Get with Our Money?

We get people of course—soldiers, sailors, airmen, and airwomen. They are the most expensive part of the defense budget. Then we get hardware of roughly two kinds—big-ticket items, like aircraft carriers and bombers, and small-ticket items, like hammers and screwdrivers. Each of these kinds of hardware has its own politics. Finally, we get "readiness"—training, supplies, munitions, fuel, and food.

The United States has tried to decide whether to build interceptors like this one to shoot down incoming missiles from enemies.

Women in training for the armed forces.

bit difficult to say, since even personnel far from the main fighting can be hit by an enemy bomb or artillery shell.) In 1993 Congress ended the legal ban on assigning women to navy combat ships and air force fighter jets, and by 1994 between four hundred and five hundred women were serving on three aircraft carriers. Congress must still be consulted in advance if women are to serve in ground combat forces (such as in front-line infantry or tank units), but soon they may be in those positions as well.

The presence of homosexuals in the military has proved much harder to resolve. Until 1993 it was the long-standing policy of the U.S. armed forces to bar homosexuals from entering the military and to discharge them if they were discovered serving. Gay and lesbian rights organizations had long protested this exclusion. In 1993 a gay soldier won a lawsuit against the army for having discharged him; he settled for back pay and retirement benefits in exchange for a promise not to reenlist. In 1993 a judge ordered the navy to reinstate a discharged sailor who had revealed on national television that he was a homosexual. In response to the growing controversy presidential candidate Bill Clinton promised to lift the official ban on gays and lesbians serving in the military if he were elected to office.

Once in office he discovered that it was not that easy. Many members of the armed forces believed that knowingly serving alongside and living in close quarters with gays and lesbians would create unnecessary tension and harm military morale and troop solidarity. The Joint Chiefs of Staff opposed lifting the ban, and several key members of Congress said they would

try to pass a law reaffirming it. President Clinton was forced to settle for a compromise: "don't ask, don't tell." Under this policy persons entering or serving in the military will not be asked to reveal their sexual orientation and will be allowed to serve provided they do not engage in homosexual conduct. If a person says he or she is a homosexual, it will not be automatic grounds for discharge, but it may be grounds for launching an investigation to see whether rules against homosexual conduct have been violated.

In 1994 the new Pentagon rules designed to implement "don't ask, don't tell" went into effect, but they created their own problems. What if heterosexuals harass gays without asking if they are gay? What if a gay or lesbian doesn't tell but his or her commanding officer finds out anyway?

■ **Big Ticket Items**   Whenever the Pentagon buys a new submarine, airplane, or missile, we hear about **cost overruns.** In the 1950s actual costs were three times greater than estimated costs; by the 1960s things were only slightly better—actual costs were twice estimated costs.[45]

There are five main reasons for these overruns. First, it is hard to know in advance what something that has never existed before will cost once you build it. People who have remodeled their homes know this all too well. So do government officials who build new subways or congressional office buildings. It is no different with a B-2 bomber.

Second, people who want to persuade Congress to appropriate money for a new airplane or submarine have an incentive to underestimate the cost. To get the weapon approved, its sponsors tell Congress how little it will cost; once the weapon is under construction, the sponsors go back to Congress for additional money to cover "unexpected" cost increases.

Third, the Pentagon officials who decide what kind of new aircraft they want are drawn from the ranks of those who will fly it. These officers naturally want the best airplane (or ship or tank) that money can buy. As air force general Carl "Tooey" Spaatz once put it, "A second-best aircraft is like a second-best poker hand. No damn good."[46] But what exactly is the "best" airplane? Is it the fastest one? Or the most maneuverable one? Or the most reliable one? Or the one with the longest range? Pentagon officials have a tendency to answer, "All of the above." Of course, trying to produce all of the above is incredibly expensive (and sometimes impossible).

Gays campaign for greater acceptance in the armed forces.

But asking for the expensive (or the impossible) is understandable, given that the air force officers who buy it will also fly it. This tendency to ask for everything at once is called **gold plating.**

Fourth, many new weapons are purchased from a single contractor. This is called sole-sourcing. A contractor is hired to design, develop, and build an airplane. As a result there is no competition, and so the manufacturer has no strong incentive to control costs. And if the sole manufacturer gets into financial trouble, the government, seeking to avoid a shutdown of all production, has an incentive to bail the company out.

Fifth, when Congress wants to cut the military budget, it often does so not by canceling a new weapons system but by stretching out the number of years during which it is purchased. Say that Congress wants to buy one hundred F-14s, twenty-five a year for four years. To give the appearance of cutting the budget, it will decide to buy only fifteen the first year and take five years to buy the rest. Or it will authorize the construction of twenty now and then ask again next year for the authority to build more. But start-and-stop production decisions and stretching out production over more years drives up the cost of building each unit. If Ford built cars this way, it would go broke.

There are ways to cope with four of these five problems. You cannot do much about the first, ignorance, but you can do something about low estimates, gold plating, sole-sourcing, and stretch-outs. If the Pentagon would give realistic cost estimates initially (perhaps verified by another agency); if it would ask for weapons that meet a few critical performance requirements instead of every requirement that can be thought of; if two or more manufacturers were to compete in designing, developing, and manufacturing new weapons; and if Congress were to stop trying to "cut" the budget using the smoke-and-mirrors technique of stretch-outs, then we would hear a lot less about cost overruns.

Some of these things are being done. There is more competition and less sole-sourcing in weapons procurement today than once was the case.[47] But the political incentives to avoid other changes are very powerful. Pentagon officers will always want "the best." They will always have an incentive to understate costs. Congress will always be tempted to use stretch-outs as a way of avoiding hard budget choices.

■ **Small Ticket Items**   It may be easy to understand why jet fighters cost so much, but what about $435 hammers?

In fact there never was a $435 hammer. It was a myth. The myth grew out of a complicated Pentagon accounting procedure that was exploited for publicity purposes by a member of Congress who thought he had found a hot issue.

The issue in buying small-ticket items is not the hammer problem, it is the coffee maker problem. Everybody knows what a hammer is and where to buy one—for about $20, tops. But a coffee maker, *if it is especially designed to function on a military plane*, is another matter. If the plane is going to lurch about in rough air, if the coffee maker has to fit into an odd place, it will occur to somebody in the Pentagon that what is needed is a specially designed coffee maker.

Once somebody thinks like that, the coffee maker is purchased in the same way as a new jet fighter, and with results just as bad. The design is gold-plated (for example, "Let's have a coffee maker that can fly upside down"), the contract is let out to a sole source with no competition, the cost is underestimated, and the production run is limited to ten coffee makers. The result? A coffee maker that costs $7,600.[48]

■ **Readiness**   Presumably we have a peacetime military so that we will be ready for wartime. Presumably, therefore, the peacetime forces will devote a lot of their time and money to improving their readiness.

Not necessarily. The politics of defense spending is such that readiness often is given a very low priority. Here is why.

Client politics influences the decision. In 1990 Congress was willing to cut almost anything, provided it wasn't built or stationed in some member's district. That doesn't leave much. Plans to stop producing F-14 fighters for the navy were opposed by members from Long Island, where the Grumman manufacturing plant is located. Plans to kill the Osprey aircraft for the Marines were opposed by members from the places where it was to be built. Plans to close bases were opposed by every member with a base in his or her district.

That leaves training and readiness. These things, essential to military effectiveness, have no constituencies and hence few congressional defenders. When forced to choose, the services themselves often prefer to allocate scarce dollars to developing and buying new weapons than to spending for readiness. Moreover, the savings from buying less fuel or having fewer exercises shows up right away, while the savings from canceling an aircraft carrier may not show up for years. Not surprisingly, training and readiness are usually what get the ax.

■ **Bases** At one time the opening and closing of military bases was pure client politics, which meant that a lot of bases were opened and hardly any were closed. Almost every member of Congress fought to get a base in his or her district, and *every* member fought to keep an existing base open. Even the biggest congressional critics of the U.S. military, people who would vote to take a gun out of a soldier's hand, would fight hard to keep bases in their districts open and operating.

In 1988 Congress finally concluded that no base would ever be closed unless the system for making decisions was changed. It created a Commission on Base Realignment and Closure, consisting of private citizens (originally twelve, later eight) who would consider recommendations from the secretary of defense. By law Congress would have to vote within forty-five days for or against the commission's list as a whole, without having a chance to amend it. In 1989 Congress considered the commission's first report, which called for closing eighty-six bases and slimming down five others. With no chance to pick the bases the members wanted to protect and knowing that the country had more bases than it needed,

Congress let the report stand, and the closings began.

In 1991 it went through the same process again, finally voting to accept (technically, voting not to block) a commission report calling for closing thirty-four more bases and altering many others.

Congress, it appears, has finally figured out how to make some decisions that most members know are right but that each member individually finds it politically necessary to oppose. But opposition to base closings remains strong enough to create congressional resistance to forming more Base Realignment and Closure commissions. In 2001, Congress authorized a new one but told it not to report until 2005.

The Structure of Defense Decision-Making

The formal structure within which decisions about national defense are made was in large part created after World War II, but it reflects concerns that go back at least to the time of the Founding. Chief among these is the persistent desire by citizens to ensure civilian control over the military.

The National Security Act of 1947 and its subsequent amendments created the Department of Defense. It is headed by the secretary of defense, under whom serve the secretaries of the army, the air force, and the navy as well as the Joint Chiefs of Staff. The secretary of defense, who must be a civilian (though one former general, George C. Marshall, was allowed by Congress to be the secretary), exercises, on behalf of the president, command authority over the defense establishment. The secretary of the army, the secretary of the navy,* and the secretary of the air force also are civilians and are subordinate to the secretary of defense. Unlike him, they do not attend cabinet meetings or sit on the National Security Council. In essense they manage the "housekeeping" functions of the various armed services, under the general direction of the secretary of defense and his deputy and assistant secretaries of defense.

The four armed services are separate entities; by law they cannot be merged or commanded by a

---

*The secretary of the navy manages two services, the navy and the Marine Corps.

single military officer, and each has the right to communicate directly with Congress. There are two reasons for having separate uniformed services functioning within a single department: the fear of many citizens that a unified military force might become too powerful politically, and the desire of each service to preserve its traditional independence and autonomy. The result, of course, is a good deal of interservice rivalry and bickering, but this is precisely what Congress intended when it created the Department of Defense. Rivalry and bickering, it was felt, would ensure that Congress would receive the maximum amount of information about military affairs and would enjoy the largest opportunity to affect military decisions.

Since the end of World War II Congress has aimed both to retain a significant measure of control over the military's decision-making and to ensure the adequacy of the nation's defenses. Congress does not want a single military command headed by an all-powerful general or admiral, but neither does it want the services to be so autonomous or their heads so equal that coordination and efficiency suffer. In 1986 Congress passed and the president signed a defense reorganization plan known as the Goldwater-Nichols Act, which increased the power of the officers who coordinate the activities of the different services. The 1947 structure was left in place, but with revised procedures.

Joint Chiefs of Staff

The Joint Chiefs of Staff (JCS) is a committee consisting of the uniformed heads of each of the military services (the army, navy, air force, and Marine Corps), plus a chairman and a (nonvoting) vice chairman, also military officers, who are appointed by the president and confirmed by the Senate. The JCS does not have command authority over troops, but it plays a key role in national defense planning. Since 1986 the chairman of the Joint Chiefs has been designated the president's principal military adviser, in an effort to give him more influence over the JCS.

Assisting the JCS is the Joint Staff, consisting of several hundred officers from each of the four services. The staff draws up plans for various military contingencies. Before 1986 each staff member was loyal to the service whose uniform he or she wore. As a result the staff was often "joint" in name only, since few members were willing to take a position opposed by their service for fear of being passed over for promotion. The 1986 law changed this in two ways: First, it gave the chairman of the JCS control over the Joint Staff; now it works for the chairman, not for the JCS as a group. Second, it required the secretary of defense to establish guidelines to ensure that officers assigned to the Joint Staff (or to other interservice bodies) are promoted at the same rate as officers whose careers are spent entirely with their own services.

The Services

Each military service is headed by a civilian secretary—one for the army, the navy (including the Marine Corps), and the air force—plus a senior military officer: the chief of staff of the army, the chief of naval operations, the commandant of the Marine Corps, and the chief of staff of the air force. The civilian secretaries are in charge of purchasing, auditing, congressional relations, and public affairs. The military chiefs oversee the discipline and training of their uniformed forces and in addition represent their services on the Joint Chiefs of Staff.

The Chain of Command

Under the Constitution the president is the commander in chief of the armed forces. The chain of command runs from him to the secretary of defense (also a civilian), and from him to the various unified and specified commands. These orders may be transmitted through the Joint Chiefs of Staff or its chairman, but by law the chairman of the JCS does not have command authority over the combat forces. Civilians are in charge at the top to protect against excessive concentration of power.

No one yet knows how well the 1986 changes will work, though many analysts viewed the quick victory in the 1991 Persian Gulf War as evidence of its success. Critics of the Pentagon have been urging changes along these lines at least since 1947. But others say that unless the armed services are actually merged, interservice rivalry will continue. Still others argue that even the coordination achieved by the 1986 act is excessive. The country, in their view, is better served by having wholly autonomous services. What is striking is that so many members of Congress who once would have insisted on the anti-coordination view voted for the 1986 law, thereby indicating a greater willingness to permit some degree of central military leadership.

Spending for the War on Terrorism

For a long time, what we bought with our defense dollars was not hard to justify. In the Second World War we fought massive armies on the ground; during the cold war we prepared for the possibility of fighting such an army on the ground. And so we bought artillery and tanks and big ships with which to move those things.

But in the new war on terrorism, a war that is likely to last many years, we will probably be fighting small groups of people who are hidden in large countries with which we are friendly, such as the Philippines, or who control parts of large countries in which we have potential allies, such as Afghanistan.

The war against the Taliban in Afghanistan was a completely new experience for America. We relied on special forces, such as the Green Berets or the Delta Force from the army and the Seals from the navy, soldiers that are trained to operate in hostile and distant places. They were linked by radios and computers to aircraft carrying precision-guided bombs and rockets that were vastly more accurate than anything anyone had used before. They searched remote and dangerous caves in alliance with local guerilla fighters. We did not deploy any tank battalions or fire any big guns. And we counted on many different services—army, navy, Marines, and air force—working together in close harmony.

But traditionally our military operations have not involved special forces, alliances with guerrillas, or close interservice cooperation. Usually we have fought using four different military services performing different tasks in different places. As a result, each service has developed its own tactics, its own weapons, and its own communications systems.

Now that has to change, and of course the change has begun. But it moves slowly because each service is independent of every other one and until recently did not take the idea of joint operations very seriously. The Joint Chiefs of Staff, made up of the top commanders of each of the four services, has customarily recommended policies that will benefit all services equally and, if cuts must be made, recommended cuts that hurt all services equally.

At one time each military service was overseen by a separate congressional committee in the House and Senate. Today these committees have been merged into a House Armed Services Committee and a Senate Armed Services Committee, but on these committees there remain powerful advocates of each individual service.

Today the secretary of defense must find ways of transforming the military into an organization that will be effective at fighting terrorists while not neglecting the other roles it must play, such as coping with missile attacks by hostile nations. This means canceling some weapons systems that would only be of value if we were to fight the (now nonexistent) Soviet Union in a massive land battle. But these weapons have strong defenders in the military and among members of Congress who represent the districts where they will be manufactured. (When Dick Cheney was secretary of defense, he tried to cancel the V-22 Osprey aircraft, but Congress ignored him and put it back in the budget.) The new war against terrorism also means reorganizing the military so that many of its members can be sent immediately to distant places to fight terrorists who have suddenly appeared.

Washington is used to debates about big new weapons. We have had major quarrels about building the B-1 and B-2 bombers, aircraft carriers and submarines, the MX missile, the M1 tank, and new high-performance aircraft. The longest war has been over the Strategic Defense Initiative (SDI), something its critics call the Star Wars plan. It is an effort to find ways of destroying incoming enemy missiles. The issue arose in the Reagan administration in the 1980s and continues to be debated. It causes not only major scientific and philosophical quarrels but reluctance among some parts of the military itself. If you head the air force, you may feel that the country would be best defended against missile attacks by threatening other countries with our own missile attacks. This doctrine of "mutual assured destruction" (MAD) was the basis for our standoff against the old Soviet Union. Were we to continue a MAD approach, the air force budget for missiles and bombers would remain high, but if we produced a successful SDI the need for so many missile and bombers would lessen and the air force budget might be cut. Defenders of SDI point out that while Soviet leaders were suitably fearful of an American attack, the heads of some smaller rogue nations today may not be so fearful, and so SDI will become even more important. MAD works against rational leaders, not against fanatics.

American Hostages Begin Second Year of Captivity

Families Urge President to Negotiate Freedom

July 13
WASHINGTON

The families of the six American hostages held captive in the Middle East today criticized the president for failing to win their release . . .

MEMORANDUM

To: The president
From: National security adviser
Subject: Hostages

The six Americans held hostage in the Middle East are beginning their second year of captivity. One, a CIA officer, is undergoing torture. It has been the policy of this administration not to negotiate with terrorists. Criticism of this refusal is being heard from hostage families and their sympathizers. The terrorist groups are demanding that we end our support of Israel. A government in the region has secretly indicated that, in exchange for military supplies, it may be able to help win the release of "some" hostages.

Your options:

1. Maintain the "no-negotiations" policy but use quiet diplomacy with friendly nations in the region to see whether they can intercede with the terrorist groups on behalf of the hostages.
Advantages: (a) Our "no-negotiations" policy remains credible, and this will deter other terrorist groups from thinking that they can win concessions by capturing Americans. (b) This policy is consistent with our insistence that U.S. allies not negotiate with terrorists.
Disadvantages: (a) There is no evidence that our traditional policy will get the hostages released. (b) Public sympathy for the hostages may increase, and this will lead to more criticism of this administration for failing to free captive Americans.

2. Secretly exchange arms for the release of Americans.
Advantages: (a) Some or all hostages may be released. (b) We may earn the goodwill of more moderate elements in the area and thereby increase our influence there.
Disadvantages: (a) We may deliver arms and no hostages will be released. (b) If secret arms deliveries become public, we will be heavily criticized for abandoning our "no-negotiations" policy.

3. Use military units to find and free the hostages.
Advantage: The hostages may be freed without our having to make any concessions.
Disadvantages: (a) The military is not optimistic that it can find and free the hostages, who are being kept in hidden, scattered sites. (b) The hostages may be killed during the rescue effort.

Your decision:
Option 1 _____ Option 2 _____ Option 3 _____

Now Washington must also take on equally important battles over the design of the armed services and the question of who gets to do what job. And it must do this knowing that these changes will cost a lot of money.

Summary

The great issues of national diplomacy and military policy are shaped by majoritarian politics. The president is the dominant figure, political ideology is important, and interest groups are central only to those issues—such as free trade and the allocation of military contracts—that engage their interests.

Majority opinion is weakly defined. In general it approves of the United States playing an international role but in particular cases would like Americans to stay home and mind their own business. But when America is caught up in a crisis or the president sends troops overseas, the country and the troops are strongly supported.

Elite opinion plays a more powerful role, but it is divided into four worldviews: isolationism, containment, disengagement, and human rights. The first is less common now than once was the case. Proponents of the remaining three would be deeply at odds if they were confronted today with a decision of whether we should stay in Vietnam, drive Iraqi troops out of Kuwait, give aid to Bosnia, or launch an air campaign in Kosovo.

Foreign and military decision-making is organized to give civilians control. The president is assisted chiefly by the National Security Council and the secretaries of state and defense. Civilian control of the military is vested in the president, who issues orders not through military officers but through the secretary of defense. The Joint Chiefs of Staff is a planning and advisory body.

When the military budget is developed, it tends to abide by majoritarian politics. But when it is spent on the armed services and military contractors, interest group politics intervenes.

Reconsidering the Enduring Questions

1. *How can a democracy maintain enough secrecy to conduct a good foreign policy?*

   By and large, it can't. In an open society, especially one with checks and balances in government, secrecy is almost impossible to maintain. But it remains to be seen just how important secrecy is. Authoritarian regimes that find it easy to keep secrets often make terrible foreign policy mistakes (as when Hitler invaded Russia or Iraq invaded Kuwait). Democratic regimes may tell everybody what they are going to do, but often telling them makes little difference (as when the United States and its allies expelled Iraq from Kuwait or defeated the Taliban in Afghanistan). Secrets are often important, but the need for them has to be assessed on a case-by-case basis.

2. *Should our foreign policy reflect what is in America's interests or should it be based on some conception of human rights?*

   In many cases these two positions represent false choices because what is in America's interests often requires dealing with governments that respect human rights. But in some cases we have to make a tough choice, as when we aid one authoritarian regime that is struggling with another. When we do that, it is clear that we ought to support the regime that is helpful to this country.

World Wide Web Resources

- U.S. Army: www.army.mil
- U.S. Air Force: www.af.mil
- U.S. Navy: www.navy.mil

- Central Intelligence Agency: www.odci.gov
- Department of State: www.state.gov

Key Terms

iron curtain *p. 566*
cold war *p. 566*
worldviews *p. 566*
isolationism *p. 567*
domino theory *p. 567*

containment (or antiappeasement)
  p. 568
disengagement *p. 568*
Third World *p. 569*
human rights *p. 569*

military-industrial complex *p. 572*
cost overruns *p. 576*
gold plating *p. 577*

Suggested Readings

Allison, Graham T. *Essence of Decision: Explaining the Cuban Missile Crisis.* Boston: Little, Brown, 1971. Shows how the decision made by a president during a major crisis was shaped by bureaucratic and organizational factors.

Kissinger, Henry. *White House Years.* Boston: Little, Brown, 1979. A brilliant insider's account of the politics and tactics of "high diplomacy" during the Nixon administration.

Mead, Walter Russell. *Special Providence.* New York: Knopf, 2001. Argues that American foreign policy, though often criticized, has been remarkably successful.

Mueller, John E. *War, Presidents, and Public Opinion.* New York: Wiley, 1973. Best summary of the relationship between presidential foreign policy decisions and public opinion.

Silverstein, Gordon. *Imbalance of Powers: Constitutional Interpretation and the Making of American Foreign Policy.* New York: Oxford University Press, 1996. Argues that the president has not yielded his authority over foreign policy to Congress.

Weissman, Stephen R. *A Culture of Deference: Congress's Failure of Leadership in Foreign Policy.* New York: Basic Books, 1995. Takes a view opposite that of Silverstein: Congress defers too much to the president in foreign policy.

Wittkopf, Eugene R. *Faces of Internationalism: Public Opinion and American Foreign Policy* (Durham, N.C.: Duke University Press, 1990). A useful review of public opinion toward America's international roles.

Environmental Policy

Enduring Questions

1. If we wish to have cleaner air and water, how far can we go in making them cleaner when the cost of each additional gain goes up?
2. What is the best way for the government to achieve an environmental goal: by issuing orders or offering incentives?

Everybody loves the environment. A large majority of the American public believes that the government should do more to protect it. Over 80 percent of college freshmen believe that the government is not doing enough to control pollution, far more than the number who think the government is doing too little about disarmament, protecting the consumer, or controlling handguns.[1] No one wants to be called a "polluter."

Why, then, is environmental policy so controversial? There are three reasons. First, every governmental policy, including one established to protect the environment, creates both winners and losers. The losers are the people who must pay the costs without getting enough of the benefits. Sometimes those losers are influential interest groups. But sometimes the losers are average citizens. They may love the environment, but not enough to change the way they live in order to enhance it. For example, automobile exhausts are a major cause of smog, but not many people like the idea of being told to leave their cars at home and take the bus to work.

Second, many environmental issues are enmeshed in scientific uncertainty: the experts either do not know or they disagree about what is happening and how to change it. For example, some people worry that society is burning so much fuel (thus producing a lot of carbon dioxide) and cutting down so many trees (thus reducing the plants available to convert carbon dioxide back into oxygen) that the earth will soon become a greenhouse: the excess carbon dioxide in the earth's atmosphere will prevent heat from escaping, and so the earth will get warmer, with disastrous effects for humanity. But scientists do not know how large the greenhouse effect is, whether it will lead to a harmful amount of global warming, or (if it will) what should be done about it.[2]

Third, much environmental policy takes the form of entrepreneurial politics—mobilizing decision-makers with strong, often emotional appeals in order to overcome the political advantages of the client groups that oppose a change. To make these appeals, people who want change must stir up controversy and find villains. Many times this produces desirable changes. But it can also lead to distorted priorities. For example, it is much easier to make dramatic and politically powerful arguments about a pesticide that causes a minute increase in the risk of cancer than it is to dramatize the runoff into our rivers and oceans of polluted water from farms and city streets.

The American Context

Environmental policy, like welfare policy, is shaped by the unique features of American politics. Almost every industrialized nation has rules to protect the environment, but in this country those rules are designed and enforced in a way that would be baffling to someone in, say, Sweden or England.

First, environmental policy making in the United States is much more adversarial than it is in most European nations. In this country there have been bitter and lasting conflicts over the contents of the Clean Air Act. Minimum auto emissions standards are uniform across the nation, regardless of local conditions (states can set higher standards if they wish). Many rules for improving air and water quality have strict deadlines and require expensive technology. Hundreds of inspectors enforce these rules, and hundreds of lawyers bring countless lawsuits to support or challenge this enforcement. Government

and business leaders have frequently denounced each other for being unreasonable or insensitive. So antagonistic are the interests involved in environmental policy that it took thirteen years, from 1977 to 1990, to agree on a congressional revision of the Clean Air Act.

In England, by contrast, rules designed to reduce air pollution were written by government and business leaders acting cooperatively. The rules are neither rigid nor nationally uniform; they are flexible and allow plenty of exceptions to deal with local variations in business needs. Compliance with the rules depends mostly on voluntary action, not formal enforcement. Lawsuits are rare. Business and government officials do not routinely accuse each other of being unreasonable. You might think that all this sweetness and light were the result of having meaningless rules, but not so. As David Vogel has shown, the improvement in air and water quality in England has been at least as great as, if not greater than, that in the United States.[3]

A second feature of environmental policy here is that, as in so many other policy areas, what is done depends heavily on the states. Though there are uniform national air quality standards, how those standards are achieved is left to the states (subject to certain federal controls). Though sewage treatment plants are in large measure paid for by Washington, they are designed, built, and operated by state and local governments. Though the federal government decrees that radioactive waste must be properly disposed of somewhere, the states have a big voice in where that is. When Congress decided in 1982 to select places in which to dispose of such waste, it announced that sites would be chosen on the basis of "science." But of course no state wanted to get such waste, so all objected. In the congressional committee that made the final decision in 1988, Nevada had the least influence, and so Nevada got the waste. In a federal system of government, "science" rarely makes allocative decisions; local politics usually does.

Federalism reinforces adversarial politics: one of the reasons environmental issues are so contentious in this country is that cities and states fight over what standards should apply where. But federalism is not the whole story. The separation of powers guarantees that almost anybody who wants to wield influence over environmental policy will have an opportunity to do so. In England and in most

European nations, the centralized, parliamentary form of government means that the opponents of a policy have less leverage.*

It would take a book almost as long as this one to describe all the environmental laws and regulations now in effect in this country and to discuss the endless controversies over how those rules should be changed or expanded. In Table 21.1 you can find a summary of some of the more important federal laws governing air and water pollution, environmental impact statements, and open spaces.

In this chapter we want to explain how environmental policy is made. Controversies over controlling pollution from stationary sources, such as factories and power plants, take the form of *entrepreneurial politics*—many people hope to benefit from rules that impose costs on a few firms. Policies intended to reduce air pollution caused by automobiles involve *majoritarian politics*—many people hope to benefit, but many people (anyone who owns a car) will have to pay the cost. The fight over acid rain has largely been a case of *interest group politics*—regions hurt by acid rain (mainly in the Northeast) argue with regions that produce a lot of acid rain (mainly in the Midwest) about who should pay. Finally, there are examples of *client politics* at work—for example, when farmers manage to minimize federal controls over the use of pesticides. Most people are unaware of what food contains what pesticide or which, if any, are harmful; farmers are keenly aware of the economic benefits of pesticides and are well organized to defend them.

Entrepreneurial Politics: Global Warming

Entrepreneurial politics created the environmental movement. When an offshore well spewed thousands of gallons of oil onto the beaches of Santa Barbara, California, at the very time (January 1969) when protest politics was in the air, it became difficult or impossible for the government or business

Table 21.1 Major Federal Environmental Laws

1963	Clean Air Act
1964	Wilderness Act
1965	Highway Beautification Act
	Water Quality Act
1967	Air Quality Act
1968	Wild and Scenic Rivers Act
1969	National Environmental Policy Act
	Endangered Species Conservation Act
1970	Clean Air Amendments
	Water Quality Improvement Act
1972	Federal Water Pollution Control Act
	Marine Mammal Protection Act
	Marine Protection, Research, and Sanctuaries Act
	Coastal Zone Management Act
	Federal Environmental Pesticide Control Act
	Noise Control Act
1973	Endangered Species Act
1974	Safe Drinking Water Act
1976	Federal Land Policy and Management Act
	National Forest Management Act
	Resource Conservation and Recovery Act
	Toxic Substances Control Act
1977	Clean Air Act Amendments
	Clean Water Act
	Surface Mining Control and Reclamation Act
1978	Outer Continental Shelf Lands Act Amendments
1980	Comprehensive Environmental Response, Compensation, and Liability Act ("Superfund")
	Alaska National Interest Lands Conservation Act
1984	Hazardous and Solid Waste Amendments
1986	Safe Drinking Water Amendments
	Superfund Amendments and Reauthorization Act
1987	Water Quality Act
1988	Endangered Species Act Reauthorization
	Federal Insecticide, Fungicide, and Rodenticide Act Amendments
1990	Clean Air Act Amendments
	Pollution Prevention Act

Source: Congressional Quarterly Weekly Report (January 20, 1990): 154.

---

*Here, environmental pressures are brought by interest groups; in Europe, where such groups have less influence, environmentalists form or enter political parties so as to be represented in the legislature.

firms to resist the demand that threats to our natural surroundings be curtailed. The emerging environmental movement created an occasion—Earth Day, first celebrated on April 22, 1970—to celebrate its beginning.

The movement was hugely successful. In 1970 President Nixon created the Environmental Protection Agency (EPA) and Congress toughened the existing Clean Air Act and passed the Water Quality Improvement Act. Two years later it passed laws designed to clean up the water; three years later it adopted the Endangered Species Act. New laws were passed right into the 1990s (see Table 21.1). Existing environmental organizations grew in size, and new ones were formed. Public opinion rallied around environmental slogans.

It is a foolish politician who today opposes environmentalism. And that creates a problem, because not all environmental issues are equally deserving of support. Take the case of global warming.

The phrase means that gases, such as carbon dioxide, produced by people when they burn fossil fuels—wood, oil, or coal—get trapped in the atmosphere and cause the earth's temperature to rise. When the temperature goes up, bad things may follow—floods on coastal areas as the polar ice caps melt, wilder weather as more storms are created, and the spread of tropical diseases to North America. Some politicians say that "all" or "almost all" scientists know that global warming will occur in ways that hurt humankind.

In fact neither all nor almost all scientists believe this theory. The scientific community is deeply divided over the issue. Most scientists agree that the earth has gotten a bit warmer over the past century. But from there on profound disagreements exist. Activist scientists say that the earth is getting warmer; skeptical ones note that the earth's atmosphere has been getting cooler. Activists say that fossil-fuel gases are making the earth warmer; skeptics rejoin that the earth's temperature regularly changes from natural causes, such as changes in the sun's production of heat. Activists say that the sea will rise because of melting ice caps; skeptics respond that the ice caps are not melting. Activists say that their computer models prove that the earth will get warmer in the future; skeptics rejoin that these models can't even explain temperature changes that have occurred in the past. Activists say that a warmer earth will be bad for humankind; skeptics say that a warmer earth will make it easier to grow crops and feed people. Activists say that we should act now, despite scientific doubts; skeptics say that we should learn more before doing anything. Surveys of professional meteorologists suggest that the skeptics outnumber the activists.[4]

Outnumbered or not, the activists have had the greatest influence thus far. In 1997 the United States signed the Kyoto Protocol in which it pledged to lower emissions of greenhouse gases (such as carbon dioxide) by 7 percent below 1990 levels. By the years 2008–2012 that means a reduction of more than 30 percent below the levels that would otherwise occur. Undeveloped countries such as Brazil, China, India, and Mexico will not be required to cut their emissions. Given the large cuts that the American economy would have to endure, many business firms are worried about the effects of the Kyoto Protocol. In 2001 President Bush announced that he opposed the treaty; in 2002, he proposed some alternative policies.

As with most kinds of entrepreneurial politics, global warming has resulted in a conflict among elites who often base their arguments on ideology as much as on facts. Environmental activists raise money with scary statements about the harm global warming will cause; conservatives raise money with scary statements about the economic pain an American cut in greenhouse gases will cause.[5] But given the popularity of "the environment" as an issue, the activists dominate the discussion, and politicians can only with great difficulty criticize their claims.

Another environmental example of entrepreneurial politics is the Endangered Species Act. Passed in 1973, it forbids buying or selling a bird, fish, animal, or plant that the government regards as "endangered"—that is, likely to become extinct unless it receives special protection—or engaging in any economic activity (such as building a dam or running a farm) that would harm an endangered species. Currently there are more than six hundred species on the protected list; about half are plants. The regulations forbid not only killing a protected species but also adversely affecting its habitat.

Firms and government agencies that wish to build a dam, bridge, factory, or farm in an area where an endangered species lives must comply with federal regulations. The complaints of such clients about these regulations are outweighed by the public support for the law. Sometimes the law preserves a creature, such as the bald eagle, that almost everyone admires; sometimes it protects a creature, such as the snail darter, that no one has ever heard of.

Senate Debates Endangered Species Law

May 8
WASHINGTON, D.C.

The Senate Committee on Environment and Public Works held hearings today in an effort to decide how, if at all, it should modify the law that protects endangered species. The chairman said . . .

MEMORANDUM

To: Senator Diane Gray
From: Michael Jordan, legislative assistant

Endangered species have been protected by federal laws since 1973. People now disagree about the value and effectiveness of these enactments.

Arguments for keeping or strengthening the law:

1. The law has helped preserve some endangered species, such as the condor.
2. It is essential that humans preserve biodiversity, in part because we owe it to nature and in part because people may derive medical and other benefits from plants that are now endangered.
3. The earth is losing species at an alarming rate.

Arguments against keeping the present law:

1. Some species, such as the condor or the ocelot, may be worth preserving, but surely not the pocket mouse, snail darter, or pine barren tree frog. There are now over one thousand species labeled "endangered."
2. The law does not take into account the harm to farmers, loggers, or home builders that results from threatening legitimate activities with demands that some species be protected.
3. The law has generally failed to protect any species.

Your decision:
Favor law _____
Wish to change or abolish law _____

Major Environmental Laws

Smog Clean Air Act (passed in 1970; amended in 1977 and 1990)

- **Stationary sources:** EPA sets national air quality standards; states must develop plans to attain them. If state plan is inadequate, EPA sets a federal plan. Local sources that emit more than a certain amount of pollutants must install pollution control equipment.
- **Gasoline-powered vehicles:** Between 1970 and 1990, pollution from cars was cut by between 60 and 80 percent. Between 1991 and 1998 there was another 30 percent reduction. All states must have an auto pollution inspection system.
- **Cities:** Classifies cities in terms of how severe their smog problem is and sets deadlines for meeting federal standards.

Water Clean Water Acts of various years state that there is to be no discharge of wastewater into lakes and streams without a federal permit; to get a permit, cities and factories must meet federal discharge standards.

Toxic Wastes EPA is to clean up abandoned dump sites with money raised by a tax on the chemical and petroleum industries and from general revenues. (Many thousands of such sites exist.)

Environmental Impact Statements Since 1969, any federal agency planning a project that would significantly affect the human environment must prepare in advance an environmental impact statement (EIS).

Acid Rain The Clean Air Act of 1990 requires a reduction of 10 million tons of sulfur dioxide (mostly from electric-generating plants that burn coal) by 1995. The biggest sources must acquire government allowances (which can be traded among firms) setting emission limits.

Majoritarian Politics: Pollution from Automobiles

The Clean Air Act of 1970 imposed tough restrictions on the amount of pollutants that could come out of automobile tail pipes. Indeed, most of the debate over that bill centered on this issue.

Initially the auto emissions control rules followed the pattern of entrepreneurial politics: an aroused public with media support demanded that automobile companies be required to make their cars less polluting. It seemed to be "the public" against "the interests," and the public won: by 1975 new cars would have to produce 90 percent less of two pollutants (hydrocarbons and carbon monoxide), and by 1976 achieve a 90 percent reduction in another (nitrous oxides). This was a tall order. There was no time to redesign automobile engines or to find an alternative to the internal combustion engine; it would be necessary to install devices (called catalytic converters) on exhaust pipes that would transform pollutants into harmless gases.

But a little-noticed provision in the 1970 law soon shoved the battle over automobile pollution into the arena of majoritarian politics. That provision required states to develop land-use and transportation rules to help attain air quality standards. What that meant in practice was that in any area where smog was still a problem, even after emission controls had been placed on new cars, there would have to be rules restricting the public's use of cars.

There was no way cities such as Denver, Los Angeles, and New York could get rid of smog just by requiring people to buy less-polluting cars—the increase in the number of cars or in the number of miles driven in those places outweighed the gain from making the average car less polluting. That meant that the government would have to impose such unpopular measures as bans on downtown parking, mandatory use of buses and carpools, and even gasoline rationing.

Efforts to do this failed. Popular opposition to such rules was too great, and the few such rules that were put into place didn't work. Congress reacted by postponing the deadlines by which air quality standards in cities would have to be met; the EPA reacted by abandoning any serious effort to tell people when and where they could drive.[6]

Even the effort to clean up the exhausts of new cars ran into opposition. Some people didn't like the higher cost of cars with catalytic converters; others didn't like the loss in horsepower that these converters caused (many people disconnected them). The United Auto Workers union began to worry that antismog rules would hurt the U.S. auto industry and cost them their jobs. Congress took note of these complaints and decided that despite a lot of effort, new cars could not meet the 90 percent emission reduction standard by 1975–1976, and so in 1977 it amended the Clean Air Act to extend these deadlines by up to six years.

The Clean Air Act, when revised again in 1990, set new, tougher auto emission control standards—but it pushed back the deadline for compliance. It reiterated the need for getting rid of smog in the smoggiest cities and proposed a number of ways to do it—but it set the deadline for compliance in the worst area (Los Angeles) at twenty years in the future.

The public will support tough environmental laws when somebody else pays or when the costs are hidden (as in the price of a car); it will not give as much support when it believes that it is paying, especially when the payment takes the form of changing how and when it uses the family car. Here are more examples of each kind of majoritarian politics.

Everyone wants clean air, but few people are willing to give up the personal freedom that their automobiles afford them.

■ Majoritarian Politics When People Believe the Costs Are Low

The National Environmental Policy Act (NEPA), passed in 1969, contained a provision requiring that an **environmental impact statement** (EIS) be written before any federal agency undertakes an activity that will "significantly" affect the quality of the human environment. (Similar laws have been passed in many states, affecting not only what government does but what private developers do.) Because it required only a "statement" rather than some specific action and because it was a pro-environment law, NEPA passed by overwhelming majorities.

As it turned out, the EIS provision was hardly innocuous. Opponents of virtually any government-sponsored project have used the EIS as a way of blocking, changing, or delaying the project. Hundreds of lawsuits have been filed to challenge this or that provision of an EIS or to claim that a project was not supported by a satisfactory EIS. In this way environmental activists have challenged the Alaska pipeline, a Florida canal, and several nuclear power plants, as well as countless dams, bridges, highways, and office buildings. Usually the agency's plan is upheld, but this does not mean that the EIS is unimportant: the EIS induces the agency to think through what it is doing, and it gives critics a chance to examine, and often to negotiate, the content of those plans.

Despite the grumbling of many people adversely affected by fights over an EIS (someone once complained that Moses would never have been able to part the Red Sea if he had had to file an EIS first), popular support for it remains strong because the public at large does not believe that it is paying a high price and does believe that it is gaining a significant benefit.

■ Majoritarian Politics When People Believe the Costs Are High

From time to time someone proposes that gasoline taxes be raised sharply. Such taxes would discourage driving, and this not only would conserve fuel but also would reduce smog. Almost everyone would pay, but almost everyone would benefit. However, it is only with great difficulty that the public can be persuaded to support such taxes. The reason is that the people pay the tax first, and the benefit, if any, comes later. Unlike Social Security, where the taxes we pay now support cash benefits we get later, gasoline taxes support noncash benefits (cleaner air, less congestion) that many people doubt will ever appear or, if they do, will not be meaningful to them.[7]

When gasoline taxes have been raised, it has usually been because the politicians did not push the tax hike as an environmental measure. Instead they promised that in return for paying higher taxes the public would receive some concrete benefits—more highways, more buses, or a reduction in the federal deficit (as happened with the gas tax hike of 1990 and again in 1993).

Interest Group Politics: Acid Rain

Sometimes the rain, snow, or dust particles that fall onto the land are acidic. This is called **acid rain.** One source of that acid precipitation is burning fuel, such as certain types of coal, that contains a lot of sulfur. Some of the sulfur (along with nitrogen) will turn into sulfuric (or nitric) acid as it comes to earth. Steel mills and electric power plants that burn high-sulfur coal are concentrated in the Midwest and Great Lakes regions of the United States. The prevailing winds tend to carry those sulfurous fumes eastward, where some fall to the ground.

That much seems certain. Everything else has been surrounded by controversy. Many lakes and rivers in the eastern United States and in Canada have become more acidic, and some forests in these areas have died back. Some part of this is the result of acid rain from industrial smokestacks, but some part of it is also the result of naturally occurring acids in the soils and rainfall. How much of the acidification is man-made and how much is a result of the actions of Mother Nature is unclear. Some lakes are not affected by acid rain; some are. Why some are affected more than others is unclear. The long-term effects of higher acid levels in lakes and forests are also unclear.

These scientific uncertainties were important because they provided some support for each side in a fierce interest group battle. Residents of Canada

and New England complained bitterly of the loss of forests and the acidification of lakes, blaming it on midwestern smokestacks. Midwestern businesses, labor unions, and politicians denied that their smokestacks were the major cause of the problem (if, indeed, there was a problem) and argued that, even if they were the cause, they shouldn't have to pay the cost of cleaning up the problem.

Here was a classic case of two well-organized parties, one hoping to reap benefits and the other fearing to pay costs, locked in a struggle over a policy proposal. Even before people were aware that acid rain might be a problem, these two groups were fighting over how, if at all, sulfur emissions should be reduced.

An attempt to deal with the issue in 1977 reflected the kind of bizarre compromises that sometimes result when politically opposed forces have to be reconciled. There were essentially two alternatives. One was to require power plants to burn low-sulfur coal. This would undoubtedly cut back on sulfur emissions, but it would cost money, because, as can be seen in the map on page 593, low-sulfur coal is mined mostly in the West, hundreds of miles away from the midwestern coal-burning industries. The other way would be to require power plants to install scrubbers—complicated and very expensive devices that would take sulfurous fumes out of the gas before it came out of the smokestack. In addition to their cost, the trouble with scrubbers was that they didn't always work and that they generated a lot of unpleasant sludge that would have to be hauled away and buried somewhere. Their great advantage, however, was that they would allow midwestern utilities to continue their practice of using cheap, high-sulfur coal.

Congress voted for the scrubbers for all new coal-burning plants, even if they burned low-sulfur coal. In the opinion of most economists, this was the wrong decision,[8] but it had four great political advantages. First, the jobs of miners in high-sulfur coal mines would be protected. They had powerful allies in Congress. Second, environmentalists liked scrubbers, which they seemed to regard as a definitive, technological "solution" to the problem, an approach far preferable to relying on incentives to induce power plants to buy low-sulfur coal. Third, scrubber manufacturers liked the idea, for obvious reasons. Finally, some eastern governors liked scrubbers because if all new plants had to have them, it

The Politics of Energy: Sources of Fossil Fuels in the United States

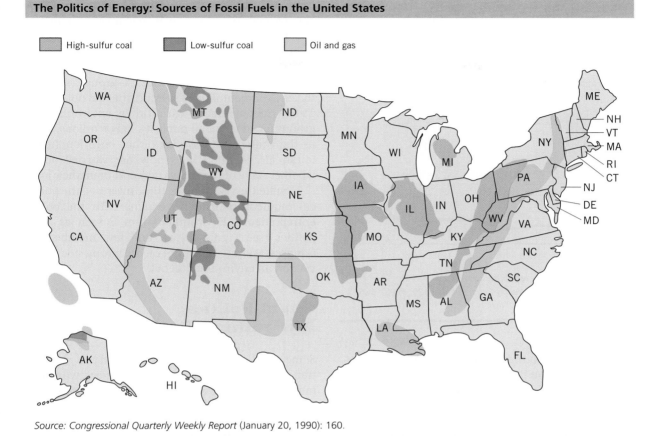

☐ High-sulfur coal   ☐ Low-sulfur coal   ☐ Oil and gas

Source: Congressional Quarterly Weekly Report (January 20, 1990): 160.

would be more costly, and thus less likely, for existing factories in their states to close down and move into the West.

The 1977 law in effect required scrubbers on all new coal-burning plants—even ones located right next to mines where they could get low-sulfur coal. As two scholars later described the law, it seemed to produce "clean coal and dirty air."[9]

The 1977 bill did not solve much. Many of the scrubbers, as predicted, didn't work very well. And there remained the question of what to do about existing power plants and factories. In the early 1980s the Reagan administration took the position that too little was known to warrant strong action; more research was needed first. The Canadian government and members of Congress from the Northeast took a very different view, demanding that something be done immediately.

For thirteen years there was a political stalemate in Congress, as is often the case when strongly opposed interest groups fight it out. And when a solution was finally agreed upon, it was a compromise. President Bush the elder proposed a two-step regulation. In the first phase 111 power plants would be required to reduce their emission of sulfur by a fixed amount. They could decide for themselves how to do it: buy low-sulfur coal, install scrubbers, or use some other technology. This would be done by 1995. In the second phase, with a deadline in the year 2000, there would be sharper emission reductions for many more plants, and this would probably require the use of scrubbers. To create some flexibility in how much each utility must cut its emissions, a system of sulfur dioxide allowances that could be bought and sold was established. Coal miners complained that they would lose jobs during

Figure 21.1   Government Regulation

QUESTION   *In general do you think there is too much, too little . . .
government regulation and involvement in the area of environmental
protection?**

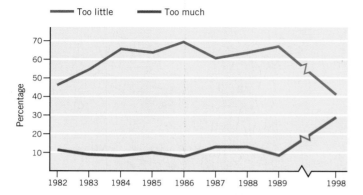

*Others responded "right amount" or "don't know."
Source: Congressional Quarterly Weekly Report (January 20, 1990): 185,
updated with Wirthlin Worldwide Survey.

phase one, and so they were promised some finan-cial compensation if they were laid off as a result of their employers' complying with the new limits. This compromise became part of the Clean Air Act of 1990.

Interest group politics permeates many aspects of environmental policy making. When cities or states consider land-use controls and zoning ordinances, they are weighing the competing demands of estab-lished residents (who often want as little new growth in their communities as possible) against demands of developers who want to build additional housing.

Interest group politics often lacks the moral fer-vor of entrepreneurial politics and rarely taps the deep streams of public opinion that are reflected in majoritarian politics. As environmental policy has become more complex and as people have adjusted to existing laws, however, new interest groups have been formed that have a stake in how things are done. As a result it becomes harder and harder to change existing policies. The heady victories of the early 1970s are hard to duplicate today because groups that were once unorganized are now well organized.

For example, there is now a large and growing industry that makes products designed to improve the environment. As we saw in the acid rain contro-versy, industry can play an important role in sup-porting laws that favor their machines, whether or not they are the best solution to the problem. Industry is far better organized today than in 1970 to use its employees and political allies to defend its interests. Similarly, public-interest groups, such as the Environmental Defense Fund, that did not exist in 1965 now compete with other environmental groups for money and publicity. Labor unions, such as the United Auto Workers, that once fought for tough air pollution laws now are worried about whether some of these laws may cost them their jobs.

Despite the rise of all of these interests, the politi-cal momentum usually remains with the policy entrepreneurs. Environmentalism is seen as good politics (see Figure 21.1), and few members of Congress want to be caught on the wrong side of the vote on an environmental bill.

Client Politics: Agricultural Pesticides

Some client groups have so far escaped this momen-tum. One such group is organized farmers, who have more or less successfully resisted efforts to restrict, sharply, the use of pesticides or to control the runoff of pesticides from farmlands.

For a while it seemed as though farmers would also fall before the assaults of policy entrepreneurs. When Rachel Carson published *Silent Spring* in 1962, she set off a public outcry about the harm to wildlife caused by the indiscriminate use of DDT, a common pesticide. In 1972 the EPA banned the use of DDT.

That same year Congress directed the EPA to eval-uate the safety of all pesticides on the market; unsafe ones were to be removed. However, that is easier said than done. One reason is that there are over fifty thousand pesticides now in use, with five thousand new ones introduced every year.[10] Testing all of these chemicals is a huge, vastly expensive, and very time-consuming job, especially since any health effects on people may not be observed for several years.[11] Another reason is that pesticides have many benefi-cial uses; therefore someone has to balance the gains and the risks of using a given pesticide and compare the relative gains and risks of two similar pesticides.

But even if the science were easy, the politics would not be. American farmers are the most

Pesticides help grow better crops but some worry they may harm the environment.

Environmentalists have used the protection of an endangered species, such as the spotted owl, as a way of reducing timber harvests.

productive in the world, and most of them believe that they cannot achieve that output (and thus their present incomes) without using pesticides. These farmers are well organized to express their interests and well represented in Congress (especially on the House and Senate Agricultural Committees). Complicating matters is the fact that the subsidies the taxpayers give to farmers often encourage them to produce more food than they can sell and thus to use more pesticides than they really need. Though many of these chemicals do not remain in the crops that are harvested, large amounts sink into the soil, contaminating water supplies. But these problems are largely invisible to the public and are much harder to dramatize than, say, the discovery of a toxic waste dump like that at Love Canal, New York.

Though attacked by environmental organizations, farm groups have been generally successful at practicing client politics. The EPA's budget for reviewing pesticides has been kept small (the long-time chairman of the House Appropriations Committee, Jamie Whitten, was a supporter of farmers and a critic of environmentalists).[12] Very few pesticides have been taken off the market, and

those that have been removed have tended to be ones that, because they were involved in some incident receiving heavy media coverage (such as the effect of DDT on birds), easily fell prey to entrepreneurial politics.

One of the reasons client politics has been able to protect the use of pesticides despite a political atmosphere that heavily favors environmental safety is that in fact pesticides have trivial effects on long-term human health problems, such as cancer. The most scholarly studies of the tendency of pesticides to cause cancer suggest that they are "unimportant" because "there is no convincing evidence" that they produce cancer.[13]

A similar kind of client politics exists in the timber industry. Wood product companies and loggers want access to forests under the control of the U.S. Forest Service. Though only 13 percent of all cut timber comes from these forests and two-thirds of the U.S. forest system is already off-limits to logging, environmentalists want further restrictions, especially to prevent clear-cutting (cutting down all the trees in a given area) and to prevent harvesting trees from the old-growth forests of Oregon and

WHO GOVERNS? TO WHAT ENDS?

> ### Superfund: Cleaning Up Toxic Wastes

During the 1970s hazardous waste sites were discovered all across America. Dangerous chemicals, many used decades before anybody worried about the environment and in some cases involving substances no one knew to be toxic, were found in the soil and near drinking water. These new investigations understandably alarmed many people. They and their legislators wanted this junk cleaned up.

What could be simpler? Find the dangerous stuff and take it out. In 1980 President Carter signed the Comprehensive Environmental Response, Compensation, and Liability Act (CERCLA), commonly known as Superfund. The law did two things: First, it taxed chemical and petroleum industries and put the proceeds, along with general tax revenues, into a trust fund to pay for cleaning up abandoned hazardous waste sites. Second, the law gave the government the power to sue any person or company (if they could be found) that had dumped the waste. In 1986 the law was strengthened when President Reagan signed a bill that gave the Environmental Protection Agency (EPA) more power and increased the size of Superfund to $8.5 billion.

But a decade later little had been done. Only 14 of 1,200 known hazardous waste sites had been cleaned up. By 2000 there were more than 2,000 waste sites that had not been treated. What had gone wrong?

First, finding and suing the responsible parties was very difficult. These "potentially responsible parties" included present and past owners of a site, their insurance companies, and any firm that deposited waste long before a law had been passed saying that it was illegal. Some companies had dumped the junk knowingly, others by accident; still others had long since gone out of business or were bankrupt. Finding them and getting them to pay were slow and difficult processes. As a result a lot of the Superfund money went to hire lawyers, not waste removers.

Second, it is complicated and time-consuming to clean up a site. Some sites had become big industrial plants or suburban housing developments. The EPA never had a staff equal to these high demands. There was a rapid turnover in EPA Superfund managers.

Third, as the environmental lobby got stronger, it put more and more pressure on the EPA to expand the list of hazardous sites and raise the standard for what constituted a cleaned-up site. No one seemed to be interested in developing a clear list of top-priority sites; instead the whole list just got longer.

Nobody wants to live on a toxic waste site. But how do you clean it up? Just by hiring more lawyers to sue more people? The Superfund problem highlights the difficulty of designing an effective strategy and a good administrative system for doing what almost everyone wants done.

Washington. But Congress has generally supported the timber industry, ordering the Forest Service to sell harvesting rights at below-market prices, in effect subsidizing the industry. Some activists hope to convert this client politics into entrepreneurial politics by demanding that clear-cutting in certain forests be stopped in order to protect endangered species, such as the spotted owl.

The Environmental Uncertainties

Making environmental policy strikes many people as easy—identify a problem, raise a fuss, defeat "the interests," and enjoy the benefits. In fact it is much harder than that to have a sane environmental policy.

First, what is the problem? Nobody likes smog, and human waste or oil slicks floating off our beaches are obviously bad. But many other problems are much less clear-cut. Science doesn't know whether we are experiencing a dangerous level of global warming or how bad the greenhouse effect is, if it exists at all. Pesticides that cause cancer in animals when given in megadoses may or may not cause cancer in people when absorbed in nominal amounts.

Second, if there is a problem, what goals do we want to achieve? We want reasonably clean air and water, of course, but how clean is reasonably clean? Since the cost of removing from the air the last 10 percent of some pollutants is often greater than the cost of removing the first 90 percent, how clean is clean enough? If making air and water cleaner is costly in terms of jobs, energy, and economic growth, how big a price are we willing to pay? When the cost of gasoline shot up in 1973–1974, many voters became much less interested in nonpolluting cars if the devices that reduced the pollution also reduced the cars' gas mileage.

Third, how do we want to achieve our goals? Issuing rules and enforcing them in court often seem the easiest things to do, but they are not always the wisest. That **command-and-control strategy** assumes that the rule makers and rule enforcers know how to achieve the greatest environmental gain at the least cost. In fact no one knows how to do that, because local circumstances, technological problems, and economic costs are so complex. Under what circumstances can we use incentives and market prices to get people voluntarily to clean up their act by using their own imagination?

All of these uncertainties have become part of the endless political controversies surrounding the administration of the Environmental Protection Agency. For example:

■ **What Is the Problem?**   The EPA was given the responsibility to administer certain laws governing air, water, and pesticides (among others). But it is rarely left alone to define these problems; any new environmental scandal leads to popular and congressional demands that it drop everything and solve that crisis. When toxic chemicals were found at Love Canal and Virginia Beach, these dramatic discoveries put other, less dramatic, but often more important problems on the back burner.

Cleaning up the more than 1,200 major toxic waste sites nationwide will take decades.

■ **What Are the Costs and Benefits?**   Everyone wants a healthy environment, but people do not distinguish accurately between realistic and unrealistic threats or between reasonable and unreasonable costs. The biggest scare is cancer, even though every form of cancer has been steadily declining for many years (except lung cancer, which is caused primarily by smoking, not environmental hazards). People fear the unknown—many are afraid of flying, for example, even though flying is vastly safer than driving. People fear strange threats, such as toxic chemicals, even though they may never hurt anyone. People applaud dramatic governmental steps without asking whether they actually help anyone. For example, the government has mandated that all asbestos must be removed from public school buildings. Though intense exposure to asbestos can cause health problems, removing all the asbestos from old school buildings helps almost no one and may hurt the asbestos removers. The problem for government officials is to keep policies aimed at real risks—they do exist—and not to be diverted by popular concerns over unreal ones. In a free society, that is not easy.

■ **What Are Our Goals?**   When the EPA was told by Congress to eliminate *all* pollutants entering our waterways by 1985, to cut auto emissions by 90 percent within five years, and to eliminate smog in *all* cities, Congress should have known that these goals were utterly unrealistic. When the EPA realized that it could not achieve these goals, it was forced to ask for extensions in deadlines and for revisions in laws. This gave it the appearance of knuckling under to industry pressure.[14]

■ **How Do We Achieve Our Goals?**   Initially the EPA was zealous about using a command-and-control strategy to improve air and water quality. For example, to reduce water pollution discharged from factories, the EPA issued rules broken down into 642 industry subcategories, and even then there was a lot of local variation that it could not take into account. When the cost of doing this sort of thing got out of control, the EPA during the Carter administration began to devise incentives to replace some rules. These included offsets, bubbles, and banks:

- **Offsets.** If a company wants to open a new plant in an area with polluted air, it can do so if the pollution it generates is offset by a reduction in pollution from another source in that area. To achieve that reduction, the new company may buy an existing company and close it down.
- **Bubble standard.** A bubble is the total amount of air pollution that can come from a given factory. A company is free to decide which specific sources within that factory must be reduced and how to meet the bubble standard.
- **Pollution allowances (or banks).** If a company reduces its polluting emissions by more than the law requires, it can either use this excess to cover a future plant expansion or sell it to another company as an offset.

Once, only affected businesses complained about the high cost, slow progress, and legal complexity of environmental regulations. Increasingly, however, pro-environment interest groups and the government itself have become aware of the difficulties that arise when the government relies on a command-and-control strategy that is indifferent to costs and excessively reliant on lawsuits.

When the Clinton administration took office in 1993, it had the strong support of environmentalists. Vice President Gore was a visible and influential supporter of environmental protection; he had even written a book on the subject. Secretary of the Interior Bruce Babbitt was also a staunch environmentalist. But instead of just pushing ahead with more command-and-control policies, the new administration began to reexamine these approaches. It suggested, for example, that the Superfund law, intended to clean up toxic waste dumps, was in fact not cleaning up many sites; instead it was encouraging armies of lawyers to bring lengthy and costly lawsuits to determine who was responsible for the toxic waste. The administration tried to amend the law, but without much success.

American politics, though often messy, confusing, and conflict-ridden, sometimes changes as people learn from their experiences. Indeed, our political system causes learning (and undergoes change) precisely *because* it is messy, confusing, and conflict-ridden. Problems that once looked simple ("There is too much pollution") and policies that once sounded straightforward ("We'll tell people to stop polluting") must often be tempered and modified once they are tested by the complexities of reality.

The Results

Though Americans think that their environment has gotten worse, in fact many aspects of it have gotten better since 1970. There is now much less carbon monoxide, sulfur dioxide, and lead in the atmosphere than once was the case. It is less clear whether there have been equally noticeable improvements in water quality, in large part because much of the gunk that flows into our rivers, lakes, and oceans does not come from some fixed source (such as a sewer) that can be easily isolated; a lot comes from runoff from the ground as a result of rain washing pollutants off urban streets and farmlands and into the water.

Hazardous waste is found at thousands of known locations (and perhaps hundreds more unknown ones). The cleanup job is so great that it will be years before much progress can be shown. Getting big reductions in dangerous pesticides requires first reaching agreement on what is a dangerous pesticide and then finding a way of minimizing the harm to agriculture that would be caused by the reduction.

Summary

nvironmental issues illustrate all four styles of policy-making.

Entrepreneurial politics: an unorganized public is to benefit at the expense of a well-organized group. An example is the effort to reduce what some think is global warming. Such politics requires mobilizing the media, dramatizing the issue, and convincing members of Congress that their political reputations will suffer if they do not cast the right vote. To prevent client groups from taking over the implementation of these laws, the bills are written to make it easy to use the courts to force action.

Majoritarian politics: an unorganized public is to benefit at its own expense. Examples include reducing auto emissions by imposing transportation controls, raising gasoline taxes, and requiring environmental impact statements. Interest groups tend not to be the decisive players. Whether the proposal wins or loses depends on how the public generally evaluates the costs. They like environmental impact statements but oppose higher gasoline taxes and restrictions on private automobile use. Dramatizing a crisis tends to be less effective because the public at large, and not some small interest, must pay for any benefits.

Interest group politics: two organized groups with a material stake in the outcome fight over who will pay and who will benefit. An example is the controlling of acid rain. When faced with two or more powerful interests, Congress tends not to pass broad, sweeping bills but to find workable compromises.

Client politics: an organized group gets a benefit; an unorganized public must pay. Examples include the use of agricultural pesticides and timber cutting in U.S. forests. Client politics depends on the client group's having strategically placed allies in Congress and on its potential opponents' being unable to convert this policy system into a pattern of entrepreneurial politics (by dramatizing a crisis, for example).

In general, entrepreneurial politics has played the dominant role in most environmental issues. The prevalence of entrepreneurial politics in this arena is largely due to (1) the success of policy entrepreneurs in sensitizing public opinion to these matters and (2) the growth of a variety of public-interest lobbies with close ties to the media and with the ability to threaten recalcitrant legislators with attacks on their reputations.

Unlike economic or welfare issues, environmental issues lend themselves to entrepreneurial politics because the problems can be portrayed in life-threatening terms, the goals can be related to what most people believe is the good life, and the costs can be minimized, deferred, or (seemingly) placed on small groups.

Reconsidering the Enduring Questions

1. If we wish to have cleaner air and water, how far can we go in making them cleaner when the cost of each additional gain goes up?

Not as far as some people would like. We have cut the pollutants coming out of cars dramatically, but it will cost a lot to cut them to zero. The key question is whether spending scarce dollars that way makes more sense than spending the same amount of money on something else, like preventing diseases or funding schools. Choosing between spending money on clean air, less disease, and better schools may strike some readers as wrongheaded; shouldn't we have all of these? But governing means using limited resources to deal with many different desires. It is almost impossible to have air that is entirely clean (natural fires and dust storms will make it dirty), and

even reducing auto pollutants to zero will have to await the invention of engines powered by things like fuel cells that have as a waste product only water. If we spend huge sums on making air or water entirely pure, we will inevitably be spending less on something else that we also want. Americans love the environment, but even for things we love we have to worry about costs.

2. What is the best way for the government to achieve an environmental goal: by issuing orders or offering incentives?

For a lot of people, issuing orders makes sense. That way we tell people what they have to do and can punish them if they don't do it. But for most economists and policy analysts, incentives make more sense because they give people the opportunity to choose the most efficient way to help the environment. For example, we can tell utilities not to let any sulphur dioxide out of their smokestacks, but that may impose huge costs on utilities that already produce very little sulphur dioxide or even drive them out of business. If instead we tell utilities they will get rewards for reducing pollutants, those that can do so easily will make big changes and, if they reduce them by more than a specified amount, will be allowed to sell the extra gains to another company to help it meet its goals. Still, when the gains are huge and the costs minimal, issuing orders makes sense.

World Wide Web Resources

- Environmental Protection Agency: www.epa.gov
- Environmental activists
  Environmental Defense Fund: www.edf.org
  Natural Resources Defense Council:
  www.nrdc.org
  Sierra Club: www.sierraclub.org

- Environmental skeptics
  American Enterprise Institute: www.aei.org
  Competitive Enterprise Institute: www.cei.org
  Oregon Institute: www.oism.org/pproject/

Key Terms

environmental impact statement
  p. 591
acid rain *p. 592*

command-and-control strategy
  p. 597
offsets *p. 598*

bubble standard *p. 598*
pollution allowances (or banks)
  p. 598

Suggested Readings

Easterbrook, Gregg. *A Moment on Earth.* New York: Viking, 1995. A comprehensive account of what we have accomplished and what remains to be done regarding the environment, written by a hard-headed environmentalist.

Gore, Al. *Earth in the Balance.* Boston: Houghton Mifflin, 2000. Revised edition of a pro-environment argument first written when Gore was a senator.

Landy, Mark K., Marc J. Roberts, and Stephen R. Thomas. *The Environmental Protection Agency: Asking the Wrong Questions.* New York: Oxford University Press, 1990. Careful review of how the EPA tries to manage complex environmental problems under laws and policies that force it to focus on "what causes cancer."

Lomborg, Bjørn. *The Skeptical Environmentalist.* Cambridge: Cambridge University Press, 2001. A scholarly criticism, written by a liberal, of claims about growing harm to the environment.

Mendelsohn, Robert. *The Greening of Global Warming.* Washington, D.C.: American Enterprise Institute, 1999. A critique of global warming theories.

Rosenbaum, Walter A. *Environmental Politics and Policy.* 4th ed. Washington, D.C.: Congressional Quarterly Press, 1998. Analysis of the politics of environmental issues, including air and water pollution, the use of chemicals, nuclear power, and preserving outer space.

Vogel, David. *National Style of Regulation: Environmental Policy in Great Britain and the United States.* Ithaca, N.Y.: Cornell University Press, 1986. An explanation of why environmental politics in the United States is so adversarial.

PART V

The Nature of American Democracy

*Justice is the end of government. It is the end of civil society.
It ever has been and ever will be pursued until it be obtained,
or until liberty be lost in the pursuit.*

FEDERALIST No. 51

Who Governs? To What Ends?

Enduring Questions

1. Why has the federal government become bigger and more complicated?
2. What would our national government be like if it were based on a parliamentary system?

As we stated at the start of this book, there are two questions about politics: Who governs? To what ends? This concluding chapter constitutes our best contemporary answer to these two most enduring questions as they relate to American politics, past and present. You can begin to answer them yourself. Just ask almost any contemporary American about how to fix a social or economic problem, and he or she will start talking about what the president and Congress should do. People worry about crime, abortion, drug abuse, civil rights, campaign finance, sexual status, gun control, school quality, the environment, and the homeless, and they debate one another about what policy Washington should have on these matters. We are all quite used to this. But until a half century ago, such chatter would have been nonsense.

Restraints on the Growth of Government

When Dwight Eisenhower was president, none of these issues except civil rights was even thought to be a matter for federal policy, and on civil rights

603

Congress didn't do very much. Our national political agenda was very short. During the Eisenhower administration we decided to build an interstate highway system, admit Alaska and Hawaii into the union, and fight over the power of labor unions. For *eight years* these were about the only major domestic political issues. The rest of the time Washington worried about foreign affairs.

This was about what the Founders had expected, though many of them would have objected to some things that were done in the Eisenhower administration. Some would have thought Washington shouldn't build any highways because the Constitution did not authorize Congress to make laws about such matters. The federal government, in their view, should limit itself to war, peace, interstate commerce, establishing a national currency, and delivering the mail. And for a long time, the prevailing interpretation of the Constitution sharply limited what policies the federal government could adopt. The Supreme Court restricted the authority of the government to regulate business and prevented it from levying an income tax. Most important, the Supreme Court refused, with some exceptions, to allow the delegation of broad discretionary power to administrative agencies.

The Supreme Court could not have maintained this position for as long as it did if it had acted in the teeth of popular opposition. But popular opinion was also against the growth of government. It was not thought legitimate for the federal government to intervene deeply in the economy (even the American Federation of Labor, led by Samuel Gompers, resisted federal involvement in labor-management issues). It was certainly not thought proper for Washington to upset racial segregation as it was practiced in both the North and the South. It took constitutional amendments to persuade Congress that it had the authority to levy an income tax or to prohibit the sale of alcoholic beverages. Even in the 1930s public opinion polls showed that as many as half the voters were skeptical of a federal unemployment compensation program.

That was the Old System. Today, under the New System, federal politics is not about some small list of problems thought to be truly national; it is about practically everything. It is almost impossible to think of a problem about which Washington has no policy at all or around which it does not carry on intense debates. Listen to radio talk shows and they will be about why Washington has a good or bad policy about almost every issue you can imagine.

What is puzzling about this change from the Old System to the New System is that the Constitution is filled with arrangements designed to make it hard, not easy, for the federal government to act. The separation of powers permits the president, Congress, and the courts to check one another; federalism guarantees that states will have an important role to play; and the division of legislative authority between the House and the Senate ensures that each body will be inclined to block the other. To get a new law passed, you have to please a large number of political actors; to get a new one blocked, you only have to convince one congressional committee.

That system made the national government relatively unimportant for many decades. Until well into the twentieth century, governors and mayors were more important than the president. Most members of Congress did not serve more than one or two terms in Washington; there didn't seem to be much point in becoming a career legislator because Congress didn't do much, didn't pay much, and wasn't in session for very long.

Relaxing the Restraints

As we have said, the constraints on federal action have now weakened or disappeared altogether. First, the courts have altered their interpretation of the Constitution in ways that have not only permitted but sometimes even required government action. The Bill of Rights has been extended so that almost all its important provisions are now regarded as applying to the states (by having been incorporated into the due process clause of the Fourteenth Amendment). This means that a citizen can use the federal courts to alter state policy to a greater degree than ever before. (Overturning state laws that ban abortions or require racially separate schools are two important examples of this change.) The special protection that the courts once granted property rights has been substantially reduced so that business can be regulated to a greater degree than previously. The Court has permitted Congress to give broad discretionary powers to administrative agencies, allowing bureaucrats to make decisions that once only Congress could make.

Second, public opinion has changed in ways that support an expanded role for the federal government. The public demanded action to deal with the Great Depression (the programs that resulted, such as Social Security, survived in part because the Supreme Court changed its mind about the permissible scope of federal action). Political elites changed their minds faster than the average citizen. Well-educated, politically active people began demanding federal policies regarding civil rights, public welfare, environmental protection, consumer safety, and foreign aid well before the average citizen became concerned with such things.

Once in place, most of these programs proved popular, so their continuance was supported by mass as well as elite opinion. The cumulative effect of this process was to blur, if not erase altogether, the line that once defined what the government had the authority to do. At one time a new proposal was debated in terms of whether it was *legitimate* for the federal government to do it all. Federal aid to education, for example, was usually opposed because many people feared it would lead to federal control of local schools. But after so many programs (including federal aid to education) had been passed, people stopped arguing about whether a certain policy was legitimate and argued instead about whether it was *effective*.

Third, political resources have become more widely distributed. The number and variety of interest groups have increased enormously. The funds available from foundations for organizations pursuing specific causes have grown. It is now easier to get access to the federal courts than formerly was the case, and once in the courts the plaintiffs are more likely to encounter judges who believe that the law and the Constitution should be interpreted broadly to permit particular goals (for example, prison reform) to be attained by legal rather than legislative means. Hundreds of magazines, newsletters, and World Wide Web pages have arisen to provide policy information to specialized segments of opinion. The techniques of mass protest, linked to the desire of television to show visually interesting accounts of social conflict, have been perfected in ways that convey the beliefs of a few into the living rooms of millions.

Campaign-finance laws and court rulings have given legal status and constitutional protection to thousands of political-action committees (PACs) that raise and spend tens of millions of dollars from millions of small contributors. College education, once the privilege of a tiny minority, has become the com-

The growth of the federal government is symbolized by its building the remarkable Hoover Dam across the Colorado River.

mon experience of millions of people, so that the effects of college—in encouraging political participation and in shaping political beliefs (usually in a liberal direction)—are now widely shared. The ability of candidates to win nomination for office no longer depends on their ability to curry favor with a few powerful bosses; it now reflects their skill at raising money, mobilizing friends and activists, cultivating a media image, and winning a primary election.

So great have been the changes in the politics of policy making in this country starting in the 1930s that we can refer, with only slight exaggeration, to one policy-making system having been replaced by another (see box on page 606).

The Old System

The Old System had a small agenda. Though people voted at a high rate and often took part in torchlight parades and other mass political events, political leadership was professionalized in the sense that the leadership circle was small, access to it was difficult, and the activists in social movements were generally kept out. Only a few major issues were under discussion at any time. A member of Congress had a small staff (if any at all), dealt with his or her colleagues on a personal basis, deferred to the prestige of House and Senate leaders, and tended to become part of some stable coalition (the farm bloc, the labor bloc, the southern bloc) that persisted across many issues.

How American Politics Has Changed

Old System		New System
	Congress	
Chairmen relatively strong		Chairmen relatively weak
Small staffs		Large staffs
Few subcommittees		Many subcommittees
	Interest Groups	
A few large blocs (farmers, business, labor)		Many diverse interests that form ad hoc coalitions
Rely on "insider" lobbying		Mobilize grassroots
	Presidency	
Small staff		Large staff
Reaches public via press conferences		Reaches public via radio and television
	Courts	
Allow government to exercise few economic powers		Allow government to exercise broad economic power
Take narrow view of individual freedoms		Take broad view of individual freedoms
	Political Parties	
Dominated by state and local party leaders meeting in conventions		Dominated by activists chosen in primaries and caucuses
	Policy Agenda	
Brief		Long
	Key Question	
Should the federal government enter a new policy area?		How can we fix and pay for an existing policy?
	Key Issue	
Would a new federal program abridge states' rights?		Would a new federal program prove popular?

When someone proposed adding a new issue to the public agenda, a major debate often arose over whether it was legitimate for the federal government to take action at all on the matter. A dominant theme in this debate was the importance of "states' rights." Except in wartime, or during a very brief period when the nation expressed interest in acquiring colonies, the focus of policy debate was on domestic affairs. Members of Congress saw these domestic issues largely in terms of their effect on local constituencies. The presidency was small and somewhat personal; there was only a rudimentary White House staff. The president would cultivate the press, but there was a clear understanding that what he said in a press conference was never to be quoted directly.

For the government to take bold action under this system, the nation usually had to be facing a crisis. War presented such crisis, and so the federal government during the Civil War and World Wars I and II acquired extraordinary powers to conscript soldiers, control industrial production, regulate the flow of information to citizens, and restrict the scope of personal liberty. Each succeeding crisis left the government bureaucracy somewhat larger than it had been before, but when the crisis ended, the exercise of extraordinary powers ended. Once again, the agenda of political issues became small, and legislators argued about whether it was legitimate for the government to enter some new policy area, such as civil rights or industrial regulation.

The New System

The New System began in the 1930s but did not take its present form until the 1970s. It is characterized by a large policy agenda, the end of the debate over the legitimacy of government action (except in the area of First Amendment freedoms), the diffusion and decentralization of power in Congress, and the multiplication of interest groups. The government has grown so large that it has a policy on almost every conceivable subject, and so the debate in Washington is less often about whether it is right and prudent to take some bold new step and more often about how the government can best cope with the strains and problems that arise from implementing existing policies. As someone once said, the federal government is now more concerned with managing than with ruling.

For example, in 1935 Congress debated whether the nation should have a Social Security system at all; in the 1980s it debated whether the system could best be kept solvent by raising taxes or by cutting benefits; in the late 1990s it debated whether some part of each person's Social Security payments could be invested in the stock market. In the 1960s Congress argued over whether there should be any federal civil rights laws at all; by the 1980s and 1990s it was arguing over whether those laws should be administered in a way that simply eliminated legal barriers to equal opportunity for racial minorities or in a way (by affirmative action) that made up for the disadvantages that burdened such minorities in the past. As late as the 1950s the president and Congress argued over whether it was right to adopt a new program if it meant that the government had to borrow money to pay for it. As late as the 1960s many members of Congress believed the federal government had no business paying for the health care of its citizens; today hardly anyone argues against having Medicare but many worry about how best to control its rising cost.

The differences between the Old and New Systems should not be exaggerated. The Constitution still makes it easier for Congress to block the proposals of the president, or for some committee of

Federal rules since the mid-1960s have regulated how workers in factories should be protected.

Congress to defeat the preferences of the majority of Congress, than in almost any other democratic government. The system of checks and balances operates as before. The essential differences between the Old and the New Systems are these:

1. Under the Old System, the checks and balances made it difficult for the federal government to *start* a new program, and so the government remained relatively small. Under the New System, these checks and balances made it hard to *change* what the government is already doing, and so the government remains large.
2. Under the Old System, power was *somewhat centralized* in the hands of party and congressional leaders. There was still plenty of conflict, but the number of people who had to agree before something could be done was not large. Under the New System, power is much more *decentralized*, and so it is harder to resolve conflict because so many more people—party activists, interest group leaders, individual members of Congress, heads of government agencies—must agree.

The transition from the Old to the New System occurred chiefly during two periods in American politics. The first was in the early 1930s when a catastrophic depression led the government to explore new ways of helping the needy, regulating business, and preventing a recurrence of the disaster. Franklin Roosevelt's New Deal was the result. The huge majorities enjoyed by the Democrats in Congress, coupled with popular demands to solve the problem, led to a vast outpouring of new legislation and the creation of dozens of new government agencies. Though initially the Supreme Court struck down some of these measures as unconstitutional, a key member of the Court changed his mind and others retired from the bench; by the late 1930s the Court had virtually ceased opposing any economic legislation.

The second period was in the mid-1960s, a time of prosperity. There was no crisis akin to the Great Depression or World War II, but two events helped change the face of American politics. One was an intellectual and popular ferment that we now refer to as the spirit of "the sixties"—a militant civil rights movement, student activism on college campuses aimed at resisting the Vietnam War, growing concern about threats to the environment, the popular appeal of Ralph Nader and his consumer-protection movement, and an optimism among many political and intellectual leaders that the government could solve whatever problems it was willing to address. The other was the 1964 election that returned Lyndon Johnson to the presidency with a larger share of the popular vote than any other president in modern times. Johnson swept into office and with him, liberal Democratic majorities in both the House and Senate.

The combination of organized demands for new policies, elite optimism about the likely success of those policies, and extraordinary majorities in Congress meant that President Johnson was able, for a few years, to get almost any program he wanted enacted into law. So large were his majorities in Congress that the conservative coalition of Republicans and southern Democrats was no longer large enough to block action; northern Democratic liberals were sufficiently numerous in the House and Senate to take control of both bodies. And so much of Johnson's "Great Society" legislation became law. This included the passage of Medicare (to help pay the medical bills of retired people) and Medicaid (to help pay the medical bills of people on welfare), greatly expanded federal aid to the states to assist them in fighting crime, rebuilding slums, and running transit systems, the enactment of major civil rights laws and of a program to provide federal aid to local schools, the creation of a "War on Poverty" that included various job-training and community-

action agencies, and the enactment of a variety of laws regulating business for the purpose of reducing auto fatalities, improving the safety and health of industrial workers, cutting back on pollutants entering the atmosphere, and safeguarding consumers from harmful products.

These two periods—the early 1930s and the mid-1960s—changed the political landscape in America. Of the two, the latter was perhaps the more important, for not only did it witness the passage of so much unprecedented legislation, but also it saw major changes in the pattern of political leadership. It was during this time that the great majority of the members of the House of Representatives came to enjoy relatively secure seats, the primary elections came to supplant party conventions as the decisive means of selecting presidential candidates, interest groups increased greatly in number, and television began to play an important role in shaping the political agenda and perhaps influencing the kinds of candidates that are nominated.

Consequences of Activist Government

One way of describing the New System is to call it an "activist" government. It is tempting to make a sweeping judgment about such a government, either praising it because it serves a variety of popular needs or condemning it because it is a bureaucratic affliction. Such generalizations are not entirely empty, but neither are they very helpful. The worth of any given program, or of any collection of programs, can be assessed only by a careful consideration of its costs and benefits, of its effects and side effects. But we may discover some general political consequences of the enlarged scope of government activity.

First, as the government gets bigger, its members must spend more time managing the consequences—intended and unintended—of existing programs and less time debating at length new ideas. As a result, all parts of the government, not just the executive agencies, become more bureaucratized. The White House Office and the Office of Management and Budget (OMB) grow in size and influence, as do the staffs of Congress. At the same time, private organizations (corporations, unions, universities) that deal with the government must also become more bureaucratic. The government hires more people when it is running eighty programs concerned with employment than when it is running two. By the same token, a private employer will hire (and give power to) more people when it is complying with eighty sets of regulations than when it is complying with two.

Second, the more government does, the more it will appear to be acting in inconsistent, uncoordinated, and cumbersome ways. When people complain of red tape, bureaucracy, stalemates, and confusion, they often assume that these irritants are caused by incompetent or self-seeking public officials. There is incompetence and self-interest in government just as in every other part of society, but these character traits are not the chief cause of the problem. As citizens, we want many different and often conflicting things. The result is the rise of competing policies, the division of labor among separate administrative agencies, the diffusion of accountability and control, and the multiplication of paperwork. And because Americans are especially energetic about asserting their rights, we must add to the above list of problems the regular use of the courts to challenge policies that we do not like.

Third, an activist government is less susceptible to control by electoral activity than a passive one. When the people in Washington did little, elections made a larger difference in policy than when they began to do a lot. We have pointed out in this book the extent to which both political parties and voter turnout have declined. There are many reasons for this, but an important one is often forgotten. If elections make less of a difference—because the few people for whom one votes can do little to alter the ongoing programs of government—then it may make sense for people to spend less time on party or electoral activities and more on interest group activities aimed at specific agencies and programs.

The rapid increase in the number and variety of interest groups and their enlarged role in government are not pathological. They are a rational response to the fact that elected officials can tend to only a few things, and therefore we must direct our energies at the appointed officials (and judges) who tend to all other government matters. Every president tries to accomplish more, usually by trying to reorganize the executive branch. But no president and no reorganization plan can affect more than a tiny fraction of the millions of federal employees and thousands of government programs. "Coordination" from the top can at best occur selectively, for a few issues of exceptional importance.

Ronald Reagan learned this when he took office in 1981 after promising to reduce the size of government. He did persuade Congress to cut taxes, but his plans to cut domestic spending resulted in only small declines in some programs and actual increases in many others. Though some programs, such as public housing, were hard hit, most were not, and agricultural subsidies increased dramatically.

When George W. Bush became president in 2001, his philosophy was summarized by the phrase "compassionate conservatism," words that implied that, though he was a conservative, he was not much interested in simply cutting the size of the federal government. And while in office, he proposed programs that would increase spending on many programs. His actions suggest a fact; cutting down on what Washington does is virtually impossible because the people want so much of what it does.

Finally, the more government tries to do, the more things it will be held responsible for and the greater the risk of failure. From time to time in the nineteenth century, the business cycle made many people unhappy with the federal government—recall the rise of various protest parties—though then the government did very little. If federal officials were lucky, popular support would rise as soon as economic conditions improved. If they were unlucky and a depression lasted into the election campaign, they would be thrown out of office. Today, however, the government—and the president in particular—is held responsible for crime, drug abuse, abortion, civil rights, the environment, the elderly, the status of women, the decay of central cities, the price of gasoline, and international tensions in half a dozen places on the globe.

No government and no president can do well on all or even most of these matters most of the time. Indeed, most of these problems, such as crime, may be totally beyond the reach of the federal government, no matter what its policy. It should not be surprising, therefore, that opinion surveys taken since the early 1960s have shown a steep decline in public confidence in government. There is no reason to believe that this represents a loss of faith in our form of government or even in the design of its institutions, but it clearly reflects a disappointment in, and even cynicism about, the performance of government.

Disenchantment with government performance is not unique to the United States; it appears to be a feature of almost every political system in which public opinion is accurately measured. The disenchantment is in fact probably greater elsewhere. Americans who complain of high taxes might feel somewhat differently if they lived in Sweden, where taxes are nearly twice as high as here. Those who grouse about bureaucrats in this country probably have never dealt with the massive, centralized bureaucracies of Italy or France. People who are annoyed by congestion, pollution, and inflation ought to arrange a trip to Rome, Mexico City, or Tokyo. However frustrating private life and public affairs may be in this country, every year thousands living in other nations become immigrants to this country. Few Americans choose to emigrate to other places.

The enormous expansion of the scope and goals of the federal government has not been random or unguided. The government has tended to enlarge its powers more in some directions than in others; certain kinds of goals have been served more frequently than others. Though many factors shape this process of selection, two are of special importance. One is our constitutional structure, the other our political culture.

The Influence of Structure

To see the influence of structure, it is necessary to perform a mental experiment. Suppose that the Founders had adopted a centralized, parliamentary regime instead of a decentralized, congressional one. They had the British model right before their eyes. Every other European democracy adopted it. What difference would it have made had we followed the British example?

No one can be certain, of course, because the United States and Great Britain differ in many ways, and not just in their political forms. At best our mental experiment will be an educated guess. But the following possibilities seem plausible.

A parliamentary regime of the British sort centralizes power in the hands of an elected prime minister with a disciplined partisan majority in the legislature and frees him or her from most of the constraints created by independent congressional committees or independent, activist courts. Had the Framers adopted a parliamentary system, we might see these features in the political life of the United States today:

* *Quicker adoption of majoritarian policies, such as those in the area of social welfare.* Broad popular desires would be translated sooner into national policy when they are highly salient and conform to the views of party leaders.
* *More centralization of bureaucratic authority—more national planning, less local autonomy.* More decisions would be made bureaucratically, both because bureaucracies would be proportionately larger and because they would have wider discretionary authority delegated to them. (If the prime minister heads *both* the executive branch and the legislature, he or she sees no reason why decisions cannot be made as easily in one place as the other.) Local authorities would not have been able to prevent groups of citizens (such as African Americans) from voting or otherwise participating in public life by maintaining segregated facilities at the local level.
* *Fewer opportunities for citizens to challenge or block government policies of which they disapprove.* Without independent and activist courts, without local centers (state and city) of autonomous power, U.S. citizens would have less of a chance to organize to stop a highway or an urban-renewal project, for example, and hence fewer citizen organizations with these and similar purposes would exist.
* *Greater executive control of government.* If a situation like Watergate occurred, we would never know about it. No legislative investigating committees would be sufficiently independent of executive control to be able to investigate claims of executive wrongdoing.
* *Similar foreign policy.* We probably would have fought in about the same number of wars and under pretty much the same circumstances.
* *Higher and more centralized taxation.* Taxes would be higher, and a larger share of our tax money would be collected at the national level. Thus we would find it harder to wage a "tax revolt" (since it is easier to block local spending decisions than national ones).

If this list of guesses is even approximately correct, it means that you would get more of some things that you want and less of others. In general it would have been easier for temporary majorities to govern and harder for individuals and groups to protect their interests.

The Founders would probably not be surprised at this list of differences. Though they could not have foreseen all the events and issues that would have led to these outcomes, they would have understood them, because they thought that they were creating a system designed to keep central power weak and to enhance local and citizen power. They would have been amazed, of course, at the extent to which central power has been enhanced and local power weakened in the United States, but if they visited Europe, they would learn that by comparison American politics remains far more sensitive to local concerns than does politics abroad.

The Influence of Ideas

The broadly shared political culture of Americans has also influenced the policies adopted by the U.S. government. Paramount among these attitudes is the preoccupation with rights. More than the citizens of perhaps any other nation, Americans define their relations with one another and with political authority in terms of rights. The civil liberties protected by the Bill of Rights have been assiduously defended and their interpretation significantly broadened even while the power of government has been growing.

For example, we expect that the groups affected by any government program will have a right to play a role in shaping and administering that program. In consequence interest groups have proliferated. We think that citizens should have the right to select the nominees of political parties as well as to choose between the parties; hence primary elections have largely replaced party conventions in selecting candidates. Individual members of Congress assert their rights, and thus the power of congressional leaders and committee chairmen has steadily diminished. We probably use the courts more frequently than the citizens of any other nation to make or change public policy; in doing so, we are asserting one set of rights against a competing set. The procedural rules that set forth how government is to act—the Freedom of Information Act, the Privacy Act, the Administrative Procedure Act—are more complex and demanding than the rules under which any other democratic government must operate. Each rule exists because it embodies what somebody has claimed to be a right: the right to know information, to maintain one's privacy, to participate in making decisions, and to bring suit against rival parties.

A policy dilemma: Nuclear power plants reduce our dependence on foreign and nonrenewable energy sources but sharpen our concerns over safety.

The more vigorously we assert our rights, the harder it is to make government decisions or to manage large institutions. We recognize this when we grumble about red tape and bureaucratic confusion, but we rarely give much support to proposals to centralize authority or simplify decision-making. We seem to accept whatever it costs in efficiency or effectiveness in order to maintain the capacity for asserting our rights.

We do not always agree on which rights are most important, however. In addition to the influence of the widely shared commitment to rights generally, government is also shaped by the views that certain political elites have about which rights ought to be given the highest priority. Elite opinion tends to favor freedom of expression over freedom to manage or dispose of property. Mass opinion, though it has changed a good deal in the last few decades, is less committed to the preferred position of freedom of expression. Rank-and-file citizens often complain that what the elite calls essential liberty should instead be regarded as excessive permissiveness. People who own or manage property often lament the extent to which the rights governing its use have declined.

The changes in the relative security of personal and property freedom are linked to a fundamental and enduring tension in American thought.

Tocqueville said it best: Americans, he wrote, "are far more ardently and tenaciously attached to equality than to freedom." Though democratic communities have a "natural taste for freedom," that freedom is hard to preserve, because its excesses are immediate and obvious and its advantages are remote and uncertain. The advantages of equality, on the other hand, are readily apparent, and its costs are obscure

and deferred.[1] For example, Americans believe in free speech, but most of us rarely take advantage of that right and notice the problem only when somebody says something we don't like. We have to remind ourselves that freedom has to be protected even when it does not help us directly. By contrast, we notice equality immediately, as when everybody of a certain age gets Social Security even when they are already rich. Equality makes us feel comfortable even if a few people don't need the benefits they are getting.

Tocqueville may have underestimated the extent to which political liberties would endure, because he did not foresee the determination of the courts to resist, in the long run if not the short, the passions of temporary majorities seeking to curtail such liberties. But he did not underestimate the extent to which in the economic and social realms Americans would decide that improving the conditions of life would justify restrictions on the right to dispose of property and to manage private institutions. At first the conflict was between liberty and equality of opportunity; more recently it has become a conflict—among political elites if not within the citizenry itself—between equality of opportunity and equality of results.

The fact that decisions can be influenced by opinions about rights indicates that decisions can be influenced by opinions generally. As the political system has become more fragmented and more individualized as a result of our collective assertion of rights, it has come more under the sway of ideas. When political parties were strong and congressional leadership was centralized (as in the latter part of the nineteenth and the early part of the twentieth centuries), gaining access to the decision-making process in Washington was difficult, and the number of new ideas that stood a chance of adoption was small. However, those proposals that could command leadership support were more easily adopted: though there were powerful organizations that could say no, those same organizations could also say yes.

Today these and other institutions are fragmented and in disarray. Individual members of Congress are far more important than congressional leaders. Political parties no longer control nominations for office. The media have given candidates direct access to the voters; campaign finance laws have restricted, but not eliminated, the influence that interest groups can wield by spending money. Forming new, issue-oriented lobbying groups is much easier today

Not only do interest groups promote government policies, such policies stimulate interest groups. The National Rifle Association had little interest in federal regulations until gun control became a big issue.

than formerly, thanks to the capability of computers and direct-mail advertising.

These idea-based changes in institutions affect how policy is made. When there is widespread enthusiasm for an idea—especially among political elites but also in the public at large—new programs can be formulated and adopted with great speed. This happened when Lyndon Johnson's Great Society legislation was proposed, when the environmental and consumer protection laws first arrived on the public agenda, and when campaign finance reform was proposed in the wake of Watergate. So long as such symbols have a powerful appeal, so long as a consensus persists, change is possible. But when these ideas lose their appeal—or are challenged by new ideas—the competing pressures make change extremely difficult. Environmentalism today is challenged by concerns about creating jobs and economic growth; social legislation is challenged by skepticism about its effectiveness and concern over its cost; campaign finance reforms are, to some critics, merely devices for protecting incumbents.

This may all seem obvious to a reader raised in the world of contemporary politics. But it is different in degree if not in kind from the way in which politics was once carried out. In the 1920s, the 1930s, the 1940s, and even the 1950s, people described politics as a process of bargaining among organized interests, or "blocs," representing business, farming, labor, ethnic, and professional groups. With the expansion of the scope of government policy, there are no longer a few major blocs that sit astride the policy process. Instead thousands of highly specialized interests and constituencies seek above all to protect whatever benefits, intangible as well as tangible, they get from government.

We have a large government—and large expectations about what it can achieve. But the government finds it increasingly difficult to satisfy those expectations. The public's acceptance of an activist role for government has been accompanied by a decline in public confidence in those who manage that government. We expect more and more from government but are less and less certain that we will get it, or get it in a form and at a cost that we find acceptable. This perhaps constitutes the greatest challenge to statesmanship in the years ahead: to find a way to serve the true interests of the people while restoring and retaining their confidence in the legitimacy of government itself.

The "Rules" of Politics

Some "Rules" of Politics

Here are some generalizations about American politics, distilled from what has been said in this book, and offered in nervous awareness that our political system has a way of proving everybody wrong. (Before the 1960s it was a "rule" of politics that no Catholic could be elected president. John F. Kennedy took care of that.)

- Policies, once adopted, tend to persist whatever their value. (It is easier to start new programs than to end old ones.)

- Almost all electoral politics is local politics. (Members of Congress who forget "home base" tend not to remain in Congress for long.)

- Whatever the size of their staff and budget, Congress and the White House will always be overworked. (More resources produce more work, which requires more resources.)

- Each branch of government tends to emulate the others. (Congress will become more bureaucratized to cope with an executive branch that becomes more bureaucratized; judges will become more activist as Congress becomes more activist.)

- Proposals that seem to confer widespread and immediate benefits will be enacted whatever their long-term costs.

- Proposals that seem to confer delayed benefits will be enacted only if their costs are unknown, concealed, or deferred.

- Nobody—businesspeople, bureaucrats, members of Congress, judges, professors—likes competition, and everybody will do whatever he or she can to reduce or eliminate it.

- "Planning" in government takes place after a crisis takes place.

- The mass media never cover a story about things that are going well. Thus the number of "problems" in society is a function of the number of reporters.

- If you want something, you are claiming a right; if your opponent wants something, he or she is protecting a vested interest.

Reconsidering the Enduring Questions

1. *Why has the federal government become bigger and more complicated?*

   The obvious answer is that people want more from government. But that answer is not enough, because for most of our history the federal government did very little. The reason was in part that the people did not ask it to do that much and in part that constitutional restraints would not have allowed the government to do everything the public wanted. The Supreme Court, until the 1930s, would not have allowed Congress to pass many laws that we now take for granted. These restraints have ended. One reason was the Great Depression that led Washington for the first time to try to play a major role in stimulating the economy, and the Supreme Court allowed these things to happen. Another was the period of heightened expectations that came in the 1960s and the arrival in Washington of President Lyndon Johnson with huge, liberal majorities in the House and Senate.

   Now the government was ready to try almost anything. Even so, the system of checks and balances has kept our national government from growing as rapidly as that of many democratic nations that have parliamentary regimes.

2. *What would our national government be like if it were based on a parliamentary system?*

   No doubt it would be very different from what it is today, though exactly what would have changed is a matter of speculation. If we had had a British style of government we would probably have seen the following: quicker adoption of broad new policies favored by temporary majorities in areas such as welfare and health care; more national power and less local authority over schools, the police, and land-use control; higher rates of taxation to pay for these things; and fewer chances for small groups of citizens to block changes they did not like.

UNDERSTANDING THE 2004 ELECTION

Table of Contents

Introduction: The Most Important Presidential Election Ever?

The stakes in the 2004 presidential election were extraordinarily high. Indeed, Vice President Dick Cheney called the election "one of the most important, not just in our lives but in our history."[1] Of course, hyperbolic claims of historical significance occur every four years.[2] But the choice between Republican President George W. Bush and Democratic Senator John F. Kerry in 2004 did seem far more consequential than the typical presidential election.

The economy garnered a great deal of attention, in part because the Bush administration was likely to become the first since Herbert Hoover's (1929-1933) in which a net job loss occurred during a four-year term. The budget deficit, coming on the heels of a surplus just four years prior, also prompted some discussion. For his part, President Bush emphasized tax cuts that he claimed were stimulating the economy and rapidly creating new jobs. A focus on the economy, of course, is not unique in presidential politics. The parties' conflicting views of economic stewardship make for a recurring theme at election time.

Terrorism was an equally salient issue during the election. Indeed, numerous polls during the campaign showed that terrorism and the economy/jobs were ranked as the most important issue facing the nation by roughly equal numbers of voters.[3] In some ways, the "war on terror" played a role similar to that of the Cold War during past elections. As before, a general and constant concern (or even fear) about the security of the nation served as the backdrop for the campaign.

Voters tended to think Senator Kerry would be better at handling the economy, while they trusted President Bush more to handle terrorism.[4] That helps explain why the election was so close throughout much of the campaign. To the extent that voters had these issues in mind as they went to the polls, their choice appeared to be between changing directions on the economy and staying the course on combating terrorism.

What was most unique about 2004, however, was the fact that the United States was at war. Only three presidential elections since World War II have been held during war (1952, 1968, 1972).[5] The war in Iraq was the wildcard issue of the election, though in polls it rarely ranked higher than third among the most pressing issues of the day. One of the questions for voters was whether Iraq was a necessary extension of the broader war on terror, as the Bush campaign maintained, or a war of choice and a distraction from the fight against terror, as the Kerry campaign alleged. With voters so evenly divided between the economy and terrorism, the ultimate decision of many voters would hinge on an answer to that question.

In addition, the management of the war in Iraq was at issue, as were competing visions of how to end the war, though the differences were more of emphasis than of specific proposals. In fact, neither candidate had a clear plan to "win the peace." Senator Kerry argued that the operation had to be internationalized, which he insisted could only happen with a change in American leadership. President Bush maintained that freedom and democracy in Iraq required the defeat of the insurgency, something he argued would only happen under his resolute guidance.

Finally, the Vietnam War was present throughout the election as a sub-theme. Most obviously, Senator Kerry's and President Bush's military records during Vietnam became a topic of much discussion. In particular, Senator Kerry faced savage attacks on his war record and his anti-war activities. And questions were once again raised about President Bush's National Guard service. Vietnam also served as an analogy for the Iraq War. Was the war becoming a "quagmire?" Would it be necessary to reinstate the draft?

In the end, the direction of the economy, success against terrorism, and peace and stability in Iraq – if not our collective coming to grips with the memory of the Vietnam era – were thought to be dependent upon the outcome of the 2004 election. It does seem that few elections in American history have had stakes that high. And the intensity of feeling on both sides of the political divide certainly suggested a significance not felt since 1968, at the height of the Vietnam War.

The Presidential Nomination Process

In 2004, President Bush faced no Republican opposition to his re-nomination. With no candidates running against him in the primaries, he was able to save all the money he raised to spend against the presumptive Democratic nominee as soon as one emerged. By January 1, 2004, the Bush campaign had raised over $132 million.[6] That's more than he had collected during the entire nomination phase in 2000.[7] In the end, he raised over $250 million for his reelection bid, all of which would eventually be spent against John Kerry.[8]

The Democratic field for president was crowded, to say the least. The first candidate to enter the race was former Vermont Governor Howard Dean, who announced his candidacy on May 31, 2002. Massachusetts Senator John Kerry followed Dean into the contest nearly six months later (announcing on December 1, 2002). In the middle of December, a question on every political observer's mind – would the 2000 Democratic nominee, Al Gore, once again seek the party's nomination? – was answered when the former Vice President announced on "60 Minutes" that he would not enter the race. In every poll taken prior to that point, Gore led the Democratic field, usually by comfortable margins. Of course, that had more to do with name recognition than real support for Gore; nevertheless he would have been the presumptive favorite had he decided to run.

Gore's decision paved the way for a number of other candidates to throw their hats into the ring. In particular, the Democratic Party's 2000 vice presidential nominee, Senator Joe Lieberman (CT), entered the race within a month of Gore's announcement. In January and February of 2003, the field grew rapidly with Senator John Edwards (NC), Reverend Al Sharpton (NY), Representative Dennis Kucinich (OH), former House Minority Leader Richard Gephardt (MO), former Senator Carol Moseley Braun (IL), and Senator Bob Graham (FL) announcing their bids. One final candidate, retired four-star general Wesley Clark, entered the race on September 17, 2003, bringing the total number of Democratic candidates to ten.[9]

The race began with Joe Lieberman in the lead. As with earlier polls showing Gore ahead of the pack, Lieberman's early lead was likely due to the name recognition he had built as part of the national ticket in 2000. According to an ABC News/*Washington Post* poll in January 2003, Lieberman had support from 27 percent of the respondents, followed by Dick Gephardt (with 14 percent), John Edwards (11 percent) and John Kerry (10 percent).[10] At that point in the race, Howard Dean was in eighth place among eight named candidates, including Al Sharpton, with just 1 percent support.[11]

It wasn't likely that Joe Lieberman would maintain a lead for long, given his relative cultural conservatism and hawkish support for the war in Iraq. Democratic caucus and primary voters are more liberal than the average Democrat and there was opposition to the war in Iraq right from the beginning among many Democratic activists.[12] In fact, by July of 2003, Lieberman, Kerry, Gephardt and Dean were locked in a virtual four-way tie for first place (garnering support from 16, 14, 12, and 10 percent of respondents respectively).[13]

The period from January to late summer 2003 witnessed a fairly dramatic change in the political landscape in the United States. The previous October, President Bush had asked Congress for authority to use military force, if "necessary and appropriate," to "defend the national security of the United States" and "enforce all relevant United Nations Security Council resolutions regarding Iraq."[14] Senators Kerry, Edwards and Lieberman and Representative Gephardt each voted in favor of that authority.[15] By January or February of 2003, however, only Lieberman unequivocally defended his vote. The other candidates who had voted "yes" on the resolution began to walk a fine line between support for the goal of disarming Iraq and opposition to the *way* in which the President was proceeding towards war. Of these four candidates, Kerry was perhaps the most critical of the Bush Administration's approach to the war. In a speech at Georgetown University on January 23, 2003, Kerry rebuked the administration's rush to war and its "blustering unilateralism" and argued that Bush had "no plan to win the peace."[16]

All of the other candidates in the race at that time had opposed military action in Iraq, though only one would prove to be a viable candidate. Howard Dean, who had started the race at the bottom of the heap, began vigorously critiquing the President's war plans in early 2003. In a speech in February, he argued that Bush was pursuing "the wrong war at the wrong time" and urged the administration to give the United Nations weapons inspectors more time to investigate claims of Iraqi weapons of mass destruction.[17] In addition, Dean criticized his Democratic opponents for voting to authorize the war. The latter criticism would eventually help him catapult to the front of the pack.

When the war began on March 19, 2003, public support for the President's decision was high. Two days before the invasion began, an ABC News/*Washington Post* Poll found that 71 percent of the respondents supported going to war in Iraq. That was a twelve-point jump in just two weeks.[18] President Bush's approval rating similarly soared; in one month, from roughly two weeks before the war began to two weeks after, the number of those who approved of how he was handling his job as president went from 56 percent to 73 percent.[19]

The military achieved a quick and decisive victory for the United States and those allied forces that took part in the invasion. By May 2, President Bush had declared that "major combat operations in

Iraq have ended" and referred to the "battle of Iraq" as "one victory in a war on terror that began on September 11, 2001, and still goes on."[20] Almost immediately, however, the situation in Iraq seemed to be less positive than the Bush Administration had suggested it would be. Looting of government buildings and museums was rampant, delays in rebuilding basic infrastructure frustrated Iraqis, and the security situation deteriorated rapidly. Furthermore, it was beginning to appear as though there were no weapons of mass destruction in Iraq. As this had been the cornerstone of the argument for going to war in the first place, the Bush Administration was suddenly on the defensive. As the title of one newspaper editorial put it in the middle of the summer, "The War in Iraq, Alive and Unwell; A Final Victory Parade is Far Away, and Bush Faces a Credibility Canyon."[21]

By July 2003, "the postwar environment [had become] a serious political liability for Bush" and Democrats were stepping up their criticisms.[22] The Democratic National Committee, for instance, unveiled a television ad on July 10th suggesting that the Bush Administration had misled the country in the run-up to war. Among the Democratic candidates, none was as vociferous as Howard Dean. As the summer wore on, confidence in the President's policy on Iraq waned and support among Democrats for Dean increased, if only slightly. A CNN/*USA Today*/Gallup Poll from September showed Lieberman still in the lead at 18 percent, with Gephardt and Dean tied for second at 15 percent each.[23] Kerry appeared to have hit a ceiling in his support, garnering only 12 percent in the same poll.

Perhaps more important to Dean at that stage of the campaign was the headway he was making in fundraising. He had clearly touched a nerve among activists and his campaign's bank account was the beneficiary. Though he had begun 2003 with only $157,000, he raised more money than any other candidate in the second quarter of the year and his fundraising totals skyrocketed in the third quarter (July 1 – September 30), setting a record for Democratic fundraising in a single quarter.[24] He would go on to break his own record in the fourth quarter; in fact, he was the only major candidate to have increased his fundraising totals in each successive quarter 2003. Table 1 indicates just how dominant Dean was at fundraising in the last half of 2003.

Table 1: 2003 Fundraising Totals of the Major Democratic Candidates for President, in Millions

	Q1	Q2	Q3	Q4	`03 Total
Kerry	$7.0	$5.9	$4.0	$5.3	$22.2
Edwards	$7.4	$4.5	$2.6	$1.9	$16.4
Dean	$2.6	$7.6	$14.8	$16.0	$41.0
Lieberman	$3.0	$5.1	$3.6	$2.2	$13.9
Gephardt	$5.9	$3.9	$3.8	$3.0	$16.6

Source: Compiled from data available at www.politicalmoneyline.com

Much of Dean's success was based on an innovative use of the Internet. Indeed, about half of the money given to Dean in the third quarter of 2003 was contributed on-line.[25] But the Dean campaign also used the Internet for non-fundraising activities. For instance, the campaign used the Meetup.com website to help Dean supporters in cities and towns throughout the country find one another and organize to help the campaign. The Dean campaign was also the first to create a blog ("Blog for America").[26]

As fall approached, Dean had clearly established more momentum than any other Democratic candidate in the race. During the same week in early August, Dean made the covers of both *Time* and *Newsweek*, and he began the fourth quarter (October 1 – December 31) with roughly $5 million more in the bank than any other candidate.[27] Becoming the front-runner, however, would not only make him the target of other candidates, but would increase the media scrutiny of his candidacy.

On September 17, 2003, the same day that Senator Edwards formally announced his candidacy, retired general Wesley Clark decided to throw his hat into the ring. Supporters had been attempting to "draft" Clark for months, and his entrance into the race changed the dynamics immediately. In a September 3rd-5th Zogby poll that found Dean to be leading the Democratic field with 16 percent support, Clark was polling at 3 percent. Just two and a half weeks later, Clark had drawn even with Dean, at 12 percent each.[28] Though his resume was impressive – Rhodes Scholar, four-star general, supreme commander of NATO – Clark would eventually fade as a candidate because of his late start, superficial command of domestic policy, and a host of concerns about his political skill.

As Dean's fundraising success continued in the forth quarter, he faced a decision concerning presidential "matching funds." According to the partial public funding system in place for presidential nominations, candidates that agree to abide by certain fundraising restrictions (beyond those established for all federal candidates) are eligible to receive public campaign funds from the government. To qualify, candidates must collect $100,000 by raising $5,000 in twenty states in increments of $250 or less. Once eligible, candidates can receive a dollar-for-dollar match for each contribution up to $250, with a limit on the total amount of matching funds provided (equal to half the national spending limit). In exchange for public funds, candidates agree to abide by state-by-state and national spending limits; in 2004, the national limit was $45 million.

The Dean campaign had been raising so much money in 2003 that they were confident they could raise more than $45 million through private contributions. More importantly, they wanted to be able to raise and spend unlimited amounts of money against George Bush in the event that Dean wrapped up the Democratic nomination early in 2004. A candidate who accepted matching funds would have his hands tied after the primaries, long before public funds for the general election were provided. Earlier in the campaign, Dean had promised to participate in the public funding system, so a decision to opt out at that stage of the process might draw criticism. To blunt that criticism, Dean decided to poll his supporters. In early November, the campaign e-mailed nearly 500,000 supports to ask them to help him make a decision. The response was positive and within days, Dean became the first Democrat to ever decline presidential matching funds.[29]

With his campaign flagging just as Dean's was on the rise, John Kerry made a number of big decisions in November. To begin with, he replaced his campaign manager in the hope that a fresh face would kick-start his campaign. A more significant decision – though just how significant wasn't known at the time – was to follow Dean's lead and opt out of the matching fund system. By December, that decision looked foolhardy. Kerry's financial situation had deteriorated to such an extent that he mortgaged his home to loan the campaign $6 million.

However, Kerry was in a better position than it appeared as the January 19, 2004, Iowa caucuses approached. For one thing, some polls suggested that a majority of "Democratic voters in three states with early primaries or caucuses [said] they prefer a presidential nominee who supported military action against Iraq but criticized President Bush for failing to assemble international support."[30] That was precisely John Kerry's position. Though Dean had capitalized on anti-war sentiment among many Democratic activists, it appeared that rank-and-file Democrats preferred a more balanced approach.

Furthermore, the Dean campaign was faced with a number of controversial statements made by the candidate himself, including a claim to "want to be the candidate for guys with Confederate flags in their pickup trucks;" calling a conspiratorial charge about the 9/11 attacks an "interesting theory;" arguing that the capture of Saddam Hussein in December "has not made American safer;" and implying that Osama bin Laden deserved a jury trial at which his guilt should not be prejudged.[31] Dean was also forced to explain a comment he had made about the sealing of his gubernatorial papers for ten years, which suggested that something embarrassing might be in the record.

Still, Dean's campaign got what was thought to be a giant boost in early December when Al Gore announced his endorsement of Dean. Though an endorsement from an establishment Democrat could have been viewed as undermining Dean's appeal as an outsider, it was ultimately seen as way for Dean to gain credibility.[32] As the holidays approached, Dean had surged ahead of his rivals, garnering the support of 31 percent of respondents in an ABC News/*Washington Post* poll.[33] His rivals were all in the single digits.

On the eve of the Iowa caucuses, then, it looked as though the only real race was for second place. In the final debate before the caucuses, Dean's opponents had even urged Democrats not to "have a coronation."[34] Dean not only had momentum, he was reported to have built a "juggernaut" in Iowa, and his organization was said to be unmatched.[35] Gephardt, too, had a strong organization, which is crucial in states that hold caucuses. Getting people to attend these extended meetings is difficult work and it requires an army of volunteers "on the ground" to identify the candidate's supporters and turn them out on caucus day.

Somehow, the "Perfect Storm," as the Dean corps of volunteers was dubbed, turned out to be little more than a cloudy sky. On the day of the Iowa caucus, January 19, 2004, Kerry amazingly surged ahead to win with 38 percent of the attendees, followed (almost as surprisingly) by John Edwards, who received the support of 32 percent of caucus-goers.[36] Dean came in a distant third. Adding insult to injury, Dean's attempt to motivate his supporters at a post-caucus rally resulted in the "Dean Scream," a list of upcoming primary states that Dean shouted into the microphone, capped off with a yelp. That episode was reportedly replayed 633 times in four days on network and cable news shows.[37] To many potential voters, the "Dean Scream" made the candidate look desperate at best, and unstable at worst.

While the Dean campaign was not as well oiled as nearly everyone had assumed, the Kerry campaign had quietly built a very effective operation. They had, according to one campaign recap, "coordinated the needs of Iowa with the candidate's message and appearances."[38] In addition, an emotional reunion just days before the caucuses might have had an impact on the fortunes of the Kerry campaign. A former comrade of Kerry's, whose life he had saved in Vietnam and whom he had not seen in thirty-five years, traveled from California to help the campaign. Their tearful reunion dominated media coverage during the weekend before the vote. In the end, Kerry ended up with more support from anti-war voters than did Dean.[39] The movement of voters from Dean to Kerry was humorously captured in an Iowa campaign button that read, "Dated Dean, Married Kerry."

Having won the nation's first caucus in Iowa, Kerry went on to capture another quick victory eight days later, winning the nation's first primary in New Hampshire with 38 percent of the vote to Dean's 28 percent.[40] With victories in the first two contests under his belt, Kerry gained the momentum to take him to a commanding lead in the battle for the nomination. Indeed, he only lost in four states along the way (to Edwards in North and South Carolina, to Dean in Vermont, and to Clark in Oklahoma). By March, Kerry had become the presumptive nominee of the Democratic Party. And the general election campaign began in earnest.

The Run-Up to the Conventions

Officially, of course, Kerry would not become the party's nominee until the Democratic National Convention at the end of July. But his attention turned to President Bush almost immediately after it became obvious that he would head the Democratic ticket. To challenge Bush, Kerry began raising significant sums of money. Because he had opted out of the public funding system for the nomination phase, Kerry was legally allowed to raise unlimited money until he accepted public funding for the general election upon his official nomination. President Bush had also opted out of the public funding system during the primaries. As a result, the two candidates would eventually raise and spend unprecedented amounts of money.

Though Bush raised more than Kerry overall (by one count, $272.6 million to $249.3 million[41]), Kerry collected more contributions in 2004 (roughly $223.8 million to $139.8 million[42]). In fact, Kerry raised over $30 million per month for five straight months, including $44.2 million in March and $48.3 million in July.[43] Much of Kerry's success, like Dean's before him, was attributable to an aggressive Internet fundraising effort. Kerry eventually raised about $82 million on-line, compared to Bush's $14 million.[44]

Kerry and Bush would use at least some of this money to attack each other during the spring and summer. Traditionally, the general election campaign is said to begin on Labor Day, but in 2004 the campaign began long before that. Both campaigns were running ads in March, though Kerry had been attacking Bush in ads during the primaries.[45]

The issue agenda was not fully formed in the spring and summer, of course, but a number of events took place during those months that would foreshadow the fall campaign.[46] On March 24th, former White House anti-terrorism advisor Richard Clarke testified before the 9/11 Commission and criticized the Bush Administration's efforts to combat terrorism prior to the September 11, 2001, attacks. The President and Vice President were questioned together, and in person, by some of the commissioners on April 28th. In July, the Commission released its final report finding no significant links between Iraq and September 11, or between Saddam Hussein and al-Qaeda.[47] The Commission's hearings and its report served to remind voters of the threat of terrorism and the tragedy of September 11, which played to President Bush's strengths as the more trusted candidate on security issues, but also raised questions about the President's credibility that Kerry attempted to exploit throughout the campaign.[48]

Bad news out of Iraq continued to be reported as well. In March, news organizations reported allegations of widespread prisoner abuse by military personnel at Abu Ghraib, causing a firestorm of criticism and congressional hearings (and later, trials and guilty pleas from several of the soldiers involved). In May, videotape of Iraqi insurgents beheading American contractor Nicholas Berg was released. Throughout the campaign, militants kidnapped and beheaded a number of other American and allied civilians.

On the domestic front, jobs reports were better than expected in March, April and May, but worse than expected in June and July (with only 32,000 jobs added in July).[49] With respect to social policy, gay marriage emerged as the year's hot-button issue. In February, the Supreme Judicial Court of Massachusetts declared that same-sex couples in the state must be given the right to marry. Simultaneously, San Francisco mayor Gavin Newsom defied California state law and ordered the city to issue marriage licenses to same-sex couples. Later that month, President Bush announced that he would support a constitutional amendment defining marriage as "a union between one man and one woman."[50] Kerry's position on the issue was identical to that of Vice President Cheney. He made it clear that he thought the term 'marriage' should apply only to a union between a man and a woman, but he opposed a constitutional amendment, preferring to let the states decide the issue for themselves. The President's position – and the images on television of same-sex couples getting married - would prove to be beneficial to Bush in helping to motivate social conservatives to go the polls on Election Day.

In early July, Kerry completed his ticket by choosing North Carolina Senator, and former primary foe, John Edwards as his running mate. The pick was widely praised among Democrats, since Edwards was seen as optimistic, energetic, articulate and charismatic. Given Edwards's background as a trial attorney, Republicans were quick to attack, blaming lawyers for, among other things, the high cost of medical malpractice insurance. Nevertheless, polls showed a considerable bounce for Kerry after his announcement of Edwards as the vice presidential choice.[51]

The Democratic and Republican National Conventions

Nowadays, the parties' national conventions are more like pep rallies than meetings to take care of party business. There are no surprises and very little drama because each party runs a tightly controlled event intended give the party and its presidential ticket a positive image as they begin the general election campaign season. Nevertheless, the themes of the candidates' campaigns are often foreshadowed at the conventions, and the shape of the upcoming presidential race is previewed.

The Democratic National Convention began on July 26, 2004, and it was clear from the outset that the tone of the convention would be positive. Democrats sought to portray themselves as a united party and emphasized "change, diversity, moderation and optimism designed to appeal to independent swing voters."[52] Though there were clearly criticisms of President Bush, most pointedly by Reverend Al Sharpton, most speakers focused on the qualities of John Kerry more than the deficiencies of George Bush.

More than anything else, the convention was intended to bolster Kerry's image as a credible alternative to Bush as commander-in-chief. In a time of war and facing the threat of terrorism, Democrats believed that voters would want reassurances that Kerry would be strong in defending the country. As such, Kerry's experience in Vietnam at the end of the 1960s became the focal point of the convention. He arrived at the convention in Boston the night before his nomination on a boat surrounded by his former Vietnam crewmates. The next evening, those same crewmates would join him on stage as he entered the hall to give his acceptance speech, which began, "I'm John Kerry, and I'm reporting for duty."[53]

As the convention ended, Kerry faced a serious strategic challenge. Presidential general election candidates are given public funds for their campaigns immediately upon receiving their parties' nominations. At that point, they are prohibited from raising private funds for their campaign (though they do fundraise for their parties) and are limited to spending the amount they're given (which was $75 million this year). That meant that Kerry would get his money on July 30th but, because the Republican National Convention wasn't held until the beginning of September, Bush wouldn't get his money until September 3rd. Not only did Bush have an additional five weeks to raise and spend private dollars, he had only eight and a half weeks to spend his $75 million of public funds, while Kerry had to stretch his over thirteen and a half weeks.

In fact, the Kerry campaign had considered delaying his acceptance of the nomination until later in August or asking the Federal Election Commission to give him permission to continue raising private contributions in August. Ultimately, the campaign decided against such a move, in part because of the public relations damage it might create.[54] To make up for Kerry's absence on the airwaves, the Democratic National Committee and various left-leaning independent organizations spent millions on Kerry's behalf during that month.[55] Nevertheless, Kerry's financial disadvantage in August had considerable consequences for his campaign.

The heavy reliance on Kerry's Vietnam heroics was intended, as noted earlier, to solidify his image as a strong defender of the country. However, part of his Vietnam era record was purposely ignored. When Kerry returned from Vietnam, he became a leader of the anti-war organization Vietnam Veterans Against the War. As such, he was asked to give testimony to the Senate Foreign Relations Committee in 1971. At that hearing, he reported on allegations of war crimes that had been made at the "Winter Soldier Investigation" in Detroit a few months earlier.[56] Though the campaign might have been able to frame Kerry's testimony as an act of courage and conscience and, therefore, of character, it apparently decided that voters would view any mention of this part of his biography negatively. This left a rather large gap in Kerry's story for his opponents to fill.

Within days of the end of the Democratic National Convention, the Swift Boat Veterans for Truth, an independently-organized advocacy group formed by Vietnam veterans opposed to Kerry's campaign, set about doing just that, buying limited TV ad time in three states to run an attack ad against Kerry. Interestingly, the group's first ad challenged Kerry's status as a war hero, not his 1971 testimony. The group claimed that Kerry had lied to get his first Purple Heart and that he didn't deserve his Bronze Star. Though the evidence for such claims was sparse,[57] the ad garnered a great deal of attention, helped the group raise additional money, and put Kerry on the defensive.[58] Swift Boat Veterans for Truth would keep up their attacks, eventually focusing on Kerry's anti-war activity. For its part, the Kerry campaign was slow to react to the group, in part because it didn't have the resources to do so and in part because it didn't want to dignify the attacks with a response. By not responding, however, Kerry might have allowed the group to do damage to his campaign (though the evidence here is mixed).[59] His message was certainly drowned out during this period, and the typical post-convention "bounce" in the polls never fully materialized.[60]

Kerry did charge that the Bush campaign was coordinating efforts with the Swift Boat Veterans for Truth.[61] Under campaign finance laws, coordination between independent groups and campaigns is illegal. There was, in fact, little evidence of such coordination, though the Bush campaign's chief outside counsel was forced to resign over the matter.[62]

Faced with questions about whether or not he would condemn the independent ads attacking Kerry, President Bush chose to call for an end to advertising by all groups like the Swift Boat Veterans. These groups, called 527s because of the section of the Internal Revenue Code governing this particular kind of tax-exempt organization, exploited a major loophole in campaign finance reforms that went into effect for the first time in 2004. Though the Bipartisan Campaign Reform Act (BCRA) bars parties from raising "soft money" – unlimited contributions from corporations, unions and wealthy individuals – political action committees (PACs) and independent organizations (like 527s) are still allowed to collect these contributions. Under BCRA, PACs cannot use such money to run ads mentioning a federal candidate sixty days before a general election. Instead, they have to use "hard money" – limited contributions from individuals – to air their ads. But 527s occupy a unique place: they aren't PACs, so they maintain that they are not bound by BCRA's restrictions. In May, the Federal Election Commission decided not to force 527s to play by BCRA's rules for 2004, but said it would eventually clarify regulations for these groups' future activities.[63]

As a result, 527 organizations played a large role in the 2004 campaign. Initially, Kerry enjoyed a distinct advantage among 527s. In the spring and summer, liberal groups like the Media Fund, America Coming Together, and MoveOn.org raised and spent more than $60 million attacking Bush. However, Republican-leaning groups like the Swift Boat Veterans and Progress for America caught up, and eventually surpassed, their Democratic counterparts. In fact, groups loyal to President Bush spent nearly $30 million on television ads in the last three weeks of the campaign.[64] It is difficult to know what impact 527s had, but given their ability to produce ads that are more provocative than party or candidate ads, they certainly garnered a significant amount of attention.

The GOP's convention began on August 30th with a dramatically different tone than the Democrats' gathering. For one thing, the Republicans were clearly going to remind voters again and again about the attacks of September 11th. They vigorously defended President Bush's decision to invade Iraq, thereby establishing Bush as a wartime commander-in-chief. But they were also going to directly challenge John Kerry's ability to lead in a time of insecurity, as former New York City Mayor Rudolph Giuliani did on the first evening of the convention.[65]

Ultimately, the Republican message at the convention was the Bush message throughout the campaign. As Ron Brownstein wrote in the *Los Angeles Times*, "President Bush's case for reelection [could be reduced] to virtually a single argument: Bush would be tough and resolute in the war on terrorism and Kerry would be neither."[66] During the convention Bush was repeatedly portrayed as a decisive leader while Kerry was said to be weak, liberal, and inconsistent. At least as judged by the polls, the convention was a success.[67] Bush entered the fall campaign clearly ahead of Kerry.

The General Election Campaign

For most of the race, Bush campaign efforts were directed at labeling Kerry a "flip-flopper." Initially, the Bush staff was unsure of whether to emphasize Kerry's inconsistencies or to point to his liberal voting record in the Senate. It would be hard to do both, since being extremely liberal and yet constantly changing positions seems impossible. But Kerry gave the Bush campaign a "gift," according to media consultant Mark McKinnon, when he explained his vote against $87 billion of military spending for Iraq by saying, "I actually did vote for the $87 billion – before I voted against it."[68] At that point, apparently, the Bush campaign decided it could get more mileage out of the flip-flop charge. Nevertheless, the "L-word" (liberal) would make an appearance again late in the campaign.

As Labor Day came and went, the Bush strategy solidified. But John Kerry's message remained muddled. He obviously wanted to counter the charge that he was not strong enough to be commander-in-chief, but the Swift Boat Veterans and the Republican convention raised questions about his ability to protect the country. Equally damaging, the flip-flop charge appeared to be sticking. Furthermore, because the Democrats had not spent much time attacking President Bush during their convention, it wasn't entirely clear how Kerry wanted to portray Bush. At various times, the campaign had suggested that Bush was incompetent, stubborn, wrong, or out of touch. While the Kerry campaign may have wanted to say that he was all of these, it is far more effective to have a single, simple message. To add to the confusion, Kerry continued to focus on both Iraq and the economy, shifting emphasis as the news warranted (which certainly did nothing to counter Bush's claim that he was indecisive). By the end of September, the campaign had not even settled on a slogan.

Bush entered the first presidential debate on September 30 with a considerable lead in the polls.[69] His campaign had negotiated for that debate to focus on foreign policy, which was widely perceived to be Bush's strong suit, and the campaign hoped they could slam the door on Kerry's chances right off the bat. Instead, the first debate got Kerry back in the game as he clearly defeated the president based on post-debate polls. In fact, while only 37 percent of respondents to a *USA Today*/CNN/Gallup Poll thought Bush won, 53 percent thought Kerry did a better job.[70] Many viewers thought the President reacted testily to pointed criticism from Kerry, while Kerry sounded "confident and cogent talking about issues widely seen as Republican strengths."[71] Within days of the debate, Kerry had moved back into a dead-heat with the President in at least one poll.[72]

The second debate (on October 8th) was scored a draw according to the first post-debate polls, but Kerry won the third debate (October 13th) handily.[73] Nevertheless, the trends in the polls following the debates showed Bush moving slightly ahead of Kerry.[74] It's not entirely clear what caused this seemly-contradictory result, though it might very well have been fall-out from Kerry's reference to the daughter of Vice President Cheney in the third debate. In response to a question about whether or not the candidates thought homosexuality was a choice, Kerry suggested, "If you were to talk to Dick Cheney's daughter, who is a lesbian, she would tell you that she's being who she was, she's being who she was born as."[75] The Cheneys criticized Kerry for pulling such a "cheap and tawdry political trick," as Lynn Cheney called the comment.[76] The Kerry campaign tried to answer the criticism by saying that it was the Vice President who first mentioned his daughter's sexuality in the campaign; and, further, that Cheney had thanked John Edwards for saying much the same thing as Kerry had during the Vice Presidential debate.[77] Nevertheless, though Kerry won the debate, his ability to capitalize on that victory was hampered by the discussion of the "Mary Cheney incident" for days afterward.

As the campaign headed into the final stretch, the candidates sharpened their rhetoric and tweaked their messages. The Bush campaign continued to focus on national security and suggested that a Kerry victory would put the United States in jeopardy of another terrorist attack. Kerry argued that Bush had been a disaster on a number of fronts, from the failure to capture Osama bin Laden, to the difficulties in Iraq, to a net loss of jobs for the first time in over 70 years. In a nutshell, Bush told voters that a Kerry presidency was too risky and Kerry argued, as challengers often do, that it was time for change.

Beyond those basic messages, the two campaigns focused on a different set of voters. The Bush strategy was to mobilize his base of supporters, particularly conservative evangelical Christians. This was most evident in Bush's use of the phrase "Massachusetts liberal," rather than "flip-flopper," to describe Kerry late in the campaign.[78] For Kerry, the goal was to reach undecided voters with last minute appeals that might still influence their votes. Of course, Democrats put great effort and resources into their get-out-the-vote operation. But the Kerry message in the closing days was intended to appeal to swing voters.[79]

In the last month of the race, the campaigns spent most of their time and money in the roughly ten battleground states that polls showed were still too close to call. At the beginning of the year, both campaigns suggested that as many as eighteen states were "in play." But as the year wore on, the field narrowed to Colorado, Florida, Iowa, Michigan, Minnesota, New Mexico, Nevada, Ohio, Pennsylvania, and Wisconsin.[80] To that list, many would have added New Hampshire, and a few other states popped up as potentially close contests, including West Virginia and Arkansas. Even Hawaii, usually safely Democratic, got visits from Al Gore and Vice President Cheney because late polls showed the state deadlocked between Kerry and Bush. Given the closeness of the national Electoral College picture, any state, no matter how small, was on the radar screens of the two campaigns if they had reason to believe it could go either way. The real battles, though, were in Ohio and Florida, which polls showed to be close and which have a substantial number of electoral votes each.

Campaign observers often talk about the possibility of an "October surprise" occurring late in a campaign that could dramatically change the dynamics in favor of one of the candidates. In 2000, for example, a story about George W. Bush's drunk driving arrest 25 years before broke just days before the election. In 2004, many speculated that Osama bin Laden might be captured in the final weeks, giving President Bush a big boost. As it turned out, there was no October surprise, though two stories garnered a great deal of attention in the last week. First, the *New York Times* broke a story on October 25th about explosives that had gone missing in Iraq after the U.S. military invasion.[81] The White House disputed the report, but the issue dominated the news – and the campaigns – for days, since it was believed that those explosives were being used in attacks against American and allied military personnel in Iraq.[82] Then, on the Friday before the election, a new videotape of Osama bin Laden was released. It was unclear exactly how that tape would affect the campaigns. On the one hand, anything that served to remind voters of terrorism fit perfectly with the Bush campaign's strategy. On the other, the appearance of bin Laden reinforced Kerry's claims of Bush's mishandling of the hunt for the al Qaeda leader.

The campaigns entered Election Day in a statistical tie, but there were discouraging signs for the president. To begin with, his percentage of the vote in most polls had been consistently below 50 percent. Conventional wisdom among political analysts was that an incumbent below 50 percent in the polls is in trouble because voters undecided late in the campaign supposedly break decidedly in the challenger's direction.[83] Furthermore, the president's job approval rating had also been below 50 percent for some time, though in one poll it had risen to 49 percent on the eve of the election, up from 44 percent just two weeks prior.[84] Finally, the voters' perception of the direction in which the country was heading was not positive. Nevertheless, Bush seemed to have roughly a two-point lead in most polls (well within the margin of error for most polls) as the campaign wound down.

If the polls suggested he was a bit behind, the Electoral College map looked better for Kerry. The possibility of another Electoral College winner but popular vote loser (as in 2000) seemed increasingly plausible. Indeed, late in the afternoon on Election Day, pollster John Zogby made just such a prediction (giving Kerry at least 311 electoral votes, but Bush the popular vote by less than a point).[85]

The Results

Prior to the 2004 election, there had been considerable hand-wringing about the possibility of another disputed election in which the results were not know for some time after Election Day. Both parties prepared for such a situation, and the Democrats lined up 10,000 lawyers to help with recounts and challenges in key states.[86] New regulations for election administration meant that there was likely to be confusion at polling places as voters and election officials confronted unfamiliar processes for the first time. In particular, provisional ballots, which by law must be offered to any would-be voter whose name doesn't appear on registered voter rolls, were causing a great deal of concern.[87]

Nevertheless, Election Day, November 2, started off smoothly, and turnout at the polls was reportedly heavy. Given how hotly contested the campaign had been, and how high emotions on both side were running, this was no surprise. According to one poll, 81 percent of registered voters said they were very interested in this election, compared to 58 percent who said the same in 2000.[88] In the end, turnout in 2004 was higher than any year since 1968, coming in at nearly 60 percent of eligible voters.[89] Among those 18 to 29 years old, turnout increased by 9.3 percentage points.[90] According to exit polls, however, their share of the entire electorate didn't change from 2000 levels because turnout increased to roughly the same degree among *all* age groups.

By midday on Election Day, John Kerry had some reason to be optimistic. To begin with, most observers believed that a heavy turnout in crucial states would benefit Kerry. Furthermore, early exit polls leaked to Internet websites and blogs showed him with leads in most battleground states, including narrow margins in Ohio and Florida.[91] As the results began to roll in, however, the situation looked more positive for Bush.

In the first major developments of the evening, Kerry was declared the winner in Pennsylvania, but lost in Florida. That would mean the election would be determined by the outcome in Ohio (assuming Kerry held on to win Michigan and Wisconsin, which he did). But Ohio remained too close to call until the next day.[92] Eventually, a few media outlets would call the state for Bush on election night, but Kerry didn't concede and John Edwards addressed supporters by saying, "We've waited four years for this victory, and we can wait one more night."[93]

Democrats were hoping that the number of provisional ballots left to be counted in Ohio would be significantly more than the margin between Bush and Kerry. By morning, however, that seemed highly unlikely; Bush maintained a lead of over 135,000 votes with an estimated 150,000 provisional ballots uncounted.[94] The race for Ohio – and the presidency – was over, and George W. Bush had been reelected. In the end, Bush received 286 electoral votes (to Kerry's 252) and garnered 51 percent of the popular vote (to Kerry's 48%; 1% went to Independent candidate Ralph Nader).[95]

Obviously, terrorism, the war in Iraq, and jobs and the economy weighed heavily on voters minds. Those issues were the most important to 19, 15, and 20 percent of the electorate, respectively, according to the exit polls.[96] Surprisingly, the issue that a plurality of voters (22 percent) listed as most important was "moral values." Though there is some reason to doubt these results due to the wording of the exit poll question,[97] clearly many voters were motivated by their positions on issues of morality, particularly gay marriage (which was on the ballot in the form of state measures to ban it in eleven states).

Bush won among those who chose moral values as the most important issue by a margin of 80 percent to 18 percent. He also beat Kerry among those listing terrorism first (86 percent to 14 percent). Kerry, on the other hand, won among those picking Iraq (73 percent to 26 percent) and the economy/jobs (80 percent to 18 percent).

Even if terrorism wasn't foremost in the minds of voters, it certainly set the stage for the election. The Bush campaign did its best to keep the issue front and center and the bin Laden videotape served to remind voters that groups seeking to harm the United States are still active throughout the world. Concerns about terrorism even spawned theories about a new group of swing voters dubbed "security moms."[98] These mostly suburban women with children were thought to be an important constituency because they often vote Democratic but appeared to be defecting to President Bush. If they did so in large numbers, they would not only help close the gender gap that has existed for over twenty years in American politics, but they might very well decide the outcome of the election. As it turns out, the existence of this group of voters might have been a myth[99] (and the gender gap narrowed only slightly from its 2000 level). Nevertheless, the discussion of an important set of voters who were thought to be placing terrorism above their ordinary concerns signaled an environment in which President Bush had a distinct advantage.

Ultimately, turnout may very well have been the key to this election. Both sides put in place an unprecedented effort to get their voters to the polls. Democrats claimed to have 250,000 get-out-the-vote volunteers in the battleground states, and Republicans claimed 300,000 in Wisconsin, Minnesota, Florida and Ohio alone.[100] Democrats typically have an advantage in getting their voters to the polls. But the Bush strategy of appealing directly to – and expanding – the Republican base, a strategy crafted by Bush adviser Karl Rove, was designed to erase that advantage. It appears to have been successful. In 2000, 39 percent of those who voted on Election Day were Democrats, while 35 percent were Republicans.[101] This year, Democrats and Republicans made up 37 percent each. Because Republicans "defect" – or vote for a candidate of a party other than their own – less than Democrats, George Bush was able to edge out John Kerry to win reelection.

The Republicans not only increased the participation rate of their base, they also helped Bush add to his 2000 vote totals among some key voting constituencies. For instance, Bush gained five percentage points among women (to 48 percent in 2004), nine points among Latinos (to 44 percent), seven points among those 60 years old and older (to 54 percent), ten points among those without a high school degree (to 49 percent), five points among Catholics and six among Jews (to 52 percent and 25 percent, respectively), and ten points among those living in urban areas (to 45 percent). Though majorities in most of these groups still gave their support to Kerry, the increase in Bush's margins was certainly beneficial to the President in winning a close election and was enough to give him a slight majority of the popular vote.

House and Senate Races

In a presidential election year, most of the media attention is paid to the national candidates. As a result, congressional races are overshadowed. Nevertheless, there were some noteworthy develops in House and Senate elections that deserve brief mention.

Republicans began the 2004 election cycle with 51 seats in the Senate to the Democrats' 48 (plus one Independent who caucuses with the Democrats). In the House of Representatives, Republicans held a 227 to 205 (plus one Independent) advantage, with two vacancies. Republicans were poised to add to their margins in both chambers, but this was particularly true in the House, where a rare second round of redistricting in Texas made five incumbent Democrats vulnerable.[102] Two of those were forced to face off against Republican incumbents.

As usual, there were very few competitive districts in the House in 2004. One election preview identified only 33 such races; in other words, more than 90 percent of seats were safe for one party or the other.[103] Ultimately, only seven incumbents lost their reelection bids; four of those were Texas Democrats while only two were Republican. As of this writing, Republicans had increased their number of seats in the House to 231 and Democrats had fallen to 201 (plus one Independent).[104]

In the Senate, 34 seats were up for election, 19 of which were held by Democrats and 15 by Republicans. Five of the Democratic seats were considered "highly vulnerable," with one "likely [to] switch" and another simply "vulnerable." Only three Republicans seats were "highly vulnerable," with one "likely [to] switch."[105] As a result, the Democrats faced the difficult challenge of trying to pick up two seats (in order to gain a majority in the Senate) while defending more seats, and holding on to more vulnerable seats, than the Republicans.

When all the results were in, Republicans wound up with 55 seats in the Senate to the Democrats' 45 (including one Independent), a net gain of four seats for Republicans. The GOP lost open seats in Colorado and Illinois, where newcomer and Democratic National Convention keynote speaker Barack Obama beat conservative Republican Alan Keyes. As expected, Democrats lost the open seat of Zell Miller (GA), who served as the keynote speaker at the Republican National Convention, much to the consternation of Democrats. But Democrats also lost all five of their "highly vulnerable" seats, including those in Florida, Louisiana, and North and South Carolina.

Most notable, however, was the loss of Senate Minority Leader Tom Daschle (SD). That race had been particularly hard fought, with over $40 million spent by the two candidates. Daschle was the only incumbent senator to lose in 2004 and the first Senate leader to lose a reelection bid since 1952.[106]

Conclusion

November 2, 2004, was a good day for Republicans. Their gains in the House and Senate gave them breathing room for implementing their legislative agenda. While their Senate majority was short of the magical 60 seats – which would enable them to stop Democratic filibusters – their defeat of Tom Daschle was a symbolic show of dominance.

Most important for Republicans, however, was the reelection of George W. Bush. With a relatively uncontroversial Electoral College victory and a majority of the popular vote, Bush supporters felt vindicated. Though the race was extremely close, President Bush moved quickly to claim a mandate. He certainly begins his second term with more political capital than he began his first term. Democrats, meanwhile, are faced with the challenge of rebuilding to be competitive in the midterm elections of 2006 and the presidential election of 2008.

[1] Dick Cheney, speech accepting the Republican nomination for Vice President, September 1, 2004, www.gopconvention.com/cgi-data/speeches/files/gp97u7nje4458h0g3ieg9925411525kb.shtml (accessed October 8, 2004).

[2] Even the now-unremarkable 1988 election was called "the most important choice in a generation" (see Roy Rivenburg, "The most overused superlative ever," *Los Angeles Times*, August 2, 2004, E5. LexisNexis Academic, October 8, 2004).

[3] See, for example, "Fox News/Opinion Dynamics Poll," September 9, 2004, www.foxnews.com/projects/pdf/090904_poll.pdf (accessed October 9, 2004); and "USA Today/CNN/Gallup poll results," October 4, 2004, www.usatoday.com/news/politicselections/nation/polls/usatodaypolls.htm (accessed October 9, 2004).

[4] "USA Today/CNN/Gallup Poll results," October 4, 2004.

[5] See Michael Cornfield, "Elections during war," *Campaigns & Elections*, October 2001, 39.

[6] See www.politicalmoneyline.com/cgi-win/pml1_sql_efview.exe?DoFn=C003869872004&server=PML2 (accessed October 10, 2004).

[7] In 2000, Bush raised over $94 million. John C. Green and Nathan S. Bigelow. 2002. "The 2000 Presidential Nominations: The Costs of Innovation." In *Financing the 2000 Election*, ed. David B. Magleby. Washington, DC: Brookings Institution Press.

[8] See www.politicalmoneyline.com/cgi-win/pml1_sql_PRESIDENTIAL.exe?DoFn=2004 (accessed October 10, 2004).

[9] Information on candidates and their announcement dates was taken from "America Votes 2004: The Primaries: The Candidates" www.cnn.com/ELECTION/2004/special/president/candidates/whos.in.out.html (accessed October 10, 2004).

[10] ABCNews/*Washington Post* Poll. Jan. 16-20, 2003. www.pollingreport.com/wh04dem2.htm (accessed October 18, 2004).

[11] *The Los Angeles Times* Poll. Jan. 30-Feb. 2, 2003. www.pollingreport.com/wh04dem2.htm (accessed October 18, 2004).

[12] Among all self-identified Democrats, support for the war was high, though not as high as the levels of support among Republicans. Whereas 95 percent of Republicans supported President Bush's decision to invade Iraq, 70 percent of Democrats did the same. *The Los Angeles Times* Poll. April 2-3, 2003. www.pollingreport.com/iraq5.htm (accessed October 19, 2004).

[13] *Time*/CNN Poll conducted by Harris Interactive. July 16-17, 2003. www.pollingreport.com/wh04dem2.htm (accessed October 18, 2004).

[14] "Congressional Joint Resolution to Authorize Use of Force Against Iraq," October 11, 2002. http://www.washingtonpost.com/ac2/wp-dyn?pagename=article&contentId=A9570-2002Oct10&notFound=true (accessed October 19, 2004).

[15] The only other elected officials in the race – Senator Bob Graham and Representative Dennis Kucinich – voted against the resolution.

[16] Quoted in David Von Drehle, "Kerry Says Bush 'Rush to War' Imperils U.S. Alliances," *The Washington Post*, January 24, 2003, A3. LexisNexis Academic, October 19, 2004.

[17] Dan Balz, "Dean Speech to Critique Plans for War on Iraq," *The Washington Post*, February 17, 2003, A24. LexisNexis Academic, October 19, 2004.

[18] ABCNews/*Washington Post* Poll. March 17, 2003. www.pollingreport.com/wh04dem2.htm (accessed October 18, 2004).

[19] CBS News/*New York Times* Poll. Oct. 14-17, 2004. www.pollingreport.com/BushJob.htm (accessed October 19, 2004).

[20] "Bush calls end to 'major combat.'" CNN.com, May 2, 2003 (accessed October 19, 2004).

[21] Editorial, *Pittsburgh Post-Gazette*, July 7, 2003, A13. LexisNexis Academic, October 19, 2004.

[22] Anne E. Kornblut, "Rebuilding Iraq; Democrats see a Crack in the Bush Armor," *The Boston Globe*, July 18, 2003, A1. LexisNexis Academic, October 19, 2004.

[23] CNN/*USA Today*/Gallup Poll. Sept. 8-10, 2003. www.pollingreport.com/BushJob.htm (accessed October 19, 2004).

[24] Julia Malone, "Dean fund-raising sets party record; small donors give $15 million, most through Internet," *The Atlanta Journal-Constitution*, October 16, 2003, A3. LexisNexis Academic, October 22, 2004.

[25] Convio, "Using the Internet to Raise Funds and Mobilize Supporters: Lessons Nonprofits Can Learn from the Dean for America Presidential Campaign," December 2003. Convio.com (accessed October 22, 2004).

[26] See Alexis Rice, "Campaigns Online: The Profound Impact of the Internet, Blogs, and E-Technologies in Presidential Political Campaigning," Center for the Study of American Government, Johns Hopkins University, January 2004. CampaignsOnline.org (accessed October 22, 2004).

[27] www.politicalmoneyline.com (accessed October 22, 2004).

[28] Zogby America Poll. November 3-5, 2003. www.polingreport.com/wh04dem.htm (accessed October 18, 2004).

[29] Glen Justice, "Dean Rejects Public Financing in Primaries," *The New York Times*, November 9, 2003, A28. LexisNexis Academic, October 22, 2004.

[30] Dan Balz, "Voters Describe Ideal Nominee: Democrats in Poll Want a Candidate Who Backed Iraq War," *The Washington Post*, October 17, 2003, A9. LexisNexis Academic, October 19, 2004.

[31] As quoted in Roger Simon, "Turning Point," *U.S. News & World Report*, July 19, 2004. LexisNexis Academic, October 18, 2004.

[32] Dan Balz, "Gore Will Endorse Dean; An Insider Boost for An Outsider Candidacy," *The Washington Post*, December 9, 2003, A1. LexisNexis Academic, October 19, 2004.

[33] ABC News/*Washington Post* Poll. December 18-21, 2003. www.polingreport.com/wh04dem.htm (accessed October 18, 2004).

[34] Dan Balz, "Democratic Rivals Dismiss Dean's Chances; In Final Debate, They Assert That Race for Presidential Nomination is Not Over," *The Washington Post*, December 10, 2003, A8. LexisNexis Academic, October 19, 2004.

[35] See Simon.

[36] *Congressional Quarterly*, "2004 Primary and Caucus Results," CQ Democratic Convention Guide, July 2004, 28.

[37] David Bauder, "Fallout from Dean's scream on news networks: Get used to it," The Associated Press, February 6, 2004. LexisNexis Academic, November 1, 2004.

[38] Simon.

[39] Simon.

[40] *Congressional Quarterly*.

[41] http://www.politicalmoneyline.com/cgi-win/pml1_sql_PRESIDENTIAL.exe?DoFn=2004 (accessed November 6, 2004).

[42] Calculations based on candidate data at www.politicalmoneyline.com (accessed November 6, 2004).

[43] http://www.politicalmoneyline.com/cgi-win/pml1_sql_efview.exe?DoFn=C003836532004&server=PML2 (accessed November 6, 2004).

[44] Glen Justice, "Kerry Kept Money Coming With the Internet as His ATM," *The New York Times*, November 6, 2004, http://www.nytimes.com/2004/11/06/politics/campaign/06internet.html (accessed November 6, 2004).

[45] For a list of Kerry and Bush ads, see http://www2.gwu.edu/~action/2004/ads04/kerrads.html and http://www2.gwu.edu/~action/2004/ads04/bushads04.html, respectively (accessed November 6, 2004). For a list of Kerry primary ads, see http://www2.gwu.edu/~action/2004/ads04/kerradsprim.html (accessed November 6, 2004).

[46] A timeline of major events can be found on page A2 of the *USA Today* for November 3, 2004.

[47] Philip Shenon, "9/11 Report Is Said to Dismiss Iraq-Qaeda Alliance," *The New York Times*, July 12, 2004, A12. LexisNexis Academic, November 7, 2004. The entire report can be found at http://www.gpoaccess.gov/911/ (accessed November 6, 2004).

[48] Dana Milbank, "9/11 Panel's Findings Vault Bush Credibility to Campaign Forefront," *Washington Post*, June 20, 2004, A1, http://www.washingtonpost.com/wp-dyn/articles/A54702-2004Jun19.html (accessed November 6, 2004).

[49] "Major events."

[50] Deb Riechmann, "Bush to support constitutional amendment prohibiting marriages between same-sex partners," Associated Press, February 24, 2004, http://sfgate.com/cgi-bin/article.cgi?f=/news/a/2004/02/24/national1010EST0552.DTL (accessed November 6, 2004).

[51] See http://www.realclearpolitics.com/Presidential_04/chart3way.html (accessed November 6, 2004).

[52] Paul West, "In lauding Kerry, speakers seek swing voters; Themes of change, diversity, moderation, optimism prevail," *The Baltimore Sun*, July 28, 2004, 1A. LexisNexis Academic, November 7, 2004.

[53] Bill Lambrecht , "Kerry paints self-portrait of tough commander in chief," *St. Louis Post-Dispatch*, July 30, 2004, A1. LexisNexis Academic, November 5, 2004.

[54] Patrick Healy and Rick Klein, "Kerry may delay official nomination move would be advantage in spending race," *The Boston Globe*, May 22, 2004, A1. LexisNexis Academic, November 5, 2004; and Glen Johnson and Patrick Healy, "Kerry Rules out delaying tactic ok's hub nomination; may challenge FEC rule," *The Boston Globe*, May 27, 2004, A1. LexisNexis Academic, November 5, 2004.

[55] Mark Memmott, "Anti-Bush groups make up for ad gap," *USA Today*, August 4, 2004, 2A. LexisNexis Academic, November 5, 2004.

[56] David M. Halbfinger, "Three decades later, Vietnam remains a hot issue," *The New York Times*, August 29, 2004, A26. LexisNexis Academic, November 5, 2004; and Michael Dobbs, "After decades, renewed war on old conflict," *The Washington Post*, August 28, 2004, A1. LexisNexis Academic, November 5, 2004.

[57] See Michael Dobbs, "Swift Boat Accounts Incomplete; Critics Fail to Disprove Kerry's Version of Vietnam War Episode," *The Washington Post*, August 22, 2004, A1, http://www.washingtonpost.com/ac2/wp-dyn/A21239-2004Aug21 (accessed August 23, 2004); and FactCheck.org, "Republican-funded Group Attacks Kerry's Record," August 6, 2004 (modified August 22, 2004), http://www.factcheck.org/article231.html (accessed August 23, 2004).

[58] Tom Infield, "Anti-Kerry group sees rise in donations after airing ads," Knight Ridder/Tribune News Service, August 14, 2004. LexisNexis Academic, August 23, 2004.

[59] Adam Nagourney, "Kerry Might Pay Price for Failing to Strike Back Quickly," *The New York Times*, August 21, 2004, http://www.nytimes.com/2004/08/21/politics/campaign/21assess.html (accessed August 23, 2004). For evidence that the Swift Boat Veterans for Truth ads had limited, if
any, effect, see David W. Moore, "No Change in Presidential Race Despite Attack Ads," The Gallup Organization, August 27, 2004, www.gallup.com/content/print.aspx?ci=12823 (accessed
September 1, 2004); and Annenberg Public Policy Center, "Pluralities of Public, Independents Believe Bush Campaign Is Behind Swift Boat Veterans' Ads, Annenberg Data Show," August 27, 2004, www.naes04.org (accessed September 1, 2004).

[60] Richard Morin and Dan Balz, "Convention gives Kerry slight lead over Bush," *The Washington Post*,"August 3, 2004, A1. LexisNexis Academic, November 5, 2004.

[61] Glen Justic and Jim Rutenberg, "Kerry is filing a complaint against Swift Boat group," *The New York Times*, August 21, 2004, A10. LexisNexis Academic, November 5, 2004.

[62] Dan Balz and Thomas B. Edsall, "Lawyer quits Bush-Cheney organization; campaigns spar over ties to outside funding groups," *The Washington Post*, August 26, 2004, A1. LexisNexis Academic, November 5, 2004.

[63] See Thomas B. Edsall, "In boost for Democrats, FEC rejects proposed limits on small donors," *The Washington Post*, May 14, 2004, A9. LexisNexis Academic, November 5, 2004; and Thomas B. Edsall, "FEC votes to curb nonparty donations; stricter rules will go into effect in January," *The Washington Post*, August 20, 2004, A6. LexisNexis Academic, November 5, 2004.

[64] Jeffrey H. Birnbaum and Thomas B. Edsall, "At the end, Pro-GOP '527's' outspent their counterparts," *The Washington Post*, November 6, 2004, A6. LexisNexis Academic, November 5, 2004.

[65] Adam Nagourney, "Guiliani lauds Bush's leadership on terror," *The New York Times*, August 31, 2004, A1. LexisNexis Academic, November 5, 2004.

[66] Ronald Borwnstein, "GOP locks in on theme, and opens fire on Kerry," *Los Angeles Times*, September 2, 2004, A23. LexisNexis Academic, November 5, 2004.

[67] Richard Benedetto and Judy Keen, "Upbeat Bush campaign rides convention 'bounce,'" *USA Today*, September 7, 2004, 10A. LexisNexis Academic, November 5, 2004.

[68] Jodi Wilgoren, "Kerry's words, and Bush's use of them, offer valuable lesson in '04 campaigning," *The New York Times*, May 8, 2004, A14. LexisNexis Academic, November 5, 2004.

[69] See http://www.realclearpolitics.com/Presidential_04/chart3way.html (accessed November 6, 2004).

[70] *USA Today*, "*USA Today*/CNN/Gallup post-debate poll results," October 14, 2004, http://www.usatoday.com/news/polls/tables/live/2004-10-14-poll.htm (accessed November 7, 2004).

[71] Michael Powell, "The battle, if not the war, to Kerry; Bush hit off-notes with debate viewers," *The Washington Post*, October 2, 2004, A1. LexisNexis Academic, November 8, 2004.

[72] Susan Page, "Bush, Kerry in a draw, poll says," *USA Today*, October 4, 2004, 1A. LexisNexis Academic, November 8, 2004.

[73] See "*USA Today*/CNN/Gallup post-debate poll results."

[74] See http://www.realclearpolitics.com/Presidential_04/chart3way.html (accessed November 6, 2004).

[75] Michael Laris and Mike Allen, "Cheney's steamed at Kerry reference to daughter; Republicans jump on statement in final Presidential debate; Democrats issue a clarification," *The Washington Post*, October 15, 2004, A8. LexisNexis Academic, November 8, 2004.

[76] David Stout, "Cheney criticizes Kerry for mentioning daughter," *The New York Times*, October 15, 2004, A21. LexisNexis Academic, November 8, 2004.

[77] Stout.

[78] Julie Mason, "Election 2004; candidates narrow their strategies; Bush puts focus on U.S. security; Kerry working on undecided voters," *The Houston Chronicle*, October 24, 2004, A15. LexisNexis Academic, November 8, 2004.

[79] Dana Milbank, "Diverse tactics on the stump; as Bush pumps up his base; Kerry aims for middle," *The Washington Post*, October 12, 2004, A1. LexisNexis Academic, November 8, 2004; and Dan Balz and Jim VandeHei, "Bush, Kerry return to trail and take different tracks," *The Washington Post*, October 10, 2004, A1. LexisNexis Academic, November 8, 2004.

[80] Nielsen Monitor-Plus and the University of Wisconsin Advertising Project, "Presidential TV Advertising Battle Narrows to Just Ten Battleground States, Florida and Ohio Center of the Ads Storm," October 12, 2004, http://polisci.wisc.edu/tvadvertising/Press_Releases/Press_Release_PDFs/Release 2004 October 12th.pdf (accessed October 14, 2004).

[81] James Glanz, William J. Broad, and David E. Sanger, "Huge cache of explosives vanished from site in Iraq," *The New York Times*, October 25, 2004, A1. LexisNexis Academic, November 8, 2004.

[82] David E. Sanger, "Iraq explosives become issue in campaign," *The New York Times*, October 26, 2004, A1. LexisNexis Academic, November 8, 2004.

[83] See http://www.mysterypollster.com/main/incumbent_rule/index.html (accessed November 10, 2004) for a discussion of this.

[84] CBS News/*New York Times* Poll, October 28-30, 2004, http://www.pollingreport.com/bushjob2.htm (accessed November 8, 2004).

[85] See http://www.professorbainbridge.com/2004/11/zogbys_predicti.html (accessed November 8, 2004).

[86] John Wildermuth, "Parties anticipate chaotic election; observers mobilize for big day, lawyers prepare for fallout," *San Francisco Chronicle*, September 18, 2004, http://www.sfgate.com/cgi-bin/article.cgi?file=/c/a/2004/09/18/MNGN78R6PT1.DTL (accessed November 8, 2004); and Anne Gearan, "Party lawyers prepare for post-election day trauma," *USA Today*, September 20, 2004, http://www.usatoday.com/news/politicselections/nation/president/2004-09-20-election-lawyers_x.htm (accessed November 8, 2004).

[87] Ford Fessenden, "A rule to avert balloting woes adds to them," *The New York Times*, August 6, 2004, http://www.nytimes.com/2004/08/06/politics/campaign/06vote.html (accessed November 8, 2004); and Jim Drinkard, "Standby ballots already disputed; election officials fear new 'hanging chads'," *USA Today*, October 11, 2004, http://www.usatoday.com/printedition/news/20041011/1a_lede11.art.htm (accessed November 8, 2004).

[88] Marist College Institute for Public Opinion, "National Poll: Campaign 2004, Election Eve Results," November 1, 2004, http://www.maristpoll.marist.edu/usapolls/PZ041102.htm (accessed November 8, 2004).

[89] CNN, "Voter turnout highest since 1968," CNN.com, November 3, 2004, http://www.cnn.com/2004/ALLPOLITICS/11/03/voter.turnout.ap/ (accessed November 3, 2004).

[90] The Center for Information & Research on Civic Learning & Engagement, "Youth Turnout Up Sharply in 2004," November 3, 2004, http://www.civicyouth.org/PopUps/Release_Turnout2004.pdf (accessed November 7, 2004).

[91] See http://www.slate.com/id/2109053/ (accessed November 2 and 8, 2004).

[92] Jim Rutenberg, "Early night for viewers becomes cliffhanger," *The New York Times*, November 3, 2004, A1. LexisNexis Academic, November 8, 2004.

[93] Mark Z. Barabak, "Election 2004: The White House; Ohio up for grabs; Bush has slim lead; in heavy turnout, California ok's stem cell initiative," *Los Angeles Times*, November 3, 2004, A1. LexisNexis Academic, November 8, 2004.

[94] Dennis Cauchon, "The election won't be over in Ohio for weeks," *USA Today*, November 4, 2004, A13. LexisNexis Academic, November 8, 2004.

[95] See http://www.washingtonpost.com/wp-srv/elections/2004/page/295001/ (accessed November 8, 2004).

[96] Exit poll results can be found at http://www.cnn.com/ELECTION/2004/pages/results/states/US/P/00/epolls.0.html (accessed November 8, 2004).

[97] Jim Rutenberg, "Poll Question Stirs Debate on Meaning of 'Values'," *The New York Times*, November 6, 2004, http://www.nytimes.com/2004/11/06/politics/campaign/06poll.html?pagewanted=all (accessed November 6, 2004).

[98] Michelle Malkin, "Candidates ignore 'security moms,' at their peril," *USA Today*, July 21, 2004, A11. LexisNexis Academic, November 9, 2004.

[99] Richard Morin and Dan Balz, "'Security Mom' Bloc Proves Hard to Find; The Phenomenon May Be a Myth," *The Washington Post*, October 1, 2004, A5. LexisNexis Academic, November 9, 2004.

[100] Bill Nichols, "Mad dash to get out the vote," *USA Today*, November 2, 2004, A1. LexisNexis Academic, November 9, 2004.

[101] See the 2000 exit poll results, http://www.cnn.com/ELECTION/2000/results/index.epolls.html (accessed November 9, 2004).

[102] Associated Press, "Texas Redistricting Fight Not Over," CBSNews.com, October 18, 2004, http://www.cbsnews.com/stories/2004/10/18/politics/main649927.shtml (accessed November 9, 2004); and Amy Walter, "House GOP Still Confident," *National Journal: The Cook Election Preview*, August 28, 2004: 19.

[103] Walters, 20.

[104] Two races in Louisiana were undetermined as of this writing and would be decided by run-offs in December 2004.

[105] Jennifer E. Duffy, "The Democrats' Tough Task," *National Journal: The Cook Election Preview*, August 28, 2004: 12.

[106] Josh White, "Daschle Trailing in Tight Race; Minority Leader Vies to Keep His Seat," *The Washington Post*, November 3, 2004, A25, http://www.washingtonpost.com/wp-dyn/articles/A20758-2004Nov3.html (accessed November 9, 2004).

THE DECLARATION OF INDEPENDENCE

In Congress, July 4, 1776

The Unanimous Declaration of the Thirteen United States of America

When, in the course of human events, it becomes necessary for one people to dissolve the political bands which have connected them with another, and to assume, among the powers of the earth, the separate and equal station to which the laws of nature and of nature's God entitle them, a decent respect to the opinions of mankind requires that they should declare the causes which impel them to the separation.

We hold these truths to be self-evident: That all men are created equal; that they are endowed by their Creator with certain unalienable rights; that among these are life, liberty, and the pursuit of happiness; that, to secure these rights, governments are instituted among men, deriving their just powers from the consent of the governed; that whenever any form of government becomes destructive of these ends, it is the right of the people to alter or to abolish it, and to institute new government, laying its foundation on such principles, and organizing its power in such form, as to them shall seem most likely to effect their safety and happiness. Prudence, indeed, will dictate that governments long established should not be changed for light and transient causes; and accordingly all experience hath shown that mankind are more disposed to suffer, while evils are sufferable, than to right themselves by abolishing the forms to which they are accustomed. But when a long train of abuses and usurpations, pursuing invariably the same object, evinces a design to reduce them under absolute despotism, it is their right, it is their duty, to throw off such government, and to provide new guards for their future security. Such has been the patient sufferance of these colonies; and such is now the necessity which constrains them to alter their former systems of government. The history of the present King of Great Britain is a history of repeated injuries and usurpations, all having in direct object the establishment of an absolute tyranny over these states. To prove this, let facts be submitted to a candid world.

He has refused to assent to laws, the most wholesome and necessary for the public good.

He has forbidden his governors to pass laws of immediate and pressing importance, unless suspended in their operation till his assent should be obtained; and, when so suspended, he has utterly neglected to attend to them.

He has refused to pass other laws for the accommodation of large districts of people, unless those people would relinquish the right of representation in the legislature, a right inestimable to them, and formidable to tyrants only.

He has called together legislative bodies at places unusual, uncomfortable, and distant from the depository of their public records, for the sole purpose of fatiguing them into compliance with his measures.

He has dissolved representative houses repeatedly, for opposing, with manly firmness, his invasions on the rights of the people.

He has refused for a long time, after such dissolutions, to cause others to be elected; whereby the legislative powers, incapable of annihilation, have returned to the people at large for their exercise; the state remaining, in the mean time, exposed to all dangers of invasions from without and convulsions within.

He has endeavored to prevent the population of these states; for that purpose obstructing the laws for naturalization of foreigners; refusing to pass others to encourage their migration hither, and raising the conditions of new appropriations of lands.

He has obstructed the administration of justice, by refusing his assent to laws for establishing judiciary powers.

He has made judges dependent on his will alone, for the tenure of their offices, and the amount and payment of their salaries.

He has erected a multitude of new offices, and sent hither swarms of officers to harass our people, and eat out their substance.

He has kept among us, in times of peace, standing armies, without the consent of our legislatures.

He has affected to render the military independent of, and superior to, the civil power.

He has combined with others to subject us to a jurisdiction foreign to our constitution, and unacknowledged by our laws, giving his assent to their acts of pretended legislation:

For quartering large bodies of armed troops among us:

For protecting them, by a mock trial, from punishment for any murders which they should commit on the inhabitants of these states;

For cutting off our trade with all parts of the world;

For imposing taxes on us without our consent;

For depriving us, in many cases, of the benefits of trial by jury;

For transporting us beyond seas, to be tried for pretended offenses;

For abolishing the free system of English laws in a neighboring province, establishing therein an arbitrary government, and enlarging its boundaries, so as to render it at once an example and fit instrument for introducing the same absolute rule into these colonies;

For taking away our charters, abolishing our most valuable laws, and altering fundamentally the forms of our governments;

For suspending our own legislatures, and declaring themselves invested with power to legislate for us in all cases whatsoever.

He has abdicated government here, by declaring us out of his protection and waging war against us.

He has plundered our seas, ravaged our coasts, burned our towns, and destroyed the lives of our people.

He is at this time transporting large armies of foreign mercenaries to complete the works of death, desolation, and tyranny already begun with circumstances of cruelty and perfidy scarcely paralleled in the most barbarous ages, and totally unworthy the head of a civilized nation.

He has constrained our fellow-citizens, taken captive on the high seas, to bear arms against their country, to become the executioners of their friends and brethren, or to fall themselves by their hands.

He has excited domestic insurrection among us, and has endeavored to bring on the inhabitants of our frontiers the merciless Indian savages, whose known rule of warfare is an undistinguished destruction of all ages, sexes, and conditions.

In every stage of these oppressions we have petitioned for redress in the most humble terms; our repeated petitions have been answered only by repeated injury. A prince, whose character is thus marked by every act which may define a tyrant, is unfit to be the ruler of a free people.

Nor have we been wanting in our attentions to our British brethren. We have warned them, from time to time, of attempts by their Legislature to extend an unwarrantable jurisdiction over us. We have reminded them of the circumstances of our emigration and settlement here. We have appealed to their native justice and magnanimity; and we have conjured them, by the ties of our common kindred, to disavow these usurpations, which would inevitably interrupt our connections and correspondence. They, too, have been deaf to the voice of justice and of consanguinity. We must, therefore, acquiesce in the necessity which denounces our separation, and hold them, as we hold the rest of mankind, enemies in war, in peace friends.

We, therefore, the representatives of the United States of America, in General Congress assembled, appealing to the Supreme Judge of the world for the rectitude of our intentions, do, in the name and by the authority of the good people of these colonies, solemnly publish and declare, that these United Colonies are, and of right ought to be, FREE AND INDEPENDENT STATES; that they are absolved from all allegiance to the British crown, and that all political connection between them and the state of Great Britain is, and ought to be, totally dissolved; and that, as free and independent states, they have full power to levy war, conclude peace, contract alliances, establish commerce, and do all other acts and things which independent states may of right do. And for the support of this declaration, with a firm reliance on the protection of Divine Providence, we mutually pledge to each other our lives, our fortunes, and our sacred honor.

JOHN HANCOCK [*President*]
[*and fifty-five others*]

THE CONSTITUTION OF THE UNITED STATES

Preamble

We the People of the United States, in Order to form a more perfect Union, establish Justice, insure domestic Tranquility, provide for the common defence, promote the general Welfare, and secure the Blessings of Liberty to ourselves and our Posterity, do ordain and establish this Constitution for the United States of America.

ARTICLE I.

Bicameral Congress

Section 1. All legislative Powers herein granted shall be vested in a Congress of the United States, which shall consist of a Senate and House of Representatives.

Membership of the House

Section 2. The House of Representatives shall be composed of Members chosen every second Year by the People of the several States, and the Electors in each State shall have the Qualifications requisite for Electors of the most numerous Branch of the State Legislature.

No person shall be a Representative who shall not have attained to the age of twenty five Years, and been seven Years a Citizen of the United States, and who shall not, when elected, be an Inhabitant of that State in which he shall be chosen.

Representatives and direct Taxes shall be apportioned among the several States which may be included within this Union, according to their respective Numbers, which shall be determined by adding to the whole Number of free Persons, including those bound to Service for a Term of Years, and excluding Indians not taxed, three fifths of all other Persons.[1] The actual Enumeration shall be made within three Years after the first Meeting of the Congress of the United States, and within every subsequent Term of ten Years, in such Manner as they shall by Law direct. The Number of Representatives shall not exceed one for every thirty Thousand, but each State shall have at Least one Representative; and until such enumeration shall be made, the State of New Hampshire shall be entitled to chuse three, Massachusetts eight, Rhode-Island and Providence Plantations one, Connecticut five, New-York six, New Jersey four, Pennsylvania eight, Delaware one, Maryland six, Virginia ten, North Carolina five, South Carolina five, and Georgia three.

When vacancies happen in the Representation from any State, the Executive Authority thereof shall issue Writs of Election to fill such Vacancies.

Power to impeach

The House of Representatives shall chuse their Speaker and other Officers; and shall have the sole Power of Impeachment.

Membership of the Senate

Section 3. The Senate of the United States shall be composed of two Senators from each State, *chosen by the Legislature thereof,*[2] for six Years; and each Senator shall have one Vote.

NOTE: The topical headings are not part of the original Constitution. Excluding the Preamble and Closing, those portions set in italic type have been superseded or changed by later amendments.
1. Changed by the Fourteenth Amendment, section 2.
2. Changed by the Seventeenth Amendment.

Immediately after they shall be assembled in Consequence of the first Election, they shall be divided as equally as may be into three Classes. The Seats of the Senators of the first class shall be vacated at the Expiration of the second Year, of the second Class at the Expiration of the fourth Year, and of the third Class at the Expiration of the sixth Year, so that one third may be chosen every second Year; *and if Vacancies happen by Resignation, or otherwise, during the Recess of the Legislature of any State, the Executive thereof may make temporary Appointments until the next Meeting of the Legislature, which shall then fill such Vacancies.* [3]

No Person shall be a Senator who shall not have attained to the Age of thirty Years, and been nine Years a Citizen of the United States, and who shall not, when elected, be an Inhabitant of that State for which he shall be chosen.

The Vice President of the United States shall be President of the Senate, but shall have no Vote, unless they be equally divided.

The Senate shall chuse their other Officers, and also a President pro tempore, in the Absence of the Vice President, or when he shall exercise the Office of President of the United States.

Power to try impeachments

The Senate shall have the sole Power to try all Impeachments. When sitting for that Purpose, they shall be on Oath or Affirmation. When the President of the United States is tried the Chief Justice shall preside: And no Person shall be convicted without the Concurrence of two thirds of the Members present.

Judgment in Cases of Impeachment shall not extend further than to removal from Office, and disqualification to hold and enjoy any Office of honor, Trust or Profit under the United States: but the Party convicted shall nevertheless be liable and subject to Indictment, Trial, Judgment and Punishment, according to Law.

Laws governing elections

Section 4.   The Times, Places and Manner of holding Elections for Senators and Representatives, shall be prescribed in each State by the Legislature thereof; but the Congress may at any time by Law make or alter such Regulations, except as to the Places of chusing Senators.

The Congress shall assemble at least once in every Year, and such Meeting shall be on the *first Monday in December, unless they shall by Law appoint a different Day.* [4]

Rules of Congress

Section 5.   Each House shall be the Judge of the Elections, Returns and Qualifications of its own Members, and a Majority of each shall constitute a Quorum to do Business; but a smaller number may adjourn from day to day, and may be authorized to compel the Attendance of absent Members, in such Manner, and under such Penalties as each House may provide.

Each House may determine the Rules of its Proceedings, punish its Members for disorderly Behaviour, and, with the Concurrence of two thirds, expel a Member.

Each House shall keep a Journal of its Proceedings, and from time to time publish the same, excepting such Parts as may in their Judgment require Secrecy; and the Yeas and Nays of the Members of either House on any question shall, at the Desire of one fifth of those Present, be entered on the Journal.

---

3. Changed by the Seventeenth Amendment.
4. Changed by the Twentieth Amendment, section 2.

Neither House, during the Session of Congress, shall, without the Consent of the other, adjourn for more than three days, nor to any other Place than that in which the two Houses shall be sitting.

Salaries and
immunities of members

Section 6.   The Senators and Representatives shall receive a Compensation for their Services, to be ascertained by Law, and paid out of the Treasury of the United States. They shall in all Cases, except Treason, Felony and Breach of the Peace, be privileged from Arrest during their Attendance at the Session of their respective Houses, and in going to and returning from the same; and for any Speech or Debate in either House, they shall not be questioned in any other Place.

Bar on members of Congress
holding federal appointive
office

No Senator or Representative shall, during the Time for which he was elected, be appointed to any civil Office under the Authority of the United States, which shall have been created, or the Emoluments whereof shall have been encreased during such time; and no Person holding any Office under the United States, shall be a Member of either House during his Continuance in Office.

Money bills originate in
House

Section 7.   All Bills for raising Revenue shall originate in the House of Representatives; but the Senate may propose or concur with Amendments as on other Bills.

Procedure for enacting
laws; veto power

Every Bill which shall have passed the House of Representatives and the Senate, shall, before it become a Law, be presented to the President of the United States; If he approve he shall sign it, but if not he shall return it, with Objections to that House in which it shall have originated, who shall enter the Objections at large on their Journal, and proceed to reconsider it. If after such Reconsideration two thirds of that House shall agree to pass the Bill, it shall be sent, together with the Objections, to the other House, by which it shall likewise be reconsidered, and if approved by two thirds of that House, it shall become a Law. But in all such Cases the Votes of both Houses shall be determined by yeas and Nays, and the Names of the Persons voting for and against the Bill shall be entered on the Journal of each House respectively. If any Bill shall not be returned by the President within ten Days (Sundays excepted) after it shall have been presented to him, the Same shall be a Law, in like Manner, as if he had signed it, unless the Congress by their Adjournment prevent its Return, in which Case it shall not be a Law.

Every Order, Resolution, or Vote to which the Concurrence of the Senate and House of Representatives may be necessary (except on a question of Adjournment) shall be presented to the President of the United States; and before the Same shall take Effect, shall be approved by him, or being disapproved by him, shall be repassed by two thirds of the Senate and House of Representatives, according to the Rules and Limitations prescribed in the Case of a Bill.

Powers of Congress
—*taxes*

Section 8.   The Congress shall have Power To lay and Collect Taxes, Duties, Imposts and Excises, to pay the Debts and provide for the common Defence and general Welfare of the United States; but all Duties, Imposts and Excises shall be uniform throughout the United States.

—*borrowing*

To borrow Money on the credit of the United States;

—*regulation of commerce*

To regulate Commerce with foreign Nations, and among the several States, and with the Indian Tribes;

—*naturalization and bankruptcy*

To establish an uniform Rule of Naturalization, and uniform Laws on the subject of Bankruptcies throughout the United States;

—money

To coin Money, regulate the Value thereof, and of foreign Coin, and fix the Standard of Weights and Measures;

—counterfeiting

To provide for the Punishment of counterfeiting the Securities and current Coin of the United States;

—post office

To establish Post Offices and post Roads;

—patents and copyrights

To promote the Progress of Science and useful Arts, by securing for limited Times to Authors and Inventors the exclusive Right to their respective Writings and Discoveries;

—create courts

To constitute Tribunals inferior to the Supreme Court;

—punish piracies

To define and punish Piracies and Felonies committed on the high Seas, and Offences against the Law of Nations;

—declare war

To declare War, grant Letters of Marque and Reprisal, and make Rules concerning Captures on Land and Water;

—create army and navy

To raise and support Armies, but no Appropriation of Money to that Use shall be for a longer Term than two Years;

To provide and maintain a Navy;

To make Rules for the Government and Regulation of the land and naval Forces;

—call the militia

To provide for calling forth the Militia to execute the Laws of the Union, suppress Insurrections and repel Invasions;

To provide for organizing, arming, and disciplining, the Militia, and for governing such Part of them as may be employed in the Service of the United States, reserving to the States respectively, the Appointment of the Officers, and the Authority of training the Militia according to the discipline prescribed by Congress;

—govern District of Columbia

To exercise exclusive Legislation in all Cases whatsoever, over such District (not exceeding ten Miles square) as may, by Cession of Particular States, and the Acceptance of Congress, become the Seat of the Government of the United States, and to exercise like Authority over all Places purchased by the Consent of the Legislature of the State in which the Same shall be, for the Erection of Forts, Magazines, Arsenals, dock-Yards and other needful Buildings;—And

—"necessary-and-proper" clause

To make all Laws which shall be necessary and proper for carrying into Execution the foregoing Powers, and all other Powers vested by this Constitution in the Government of the United States, or in any Department or Officer thereof.

Restrictions on powers of Congress

—slave trade

Section 9.   The Migration or Importation of such Persons as any of the States now existing shall think proper to admit, shall not be prohibited by the Congress prior to the Year one thousand eight hundred and eight, but a Tax or duty may be imposed on such Importation, not exceeding ten dollars for each Person.

—habeas corpus

The Privilege of the Writ of Habeas Corpus shall not be suspended, unless when in Cases of Rebellion or Invasion the public Safety may require it.

—no bill of attainder or ex post facto law

No bill of Attainder or ex post facto Law shall be passed.

No Capitation, or other direct, Tax shall be laid, *unless in Proportion to the Census or Enumeration herein before directed to be taken.*[5]

—no interstate tariffs

No Tax or Duty shall be laid on Articles exported from any State.

—no preferential treatment for some states

No Preference shall be given by any Regulation of Commerce or Revenue to the Ports of one State over those of another; nor shall Vessels bound to, or from, one State, be obliged to enter, clear or pay Duties in another.

---

5. Changed by the Sixteenth Amendment.

—*appropriations*

No Money shall be drawn from the Treasury, but in Consequence of Appropriations made by Law; and a regular Statement and Account of the Receipts and Expenditures of all public Money shall be published from time to time.

—*no titles of nobility*

No Title of Nobility shall be granted by the United States: And no Person holding any Office of Profit or Trust under them, shall, without the Consent of the Congress, accept of any present, Emolument, Office, or Title, of any kind whatever, from any King, Prince, or foreign State.

Restrictions on powers of states

Section 10.   No State shall enter into any Treaty, Alliance, or Confederation; grant Letters of Marque and Reprisal; coin Money; emit Bills of Credit; make any Thing but gold and silver Coin a Tender in Payment of Debts; pass any Bill of Attainder, ex post facto Law, or Law impairing the Obligation of Contracts, or grant any Title of Nobility.

No State shall, without the Consent of Congress, lay any Imposts or Duties on Imports or Exports, except what may be absolutely necessary for executing its inspection Laws; and the net Produce of all Duties and Imposts, laid by any State on Imports or Exports, shall be for the Use of the Treasury of the United States; and all such Laws shall be subject to the Revision and Controul of the Congress.

No State shall, without the Consent of Congress, lay any Duty of Tonnage, keep Troops, or Ships of War in time of Peace, enter into any Agreement or Compact with another State, or with a foreign Power, or engage in War, unless actually invaded, or in such imminent Danger as will not admit of delay.

ARTICLE II.

Office of president

Section 1.   The executive Power shall be vested in a President of the United States of America. He shall hold his Office during the Term of four Years, and, together with the Vice President, chosen for the same Term, be elected, as follows:

Election of president

Each State shall appoint, in such Manner as the Legislature thereof may direct, a Number of Electors, equal to the whole Number of Senators and Representatives to which the State may be entitled in the Congress: but no Senator or Representative, or Person holding an Office of Trust or Profit under the United States, shall be appointed an Elector.

The Electors shall meet in their respective States, and vote by Ballot for two Persons, of whom one at least shall not be an Inhabitant of the same State with themselves. And they shall make a List of all the Persons voted for, and of the Number of Votes for each; which List they shall sign and certify, and transmit sealed to the Seat of the Government of the United States, directed to the President of the Senate. The President of the Senate shall, in the Presence of the Senate and House of Representatives, open all the Certificates, and the Votes shall then be counted. The Person having the greatest Number of Votes shall be the President, if such Number be a Majority of the whole Number of Electors appointed; and if there be more than one who have such Majority, and have an equal Number of Votes, then the House of Representatives shall immediately chuse by Ballot one of them for President; and if no Person have a Majority, then from the five highest on the List said House shall in like Manner chuse the President. But in chusing the President, the Votes shall be taken by States, the Representation from each State having one Vote; a quorum for this Purpose shall consist of a Member or Members from two thirds of the States, and a Majority of all the States shall be necessary to a Choice. In every Case, after the Choice of the President, the Person having the greatest Number of Votes of the Electors shall be the Vice President. But if there should remain two or more who have equal Votes, the Senate shall chuse from them by Ballot the Vice President.[6]

The Congress may determine the Time of chusing the Electors, and the Day on which they shall give their Votes, which Day shall be the same throughout the United States.

Requirements to be president

No Person except a natural born Citizen, or a Citizen of the United States, at the time of the Adoption of this Constitution, shall be eligible to the Office of President; neither shall any person be eligible to that Office who shall not have attained to the Age of thirty five Years, and been fourteen Years a Resident within the United States.

In Case of the Removal of the President from Office, or of his Death, Resignation, or Inability to discharge the Powers and Duties of the said Office, the Same shall devolve on the Vice President, and the Congress may by Law provide for the Case of Removal, Death, Resignation or Inability, both of the President and Vice President, declaring what Officer shall then act as President, and such Officer shall act accordingly, until the Disability be removed, or a President shall be elected.[7]

Pay of president

The President shall, at stated Times, receive for his Services, a Compensation, which shall neither be increased nor diminished during the Period for which he shall have been elected, and he shall not receive within that Period any other Emolument from the United States, or any of them.

Before he enter on the Execution of his Office, he shall take the following Oath or Affirmation:—"I do solemnly swear (or affirm) that I will faithfully execute the Office of President of the United States, and will to the best of my Ability preserve, protect and defend the Constitution of the United States."

Powers of president
—*commander in chief*

Section 2.   The President shall be Commander in Chief of the Army and Navy of the United States, and of the Militia of the several States, when called into the actual Service of the United States; he may require the Opinion, in writing, of the principal Officer in each of the executive Departments, upon any Subject relating to the Duties of their respective Offices, and he shall have Power to grant Reprieves and Pardons for Offences against the United States, except in Cases of Impeachment.

—*pardons*

—*treaties and appointments*

He shall have Power, by and with the Advice and Consent of the Senate, to make Treaties, provided two thirds of the Senators present concur; and he shall nominate, and by and with the Advice and Consent of the Senate, shall appoint Ambassadors, other public Ministers and Consuls, Judges of the supreme Court, and all other Officers of the United States, whose Appointments are not herein otherwise provided for, and which shall be established by Law: but the Congress may by Law vest the Appointment of such inferior Officers, as they think proper, in the President alone, in the Courts of Law, or in the Heads of Departments.

The President shall have Power to fill up all Vacancies that may happen during the Recess of the Senate, by granting Commissions which shall expire at the End of their next Session.

Relations of president with Congress

Section 3.   He shall from time to time give to the Congress Information of the State of the Union, and recommend to their Consideration such Measures as he

---

6. Superseded by the Twelfth Amendment.
7. Modified by the Twenty-fifth Amendment.

shall judge necessary and expedient; he may, on extraordinary Occasions, convene both Houses, or either of them, and in Case of Disagreement between them, with Respect to the Time of Adjournment, he may adjourn them to such Time as he shall think proper; he shall receive Ambassadors and other public Ministers; he shall take Care that the Laws be faithfully executed, and shall Commission all the Officers of the United States.

Impeachment

Section 4.   The President, Vice President and all civil Officers of the United States, shall be removed from Office on Impeachment for, and Conviction of, Treason, Bribery, or other high Crimes and Misdemeanors.

ARTICLE III.

Federal courts

Section 1.   The judicial Power of the United States, shall be vested in one supreme Court, and in such inferior Courts as the Congress may from time to time ordain and establish. The Judges, both of the supreme and inferior Courts, shall hold their Offices during good Behaviour, and shall, at stated Times, receive for their Services, a Compensation, which shall not be diminished during their Continuance in Office.

Jurisdiction of courts

Section 2.   The judicial Power shall extend to all Cases, in Law and Equity, arising under this Constitution, the Laws of the United States, and Treaties made, or which shall be made, under their Authority;—to all Cases affecting Ambassadors, other public Ministers and Consuls;—to all Cases of admiralty and maritime Jurisdiction;—to Controversies to which the United States shall be a Party;—to Controversies between two or more States;—*between a State and Citizens of another State;*[8]—between Citizens of different States;—between Citizens of the same State claiming Lands under Grants of different States, and between a State, or the Citizens thereof, and foreign States, Citizens or Subjects.

—*original*

In all Cases affecting Ambassadors, other public Ministers and Consuls, and those in which a State shall be Party, the supreme Court shall have original Jurisdiction. In all the other Cases before mentioned, the supreme Court shall have

—*appellate*

appellate Jurisdiction, both as to Law and Fact, with such Exceptions, and under such Regulations as the Congress shall make.

The Trial of all Crimes, except in Cases of Impeachment, shall be by Jury; and such Trial shall be held in the State where the said Crimes shall have been committed; but when not committed within any State, the Trial shall be at such Place or Places as the Congress may by Law have directed.

Treason

Section 3.   Treason against the United States, shall consist only in levying War against them, or in adhering to their Enemies, giving them Aid and Comfort. No Person shall be convicted of Treason unless on the Testimony of two Witnesses to the same overt Act, or on Confession in open Court.

The Congress shall have Power to declare the Punishment of Treason, but no Attainder of Treason shall work Corruption of Blood, or Forfeiture except during the Life of the Person attainted.

---

8. Modified by the Eleventh Amendment.

ARTICLE IV.

Full faith and credit

Section 1.   Full Faith and Credit shall be given in each State to the public Acts, Records, and judicial Proceedings of every other State. And the Congress may by general Laws prescribe the Manner in which such Acts, Records and Proceedings shall be proved, and the Effect thereof.

Privileges and immunities

Section 2.   The Citizens of each State shall be entitled to all Privileges and Immunities of Citizens in the several States.

Extradition

A person charged in any State with Treason, Felony, or other Crime, who shall flee from Justice, and be found in another State, shall on Demand of the executive Authority of the State from which he fled, be delivered up, to be removed to the State having Jurisdiction of the Crime.

No Person held to Service or Labour in one State, under the Laws thereof, escaping into another, shall, in Consequence of any Law or Regulation therein, be discharged from such Service or Labour, but shall be delivered up on Claim of the Party to whom such Service or Labour may be due.[9]

Creation of new states

Section 3.   New States may be admitted by the Congress into this Union; but no new State shall be formed or erected within the Jurisdiction of any other State; nor any State be formed by the Junction of two or more States, or Parts of States, without the Consent of the Legislatures of the States concerned as well as of the Congress.

Governing territories

The Congress shall have Power to dispose of and make all needful Rules and Regulations respecting the Territory or other Property belonging to the United States; and nothing in this Constitution shall be so construed as to Prejudice any Claims of the United States, or of any particular State.

Protection of states

Section 4.   The United States shall guarantee to every State in this Union a Republican Form of Government, and shall protect each of them against Invasion; and on Application of the Legislature, or of the Executive (when the Legislature cannot be convened) against domestic Violence.

ARTICLE V.

Amending the Constitution

The Congress, whenever two thirds of both Houses shall deem it necessary, shall propose Amendments to this Constitution, or, on the Application of the Legislatures of two thirds of the several States, shall call a Convention for proposing Amendments, which, in either Case, shall be valid to all Intents and Purposes, as Part of this Constitution, when ratified by the Legislatures of three fourths of the several States, or by Conventions in three fourths thereof, as the one or the other Mode of Ratification may be proposed by the Congress; Provided that no Amendment which may be made prior to the Year One thousand eight hundred and eight shall in any Manner alter the first and fourth Clauses in the Ninth Section of the first Article; and that no State, without its Consent, shall be deprived of its equal Suffrage in the Senate.

---

9. Changed by the Thirteenth Amendment.

ARTICLE VI.

Assumption of debts of
Confederation

All Debts contracted and Engagements entered into, before the Adoption of this Constitution, shall be as valid against the United States under this Constitution, as under the Confederation.

Supremacy of federal laws and
treaties

This Constitution, and the Laws of the United States which shall be made in Pursuance thereof; and all Treaties made, or which shall be made, under the Authority of the United States, shall be the Supreme Law of the Land; and the Judges in every State shall be bound thereby, any Thing in the Constitution or Laws of any State to the Contrary notwithstanding.

No religious test

The Senators and Representatives before mentioned, and the Members of the several State Legislatures, and all executive and judicial Officers, both of the United States and of the several States, shall be bound by Oath or Affirmation, to support this Constitution; but no religious Test shall ever be required as a Qualification to any Office or public Trust under the United States.

ARTICLE VII.

Ratification procedure

The Ratification of the Conventions of nine States, shall be sufficient for the Establishment of this Constitution between the States so ratifying the Same.

Done in Convention by the Unanimous Consent of the States present the Seventeenth Day of September in the Year of our Lord one thousand seven hundred and Eighty seven and of the Independence of the United States of America the Twelfth In witness whereof We have hereunto subscribed our Names,

G⁰.ASHINGTON—*Presid*ᵗ.
and deputy from Virginia

New Hampshire	{ JOHN LANGDON NICHOLAS GILMAN	*Connecticut*	{ Wᴹ SAMᴸ JOHNSON ROGER SHERMAN
Massachusetts	{ NATHANIEL GORHAM RUFUS KING	*New York*	ALEXANDER HAMILTON
New Jersey	{ WIL: LIVINGSTON DAVID BREARLEY Wᴹ PATERSON JONA: DAYTON	*Maryland*	{ JAMES MᶜHENRY DAN OF Sᵀ THOˢ JENIFER DANᴸ CARROLL
		Virginia	{ JOHN BLAIR— JAMES MADISON JR.
Pennsylvania	{ B FRANKLIN THOMAS MIFFLIN ROBᵀ MORRIS GEO. CLYMER THOˢ FITZSIMONS JARED INGERSOLL JAMES WILSON GOUV MORRIS	*North Carolina*	{ Wᴹ BLOUNT RICHᴰ DOBBS SPAIGHT HU WILLIAMSON
		South Carolina	{ J. RUTLEDGE CHARLES COTESWORTH PINCKNEY CHARLES PINCKNEY PIERCE BUTLER

		Georgia	
	GEO: READ		WILLIAM FEW
	GUNNING BEDFORD jun		ABR BALDWIN
Delaware	JOHN DICKINSON		
	RICHARD BASSETT		
	JACO: BROOM		

[The first ten amendments, known as the "Bill of Rights," were ratified in 1791.]

AMENDMENT I.

Freedom of religion, speech, press, assembly

Congress shall make no law respecting an establishment of religion, or prohibiting the free exercise thereof, or abridging the freedom of speech, or of the press; or the right of the people peaceably to assemble, and to petition the Government for a redress of grievances.

AMENDMENT II.

Right to bear arms

A well regulated Militia, being necessary to the security of a free State, the right of the people to keep and bear Arms, shall not be infringed.

AMENDMENT III.

Quartering troops in private homes

No Soldier shall, in time of peace be quartered in any house without the consent of the Owner, nor in time of war, but in a manner to be prescribed by law.

AMENDMENT IV.

Prohibition against unreasonable searches and seizures

The right of the people to be secure in their persons, houses, papers, and effects, against unreasonable searches and seizures, shall not be violated, and no Warrants shall issue, but upon probable cause, supported by Oath or affirmation, and particularly describing the place to be searched, and the persons or things to be seized.

AMENDMENT V.

Right when accused; "due-process" clause

No person shall be held to answer for a capital, or otherwise infamous crime, unless on a presentment or indictment of a Grand Jury, except in cases arising in the land or naval forces, or in the Militia, when in actual service in time of War or public danger; nor shall any person be subject for the same offence to be twice put in jeopardy of life or limb; nor shall be compelled in any criminal case to be a witness against himself, nor be deprived of life, liberty, or property, without due process of law, nor shall private property be taken for public use, without just compensation.

AMENDMENT VI.

Rights when on trial

In all criminal prosecutions, the accused shall enjoy the right to a speedy and public trial, by an impartial jury of the State and district wherein the crime shall have been committed, which district shall have been previously ascertained by law, and to be informed of the nature and cause of the accusation; to be confronted with the witnesses against him; to have compulsory process for obtaining witnesses in his favor, and to have the Assistance of Counsel for his defence.

AMENDMENT VII.

Common-law suits

In Suits at common law, where the value in controversy shall exceed twenty dollars, the right of trial by jury shall be preserved, and no fact tried by a jury, shall be otherwise reexamined in any Court of the United States, than according to the rules of the common law.

AMENDMENT VIII.

Bail; no "cruel and unusual" punishments

Excessive bail shall not be required, nor excessive fines imposed, nor cruel and unusual punishments inflicted.

AMENDMENT IX.

Unenumerated rights protected

The enumeration in the Constitution, of certain rights, shall not be construed to deny or disparage others retained by the people.

AMENDMENT X.

Powers reserved for states

The powers not delegated to the United States by the Constitution, nor prohibited by it to the States, are reserved to the States respectively, or to the people.

AMENDMENT XI.
[*Ratified in 1795.*]

Limits on suits against states

The Judicial power of the United States shall not be construed to extend to any suit in law or equity, commenced or prosecuted against one of the United States by Citizens of another state, or by Citizens or Subjects of any Foreign State.

AMENDMENT XII.
[*Ratified in 1804.*]

Revision of electoral-college procedure

The Electors shall meet in their respective states and vote by ballot for President and Vice President, one of whom, at least, shall not be an inhabitant of the same state with themselves; they shall name in their ballots the person voted for as President, and in distinct ballots the person voted for as Vice President, and they shall make distinct lists of all persons voted for as President, and of all persons voted for as Vice President, and of the number of votes for each, which lists they shall sign and certify, and transmit sealed to the seat of government of the United States, directed to the President of the Senate;—The President of the Senate shall, in the presence of the Senate and House of Representatives, open all the certificates and the votes shall then be counted;—The person having the greatest number of votes for President, shall be the President, if such number be a majority of the whole number of Electors appointed; and if no person have such majority, then from the persons having the highest numbers not exceeding three on the list of those voted for as President, the House of Representatives shall choose immediately, by ballot, the President. But in choosing the President, the votes shall be taken by states, the representation from each state having one vote; a quorum for this purpose shall consist of a member or members from two-thirds of the states, and a majority of all the states shall be necessary to a choice. *And if the House of Representatives shall not choose a President whenever the right of choice shall devolve upon them, before the fourth day of March next following, then the Vice President shall act as President, as in the case of the death or other constitutional disability of the President.*—[10] The person having the greatest number of votes as Vice President, shall be the Vice President, if such number be a majority of the whole number of Electors appointed, and if no person have a majority, then from the two highest numbers on the list, the Senate shall choose the Vice President; a quorum for the purpose shall consist of two-thirds of the whole number of Senators, and a majority of the whole number shall be necessary to a choice. But no person constitutionally ineligible to the office of President shall be eligible to that of Vice President of the United States.

AMENDMENT XIII.
[*Ratified in 1865.*]

Slavery prohibited

Section 1.   Neither slavery nor involuntary servitude, except as a punishment for crime whereof the party shall have been duly convicted, shall exist within the United States, or any place subject to their jurisdiction.

Section 2.   Congress shall have power to enforce this article by appropriate legislation.

AMENDMENT XIV.
[*Ratified in 1868.*]

Ex-slaves made citizens

Section 1.   All persons born or naturalized in the United States and subject to the jurisdiction thereof, are citizens of the United States and of the State wherein they reside. No State shall make or enforce any law which shall abridge the privileges or immunities of citizens of the United States; nor shall any State deprive any person of life, liberty, or property, without due process of law; nor deny to any person within its jurisdiction the equal protection of the laws.

"Due-process" clause applied to states

"Equal-protection" clause

Reduction in congressional representation for states denying adult males the right to vote

Section 2.   Representatives shall be apportioned among the several States according to their respective numbers, counting the whole number of persons in each State, excluding Indians not taxed. But when the right to vote at any election for the choice of electors for President and Vice President of the United States, Representatives in Congress, the Executive and Judicial officers of a State, or the members of the Legislature thereof, is denied to any of the male inhabitants of such State, being *twenty-one*[11] years of age and citizens of the United States, or in any way abridged, except for participation in rebellion, or other crime, the basis of representation therein shall be reduced in the proportion which the number of such male citizens shall bear to the whole number of male citizens twenty-one years of age in such State.

Southern rebels denied federal office

Section 3.   No person shall be a Senator or Representative in Congress, or elector of President and Vice President, or hold any office, civil or military, under the

---

10. Changed by the Twentieth Amendment, section 3.
11. Changed by the Twenty-sixth Amendment.

United States, or under any State, who, having previously taken an oath, as a member of Congress, or as an officer of the United States, or as a member of any State legislature, or as an executive or judicial officer of any State, to support the Constitution of the United States, shall have engaged in insurrection or rebellion against the same, or given aid or comfort to the enemies thereof. But Congress may by a vote of two-thirds of each House, remove such disability.

Rebel debts repudiated

Section 4.   The validity of the public debt of the United States, authorized by law, including debts incurred for payment of pensions and bounties for services in suppressing insurrection or rebellion, shall not be questioned. But neither the United States nor any State shall assume or pay any debt or obligation incurred in aid of insurrection or rebellion against the United States, or any claim for the loss or emancipation of any slave; but all such debts, obligations and claims shall be held illegal and void.

Section 5.   The Congress shall have power to enforce, by appropriate legislation, the provisions of this article.

AMENDMENT XV.
[Ratified in 1870.]

Blacks given right to vote

Section 1.   The right of citizens of the United States to vote shall not be denied or abridged by the United States or by any State on account of race, color, or previous condition of servitude.

Section 2.   The Congress shall have power to enforce this article by appropriate legislation.

AMENDMENT XVI.
[Ratified in 1913.]

Authorizes federal income tax

The Congress shall have power to lay and collect taxes on incomes, from whatever source derived, without apportionment among the several States, and without regard to any census or enumeration.

AMENDMENT XVII.
[Ratified in 1913.]

Requires popular election of senators

The Senate of the United States shall be composed of two Senators from each State, elected by the people thereof, for six years; and each Senator shall have one vote. The electors in each State shall have the qualifications requisite for electors of the most numerous branch of the State legislatures.

When vacancies happen in the representation of any State in the Senate, the executive authority of such State shall issue writs of election to fill such vacancies: Provided, That the legislature of any State may empower the executive thereof to make temporary appointments until the people fill the vacancies by election as the legislature may direct.

This amendment shall not be so construed as to affect the election or term of any Senator chosen before it becomes valid as part of the Constitution.

AMENDMENT XVIII.
[*Ratified in 1919.*]

Prohibits manufacture and sale
of liquor

Section 1.   *After one year from the ratification of this article the manufacture, sale, or transportation of intoxicating liquors within, the importation thereof into, or the exportation thereof from the United States and all territory subject to the jurisdiction thereof for beverage purposes is hereby prohibited.*

Section 2.   *The Congress and the several States shall have concurrent power to enforce this article by appropriate legislation.*

Section 3.   *This article shall be inoperative unless it shall have been ratified as an amendment to the Constitution by the legislatures of the several States, as provided in the Constitution, within seven years from the date of the submission hereof to the States by the Congress.*[12]

AMENDMENT XIX.
[*Ratified in 1920.*]

Right to vote for women

The right of citizens of the United States to vote shall not be denied or abridged by the United States or by any State on account of sex.
    Congress shall have power to enforce this article by appropriate legislation.

AMENDMENT XX.
[*Ratified in 1933.*]

Federal terms of office to begin
in January

Section 1.   The terms of the President and Vice President shall end at noon on the 20th day of January, and the terms of Senators and Representatives at noon on the 3d day of January, of the years in which such terms would have ended if this article had not been ratified; and the terms of their successors shall then begin.

Section 2.   The Congress shall assemble at least once in every year, and such meeting shall begin at noon on the 3d day of January, unless they shall by law appoint a different day.

Emergency presidential
succession

Section 3.   If, at the time fixed for the beginning of the term of the President, the President elect shall have died, the Vice President elect shall become President. If a President shall not have been chosen before the time fixed for the beginning of his term, or if the President elect shall have failed to qualify, then the Vice President elect shall act as President until a President shall have qualified; and the Congress may by law provide for the case wherein neither a President elect nor a Vice President elect shall have qualified, declaring who shall then act as President, or the manner in which one who is to act shall be selected, and such person shall act accordingly until a President or Vice President shall have qualified.

---

12. Repealed by the Twenty-first Amendment.

Section 4.   The Congress may by law provide for the case of the death of any of the persons from whom the House of Representatives may choose a President whenever the right of choice shall have devolved upon them, and for the case of the death of any of the persons from whom the Senate may choose a Vice President whenever the right of choice shall have devolved upon them.

Section 5.   Sections 1 and 2 shall take effect on the 15th day of October following the ratification of this article.

Section 6.   This article shall be inoperative unless it shall have been ratified as an amendment to the Constitution by the legislatures of three-fourths of the several States within seven years from the date of its submission.

AMENDMENT XXI.
[*Ratified in 1933.*]

Repeals Prohibition

Section 1.   The eighteenth article of amendment to the Constitution of the United States is hereby repealed.

Section 2.   The transportation or importation into any State, Territory, or possession of the United States for delivery or use therein of intoxicating liquors, in violation of the laws thereof, is hereby prohibited.

Section 3.   This article shall be inoperative unless it shall have been ratified as an amendment to the Constitution by conventions in the several States, as provided in the Constitution, within seven years from the date of submission hereof to the States by the Congress.

AMENDMENT XXII.
[*Ratified in 1951.*]

Two-term limit for president

Section 1.   No person shall be elected to the office of the President more than twice, and no person who has held the office of President, or acted as President, for more than two years of a term to which some other person was elected President shall be elected to the office of President more than once. But this Article shall not apply to any person holding the office of President when this Article was proposed by the Congress, and shall not prevent any person who may be holding the office of President, or acting as President, during the term within which this Article becomes operative from holding the office of President or acting as President during the remainder of such term.

Section 2.   This Article shall be inoperative unless it shall have been ratified as an amendment to the Constitution by the legislatures of three-fourths of the several States within seven years from the date of its submission to the States by the Congress.

AMENDMENT XXIII.
[*Ratified in 1961.*]

Right to vote for president in District of Columbia

Section 1.   The District constituting the seat of Government of the United States shall appoint in such manner as the Congress may direct:

A number of electors of President and Vice President equal to the whole number of Senators and Representatives in Congress to which the District would be entitled if it were a State, but in no event more than the least populous State; they shall be in addition to those appointed by the States, but they shall be considered, for the purposes of the election of President and Vice President, to be electors appointed by a State; and they shall meet in the District and perform such duties as provided by the twelfth article of amendment.

Section 2.   The Congress shall have power to enforce this article by appropriate legislation.

AMENDMENT XXIV.
[Ratified in 1964.]

Prohibits poll taxes in federal elections

Section 1.   The right of citizens of the United States to vote in any primary or other election for President or Vice President, for electors for President or Vice President, or for Senator or Representative in Congress, shall not be denied or abridged by the United States or any State by reason of failure to pay any poll tax or other tax.

Section 2.   The Congress shall have the power to enforce this article by appropriate legislation.

AMENDMENT XXV.
[Ratified in 1967.]

Presidential disability and succession

Section 1.   In case of the removal of the President from office or of his death or resignation, the Vice President shall become President.

Section 2.   Whenever there is a vacancy in the office of the Vice President, the President shall nominate a Vice President who shall take office upon confirmation by a majority vote of both Houses of Congress.

Section 3.   Whenever the President transmits to the President pro tempore of the Senate and the Speaker of the House of Representatives his written declaration that he is unable to discharge the powers and duties of his office, and until he transmits to them a written declaration to the contrary, such powers and duties shall be discharged by the Vice President as Acting President.

Section 4.   Whenever the Vice President and a majority of either the principal officers of the executive departments or of such other body as Congress may by law provide, transmit to the President pro tempore of the Senate and the Speaker of the House of Representatives their written declaration that the President is unable to discharge the powers and duties of his office, the Vice President shall immediately assume the powers and duties of the office as Acting President.

Thereafter, when the President transmits to the President pro tempore of the Senate and the Speaker of the House of Representatives his written declaration that no inability exists, he shall resume the powers and duties of his office unless the Vice President and a majority of either the principal officers of the executive department[s] or of such other body as Congress may by law provide, transmit within four days to the President pro tempore of the Senate and the Speaker of the House of Representatives their written declaration that the President is unable to discharge the powers and duties of his office. Thereupon Congress shall decide the issue, assembling within forty-eight hours for that purpose if not in session. If the Congress, within twenty-one days after receipt of the latter written declaration, or, if Congress is not in session, within twenty-one days after Congress is required to assemble, determines by two-thirds vote of both Houses that the President is unable to discharge the powers and duties of his office, the Vice President shall continue to discharge the same as Acting President; otherwise, the President shall resume the powers and duties of his office.

AMENDMENT XXVI.
[*Ratified in 1971.*]

Voting age lowered to eighteen

Section 1. The right of citizens of the United States, who are eighteen years of age or older, to vote shall not be denied or abridged by the United States or by any State on account of age.

Section 2. The Congress shall have power to enforce this article by appropriate legislation.

AMENDMENT XXVII.
[*Ratified in 1992.*]

Congressional pay raises

No law varying the compensation for the services of the Senators and Representatives shall take effect, until an election of Representatives shall have intervened.

The Federalist No. 10

November 22, 1787

James Madison

TO THE PEOPLE OF THE STATE OF NEW YORK.

Among the numerous advantages promised by a well constructed Union, none deserves to be more accurately developed than its tendency to break and control the violence of faction. The friend of popular governments, never finds himself so much alarmed for their character and fate, as when he contemplates their propensity to this dangerous vice. He will not fail therefore to set a due value on any plan which, without violating the principles to which he is attached, provides a proper cure for it. The instability, injustice and confusion introduced into the public councils, have in truth been the mortal diseases under which popular governments have every where perished; as they continue to be the favorite and fruitful topics from which the adversaries to liberty derive their most specious declamations. The valuable improvements made by the American Constitutions on the popular models, both ancient and modern, cannot certainly be too much admired; but it would be an unwarrantable partiality, to contend that they have as effectually obviated the danger on this side as was wished and expected. Complaints are every where heard from our most considerate and virtuous citizens, equally the friends of public and private faith, and of public and personal liberty; that our governments are too unstable; that the public good is disregarded in the conflicts of rival parties; and that measures are too often decided, not according to the rules of justice, and the rights of the minor party; but by the superior force of an interested and over-bearing majority. However anxiously we may wish that these complaints had no foundation, the evidence of known facts will not permit us to deny that they are in some degree true. It will be found indeed, on a candid review of our situation, that some of the distresses under which we labor, have been erroneously charged on the operation of our governments; but it will be found, at the same time, that other causes will not alone account for many of our heaviest misfortunes; and particularly, for that prevailing and increasing distrust of public engagements, and alarm for private rights, which are echoed from one end of the continent to the other. These must be chiefly, if not wholly, effects of the unsteadiness and injustice, with which a factious spirit has tainted our public administrations.

By a faction I understand a number of citizens, whether amounting to a majority or minority of the whole, who are united and actuated by some common impulse of passion, or of interest, adverse to the rights of other citizens, or to the permanent and aggregate interests of the community.

There are two methods of curing the mischiefs of faction: the one, by removing its causes; the other, by controlling its effects.

There are again two methods of removing the causes of faction: the one by destroying the liberty which is essential to its existence; the other, by giving to every citizen the same opinions, the same passions, and the same interests.

It could never be more truly said than of the first remedy, that it is worse than the disease. Liberty is to faction, what air is to fire, an aliment without which it instantly expires. But it could not be a less folly to abolish liberty, which is essential to political life, because it nourishes faction, than it would be to wish the annihilation of air, which is essential to animal life, because it imparts to fire its destructive agency.

The second expedient is as impracticable, as the first would be unwise. As long as the reason of man continues fallible, and he is at liberty to exercise it, different opinions will be formed. As long as the connection subsists between his reason and his self-love, his opinions and his passions will have a reciprocal influence on each other; and the former will be objects to which the latter will attach themselves. The diversity in the faculties of men from which the rights of property originate, is not less an insuperable obstacle to a uniformity of interests. The protection of these faculties is the first object of Government. From the protection of different and unequal faculties of acquiring property, the possession of different degrees and kinds of property immediately results: and from the influence of these on the sentiments and views of the respective proprietors, ensues a division of the society into different interests and parties.

The latent causes of faction are thus sown in the nature of man; and we see them every where brought into different degrees of activity, according to the different circumstances of civil society. A zeal for different opinions concerning religion, concerning Government and many other points, as well of speculation as of practice; an attachment to different leaders ambitiously contending for pre-eminence and power; or to persons of other descriptions whose fortunes have been interesting to the human passions, have in turn divided mankind into parties, inflamed them with mutual animosity, and rendered them much more disposed to vex and oppress each other, than to cooperate for their common good. So strong is this propensity of mankind to fall into mutual animosities, that where no substantial occasion presents itself, the most frivolous and fanciful distinctions have been sufficient to kindle their unfriendly passions, and excite their most violent conflicts. But the most common and durable source of factions, has been the various and unequal distribution of property. Those who hold, and those who are without property, have ever formed distinct interests in society. Those who are creditors, and those who are debtors, fall under a like discrimination. A landed interest, a manufacturing interest, a mercantile interest, a monied interest, with many lesser interests, grow up of necessity in civilized nations, and divide them into different classes, actuated by different sentiments and views. The regulation of these various and interfering interests forms the principal task of modern Legislation, and involves the spirit of party and faction in the necessary and ordinary operations of Government.

No man is allowed to be judge in his own cause; because his interest would certainly bias his judgment, and, not improbably, corrupt his integrity. With equal, nay with greater reason, a body of men, are unfit to be judges and parties, at the same time; yet, what are many of the most important acts of legislation, but so many judicial determinations, not indeed concerning the rights of single persons, but concerning the rights of large bodies of citizens, and what are the different classes of legislators, but advocates and parties to the causes which they determine? Is a law proposed concerning private debts? It is a question to which the creditors are parties on one side, and the debtors on the other. Justice ought to hold the balance between them. Yet the parties are and must be themselves the judges; and the most numerous party, or, in other words, the most powerful faction must be expected to prevail. Shall domestic manufactures be encouraged, and in what degree, by restrictions on foreign manufactures? are questions which would be differently decided by the landed and the manufacturing classes; and probably by neither, with a sole regard to justice and the public good. The apportionment of taxes on the various descriptions of property, is an act which seems to require the most exact impartiality; yet, there is perhaps no legislative act in which greater opportunity and temptation are given to a predominant party, to trample on the rules of justice. Every shilling with which they over-burden the inferior number, is a shilling saved to their own pockets.

It is in vain to say, that enlightened statesmen will be able to adjust these clashing interests, and render them all subservient to the public good. Enlightened statesmen will not always be at the helm: Nor, in many cases, can such an adjustment be made at all, without taking into view indirect and remote considerations, which will rarely prevail over the immediate interest which one party may find in disregarding the rights of another, or the good of the whole.

The inference to which we are brought, is, that the *causes* of faction cannot be removed; and that relief is only to be sought in the means of controlling its *effects*.

If a faction consists of less than a majority, relief is supplied by the republican principle, which enables the majority to defeat its sinister views by regular vote: It may clog the administration, it may convulse the society; but it will be unable to execute and mask its violence under the forms of the Constitution. When a majority is included in a faction, the form of popular government on the other hand enables it to sacrifice to its ruling passion or interest, both the public good and the rights of other citizens. To secure the public good, and private rights, against the danger of such a faction, and at the same time to preserve the spirit and the form of popular government, is then the great object to which our inquiries are directed: Let me add that it is the great desideratum, by which alone this form of government can be rescued from the opprobrium under which it has so long labored, and be recommended to the esteem and adoption of mankind.

By what means is this object attainable? Evidently by one of two only. Either the existence of the same passion or interest in a majority at the same time, must be prevented; or the majority, having such co-existent passion or interest, must be rendered, by their number and local situation, unable to concert and carry into effect schemes of oppression. If the impulse and the opportunity be suffered to coincide, we well know that neither moral nor religious motives can be relied on as an adequate control. They are not found to be such on the injustice and violence of individuals, and lose their efficacy in proportion to the number combined together; that is, in proportion as their efficacy becomes needful.

From this view of the subject, it may be concluded, that a pure Democracy, by which I mean, a Society, consisting of a small number of citizens, who assemble and administer the Government in person, can admit of no cure for the mischiefs of faction. A common passion or interest will, in almost every case, be felt by a majority of the whole; a communication and concert results from the form of Government itself; and there is nothing to check the inducements to sacrifice the weaker party, or an obnoxious individual. Hence it is, that such Democracies have ever been spectacles of turbulence and contention; have ever been found incompatible with personal security, or the rights of property; and have in general been as short in their lives, as they have been violent in their deaths. Theoretic politicians, who have patronized this species of Government, have erroneously supposed, that by reducing mankind to a perfect equality in their political rights, they would, at the same time, be perfectly equalized and assimilated in their possessions, their opinions, and their passions.

A republic, by which I mean a government in which the scheme of representation takes place, opens a different prospect, and promises the cure for which we are seeking. Let us examine the points in which it varies from pure democracy, and we shall comprehend both the nature of the cure and the efficacy which it must derive from the union.

The two great points of difference, between a democracy and a republic, are, first, the delegation of the government, in the latter, to a small number of citizens, elected by the rest; secondly, the greater number of citizens, and greater sphere of country, over which the latter may be extended.

The effect of the first difference is, on the one hand, to refine and enlarge the public views, by passing them through the medium of a chosen body of citizens, whose wisdom may best discern the true interest of their country, and whose patriotism and love of justice, will be least likely to sacrifice it to temporary or partial considerations. Under such a regulation, it may well happen, that the public voice, pronounced by the representatives of the people, will be more consonant to the public good, than if pronounced by the people themselves, convened for the purpose. On the other hand the effect may be inverted. Men of factious tempers, of local prejudices, or of sinister designs, may by intrigue, by corruption, or by other means, first obtain the suffrages, and then betray the interest of the people. The question resulting is, whether small or extensive republics are most favorable to the election of proper guardians of the public weal, and it is clearly decided in favor of the latter by two obvious considerations.

In the first place, it is to be remarked that, however small the republic may be, the representatives must be raised to a certain number, in order to guard against the cabals of a few; and that however large it may be, they must be limited to a certain number, in order to guard against the confusion of a multitude. Hence, the number of representatives in the two cases not being in proportion to that of the constituents, and being proportionally greatest in the small republic, it follows, that if the proportion of fit characters be not less in the large than in the small republic, the former will present a greater option, and consequently a greater probability of a fit choice.

In the next place, as each Representative will be chosen by a greater number of citizens in the large than in the small Republic, it will be more difficult for unworthy candidates to practise with success the vicious arts, by which elections are too often carried; and the suffrages of the people being more free, will be more likely to center on men who possess the most attractive merit, and the most diffusive and established characters.

It must be confessed, that in this, as in most other cases, there is a mean, on both sides of which inconveniences will be found to lie. By enlarging too much the number of electors, you render the representatives too little acquainted with all their local circumstances and lesser interests; as by reducing it too much, you render him unduly attached to these, and too little fit to comprehend and pursue great and national objects. The Federal Constitution forms a happy combination in this respect; the great and aggregate interests being referred to the national, the local and particular, to the state legislatures.

The other point of difference is, the greater number of citizens and extent of territory which may be brought within the compass of Republican, than of Democratic Government; and it is this circumstance principally which renders factious combinations less to be dreaded in the former, than in the latter. The smaller the society, the fewer probably will be the distinct parties and interests composing it; the fewer the distinct parties and interests, the more frequently will a majority be found of the same party; and the smaller the number of individuals composing a majority, and the smaller the compass within which they are placed, the more easily they will concert and execute their plans of oppression. Extend the sphere, and you take in a greater variety of parties and interests; you make it less probable that a majority of the whole will have a common motive to invade the rights of other citizens; or if such a common motive exists, it will be more difficult for all who feel it to discover their own strength, and to act in unison with each other. Besides other impediments, it may be remarked, that where there is a consciousness of unjust or dishonorable purposes, communication is always checked by distrust, in proportion to the number whose concurrence is necessary.

Hence it clearly appears, that the same advantage, which a Republic has over a Democracy, in controlling the effects of factions, is enjoyed by a large over a small Republic—is enjoyed by the Union over the States composing it. Does this advantage consist in the substitution of Representatives, whose enlightened views and virtuous sentiments render them superior to local prejudices, and to schemes of injustice? It will not be denied, that the Representation of the Union will be most likely to possess these requisite endowments. Does it consist in the greater security afforded by a greater variety of parties, against the event of any one party being able to outnumber and oppress the rest? In an equal degree does the increase variety of parties, comprised within the Union, increase this security? Does it, in fine, consist in the greater obstacles opposed to the concert and accomplishment of the secret wishes of an unjust and interested majority? Here, again, the extent of the Union gives it the most palpable advantage.

The influence of factious leaders may kindle a flame within their particular States, but will be unable to spread a general conflagration through the other States: a religious sect, may degenerate into a political faction in a part of the Confederacy but the variety of sects dispersed over the entire face of it, must secure the national Councils against any danger from that source: a rage for paper money, for an abolition of debts, for an equal division of property, or for any other improper or wicked project, will be less apt to pervade the whole body of the Union, than a particular member of it; in the same proportion as such a malady is more likely to taint a particular county or district, than an entire State.

In the extent and proper structure of the Union, therefore, we behold a Republican remedy for the diseases most incident to Republican Government. And according to the degree of pleasure and pride, we feel in being Republicans, ought to be our zeal in cherishing the spirit, and supporting the character of Federalists.

PUBLIUS

THE FEDERALIST NO. 51

February 6, 1788

James Madison

TO THE PEOPLE OF THE STATE OF NEW YORK.

To what expedient then shall we finally resort for maintaining in practice the necessary partition of power among the several departments, as laid down in the constitution? The only answer that can be given is, that as all these exterior provisions are found to be inadequate, the defect must be supplied, by so contriving the interior structure of the government, as that its several constituent parts may, by their mutual relations, be the means of keeping each other in their proper places. Without presuming to undertake a full development of this important idea, I will hazard a few general observations, which may perhaps place it in a clearer light, and enable us to form a more correct judgment of the principles and structure of the government planned by the convention.

In order to lay a due foundation for that separate and distinct exercise of the different powers of government, which to a certain extent, is admitted on all hands to be essential to the preservation of liberty, it is evident that each department should have a will of its own; and consequently should be so constituted, that the members of each should have as little agency as possible in the appointment of the members of the others. Were this principle rigorously adhered to, it would require that all the appointments for the supreme executive, legislative, and judiciary magistracies, should be drawn from the same fountain of authority, the people, through channels, having no communication whatever with one another. Perhaps such a plan of constructing the several departments would be less difficult in practice than in it may in contemplation appear. Some difficulties however, and some additional expense, would attend the execution of it. Some deviations therefore from the principle must be admitted. In the constitution of the judiciary department in particular, it might be inexpedient to insist rigorously on the principle; first, because peculiar qualifications being essential in the members, the primary consideration ought to be to select that mode of choice, which best secures these qualifications; secondly, because the permanent tenure by which the appointments are held in that department, must soon destroy all sense of dependence on the authority conferring them.

It is equally evident that the members of each department should be as little dependent as possible on those of the others, for the emoluments annexed to their offices. Were the executive magistrate, or the judges, not independent of the legislature in this particular, their independence in every other would be merely nominal.

But the great security against a gradual concentration of the several powers in the same department, consists in giving to those who administer each department, the necessary constitutional means, and personal motives, to resist encroachments of the others. The provision for defense must in this, as in all other cases, be made commensurate to the danger of attack. Ambition must be made to counteract ambition. The interest of the man must be connected with the constitutional right of the place. It may be a reflection on human nature, that such devices should be necessary to control the abuses of government. But what is government itself but the greatest of all reflections on human nature? If men were angels, no government would be necessary. If angels were to govern men, neither external nor internal controls on government would be necessary. In framing a government which is to be administered by men over men, the great difficulty lies in this: You must first enable the government to control the governed; and in the next place, oblige it to control itself. A dependence on the people is no doubt the primary control on the government; but experience has taught mankind the necessity of auxiliary precautions.

This policy of supplying by opposite and rival interests, the defect of better motives, might be traced through the whole system of human affairs, private as well as public. We see it particularly displayed in all the subordinate distributions of power; where the constant aim is to divide and arrange the several offices in such a manner as that each may be a check on the other; that the private interest of every individual, may be a sentinel over the public rights. These inventions of prudence cannot be less requisite in the distribution of the supreme powers of the state.

But it is not possible to give each department an equal power of self defense. In republican government the legislative authority, necessarily, predominates. The remedy for this inconvenience is, to divide the legislative into different branches; and to render them by different modes of election, and different principles of action, as little connected with each other, as the nature of their common functions, and their common dependence on the society, will admit. It may even be necessary to guard against dangerous encroachments by still further precautions. As the weight of the legislative authority requires that it should be thus divided, the weakness of the executive may require, on the other hand, that it should be fortified. An absolute negative, on the legislature, appears at first view to be the natural defense with which the executive magistrate should be armed. But perhaps it would be neither altogether safe, nor alone sufficient. On ordinary occasions, it might not be exerted with the requisite firmness, and on extraordinary occasions, it might be prefidiously abused. May not this defect of an absolute negative be supplied, by some qualified connection between this weaker department, and the weaker branch of the stronger department, by which the latter may be led to support the constitutional rights of the former, without being too much detached from the rights of its own department?

If the principles on which these observations are founded be just, as I persuade myself they are, and they be applied as a criterion, to the several state constitutions, and to the federal constitution, it will be found, that if the latter does not perfectly correspond with them, the former are infinitely less able to bear such a test.

There are moreover two considerations particularly applicable to the federal system of America, which place the system in a very interesting point of view.

First. In a single republic, all the power surrendered by the people, is submitted to the administration of a single government; and usurpations are guarded against by a division of the government into distinct and separate departments. In the compound republic of America, the power surrendered by the people, is first divided between two distinct governments, and then the portion allotted to each, subdivided among distinct and separate departments. Hence a double security arises to the rights of the people. The different governments will control each other; at the same time that each will be controlled by itself.

Second. It is of great importance in a republic, not only to guard the society against the oppression of its rulers; but to guard one part of the society against the injustice of the other part. Different interests necessarily exist in different classes of citizens. If a majority be united by a common interest, the rights of the minority will be insecure. There are but two methods of providing against this evil: The one by creating a will in the community independent of the majority, that is, of the society itself, the other by comprehending in the society so many separate descriptions of citizens, as will render an unjust combination of a majority of the whole, very improbable, if not impracticable. The first method prevails in all governments possessing an hereditary or self appointed authority. This at best is but a precarious security; because a power independent of the society may as well espouse the unjust views of the major, as the rightful interests, of the minor party, and may possibly be turned against both parties. The second method will be exemplified in the federal republic of the United States. While all authority in it will be derived from and dependent on the society, the society itself will be broken into so many parts, interests and classes of citizens, that the rights of individuals or of the minority, will be in little danger from interested combinations of the majority. In a free government, the security for civil rights must be the same as for religious rights. It consists in the one case in the multiplicity of interests, and in the other, in the multiplicity of sects. The degree of security in both cases will depend on the number of interests and sects; and this may be presumed to depend on the extent of country and number of people comprehended under the same government. This view of the subject must particularly recommend a proper federal system to all the sincere and considerate friends of republican government: Since it shows that in exact proportion as the territory of the union may be formed into more circumscribed confederacies or states, oppressive combinations of a majority will be facilitated, the best security under the republican form, for the rights of every class of citizens, will be diminished; and consequently, the stability and independence of some member of the government, the only other security, must be proportionally increased. Justice is the end of government. It is the end of civil society. It ever has been, and ever will be pursued, until it be obtained, or until liberty be lost in the pursuit. In a society under the forms of which the stronger faction can readily unite and oppress the weaker, anarchy may as truly be said to reign, as in a state of nature where the weaker individual is not secured against the violence of the stronger: And as in the latter state even the stronger individuals are prompted by the uncertainty of their condition, to submit to a government which may protect the weak as well as themselves: So in the former state, will the more powerful factions or parties be gradually induced by a like motive, to wish for a government which will protect all parties, the weaker as well as the more powerful. It can be little doubted, that if the state of Rhode Island was separated from the confederacy, and left to itself, the insecurity of rights under the popular form of government within such narrow limits, would be displayed by such reiterated oppressions of factious majorities, that some power altogether independent of the people would soon be called for by the voice of the very factions whose misrule had proved the necessity of it. In the extended republic of the United States, and among the great variety of interests, parties and sects which it embraces, a coalition of a majority of the whole society could seldom take place on any other principles than those of justice and the general good; and there being thus less danger to a minor from the will of the major party, there must be less pretext also, to provide for the security of the former, by introducing into the government a will not dependent on the latter; or in other words, a will independent of the society itself. It is no less certain than it is important, notwithstanding the contrary opinions which have been entertained, that the larger the society, provided it lie within a practicable sphere, the more duly capable it will be of self government. And happily for the *republican cause*, the practicable sphere may be carried to a very great extent, by a judicious modification and mixture of the *federal principle.*

PUBLIUS

PRESIDENTS AND CONGRESSES, 1789–2000

Year	President and vice president	Party of president	Congress	House Majority party	House Minority party	Senate Majority party	Senate Minority party
1789–1797	**George Washington** John Adams	None	1st 2d 3d 4th	38 Admin 37 Fed 57 Dem-Rep 54 Fed	26 Opp 33 Dem-Rep 48 Fed 52 Dem-Rep	17 Admin 16 Fed 17 Fed 19 Fed	9 Opp 13 Dem-Rep 13 Dem-Rep 13 Dem-Rep
1797–1801	**John Adams** Thomas Jefferson	Federalist	5th 6th	58 Fed 64 Fed	48 Dem-Rep 42 Dem-Rep	20 Fed 19 Fed	12 Dem-Rep 13 Dem-Rep
1801–1809	**Thomas Jefferson** Aaron Burr (to 1805) George Clinton (to 1809)	Dem-Rep	7th 8th 9th 10th	69 Dem-Rep 102 Dem-Rep 116 Dem-Rep 118 Dem-Rep	36 Fed 39 Fed 25 Fed 24 Fed	18 Dem-Rep 25 Dem-Rep 27 Dem-Rep 28 Dem-Rep	13 Fed 9 Fed 7 Fed 6 Fed
1809–1817	**James Madison** George Clinton (to 1813) Elbridge Gerry (to 1817)	Dem-Rep	11th 12th 13th 14th	94 Dem-Rep 108 Dem-Rep 112 Dem-Rep 117 Dem-Rep	48 Fed 36 Fed 68 Fed 65 Fed	28 Dem-Rep 30 Dem-Rep 27 Dem-Rep 25 Dem-Rep	6 Fed 6 Fed 9 Fed 11 Fed
1817–1825	**James Monroe** Daniel D. Tompkins	Dem-Rep	15th 16th 17th 18th	141 Dem-Rep 156 Dem-Rep 158 Dem-Rep 187 Dem-Rep	42 Fed 27 Fed 25 Fed 26 Fed	34 Dem-Rep 35 Dem-Rep 44 Dem-Rep 44 Dem-Rep	10 Fed 7 Fed 4 Fed 4 Fed
1825–1829	**John Quincy Adams** John C. Calhoun	Nat-Rep	19th 20th	105 Admin 119 Jack	97 Jack 94 Admin	26 Admin 28 Jack	20 Jack 20 Admin
1829–1837	**Andrew Jackson** John C. Calhoun (to 1833) Martin Van Buren (to 1837)	Democrat	21st 22d 23d 24th	139 Dem 141 Dem 147 Dem 145 Dem	74 Nat Rep 58 Nat Rep 53 AntiMas 98 Whig	26 Dem 25 Dem 20 Dem 27 Dem	22 Nat Rep 21 Nat Rep 20 Nat Rep 25 Whig
1837–1841	**Martin Van Buren** Richard M. Johnson	Democrat	25th 26th	108 Dem 124 Dem	107 Whig 118 Whig	30 Dem 28 Dem	18 Whig 22 Whig
1841	**William H. Harrison*** John Tyler	Whig					
1841–1845	**John Tyler** (VP vacant)	Whig	27th 28th	133 Whig 142 Dem	102 Dem 79 Whig	28 Whig 28 Whig	22 Dem 25 Dem
1845–1849	**James K. Polk** George M. Dallas	Democrat	29th 30th	143 Dem 115 Whig	77 Whig 108 Dem	31 Dem 36 Dem	25 Whig 21 Whig
1849–1850	**Zachary Taylor*** Millard Fillmore	Whig	31st	112 Dem	109 Whig	35 Dem	25 Whig
1850–1853	**Millard Fillmore** (VP vacant)	Whig	32d	140 Dem	88 Whig	35 Dem	24 Whig
1853–1857	**Franklin Pierce** William R. King	Democrat	33d 34th	159 Dem 108 Rep	71 Whig 83 Dem	38 Dem 40 Dem	22 Whig 15 Rep

NOTES: Only members of two major parties in Congress are shown; omitted are independents, members of minor parties, and vacancies.

Party balance as of beginning of Congress.

Congresses in which one or both houses are controlled by party other than that of the president are shown in color.

During administration of George Washington and (in part) John Quincy Adams, Congress was not organized by formal parties; the split shown is between supporters and opponents of the administration.

ABBREVIATIONS: **Admin** = Administration supporters; **AntiMas** = Anti-Masonic; **Dem** = Democratic; **Dem-Rep** = Democratic-Republican; **Fed** = Federalist; **Jack** = Jacksonian Democrats; **Nat Rep** = National Republican; **Opp** = Opponents of administration; **Rep** = Republican; **Union** = Unionist; **Whig** = Whig.

* Died in office.

Year	President and vice president	Party of president	Congress	House		Senate	
				Majority party	Minority party	Majority party	Minority party
1857–1861	**James Buchanan**	Democrat	35th	118 Dem	92 Rep	36 Dem	20 Rep
	John C. Breckinridge		36th	114 Rep	92 Dem	36 Dem	26 Rep
1861–1865	**Abraham Lincoln***	Republican	37th	105 Rep	43 Dem	31 Rep	10 Dem
	Hannibal Hamlin (to 1865)		38th	102 Rep	75 Dem	36 Rep	9 Dem
	Andrew Johnson (1865)						
1865–1869	**Andrew Johnson**	Republican	39th	149 Union	42 Dem	42 Union	10 Dem
	(VP vacant)		40th	143 Rep	49 Dem	42 Rep	11 Dem
1869–1877	**Ulysses S. Grant**	Republican	41st	149 Rep	63 Dem	56 Rep	11 Dem
	Schuyler Colfax (to 1873)		42d	134 Rep	104 Dem	52 Rep	17 Dem
	Henry Wilson (to 1877)		43d	194 Rep	92 Dem	49 Rep	19 Dem
			44th	169 Dem	109 Rep	45 Rep	29 Dem
1877–1881	**Rutherford B. Hayes**	Republican	45th	153 Dem	140 Rep	39 Rep	36 Dem
	William A. Wheeler		46th	149 Dem	130 Rep	42 Dem	33 Rep
1881	**James A. Garfield***	Republican	47th	147 Rep	135 Dem	37 Rep	37 Dem
	Chester A. Arthur						
1881–1885	**Chester A. Arthur**	Republican	48th	197 Dem	118 Rep	38 Rep	36 Dem
	(VP vacant)						
1885–1889	**Grover Cleveland**	Democrat	49th	183 Dem	140 Rep	43 Rep	34 Dem
	Thomas A. Hendricks		50th	169 Dem	152 Rep	39 Rep	37 Dem
1889–1893	**Benjamin Harrison**	Republican	51st	166 Rep	159 Dem	39 Rep	37 Dem
	Levi P. Morton		52d	235 Dem	88 Rep	47 Rep	39 Dem
1893–1897	**Grover Cleveland**	Democrat	53d	218 Dem	127 Rep	44 Dem	38 Rep
	Adlai E. Stevenson		54th	244 Rep	105 Dem	43 Rep	39 Dem
1897–1901	**William McKinley***	Republican	55th	204 Rep	113 Dem	47 Rep	34 Dem
	Garret A. Hobart (to 1901)		56th	185 Rep	163 Dem	53 Rep	26 Dem
	Theodore Roosevelt (1901)						
1901–1909	**Theodore Roosevelt**	Republican	57th	197 Rep	151 Dem	55 Rep	31 Dem
	(VP vacant, 1901–1905)		58th	208 Rep	178 Dem	57 Rep	33 Dem
	Charles W. Fairbanks		59th	250 Rep	136 Dem	57 Rep	33 Dem
	(1905–1909)		60th	222 Rep	164 Dem	61 Rep	31 Dem
1909–1913	**William Howard Taft**	Republican	61st	219 Rep	172 Dem	61 Rep	32 Dem
	James S. Sherman		62d	228 Dem	161 Rep	51 Rep	41 Dem
1913–1921	**Woodrow Wilson**	Democrat	63d	291 Dem	127 Rep	51 Dem	44 Rep
	Thomas R. Marshall		64th	230 Dem	196 Rep	56 Dem	40 Rep
			65th	216 Dem	210 Rep	53 Dem	42 Rep
			66th	240 Rep	190 Dem	49 Rep	47 Dem
1921–1923	**Warren G. Harding***	Republican	67th	301 Rep	131 Dem	59 Rep	37 Dem
	Calvin Coolidge						
1923–1929	**Calvin Coolidge**	Republican	68th	225 Rep	205 Dem	51 Rep	43 Dem
	(VP vacant, 1923–1925)		69th	247 Rep	183 Dem	56 Rep	39 Dem
	Charles G. Dawes		70th	237 Rep	195 Dem	49 Rep	46 Dem
	(1925–1929)						
1929–1933	**Herbert Hoover**	Republican	71st	267 Rep	167 Dem	56 Rep	39 Dem
	Charles Curtis		72d	220 Dem	214 Rep	48 Rep	47 Dem
1933–1945	**Franklin D. Roosevelt***	Democrat	73d	310 Dem	117 Rep	60 Dem	35 Rep
	John N. Garner		74th	319 Dem	103 Rep	69 Dem	25 Rep
	(1933–1941)		75th	331 Dem	89 Rep	76 Dem	16 Rep
	Henry A. Wallace		76th	261 Dem	164 Rep	69 Dem	23 Rep
	(1941–1945)		77th	268 Dem	162 Rep	66 Dem	28 Rep
	Harry S Truman (1945)		78th	218 Dem	208 Rep	58 Dem	37 Rep
1945–1953	**Harry S Truman**	Democrat	79th	242 Dem	190 Rep	56 Dem	38 Rep
	(VP vacant, 1945–1949)		80th	245 Rep	188 Dem	51 Rep	45 Dem
	Alben W. Barkley		81st	263 Dem	171 Rep	54 Dem	42 Rep
	(1949–1953)		82d	234 Dem	199 Rep	49 Dem	47 Rep

* Died in office.

Year	President and vice president	Party of president	Congress	House Majority party	House Minority party	Senate Majority party	Senate Minority party
1953–1961	**Dwight D. Eisenhower** Richard M. Nixon	Republican	83d 84th 85th 86th	221 Rep 232 Dem 233 Dem 283 Dem	211 Dem 203 Rep 200 Rep 153 Rep	48 Rep 48 Dem 49 Dem 64 Dem	47 Dem 47 Rep 47 Rep 34 Rep
1961–1963	**John F. Kennedy*** Lyndon B. Johnson	Democrat	87th	263 Dem	174 Rep	65 Dem	35 Rep
1963–1969	**Lyndon B. Johnson** (VP vacant, 1963–1965) Hubert H. Humphrey (1965–1969)	Democrat	88th 89th 90th	258 Dem 295 Dem 247 Dem	177 Rep 140 Rep 187 Rep	67 Dem 68 Dem 64 Dem	33 Rep 32 Rep 36 Rep
1969–1974	**Richard M. Nixon†** Spiro T. Agnew†† Gerald R. Ford§	Republican	91st 92d	243 Dem 254 Dem	192 Rep 180 Rep	57 Dem 54 Dem	43 Rep 44 Rep
1974–1977	**Gerald R. Ford** Nelson A. Rockefeller§	Republican	93d 94th	239 Dem 291 Dem	192 Rep 144 Rep	56 Dem 60 Dem	42 Rep 37 Rep
1977–1981	**Jimmy Carter** Walter Mondale	Democrat	95th 96th	292 Dem 276 Dem	143 Rep 157 Rep	61 Dem 58 Dem	38 Rep 41 Rep
1981–1989	**Ronald Reagan** George Bush	Republican	97th 98th 99th 100th	243 Dem 269 Dem 253 Dem 257 Dem	192 Rep 165 Rep 182 Rep 178 Rep	53 Rep 54 Rep 53 Rep 54 Dem	46 Dem 46 Dem 47 Dem 46 Rep
1989–1993	**George Bush** Dan Quayle	Republican	101st 102d	262 Dem 267 Dem	173 Rep 167 Rep	55 Dem 56 Dem	45 Rep 44 Rep
1993–2000	**Bill Clinton** Albert Gore, Jr.	Democrat	103d 104th 105th 106th	258 Dem 230 Rep 228 Rep 223 Rep	176 Rep 204 Dem 206 Dem 211 Dem	57 Dem 53 Rep 55 Rep 54 Rep	43 Rep 47 Dem 45 Dem 46 Dem
2000	**George W. Bush** Dick Cheney	Republican	107th 108th	220 Rep 229 Rep	215 Dem 204 Dem	50 Rep 51 Rep	50 Dem 48 Dem

*Died in office.   †Resigned from the presidency.   ††Resigned from the vice presidency.   §Appointed vice president.

GLOSSARY

Acid rain   Precipitation in the form of rain, snow, or dust particles, the increased acidity of which is caused by environmental factors such as pollutants released into the atmosphere. (21)

Activist approach   The view that judges should discern the general principles underlying the Constitution and its often vague language and assess how best to apply them in contemporary circumstances, in some cases with the guidance of moral or economic philosophy. (14)

Activists   Individuals, usually outside of government, who actively promote a political party, philosophy, or issue they care about. (6)

Ad hoc structure   A method of organizing a president's staff in which several task forces, committees, and informal groups of friends and advisers deal directly with the president. (12)

Adversarial press   A national press that is suspicious of officialdom and eager to break an embarrassing story about a public official. (10)

Affirmative action   The requirement, imposed by law or administrative regulation, that an organization (business firm, government agency, labor union, school, or college) take positive steps to increase the number or proportion of women, African Americans, or other minorities in its membership. (19)

Amendments   Changes in, or additions to, the U.S. Constitution. Amendments are proposed by a two-thirds vote of both houses of Congress or by a convention called by Congress at the request of two-thirds of the state legislatures and ratified by approval of three-fourths of the states. (2)

Amicus curiae   A Latin term meaning "a friend of the court." Refers to interested groups or individuals, not directly involved in a suit, who may file legal briefs or make oral arguments in support of one side. (14)

Annual authorizations   *See* Authorization legislation (13)

Antifederalists   Opponents of a strong central government who campaigned against ratification of the Constitution in favor of a confederation of largely independent states. Antifederalists successfully marshaled public support for a federal bill of rights. After ratification, they formed a political party to support states' rights. *See also* Federalists (2)

Appropriation   A legislative grant of money to finance a government program. *See also* Authorization legislation (13)

Articles of Confederation   A constitution drafted by the newly independent states in 1777 and ratified in 1781. It created a weak national government that could not levy taxes or regulate commerce. In 1789 it was replaced by our current Constitution in order to create a stronger national government. (2)

Assistance program   A government program financed by general income taxes that provides benefits to poor citizens without requiring contributions from them. (17)

Australian ballot   A government-printed ballot of uniform size and shape to be cast in secret that was adopted by many states around 1890 in order to reduce the voting fraud associated with party-printed ballots cast in public. (6)

Authority   The right to use power. (1)

Authorization legislation   Legislative permission to begin or continue a government program or agency. An authorization bill may grant permission to spend a certain sum of money, but that money does not ordinarily become available unless it is also appropriated. Authorizations may be annual, multiyear, or permanent. *See also* Appropriation (13)

Background story (news)   A public official's explanation of current policy provided to the press on the condition that the source remain anonymous. (10)

Benefit   Any satisfaction, monetary or nonmonetary, that people believe they will enjoy if a policy is adopted. *See also* Cost (15)

Bicameral legislature   A lawmaking body made up of two chambers or parts. The U.S. Congress is a bicameral legislature composed of the Senate and the House of Representatives. (11)

Bill of attainder   A law that declares a person, without a trial, to be guilty of a crime. The state legislatures and Congress are forbidden to pass such acts by Article I of the Constitution. (2)

Bill of rights   A list of individual rights and liberties, such as freedom of speech, religion, and the press. (2)

Blanket primary   A primary election that permits all voters, regardless of party, to choose candidates. A Democratic voter, for example, can vote in a blanket primary for both Democratic and Republican candidates for nomination. (8)

Block grants   Grants of money from the federal government to states for programs in certain general areas rather than for specific kinds of programs. *See also* Grants-in-aid; Categorical grants (3)

Boycott   A concerted effort to get people to stop buying goods and services from a company or person in order to punish that company or to coerce its owner into changing policies. (15)

Brief   A legal document prepared by an attorney representing a party before a court. The document sets forth the facts of the case, summarizes the law, gives the arguments for its side, and discusses other relevant cases. (14)

Bubble standard   The total amount of air pollution that can come from a given factory. A company is free to decide which specific sources within that factory must be reduced and how to meet the bubble standard. (21)

Budget   A document that announces how much the government will collect in taxes and spend in revenues and how those expenditures will be allocated among various programs. (16)

Budget deficit   A situation in which the government spends more money than it takes in from taxes and fees. (16)

Budget resolution   A proposal submitted by the House and Senate budget committees to their respective chambers recommending a total budget ceiling and a ceiling for each of several spending areas (such as health or defense) for the current fiscal year. These budget resolutions are intended to guide the work of each legislative committee as it decides what to spend in its area. (16)

Budget surplus   A situation in which the government takes in more money than it spends. (16)

Bureaucracy   A large, complex organization composed of appointed officials. The department and agencies of the U.S. government make up the federal bureaucracy. (13)

Bureaucrats   The appointed officials who operate government agencies from day to day. (1)

Cabinet   By custom, the cabinet includes the heads of the fourteen major executive departments. (12)

Categorical grants   Federal grants for specific purposes defined by federal law: to build an airport, for example, or to make welfare payments to low-income mothers. Such grants usually require that the state or locality put up money to "match" some part of the federal grants, though the amount of matching funds can be quite small. *See also* Grants-in-aid; Block grants (3)

Caucus (congressional)   An association of members of Congress created to advocate a political ideology or a regional, ethnic, or economic interest. (7, 11)

Checks and balances   The power of the legislature, executive, and judicial branches of government to block some acts by the other two branches. *See also* Separation of powers (2)

Christmas tree bill   *See* Rider (11)

Circular structure   A method of organizing a president's staff in which several presidential assistants report directly to the president. (12)

City   A municipal corporation or municipality that has been chartered by a state to exercise certain defined powers and provide certain specific services. (3)

Civic competence   A belief that one can affect government policies. (4)

Civic duty   A belief that one has an obligation to participate in civic and political affairs. (4)

Civil law   The body of rules defining relationships among private citizens. It consists of both statutes and the accumulated customary law embodied in judicial decisions (the "common law"). *See also* Criminal law (14)

Civil rights   The rights of citizens to vote, to receive equal treatment before the law, and to share equally with other citizens the benefits of public facilities (such as schools). (19)

Class-action suit   A case brought into court by a person on behalf of not only himself or herself but all other persons in the country under similar circumstances. For example, in *Brown v. Board of Education of Topeka, Kansas*, the Supreme Court decided that not only Linda Brown but all others similarly situated had the right to attend a local public school of their choice without regard to race. (14)

Class consciousness   An awareness of belonging to a particular socioeconomic class whose interests are different from those of others. Usually used in reference to workers who view their interests as opposite those of managers and business owners. (4)

Clear-and-present-danger test   A legal interpretation that reconciled two views of the First Amendment right of free speech, the first that Congress could not pass any law to restrict speech and the second that it could punish harms caused by speech. Proposed by Supreme Court justice Oliver Wendell Holmes in 1919, it held that Congress could punish only speech that created a "clear and present danger" of bringing about the actions that Congress is authorized to prevent. (18)

Client politics   The politics of policy-making in which some small group receives the benefits of the policy and the public at large bears the costs. Only those who benefit have an incentive to organize and press their case. (15, 17)

Closed primary   A primary election limited to registered party members. Prevents members of other parties from crossing over to influence the nomination of an opposing party's candidate. *See also* Open primary; Primary election (8)

Closed rule   An order from the House Rules Committee that sets a time limit on debate and forbids a particular bill from being amended on the legislative floor. *See also* Open rule; Restrictive rule (11)

Cloture rule   A rule used by the Senate to end or limit debate. Designed to prevent "talking a bill to death" by filibuster. For a bill to pass in the Senate, three-fifths of the entire Senate membership (or sixty senators) must vote for it. *See also* Filibuster (11)

Coalition   An alliance among different interest groups (factions) or parties to achieve some political goal. An example is the coalition sometimes formed between Republicans and conservative Democrats. (2)

Coattails   The tendency of lesser-known or weaker candidates to profit in an election by the presence on the ticket of a more popular candidate. (8)

Cold war   Refers to the nonmilitary struggle between the United States (and its allies) and the former Soviet Union (and its allies) following World War II. (A cold war is distinguished from a *hot or shooting war*.) (20)

Command-and-control strategy   A strategy to improve air and water quality, involving the setting of detailed pollution standards and rules. (21)

Committee clearance   The ability of a congressional committee to review and approve certain agency decisions in advance and without passing a law. Such approval is not legally binding on the agency, but few agency heads will ignore the expressed wishes of committees. (13)

Compensatory action   An action designed to help members of disadvantaged groups, especially minorities and women, catch up, usually by giving them extra education, training, or services. (19)

Competitive service   The government offices to which people are appointed on the grounds of merit as ascertained by a written examination or by having met certain selection criteria (such as training, educational attainments, or prior experience). (13)

Concurrent resolution   An expression of congressional opinion without the force of law that requires the approval of both the House and Senate but not of the president. Used to settle housekeeping and procedural matters that affect both houses. *See also* Simple resolution; Joint resolution (11)

Concurring opinion   A Supreme Court opinion by one or more justices who agree with the majority's conclusion but for different reasons. *See also* Opinion of the Court; Dissenting opinion (14)

Conditions of aid   Federal rules attached to the grants that states receive. States must agree to abide by these rules in order to receive the grants. (3)

Confederation or confederal system   A political system in which states or regional governments retain ultimate authority except for those powers that they expressly delegate to a central government. The United States was a confederation from

1776 to 1787 under the Articles of Confederation. *See also* Federalism; Unitary system (3)

Conference committee   *See* Joint committees (11)

Congressional campaign committee   A party committee in Congress that provides funds to members who are running for reelection or to would-be members running for an open seat or challenging a candidate from the opposition party. (7)

Conservative   In general a person who favors more limited and local government, less government regulation of markets, more social conformity to traditional norms and values, and tougher policies toward criminals. *See also* Liberal (5)

Conservative coalition   An alliance between Republicans and conservative Democrats. (11)

Constitutional Convention   A meeting of delegates in 1787 to revise the Articles of Confederation, which produced a totally new constitution still in use today. (2)

Constitutional court   A federal court exercising the judicial powers found in Article III of the Constitution and whose judges are given constitutional protection: they may not be fired (they serve during "good behavior"), nor may their salaries be reduced while they are in office. The most important constitutional courts are the Supreme Court, the ninety-four district courts, and the courts of appeals (one in each of eleven regions plus one in the District of Columbia). *See also* District courts; Courts of appeals; Federal-question cases (14)

Containment (or antiappeasment)   The view that the United States should contain aggressive nations (such as the former Soviet Union). *See also* Isolationism (20)

Cost   Any burden, monetary or nonmonetary, that some people must bear, or think that they must bear, if a policy is adopted. *See also* Benefit (15)

Cost overruns   Actual costs that are several times greater than estimated costs. These occur frequently among private contractors producing new weapons for the Pentagon. (20)

County   The largest territorial unit between a city and a town. (3)

Courts of appeals   The federal courts with authority to review decisions by federal district courts, regulatory commissions, and certain other federal courts. Such courts have no original jurisdiction; they can hear only appeals. There are a total of twelve courts of appeals in the United States and its territories. *See also* Constitutional court; District courts (14)

Criminal law   The body of rules defining offenses that, though they harm an individual (such as murder, rape, and robbery), are considered to be offenses against society as a whole and as a consequence warrant punishment by and in the name of society. *See also* Civil law (14)

Critical or realigning periods   Periods during which a sharp, lasting shift occurs in the popular coalition supporting one or both parties. The issues that separate the two parties change, and so the kinds of voters supporting each party change. (7)

Cue (political)   A signal telling a congressional representative what values (e.g., liberal or conservative) are at stake in a vote—who is for, who against a proposal—and how that issue fits into his or her own set of political beliefs or party agenda. (9)

***De facto* segregation**   Racial segregation in schools that occurs not because of laws or administrative decisions, but as a result of patterns of residential settlement. To the extent that blacks and whites live in separate neighborhoods, neighborhood schools will often be segregated *de facto*. *See also* De jure segregation (19)

***De jure* segregation**   Racial segregation that occurs because of laws or administrative decisions by public agencies. When state laws, for example, required blacks and whites to attend separate schools or sit in separate sections of a bus, *de jure* segregation resulted. *See also* De facto segregation (19)

Delegate model   The view that an elected representative should represent the opinions of his or her constituents. (12)

Democracy   A term used to describe a political system in which the people are said to rule, directly or indirectly. *See also* Direct or participatory democracy; Representative democracy (1)

Descriptive representation   A correspondence between the demographic characteristics of representatives and those of their constituents. (11)

Devolution   The current effort to scale back the size and activities of the national government and to shift responsibility for a wide range of domestic programs from Washington to the states. In recent years these areas have included welfare, health care, and job training. (3)

Dillon's rule   A legal principle that holds that the terms of city charters are to be interpreted narrowly. Under this rule (named after a lawyer who wrote a book on the subject in 1911) a municipal corporation can exercise only those powers expressly given it or those powers necessarily implied by, or essential to the accomplishment of, these stated powers. (3)

Direct or participatory democracy   A political system in which all or most citizens participate directly by either holding office or making policy. The town meeting, in which citizens vote on major issues, is an example of participatory democracy. (1, 12)

Discharge petition   A device by which any member of the House, after a committee has had a bill for thirty days, may petition to have it brought to the floor. If a majority of the members agree, the bill is discharged from the committee. The discharge petition was designed to prevent a committee from killing a bill by holding it for too long. (11)

Discretionary authority   The extent to which appointed bureaucrats can choose courses of action and make policies that are not spelled out in advance by laws. (13)

Disengagement   A view that U.S. involvement in Vietnam had led to a military defeat and political disaster and that further similar involvements should be avoided. Also known as "new isolationism." *See also* Isolationism; Containment (20)

Dissenting opinion   A Supreme Court opinion by one or more justices in the minority to explain the minority's disagreement with the Court's ruling. *See also* Opinion of the Court; Concurring opinion (14)

District courts   The lowest federal courts where federal cases begin. They are the only federal courts where trials are held. There are a total of ninety-four district courts in the United States and its territories. *See also* Courts of appeals; Constitutional court; Federal-question cases (14)

Diversity cases   Cases involving citizens of different states over which the federal courts have jurisdiction as described in the Constitution. *See also* Federal-question cases (14)

Divided government   A government in which one party controls the White House and another party controls one or both houses of Congress. *See also* Unified government (12)

Division vote   A congressional voting procedure in which members stand and are counted. *See also* Voice vote; Teller vote; Roll-call vote (11)

Domino theory   An influential theory first articulated by President Eisenhower holding that if an important nation were to fall into communist hands, other neighboring countries would follow suit. Eisenhower used the metaphor of a row of dominoes falling in sequence to illustrate his point. (20)

Double-tracking   A procedure to keep the Senate going during a filibuster in which the disputed bill is shelved temporarily so that the Senate can get on with other business. *See also* Filibuster; Cloture rule (11)

Dual federalism   A constitutional theory that the national government and the state governments each have defined areas of authority, especially over commerce. (3)

Due-process clause   Protection against arbitrary deprivation of life, liberty, or property as guaranteed in the Fifth and Fourteenth Amendments. (18)

Earned Income Tax Credit   A provision of a 1975 tax law that entitles working families with children to receive money from the government if their total income falls below a certain level. (17)

Economic planning   An economic philosophy that assumes that the government should plan, in varying ways, some part of the country's economic activity. For instance, in times of high inflation, it suggests that the government regulate the maximum prices that can be charged and wages that can be paid, at least in the larger industries. Another form of planning, called *industrial policy*, would have the government planning or subsidizing investments in industries that need to recover or in new industries that could replace them. (16)

Elite   An identifiable group of persons who possess a disproportionate share of some valued resource—such as money or political power. (1)

Entitlement   A claim for government funds that cannot be abridged without violating the rights of the claimant; for example, Social Security benefits or payments on a contract. (16)

Entrepreneurial politics   Policies benefiting society as a whole or some large part that impose a substantial cost on some small identifiable segment of society. *See also* Policy entrepreneurs (15)

Environmental impact statement   A report required by federal law that assesses the possible effect of a project on the environment if the project is subsidized in whole or part by federal funds. (21)

Equality of opportunity   A view that it is wrong to use race or sex either to discriminate against or give preferential treatment to minorities or women. *See also* Reverse discrimination (19)

Equal time rule   A rule of the Federal Communications Commission (FCC) stating that if a broadcaster sells time to one candidate for office, he or she must be willing to sell equal time to opposing candidates. (10)

Establishment clause   A clause in the First Amendment to the Constitution stating that Congress shall make no law "respecting an establishment of religion." (18)

Exclusionary rule   A rule that holds that evidence gathered in violation of the Constitution cannot be used in a trial. The rule has been used to implement two provisions of the Bill of Rights—the right to be free from unreasonable searches or seizures (Fourth Amendment) and the right not to be compelled to give evidence against oneself (Fifth Amendment). *See also* Good-faith exception (18)

Ex post facto law   *Ex post facto* is a Latin term meaning "after the fact." A law that makes criminal an act that was legal when it was committed, that increases the penalty for a crime after it has been committed, or that changes the rules of evidence to make conviction easier; a retroactive criminal law. The state legislatures and Congress are forbidden to pass such laws by Article I of the Constitution. (2)

External efficacy   *See* Political efficacy. (4)

Faction   According to James Madison, a group of people who seek to influence public policy in ways contrary to the public good. (2)

Fairness doctrine   A former rule of the Federal Communications Commission (FCC) that required broadcasters to give time to opposing views if they broadcast a program giving one side of a controversial issue. (10)

Feature stories   Media reports about public events knowable to any reporter who cares to inquire, but involving acts and statements not routinely covered by a group of reporters. Thus a reporter must take the initiative and select a particular event as newsworthy, decide to write about it, and persuade an editor to run it. (10)

Federalism   A political system in which ultimate authority is shared between a central government and state or regional governments. *See also* Confederation; Unitary system (2, 3)

Federalist papers   A series of eighty-five essays written by Alexander Hamilton, James Madison, and John Jay (all using the name "Publius") that were published in New York newspapers in 1787–1788 to convince New Yorkers to adopt the newly proposed Constitution. They are classics of American constitutional and political thought. (2)

Federalists   Supporters of a stronger central government who advocated ratification of the Constitution. After ratification they founded a political party supporting a strong executive and Alexander Hamilton's economic policies. *See also* Antifederalists (2)

Federal-question cases   Cases concerning the Constitution, federal law, or treaties over which the federal courts have jurisdiction as described in the Constitution. *See also* Diversity cases (14)

Federal regime   A political system in which local units of government have a specially protected existence and can make final decisions over some governmental activities. (3)

Federal system   A system in which sovereignty is shared so that on some matters the national government is supreme and on others the state, regional, or provincial governments are supreme. (3)

Fee shifting   A law or rule that allows the plaintiff (the party that initiates the lawsuit) to collect its legal costs from the defendant if the defendant loses. *See also* Plaintiff (14)

Filibuster   An attempt to defeat a bill in the Senate by talking indefinitely, thus preventing the Senate from taking action on the bill. (11)

Fiscal policy   An attempt to use taxes and expenditures to affect the economy. (16)

Fiscal year (FY)   The period from October 1 to September 30 for which government appropriations are made and federal books are kept. A fiscal year is named after the year in which it ends—thus "fiscal 1995" (or "FY 95") refers to the twelve-month period ending September 30, 1995. (16)

Franking privilege   The ability of members of Congress to mail letters to their constituents free of charge by substituting their facsimile signature (frank) for postage. (11)

Freedom of expression The constitutional rights of Americans to "freedom of speech, or of the press, or the right of people peaceably to assemble, and to petition the government for a redress of grievances" as outlined in the First Amendment to the Constitution. (18)

Freedom of religion The religious rights of Americans outlined in the First Amendment to the Constitution. The amendment states that "Congress shall make no law respecting an establishment of religion; or abridging the free exercise thereof." (18)

Free-exercise clause A clause in the First Amendment to the Constitution stating that Congress shall make no law prohibiting the "free exercise" of religion. (18)

Gender gap Differences in the political views and voting behavior of men and women. (5)

General-act charter A charter that applies to a number of cities that fall within a certain classification, usually based on city population. Thus in some states all cities with populations over 100,000 are governed on the basis of one charter, while all cities with populations between 50,000 and 99,999 are governed by a different one. *See also* Special-act charter (3)

General election An election used to fill an elective office. *See also* Primary election (8)

Gerrymandering Drawing the boundaries of political districts in bizarre or unusual shapes to make it easy for candidates of the party in power to win elections in those districts. (8)

Gold plating The tendency of Pentagon officials to ask weapons contractors to meet excessively high requirements. (20)

Good-faith exception Admission at a trial of evidence that is gathered in violation of the Constitution if the violation results from a technical or minor error. *See also* Exclusionary rule (18)

Grandfather clause A clause added to registration laws allowing people who did not meet registration requirements to vote if they or their ancestors had voted before 1867 (before African Americans were legally allowed to vote). This was to exempt poor and illiterate whites from registration requirements established to keep former slaves from voting. The Supreme Court declared the practice unconstitutional in 1915. (6)

Grants-in-aid Federal funds provided to states and localities. Grants-in-aid are typically provided for airports, highways, education, and major welfare services. *See also* Categorical grants; Block grants (3)

Great Compromise A compromise at the Constitutional Convention in 1787 that reconciled the interests of small and large states by allowing the former to predominate in the Senate and the latter in the House. Under the agreement each state received two representatives in the Senate, regardless of size, but was allotted representatives on the basis of population in the House. (2)

Home-rule charter A charter that allows the city government to do anything that is not prohibited by the charter or by state law. (3)

Human rights In foreign policy, the view that our government should act to enhance the rights of people living in other countries. (20)

Ideological interest groups Political organizations that attract members by appealing to their political convictions with coherent sets of (usually) controversial principles. (9)

Ideological party A party that values principled stands on issues above all else, including winning. It claims to have a comprehensive view of American society and government radically different from that of the established parties. (7)

Impeachment A formal accusation against a public official by the lower house of a legislative body. Impeachment is merely an accusation and not a conviction. Only two presidents, Andrew Johnson in 1868 and Bill Clinton in 1998, were ever impeached. They were not, however, convicted, for the Senate failed to obtain the necessary two-thirds vote required for conviction. (12)

Incentive A valued benefit obtained by joining a political organization. (9)

Income strategy A policy of giving poor people money to help lift them out of poverty. (17)

Incumbent The person currently in office. (8)

Independent expenditure Spending by political action committees on political matters that is done directly and not by giving money to a candidate or party. (8)

Industrial policy *See* Economic planning (16)

In forma pauperis A procedure whereby a poor person can file and be heard in court as a pauper, free of charge. (14)

Initiative A procedure allowing voters to submit a proposed law to a popular vote by obtaining a required number of signatures. *See also* Referendum (3)

Insider stories Information not usually made public that becomes public because someone with inside knowledge tells a reporter. The reporter may have worked hard to learn these facts, in which case it is called "investigative reporting," or some official may have wanted a story to get out, in which case it is called a "leak." (10)

Insurance program A self-financing government program based on contributions that provide benefits to unemployed or retired persons. (17)

Interest group An organization of people sharing a common interest or goal that seeks to influence the making of public policy. (9)

Interest group politics The politics of policy-making in which one small group bears the costs of the policy and another small group receives the benefits. Each group has an incentive to organize and to press its interest. *See also* Majoritarian politics; Client politics (15)

Internal efficacy *See* Political efficacy (4)

Iron curtain A metaphor first used by Winston Churchill to describe a military and political barrier maintained by the former Soviet Union to prevent free travel and communication between Eastern and Western Europe. (20)

Iron triangle A close relationship between an agency, a congressional committee, and an interest group that often becomes a mutually advantageous alliance. *See also* Issue network; Client politics (13)

Isolationism The view that the United States should withdraw from world affairs, limit foreign aid, and avoid involvement in foreign wars. *See also* Containment (20)

Issue network A network of people in Washington-based interest groups, on congressional staffs, in universities and think tanks, and in the mass media who regularly discuss and advocate public policies—say, health care or auto safety. Such networks are split along political, ideological, and economic lines. (13)

Jim Crow   A slang expression for African Americans that emerged in the 1820s and came to signify the laws and governmental practices designed to segregate blacks from whites, especially in the American South. (19)

John Q. Public   Colloquial term for average citizens and what they want or believe. (5)

Joint committees   Committees on which both representatives and senators serve. An especially important kind of joint committee is the *conference committee*, made up of representatives and senators appointed to resolve differences in the Senate and House versions of the same piece of legislation before final passage. *See also* Standing committees (11)

Joint resolution   A formal expression of congressional opinion that must be approved by both houses of Congress and by the president. Joint resolutions proposing a constitutional amendment need not be signed by the president. *See also* Concurrent resolution; Simple resolution (11)

Judicial review   The power of the courts to declare acts of the legislature and of the executive to be unconstitutional and hence null and void. (2, 14)

Keynesianism   An economic philosophy that assumes that the market will not automatically operate at a full-employment, low-inflation level. It suggests that the government should intervene to create the right level of demand by pumping more money into the economy (when demand is low) and taking it out (when demand is too great). (16)

Laissez-faire   An economic theory that government should not regulate or interfere with commerce. (13)

Lame duck   A politician who is still in office after having lost a reelection bid. (12)

Legislative court   A court that is created by Congress for some specialized purpose and staffed with judges who do not enjoy the protection of Article III of the Constitution. Legislative courts include the Court of Military Appeals and the territorial courts. (14)

Legislative veto   The rejection of a presidential or administrative-agency action by a vote of one or both houses of Congress without the consent of the president. In 1983 the Supreme Court declared the legislative veto to be unconstitutional. (12, 13)

Legitimacy   Political authority conferred by law, public opinion, or constitution. (1)

Libel   A written statement that falsely injures the reputation of another person. (18)

Liberal   In general, a person who favors a more active federal government for regulating business, supporting social welfare, and protecting minority rights, but who prefers less regulation of private social conduct. *See also* Conservative (5)

Libertarians   People who wish to maximize personal liberty on both economic and social issues. They prefer a small, weak government that has little control over either the economy or the personal lives of citizens. (5)

Line-item veto   The power of an executive to veto some provisions in an appropriations bill while approving others. The president does not have the right to exercise a line-item veto and must approve or reject an entire appropriations bill. *See also* Pocket veto; Veto message (2, 12)

Literacy test   A requirement that citizens pass a literacy test in order to register to vote. It was established by many states to prevent former slaves (most of whom were illiterate) from voting. Illiterate whites were allowed to vote by a "grandfather clause" added to the law saying that a person could vote, even though he did not meet the legal requirements, if he or his ancestors voted before 1867. (6)

Litmus test   In chemistry a way of finding out whether a liquid is acid or alkaline. The term is used in politics to mean a test of ideological purity, a way of finding out whether a person is a dyed-in-the-wool liberal or conservative or what his or her views are on a controversial question. (14)

Loaded language   Words that reflect a value judgment, used to persuade the listener without making an argument. For example, if someone likes a politician, he might call him "the esteemed Senator Smith"; if he doesn't like him, he might refer to him as "that right-wing or radical senator." (10)

Lobby   An interest group organized to influence government decisions, especially legislation. To *lobby* is to attempt to influence such decisions. A *lobbyist* is a person attempting to influence government decisions on behalf of the group. (9)

Lobbyist   *See* Lobby (9)

Logrolling   Mutual aid among politicians, whereby one legislator supports another's pet project in return for the latter's support of his. The expression dates from the days when American pioneers needed help from neighbors in moving logs off of land to be farmed. (15)

Majoritarian politics   The politics of policy-making in which almost everybody benefits from a policy and almost everybody pays for it. *See also* Interest group politics; Client politics (15, 17)

Majority leader   The legislative leader elected by party members holding the majority of seats in the House of Representatives or the Senate. *See also* Minority leader (11)

Majority-minority districts   Congressional districts designed to make it easier for citizens of a racial or ethnic minority to elect representatives. (11)

Malapportionment   Drawing the boundaries of political districts so that districts are very unequal in population. (8)

Mandates   Rules imposed by the federal government on the states as conditions for obtaining federal grants or requirements that the states pay the costs of certain nationally defined programs. (3)

Marginal districts   Political districts in which candidates elected to the House of Representatives win in close elections, typically with less than 55 percent of the vote. (11)

Market (television)   An area easily reached by a television signal. There are about two hundred such markets in the country. (10)

Marxists   People who believe that those who control the economic system also control the political one. (1)

Material incentives   Benefits that have monetary value, including money, gifts, services, or discounts received as a result of one's membership in an organization. (9)

McCarthyism   Charges that unfairly or dishonestly tarnish the motives, attack the patriotism, or violate the rights of individuals, especially of political opponents. Refers to the numerous unsubstantiated accusations of communism made against public and private individuals by Senator Joseph McCarthy in the 1950s. (18)

Means test   An income qualification that determines whether one is eligible for benefits under government programs reserved for lower-income groups. (17)

Middle America A phrase coined by Joseph Kraft in a 1968 newspaper column to refer to Americans who have moved out of poverty but are not yet affluent and who cherish traditional middle-class values. (5)

Military-industrial complex An alleged alliance among key military, governmental, and corporate decision-makers involved in weapons procurement and military support systems. The phrase was coined by Dwight D. Eisenhower, who warned Americans about its dangers. (20)

Minority leader The legislative leader elected by party members holding a minority of seats in the House of Representatives or the Senate. *See also* Majority leader (11)

Monetarism An economic philosophy that assumes inflation occurs when there is too much money chasing too few goods. Monetarism suggests that the proper thing for government to do is to have a steady, predictable increase in the money supply at a rate about equal to the growth in the economy's productivity. (16)

Monetary policy An attempt to alter the amount of money in circulation and the price of money (the interest rate) to affect the economy. (16)

Motor-voter law A bill passed by Congress in 1993 to make it easier for Americans to register to vote. The law, which went into effect in 1995, requires states to allow voter registration by mail, when one applies for a driver's license, and at state offices that serve the disabled or poor. (6)

Muckraker A journalist who searches through the activities of public officials and organizations seeking to expose conduct contrary to the public interest. The term was first used by President Theodore Roosevelt in 1906 to warn that antibusiness journalism, while valuable, could be excessively negative. (10)

Mugwumps or progressives The faction in the Republican party of the 1890s to the 1910s composed of reformers who opposed the use of patronage and party bosses and favored the leadership of experts. After 1910 they evolved into a nonpartisan "good government" movement that sought to open up the political system and curb the abuses of parties. *See also* Political machine (7)

Multiple referral A congressional process whereby a bill may be referred to several committees that consider it simultaneously in whole or in part. For instance, the 1988 trade bill was considered by fourteen committees in the House and nine in the Senate simultaneously. (11)

Municipal corporation or municipality A legal term for a city. It is chartered by the state to exercise certain powers and provide certain services. *See also* Special-act charter; General-act charter (3)

Name-request job A job to be filled by a person whom a government agency has identified by name. (13)

National chairman A paid, full-time manager of a party's day-to-day work who is elected by the national committee. (7)

National committee A committee of delegates from each state and territory that runs party affairs between national conventions. (7)

National convention A meeting of party delegates elected in state primaries, caucuses, or conventions that is held every four years. Its primary purpose is to nominate presidential and vice-presidential candidates and to ratify a campaign platform. (7)

"Necessary and proper" clause The final paragraph of Article I, section 8, of the Constitution, which authorizes Congress to pass all laws "necessary and proper" to carry out the enumerated powers. Sometimes called the "elastic clause" because of the flexibility that it provides to Congress. (3)

Nonviolent civil disobedience A philosophy of opposing a law one considers unjust by peacefully violating it and allowing oneself to be punished as a result. (19)

Norm A standard of right or proper conduct that helps determine the range of acceptable social behavior and policy options. (5)

Nullification A theory first advanced by James Madison and Thomas Jefferson that the states had the right to "nullify" (that is, declare null and void) a federal law that, in the states' opinion, violated the Constitution. The theory was revived by John C. Calhoun of South Carolina in opposition to federal efforts to restrict slavery. The North's victory in the Civil War determined once and for all that the federal Union is indissoluble and that states cannot declare acts of Congress unconstitutional, a view later confirmed by the Supreme Court. (3)

Office-bloc ballot A ballot listing all candidates for a given office under the name of that office; also called a "Massachusetts" ballot. *See also* Party-column ballot (8)

Offsets An environmental rule that a company in an area with polluted air can offset its own pollution by reducing pollution from another source in the area. For instance, an older company that can't afford to pay for new antipollution technologies may buy pollution credits from a newer company that has reduced its source of pollution below the levels required by law. (21)

Open primary A primary election that permits voters to choose on election day the primary in which they wish to vote. They may vote for candidates of only one party. *See also* Blanket primary; Closed primary; Primary election (8)

Open rule An order from the House Rules Committee that permits a bill to be amended on the legislative floor. *See also* Closed rule; Restrictive rule (11)

Opinion of the Court A Supreme Court opinion written by one or more justices in the majority to explain the decision in a case. *See also* Concurring opinion; Dissenting opinion (14)

Ordinance A law passed and enforced by a city government. (3)

Orthodox People who believe that moral rules are derived from the commands of God or the laws of nature; these commands and laws are relatively clear, unchanging, and independent of individual moral preferences. They are likely to believe that traditional morality is more important than individual liberty and should be enforced by government and communal norms. *See also* Progressive (4)

Party-column ballot A ballot listing all candidates of a given party together under the name of that party; also called an "Indiana" ballot. *See also* Office-bloc ballot (8)

Party polarization A vote in which a majority of Democratic legislators oppose a majority of Republican legislators. (11)

Per curiam opinion A brief, unsigned opinion issued by the Supreme Court to explain its ruling. *See also* Opinion of the Court (14)

Perks A short form of *perquisites*, meaning "fringe benefits of office." Among the perks of political office for high-ranking officials are limousines, expense accounts, free air travel, fancy offices, and staff assistants. (12)

Personal following   The political support provided to a candidate on the basis of personal popularity and networks. (7)

Plaintiff   The party that initiates a lawsuit to obtain a remedy for an injury to his or her rights. (14)

Pluralist   A theory that competition among all affected interests shapes public policy. (1)

Plurality system   An electoral system, used in almost all American elections, in which the winner is the person who gets the most votes, even if he or she does not receive a majority of the votes. (7)

Pocket veto   One of two ways for a president to disapprove a bill sent to him by Congress. If the president does not sign the bill within ten days of his receiving it and Congress has adjourned within that time, the bill does not become a law. *See also* Veto message; Line-item veto (12)

Police power   The power of a state to promote health, safety, and morals. (3)

Policy entrepreneurs   Those in and out of government who find ways of pulling together a legislative majority on behalf of unorganized interests. *See also* Entrepreneurial politics (15)

Political action committee (PAC)   A committee set up by and representing a corporation, labor union, or special-interest group that raises and spends campaign contributions on behalf of one or more candidates or causes. (8)

Political agenda   A set of issues thought by the public or those in power to merit action by the government. (15)

Political cue   *See* Cue (political) (9)

Political culture   A broadly shared way of thinking about political and economic life that reflects fundamental assumptions about how government should operate. It is distinct from *political ideology*, which refers to a more or less consistent set of views about the policies government ought to follow. Up to a point people sharing a common political culture can disagree about ideology. *See also* Political ideology (4)

Political editorializing rule   A rule of the Federal Communications Commission that if a broadcaster endorses a candidate, the opposing candidate has a right to reply. (10)

Political efficacy   A citizen's belief that he or she can understand and influence political affairs. This sense is divided into two parts—internal efficacy (confidence in a citizen's own abilities to understand and take part in political affairs) and external efficacy (a belief that the system will respond to a citizen's demands). (4)

Political elite   *See* Elite (5)

Political ideology   A more or less consistent set of views as to the policies government ought to pursue. *See also* Political culture (4, 5)

Political machine   A party organization that recruits its members by dispensing *patronage*—tangible incentives such as money, political jobs, or an opportunity to get favors from government—and that is characterized by a high degree of leadership control over member activity. (7)

Political party   A group that seeks to elect candidates to public office by supplying them with a label—a "party identification"—by which they are known to the electorate. (7)

Political question   An issue that the Supreme Court refuses to consider because it believes the Constitution has left it entirely to another branch to decide. Its view of such issues may change over time, however. For example, until the 1960s the Court refused to hear cases about the size of congressional districts, no matter how unequal their populations. In 1962, however, it decided that it was authorized to review the constitutional implications of this issue. (14)

Political subculture   Fundamental assumptions about how the political process should operate that distinguish citizens by region, religion, or other characteristics. (4)

Poll   A survey of public opinion. *See also* Random sample (5)

Poll tax   A requirement that citizens pay a tax in order to register to vote. It was adopted by many states to prevent former slaves (most of whom were poor) from voting. It is now unconstitutional. *See also* Grandfather clause; Literacy test (6)

Pollution allowances (or banks)   A reduction in pollution below that required by law that can be used to cover a future plant expansion or sold to another company whose pollution emissions are above the legal requirements. (21)

Populists   People who hold liberal views on economic matters and conservative ones on social matters. They prefer a strong government that will reduce economic inequality, regulate businesses, and impose stricter social and criminal sanctions. The name and views have their origins in an agriculturally based social movement and party of the 1880s and 1890s that sought to curb the power of influential economic interests. (5)

Pork-barrel legislation   Legislation that gives tangible benefits (highways, dams, post offices) to constituents in several districts or states in the hope of winning their votes in return. (11)

Pork-barrel projects   *See* Pork-barrel legislation (15)

Position issue   An issue dividing the electorate on which rival parties adopt different policy positions to attract voters. *See also* Valence issue (8)

Power   The ability of one person to get another person to act in accordance with the first person's intentions. (1)

Presidential primary   *See* Primary election (8)

Price and wage controls   *See* Economic planning (16)

Primary election   An election prior to the general election in which voters select the candidates who will run on each party's ticket. Before presidential elections, a *presidential primary* is held to select delegates to the presidential nominating conventions of the major parties. *See also* Closed primary; Open primary (8)

Prior restraint   The traditional view of the press's free speech rights as expressed by William Blackstone, the great English jurist. According to this view the press is guaranteed freedom from censorship—that is, rules telling it in advance what it can publish. After publication, however, the government can punish the press for material that is judged libelous or obscene. (18)

Private bill   A legislative bill that deals only with specific, private, personal, or local matters rather than with general legislative affairs. The main kinds include immigration and naturalization bills (referring to particular individuals) and personal-claim bills. *See also* Public bill (11)

Probable cause   *See* Search warrant (18)

Process regulation   Rules regulating manufacturing or industrial processes, usually aimed at improving consumer or worker safety and reducing environmental damage. (15)

Progressive   A person who believes that moral rules are derived in part from an individual's beliefs and the circumstances of modern life. Progressives are likely to favor government tolerance and protection of individual choice. (4)

Prospective voting   Voting for a candidate because one favors his or her ideas for addressing issues after the election. (*Prospective* means "forward-looking.") *See also* Retrospective voting (8)

Public bill   A legislative bill that deals with matters of general concern. A bill involving defense expenditures is a public bill; a bill pertaining to an individual's becoming a naturalized citizen is not. *See also* Private bill (11)

Public-interest lobby   A political organization the stated goals of which will principally benefit nonmembers. (9)

Purposive incentive   The benefit that comes from serving a cause or principle from which one does not personally benefit. (9)

Pyramid structure   A method of organizing a president's staff in which most presidential assistants report through a hierarchy to the president's chief of staff. (12)

Quorum   The minimum number of members who must be present for business to be conducted in Congress. (11)

Quorum call   A calling of the roll in either house of Congress to see whether the number of representatives in attendance meets the minimum number required to conduct official business. (11)

Random sample   A sample selected in such a way that any member of the population being surveyed (e.g., all adults or voters) has an equal chance of being interviewed. (5)

Ratings   An assessment of a representative's voting record on issues important to an interest group. Such ratings are designed to generate public support for or opposition to a legislator. (9)

Reaganomics   The federal economic policies of the Reagan administration, elected in 1981. These policies combined a monetarist fiscal policy, supply-side tax cuts, and domestic budget cutting. Their goal was to reduce the size of the federal government and stimulate economic growth. *See also* Supply-side theory; Monetarism (16)

Recall   A procedure, in effect in over twenty states, whereby the voters can vote to remove an elected official from office. (3)

Red tape   Complex bureaucratic rules and procedures that must be followed to get something done. (13)

Referendum   The practice of submitting a law to a popular vote at election time. The law may be proposed by a voter's initiative or by the legislature. *See also* Initiative (3)

Registered voters   People who are registered to vote. While almost all adult American citizens are theoretically eligible to vote, only those who have completed a registration form by the required date may do so. (6)

Religious tradition   The moral teachings of religious institutions on religious, social, and economic issues. (5)

Remedy   A judicial order preventing or redressing a wrong or enforcing a right. (14)

Representative democracy   A political system in which leaders and representatives acquire political power by means of a competitive struggle for the people's vote. This is the form of government used by nations that are called democratic. (1, 12)

Republic   A form of democracy in which power is vested in representatives selected by means of popular competitive elections. *See also* Representative democracy (2)

Restrictive rule   An order from the House Rules Committee that permits certain kinds of amendments but not others to be made into a bill on the legislative floor. *See also* Closed rule; Open rule (11)

Retrospective voting   Voting for or against the candidate or party in office because one likes or dislikes how things have gone in the recent past. (*Retrospective* means "backward-looking.") *See also* Prospective voting (8)

Revenue sharing   A law providing for the distribution of a fixed amount or share of federal tax revenues to the states for spending on almost any government purpose. Distribution was intended to send more money to poorer, heavily taxed states and less to richer, lightly taxed ones. The program was ended in 1986. (3)

Reverse discrimination   Using race or sex to give preferential treatment to some people. (19)

Rider   An amendment on a matter unrelated to a bill that is added to the bill so that it will "ride" to passage through the Congress. When a bill has lots of riders, it is called a Christmas tree bill. (11)

Right-of-reply rule   A rule of the Federal Communications Commission that if a person is attacked on a broadcast (other than in a regular news program), that person has the right to reply over that same station. (10)

Roll-call vote   A congressional voting procedure that consists of members answering "yea" or "nay" to their names. When roll calls were handled orally, it was a time-consuming process in the House. Since 1973 an electronic voting system permits each House member to record his or her vote and learn the total automatically. *See also* Voice vote; Division vote; Teller vote (11)

Routine stories   Media reports about public events that are regularly covered by reporters and that involve simple, easily described acts or statements. For example, the president takes a trip or Congress passes a bill. (10)

Runoff primary   A second primary election held in some states when no candidate receives a majority of the votes in the first primary; the runoff is between the two candidates with the most votes. Runoff primaries are common in the South. (8)

Safe districts   Districts in which incumbents win by margins of 55 percent or more. (11)

Sampling error   The difference between the results of two surveys or samples. For example, if one random sample shows that 60 percent of all Americans like cats and another random sample taken at the same time shows that 65 percent do, the sampling error is 5 percent. (5)

School district   A special-district government responsible for administering public schools. (3)

Search warrant   An order from a judge authorizing the search of a place; the order must describe what is to be searched and seized, and the judge can issue it only if he or she is persuaded by the police that good reason (probable cause) exists that a crime has been committed and that the evidence bearing on the crime will be found at a certain location. (18)

Second-order devolution   The flow of power and responsibility from states to local governments. (3)

Select committees   Congressional committees appointed for a limited time and purpose. *See also* Standing committees; Joint committees (11)

Selective attention   Paying attention only to those parts of a newspaper or broadcast story with which one agrees. Studies suggest that this is how people view political ads on television. (10)

Separate-but-equal doctrine   The doctrine established in *Plessy v. Ferguson* (1896), in which the Supreme Court ruled that a state could provide "separate but equal" facilities for African Americans. (19)

Separation of powers   A principle of American government whereby constitutional authority is shared by three separate branches of government—the legislative, the executive, and the judicial. *See also* Checks and balances (2)

Sequential referral   A congressional process by which a Speaker may send a bill to a second committee after the first is finished acting, or may refer parts of a bill to separate committees. (11)

Sequester   Automatic, across-the-board cuts in certain federal programs that are triggered by law when Congress and the president cannot agree on a spending plan. (16)

Service strategy   A policy of providing poor people with education and job training to help lift them out of poverty. (17)

Shays's Rebellion   A rebellion in 1787 led by Daniel Shays and other ex–Revolutionary War soldiers and officers to prevent foreclosures of farms as a result of high interest rates and taxes. The revolt highlighted the weaknesses of the Confederation and bolstered support for a stronger national government. (2)

Silent majority   A phrase used to describe people, whatever their economic status, who uphold traditional values, especially against the counterculture of the 1960s. (5)

Simple resolution   An expression of opinion either in the House of Representatives or the Senate to settle housekeeping or procedural matters in either body. Such expressions are not signed by the president and do not have the force of law. *See also* Concurrent resolution; Joint resolution (11)

Social movement   A widely shared demand for change in some aspect of the social or political order. The civil rights movement of the 1960s was such an event, as are broadly based religious revivals. A social movement may have liberal or conservative goals. (9)

Social status   A measure of one's social standing obtained by combining factors such as education, income, and occupation. (5)

Soft money   Funds solicited from individuals, corporations, and unions that are spent on party activities, such as voter-registration campaigns and voting drives, rather than on behalf of a specific candidate. These funds need not be reported to the Federal Election Commission. (8)

Solidary incentives   The social rewards that lead people to join local or state political organizations. People who find politics fun and want to meet others who share their interests are said to respond to solidary incentives. (7, 9)

Sophomore surge   An increase in the votes that congressional candidates usually get when they first run for reelection. (8)

Sound bite   A brief statement no longer than a few seconds used on a radio or television news broadcast. (10)

Sovereign immunity   A doctrine that a citizen cannot sue the government without its consent. By statute Congress has given its consent for the government to be sued in many cases involving a dispute over a contract or damage done as a result of negligence. (14)

Sovereignty   Supreme or ultimate political authority; a sovereign government is one that is legally and politically independent of any other government. (3)

Special-act charter   A charter that denies the powers of a certain named city and lists what the city can and cannot do. *See also* General-act charter (3)

Special-district government or authority   A local or regional government with responsibility for some single function such as administering schools, handling sewage, or managing airports. (3)

Split ticket   Voting for candidates of different parties for various offices in the same election. For example, voting for a Republican for senator and a Democrat for president. *See also* Straight ticket (7)

Spoils system   Another phrase for political patronage—that is, the practice of giving the fruits of a party's victory, such as jobs and contracts, to the loyal members of that party. (13)

Sponsored party   A local or state political party that is largely staffed and funded by another organization with established networks in the community. One example is the Democratic party in and around Detroit, which has been developed, led, and to a degree financed by the political-action arm of the United Auto Workers. (7)

Standing   A legal concept establishing who is entitled to bring a lawsuit to court. For example, an individual must ordinarily show personal harm in order to acquire standing and be heard in court. (14)

Standing committees   Permanently established legislative committees that consider and are responsible for legislation within a certain subject area. Examples are the House Ways and Means Committee and the Senate Judiciary Committee. *See also* Select committees; Joint committees (11)

Stare decisis   A Latin term meaning "let the decision stand." The practice of basing judicial decisions on precedents established in similar cases decided in the past. (14)

Straight ticket   Voting for candidates who are all of the same party. For example, voting for Republican candidates for senator, representative, and president. *See also* Split ticket (7)

Strict-constructionist approach   The view that judges should decide cases on the basis of the language of the Constitution. (14)

Strict scrutiny   The standard by which the Supreme Court judges classifications based on race. To be accepted such a classification must be closely related to a "compelling" public purpose. (19)

Substantive representation   The correspondence between representatives' opinions and those of their constituents. *See also* Descriptive representation (11)

Superdelegates   Party leaders and elected officials who become delegates to the national convention without having to run in primaries or caucuses. Party rules determine the percentage of delegate seats reserved for party officials. (7)

Supply-side theory   An economic philosophy that holds that sharply cutting taxes will increase the incentive people have to work, save, and invest. Greater investments will lead to more jobs, a more productive economy, and more tax revenues for the government. (16)

Suspect classifications   Classifications of people on the basis of their race and ethnicity. The courts have ruled that laws classifying people on these grounds will be subject to "strict scrutiny." (19)

Symbolic speech   An act that conveys a political message, such as burning a draft card to protest the draft. (18)

Teller vote   A congressional voting procedure in which members pass between two tellers, the "yeas" first and then the "nays." Since 1971 the identities of members in a teller vote can be "recorded." *See also* Voice vote; Division vote; Roll-call vote (11)

Third-order devolution   The use of nongovernmental organizations to implement public policy. (3)

Third World   Originally a French term *(tiers monde)* referring to nations neutral in the cold war between the United States and the former Soviet Union. The term now refers to the group of developing nations in Africa, Asia, Latin America, and the Middle East. *See also* Cold war (20)

Town or township   A subunit of county government in many eastern and Midwestern states. (3)

Trial balloon   Information provided to the media by an anonymous public official as a way of testing the public reaction to a possible policy or appointment. (10)

Trustee approach   The view that an elected representative should act on his or her own best judgment of what public policy requires. (12)

Trust funds   Funds for government programs that are collected and spent outside the regular government budget; the amounts are determined by preexisting law rather than by annual appropriations. The Social Security trust fund is the largest of these. *See also* Appropriation (13)

Two-party system   An electoral system with two dominant parties that compete in state or national elections. Third parties have little chance of winning. (7)

Unalienable   Based on nature and Providence rather than on the preferences of people. (2)

Unified government   A government in which the same party controls both the White House and both houses of Congress. When Bill Clinton became president in 1993, it was the first time since 1981 (and only the second time since 1969) that the same party was in charge of the presidency and Congress. *See also* Divided government (12)

Unitary system   A system in which sovereignty is wholly in the hands of the national government so that subnational political units are dependent on its will. *See also* Federalism; Federal system (3)

Valence issue   An issue on which voters distinguish rival parties by the degree to which they associate each party or candidate with conditions, goals, or symbols the electorate universally approves or disapproves of. Examples of such issues are economic prosperity and political corruption. *See also* Position issue (8)

Veto message   One of two ways for a president to disapprove a bill sent to him by Congress. The veto message must be sent to Congress within ten days after the president receives the bill. *See also* Pocket veto; Line-item veto (12)

Voice vote   A congressional voting procedure in which members shout "yea" in approval or "nay" in disapproval; allows members to vote quickly or anonymously on bills. *See also* Division vote; Teller vote; Roll-call vote (11)

Voting-age population   The citizens who are eligible to vote after reaching a minimum age requirement. In the United States a citizen must be at least eighteen years old in order to vote. (6)

Wall-of-separation principle   A Supreme Court interpretation of the establishment clause in the First Amendment that prevents government involvement with religion, even on a nonpreferential basis. (18)

Whip   A senator or representative who helps the party leader stay informed about what party members are thinking, rounds up members when important votes are to be taken, and attempts to keep a nose count on how the voting on controversial issues is likely to go. (11)

White primary   The practice of keeping African Americans from voting in primary elections (at the time, the only meaningful election in the one-party South was the Democratic primary) through arbitrary implementation of registration requirements and intimidation. Such practices were declared unconstitutional in 1944. (6)

Work ethic   A belief in the importance of hard work and personal achievement. (4)

Worldviews   More or less comprehensive mental pictures of the critical problems facing the United States in the world and of the appropriate and inappropriate ways of responding to these problems. (20)

Writ of certiorari   A Latin term meaning "made more certain." An order issued by a higher court to a lower court to send up the record of a case for review. Most cases reach the Supreme Court through the writ of certiorari, issued when at least four of the nine justices feel that the case should be reviewed. (14)

Writ of habeas corpus   A Latin term meaning "you shall have the body." A court order directing a police officer, sheriff, or warden who has a person in custody to bring the prisoner before a judge and show sufficient cause for his or her detention. The writ of habeas corpus was designed to prevent illegal arrests and imprisonment. (2)

Chapter 1 *The Study of American Government*

1. Aristotle, *Politics*, iv, 4, 1290^b. More precisely, Aristotle's definition was this: Democracy is a "constitution in which the free-born and poor control the government—being at the same time a majority." He distinguished this from an oligarchy, "in which the rich and well-born control the government—being at the same time a minority." Aristotle listed several varieties of democracy, depending on whether, for example, there was a property qualification for citizenship.
2. Joseph A. Schumpeter, *Capitalism, Socialism, and Democracy*, 3d ed. (New York: Harper Torchbooks, 1950), 269. (First published in 1942.)
3. Karl Marx and Friedrich Engels, "The Manifesto of the Communist Party," in *The Marx-Engels Reader*, 2d ed., ed. Robert C. Tucker (New York: Norton, 1978), 469–500.
4. C. Wright Mills, *The Power Elite* (New York: Oxford University Press, 1956).
5. H. H. Gerth and C. Wright Mills, eds., *From Max Weber: Essays in Sociology* (London: Routledge and Kegan Paul, 1948), 232–235.
6. Among the authors whose interpretations of American politics are essentially pluralist is David B. Truman, *The Governmental Process*, 2d ed. (New York: Knopf, 1971).
7. Alexis de Tocqueville, *Democracy in America*, vol. 2, ed. Phillips Bradley (New York: Knopf, 1951), book 2, ch. 8, 122.
8. Derek C. Bok and John T. Dunlop, *Labor and the American Community* (New York: Simon and Schuster, 1970), 134.

Chapter 2 *The Constitution*

1. Quoted in Bernard Bailyn, *The Ideological Origins of the American Revolution* (Cambridge: Harvard University Press, 1967), 61, n. 6.
2. Quoted in Bailyn, ibid., 135–137.
3. Quoted in Bailyn, ibid., 77.
4. Quoted in Bailyn, ibid., 160.
5. *Federalist* No. 37.
6. Gordon S. Wood, *The Creation of the American Republic* (Chapel Hill: University of North Carolina Press, 1969). See also *Federalist* No. 49.
7. Letter of George Washington to Henry Lee (October 31, 1787), in *Writings of George Washington*, vol. 29, ed. John C. Fitzpatrick (Washington, D.C.: Government Printing Office, 1939), 34.
8. Letters of Thomas Jefferson to James Madison (January 30, 1787) and to Colonel William S. Smith (November 13, 1787), in *Jefferson Himself*, ed. Bernard Mayo (Boston: Houghton Mifflin, 1942), 145.
9. *Federalist* No. 51.
10. *Federalist* No. 48.

11. *Federalist* No. 51.
12. Ibid.
13. Ibid.
14. "The Address and Reasons of Dissent of the Minority of the State of Pennsylvania to Their Constituents," in *The Anti-Federalist*, ed. Cecelia Kenyon (Indianapolis: Bobbs-Merrill, 1966), 39.
15. Max Farrand, *The Framing of the Constitution of the United States* (New Haven, Conn.: Yale University Press, 1913), 185.
16. See, for example, John Hope Franklin, *Racial Equality in America* (Chicago: University of Chicago Press, 1976), ch. 1, esp. 12–20.
17. Max Farrand, *The Records of the Federal Convention of 1787*, 4 vols. (New Haven, Conn.: Yale University Press, 1911–1937).
18. Theodore J. Lowi, *American Government: Incomplete Conquest* (Hinsdale, Ill.: Dryden Press, 1976), 97.
19. Article I, section 2, para. 3.
20. Article I, section 9, para. 1.
21. Article IV, section 2, para. 3
22. Charles A. Beard, *An Economic Interpretation of the Constitution* (New York: Macmillan, 1913), esp. 26–51, 149–151, 324–325.
23. Forrest McDonald, *We the People* (Chicago: University of Chicago Press, 1958); Robert E. Brown, *Charles Beard and the Constitution* (Princeton: Princeton University Press, 1956).
24. Robert A. McGuire, "Constitution Making: A Rational Choice Model of the Federal Convention of 1787," *American Journal of Political Science* 32 (May 1988): 483–522. See also Forrest McDonald, *Novus Ordo Seclorum* (Lawrence: University of Kansas Press, 1985), 221.
25. McDonald, *Novus Ordo Seclorum*, 202–221.
26. Robert A. McGuire and Robert L. Ohsfeldt, "Economic Interests and the American Constitution: A Quantitative Rehabilitation of Charles A. Beard," *Journal of Economic History* 44 (June 1984): 509–519.
27. Lloyd N. Cutler, "To Form a Government," *Foreign Affairs* (Fall 1980): 126–143.

Chapter 3 *Federalism*

1. Woodrow Wilson, *Constitutional Government in the United States* (New York: Columbia University Press, 1961), 173. (First published in 1908.)
2. David B. Truman, "Federalism and the Party System," in *Federalism: Mature and Emergent*, ed. Arthur MacMahon (Garden City, N.Y.: Doubleday, 1955), 123.
3. Ibid.
4. Harold J. Laski, "The Obsolescence of Federalism," *New Republic* (May 3, 1939): 367–369.

5. William A. Riker, *Federalism: Origin, Operation, Significance* (Boston: Little, Brown, 1964), 154.
6. Daniel J. Elazar, *American Federalism: A View from the States* (New York: Crowell, 1966), 216.
7. Martin Diamond, "The Federalists' View of Federalism," in *Essays in Federalism*, ed. George C. S. Benson (Claremont, Calif.: Institute for Studies in Federalism, 1961), 21–64; and Samuel H. Beer, "Federalism, Nationalism, and Democracy in America," *American Political Science Review* 72 (March 1978): 9–21.
8. *United States v. Sprague*, 282 U.S. 716 (1931).
9. *Garcia v. San Antonio Metropolitan Transit Authority*, 105 S. Ct. 1005 (1985), overruling *National League of Cities v. Usery*, 426 U.S. 833 (1976).
10. *McCulloch v. Maryland*, 4 Wheat. 316 (1819).
11. *Pollock v. Farmers' Loan & Trust Co.*, 157 U.S. 429 (1895); *South Carolina v. Baker*, No. 94 (1988).
12. *Texas v. White*, 7 Wall. 700 (1869).
13. *Champion v. Ames*, 188 U.S. 321 (1903).
14. *Hoke v. United States*, 227 U.S. 308 (1913).
15. *Clark Distilling Co. v. W. Md. Ry.*, 242 U.S. 311 (1917).
16. *Hipolite Egg Co. v. United States*, 220 U.S. 45 (1911).
17. *United States v. E. C. Knight Co.*, 156 U.S. 1 (1895).
18. *Paul v. Virginia*, 8 Wall. 168 (1869).
19. *Veazie Bank v. Fenno*, 8 Wall. 533 (1869).
20. *Brown v. Maryland*, 12 Wheat. 419 (1827).
21. *Wickard v. Filburn*, 317 U.S. 111 (1942); *NLRB v. Jones & Laughlin Steel Corp.*, 301 U.S. 58 (1937).
22. *Kirschbaum Co. v. Walling*, 316 U.S. 517 (1942).
23. *Goldfarb v. Virginia State Bar*, 421 U.S. 773 (1975); *Flood v. Kuhn*, 407 U.S. 258 (1972).
24. *United States v. California*, 332 U.S. 19 (1947).
25. Morton Grodzins, *The American System* (Chicago: Rand McNally, 1966), 49–50.
26. Max Sawicky, Economic Policy Institute Brief #176, Washington, D.C., February 14, 2002; U.S. Office of Management and Budget, *Summary Composition of Total Outlays for Grants to State and Local Governments, 1940–2001* (Washington, D.C.: Government Printing Office, 2002).
27. Morton Keller, *Affairs of State* (Cambridge: Harvard University Press, 1977), 310, 381–382.
28. Edward C. Banfield, "Making a New Federal Program: Model Cities, 1964–1968," in *Policy and Politics in America*, ed. Allan P. Sindler (Boston: Little, Brown, 1973), 124–158.

29. Samuel H. Beer, "The Modernization of American Federalism," *Publius* 3 (Fall 1973): esp. 74–79; and Beer, "Federalism," 18–19.

30. R. Douglas Arnold, "The Local Roots of Domestic Policy," in *The New Congress*, ed. Thomas E. Mann and Norman J. Ornstein (Washington, D.C.: American Enterprise Institute, 1981), 268.

31. Congressional Budget Office, *Federal Constraints on State and Local Government Actions* (Washington, D.C.: Government Printing Office, 1979).

32. *Federally Induced Costs Affecting State and Local Governments* (U.S. Advisory Commission on Intergovernmental Relations, September 1994).

33. Richard P. Nathan and Fred Doolittle, *Reagan and the States* (Princeton, N.J.: Princeton University Press, 1987), 7.

34. George Peterson et al., *The Reagan Block Grants: What Have We Learned?* (Washington, D.C.: Urban Institute Press, 1986), 21–27.

35. Data from State Capacity Study, Nelson A. Rockefeller Institute of Government, SUNY-Albany, March 2002.

36. R. Kent Weaver, "Deficits and Devolution in the 104th Congress," unpublished draft paper, Washington, D.C., Brookings Institution, April 1996.

37. *The Public Perspective* (April/May 1995): 5.

Chapter 4   *American Political Culture*

1. Alexis de Tocqueville, *Democracy in America*, ed. Phillips Bradley (New York: Knopf, 1951), vol. 1, 288. (First published in 1835.)

2. Ibid., vol. 1, 319–320.

3. Ibid., 319.

4. Donald J. Devine, *The Political Culture of the United States* (Boston: Little, Brown, 1972), 185; Herbert McClosky and John Zaller, *The American Ethos: Public Attitudes Toward Capitalism and Democracy* (Cambridge: Harvard University Press, 1984), ch. 3, esp. 74–75.

5. Herbert McClosky and John Zaller, *The American Ethos* (Cambridge, MA: Harvard University Press, 1984), 74–77.

6. Ibid., 66.

7. Gunnar Myrdal, *An American Dilemma: The Negro Problem in Modern Democracy* (New York: Harper, 1944), intro. and ch. 1.

8. Frank R. Westie, "The American Dilemma: An Empirical Test," *American Sociological Review* 30 (August 1965): 536–537.

9. Eric L. McKitrick, "Party Politics and the Union and Confederate War Efforts," in *The American Party Systems*, ed. William Nisbet Chambers and Walter Dean Burnham, 2d ed. (New York: Oxford University Press, 1975), 117–121.

10. McClosky and Zaller, 174.

11. Sidney Verba and Gary R. Orren, *Equality in America: The View from the Top* (Cambridge: Harvard University Press, 1985), 146–147.

12. McClosky and Zaller, 82–84.

13. Ibid., 93, 95.

14. Verba and Orren, *Equality in America*, 74; McClosky and Zaller, *The American Ethos*, 126.

15. Verba and Orren, *Equality in America*, 72, 254.

16. Donald Kinder and David Sears, "Symbolic Racism Versus Racial Threats to the Good Life," *Journal of Personality and Social Psychology* 40 (1981): 414–431.

17. Paul M. Sniderman and Michael Gray Hagen, *Race and Inequality: A Study in American Values* (Chatham, N.J.: Chatham House, 1985), 111.

18. Ibid., 37–38.

19. Theodore Caplow and Howard M. Bahr, "Half a Century of Change in Adolescent Attitudes: A Replication of a Middletown Survey by the Lynds," *Public Opinion Quarterly* 43 (1979): 1–17, table 1.

20. Thomas J. Anton, "Policy-Making and Political Culture in Sweden," *Scandinavian Political Studies* 4 (1969): 88–100; M. Donald Hancock, *Sweden: The Politics of Post-Industrial Change* (Hinsdale, Ill.: Dryden Press, 1972); Sten Johansson, "Liberal-Democratic Theory and Political Processes," in *Readings in the Swedish Class Structure*, ed. Richard Scarse (New York: Pergamon Press, 1976); Steven J. Kelman, *Regulating America, Regulating Sweden: A Comparative Study of Occupational Safety and Health Policy* (Cambridge, Mass.: MIT Press, 1981), 118–123.

21. Lewis Austin, *Saints and Samurai: The Political Culture of American and Japanese Elites* (New Haven, Conn.: Yale University Press, 1975).

22. Gabriel Almond and Sidney Verba, *The Civic Culture* (Princeton, N.J.: Princeton University Press, 1963), 169, 185. See also Gabriel Almond and Sidney Verba, eds., *The Civic Culture Revisited* (Boston: Little, Brown, 1980).

23. Sidney Verba et al., *Voice and Equality: Civic Voluntarism in American Politics* (Cambridge: Harvard University Press, 1995), 69, 70.

24. Kenneth Newton and Pipa Norris, "Confidence in Public Institutions: Faith, Culture or Performance?," paper presented at the Annual Meeting of the American Political Science Association, Atlanta, Ga., September 1999, tables 8.1 and 8.3.

25. Paul M. Sniderman, *A Question of Loyalty* (Berkeley: University of California Press, 1981).

26. Verba and Orren, *Equality in America*, 255.

27. George Gallup, Jr., and Thomas Jones, *The Next American Spirituality: Finding God in the Twenty-First Century* (Colorado Springs, Colo.: Cook, 2000); Kenneth D. Wald, *Religion and Politics in the United States*, 3d ed. (Washington, D.C.: Congressional Quarterly Press, 1997); Samuel P. Huntington, *American Politics: The Promise of Disharmony* (Cambridge: Harvard University Press, 1981), 154–166; Seymour Martin Lipset, *The First New Nation* (New York: Doubleday Anchor Books, 1967), 170, 171.

28. Gallup and Jones, *The Next American Spirituality*, 25.

29. Ibid., 94.

30. Ram A. Cnaan et al., *The Newer Deal: Religion and Social Work in Partnership* (New York: Colombia University Press, 1999).

31. Robert D. Putnam, "Bowling Alone: America's Declining Social Capital," *Journal of Democracy* (January 1995): 65–78.

32. C. Everett Ladd, "The Data Just Don't Show Erosion of America's 'Social Capital,'" *The Public Perspective* (June/July 1996): 5–22; Robert J. Samuelson, "Bowling Alone Is Bunk," *Washington Post* (April 10, 1996): 19.

33. Ladd, op. cit. Ladd, reporting data from the National Opinion Research Center.

34. Ibid; *Gallup Monthly Poll* (January 1995), 20; *Gallup Monthly Poll* (January 1996), 22.

35. *Better Together*, Report of the Saguaro Seminar, Cambridge, Massachusetts, John F. Kennedy School of Government, Harvard University, 2002, 51. Also see Robert D. Putnam, *Bowling Alone: The Collapse and Renewal of American Community* (New York: Simon and Shuster, 2000).

36. Pew Center for the People and the Press, *Religion and Politics: The Ambivalent Majority* (Author: Washington, D.C., 2000).

37. Pew Forum on Religion and Public Life, *Lift Every Voice: A Report on Religion in American Public Life 2002* (Author: Washington, D.C., 2001).

38. Pew Center for the People, *Religion and Politics.*

39. Max Weber, *The Protestant Ethic and the Spirit of Capitalism*, trans. Talcott Parsons (New York: Scribner's, 1930). (First published in 1904.)

40. Erik H. Erikson, *Childhood and Society* (New York: Norton, 1950), ch. 8.

41. The phrase "culture war" is from James Davison Hunter, *Culture Wars: The Struggle to Define America* (New York: Basic Books, 1991). This discussion draws heavily on Professor Hunter's analysis.

42. Ibid., 96–97, 116–117. See also Robert Lerner, Stanley Rotham, and S. Robert Lichter, "Christian Religious Elites," *Public Opinion* 11 (March/April 1989): 54–58.

43. Gary Orren, "Fall From Grace: The Public's Loss of Faith in Government," in Joseph Nye, Jr., Philip D. Zelikow, and David C. King, eds., *Why People Don't Trust Government* (Cambridge, MA: Harvard University Press, 1997), 77–107, and Robert J. Blendon, et al., "Changing Attitudes in America," in *ibid.*, 205–16.

44. Ibid.

45. The Gallup Organization, *Poll Releases* (June 19, 1997), 3–6.

46. The Gallup Organization, *Social Audit* (June 1997), 14; George Gallup, Jr., and D. Michael Lindsay, *Surveying the Religious Landscape: Trends in U.S. Beliefs* (Harrisburg, Pa.: Morehouse Publishing, 1999), 53.

47. Samuel H. Barnes and Max Kaase, eds., *Political Action: Mass Participation in Five Democracies* (Beverly Hills, Calif.: Sage, 1979), 541–542, 574.

48. Marc J. Hetherington, "The Effect of Political Trust on the Presidential Vote, 1968–96," *American Political Science Review*, 93 (June 1999): 311–327.

49. James W. Prothro and Charles M. Grigg, "Fundamental Principles of Democracy: Bases of Agreement and Disagreement," *Journal of Politics* 22 (Spring 1960): 275–294.

50. Herbert McClosky and Alida Brill, *Dimensions of Tolerance: What Americans Believe About Civil Liberties* (New York: Russell Sage Foundation, 1983), 124.

51. Ibid., 62, 66, 70, 118, 131.

52. Ibid., 435; James A. Davis, "Communism, Cohorts, and Categories: American Tolerance in 1954 and 1972–1973," *American Journal of Sociology* 81 (1975): 491–513; and Clyde A. Nunn, Harry J. Crockett, Jr., and J. Allen Williams, Jr., *Tolerance for Nonconformity: A National Survey of Changing Commitment to Civil Liberties* (San Francisco: Jossey-Bass, 1978). But compare the different conclusion in John L. Sullivan, James Piereson, and George E. Marcus, *Political Tolerance and American Democracy* (Chicago: University of Chicago Press, 1982).

53. See, for example, John L. Sullivan, James Piereson, and George F. Marcus, *Political Tolerance and American Democracy* (Chicago, IL: University of Chicago Press, 1982), 194–202.

Chapter 5   *Public Opinion*

1. George W. Bishop, Alfred J. Tuchfarber, and Robert W. Oldendick, "1984: How Much Can We Manipulate and Control People's Answers to Public Opinion Surveys?" paper delivered at the 1984 annual meeting of the American Political Science Association; Howard Schuman and S. Presser, *Questions and Answers in Attitude Surveys* (New York: Academic Press, 1981), ch. 5.

2. Robert Weissberg, "The Problem with Polling," *Public Interest*, no. 148 (Summer 2002): 37–48.

3. M. Kent Jennings and Richard G. Niemi, "The Transmission of Political Values from Parent to Child," *American Political Science Review* 62 (March 1968): 173; Robert D. Hess and Judith V. Tomey, *The Development of Political Attitudes in Children* (Chicago: Aldine, 1967), 90.

4. Several studies of child-parent agreement on party preference are summarized in David O. Sears, "Political Behavior," in *The Handbook of Social Psychology*, ed. Gardner Lindzey and Elliot Aronson, 2d ed. (Reading, Mass.: Addison-Wesley, 1969), vol. 5, 376.

5. Norman H. Nie, Sidney Verba, and John R. Petrocik, *The Changing American Voter* (Cambridge: Harvard University Press, 1976), ch. 4.

6. Robert S. Erikson and Norman R. Luttbeg, *American Public Opinion: Its Origins, Content, and Impact* (New York: Wiley, 1973), 197; and Seymour Martin Lipset, *Revolution and Counterrevolution*, rev. ed. (Garden City, N.Y.: Doubleday Anchor Books, 1970), 338–342;

David B. Brinkerhoff et. al, *Essentials of Sociology, Media Edition* (Belmont, CA: Wadsworth/Thompson Learning, 2002). Micro Case, "Politics, Religion, and the Culture War," rows 26 and 35, column 2.

7. Karen M. Kaufman and John R. Petrocik, "The Changing Politics of American Men: Understanding the Sources of the Gender Gap," *American Journal of Political Science* 43 (1999): 864–887.

8. *The Los Angeles Times* Poll, November 7, 2001, based on interviews with 8,132 voters as they exited 140 polling places across the nation.

9. Alexander M. Astin, *Four Critical Years: Effects of College on Beliefs, Attitudes, and Knowledge* (San Francisco: Jossey-Bass, 1978), 36–38.

10. Institute of Politics, Harvard University, *Campaign '84 and Beyond* (1986), 12.

11. Erikson and Luttbeg, *American Public Opinion*, 138; Terry S. Weiner and Bruce K. Eckland, "Education and Political Party: The Effects of College or Social Class?" *American Journal of Sociology* 84 (1979): 911–928.

12. Astin, *Four Critical Years*, 38.

13. John Zaller, "Information, Values, and Opinion," *American Political Science Review*, 85 (1991): 1215–1238.

14. Everett Carl Ladd, Jr., and Seymour Martin Lipset, *The Divided Academy: Professors and Politics* (New York: McGraw-Hill, 1975), 26–27, 55–67, 184–190.

15. *Statistical Abstract of the United States, 2000.*

16. J. L. Spaeth and Andrew M. Greeley, *Recent Alumni and Higher Education* (New York: McGraw-Hill, 1970), 100–110; and Erland Nelson, "Persistence of Attitudes of College Students Fourteen Years Later," *Psychological Monographs* 68 (1954): 1–13.

17. Kenneth A. Feldman and Theodore M. Newcomb, *The Impact of College on Students* (San Francisco: Jossey-Bass, 1969), vol. 1, 99–100, 312–320.

18. John McAdams, "Testing the Theory of the New Class," *Sociological Quarterly* 28 (1987): 23–49.

19. M. Kent Jennings, "Residues of a Movement: The Aging of the American Protest Generation," *American Political Science Review* 81 (1987): 367–382.

20. Kay Lehman Schlozman and Sidney Verba, *Insult to Injury: Unemployment, Class, and Political Response* (Cambridge: Harvard University Press, 1979), 115–118; David Butler and Donald Stokes, *Political Change in Great Britain* (New York: St. Martin's Press, 1969), 70, 77; Erikson and Luttbeg, *American Public Opinion*, 184; *National Journal* (November 8, 1980), 1878.

21. V. O. Key, Jr., *Public Opinion and American Democracy* (New York: Knopf, 1961), 122–138.

22. Richard E. Dawson, *Public Opinion and Contemporary Disarray* (New York: Harper & Row, 1973), ch. 4.

23. Paul Starobin, "Party Hoppers," *National Journal* (February 7, 1998): 277, 278.

24. David A. Bositis, *Public Opinion 1998: Political Attitudes* (Washington, D.C.: Joint Center

for Political and Economic Studies (October 1998), table 18A.

25. *The American Enterprise* (November/December 1998): 91, reporting data from a *Time*/CNN survey, August 1997.

26. David A. Bositis, foreword by Eddie N. Williams, *Dividing Generations: The Transformation of African American Policy Views* (Washington, D.C.: Joint Center for Political and Economic Studies, 2001).

27. Bruce Cain and Roderick Kiewiet, "California's Coming Minority Majority" *Public Opinion* (February/March 1986) 50–52.

28. Lisa J. Montoya et al., "Latina Politics: Gender, Participation, and Leadership," *PS: Political Science and Politics* 33 (September 2000): 557.

29. Cain and Kiewiet, "California's Coming Minority Majority," 50–52.

30. F. Chris Garcia et al., "The Effects of Ethnic Partisanship on Electoral Behavior: An Analysis and Comparison of Latino and Anglo Voting in the 1988 United States Presidential Election," paper delivered at the Annual Meeting of the American Political Science Association, September 3–6, 1992.

31. Michael Barone, "We've Been Here Before: Ethnicity and America, 1900 and 2000," Bradley Lecture, American Enterprise Institute, October 4, 1999, 21, 22.

32. Meenekski Bose, using data from the ICPSR *1992 American National Election Survey*, University of Michigan.

33. Nie, Verba, and Petrocik, *The Changing American Voter*, 247–250.

34. *The American Enterprise* (January/February 1999): 51, citing surveys by CBS/*New York Times*.

35. Philip E. Converse, "The Nature of Belief Systems in Mass Publics," in *Ideology and Discontent*, ed. David Apter (Glencoe, Ill.: Free Press, 1964), 206–261.

36. Christopher H. Achen, "Mass Political Attitudes and the Survey Response," *American Political Science Review* 69 (December 1975): 1218–1231.

37. Seymour Martin Lipset and Earl Raab, *The Politics of Unreason* (New York: Harper & Row, 1970), ch. 11; James A. Stimson, "Belief Systems: Constraint, Complexity, and the 1972 Election," *American Journal of Political Science* 19 (1975): 393–417; and Herbert McClosky and John Zaller, *The American Ethos* (Cambridge: Harvard University Press, 1984), ch. 8.

38. William S. Maddox and Stuart A. Lilie, *Beyond Liberal and Conservative* (Washington, D.C.: Cato Institute, 1984), 5, 68, 96, 104.

39. Estimates of size of four groups averaged from 1993–1994 data presented by Everett Carll Ladd, "A New View of the Electorate," *The American Enterprise* (May/June 1994): 91.

40. Zaller, "Information," and Stimson, "Belief Systems." See also Allen H. Barton and R. Wayne Parsons, "Measuring Belief System Structures," *Public Opinion Quarterly* 41 (1977): 159–180.

41. Gary C. Jacobson, "The Electoral Basis of Partisan Polarization in Congress," paper delivered at the annual meeting of the American Political Science Association, August 31–September 3, 2000.

42. Larry M. Bartels, "Partisanship and Voting Behavior, 1952–1996," *American Journal of Political Science* 44 (2000): 35–50.

43. Melissa P. Collie and John Lyman Mason, "The Electoral Connection Between Party and Constituency Reconsidered: Evidence from the U.S. House of Representatives, 1972–1994," in *Continuity and Change in House Elections*, ed. David W. Brady et al. (Stanford, Calif.: Hoover Institution, 2000).

44. John McAdams, "Testing the Theory of the New Class," *Sociological Quarterly* 28 (1987): 23–49.

45. Seymour Martin Lipset and David Riesman, *Education and Politics at Harvard* (New York: McGraw-Hill, 1975), ch. 8.

46. McAdams, "Testing."

47. Ibid.

48. John Zaller, *The Nature and Origins of Mass Opinion* (Cambridge: Cambridge University Press, 1992).

49. Lawrence R. Jacobs and Robert Y. Shapiro, "Debunking the Myth of the Pandering Politician," *The Public Perspective* (April/May 1997): 3–5.

Chapter 6   *Political Participation*

1. David Glass, Peverill Squire, and Raymond Wolfinger, "Voter Turnout: An International Comparison," *Public Opinion* (December/January 1984): 49–55. See also G. Bingham Powell, Jr., "Voting Turnout in Thirty Democracies: Partisan, Legal, and Socio-Economic Influences," in *Electoral Participation: A Comparative Analysis*, ed. Richard Rose (Beverly Hills, Calif.: Sage Publications, 1980).

2. Stephen Knack, "Drivers Wanted: Motor Voter and the Election of 1996," *PS: Political Science* (June 1999): 237.

3. Ibid.; and *Congressional Quarterly Weekly* (October 24, 1998): 2881.

4. Knack, "Drivers Wanted," 238.

5. Ibid., 242.

6. Raymond E. Wolfinger and Jonathan Hoffman, "Registering and Voting with Motor Voter," *PS: Political Science and Politics*, 34 (March 2001): 90.

7. Morton Keller, *Affairs of State* (Cambridge: Harvard University Press, 1977), 523.

8. *United States v. Reese*, 92 U.S. 214 (1876); *United States v. Cruikshank*, 92 U.S. 556 (1876); and *Ex parte Yarbrough*, 110 U.S. 651 (1884).

9. *Guinn and Beall v. United States*, 238 U.S. 347 (1915).

10. *Smith v. Allwright*, 321 U.S. 649 (1944).

11. *Schnell v. Davis*, 336 U.S. 933 (1949).

12. *Congress and the Nation, vol. 3: 1969–1972* (Washington, D.C.: Congressional Quarterly, 1973), 1006; and *Statistical Abstract of the United States, 1975*, 450.

13. U.S. Bureau of the Census; and Elizabeth Crowley, "More Young People Turn Away from Politics," *Wall Street Journal* (June 16, 1999).

14. Crowley, "More Young People," citing data from the Pew Research Center.

15. Paul Wellstone, quoted in ibid.

16. *Historical Statistics of the United States: Colonial Times to 1970*, part 2, 1071–1072.

17. Walter Dean Burnham, "The Changing Shape of the American Political Universe," *American Political Science Review* 59 (March 1965): 11; and William H. Flanigan and Nancy H. Zingale, *Political Behavior of the American Electorate*, 3d ed. (Boston: Allyn and Bacon, 1975), 15.

18. Burnham, "Changing Shape;" E. E. Schattschneider, *The Semisovereign People* (New York: Holt, Rinehart and Winston, 1960), chs. 5, 6.

19. Philip E. Converse, "Change in the American Electorate," in *The Human Meaning of Social Change*, ed. Angus Campbell and Philip E. Converse (New York: Russell Sage Foundation, 1972), 263–338.

20. Michael P. McDonald and Samuel L. Popkin, "The Myth of the Vanishing Voter," *American Political Science Review* 95 (December 2001): table 1, 966.

21. Ibid.

22. Raymond Wolfinger and Benjamen Highton, "What If They Gave an Election and Everyone Came?" Public Affairs Report, Institute of Governmental Studies, University of California at Berkeley, June 1999, 11–13.

23. Ibid., 13.

24. Ibid.

25. Sidney Verba and Norman H. Nie, *Participation in America* (New York: Harper & Row, 1972), 30. See also Aage R. Clausen, "Response Validity: Vote Report," *Public Opinion Quarterly*, 32 (1968–1969): 588–606.

26. Michael W. Traugott and John P. Katosh, "Response Validity in Surveys of Voting Behavior," *Public Opinion Quarterly* 43 (1979): 359–377; Aage R. Clausen, "Response Validity: Vote Report," *Public Opinion Quarterly* 32 (1969): 588–606.

27. Sidney Verba et al., *Voice and Equality: Civic Voluntarism in American Politics* (Cambridge: Harvard University Press, 1995), 79.

28. Ibid., 77.

29. Sidney Verba and Norman H. Nie, *Participation in America* (New York: Harper and Row, 1972), ch. 6.

30. Lester W. Milbrath and M. I. Goel, *Political Participation*, 2d ed. (Chicago: Rand McNally, 1977); Raymond E. Wolfinger and Steven J. Rosenstone, *Who Votes?* (New Haven, Conn.: Yale University Press, 1980); W. Russell Neuman, *The Paradox of Mass Voting* (Cambridge: Harvard University Press, 1986), ch. 4.

31. Wolfinger and Rosenstone, *Who Votes?*, esp. 102, and John P. Katosh and Michael W. Traugott, "Costs and Values in the Calculus of Voting," *American Journal of Political Science* 26 (1982): 361–376.

32. David C. Leege and Lyman A Kellstedt, *Rediscovering the Religious Factor in American Politics* (Armonk, N.Y.: M. E. Sharpe, 1993), 129–131.

33. Verba and Nie, *Participation in America* 151–157; Milbrath and Goel, *Political Participation*, 120.

34. Jack Citrin, "The Alienated Voter," *Taxing and Spending* (October 1978), 1–7; Austin Ranney, "Nonvoting Is Not a Social Disease," *Public Opinion* (October/November 1983): 16–19; Glass, Squire, and Wolfinger, "Voter Turnout."

35. *Dunn v. Blumstein*, 405 U.S. 330 (1972).

36. Wolfinger and Rosenstone, *Who Votes?*

37. Richard G. Smolka, *Election Day Registration: The Minnesota and Wisconsin Experience* (Washington, D.C.: American Enterprise Institute, 1977), 5.

38. Gary R. Orren, "The Linkage of Policy to Participation," in *Presidential Selection*, ed. Alexander Heard and Michael Nelson (Durham, N.C.: Duke University Press, 1987).

39. Glass, Squire, and Wolfinger, "Voter Turnout," 52.

40. Powell, "Voting Turnout"; Robert W. Jackman, "Political Institutions and Voter Turnout in Industrial Democracies," *American Political Science Review* 81 (1987): 405–423.

41. Roy Texeira, "Will The Real Nonvoter Please Stand Up?" *Public Opinion* (July/August 1988): 43; Texeira, "Registration and Turnout," *Public Opinion* (January/February 1989): 12.

42. Richard A. Brody, "The Puzzle of Political Participation in America," in *The New American Political System*, ed. Anthony King (Washington, D.C.: American Enterprise Institute, 1978): 315–323.

43. Richard Smolka, quoted in William J. Crotty, *Political Reform and the American Experiment* (New York: Crowell, 1977), 86–87.

44. For Japan: The Society for Promotion of Clear Elections, *Survey of 34th General Election, 1976*. See Gary Orren, "Political Participation and Public Policy: The Case for Institutional Reform," Cambridge, Mass., November 1985, 16A. For U.S. and Sweden: Samuel P. Huntington and Joan M. Nelson, *No Easy Choice* (Cambridge: Harvard University Press, 1976), 88.

45. Sidney Verba et al., "Race, Ethnicity, and the Resources for Participation: The Role of Religion," paper delivered at the 1992 annual meeting of the American Political Science Association, September 3–6, 1992.

Chapter 7   *Political Parties*

1. Leon D. Epstein, "Political Parties," in *Handbook of Political Science*, ed. Fred I. Greenstein and Nelson W. Polsby (Reading, Mass.: Addison-Wesley, 1975), vol. 4, 230.

2. Quoted in Henry Adams, *History of the United States of America During the Administrations of Jefferson and Madison*, ed. Ernest Samuels, abridged edition (Chicago: University of Chicago Press, 1967), 147.

3. Walter Dean Burnham, *Critical Elections and the Mainsprings of American Politics* (New York: Norton, 1970), 10.

4. James L. Sundquist, *Dynamics of the Party System* (Washington, D.C.: Brookings Institution, 1973), ch. 7.
5. Edward G. Carmines and James A. Stimson, "Issue Evolution, Population Replacement, and Normal Partisan Change," *American Political Science Review* 75 (March 1981): 107–118; and Gregory Markus, "Political Attitudes in an Election Year," *American Political Science Review* 76 (September 1982): 538–560.
6. Ray Wolfinger and Michael G. Hagen, "Republican Prospects: Southern Comfort," *Public Opinion* (October/November 1985): 8–13. But compare Richard Scammon and James A. Barnes, "Republican Prospects: Southern Discomfort," *Public Opinion* (October/November 1985): 14–17.
7. Jerold G. Rusk, "The Effect of the Australian Ballot Reform on Split-Ticket Voting: 1876–1908." *American Political Science Review* 64 (December 1970): 1220–1238.
8. Robert Kuttner, "Fat and Sassy," *The New Republic* (February 23, 1987): 21–23.
9. Morton Keller, *Affairs of State* (Cambridge: Harvard University Press, 1977), 239.
10. Quoted in Keller, ibid., 256.
11. Martin Shefter, "Parties, Bureaucracy, and Political Change in the United States," in *The Development of Political Parties*, Sage Electoral Studies Yearbook, vol. 4, ed. Louis Maisel and Joseph Cooper (Beverly Hills, Calif.: Sage Publications, 1978).
12. James Q. Wilson, *The Amateur Democrat: Club Politics in Three Cities* (Chicago: University of Chicago Press, 1962).
13. Samuel J. Eldersveld, *Political Parties: A Behavioral Analysis* (Chicago: Rand McNally, 1964), 278, 287.
14. Robert H. Salisbury, "The Urban Party Organization Member," *Public Opinion Quarterly* 29 (Winter 1965–1966): 550–564.
15. Ibid., 557, 559.
16. Eldersveld, *Political Parties;* and J. David Greenstone, *Labor in American Politics* (New York: Knopf, 1969), 187.
17. David R. Mayhew, *Placing Parties in American Politics* (Princeton, N.J.: Princeton University Press, 1986), chs. 2, 3.
18. *Boston Globe* (July 9, 1984): 1.
19. William Nisbet Chambers and Walter Dean Burnham, eds., *The American Party Systems: Stages of Political Development*, 2d ed. (New York: Oxford University Press, 1975), 6.
20. *Williams v. Rhodes*, 393 U.S. 23 (1968).
21. James Q. Wilson, *Political Organizations* (New York: Basic Books, 1973), ch. 12; and Samuel Stouffer, *Communism, Conformity, and Civil Liberties* (Garden City, N.Y.: Doubleday, 1955).
22. Updated from Jeane Kirkpatrick, *The New Presidential Elite* (New York: Russell Sage Foundation and Twentieth Century Fund, 1976), 297–315.
23. Nelson W. Polsby, *Consequences of Party Reform* (New York: Oxford University Press, 1983), 9–11, 64.

24. Ibid., 158. But compare John G. Geer, "Voting in Presidential Primaries," paper delivered to the 1984 annual meeting of the American Political Science Association.
25. Center for the Study of the American Electorate, April 2000.
26. Michael J. Malbin, "Democratic Party Rules Are Made to Be Broken," *National Journal* (August 23, 1980): 1388.

Chapter 8 *Elections and Campaigns*

1. *Wesberry v. Sanders*, 376 U.S. 1 (1964).
2. Richard F. Fenno, Jr. "U.S. House Members and Their Constituencies: An Exploration," *American Political Science Review* 71 (September 1977): 883–917, esp. 914.
3. John A. Ferejohn, *Pork Barrel Politics* (Stanford, Calif.: Stanford University Press, 1974).
4. Douglas Arnold, *Congress and the Bureaucracy* (New Haven, Conn.: Yale University Press, 1979).
5. Fred Barnes, "Charade on Main Street," *The New Republic* (June 15, 1987): 15–17. See also Hugh Winebrenner, *The Iowa Precinct Caucuses: The Making of a Media Event* (Ames: Iowa State University Press, 1987).
6. Arthur H. Miller et al., "A Majority Party in Disarray: Policy Polarization in the 1972 Election," *American Political Science Review* 70 (1976): 757.
7. Donald E. Stokes and John J. DiIulio, Jr., "Valence Politics in Modern Elections," in *The 1992 Elections*, ed. Michael J. Nelson (Washington, D.C.: Congressional Quarterly Press, 1993), ch. 1.
8. Michael Kelley, "The Making of a First Family: A Blueprint," *New York Times* (November 14, 1992): 1, 9.
9. Ibid.
10. Thomas E. Patterson and Robert D. McClure, *The Unseeing Eye: The Myth of Television Power in National Politics* (New York: Putnam, 1976); and Xandra Kayden, *Campaign Organization* (Lexington, Mass.: D. C. Heath, 1978), ch. 6.
11. Gerald M. Pomper et al., *The Election of 1980* (Chatham, N.J.: Chatham House, 1981), 75, 105–107.
12. John J. DiIulio, Jr., "Valence Voters Are Not Fools," in *The 1996 Elections*, ed. Michael J. Nelson (Washington, D.C.: Congressional Quarterly Press, 1997), ch. 10.
13. Gary C. Jacobson, *The Politics of Congressional Elections*, 2d ed. (Boston: Little, Brown, 1987), 49.
14. Donald Philip Green and Jonathan S. Krasno, "Salvation for the Spendthrift Incumbent: Reestimating the Effects of Campaign Spending in House Elections," *American Journal of Political Science* 32 (1988): 884–960; Stephen Ansolabehre, "Winning Is Easy but It Sure Ain't Cheap," Working Paper 90–1, Center for American Politics and Public Policy, UCLA, 1990; Robert S. Erickson and Thomas R. Palfrey, "The Puzzle of Incumbent Spending in Congressional Elections," *Social Science*

Working Paper 806, California Institute of Technology, August 1992.
15. Angus Campbell, Philip E. Converse, Warren E. Miller, and Donald E. Stokes, *The American Voter* (New York: Wiley, 1960), ch. 8.
16. V. O. Key, Jr., *The Responsible Electorate* (Cambridge: Harvard University Press, 1966).
17. Morris P. Fiorina, *Retrospective Voting in American National Elections* (New Haven, Conn.: Yale University Press, 1981).
18. Jay P. Greene, "Forewarned Before Forecast: Presidential Election Forecasting Models and the 1992 Election," *P.S.: Political Science and Politics* (March 1993): 20.
19. In 1988 Dukakis led Bush by 17 percent in polls taken shortly after Dukakis was nominated, only to see Bush win handily. In 1980 Carter led Reagan in the early polls.
20. Paul Freedman and Ken Goldstein, "Measuring Media Exposure and the Effects of Negative Campaign Ads," *American Journal of Political Science* 43 (October 1999): 1189–1208.
21. Robert Axelrod, "Where the Votes Come From: An Analysis of Electoral Coalitions, 1952–1968," *American Political Science Review* 66 (1972): 11–20; and Axelrod, "Communication," *American Political Science Review* 68 (1974): 718–719.
22. Gerald M. Pomper, *Elections in America* (New York: Dodd, Mead, 1971), 178.
23. Benjamin Ginsberg, "Elections and Public Policy," *American Political Science Review* 70 (March 1976): 41–49.

Chapter 9 *Interest Groups*

1. L. Harmon Zeigler and Hendrik van Dalen, "Interest Groups in the States," in *Politics in the American States*, ed. Herbert Jacob and Kenneth N. Vines, 2d ed. (Boston: Little, Brown, 1974), 122–160; and Edward C. Banfield and James Q. Wilson, *City Politics* (Cambridge: Harvard University Press, 1963), chs. 18, 19.
2. Joseph LaPalombara, *Interest Groups in Italian Politics* (Princeton, N.J.: Princeton University Press, 1964).
3. Kay Lehman Schlozman and John T. Tierney, "More of the Same: Washington Pressure Group Activity in a Decade of Change," *Journal of Politics* 45 (1983): 356.
4. The use of injunctions in labor disputes was restricted by the Norris-LaGuardia Act of 1932; the rights to collective bargaining and to the union shop were guaranteed by the Wagner Act of 1935.
5. *Historical Statistics of the United States, Colonial Times to 1970*, vol. 1, 386.
6. The distinction is drawn from Kay Lehman Schlozman and John T. Tierney, *Organized Interests and American Democracy* (New York: Harper and Row, 1985).
7. Jeffrey M. Berry, *The Interest Group Society* (Boston: Little, Brown, 1984), 20–21.
8. Ibid., 24, 130.
9. Gabriel A. Almond and Sidney Verba, *The Civic Culture* (Princeton, N.J.: Princeton University

Press, 1963), 302; Derek C. Bok and John T. Dunlop, *Labor and the American Community* (New York: Simon and Schuster, 1970), 49; *Statistical Abstract of the United States, 1975,* 373.

10. Almond and Verba, *The Civic Culture,* 194.
11. Ibid., 207.
12. Mancur Olson, Jr., *The Logic of Collective Action* (Cambridge: Harvard University Press, 1965), 153–157.
13. Bok and Dunlop, *Labor,* 134.
14. Henry J. Pratt, *The Liberalization of American Protestantism* (Detroit: Wayne State University Press, 1972), ch. 12; Gerhard Lenski, *The Religious Factor* (Garden City, N.Y.: Doubleday, 1961), ch. 4.
15. Jane J. Mansbridge, *Why We Lost the ERA* (Chicago: University of Chicago Press, 1986), ch. 10.
16. Joyce Gelb and Marian Lief Palley, *Women and Public Choices* (Princeton, N.J.: Princeton University Press, 1982), ch. 3; Jo Freeman, *The Politics of Women's Liberation* (New York: McKay, 1975), ch. 3; Maren Lockwood Carden, "The Proliferation of a Social Movement: Ideology and Individual Incentives in the Contemporary Feminist Movement," *Research in Social Movements* 1 (1978): 179–196; and Dom Bonafede, "Still a Long Way to Go," *National Journal* (September 13, 1986): 2175–2179.
17. *Statistical Abstract of the United States,* 2000, 445; Mansbridge, *Why We Lost, 130–131.*
18. Jeffrey M. Berry, *Lobbying for the People* (Princeton, N.J.: Princeton University Press, 1977), 71–76.
19. Berry, *Interest Group Society,* 88.
20. Schlozman and Tierney, *Organized Interests and American Democracy,* table 5-4.
21. *New York Times* (December 8, 1983): 1.
22. Raymond A. Bauer, Ithiel de Sola Pool, and Lewis Anthony Dexter, *American Business and Public Policy* (New York: Atherton, 1963), ch. 30.
23. Berry, *Lobbying for the People,* 136–140.
24. Margaret Ann Latus, "Assessing Ideological PACs: From Outrage to Understanding," in *Money and Politics in the United States,* ed. Michael J. Malbin (Chatham, N.J.: Chatham House, 1984), 143; data supplied by the Federal Election Commission, March 1992.
25. Latus, *Assessing,* 144.
26. Malbin, *Money and Politics,* table A.8, 290–291.
27. Michael J. Malbin, "Looking Back at the Future of Campaign Finance Reform: Interest Groups and American Elections," in Malbin, *Money and Politics,* 248; James B. Kau and Paul H. Rubin, *Congressmen, Constituents and Contributors* (Boston: Martinus Nijhoff, 1982); Henry W. Chappell, Jr., "Campaign Contributions and Voting on the Cargo Preference Bill: A Comparison of Simultaneous Models," *Public Choice* 36 (1981): 301–312; W. P. Welch, "Campaign Contributions and Voting: Milk Money and Dairy Price Supports," *Western Political Quarterly* 35 (1982): 478–495; John R. Wright,

"PACs, Contributions, and Roll Calls: An Organizational Perspective," *American Political Science Review* 79 (1985): 400–414. But compare Benjamin Ginsberg and John C. Green, "The Best Congress Money Can Buy," in *Do Elections Matter?,* ed. Benjamin Ginsberg and Alan Stone (Armonk, N.Y.: M. E. Sharpe, 1986), 75–89.
28. William T. Gormley, "A Test of the Revolving Door Hypothesis at the FCC," *American Journal of Political Science* 23 (1979): 665–683; Paul J. Quirk, *Industry Influence in Federal Regulatory Agencies* (Princeton, N.J.: Princeton University Press, 1981); Jeffrey E. Cohen, "The Dynamics of the 'Revolving Door' on the FCC," *American Journal of Political Science* 30 (1986): 689–708.
29. Suzanne Weaver, *Decision to Prosecute* (Cambridge, Mass.: MIT Press, 1977), 154–163.
30. *United States v. Harriss,* 347 U.S. 612 (1954).
31. *United States Code,* Title 26, section 501(c)(3).

Chapter 10   *The Media*

1. R. L. Lowenstein, *World Press Freedom, 1966* (Columbia, Mo.: Freedom of Information Center, 1967), publication No. 11.
2. D. E. Butler, "Why American Political Reporting Is Better Than England's," *Harper's* (May 1963): 15–25.
3. *New York Times* (March 15, 1975).
4. *New York Times* (January 28, 1974).
5. Douglass Cater, *The Fourth Branch of Government* (Boston: Houghton Mifflin, 1959), 76; and William L. Rivers, "The Press as a Communication System," in *Handbook of Communication,* ed. Ithiel de Sola Pool et al. (Chicago: Rand McNally, 1973), 522–526.
6. Quoted in F. L. Mort, *American Journalism, 1690–1960,* 3d ed. (New York: Macmillan, 1962), 529, as cited in Rivers, "The Press," 526.
7. Center for Media and Public Affairs, "The Incredible Shrinking Sound Bite," Press Release, Washington, D.C., September 28, 2000.
8. Edward Jay Epstein, *News from Nowhere: Television and the News* (New York: Random House, 1973), 37.
9. Allen H. Barton, "Consensus and Conflict Among American Leaders," *Public Opinion Quarterly* 38 (Winter 1974–1975): 507–530.
10. Paul H. Weaver, "The New Journalism and the Old—Thoughts After Watergate," *The Public Interest* (Spring 1974): 67–88.
11. *Near v. Minnesota,* 283 U.S. 697 (1931).
12. *New York Times v. United States,* 403 U.S. 713 (1971).
13. *New York Times v. Sullivan,* 376 U.S. 254 (1964).
14. *Miami Herald Publishing Co. v. Tornillo,* 418 U.S. 241 (1974).
15. *Yates v. United States,* 354 U.S. 298 (1957).
16. *Branzburg v. Hayes,* 408 U.S. 665 (1972).
17. *Zurcher v. Stanford Daily,* 436 U.S. 547 (1978), overturned by the Privacy Protection Act of 1980 (P.L. 96–440).
18. *National Journal* (April 16, 1983): 787.

19. Benjamin I. Page, "The Media as Political Actors," *PS: Political Science & Politics* (March 1996): 21.
20. Thomas E. Patterson and Robert D. McClure, *The Unseeing Eye: The Myth of Television Power in National Elections* (New York: Putnam, 1976); and Herbert Asher, *Presidential Elections and American Politics* (Homewood, Ill.: Dorsey Press, 1976), 239–240 (and studies cited therein).
21. David O. Sears and Richard E. Whitney, "Political Persuasion," in Pool, *Handbook of Communication,* 253–289.
22. Robert S. Erickson, "The Influence of Newspaper Endorsements in Presidential Elections: The Case of 1964," *American Journal of Political Science* 20 (May 1976): 207–233.
23. Maxwell E. McCombs and Donald R. Shaw, "The Agenda Setting Function of the Mass Media," *Public Opinion Quarterly* 36 (Summer 1972): 176–187; Shanto Iyengar and Donald R. Kinder, *News That Matters* (Chicago: University of Chicago Press, 1987).
24. G. Ray Funkhouser, "The Issues of the Sixties," *Public Opinion Quarterly* 37 (Spring 1973): 62–75.
25. Joseph Wagner, "Media Do Make a Difference: The Differential Impact of Mass Media in the 1976 Presidential Race," *American Journal of Political Science* 27 (August 1983): 407–430.
26. Benjamin I. Page, Robert Y. Shapiro, and Glenn R. Dempsey, "What Moves Public Opinion?" *American Political Science Review* 81 (March 1987): 23–43.
27. George Jergens, "Theodore Roosevelt and the Press," *Daedalus* (Fall 1982): 113–133; and Henry Fairlie, "The Rise of the Press Secretary," *New Republic* (March 18, 1978): 20–23.
28. Michael J. Robinson, "A Twentieth Century Medium in a Nineteenth Century Legislature: The Effects of Television on the American Congress," in *Congress in Change,* ed. Norman J. Ornstein (New York: Praeger, 1975), 240–261.
29. S. Robert Lichter and Stanley Rothman, "Media and Business Elites," *Public Opinion* (October/November 1981): 42–46.
30. Robert Lichter, "Consistently Liberal: But Does It Matter?," *Forbes Media Critic,* Fall 1996, 26–39.
31. Michael J. Robinson, "Just How Liberal Is the News? 1980 Revisited," *Public Opinion* (February/March 1983): 55–60; Maura Clancey and Michael J. Robinson, "The Media in Campaign '84: General Election Coverage," *Public Opinion* (December/January 1985); Elizabeth Kolbet, "Maybe the Media Did Treat Bush Harshly," *New York Times* (November 22, 1992): E2.
32. Peter Braestrup, *Big Story,* 2 vols. (Boulder, Colo.: Westview Press, 1977).
33. S. Robert Lichter, Stanley Rothman, and Linda S. Lichter, *The Media Elite* (Bethesda, Md.: Adler and Adler, 1986).
34. Pew Research Center for the People and the Press, "Media Seen as Fair, But Tilting to

Gore," Press Release, Washington, D.C., October 15, 2000.

35. Center for Media and Public Affairs, "Public to Press: Keep in Touch!," Press Release, Washington, D.C., 1996.

36. Pew Center for the People and the Press, "Terror Coverage Boost News Media's Images," Press Release, November 28, 2001.

37. Will Lester, "Poll: Interest in News Stabilizes," *The Macon Telegraph* (June 9, 2002).

Chapter 11   *Congress*

1. H. Douglas Price, "Careers and Committees in the American Congress," in *The History of Parliamentary Behavior*, ed. William O. Aydelotte (Princeton, N.J.: Princeton University Press, 1977), 28–62; John F. Bibby, Thomas E. Mann, and Norman J. Ornstein, *Vital Statistics on Congress, 1980* (Washington, D.C.: American Enterprise Institute, 1980), 53–54; Thomas E. Cavanaugh, "The Dispersion of Authority in the House of Representatives," *Political Science Quarterly* 97 (1982–1983): 625–626; *Congressional Quarterly Weekly Reports.*

2. David R. Mayhew, *Congress: The Electoral Connection* (New Haven, Conn.: Yale University Press, 1974); Bibby, Mann, and Ornstein, *Vital Statistics*, 14–15.

3. Mayhew, *Congress*; Morris P. Fiorina, *Congress: Keystone of the Washington Establishment* (New Haven, Conn.: Yale University Press, 1977).

4. Rhodes Cook, "House Republicans Scored a Quiet Victory in '92," *Congressional Quarterly* (April 17, 1993): 966.

5. Bruce E. Cain and David Butler, "Redrawing District Lines: What's Going On and What's at Stake," *The American Enterprise* (July/August 1991): 37.

6. Gary C. Jacobson, "The Persistence of Democratic House Majorities: Structure or Politics," paper delivered at the 1990 annual meeting of the American Political Science Association, San Francisco, August 30–September 2, 1990, 2.

7. Warren E. Miller and Donald E. Stokes, "Constituency Influence in Congress," in *Elections and the Political Order*, ed. Angus Campbell et al. (New York: Wiley, 1966), 359.

8. John E. Jackson, *Constituencies and Leaders in Congress* (Cambridge: Harvard University Press, 1974).

9. Jerrold E. Schneider, *Ideological Coalitions in Congress* (Westport, Conn.: Greenwood Press, 1979), 134, 195.

10. Michael Foley, *The New Senate: Liberal Influence on a Conservative Institution, 1959–1972* (New Haven, Conn.: Yale University Press, 1980), 242.

11. Tim Groseclose, Steven D. Levitt, and James M. Snyder, Jr., "Comparing Interest Group Scores Across Time and Chambers," *American Political Science Review* 93 (1999): 33–50.

12. *Congressional Quarterly Weekly Report* (December 3, 1994): 3430–3435.

13. In 1993 the 103d Congress also contained a lot of newly elected Democratic members eager to change House rules. They voted for the old rules and procedures, however, because that is what their party leaders wanted.

14. Barbara Sinclair, *The Transformation of the United States Senate* (Baltimore: Johns Hopkins University Press, 1989).

15. Norman J. Ornstein, Thomas E. Mann, and Michael J. Malbin, *Vital Statistics on Congress, 1995–1996* (Washington, D.C.: Congressional Quarterly Press, 1996), 199–200.

16. Gary C. Jacobson, "The Electoral Basis of Partisan Polarization in Congress," paper delivered at the annual meeting of the American Political Science Association, August 31–September 3, 2002; Larry M. Bartels, "Partisanship and Voting Behavior, 1952–1996," *American Journal of Political Science* 44 (2000): 35–50.

17. Marc J. Hetherington, "Resurgent Mass Partisanship: The Role of Elite Polarization," *American Political Science Review* 95 (2001): 619–631.

18. Susan Webb Hammond, "Congressional Caucuses in the 104th Congress," chapter in *Congress Reconsidered*, ed. Lawrence C. Dodd and Bruce I. Oppenheimer, 6th ed. (Washington, D.C.: Congressional Quarterly Press, 1997), 6.

19. Ibid., 34.

20. Steven S. Smith, "Revolution in the House: Why Don't We Do It on the Floor?" discussion paper no. 5, Brookings Institution, Washington, D.C., September 1986.

21. Richard F. Fenno, Jr., *Congressmen in Committees* (Boston: Little, Brown, 1973).

22. Michael J. Malbin, "Delegation, Deliberation, and the New Role of Congressional Staff," in *The New Congress*, ed. Thomas E. Mann and Norman J. Ornstein (Washington, D.C.: American Enterprise Institute, 1981), 134–177, esp. 170–171.

23. Lawrence H. Chamberlain, "The President, Congress, and Legislation," in *The Presidency*, ed. Aaron Wildavsky (Boston: Little, Brown, 1969), 444–445; Ronald C. Moe and Steven C. Teel, "Congress as a Policy-Maker: A Necessary Reappraisal," *Political Science Quarterly* 85 (September 1970): 443–470.

24. Richard E. Cohen, "Challenging the House's Traffic Cop," *National Journal* (April 4, 1993): 1002.

25. Thomas E. Mann and Norman J. Ornstein, *Renewing Congress: A Second Report* (Washington, D.C.: American Enterprise Institute, 1993), 49.

26. Malcolm E. Jewell and Samuel C. Patterson, *The Legislative Process in the United States*, 3d ed. (New York: Random House, 1977), 439.

27. Mann and Ornstein, *Renewing Congress*, 71–72.

28. Ibid., 72.

29. Dennis F. Thompson, *Ethics in Congress: From Individual to Institutional Corruption* (Washington, D.C.: Brookings Institution, 1995), 191.

Chapter 12   *The Presidency*

1. Jean Blondel, *An Introduction to Comparative Government* (New York: Praeger, 1969), as cited in Nelson W. Polsby, "Legislatures," in *Handbook of Political Science*, ed. Fred I. Greenstein and Nelson W. Polsby (Reading, Mass.: Addison-Wesley, 1975), vol. 5, 275.

2. Donald F. Kettl, *Deficit Politics: Public Budgeting in Its Institutional and Historical Context* (New York: Macmillan, 1992), 13.

3. Morris P. Fiorina, *Divided Government* (New York: Macmillan, 1992), 86–111.

4. David Mayhew, *Divided We Govern: Party Control, Lawmaking, and Investigations, 1946–1990* (New Haven, Conn.: Yale University Press, 1991), 76.

5. Mark A. Peterson, *Legislating Together: The White House and Congress from Eisenhower to Reagan* (Cambridge: Harvard University Press, 1990).

6. Richard E. Cohen, *Washington at Work: Back Rooms and Clean Air* (New York: Macmillan, 1992), 154–155.

7. Ibid., 169.

8. Kettl, *Deficit Politics*, 138.

9. Woodrow Wilson, *Congressional Government* (New York: Meridian Books, 1956), 167–168, 170. (First published in 1885.)

10. Stephen Hess, *Organizing the Presidency* (Washington, D.C.: Brookings Institution, 1976), 3; R. W. Apple, "Clinton's Refocusing," *New York Times* (May 6, 1993): A22; Michael K. Frisby, "Power Switch," *Wall Street Journal* (March 26, 1993): A1, A7.

11. David T. Stanley et al., *Men Who Govern* (Washington, D.C.: Brookings Institution, 1967), 41–42, 50.

12. Daniel J. Elazar, "Which Road to the Presidency?" in *The Presidency*, ed. Aaron Wildavsky (Boston: Little, Brown, 1969), 340.

13. Richard E. Neustadt, *Presidential Power*, rev. ed. (New York: Wiley, 1976), ch. 4.

14. Walter D. Burnham, "Insulation and Responsiveness in Congressional Elections," *Political Science Quarterly* 90 (Fall 1975): 412–413; George C. Edwards III, *Presidential Influence in Congress* (San Francisco: Freeman, 1980), 70–78; Warren E. Miller, "Presidential Coattails: A Study in Political Myth and Methodology," *Public Opinion Quarterly* 19 (Winter 1955–1956): 368; and Miller, "The Motivational Basis for Straight and Split Ticket Voting," *American Political Science Review* 51 (June 1957): 293–312.

15. *Clinton v. City of New York*, 118 S.Ct. 2091 (1998).

16. *Marbury v. Madison*, 1 Cranch 137 (1803).

17. *United States v. Nixon*, 418 U.S. 683 (1974).

18. *Clinton v. Jones*, 520 U.S. 681 (1997); *In Re Grand Jury Subpoena Duces Tecum*, 112 F.3d 910 (1997); *In Re Sealed Case*, 121 F.3d 729 (1997).

19. Marcus Cunliffe, *American Presidents and the Presidency* (New York: American Heritage Press/McGraw-Hill, 1972), 63, 65.

20. Ibid., 214.

21. Adapted from Paul C. Light, *The President's Agenda* (Baltimore, Md.: Johns Hopkins University Press, 1982), 217–225.

Chapter 13 *The Bureaucracy*

1. Charles E. Lindblom, *Politics and Markets* (New York: Basic Books, 1977), 114.
2. Article II, section 2, para. 2.
3. Article II, section 3.
4. Calculated from data in *Historical Statistics of the United States: Colonial Times to 1970* (Washington, D.C.: Government Printing Office, 1975), vol. 2, 1102–1103.
5. *Panama Refining Co. v. Ryan*, 293 U.S. 388 (1935).
6. *Hampton Jr. & Co. v. United States*, 276 U.S. 394 (1928).
7. Edward S. Corwin, *The Constitution and What It Means Today*, 13th ed. (Princeton, N.J.: Princeton University Press, 1973), 151.
8. Bruce D. Porter, "Parkinson's Law Revisited: War and the Growth of American Government," *Public Interest* (Summer 1980): 50–68.
9. See the cases cited in Corwin, *The Constitution*, 8.
10. *U.S. Statutes*, vol. 84, sec. 799 (1970).
11. *Historical Statistics of the United States*, vol. 2, 1107.
12. Donald F. Kettl et al., *Civil Service Reform: Building a Government That Works* (Washington, D.C.: Brookings Institution, 1996), 18.
13. Ibid., 15.
14. Hugh Heclo, "Issue Networks and the Executive Establishment," in *The New American Political System*, ed. Anthony King (Washington, D.C.: American Enterprise Institute, 1978), 87–124.
15. Quoted in Hugh Heclo, *A Government of Strangers* (Washington, D.C.: Brookings Institution, 1977), 225.
16. Alexis Simendinger, "Of the People, for the People," *National Journal* (April 18, 1998): 852–855. Data from the Pew Charitable Trusts Research Center for the People and the Press.
17. Stanley Rothman and S. Robert Lichter, "How Liberal Are Bureaucrats?" *Regulation* (November/December, 1983): 17–18.
18. Kenneth Meier and Lloyd Nigro, "Representative Bureaucracy and Policy References: A Study of the Attitudes of Federal Executives," *Public Administration Review* 36 (July/August 1976): 458–467; Bernard Mennis, *American Foreign Policy Officials* (Columbus: Ohio State University Press, 1971).
19. Joel D. Aberbach and Bert A. Rockman, "Clashing Beliefs Within the Executive Branch: The Nixon Administration Bureaucracy," *American Political Science Review* 70 (June 1976): 456–468.
20. David Stockman, *The Triumph of Politics* (New York: Harper and Row, 1986).
21. James Q. Wilson, *Bureaucracy* (New York: Basic Books, 1989), ch. 6.
22. Heclo, "Issue Networks and the Executive Establishment," 87–124.

23. Richard F. Fenno, Jr., *The Power of the Purse* (Boston: Little, Brown, 1966), 450, 597.
24. John E. Schwartz and L. Earl Shaw, *The United States Congress in Comparative Perspective* (Hinsdale, Ill.: Dryden Press, 1976), 262–263; *National Journal* (July 4, 1981): 1211–1214.
25. *Immigration and Naturalization Service v. Chadha*, 103 S. Ct. 2764 (1983); *Maine v. Thiboutot*, 100 S. Ct. 2502 (1980).
26. See cases cited in Corwin, *The Constitution*, 22.
27. Steven Kelman, "The Grace Commission: How Much Waste in Government?" *Public Interest* (Winter 1985): 62–87.
28. Daniel Katz et al., *Bureaucratic Encounters* (Ann Arbor: Survey Research Center, University of Michigan, 1975), 63–69, 118–120, 184–188.
29. *From Red Tape to Results: Creating a Government That Works Better and Costs Less*, report of the National Performance Review, Vice President Al Gore, September 7, 1993.

Chapter 14 *The Judiciary*

1. Henry J. Abraham, *The Judicial Process*, 3d ed. (New York: Oxford University Press, 1975), 279–280.
2. Robert G. McCloskey, *The American Supreme Court* (Chicago: University of Chicago Press, 1960), 27.
3. *Marbury v. Madison*, 5 U.S. 137 (1803); and *McCulloch v. Maryland*, 17 U.S. 316 (1819).
4. *Martin v. Hunter's Lessee*, 14 U.S. 304 (1816); and *Cohens v. Virginia*, 19 U.S. (1821).
5. *Gibbons v. Ogden*, 22 U.S. (1824).
6. Quoted in Albert J. Beveridge, *The Life of John Marshall* (Boston: Houghton Mifflin, 1919), vol. 4, 551.
7. *Dred Scott v. Sandford*, 60 U.S. 393 (1857).
8. Abraham, *The Judicial Process*, 286.
9. *In re Debs*, 158 U.S. 564 (1895).
10. *Pollock v. Farmers' Loan & Trust Co.*, 157 U.S. 429 (1895).
11. *United States v. Knight*, 156 U.S. 1 (1895).
12. *Cincinnati, N.O. & T.P. Railway Co. v. Interstate Commerce Commission*, 162 U.S. 184 (1896).
13. *Hammer v. Dagenhart*, 247 U.S. 251 (1918).
14. *Lochner v. New York*, 198 U.S. 45 (1905).
15. McCloskey, *The American Supreme Court*, 151.
16. *Munn v. Illinois*, 94 U.S. 113 (1877).
17. *Dayton-Goose Creek Railway Co. v. United States*, 263 U.S. 456 (1924).
18. *Atchison, Topeka, and Santa Fe Railroad Co. v. Matthews*, 174 U.S. 96 (1899).
19. *Mugler v. Kansas*, 123 U.S. 623 (1887).
20. *St. Louis Consolidated Coal Co. v. Illinois*, 185 U.S. 203 (1902).
21. *New York Central Railroad Co. v. White*, 243 U.S. 188 (1917).
22. *German Alliance Insurance Co. v. Lewis*, 233 U.S. 389 (1914).
23. Morton Keller, *Affairs of State* (Cambridge: Harvard University Press, 1977), 369. See also Mary Cornelia Porter, "That Commerce Shall Be Free: A New Look at the Old Laissez-Faire Court," in *The Supreme Court Review*, ed. Philip B. Kurland (Chicago: University of Chicago Press, 1976), 135–159.

24. *Chief of Capitol Police v. Jeannette Rankin Brigade*, 409 U.S. 972 (1972).
25. *Aptheker v. Secretary of State*, 378 U.S. 500 (1964).
26. *Trop v. Dulles*, 356 U.S. 86 (1958); *Afroyim v. Rusk*, 387 U.S. 253 (1967); and *Schneider v. Rusk*, 377 U.S. 163 (1964).
27. *Lamont v. Postmaster General*, 381 U.S. 301 (1965); and *Blount v. Rizzi*, 400 U.S. 410 (1971).
28. *Richardson v. Davis*, 409 U.S. 1069 (1972); *U.S. Department of Agriculture v. Murry*, 413 U.S. 508 (1973); *Jimenez v. Weinberger*, 417 U.S. 628 (1974); and *Washington v. Legrant*, 394 U.S. 618 (1969).
29. *United States v. Lopez*, 514 U.S. 549 (1995).
30. *Seminole Tribe of Florida v. Florida*, 517 U.S. 44 (1996); *Alden v. Maine*, 527 U.S. 706 (1999); *Florida v. College Savings Bank*, 527 U.S. 627 (1999).
31. Robert A. Carp and C. I. Rowland, *Policymaking and Politics in the Federal District Courts* (Knoxville: University of Tennessee Press, 1983), 38; Sheldon Goldman, "Voting Behavior on the United States Courts of Appeals, Revisited," *American Political Science Review* 69 (1975): 491–506; C. Heal Tate, "Personal Attribute Models of the Voting Behavior of U.S. Supreme Court Justices," *American Political Science Review* 75 (1981): 355–367.
32. Daniel R. Pinello, "Linking Party to Judicial Ideology in American Courts: A Meta-analysis," *Justice System Journal* 20 (1999): 219–254.
33. *United States v. Lanza*, 260 U.S. 377 (1922). Cf. *Abbate v. United States*, 359 U.S. 187 (1959); and *Bartkus v. Illinois*, 359 U.S. 121 (1989).
34. *Gideon v. Wainwright*, 372 U.S. 335 (1963). The story is told in Anthony Lewis, *Gideon's Trumpet* (New York: Random House, 1964).
35. Erwin Griswold, "Rationing Justice: The Supreme Court's Case Load and What the Court Does Not Do," *Cornell Law Review* 60 (1975): 335–354.
36. Joseph Weis, Jr., "Disconnecting the Overloaded Circuits—A Plan for a Unified Court of Appeals," *St. Louis University Law Journal* 39 (1995): 455.
37. *Alyeska Pipeline Service Co. v. Wilderness Society*, 421 U.S. 240 (1975).
38. *Flast v. Cohen*, 392 U.S. 83 (1968), which modified the earlier *Frothingham v. Mellon*, 262 U.S. 447 (1923); *United States v. Richardson*, 418 U.S. 166 (1947).
39. *Brown v. Board of Education of Topeka*, 347 U.S. 483 (1954).
40. *Baker v. Carr*, 369 U.S. 186 (1962).
41. See Louise Weinberg, "A New Judicial Federalism?" *Daedalus* (Winter 1978): 129–141.
42. Quoted in Abraham, *The Judicial Process*, 330.
43. Carolyn D. Richmond, "The Rehnquist Court: What Is in Store for Constitutional Precedent?" *New York Law Review* 39 (1994): 511.
44. *Colegrove v. Green*, 328 U.S. 549 (1946).
45. The Court abandoned the "political question" doctrine in *Baker v. Carr*, 369 U.S. 186 (1962), and began to change congressional-

district apportionment in *Wesberry v. Sanders*, 376 U.S. 1 (1964).

46. Donald L. Horowitz, *The Courts and Social Policy* (Washington, D.C.: Brookings Institution, 1977), 6.

47. *Gates v. Collier*, 349 F. Supp. 881 (1972).

48. *Lau v. Nichols*, 414 U.S. 563 (1974).

49. Jane Burnbaum, "Guilty! Too Many Lawyers and Too Much Litigation," *Business Week* (April 13, 1992), 60–61.

50. Joel B. Grossman and Austin Sarat, "Litigation in the Federal Courts: A Comparative Perspective," *Law and Society Review* 9 (Winter 1975): 321–346.

51. Administrative Office of the U.S. Courts, *Annual Report, 1988*, 109.

52. Jack W. Peltason, *Fifty-eight Lonely Men: Southern Federal Judges and School Desegregation* (New York: Harcourt Brace, 1961).

53. Anthony Patridge and William B. Eldridge, *The Second Circuit Sentencing Study* (Washington, D.C.: Federal Judicial Center, 1974).

54. *Abington School District v. Schempp*, 374 U.S. 203 (1963).

55. Robert H. Birkby, "The Supreme Court and the Bible Belt," *Midwest Journal of Political Science* 10 (1966): 3.

56. Cless R. Sunstein, "Impeaching the President," *University of Pennsylvania Law Review* 147 (1998): 279.

57. *United States v. Butler*, 297 U.S. 1 (1936).

58. *Ex parte McCardle*, 74 U.S. 506 (1869).

59. Walter F. Murphy, *Congress and the Court* (Chicago: University of Chicago Press, 1962); and C. Herman Pritchett, *Congress Versus the Supreme Court* (Minneapolis: University of Minnesota Press, 1961).

60. Gregory A. Caldeira, "Neither the Purse nor the Sword: Dynamics of Public Confidence in the U.S. Supreme Court," *American Political Science Review* 80 (1986): 1209–1226. See also Joseph T. Tannenhaus and Walter F. Murphy, "Patterns of Public Support for the Supreme Court: A Panel Study," *Journal of Politics* 43 (1981): 24–39.

Chapter 15   *The Policy-Making Process*

1. E. E. Schattschneider, *The Semisovereign People* (New York: Holt, Rinehart and Winston, 1960), 68.

2. Jack L. Walker, "Setting the Agenda in the U.S. Senate: A Theory of Problem Selection," *British Journal of Political Science* 7 (1977): 343, 441.

3. *Statistical Abstract of the United States, 1975* (Washington, D.C.: Government Printing Office, 1975), 342–343, 349.

4. Alexis de Tocqueville, *The Old Regime and the French Revolution*, trans. Gilbert Stuart (Garden City, N.Y.: Doubleday Anchor Books, 1955), 176–177. (First published in 1856.)

5. David O. Sears and J. B. McConahay, *The Politics of Violence* (Boston: Houghton Mifflin, 1973). Compare Abraham H. Miller et al., "The New Urban Blacks," *Ethnicity* 3 (1976): 338–367.

6. Daniel Patrick Moynihan, *Maximum Feasible Misunderstanding* (New York: Free Press, 1969), ch. 2.

7. Nelson W. Polsby, "Goodbye to the Senate's Inner Club," in *Congress in Change: Evolution and Reform*, ed. Norman J. Ornstein (New York: Praeger, 1975), 208–215.

8. *Federalist No. 62*.

9. Walker, "Setting the Agenda," 434, 439, 441.

10. This is a revised version of a theory originally presented in James Q. Wilson, *Political Organizations* (New York: Basic Books, 1973), ch. 16. There are other ways of classifying public policies, notably that of Theodore J. Lowi, "American Business, Public Policy, Case Studies, and Political Theory," *World Politics* 16 (July 1964).

11. Donald F. Kettl, *Sharing Power: Public Governance and Private Markets* (Washington, D.C.: Brookings Institution, 1993); Lawrence J. Hajna, "Superfund: Costly Program Under Fire," *Courier-Post* (February 13, 1994): 6A.

12. Edward S. Greenberg, *Serving the Few: Corporate Capitalism and the Bias of Government Policy* (New York: Wiley, 1974).

13. Charles E. Lindblom, *Politics and Markets* (New York: Basic Books, 1977).

14. Joseph Schumpeter, *Capitalism, Socialism, and Democracy* (New York: Harper and Row, 1950).

15. Louis Galambos, *The Public Image of Big Business in America, 1880–1940* (Baltimore: Johns Hopkins University Press, 1975).

16. Suzanne Weaver, *Decision to Prosecute: Organization and Public Policy in the Antitrust Division* (Cambridge, Mass.: MIT Press, 1977); Robert H. Bork, *The Antitrust Paradox* (New York: Basic Books, 1978).

17. Richard A. Posner, *Antitrust Law: An Economic Perspective* (Chicago: University of Chicago Press, 1976), 25.

18. Alan L. Seltzer, "Woodrow Wilson as 'Corporate-Liberal': Toward a Reconsideration of Left Revisionist Historiography," *Western Political Quarterly* 30 (June 1977): 183–212.

19. Weaver, *Decision to Prosecute*; and Robert A. Katzmann, *Regulatory Bureaucracy: The Federal Trade Commission and Antitrust Policy* (Cambridge, Mass.: MIT Press, 1980).

20. Charles R. Plott, "Occupational Self-Regulation: A Case Study of the Oklahoma Dry Cleaners," *Journal of Law and Economics* 8 (October 1965): 195–222.

21. Paul H. MacAvoy, ed., *Federal Milk Marketing Orders and Price Supports* (Washington, D.C.: American Enterprise Institute, 1977).

22. Ibid., 111.

23. *Congressional Quarterly Weekly Report* (April 21, 1990): 1184–1188.

24. Pietro Nivola, "The New Pork Barrel," *Brookings Review* (Winter 1998): 6–13.

25. Upton Sinclair, *The Jungle* (New York: Doubleday, Page and Co., 1906).

26. Mark V. Nadel, *The Politics of Consumer Protection* (Indianapolis, Ind.: Bobbs-Merrill, 1971), 143–144.

27. Alfred A. Marcus, *Promise and Performance: Choosing and Implementing an Environmental Policy* (Westport, Conn.: Greenwood Press, 1980).

28. Nadel, *Politics*, 66–80.

29. Martha Derthick and Paul J. Quirk, *The Politics of Deregulation* (Washington, D.C.: Brookings Institution, 1985).

30. Executive Orders 11821 (1974), 12044 (1978), and 12291 (1981).

Chapter 16   *Economic Policy*

1. *New York Times* (July 4, 1999): 5; *National Journal* (January 30, 1999): 251.

2. Edward R. Tufte, *Political Control of the Economy* (Princeton, N.J.: Princeton University Press, 1978): 84; Douglas A. Hibbs, Jr., "The Mass Public and Macroeconomic Performance: The Dynamics of Public Opinion Toward Unemployment and Inflation," *American Journal of Political Science* 23 (1979): 705–731.

3. D. Roderick Kiewiet, *Macroeconomics and Micropolitics: The Electoral Effect of Economic Issues* (Chicago: University of Chicago Press, 1983); Morris P. Fiorina, "Economic Retrospective Voting in American National Elections: A Micro-Analysis," *American Journal of Political Science* 22 (1978): 426–443; Donald R. Kinder and D. Roderick Kiewiet, "Sociotropic Politics: The American Case," *British Journal of Political Science* 11 (1981): 129–161.

4. *New York Times*/CBS News poll cited in Douglas A. Hibbs, Jr., "President Reagan's Mandate from the 1980 Elections: A Shift to the Right?" *American Politics Quarterly* 10 (1982): 387–420.

5. Hibbs, "The Mass Public."

6. Ibid.

7. Kiewiet, *Macroeconomics and Micropolitics*.

8. Michael S. Lewis-Beck, "Comparative Economic Voting: Britain, France, Germany, Italy," *American Journal of Political Science* 30 (1986): 315–346.

9. Douglas A. Hibbs, Jr., "Political Parties and Macroeconomic Policy," *American Political Science Review* 71 (1977): 1467–1487.

10. Kiewiet, *Macroeconomics and Micropolitics*, 69.

11. *Pollock v. Farmers' Loan & Trust Co.*, 157 U.S. 429, 158 U.S. 601 (1895).

12. NBC News/*Wall Street Journal* poll, as reported in *National Journal* (July 12, 1986): 1741.

Chapter 17   *Social Welfare*

1. For a general discussion see Charles E. Gilbert, "Welfare Policy," in *Handbook of Political Science*, ed. Fred I. Greenstein and Nelson W. Polsby (Reading, Mass.: Addison-Wesley, 1975), vol. 6, ch. 4.

2. *Congress and the Nation, 1945–1964* (Washington, D.C.: Congressional Quarterly Service, 1965), 1225.

3. Harold E. Raynes, *Social Security in Britain: A History* (London: Pitman, 1960), ch. 18. See also Hugh Heclo, *Modern Social Politics in Britain and Sweden* (New Haven, Conn.: Yale University Press, 1974).

4. Histories of the 1935 act include Edwin E. Witte, *The Development of the Social Security Act* (Madison: University of Wisconsin Press, 1962). A different view, offering a neo-Marxist interpretation of the act, can be found in Frances Fox Piven and Richard A. Cloward, *Regulating the Poor* (New York: Pantheon, 1971).

5. The development of Medicare is described in Theodore Marmor, "Doctors, Politics, and Health Insurance for the Aged: The Enactment of Medicare," in *Cases in Contemporary American Government*, ed. Allan Sindler (Boston: Little, Brown, 1969).

6. Charles R. Morris, *Too Much of a Good Thing? Why Health Care Spending Won't Make Us Sick* (New York: The Century Foundation, 2000), 57.

7. Rick Blizzard, "Why Are Healthcare Issues Gridlocked?" Gallup Tuesday Briefing, June 25, 2002.

8. Michael Harrington, *The Other America* (Baltimore: Penguin Books, 1962).

9. Michael E. Schiltz, *Public Attitudes Toward Social Security, 1935–1965*, Research Report No. 3, Social Security Administration, U.S. Department of Health, Education, and Welfare (Washington, D.C.: Government Printing Office, 1970), 36, 98, 128, 140.

10. Ibid., ch. 4, 154–165

11. Charles Murray, *Losing Ground: American Social Policy, 1950–1980* (New York: Basic Books, 1984). A critique of Murray is William J. Wilson, *The Truly Disadvantaged* (Chicago: University of Chicago Press, 1987), esp. chs. 3 and 4.

Chapter 18   *Civil Liberties*

1. *Zamora v. Pomeroy*, 639 F.2d 662 (1981); *Goss v. Lopez*, 419 U.S. 565 (1975); *Tinker v. Des Moines Community School District*, 393 U.S. 503 (1969); *Smith v. Goguen*, 415 U.S. 566 (1974); *New Jersey v. T.L.O.*, 469 U.S. 325 (1985).

2. *Sheppard v. Maxwell*, 384 U.S. 333 (1966); *New York Times Co. v. United States*, 403 U.S. 713 (1971); *Kunz v. New York*, 340 U.S. 290 (1951).

3. William Blackstone, *Commentaries*, vol. 4 (1765), 151–152.

4. Jefferson's remarks are from a letter to Abigail Adams (quoted in Walter Berns, *The First Amendment and the Future of American Democracy* [New York: Basic Books, 1976], 82 and from a letter to Thomas McKean, governor of Pennsylvania, February 19, 1803 (Paul L. Ford, ed., *The Writings of Thomas Jefferson: 1801–1806*, vol. 8 [New York: Putnam, 1897], 218.

5. *Schenck v. United States*, 249 U.S. 47 (1919), 52.

6. *Gitlow v. New York*, 268 U.S. 652 (1925), 666.

7. *Fiske v. Kansas*, 274 U.S. 380 (1927); *Stromberg v. California*, 283 U.S. 359 (1931); *Near v. Minnesota*, 283 U.S. 697 (1931); *De Jonge v. Oregon*, 299 U.S. 353 (1937).

8. *Dennis v. United States*, 341 U.S. 494 (1951), 510ff. The test was first formulated by Judge Learned Hand of the court of appeals: see *Dennis v. United States*, 183 F.2d 201 (1950), 212.

9. *Yates v. United States*, 354 U.S. 298 (1957).

10. *Brandenburg v. Ohio*, 395 U.S. 444 (1969).

11. *Village of Skokie v. National Socialist Party*, 432 U.S. 43 (1977); 366 N.E.2d 349 (1977); and 373 N.E.2d 21 (1978).

12. *R.A.V. v. City of St. Paul*, 112 S. Ct. 2538 (1992).

13. *Wisconsin v. Mitchell*, No. 92–515 (1993).

14. C. Herman Pritchett, *Constitutional Civil Liberties* (Englewood Cliffs, N.J.: Prentice-Hall, 1984), 100.

15. *New York Times v. Sullivan*, 376 U.S. 254 (1964); but compare *Time, Inc. v. Firestone*, 424 U.S. 448 (1976).

16. Henry J. Abraham, *Freedom and the Court*, 4th ed. (New York: Oxford University Press, 1982), 193, fn 189.

17. Justice Stewart's famous remark was made in his concurring opinion in *Jacobellis v. Ohio*, 378 U.S. 184 (1964), 197.

18. *Miller v. California*, 413 U.S. 15 (1973).

19. *Jenkins v. Georgia*, 418 U.S. 153 (1974).

20. *Schad v. Borough of Mt. Ephraim*, 452 U.S. 61 (1981).

21. *Barnes v. Glen Theatre*, 111 S. Ct. 2456 (1991).

22. *American Booksellers Association v. Hudnut*, 771 F.2d 323 (1985), affirmed at 475 U.S. 1001 (1986).

23. *Renton v. Playtime Theatres*, 475 U.S. 41 (1986). See also *Young v. American Mini-Theatres, Inc.*, 427 U.S. 50 (1976).

24. *Reno v. American Civil Liberties Union*, 521 U.S. 844 (1997); *Ashcroft v. Free Speech Coalition*, 122 S. Ct. 1389 (2002).

25. *United States v. O'Brien*, 391 U.S. 367 (1968).

26. *Texas v. Johnson*, 109 S. Ct. 2533 (1989).

27. The Court had earlier held unconstitutional statutes that made it illegal to mutilate the flag (*Street v. New York*, 394 U.S. 576 [1967]), deface the flag (*Spence v. Washington*, 418 U.S. 405 [1974]), or treat the flag contemptuously by, for example, sewing it to the seat of your pants (*Smith v. Goguen*, 415 U.S. 566 [1974]). *U.S. v. Eichman*, 496 U.S. 310 (1990).

28. *First National Bank of Boston v. Bellotti*, 435 U.S. 765 (1978); *Federal Election Commission v. Massachusetts Citizens for Life, Inc.*, 479 U.S. 238 (1986).

29. *44 Liquormart v. Rhode Island*, 116 S. Ct. 1495 (1996); *Greater New Orleans Broadcasting Association v. United States*, 119 S. Ct. 1923 (1999).

30. *Pacific Gas and Electric Co. v. Public Utilities Commission*, 475 U.S. 1 (1986). Some limitations on corporate speech have been upheld, including a state law prohibiting a firm from spending money on candidates for elective office. *Austin v. Michigan Chamber of Commerce*, 100 S. Ct. 1391 (1990).

31. *Board of Trustees of the State University of New York v. Fox*, 492 U.S. 469 (1989).

32. *Bates v. State Bar of Arizona*, 433 U.S. 350 (1977); *Edenfield v. Bane*, 113 S. Ct. 1792 (1993).

33. *Hazelwood School District v. Kuhlmeier, et al.*, 484 U.S. 260 (1988).

34. *Murdock v. Pennsylvania*, 319 U.S. 105 (1943).

35. *Church of the Lukumi Babalu Aye v. City of Hialeah*, No. 91–948 (1993).

36. *Reynolds v. United States*, 98 U.S. 145 (1878).

37. *Jacobson v. Massachusetts*, 197 U.S. 11 (1905).

38. *Employment Division, Department of Human Resources of Oregon v. Smith*, 110 S. Ct. 1595 (1990).

39. *Society for Krishna Consciousness v. Lee*, 112 S. Ct. 2701 (1992).

40. *Welsh v. United States*, 398 U.S. 333 (1970); Pritchett, *Constitutional Civil Liberties*, 140–141.

41. *Sherbert v. Verner*, 374 U.S. 398 (1963); *Wisconsin v. Yoder*, 406 U.S. 205 (1972); *Hobbie v. Unemployment Appeals Commission of Florida*, 480 U.S. 136 (1987); *Estate of Thornton v. Caldor, Inc.*, 472 U.S. 703 (1985).

42. Berns, *The First Amendment*.

43. Pritchett, *Constitutional Civil Liberties*, 145–147.

44. *Everson v. Board of Education*, 330 U.S. 1 (1947).

45. *Engel v. Vitale*, 370 U.S. 421 (1962).

46. *Lubbock Independent School District v. Lubbock Civil Liberties Union*, 669 F.2d 1038.

47. *School District of Abington Township v. Schempp*, 374 U.S. 203 (1963).

48. *Lee v. Weisman*, 112 S. Ct. 2649 (1992); *Santa Fe Independent School District v. Jane Doe*, 530 U.S. 290 (2000).

49. *Epperson v. Arkansas*, 393 U.S. 97 (1968); *McLean v. Arkansas Board of Education*, 529 F. Supp. 1255 (1982).

50. *McCollum v. Board of Education*, 333 U.S. 203 (1948); *Zorach v. Clauson*, 343 U.S. 306 (1952).

51. *Tilton v. Richardson*, 403 U.S. 672 (1971).

52. *Board of Education v. Allen*, 392 U.S. 236 (1968).

53. *Walz v. Tax Commission*, 397 U.S. 664 (1970).

54. *Mueller v. Allen*, 463 U.S. 388 (1983).

55. *Zobrest v. Catalina Foothills School District*, 509 U.S. 1 (1993); *Mitchell v. Helms*, 2000 Lexis 4485.

56. *Lemon v. Kurtzman*, 403 U.S. 602 (1971).

57. *Committee for Public Education v. Nyquist*, 413 U.S. 756 (1973).

58. *Meek v. Pittenger*, 421 U.S. 349 (1975); *Wolman v. Walter*, 433 U.S. 229 (1977).

59. *Edwards v. Aguillard*, 482 U.S. 578 (1987); *Board of Education of Kiryas Joel Village School v. Louis Grumet*, 114 S. Ct. 2481 (1994).

60. *Agostini v. Felton*, 521 U.S. 203 (1997) overruled *Aguilar v. Felton*, 473 U.S. 402 (1985).

61. *Lemon v. Kurtzman*, 403 U.S. 602 (1971).

62. *Lynch v. Donelly*, 465 U.S. 668 (1984); *Allegheny v. ACLU*, 109 S. Ct. 3086 (1989).

63. *Marsh v. Chambers*, 492 U.S. 573 (1983).

64. Yale Kamisar, "Does (Did) (Should) the Exclusionary Rule Rest on a 'Principled Basis' Rather Than an 'Empirical Proposition'?" *Creighton Law Review* 16 (1982–1983): 565–667.

65. *Wolf v. Colorado*, 338 U.S. 25 (1949).

66. *Mapp v. Ohio*, 367 U.S. 643 (1961).
67. *Chimel v. California*, 395 U.S. 752 (1969).
68. *Washington v. Chrisman*, 455 U.S. 1 (1982).
69. *Oliver v. United States*, 466 U.S. 170 (1984).
70. *Arkansas v. Sanders*, 442 U.S. 753 (1979); *Robbins v. California*, 453 U.S. 420 (1981).
71. *United States v. Ross*, 456 U.S. 798 (1982); *Maryland v. Dyson*, 199 S. Ct. 2013 (1999); *Wyoming v. Houghton*, 119 S. Ct. 1297 (1999); *Whren v. United States*, 517 U.S. 806 (1996).
72. *Winston v. Lee*, 470 U.S. 753 (1985).
73. *South Dakota v. Neville*, 459 U.S. 553 (1983); *Schmerber v. California*, 384 U.S. 757 (1966).
74. *United States v. Dunn*, 480 U.S. 294 (1987); *California v. Ciraolo*, 476 U.S. 207 (1986); *California v. Carney*, 471 U.S. 386 (1985).
75. *O'Connor v. Ortega*, 480 U.S. 709 (1987).
76. *Bowers v. Hardwick*, 478 U.S. 186 (1986).
77. *Escobedo v. Illinois*, 378 U.S. 478 (1964); *Miranda v. Arizona*, 384 U.S. 436 (1966).
78. *Malloy v. Hogan*, 378 U.S. 1 (1964).
79. *Miranda v. Arizona*, 384 U.S. 436 (1966).
80. *Gilbert v. California*, 388 U.S. 263 (1967); *Kirby v. Illinois*, 406 U.S. 682 (1972).
81. *Estelle v. Smith*, 451 U.S. 454 (1981).
82. *Brewer v. Williams*, 430 U.S. 387 (1977).
83. *Illinois v. Perkins*, 496 U.S. 292 (1990).
84. *Dickerson v. United States*, 166 F.3d 667 (1999).
85. *Dickerson v. United States*, 120 S. Ct. 2326 (2000).
86. *Fare v. Michael C.*, 442 U.S. 707 (1979).
87. *United States v. Leon*, 468 U.S. 897 (1984); *Massachusetts v. Sheppard*, 468 U.S. 981 (1984).
88. *New York v. Quarles*, 467 U.S. 649 (1984). See also *Arizona v. Fulminante*, 111 S. Ct. 1246 (1991).
89. *Nix v. Williams*, 467 U.S. 431 (1984).
90. Ex parte Quirin, 317 U.S. 1 (1942).

Chapter 19 *Civil Rights*

1. *United States v. Carolene Products Co.*, 304 U.S. 144 (1938); *San Antonio Independent School District v. Rodriguez*, 411 U.S. 1 (1973).
2. Gunnar Myrdal, *An American Dilemma* (New York: Harper, 1944), ch. 27.
3. Richard Kluger, *Simple Justice* (New York: Random House/Vintage Books, 1977), 89–90.
4. Paul B. Sheatsley, "White Attitudes Toward the Negro," in *The Negro American*, ed. Talcott Parsons and Kenneth B. Clark (Boston: Houghton Mifflin, 1966), 305, 308, 317.
5. *Strauder v. West Virginia*, 100 U.S. 303 (1880).
6. *Civil Rights Cases*, 109 U.S. 3 (1883).
7. *Plessy v. Ferguson*, 163 U.S. 537 (1896).
8. *Cumming v. Richmond County Board of Education*, 175 U.S. 528 (1899).
9. *Missouri ex rel. Gaines v. Canada*, 305 U.S. 337 (1938).
10. *Sipuel v. Board of Regents of the University of Oklahoma*, 332 U.S. 631 (1948).
11. *Sweatt v. Painter*, 339 U.S. 629 (1950); *McLaurin v. Oklahoma State Regents for Higher Education*, 339 U.S. 637 (1950).

12. *Brown v. Board of Education of Topeka*, 347 U.S. 483 (1954).
13. *Brown v. Board of Education of Topeka*, 349 U.S. 294 (1955). This case is often referred to as "Brown II."
14. Frederick S. Mosteller and Daniel P. Moynihan, eds., *On Equality of Educational Opportunity* (New York: Random House, 1972), 60–62.
15. *Brown v. Board of Education of Topeka*, 347 U.S. 483 (1954).
16. C. Herman Pritchett, *Constitutional Civil Liberties* (Englewood Cliffs, N.J.: Prentice-Hall, 1984), 250–251, 261.
17. *Green et al. v. County School Board of New Kent County*, 391 U.S. 430 (1968).
18. *Swann v. Charlotte-Mecklenburg Board of Education*, 402 U.S. 1 (1971).
19. Busing *within* the central city was upheld in *Armour v. Nix*, 446 U.S. 930 (1980); *Keyes v. School District No. 1*, Denver, 413 U.S. 189 (1973); *Milliken v. Bradley*, 418 U.S. 717 (1974); *Board of School Commissioners of Indianapolis v. Buckley*, 429 U.S. 1068 (1977); and *School Board of Richmond v. State Board of Education*, 412 U.S. 92 (1972). Busing *across* city lines was upheld in *Evans v. Buchanan*, 423 U.S. 963 (1975), and *Board of Education v. Newburg Area Council*, 421 U.S. 931 (1975).
20. *Pasadena City Board of Education v. Spangler*, 427 U.S. 424 (1976).
21. See, for example, Herbert McClosky and John Zaller, *The American Ethos* (Cambridge: Harvard University Press, 1984), 92, 100; and data reported in Chapter 5 of this text.
22. NES, *1952–1990 Cumulative Data File*, *1992 NES Pre/Post Election Study* (1992).
23. *Freeman v. Pitts*, 112 S. Ct. 1430 (1992).
24. Robert S. Erikson and Norman R. Luttbeg, *American Public Opinion* (New York: Wiley, 1973), 49; Hazel Erskine, "The Polls: Demonstrations and Race Riots," *Public Opinion Quarterly* 31 (Winter 1967–1968): 654–677.
25. Howard Schuman, Charlotte Steeh, and Lawrence Bobo, *Racial Attitudes in America* (Cambridge: Harvard University Press, 1985), 69, 78–79.
26. Ibid., 102, 110, 127–135.
27. *Grove City College v. Bell*, 465 U.S. 555 (1984).
28. *United States v. Armstrong*, 116 S. Ct. 1480 (1996).
29. *Mueller v. Oregon*, 208 U.S. 412 (1908).
30. Equal Pay Act of 1963; Civil Rights Act of 1964, Title VII, and 1978 amendments thereto; Education Amendments of 1972, Title IX.
31. *Reed v. Reed*, 404 U.S. 71 (1971).
32. *Frontiero v. Richardson*, 411 U.S. 677 (1973).
33. *Stanton v. Stanton*, 421 U.S. 7 (1975).
34. *Craig v. Boren*, 429 U.S. 190 (1976).
35. *Dothard v. Rawlinson*, 433 U.S. 321 (1977).
36. *Cleveland Board of Education v. LaFleur*, 414 U.S. 632 (1974).
37. *Fortin v. Darlington Little League*, 514 F.2d 344 (1975).
38. *Roberts v. United States Jaycees*, 468 U.S. 609 (1984); *Board of Directors Rotary International v. Rotary Club of Duarte*, 481 U.S. 537 (1987).

39. *Arizona Governing Committee for Tax Deferred Annuity and Deferred Compensation Plans v. Norris*, 463 U.S. 1073 (1983).
40. *E.E.O.C. v. Madison Community Unit School District No. 12*, 818 F.2d 577 (1987).
41. *Michael M. v. Superior Court*, 450 U.S. 464 (1981).
42. *Vorchheimer v. School District of Philadelphia*, 430 U.S. 703 (1977).
43. *Kahn v. Shevin*, 416 U.S. 351 (1974).
44. *Schlesinger v. Ballard*, 419 U.S. 498 (1975).
45. *Bennett v. Dyer's Chop House*, 350 F. Supp. 153 (1972); *Morris v. Michigan State Board of Education*, 472 F.2d 1207 (1973); *Fitzgerald v. Porter Memorial Hospital*, 523 F.2d 716 (1975); *Kruzel v. Podell*, 226 N.W.2d 458 (1975).
46. *United States v. Virginia*, 116 S. Ct. 2264 (1996).
47. *Rostker v. Goldberg*, 453 U.S. 57 (1981).
48. *Gebser v. Lago Vista School District*, 118 S. Ct. 1989 (1998); *Faragher v. Boca Raton*, 118 S. Ct. 2275 (1998); *Burlington Industries v. Ellerth*, 118 S. Ct. 2257 (1998).
49. *Roe v. Wade*, 410 U.S. 113 (1973).
50. *Harris v. McRae*, 448 U.S. 297 (1980); *Beal v. Doe*, 432 U.S. 438 (1977); *Maher v. Roe*, 432 U.S. 464 (1977).
51. *Planned Parenthood Federation of Central Missouri v. Danforth*, 428 U.S. 52 (1976); *Bellotti v. Baird*, 443 U.S. 622 (1979); *Akron v. Akron Center for Reproductive Health*, 462 U.S. 416 (1983); *Thornburgh v. American College of Obstetricians and Gynecologists*, 476 U.S. 747 (1986). But compare with *Planned Parenthood Association of Kansas City v. Ashcroft*, 462 U.S. 476 (1983).
52. *Planned Parenthood v. Casey*, 112 S. Ct. 2791 (1992).
53. *Schenck v. Pro-Choice Network of Western New York*, 519 U.S. 357 (1997).
54. For an argument in support of a color-blind Constitution, see Andrew Kull, *The Color-Blind Constitution* (Cambridge: Harvard University Press, 1992).
55. *Regents of the University of California v. Bakke*, 438 U.S. 265 (1978).
56. *Fullilove v. Klutznick*, 448 U.S. 448 (1980).
57. *City of Richmond v. J.A. Croson Co.*, 488 U.S. 469 (1989).
58. *Metro Broadcasting v. FCC*, 497 U.S. 547 (1990).
59. *Northeastern Florida Contractors v. Jacksonville*, No. 91–1721 (1993).
60. *Firefighters Local Union No. 1784 v. Stotts*, 467 U.S. 561 (1984); *Wygant v. Jackson Board of Education*, 476 U.S. 267 (1986); *City of Richmond v. J.A. Croson Co.*, 488 U.S. 469 (1989).
61. *Local No. 28 of the Sheet Metal Workers' International Association v. Equal Employment Opportunity Commission*, 478 U.S. 421 (1986); *Wards Cove Packing Co. v. Atonio*, 490 U.S. 642 (1989); *Price Waterhouse v. Hopkins*, 490 U.S. 228 (1989). (Note: *Wards Cove* and *Price* were both superseded in part by the Civil Rights Act of 1991.)
62. *Fullilove v. Klutznick*, 448 U.S. 448 (1980); *Metro Broadcasting v. FCC*, 497 U.S. 547 (1990).

63. *United Steelworkers of America v. Weber*, 443 U.S. 193 (1979); *Johnson v. Santa Clara County Transportation Agency*, 480 U.S. 616 (1987).

64. *Wygant v. Jackson Board of Education*, 476 U.S. 267 (1986); *U.S. v. Paradise*, 480 U.S. 149 (1987).

65. Seymour Martin Lipset and William Schneider, "An Emerging National Consensus," *The New Republic* (October 15, 1977): 8–9.

66. John R. Bunzel. "Affirmative Re-Actions," *Public Opinion* (February/March 1986): 45–49; *New York Times* (December 14, 1997).

67. *Hopwood v. State of Texas*, 78 F. 3d 932 (1996); *Texas v. Hopwood*, 135 L.Ed.2d 1095 (1996).

68. *Adarand Constructors v. Pena*, 115 S. Ct. 2097 (1995).

69. *Bowers v. Hardwick*, 478 U.S. 186 (1986).

70. *Romer v. Evans*, 116 S. Ct. 1620 (1996).

71. *Boy Scouts of America v. Dale*, 1205. Ct. 2446 (2000).

72. *Hurley v. Irish-American Gay Group*, 515 U.S. 557 (1995).

Chapter 20 *Foreign and Military Policy*

1. Alexis de Tocqueville, *Democracy in America*, vol. 1, ed. Phillips Bradley (New York: Knopf, 1951), 235.

2. Richard Lau, Thad A. Brown, and David O. Sears, "Self-Interest and Civilians' Attitudes Toward the Vietnam War," *Public Opinion Quarterly* 42 (1978): 464–481.

3. Edward S. Corwin, *The President: Office and Powers* (New York: New York University Press, 1940), 200.

4. Louis Henkin, *Foreign Affairs and the Constitution* (New York: Norton, 1972), 53; 306, n 43.

5. Louis W. Koenig, *The Chief Executive*, 3d ed. (New York: Harcourt Brace Jovanovich, 1975), 217.

6. Louis Fisher, *President and Congress* (New York: Free Press, 1972), 45; *United States v. Belmont*, 301 U.S. 324 (1937).

7. Aaron Wildavsky, "The Two Presidencies," in *The Presidency*, ed. Wildavsky (Boston: Little, Brown, 1969), 231.

8. Loch Johnson and James M. McCormick, "The Making of International Agreements: A Reappraisal of Congressional Involvement," *Journal of Politics*, 40 (1978), 468–478.

9. Bernard E. Brown, "The Decision to End the Algerian War," in *Cases in Comparative Politics*, ed. James B. Christoph (Boston: Little, Brown, 1965), 154–180; Roy C. Macridis, "De Gaulle and NATO," in *Modern European Governments*, ed. Macridis (Englewood Cliffs, N.J.: Prentice-Hall, 1967), 92–115; and John E. Schwartz and L. Earl Shaw, op. cit., 235–236.

10. Peter G. Richards, *Parliament and Foreign Affairs* (London: George Allen and Unwin, 1967), 37–38; John Schwartz and Earl Shaw, *The United States Congress in Comparative Perspective* (Hinsdale, Ill.: Dryden Press, 1976), 235.

11. Arthur M. Schlesinger, Jr., *A Thousand Days: John F. Kennedy in the White House* (Boston: Houghton Mifflin, 1965), chs. 30, 31. Schlesinger, at p. 841, described Kennedy's

actions as a "brilliantly controlled," "matchlessly calibrated" combination of "nerve and wisdom." His view of Nixon's actions was a good deal less charitable in *The Imperial Presidency* (Boston: Houghton Mifflin, 1974), ch. 7.

12. *United States v. Curtiss-Wright Export Co.*, 299 U.S. 304 (1936).

13. *Mitchell v. Laird*, 488 F.2d 611 (1973).

14. *Prize Cases*, 67 U.S. 635 (1863); *Mora v. McNamara*, 389 U.S. 934 (1964); *Massachusetts v. Laird*, 400 U.S. 886 (1970).

15. *Dames and Moore v. Regan*, 435 U.S. 654 (1981).

16. *Korematsu v. United States*, 323 U.S. 214 (1944).

17. *Youngstown Sheet & Tube Co. v. Sawyer*, 343 U.S. 579 (1952).

18. *Immigration and Naturalization Service v. Chadha*, 103 S. Ct. 2764 (1983).

19. Robert S. Erikson and Norman R. Luttbeg, *American Public Opinion* (New York: Wiley, 1973), 50–51.

20. William R. Caspary, "The 'Mood Theory': A Study of Public Opinion and Foreign Policy," *American Political Science Review* 64 (June 1970): 536–547.

21. Erikson and Luttbeg, *American Public Opinion*, 52.

22. John E. Mueller, *War, Presidents, and Public Opinion* (New York: Wiley, 1973), 110.

23. Ibid., 112.

24. Milton J. Rosenberg, Sidney Verba, and Philip E. Converse, *Vietnam and the Silent Majority* (New York: Harper and Row, 1970), 26–27.

25. Erikson and Luttbeg, *American Public Opinion*, 155.

26. John R. Oneal and Brad Lian, "Presidents, the Use of Military Force, and Public Opinion," Working Papers in International Security I–92–8, Hoover Institution, Stanford, Calif. (July 1992).

27. Benjamin C. Schwarz, *Casualities, Public Opinion, and U.S. Military Intervention* (Santa Monica, Calif.: RAND, 1994).

28. Mueller, *War, Presidents, and Public Opinion*, 45–47, 169.

29. ABC/*Washington Post* poll as cited in *National Journal* (July 28, 1984): 1450.

30. Everett Carll Ladd, "Since World War II, Americans Have Persistently Looked Outward," *The Public Perspective* (August/September 1997): 5–34.

31. Howard Schuman, "Two Sources of Antiwar Sentiment in America," *American Journal of Sociology* 78 (1973): 513–536.

32. Philip E. Converse, Warren E. Miller, Jerrold G. Rusk, and Arthur C. Wolfe, "Continuity and Change in American Politics," *American Political Science Review* 63 (December 1969): 1083–1105; John P. Robinson, "Public Reaction to Political Protest: Chicago, 1968," *Public Opinion Quarterly* 34 (Spring 1970): 1–9.

33. James D. Wright, "Life, Time, and the Fortunes of War," *Transaction* 9 (January 1972).

34. John E. Rielly, *American Public Opinion and U.S. Foreign Policy, 1999* (Chicago: Chicago Council on Foreign Relations, 1999).

35. X, "The Sources of Soviet Conduct," *Foreign Affairs* 25 (July 1947): 566.

36. Walter Lippmann, *The Cold War* (New York: Harper Brothers, 1947).

37. Erikson and Luttbeg, *American Public Opinion*, 52.

38. Mueller, *War, Presidents, and Public Opinion*, 40.

39. Michael Roskin, "From Pearl Harbor to Vietnam: Shifting Generational Paradigms and Foreign Policy," *Political Science Quarterly* 89 (Fall 1974): 567.

40. Frank L. Klingberg, "The Historical Alternation of Moods in American Foreign Policy," *World Politics* 4 (1952): 239–273.

41. Roskin, "From Pearl Harbor," 567.

42. *American Public Opinion and U.S. Foreign Policy, 1987* (Chicago: Chicago Council on Foreign Relations, 1987), 33.

43. Stanley Lieberson, "An Empirical Study of Military-Industrial Linkages," in *Testing the Theory of the Military Industrial Complex*, ed. Steven Rosen (Lexington, Mass.: D.C. Heath/Lexington Books, 1973), 74.

44. Arnold Kanter, "Congress and the Defense Budget: 1960–1970," *American Political Science Review* 66 (1972): 129–143.

45. Robert J. Art, "Why We Overspend and Underaccomplish: Weapons Procurement and the Military-Industrial Complex," in Rosen, *Testing the Theory*, 249.

46. Quoted in Robert J. Art, *The TFX Decision: McNamara and the Military* (Boston: Little, Brown, 1968), 126.

47. Bill Keller, "Competition: A Pentagon Battlefield," *New York Times* (May 12, 1985), section 3, p. 1.

48. James Fairhall, "The Case for the $435 Hammer," *Washington Monthly* (January 1987): 50.

Chapter 21 *Environmental Policy*

1. Alexander W. Astin et al., *The American Freshman: National Norms for 1989* (Los Angeles: UCLA Graduate School of Education, 1989), 89.

2. On the greenhouse effect, see Philip D. Jones and Tom L. Wigley, "Global Warming Trends," *Scientific American* (August 1990): 84–91; Gordon J. MacDonald, "Scientific Basis for the Greenhouse Effect," *Journal of Policy Analysis and Management* 7 (1988): 425–444; S. Fred Singer, *Global Warming: Do We Know Enough to Act?* Paper 104, Center for the Study of American Business, Washington University (March 1991).

3. David Vogel, *National Styles of Regulation* (Ithaca, N.Y.: Cornell University Press, 1986), 19–30.

4. For arguments by activists, see Albert Gore, *Earth in the Balance* (Boston: Houghton Mifflin, 1992), and Stephen Schneider, *Global Warming* (San Francisco: Sierra Club Books, 1989). For arguments by skeptics, see Gregg Easterbrook, *A Moment on the Earth* (New York: Viking, 1995), ch. 17; Frederick Seitz et al., "Environmental Effects of Increased Atmospheric Carbon Dioxide," on the World

Wide Web at www.oism.org/project; and Patrick J. Michaels, "Global Deception," Policy Study 146, Center for the Study of American Business, Washington University (1998).

5. Easterbrook, *A Moment*, 309.

6. R. Shep Melnick, *Regulation and the Courts: The Case of the Clean Air Act* (Washington, D.C.: Brookings Institution, 1983), ch. 9.

7. Pietro S. Nivola, *The Politics of Energy Conservation* (Washington, D.C.: Brookings Institution, 1986), 11–12, 244–247.

8. Robert W. Crandall, "Pollution, Environmentalists, and the Coal Lobby," in *The Political Economy of Deregulation*, ed. Roger G. Noll and Bruce M. Own (Washington, D.C.: American Enterprise Institute, 1983), 84–96; Crandall, *Controlling Industrial Pollution* (Washington, D.C.: Brookings Institution, 1983).

9. Bruce A. Ackerman and William T. Hassler, *Clear Coal/Dirty Air* (New Haven, Conn.: Yale University Press, 1981).

10. Robert Dorfman, "Lessons of Pesticide Regulation," in *Reform of Environmental Regulation*, ed. Wesley A. Magat (Cambridge, Mass.: Ballinger, 1982), 13–30.

11. Easterbrook, *A Moment*, 386–395.

12. *Congressional Quarterly Weekly Report* (January 12, 1990): 166–170.

13. Richard Doll and Richard Peto, "The Causes of Cancer," *Journal of the National Cancer Institute* 66 (1981); World Cancer Research Fund, *Food, Nutrition, and the Prevention of Cancer* (Washington, D.C.: American Institute for Cancer Research, 1997).

14. R. Shep Melnick, "Deadlines, Cynicism, and Common Sense," *The Brookings Review* (Fall 1983): 21–24.

Chapter 22 *Who Governs? To What Ends?*

1. Alexis de Tocqueville, *Democracy in America*, vol. 2, ed. Phillips Bradley (New York: Knopf, 1951), book 2, ch. 1.

PHOTO CREDITS